2014

WINFIELD AND JOLOWICZ ON TORT

NINETEENTH EDITION

EDWIN PEEL
Fellow of Keble College and Professor of Law, Oxford University

JAMES GOUDKAMP
*Fellow of Keble College and Associate Professor of Law,
Oxford University*

SWEET & MAXWELL

 THOMSON REUTERS

First Edition	(1937) The Author
Second Edition	(1943) The Author
Third Edition	(1946) The Author
Fourth Edition	(1948) The Author
Fifth Edition	(1950) The Author
Sixth Edition	(1954) T. Ellis Lewis
Seventh edition	(1963) J.A. Jolowicz and T. Ellis Lewis
Eighth Edition	(1967) J.A. Jolowicz with T. Ellis Lewis
Ninth Edition	(1971) J.A. Jolowicz with T. Ellis Lewis and D.M. Harris
Tenth Edition	(1975) W.V.H. Rogers
Eleventh Edition	(1979) W.V.H. Rogers
Twelfth Edition	(1984) W.V.H. Rogers
Thirteenth Edition	(1989) W.V.H. Rogers
Fourteenth Edition	(1994) W.V.H. Rogers
Fifteenth Edition	(1998) W.V.H. Rogers
Sixteenth Edition	(2002) W.V.H. Rogers
Seventeenth Edition	(2006) W.V.H. Rogers
Eighteenth Edition	(2010) W.V.H. Rogers

Published in 2014 by Thomson Reuters (Professional) UK Limited
trading as Sweet & Maxwell, Friars House, 160 Blackfriars Road, London SE1 8EZ
(Registered in England & Wales, Company No 1679046.
Registered Office and address for service: 2nd Floor, 1 Mark Square, Leonard Street,
London EC2A 4EG)

For further information on our products and services, visit *www.sweetandmaxwell.co.uk*

Typeset by Letterpart Limited, Caterham on the Hill, Surrey CR3 5XL
Printed and bound in Great Britain by CPI Group (UK) Ltd, Croydon CR0 4YY.

No natural forests were destroyed to make this product; only farmed timber was used and
re-planted.

A CIP catalogue record of this book is available for the British Library.

ISBN 978-0-414-02565-3

Thomson Reuters and the Thomson Reuters logo are trademarks of Thomson Reuters.

Sweet & Maxwell ® is a registered trademark of Thomson Reuters (Professional) UK
Limited.

Preface to the Nineteenth Edition

We begin this preface by paying tribute to our predecessor as author, Horton Rogers. One of us had the good fortune to know Horton Rogers as mentor and colleague, albeit briefly, and that has been acknowledged elsewhere. On this occasion, we confine ourselves to recognising his work on this book, which has spanned 40 years. In that time he has been responsible for nine editions, which is the same as the combined output of all of the previous authors. It is typical of his modesty that we received no request that he should be added as an eponymous author; we would not have demurred.

The first edition of this book appeared shortly after the momentous decision in *Donoghue v Stevenson* and, by the time that Horton Rogers took over its authorship in 1975, the law of negligence, and of many other torts, had undergone rapid development. The rate of change continued to accelerate in the decades immediately following 1975 (in the preface to the eighteenth edition *Home Office v Dorset Yacht Co Ltd* was singled out as the first engagement in a 40-year "Duty of Care War"), due partly to major developments in the field of human rights. The fact that Horton was writing about a rapidly moving target, coupled with a tremendous increase in the volume of case law over the period of his authorship, must have made the process of updating this book a monumental task. Nevertheless, all of the changes were woven expertly and deftly into the text without sacrificing the clarity and insightful analysis for which Horton Rogers was well known, as a result of his work on this book and by his many other publications.

Our predecessor would be the first to admit that for several editions under his watch the law had the irritating habit of undergoing major development shortly after the text had been submitted, but before publication. This was often too much to cater for at the proofs stage. As a result, the prefaces of several editions became masterfully concise mini-chapters regarding the way in which parts of the book should be read in the light of such developments. Mercifully, we have been spared the need to deal with any major development in this preface. However, this is not to say that the law has stood still since the eighteenth edition; it has, rather, conveniently chosen to move on in the period prior to submission of the text.

In terms of legislation, the most significant developments have been the coming into force of the Defamation Act 2013 and an amendment to s.47(2) of the Health and Safety at Work etc. Act 1974. The former has been much heralded and has required a major rewriting of the chapter on Defamation (Ch.13). The latter is, arguably, of much greater practical significance leading as it does to a reversal in the presumption of actionability for breach of health and safety regulations. The potential significance of this still very recent development is considered in Chs 8 and 9.

Over 250 new cases are referred to in this edition and many more than that were read. In some of the decisions that have been incorporated into the book the courts have continued to explore the limits of liability in negligence and, in particular, the law relating to causation. One significant development in this regard is the decision of the Supreme Court in *Sienkiewicz v Greif (UK) Ltd*, but perhaps less so for its confirmation of the approach to mesothelioma claims than for the observations of the Justices on other ways of resolving the question of causation in different types of claims based on epidemiological or statistical evidence. *Sienkiewicz* may, however, be overshadowed by the anticipated decision of the Supreme Court in *International Energy Group Ltd v Zurich Insurance Plc UK Branch*. For now, this edition takes note of the decision of the Court of Appeal, itself based on observations made by the Supreme Court in *Durham v BAI (Run Off) Ltd v Independent Insurance Co Ltd*concerning the correct interpretation of *Barker v Corus UK Ltd*. These decisions and several others have necessitated a significant rewriting of parts of the chapter on causation and remoteness (Ch.7).

One area of law which has certainly been "on the move" since the last edition is vicarious liability. This is precisely the phrase used by Lord Phillips in *Child Catholic Welfare Society v Institute of the Brothers of the Christian Schools* to describe the developments that have taken the doctrine beyond the traditional employment context. That case was shortly followed by the decision of the Supreme Court in *Woodland v Essex CC* to extend the scope of non-delegable duties of care. These decisions and others that have reassessed the scope of liability for the wrongs of others required that significant revisions be made to the chapter on Vicarious Liability (Ch.21).

Relatively late on in the process of writing this edition the Supreme Court delivered its decision in *Coventry v Lawrence*, a case which raised many contentious issues in the law of nuisance. The chapter on Nuisance (Ch.15) has been rewritten to reflect that decision (some consequential changes were also made to the chapter on Remedies (Ch.23), but given the radical nature of some of the solutions adopted, and suggested for the future (most notably, the appropriate remedy), further decisions in this area are very likely).

Other decisions of note at the highest level and the chapters which have been partially rewritten as a result are: *Jones v Kaney*, removing the immunity in negligence of expert witnesses (Duty of Care, Ch.5); *Baker v Quantum Clothing Group Ltd* (Breach of Duty, Ch.6, and Breach of Statutory Duty, Ch.8); *Smith v Ministry of Defence* on the liability of the government to members of the armed forces injured while on duty (Duty of Care, Ch.5); *Rabone v Pennine Care NHS Trust* (Duty of Care, Ch.5); *AB v Ministry of Defence* on limitation (Defences, Ch.26); *Hayes v Willoughby*, *R (Lumba) v Secretary of State for the Home Department* and *R (Kambadzi) v Secretary of State for the Home Department* (Trespass to the Person and Related Matters, Ch.4); *Bocardo SA v Star Energy*

UK Onshore Ltd(Trespass to Land, Ch.14); and *Crawford Adjusters Ltd v Sagicor Insurance Ltd* on the tort of malicious prosecution (Abuse of Legal Procedure, Ch.20).

In relation to the Court of Appeal, the decision in *International Energy Group Ltd v Zurich Insurance Plc UK Branch*has already been noted. Others of note include *Chandler v Cape Plc* on the duties of care that a parent company may owe to those affected by the conduct of a subsidiary (Duty of Care, Ch.5; Capacity, Ch.25); *Everett v Comojo (UK) Ltd* on liability for third parties (Duty of Care, Ch.5); *E v English Province of Our Lady of Charity* (Vicarious Liability, Ch.20); *Delaney v Pickett* and *Joyce v O'Brien* on illegality (Defences, Ch.26); *Goldsmith v Patchcott* and *Turnbull v Warrener* (Animals, Ch.17); *Gore v Stannard* on liability for fire (*Rylands v Fletcher*, Ch.16); *Hide v Steeplechase Co (Cheltenham) Ltd* (Breach of Statutory Duty, Ch.8); *Scullion v Bank of Scotland Plc* (Liability for Statements, Ch.12); *Tamiz v Google Inc* (Defamation, Privacy and Related Matters, Ch.13); and *Swift v Secretary of State for Justice* and *Haxton v Philips Electronics UK Ltd* (Death in Relation to Tort, Ch.24).

As authors, we have our own personal favourites. *Geary v JD Wetherspoon Plc* (Liability for Land and Structures, Ch.10) is notable for making real the well-known dictum of Scrutton LJ in *The Carlgarth* that "[w]hen you invite a person into your house to use the staircase you do not invite him to slide down the bannisters". Although it was not necessary to include it in the text, one of the authors welcomed the nostalgia of *Scout Association v Barnes* in being reminded of the game he also played as a scout, but without the modification which led to unfortunate consequences in that case. But pride of place must go to *Dufosse v Melbry Events Ltd* in which Rix LJ was able to conclude his judgment, entirely legitimately on the facts of the case, as follows: "[T]he learned district judge took an overly benevolent view of the performance by Santa and the Elf of their duties in this case and I would allow the appeal."

As new authors, we have taken the opportunity to consider whether the time may be right to make any structural changes to the organisation of the book, but we have confined ourselves to just a few. The chapter that previously covered both Duty of Care and Breach of Duty has been divided into two, partly because of the enormous size of the combined chapter. The chapter which previously covered Causation, Remoteness and Contributory Negligence is now confined to the first two of those topics and the treatment of contributory negligence has been moved to the chapter on Remedies; not all will agree with that change. The two previous chapters on Defences and Extinction of Liability in Tort have been merged. Within each chapter, two stylistic changes have been introduced: headings and sub-headings have been revised to limit them to a maximum of three levels; and, where possible, any paragraph that makes a distinct point contains an opening sentence or phrase in bold type that indicates the point concerned. We hope that these changes will assist the reader who is looking for material on a particular matter.

This edition is considerably shorter than the previous edition, which ran to over 1,200 pages. There are several reasons for this reduction in length, the more important of which are as follows. First, some areas of law have been simplified or consolidated and this has permitted them to be treated within a shorter compass. Secondly, legislation has in some instances swept away vast swathes of authority and has not as yet been the subject of judicial exposition (especially the Defamation Act 2013). Thirdly, some of the organisational changes that we mentioned in the previous paragraph have allowed considerable savings to be made in terms of the number of words used.

We divided the burden of the new edition roughly equally between us. However, despite this division we both take joint and several responsibility for the entire project. Each of us made revisions to drafts of the chapters for which we took primary responsibility in the light of the comments of the other. Nevertheless, primarily because collaborative work invariably involves a degree of compromise and consequently the need to deviate from ideas that we have expressed elsewhere, we felt that it may be useful to identify the chapters to which each of us attended in the first instance. Edwin Peel attended to Chs 7–12, 14–22 and 25. James Goudkamp dealt with Chs 1–6, 13, 23, 24 and 26.

Our thanks are due to many people. In particular, Edwin Peel would like to thank his family for their patience and understanding which they continue to extend to him without complaint, but with love and affection. James Goudkamp is grateful to his parents, who have shown him endless support. Our collective thanks are due to the publishers who have also been required to extend a degree of patience; in particular to the Senior Publishing Editor, Nicola Thurlow and to the House Editor, Bethany Tasker.

We have sought to state the law as at the date of this Preface. For those who are intrigued by the relevance of the cover image to a book on the law of torts, please refer to Ch.10, footnote 90.

WEP

JG

Keble College, Oxford

22 June 2014

TABLE OF CONTENTS

12. LIABILITY FOR STATEMENTS

13. DEFAMATION, PRIVACY AND RELATED MATTERS

14. TRESPASS TO LAND

15. NUISANCE

16. THE RULE IN RYLANDS V FLETCHER

17. ANIMALS

18. INTERFERENCE WITH GOODS

19. INTERFERENCE WITH CONTRACT OR BUSINESS

20. ABUSE OF LEGAL PROCEDURE

21. VICARIOUS LIABILITY

TABLE OF CASES

TABLE OF STATUTES

Australia

Germany

Ireland

Scotland

New Zealand

United States

TABLE OF STATUTORY INSTRUMENTS

TABLE OF CONVENTIONS AND EUROPEAN LEGISLATION

CHAPTER 1

INTRODUCTION

1. Nature and Functions of the Law of Tort

A. Aims of the Law of Tort

1–001 Numerous attempts have been made to define a "tort" with varying degrees of lack of success. We will begin, therefore, with a general description rather than with a definition and must be content for the moment to sacrifice accuracy and completeness for the sake of simplicity. Having given a very broad description of the role of the law of tort we can then turn to the problem of formal definition, and finally look at the relationship of the tort system with certain other legal and social institutions pursuing similar ends.

1–002 It is not possible to assign any one aim to the law of tort, which is not surprising when one considers that the subject comprehends situations as disparate as A carelessly running B down in the street; C calling D a thief; E giving bad investment advice to F; G failing to diagnose H's dyslexia at school; and I selling J's car when he has no authority to do so. At a very general level, however, we may say that tort law is concerned with allocating responsibility for certain types of losses. It is obvious that in any society of people living together numerous conflicts of interest will arise and the actions of one person or group of persons will from time to time cause or threaten damage to others. This damage may take many forms—injury to the person, damage to physical property, damage to financial interests, injury to reputation and so on—and whenever a person suffers damage at the hands of another person, especially if it is serious, he is inclined to look to the law for redress. If the law grants redress, some person or group of persons will be required to do or refrain from doing something. This redress may take various forms. In the great majority of tort actions the claimant is seeking monetary compensation (damages) for the injury he has suffered, and this fact strongly emphasises the function of tort in allocating or redistributing loss. In many cases, however, the claimant is seeking an injunction to prevent the occurrence of harm in the future and in this area the direct "preventive" function of tort predominates.[1] An injunction is usually the primary remedy sought, for example, in cases of private nuisance (wrongful interference with the enjoyment of land) and the so-called "economic torts" such as inducing breach of contract. This is not because damages are unavailable (they clearly are) but because the defendant is engaged in a continuing act and the damage suffered by the claimant may not yet have occurred or may be suffered over a long period of time. Even when the claim is for damages in respect of a completed wrong, the role of tort cannot only be squared with the idea of compensation. Thus, there are some situations in which the law imposes upon the defendant an obligation to disgorge the profits he has made from his wrongdoing, whether or not the claimant has suffered any loss. In a few situations, where exemplary damages are awarded, the idea of compensation is dropped in favour of overt punishment; but much more frequently there are substantial awards of damages (nominally compensatory) for matters like injury to reputation and interference with liberty, which one cannot

---

[1] An award of damages against A may also have a "preventive" function in deterring B from behaving in the same way, but how far this works is controversial: see paras 1–035—1–037.

even begin to quantify in mathematical terms. A couple of nights of wrongful detention in the police station may attract more damages than a broken arm, and a libel in a national newspaper more than the loss of that arm. In these cases the law is performing a complex function incorporating vindication, deterrence and appeasement.[2] Some tort actions (for example, some claims for trespass to land) may be brought mainly as a method of obtaining a declaration of rights, notwithstanding the availability under modern procedure of a specific remedy of that nature. Associated with this is what a Canadian judge, Linden J, has called the "Ombudsman" function of tort,[3] under which those responsible for losses (typically corporations whose activities cause major disasters) may be called upon to answer in public for their activities. Now it is clear that it is not a function of tort law to provide an alternative route to a public inquiry but there are certainly cases which come close to that. In *Ashley v Chief Constable of Sussex Police*[4] A had been shot dead by a police officer in a drugs raid. The officer was acquitted on a charge of murder and the Chief Constable conceded liability for negligence in a civil claim by A's family and estate. The majority of the House of Lords rejected an application to strike out as an abuse of process the alternative cause of action based upon trespass to the person even though it was accepted that in the circumstances no greater damages could be obtained under this action than under that on which the defendants were prepared to concede liability. It was a fair inference that the family's purpose was to obtain a finding that the deceased had not merely been the victim of organisational negligence in the planning of the raid but that he had been unlawfully killed, but they had pleaded a valid cause of action and the fact that they would recover no more damages for it did not mean that they had no legitimate interest in pressing it. As Lord Rodger observed: "the very fact that the chief constable remains understandably concerned to defend the claim of [trespass] tends to confirm that the claimants may remain, equally understandably, concerned to pursue that claim."[5] There have also been cases in which a civil claim has been brought in order to provoke the prosecuting authorities into acting.[6] It is perhaps unkind to call tort the dustbin of the law of obligations, but it is certainly the great residuary category. No one theory explains the whole of the law.

B. Definition of Tortious Liability

Winfield's definition of tort was as follows: "Tortious liability arises from the breach of a duty primarily fixed by law; this duty is towards persons generally and its breach is redressible by an action for unliquidated damages." In framing this definition Winfield was not seeking to indicate what conduct is and what is

1–003

---

[2] Vindication of rights may play a role even in cases of negligence. See, e.g. the award of damages in *Rees v Darlington Memorial Hospital NHS Trust* [2003] UKHL 52; [2004] 1 A.C. 309 (see para.25–021) and the modification of causation principles in *Chester v Afshar* [2004] UKHL 41; [2005] 1 A.C. 134 (see para.7–062).

[3] Linden (1973) 51 Can. B. Rev. 155.

[4] [2008] UKHL 25; [2008] 1 A.C. 962.

[5] [2008] UKHL 25; [2008] 1 A.C. 962 at [69].

[6] See *Halford v Brookes* [1991] 1 W.L.R. 428 (successful civil action arising from murder; defendant subsequently prosecuted and convicted: *The Times*, August 1, 1996).

not sufficient to involve a person in tortious liability, but merely to distinguish tort from certain other branches of law.[7] As we shall see, it cannot be accepted as entirely accurate but it has the merit of brevity and contains elements which deserve continuing emphasis. It is true that a cause of action in modern law is merely a factual situation the existence of which enables the claimant to obtain a remedy from the court[8] so he is certainly not in the position he was in 200 years ago of having to choose the right "form of action" to fit his claim. Nonetheless, even the comparatively lax modern style of pleading requires the claimant to set out the elements of the claim which he seeks to establish, and in practice this will nearly always involve identifying the tort or other cause of action on which he relies. The third element of Winfield's definition (which is convenient to mention first) is that the breach of duty is redressable by an action for unliquidated damages. A claim is said to be "liquidated" when it is for a fixed, inelastic sum[9] or one which is calculable by the mere process of arithmetic.[10] It is not, of course, a sufficient test of tort liability that the remedy is unliquidated damages—for these are also the primary remedy for breach of contract—but it seems to be a necessary one. If the claimant cannot recover unliquidated damages then whatever claim he may have, it is not for tort.

Winfield would now be forced to retreat from the claim that if a duty is towards a specific person or specific persons it cannot arise from tort,[11] but there is probably still some substance in his contention that the element of generality was an important factor in the definition. It is arguable that everything depends upon the level of abstraction at which the duty is expressed. It can be truly stated that by virtue of the law of tort D is under a duty not to convert to his own use the goods of anybody else, while D's contractual duty to deliver goods which D has sold is owed only to the person to whom D has sold them but this is to compare two statements at different levels. Just as D has a general duty not to commit the tort of conversion, so D has a general duty not to commit breaches of contract. If, on the other hand, we descend to the particular, then just as D's duty to deliver certain goods is owed only to their buyer, so also D's duty not to convert certain goods to D's own use is owed only to the person in possession, or having the immediate right to possession, of them.

---

[7] Many lawyers have endeavoured, like Winfield, to define a "tort" by distinguishing it from related concepts. This approach to definition led Wigmore to remark: "Never did a Name so obstruct a true understanding of the Thing. To such a plight has it brought us that a favorite mode of defining a Tort is to declare merely that it is not a Contract. As if a man were to define Chemistry by pointing out that it is not Physics nor Mathematics!": Wigmore, *Select Cases on the Law of Torts* (1912), p.vii. But see *R. v Secretary of State, Ex p. Factortame Ltd (No.7)* [2001] 1 W.L.R. 942 at 965.

[8] *Letang v Cooper* [1965] 1 Q.B. 232 at 244.

[9] But the fact that the claimant claims a specific sum in his pleadings (e.g. £5,000 as the value of a wrecked car) does not make it liquidated.

[10] For example, the price of goods sold and delivered at so much a unit or wages at so much a week.

[11] Stevens, *Torts and* Rights (2007).

C. Tort and Contract

Overlap between tort and contract. From a practical lawyer's point of view   1–004
there may be a considerable overlap in any factual situation between the law of
contract and the law of tort. For example, a claim for damages arising from a
defective product may involve a complex web of issues under the Sale of Goods
Act 1979, the law of misrepresentation and collateral warranty, the tort of
negligence, the Consumer Protection Act 1987 and a chain of contractual
indemnities among retailer, middleman and manufacturer.[12] It is unlikely that any
legal system can ever cut loose from general conceptual classifications such as
"contract" and "tort" (at any rate they seem to be found everywhere) but the
student will quickly come to recognise that the boundary must sometimes be
crossed in the solution of a problem. It has long been trite law that a defendant
may be liable on the same facts in contract to A and in tort to B (notwithstanding
privity of contract);[13] it is now, after a period of uncertainty, also clearly
established that there may be concurrent contractual and tortious liability to the
same claimant, though he may not, of course, recover damages twice over.
However, before we examine these propositions further we must make some
attempt at formally distinguishing the two heads of liability.

Source of the duty. It was Winfield's view that tortious duties exist by virtue of   1–005
the law itself and are not dependent upon the agreement or consent of the persons
subjected to them. D is under a duty not to assault C, not to slander C and not to
trespass on C's land because the law says that D is under such a duty and not
because D has agreed with C to undertake such a duty. Winfield therefore
considered that tortious liability could for this reason be distinguished from
contractual liability and from liability on bailment, neither of which can exist
independently of the parties, or at least of the defendant's agreement or consent.
There are, however, several instances of what is undoubtedly tortious liability for
the existence of which some prior consent, undertaking or assumption of
responsibility on the part of the defendant is essential. The liability of the
occupier of premises to his visitor, for example, which is now governed by the
Occupiers' Liability Act 1957, is based upon breach of a duty of care owed by the
occupier to persons whom he has permitted to enter upon his premises. The duty
owed to trespassers, i.e. persons who enter without his consent, is not the same.[14]
Again, the duty of care owed by a person who gives gratuitous advice upon a
serious occasion is, doubtless, a tortious one,[15] but its existence is dependent
upon the adviser's agreement to give the advice, if not necessarily upon his
agreement to accept legal responsibility for it. Still more difficult is the fact that
in some situations an undertaking (whether or not by contract) by A to B to
perform a service, the object of which is to confer a benefit upon C, may give rise

---

[12] See, e.g. *Lexmead (Basingstoke) v Lewis* [1982] A.C. 225.
[13] Modified by the Contracts (Rights of Third Parties) Act 1999, but it is still the *basic* rule that only
a party to a contract may sue or be sued on it.
[14] See para.10–034.
[15] But a close relationship between adviser and advisee is required and for this purpose the
relationship has been described as "equivalent to contract": *Hedley Byrne & Co Ltd v Heller &
Partners Ltd* [1964] A.C. 465 at 530.

to liability in tort to C.[16]   Not only is it untrue that all tortious duties arise independently of the will of the defendant, but it is equally not true that contractual duties are always dependent upon that will. Apart from the obvious point that the duty not to break one's contracts is itself a duty imposed by the law, it is also the case that contractual liability may exist even in the absence of any true consent between the parties. Whether or not there is a contract normally depends upon the outward manifestations of agreement by the parties, not on their subjective states of mind.[17]

1–006   **Content of the duty.** Another mode of differentiation between tortious and contractual liability is to be found in the proposition that in tort the content of the duties is fixed by the law whereas the content of contractual duties is fixed by the contract itself. If D consents to C's entry upon his premises then the duty which D owes to C is the duty fixed by the Occupiers' Liability Act 1957, i.e. by the law itself, but whether, for example, D's duty is to deliver to C 10 or 20 tons of coal can only be discovered from the contract between C and D. Even this distinction, however, is by no means always valid, for today in many cases the content of contractual duties is also fixed by the law. Statute provides, for example, that certain quite specific obligations shall be contained in contracts for the sale or hire-purchase of goods and cannot be excluded;[18] and it is now no longer true, as perhaps it once was, that implied terms in a contract, in the absence of a statutory rule, are always to be based upon the presumed intention of the parties.[19] Conversely, there are tortious duties which are subject to variation by agreement, whether or not that agreement amounts in law to a contract between the parties.[20]

1–007   **Aims of contract and tort.** Another basis for distinguishing between contract and tort may be sought in the aims of the two heads of liability. Arguably, the "core" of contract is the idea of enforcing promises, whereas tort aims principally at the prevention or compensation of harms, and this difference of function has two principal consequences. First, that a mere failure to act will not usually be actionable in tort, for that would be to set at naught the rule that even a positive promise will not give rise to legal liability unless it is intended as legally binding and supported by consideration or the formality of a deed. The second consequence is that damages cannot be claimed in tort for a "loss of expectation". Damages in contract put the claimant in the position he would have been in had the contract been performed, whereas damages in tort put him in the position he would have been in had the tort not been committed. However, this basis for distinguishing between contract and tort is imperfect. For one thing, failure to receive the benefits promised under a contract might be regarded as "harm".[21] Furthermore, there are instances where liability in tort arises for failing to confer

---

[16] See para.5–049.
[17] See, e.g. *Smith v Hughes* (1871) L.R. 6 Q.B. 597 at 607.
[18] Sale of Goods Act 1979; Unfair Contract Terms Act 1977.
[19] *Lister v Romford Ice and Cold Storage Co Ltd* [1957] A.C. 555 at 594; *Liverpool CC v Irwin* [1977] A.C. 239 at 257–258.
[20] Occupiers' Liability Act 1957 s.2(1); *Ashdown v Samuel Williams & Sons Ltd* [1957] 1 Q.B. 409. This case would be decided differently since the Unfair Contract Terms Act 1977 but is still illustrative of the general principle of law.
[21] See Burrows, *Understanding the Law of Obligations* (1998), Ch.1, who adopts the idea of "wrongful interference" as the hallmark of tort in order to avoid this overlap.

a benefit on others in the sense of failing to protect their safety. Some of these are of very long standing, for example, the duty of an occupier to take steps to ensure that his visitors are not harmed by dangers on his land, even if those are not of his making. As to damages, the law of contract puts the claimant in the position he would have been entitled to occupy (subject to the law of remoteness) as a result of the transaction agreed between the parties. While it is clear that (assuming the claim in tort to arise from some transaction between the parties) tort does not do that, the distinction is less fundamental than might appear. If a surgeon operates negligently on a curable condition and leaves the condition incurable, the patient recovers damages on the basis that with careful surgery he would have been cured; if a solicitor negligently fails to carry out X's instructions to make a will in favour of C, C can recover as damages the value of the lost legacy;[22] and if the seller of property fraudulently[23] induces the claimant to buy it, while the claimant cannot recover as damages the profits he would have made if the representation had been true, he may be able to recover the profits he would have earned by laying out his money elsewhere.[24]

D. Concurrent Liability in Tort and Contract

Three-party situations. We now return to the point that contractual and tortious duties may co-exist on the same facts. The proposition that D may incur liability in tort to C from a matter or transaction in respect of which D had a contract with B was clearly established in *Donoghue v Stevenson*,[25] which is the basis of the manufacturer's common law liability in tort to the ultimate consumer.[26] It is noteworthy that the action in negligence rests upon the existence of a duty of care owed by the defendant to the claimant and in the last resort this is determined by the court's perception of what is fair, just and reasonable, and on that issue the contractual context in which the events take place will often be relevant. For example, it has been held that a building sub-contractor was not liable in negligence for damage to the works when the main contract provided that they were to be at the risk of and insurable by the building owner,[27] and an agent answering inquiries on behalf of his principal is not personally liable in negligence in respect of their accuracy unless he has assumed some direct responsibility.[28] Similarly, too great a readiness to hold that a director owes a personal duty of care to persons with whom his company has dealings risks setting at naught the protection of limited liability.[29]

1–008

---

[22] *White v Jones* [1995] 2 A.C. 207, see para.5–054.

[23] Fraud (deceit) is a tort and subject to the tort measure of damages: see para.12–019.

[24] *East v Maurer* [1991] 1 W.L.R. 461. But see *Clef Aquitaine SARL v Laporte Materials (Barrow) Ltd* [2001] Q.B. 488.

[25] [1932] A.C. 562.

[26] See Ch.11.

[27] *Norwich CC v Harvey* [1989] 1 W.L.R. 828.

[28] *Gran Gelato Ltd v Richcliff (Group) Ltd* [1992] Ch. 560 (the principal will be responsible to the claimant for the acts of the agent and may recover an indemnity under his contract with the agent. The point is significant for the claimant where the principal is insolvent). See para.12–032.

[29] See para.25–033.

1–009 **Two-party situations.** Where it is alleged that the defendant owes concurrent duties in contract and tort to the *same* person, some legal systems have a doctrine (known in French law as *non cumul des obligations*) that this is not possible.[30] Though there were signs of this in England in earlier days,[31] the weight of the modern case law was the other way and the "concurrence" approach was decisively affirmed by the House of Lords in *Henderson v Merrett Syndicates Ltd*,[32] where it was held that Names at Lloyd's might sue members' agents (with whom they had a contract) for negligence as well as for breach of contract in the management of underwriting business so as to gain the advantage of the longer time limit under the Latent Damage Act 1986.[33] As Lord Goff put it:[34]

> "the result may be untidy; but, given that the tortious duty is imposed by the general law, and the contractual duty is attributable to the will of the parties, I do not find it objectionable that the claimant may be entitled to take advantage of the remedy which is most advantageous to him."[35]

Thus, for example, concurrent liability arises between carrier and passenger, doctor and (private) patient, solicitor and client, and employer and employee.

1–010 **Effect of allocation of responsibility by contract.** Usually, concurrent liability will not affect the substantive duty that the defendant owes: the duty will be the same in tort and contract. For example, a doctor's duty in tort is to exercise proper professional care and skill and the implied terms in his contract are the same:[36] he does not impliedly warrant that he will effect a cure, though theoretically he may do so by an express promise to that effect.[37] However, there have been several cases in which attempts have been made to use the duty in tort to override the allocation of responsibility between the parties by contract. If the contract were to provide expressly that the defendant was not liable for "risk X" then (subject to the effect of the Unfair Contract Terms Act 1977 upon that term) it would be absurd to allow a tort duty to intrude and contradict that allocation.[38] The same must be true where there is an implied term in the contract that the defendant is not to be liable for "X" (or, as it would be more likely to be expressed, there is no implied term that he should be liable for that risk).[39]

---

[30] See generally Weir in XI International Encyclopaedia of Comparative Law, Ch.12.

[31] See, e.g. *Groom v Crocker* [1939] 1 K.B. 194; *Bagot v Stevens Scanlan & Co Ltd* [1966] 1 Q.B. 197.

[32] [1995] 2 A.C. 145.

[33] See para.26–093.

[34] [1995] 2 A.C. 145 at 194.

[35] This seems to be a general trend: *BG Checo International Ltd v BC Hydro and Power Authority* (1993) 99 D.L.R. (4th) 577; *Bryan v Maloney* (1995) 182 C.L.R. 163 at 609; *Dairy Containers Ltd v NZI Bank Ltd* [1995] 2 N.Z.L.R. 30.

[36] The implied term in a contract for the supply of a service where the supplier acts in the course of a business (which includes a profession) is found in the Supply of Goods and Services Act 1982 s.13, restating the common law.

[37] *Thake v Maurice* [1986] Q.B. 644 shows that a court will require very clear evidence to establish such a warranty against a doctor.

[38] *Norwich CC v Harvey* [1989] 1 W.L.R. 828, in the three-party situation.

[39] *National Bank of Greece S.A. v Pinios Shipping Co No.1* [1989] 3 W.L.R. 185 (on appeal, but not on this point: [1990] 1 A.C. 637); *Bank of Nova Scotia v Hellenic Mutual War Risks Association (Bermuda) Ltd* [1990] 1 Q.B. 818 reversed on the construction of the contract: [1992] 1 A.C. 233.

Instances where the courts regard the situation as the province of the law of contract. Even where the parties are not in a contractual relationship restraint may have to be exercised because sound policy may suggest that the matter should be left entirely to contract law. Thus building contracts are commonly made by a tendering process and contract law has reasonably clear rules about this. The basic principle is that the person who invites tenders has complete discretion as to which bidder shall get the contract. This may be modified in some cases by a finding that there was a promise (a collateral contract) to accept the "best" bid; or at least a promise to give honest consideration to all conforming bids; and where public works are involved there may be statutory requirements which displace the general law. There would be a serious risk of disruption of these principles if we allowed contentions that the invitor owed a "duty of care" to bidders, still more if we allowed such arguments to be advanced by sub-contractors associated with unsuccessful bidders.[40]

1–011

E. Tort and Unjust Enrichment

The law of unjust enrichment is concerned with situations where one person has been unjustly enriched at the expense of another. The paradigm example of liability arising in this branch of the law is that to repay money which has been paid under a mistake of fact. Suppose that C mistakenly deposits £100 in D's bank account thinking that he was depositing the money in X's account. D is under a duty to return the money to C. The liability is distinct from liability in tort because the liability does not depend on any breach of duty. D does not owe C any duty not to accept money from C.[41]

1–012

F. Tort and Equitable Wrongs

Wrongs that are redressable in equity include breach of trust and breach of fiduciary duty. A breach of trust occurs, for example, where a trustee misapplies trust property. A breach of fiduciary duty is committed, for instance, where a solicitor who is acting for a client in respect of a commercial opportunity seizes that opportunity for himself. Liability for equitable wrongs can arise concurrently with liability in tort. Equitable wrongs are distinct, at least historically, from torts. In earlier times, equitable wrongs were actionable only in the chancery courts whereas proceedings in tort were commenced in the common law courts. However, the fact that equitable wrongs depend upon a breach of duty owed to the claimant has led some authors to argue that they should be regarded as torts.[42] This view is now arguably dominant among theorists, although it certainly does not command universal support. It has been argued, for example, that torts and

1–013

---

[40] See *Design Services Ltd v Canada* [2008] SCC 22; [2008] 1 S.C.R. 737.
[41] See Birks, "The Concept of a Civil Wrong" in Owen (ed.), *Philosophical Foundations of Tort Law* (1995).
[42] Birks, "The Concept of a Civil Wrong" in Owen (ed.), *Philosophical Foundations of Tort Law* (1995); Edelman (2002) 10 T.L.J. 64.

equitable wrongs are distinct on the ground that the former are concerned with the correction of losses whereas the latter are aimed at the diversion of wrongful gains.[43]

Perhaps the time is approaching to assimilate equitable wrongdoing with the law of tort but the force of history is powerful in English law and for the moment it is probably safer to say that the streams run in different channels even though the patterns they produce may have similarities. Even now, although law and equity have long been fused and questions relating to equitable wrongs may incidentally arise in tort cases, actions arising from equitable wrongs are allocated to the Chancery Division of the High Court. The distinctiveness of equity (at least at a theoretical level) has been affirmed in situations which might have been absorbed into the tort of negligence. Thus a mortgagee of property exercising a power of sale may have to take care to obtain a proper price and a receiver who carries on a debtor's business for the creditor may have to run it properly, but these duties are owed in equity and not in negligence on the basis of "neighbourhood".[44]

G. Tort and Bailment

1–014   A bailment involves one person taking custody of another person's goods. The person who delivers the goods is called a "bailor". The person to whom they are delivered is the "bailee". Common examples of bailment are hire of goods (such as hiring a car from a garage); gratuitous loan of goods (such as lending this book to a friend); and pawn or pledge. In very many cases, the delivery is on a condition, express or implied, that the goods shall be restored to the bailor as soon as the purpose for which they are bailed is completed, but it seems that this is not a necessary condition. For example, a standard hire-purchase agreement involves a bailment followed by an option to purchase and if the hire charges and option fee are paid the purpose of the exercise is that the bailee should become the owner. If the bailee misuses or damages the goods he is, of course, liable in a civil action to the bailor. Is this liability to be distinguished from liability in tort? Many bailments arise out of a contract, but it is undoubtedly possible for bailment to exist without a contract and where this is the case, as in the gratuitous loan of something for the use of the borrower, what is the nature of the liability? Winfield's opinion was that the bailee's liability is not tortious because, he said, the duty arises from a relation, that of bailor and bailee, which is created by the parties. No one need be a bailee if he does not wish to be one and no one can have

---

[43] Gardner (2012) 39 F. St. U.L. Rev. 43.

[44] *Downsview Nominees Ltd v First City Corp Ltd* [1993] A.C. 295; *Medforth v Blake* [2000] Ch. 86. But see the remark of Scott V.C. at [2000] Ch. 86 at 102: "I do not accept that there is any difference between the answer that would be given by the common law to the question what duties are owed by a receiver managing a mortgaged property to those interested in the equity of redemption and the answer that would be given by equity to that question. I do not, for my part, think it matters one jot whether the duty is expressed as a common law duty or as a duty in equity. The result is the same. The origin of the receiver's duty, like the mortgagee's duty, lies, however, in equity and we might as well continue to refer to it as a duty in equity." A liquidator or administrator owes no duty to individual creditors: *Hague v Nam Tai Electronics* [2008] UKPC 13; [2008] B.C.C. 295; *Kyrris v Oldham* [2003] EWCA Civ 1506; [2004] 1 B.C.L.C. 305.

liability for the safe custody of goods thrust upon him against his will.[45] It is certainly true that a person cannot be subjected to the duties of a bailee without his consent but as we have already seen, there are duties which are undoubtedly tortious and which can only exist if there has been some prior agreement between the parties, so it may be argued that there is no good reason for distinguishing the common law duties of a bailee from duties of this kind. Assumption of responsibility has been an important idea in the expansion of the modern law of negligence[46] but a little before this occurred it was said on high authority that the obligation of the bailee "arises because the taking of possession in the circumstances involves an assumption of responsibility for the safe keeping of the goods".[47] Furthermore, while it is a requirement of a bailment that the bailee voluntarily takes custody of the goods, it seems that it is not necessary that the bailor should consent to their custody.[48] If the bailor's claim is necessarily founded upon some specific provision in a contract, then, no doubt, the bailee's liability is not tortious but contractual; but if the bailor's claim rests upon a breach by the bailee of one of the bailee's common law duties, then might one not contend that his liability is as much attributable to the law of tort as is the claim of a visitor against the occupier of premises under the Occupiers' Liability Act 1957?[49] However, the Court of Appeal has held that a gratuitous bailment may create a legal obligation independent of that in tort, though on the facts there was also a parallel liability under that head.[50] Sometimes the legislature lays down rules by reference to the contract/tort distinction and no other. For example, the legislation on limitation of actions contains elaborate provisions on contract and tort but says nothing about bailment. The courts have nevertheless managed to accommodate bailment cases within this structure.[51] All this is typical of the common law's willingness to be pragmatic about "classification" and to admit parallel causes of action.

H. Tort and Crime

Crime and tort overlap. Many torts are also crimes, sometimes with the same names and with similar elements (for example, assault and battery) and sometimes a civil action in tort is deduced from the existence of a statute creating   **1–015**

---

[45] See para.18–017. Winfield's view is set out in full in *The Province of the Law of Tort*, 2nd edn (1968), Ch.5, where he makes the point that bailment is more fittingly regarded as a distinct branch of the law of property under the title "Possession" than as appropriate to either the law of contract or the law of tort.

[46] See para.5–049.

[47] *Gilchrist Watt & Sanderson Pty Ltd v York Products Pty Ltd* [1970] 1 W.L.R. 1262 at 1268.

[48] *KH Enterprise v Pioneer Container* [1994] 2 A.C. 324.

[49] *Turner v Stallibrass* [1898] 1 Q.B. 56 at 59; *Morris v C.W. Martin & Sons Ltd* [1966] 1 Q.B. 716; *Chesworth v Farrar* [1967] 1 Q.B. 407; *Gilchrist, Watt and Sanderson Pty Ltd v York Products Pty Ltd* [1970] 1 W.L.R. 1262.

[50] *Yearworth v North Bristol NHS Trust* [2009] EWCA Civ 37; [2009] 3 W.L.R. 118. Where the bailment involves specific undertakings by the bailee the measure of damages may be more akin to that in contract than tort: at [50].

[51] See, e.g. *Chesworth v Farrar* [1967] 1 Q.B. 407. See also *American Express Co v British Airways Board* [1983] 1 W.L.R. 701 (protection from action in tort under Post Office Act 1969 extended to bailment or the legislation would be ineffective).

a criminal offence.[52] The more serious, "traditional" criminal offences are likely to amount to torts[53] provided there is a victim.[54] There is no real difficulty in distinguishing criminal prosecutions from action in tort, if only because they are tried in different courts by different procedures. Generally, criminal proceedings are brought by the Crown Prosecution Service or some authorised body and although a private prosecution is still possible, the object of the proceedings in any case is the imposition of some sanction in the nature of punishment, for example, imprisonment or a pecuniary fine, even though the sanction imposed may have a reformative rather than a strictly punitive purpose. Nevertheless, there are functional overlaps between the two categories. At least some of tort law, like crime, has the purpose of deterrence and in a very limited class of cases tort imposes overt punishment upon defendants in the shape of exemplary damages.[55] On the other side, criminal proceedings may lead to a compensation order in favour of the victim. In this respect the distinction between crime and tort has become more blurred, though since tort originated in trespass, which to our eyes was in medieval times quasi-criminal, the law may only be returning to its roots. Furthermore, the compensatory sums awarded under these provisions are, until the court specifies their exact amount, quite uncertain and are therefore just as "unliquidated" as are damages in tort. There is, however, one peculiarity which marks them off from damages in tort. In every case they are obtainable only as a result of a process the primary purpose of which, when it is initiated, is the imposition of punishment, or something in the nature of punishment. In crime, the award of compensation is ancillary to the criminal process: in tort it is normally its very object.

It should also be borne in mind that criminal proceedings may act in an auxiliary role to a civil case. For example, a prosecution in respect of a traffic accident is likely to take place before any trial or settlement of a civil action arising from it and a conviction may be used as evidence of negligence in the civil action.

I.   A Law of Obligations?

1–016   The foregoing discussion has hopefully made it clear that it is not easy to separate tort law from certain other areas of the law, particularly the law of contract and that part of the law of equity that provides for wrongs. Would it not, therefore, be advantageous to bring the rules that provide for civil liability together in one book under some such title as "The Law of Obligations"? There is a great deal to be said for this and it will be essential where one aims at a study of a particular factual area of legal liability, such as product liability or professional negligence. However, the practicality of the exercise depends on the level of detail required. A general book on the law of obligations risks becoming unmanageably large. Furthermore, while there are undoubtedly points at which our legal categories interconnect and cross, and it is vital that the lawyer should grasp the implications

---

[52]   See Ch.8.
[53]   But not always, e.g. perjury: para.20–023.
[54]   There is no law of "attempted tort".
[55]   See para.23–012.

of this, there are also large areas where they travel alone. The law of tort is concerned with the incidence of liability.[56] Books on contract or on equity are, no doubt, concerned with the incidence of liability for loss or damage suffered, as are those on tort, but there, liability only forms a part, and sometimes a small part, of their subject-matter. Equally, if not more important, are such questions as the ways in which a contract may be concluded or a trust set up, the various modes of discharge or dissolution and the nature of the property rights these institutions may create. But the central question for the law of tort is always that of liability, and it is this which really forms the link between the various topics covered in this book. We are not here concerned with the creation of legal relationships or rights of property, though it may be necessary to mention them incidentally from time to time.

2. FOUNDATION OF TORTIOUS LIABILITY

Law of tort or law of torts? Winfield's definition of tortious liability has been criticised on the ground that it is formal, not material, and does nothing to indicate the lawfulness or otherwise of a given act. However, Winfield did devote several pages of early editions of this work to discussion of a familiar controversy concerning the foundation of tortious liability which has some bearing on the problem of a material definition. Salmond had asked:[57]

1–017

> "Does the law of torts consist of a fundamental general principle that it is wrongful to cause harm to other persons in the absence of some specific ground of justification or excuse, or does it consist of a number of specific rules prohibiting certain kinds of harmful activity, and leaving all the residue outside the sphere of legal responsibility?"

Put differently, the question is whether we have a law of tort, or a law of torts. Winfield chose the second alternative.[58] From the point of view of the practical lawyer concerned with the law at a particular moment there can be no doubt that the second view is the correct one: for example, a recording company was held to have no civil action in respect of "bootlegging" of its artists' performances where it was unable to prove any of the economic torts or the distinct tort of breach of statutory duty,[59] even though the defendants' conduct was criminal and no justification for it could be offered. Despite occasional judicial canvassing of the idea,[60] English law has not adopted what in the United States is known as the

---

[56] In this sense, tort most closely resembles crime.

[57] Salmond, *Law of Torts*, 2nd edn (1910), pp.8–9.

[58] To take two modern examples, in *Furniss v Fitchett* [1958] N.Z.L.R. 396 at 401, Barrowclough CJ said: "The well-known torts do not have their origin in any all-embracing principle of tortious liability." In *Bollinger v Costa Brava Wine Co Ltd* [1960] Ch. 262 at 283, Danckwerts J said: "The substance of [the argument for the defendants] was that, before a person can recover for loss which he suffered from another person's act, it must be shown that his case falls within the class of actionable wrongs. But the law may be thought to have failed if it can offer no remedy for the deliberate act of one person which causes damage to the property of another."

[59] *RCA Corp v Pollard* [1983] Ch. 135. See also *Dunlop v Woollahra MC* [1982] A.C. 158; *Lonrho Ltd v Shell Petroleum Co Ltd (No.2)* [1982] A.C. 173.

[60] For example, *The Mogul Steamship Co Ltd v McGregor Gow & Co* (1889) 23 Q.B.D. 598 at 663. The High Court of Australia's flirtation in *Beaudesert SC v Smith* (1966) 120 C.L.R. 145 with the

"prima facie tort theory" whereby "the intentional infliction of temporal damages is a cause of action, which, as a matter of substantive law, whatever may be the form of pleading, requires a justification if the defendant is to escape".[61] Nevertheless, it should be noted that we have for a good many years had something very close to a generalised principle of liability in situations where the defendant's purpose is the infliction of physical harm[62] on the claimant,[63] and despite the caution which characterises the courts' attitude to the duty of care in negligence[64] it will be an unusual case in which the defendant is not liable where his act has caused foreseeable physical damage to the claimant or his property.

1–018 **A general principle underpinning tortious liability?** Despite Winfield's embrace of the "law of torts" view as a practical, day-to-day matter,[65] he contended that from a broader outlook there was validity in the theory of a fundamental general principle of liability, for if we take the view, as we must, that the law of tort has grown for centuries, and is still growing, then some such principle seems to be at the back of it. It is the difference between treating a tree as inanimate for the practical purposes of the moment (for example, for the purpose of avoiding collision with it, it is as lifeless as a block of marble) and realising that it is animate because we know that it has grown and is still growing. The caution and slowness which usually mark the creation of new rules by the judges tend to mask the fact that they have been created, for they have often come into existence only by a series of analogical extensions spread over a long period of time. To vary the metaphor, the process has resembled the sluggish movement of the glacier rather than the catastrophic charge of the avalanche but when once a new tort has come into being, it might fairly seem to have done so, if the whole history of its development is taken into account, in virtue of the principle that unjustifiable harm is tortious.[66]

1–019 **An attempt to find some middle ground.** Since the supporters of the second view do not deny that the law of tort is capable of development, or even that new heads of liability can come into existence, and since the supporters of the first view admit that no action will lie if the conduct which caused the harm was justifiable, the difference between them is perhaps less than is sometimes supposed. Summing up his investigation into the controversy, Professor Glanville Williams said this:[67]

---

principle that independently of the "nominate" torts "a person who suffers harm or loss as the inevitable consequence of the unlawful, intentional and positive acts of another is entitled to recover damages from the other" no longer represents the law there: *Northern Territory of Australia v Mengel* (1995) 185 C.L.R. 307.

[61] *Aikens v State of Wisconsin* 195 U.S. 194 at 204 (1904) per Holmes J. But see Dobbs (1980) 34 Ark. L. Rev. 335.

[62] The American doctrine was primarily focused on interference with economic interests. We have had similar problems in attempting to generalise the economic torts.

[63] *Wilkinson v Downton* [1897] 2 Q.B. 57, see para.4–031.

[64] See para.5–020.

[65] For an entertaining perspective on the fissiparous nature of the common law of torts, see Rudden (1991–92) 6/7 *Tulane Civil Law Forum* 105.

[66] Damage for which compensation is not recoverable is known as *damnum sine injuria*; where a tort is actionable per se (without proof of loss, e.g. trespass) there is said to be *injuria sine damno*.

[67] Williams (1939) 7 C.L.J. 131.

"The first school has shown that the rules of liability are very wide. The second school has shown that some rules of absence of liability are also very wide. Neither school has shown that there is any general rule, whether of liability or of non-liability, to cover novel cases that have not yet received the attention of the Courts. In a case of first impression—that is, a case that falls under no established rule or that falls equally under two conflicting rules—there is no ultimate principle directing the Court to find for one party or the other . . . Why should we not settle the argument by saying simply that there are some general rules creating liability . . . and some equally general rules exempting from liability . . . Between the two is a stretch of disputed territory, with the Courts as an unbiased boundary commission. If, in an unprovided case, the decision passes for the claimant, it will be not because of a general theory of liability but because the court feels that here is a case in which existing principles of liability may properly be extended."

3. Tort and Other Sources of Compensation

As will be seen, much of the law of tort in practice is concerned with the problem of accidental injury to the person or damage to property, and the general approach of the law to these problems rests on two broad principles. Both are subject to many exceptions and qualifications but by and large it is the case (1) that the victim of accidental injury or damage is entitled to redress through the law of tort if, and only if, his loss was caused by the fault of the defendant or those for whose fault the defendant must answer, and (2) that the redress due from the defendant whose liability is established should be "full" or should, in other words, be as nearly equivalent as money can be to the claimant's loss. Nevertheless, even in those accidents which can be attributed to another's fault, the role played by the law of tort should not be exaggerated. A century or so ago the law of tort was probably the primary vehicle of compensation, but poverty, ignorance or economic pressure deprived many injured persons of access to the law and threw them back on the Poor Law, charity or the assistance of a trade union or friendly society. In more recent times the development of insurance and social security has tended to relegate tort law to a more secondary role. We must, therefore, turn to look at some of these other sources of compensation and their relationship with the law of tort and in doing so consider further some of the assumptions which underpin the tort system.

1–020

A. Damage to Property: Tort and Insurance

Types of insurance. There is little in the way of state provision for loss or damage to property,[68] which obviously occupies a much lower position of priority than personal injury.[69] Private insurance is, however, of very great significance in relation to property damage. Insurance takes two basic forms: "loss" or "first party" insurance and "liability" or "third party" insurance. Under the first, the

1–021

---

[68] However, the Riot (Damages) Act 1886 makes the police authority liable for property damage caused by a riot within its area, presumably on the basis that it has failed to uphold order. The Act can be relied on by a company carrying out public functions on a "contracted out" basis: *Yarl's Wood Immigration Ltd v Bedfordshire Police Authority* [2009] EWCA Civ 1110; [2010] Q.B. 698.

[69] In an emergency such as flood or fire the social security authorities would assist with clothing, bedding and other immediate needs. Provision may sometimes be made on an ad hoc basis for widespread disasters. For various mechanisms, see Faure and Hartlief, *Financial Compensation for Victims of Catastrophies* (2006).

owner of property has cover against loss or damage to specified property from the risks described in the policy, such as fire, flood and theft, whether or not the loss occurs through the fault of any other person.[70] Under the second, the insured himself is covered against legal liability which he may incur to a third party, and the establishment of such liability by the third party, not merely loss suffered by the third party, is an essential prerequisite to a claim on the policy. A good example of a policy combining both types of cover is a motor "comprehensive" policy,[71] which will: (a) cover the insured against legal liability to other road users and passengers; and (b) entitle the insured to claim from his insurer the cost of repairs should his vehicle be damaged or the value of the vehicle if it becomes a "write-off".[72]

1–022   **Subrogation.** Loss insurance is of very great significance in relation to damage to property. A fundamental principle of the law on loss insurance is that it is irrelevant to tort liability.[73] If D damages C's property and this is fully covered by an insurance policy, that in no way precludes C suing D for the cost of repairing the property.[74] Indeed, even if C has collected on his insurance that would not provide D with a defence.[75] In fact, it is inconceivable that C would sue in the latter case because, property loss policies generally being contracts of indemnity, he would then have to reimburse the insurer with the damages recovered. A more likely outcome is that the insurer will exercise his right to be subrogated to C's rights against D, and sue D (in reality probably D's liability insurers) in C's name.[76]

The opportunities for an effective exercise of the insurer's rights of subrogation may vary considerably from one type of case to another. In marine cases the right is probably commonly exercised because the size of the individual claim makes it worthwhile to do so; in home and contents insurance subrogation is probably almost nonexistent since if the loss is anyone's fault it is likely to be the householder's (against whom it cannot be exercised) or that of persons, like burglars, who will not be worth pursuing. In the case of road accidents, repairing or replacing vehicles probably represents insurers' largest single cost. For many

---

[70] Indeed, the insured could normally claim on the policy even if the property was damaged through his own negligence (but not his own deliberate act) though the policy may restrict cover in certain circumstances, for example, where the key is left in the car and it is then stolen.

[71] The majority of motor policies are comprehensive, though all that is required by law is cover against liability for personal injuries and, from 1989, property damage to third parties. A standard householder's policy will also combine both loss and liability insurance.

[72] The fact that the accident is the insured's own fault will not prevent a claim under (b), though there will normally be conditions as to the use of the vehicle and its maintenance in a roadworthy condition, breach of which will entitle the insurer to repudiate liability. In no circumstances can the insured claim under (a) in respect of his own injuries, though many policies contain a limited element of "no-fault" loss insurance for injury to driver and passengers.

[73] See para.23–121. And in relation to "collateral benefits" in personal injury cases (a similar issue), see para.23–085.

[74] Informal settlements of minor motor claims without calling on the insurance are probably quite common because of the concern of both parties to maintain their no claims bonuses.

[75] *Bee v Jenson* [2007] EWCA Civ 923; [2007] 4 All E.R. 791 (hire charges). But it might have an impact on costs: *Hobbs v Marlowe* [1978] A.C. 16.

[76] See *Castellain v Preston* (1883) 11 Q.B.D. 380; *Caledonia North Sea Ltd v British Telecommunications Plc* [2002] UKHL 4; [2002] S.C. (H.L.) 117 (a case of subrogation of a liability insurer).

years nearly all motor insurers operated a "knock for knock" agreement, so that if there was a collision between car A, comprehensively insured by Company X, and car B, insured by Company Y, and the accident was caused by the fault of car A and led to damage to both vehicles, each insurer would bear its own loss in respect of the vehicle it insured and would not pursue subrogation rights against the other in that other's capacity as liability insurer. There has been no such general agreement since 1994, though that does not mean that subrogation rights will be regularly pursued.

It can be argued that to allow a tort claim in respect of property damage when loss insurance is widely held or easily available is wasteful and that this is compounded by subrogation litigation, which only shifts money around the system from one insurer to another. On the other hand, it would require a pretty major change in our intuitive ideas of justice to take away C's right to claim against D when D's fault has damaged C's property, and there would still remain the problem of uninsured losses, whether by total absence of cover,[77] inadequate cover or "excess" thresholds.[78] If, as is likely, the subrogation system is of limited application in smaller cases, it may be thought that the continued operation of tort law in large claims is not a serious social problem.

Impact of insurance and insurability. No one has yet gone so far as to hold that the fact that the claimant is insured is in itself enough to defeat his claim but the presence (or likely presence) of loss insurance has sometimes, rightly or wrongly, been used in combination with other factors to reach that conclusion.[79] We may note, on the other side of the equation, that the fact that D has (or is likely to have) liability cover is equally not generally thought to be a good reason for making him liable but that, too, has sometimes been a strong influence in favour of liability.[80]   1–023

B.   Personal Injuries and Death

The Royal Commission under Lord Pearson[81] reported in 1978, that tort law accounted for no more than one-quarter of the total amount of money which was then paid in respect of compensation for personal injury. There is no reason to believe that tort has advanced from the second rank in the intervening years. Private insurance plays a role here, too, but the major player is social security. However, what is true of the whole system is not necessarily true of part of it. For   1–024

---

[77] Compulsion to insure one's property could hardly be justified.

[78] In motor cases the loss of no claims bonus is also a significant factor.

[79] See, e.g. Lord Denning MR in *Lamb v Camden LBC* [1981] Q.B. 625 at 637–638, though his Lordship was probably wrong on the facts to assume that there was cover. In *Norwich CC v Harvey* [1989] 1 W.L.R. 828 the fact that D was in a chain of building contracts, one of which, between C and X, required C to maintain insurance on the works, was held to be a good reason for holding D not liable to C.

[80] Again, most notably, Lord Denning MR in *Nettleship v Weston* [1971] 2 Q.B. 691, see para.6–009. In German law a person who is immune from liability because of mental disorder may nevertheless be ordered to pay compensation if he has sufficient assets: BGB §829. This includes having compulsory liability insurance.

[81] Royal Commission, *Royal Commission on Civil Liability and Compensation for Personal Injury* (1978), Cmnd.7054.

example, tort damages play a very small role with regard to accidents in the home (one of the largest categories) simply because there is rarely anyone on whom to pin liability; on the other hand, quite a high proportion of road accident victims recover under the tort system (such accidents are rarely no one's fault[82] and insurance is compulsory).

C.   Private Insurance, Occupational Pensions, etc.

1–025   Three main types of insurance give protection against death or injury regardless of whether the death or injury was caused by fault: life insurance, personal accident insurance and permanent health insurance. The first is without doubt the most important: personal accident and permanent health insurance are a good deal less common, the Pearson Commission's personal injury survey finding that such cover contributed only about 6 per cent to accident compensation. Probably the main source of short-term income replacement is employers' occupational sick pay schemes. Individual schemes vary in detail but replace all or part of lost income for a maximum period which may be related to length of service but which rarely exceeds six months. In cases of death or long-term injury leading to premature retirement a payment may be made under an occupational pension scheme. The chance of receipt of any one or more of the above benefits is heavily influenced by the social class of the victim and the nature of his employment, but it will readily be appreciated that some accident victims or their dependants stand to get very large sums from such sources and it may be asked to what extent such receipts are taken into account in assessing tort damages for loss of earnings.[83] The question is complex and will be considered in more detail later,[84] but the broad answer is that the courts will ignore all charitable and comparable payments, all proceeds of private insurance and all occupational pension scheme payments but will make a deduction in respect of sick pay. Quite apart, therefore, from social security benefits, there is a strong possibility that some accident victims who are successful in a tort claim will receive more than they have lost in income.

D.   Social Security

1–026   The social security system is highly complex and it would be impossible to summarise it satisfactorily here. It is not even easy to define what "the system" is. The Criminal Injuries Compensation Scheme, for example, is a major provider of state assistance to a group of victims of misfortune, but it has not, since its inception, been within the legal framework of benefits nor has it been administered by the Department of Work and Pensions. With respect to benefits

---

[82] It may of course be entirely the victim's fault, which bars any claim.

[83] The question usually arises in this way because the payment of such benefits nearly always precedes the recovery of tort damages. If the issue arose of whether tort damages were to be taken into account in assessing payments under the insurance policy or the pension scheme, everything would depend upon the construction of the contract. Tort damages, however, would almost invariably have no effect on payments of life or personal accident policies.

[84] See para.23–085.

usually regarded as being in this category we still have to draw a distinction between industrial and non-industrial injuries.

i. Non-industrial Injuries

Some benefits (for example, income support and housing benefit) are simply based on the fact that the recipient's means are below bare subsistence level and they have no connection with injury—though an accident victim may receive them if the conditions are satisfied. Otherwise, non-industrial injury cases are dealt with in the same way as sickness and the primary short-term benefit is in fact now paid by employers in the form of "statutory sick pay" for up to 28 weeks. When the statutory sick pay entitlement has been exhausted it is replaced by employment and support allowance. In addition, a claimant who needs constant care or assistance or is unable to walk may receive disability living allowance or attendance allowance.[85]

1–027

ii. Industrial Injuries

The Workmen's Compensation Act 1897 introduced into English law the first important type of accident compensation not based on the law of tort. Under that Act, workers injured in various types of employment could recover compensation for personal injury "arising out of and in the course of employment". Unlike the modern system of industrial injury benefits, however, this compensation was payable by the employer and was recoverable by action in the courts. With the implementation of the Beveridge Report's recommendations[86] the Workmen's Compensation Scheme was abolished and replaced by a system of benefits payable by the state for such accidents and diseases.[87] The Industrial Injuries Scheme now covers industrial injuries (including certain prescribed diseases) and provides for payment of "disablement benefit" to the injured worker. The basic condition of award is that the injury was caused by an accident "arising out of and in the course of employment". Injuries with short-term effects are excluded by the rule that disablement benefit is not payable for the first 15 weeks after the accident. It is most important to note that disablement benefit is not necessarily looked upon as a method of replacement of lost earnings but is based upon an objective assessment of disablement, fixed on a percentage basis either by regulations or by a medical board. For example, the regulations provide that loss of sight of one eye amounts to a 30 per cent disablement so that the victim receives proportionate benefit even though his earnings may not be affected at all. The system employs thresholds, which has the effect of making tort claims more important in smaller cases. Disablement benefit takes the form of a pension. Payments in respect of industrial injuries are higher than in the case of other

1–028

---

[85] In a very serious case, the sums involved can be very large. In *Freeman v Lockett* [2006] EWHC 102 (QB); [2006] P.I.Q.R. P340 the claimant was receiving over £50,000 a year in respect of domiciliary care.
[86] Beveridge Report (1942), Cmd.6404.
[87] National Insurance (Industrial Injuries) Act 1946. There may of course be further provision in particular employments, e.g. the Police (Injury Benefit) Regulations 2006 (SI 2006/932).

accidents, and in some cases payments may be made even though there is no interruption of employment and earnings are unaffected.

E. Recovery of Social Security Payments

1–029 The question of offsetting social security payments against damages where a tort claim succeeds is governed by statute and is dealt with later.[88] Briefly, in the case of personal injuries social security payments paid in the initial five-year period after the accident are deducted by the defendant, who must reimburse the Secretary of State. In this context the reader should also remember the reimbursement extends to the cost of providing medical services. The cost attributable for the National Health Service and the personal social services to accidental death, injury and industrial disease is probably considerably more than the social security payments made in respect of such losses. Subrogation or reimbursement of healthcare providers has long been found in several other legal systems and there was, for a long while, a limited right of recourse by the health service in road accident cases—this has now been extended more widely.[89]

4. PAYING FOR THE TORT SYSTEM

1–030 **Who pays damages?** Who pays for the damages awards (and settlement monies in the case of claims that are not litigated)? In the case of personal injuries, the great majority of claims are brought against defendants who are insured against liability. This means that the bill for damages awards is met by the premium paying population. In other words, the tort system is financed by the public. Because they are insured, wrongdoers almost never pay. These basic facts about the cost of the tort system have profound implications in relation to its rationales, as will be seen later.[90]

1–031 **Conditional fee agreements.** As observed in the previous paragraph, it is the public that foots the bill for damages awards. However, who pays for legal costs and disbursements incurred in pursuing a claim? A full answer to this question would be very lengthy, and it is impractical to go into the details here. What follows is a highly compact description of the relevant law and practice. Typically, claimants seeking compensation for personal injuries enter into a "conditional fee agreement" (CFA) with their lawyer, pursuant to which the lawyer agrees to charge the claimant for the cost of the legal services and disbursements in the event that the claim is successful (success is defined as obtaining damages in any amount, however small).[91] CFAs are also known as "no win no fee" agreements. In return for taking the risk that he will not be paid, the lawyer is entitled to a success fee if the claimant succeeds. The maximum success fee that can be charged depends on the type of proceedings and the stage of the litigation at which the case is at.

---

[88] See para.23–091.
[89] See para.23–091.
[90] See paras 1–036, 1–038.
[91] Courts and Legal Services Act 1990 s.58.

Damages-based agreements. Provision has recently been made for claimants to enter into damages-based agreements (DBAs) with their lawyers.[92] DBAs are also no-win-no-fee agreements, so that the lawyer carries the cost of pursuing the claim. However, instead of a taking their normal hourly fee plus a success fee if the case is won, which is what occurs where a CFA is used, under a DBA the lawyer will charge the claimant a proportion of the damages up to a maximum of 25 per cent.[93] DBAs are sometimes referred to as "contingency fee agreements". They are likely to be offered by lawyers only in high value claims.

1–032

Costs shifting. If the claim is successful, the defendant (or, more often, the defendant's insurer) is liable to pay the claimant's costs. An important qualification to this rule is that the success fee under a CFA is not recoverable as costs.[94] If the claim is unsuccessful, the claimant's lawyer, whether he is acting on a CFA or a DBA, charges the claimant nothing. Generally speaking, claimants are not required to pay the defendant's costs if the claim is unsuccessful. Thus, the cost shifting rule works only in one direction (it is known as "one-way costs shifting"). Where, exceptionally, claimants are required to pay the defendant's costs, their costs liability only extends to the value of any orders for damages made in favour of the claimant.[95] To guard against the risk of having to pay the defendant's costs in the event that the claim is unsuccessful claimants may take out an insurance policy to cover this risk. This premium, which is normally paid after the claim has been concluded, is not recoverable as costs.[96]

1–033

5.   CRITICISMS OF THE TORT SYSTEM IN THE CONTEXT OF PERSONAL INJURIES

A.   The "Fault Principle"

Though overall the law of tort is by no means the most important vehicle for accident compensation, an accident victim who can make out a tort claim stands to recover very substantially more than one who cannot, partly because of the rules about deductibility of other compensation payments from tort damages and partly because tort damages, unlike social security payments, are subject to no financial limits and take into account matters like pain and suffering, loss of amenity, loss of promotion prospects and extra expenses incurred as a result of the injury. The claimant in a tort action must generally show that his injuries were caused by the defendant's fault. This rule is known as the "fault principle". What justification is there for the fault principle, and what objections lie in respect of it?

1–034

---

[92] Courts and Legal Services Act 1990 s.58AA; Damages-Based Agreements Regulations 2013.

[93] Damages-Based Agreements Regulations 2013 cl.4(2).

[94] Courts and Legal Services Act 1990 s.58(6).

[95] CPR Pt 44.14(1).

[96] Courts and Legal Services Act 1990 s.58C.

B. Tort and Deterrence

1–035 **How precise is the guidance given by tort law?** The principle that a person should be called upon to pay for damage caused by his fault may be thought to have an affinity with the criminal law (which the law of tort as a whole certainly did have much earlier in its history) in the sense that one of its purposes is to deter harmful conduct. It is certainly true that at least some parts of the law dealing with premeditated conduct serve this purpose. It is, however, more controversial how far there is any effective deterrent force in those parts of the law relating to accidental injury, where liability is based upon negligence. There are two main reason for this. First, a generalised instruction to people to take care, which is all that the law gives, is arguably of little practical use in guiding their behaviour in a given situation. Certain driving practices, for example driving at 60mph down a crowded shopping street, could be recognised as negligent by ordinary people without any judicial assistance, but the majority of cases do not present such clear-cut issues and the number of variable factors is so great that each case will turn on its own facts. The force of this criticism probably depends on the context. It is particularly strong in the case of road accidents, where the activity is, in the case of an experienced driver, largely instinctive and where a momentary lapse of attention can lead to catastrophic results with few realistic possibilities of taking other precautions to minimise or avoid the risk.[97] Where, however, the accident arises from an alleged defect in a system of work or the organisation of a business, it is possible that a tort judgment may play a part in exposing the risk and leading others to take measures to prevent recurrence, whether voluntarily or at the insistence of their insurers.

1–036 **The impact of insurance.** The second reason why the deterrence argument is of limited force relates to the sources from which damages are in fact paid. If it were the case that tort damages were paid out of the tortfeasor's own resources it could hardly be denied that the threat of legal liability would deter,[98] but in practice damages are, far more often than not, paid by an insurer[99] rather than by the tortfeasor himself,[100] which undoubtedly blunts the deterrent edge. Liability insurance is now actually compulsory so far as concerns road accidents affecting

---

[97] Several surveys have found a correlation between the introduction of "no fault" motor schemes and increased accident rates: Landes (1982) 25 J.L. & Econ. 49; McEwin (1989) 9 Intl. Rev. L. & Econ. 13; Sloan (1994) 14 Intl. Rev. L. & Econ. 53. However, the figures may be affected by factors unrelated to tort liability, e.g. guarantees of compensation to drivers (thereby reducing the self-preservation deterrent), changes in traffic laws, reporting or car use patterns.

[98] "If it were not for insurance, the common law would operate with intolerable harshness in its application to driving": *Imbree v McNeilly* [2008] HCA 40; (2008) 236 C.L.R. 510 at [23] per Gleeson CJ. Damages may be much larger than any fine likely to be imposed by a criminal court for comparable conduct.

[99] The general position is that the claim is against the insured tortfeasor in person, though of course in practice his insurer will handle the claim. However, in the case of motor claims there is, without prejudice to the claim against the tortfeasor, a direct right of action against the insurer: European Communities (Rights Against Insurers) Regulations (SI 2002/3061), implementing Directive 2000/26.

[100] See Lewis [2005] J.P.I.L. 1. However, some large organisations, public and private, act as self-insurers. The National Health Service Litigation Authority administers a risk-pooling scheme for NHS Trusts.

third parties[101] and most work accidents[102] and to meet the problem of the uninsured driver[103] there is an agreement under which the Motor Insurers' Bureau (i.e. the road traffic insurers acting collectively) satisfies claims.[104] Of course, the presence of insurance does not necessarily altogether take away the deterrent effect, for the premium may be related not only to the general risk presented by the activity or the actor (the nature of the employer's trade or the age of the driver) but the record of the particular insured. However, the setting of insurance premiums may depend on many factors and while, say, motor premiums are quite strongly "experience-related",[105] this appears to be less so in relation to employers' liability. Where the defendant is in the business of supplying goods or services to the public, the cost of obtaining insurance cover (or of paying damages if he carries his own risk) will be reflected in the price charged to the public or in a reduced profit margin so that those who actually pay it are either the consumers or the shareholders or both. Nevertheless, the overall cost of the harmful conduct is still (in theory) reduced because if others can provide similar goods and services without this additional cost they will gain an increased share of the market.

Deterrence is not only produced of course by the threat of direct imposition of a financial penalty. It is perfectly possible that a person may be induced to take greater care by, among other things, the harm to his reputation which may be caused by a successful tort suit against him.[106] Again, this effect would probably only be produced in certain fields of liability such as professional negligence, injuries caused by defective products and work injuries. While experience shows that a powerful force of public opinion can be mobilised against a drug company which was alleged to have produced a drug which had injured children, it is very unlikely that people would take much interest in a road accident caused by one of its delivery vans. In any event, a large corporate defendant which has the wherewithal is capable of avoiding much adverse publicity by an out-of-court settlement (the details of which will be confidential), and the speed with which substantial compensation has been offered in the wake of some mass disasters

---

[101] Road Traffic Act 1988 s.143, replacing earlier legislation and, from the end of 1988, extended to cover property damage as well as personal injury. Cover must be unlimited in respect of personal injury but is generally only up to £20 million in respect of property damage.

[102] Employers' Liability (Compulsory Insurance) Act 1969 s.1.

[103] i.e. where there is no policy at all. Where there is a policy and the car is driven by a person not entitled to drive it (even if he has unlawfully taken the car) the insurer must pay: see, e.g. *Miller v Hales* [2006] EWHC 1529 (QB); [2007] Lloyd's Rep. I.R. 54.

[104] There is a supplementary agreement covering claims by untraced drivers. The agreements are not strictly enforceable by the claimant, but the Bureau will never take the point. The Bureau may require the claimant to pursue any claims at law that he may have or to assign claims to it, but the existence of the Bureau means that we are far less likely than some countries to have tort claims against third parties who are in some way involved in the events leading up to an accident with an uninsured driver (see, e.g. *Childs v Desormeaux* [2006] SCC 18; [2006] 1 S.C.R. 643). By virtue of Directive 84/5 the agreements must provide protection equivalent to that which would be available against an insured and identified driver: *Byrne v MIB* [2008] EWCA Civ 574; [2009] Q.B. 66 (shorter time limit under untraced drivers' agreement).

[105] But the greater part of motor insurance premiums go to pay for property damage, which, in the case of damage to the insured's own car, has nothing to do with tort.

[106] See Linden (1973) 51 Can. Bar Rev. 155.

suggests that in practice the victim's chances of recovery are in direct proportion to the scale of the accident and, hence, the amount of public attention it receives.

1–037   **Conclusions.** We may conclude, therefore, that the prospect of tort liability will have some influence on conduct but that this influence is variable and limited. Even if it had a greater deterrent effect it would not necessarily justify a fault-based system, for strict liability would, presumably, have just as great an effect. Professor Gary Schwartz, after a survey of the empirical evidence in the United States, concluded that: "[T]he information suggests that the strong form of the deterrence argument is in error. Yet it provides support for that argument in its moderate form: sector-by-sector tort law provides something significant by way of deterrence."[107]

Our ambivalence on this surfaces in judicial decisions here. Thus Staughton LJ said in 1994 that:[108]

> "One advantage that is claimed for imposing a duty of care is that it encourages people not to be negligent. I very much doubt if that is the case. The great expansion of tortious liability over the last hundred and fifty years has had the remarkable feature that the direct financial consequences almost invariably fall on someone whose purse is assumed to be bottomless, such as an insurance company or a large commercial concern or an organ of central or local government."

However, in the same case Sir Thomas Bingham MR said that he could not "accept, as a general proposition, that the imposition of a duty of care makes no contribution to the maintenance of high standards. The common belief that the imposition of such a duty may lead to overkill[109] is not easily reconciled with the suggestion that it has no effect".[110]

C.   Tort and Responsibility

1–038   **Calling wrongdoers to account.** Another argument in favour of a tort system based on fault (or at least of a tort system, as opposed to other mechanisms of compensation) is still more difficult to assess but cannot be dismissed out of hand on that basis. It is that the notion of responsibility is a powerful, intuitive factor in people's attitudes to accidents and that there is a deep-seated idea that those who have caused damage to others should pay:[111] "corrective justice" requires that those who have caused harm to others should correct what they have done and in practice, in most cases, the payment of money is the only practical correction available. This argument is not necessarily rebutted by the fact that the money may come from an insurer; indeed, since few awards of damages would otherwise be paid, it might be regarded as buttressing it. Of course there is no logical reason why such a duty to correct harm should arise only where the

---

[107] Schwartz (1994) 42 U.C.L.A. Law Rev. 377. He is speaking in a context in which the predominant requirement is "fault" but with a major enclave of strict product liability.

[108] *M v Newham LBC* [1994] 4 All E.R. 602 at 631 (on appeal sub nom. *X v Bedfordshire CC* [1995] 2 A.C. 633, see para.5–072).

[109] For example, "defensive medicine".

[110] *M* [1994] 4 All E.R. 602 at 619.

[111] For exploration of this idea see Goudkamp (2004) 28 M.U.L.R. 343.

defendant is at fault (though it seems inevitable that there should be a minimum requirement that he has caused the harm). However, even if it is only the product of a long-standing system dominated by fault, one may confidently say that the call for the duty to correct harm is stronger where there is fault.

One objection to the foregoing is that the tort system is a crude mechanism for apportioning blame. For example, it ignores massive disproportions that can occur between the defendant's negligence and the consequences for which he is obliged to pay. Suppose two drivers career off the motorway on to a railway track below and cause a train wreck in which there are dozens of casualties. The first has had no sleep the night before and knows full well that he is unfit to drive; the second merely commits a momentary piece of inattention. As far as tort law is concerned the outcome of both cases is the same: the driver (in reality his insurer) pays all the resulting damages in full. The example can be extended. Suppose that the first driver's car slides off the railway track with the result being that the train wreck does not occur. He will incur no liability whatsoever despite the fact that he is more culpable than the second driver.

Other ways of holding wrongdoers responsible. There may be more effective and efficient means of requiring wrongdoers to account for what they did. The most obvious is the criminal law. The criminal law's response to negligently caused harm is more partial than that of the civil law: there are fairly comprehensive sanctions on careless conduct on the road and (as far as employers are concerned) at work, but there are other areas of activity (medical treatment, for example) where the criminal law only operates if the fault is very bad and death ensues. A surgeon who kills his patient by gross negligence commits manslaughter; one who by the same means renders him quadriplegic commits no offence at all. That, of course, is not the whole story, for the surgeon is exposed to disciplinary proceedings, and since the outcome of these may be exclusion from the profession (whereas any tort damages will be paid by the hospital trust or insurer) they are a far more effective sanction. Again, however, the system operates in a random way: there is no equivalent of the General Medical Council for plumbers or electricians. In other cases, where there is a major disaster, there will commonly be a public inquiry and that may "point the finger" more effectively than a civil suit. Certainly it will avoid the underlying flaw in the argument that the "day in court" in a civil suit ensures accountability—the simple fact of an out-of-court settlement will avoid that.

1–039

D. Expense and Inefficiency

The cost of administering the tort system. The tort system based upon fault is undoubtedly expensive to administer when compared with, say, social security, and this might be thought to be a serious defect in it. The Pearson Commission estimated that in personal injury claims the cost of operation was about 85 per cent of the value of compensation paid through the tort system, whereas the corresponding figure for social security was about 11 per cent.[112] Up-to-date,

1–040

---

[112] The figures, however, favour social security because they conceal the fact that the cost of collection of contributions falls outside the account, i.e. on employers. The estimate by the Civil

across the board figures are hard to come by and there is of course likely to be a substantial difference between a claim which settles early and one which goes to trial. The relative cost of the system as a whole has probably increased substantially in the last 10 or 15 years, probably because of the new methods of funding claims which have been outlined above.[113] Most claims are for comparatively small amounts of money and then even fairly minimal legal input will loom quite large in the equation; the amount of costs incurred in a settled motor claim for £2,000 is likely to be proportionately a good deal more than in one for £200,000. Claimants' costs tend to be higher than defendants', which is hardly surprising since the claimant has to make the running, but where the claim is successful (and most claims which get to the stage of proceedings being issued are) these have to be borne by the defendant. In considering these points, however, one must bear in mind that in a very large number of cases liability will not be contested at all and the cost will be generated by, for example, the issue of the quantum of damages, which would also arise if the law imposed liability without fault. So to some extent, therefore, the criticism on efficiency grounds is directed not so much at the fault system as at the *tort* system.

1–041 **Delays in the tort system.** Secondly, there is the problem of delay. The Pearson Commission concluded that delay was:

> ". . . the most important reason for dissatisfaction with the legal system . . . delay is sometimes justifiable but it can often aggravate pressure on the claimant to settle prematurely, and can be a source of worry and distress. Nor is it necessarily in the interests of the defendant. The problem of delay is also linked with the medical condition sometimes known as 'compensation neurosis'."

There has recently been a major shift of personal injury cases to the County Court (where proceedings for all lower-value claims must now be started) and the Civil Procedure Rules 1998 have led to a fundamental change in responsibility for the handling of civil litigation from the parties to the courts, based on an interventionist judicial role in case management. There is some evidence that this can actually increase costs by leading to steps being taken earlier, and therefore sometimes unnecessarily ("front-loading"), than would have been the case in the past, though it has been concluded that in a personal injury context the benefits of the changes in promoting settlement outweigh this factor. In any event, there is not a great deal that procedural reform can do about delay prior to the issue of proceedings, although some steps have been taken to address this situation by the introduction in the Civil Procedure Rules of "Pre-Action Protocols", which the parties are expected to follow prior to proceedings being commenced. The fault principle is probably responsible for causing some of the delay, since where fault is contested the parties will often undertake significant investigations into the circumstances that led to the claimant being injured.

Justice Review (Cm. 394, 1988) was that the cost of the tort system was between 50 and 70 per cent of personal injury damages awarded. According to the Association of British Insurers (*Delivering a Fair and Efficient Compensation System*, 2005) claimants' costs (which are usually higher than defendants') average 38 per cent of sums recovered in motor vehicle accident claims.

[113] See paras 1–031—1–032.

Unpredictability of outcomes. Thirdly, the unpredictability of the outcomes of claims caused by the fault principle (where the defendant denies fault, it may be hard for the claimant to predict whether the claim will succeed) may put claimants under pressure to settle their claims for amounts that are significantly less than they would receive if their claim went successfully to trial. The vast majority of personal injury claims are settled without trial, most of them without proceedings even being commenced. It is true that of claimants who make a claim most will receive some payment but many of those payments will be for substantially less than would be awarded if the matter went to trial. Since there is always some risk that the claimant's claim will founder in whole or in part at the trial, the defendant's insurers are in a position to exploit this factor by making a discount in the amount they offer in settlement.[114] This element of risk, leading to pressure to settle, is of course present in virtually all litigation but it is peculiarly powerful in the case of personal injuries because a very large part of the claimant's future wealth may be at stake. The problem is exacerbated—though the matter may be of more direct concern to the claimant's lawyers than to him—by the fact that even if the claimant wins at the trial on liability there may be a large element of irrecoverable costs if the defendant's insurers have made an accurately-calculated Part 36 offer of settlement.[115] On the other hand, a claimant may make a Pt 36 settlement offer, with penal consequences to the defendant on interest and costs if a higher award is made at trial. The claimant is also entitled to an uplift of 10 per cent in his damages (up to a maximum of £75,000).[116]

1–042

6. ALTERNATIVES

These criticisms do not complete the tally of objections to the law of tort so far as it concerns personal injury accidents, but similar problems have been encountered in other jurisdictions and there has been a widespread debate about alternative solutions. Any reform of the law governing compensation for personal injuries might adopt one of two basic solutions—an extension of strict liability (i.e. liability imposed regardless of fault), which would retain the law of tort though in a different form; and the "insurance" technique (whether private or public), which would mean the abolition or bypassing of the law of tort in whole or in part.

1–043

A. Strict Liability

Despite the continuing dominance of fault liability, the English law of tort contains certain limited principles of strict liability with regard to personal injuries. Some of these are of common law origin and of respectable antiquity, while others have been the creation of modern statutes and have either been

1–044

---

[114] See Genn, *Hard Bargaining* (1987); Phillips and Hawkins (1976) 39 M.L.R. 497.

[115] Under CPR Pt 36 the defendant may offer a sum in satisfaction of the claim. If the claimant does not accept it and the action goes to trial, the claimant bears the costs of the action from the date of the offer if his award does not exceed it.

[116] CPR Pt 36.14(3)(d). This 10 per cent uplift applies where the damages recovered are up to £500,000. The uplift is reduced to 5 per cent to the extent that damages exceed this figure.

limited in their practical importance[117] or of rather haphazard application.[118] It is unlikely that any consistent policy has been followed in the creation of these areas of strict liability, though it is perhaps possible to discern behind some of them a very hazy idea of unusual or increased risk. However, the strictness of the liability varies considerably along a spectrum from near absolute liability to little more than a reversed burden of proof, and in nearly every case the defendant may plead the contributory fault of the claimant as a defence. While there may be some merit in a system of strict liability for unusual risks it can hardly make much contribution to the accident compensation problem as a whole when common risks are left to the law of negligence. As a result of an EEC initiative one such risk has been brought into the strict liability fold, namely losses caused by defective products, though the liability is by no means absolute.[119]

Of course, a statutory strict liability is confined to cases where its specified conditions are fulfilled and may be narrower in scope than an equivalent general fault liability. Thus the Montreal Convention makes an air carrier liable without fault for bodily injury suffered by a passenger caused by accident.[120] "Bodily injury" does not, in this context, include psychiatric trauma[121] and an "accident" requires some unexpected event external to the passenger (deep vein thrombosis caused by cramped but normal seating is not an accident in this sense, nor is a fall by a passenger when the aircraft is in its normal state).[122] Nor, in this context (though not necessarily in others), can the claimant fall back on a common law duty based on failure to warn or instruct, because the Convention is an exclusive basis for the carrier's liability.[123]

As compared with the fault principle, strict liability would reduce uncertainty in the outcomes of litigation and would, by reducing the number of issues in play, expedite the proceedings, all other things being equal. Strict liability would also dramatically increase the number of accident victims who are entitled to compensation, since victims would no longer need to establish fault on the part of the defendant in order to recover. Possible objections to strict liability are that it would diminish tort law's potential to deter harmful behaviour (although this is hotly contested) and would result in an undesirable disconnect between liability and moral blameworthiness.

---

[117] The liability under the Nuclear Installations Act 1965 is probably the strictest known to English law.

[118] See, e.g. the many statutory duties arising under industrial safety legislation, some of which are considered in Ch.9.

[119] See Ch.11.

[120] For some unusual situations see *Disley v Levine* [2001] EWCA Civ 1087; [2002] 1 W.L.R. 785 and *Laroche v Spirit of Adventure (UK) Ltd* [2009] EWCA Civ 12; [2009] Q.B. 778.

[121] *Morris v KLM Royal Dutch Airlines* [2002] UKHL 7; [2002] 2 A.C. 628.

[122] *Deep Vein Thrombosis and Air Travel Group Litigation, Re* [2005] UKHL 72; [2006] 1 A.C. 495; *Povey v Qantas Airways Ltd* [2005] HCA 33; (2005) 223 C.L.R. 189; *Barclay v British Airways Plc* [2008] EWCA Civ 1419; [2010] Q.B. 187.

[123] *Sidhu v British Airways Plc* [1997] A.C. 430.

B. Compensation Schemes

Compensation schemes distinguished from the tort system. An alternative   **1–045**
approach is to replace tort liability, either in part or in full, with a compensation
scheme. Compensation schemes are a type of social security. They provide
benefits for injuries irrespective of whether the injuries were caused by
someone's fault. Unlike proceedings based on strict liability torts, they do not
involve litigation against the injurer. Instead, the claimant applies for payments
from a government administered fund. Compensation schemes, consequently,
provide far broader coverage than the tort system, which usually only awards
compensation to the "lucky" victims who are able to establish that they were
injured by the fault of an (insured) defendant. However, compensation schemes
tend to provide far lower levels of financial support than the tort system.

Ad hoc compensation schemes. Some compensation schemes are ad hoc in the   **1–046**
sense that they apply only in a particular context. Probably the most common
type of ad hoc compensation scheme is that which applies in the context of
criminal injuries. Ad hoc compensation schemes that apply to motor vehicle
accidents and workplace injuries exist in Australia and the United states. These
schemes vary greatly in the amount and range of benefits that they offer and in
the extent to which they limit the right to claim tort damages. Generally they
either do not cover non-pecuniary loss such as pain and suffering, or an
entitlement to damages in respect of such loss is subject to a threshold. It is
doubtful whether there is any logical reason why these areas have been singled
out for special treatment.

Comprehensive compensation schemes. Much more far reaching than the   **1–047**
schemes mentioned in the previous paragraph is the scheme now operating in
New Zealand. The origin of this scheme is the Report of the Woodhouse
Commission, which had been appointed to deal only with compensation for work
injuries but which felt unable to limit itself to its terms of reference and proposed
an all-embracing compensation system based on the five guiding principles of
community responsibility, comprehensive entitlement, "real" compensation
(including non-pecuniary loss), the promotion of rehabilitation, and administrative efficiency. Most of the proposals were implemented by the Accident
Compensation Act 1972.[124] The law that underpins the scheme is now to be found
mainly in the Injury Prevention, Rehabilitation and Compensation Act 2001.
Claims are handled administratively with reviews and ultimate appeals on a
question of law to the High Court and Court of Appeal.

Broadly speaking, the scheme provides cover for personal injury caused by
accidents, occupational diseases and medical "treatment injuries". Cover for
mental injury (other than that related to physical injury) is confined to cases
involving certain sexual offences and to a single work-related event which the
injured person experiences directly. As injury arising from an intentional act is

---

[124] For a full account of the current scheme see Todd (ed.), *The Law of Torts in New Zealand*, 6th edn
(2013). In Australia, a National Committee of Inquiry in 1974 proposed a scheme that would cover all
incapacity, whether caused by accident or illness, but the proposal was lost with a change of
government in 1975.

"accidental" as far as the victim is concerned, there is no need for a separate criminal injuries compensation scheme in New Zealand. The original plan envisaged the extension of the scheme to disease in general and to disability; there now seems no prospect of this happening.

Where the compensation scheme applies the right of action in tort is abolished (though it remains possible to claim exemplary damages,[125] and proceedings in tort can be brought for cases that fall outside the scheme).[126] In the case of total incapacity for work, compensation is at the rate of 80 per cent of earnings, subject to a statutory maximum. The scheme provides for fairly modest lump sum payments for non-pecuniary loss. According a low priority to non-pecuniary loss is a feature of most compensation schemes. It is no doubt true that "loss" of this description is very different from the loss of something having an obvious monetary value and that, at common law, damages for non-pecuniary loss are awarded by way of "solace for unpleasantness and misfortune" than by way of replacement of something of which a person has been deprived. It is also true that it is difficult to find a basis for the assessment of some types of non-pecuniary damage.[127] On the other hand, there is no a priori reason for saying that those who suffer pain or loss of amenity are undeserving of such solace as the payment of money can bring them. The reply to the last point is that compensation of this kind should be given to none until such time as the basic income losses of all can be restored through the chosen compensation system on the ground that a loss of income has a particularly profound impact on the person who suffers the loss.

1–048   **Obstacles to reform.** As has been discussed, compensation schemes, because they do not insist on proof that the injury was caused by someone's fault, provide for far greater coverage than the tort system albeit the payments that they offer are lower. It might be thought that a decent meal for all is preferable to a banquet for some. However, it is often complained that the level of benefits paid by compensation systems is too low. The difficulty is that public debate over medical negligence and some mass-disaster cases suggests that expectations of the "proper" level of compensation are at a level well beyond that which could be financed without significant additional taxation. This cannot be ignored if any reform is to be effected. A related difficulty is the scope of compensation schemes. It is widely felt among reformers that a rational compensation system cannot confine its coverage to accident victims, since the needs of a person under disability are not mitigated by the fact that it has arisen from illness or congenital cause rather than by accident.[128] On this view, even the comprehensive New Zealand scheme suffers from the vice of cause-related compensation. However, if we bring in illness, we enter a wholly different statistical dimension, since it is

---

[125] See, e.g. *A v Bottrill* [2002] UKPC 44; [2003] 1 A.C. 449.
[126] Hence, there is still common law litigation in New Zealand in, for example, "nervous shock" cases.
[127] See para.23–069—23–071.
[128] See Stapleton, *Disease and the Compensation Debate* (1986).

generally thought that the contribution of accidents to all forms of disability is not more than about 10 per cent.[129] The implications of this in terms of cost are obvious.

Reform in this area is as much about politics as principle, and the present system contains a whole range of firmly entrenched misconceptions about the nature and quantum of compensation, not to mention vested interests (of particular classes of victims as well as of personal injury lawyers and insurers). If there was no social security system and all persons suffering disability for non-fault reasons were condemned to utter destitution, it might be possible to raise a sufficient head of steam for a new and comprehensive approach but the basic social security system does exist and reform may well be perceived by the public as "fine tuning" brought about at the price of taking away existing rights—and there are no votes in that. Even the present social security system is proving difficult to sustain and the prospect of the additional funding necessary to support general disability compensation at more than subsistence level appears remote. There is perhaps more chance of the introduction of limited, ad hoc no-fault schemes, but these are likely to make comprehensive change even more difficult by creating further enclaves of preferential treatment.

C. First-Party Insurance

Professor Patrick Atiyah in an important contribution controversially argued in favour of abandoning the tort system (in most situations) and putting nothing in its place, thereby leaving it to the market to provide a solution to the problem of compensating accident victims.[130] Expressing his views crudely, Atiyah saw little of value in the tort system. It was not, in his eyes, a personal responsibility system given that wrongdoers almost never pay personally for the losses that they cause (it is the insurers and, hence, the premium paying public that pays). For Atiyah, tort law should therefore be seen as a system of distributive justice, and, so understood, it is a dismal failure primarily since it awards compensation not on the basis of need but based on whether the claimant happened to have been injured by the fault of an insured defendant. Compensation schemes were not, to Atiyah's mind, the way forward given that there had been a profound and world-wide reaction to bureaucratic welfare schemes. Thus, Atiyah's preference was to put nothing in the void left by the suggested abolition of tort law and to leave it up to people to buy first-party insurance cover for themselves and their families. He contended that this would ensure vastly increased coverage (since first-party insurance is not dependent upon fault). He also stressed that this solution would not be regressive since people would only buy the cover that they felt that they need. Tort law, in contrast, is a highly regressive system since wealthier people tend to stand to gain the most from it, primarily because tort law provides damages to replace lost income.

1–049

---

[129] Pearson Report, Vol.2, p.12. Of course, tort liability applies to the wrongful causing of disease and is of importance in the employment context but, despite sporadic litigation about matters like smoking diseases, hepatitis and CJD, the overall impact of tort must be small outside the employment context.
[130] Atiyah, *The Damages Lottery* (1997).

7. Tort and the Compensation Culture

1–050   **Introduction.** It is widely agreed that tort law is not a very efficient means of compensating misfortune, but one might reply that it never set out to do that, but to right wrongs. The question nevertheless arises whether, even in that more modest frame, it has not become rather out of control. We have all been brought up to believe that the United States has long been the home of rampant tort law, of multi-million dollar recoveries involving cars which did not prove crash-proof or cups of coffee which scalded the buyer. In 1991, an American writer asserted that "the American links adversity with recompense whereas the Englishman or woman accepts adversity as a routine part of life"[131] but recent events cast some doubt on the second proposition.

1–051   **Tort reform in other jurisdictions.** "Tort reform" has long been a matter of heated debate in the United States and this has led to various forms of legislative action, most commonly in the form of putting caps on damages, especially for non-pecuniary loss and exemplary damages,[132] and abolishing or modifying the traditional common law rule that each of a number of tortfeasors causing indivisible harm is liable for the whole loss.[133] More recently there has been very large scale legislative action in most Australian jurisdictions, driven by a perceived insurance crisis.[134] The New South Wales Civil Liability Act 2002 goes the furthest in most respects and contains provisions of three main types. First, some basic principles of the common law have been "restated" in a way presumably intended to render them immune from judicial tampering.[135] So, for example, under s.5I(2) a person is not liable for a risk which cannot be avoided by the exercise of reasonable care and skill (except in so far as it is appropriate to require him to warn of such a risk). In this way, at least part of the common law in this area has been "codified". Secondly, extensive provision has been made for defences,[136] including potent illegality defences[137] and claimant-intoxication defences.[138] Thirdly, the quantum of damages for personal injury has been radically reduced. Pecuniary loss damages are capped at three times average earnings.[139] Furthermore, the discount rate is set at 5 per cent,[140] twice the figure in England, something which has a dramatic effect on awards. An index-linked cap was put on non-pecuniary loss. Perhaps the impact is even greater on smaller claims. There is now no payment at all for non-pecuniary loss unless there is long-term impairment of at least 15 per cent, which cuts out many cases of the

---

[131] Kritzer [1991] J. Law & Soc. 400 at 422.

[132] Exemplary damages are usually known as punitive damages in the United States.

[133] See Dobbs, *The Law of Torts* (2000), Chs 25 and 26.

[134] Overviews of the Australian reforms are offered in Cane (2003) 27 M.U.L.R. 649; Goudkamp (2012) 28 J.P.N. 4; Luntz (2004) 35 V.U.W.L.R. 879; McDonald (2005) 27 Syd. L. Rev. 443; McDonald (2006) 14 T.L.J. 268; Underwood (2004) 12 T.L.J. 39.

[135] The High Court of Australia may fairly be said to have shown a pro-claimant inclination until the mid-90s, but that was rather reversed before the legislation. This judicial reversal of the fortunes of claimants is masterfully described in Luntz (2001) 1 O.U.C.L.J. 95.

[136] See Goudkamp in Arvind and Steele (eds), *Tort Law and the Legislature* (2013).

[137] Civil Liability Act 2002 (NSW) ss.54–54A.

[138] Civil Liability Act 2002 (NSW) s.50.

[139] Civil Liability Act 2002 (NSW) s.12.

[140] Civil Liability Act 2002 (NSW) s.14.

"trip and fall" or "whiplash injury" variety. If the impairment is more than 15 per cent but less than 33 per cent damages are not based on a percentage of the maximum, but on a reduced sliding scale, so someone with a 25 per cent impairment gets 6.5 per cent of the maximum.

The situation in England. There has recently been much discussion in England **1–052** of a supposed compensation culture and an insurance crisis.[141] Most of the debate has been conducted at a rather superficial level and exploited for political ends.[142] Following various statements by politicians and media reports that England was suffering a dramatic rise in the number of claims, an important independent study reported that the rate of claiming had actually decreased.[143] Substantial increases in liability insurance premiums are an undeniable fact but it does not follow that they are caused by the increased cost of liability, there being many influences on the level of premiums that have nothing to do with the tort system, such as the returns that insurers earn on the premiums. There is also no doubt that there is a social cost in the *perception* of a litigation-conscious society in the form of restrictions on activities which would formerly have been perceived as harmless[144]—safety overkill—something which the House of Lords strove to counter in 2003.[145] The Compensation Act 2006 also contains a rather pale imitation of the New South Wales legislation in the form of s.1:

> "1. Deterrent effect of potential liability
>   A court considering a claim in negligence or breach of statutory duty may, in determining whether the defendant should have taken particular steps to meet a standard of care (whether by taking precautions against a risk or otherwise), have regard to whether a requirement to take those steps might—
>   (a) prevent a desirable activity from being undertaken at all, to a particular extent or in a particular way, or
>   (b) discourage persons from undertaking functions in connection with a desirable activity."

Some may consider this to be a rather futile exercise in the sense that not only is it implicit or explicit in the current approach taken by the courts[146] but it is hardly

---

[141] See Goudkamp (2012) 28 J.P.N. 4; Hand (2010) 37 J.L.S. 569; Morris (2007) 70 M.L.R. 349; Mullender (2006) 22 J.P.N. 2; Williams (2005) 25 L.S. 499.

[142] See, e.g. David Davis, Shadow Home Secretary, in *The Spectator*, August 20, 2004, confusing the personal injury problem with the Human Rights Act 1998. Some estimates of the annual cost of clinical negligence to the NHS simply take the total value of all unsettled claims in the pipeline and assume that they will all succeed at 100 per cent.

[143] Lewis, Morris and Oliphant (2006) 14 T.L.J. 158.

[144] For an example, see *Hampstead Heath Winter Swimming Club v Corporation of London* [2005] EWHC 713 (Admin); [2005] 1 W.L.R. 2930.

[145] *Tomlinson v Congleton BC* [2003] UKHL 47; [2004] 1 A.C. 46, see paras 6–026, 10–014, 10–022.

[146] Section 1 was mentioned in passing in *Hopps v Mott MacDonald Ltd* [2009] EWHC 1881 (QB) at [91]–[93]; *Barnesv Scout Association* [2010] EWCA Civ 1476 at [34]; *Reynolds v Strutt & Parker LLP* [2011] EWHC 2740 (QB) at [46]; *Uren v Corporate Leisure (UK) Ltd* [2011] EWCA Civ 66 at [13]; *Sutton v Syston Rugby Football Club Ltd* [2011] EWCA Civ 1182 at [13]; *Wilkin-Shaw v Fuller* [2012] EWHC 1777 (QB) at [41]–[46]; *Uren v Corporate Leisure (UK) Ltd* [2013] EWHC 353 (QB) at [75]. The view that emerges from these cases is that s.1 adds nothing to the common law.

of such strength as to deter a court determined to go in the opposite direction (unlikely as that may be).[147]

---

[147] Fulbrook, *Outdoor Activities, Negligence and the Law* (2005) is an interesting and detailed examination of the "law in action" in the context of outdoor activities, one of the contexts in which the charge of restriction of worthwhile activities by tort law has been most prominent.

Chapter 2

THE STRUCTURE OF TORT LAW

1. HISTORICAL INFLUENCES

The distinction between trespass and case. The law of torts did not evolve around a broad central principle of liability. Rather, it grew up, like other branches of our law, behind a screen of legal procedure. Until the mid-19th century, the question which arose when a claimant sued a defendant for some alleged injury was not "Have the claimant's rights been infringed by the defendant?" or even "Has the defendant broken some duty which he owed to the claimant?" but "Has the claimant any form of action against the defendant, and, if so, what form?" If the claimant could not fit his claim into one of the recognised forms of action, he had no legal grievance. An action was usually commenced by a royal writ issued from the Chancery, which in this sense signified not a court of law but a government department, one of whose functions was the creation and issue of these writs. It was known also as the *officina brevium* which has been conveniently translated as "the writ-shop", for a claimant could not get a writ without paying for it. For a very considerable period of our legal history the shape of the law was no more than a classification of writs. The writs that remedied the injuries which in modern times are called torts were principally the writ of trespass and the writ of trespass on the case or "case". Trespass in common parlance now signifies unauthorised entry on another person's land, but in law it has a wider signification, as it has in the King James Bible. The writ of trespass lay for injuries to land or to goods, or to the person, though "injuries" must be read in an extended sense[1] because the tort was actionable per se, that is to say, the claimant could sue even if there had been no damage as that word would normally be understood. However, it was limited to injuries which were direct and immediate and it did not extend to indirect or consequential injuries: so it was trespass for D to throw a brick at C and hit C but not if D left an unlighted pile of bricks in the alley at the side of C house's and C stumbled over them.

2–001

---

[1] The sense is the Latin *iniuria*, "wrong".

However, these indirect injuries came to be remediable through the action on the case, though this, unlike trespass, required proof of damage. These two classes of action, "trespass" and "case", existed side by side for centuries and to them we owe most of our law of tort. There were, however, definite distinctions between these two forms of action and until the 19th century it was vital for a claimant to choose correctly between them.[2] Only after the reforms of that century had broken up the cast-iron moulds of procedure did it cease to be necessary: "to canvass the niceties of the old forms of action. Remedies now depend on the substance of the right, not on whether they can be fitted into a particular framework".[3]

2–002   **The continuing significance of the forms of action.** Despite the foregoing, a basic knowledge of the forms of action is still necessary not only in order to understand the old authorities but also in order to comprehend the classification of much of the modern law.[4] As Maitland's famously observed: "The forms of action we have buried, but they still rule us from their graves".[5] In the course of time certain types of claim acquired more specific names, such as assault, battery, libel, slander, private nuisance, negligence and so on. The fact that they acquired such names was due to mere accidents of terminology traceable probably to their frequent occurrence, but they still have their roots in the ancient categories, so that even now (although trespass and case are long gone) a lawyer might explain that the reason why a claim for negligence requires proof of damage, whereas a claim for battery does not, is that the former is (or was) an action on the case, the latter one is trespass. Of course the fact that the explanation is historical does not mean that there might not then have been, and may still continue to be, a good policy reason for the distinction: those torts which are actionable per se might be regarded as concerned with the vindication of rights[6] or with situations where damage is likely but very hard to prove.[7]

2–003   **The concept of negligence is not an organising principle for tort law generally.** It was noted at the outset of this chapter that tort law did not evolve around a single comprehensive concept of wrongdoing. Can tort law as it currently stands be reduced to a central organising principle? One might get the impression from studying the modern case law that the concept of "negligence", which dominates tort law (and which dominates tort courses even more than textbooks), is such a principle but common sense and simple morality tell us that wherever there is liability for negligence there must also be liability for

---

[2] See Prichard (1964) 22 C.L.J. 234.

[3] *Nelson v Larholt* [1948] 1 K.B. 339 at 343 per Denning J.

[4] For an example see *Watkins v Secretary of State for the Home Department* [2006] UKHL 17; [2006] 2 A.C. 395 (misfeasance in a public office), discussed at para.8–030.

[5] Maitland, *Equity: A Course of Lectures* (1936), p.296. Thus the distinction between trespass to land and private nuisance still turns upon the old distinction between trespass and case. See, e.g. *Esso Petroleum Co Ltd v Southport Corp* [1956] A.C. 218.

[6] See *Ashley v CC Sussex Police* [2008] UKHL 25; [2008] 1 A.C. 962, discussed at para.1–002.

[7] However, in torts that are actionable per se the courts are nowadays quite ready to strike out a claim as an abuse of process where it is clear that the damage is trivial or nonexistent and the claim is "not worth the candle". "The claim for a shilling in damages in order to prove a point and obtain an award of costs is history": *White v Withers LLP* [2009] EWCA Civ 1122 at [72]. So in these cases it might now be better to say, not that damage is unnecessary, but that it is presumed.

intentional harm; indeed, liability for intentional wrongdoing is, and probably should be, wider than that for negligence. In the European systems both types of conduct are easily accommodated under the name of "fault", or at least they are both placed under the same heading.[8] As a practical matter one may say that fault is as much a dominant feature of tort liability here as in those systems, but to say that we had a general concept of fault would be to over-simplify the law, for our intentional torts such as battery and deceit came into existence long before any general conception of negligence, and they continue to carry some of their history with them.

There is, therefore, no doubt that we have a collection of torts rather than a single principle of liability but this does not prevent the courts creating new heads of liability to meet changing circumstances or changing perceptions of the need for protection from harm. Sometimes this may occur very suddenly, as happened in the middle of the 19th century, when the tort of inducing breach of contract was spontaneously established;[9] on other occasions the process may involve more of a synthesis of existing principles, the culmination of an evolution rather than a revolution, as happened when the foundation of the general law of negligence was laid in 1932.[10] The modern law has seen a marked development of the law of confidence and, propelled by the Human Rights Act 1998, this has now cut loose from any strict requirement that the information should have been *imparted* in confidence by the person to whom it relates. There is a growing tendency to refer to it as "misuse of private information", though it seems not quite to have become a general basis for the protection of privacy against wrongful intrusion.[11] The predominant view has been that the law of confidence rests upon equitable principles rather than upon tort but in practical terms this is perhaps a distinction without a difference, as witness the occasional judicial reference to the "tort of breach of confidence" or the "tort of misuse of private information".[12] The traffic is, of course, not all one way: a head of tortious liability may be born, acquire a name and be cut off by other developments before it reaches its prime.[13]

The need to establish a cause of action. The forms of action have long gone: for a century and a half there has been a more or less uniform process for starting all civil claims for damages. But it has not been in accordance with the tradition of the common law to analyse rights as something separate from the remedy given to the claimant. Accordingly, although the procedural restrictions of the forms of action have been abolished, it is still necessary for the claimant to establish a cause of action. It is not therefore correct to say that a person has a basic right not to have, for example, untruths told about himself, for he is only able to restrain the publication of such untruths if the circumstances in which they are

2–004

---

[8] As in the German Civil Code, BGB § 823(1): "A person who, *wilfully or negligently*, unlawfully injures the life, body, health, freedom, property or other right of another is bound to compensate him for any damage arising therefrom."

[9] *Lumley v Gye* (1853) 2 El. & Bl. 216. See para.19–006.

[10] *Donoghue v Stevenson* [1932] A.C. 562. See para.5–015. Of course, the common law judge is always reluctant to admit that a completely new departure has been made.

[11] See para.13–143.

[12] See para.13–143.

[13] This seems to be the effect of the Protection from Harassment Act 1997 (see para.4–034) upon the common law tort rather tentatively advanced in *Khorasandjian v Bush* [1993] Q.B. 727.

disseminated fall within a specific tort such as passing off, malicious falsehood or defamation.[14] To some extent this basic approach has changed under the Human Rights Act 1998, pursuant to which the court must give effect to the rights and freedoms guaranteed by the European Convention on Human Rights.[15] This guarantees, for example, the rights to life, to liberty and to the enjoyment of property but it seems that, in the medium term at least, we are more likely to rely on these to modify existing rules of tort law where necessary than to rewrite the whole rule book in terms of rights[16] rather than liabilities.

2–005 **Pleading a cause of action.** It is important to realise that the various torts are not exclusive of one another and that there is no reason why a given set of facts should not contain the elements of several of them. The claim form which initiates a civil case must contain a concise statement of the nature of the claim[17] and this is supplemented (later, except in the simplest cases) by particulars of claim which contain "a concise statement of the facts on which the claimant relies".[18] The main purpose of the exercise is to enable the opposing party to know what case is being made in sufficient detail to enable him properly to answer it.[19] Today the claimant does not necessarily have to specify the particular tort on which he wishes to rely, for the issue is whether what he alleges (in traditional terminology) "discloses a cause of action", i.e. a set of facts for which there is a legal remedy.[20] Thus, it is open to the claimant to assert that the factual situation gives rise to a basis of liability which has never before been expressly recognised. In practice, however, it is normally prudent, and may in practical terms be essential for the claimant, to identify by name the cause of action on which he relies: judges are presumed to know the law, but they are entitled to and should receive the assistance of counsel. Furthermore, subject to the court's power to allow amendment of pleadings (probably now to be exercised less generously than in the past) no one is allowed to lead evidence of facts which he has not pleaded. If the facts alleged in the claim do not show a sustainable legal basis for the claim even if they are all proven, the defendant may apply to have the claim struck out[21] or apply for summary judgment on the ground that the claim has no reasonable prospect of success.[22] So, what is necessary to get to trial is that the facts alleged should include those essential to liability under at least

---

[14] *Kingdom of Spain v Christie, Manson & Woods Ltd* [1986] 1 W.L.R. 1120 at 1129.

[15] See para.2–010.

[16] In *Watkins v Secretary of State for the Home Department* [2006] UKHL 17; [2006] 2 A.C. 395 the court rejected an attempt to fashion an extension of tort liability based on "constitutional rights".

[17] CPR r.16.2(1)(a).

[18] CPR r.16.4(1)(a).

[19] *British Airways Pension Trustees Ltd v Sir Robert McAlpine & Sons Ltd* (1994) 45 Con. L.R. 1 at 4.

[20] *Letang v Cooper* [1965] 1 Q.B. 232 at 242–244, where Diplock LJ states that a "cause of action" is simply a factual situation the existence of which entitles one person to obtain from the court a remedy against another person. An alternative definition is, "every fact [though not every piece of evidence] which it would be necessary for the plaintiff to prove, if traversed, in order to support his right to the judgment of the court": *Read v Brown* (1888) 22 Q.B.D. 128 at 131. See also *Black v Yates* [1992] Q.B. 526.

[21] CPR r.3.4.2(a). This is the successor of what in former times was known as the demurrer procedure.

[22] CPR r.24.2(a)(i).

one tort, without at the same time including any which are fatal to that liability. For this purpose the court is not concerned with evidence, i.e. with whether the facts alleged can be proven, but with whether the facts if proven can realistically be regarded[23] as being the possible basis of a claim.[24] However, the whole sequence of events leading up to the claimant's damage may include the essentials of more than one tort, and where this is so the position is simply that there is more than one reason why the claimant should succeed.

Put simply, therefore, it is necessary for counsel for the claimant, in settling the particulars of claim, to plead all the facts which are essential to the particular tort or torts on which he intends to rely. One cannot, however, simply plead all the facts which led up to the claimant's injury, for this would be to go back to the creation of the world. One is bound to select from the whole complex of facts those which are relevant to the client's claim in point of law and this, of course, one cannot do save by reference to particular torts which are recognised (or at least which one hopes to convince the court should be recognised). Suppose that the defendant has orally stated of the claimant, a shopkeeper, that the claimant habitually sells goods which he knows to have been stolen. Here the defendant's words prima facie fall under the tort known as "slander of title" or "malicious falsehood"[25] and also within the tort of defamation.[26] Now it is not normally an essential element of the tort of defamation that the defendant should have used the words maliciously, but this is an essential element of malicious falsehood. If, therefore, the claimant wishes to make use in argument of that tort he must allege in his pleading that the defendant acted with malice. Otherwise, even though the defendant was in fact malicious, he will be precluded from proving this at the trial and so will fail to bring his case within malicious falsehood. He will thus lose the advantage of an alternative line of argument which, on the facts as they actually occurred, should have been open to him.[27] The claimant may, of course, have practical reasons for not pursuing all the causes of action available. In *Joyce v Sengupta*[28] a statement published about the claimant was clearly defamatory on its face but the claimant sued only for the tort of malicious falsehood because legal aid was then available for the tort but not available for defamation.[29] An argument that this was an abuse of the process of the court was rejected, for:[30]

---

[23] It is not necessary for the court to be satisfied that the claim *will* succeed as a matter of law and it is undesirable to decide complex issues of law on hypothetical facts: *Farah v British Airways Plc, The Times*, January 26, 2000.

[24] However, under CPR Pt 24, where the issue is simply whether the claimant has a real prospect of success, the defendant may seek summary judgment on the ground that the evidence available to the claimant is too weak. See *Three Rivers DC v Bank of England (No.3)* [2001] UKHL 16; [2003] 2 A.C. 1, especially the speech of Lord Hutton at [120], where the distinction is drawn between the "attack on the pleadings" point and the "no real prospects of success" point.

[25] See para.13–131.

[26] See para.13–001.

[27] But compare *Cornwall Gardens Pte Ltd v RO Garrard & Co Ltd* [2001] EWCA Civ 699, where the court refused to allow the claimant to dress up what was in substance a claim for malicious falsehood as one for interference with rights by unlawful means, in order to escape the limitation period.

[28] [1993] 1 W.L.R. 337.

[29] See also *Spring v Guardian Assurance Plc* [1995] 2 A.C. 296 (claim for negligence as a way of sidestepping privilege blocking defamation claim): discussed in para.11–033.

[30] *Joyce* [1993] 1 W.L.R. 337 at 342–343 per Nicholls VC.

"When more than one cause of action is available to him, a plaintiff may choose which he will pursue. Usually, he pursues all available causes of action, but he is not obliged to do so. He may pursue one to the exclusion of another . . . I have never heard it suggested before that a plaintiff is not entitled to proceed in this way . . . [or] that he must pursue the most appropriate remedy."

We may say, therefore, that the law of tort is divided over the various torts which we are now to consider, but life itself is not similarly divided. The law of tort may say: "If A, B and C, then liability in negligence" and also "If A, B and D, then liability in private nuisance". Life may produce A, B, C, D, E, F, G and H. If it does, and assuming E, F, G, and H to be legally irrelevant, the claimant should plead and prove A, B, C, D. If he does he is entitled to succeed under the rules both of negligence and of private nuisance but this conclusion cannot, of course, be reached by one who is not familiar with the essentials of each particular tort.

2. NEW INFLUENCES ON ENGLISH TORT LAW

A. The European Convention on Human Rights and the Human Rights Act

2–006   **The European Convention on Human Rights.** Our courts have tended to look not for inspiration to Europe but to the Commonwealth and, to a lesser extent, the United States; but we are also now part of a complex of European institutions which have a political as well as an economic agenda and this has implications for the development of tort law. Of most immediate concern is the impact of the European Convention on Human Rights and Fundamental Freedoms. The United Kingdom was the first state to ratify the Convention, signed in Rome in 1950. The Convention binds its signatories to secure to citizens the rights and freedoms defined in it but does not require that a state incorporate the Convention in domestic law. A person who claims to be a victim of a violation of the Convention might, however, petition the European Commission of Human Rights in Strasbourg and if that body finds the complaint admissible (one condition of which is the exhaustion of local remedies) the case will go before the European Court of Human Rights. If the Court finds that there has been a violation of the Convention it can award the applicant monetary compensation as "just satisfaction".[31] It has no power to undo what had been done on the domestic plane (e.g. a criminal conviction or dismissal from employment) but if the state of domestic law had led to the violation or prevented any local remedy for it, the Government will feel obliged to correct that.

2–007   **The Human Rights Act generally.** The Human Rights Act 1998 was enacted in order to guarantee the rights provided for in the Convention. The Act has spawned a vast literature, and it is well beyond the scope of this book to engage with that literature, much of which has little relevance to tort law.[32] However, it is convenient to offer some general observations regarding the Act. It is important to bear in mind throughout this discussion that, strictly speaking, the Act does not

---

[31] Article 41.
[32] Although, see Hoffman (ed.), *The Impact of the UK Human Rights Act on Private Law* (2011).

"incorporate" the Convention into English law (the Convention is an international treaty).[33] The rights created by the Act are domestic ones.

The interpretation of legislation. The core of the Act from a constitutional point of view is perhaps the provisions that deal with legislation. Under s.3 the court is required to read primary and subordinate legislation in a way compatible with Convention rights, *so far as it is possible to do so*. To avoid the effect of s.3 there must be a clear indication of an intention to legislate incompatibly with the Convention.[34] In that event, the court has no power to strike down primary legislation but may (at the level of the High Court or above) make a declaration of incompatibility under s.4.[35] This has no effect on the outcome of the suit in which the issue is raised, nor does it require the Government to take remedial action, though a fast-track legislative procedure is available if it chooses to do so.[36]

2–008

The duty of public authorities to act compatibly with Convention rights. Perhaps of greater relevance to tort law are the provisions of the Act that are concerned with the acts of "public authorities". There is no comprehensive definition of a public authority in the Act. But a public authority is defined to include a court or tribunal or "any person certain of whose functions are functions of a public nature".[37] The mere fact that a body has functions some of which are of a public nature is not sufficient to make it a public authority in respect of its acts that are of a private nature.[38] The basic principle is that it is unlawful for a public authority to act in a way which is incompatible with a Convention right.[39] The victim of such an unlawful act may bring proceedings in which a court "may grant such relief or remedy, or make such order, within its powers as it considers just and appropriate."[40] The relief may include an award of damages but only if, taking account of all the circumstances of the case (including any other relief granted), such an award "is necessary to afford just satisfaction to the person in whose favour it is made".[41] The court is directed, on the issue of damages, to

2–009

---

[33] *McKerr, Re* [2004] UKHL 12; [2004] 1 W.L.R. 807 at [65] per Lord Hoffmann.

[34] See *R v A (No.2)* [2001] UKHL 25; [2002] 1 A.C. 45 at [44].

[35] As to subordinate legislation, see Human Rights Act 1998 s.4(4).

[36] Human Rights Act 1998 s.10 and Sch.2.

[37] Human Rights Act 1998 s.6(3). But not Parliament.

[38] Human Rights Act 1998 s.6(5). For discussion see *Aston Cantlow PCC v Wallbank* [2003] UKHL 37; [2004] 1 A.C. 546. Regarding the difference between the public and private acts of a body consider, e.g. a security firm which: (a) operates a prison under contract with the state; and (b) guards private premises: *Quaquah v Group 4 Securities Ltd (No.2)* [2003] EWHC 1504 (QB); *The Times*, June 27, 2001.

[39] Convention rights are those set out in arts 2 to 12 and 14 of the Convention and certain rights governed by the First and Sixth Protocols. See Clayton and Tomlinson, *The Law of Human Rights*, 2nd edn (2009); Lester, Pannick and Herberg, *Human Rights Law and Practice*, 3rd edn (2009); Beatson, Grosz, Hickman, Singh and Palmer, *Human Rights: Judicial Protection in the United Kingdom* (2008).

[40] Human Rights Act 1998 s.8(1).

[41] Human Rights Act 1998 s.8(3).

have regard to the principles applied by the European Court of Human Rights, and that body has quite frequently considered the vindication of the right as sufficient satisfaction.[42]

2–010   **The position of courts.**Although a court is a public authority for the purposes of the Act, a claim in respect of a judicial act is only to be brought by way of appeal (or in some cases judicial review) and damages may not be awarded in respect of judicial acts done in good faith except with regard to wrongful detention under art.5(5) of the Convention.[43] However, that takes us to the central area of difficulty in mapping the relationship of the Act, the Convention and the common law of tort. Despite the fact that the act of a court may not be subject to an award of damages, because a court is a public authority it must not act in a way that is incompatible with the Convention. Does that mean that a court, in declaring and applying the common law, is required to proceed in a way which is compatible with the Convention rights?[44] Or, is it enough that they simply give effect to the Convention rights by means of the mechanisms created by the Act? The first approach would have very significant implications: it would make the common law a subsidiary regime shaped by the Convention, which is expressed in terms of very broad, general rights quite different from the common law's method of building up principle from case to case; and, since it is plain that the international obligations under the Convention may extend to creating and implementing a legal regime which protects the right in question against acts in the private sphere,[45] it would have the potential to create new causes of action against private persons, even though the Act applies only to public authorities. The broad approach would arguably be inconsistent with the doctrine of precedent, since it would give a trial judge a "trump card" (at least where the matter in question had not been considered by a higher court in the context of the Convention) which would enable him to escape otherwise binding decisions. The courts have been reluctant to supply clear guidance on the precise effect of the Act on the development of the common law.

2–011   **Overlap between Convention rights and common law rights.** There is a considerable overlap between the rights guaranteed by the Convention and the rights recognised by the common law. To a large degree, therefore, the existing common law fulfils the Convention requirements without more—the Convention, after all, is primarily an international instrument designed to ensure compliance by States with basic standards of protection and it would be surprising if none of them had achieved that in any area before the Convention. For example, art.5.2 provides: "Everyone who is arrested shall be informed promptly, in a language which he understands, of the reason for his arrest and of any charge against him." At common law (and under the Police and Criminal Evidence Act 1984) a person

---

[42]   *R. (on the application of Greenfield) v Secretary of State for the Home Dept* [2005] UKHL 14; [2005] 1 W.L.R. 673; *Gillan v United Kingdom* [2010] ECHR 4158/05; (2010) 50 E.H.R.R. 1105. See generally, *Damages under the Human Rights Act 1998* (2000) Law Com. No.266.

[43]   Human Rights Act 1998 s.9.

[44]   On this point see Young, "Mapping Horizontal Effect" in Hoffman (ed.), *The Impact of the UK Human Rights Act on Private Law*(2011), p.16.

[45]   *Airey v Ireland* (1979) 2 E.H.R.R. 305; *X v Netherlands* (1985) 8 E.H.R.R. 235; *Johnston v Ireland* (1986) 9 E.H.R.R. 203.

arrested has a similar right to be informed of the reason for his arrest[46] and if he is not, he has a claim for the tort of false imprisonment, which may lead to the award of substantial damages. However, some infringements of the Convention rights by a public body would not be a tort under the common law. For example, under art.8.1 everyone has the "right to respect for his private and family life, his home and his correspondence".[47] Now although the English common law of torts has always protected privacy in various indirect ways[48] and the law of confidence has been developed into a wrong of misuse of private information, which covers much of the ground, there is no general tort of infringement of privacy under that name. However, where the defendant is a public authority there is now a statutory wrong under the Act. This is not an action in tort for breach of statutory duty,[49] because the remedy in damages is discretionary and even where they are awarded they will be in line with the Strasbourg practice, not that of English courts in tort cases, but otherwise there is some similarity with such an action.[50] It would be impracticable in this book to provide a full account of the various Convention rights but it will be necessary to refer to them when they overlap with or qualify the common law.

Restriction of common law rights by the Convention. Sometimes a Convention right does not so much create a cause of action as militate against an existing liability at common law—for example, the right of freedom of expression under art.10 has at least the potential to restrict the ability of the law to impose liability for defamation. In such a situation the court really has no choice but to alter the common law to make it compatible with the Convention. In one case a judge declined as a result of art.10 to apply the common law rule of strict liability in "mistaken identity" libel cases even though that rule was supported by decisions of the Court of Appeal and the House of Lords before the Act (and indeed before the Convention).[51]

2–012

Parallel regimes. Where the Convention protects a right which is not protected by the common law of tort the general tendency since the Human Rights Act 1998 has been to take the line that there may be two parallel regimes governing the situation and the court's duty not to act inconsistently with the Convention is fulfilled by its giving a remedy, via the Act, for the infringement of the Convention right itself, even if one is denied under the common law. In *Wainwright v Home Office*[52] where the events took place before the Act, the House of Lords declined to create a "high level" general tort of invasion of privacy, despite art.8, which provides for a right to private and family life. Lord Hoffmann remarked that a:[53]

2–013

---

[46] See para.26–054.
[47] Subject to art.8.2, which allows lawful interference which is necessary in a democratic society for national security, the prevention of crime, etc.
[48] See para.13–143.
[49] See Ch.8.
[50] See *Damages under the Human Rights Act 1998* (2000) Law Com. No.266 at [4.20] ("in effect a form of action for breach of statutory duty").
[51] *O'Shea v MGN Ltd* [2001] E.M.L.R. 40, see para.13–018.
[52] [2003] UKHL 53; [2004] 2 A.C. 406.
[53] [2003] UKHL 53; [2004] 2 A.C. 406 at [52].

"[F]inding that there was a breach of article 8 will only demonstrate that there was a gap in the English remedies for invasion of privacy which has since been filled by sections 6 and 7 of the 1998 Act. It does not require that the courts should provide an alternative remedy which distorts the principles of the common law."

2–014 **Actions available under the Human Rights Act do not necessarily mirror common law rights.** In *Smith v Chief Constable of Sussex Police*[54] the House of Lords held that the common law rule that the police owed no actionable duty to protect individuals from crime[55] remained intact notwithstanding the positive duty in art.2 of the Convention to protect life. This reveals that the duties created by art.2 are not simply a mirror image of the duties created by the tort of negligence. The primary focus of art.2 is upon the need for public authorities to have suitable systems in place to protect citizens—the provision of a criminal law and police services, the assessment of detained persons for suicide risk and so on.[56] Even if these requirements are fulfilled there may be an "operational" duty to take further steps to protect an individual but then the Strasbourg jurisprudence on art.2 requires the public authority to have reason to know of a "real and immediate risk" to life and while this cannot be equated with "gross negligence" it is nonetheless a stringent test and it should not be assumed that it is satisfied in every case where, a duty of care being established, there would be negligence at common law.[57] Thus, a public hospital is a "public authority" for the purposes of the Human Rights Act and it must take steps to secure competent staff and adequate equipment and safety systems, but there is no liability under art.2 for every negligent treatment error which would lead to liability at common law.[58] However, while medical negligence is not normally a breach of art.2, there is an exception where the negligence is a failure to allow a psychiatric patient who is known to present a real and immediate risk of suicide to go home.[59] The mere fact that the defendant is a public authority that could have prevented harm from occurring does not necessarily mean that it is in breach of art.2, because the matter in question may fall within the scope of the activities of another authority.[60]

B. A European Tort Law?

2–015 **The search for Europe-wide principles.** Private law is outside the competence of the European Union, though certain of its functions, most notably that of consumer protection, have produced pockets of "European tort law" if we may use that phrase, on matters like product liability[61] and unfair contract terms. However, in the last 20 years there has been a remarkable amount of academic activity directed towards framing Europe-wide principles of private law. A

---

[54] [2008] UKHL 50; [2009] A.C. 225.
[55] See para.5–029.
[56] *Mitchell v Glasgow CC* [2009] UKHL 11; [2009] A.C. 874 at [66].
[57] *Van Colle v CC Hertfordshire Police* [2008] UKHL 50; [2009] A.C. 225; *Savage v South Essex Partnership NHS Foundation Trust* [2008] UKHL 74; [2009] A.C. 681.
[58] *Savage v South Essex Partnership NHS Foundation Trust* [2008] UKHL 74; [2009] 1 A.C. 681.
[59] *Rabone v Pennine Care NHS Trust* [2012] UKSC 2; [2012] 2 A.C. 72.
[60] *Mitchell* [2009] UKHL 11; [2009] 1 A.C. 874 at [68].
[61] See Ch.11.

"European Group on Tort Law" produced a series of surveys of particular aspects of tort law which culminated in a volume of Principles.[62] A study group on a European Civil Code was active on a broader front in preparing principles of private law and combined with a number of other groups to produce in 2008 *Principles, Definitions and Model Rules of European Private Law*, the "Draft Common Frame of Reference" (DCFR). The DCFR is an "enigmatic concept".[63] It declares itself to be "an academic, not a politically authorised text"[64] but in the past the European Parliament has declared itself in favour of a European Civil Code[65] and the Commission has spoken in terms of a common frame of reference being used as a "legislator's toolbox", at least in the area of consumer law (though in that case it is difficult to see why it contains material on general tort law, commercial agency and unjust enrichment). People have also spoken of an "optional civil code" but while that idea has real content in relation to contracts, the option idea would seem rather unsuitable to tort.

Obstacles to unification. It is a truism of comparative law that the results in different systems are often rather similar, though the routes by which they are reached may be different. Let us take the provisions from the DCFR and the Principles of European Tort Law which deal with a broadly similar issue.   **2–016**

"DCFR:
  VI.–2:101 Meaning of legally relevant damage
(1)   Loss, whether economic or non-economic, or injury is legally relevant damage if:
    (a)   one of the following rules of this Chapter so provides;
    (b)   the loss or injury results from a violation of a right otherwise conferred by the law; or
    (c)   the loss or injury results from a violation of an interest worthy of legal protection.
(2)   In any case covered only by sub-paragraphs (b) or (c) of paragraph (1) loss or injury constitutes legally relevant damage only if it would be fair and reasonable for there to be a right to reparation . . .
(3)   In considering whether it would be fair and reasonable for there to be a right to reparation . . . regard is to be had to the ground of accountability, to the nature and proximity of the damage . . . , to the reasonable expectations of the person who suffers . . . the damage, and to considerations of public policy."

"Principles of European Tort Law:
  Art. 2:102. Protected interests
(1)   The scope of protection of an interest depends on its nature; the higher its value, the precision of its definition and its obviousness, the more extensive is its protection.
(2)   Life, bodily or mental integrity, human dignity and liberty enjoy the most extensive protection.
(3)   Extensive protection is granted to property rights, including those in intangible property.
(4)   Protection of pure economic interests or contractual relationships may be more limited in scope. In such cases, due regard must be had especially to the proximity between the actor and the endangered person, or to the fact that the actor is aware of the fact that he will cause damage even though his interests are necessarily valued lower than those of the victim.

---

[62] European Group on Tort Law, *Principles of European Tort Law* (2005).
[63] Eidenmüller, Faust, Grigoleit, Jansen, Wagner, Zimmermann (2008) 28 O.J.L.S. 659 at 661.
[64] Introduction, para.4.
[65] Resolution of May 1989.

(5)   The scope of protection may also be affected by the nature of liability, so that an interest may receive more extensive protection against intentional harm than in other cases.

(6)   In determining the scope of protection, the interests of the actor, especially in liberty of action and in exercising his rights, as well as public interests also have to be taken into consideration."

Those who progress through this book will be able to recognise, even if "through a glass darkly", a good deal of this in current English tort law, in particular the approach to the duty of care and the differing extent of protection of certain interests according to whether we are dealing with negligent or intentional conduct, though there are of course provisions in both drafts which are simply incompatible with current English law. However, some of those incompatibilities (most obviously the absence in England of strict liability for motor accidents) are really political rather than issues of legal doctrine. Nor are the incompatibilities a case of "English law v the Rest". The idea that "the Civil Law" is some monolithic unity is far from the truth: thus acceptance of either set of proposals would, for example, require German law to take a fundamentally different approach to liability for employees and neither draft contains anything resembling the French liability for damage done by things, a most distinctive feature of French tort law. A more important question is whether, even if such substantive problems could be overcome, any "unification" of tort law in Europe (which is always there in the background, even if everyone involved in these projects seems to want to distance himself from such an idea) is at all feasible. The legal cultures are very different even if they all embrace much the same principles at the highest level of abstraction. Thus the extracts above seem to assume open exposition and discussion at the highest level which are quite familiar in English judgments (and indeed in German ones) but which are quite alien to the tradition of the Cour de Cassation in France, where the tradition is that one must give reasons but not explain the reasons. Although English appellate procedures have become markedly more "paper-based" in recent years the fundamental idea of the oral trial which settles all issues between the parties is still the underlying foundation of the procedural system, even though most cases are of course settled; and matters which on the face of it have nothing to do with substantive law may have major implications for the substantive principles. For example, in English civil cases the standard of proof is on a balance of probabilities: if something is shown to be just more likely than not it is treated as having been conclusively established for most purposes. In some European systems on the other hand the damage must be proved with "certainty".[66] It would be wrong to equate this with the English "beyond a reasonable doubt" of the criminal standard and it is hard to pin down. However, it does seem more onerous than the balance of probability standard. That has obvious implications for the approach the particular system will take to the substantive law issue of claims based on "loss of a chance". One must also not forget the considerable uncertainty which would result from unification, and the massive burden of re-education, not to mention the natural human fondness for the familiar. Perhaps

---

[66] Thus in the *Principles of European Tort Law* art.2:105 damage "must be proved according to normal [national] procedural standards".

most important of all is the fact that even if everyone adopted the same text, how would one prevent the system simply breaking up very quickly by divergences in local interpretation? In a few very narrow areas of private law (principally matters of jurisdiction) the European Court of Justice acts as the ultimate appellate court for an "autonomous" European law but it is inconceivable that we could have a Supreme Court of Private Law for the whole of Europe or that we could expect local courts to keep up with legal developments in all the other countries.

The prospect of unification. It seems unlikely that there will be wholesale unification or harmonisation in the foreseeable future (even of the law of contract, which might appear more desirable and which would probably be a good deal easier than in the case of tort). If EU legislators in their activities impinging on private law do make substantial use of the DCFR as a legislative toolbox then that will have an impact on English law. However, even if nothing like this happens and these documents and proposals remain academic texts, it must also be borne in mind that for a century the English courts have been "comparatists" in the sense that they have been willing to look at developments in other common law countries and in the last 20 years at the highest level they have shown an increasing inclination to look at civil law systems.[67] So it is not inconceivable that at the highest level English courts might make "voluntary" use of things like the DCFR.

2–017

3. STRUCTURE OF THE BOOK

Tort theorists have long debated how torts should be categorised. By and large, two schemas vie for acceptance. One arranges torts according to the different forms of liability. This arrangement, which was famously suggested by Oliver Wendell Holmes,[68] yields the following threefold classification: torts that require proof of a state of mind, torts that are susceptible to commission by negligence and torts that impose liability regardless of whether or not the defendant is at fault. The other schema organises torts in terms of the rights that they protect.[69] So systematised, torts are herded together according to whether they vindicate rights in bodily integrity, possession of tangible property, reputation, economic relations and so on.[70] The order followed in the succeeding chapters of this book adheres strictly to neither course but has as its principal aim no more than the avoidance, so far as reasonably possible, of repetition and of references forward

2–018

---

[67] Three well-known examples are *Henderson v Merrett Syndicates Ltd* [1995] 2 A.C. 145, *White v Jones* [1995] 2 A.C. 207 and *Fairchild v Glenhaven Funeral Services Ltd* [2002] UKHL 22; [2003] 1 A.C. 32. Such overt external references, even to another civil law system, would be very unusual in Europe.

[68] This schema was proposed in an anonymous article ((1873) 7 Am. L. Rev. 652). Holmes is generally credited as the author.

[69] This approach is usually associated with Pollock: see Pollock, *The Law of Torts* (1887), pp.6–12. It is endorsed in Robert Stevens: Stevens, *Torts and Rights* (2007), Ch.13, especially at pp.296–300.

[70] For analysis of these and other ways of classifying torts see Keeton, Dobbs, Keeton and Owen (eds), *Prosser and Keeton on Torts*, 5th edn (1984), pp.31–33. Several commentators have expressed doubts about the usefulness of categorising torts: see, e.g. Friedman, *The Law of Torts in Canada*, 2nd edn (2002), p.26.

to later chapters. The object is comprehensibility and the convenience of the reader who wants to begin at the beginning and go on to the end. The result is not, therefore, "scientific". If it is convenient, that is enough.

4. Torts Not Treated in this Book

2–019   There are some wrongs which are certainly torts but which are outside the scope of an elementary book on tort law. First, there are those matters which are commonly treated as specialised legal subjects in their own right. Technically speaking, actions for infringement of the intellectual property rights of copyright, patents, and trademarks are actions in tort (albeit statutory) but these matters are far too specialised and complex for inclusion in a book of this kind and the statutory causes of action for wrongful discrimination are best looked at in the context of employment law, where they most commonly arise.[71] Then there is a range of minor tort causes of action based on the common law.[72] For example, there is a group of wrongs concerned with interference with a franchise—a royal privilege, or branch of the Queen's prerogative, subsisting in the hands of a subject.[73] The forms of it are various, but examples are the franchise of a number of persons to be incorporated and subsist as a body politic; franchises to have waifs, wrecks, strays, royal fish; and franchises to hold markets or fairs, and to take tolls for bridges and ferries.[74] In another sense, "franchise" signifies the right to vote at a parliamentary or municipal election. In the famous case of *Ashby v White*,[75] a returning officer was held liable in damages for wrongfully refusing to take the claimant's vote at a parliamentary election. From this point of view the case is now wholly obsolete since by statute the remedy is criminal not civil,[76] but it remains a relevant authority on the tort of breach of statutory duty. Sometimes Parliament may sweep away whole areas of tort law, as happened with the group of torts which related to interference with family relationships.[77] Others may be preserved like legal fossils, the social circumstances which underlay them having passed away, for the time being at least. An example is usurpation of a public office.

---

[71] But note that these may overlap on the facts with common law claims: see *Farah v MPC* [1998] Q.B. 65 at 69.

[72] See Rudden (1991–92) 6–7 Tulane Civ. L.F. 105.

[73] Blackstone, Comm, ii, 37.

[74] Some of this is by no means obsolete, see, e.g. *Iveagh v Martin* [1961] 1 Q.B. 232; *Wyld v Silver* [1963] 1 Q.B. 169; *Sevenoaks DC v Patullo & Vinson Ltd* [1984] Ch. 211.

[75] (1703) 2 Ld. Raym. 938; 92 E.R. 126.

[76] Representation of the People Act 1985.

[77] Law Reform (Miscellaneous Provisions) Act 1970 ss.4–15; Administration of Justice Act 1982 s.2

CHAPTER 3

FOUNDATIONAL CONCEPTS IN TORT LAW

Introduction. Some torts require proof of fault, which means acting with a   3–001
particular state of mind (usually with an intention to bring about a particular
result) or failing to take as much care as the reasonable person would have taken
(negligence). Other torts impose strict liability. In the case of strict liability torts,
proof of fault on the part of the defendant is not required. These three
concepts—intention, negligence and strict liability—are regularly encountered
throughout this book. They are foundational ideas in the law of torts.
Accordingly, it is useful to look at them jointly before progressing further. To
properly understand these concepts, it is necessary to distinguish them from the
ideas of motive and malice, and so a few words will also be said about motive
and malice.

1. INTENTION

Intention is inferred from conduct. Some torts require proof that the defendant   3–002
acted with a particular intention. It is, of course, impossible for the law to do
more than to infer a person's intention, or indeed any other mental state, from his
conduct. Intention is simply not amenable to direct proof. Centuries ago, Brian CJ
said: "It is common knowledge that the thought of man shall not be tried, for the
Devil himself knoweth not the thought of man."[1] It is true that Bowen LJ in 1885
said that "the state of a man's mind is as much a fact as the state of his
digestion".[2] However, there is no contradiction in these dicta. Brian CJ's point
merely meant that no one can know for certain what passes in the mind of another
person. Brian CJ would certainly not have dissented from the proposition that
what a person thinks must be deduced from what he says and does, and that is all
that Bowen LJ meant.

---

[1] Year Book Pasch. 17 Edw. 4, fol. 2, pl. 2.
[2] *Edgington v Fitzmaurice* (1885) 29 Ch. D. 459 at 483.

3–003   **Intention in general terms.** Everyone agrees that a person intends to bring about a consequence if it is his goal to cause it, but beyond that it is probably not possible to lay down any universal definition of intention for the purposes of tort. In crime, the law is that the trier of fact is entitled (but not, it seems, required) to infer intention where the defendant was aware that the harm was "virtually certain" to result from his act.[3]

3–004   **Intention is an under-analysed concept in tort law.** Whereas criminal theorists have spent much time exploring the concept of intention in the criminal law,[4] there has been much less discussion of intention in the tort context.[5] There are probably several reasons for this situation. First, actions in tort against persons who intend to cause harm are relatively rare. This is likely because it is often not worth suing such persons, who will usually be without relevant insurance. Secondly, although D acted intentionally, the claimant may sometimes be able to recover in the tort of negligence. This reduces the need for the courts to grapple with the concept of intention. Thirdly, intention is not an element of many torts. Even when intention is needed, tort law often only requires that the initial interference with the claimant be intended, and does not insist that the defendant intend the consequences of that interference. For instance, if A hits B intending some slight harm but B suffers greater harm A is responsible for the greater harm regardless of whether he intends it.[6] Indeed, the defendant is liable for the greater harm even if it is the result of some unusual susceptibility of the claimant, a principle developed primarily in the context of negligence[7] but applying with even more force to intentional wrongdoers.[8]

3–005   **The concept of intention to relation to specific torts.** The concept of intention has been given a specific definition in relation to particular causes of action. In one tort, conspiracy to injure, intention has the very narrow meaning of single-minded purpose to do harm, so that the defendant does not "intend" even what he foresees as inevitable if his purpose is to advance his own interests.[9] Other torts in the area of unlawful interference with economic interests now require either that very narrow "purpose" intention *or* that the defendant acts so as to cause harm to the claimant as the means to some other end which it is his purpose to achieve: the claimant must therefore be the "target" of the defendant's actions.[10] In the context of trespass to land it has been said that indifference to a risk that trespass will occur by animals in the defendant's charge amounts to intention[11] and it is thought that the same approach should be taken in all the trespass torts: if D throws his coffee dregs out of the window of his office, knowing that others may be passing, that should be trespass if anyone is hit,

---

[3] *R. v Woollin* [1999] 1 A.C. 82.

[4] See, e.g. Duff, *Intention, Agency and Criminal Liability* (1990).

[5] But see Finnis in Owen (ed.), *Philosophical Foundations of Tort Law* (1995), p.229; Cane (2000) 20 O.J.L.S. 533; Hylton (2010) 44 Val. U.L. Rev. 1217.

[6] *Wainwright v Home Office* [2001] EWCA Civ 2081; [2002] Q.B. 1334 at [69] (on appeal [2003] UKHL 53; [2004] 2 A.C. 406).

[7] See para.7–038.

[8] *Allan v New Mount Sinai Hospital* (1980) 109 D.L.R. (3d) 634.

[9] See para.19–037.

[10] See para.19–026.

[11] *League Against Cruel Sports v Scott* [1986] Q.B. 240 at 252.

whether the street is so crowded that it is a virtual certainty or is comparatively unfrequented.[12] To take another example, consider the case of someone who places a bomb for political reasons; he may give a warning on the basis of which the emergency services may be expected to act and he may not "intend" personal injury in the sense of desiring it but he can hardly deny that he appreciates the real risk of something going wrong.[13] This is the state of mind referred to in the criminal law as "recklessness", that is to say, the wrongdoer is conscious of the risk he is taking.[14] Where recklessness as to consequences will do in tort, so too will recklessness as to circumstances. Thus, the tort of misfeasance in a public office is committed when a public officer acts knowingly outside the scope of his powers with the intent that the claimant will thereby be injured or if he is recklessly indifferent to the legality of his acts and the damage he may inflict on the claimant.[15]

2. NEGLIGENCE

Negligence is both a tort and a type of fault. The word "negligence" has two   3–006
meanings in the law of torts. First, "negligence" is an independent tort. Secondly, "negligence" is a type of fault. What we are concerned with at this point is negligence as a form of fault, and the focus will be on distinguishing it from intention.

Negligence as a form of fault is a type of conduct. Negligence qua species of   3–007
fault refers to a failure to take as much care as the hypothetical reasonable person in the defendant's position would have taken in the circumstances. It is, in other words, a falling short of the standard of care set by the reasonable person. The process of determining whether the defendant was negligent involves, therefore, comparing the defendant's conduct with that of the reasonable person. It is important to note that this means that negligence is a type of conduct rather than a state of mind.[16] It is not required that a defendant be inadvertent (i.e. have a blank mind) with respect to a particular risk of injury in order to be negligent in relation to that risk. On the contrary, people who consciously run risks may be negligent with respect to those risks. An illustration of advertent risk-taking constituting negligence can be found in *Vaughan v Menlove*,[17] where the defendant had been warned that his haystack was likely to overheat and catch

---

[12] *Bici v Ministry of Defence* [2004] EWHC 786 (QB).
[13] *Breslin v McKenna* [2009] NIQB 50.
[14] Though using "intention" to embrace this state of mind is convenient it is open to criticism as being wider than the proper usage. As Finnis points out, lecturers know that what they say will inevitably confuse some of their audience, but it would be difficult to say that they intend to do so: Finnis in Owen (ed.), *Philosophical Foundations of Tort Law* (1995), p.229.
[15] *Three Rivers DC v Bank of England (No.3)* [2001] UKHL 16; [2003] 2 A.C. 1. See also *White v White* [2001] UKHL 9; [2001] 2 All E.R. 43 (a requirement that a person "knows" something will generally be satisfied if he suspects that it is so but takes the attitude that he will not ask further because he would rather not know).
[16] The mental and conduct theories of negligence are compared in Goudkamp (2004) 28 M.U.L.R 343 at 349–351.
[17] (1837) 3 Bing NC 468; 132 E.R. 490.

fire, which might spread to his neighbour's land. The defendant said that he would "chance it" and he was found to be negligent when the haystack caught fire.

3–008 **Overlap between negligence and subjective forms of fault.** The fact that negligence is a type of conduct means that there is a degree of overlap between the concepts of negligence on the one hand and those of intention and recklessness on the other, the latter being states of mind. It is perfectly possible for a defendant who acts intentionally or recklessly to also act negligently. Provided that the defendant's conduct is conduct in which the reasonable person would not have engaged, the defendant will be negligent, irrespective of whether the defendant proceeds with the intention to cause a particular result, or is reckless with regard to a given risk.

3–009 **"Reasonable" and the "reasonable person".** It is convenient to provide an explanation of the terms "reasonable" and "reasonable person". They recur so frequently in the law of tort, and indeed in every branch of the law, that their meaning must be grasped at the outset. Negligence as a species of fault is synonymous with acting unreasonably, and the question of whether a person has acted unreasonably is determined by reference to the concept of the reasonable person. The reasonable person always acts reasonably, and so acting unreasonably means acting other than as the reasonable person would have acted. The reasonable person is, of course, an abstraction. Lord Bowen visualised the reasonable person as "the man on the Clapham omnibus".[18] An American writer said that the reasonable person is "the man who takes the magazines home, and in the evening pushes the lawn-mower in his shirt sleeves".[19] It will be noticed that the two passages that have just been quoted refer to the "reasonable man." Until relatively recently, the tendency of the courts and writers was to speak of the "reasonable man" rather than the "reasonable person". As a matter of strict legal principle, these labelling practices were of no importance. It was simply a matter of convention, and the norm today is to speak of the "reasonable person".

3–010 **Degrees of negligence.** For the purposes of determining whether the defendant is guilty of negligence, it is irrelevant whether the defendant fell well below the standard of the reasonable person or just short of it:[20] the defendant has reached a single required standard or he has not.[21] However, the gravity of the defendant's negligence can be relevant in various other ways. For example, it can have a bearing on whether exemplary damages should be ordered, and their quantum. It can also be relevant where contributory negligence or contribution is in issue. This is because, when damages are apportioned, it is necessary to compare the defendant's conduct with another person's conduct (either the claimant or another defendant).

---

[18] Attributed to Lord Bowen in *McQuire v Western Morning News Co Ltd* [1903] 2 K.B. 100 at 109.
[19] Cited by Greer LJ in *Hall v Brooklands Auto Racing Club* [1933] 1 K.B. 205 at 224.
[20] See Nolan (2013) 72 C.L.J. 651 at 672–687.
[21] "Generally speaking in civil cases 'gross' negligence has no more effect that [sic] negligence without an opprobrious epithet": *Caswell v Powell Duffryn Associated Collieries Ltd* [1940] A.C. 152 at 175 per Lord Wright. To similar effect see *Wilson v Brett* (1843) 11 M. & W. 113 at 116; 152 E.R. 737 at 739.

3. STRICT LIABILITY

A defendant may be liable in some torts irrespective of whether he was at fault. **3–011**
Such torts impose strict liability. They lack a fault element, such as intention or
negligence. It is important to note that strict liability means liability *regardless* of
whether the defendant is at fault. Strict liability torts do not require proof that the
defendant was not at fault, and hence it is technically incorrect to say that strict
liability is liability without fault. No tort requires proof that the defendant was not
at fault. Very often, a defendant who is held strictly liable will in fact be at fault,
but the claimant is not required to establish fault on the part of the defendant in
order to make out his action.

4. MOTIVE AND MALICE

The general irrelevance of motive. Motive signifies a person's reasons for **3–012**
committing a particular act. Motive is generally irrelevant in tort law, although
there are, as always, exceptions. The mere fact that a defendant was virtuously
motivated is, in principle, insufficient to exonerate him from liability if all of the
elements of a tort are present. Similarly, if conduct is lawful apart from motive, a
bad motive will not make the defendant liable. The general irrelevancy of evil
motive was affirmed by the House of Lords in *Bradford Corp v Pickles*.[22] Pickles
was annoyed at the refusal of the claimant corporation to purchase his land in
connection with a scheme to supply water to the inhabitants of a town. In
revenge, he sank a shaft on his land. The water which percolated through his land
in unknown and undefined channels from the land of the corporation on a higher
level was consequently discoloured and diminished when it passed again to the
lower land of the corporation. For this injury Pickles was held not liable. "It is the
act", said Lord Macnaghten, "not the motive for the act, that must be regarded. If
the act, apart from motive, gives rise merely to damage without legal injury, the
motive, however reprehensible it may be, will not supply that element". [23] Three
years later this was again emphasised by the House of Lords in *Allen v Flood*[24]
and, for better or worse, it remains the general rule today. As we shall see,
however, there are certain exceptional cases in which the evil motive of the
defendant, if established, will tip the scales of liability against him.[25]

Mixed motive. It is often the case that a person has more than one reason for **3–013**
doing a particular act. In other words, motive is often mixed. When this is the
case, the law generally regards a person's dominant purpose as his motive[26]
when, exceptionally, motive is relevant.

Malice. The term "malice" is used in several different ways in the law of torts. It **3–014**
may mean what the layperson usually takes it to be—evil motive or spite—or the

---

[22] [1895] A.C. 587.
[23] [1895] A.C. 587 at 601. See further as to this case, para.15–022.
[24] [1898] A.C. 1.
[25] The principal exceptions are misfeasance in a public office (see *Three Rivers* 2003] 2 A.C. 1 at 191
and Ch.8) and malicious prosecution (see Ch.20).
[26] *Hayes v Willoughby* [2013] UKSC 17; [2013] 1 W.L.R. 935 at [17].

purpose of causing harm to someone. Alternatively, it may simply signify doing an act wilfully without justification or excuse. The last two senses have really nothing to do with motive but refer to intention, a term which ought to be confined to advertence to conduct and its consequences, and which is quite colourless as to the motive which influences the actor. The meaning of malice has to be considered in the context of each tort where it is said to be relevant—for example, defamation, malicious prosecution and misfeasance in a public office.

CHAPTER 4

TRESPASS TO THE PERSON AND RELATED MATTERS

1.   INTRODUCTION

The law of torts recognises several actions in trespass. This chapter deals with the **4–001** action in trespass to the person. The other actions in trespass—trespass to land and trespass to chattels—are addressed later.[1] There are three main forms of trespass to the person, namely, assault, battery and false imprisonment.[2] These forms of trespass are sometimes referred to as torts in their own right. However, it is clear that they exist under the umbrella of trespass to the person, and so references to trespass to the person encompass assault, battery and false imprisonment. After exploring the forms of trespass to the person, three further related actions will be dealt with. These are the action in *Wilkinson v Downton*, which deals with intentional harm that does not constitute a trespass to the person because of the indirect way in which it was inflicted, and the statutory causes of action for harassment provided for in the Protection from Harassment Act 1997 and the Equality Act 2010.

2.   GENERAL PRINCIPLES OF TRESPASS TO THE PERSON

Trespass to the person requires direct interference with a person's body or **4–002** **liberty.** Trespass to the person involves direct interference with another person's body or freedom of movement. What precisely "directness" means is difficult to say. The classic example involves throwing a log into a highway. The requisite

---

[1] See Ch.14 and Ch.18.
[2] Trespass to the person was also the parent of some torts, now abolished, which protected family and service relationships: see para.2–019.

directness is present if the log hits a passer-by, but absent if the passer-by were to stumble on the log. The broad idea of the notion is easy enough to understand in the case of battery, where it seems to mean something in the nature of a blow (though even that may be hard to define with precision).[3] It is more difficult to give directness a clear meaning in relation to assault and false imprisonment: assault requires no physical contact and may, it seems, be committed by making threats over the telephone,[4] and while the obvious form of false imprisonment is physical seizure of the claimant by a police officer, it is clear that false imprisonment is equally committed if the claimant submits to a legal authority asserted by the officer.[5] In neither assault nor false imprisonment is there much meaning in "directness", save that both situations involve a threat, express or implied, of the infliction of force, though in false imprisonment it is qualified.

4–003   **The direct/indirect distinction is drawn elsewhere in tort law.** A distinction between what is "direct" and "indirect" is found in other parts of tort law. For example, at one time the leading test of remoteness of damage[6] was based on the theory that the defendant was liable for directly inflicted harm even though it was unforeseeable. It seems unlikely that "direct" had precisely the same meaning there as it does here. More recently, a majority of the House of Lords drew a distinction between the direct and indirect infliction of physical harm by negligence, a duty of care with regard to the former being easier to establish than with regard to the latter,[7] but there is no overt suggestion that the distinction is meant to reflect the concept of directness in the trespass torts.

4–004   **The requirement of intention.** Historically, the claimant did not need to prove fault on the part of the defendant to succeed in an action in trespass. The law in this regard underwent a significant change in the Twentieth Century principally as a result of two decisions. The first of these decisions is *Fowler v Lanning*.[8] In this case Diplock J held that where the contact with the claimant was unintentional the claimant was required to plead and prove that the defendant had acted negligently. Accordingly, the statement of claim, which recorded laconically that "the defendant shot the plaintiff", was struck out as disclosing no cause of action since it lacked an allegation of intention or negligence. *Fowler* was concerned only with the burden of proof as reflected in the principles of pleading: it did not hold that there could not be a negligent trespass. The second important decision is *Letang v Cooper*.[9] The defendant in this case drove his car over the legs of the claimant, who was sunbathing on a piece of grass outside a hotel where cars were parked. The claimant did not commence proceedings until more than three years had passed, which meant that a claim for negligence was statute-barred,[10] but she argued that she had an alternative claim in trespass, which was not statute-barred, the general tort limitation period being six years.

---

[3] See para.4–010.
[4] See para.4–020.
[5] See para.4–024.
[6] See para 7–031.
[7] *Marc Rich v Bishop Rock Marine* [1996] A.C. 211, see para.5–031.
[8] [1959] 1 Q.B. 426.
[9] [1965] 1 Q.B. 232.
[10] Nowadays the court might simply "disapply" the limitation period: see para.26–098.

This argument was rejected by the Court of Appeal for two reasons. One was that the three-year period prescribed by statute applied to all claims for personal injuries no matter what the cause of action.[11] However, the other reason is not a mere matter of statutory interpretation and concerns the structure of the law in this area. Lord Denning MR (with whom Danckwerts LJ agreed) expressed his agreement with *Fowler v Lanning* but added: "I would go this one step further: when the injury is not inflicted intentionally, but negligently, I would say the only cause of action is negligence and not trespass."[12] It seems, therefore, that trespass to the person is a tort only of intention (including within that term "subjective recklessness").[13] Diplock LJ would not have gone quite so far. He considered that trespass could be committed negligently but where the trespass was negligent the claimant would need to plead and prove negligence and also that the contact with his body caused damage. In other words, Diplock LJ thought that it was possible to commit trespass negligently but that the victim of a negligent trespass would gain no advantage from framing his claim in trespass. Trespass liability becomes merely an alternative label for some cases of negligence. Although the matter has not been fully explored in England since *Letang v Cooper*,[14] the net result appears to be that the action for unintentional trespass to the person has disappeared in practice (for Diplock LJ) or even in name (for Lord Denning MR).[15]

Trespass to the person is actionable per se. Damage is not an element of trespass to the person: the tort is actionable per se. It is therefore irrelevant to liability in this tort whether the claimant suffered any damage as a result of the defendant's actions. Because there is no damage element, it is unnecessary to consider any issues of causation in determining whether liability arises.[16]   **4–005**

Intersection with the criminal law. Trespass to the person is a crime as well as   **4–006**
a tort. Consequently, judges deciding proceedings in tort based on trespass to the person often refer to criminal law cases and vice versa. To a great degree, the relevant principles are the same in both contexts, but it should not be assumed that this is universally the case.[17] The criminal justice system may provide compensation in respect of acts of trespass,[18] although discussion of such relief is beyond the scope of this book. In comparison with the volume of offences against

---

[11] This view was subsequently declared to be wrong but has now been restored to favour. See para.26–098.

[12] [1965] 1 Q.B. 232 at 240.

[13] As to this, see para.3–005.

[14] In *Wilson v Pringle* [1987] Q.B. 237, the Court of Appeal referred to the necessity for the touching in trespass to be "deliberate" and that is really the only view reconcilable with the requirement of hostility emphasised in that case.

[15] See *Bici v MoD* [2004] EWHC 786 (QB); *The Times*, June 11, 2004, where Elias J held that intention or subjective recklessness was required.

[16] *R. (on the application of Lumba) v Secretary of State for the Home Department* [2011] UKSC 12; [2012] 1 A.C. 245 at [64]–[65]; *R (on the application of Kambadzi) v Secretary of State for the Home Department* [2011] UKSC 23; [2011] 1 W.L.R. 1299.

[17] There is perhaps a certain ambivalence in *R. v Barnes* [2004] EWCA Crim 3246; [2005] 1 W.L.R. 910 on whether the court is simply giving advice on prosecutorial policy or stating substantive differences between tort and crime.

[18] For example, criminal courts in sentencing an offender may order the offender to pay compensation.

the person handled by the criminal courts or the number of civil actions for negligence, civil actions for trespass to the person are not common. No doubt this has always been so, for in trivial cases the claimant is likely to hesitate at the risks of civil litigation once tempers have cooled, and in serious cases the defendant may well not be worth pursuing. However, as we have seen, civil suits are sometimes brought for rather indirect motives, for example, to make a "point of principle" or to get an individual investigation or to provoke the prosecution authorities into acting.[19] In other cases there may be the prospect of recovering large damages because, from a civil point of view, someone is vicariously liable for the act of the wrongdoer, even though it amounts to a crime. The best example is the large number of actions that have been brought in respect of abuse in children's homes, sometimes many years after the event.[20]

3. BATTERY

4–007 **Elements of battery.** The elements of battery are as follows: (1) an act; (2) by which contact is made with the claimant's body; (3) the contact must be direct; (4) the contact with the claimant's body must be hostile; and (5) the claimant did not consent to the contact. Note that, since battery is actionable per se, its lacks a damage element. It is irrelevant to liability in battery whether the claimant suffered any damage.

4–008 **Terminology.** It is frequently the case, both inside and outside of the law, for the word "assault" to be used to refer both to assaults and to batteries. Technically, an assault, as will be explained later, involves causing someone to apprehend that they will suffer a battery.[21] In this chapter the word "assault" will be used in its strict sense. So, to throw water at a person is an assault but if any drops fall upon him it is battery.[22]

4–009 **The act element.** For a battery to be committed there must be an act by the defendant that involves contact with the claimant. D does not commit battery against C if X seizes D's arm and uses it like a club to hit C (X and X alone is liable in this scenario). The act need be intentional only as to the contact, and an intention to cause harm is not required. Thus, if D pushes C into a swimming pool and injury occurs, then, assuming D's act to be "hostile", D is liable regardless of whether the injury was desired or foreseen by D.[23]

4–010 **The contact element.** Any contact with the body of the claimant (or his clothing) is sufficient to amount to a battery. Thus, in *Cole v Turner* Lord Holt CJ said that, "the least touching of another in anger is a battery".[24] The contact does not have to involve literally the defendant's body coming into contact with the claimant's body. There is a battery when the defendant shoots the claimant from a distance

---

[19] See para.1–002.
[20] The limitation difficulties in these cases were ameliorated by *A v Hoare* [2008] UKHL 6; [2008] 1 A.C. 844, see para.26–098.
[21] See para.4–018.
[22] *Pursell v Horne* (1838) 3 N. & P. 564.
[23] *Wilson v Pringle* [1987] Q.B. 237 at 249; *Williams v Humphrey, The Times*, February 20, 1975.
[24] (1704) 6 Mod. 149 at 149.

just as much as when he strikes him with his fist and the same is probably true when the defendant deliberately collides with the car in which the claimant is sitting, shaking him up.[25] It is unclear whether the infliction of such things as heat, light[26] or smoke[27] on a person constitutes a battery, although they probably do not. Smoke is, from a scientific point of view, particulate matter but for the purposes of trespass to land it has been treated as an intangible and therefore falling into the realm of nuisance. Mere passive obstruction has been said not to be a battery,[28] although in a criminal case there was held to be a battery where the defendant innocently drove his car on to the victim's foot and declined to move it.[29]

The contact must be direct. As has already been mentioned, in order for a   **4–011**
battery to be committed the defendant must come into direct contact with the claimant.[30] Depending on the view one takes of this requirement it may not be battery if D smears dirt on a towel hoping that C will use it to wipe his face. The tendency in the criminal law seems to be to give a broad meaning to the word "directly". Putting acid in a dryer so that it injured the next person to use it was held to amount to a battery.[31] In *Haystead v Chief Constable of Derbyshire*[32] the defendant struck a woman in the face, with the result that the baby she was holding fell to the floor. The defendant was charged with an offence of assault (which in this context includes battery) on the baby and his conviction was upheld by the Divisional Court on the basis that:[33]

> "[T]he movement of W whereby she lost hold of the child was entirely and immediately the result of the [defendant's] action in punching her. There is no difference in logic or good sense between the facts of this case and one where the defendant might have used a weapon to fell the child to the floor, save only that this is a case of reckless and not intentional battery."

Of course in the civil law, if the baby had been injured, there would have been the plainest possible case of negligence even if the defendant had never given any thought to the likely effect on the baby.

The contact must be hostile. Life would be too difficult if the law did not place   **4–012**
limits on the types of bodily contact that were actionable. However, the courts have struggled to identify appropriate limits. In *Collins v Wilcock*[34] Robert Goff LJ said that bodily contact was not actionable if it was generally acceptable in the

---

[25] *Clark v State* 746 So. 2d 1237 (Fla. 1999).

[26] Photographing a person is not an assault: *Murray v Ministry of Defence* [1985] 12 N.I.J.B. 12; *Kaye v Robertson* [1991] F.S.R. 62.

[27] "Second-hand smoking" claims in this country have tended to be against employers for negligence in allowing smoking to injure the claimant employee's health.

[28] *Innes v Wylie* (1844) 1 C. & K. 257 at 263.

[29] *Fagan v MPC* [1969] 1 Q.B. 439.

[30] See para.4–010.

[31] *DPP v K* (1990) 1 W.L.R. 1067 (offence of "assault" under s.47 of the Offences Against the Person Act 1861). In *Breslin v McKenna* [2009] NIQB 50 (a civil action) planting a bomb set to go off later was held to be trespass.

[32] [2000] 2 Cr. App. R. 339.

[33] [2000] 2 Cr. App. R. 339 at [30]. The court did not consider an alternative approach based on "transferred malice" but was dubious about its success.

[34] [1984] 1 W.L.R. 1172.

ordinary conduct of everyday life.[35] This is more satisfactory than the somewhat artificial approach whereby a person is deemed to consent to the multitude of minor contacts which take place in, for example, a crowded bus. Of course, the absence of consent is often relevant in the sense that it is open to a person to make it plain that he objects to contact that most people find trivial and thereby render actionable what would not be so if done to others, but there must be limits on this: the passenger on the crowded bus can hardly be allowed to appropriate to himself a disproportionate share of the space available because he objects to being touched by others. In *Wilson v Pringle*,[36] however, the Court of Appeal, while not rejecting what was said in *Collins*, laid down the rule that a battery involves a "hostile" touching. The actual decision was that the trial judge had fallen into error in granting summary judgment to the claimant where the defendant, a schoolboy, had on his own admission pulled the claimant's bag from his shoulder and thereby caused him to fall to the ground and injure himself. Such horseplay, it seems, may or may not be battery, according to whether the tribunal of fact can discern the ingredient of "hostility". However, since the court expressly said that hostility did not require ill will or malevolence, the requirement seems hardly to mean any more than that the defendant has interfered in a way to which the claimant might object. Perhaps the closest we can get to the central idea is to say that the interference must be "offensive" in the sense that it infringes the claimant's right to be physically inviolate, to be "let alone". To say, however, that there must be something offensive to dignity seems to be going too far, at least if *Nash v Sheen*[37] is correctly decided. In that case it was held to be battery where the claimant went to a hairdresser for a permanent wave and the defendant, without her consent, applied a tone rinse which produced a skin reaction. Even this rather vague formulation may not cover every case: for example, indecent touching of a small child is clearly a battery even though the child may have insufficient understanding to "take offence". Whatever the theoretical basis of liability, we can say that touching another in the course of conversation or to gain his attention[38] is not a battery. Even some persistence may be justifiable, for:[39]

"[T]he lost or distressed may surely be permitted a second touch, or possibly even more, on a reluctant or impervious sleeve or shoulder, as may a person who is acting reasonably in the exercise of a duty. In each case, the test must be whether the physical contact so persisted in has in the circumstances gone beyond generally accepted standards of conduct."

Into the assessment of this must enter not only any limitations laid down by the claimant but also the relationship (or lack of it) between the parties. An embrace of a complete stranger may be a battery; an embrace in an attempt to settle a lovers' quarrel may not be.

---

[35] See also the same judge in *F v West Berkshire HA* [1990] 2 A.C. 1. *Collins* was applied in *McMillan v CPS* [2008] EWHC 1457 (Admin).

[36] [1987] Q.B. 237.

[37] *The Times*, March 13, 1953.

[38] *Wiffin v Kincard* (1807) 2 Bos. & Pul. 471; *Coward v Baddeley* (1859) 4 H. & N. 478.

[39] *Collins v Wilcock* [1984] 1 W.L.R. 1172 at 1178.

The contact must be non-consensual. Where the claimant consents to the contact there is no battery[40] and the same is true where the claimant, though not in fact consenting, so conducts himself so as to lead the defendant reasonably to believe that consent exists.[41] Whether or not the claimant in fact consents is, therefore, determined objectively, that is to say, by what the reasonable person would conclude given the claimant's behaviour.

4–013

The right to bodily integrity is absolute. Subject to any defences, an adult with full capacity has an absolute right to the inviolability of his body and therefore has an absolute right to choose whether or not to consent to medical treatment, even if the treatment is necessary to save his life,[42] or, in the case of a pregnant woman, the life of her unborn child.[43] Similarly, an adult of full capacity has the right to choose whether to eat or not: "Even if the refusal is tantamount to suicide, as in the case of a hunger strike, he cannot be compelled to eat or forcibly fed."[44] The same seems to be true even if the would-be suicide is a prisoner in lawful custody and the practice of forcible feeding, which was followed when suicide and attempted suicide were crimes,[45] has ceased: imprisonment limits a person's autonomy but does not deprive him of the power to choose to end his life.[46] Nor can the defendant contend that his well-meaning life-saving acts should attract only nominal damages, for that would be to make the principle of autonomy no more than symbolic. Thus, in Canada damages of CAN $20,000 were awarded where the defendants ignored the claimant's known religious objections to a blood transfusion.[47]

4–014

Consent and capacity. These principles apply if the claimant has full capacity[48] to make decisions regarding his wellbeing. The issue of capacity usually arises in

4–015

---

[40] It seems that the claimant has to prove absence of consent: see para.25–003. Regarding the relationship between consent and "offensiveness", see *Non-Marine Underwriters at Lloyd's v Scalera* [2000] SCC 24; [2000] 1 S.C.R. 551.

[41] See, e.g. *O'Brien v Cunard SS Co* 28 N.E. 266 (Mass. 1891) (holding up arm in vaccination line).

[42] *St George's Healthcare NHS Trust v S* [1999] Fam. 26; *Airedale NHS Trust v Bland* [1993] A.C. 789 at 891; *T (Adult, Refusal of Treatment), Re* [1993] Fam. 95; *A (Children) (Conjoined Twins: Surgical Separation), Re* [2001] Fam. 147; *R. (on the application of Burke) v General Medical Council* [2005] EWCA Civ 1003; [2005] 3 W.L.R. 1132.

[43] *St George's Healthcare NHS Trust v S* [1999] Fam. 26; and see *Winnipeg Child and Family Services v G* [1997] 3 S.C.R. 925 (mentally competent woman addicted to glue sniffing). It is not possible to sidestep the problem via the wardship procedure for that does not arise until the child is born: *F (in utero), Re* [1988] Fam. 122.

[44] *B v Croydon HA* [1995] Fam. 133 at 137.

[45] See *Leigh v Gladstone* (1909) 26 T.L.R. 139.

[46] This seems clearly to be accepted in *Reeves v MPC* [2001] 1 A.C. 360, though that case involved the question of whether the gaoler could be liable to the prisoner for failing to take steps to ensure that the suicide was not facilitated: see para.5–047. In *Secretary of State for the Home Dept v Robb* [1995] Fam. 127, a declaration was granted that the prison authorities might lawfully abide by the prisoner's refusal to take food. However, despite the negative form of the declaration the tenor of the judgment is plainly that the prison authorities would have been behaving unlawfully if they had chosen *not* to abide by the prisoner's decision.

[47] *Malette v Shulman* (1990) 67 D.L.R. (4th) 321. Cf. *B v An NHS Hospital Trust* [2002] EWHC 429 (Fam.); [2002] 2 All E.R. 449, where the claimant sought only nominal damages and £100 was awarded.

[48] Even where the claimant has the mental capacity to give a valid consent, any consent must be given freely and not under threats or improper pressure or undue influence. See *T (Adult, Refusal of*

the context of medical care and treatment and the law is mostly found in the Mental Capacity Act 2005, though the law created by that Act is generally similar to the common law. A detailed analysis of the Act is beyond the scope of this book, and readers are advised to consult specialised works in the area. However, it is convenient to make some general observations. The Act does not confer any right to impose treatment unless the person lacks capacity (or, in certain cases, is reasonably believed to lack it) and it is presumed that a person has capacity unless the contrary is shown. A person is not to be treated as lacking capacity merely because the decision that he makes is an unwise one.[49] A person lacks capacity in relation to any matter[50] "if at the material time he is unable to make a decision for himself in relation to the matter because of an impairment of, or a disturbance in the functioning of, the mind or brain".[51] If this requirement is fulfilled then any act done for or decision made for or on behalf of the incapable person must be in his "best interests",[52] though provided the person doing the act or making the decision complies with the requirements of s.4 (which sets out factors that the defendant must consider) it is sufficient if he reasonably believes that it is in the best interests of the person concerned.[53] The Act is not confined to acts of medical care or treatment but this is specifically dealt with by s.5. If the person doing the act has reasonably concluded, after making proper inquiries, that the person concerned lacks capacity and reasonably believes that it will be in his best interests, then he does not incur any liability in relation to the act that he would not have incurred if the person treated had had capacity and had consented.[54] So if C is brought into hospital in a coma and life-saving treatment, which cannot be postponed until he regains consciousness,[55] is administered to him by D, D will have a defence to any action for battery. If a person is not unconscious but, say, suffering from mental disorder, it may be necessary to "restrain" him, that is to say, to use or threaten force or restrict his liberty of movement.[56] If that is the case then the person doing the act must also comply with two further conditions set out in s.6: (1) that he reasonably believes it is

---

Treatment), Re [1993] Fam. 95 (mother's religious influence). It seems possible that nowadays a case like *Latter v Braddell* (1881) 50 L.J.Q.B. 448 (housemaid compelled to submit to medical examination on suspicion of pregnancy) would go the other way and that threats of violence would not be required. In *Wainwright v Home Office* [2003] UKHL 53; [2004] 2 A.C. 406 this issue was not pursued because the limits on the strip-search procedure to which the claimant was said to have consented were exceeded by the defendants.

[49] Mental Capacity Act 2005 s.1. The mere fact that a person is mentally ill does not necessarily mean that he lacks capacity.

[50] Clearly there will be many cases in which a person has full capacity to decide matters relating to issue A but not issue B.

[51] Mental Capacity Act 2005 s.2(1). This may be permanent or temporary. The definition is amplified by s.3 by reference to understanding, retaining and using information and communication decisions.

[52] Mental Capacity Act 2005 s.1(5).

[53] Mental Capacity Act 2005 s.4(9).

[54] Mental Capacity Act 2005 s.5(2).

[55] If it can be, the person administering the treatment is likely to fall foul of s.4(3).

[56] Mental Capacity Act 2005 s.6(4). This section does not cover "deprivation of liberty" under art.5 of the European Convention on Human Rights. Restraint amounting to this is governed ss.4A, 4B and 16A and by Sch.A1. For discussion of the concept of "deprivation of liberty" in this context see *P v Cheshire West and Chester Council* [2014] UKSC 19; [2014] 2 W.L.R. 642.

necessary to do the act to prevent harm to the person subjected to it; and (2) the act is a proportionate response to the likelihood of harm and its potential seriousness.[57]

Advance decisions to refuse treatment. The Act contains, in ss.24–26, provisions on "advance decisions to refuse treatment", that is to say, decisions made by a person with capacity that, if he becomes incapable at some time in the future, treatments specified by him may not be carried out or continued. Such a decision is only applicable to life-sustaining treatment if: (1) it is in writing, signed by the person and witnessed; and (2) contains an express statement that it is to apply even if there is a risk to life.[58] However, while going against an advance declaration complying with s.25 automatically makes the treatment wrongful,[59] where there is no such declaration the wishes of the patient are a factor to be considered[60] but the ultimate question is whether the doctor reasonably believes that he is acting in the patient's best interests.[61]

4–016

Consent and children. A minor who has reached the age of 16 years may give a valid consent to medical treatment under s.8 of the Family Law Reform Act 1969 and he may do so at common law below that age provided that he is capable of a full understanding of the consequences.[62] In these cases the child's power to consent to treatment is concurrent with that of the parents[63] and a parental consent may render lawful treatment to which the child objects,[64] though no doctor can be compelled to administer treatment and in deciding whether or not to do so the doctor will be influenced by the child's wishes. When the child has the capacity to give a valid consent and does so, the parents' objection to the treatment will not invalidate the child's consent.[65] In all cases involving a minor the court has an inherent jurisdiction to override both the child's objection to treatment and the child's consent to treatment.[66] In the case of young children the consent of the parents or guardian to medical treatment which is reasonably

4–017

---

[57] For discussion see *ZH v Metropolitan Police Commission* [2013] EWCA Civ 69; [2013] 3 All E.R. 113.

[58] Mental Capacity Act 2005 s.25(5)–(6).

[59] This is the effect of s.26(1).

[60] Mental Capacity Act 2005 s.4(6)(a).

[61] This is the approach taken to s.4 in the context of making a will for an incapable person in *Re P (Statutory Will)* [2009] EWHC 163 (Ch); [2010] Ch. 33 at [42]: "[A]lthough the fact that P makes an unwise decision does not on its own give rise to any inference of incapacity . . . , once the decision-making power shifts to a third party (whether a carer, deputy or the court) I cannot see that it would be a proper exercise for the third party decision-maker consciously to make an unwise decision merely because P would have done so."

[62] *Gillick v West Norfolk AHA* [1986] A.C. 112.

[63] *R, Re* [1992] Fam. 11.

[64] This is the effect of s.8(3) of the 1969 Act: *W, Re* [1993] Fam. 64.

[65] *W, Re* [1993] Fam. 64.

[66] Where the child has no capacity to consent the doctor should respect the parents' refusal to consent, but may apply to the court, which may override the parents' decision: *A (Children) (Conjoined Twins: Surgical Separation), Re* [2001] Fam. 147. The Mental Capacity Act 2005 has no relevance in such cases because although the child lacks capacity it is not because of "an impairment of, or a disturbance in the functioning of, the mind or brain" (s.2(1)).

necessary or to procedures which, though not therapeutic, are generally acceptable,[67] constitutes a valid consent on behalf of the child.

4. ASSAULT

4–018   **Definition of assault and relationship to battery.** Assault requires no contact because its essence is conduct which leads the claimant to apprehend the application of force. In the majority of cases an assault precedes a battery, perhaps by only a very brief interval, but there are examples of battery in which the claimant has no opportunity of experiencing any apprehension before the force is applied, for example, a blow from behind inflicted by an unseen assailant.[68] Just as there can be a battery without an assault, so also there can be an assault without a battery, as where the defendant does not carry out his threat or even has no intention of doing so but knows that the claimant is unaware of this.[69] There is similarly an assault without a battery if the blow is intercepted or prevented by some third person. In *Stephens v Myers*[70] the defendant, advancing with clenched fist upon the claimant at a parish meeting, was stopped by the churchwarden, who sat nearby the claimant. The defendant was held to be liable for assault.

4–019   **The claimant must apprehend the application of force.** It is irrelevant that the claimant is courageous and is not frightened by the threat or that he could easily defeat the defendant's attack: "apprehend" is used in the sense of "expect". The claimant must, however, have reason to apprehend that the defendant has the capacity to carry out the threat immediately.[71] It would not be an assault for the defendant to wave his fist (as opposed to pointing a gun) at the claimant on a passing train, nor where the claimant was under the effective protection of the police.[72] Pointing a loaded pistol at someone is of course an assault. The same is true even if the pistol is unloaded,[73] unless the claimant knows this (or unless his

---

[67] For example, testing of blood to determine paternity (*S v McC* [1972] A.C. 24); ritual circumcision or ear-piercing (*R. v Brown* [1994] 1 A.C. 212 at 231) but not tattooing: Tattooing of Minors Act 1969. A parent clearly could not give a valid consent to the sterilisation of a minor (as opposed to a necessary therapeutic procedure of which sterility was a by product). Where it is thought that sterilisation would be in the best interests of a minor because of mental incapacity the leave of the court should be sought, as in the case of a mentally incompetent adult.

[68] A Biblical instance in point is the slaying of Sisera by Jael, the wife of Heber the Kenite. She drove a tent-peg through his head while he was asleep. The shooting of FB in *Bici v MoD* [2004] EWHC 786 (QB); *The Times*, June 11, 2004 seems to be a modern example.

[69] For example, *Herbert v Misuga* (1994) 111 D.L.R. (4th) 193.

[70] (1840) 4 Car. & P. 349; 172 E.R. 735.

[71] See, e.g. *Mbasogo v Logo Ltd* [2006] EWCA Civ 1370; [2007] Q.B. 846 (presence of coup plotters in city insufficient); *Darwish v Egyptair Ltd* [2006] EWHC 1399 (QB). Holding out a baton in such a way as to show an intention to prevent the claimant's exit was an assault in *Hepburn v CC Thames Valley* [2002] EWCA Civ 1841; *The Times*, December 19, 2002.

[72] What is sufficiently "immediate" is a question of fact. In *Thomas v NUM (South Wales Area)* [1986] Ch. 20 it was held that the immediacy requirement was not satisfied where pickets who were held back by a police cordon made violent threats and gestures at persons going into work in vehicles.

[73] Cf. *Blake v Barnard* (1840) 9 Car. & P. 626 at 628; 173 E.R. 985 at 986.

distance from the weapon is so great that any reasonable person would have realised he was out of range, in which case there would be no assault even if it was loaded).[74]

An assault may be committed by threatening words. Threatening words alone may be actionable, according to the House of Lords in *R. v Ireland*.[75] This was a criminal case, but there seems no reason to doubt that the reasoning also applies to tort. Hence threats on the telephone may be an assault provided the claimant has reason to believe that they may be carried out in the sufficiently near future to qualify as "immediate".[76] In fact the House in *Ireland* went further and held that an assault could be committed by malicious silent telephone calls. The defendant's purpose was to convey a message to the victim just as surely as if he had spoken to her. In Lord Steyn's words: "The victim is assailed by uncertainty about his intentions. Fear may dominate her emotions, and it may be the fear that the caller's arrival at her door may be imminent. She may fear the *possibility* of immediate personal violence."[77]

4–020

Conditional threats. While words alone may constitute an assault, they may also negate the threatening nature of a gesture which would otherwise be an assault. In *Tubervell v Savage*[78] D laid his hand on his sword and said to C: "If it were not assize time, I would not take such language from you." This was a conditional threat. As it was assize time, D, as his words made clear, did not intend to make good on the threat.[79] Similarly it would be no assault if a landowner were to insist that a trespasser leave his land and show that he would use reasonable force in the event of a refusal; but the highwayman could not defend an action for assault by showing that he offered the claimant the opportunity to escape violence by handing over his money.

4–021

Alternative relief where the threat is not immediate. Where the threat lacks the quality of immediacy necessary for an assault, it does not follow that there is no remedy. First, if the claimant suffers actual damage (for example, psychiatric illness) as a result of a threat of unlawful action, he may have a claim on the basis exemplified in *Wilkinson v Downton*[80] or, perhaps, intimidation.[81] More important in practice is likely to be the Protection from Harassment Act 1997.[82]

4–022

---

[74] See the *Restatement*, 2d, § 29.

[75] [1998] A.C. 147.

[76] [1998] A.C. 147 at 162, Lord Steyn refers to a threat which is to be carried out "in a minute or two". No doubt that should not be taken as the outer limit of "immediate" but it is submitted that a threat in a call which the claimant knows is coming from Australia is not an assault.

[77] [1998] A.C. 147 at 162 (emphasis in original).

[78] (1669) 1 Mod. 3; 86 E.R. 684.

[79] Cf. *R. v Light* (1857) Dears & B. 332; 169 E.R. 1029.

[80] See para.4–031.

[81] See para.19–029.

[82] See para.4–034.

5.   FALSE IMPRISONMENT

4–023   **Definition of false imprisonment.** A defendant commits false imprisonment where he directly and intentionally imprisons the claimant.[83] Both "false" and "imprisonment" are somewhat misleading terms. "False" here does not necessarily signify "mendacious" or "fallacious". It is used in the less common sense of "erroneous" or "wrong" and it is quite possible to commit the tort without "imprisonment" of a person in the common acceptance of that term. In fact, neither physical contact nor anything resembling a prison is necessary. If a lecturer locks his class in the lecture room after the usual time for dismissal has arrived, that is false imprisonment; so, too, if a person be restrained from leaving his own house or any part of it,[84] or be forcibly detained in the public streets.[85]

4–024   **False imprisonment requires the absence of consent.** There is no false imprisonment where the claimant consents, but he is not to be taken as consenting simply because he does not resist by force.[86] A difficult line must be drawn between consent on the one hand and peaceful but unwilling submission to express or implied threats of force or asserted legal authority (whether valid or not) on the other.[87]

4–025   **State of mind of the defendant.** The law regarding the required state of mind on the part of the defendant is not especially clear. Historically, there was something to be said for the view that negligence would suffice (for example, locking a room without checking whether there is anyone inside) but false imprisonment is a species of trespass to the person and intention is probably now required for all forms of this wrong.

4–026   **Relevance of knowledge by the claimant of his imprisonment.** In *Grainger v Hill*[88] it was held that imprisonment is possible even if the claimant is so ill that he could not have moved anyway. In *Meering v Grahame-White Aviation Co Ltd*[89] the court went much further by holding that the tort is committed even if the claimant did not know that he was being detained. The claimant in this case was suspected of stealing a keg of varnish from the defendants, his employers. He was asked by two of their policemen to go with them to the company's office. He agreed to do so and at his suggestion they took a short cut there. On arrival the claimant was taken or invited to go to the waiting room, and the two policemen remained nearby. In an action for false imprisonment the defendants pleaded that the claimant was perfectly free to go where he liked, that he knew it and that he

---

[83] *R. (on the application of Lumba) v Secretary of State for the Home Department* [2011] UKSC 12; [2012] 1 A.C. 245 at [65].

[84] *Warner v Riddiford* (1858) 4 C.B. (N.S.) 180; 140 E.R. 1052.

[85] Blackstone, Comm., iii, 127.

[86] He is entitled to resist by force (*Hepburn v CC Thames Valley* [2002] EWCA Civ 1841; *The Times*, 19 December) but resistance to arrest is generally unwise, because the arrest may turn out to be lawful.

[87] Thus, there is no false imprisonment when the claimant complies with a police request to accompany them to the police station, but the tort is committed if the "request" is made in such a manner as to lead the claimant to believe he has no choice in the matter: *Myer Stores Ltd v Soo* [1991] 2 V.R. 597.

[88] (1838) 4 Bing. N.C. 212; 132 E.R. 769.

[89] (1920) 122 L.T. 44.

did not desire to leave. However, a majority of the Court of Appeal held that the defendants were liable because the claimant from the moment that he came under the influence of the police was no longer a free man. Atkin LJ said:[90]

"It appears to me that a person could be imprisoned without his knowing it. I think a person can be imprisoned while he is asleep, while he is in a state of drunkenness, while he is unconscious, and while he is a lunatic. Those are cases where it seems to me that the person might properly complain if he were imprisoned, though the imprisonment began and ceased while he was in that state. Of course, the damages might be diminished and would be affected by the question whether he was conscious of it or not."

Atkin LJ's ground for this opinion was that, although a person might not know he was imprisoned, his captors might be boasting elsewhere that he was.[91] This point might be regarded as more relevant to defamation than to false imprisonment, but Atkin LJ's view has been approved, obiter,[92] by the House of Lords in an appeal from Northern Ireland, *Murray v Ministry of Defence*,[93] although with the rider that a person who is unaware that he has been falsely imprisoned and has suffered no harm can normally[94] expect to recover no more than nominal damages. The basis of the law as stated in *Meering* and *Murray* is no doubt that personal liberty is supremely important so that interference with it must be deterred even where there is neither consciousness nor harm. There must, however, be a detention. A patient who is in a coma after an accident is not "detained" by the hospital. A more difficult case is *R. v Bournewood etc. NHS Trust*.[95] In this matter a man who suffered from severe mental disabilities and who became agitated was admitted to the defendant hospital as a "voluntary" patient. The court held that the hospital's actions were justified at common law by necessity. The majority were of the view that he was not "detained" by being kept in an unlocked ward, even though he was sedated and closely supervised and, if he had attempted to leave, the hospital would have considered his compulsory detention under the Mental Health Act 1983.[96]

The restraint must be complete. The tort of false imprisonment is not committed unless motion be restrained in every direction. In *Bird v Jones*[97] the defendants wrongfully enclosed part of the public footway on Hammersmith Bridge, put seats in it for the use of spectators of a regatta on the river, and

4–027

---

[90] *Meering* (1920) 122 L.T. 44 at 53.
[91] (1920) 122 L.T. 44 at 53–54.
[92] On the facts the claimant was aware she was under restraint.
[93] [1988] 1 W.L.R. 692; *Herring v Boyle* (1834) 1 Cr. M. & R. 377 must be regarded as wrongly decided.
[94] Perhaps this is intended as a reference to the possibility of exemplary damages where there is arbitrary, oppressive or unconstitutional action: see para.23–014. However, a person who is aware that he is detained is imprisoned during periods thereafter when he is asleep: *Roberts v CC Cheshire* [1999] 1 W.L.R. 662.
[95] *R. v Bournewood etc. NHS Trust* [1999] 1 A.C. 458.
[96] Cf. Lord Steyn, dissenting on this issue: "The suggestion that L was free to go is a fairy tale" ([1999] 1 A.C. 458 at 495). Even the majority, however, were of the view that he was detained while being taken to the hospital by ambulance. The European Court of Human Rights held that he had been deprived of his liberty for the purposes of art.5 of the Convention: *HL v United Kingdom* (2004) 40 E.H.R.R. 761. While it did not—indeed could not—question the correctness of the decision on false imprisonment, the difference seems odd.
[97] (1845) 7 Q.B. 742.

charged for admission to the enclosure. The claimant insisted on passing along this part of the footpath, and climbed over the fence of the enclosure without paying the charge. The defendants refused to let him go forward, but he was told that he might go back into the carriageway and cross to the other side of the bridge if he wished. He declined to do so and remained in the enclosure for half an hour. The defendants were held not to have committed false imprisonment.[98] What will amount to a complete restraint must be a question of degree. A person would plainly be imprisoned if locked inside a large building,[99] even though he had full freedom to roam around inside it, and it has been suggested that unlawful conscription is theoretically capable of being false imprisonment[100] but it seems unlikely that an action for false imprisonment would lie if, for example, the claimant was wrongfully prevented from leaving this country.[101] If, however, there is a total restraint upon the claimant's liberty, that is false imprisonment even though it lasts for only a brief period of time. This means that many acts which are "primarily" battery may also involve false imprisonment, as where C is raped by D.

4–028   **Means of escape.** If a person has reasonable[102] means of escape, but does not know it, it is submitted that his detention is nevertheless false imprisonment unless any reasonable person would have realised that he had an available outlet. Thus, if D pretends to turn the key of the door of a room in which you are situated and take away the key, it would seem unreasonable if you made no attempt to see whether the door was in fact locked. A more difficult case is that in which you have a duplicate key in your pocket but have forgotten its existence. A reasonable person may suffer from a lapse of memory.

4–029   **Reasonable condition.** It is not false imprisonment to prevent a person from leaving your premises because he will not fulfil a reasonable condition subject to which he entered them. In *Robinson v Balmain Ferry Co Ltd*[103] the claimant paid a penny for entry to the defendants' wharf from which he proposed to cross the river by one of the defendants' ferry boats. A boat had just gone and, as there was not another one for 20 minutes, the claimant wished to leave the wharf and was directed to the turnstile which was its exit. There he refused to pay another penny which was chargeable for exit, as was stated on a noticeboard, and the defendant declined to let him leave the wharf unless he did pay. The Privy Council held that

---

[98] But if the claimant suffers damage by being prevented from going in a certain direction (e.g. misses an important appointment), an action in negligence might lie. Obstruction of the highway may be a public nuisance even though the claimant is not totally detained.

[99] Or marooned on an island: Napoleon was certainly imprisoned on St Helena. Cf. *Guzzardi v Italy* (1980) 3 E.H.R.R. 333. By these standards detaining people in Oxford Circus plainly constitutes imprisonment: *Austin v MPC* [2007] EWCA Civ 989; [2008] Q.B. 660 (on appeal on other issues [2009] UKHL 5; [2009] 1 A.C. 564).

[100] *Pritchard v MoD* [1995] C.L.Y. 4726.

[101] See *Louis v Commonwealth* (1986) 87 F.L.R. 277. Protocol 4, art.2 of the European Convention on Human Rights guarantees the rights to liberty of movement and to leave a country, but these have not been enacted by the Human Rights Act 1998. There is no common law tort of imposing exile upon a person, even though it is forbidden by Magna Carta. It is necessary to show trespass to the person or some other tort: *Chagos Islanders v Attorney General* [2004] EWCA Civ 997.

[102] See *McFadzean v Construction Forestry Mining and Energy Union* [2007] VSCA 289 for extensive discussion.

[103] [1910] A.C. 295.

this was not false imprisonment: "There is no law requiring the defendants to make the exit from their premises gratuitous to people who come there upon a definite contract which involves their leaving the wharf by another way . . . The question whether the notice which was affixed to these premises was brought home to the knowledge of the plaintiff is immaterial, because the notice itself is immaterial."[104] The court regarded the charge of a penny for exit as reasonable. It must be stressed that it was crucial to the decision in this case that the claimant had contracted to leave the wharf by a different route. Nonetheless, the decision is a strong one because it amounts, in effect, to recognising extra-judicial imprisonment as a method of enforcing contractual rights.[105]

Liability in false imprisonment distinguished from abuse of legal procedure.   **4–030**
A defendant may be liable for false imprisonment even though he did not personally detain the claimant provided that he acted through an intermediary who exercised no independent discretion of his own. In *Austin v Dowling*[106] a police inspector refused to take the responsibility of arresting B on a charge made by A, but finally arrested B when A signed the charge sheet. It was held that A could be liable for false imprisonment. There can, however, be no false imprisonment if a discretion is interposed between the defendant's act and the claimant's detention. If, for example, A makes a charge against B before a magistrate and the magistrate then decides to order the arrest of B, A has set in motion not a ministerial but a judicial officer exercising a discretion of his own and A cannot be liable for false imprisonment.[107] In modern conditions it is very likely that where the police make an arrest on the basis of information or a complaint they will be held to be exercising an independent discretion[108] but that is not inevitably so, as for example, where there is a request or encouragement to arrest on information provided solely by the defendant.[109] The liability of an informant for abuse of legal procedure[110] is an entirely different matter which is considered in detail in a later chapter.[111]

---

[104] [1910] A.C. 295 at 299. Cf. Viscount Haldane LC in *Herd v Weardale Steel Co Ltd* [1915] A.C. 67 at 72.

[105] A right denied in *Bahner v Marwest Hotel* (1970) 12 D.L.R. (3d) 646. The claimant in *Robinson's* case was, after a short time, allowed to leave by squeezing past the turnstile. Could the defendants have kept there indefinitely?

[106] (1870) L.R. 5 C.P. 534.

[107] (1870) L.R. 5 C.P. 534 at 540 per Willes J; *Sewell v National Telephone Co Ltd* [1907] 1 K.B. 557.

[108] See, e.g. *Davidson v CC North Wales* [1994] 2 All E.R. 597 (so held even though the informant was a store detective).

[109] *Ahmed v Shafique* [2009] EWHC 618 (QB). Cf. *Coles Myer Ltd v Webster* [2009] NSWCA 299 (invention of allegation led to liability).

[110] A claim for defamation will fail because it is now held that even a malicious informant is protected by absolute privilege: see para.13–058.

[111] See Ch.20.

6. ACTS INTENDED TO CAUSE PHYSICAL HARM OTHER THAN TRESPASS TO THE PERSON

4–031   **The action in Wilkinson v Downton.** The action in trespass is confined to the intentional and direct infliction of harm. So what is the position in the situation where the harm is intentionally but indirectly inflicted—surreptitious poisoning, for example? For many years it has been customary to say that liability would arise in such a case based on the principle established in *Wilkinson v Downton*.[112] In this case the defendant, by way of a practical joke, falsely told the claimant, a married woman, that her husband had met with an accident in which both his legs had been broken. This caused the claimant, who was found to be a person of normal fortitude, to suffer a violent shock "producing vomiting and other more serious and permanent physical consequences at one time threatening her reason, and entailing weeks of suffering and incapacity." In holding D liable to C, Wright J said that: "[T]he defendant has . . . wilfully done an act calculated to cause physical harm to the plaintiff – that is to say, to infringe her legal right to safety, and has in fact thereby caused physical harm to her. That proposition without more appears to me to state a good cause of action, there being no justification alleged for the act."[113] The principle was approved and applied by the Court of Appeal on somewhat similar facts in *Janvier v Sweeney*[114] where a private detective, in order to get papers from the claimant, falsely represented that he was a police officer and that she was in danger of arrest for association with a German spy, thereby causing her psychiatric trauma.

4–032   **The fault element.** One difficulty with *Wilkinson v Downton* is that it is doubtful whether the case really imposes liability for intentionally caused harm given that it is most unlikely that the defendant in that case intended to produce the result which he did or even foresaw it. Indeed, Wright J.'s judgment implies that he did not.[115] Essentially, Wright J imputed an intention to the defendant. Note also that the phrase "calculated to cause harm" is ambiguous. It could refer to harm that is actually contemplated or intended by the defendant or to harm which a reasonable person would foresee as a probable result and it is the latter which fits the facts.[116] If "calculated to cause harm" merely refers to negligence, it is doubtful whether the action in *Wilkinson v Downton* really establishes a separate tort.

4–033   **Historical explanation for the decision.** A few years before *Wilkinson v Downton*, the Privy Council in *Victorian Ry Commrs v Coultas*[117] had held that "nervous shock" was not a recoverable head of damage in a claim arising from a

---

[112] *Wilkinson v Downton* [1897] 2 Q.B. 57.
[113] [1897] 2 Q.B. 57 at 58–59. Described by Stuart-Smith LJ in *W v Essex CC* [1999] Fam. 90 at 114 as a "peculiar tort".
[114] [1919] 2 K.B. 316.
[115] [1897] 2 Q.B. 57 at 59. See also *Wong v Parkside Health NHS Trust* [2001] EWCA Civ 1721; [2003] 3 All E.R. 932 at [8].
[116] Cf. *Hall v Gwent Healthcare NHS Trust* [2005] EWCA Civ 919, an even more terrible warning against practical jokes, where the lies were told to a third person who inflicted the damage and which would not even have passed the latter threshold.
[117] (1888) 13 App. Cas. 222.

negligent act. Wright J really seems to have been concerned to escape the shackles of that case by declining to apply it to an imputed or "deemed" intention. Although liability for nervous shock is still very different from that for other forms of injury arising from negligence,[118] the *Coultas* restriction disappeared from the law within a few years of *Wilkinson v Downton* and it has been said in *Wainwright v Home Office* that "there is no point in arguing about whether the injury was in some sense intentional if negligence will do just as well" and that *Wilkinson v Downton* "has no leading role in the modern law".[119] This, however, seems to go too far. Many other cases could be imagined where the source of the harm is something other than a statement or where the harm is something other than psychiatric injury. For example, D might scare a person into nervous shock by dressing up as a ghost[120] or subject the claimant to some terrifying spectacle.[121] Nor need the principle be confined to shock. If D suddenly shouts at a child who is descending a difficult staircase, intending the child to fall, D is surely liable if the child falls and breaks his neck. The administration of a noxious drug to an unwitting victim might be another illustration, assuming that it is not battery because the directness requirement is unsatisfied (if accompanied by false representations it might also be the tort of deceit).[122] It is also unclear whether nothing would change were the action in *Wilkinson v Downton* absorbed by the tort of negligence. For instance, the law of damages may differ: it is far from clear that aggravated damages are available for negligence and exemplary damages certainly are not, but sometimes they are where the defendant acts intentionally.[123]

---

[118] See para.5–081.

[119] [2003] UKHL 53; [2004] 2 A.C. 406 at [41]. However, it was applied in *C v D* [2006] EWHC 166 (QB) where the defendant was found to be reckless as to the causing of psychiatric injury.

[120] Although a claim for shock based on negligence by a person who is abnormally susceptible may not be sustainable (see para.5–089) there is no reason to apply such a rule to wilful conduct, even, perhaps, if D is not aware of C's susceptibility.

[121] See *Blakely v Shortal's Estate* 20 N.W. 2d 28 (1945) (D cut his throat in C's kitchen). Cf. *Bunyan v Jordan* (1937) 57 C.L.R. 1 and *Bradley v Wingnut Films Ltd* [1994] E.M.L.R. 195 (where it was found that the defendants had no reason to anticipate causing shock). Liability for negligence is well established where, in C's presence, D negligently kills or injures (or even puts in danger) C's loved one (see para.5–089). A fortiori, there must be liability where D wilfully harms the loved one. See, e.g. *Johnson v Commonwealth* (1927) 27 S.R. (N.S.W.) 133. One might question whether, in view of D's wilful behaviour one should insist in such cases on a tie of love and affection between C and the person attacked.

[122] In *Wilkinson v Downton* the claimant recovered a total of £100 1s. 1012d., the 1s. 1012d being recovered in deceit as representing the cost of the railway fares of persons she sent to her husband's aid. Similarly the principle might in some cases extend to the intentional infection of another person with disease. See *R. v Dica* [2004] EWCA Crim 1103; [2004] Q.B. 1257, discussed in para.26–014.

[123] On aggravated and exemplary damages see Ch.23.

7.   PROTECTION FROM HARASSMENT ACT 1997

4–034   **Provision for a civil action.** Section 1 of the Protection from Harassment Act 1997 makes it an offence to pursue a course of conduct[124] which the defendant knows or ought to know[125] amounts to harassment of another.[126] By s.3 this is civilly actionable,[127] leading to "damages . . . for (among other things) any anxiety caused by the harassment and any financial loss resulting from the harassment".[128] Damages may, therefore, be awarded for the sort of psychiatric damage that was suffered by the victim in *R. v Ireland*,[129] but also for lesser degrees of psychic disturbance.[130] An injunction may also be granted in respect of future conduct.[131]

4–035   **The meaning of "course of conduct".** A "course of conduct" must involve conduct on at least two occasions.[132] Putting a person in fear of violence on at least two occasions by a course of conduct is a more serious offence under the Act but is not made civilly actionable as such. Plainly, however, the greater includes the lesser and such conduct will fall under the general crime of harassment and will therefore be civilly actionable by that route.

4–036   **The meaning of "harassment".** The Act does not contain a detailed definition of harassment. It has been said that one has to draw a distinction between conduct which is "unattractive, even unreasonable, and conduct which is oppressive and unacceptable"[133] and in doing this one must take account of the context in which

---

[124] Conduct includes speech: s.7(3).

[125] But this is to be decided without reference to any mental illness or characteristic of the accused: *R. v C* [2001] EWCA Crim 1251; *The Times*, June 14, 2001; *Banks v Ablex Ltd* [2005] EWCA Civ 173; [2005] I.C.R. 819.

[126] A corporate body is incapable of being harassed within the meaning of the Act: *Daiichi UK Ltd v Stop Huntington Animal Cruelty* [2003] EWHC 2337 (QB); [2004] 1 W.L.R. 1503 (but see *SmithKlineBeecham Plc v Avery* [2009] EWHC 1488 (QB)).

[127] For an attempt to enumerate the elements of the action, see *Dowson v Chief Constable of Northumbria Police* [2010] EWHC 2612 (QB) at [142].

[128] In accordance with general principle an employer is vicariously liable for conduct by an employee which contravenes the Act, including conduct directed at fellow employees, provided there is a sufficiently close connection between the conduct and the employment: *Majrowski v Guy's and St. Thomas's NHS Trusts* [2006] UKHL 34; [2007] 1 A.C. 224. The standard of proof in civil cases is the ordinary civil one of a balance of probabilities: *Jones v Hipgrave* [2004] EWHC 2901 (QB). The "only real difference between the crime of s.2 and the tort of s.3 is standard of proof": *Ferguson v British Gas Trading Ltd* [2009] EWCA Civ 46; [2010] 1 W.L.R. 785 at [17].

[129] See para.4–020.

[130] *S & D Property Investments Ltd v Nisbet* [2009] EWHC 1726 (Ch). However, such damages are likely to be modest: at [76].

[131] The exercise of this power in a proper case does not infringe art.10 of the European Convention on Human Rights: *Howlett v Holding* [2006] EWHC 41 (QB).

[132] By s.1(1A), where the harassment is of two or more persons there need only be conduct on one occasion in relation to each person, but s.1(1A) does not give rise to a civil claim for damages. Section 1(3) provides that the Act does not apply to a course of conduct pursued for the purpose of preventing or detecting crime but it has been suggested that in the light of the Human Rights Act 1998 s.1(3) contains a requirement of necessity or proportionality: *KD v CC Hampshire* [2005] EWHC 2550 (QB). In any event it does not give carte blanche to any citizen to set up as a vigilante: *Howlett v Holding* [2006] EWHC 41 (QB).

[133] *Majrowski v Guy's and St Thomas's NHS Trusts* [2006] UKHL 34; [2007] 1 A.C. 224 at [30].

the conduct takes place.[134] For a course of conduct to constitute harassment it must "go beyond annoyances or irritations, and beyond the ordinary banter and badinage of life".[135] According to Lord Sumption SCJ in *Hayes v Willoughby*: "Harassment is a persistent and deliberate course of unreasonable and oppressive conduct, targeted at another person, which is calculated to and does cause that person alarm, fear or distress."[136] It has been held that chanting intended to disrupt a graduation ceremony was not harassment because there was insufficient evidence that anyone was "alarmed, distressed, threatened or frightened" even though they were annoyed, though the line between distress and annoyance may be hard to draw.[137] At any rate harassment goes well beyond causing fear of violence. It is capable of embracing, for example, persistent following, questioning or "doorstepping" by journalists; methods of debt collection which are humiliating, threatening or distressing[138] or persistent unjustified demands for payment;[139] newspaper articles[140] abusive letters[141] or other publications;[142] uploading to the internet explicit photographs of the claimant;[143] bullying in the workplace,[144] bombarding the claimant with text messages or emails;[145] or conduct in the course of a neighbour dispute which is designed to distress,[146] for example, playing loud music or banging on walls. In determining whether a "course of conduct" constitutes harassment it is necessary to look at the course of conduct as a whole.[147] The context in which the conduct occurs is also potentially significant. Gage LJ said in *Sunderland CC v Conn* that: "What might not be harassment on the factory floor or in the barrack room might well be harassment in the hospital ward and vice versa."[148]

The defendant's state of mind. The defendant must know or ought to know that the course of conduct constitutes harassment. The claimant's characteristics are relevant in this connection.[149] Harassment in its ordinary sense seems to imply

4–037

---

[134] *Conn v Sunderland CC* [2007] EWCA Civ 1492; [2008] I.R.L.R. 324.

[135] *Iqbal v Dean Manson Solicitors* [2011] EWCA Civ 123 at [42].

[136] [2013] UKSC 17; [2013] 1 W.L.R. 935 at [1].

[137] *University of Oxford v Broughton* [2008] EWHC 75 (QB) (an application for an interim injunction); but an injunction had earlier been granted against disruption of examinations: at [25].

[138] *S & D Property Investments* [2009] EWHC 1726 (Ch). This may enable the claimant to set off the damages against the debt sought to be enforced.

[139] *Allen v Southwark LBC* [2008] EWCA Civ 1478; *Ferguson v British Gas Trading Ltd* [2009] EWCA Civ 46; [2010] 1 W.L.R. 785.

[140] *Thomas v News Group Newspapers Ltd* [2001] EWCA Civ 1233; [2002] E.M.L.R. 4. But press criticism which is robust and likely to cause distress is not harassment unless it is an abuse of press freedom.

[141] *Iqbal v Dean Manson Solicitors* [2011] EWCA Civ 123 at [31].

[142] *Howlett v Holding* [2006] EWHC 41 (QB).

[143] *AMP v Persons Unknown* [2011] EWHC 3454 (TCC).

[144] *Majrowski v Guy's and St Thomas's NHS Trust* [2006] UKHL 34; [2007] 1 A.C. 224.

[145] *APW v WPA* [2012] EWHC 3151 (QB).

[146] *Jones v Ruth* [2011] EWCA Civ 804; [2012] 1 All E.R. 490.

[147] *Iqbal v Dean Manson Solicitors* [2011] EWCA Civ 123 at [31].

[148] [2007] EWCA Civ 1492; [2008] I.R.L.R. 324 at [12].

[149] *Banks v Ablex Ltd* [2005] EWCA Civ 173; [2005] I.C.R. 819 at [26].

something sustained and intended to distress.[150] So if D quarrels with C in 2010 and makes an abusive telephone call to him on that occasion and this is repeated in 2011, but as a result of a wholly independent quarrel, that would not, it is submitted, fall within the Act.[151] Nor would one describe the constant playing of loud music, caused not by spite but by selfish indifference to neighbours, as harassment,[152] though it may amount to a common law nuisance and an offence under other legislation governing noise. Although, for the reasons that have been given, it appears that the very concept of harassment means that the defendant must act with a certain intention,[153] it is unnecessary for the defendant to foresee that his conduct will cause the claimant to suffer damage.[154] Foreseeability of damage is not an element of the action.

4–038   **Defence of preventing or detecting a crime.** Section 1(3)(a) of the Act provides for a defence to liability where the defendant was acting "for the purpose of preventing or detecting a crime." The main aim of this provision is to shield statutory authorities from liability as a result of acts taken in connection with law enforcement, but it applies equally to private citizens.[155] In order for this defence to apply, it is unnecessary that the defendant establish that his conduct was reasonable according to the standard of the reasonable person. The word "purpose" in s.1(3)(a) refers to a subjective state of mind.[156] Nevertheless, the defence is not solely contingent upon the defendant's thought processes. It is subject to a test of "rationality". Lord Sumption SCJ in *Hayes v Willoughby* explained that this test "imports a requirement of good faith, a requirement that there should be some logical connection between the evidence and the ostensible reasons for the decision, and (which will usually amount to the same thing) an absence of arbitrariness, of capriciousness or of reasoning so outrageous in its defiance of logic as to be perverse".[157] This means that the defendant "must have thought rationally about the material suggesting the possibility of criminality and formed the view that the conduct said to constitute harassment was appropriate for the purpose of preventing or detecting it".[158] An irrational, obsessive vendetta will not satisfy these requirements. The "purpose" that matters in relation to the

---

[150] The conduct must be targeted at an individual: *Thomas v News Group Newspapers Ltd* [2001] EWCA Civ 1233; [2002] E.M.L.R. 4 at [30] but presumably in an employment context this condition might be satisfied if the claimant made it known that he objected to persistent conduct not particularly directed at him.

[151] Even where the incidents arise out of the same matter, it has been said that the fewer the incidents and the wider apart they are, the less likely they are to constitute harassment: *Lau v DPP*, *The Times*, March 29, 2000.

[152] Section 1(2) provides that: "[T]he person whose course of conduct is in question ought to know that it amounts to harassment of another if a reasonable person in possession of the same information would think the course of conduct amounted to harassment of the other." This would cover, e.g. conduct directed at the victim which the defendant regards as a joke but which a reasonable person would regard as going beyond that.

[153] Cf. *Trimingham v Associated Newspapers* [2012] EWHC 1296 (QB); [2012] 4 All E.R. 717 at [67]: "The 1997 Act does not require intent."

[154] *Jones v Ruth* [2011] EWCA Civ 804; [2012] 1 All E.R. 490.

[155] *Hayes v Willoughby* [2013] UKSC 17; [2013] 1 W.L.R. 935 at [13].

[156] *Hayes v Willoughby* [2013] UKSC 17; [2013] 1 W.L.R. 935 at [14].

[157] [2013] UKSC 17; [2013] 1 W.L.R. 935 at [14].

[158] [2013] UKSC 17; [2013] 1 W.L.R. 935 at [15].

defence is the defendant's dominant purpose.[159] Accordingly, the defence will not be excluded merely because the defendant had aims other than that of preventing or detecting a crime.

Criminal proceedings. If there are criminal proceedings for harassment, the court dealing with the offender may make a restraining order prohibiting the defendant from doing anything described in the order[160] and in practice this seems likely to be more important than civil claims under the Act for an injunction.   **4–039**

8. HARASSMENT UNDER THE EQUALITY ACT 2010

The Equality Act 2010 provides for further statutory cause of action for harassment.[161] The relevant provisions of this Act are lengthy and convoluted. Little will be said about them here, partly for this reason, but mainly because the Act only recently came into force and is in need of judicial development and elaboration. By contrast with the Protection from Harassment Act 1997, the Equality Act 2010, in s.26, provides a detailed definition of harassment. The definition is in two parts.[162] The first part requires that there must be "unwanted contact related to a relevant protected characteristic". These characteristics are age, disability, gender reassignment, race, religion or belief, sex and sexual orientation.[163] The second part requires that the conduct has the purpose of effect of violating the victim's dignity or "creating an intimidating, hostile, degrading, humiliating or offensive environment" for the victim. A major point of distinction between the action provided for by the Equality Act 2010 and the action created by the Protection from Harassment Act 1997 is that whereas the latter is available against all persons, the former lies against only certain persons, including employers, providers of public services, those who perform public functions, people who dispose of or manage premises, and providers of education. Another difference between the two actions is that behaviour can constitute harassment under the Equality Act 2010 even though it does not constitute a "course of conduct". A one-off act is capable of triggering liability under that Act. Conversely, as explained above,[164] an action under the Protection from Harassment Act 1997 is available only if there is conduct that occurs on at least two occasions.   **4–040**

---

[159] [2013] UKSC 17; [2013] 1 W.L.R. 935 at [17], [21].
[160] See s.5.
[161] Section 119.
[162] Section 26(1).
[163] Section 26(5).
[164] See para.4–035.

CHAPTER 5

NEGLIGENCE: DUTY OF CARE

vi.   Other Situations   **5–095**

1.   THE TORT OF NEGLIGENCE

5–001   **The tort of negligence.** This chapter is the first of several that analyse the tort of negligence. This chapter is about the duty of care concept. However, it is convenient to first make some general observations about the tort and the elements that constitute it.

5–002   **The elements of the tort.** The tort of negligence is by a very substantial margin the most important tort in terms of the volume of cases before the courts. It is a matter of some regret, therefore, that there is not insignificant doubt as to its elements. Judges and commentators describe its elements in an astonishing diversity of ways.[1] However, for present purposes, we will not engage with this issue. One conventional list of the elements of the tort of negligence, and the one that we will use for the purposes of this book, is as follows. The elements of the tort are: (1) a duty of care owed by D to C; (2) a breach of that duty; and (3) non-remote damage caused by the breach of duty. This chapter deals with the first element. The second and third elements are discussed in Ch.7 and Ch.8 respectively.

5–003   **The elements overlap.** A central point to note at the outset is that these three elements overlap. This is partly because, as will be explained, the concept of foreseeability plays a role in relation to all of them.[2] It has been said that "they are simply three different ways of looking at the same problem".[3] Suppose, for example, that D jostles X, causing X to drop something and this sets off a very unexpected train of events which causes injury to C, standing many feet away.[4] If one wished to hold that D was not liable to C, one might say that D owed him no duty of care because he could not foresee injury to him; or that he owed him a duty of care but had not broken it because he could not foresee that his conduct would cause C harm; or that he owed him a duty of care and had broken it but the damage was not legally attributable to him because no one could have foreseen it. The orthodox answer is the first (which has the advantage of solving the case at the first step), but they are all plausible and some may think that the second is the most convincing. Nevertheless, while it must always be borne in mind that the three elements overlap and their separation is artificial in some cases, this structure does accord with the way in which most cases are approached by the English courts. However, because we use words in a rather loose way, we must be alert that we do not, merely because the word "duty" is used, put the legal issue in the wrong box. For example, there is no doubt that the user of a vehicle is liable to other road users if an accident occurs because the vehicle is not kept in roadworthy condition. Suppose that in a particular case a road accident is caused by a burst tyre, that the defect in the tyre would have been observed if the user had checked his car before setting off on Tuesday but that the court rejects the

---

[1] See Owen (2007) 35 Hofstra L. Rev. 1671.
[2] See paras 5–027, 6–020.
[3] *Roe v Minister of Health* [1954] 2 Q.B. 66 at 86 per Denning LJ.
[4] See *Palsgraf v Long Island R.R.* 162 N.E. 99 (N.Y. 1928), discussed at para.5–007.

claim because the defendant had checked the tyres on Monday, as he always did. One might very well say that the defendant "owed no duty to check the tyres before each trip", but the issue is clearly one of breach ((2) above) not of duty of care. It is self-evident that he owes other road users a duty to take care for their safety and that this includes the maintenance of the vehicle; what we are concerned with is how he must behave in order to fulfil it.[5] It is also important to be aware of the relationship between elements (1) and (3). It has been said to be meaningless to ask whether a defendant owes the claimant a duty of care without also considering the type of damage in question.[6] This is because a defendant may be under a duty to safeguard the claimant against one type of damage (for example, physical damage to his property) but not another type of damage (for example, pure economic loss).

Sequence of the elements. It is conventional for the courts to consider the elements of negligence in sequence, beginning with duty of care,[7] then moving on to breach and finally considering whether non-remote damage was caused by the breach. Taking elements of actions in a given order can provide judicial decisions with increased structure and help to ensure that elements are not overlooked. It is critical for this reason that judges (and commentators) identify clearly the ingredients of actions. But it is unclear whether there is any deeper significance to the order in which the courts address the elements of the tort of negligence. Kirby J in the Australian case of *Neindorf v Junkovic* suggested that the order in which the elements are tackled is important for the following reason:[8]

5–004

> "Generally speaking, each of the constituent elements of the tort of negligence – duty, breach and damage – considered *seriatim*, progressively increases the specificity of the inquiry into how the incident occurred and the way in which damage was sustained. The broadest and most general level of analysis occurs at the duty stage. Here, the inquiry is primarily concerned with whether injury to the plaintiff or a class of persons to whom the plaintiff belongs, was reasonably foreseeable. With respect to the breach element, the inquiry is directed, in part, to whether a reasonable person in the defendant's position would have foreseen the risk of injury to the plaintiff. Finally, the damage element is the most specific. The issue here is whether the damage sustained as a result of the breach of duty was of a kind which was reasonably foreseeable."

Conceptual significance of organising the tort of negligence into discrete elements. If an action in negligence is rejected, it must be because one or more of the three elements that constitute the action is missing or because a defence applies. Defences are treated in a later chapter,[9] and nothing more will be said about them now. Assuming that an action is rejected on account of the absence of one of the elements of the action, does it matter which element is missing? Judges have sometimes said that it does not matter. For example, in *Vellino v Chief Constable of Greater Manchester* the Court of Appeal said that it was

5–005

---

[5] Instances where the court wrongly treated a breach case as a duty case include *Orange v Chief Constable of West Yorkshire Police*[2001] EWCA Civ 611; [2002] Q.B. 347; *Fernquest v City & County of Swansea* [2011] EWCA Civ 1712.

[6] *Caparo Industries Plc v Dickman* [1990] 2 A.C. 605 at 627; *S v Gloucestershire CC* [2001] 2 W.L.R. 909 at 932.

[7] "[D]uty is the threshold question": Robertson (2012) 33 O.J.L.S. 1 at 2.

[8] [2005] HCA 75; 80 A.L.J.R. 341 at [55] (footnotes omitted).

[9] See Ch.26.

unimportant whether the action in that case was rejected on the grounds of no duty, no breach or no causation.[10] It is doubtful whether this is correct. There are several reasons why actions are organised into elements: it is thought to aid understanding of the nature of the action, to help to ensure that cases that are based on a given action are dealt with consistently and to act as a safeguard against the risk that judges will forget to address important questions. The approach of the court in *Vellino* fails to recognise the clear advantages to breaking causes of actions into elements.

2. DUTY OF CARE: GENERAL PRINCIPLES

A. Introduction

5–006   **A duty of care is an essential element of the tort of negligence.** A person will not be liable in the tort of negligence for every careless act. Indeed, a person will not incur liability even for every careless act that causes damage. Rather, a person will only incur liability for negligence that causes damage if he is under a legal duty to take care. This point was famously encapsulated by Lord Esher MR when he said: "A man is entitled to be as negligent as he pleases to the whole world if he owes no duty to them."[11]

5–007   **The duty of care must be owed to the claimant.** The duty of care must be owed specifically to the claimant. Negligence "in the air" or towards some other person is not enough: the claimant cannot build on a duty of care owed, or a wrong committed, to someone else.[12] The point is graphically illustrated by the famous United States case of *Palsgraf v Long Island Railroad*.[13] The facts as presented to the New York Court of Appeals were that the defendants' servants negligently pushed X, who was attempting to board a moving train, and caused him to drop a package containing "fireworks". The resulting explosion knocked over some scales, many feet away, which struck the claimant, injuring her. A majority of the court found for the defendants. It might well have been that the defendants' servants were negligent with regard to X, at least as far as his property was concerned, but there was nothing in the appearance of the package to suggest even to the most cautious mind that it would cause a violent explosion and hence injury to the claimant. In the words of Cardozo CJ:[14]

> "If no hazard was apparent to the eye of ordinary vigilance, an act innocent and harmless, at least to outward seeming, with reference to [claimant], did not take to itself the quality of a tort because it happened to be a wrong, though apparently not one involving the risk of bodily insecurity, with reference to some one [sic] else . . ."

5–008   **Terminology.** It has been complained that the duty of care is not really a duty at all and, hence, it is misleading and confusing to use the language of duty in this

---

[10] [2001] EWCA Civ 1249; [2002] 1 W.L.R. 218 at [35], [59], [62].
[11] *Le Lievre v Gould* [1893] 1 Q.B. 491 at 497.
[12] *Bourhill v Young* [1983] A.C. 92 at 108 per Lord Wright.
[13] 162 N.E. 99 (N.Y. 1928).
[14] 162 N.E. 99 at 99 (N.Y. 1928).

context.[15] According to a famous analysis by Hohfeld, the idea of a duty correlates with that of a right.[16] However, it is doubtful whether the mere fact that one is owed a duty of care by D means that one has a right good against D. Strictly speaking, one has no right good against D until D acts unreasonably with respect to your safety and causes you damage as a result.

Duty of care as a control device. A general liability for carelessly causing harm to others would, at least as things are perceived by the courts, be too onerous for a practical system of law and we shall see that there are areas of activity and types of loss where the law of negligence does not intervene or intervenes only in a limited way. Thus there is, for instance, no general liability for failing to assist or protect others.[17] Nor is there generally liability in respect of negligently inflicted pure economic loss.[18] What was said by du Parcq LJ in 1946 is as true now as it was then (even though the range of recognised duties has increased substantially in the intervening years), namely, that:[19]

> "[I]t is not true to say that whenever a man finds himself in such a position that unless he does a certain act another person may suffer, or that if he does something another person will suffer, then it is his duty in the one case to be careful to do the act and in the other case to be careful not to do the act."

Duty is the primary "control device"[20] which allows the courts to keep liability for negligence within what they regard as acceptable limits and the controversies which have centred around the criteria for the existence of a duty reflect differences of opinion as to the proper ambit of liability for negligence.

The two functions performed by the duty of care concept. The concept of the duty of care is arguably something of an arcane mystery. An Australian judge in 1998, having referred to the foundational speech of Lord Atkin in *Donoghue v Stevenson*,[21] remarked that, "the modern abundance of authority [on the duty of care] . . . would not make Lord Atkin much wiser".[22] Academic writers have been searing of their criticism of the quality of judicial reasoning in this area.[23] Nevertheless, much difficulty will be avoided if it is grasped at the outset that duty is fulfilling two functions. It is true that the question in every case in which the existence of a duty of care is contested is "did *this* defendant owe a duty of care to *this* claimant?" (the first function) for the courts do not decide academic issues, but disputes between parties. Nevertheless, in most of the cases regarding the duty concept the courts have been concerned with broader questions which transcend the particular dispute and which are essentially concerned with whether, and if so how far, the law of negligence should operate in a situation of

5–009

5–010

---

[15] See Nolan (2013) 129 L.Q.R. 559 at 561–563.
[16] Hohfeld (1913) 23 Yale L.J. 16 at 32.
[17] See para.5–039.
[18] See para.5–059
[19] *Deyong v Shenburn* [1946] K.B. 227 at 233.
[20] This famous phrase was coined by Fleming: see Fleming (1953) 31 Can. B. Rev. 471.
[21] See para.5–015.
[22] Priestley JA in *Avenhouse v Hornsby SC* (1998) 44 N.S.W.L.R. 1.
[23] See, e.g. Stapleton in Cane and Stapleton (eds), *The Law of Obligations* (1998), p.59; Nolan (2013) 129 L.Q.R. 559.

a particular type (the second function). Discussion is therefore couched in terms of general categories, such as "Is there a duty of care not to cause pure economic loss by statements?" or "Is there a duty to prevent a third party from inflicting harm on another?" and the court is essentially concerned with mapping the limits of the law of negligence and identifying those areas in which there are factors which suggest that the law should not give a remedy for negligent conduct or at least should do so only to a limited extent. It was, therefore, perfectly possible for the House of Lords in *Hedley Byrne & Co Ltd v Heller & Partners Ltd*[24] to decide: (1) that there was a duty of care recognised by English law in respect of statements; but (2) no duty was owed on the facts by the defendant to the claimant.[25] The twin functions served by the duty of care concept means that the court is not concerned only with doing justice as between the parties to a particular case, but in all cases of that type. As Lord Browne-Wilkinson explained in *Barrett v Enfield LBC*: "Once the decision is taken that, say, company auditors though liable to shareholders for negligent auditing are not liable to those proposing to invest in the company . . . that decision will apply to all future cases of the same kind."[26]

5–011   **Duty of care as a preliminary issue.** Accordingly, to traditional thinking the duty issue is often suitable to be dealt with on a striking out application or as a preliminary issue, where the case would be decided on the assumption that the facts alleged by the claimant could be proved at the trial. For a while it looked as if this expedited procedure would be blocked altogether by the fair trial guarantee in art.6 of the European Convention on Human Rights. It now seems clear that this is not so and that it is legitimate, in the context of art.6, for the substantive law to lay down that liability may be excluded in all situations of a particular type so long as that is a proper and proportionate response to what it conceives to be the needs of public policy. However, the question of whether a duty was owed may not lend itself to "bright line" rules established without close examination of the facts[27] and this is particularly so:[28]

> "[I]n an area of the law which [is] uncertain and developing . . . [where] it is not normally appropriate to strike out . . . [I]t is of great importance that such development should be on the basis of actual facts found at trial not on hypothetical facts assumed (possibly wrongly) to be true for the purpose of the strike out."

On the other hand, where the matter can be dealt with at a preliminary stage as an issue of law the court should not hesitate to do so.[29] The Civil Procedure Rules enable these matters to be dealt with in a rather more flexible way than was once the case. There is no longer any complete embargo on adducing evidence on a striking out application and in the alternative the defendant may apply for

---

[24] *Hedley Byrne & Co Ltd v Heller & Partners Ltd* [1964] A.C. 465, see para.12–024.

[25] On the facts this was because of a disclaimer and disclaimers are no longer automatically valid (see para.12–044).

[26] *Barrett v Enfield LBC* [2001] 2 A.C. 550 at 560. See also *Cooper v Hobart* [2001] SCC 79; [2001] 3 S.C.R. 537 at [37].

[27] Even "quite feeble" particulars of negligence may prevent a striking out: *Strickland v Hertfordshire CC* [2003] EWHC 287 (QB).

[28] *Barrett v Enfield LBC* [2001] 2 A.C. 550 at 557 per Lord Browne-Wilkinson.

[29] *Kent v Griffiths* [2001] Q.B. 36 at 51.

summary judgment on the ground that the case has no real prospect of success, which extends further than objections to the pleaded case.[30] By proper use of these procedures it may be possible to dispose of weak claims without a full trial in a manner which satisfies the requirements of art.6.[31]

There is generally a duty of care in cases of physical damage directly caused by an act. The issue of duty arises comparatively rarely in the day-to-day business of the courts and tends to be the preserve of the Court of Appeal and the Supreme Court. Most cases of negligence arise from acts directly causing physical damage to persons or property and there the law is much more straightforward. No one would think of opening a running-down case by citing authorities to show that a duty of care was owed by a driver to a pedestrian.[32] In *Caparo Industries Plc v Dickman*[33] Lord Oliver said that in the case of physical damage directly caused by the defendant, "the existence of the nexus [of duty] between the careless defendant and the injured plaintiff can rarely give rise to any difficulty".[34] Of course, it would be going too far to say that there is a universal duty in respect of foreseeable physical damage. Nevertheless, it remains true that in physical damage cases involving an act rather than an omission there are few "duty" problems. It would, therefore, be wrong to envisage negligence as a sea of non-liability surrounding areas of liability. If anything, the true picture is the reverse, for as Lord Goff said, "the broad general principle of liability for foreseeable damage is so widely applicable that the function of the duty of care is not so much to identify cases where liability is imposed as to identify those where it is not".[35]

5–012

It must be demonstrated that a duty of care arises on the particular facts of the case. If, however, a duty does exist in the general sense then there may be an issue whether it is applicable to the particular facts before the court or, as it is sometimes said, whether it was owed to the particular claimant. For example, the House of Lords in *Donoghue v Stevenson*[36] was concerned with the general question whether a manufacturer owed a duty of care to the ultimate user of his products and the conclusion was that he did. If, however, the product had been stolen from his factory and taken to Australia where, many years later, it caused injury to C, then it might be a difficult question to determine whether a duty was owed to C, that is to say, whether C was a foreseeable victim of the initial negligence in manufacture.

5–013

Established duty of care categories and novel duties. Many duties of care are long established (for example, the duties owed by drivers to other road users and the duties that employers owe to their employees). Others are of more recent vintage but nonetheless firmly fixed in the law, though they may still be in the

5–014

[30] *Sutradhar v National Environment Research Council* [2006] UKHL 33; [2006] 4 All E.R. 490.

[31] *S v Gloucestershire CC* [2001] 2 W.L.R. 909, especially at 935–937.

[32] Compare *Langley v Dray* [1998] P.I.Q.R. P314, an unsuccessful attempt to complicate a simple road traffic case with a duty issue.

[33] [1990] 2 A.C. 605 at 633.

[34] See also *Mobil Oil Hong Kong Ltd v Hong Kong United Dockyards Ltd* [1991] 2 Lloyd's Rep. 309 at 328; *Sandhar v Dept of Transport* [2004] EWCA Civ 1440; [2005] P.I.Q.R. P13 at [38]

[35] *Smith v Littlewoods Organisation Ltd* [1987] A.C. 241 at 280.

[36] *Donoghue v Stevenson* [1932] A.C. 562, see para.5–015.

course of development (for example, the duty of a person who has "assumed responsibility" for a task[37]). In a novel case the court must take a decision as to whether a new duty should be recognised.[38] Is there any principle to guide it in this task? Three periods in the history of the law must be distinguished.

B. Law Prior to *Anns v Merton*

5–015   **Donoghue v Stevenson.** The first attempt to formulate a general principle was made by Brett MR in *Heaven v Pender*[39] but by far the most important generalisation is that of Lord Atkin in *Donoghue v Stevenson*.[40] In the latter case a manufacturer sold ginger beer in an opaque bottle to a retailer. The retailer resold it to A, who treated a young woman of her acquaintance with its contents. It was alleged that these included the decomposed remains of a snail which had found its way into the bottle at the factory. The young woman alleged that she became seriously ill as a result and sued the manufacturer for negligence. The doctrine of privity of contract prevented her bringing a claim founded upon breach of a warranty in a contract of sale, but a majority of the House of Lords held that the manufacturer owed her a duty to take care that the bottle did not contain noxious matter and that he would be liable in tort if that duty was broken. Lord Atkin said:[41]

> "In English law there must be, and is, some general conception of relations giving rise to a duty of care, of which the particular cases found in the books are instances. The liability for negligence, whether you style it such or treat it as in other systems as a species of 'culpa,' is no doubt based upon a general public sentiment of moral wrongdoing for which the offender must pay. But acts or omissions which any moral code would censure cannot, in a practical world, be treated so as to give a right to every person injured by them to demand relief. In this way rules of law arise which limit the range of complainants and the extent of their remedy. The rule that you are to love your neighbour becomes in law, you must not injure your neighbour; and the lawyer's question, Who is my neighbour? receives a restricted reply. You must take reasonable care to avoid acts or omissions which you can reasonably foresee would be likely to injure your neighbour. Who, then, in law is my neighbour? The answer seems to be—persons who are so closely and directly affected by my act that I ought reasonably to have them in contemplation as being so affected when I am directing my mind to the acts or omissions which are called in question."

5–016   **Limited initial significance of the neighbour principle.** There could be no denying that *Donoghue v Stevenson* established that manufacturers owe a duty not to cause physical damage to the ultimate consumers of their products but it

---

[37] See para.5–049.

[38] An extreme view was once advanced that liability for negligence could only exist where there was a duty recognised by previous judicial decision. See Landon (1941) 57 L.Q.R. 183: "Negligence is not actionable unless the duty to be careful exists. And the duty to be careful exists where the wisdom of our ancestors has deemed that it shall exist." There are echoes of this in the dissent of Viscount Dilhorne in *Home Office v Dorset Yacht Co Ltd* [1970] A.C. 1004 but it is quite inconsistent with the modern law. To emphasise the need for respect for precedent, as the courts now do (see para.5–020) is not the same thing as saying that new duties cannot be created: *Mills v Winchester Diocesan Board* [1989] 1 All E.R. 317 at 332.

[39] (1883) 11 Q.B.D. 503 at 509.

[40] [1932] A.C. 562. For the history of the litigation and of Mrs Donoghue, see Rodger [1988] C.L.P. 1.

[41] [1932] A.C. 562 at 580.

seems plain from the structure of Lord Atkin's speech that what we may call the "neighbour principle" was a vital step on the road to this general conclusion of law, not merely a test for determining whether the claimant was a foreseeable victim of the defendant's negligence, an issue which was anyway not before the House of Lords in any meaningful sense.[42] Nevertheless for a long time there was a marked judicial reluctance to accept that the "neighbour principle" had much relevance to determining whether a duty of care might exist in other areas of activity. There continued to be no duty of care in respect of making statements or in disposing of tumbledown houses—words were not like deeds and a dwelling was inherently different from a ginger beer bottle. Certainly new "duty situations" continued to be recognised, for as Lord Macmillan had said in *Donoghue v Stevenson*, "the categories of negligence are never closed"[43] but little reliance was placed upon this generalised concept.

C.   Law as Stated in *Anns v Merton*

The Anns test. In *Home Office v Dorset Yacht Co Ltd*[44] Lord Reid suggested that   **5–017**
the time had come to regard the "neighbour principle" of *Donoghue v Stevenson* as applicable in all cases where there was no justification or valid explanation for its exclusion. The suggestion was taken up by the House of Lords in *Anns v Merton LBC*,[45] in particular in the speech of Lord Wilberforce, who said[46] that the matter should be approached in two stages.[47] First, one must ask whether there was a sufficient relationship of "proximity or neighbourhood" between claimant and defendant such that, in the defendant's reasonable contemplation, carelessness on his part might cause damage to the claimant. If so, a prima facie duty of care arose. Then, at the second stage, it was necessary to consider whether there were any considerations which ought to "negative, or to reduce or limit" that duty.[48] This rationalisation of the law was eagerly used in several cases to attack previously well-entrenched principles of non-liability. One of the most radical manifestations of this expansive reliance on *Anns* was *Junior Books Ltd v Veitchi Co Ltd*[49] where a majority of the House of Lords in dealing with a loss which, at least on one view, was purely economic in nature, imposed a liability which appeared to conflict with hitherto well-established principles.[50]

---

[42] The case came before the House of Lords from Scotland as what in modern English procedural terms would be called a preliminary issue of law (see CPR r.3.1(2)) and no trial of the truth of the averments seems to have taken place: see Rodger [1988] C.L.P. 1 and Heuston (1957) 20 M.L.R. 2.

[43] [1932] A.C. 562 at 619.

[44] [1970] A.C. 1004 at 1027.

[45] [1978] A.C. 728.

[46] [1978] A.C. 728 at 751–752.

[47] This test has been severely criticised. Stevens described its embrace as "the greatest 20th century judicial disaster in the law of torts": Stevens in Degeling, Edelman and Goudkamp (eds), *Torts in Commercial Law* (2011), p.53.

[48] Whether as to its scope or the class of persons to whom it was owed or the damages to which a breach of it might give rise.

[49] [1983] 1 A.C. 520.

[50] The case is dealt with more fully at para.5–064.

D. Present Law

5–018 **The retreat from the Anns test.** After three decisions at the highest level in the mid-1980s which had cast doubts on the *Anns* approach,[51] the decisive case in the "counter-revolution" was probably the decision of the Privy Council in *Yuen Kun Yeu v Attorney General of Hong Kong*,[52] in which *Anns* was subjected to reinterpretation.[53] A statutory officer, the Commissioner of Deposit-taking Companies, registered as a deposit-taker a company that subsequently went into liquidation with the result being that the claimants lost money that they had deposited with it. They alleged that the Commissioner knew or ought to have known that the affairs of the company were being conducted fraudulently and speculatively, that he failed to exercise his statutory powers of supervision so as to secure that the company complied with its obligations and that he should either never have registered the company or have revoked its registration. On a preliminary issue of law and assuming these allegations to be well founded, the Privy Council upheld the judgment of the Hong Kong Court of Appeal in favour of the Commissioner. It is hard to take exception to the decision itself, even though the Commissioner's function was of course the protection of depositors, for the facts were replete with characteristics which have been relied upon in many other cases as justifying the denial of a duty. The loss was purely economic in nature; the claimants were unascertained members of a huge class of persons depositing money with Hong Kong financial institutions and had no "special relationship" with the Commissioner; the loss had been directly inflicted by the wrongful act of a third party and there is no general duty to confer protection against such loss; the Commissioner had neither the legal power nor the resources to control the day-to-day running of the many companies subject to this jurisdiction so that no duty which could fairly and practicably be imposed on him would be likely to forestall fraud by those determined to practise it; and the failure of the legislature to impose a civil sanction in the legislation was at least a pointer towards rejecting a common law duty of care. No doubt a court faithfully applying *Anns v Merton* might have rejected a duty at the second stage on any or all of these grounds[54] but the Privy Council held that it was not necessary to pass beyond the first stage because these were matters which on a proper view of the law were part of the notion of "proximity". There were, said the Privy Council, two possible interpretations of the first stage of the *Anns* formula: the first was that proximity meant merely reasonable foreseeability of injury, all matters of "policy" then being relegated to the second stage; the other, which was favoured by the Privy Council, was that proximity included other factors which should enter into the decision whether a duty of care should be imposed.

---

[51] *Governors of the Peabody Donation Fund v Sir Lindsay Parkinson Ltd* [1985] A.C. 210; *Candlewood Navigation Corp v Mitsui OSK Lines* [1986] A.C. 1; *Leigh and Sillavan Ltd v Aliakmon Shipping Co Ltd* [1986] A.C. 786.

[52] [1988] A.C. 175.

[53] The *Anns* test still has its defenders. A modified version of it is usually used in Canada: *Fullowka v Pinkerton's of Canada Ltd* [2010] SCC 5; [2010] 1 S.C.R. 132 at [18]. For an attempt to rehabilitate the *Anns* test see Robertson (2011) 127 L.Q.R. 370.

[54] As, indeed, Huggins VP and Fuad JA in the Hong Kong Court of Appeal had done: [1986] L.R.C. (Comm.) 300. See also *Mills v Winchester Diocesan Board* [1989] 2 All E.R. 317.

Three general "tests" for the existence of a duty of care. Since *Yuen Kun Yeu*   **5–019**
the stream of authority has flowed unabated and at present it is possible to
identify three approaches to the question of the determination of the duty of care:
(1) the tripartite test in *Caparo Industries Plc v Dickman*,[55] which asks whether
the harm was foreseeable, whether there was sufficient proximity between the
parties and whether the imposition of a duty of care would be "fair, just and
reasonable"; (2) the test which asks whether the defendant has "assumed
responsibility" to the claimant with regard to the matter from which the harm
arises; and (3) the "incremental test", whereby the law should develop novel
categories of negligence incrementally and by analogy with established
categories.[56] None of these tests can be mechanically applied to determine all
cases that might come before the courts and, as a result, the courts have warned
that: "[T]he unhappy experience with the rule so elegantly formulated by Lord
Wilberforce in *Anns v Merton London Borough Council* . . . suggests that
appellate judges should follow the philosopher's advice to 'Seek simplicity, and
distrust it'."[57]

Interplay between the tests. All three tests were considered at length by the   **5–020**
House of Lords in *Customs and Excise Commissioners v Barclays Bank Plc*.[58]
The claimants had obtained a freezing order against the assets of two companies
in respect of outstanding tax. This was served on the Bank, which wrote in
acknowledgment of its obligation to obey but before that letter was received
(indeed, probably before it was sent) the companies managed to withdraw large
sums, which were irrecoverable. The House of Lords held that the Bank did not
owe a duty of care to the claimants. None of the judgments purports to article any
universal test, though one can probably say that the incremental approach cannot
be regarded as a solvent in its own right because it gives no indication of where
the increments should stop—one might simply reach a radically different result in
three steps rather than one leap. However, it is not without value as a reminder
that "caution and analogical reasoning are generally valuable accompaniments to
judicial activity" and as a cross-check against the other approaches.[59] Assumption
of responsibility came to prominence in the context of liability for statements and
it was subsequently extended to cases in which the defendant undertook to

---

[55] [1990] 2 A.C. 605.
[56] It has been pointed out that "incrementalism" can apply "the other way round" so that it will be
"particularly difficult to establish a duty of care in a situation closely analogous to one where the law
has already denied the existence of such a duty": *M v MPC* [2007] EWCA Civ 1361 at [41]. Consider
also *Home Office v Mohammed* [2011] EWCA Civ 351; [2011] 1 W.L.R. 2862 at [27].
[57] *Customs and Excise Commissioners v Barclays Bank Plc* [2006] UKHL 28; [2007] 1 A.C. 181 at
[51] per Lord Rodger. What was said in Australia a few years ago is true here: "What the . . . shifts in
authority over fairly short periods demonstrate is the unlikelihood that any [judge] who tackles the
subject, even in a final court of appeal, can claim thereafter a personal revelation of an ultimate and
permanent value against which later responses must suffer in comparison": *Vairy v Wyong SC* [2005]
HCA 62; (2005) 223 C.L.R. 422 at [67]. For an even bleaker view see Hayne J in *Brodie v Singleton
SC* [2001] HCA 29; (2001) 206 C.L.R. 512 at [318]
[58] [2006] UKHL 28; [2007] 1 A.C. 181.
[59] [2006] UKHL 28; [2007] 1 A.C. 181 at [84], [93]. Further, "the closer the facts of the case in issue
to those of a case in which a duty of care has been held to exist, the readier a court will be . . . to find
that there has been an assumption of responsibility or that the proximity and policy conditions of the
threefold test are satisfied. The converse is also true": at [7].

perform a task for the claimant (it is hardly suitable for the general run of cases in which there has been no contact between the parties before the harm is suffered);[60] and because the loss in such cases tends to be purely economic rather than physical, it remains prominent where that type of loss is in issue. However, it is not confined to such cases, nor is it a universal solvent of them. Thus *Caparo Industries Plc v Dickman*, the leading case on the tripartite test, was itself a statement case involving pure economic loss; and in *Spring v Guardian Assurance*,[61] a case of a statement made to a third party, one member of the majority relied on assumption of responsibility but the others upon the tripartite test. Voluntary assumption of responsibility does not require that the defendant should actually intend to be legally liable for what he says or does, it is assessed objectively,[62] but on the facts of *Customs and Excise Commissioners*, a pure economic loss case, it clearly could not be satisfied—the Bank had no choice, it was bound by law to comply with the order and was potentially liable for contempt if it did not (though on the facts its error did not attract that penalty). That, however, was not the end of the matter, for the decision in favour of the Bank was ultimately based on the tripartite test. The dissipation of the account was certainly foreseeable, but whether or not the "notoriously elusive"[63] proximity requirement was satisfied, it would not be fair, just and reasonable to impose liability. This was, according to the House of Lords, a case where the liability was modest in relation to the defendants' resources and, unlike in many other pure economic loss cases, the amount of potential liability was known, but one might conceive of others where non-compliance with an order in a manner which would constitute negligence but not attract the penalties for contempt would involve a ruinous liability. It was to the contempt jurisdiction and not to the law of negligence that one should look for the sanctions attached to freezing orders. Lord Mance said:[64]

> "The common law has . . . developed a system offering very significant protection for claimants, together with very considerable incentives, backed by ample sanctions, for banks and other third parties to do their best to comply. Having imposed such an obligation on a third party, I do not consider that it should go further by imposing a duty on the third party towards a claimant to take care to prevent abstractions committed by the defendant in breach of a freezing order. This would not be analogous with or incremental to any previous development of the law. The position as it is without any such duty of care seems to me to represent a fair and normally effective balance between the respective interests involved."

Lord Hoffmann thought there was a close analogy with a statutory duty which did not give rise to civil liability and which could not automatically be made the foundation of a common law duty of care: "[Y]ou cannot derive a common law

---

[60] So it surprising that Lord Hoffmann says at [37] that *Henderson v Merrett Syndicates* [1995] 2 A.C. 145 (a "task" case) was: "a re-run of *Donoghue* in a claim for economic loss. . . . To say that the managing agents assumed a responsibility to the Names to take care not to accept unreasonable risks is little different from saying that a manufacturer of ginger beer assumes a responsibility to consumers to take care to keep snails out of his bottles."

[61] [1995] 2 A.C. 296, see para.12–051.

[62] *Customs and Excise Commissioners v Barclays Bank Plc* [2006] UKHL 28; [2007] 1 A.C. 181 at [5], [73], [86].

[63] [2006] UKHL 28; [2007] 1 A.C. 181 at [15] per Lord Bingham.

[64] [2006] UKHL 28; [2007] 1 A.C. 181 at [113].

duty of care directly from a statutory duty. Likewise, as it seems to me, you cannot derive one from an order of court. The order carries its own remedies and its reach does not extend any further."[65]

The current situation. So the overall picture seems to be that assumption of responsibility, the *Caparo* tripartite test and incrementalism all have a role to play in suitable cases, perhaps in a mutually supportive way, for there are some signs of running the concepts together.[66] Indeed, this is probably inevitable. Although it has been said that if the case falls within the principle of assumption of responsibility there should be no need to embark on any further enquiry whether it is fair, just and reasonable to impose liability,[67] it may be impossible to avoid issues which figure in the tripartite test in order to determine whether there is an assumption of responsibility in the relevant sense. For example, a seller of goods clearly "assumes responsibility" in the ordinary sense of those words to deliver the goods, but the current law is that he is not liable in tort (as opposed to contract) for failing to do so. One cannot escape the ultimate question of whether it is fair, just and reasonable. Despite the foregoing, it is the tripartite test which has figured most frequently in the greatest variety of cases (some judges have said that it "applies to all claims in the modern law of negligence"[68] and that it is "the most favoured test"[69]) so we need to look more closely at it. The *Caparo* case, "though it is no rule-book, represents the modern backdrop against which to judge any putative negligence claim".[70]

5–021

The test in Caparo v Dickman. *Caparo Industries Plc v Dickman*[71] concerned the liability of an auditor for financial loss suffered by investors and is considered from this point of view in more detail below,[72] but for the moment we are concerned with what it said about the general approach to the duty of care. Recall that *Caparo* states that there are three separate steps or issues in the "duty of care" inquiry. First, it must be reasonably foreseeable that the conduct of the defendant will cause damage to the claimant. Secondly, there must be sufficient "proximity" between the parties. Thirdly: "[T]he situation [must] be one in which the court considers it fair, just and reasonable that the law should impose a duty of care of a given scope on the one party for the benefit of the other."[73]

5–022

The Caparo test is a guide rather than a precise formula. The content of the steps in the *Caparo* test and the relationship between them is imprecise and one cannot reconcile all the judgments in form even if they all point the same way in substance. It is "reaching for the moon . . . to expect to accommodate every

5–023

---

[65] [2006] UKHL 28; [2007] 1 A.C. 181 at [39].
[66] Lord Hoffmann at [35], Lord Rodger at [65]–[66] and Lord Walker at [73]. This has occurred before. In *Merrett v Babb* [2001] EWCA Civ 214; [2001] Q.B. 1174 at [41] May LJ thought that the *Caparo* "strand" and the assumption of responsibility "strand" in reality merged.
[67] *Henderson v Merrett Syndicates Ltd* [1995] 2 A.C. 145 at 181.
[68] *Robinson v Chief Constable of West Yorkshire Police* [2014] EWCA Civ 15 at [40] per Hallett LJ.
[69] *Van Colle v Chief Constable of the Hertfordshire Police* [2008] UKHL 50; [2009] 1 A.C. 225 at [42] per Lord Bingham.
[70] *Connor v Surrey CC* [2010] EWCA Civ 286 at [102] per Laws LJ.
[71] [1990] 2 A.C. 605.
[72] See para.12–036.
[73] Lord Bridge in *Caparo* [1990] 2 A.C. 617.

circumstance which may arise within a single short abstract formulation"[74] and one must beware of using the ideas we do have as slogans.[75] As Lord Roskill put it in *Caparo*:[76]

> "There is no simple formula or touchstone to which recourse can be had in order to provide in every case a ready answer to the questions whether, given certain facts, the law will or will not impose liability for negligence or, in cases where such liability can be shown to exist, determine the extent of that liability. Phrases such as 'foreseeability', 'proximity', 'neighbourhood', 'just and reasonable', 'fairness' . . . will be found used from time to time in different cases. But . . . such phrases are not precise definitions. At best they are but labels or phrases descriptive of the very different factual situations which can exist in particular cases and which must be carefully examined in each case before it can be pragmatically determined[77] whether a duty of care exists and, if so, what is the scope and extent of that duty."

5–024   The *Caparo* test rarely results in the disturbance of established duty categories (and categories of case where there is no duty). Though orthodoxy may sometimes be overturned in the Supreme Court, once a duty is well established (or denied), the courts will not generally return de novo to issues like proximity and fairness, for that would be a recipe for inconsistency and uncertainty. As Hobhouse LJ explained in *Perrett v Collins*:[78]

> "It is a truism to say that any case must be decided taking into account the circumstances of the case, but where those circumstances comply with established categories of liability, a defendant should not be allowed to seek to escape from liability by appealing to some vaguer concept of justice or fairness; the law cannot be re-made for every case."

5–025   **The Caparo test is supplemented by additional rules in certain situations.** In some contexts, the courts have propounded additional and more precise rules that govern the existence of a duty of care. For example, in the case of a person who suffers psychiatric trauma from shock at injury to another it is now established that the claimant must, if he is to recover, have a sufficient relationship of love and affection with the primary victim and that he must witness the event or its immediate aftermath.[79] The relationship between such additional rules and the *Caparo* test is not entirely clear. However, it seems that they are in effect the law's standard assessments of proximity and of what is fair and reasonable in psychiatric injury cases. The more general concepts are likely to be called in aid where the court is deciding whether to venture into an entirely novel area of liability or where a "new" duty has been established and it is in the course of development.

---

[74] *Merrett v Babb* [2001] EWCA Civ 214; [2001] Q.B. 1174 at [41] per May LJ.
[75] *Customs and Excise Commissioners* [2006] UKHL 28; [2007] 1 A.C. 181 at [35].
[76] *Caparo* [1990] 2 A.C. 617 at 628.
[77] The exercise of discovering a duty of care has been described as "intensely pragmatic": *Rowling v Takaro Properties Ltd* [1988] A.C. 473 at 501.
[78] *Perrett v Collins* [1998] 2 Lloyd's Rep. 255 at 263.
[79] See para.5–088.

E.   The Stages of the *Caparo* Test

The three components of the Caparo test in detail. The analysis here shifts to   5–026
the individual parts of the *Caparo* test. The goal is to tease out precisely what
each stage involves.

i.   *Foreseeability*

The foreseeability stage of the *Caparo* test requires will be satisfied if it was   5–027
reasonable foreseeable that the claimant might be injured if the defendant was
negligent. As Lord Russell of Killowen put it, a duty of care "only arises towards
those individuals of whom it may reasonably be anticipated that they will be
affected by the act which constitutes the alleged breach".[80] This stage of the test
is rarely in issue. It is governed by several principles, which can be simply stated.
First, whether or not the claimant is foreseeable is a question of fact. Secondly, it
is not necessary that harm to the claimant specifically was foreseeable. It is
enough that the claimant is one of a class that could foreseeably be injured as a
result of negligence on the part of the defendant.[81] Thirdly, the issue of
foreseeability is tested objectively, so it is no satisfactory answer for the
defendant to say that he did not foresee that the claimant might be injured if the
reasonable person would have appreciated that risk.

ii.   *Proximity*

The concept of proximity is wider than physical nearness. As a matter of   5–028
ordinary language, the word "proximity" means "nearness", especially in a
spatial sense. There is no doubt that the courts sometimes take account of
physical distance when they talk of proximity, but the term does not merely
encompass spatial propinquity. As Lord Atkin stated in *Donoghue v Stevenson*:[82]

> "[The concept of] proximity [is] not confined to mere physical proximity, but ... extend[s] to
> such close and direct relations that the act complained of directly affects a person whom the
> person alleged to be bound to take care would know would be directly affected by his careless
> act."

Thus, it is clear that the proximity may be satisfied even though the parties are
physically distant from each other.

That which is required to establish the necessary proximity varies depending   5–029
on the type of case. A closer nexus will be required in some types of cases than
in others in order to satisfy the proximity requirement. Where the defendant has
directly caused physical harm to the claimant or his property by an act, a duty

---

[80] *Bourhill v Young* [1943] A.C. 92 at 102.
[81] He may join the class after the negligent act but before the damage is suffered: *Aiken v Stewart Wrightson Members Agency Ltd* [1995] 1 W.L.R. 1281.
[82] [1932] A.C. 562 at 581.

may readily be established by showing foreseeability and nothing else.[83] In such a case: "[I]t is enough that the plaintiff happens to be (out of the whole world) the person with whom the defendant collided or who purchased the offending ginger beer."[84] Where, however, there is a failure to act or the loss is purely economic or mental trauma or for some other reason the recognition of a duty based upon only foreseeability is perceived to be problematic, the law will, if it does not deny liability completely, insist on a substantially closer relationship between the parties. Thus while there is under the common law no general duty on D to protect C from damage which B (for whom D is not vicariously liable) wilfully chooses to do to C, there would be proximity between officers in charge of young offenders who allow them to escape and owners of property in the immediate vicinity which is damaged by the offenders during the escape.[85] The foundation of the duty is the custody of the offenders, even if the case involves a step beyond that where the defendant has custody of both the wrongdoer and the victim (for example, where one prisoner is attacked by others). However, there will not be proximity between the police and victims of crime in general. In *Hill v CC West Yorkshire*[86] a 20-year-old student was murdered by the man known as the "Yorkshire Ripper", who had committed several similar offences in Yorkshire. After his apprehension the student's estate brought an action against the police, who, it was alleged, had been guilty of negligence in failing to catch the killer and thereby prevent her murder. The House of Lords held that there was nothing to take the case out of the general rule denying a duty of care in respect of wilful wrongdoing by others: the police did not have the wrongdoer in their custody and there was no special relationship between the police and the claimant, who was a member of the public at large. The risk which the alleged negligence presented to her was no different from that presented to many thousands of young women in Yorkshire, any of whom might be the killer's victim. This was one of two alternative bases of the decision: the other was that it was undesirable to impose a duty of care in respect of the investigation of crime because it would have deleterious effects on police efficiency. Despite some earlier doubts about this in view of the Human Rights Act 1998, it has subsequently been confirmed so that there may be no liability even though the victim is identifiable to the police.[87] Neither is there any duty of care owed by the police in the course of investigating criminal conduct to witnesses of crime[88] or police informants.[89] The insistence on a close relationship between the parties is most consistently apparent in cases where the claimant complains that he has suffered loss as a result of acting on

---

[83] *Mobil Oil Hong Kong Ltd v Hong Kong United Dockyards Ltd* [1991] 1 Lloyd's Rep. 309 at 368; *Caparo Industries Plc v Dickman* [1990] 2 A.C. 605 at 632; *Customs and Excise Commissioners v Barclays Bank Plc* [2006] UKHL 28; [2007] 1 A.C. 181 at [31].

[84] *Caparo* in the Court of Appeal [1989] 1 Q.B. 653 at 686.

[85] *Home Office v Dorset Yacht Co* [1970] A.C. 1004. See further para.5–044.

[86] [1989] A.C. 53.

[87] *Osman v Ferguson* [1993] 4 All E.R. 344; *Van Colle v Chief Constable of the Hertfordshire Police* [2008] UKHL 50; [2009] 1 A.C. 225.

[88] *Brooks v Commissioner of Police of the Metropolis* [2005] UKHL 24; [2005] 1 W.L.R. 1495.

[89] *An Informer v A Chief Constable* [2012] EWCA Civ 197; [2013] Q.B. 579.

incorrect information or advice given to him by the defendant. In this situation it has been said that the relationship between the parties must be "equivalent to contract".[90]

Proximity between the defendant and the source of the harm. Sometimes the   **5–030**
concept of proximity is used to refer not to the relationship between the parties but to the relationship between the defendant and the source of harm. In *Sutradhar v National Environment Research Council*[91] the defendant Council, funded by the Overseas Development Agency, undertook a survey of the quality of water sources in Bangladesh. This tested for 31 chemical elements but not arsenic and the report said nothing about arsenic. The conventional wisdom at the time was that the presence of arsenic would be highly unlikely. Nor did it purport to be a report on potability, the purpose of the exercise being to use spare funds to increase knowledge about fish farming. The claimant (one of some 699 identified) contended that he had suffered injury to his health as a result of drinking water contaminated with arsenic. The claim went through various formulations but ended up as one based on a duty not to release a report which might give the impression that the water was free of arsenic and fit to drink. The House of Lords affirmed the decision to strike out the claim. There were cases in which persons had undertaken inspections or laid down safety requirements in respect of matters like airworthiness or medical facilities at boxing matches and liability had been imposed when these were found wanting[92] but in those cases there had been "proximity in the sense of a measure of control over . . . the potentially dangerous situation".[93] Here the defendants had no control whatever over the supply of water in Bangladesh. That was enough to find against the claimant on the duty issue.

iii.   Fair, Just and Reasonable

Illustration of the type of factors that are taken into account at the third   **5–031**
stage of the Caparo test. Even if the first and second stage of the *Caparo* test are satisfied, a duty of care may still be denied if, in the court's view, recognising a duty would not be fair, just and reasonable.[94] A good illustration of a case in which this happened, and which demonstrates the types of factors that courts take into consideration in this regard, is *Marc Rich & Co AG v Bishop Rock Marine Co Ltd*.[95] In this case the vessel *The Nicholas H* developed a crack while carrying a cargo from South America to Italy. Off Puerto Rico a surveyor employed by NKK, a marine classification society,[96] was called in by the master. The surveyor eventually pronounced that the vessel was fit to complete the voyage with temporary welding work. A few days later she sank with the total loss of the cargo. The claimants, owners of the cargo, obtained US $500,000 by settlement

---

[90]   Lord Devlin in *Hedley, Byrne v Heller & Partners* [1964] A.C. 465 at 529.
[91]   [2006] UKHL 33; [2006] 4 All E.R. 490.
[92]   See para.5–051.
[93]   [2006] UKHL 33; [2006] 4 All E.R. 490 at [38] per Lord Hoffmann.
[94]   Although three words are used it should not be thought that there will be a minute disjunctive analysis. All three words convey the same idea of "judicial policy" in slightly different ways.
[95]   [1996] A.C. 211.
[96]   These bodies inspect ships and give them certificates of seaworthiness for insurance purposes.

against the shipowners (this being the limit of their liability under the conventions governing carriage by sea) and claimed the balance of US $5.7 million from NKK. On a preliminary issue of law, for the purposes of which it was assumed that the surveyor was negligent and that the loss of the cargo was a foreseeable consequence of that negligence, a majority of the House of Lords held that NKK owed no duty of care to the cargo owners. The majority proceeded upon the assumption that the requirement of proximity was satisfied, but concluded that the cumulative effect of a number of policy factors pointed against a decision in favour of the owners. The most important of these factors related to the structure of the network of transactions involved in carriage by sea. The liability of the shipowner was limited by statute to so much per ton of the ship's tonnage and if the cargo owner were allowed to bypass this by the device of a claim against the classification society (which is beyond the protection of the tonnage limitation) such bodies would be likely to seek to pass on the cost of their liability insurance to shipowners or to seek indemnities against them, thereby disturbing the balance between cargo owners and carriers set by international convention. Even if this did not happen, another layer of insurance cover (namely, the liability cover of the classification society) would be wastefully introduced into the structure. Furthermore, there was a risk that classification societies would decline to survey high risk vessels, thereby causing potential damage to their function of acting for the public welfare in respect of safety at sea. It is important to note that the House of Lords based its decision neither upon foreseeability, nor upon any technical legal doctrine.

5–032   **Factors identified in Caparo Industries v Dickman.** While *Marc Rich* may be regarded as involving an attempt to pass liability around from a subrogated loss insurer to a defendant's liability insurer, in many cases a decision that no duty of care is owed really does mean that the loss lies where it falls. Thus in *Caparo Industries Plc v Dickman*[97] the House of Lords held that auditors of a public company owe a duty of care (by contract) only to the company and therefore to the general body of shareholders as a collectivity, but not to individual buyers of the company's shares (even if they are existing shareholders) nor to creditors of the company. Reliance on the accounts for such purposes is certainly foreseeable (Lord Bridge described it as "highly probable");[98] but that is not enough to generate a duty of care. Several reasons underlie this restrictive approach. The most obvious is a fear of a multiplicity of claims and a belief that the liability insurance market cannot in practice bear the risk of exposure to the full range of foreseeable loss arising from an inadequate audit of a major company, with the consequent risk, if a duty is imposed, of ruinous liability out of all proportion to the fault of the defendant.[99] Furthermore, there are also reasons which might be brought under the general heading of "fairness". For Lord Bridge in *Caparo*, to hold the auditor liable to anyone in the world who happens to deal with the company on the basis of the audit report is: "[T]o confer on the world at large a

---

[97] [1990] 2 A.C. 605.
[98] [1990] 2 A.C. 605 at 625.
[99] [1990] 2 A.C. 605 at 643.

quite unwarranted entitlement to appropriate for their own purposes the benefit of the expert knowledge or professional experience attributed to the maker of the statement."[100]

Vulnerability of the claimant (or lack thereof). The courts have identified vulnerability of the claimant and, conversely, the ability of the claimant to protect himself from the defendant's negligence, as an important factor to consider at the third stage of the *Caparo* test.[101] A good illustration of this can be found in McHugh J.'s reasons in *Esanda Finance v Peat Marwick Hungerford*,[102] which is another auditor case. It was held that no duty of care arose. For McHugh J a significant factor supporting this holding was the fact that investors and creditors as a group are commonly not "dependent" upon the audit. They may possess considerable financial sophistication and they:[103]   5–033

> "[A]re likely to be in a better position to know the likely extent of their losses. The investor or creditor knows the maximum extent of any likely loss. Unlike most plaintiffs in negligence cases, these investors and creditors can take steps to protect themselves against loss. Some creditors and investors will have the staff or means to investigate and verify that part of the audited person's financial affairs that is relevant to the loan or investment. They can seek verification of the report and accounts from the auditors and rely on any representations or assurances (whether for reward or otherwise) that the auditors give. Creditors can assign debts to factoring organisations and in some cases may even be able to insure their debts. They can spread the loss against successive years of revenue by making provision against bad and doubtful debts. Investors can spread their risk by diversifying their investments."

One might look askance at this logic for several reasons, one of which is that there is no evidence that it is the investors who are best positioned to avoid or absorb losses.[104] Of course, these arguments will not be applicable to some individual cases: there may be individual investors who have no sophisticated financial knowledge, no ability to spread risks and who may be ruined by reliance on the audit report but the law has to frame a rule for the generality of cases.

Whether recognising a duty of care would undermine some important public interest. Another factor to consider at the fair, just and reasonable stage of the *Caparo* test is whether recognising a duty of care would detract from some important public interest. Thus, in *Robinson v Chief Constable of West Yorkshire Police* it was held that: "claims against the police in negligence for their acts or omissions in the course of investigating and suppressing crime and apprehending offenders will fail the third stage of the Caparo test."[105] The concern is that imposing a duty would undermine the work of the police. Also as a result of this factor the state is under no duty of care to ensure a safe system of work for members of the armed forces in battle conditions.[106] Neither do individual soldiers owe a duty of care to each other during such conditions. To impose a   5–034

---

[100] [1990] 2 A.C. 605 at 621.
[101] See generally Stapleton (2003) 24 Aust. B. Rev 135.
[102] (1997) 188 C.L.R. 241. See also Stapleton (1995) 111 L.Q.R. 301.
[103] (1997) 188 C.L.R. 241 at 285.
[104] In *Spartan Steel & Alloys v Martin* [1973] 2 Q.B. 27 (see para.5–061) Lord Denning MR used a similar argument to deny a duty of care to C where C suffers pure economic loss as a result of D's interference with a public utility supply.
[105] [2014] EWCA Civ 15 at [46] per Hallett LJ.
[106] *Mulcahy v Ministry of Defence* [1996] Q.B. 732.

duty of care in this situation would not be fair, just or reasonable as imposing a duty would risk impeding the state's ability to conduct military operations. What is the situation in respect of acts done by the state in preparation for such hostilities? This issue arose in *Smith v Ministry of Defence*.[107] The claimants in this case were servicemen who had been injured in the course of military operations in Iraq or dependants of such servicemen. It was alleged that the Ministry of Defence had been negligent in failing to provide suitable equipment and training. The Ministry applied for the proceedings to be struck out due to (among other grounds) the absence of a duty of care. The Supreme Court held that the claims should not be struck out as the duty question could only be resolved once the evidence had been heard. However, it was acknowledged that it would be important to consider, in deciding whether a duty of care was owed, the public interest in the armed services being able to engage in operations without being distracted by the law of torts. As Lord Hope explained:[108]

> "[I]t is of paramount importance that the work that the armed services do in the national interest should not be impeded by having to prepare for or conduct active operations against the enemy under the threat of litigation if things should go wrong. The court [that will hear the claimants' proceedings] must be especially careful . . . to have regard to the public interest, to the unpredictable nature of armed conflict and to the inevitable risks that it gives rise to when it is striking the balance as to what is fair, just and reasonable."

5–035   **Effect of recognising a duty of care on other areas of law.** What is "fair, just and reasonable" is not merely a matter of the relationship between the parties. A factor which frequently appears in the case law is the effect of the imposition of a duty of care upon the relationship between the tort of negligence and other parts of the legal system. The courts have shown some concern lest an ever-expanding liability for negligence should eat up other rules developed by the courts and Parliament. Thus, where there is a statutory regime a: "[C]ommon law duty must not be inconsistent with the performance . . . of . . . statutory duties and powers in the manner intended by Parliament, or contrary in any other way to the presumed legislative intention."[109]

In *CBS Songs Ltd v Amstrad Consumer Electrics Plc*[110] the defendants manufactured tape-to-tape domestic audio systems which facilitated illegal copying of copyright material. In rejecting any duty of care by the manufacturers to the owners of the copyright, the House of Lords pointed out that in the copyright legislation Parliament had produced what could reasonably be regarded as a code governing the rights of copyright owners and that imposed liability only where copying had been authorised, a requirement plainly not satisfied on the facts since purchasers were warned against illegal copying by notices on the equipment. To impose liability for negligence would subvert the statutory

---

[107] [2013] UKSC 41; [2014] A.C. 52.
[108] [2013] UKSC 41; [2014] A.C. 52 at [100].
[109] *Stovin v Wise* [1996] A.C. 923 at 935 per Lord Nicholls.
[110] [1988] A.C. 1013.

regime.[111] In *Murphy v Brentwood DC*[112] this "structure of the law" argument was relied on in two ways. The House of Lords held that a builder was not liable in negligence to the owner of a house built by him in respect of defects of construction which did not cause personal injury or damage to other property (for example, the contents). Where neither of these elements was present the owner's complaint was essentially that he had acquired something which was less valuable than the price he had paid for it and the remedying of such loss was the function of the law of contract rather than negligence.[113] In addition, however, the Defective Premises Act 1972 had imposed liability upon the builder of a dwelling, transmissible from one owner to another, for just such defects of quality as were being complained of.[114] The limitation period under the statute is a fixed one of six years from completion, whereas for the common law duty it could be a good deal longer: "It would be remarkable to find that similar obligations . . . applicable to buildings of every kind and subject to no such limitations or exclusions as are imposed by the 1972 Act, could be derived from the builder's common law duty of care."[115]

However, if this approach were taken to its logical conclusion there would never be any expansion of tort law. Indeed, it would be a good deal narrower in its scope than it now is, for there is almost always some legal regime governing the situation and, if that regime gives no civil remedy in damages to the claimant, it might be argued that that reflects a proper view of public policy.[116] That this is not the law is shown dramatically by *Spring v Guardian Assurance Plc*[117] in which the House of Lords held that the writer of a reference might be under a duty of care to the subject of the reference notwithstanding that until then it had been assumed that the only liability arose in the torts of libel and malicious falsehood, both of which in such a case required proof of malice.[118] Indeed, the case illustrates a point which is perhaps rather obvious but which tends to be forgotten in discussions dominated by the need to keep liability under control. This is that what the court conceives to be fair, just and reasonable may be just as much a reason for imposing a duty of care as for denying one. The need for free and frank disclosure in references points towards a narrow rule of liability requiring malice but the interests of the subject of the reference are to be given more weight than may formerly have been the case. Against the demands of free speech:[119]

---

[111] See further *Murdoch v Department for Work and Pensions* [2010] EWHC 1988 (QB); *Home Office v Mohammed* [2011] EWCA Civ 351; [2011] 1 W.L.R. 2862; *Desmond v Chief Constable of Nottinghamshire Police* [2011] EWCA Civ 3; *B v Home Office* [2012] EWHC 226 (QB); [2012] 4 All E.R. 276 at [128].

[112] [1991] 1 A.C. 398: see para.10–049.

[113] Much was made of this point in *Robinson v P E Jones (Contractors) Ltd* [2011] EWCA Civ 9; [2012] Q.B. 44 at [84].

[114] See para.10–056.

[115] [1991] 1 A.C. 398 at 480 per Lord Bridge.

[116] See generally Cooke (1991) 107 L.Q.R. 46.

[117] [1995] 2 A.C. 296, see para.12–051.

[118] Although libel does not generally require proof of malice, it does when the occasion is one of qualified privilege and the giving of a reference is such an occasion.

[119] *Spring* [1995] 2 A.C. 296 at 326 per Lord Lowry.

"[L]ooms the probability, often amounting to a certainty, of damage to the individual, which in some cases will be serious and may indeed be irreparable. The entire prosperity and happiness of someone who is the subject of a damning reference which is given carelessly but in perfectly good faith may be irretrievably blighted."

Donoghue v Stevenson itself was a decision that, notwithstanding the restrictions imposed by privity of contract, an injured consumer required a remedy against the negligent manufacturer of a defective product.[120] Perhaps the most remarkable decision of all is that in *White v Jones*[121] holding that a solicitor in preparing a will owed a duty of care to intended beneficiaries under the will. Liability was based upon an "assumption of responsibility" by the solicitor but was carried further than in any previous case because there was no reliance by the claimants, which had been assumed to be a necessary element under that concept. What Lord Goff described as "the impulse to do practical justice"[122] was, however, an overriding consideration, for the estate in such a case has no claim against the solicitor since it has suffered no loss. Underlying the majority judgments in this case seems to be a perception that it is necessary to impose a duty of care to fulfil a quasi-disciplinary function.[123]

5–036   **Is the Caparo test satisfactory?** The *Caparo* test suffers from overwhelming problems. First, the concept of proximity is empty. It is doubtful whether it has any content. According to the Privy Council in *Yuen Kun Yeu*, proximity means, "the whole concept of necessary [i.e. necessary to produce a duty of care] relationship between the plaintiff and defendant". This formulation gives no indication as to when the parties will be in a proximate relationship. The matter can be put differently by saying that the concept of proximity refers to that which is needed in order to generate a duty of care, rather than means of discovering whether a duty of care is owed. Arguably, it a device that is used in an attempt to conceal the fact that judges are frequently engaged in the formulation of policy in this area of the law.[124] Secondly, the "fair, just and reasonable" stage is redundant since it cannot ever be "fair, just and reasonable" to impose a duty on a defendant with respect to a given claimant if the other stages of the *Caparo* test are unsatisfied. More fundamentally, the formula "fair, just and reasonable" is just an empty phrase. What is needed is an explanation of when it will be "fair, just and reasonable" to recognise a duty of care. Again, the complaint can be made that it too conceals judicial policy choices whereas it would be desirable if the relevance of policy were frankly acknowledged and the material policy considerations openly discussed. Policy choices (what Lord Goff described as "an educated reflex to facts"[125]) is an inescapable part of the judicial process[126] and it is better

---

[120] The public good is now conceived to demand a strict liability in such cases: see para.11–015.

[121] [1995] 2 A.C. 207, see para.5–054.

[122] [1995] 2 A.C. 207 at 259.

[123] See para.5–054.

[124] "[T]he concept of 'proximity' is an artificial one which depends more upon the court's perception of what is the reasonable area for the imposition of liability than upon any logical process of analogical deduction": *Alcock v Chief Constable of South Yorkshire Police* [1992] 1 A.C. 310 at 411 per Lord Oliver.

[125] *Smith v Littlewoods Organisation Ltd* [1987] A.C. 241 at 271.

[126] Cf. Stevens, *Torts and Rights* (2007), Ch.14, who argues that it is illegitimate for judges to have recourse to policy.

to recognise it as such rather than to cloud the issue by saying that, "policy need not be involved where reason and good sense . . . will point the way",[127] for these concepts are surely one and the same thing.

F. Criticism of the Duty of Care Concept

It is not only the tests that have been developed to determine whether a duty of care arises that have come in for criticism. The duty of care concept itself has been repeatedly attacked. Buckland famously described it as an "unnecessary fifth wheel on the coach, incapable of sound analysis and possibly productive of injustice".[128] Other scholars have been no less critical.[129] There is no doubt that the duty concept has spawned a great deal of litigation. The law controlling it can fairly be criticised as uncertain, and perhaps hopelessly so. A further point that can be made against the duty of care element is that many of the issues that it deals with could be considered when other elements of the action in negligence are addressed.[130] For example, the rule that the police do not owe a duty of care investigating criminal behaviour to victims of crime[131] could be reallocated to the causation element, which would see the act of the criminal that injures the victim as an intervening cause. Because most issues that are presently dealt with at the duty stage could be accommodated by other elements of the tort of negligence, the duty of care element is arguable unnecessary. It may well be that the issues that are currently dealt with by the duty element could be better handled elsewhere.

5–037

3. DUTY OF CARE: SPECIFIC PROBLEMS

Standard categories of case in which the duty of care arises as an issue. Although so far we have concentrated upon the general approach to determining whether a duty of care exists, the cases are of course concerned with producing a result on a particular set of facts. The range of situations in which the "duty issue" may arise is almost infinite but there are a number of standard situations in which it has arisen very frequently and it is necessary to say more about these since they are controlled by additional principles. Unfortunately, the categories are not watertight and there is a good deal of overlap between them so that, for example, a case concerning the activities of a public authority may also involve discussion in terms of omissions and assumption of responsibility, or even pure economic loss. With the warning, therefore, that the reader must be prepared to move between different sections (and, indeed, to refer back to the section on the general approach to duty) in order to obtain an adequate understanding of the relevant principles we turn to six of these common situations.

5–038

---

[127] *Home Office v Dorset Yacht Co Ltd* [1970] A.C. 1004 at 1039 per Lord Morris.
[128] Buckland (1935) 51 L.Q.R. 637.
[129] See, e.g. Winfield (1934) 34 Col. L. Rev. 41; Howarth [1991] C.L.J 67; Nolan (2013) 129 L.Q.R. 559.
[130] See especially Nolan (2013) 129 L.Q.R. 559.
[131] See para.5–029.

A. Omissions

5–039 **There is in general no duty to act for the benefit of others.** It is a general principle of tort law that one must take care not to cause injury to others, but there is no general duty to act for the benefit of others. The rule is that D must not harm his neighbour (misfeasance) not that D is required to save him (nonfeasance). The rule was stated starkly by Schiemann LJ in *Vellino v Chief Constable of Greater Manchester* when his Lordships said, "under our law two persons can stand asid and watch a third jump to his death: there is no legal duty to rescue".[132] There is dissatisfaction in some quarters with the suitability of the rule in modern conditions[133] and in 1987 one member of the House of Lords, while accepting the existence of the rule, said that it might one day have to be reconsidered.[134] However, in *Stovin v Wise* the rule was regarded as justifiable by both the majority and the minority in the House of Lords. Lord Hoffmann for the majority said:[135]

> "There are sound reasons why omissions require different treatment from positive conduct. It is one thing for the law to say that a person who undertakes some activity shall take reasonable care not to cause damage to others. It is another thing for the law to require that a person who is doing nothing in particular shall take steps to prevent another from suffering harm from the acts of third parties . . . or natural causes. One can put the matter in political, moral or economic terms. In political terms it is less of an invasion of freedom for the law to require him to consider the safety of others in his actions than to impose upon him a duty to rescue or protect. A moral version of this point may be called the 'Why pick on me?' argument. A duty to prevent harm to others or to render assistance to a person in danger or distress may apply to a large and indeterminate class of people who happen to be able to do something. Why should one be held liable rather than another? In economic terms, the efficient allocation of resources usually requires an activity should bear its own costs. If it benefits from being able to impose some of its costs on other people (what economists call 'externalities') the market is distorted because the activity appears cheaper than it really is. So liability to pay compensation for loss caused by negligent conduct acts as a deterrent against increasing the cost of the activity to the community and reduces externalities. But there is no similar justification for requiring a person who is not doing anything to spend money on behalf of someone else. Except in special cases (such as marine salvage) English law does not reward someone who voluntarily confers a benefit on another. So there must be some special reason why he should have to put his hand in his pocket."

The rule applies to public bodies as well as private persons. The defendants in *Stovin v Wise* were a highway authority; and where a horse fair had been held in a small town for hundreds of years the local authority was under no obligation to take steps to ensure adequate arrangements for the control of horses or that horse traders had liability insurance against the risk of visitors to the fair being injured by horses for:[136]

---

[132] [2001] EWCA Civ 1249; [2002] 1 W.L.R. 218 at [13].
[133] See, e.g. Linden (1971) 34 M.L.R. 241; Weinrib (1981) 90 Yale L.J. 247; Markesinis (1989) 105 L.Q.R. 104. Cf. Honoré in Cane and Stapleton (eds), *Essays for Patrick Atiyah*(1991).
[134] Lord Goff in *Smith v Littlewoods Organisation Ltd* [1987] A.C. 241 at 271.
[135] [1996] A.C. 923 at 943.
[136] *Glaister v Appleby in Westmorland Town Council* [2009] EWCA Civ 1325; [2010] P.I.Q.R. P6 at [46].

"[T]he general policy of the law does not extend to holding D legally to blame for injury to C caused by the negligence of T on the ground that D could have prevented it . . . . As a matter of generality, to hold a person liable to a victim for injury for which the defendant was not directly to blame, but was caused by the negligence of a third person which the defendant could have foreseen and prevented, would shift the basis of tort liability towards a system for the transfer of losses resulting from injuries not merely caused by the default of the defendant but which a defendant might have been able to prevent."

The rule is probably in practice less frequently determinative than might be thought for three reasons. The first reason is that what may from one point of view seem to be nonfeasance may be treated in law as misfeasance. Secondly, in many cases the relationship between the parties or some other factor may lead to the imposition of a duty to act. Thirdly, a defendant will usually come under a duty to act where he has created a dangerous situation, regardless of whether he was at fault for doing so.

i.   Cases Where There is Not a True Omission

An omission in the course of a wider activity is regarded as an act. An   5–040
apparent omission may be treated as an item in a chain of active conduct. A driver must take positive steps to meet emergencies which arise and no one would seriously contend that his failure to brake at a junction was an omission in the sense here discussed[137] and maintaining one's speed in a deliberate attempt to balk an overtaking driver who had "run out of road" would be treated as an act. Nonetheless, in some cases it is impossible to regard the omission as part of a course of conduct in this way. Thus in England the common understanding is (though there appears to be no case precisely in point) that refusal by a doctor in an emergency to go to the aid of a person who is not his patient would not be actionable.[138] Equally, of course, what contains elements of positive conduct may still, for the purposes of tort law be an omission. Starting something does not of itself impose a legal duty to finish it.[139] In *Stovin v Wise* the defendant road authority had resolved to improve a junction and then let the matter go to sleep. Had the work been done, the claimant would probably not have been involved in

---

[137] Rigby LJ in *Kelly v Metropolitan Ry Co* [1895] 1 Q.B. 944 at 947 said of a train driver's failure to shut off steam so that his train ran into the dead end, "the proper description of what was done was that it was a negligent act in so managing the train as to allow it to come into contact with the dead-end".

[138] In *Capital & Counties Plc v Hampshire CC* [1997] Q.B. 1004 at 1060, a case about a fire brigade, Stuart-Smith LJ, giving the judgment of the court, said that "a doctor who happened to witness a road accident . . . is not under any legal obligation to [assist], save in certain limited circumstances which are not here relevant, and the relationship of doctor and patient does not arise". What the "limited circumstances" are is not specified. However, in *Woods v Lowns* (1996) Aust. Torts Rep. 81–376 a majority of New South Wales Court of Appeal held that a doctor may be under a duty to respond to a call for help for a non-patient, although local legislation on professional conduct had some influence on the decision.

[139] In *Capital & Counties Plc v Hampshire CC* [1997] Q.B. 1004 at 1035 Stuart-Smith LJ thought that if the doctor volunteers his assistance his only duty was not to make the patient worse, but presumably that may include making him worse by dissuading others from seeking other assistance. At any rate it is plainly the law that a hospital which admits a patient must treat him, not ignore him: *R. (on the application of Burke) v GMC* [2005] EWCA Civ 1003; [2006] Q.B. 273 at [32].

the accident which took place but the accident was nevertheless caused by what the authority failed to do (improve the junction) not by anything it did.

ii. Relationships

5–041   **The law may impose a duty to act based on the relationship between the parties.** Even where there is a "true" omission the law may impose a duty to act; and it not infrequently does so. It is impossible to catalogue the situations but a number of factors which seem typically to point towards a duty of affirmative action are considered below. The situation where liability is imposed because the defendant has "assumed responsibility" for a task is considered in the following section but there is a good deal of overlap between the two categories. In most cases where a duty is imposed because there is a "special relationship" between the parties it might be said that in entering that relationship the defendant had assumed responsibility for the claimant's safety or well-being but some such assumption or relationship distinguishes the defendant from a mere stranger.

5–042   **Relationships of dependence.** A duty to act may be imposed where the claimant is under the care or control of the defendant and is incapable of protecting himself. Thus claims have succeeded against schools for failing to safeguard pupils against injury,[140] the police are liable for failure to protect a mentally disturbed person in their custody from self-inflicted harm[141] and the same is of course true of a mental hospital with regard to a patient who is a suicide risk.[142] In many of these cases the defendant will be a public authority so there is the prospect of an alternative claim, via the Human Rights Act 1998, based on art.2 of the Convention, though the primary focus of that is on the requirement that the state should ensure adequate "systems" to guard against the risk.[143] It might seem obvious as a matter of principle that a tort duty is owed by a parent to his child and this seems to be the law in England.[144] The point has been little litigated,[145] perhaps because of the likely absence of liability insurance, but it should be noted that the imposition of a duty would allow an insured defendant to claim contribution from an uninsured parent (e.g. in a case arising out of a road accident where the parent had failed to supervise the child).[146]

---

[140] On the extent to which a school may have a duty to take action to prevent bullying out of school see *Bradford-Smart v West Sussex CC* [2002] EWCA Civ 7; [2002] E.L.R. 139. While a school is under a duty to protect a pupil from physical harm in, e.g. playing sports, it is not obliged to take out accident insurance for the child, nor to advise the parents to do so: *Van Oppen v Bedford School* [1990] 1 W.L.R. 235.

[141] *Kirkham v CC Greater Manchester* [1990] 2 Q.B. 283 (as to suicide by sane persons in custody, see para.5–047).

[142] *Savage v S Essex Partnership NHS Foundation Trust* [2008] UKHL 74; [2009] 1 A.C. 681 at [47].

[143] See para.2–014.

[144] *Surtees v Kingston on Thames BC* [1992] P.I.Q.R. P101 (foster parent). See also Saville LJ in *Marc Rich & Co AG v Bishop Rock Marine* [1994] 1 W.L.R. 1071 at 1077 (no duty in stranger to save blind man from road accident, but duty in parent to prevent child running into the road).

[145] Although see *XA v YA* [2010] EWHC 1983 (QB).

[146] Hence the caution of the High Court of Australia about imposing liability in *Hahn v Conley* (1971) 126 C.L.R. 378 unless the parent has embarked on some activity.

Other relationships with the victim. The previous cases may be said to involve   **5–043**
relationships of dependence but duties of affirmative action are imposed across a
much wider range of relationships, in at least some of them probably because the
defendant gains some benefit from his relationship with the claimant. Thus, an
employer must not only take proper steps to secure safety in the workplace[147] but
must look after a worker who is injured or falls ill at work even if the employer is
not responsible for the emergency;[148] and the same is true of a carrier with regard
to his passenger.[149] Indeed, the Supreme Court of Canada has extended this so as
to hold that a private boat owner was obliged to take steps to rescue a guest who
fell overboard.[150] An occupier is under a duty to take reasonable care to ensure
that his premises are reasonably safe for the purposes for which his visitor
enters[151] and owes a duty (although a rather more restricted one) to trespassers
and both of these may clearly require positive steps, for example to do repairs or
put up warnings,[152] though the occupier is not required to prevent people from
encountering obvious risks like climbing trees or swimming in lakes.[153] However,
one cannot slip from the mere existence of a relationship to the assumption that
there is a protective duty: a social landlord who took action against an abusive
tenant was not liable when the tenant responded by killing the person who had
initiated the complaint.[154]

How far is a defendant providing an ordinary service, such as the sale of
alcohol, under a duty to protect a claimant of full age and understanding against
his own weakness? In *Barrett v Ministry of Defence*[155] the defendants operated a
military base at an isolated site in Northern Norway at which alcohol was
available cheaply and drinking was a principal recreation. The claimant's
husband died after consuming a large quantity of alcohol. The Court of Appeal
rejected the contention that the defendants were under a duty to monitor and
control the consumption of alcohol at the base, despite the fact that the
disciplinary code contained provisions designed to curb excessive consumption.
Beldam LJ, delivering the judgment of the Court of Appeal, pointed out that the

---

[147] See Ch.9. An employer may owe this duty to an employee of its subsidiary: *Chandler v Cape Plc*
[2012] EWCA Civ 525; [2012] 1 W.L.R. 3111. This duty does not require employers to arrange
accident insurance for workers abroad in a country with no developed system of motor insurance:
Reid v Rush and Tompkins Group Plc [1989] 3 All E.R. 228. Cf. *Van Oppen v Bedford School* [1990]
1 W.L.R. 235.

[148] *Kasapis v Laimos* [1959] 2 Lloyd's Rep. 378. He is under no duty to safeguard the employee's
property against theft: *Deyong v Shenburn* [1946] 1 K.B. 236.

[149] A duty to try to rescue a man overboard was conceded in *Davis v Stena Line Ltd* [2005] EWHC
420 (QB); [2005] 2 Lloyd's Rep. 13.

[150] *Horsley v Maclaren, The Ogopogo* [1971] 2 Lloyd's Rep. 410. But a taxi driver is not under a duty
to assess the sobriety of his passenger and to set him down only where a drunken person would be
safe: *Griffiths v Brown, The Times*, October 23, 1998.

[151] See, e.g. *Everett v Comojo Ltd* [2011] EWCA Civ 13; [2012] 1 W.L.R. 150 (nightclub).

[152] See generally Ch.10.

[153] See para.10–022.

[154] *Mitchell v Glasgow CC* [2009] UKHL 11; [2009] 1 A.C. 874. See also *X v Hounslow LBC* [2009]
EWCA Civ 286; [2009] P.T.S.R 1158.

[155] [1995] 1 W.L.R. 1217.

level of consumption which might put a person in danger varied considerably from person to person and that it was:[156]

> "[F]air, just and reasonable for the law to leave a responsible adult to assume responsibility for his own actions in consuming alcoholic drink. No one is better placed to judge the amount that he can safely consume or to exercise control in his own interest as well as in the interest of others. To dilute self-responsibility and to blame one adult for another's lack of self-control is neither just nor reasonable and in the development of the law of negligence is an increment too far."

The defendants were, however, liable for the death, subject to a two-thirds reduction on account of contributory negligence, because of the way in which they had dealt with the deceased after he was found in a collapsed state.[157] In *Jebson v Ministry of Defence*,[158] on the other hand, the defendants were held liable for an injury caused by their failure to supervise the claimant soldier during his return journey from an evening's drinking organised by the company commander. Perhaps that case is to be explained by the context that the soldiers were under military discipline.

The High Court of Australia has firmly rejected the view that a commercial seller of alcohol is under any tort duty to monitor the consumption of his customers or restrain them from leaving if he considers, for example, that they are unfit to drive. Such a duty would require surveillance and inquiries which would be seriously invasive of customers' autonomy and potentially destructive to peaceful social relations. Gummow, Heydon and Crennan JJ wrote:[159]

> "To encourage interference by publicans, nervous about liability, with the individual freedom of drinkers to choose how much to drink and at what pace is to take a very large step. It is a step for legislatures, not courts, and it is a step which legislatures have taken only after mature consideration. It would be paradoxical if members of the public who may deliberately wish to become intoxicated and to lose the inhibitions and self-awareness of sobriety, and for that reason are attracted to attend hotels and restaurants, were to have that desire thwarted because the tort of negligence encouraged an interfering paternalism on the part of those who run the hotels and restaurants."

There may be exceptional cases where the drinker is beyond any rational action or mentally ill but the case was not made exceptional because the drinker had asked the bar owner to store his motorcycle and then demanded it back.

5–044   **Relationship with the person who caused the harm.** A relationship between the defendant and the person who is the cause of the harm to the claimant may lead to

---

[156] [1995] 1 W.L.R. 1217 at 1224. Nor is a bookmaker under any general duty to safeguard punters against the risks of gambling: *Calvert v William Hill Credit Ltd* [2008] EWCA Civ 1427; [2009] Ch. 330.

[157] *Crocker v Sundance Northwest Resorts* (1988) 51 D.L.R. (4th) 321 and *Jordan House v Menow* (1973) 38 D.L.R. (3d) 105 were distinguished: in the first D had permitted C to take part in a ski race as well as supplying drink and in the second he had put the obviously intoxicated C out of the bar on a highway.

[158] [2000] 1 W.L.R. 2055.

[159] *CAL No 14 Pty Ltd v Scott* [2009] HCA 47; (2009) 239 C.L.R. 390 at [54]. See also *Cole v South Tweed Heads Rugby League Football Club Ltd* [2004] HCA 29; (2004) 217 C.L.R. 469.

liability to the claimant.[160] For this reason a school authority was liable for letting a small child out of school in circumstances where it was foreseeable that he would cause an accident in which a driver was killed trying to avoid him[161] and in a suitable case this may extend even to wilful wrongdoing. Thus in *Home Office v Dorset Yacht Co Ltd* authorities who failed in their duty of supervision were responsible for damage done by escaping inmates in the immediate vicinity and in the course of the escape.[162] Where the defendant has control of both the claimant and the wrongdoer (for example, in a case where there is an assault on a prisoner by fellow inmates[163]) the case for the imposition of a duty is particularly strong. In the *Dorset Yacht* case the wrongdoers were subject to a form of custody by the defendants. We have seen that the police incur no liability for failing to get wrongdoers into custody, but there may be intermediate cases where there is a duty of supervision. In *Couch v Attorney General*[164] the nominal defendant was sued as representing the New Zealand probation service on the basis that they had allowed X, during his parole from a sentence for aggravated robbery, to take up employment at premises where there were large quantities of alcohol and cash and at which he had injured the claimant and murdered three other people during the course of theft. The Supreme Court of New Zealand held that this disclosed an arguable claim of negligence, though three members of the court were of the view that the claimant would have to establish that she was a member of a class especially vulnerable in view of X's record and her position as a fellow employee.

We have seen that a person who supplies alcohol to another is entitled to assume that the other is the best judge of what he can safely consume,[165] but does the same apply if the other gets drunk and causes a road accident which injures a pedestrian? The reasoning which might deny liability to the driver does not necessarily apply to the pedestrian, who has done nothing to contribute to the accident. The matter has not been litigated here, though it has been said in the Supreme Court of Canada that "there is no doubt that commercial vendors[166] of alcohol owe a general duty of care to persons who can be expected to use the highways".[167] If this is to be the law then there may of course be serious evidentiary difficulties and in practical terms the duty cannot be a very high one, since the barman cannot be expected to keep a detailed tally of the consumption of all his customers. In an English case it has been said, obiter, that a person who

---

[160] In some cases of course the relationship (generally only that of employer and employee) between D and the wrongdoer may make D vicariously liable for the wrongdoer's act: see Ch.20, below. Here it is assumed that there is no vicarious liability, hence there must be a duty in D and breach of it by him: *Smith v Leurs* (1945) 70 C.L.R. 256.

[161] *Carmarthenshire CC v Lewis* [1955] A.C. 549.

[162] [1970] A.C. 1004.

[163] *Ellis v Home Office* [1953] 2 Q.B. 135.

[164] [2008] NZSC 45; [2008] 3 N.Z.L.R. 725. Since there is no general liability for negligence for personal injuries in New Zealand the claim was one for exemplary damages which are available there (but not here) for that tort in certain circumstances.

[165] See para.5–043.

[166] However, the Supreme Court of Canada has rejected any general duty on a private host to monitor guests' drinking at a party: *Childs v Desormeaux* [2006] SCC 18; [2006] 1 S.C.R. 643.

[167] *Stewart v Pettie* (1994) 121 D.L.R. (4th) 222 at 231. The claimant was a passenger in the car who had visited the establishment with the driver but the reasoning plainly applies to any road user. The duty was found not to have been broken.

entrusted a car to a drunk might bear liability for an accident but that a dealer who sold a car to a known alcoholic would not be liable for an accident caused by intoxication a few weeks later.[168]

5–045 **Occupiers and property owners can come under a duty to act.** An occupier is under a duty not only to his visitors but to take steps to remove a hazard on his land which threatens neighbouring property even though it has arisen from the act of nature or of a third party—property is a source of obligation as well as of rights. In principle this can extend to taking steps to prevent a third party gaining access to the property and using it to inflict damage on the claimant but wilful human conduct is not normally sufficiently likely to require the defendant to contemplate it as a reasonable probability rather than a remote possibility. So in *Smith v Littlewoods Organisation Ltd*[169] the defendants were not liable when vandals entered an empty cinema scheduled for redevelopment and caused a fire which spread to property next door.[170] Lord Griffiths said:[171]

> "So far as Littlewoods knew, there was nothing significantly different about these empty premises from tens of thousands of others up and down the country. People do not mount 24-hour guards on empty properties and the law would impose an intolerable burden if it required them to do so save in the most exceptional circumstances."

5–046 **Undertaking given by public body or service.** The traditional approach has been that a public body or service is in the same position with regard to omissions as a private person. The successful defendants in some of the leading cases were, after all, public authorities.[172] If a public authority gave an undertaking to assist and the claimant relied on that so as to change his position a duty might arise, but that argument would frequently not be open because no alternative steps were available: a person whose house is on fire is not likely to be able to assert that when the fire service said it was on its way he desisted from organising a chain of neighbours with buckets. However, the political, moral and economic arguments which are said to underpin the general rule of non-liability[173] hardly apply to a service the function of which is to guard the public against danger and that service will also be under some form of pre-existing public law duty (albeit not enforceable by a private law claim for damages) in respect of the performance of its functions. In *Kent v Griffiths*[174] the claimant suffered an asthma attack at

---

[168] Lord Goff in *Paterson Zochonis & Co Ltd v Merfarken Packaging Ltd* [1986] 3 All E.R. 522 at 540.

[169] [1987] A.C. 241.

[170] What if the claim arises from criminal injury inflicted on the premises by some third party? It would be going too far to say that an occupier can never be under a duty to protect visitors against attack: see, e.g. *Everett v Comojo Ltd*[2011] EWCA Civ 13; [2012] 1 W.L.R. 150 (nightclub). But it is unrealistic to expect the occupier to do much to prevent an assault in, say, its car park: *Modbury Triangle Shopping Centre v Anzil* [2000] HCA 61; (2000) 205 C.L.R. 254.

[171] [1987] A.C. 241 at 251. "Unless the needle that measures the probability of a particular result flowing from the conduct of a human agent is near the top of the scale it may be hard to conclude that it has risen sufficiently from the bottom to create the duty reasonably to foresee it": [1987] A.C. 241 at 261 per Lord Mackay.

[172] See, e.g. *Stovin v Wise* [1996] A.C. 923; *Capital & Counties Plc v Hampshire CC* [1997] Q.B. 1004; *Mitchell v Glasgow CC* [2009] UKHL 11; [2009] 1 A.C. 874.

[173] See para.5–039.

[174] [2001] Q.B. 36.

home. Her doctor called for an ambulance and was assured that it was on its way. In fact the ambulance did not arrive until well after the "target" time (something for which there was no explanation) and the claimant suffered a respiratory arrest, which would probably have been avoided by timely arrival of the ambulance. The doctor gave evidence that if she had been informed of the likely delay she would have had the claimant driven to hospital by other means, so a decision in favour of the claimant could easily have been reached on the basis of "undertaking and reliance", yet this figures hardly at all in the Court of Appeal's judgment. Rather the duty seems to have arisen simply from the acceptance of the call and it seems that the result would have been the same even if the claimant had been in a remote place with no alternative means of transport. The cases of the fire service[175] and the police were distinguished on the basis that their duty was owed to the public at large.[176] No doubt that explains why the police are not liable to some unidentifiable member of the public injured by a criminal whom they fail to catch but it is less easy to see why the fact that the fire service may have to take into account the risks to other property when fighting a fire necessarily means that they have no duty of care to fight it efficiently as far as the owner of the burning house is concerned. If there is to be a difference between the cases it seems better to recognise that it lies in the fact that the fire service is primarily concerned with saving property and that imposing liability would tend to inure for the benefit of subrogated fire insurers who have taken a premium to cover the risk,[177] though that would hardly justify a different result where life was at risk from the fire.

Control exercised by public service with respect to claimant. While such cases may not be easy to reconcile it does now seem to be the case that a public service may incur a duty of care in respect of an identifiable person whose protection from personal injury it can be said to have assumed. In *Reeves v Metropolitan Police Commissioner*[178] the police were held liable for negligence in failing to prevent the suicide of a sane person in custody in their cells. In fact the existence of a duty of care was never challenged and the matter was fought in the House of Lords on the issue of whether the deliberate act of the deceased broke the chain of causation[179] but the clear implication is that the defendants' concession on the issue of duty in the appeals was rightly made.[180] However, a duty to prevent others of full age and capacity from harming themselves will be rare, for "on the whole people are entitled to act as they please, even if this will inevitably lead to their own death or injury".[181] So the existence of the duty turned on the fact that the deceased was in the police cells and the police had reason to know that he was

5–047

---

[175] On the non-liability of the fire service see para.5–053.
[176] [2001] Q.B. 36 at 52.
[177] See Lord Hoffmann in *Stovin v Wise* [1996] A.C. 923 at 955.
[178] [2000] 1 A.C. 360.
[179] See para.7–057.
[180] See particularly Lord Hope at [2000] 1 A.C. 360 at 379.
[181] Lord Hope at [2000] 1 A.C. 360 at 379. "Under the domestic law of the United Kingdom there is no general legal duty on the state to prevent everyone within its jurisdiction from committing suicide": *Savage v S Essex Partnership NHS Foundation Trust* [2008] UKHL 74; [2009] 1 A.C. 681 at [25]. See also para.10–022.

a suicide risk:[182] the police are not required to take special precautions for every person in custody.[183] Nor will they owe a duty of care to prevent a person who has just been arrested escaping and injuring himself in the process.[184]

iii.   Dangerous Situation Created by Defendant

5–048   A defendant who without wrongdoing creates a source of danger comes under a duty of care to take reasonable steps to safeguard others against it. For example, if D's car breaks down on the highway D must take steps to prevent it causing danger to other traffic.[185] As Lord Scott explained:[186]

> "Sometimes the additional feature [necessary to found a duty of positive action] may be found in the manner in which the victim came to be at risk of harm or injury. If a defendant has played some causative part in the train of events that have led to the risk of injury, a duty to take reasonable steps to avert or lessen the risk may arise."

B.   Assumption of Responsibility

5–049   **Assumption of responsibility as a test for the existence of a duty of care.** In *Hedley, Byrne & Co Ltd v Heller & Partners Ltd*[187] the House of Lords held that a duty of care might be owed to take reasonable care not to cause pure economic loss by negligent misstatement. The House spoke in terms of the maker of the statement having assumed or undertaken a responsibility towards the recipient and the recipient having relied upon it. The relevance of the decision in the context of statements is considered in detail later.[188] However, while it cannot serve as a general "test" for all duty of care questions, it is clear that the broad principle of the case goes beyond liability for statements and extends to the situation where the defendant undertakes to perform a task or service for the claimant. That brings us very close to the realm of contract and that was essentially the point of *Henderson v Merrett Syndicates Ltd*.[189] The claims were brought by "Names" at Lloyd's who had incurred heavy personal liabilities arising out of alleged negligent underwriting by the managing agents of syndicates of which they were members. In some cases a "members' agent" was interposed between the Names and the managing agents so that prima facie there was no privity of contract and the claim was tort or nothing;[190] in other cases there was a direct contractual link but the Names were asserting a tort claim in

---

[182] Such a person is in that category of vulnerable groups, which also includes mental patients and conscripts, which attracts a duty of protection under art.2 of the European Convention on Human Rights: *Savage v S Essex Partnership NHS Foundation Trust* [2008] UKHL 74; [2009] 1 A.C. 681; *Rabone v Pennine Care NHS Trust* [2012] UKSC 2; [2012] 2 A.C. 72.

[183] *Orange v CC W Yorkshire* [2001] EWCA Civ 611; [2002] Q.B. 347.

[184] *Vellino v CC Greater Manchester* [2001] EWCA Civ 1249; [2002] 1 W.L.R. 218.

[185] *Wright v Lodge* [1993] 4 All E.R. 299.

[186] *Mitchell v Glasgow CC* [2009] UKHL 11; [2009] 1 A.C. 874 at [40].

[187] [1964] A.C. 465.

[188] See Ch.12.

[189] [1995] 2 A.C. 145.

[190] In fact it was held that the terms of the members' agents' contracts made them responsible to the Names for the default of underwriting agents.

order to gain the advantage of the Latent Damage Act 1986 on limitation of actions.[191] In holding that a duty of care arose in tort in both situations, Lord Goff said:[192]

> "There is in my opinion plainly an assumption of responsibility in the relevant sense by the managing agents towards the names in their syndicates. The managing agents have accepted the names as members of a syndicate under their management. They obviously hold themselves out as possessing a special expertise to advise the names on the suitability of risks to be underwritten, and of the circumstances in which, and the extent to which, reinsurance should be taken out and claims should be settled. The names, as the managing agents well knew, placed implicit reliance on that expertise, in that they gave authority to the managing agents to bind them to contracts of insurance and reinsurance and to the settlement of claims. I can see no escape from the conclusion that, in these circumstances, prima facie a duty of care is owed in tort by the managing agents to such names . . . Furthermore, since the duty rests on the principle in *Hedley, Byrne*, no problem arises from the fact that the loss suffered by the names is pure economic loss."

The loss suffered in *Henderson* is, of course, purely economic and in certain cases that is a bar to recovery,[193] but that is clearly not so under *Hedley Byrne*. Statements rarely give rise to any type of loss other than economic loss and if, in *Hedley Byrne*, the House of Lords had held that there was a duty of care in respect of statements, but that it did not extend to pure economic loss, that would have strangled the new duty at birth. So the argument that no duty of care should arise because the loss is purely economic is no more valid in an "undertaking" case than in a "statement" case.

Relationship to liability in contract. This approach does not go so far as to impose a liability exactly equivalent to that in contract because of the requirement of reliance (which is unnecessary where there is a contract supported by consideration) but nevertheless it goes a very long way down the road of creating a parallel liability in respect of services and one which is more than merely academic because it may lead to different results. For example, one of the underlying problems of *Henderson* was the fact that the claims of some claimants had become statute-barred before they knew about them and the imposition of a duty in tort enabled them to outflank the problem via the Latent Damage Act 1986. Now it may well be the case that the non-applicability of the Act to contractual negligence is not a very sensible rule anyway, but it might be argued that in the case of recent legislation the correct approach is direct amendment of the legislation rather than unsettling the boundary between contract and tort claims.[194] On the other hand, some writers take the view that in this type of case we have really moved into a different sort of obligation altogether, neither contract nor tort.[195] 5–050

Instances where assumption of responsibility test has led to the imposition of a duty of care. Since *Henderson,* assumption of responsibility has been the basis of recovery in a very wide range of situations and as we have seen it is to some 5–051

---

[191] See para.26–093.
[192] [1995] 2 A.C. 145 at 182.
[193] See para.5–059.
[194] See more generally Whittaker (1997) 17 L.S. 169.
[195] See McBride (1994) 14 L.S. 35; McBride and Hughes (1995) 15 L.S. 376.

extent a rival to the *Caparo* test as the general approach to the duty of care question. It has been used to justify (sometimes in tandem with the *Caparo* approach) the imposition of a duty of care on an educational psychologist called in by a local authority to advise on a child,[196] on the British Boxing Board of Control in respect of the adequacy of medical arrangements at fights taking place under its aegis,[197] on a referee of an amateur rugby match[198] and on a solicitor acting for a borrower to take care to ensure, for the benefit of an unrepresented lender, that the security was effective.[199]

5–052   **Whether the defendant has assumed responsibility is determined objectively.** In few, if any, of the cases in which a duty has been imposed on the ground that the defendant assumed responsibility has the defendant expressly assumed responsibility in the sense that he has recognised that he will incur a legal liability if he fails in it. This reveals that the assumption of responsibility in question is one which is based on the law's objective assessment of the situation.[200]

5–053   **Situations where the defendant is legally compelled to do something.** In order for a duty of care to be imposed on the basis of an assumption of responsibility, one must be able to say that the defendant has undertaken to "see to it" and that this is based on something more than a recognition that he is under a legal compulsion to perform the task. As we have seen, in *Customs and Excise Commissioners v Barclays Bank Plc*[201] it was held that a bank does not assume responsibility to the holder of an injunction freezing a customer's account by writing to acknowledge that he has received it: he has no choice but to obey the court's order. Of course a person may go beyond his legal duty, as in *Neil Martin Ltd v Revenue and Customs Commissioners*[202] where, although there was no actionable statutory duty on the part of the Revenue to process an application promptly and therefore no common law duty to do so could have arisen in its place, the defendants could be vicariously liable for an employee's decision to make (without authority) a declaration on the claimants' behalf. Even if there is no element of legal compulsion, care must be taken to focus on what the defendant has undertaken (or is to be deemed to have undertaken) responsibility for, otherwise we are on a slippery slope towards outflanking the basic principle that one is not required to take positive action to assist others: an employer no doubt assumes responsibility for his workers' safety but he is not to be taken as

---

[196] *Phelps v Hillingdon LBC* [2001] 2 A.C. 619.

[197] *Watson v British Boxing Board of Control Ltd* [2001] Q.B. 1134. See also *Wattleworth v Goodwood Racing Co Ltd* [2004] EWHC 140; [2004] P.I.Q.R. P25 (motor sport association advising on safety at tracks).

[198] *Vowles v Evans* [2003] EWCA Civ 318; [2003] 1 W.L.R. 1607. "Rarely if ever does the law absolve from any obligation of care a person whose acts or omissions are manifestly capable of causing physical harm to others in a structured relationship into which they have entered": at [25].

[199] *Dean v Allin & Watts* [2001] EWCA Civ 758; [2001] 2 Lloyd's Rep. 249. See also *Killick v Pricewaterhouse Coopers* [2001] Lloyd's Rep. P.N. 17 (valuation of shares).

[200] *Smith v Eric S. Bush* [1990] 1 A.C. 831 at 862; *Henderson v Merrett Syndicates Ltd* [1995] 2 A.C. 145 at 181; *Phelps v Hillingdon LBC* [2001] 2 A.C. 619 at 654.

[201] [2006] UKHL 28; [2007] 1 A.C. 181, see para.5–020.

[202] [2007] EWCA Civ 1041; [2007] S.T.C. 1802.

volunteering to act as a pensions adviser;[203] and an insurer that paid benefits under a health insurance scheme arranged with an employer did not assume responsibility to a worker in respect of the assessment of his condition—the worker's entitlement under the scheme was by contract with his employer and if he contended that the payments had been wrongfully withheld, the proper course was an action against the employer.[204] Nor do fire officers "assume responsibility" to the owners of property when they arrive at the scene of a fire.[205]

A defendant can assume responsibility without the claimant relying on the defendant. Assumption and reliance are flexible concepts but while the first may be found by implication in almost any circumstances in which a person takes on a task, reliance by the claimant is sometimes plainly absent. Such was the case in *White v Jones*.[206] A testator, having made a will disinheriting his daughters after a family quarrel, became reconciled with them and instructed the defendant solicitors to prepare a new will. There was a delay by the defendants which amounted to negligence and the testator died before the will could be made, with the result that the "old" will governed the devolution of his estate. The delay was a breach of contract to the testator but since the estate was in no way diminished in size that would have given rise only to nominal damages. Hence as far as the law of contract was concerned: "[T]he only persons who might have a valid claim (the testator and his estate) have suffered no loss, and the only person who has suffered a loss (i.e the disappointed beneficiary) has no claim."[207] A majority of the House of Lords upheld a decision in favour of the beneficiaries based on the tort of negligence.[208] On such facts, where the beneficiaries are aware of the testator's intention it might be possible to contend that they had relied on the solicitors by forbearing to put pressure on them or on the testator to finalise the matter, but the case was argued and decided on the basis that no such reliance was necessary, despite the additional objections that the solicitor's primary duty arises by contract with his client, that his negligence lay in simply failing to carry out the client's instructions, that the beneficiaries had not been deprived of anything which they possessed or to which they had any right, since the testator could have cut them out again for no reason at all[209] and that the practical result was to increase the size of the testator's bounty at the expense of the solicitors, since the legatee under the unrevoked will could plainly keep what the testator did not

5–054

---

[203] *Outram v Academy Plastics* [2000] I.R.L.R. 499. Cf. *Lennon v MPC* [2004] EWCA Civ 130; [2004] 1 W.L.R. 2694, where there was an assumption of responsibility in response to an inquiry.

[204] *Briscoe v Lubrizol* [2000] I.C.R. 694. The contract between the employer and the insurer would probably have barred a claim by the worker under the Contracts (Rights of Third Parties) Act 1999 had it been in force. In such a case the insurer is concerned to avoid litigation by individuals who may be impecunious.

[205] *Capital & Counties Plc v Hampshire CC* [1997] Q.B. 1004 at 1036. However, perhaps the ambulance service does when it books an emergency call: see para.5–046.

[206] [1995] 2 A.C. 207.

[207] *White v Jones* [1995] 2 A.C. 207 at 259 per Lord Goff.

[208] In *Hill v Van Erp* (1997) 188 C.L.R. 159 the majority of the High Court of Australia also came to the conclusion that a solicitor owed a duty to a disappointed beneficiary.

[209] The case was not one which would have attracted the Inheritance (Provision for Family and Dependants) Act 1975.

intend to give him.[210] It is rather hard to explain why persons who foreseeably rely on an auditor's report cannot sue,[211] whereas those who find that they were the object of the intended bounty of a long-lost relative can.

For Lord Goff, in the majority, the dominant factor seems to have been a strong "impulse for practical justice"[212] bolstered by a need for the law to recognise the role of solicitors in relation to testators and legatees[213] and the fact that other the major common law jurisdictions seemed all to have come down in favour of liability. His Lordship wrote:[214]

> "In my opinion, therefore, your Lordships' House should in cases such as these extend to the intended beneficiary a remedy under the *Hedley Byrne* principle by holding that the assumption of responsibility by the solicitor towards his client should be held in law to extend to the intended beneficiary who (as the solicitor can reasonably foresee) may, as a result of the solicitor's negligence, be deprived of his intended legacy in circumstances in which neither the testator nor his estate will have a remedy against the solicitor."

It must also be pointed out that such a situation does not normally involve any possibility of wide-ranging or indeterminate liability. In such a case the defendant's contemplation of the claimant is: "actual, nominate and direct. It is contemplation by contract, though of course the contract is with the testator."[215]

The reasoning of Lord Browne-Wilkinson, who delivered the other main majority judgment, is rather different.[216] "Assumption of responsibility", far from being invented in *Hedley Byrne*, was regarded as traceable to the decision in *Nocton v Lord Ashburton*[217] where, despite the general rule then prevailing that there was no duty of care in respect of information or advice, the House of Lords had accepted liability arising out of a fiduciary relationship. *Hedley Byrne* was simply the recognition of another category of special relationship which would give rise to a duty of care on the basis of assumption of responsibility. It was true that a necessary element in the liability arising from statements to the claimant was reliance by the claimant[218] for that was the only way in which the claimant could show damage, but reliance was not necessary in the case of a special

---

[210] "What is plain is that the family as a whole are better off because of the appellants' negligence": Lord Nolan [1995] 2 A.C. 207 at 293. Hence the view of some that the answer lies in a modification of the law of succession: see (1995) 111 L.Q.R. 357. Cf. (1996) 112 L.Q.R. 54.

[211] See para.5–032.

[212] [1995] 2 A.C. 207 at 259.

[213] There is a good deal of emphasis in the majority judgments on the role of the "family solicitor" and references to "individual citizens" and "persons of modest means" but it seems impossible to contend that the decision is inapplicable to, e.g. a beneficiary which is a major charity.

[214] [1995] 2 A.C. 207 at 268. Whether "all the conceptual problems . . . can be seen to fade innocuously away" (at 269) must, however, be debatable.

[215] *Ross v Caunters* [1980] Ch. 297 at 308. However, it is not wholly true to say that the quantum of the liability is certain. Suppose A intends to make a will leaving all his estate to B and A wins the National Lottery or discovers a Rembrandt in the attic. It is also possible in theory that there could be claims by persons who were unidentifiable at the time of the transaction (e.g. unborn members of a class). Lord Goff in *White v Jones* was content to leave such cases to be decided when they arose: [1995] 2 A.C. 207 at 269.

[216] However, like Lord Goff his Lordship emphasises public reliance and dependence on solicitors in relation to wills.

[217] [1914] A.C. 932.

[218] Cf. statements by the defendant about the claimant to other persons who act on them to the claimant's detriment: *Spring v Guardian Assurance White* [1995] 2 A.C. 207 at 256, see para.12–051.

relationship of the fiduciary variety: in the paradigm fiduciary relationship, that of trustee and beneficiary, a: "[T]rustee is under a duty of care to his beneficiary whether or not he has had any dealing with him: indeed he may be as yet unborn or unascertained and therefore any direct dealing would be impossible."[219] *White v Jones* fell neither within the category of fiduciary relationships nor was it a case of damage caused by a statement, but there was no reason why the law should not create new categories of "special relationships" and no reason why it should always require reliance. "What is important is not that A knows that B is consciously relying on A, but A knows that B's economic well being is dependent upon A's careful conduct of B's affairs."[220]

The claimants in White v Jones could not have recovered under the law of contract. While the liability recognised in *White v Jones* is one in tort, the assumption of responsibility has its origin in the contract with the testator[221] and in failing to carry out the instructions the solicitor breaks that contract. Arguably, a better way to deal with this type of situation is via the law of contract. However, such a radical step was beyond the powers of the House of Lords, and it has not been brought about by the Contracts (Rights of Third Parties) Act 1999. That Act allows a third party to enforce a term in a contract between others if the term purports to confer a benefit on him and there is no intention against such enforcement by the contracting parties. However, the contract between the solicitor and the testator is not one which confers a benefit on the beneficiary: the contract is a means whereby the testator may confer such a benefit by the will.[222] In some cases a party to the contract may be able to recover damages on behalf of the third party even though he (the promisee) has not suffered any loss, as where A commissions work on a building by B and then, before the breach by B, transfers the building to C,[223] but that is no help in a situation like *White v Jones* for in the building case the loss is "transferred" to C, that is to say it is one which A would have suffered if he had retained the building, whereas the loss suffered by the beneficiary (loss of the gift) is one which never could have been suffered by the testator.

5–055

The scope of the rule in White v Jones. Some developments since *White v Jones* in the factual context of that case are outlined in a later section.[224] It was, however, at first difficult to know how far *White v Jones* was to be taken—a rather narrow rule about solicitors and wills, or a "super-principle" transcending the boundaries of contract and tort? Even if it does not go as far as the second, it is now clear that, as Lord Mustill predicted in his dissent, it does not exist

5–056

---

[219] [1995] 2 A.C. 207 at 271. It is debatable whether the analogy is a good one: the trustee is dealing with the beneficiary's property.

[220] [1995] 2 A.C. 207 at 272. Cf. *Longstaff v Birtles* [2001] EWCA Civ 1219; [2002] 1 W.L.R. 470 (clear route to recovery on basis of fiduciary relationship; wrong to try to construct alternative case of assumption of responsibility).

[221] Lord Mustill's point that the contract was not merely part of the history as it was in *Donoghue v Stevenson* (see [1995] 2 A.C. 207 at 280) seems unanswerable.

[222] At any rate, that was the Law Commission's intention: Law Com. No.242 (1997) at [7.20]. It was held in *Gartside v Sheffield, Young & Ellis* [1983] 1 N.Z.L.R. 37 that the rather similar wording of the Contracts (Privity) Act 1982 s.4, did not give the beneficiary a claim.

[223] *Linden Gardens Trust Ltd v Lenesta Sludge Disposals Ltd* [1994] 1 A.C. 85.

[224] See para.5–076.

"simply to create a specialist pocket of tort law, with a special type of proximity, distinct from the main body of doctrine".[225] He said:[226]

> "[T]he present case does not as it seems to me concern a unique and limited situation, where a remedy might be granted on an ad hoc basis without causing serious harm to the general structure of the law for I cannot see anything sufficiently special about the calling of a solicitor to distinguish him from others in a much broader category."

C. Pure Economic Loss[227]

5–057 **The concept of pure economic loss.** As we have seen, much of the controversy about the role of the duty of care in negligence has arisen in cases which have involved the problem of "pure economic loss" but so far we have not examined that concept closely. The expression "pure economic loss" is liable to mislead: if a car is negligently destroyed, that is "economic" in the sense that the owner's assets are thereby diminished, but in legal terms it is classified as damage to property and the owner is entitled to its value as damages. Even if a loss is unquestionably only financial in nature, no difficulty is felt about allowing its recovery if it is a *consequence* of physical injury or damage to the claimant's property: for example, if C suffers physical injuries due to D's negligence and incurs medical expenses as a result, C will be able to recover those expenses. We are concerned here with cases in which the economic loss is not consequential upon physical injuries or property damage.

5–058 **It is sometimes unclear whether loss is purely economic or physical.** It is important to ascertain at the outset the type of loss that the claimant has sustained. This is mainly because, if it is purely economic, the claimant is likely find obstacles in his path to the recovery of damages that would not otherwise be present. While in most cases it is obvious how the claimant's damage should be categorised, there may be difficult borderline cases. It has been said that fabric would be physically damaged if it were subjected to large deposits of dust which require professional cleaning;[228] so is a gas appliance which is rendered unusable by the ingress of water;[229] and a ship is "physically damaged" if it is doused in hydrochloric acid and requires decontamination even if there is no appreciable permanent effect on the plating.[230] Contamination of land by radioactive material

---

[225] [1995] 2 A.C. 207 at 291.

[226] McHugh J dissenting in *Hill v Van Erp* (1997) 188 C.L.R. 159 asked whether an accountant commissioned to assess a business which the client was considering buying as a gift for a relative owed a duty to the relative or whether an insurance broker commissioned to effect a life insurance policy owed a duty to persons who were beneficiaries of the estate of the proposed insured. See *Hughes v Richards* [2004] EWCA Civ 266; [2004] P.N.L.R. 35.

[227] There is a vast literature on this topic. See, e.g. Cane, *Tort Law and Economic Interests*, 2nd edn (1991); Feldthusen, *Economic Negligence*, 6th edn (2012); Atiyah (1967) 83 L.Q.R. 248; Dwyer, "Negligence and Economic Loss" in Cane and Stapleton (eds), *Essays for Patrick Atiyah* (1991); McGrath (1985) 3 O.J.L.S. 350; Stapleton (1991) 107 L.Q.R. 249.

[228] *Hunter v Canary Wharf Ltd* [1996] 2 W.L.R. 348 (reversed, but not on this point, [1997] A.C. 655).

[229] *Anglian Water Services Ltd v Crawshaw Robbins Ltd* [2001] B.L.R. 173.

[230] *The Orjula* [1995] 2 Lloyd's Rep. 395. See also *Attorney General for Ontario v Fatehi* (1984) 15 D.L.R. (4th) 1323 (spilling petrol on highway requiring it to be cleaned).

requiring removal of the topsoil has been held to be physical damage.[231] It has even been held to be arguable that livestock are physically damaged when, as a result of a movement restriction imposed in a foot and mouth outbreak caused by the defendants, they cannot be sold at their intended price because they have become oversized.[232] It seems, although it is admittedly far from clear, that the courts will usually regard loss as constituting physical damage if there is tangible property that has been physically changed and that change makes it less valuable. That said, physical changes to tangible property may still count as physical damage even if the property's value is not diminished. As the Court of Appeal said:[233]

> "If a skilful painter overpaints X's daubs unasked, he inflicts property damage . . . even if the world will pay more for the canvas now than it would have done before he came on the scene. If a lump of concrete is dropped on X's car, property damage has been inflicted even if someone can persuade an avant garde gallery curator that the resultant object is a work of art worth more than X paid for the car. What if anything X can recover is a separate question which does not fall to be answered at this stage of the enquiry."

Situations in which pure economic loss is recoverable are narrowly confined. 5–059
The law of torts permits damages to be recovered for pure economic loss in tightly confined circumstances. This is for various reasons. It is possible to detect in the cases a feeling among judges that pure economic loss is less serious, all other things being equal, than physical loss. Furthermore, a single act of negligence can easily cause pure economic loss of great magnitude to many people, whereas negligent conduct that causes physical loss does not have the same potential. For example, if D causes pure economic loss to C, people from whom C bought goods might find that C buys fewer goods from them because less money is available to him, and those people might in turn have less money available to them and so on. The restrictive approach to the recovery of damages for pure economic loss is most marked in the law of negligence; there is less difficulty about its recovery in the case of intentional torts such as deceit or intentional interference with contract. This is probably a product of the fact that these torts are regarded as more blameworthy, all other things being equal, than the tort of negligence. Another significant point to note is that tort law's restrictive attitude towards the recovery of damages for pure economic loss does not feature also in the case of the law of contract. Thus, a claimant who can sue in contract will not face any special difficulty on account of the fact that the loss about which he complains is purely economic. Most claims for breach of contract involve only pure economic loss.

Pure economic loss cases frequently involve facts which in their own right 5–060
prompt the courts to be cautious before imposing a duty of care. The cases on pure economic loss concern a number of distinct situations and the same considerations of policy are not necessarily applicable to each: there is certainly

---

[231] *Blue Circle Industries Plc v MoD* [1999] Ch. 289. Cf. *Merlin v BNFL* [1990] 2 Q.B. 557.
[232] *D Pride & Partners v Institute for Animal Health* [2009] EWIIC 685 (QB) (but the claim was struck out because the movement order rather than the outbreak was the direct cause of the loss).
[233] *Jan de Nul (UK) Ltd v Axa Royal Belge SA* [2002] EWCA Civ 209; [2002] 1 Lloyd's Rep. 583 at [92].

no blanket rule forbidding the recovery of damages for negligently inflicted pure economic loss, as we have seen in connection with liability based on assumption of responsibility.[234] There are considerable difficulties in expounding the law in this area because the issue of pure economic loss frequently coincides with other factors that inhibit the imposition of a duty of care. For example, if a local authority acting under statutory powers fails to carry out an adequate inspection of a house in the course of its construction and is subsequently sued by the owner in respect of defects at least three potential "problems" arise for the owner in relation to the duty of care issue: (1) the loss suffered by the owner is purely economic in nature despite the fact that it manifests itself in physical defects in the building; (2) the authority's conduct is essentially an omission—failure to prevent the builder erecting a shoddy structure; and (3) since the local authority cannot devote infinite resources to such matters, the question arises of how far the courts will interfere with the authority's decision on allocation. Some degree of overlap is therefore inevitable in any exposition of the law. In this section we consider two situations: (1) where damage to the person or property of a third person causes pure economic loss to the claimant; and (2) where the claimant suffers pure economic loss because of defects in the quality of goods or property supplied to him.[235] The situation where pure economic loss is caused by the defendant's failure to fulfil an undertaking to perform a service has already been considered[236] and the liability for pure economic loss arising from statements is dealt with in Ch.12.

i. Pure Economic Loss Resulting from Damage to Property Belonging to a Third Party or from Injury to a Third Party

5–061   Pure economic loss suffered because of damage to a third party's person or property is generally irrecoverable for want of a duty of care. If D negligently damages X's property, X can sue D for that damage and foreseeable consequential economic loss resulting from it (for example, an unavoidable loss of revenue while the property is being repaired) but if C suffers loss because he is prevented from using that property as a result of the damage, C generally cannot sue D. Similarly, if D negligently kills X, who employs C and C thereby loses his job, or D injures X and C incurs care responsibilities to X, C cannot, at common law, recover damages from D,[237] though in the related context of loss of support from a family member there is a very major statutory modification of this.[238] The point about property damage is neatly illustrated by *Spartan Steel & Alloys Ltd v Martin & Co (Contractors) Ltd.*[239] A power cut caused by the defendants' negligence caused material to solidify in the claimants' furnace. The claimants

---

[234] See para.5–049.
[235] This is taken up in more detail in Chs 10 and 11.
[236] See para.5–049.
[237] *Islington LBC v University College London Hospital NHS Trust* [2005] EWCA Civ 596; [2006] P.I.Q.R. P3.
[238] The Fatal Accidents Act 1976, allowing the dependants of the deceased to sue the tortfeasor who caused the death: see Ch.24. There was once a common law action *per quod* in favour of a husband for injury to his wife and an employer for injury to his servant but this has been abolished.
[239] [1973] 2 Q.B. 27.

recovered the reduction in value of the solidified "melt" (which had undergone a chemical change from partial processing (property damage)) and the profit they would have made from its sale as an ingot (consequential economic loss), but they recovered nothing for the loss of profit on four further melts which would normally have been processed during the time the electricity was interrupted (pure economic loss), for this was not a consequence of any damage to their property but simply of the interruption of the electricity supply. In duty language, the defendants owed the claimants a duty in respect of damage to their property and consequential economic loss[240] but did not owe them any duty with respect to mere loss of profits unconnected therewith. Of course, property damage was the source of the whole of the claimants' loss but with regard to the lost profits on the four melts it was a consequence of damage to the property of the electricity undertaking, which had suffered no loss other than the cost of repairing the damaged cable and, perhaps, loss of revenue while the supply was interrupted. In other words, the claimant may only sue for damage to property or economic loss consequent on that if it is his property which is damaged[241]—though ownership is not necessary, possession (or even an immediate right to possession[242]) will do.[243] For this purpose an equitable owner of the property may recover, certainly if the legal owner is joined in the action and perhaps even without that formality.[244] It is not, however, enough that the claimant has merely contractual rights with respect to the property which are rendered less valuable as a result of the damage or that he has contractual obligations in respect of it which becomes more onerous.[245] If, therefore, the electricity supply in *Spartan Steel* had been speedily restored but the cooling had caused damage to the furnace, loss of production during the time taken to effect repairs to it would, it seems, have been recoverable. Equally the claimants would have succeeded if the cable, at the point at which it was severed, had been vested in them.

This approach was reaffirmed by the Privy Council in *Candlewood Navigation Corp Ltd v Mitsui OSK Lines Ltd*[246] where time charterers of a damaged vessel (who did not have possession of it) failed to recover the hire which they had to pay even when the vessel was out of action and the revenue which they lost through being unable to make use of the vessel. It will be observed that there was nothing unforeseeable about the loss to the charterers (such loss being a highly

---

[240] Consider *Network Rail Infrastructure Ltd v Conarken Group* [2011] EWCA Civ 644; [2012] 1 All E.R. (Comm.) 692.

[241] This is the reason why if an insurer insures A's property and B negligently destroys it the insurer cannot sue the wrongdoer in its own name, though it may be subrogated to A's rights

[242] *Colour Quest Ltd v Total Downstream UK Plc* [2009] EWHC 540 (Comm); [2009] 2 Lloyd's Rep. 1 and cases cited therein (upheld on this point, *Shell UK Ltd v Total UK Ltd* [2010] EWCA Civ 180; [2011] Q.B. 86).

[243] The common law always equated possession and ownership for this purpose: hence a bailee could sue for the full value of the goods bailed to him (even though his interest was limited) whether or not he would be responsible to the owner for the loss. The amount which a bailee can recover may now be restricted by statute: see para.18–035.

[244] *Shell UK Ltd v Total UK Ltd* [2010] EWCA Civ 180; [2011] Q.B. 86.

[245] *Cattle v Stockton Waterworks* (1875) L.R. 10 Q.B. 453. Thus, it would seem that fishermen who lost their livelihood as a result of oil pollution could not sue at common law: *Landcatch Ltd v International Oil Pollution Compensation Fund* [1999] 2 Lloyd's Rep. 316; *RJ Tilbury & Sons (Devon) Ltd v Alegrete Shipping Co Inc.* [2003] EWCA Civ 65; [2003] 1 Lloyd's Rep. 327.

[246] [1986] A.C. 1.

likely consequence of damage to a cargo ship) and that D escaped part of the liability which they would otherwise have incurred had the charterer been in possession of the vessel, for then the lost revenue would have been a consequence of damage to "their" property. The person from whom the charterer had hired the use of the vessel could not sue for this loss since he had not suffered it, nor did he suffer loss of hire, since the charterer had to go on paying it. Of course if the charterer had been relieved under the charter of their obligation to pay hire while the vessel was laid up, that would have been recoverable by the person from whom it had been hired. The extent of the tortfeasor's liability in such a case therefore turns on the contractual arrangements between the owner[247] of the damaged property and the person making use of it.

5–062　　**An exception to the general principle.** A principle of law of uncertain ambit qualifies the general rule above. If, as a result of the negligence of D, damage is caused to X's vessel, the owners of cargo in the vessel have to contribute rateably to expenditure necessary to meet the emergency (a "general average contribution") and a cargo owner may sue D for this even though there is no physical damage to his portion of the cargo. In the leading case Lord Roche said:[248]

> " . . . [I]f two lorries A and B are meeting one another on the road, I cannot bring myself to doubt that the driver of lorry A owes a duty to both the owner of lorry B and to the owner of goods then carried on lorry B. Those owners are engaged in a common adventure with or by means of lorry B and if lorry A is negligently driven and damages lorry B so severely, while no damage is done to the goods in it, the goods have to be unloaded for the repair of the lorry and then reloaded or carried forward in some other way and the consequent expense is (by reason of his contract or otherwise) the expense of the owner of the goods, then, in my judgment, the owner of the goods has a direct cause of action to recover such expense. No authority to the contrary was cited, and I know of none relating to land transport."

It seems that Lord Roche's "common adventure" principle is confined to the maritime context or at least to precisely analogous situations involving carriage by land and it was therefore held inapplicable to the relationship between a power generator and an electricity supplier.[249]

5–063　　**Merits and demerits of the current law.** The distinction that the law draws between pure economic loss and physical damage has been described as "Jesuitical"[250] and it has been rejected in other common law jurisdictions. The rule certainly rests in part upon the spectre of a liability, in Cardozo J's famous words, "in an indeterminate amount for an indeterminate time to an indeterminate class".[251] This risk is certainly present in the case of interruption of public utility supplies, though it has been contended that it is exaggerated because individual

---

[247] Confusingly, the claimant in *Candlewood* was the owner of the vessel. It had chartered it by demise to X (which gives possession to X) and then time chartered it back again. The claimant's losses were not suffered in its capacity as owner. In non-marine terms, a charter by demise is like hiring a self-drive van; a time (or voyage) charter is like engaging a removal firm.

[248] *Morrison SS Co Ltd v Greystoke Castle* [1947] A.C. 265 at 280.

[249] *Londonwaste Ltd v Amec Civil Engineering Ltd* (1997) 53 Con.L.R. 66; *Colour Quest Ltd v Total Downstream UK Plc* [2009] EWHC 540 (Comm); [2009] 2 Lloyd's Rep 1.

[250] *Coleridge v Miller Construction* 1997 S.L.T. 485 at 491.

[251] *Ultramares Corp v Touche* 174 N.E. 441 at 444 (1931). This decision was, actually, a negligent misstatement case, where there is no such hard and fast rule against recovery of damages for pure economic loss.

losses may be small and unlikely to lead to much litigation.[252] However, the physical consequences of an accident may be very wide ranging[253] and in that context the courts do not (at least overtly) deny a remedy because it will be available to many and may bankrupt defendants. Furthermore, the rule is applicable even in a case where there is no real risk of wide-ranging liability. The virtue the present rule does have is that it provides a mechanical and fairly easily applied test for the resolution of disputes (and hence for the avoidance of prolonged litigation[254]) and in many cases where it would produce an unjust result it may be open to a potential claimant, if he chooses to do so, to restructure his arrangements to avoid its impact.

ii.   Defects of Quality in Goods or Property Supplied

There is in general no duty of care to prevent pure economic loss caused by defects of quality in goods or property supplied. In *Muirhead v Industrial Tank Specialities Ltd*,[255] the claimant, an enterprising fishmonger, conceived a scheme to supply the market in lobsters at times of high demand by keeping them in tanks. He purchased the tanks from ITS but the pumps in the tanks failed to function properly, a large number of lobsters died and the claimant suffered loss in being unable to proceed with his project. There was a good claim for breach of contract against ITS but they were insolvent. Accordingly, the claimant sued the French manufacturers of the pumps (with whom he had no contract) alleging that they were negligent in supplying equipment which was not properly adapted for use under English voltages. Damages were recovered for the dead lobsters and for certain consequential losses but the claimant failed in his claim for the cost of the pumps and the profits that would have been made in the business had the pumps functioned properly. It is certainly the law that the manufacturer of goods owes a duty of care to ultimate consumers who are not in a contractual relationship with him[256] but this duty is not to cause damage to persons or to property and the major part of the claimant's claim in this case was that he had suffered a loss of business because the pumps were unsuitable for their purpose, a

5–064

---

[252] *New Zealand Forest Products v Attorney General* [1986] 1 N.Z.L.R. 14. In *Spartan Steel* itself it seems that there was no widespread interruption of supplies. However, for a case where more than a million households and businesses were affected (and where the pure economic loss claims failed) see *Johnson Tiles Pty Ltd v Esso Australia Pty Ltd* [2003] VSC 27.

[253] See James (1972–1973) 12 J.S.P.T.L. 105, who instances damage from nuclear installations (for which, however, there are special statutory provisions) and the London and Chicago fires. See also *The Grandcamp* [1961] 1 Lloyd's Rep. 504, where an explosion caused 500 deaths and 3,000 personal injuries. The damages were US $70 million, though on appeal it was held that the explosion was not foreseeable to the defendants.

[254] "When . . . courts formulate legal criteria by reference to indeterminate terms such as 'fair', 'just', 'just and equitable' and 'unconscionable', they inevitably extend the range of admissible evidentiary materials. Cases then take longer, are more expensive to try, and, because of the indeterminacy of such terms, settlement of cases is more difficult, practitioners often having widely differing views as to the result of cases if they are litigated. Bright line rules may be less than perfect because they are under-inclusive, but my impression is that most people who have been or are engaged in day-to-day practice of the law at the trial or advising stage prefer rules to indeterminate standards": *Perre v Apand Pty Ltd* [1999] HCA 36; (1999) 198 C.L.R. 180 at [81] per McHugh J.

[255] [1986] Q.B. 507.

[256] *Donoghue v Stevenson* [1932] A.C. 562, see para.11–002.

claim which lay in contract against ITS but not in tort against the manufacturers. Similarly in *Murphy v Brentwood DC*[257] the House of Lords ended a long period of controversy by reaffirming that defects in a building which cause it to be less valuable or even potentially dangerous constitute pure economic loss and do not at common law[258] give rise to any claim except via a contract with the defendant.[259]

A decade or so earlier the claim in *Muirhead* would probably never have been presented. What prompted it was the difficult case of *Junior Books Ltd v Veitchi Co Ltd*.[260] The defenders were engaged as sub-contractors to lay a floor in the pursuer's factory. There was no contractual relationship between the parties and the main contractors were not involved in the proceedings. The pursuers alleged that the floor was defective (though not dangerous), that this was caused by the negligence of the defenders and that they had suffered damage totalling some £207,000, being the cost of replacing the floor and various other items of consequential loss. On a preliminary issue of law, the majority of the House of Lords held that the pursuers' allegations disclosed a cause of action for negligence. Quite why this was so is unclear: certainly the pursuers were owners of the floor, but to say that this meant that there was damage to their property is tantamount to saying that supply of an article which is shoddy and breaks is actionable in negligence and that is not the law. Some saw in the case the beginnings of a major extension of liability for pure economic loss, but by subsequent interpretation it has largely been relegated to a rather narrow decision on specialised facts.[261] Lord Keith in *Murphy v Brentwood* suggested that the case fell within the *Hedley Byrne* principle and that may well be the case provided this is understood in the broad sense of "assumption of responsibility" rather than in the narrower sense governing statements of information or advice.[262] The defenders, as nominated sub-contractors, would have been chosen by the pursuers (no doubt after direct negotiations between them) and were therefore in a "uniquely proximate"[263] relationship with them, more so than is normally the case between a building owner and a sub-contractor. The relationship was not contractual but it was all but a contract. In contrast, although the ultimate user of goods no doubt "relies" on the manufacturer's producing a good and suitable product the relationship is far less proximate. However, even this explanation is not free from difficulty, though the difficulty is one that applies to almost any "assumption of responsibility" case. It is that we are

---

[257] [1991] 1 A.C. 398, see para.10–049.

[258] See the Defective Premises Act 1972, discussed at para.10–056.

[259] The Contracts (Rights of Third Parties) Act 1999 will not generally affect either of these situations because: (a) the contract will not generally purport to confer a benefit on the third party claimant; and (b) will not identify him.

[260] [1983] 1 A.C. 520.

[261] In *The Orjula* [1995] 2 Lloyd's Rep. 395 Mance J described *Junior Books* as a case that appeared to have, "joined the slumber of the uniquely distinguished from which it would be unwise to awaken it without very solid reason".

[262] In so far as the defendants "said" anything expressly or by implication in *Junior Books* it was much more akin to a promise than information or advice.

[263] Lord Bridge in *D&F Estates Ltd v Church Commissioners* [1989] A.C. 177 at 202. However, Lord Goff in *Henderson v Merrett Syndicates Ltd* [1995] 2 A.C. 145 at 196, was of the view that the case does not represent a general rule even for nominated sub-contractors.

imposing a contract-type liability between parties who have structured their relationship in such a way as not to create a contract.[264]

D. Negligence and Public Authorities[265]

i. Introduction

Basic principles. This section is concerned with liability of public authorities in the tort of negligence and, more specifically, with the circumstances in which public authorities will come under a duty of care. There are three fundamental principles in this area that need to be borne in mind throughout the discussion. The first is that a public body may incur liability in tort in the same way as a private individual. Indeed, the rule of law dictates that public authorities are equally subject to the law as private persons. The second is that an act or decision that is invalid in public law terms does not for that reason become actionable in tort. The same is generally true of an act or decision of an individual servant of a public body.[266] Thirdly, the rule that tort law does not impose duties to act for the benefit of others[267] applies equally to public bodies as it does to private persons.

5–065

The multiplicity of actions that can arise in the context of public authorities. In the context of public authorities, one needs to be aware that a claim may be presented in one or more of three alternative ways. The first possibility is a claim for breach of statutory duty. Breach of statutory duty is dealt with in a later chapter.[268] The second possibility is that the public body is itself under a duty of care, as it would be, for example, in relation to the maintenance of its vehicles or the selection of its staff. Such a duty of care may exist in parallel with a statutory duty or alone. The third possibility is that an individual human agent of the public body may owe a duty of care to the claimant for the breach of which the body may be vicariously liable. Again, this duty may exist in parallel with one or both of the other duties or alone.

5–066

ii. Justiciability

Some matters are non-justiciable. Some decisions are non-justiciable in a private law action. These may be high political decisions ("shall we go to war?") but they may also extend to decisions on the allocation of resources or the infliction of risks. To take an example based loosely on *Home Office v Dorset*

5–067

---

[264] As Robert Goff LJ admits in *Muirhead* at [1986] Q.B. 528 there is no legal reason, though it is not the practice, why a building contract should not involve direct contracts between the building owner and specialists who are normally sub-contractors.

[265] Booth and Squires, *The Negligence Liability of Public Authorities* (2006); Markesinis et al, *Tortious Liability of Statutory Bodies* (1999); Fairgrieve, Andenas and Bell, *Tort Liability of Public Authorities in Comparative Perspective* (2002); Law Commission, *Administrative Redress: Public Bodies and the Citizen*, Report No.332 (2010).

[266] But one tort is unique to public bodies and servants: misfeasance in a public office, as to which see para.8–024.

[267] See para.5–039.

[268] See Ch.8.

Yacht Co,[269] suppose that the Home Office institutes a policy of open, non-secure young offender institutions with a view to promoting the rehabilitation of young offenders. Claims in tort by neighbours of the institution whose homes are burgled by absconding offenders will plainly fail even if there is a sharp increase in burglaries in the area. This is because "the court cannot adjudicate on such policy".[270]

5–068   **The distinction between policy decisions and operational decisions.** The law attempts to distinguish between "policy" and "operational" decisions. Policy decisions are are normally inappropriate subjects for judicial scrutiny. By contrast, operational decisions will usually be justiciable. The line between the two categories cannot be sharply drawn, for the decision to do an operational act may easily involve and flow from a policy decision.[271] The very fine lines which have to be drawn may be illustrated by two immigration cases. In *W v Home Office*[272] the claimant was detained on arrival as an asylum seeker because of a low score on a test designed to assess his knowledge of his asserted country of origin. Subsequently he easily passed the test and it was discovered that he had not taken the test on the earlier occasion and that someone else's results had been placed on his file by mistake. Although this was the purest "operational" error the process of gathering information about the claimant's status was outside the scope of any private law remedy and he was owed no duty of care by the immigration service. In *R. (on the application of A) v Secretary of State for the Home Dept*[273] the claimants, having been allowed to remain for asylum reasons were, by administrative error, given a classification which prevented them claiming benefits. This was eventually corrected but there was no mechanism for making retrospective payments. It was held that the Secretary of State owed a duty to them and *W* was distinguished on the basis that there the mishandling of information took place at the stage of making the judgment whether the claimant should be allowed entry, whereas here the decision on the claimants' status had already been taken and it was merely a matter of the administrative implementation of that decision.

iii.   Duty of Care

5–069   **Introduction.** If the hurdle of justiciability can be overcome, the next issue to address is whether a duty of care exists. If the public authority concerned committed some positive act that resulted in injury to the claimant there will usually be little or no difficulty in finding that a duty of care was owed. For example, if a public authority builds a dangerous intersection that results in the claimant motorist suffering injury in a car accident it will usually be straightforward for the claimant to show that the authority owed him a duty of care. The situation is quite different where the cause of the claimant's injury was an omission by the authority to do something to protect him from some danger.

---

[269] [1970] A.C. 1004.
[270] *X v Bedfordshire CC* [1995] 2 A.C. 633 at 738.
[271] *Barrett v Enfield LBC* [2001] 2 A.C. 550 at 571.
[272] [1997] Imm. A.R. 302.
[273] [2004] EWHC 1585 (Admin).

As will be explained below, the fact that a public authority is under a statutory duty to do something is insufficient to create a tortious duty of care. The same is true of the fact that a public authority is vested with a statutory power to do something. Ultimately, the question of whether a public authority owes a duty to take positive steps to protect the claimant from some harm is decided according to the *Caparo* test. It is the third stage of that test that is most frequently in issue in this context.

The mere fact that a public body is under a statutory duty does not mean that the body owes a duty of care. As has already been noted, it is a guiding principle in this area of the law that the mere fact that a public body has committed an act or made a decision that is invalid in public law terms does not necessarily generate liability in tort. Legislation may provide that breach of a statutory duty is actionable in tort. But any such statutory duty does not itself create a duty of care.[274] A duty of care cannot "grow parasitically out of a statutory duty not intended to be owed to individuals".[275]

5–070

A public law duty to give consideration to exercising a statutory power does not generate a duty of care. In *Stovin v Wise*[276] Mr Stovin was injured in an accident at a dangerous junction caused by the negligence of Mrs Wise. The junction was dangerous because visibility was reduced by a bank of earth on the land of a third party. My Stovin recovered damages from Mrs Wise. Mrs Wise then sought a contribution[277] from Norfolk CC, which was the highway authority responsible for the junction, and a precondition of this was that the authority, if sued by Mr Stovin, would have been liable to him. There is a civilly actionable statutory duty to maintain the highway[278] but this was inapplicable because it concerns the state of repair of the roadway and the danger at the junction arose from poor visibility. There was a statutory power[279] to require the removal of an obstruction but after negotiations with the third party the authority decided to remove the bank of earth itself. However, the matter then "went to sleep" for nearly a year before the accident. The majority of the House of Lords declined to find that the Council owed a duty of care. There was no way, as Lord Hoffmann put it, in which the statutory "may" could be turned into a common law "ought".[280] Although Council could have been compelled via public law remedies to give consideration to the question of whether it should exercise the power, the duty did not give rise to a duty of care. *Stovin v Wise* was followed by the House of Lords in *Gorringe v Calderdale MBC*.[281] This case was based on a failure to erect a sign warning the claimant driver of the need to reduce her speed. Lord

5–071

---

[274] *X v Bedfordshire CC* [1995] 2 A.C. 633 at 734.

[275] *Gorringe v Calderdale MBC* [2004] UKHL 15; [2004] 1 W.L.R. 1057 at [71] per Lord Scott. See also *Sandhar v Dept of Transport* [2005] EWCA Civ 1440; [2005] P.I.Q.R. P183 at [37]; *Neil Martin Ltd v Revenue and Customs Comrs* [2007] EWCA Civ 1041; [2007] S.T.C. 1802.

[276] [1996] A.C. 923. See also para.5–039.

[277] Civil Liability (Contribution) Act 1978. See Ch.22.

[278] Highways Act 1980, see para.15–083.

[279] Highways Act 1980 s.79. The distinction between a power and a duty may not always be clear and in any event a duty may contain wide elements of discretion: *R. v CC Sussex Ex p. International Trader's Ferry Ltd* [1999] 2 A.C. 418; *Larner v Solihull MBC* [2001] P.I.Q.R. P17.

[280] [1996] A.C. 923 at 948.

[281] [2004] UKHL 15; [2004] 1 W.L.R. 1057.

Hoffmann remarked: "I find it difficult to imagine a case in which a common law duty can be founded simply upon the failure (however irrational) to provide some benefit which a public authority has power [sic] (or a public law duty) to provide."[282] Of course if the highway authority had installed misleading road markings or signs there would be no difficulty about finding it liable because it would then have created a source of danger.

5–072   **X v Bedfordshire CC.** The leading decision concerning the circumstances in which it is fair, just and reasonable to impose on public authorities a duty to act to protect a claimant from harm is *X v Bedfordshire CC*.[283] In this case children alleged that they were subjected to neglect and ill-treatment and that the authority negligently failed to take them into care. Lord Browne-Wilkinson was inclined to the view that this was a case of a justiciable decision but it was held that it would not be fair, just and reasonable to impose a duty of care for several reasons. It was said that a duty of care would cut across the statutory system for the protection of children at risk, which involves "inter-disciplinary" procedures for the authority, the police, doctors and others.[284] Furthermore, the task of the authority was a delicate one and the imposition of a duty of care might make the authority adopt defensive tactics which would be harmful to the broad body of children at risk. Other considerations that militated against the imposition of a duty of care included the fact that there was, in the opinion of the House of Lords, a high risk of vexatious complaints in this area and the fact that the statutory scheme provided remedies by way of complaint and investigation.

5–073   **Subsequent developments.** Subsequent cases show increased reluctance to deny a duty because of a background statutory context. In *Barrett v Enfield LBC*[285] the claim was in respect of alleged negligence in connection with the upbringing of a child in care. This claim this was allowed to go to trial, in line with the current tendency not to be so free with the striking out procedure.[286] The policy considerations in *X v Bedfordshire* restricting the duty of care on a local authority when deciding whether or not to take action in respect of a case of suspected child abuse did not have the same force in respect of decisions taken once the child was already in local authority care. *Phelps v Hillingdon LBC*[287] was a conjoined appeal concerning allegations of failure to provide for special educational needs. The claims were based on the vicarious liability of the defendants for the conduct of individual employees and these were not thought, for the purposes of striking out, to present any fatal conflict with the statutory framework. "Direct" claims against the defendant authorities were also regarded as arguable. Indeed, it may be that the law has changed even in the context of *X v*

---

[282] [2004] UKHL 15; [2004] 1 W.L.R. 1057 at [32].

[283] [1995] 2 A.C. 633.

[284] "To introduce into such a system a common law duty of care enforceable against only one of the participant bodies would be manifestly unfair. To impose such liability on all the participant bodies would lead to almost impossible problems of disentangling as between the respective bodies the liability, both primary and by way of contribution, of each for reaching a decision found to be negligent": [1995] 2 A.C. 633 at 750.

[285] [2001] 2 A.C. 550.

[286] See para.5–011. See also *W v Essex CC* [2001] 2 A.C. 592.

[287] *Essex CC* [2001] 2 A.C. 619. See also *Carty v Croydon LBC* [2005] EWCA Civ 19; [2005] 1 W.L.R. 2312.

Bedfordshire itself, that is, child abuse. In *D v East Berkshire Community Health NHS Trust*[288] the Court of Appeal held that in the light of subsequent developments *X v Bedfordshire* could no longer be taken as authority for the proposition that there could be no duty of care owed to children in these cases. The principal reason was that now (though not at the time of the events in *D*) arts 3 (protection against inhuman or degrading treatment) and 8 (respect for family life) are given direct effect in English law by the Human Rights Act 1998.[289] However, the appeals to the House of Lords in *D* involved claims by the parents of children taken into care, to which different considerations apply: as it will always be in the parents' interests that the child is not taken into care, there is a conflict of interest between the parents and the child and the striking out of those claims was therefore upheld by the majority of the House of Lords.

The fear that imposing a duty would lead to defensive practices. In several of the cases that have been mentioned in the present section, a factor that has often militated against the recognition of a duty of care is a fear that imposing a duty might lead some people to adopt defensive practices. This is clearly a defective basis for withholding a duty of care, most obviously because it is a consideration that weighs against the imposition of a duty in *all* cases. It does not explain cases in which a duty of care was recognised. Some judges, perhaps in recognition of this difficulty, have suggested that the problem of defensive practices can be dealt with adequately by reference to the undoubted principle that a person who fearlessly carries out his professional role will not be held to be negligent. So in *Barrett v Enfield LBC* Lord Slynn did not appear to embrace some of the alleged policy considerations with enthusiasm even in the *X v Bedfordshire* context.[290] However, some take a more sceptical view of the effectiveness of the "breach approach" to block bad claims. In *D v East Berkshire Community Health NHS Trust* Lord Brown said:[291]

5–074

> "There is always a temptation to say in all these cases that no one, whether a doctor concerned with possible child abuse, a witness or a prosecutor will ever in fact be held liable unless he has conducted himself manifestly unreasonably; it is unnecessary, therefore, to deny a duty of care, better rather to focus on the appropriate standard by which to judge whether it is breached. That, however, is to overlook two fundamental considerations: first, the insidious effect that his awareness of the proposed duty would have upon the mind and conduct of the doctor (subtly tending to the suppression of doubts and instincts which in the child's interests ought rather to be encouraged), and second, a consideration inevitably bound up with the first, the need to protect him against the risk of costly and vexing litigation, by no means invariably soundly based."

---

[288] [2003] EWCA Civ 1151; [2004] Q.B. 558. See also *B v Attorney General of New Zealand* [2003] UKPC 61; [2003] 4 All E.R. 833.
[289] The child abuse claims in *X v Bedfordshire* resulted in successful applications to the European Court of Human Rights: *Z v United Kingdom* (2002) 34 E.H.R.R. 3; *T.P. v UK* (2002) 34 E.H.R.R. 2. There were held to be breaches of arts 3 and 8, though not of art.6.
[290] See [2001] 2 A.C. 550 at 568.
[291] [2005] UKHL 23; [2005] 2 All E.R. 443 at [137].

E.   Lawyers and Negligence

5–075   **Introduction.** Solicitors will generally have a contract with their clients that will require them to exercise proper professional care and skill within the scope of the retainer. There may be no contract where the client is legally aided with a nil contribution and generally there is no contract between a barrister and a lay client[292] but there is no doubt that in these cases there is an assumption of responsibility which gives rise to the same duty in practical terms, though in tort not in contract.[293] Two matters have, however, proved controversial: the duty of the lawyer to third parties and the duty, even to his client, in the context of litigation.

i.   Third Parties

5–076   **Circumstances in which a lawyer will owe a duty under White v Jones.** The paradigm case is that where the lawyer is instructed to draw a will for X which will benefit C and fails to carry out that task properly.[294] We have seen how in *White v Jones*[295] liability was imposed in such a case on the basis of assumption of responsibility, but something more needs to be said by way of explanation of the scope of this duty. It applies as much to a financial institution offering will-making services as to a solicitor.[296] Although the duty sounds in tort the underlying basis of it is the acceptance of the client's instructions and the scope of those instructions is obviously determinative of the duty to the beneficiary. While as matter of principle there should be a duty in respect of gifts inter vivos, it has been held that there is no liability if the donor is able to rectify the error made:[297] if he chooses not to do so, the effective cause of the failure of the transaction is not the negligence of the solicitor but the decision of his client.[298] The duty extends to the drafting of the instrument[299] and its execution[300] as well

---

[292] Any rule of law (as opposed to professional conduct) forbidding a barrister entering into a contract was abolished by the Courts and Legal Services Act 1990 s.61.

[293] However, even where there is a contract there may be a parallel duty in tort: *Midland Bank Trust Co Ltd v Hett, Stubbs & Kemp* [1979] Ch. 384, approved in *Henderson v Merrett Syndicates Ltd* [1995] 2 A.C. 145.

[294] Where the will is in order and the deceased appoints A as his executor, leaving property to C, and the defendants culpably fail to carry out A's instructions to administer the estate promptly C may suffer loss because the property is not transferred to him expeditiously. However, in such a case A can sue for that loss (holding the damages in trust for C) since until the estate is administered the property is vested in A: *Chappell v Somers & Blake* [2003] EWHC 1644; [2004] Ch. 19.

[295] [1995] 2 A.C. 207, see para.5–054.

[296] *Esterhuizen v Allied Dunbar Assurance Plc* [1998] 2 F.L.R. 668.

[297] *Hemmens v Wilson Browne* [1995] Ch. 223. Cf. *Hughes v Richards* [2004] EWCA Civ 266; [2004] P.N.L.R. 35 (A engages B to set up a trust to benefit C—the job is mishandled, the fund lost and C receives no benefit, C's claim is arguable, even though it was possible that A might recover substantial damages in alternative).

[298] As to the effect of pre-death change of mind by the testator in the case of an ineffective will see *Humbleston v Martin Tolhurst Partnership* [2004] EWHC 151 (Ch); [2004] P.N.L.R. 26.

[299] *Horsefall v Haywards* [1999] Lloyd's Rep. P.N. 332; *Martin v Triggs Turner Bartons* [2009] EWHC 1920 (Ch); [2010] P.N.L.R. 3; cf. *Fraser v McArthur Stewart* [2008] CSOH 159; 2009 S.L.T. 31. Note that under s.20 of the Administration of Justice Act 1982 the court has jurisdiction, on application within six months of representation being taken out, to rectify a will so as to carry out the

as simple failure to implement the instructions.[301] There will generally be no liability to the estate because it will have suffered no loss by the bequest going to the wrong destination, but the duty to the beneficiary is an independent one so that, while there must be no double liability,[302] there may be liability to the beneficiary and liability to the estate in respect of any further loss which it suffers.[303] However, the solicitor in such a situation is not the guardian of the interests of the object of the client's bounty[304] except to the limited extent of carrying out the client's instructions. So he does not owe a duty to the beneficiary to advise the testator on arranging his affairs so as to minimise the tax impact of the transaction on the beneficiary.[305] In *Clarke v Bruce Lance & Co*[306] the defendants in 1973 had drawn up a will for the testator which left a petrol station to the claimant and some five years later they acted for the testator again in granting an option (at a fixed price) over the station to a tenant, who was virtually certain to exercise it. The claimant's claim for negligence was struck out: if the defendants had owed him any duty of care they could find themselves in the intolerable position of having to seek to dissuade their client (the testator) from having to carry through a transaction upon which he had decided. The duty to third parties is not confined to carrying out instructions in relation to wills; for example, it has been held that a solicitor acting for a borrower may be under a duty to take care to ensure, for the benefit of an unrepresented lender, that the security given is effective.[307] However, in conducting litigation or negotiating in an adversarial situation neither client nor lawyer owes a duty of care to their opponent.[308]

ii. Litigation

The lawyers' immunity and its abolition. For many years the law took the view that a lawyer conducting litigation did not owe a duty of care even to his own client in the conduct of the case in court and matters closely connected

5–077

---

intentions of the testator, if it is satisfied that the will is so expressed that it fails to carry out the testator's intentions in consequence of a clerical error or of a failure to understand his instructions. Failure to take this course may amount to failure to mitigate loss and provide a defence to the claim against the solicitor: *Walker v Geo H Medlicott & Son* [1999] 1 W.L.R. 727.

[300] *Ross v Caunters* [1980] 1 Ch. 297; *Esterhuizen v Allied Dunbar Assurance Plc* [1998] 2 F.L.R. 668 (normally insufficient to leave accurate written instructions on attestation, but cf. *Gray v Richards Butler* [2000] W.T.L.R. 143).

[301] *White v Jones* [1995] 2 A.C. 207

[302] *Corbett v Bond Pearce* [2001] EWCA Civ 531; [2001] 3 All E.R. 769.

[303] *Carr-Glyn v Frearsons* [1999] Ch. 326.

[304] It is assumed that there is no direct assumption of responsibility to the third party, e.g. by answering questions from him.

[305] *Cancer Research Campaign v Ernest Brown* [1998] P.N.L.R. 592. See also *Woodward v Wolferstans, The Times*, April 8, 1997.

[306] *Clarke v Bruce Lance & Co* [1988] 1 W.L.R. 881.

[307] *Dean v Allin & Watts* [2001] EWCA Civ 758; [2001] 2 Lloyd's Rep. 249. See also *Al Kandari v JR Brown & Co* [1988] Q.B. 665.

[308] *Business Computers International v Registrar of Companies* [1988] Ch. 229; *Connolly-Martin v D* [1999] Lloyd's Rep. P.N. 790.

therewith.[309] Various reasons were put forward for this immunity: (1) that an advocate has an overriding duty to the court and in order to ensure that the lawyer did not neglect that duty he had to be relieved of even the possibility that actions for negligence would be brought against him by a disgruntled client; (2) the difficulty or undesirability of retrying, in the action against the advocate, the issue which arose in the original litigation out of which the action arose; (3) the advocates' immunity was analogous to the immunity granted to other participants involved in court proceedings (such as judges and jurors); (4) the "cab-rank" rule whereby counsel must take any case within his field of competence; and (5) the existence of professional disciplinary procedures.[310] Now, however, the immunity has been swept away, at least in relation to claims arising out of civil proceedings, by the House of Lords in *Arthur JS Hall & Co v Simons*.[311]

The first of these reasons made no sense since a lawyer would never be found to be negligent in discharging his paramount duty to the court. The second reason was an appeal to the importance of litigation being final, but the House of Lords held that this interest could be adequately protected by the court's jurisdiction to strike out as an abuse of process actions that seek to re-litigate matters that have already been decided. The third reason is an incorrect analogy since the advocate is the only person in the court who can fairly be said to have assumed responsibility to his client. The fourth reason did not explain why solicitors (who are not required to comply with the cab-rank rule) benefited from the immunity, and the fifth reason was unable to explain why lawyers should be treated differently from other professionals. An important factor that motivated the decision to abolish the immunity, aside from the weakness of the arguments in favour of the immunity, was that it was a rule that must inevitably have been seen as lawyers giving special treatment to lawyers. There were also concerns that the immunity would have been vulnerable to potential attack under the European Convention on Human Rights. Finally, other jurisdictions with very similar legal systems[312] had rejected the rule without undue effects.

5–078 **Criminal proceedings.** None of the cases involved in the appeal in *Hall* originated from criminal proceedings but four members of the House of Lords were of the view that the traditional rule was equally inapplicable to claims arising from criminal proceedings.

5–079 **Solicitors who rely on barristers.** Where the claimant has been represented by solicitor and counsel and he sues the former the relationship between the two lawyers must be considered. A solicitor who has consulted counsel will prima

---

[309] The leading decisions of the House of Lords were *Rondel v Worsley* [1969] 1 A.C. 191 and *Saif Ali v Sydney Mitchell & Co* [1980] A.C. 198.

[310] For discussion see Goudkamp (2002) 10 Tort L. Rev. 188.

[311] [2002] 1 A.C. 615.

[312] Most notably Canada. However, the High Court of Australia has rejected *Hall v Simons* and affirmed the immunity: *D'Orta Ekenaike v Victoria Legal Aid* [2005] HCA 12; (2005) 223 C.L.R. 1. New Zealand rejected immunity in *Chamberlains v Lai* [2006] NZSC 70; [2007] 2 N.Z.L.R. 1.

facie be entitled to rely on his advice[313] (hence, it will be difficult to establish a breach of duty) but he cannot, "rely blindly and with no mind of his own on counsel's view".[314]

Other participants in the judicial process. Expert witnesses were once immune to liability in negligence but this immunity has recently also been removed.[315] Lay witnesses are immune, and this is an area where it is believed that immunity is necessary lest the witness be deterred from performing his duty to the court. The prosecutor in a criminal case is simultaneously client, lawyer and also a minister of justice but the accused as a general rule has no cause of action for negligence[316] against those engaged in prosecuting him on behalf of the community.[317] This rests on general grounds of public policy and not on the former advocate's immunity. However, in *Welsh v CC Merseyside*[318] a claim that the Crown Prosecution Service had failed to inform the court that certain offences had been taken into consideration in other proceedings was held to disclose a cause of action based upon assumption of responsibility via an undertaking given to the claimant.

5–080

F. Psychiatric Injury[319]

Terminology. The first point is one of terminology. For many years it has been customary to refer to this form of damage as "nervous shock". That has the advantage of serving as a reminder that this head of liability has in most cases required something in the nature of a traumatic response to an *event*. That is not necessarily so in some cases where the claimant is directly affected by the defendant's conduct[320] but it is still the law that the spouse of a brain-damaged accident victim who foreseeably succumbs to psychiatric illness from the strain of caring for the victim has no cause of action against the tortfeasor.[321] However, the expression seems to be falling into disuse[322] and "psychiatric injury" or "mental injury"[323] is becoming a more frequent terminology.

5–081

Reasons why psychiatric injury is treated differently from other types of personal injury. Psychiatric injury is a form of "personal injury" but it is more

5–082

---

[313] *Matrix Securities Ltd v Theodore Goddard* (1997) 147 N.L.J. 1847; *McFaddens v Platford* [2009] EWHC 126 (TCC) at [56].

[314] *Davy-Chieseman v Davy-Chieseman* [1984] Fam. 48; *Locke v Camberwell HA* [1991] 2 Med.L.R. 249; *Bond v Royal Sun Alliance* [2001] P.N.L.R. 30. Where the solicitor is liable it is likely that counsel will bear the greater share of the damages for the purposes of contribution: *Pritchard Joyce & Hinds v Batcup* [2008] EWHC 20 (QB); [2008] P.N.L.R. 18.

[315] *Jones v Kaney* [2011] UKSC 13; [2011] 2 A.C. 398.

[316] There may be liability for malicious prosecution or misfeasance in a public office (see Ch.20, and para.8–024 respectively) but these require "malice".

[317] *Elguzouli-Daf v MPC* [1995] Q.B. 335.

[318] [1993] 1 All E.R. 692.

[319] Mullany and Handford, *Tort Liability for Psychiatric Damage*, 2nd edn (2006).

[320] See para.5–095.

[321] *Alcock v CC South Yorkshire* [1992] 1 A.C. 310 at 396, 401, 416; *Jaensch v Coffey* (1984) 155 C.L.R. 549.

[322] See the criticism by Bingham LJ in *Attia v British Gas Plc* [1988] Q.B. 304 at 317.

[323] Evans LJ's preference in *Vernon v Bosley (No.1)* [1997] 1 All E.R. 577 at 597.

problematical for the law than most physical injury, and is consequently treated differently, for two reasons. First, despite advances in scientific knowledge of the working of the mind there is still a belief, right or wrong, that it presents a greater risk of inaccurate diagnosis[324] and the incidence or the basis or even the very existence of some conditions is controversial. A further difficulty is that the line between "mental" and "physical" is still not fully scientifically understood: nowadays, for example, there is support for the view that certain forms of depression are the product of physical changes in the brain[325] and if these can be produced by a sudden shock the only basis for treating such a case differently from physical lesion by impact must rest on legal policy. The current practice is to regard some injuries which are undoubtedly physical (such as a stroke or a miscarriage) but which are produced by shock as falling within the special rules in this section but in other contexts they may be equated with more direct physical harm. Secondly, while the physical effects of an accident are limited by the laws of inertia, physical injury to one person, or even the threat of it, may produce mental trauma in others, witnesses, relatives, friends and so on. "The contours of tort law are profoundly affected by distinctions between different types of damage"[326] and mental injury is as "special" as pure economic loss.

i.   A Recognised Psychiatric Illness

5–083   **It is necessary for the claimant to suffer a recognised psychiatric illness.** The early view was that mental injury unaccompanied by physical injury was not compensable at all[327] but this was discarded around the end of the 19th century, both for intentional wrongdoing[328] and for negligence,[329] though it took rather longer to reach the position where the claimant might recover damages for shock caused by endangerment of another. However, it is still the law that the sensations of fear or mental distress or grief[330] suffered as a result of negligence[331] do not in themselves give rise to a cause of action.[332] There must be some recognisable and

---

[324] However, in *Frost v CC South Yorkshire* [1997] 3 W.L.R. 1194 at 1217, Henry LJ put the risk of fraudulent shock claims as no greater than in "cases involving back injuries where there is often a wide gap between observable symptoms and complaints".

[325] See *Weaver v Delta Airlines Inc* 56 F Supp 2d 1190 (1999).

[326] *Frost v CC South Yorkshire* [1999] 2 A.C. 455 at 492 per Lord Steyn.

[327] *Victorian Ry Commissioners v Coultas* (1888) 13 App. Cas. 222.

[328] *Wilkinson v Downton* [1897] 2 Q.B. 57.

[329] *Dulieu v White* [1901] 2 K.B. 669.

[330] There is a limited statutory right of action for bereavement: see para.24–016.

[331] The position is different in the case of the intentional torts actionable per se because damages are then said to be at large. For example, in a case of libel the award of damages will reflect (though obviously not in any precise mathematical way) the distress suffered by the claimant at the publication and in a case of false arrest the damages may be aggravated by the distress suffered by the claimant because of the high-handed treatment of him. Some statutory wrongs such as race or sex discrimination and harassment also allow damages for distress.

[332] A claimant who has suffered a physical injury may in principle recover damages for the distress caused to him by the injury even though it does not amount to a recognisable psychiatric illness. In practice in the majority of cases this will be "lost" in the conventional figures for loss of amenity (see para.23–068) but, e.g. damages for facial scarring will take account of the psychological effect on the victim.

acknowledged psychiatric illness[333] (though of course a physical injury resulting from a shock—heart failure, a fall, a miscarriage—is also compensable). Thus where a claim alleged negligence in the conduct of a police disciplinary investigation the submission that actionable damage had occurred in the form of anxiety and vexation was described by the House of Lords as unsustainable[334] and claimants failed in their claim when they suffered claustrophobia and fear at being trapped in a lift.[335] A claim was also rejected where the victims of a disaster were trapped, fully conscious, for some time before they suffered a swift death from asphyxia.[336] Assuming the mental injury suffered qualifies as damage in the above rather imprecise sense, the cases have been said to: "[B]roadly divide into two categories, that is to say, those cases in which the injured plaintiff was involved, either mediately or immediately, as a participant, and those in which the plaintiff was no more than a passive and unwilling witness of injury caused to others."[337]

ii.   Claimant Physically Threatened by the Negligence—a Primary Victim

The rule in the case of primary victims. The simplest case is that where the claimant suffers shock from a reasonable fear for his own safety caused by the defendant's negligence (the "near miss"). Such a claimant can recover damages. In *Dulieu v White*[338] the claimant succeeded in a claim for shock, resulting in a miscarriage, when a horse-drawn van was negligently driven into the bar of the public house where she was serving. It is not necessary that the claimant should actually be in danger, provided he reasonably believes he is.[339] However, if the fear is not reasonably entertained (for example, if the claimant is a hysterical personality who suffers shock from the noise of a collision on the other side of the street) there is no action.[340]   **5–084**

The decision in Page v Smith. The scope of the "primary victim" category of liability was enlarged by the decision of the House of Lords in *Page v Smith*.[341] The claimant was involved in a collision caused by the defendant's negligence which caused property damage but no physical injury. However, as a result of the experience the claimant suffered a recurrence of myalgic encephalomyelitis or   **5–085**

---

[333] Among many statements of this requirement, see *Hinz v Berry* [1970] 2 Q.B. 40 at 42; *Alcock v CC South Yorkshire* [1992] 1 A.C. 310 at 401, 416; *Jaensch v Coffey* (1984) 155 C.L.R. 549 at 559, 587.

[334] *Calveley v CC Merseyside* [1989] A.C. 1228.

[335] *Reilly v Merseyside RHA* [1995] 6 Med. L.R. 246.

[336] *Hicks v CC South Yorkshire* [1992] 2 All E.R. 65. Where a person's life expectancy is shortened by an injury, distress at that is a compensable item of damage. No doubt in *Hicks* there was a momentary interval between the onset of physical injury by crushing and death but it was too short sensibly to attract this principle.

[337] *Alcock v CC South Yorkshire* [1992] 1 A.C. 310 at 407 per Lord Oliver.

[338] [1901] 2 K.B. 669.

[339] *McFarlane v EE Caledonia Ltd* [1994] 2 All E.R. 1 at 10.

[340] [1994] 2 All E.R. 1 at 11, though on the facts the Court of Appeal took the view that C was not in fact in fear for his own safety at the time. See also *Hegarty v E.E. Caledonia Ltd* [1997] 2 Lloyd's Rep. 259; *Monk v P.C. Harrington Ltd* [2008] EWHC 1879 (QB); [2009] P.I.Q.R. P3.

[341] [1996] A.C. 155. For damning criticism see Bailey and Nolan (2010) 69 C.L.J. 495.

chronic fatigue syndrome which had affected him on and off for 25 years but which now became chronic and permanent. The case was decided in the House of Lords on the basis that the circumstances of the accident were not such as to cause foreseeable psychiatric injury to a person of normal fortitude but some physical injury was plainly foreseeable from it. In the view of the majority, psychiatric injury was but a variety of the broader genus of "personal injury"[342] and therefore the claimant was entitled to recover on the basis of the "thin skull" principle. This says that once the defendant owes a duty to the claimant and is in breach of it, his liability is not limited to the injuries which were reasonably foreseeable at the time of the accident but extends to more serious injuries brought about by the claimant's pre-existing weakness.[343]

5–086   **The scope of the "primary victim" category.** The limits of *Page v Smith* are not easy to state. How stringently is the "zone of danger" to be defined? If the defendant drives furiously down a crowded street there may be hundreds of people momentarily in the zone of physical danger created by his negligence: can any of them who happens to have an "eggshell personality" sue if he suffers shock?[344] However, the case is not confined to the simple situation where D's negligence puts C in danger of injury by *accident*: thus where the negligence of the police force in failing to provide a functioning surveillance device required an officer to make repeated surreptitious visits to a car belonging to gangsters in order to make it work, the defendants were held liable when the stress of this, combined with his existing hypertension (of which they were unaware) precipitated a psychiatric condition and a stroke.[345]

It is enough, it seems, that the claimant is within the zone of physical danger even if what triggers the mental injury is the sight of what happens to others. In *Chadwick v British Transport Commission*[346] the claimant was a volunteer helper at the scene of a rail disaster and suffered mental trauma as a result. For many years this case was regarded as resting on the basis that a duty was owed to him as a rescuer but the existence of any separate category of rescuers for this purpose was rejected in *Frost v CC South Yorkshire*[347] and *Chadwick*'s case was regarded as correctly decided on the basis that the claimant had been in physical danger from the collapse of the wreckage, even though the judge[348] found that it was the horrific nature of the experience rather than fear for himself which had affected him.[349] This approach may be supported on the grounds that in some cases it may be extremely difficult to determine whether or how far the claimant suffered

---

[342] As Lord Lloyd pointed out at 190, a standard English statutory formula in the Limitation Acts and elsewhere is, "'personal injury' includes any disease and any impairment of a person's physical or mental condition".

[343] See para.7–038.

[344] *Glen v Korean Airlines Co Ltd* [2003] EWHC 643 (QB); [2003] Q.B. 1386 would provide an example but the point was not in issue in the proceedings.

[345] *Donachie v CC Greater Manchester* [2004] EWCA Civ 405; *The Times*, May 6, 2004. See also *A v Essex CC* [2003] EWCA Civ 1848; [2004] 1 W.L.R. 1881.

[346] [1967] 1 W.L.R. 912.

[347] [1999] 2 A.C. 455. See also *Young v Charles Church (Southern) Ltd* (1997) 39 B.M.L.R. 146.

[348] The father of the trial judge in *Frost*.

[349] Cf. *Hunter v British Coal* [1998] Q.B. 140, decided before *Frost*, where the claimant had been in some danger (though he was not aware of it) when he was near a defective hydrant but when the hydrant exploded and killed a workmate he was out of sight and some distance away.

shock from fear for himself or from the sight of what happened to others, and there may be cases in which there is a damaging impact on his psyche without his consciously suffering anything that could be called fear. Nevertheless, it is a mechanical approach and one can conceive of cases where it might operate in the claimant's favour even though he was at the time entirely unaware of any danger to himself.

The decision in Rothwell v Chemical & Insulating Co Ltd. Suppose that the defendant exposes the claimant to some risk of harm (a pollutant or some harmful chemical, for example) which has not caused any direct harm but the claimant's knowledge of this expose affects his mental state. Although he might be said to be in the "zone of danger", *Page v Smith* does not stretch this far. In *Rothwell v Chemical & Insulating Co Ltd*[350] one of the appellants, G, had been exposed to asbestos and developed asymptomatic pleural plaques. These did not in any way interfere with his physical health and would not themselves lead to any illness but they were a signal that asbestos had penetrated the body and that there was some more than normal risk of the development of an asbestos-related condition, something which G discovered when he was told about it by a doctor over 30 years after the exposure, though he had been concerned about the risk of developing an asbestos-related disease for years before that. That would not amount to damage which created a cause of action (suffering a risk of damage is not damage). However, G worried so much about the risk that he developed a clinical depressive condition. While it is obvious that this knowledge would cause anxiety to anyone, the case was conducted on the basis that there was no evidence that a person of reasonable fortitude would react so strongly as to become mentally ill. On that basis the House of Lords held that *Page v Smith* could not be extended to such a situation. The case is obviously very far removed on its facts from *Page*, not least because of the very long gap between the "exposure to danger" and the mental consequences of it, though the reasons for distinguishing that decision are variously expressed. Unlike *Rothwell*, *Page* was a case of psychiatric injury "arising as an immediate consequence of an obvious accident";[351] the chain of causation in *Rothwell* was "stretched far beyond that which was envisaged in *Page*";[352] and "it would be an unwarranted extension of [*Page*] to apply it to psychiatric illness caused by apprehension of the possibility of an unfavourable event which had not actually happened".[353]

The result in *Rothwell* might have been different if the pleural plaques had constituted "damage" for it is well-established that even anxiety falling short of mental illness at the consequences of a physical injury is a proper item of damages.[354] There would still, however, have been a difficulty, for the plaques themselves were not dangerous, they were simply an indication of penetration of the body by asbestos and one would be saying that: "[A] claimant with plaques would have a claim for damages for the risk that he would develop asbestosis or

5–087

---

[350] [2007] UKHL 39; [2008] A.C. 281. See also *The Creutzfeldt-Jakob Disease litigation; Group B Plaintiffs v Medical Research Council* [2000] Lloyd's Rep. Med. 161; *Fletcher v Commissioners of Public Works* [2003] 1 I.R. 465

[351] Lord Mance at [104]; "an immediate response to a past event": Lord Rodger at [95].

[352] Lord Hope at [55].

[353] Lord Hoffmann at [33].

[354] See para.22–066.

mesothelioma, when a claimant without plaques, but with exactly the same risk of developing those diseases, would have no claim."[355] It may well be impossible in such a case to disentangle the mental processes which lead to the claimant's anxiety but one may say that a wholly rational person would be worried by the exposure, not the plaques. On the other hand, given the basic premise of *Page v Smith* that physical injury and mental injury are but different forms of "personal injury" the fact that on this hypothesis some physical injury has occurred would make it impossible to avoid the application of the thin skull rule.[356]

iii.   Claimant a Witness of Danger to Others—a Secondary Victim

5–088   **Requirements where claimant is a secondary victim.** The situation here is that D's negligence causes injury to B (or puts B in danger of injury) and C (who is neither injured nor in danger) suffers shock as a result of the incident. The leading case is *Alcock v CC South Yorkshire.*[357] The 10 appellants had suffered psychiatric injury as a result of the disaster in 1989 at Hillsborough Stadium in Sheffield, in which, because of the admitted negligence of the defendants, some 95 people were crushed to death and over 400 physically injured. None of the appellants had suffered any physical injury, nor been in any danger, indeed most of them were not at the ground, though they saw part of the events on television. All whose appeals were before the House of Lords failed. The starting point is a clear assumption that there is a real need for the law to place some limitation going beyond reasonable foreseeability and medical proof of causation on the range of admissible claims. This limitation is to be found by reference to three elements: (1) the class of persons whose claims should be recognised; (2) the proximity of those persons to the accident; and (3) the means by which the trauma to the claimant is caused (though in practice heads (2) and (3) are closely related).

5–089   **The claimant must be in a relationship of close ties of love and affection with the person endangered.** As to the first element, the House of Lords rejected any arbitrary qualifying test by reference to particular relationships such as husband and wife or parent and child for, as Lord Keith pointed out:[358]

---

[355] [2007] UKHL 39; [2008] A.C. 281 at [91] per Lord Rodger.

[356] In Scotland s.1 of the Damages (Asbestos-Related Conditions) (Scotland) Act 2009 provides:

"(1) Asbestos-related pleural plaques are a personal injury which is not negligible.

(2) Accordingly, they constitute actionable harm for the purposes of an action of damages for personal injuries.

(3) Any rule of law the effect of which is that asbestos-related pleural plaques do not constitute actionable harm ceases to apply to the extent it has that effect.

(4) But nothing in this section otherwise affects any enactment or rule of law which determines whether and in what circumstances a person may be liable in damages in respect of personal injuries."

This provision has retroactive effect and clearly allows recovery for mere anxiety about plaques but damages will presumably be modest. A constitutional challenge to the legislation failed in *Axa General Insurance Ltd v HM Advocate* [2011] UKSC 46; [2012] 1 A.C. 868. In England, the Ministry of Justice on February 25, 2010, announced that it was to make payments of £5,000 to persons who had begun but not resolved claims for pleural plaques before *Rothwell* but that it was not minded to reverse that decision.

[357] [1992] 1 A.C. 310.

[358] *Alcock* [1992] 1 A.C. 310 at 397.

"[T]he kinds of relationship which may involve close ties of love and affection are numerous, and it is the existence of such ties which leads to mental disturbance when the loved one suffers a catastrophe. They may be present in family relationships or those of close friendship, and may be stronger in the case of engaged couples than in that of persons who have been married to each other for many years."

The question is therefore whether there is a sufficiently close relationship of love and affection in fact between the claimant and the person injured or threatened, subject to the practical qualifications that a sufficiently close relationship will be presumed in the case of the relationship of parent and child or husband and wife and perhaps engaged couples but the claims of remoter relatives will be scrutinised with care. The effect is that those falling outside the narrow category have to show a relationship which is more intense than that usually found. The only claimants in *Alcock* who satisfied this requirement failed on the next ground.

In *Alcock* three judges left open the possibility that a mere bystander might have a claim if the circumstances of the accident were unusually horrific, as where a petrol tanker collided with a school in session.[359] However, the Court of Appeal in *McFarlane v EE Caledonia Ltd*,[360] a case arising out of the Piper Alpha oil rig disaster, rejected this extension, on the ground that it ran counter to the general thrust of *Alcock* and would present practical problems since reactions to horrific events are subjective and variable.

Even where there is a very close relationship, the thin skull rule does not apply, so a parent who suffers a hysterical and disproportionate reaction to a minor injury to his child may fail.[361]

There must be sufficient proximity in time and space to the event that resulted in the mental injury. The second element which must be satisfied is that there must be sufficient proximity of time and space in relation to the event leading to the mental injury. This requirement was fatal to the claim in *Taylor v A Novo (UK) Ltd*.[362] The claimant in this case watched her mother unexpectedly collapse and die. The claimant's mother had been negligently injured by the defendant three weeks earlier. The Court of Appeal said that the relevant event was the accident rather than the death and that necessary proximity with the accident was lacking.

However, this requirement will be satisfied if the claimant can establish sufficient proximity to the "immediate aftermath" of the event. In *McLoughlin v O'Brian*[363] a road accident caused by the defendant's negligence killed the claimant's young daughter and caused injuries of varying severity to other of her children and to her husband. At the time the claimant was at home two miles away. An hour later the accident was reported to the claimant by a friend, who drove the claimant to the hospital in Cambridge. Upon arrival, the claimant was told of the death and saw the injured members of her family in circumstances which, it was found, were "distressing in the extreme and were capable of

5–090

---

[359] Lord Ackner's example at [1992] 1 A.C. 310 at 403. See also Lord Keith at 397 and Lord Oliver at 416.
[360] *McFarlane v EE Caledonia Ltd* [1994] 2 All E.R. 1.
[361] *Vanek v Great Atlantic etc. Co of Canada* (1999) 180 D.L.R. (4th) 748; *Mustapha v Culligan of Canada Ltd* [2008] SCC 27; [2008] 2 S.C.R. 114 (bizarre reaction to fly in bottle of water).
[362] [2013] EWCA Civ 194; [2014] Q.B. 150.
[363] [1983] 1 A.C. 410. See also *Kelly v Hennessy* [1996] 1 I.L.R.M. 321.

producing an effect going well beyond that of grief and sorrow".[364] The House of Lords held that this qualified as the "immediate aftermath" of the accident and, consequently, the proximity requirement was satisfied and the claim was upheld. *McLoughlin* was considered in *Alcock*. However, *McLoughlin* was distinguished because in *Alcock* the interval between the accident and the sight of the bodies by the claimants was longer (nine hours)[365] and (at least according to Lord Jauncey) because the purpose was formal identification, rather than aid and comfort.[366]

5–091   **The psychiatric injury must have been caused by sight or hearing of the event or its immediate aftermath.** The third element, the means by which the injury is caused, requires that it must be by sight or hearing of the event or its immediate aftermath. Notification by third parties (including newspaper or broadcast reports) will not do. In practical terms, a claimant who fails on the second element will not be able to satisfy this requirement, though it is possible that there could be a case in which the claimant was in the vicinity but failed to satisfy the third requirement. However, in *Alcock* the House of Lords did not altogether rule out the possibility of liability where the mental injury was induced by contemporaneous television transmission of the incident, two members using the example given by Nolan LJ in the Court of Appeal of a live television broadcast of a ballooning event for children, watched by parents, in which the balloon bursts into flames. In *Alcock* itself the television transmission showed the developing chaos in the stadium and no doubt provided the framework in which the fear of the claimants for their loved ones developed, but it did not show the suffering of identifiable individuals and therefore lacked the immediacy necessary to found a claim.[367] The illness must be caused by the "sudden appreciation by sight or sound of a horrifying event which violently agitated the mind".[368]

iv. Participants other than Mere Bystanders

5–092   **Rescuers.** *Frost v CC South Yorkshire*,[369] a second case that arose from the Hillsborough disaster, provides guidance as to the position of rescuers who suffer mental injury in the course of rendering assistance. This time the claimants were police officers who were not in physical danger from the crush in the pens (if they had been they would have been primary victims) but who tended the victims of the tragedy in various ways and who claimed to have suffered mental injury as a result. The House of Lords held that there was no special category of rescuers and

---

[364] [1983] 1 A.C. 410 at 417.
[365] See also *Palmer v Tees HA* [2000] P.I.Q.R. P1; *Spence v Percy* [1992] 2 Qd. R. 299.
[366] Cf. *Galli-Atkinson v Seghal* [2003] EWCA Civ 697; [2003] Lloyd's Rep. Med 285 (visit to mortuary not merely for formal identification but for claimant to convince herself of the death; body in very badly disfigured condition).
[367] "It would be inaccurate and hurtful to suggest that grief is made any the less real or deprivation more tolerable by a mere gradual realisation, but to extend liability to cover injury in such cases would be to extend the law in a direction for which there is no pressing policy and in which there is no logical stopping point": [1992] 1 A.C. 310 at 416 per Lord Oliver.
[368] *Alcock* [1992] 1 A.C. 310 at 401 per Lord Ackner. Cf. *Walters v North Glamorgan NHS Trust* [2002] EWCA Civ 1792; [2003] Lloyd's Rep. Med. 49.
[369] [1999] 2 A.C. 455.

that the police officers were subject to the controls discussed earlier that apply to secondary victims. While it is well established that a rescuer may be owed a duty of care by the person responsible for the danger,[370] that is simply because the fact that he is engaged in a rescue makes his presence foreseeable and negatives the arguments that he has assumed the risk of injury or that his intervention has broken the chain of causation; it is not a reason for equating him with a primary victim (though of course he may fall into that category)[371] and for dispensing with the requirement that he should have a relationship of love and affection with those threatened. The claims of the relatives in the same disaster had failed in *Alcock* and the House of Lords was of the view that people in general: "[W]ould think it wrong that policemen, even as part of a general class of persons who rendered assistance, should have the right to compensation for psychiatric injury out of public funds while the bereaved relatives are sent away with nothing."[372]

Employees. The claims in *Frost* were also advanced on the basis that the police officers were owed a duty of care by their employer,[373] which was responsible for the disaster. The House of Lords also rejected the proposition that a duty of care arose on this basis. Certainly the employer's duty of care may extend to cases of psychiatric injury to a worker,[374] but that does not dispense with the *Alcock* "control devices" where the claim is based on the worker's reaction to witnessing the injury or endangerment of a third party on a particular occasion.[375] Had the employment basis of the claims in *Frost* been accepted, the result would have been that the claims of the police officers would have succeeded, whereas those of ambulance crew performing the same function would have failed because their employers would not have been responsible for the disaster. The House indicated that the outcome might be different where the employer had reason to believe that a particular worker in an emergency service was susceptible to trauma from witnessing danger to others and took no steps to reduce this risk. In such a situation, it was suggested that it would be irrelevant whether the employer was responsible for the disaster.[376]

There may also be liability where the employer negligently causes the employee to think that he was an instrument of death or injury. In *Dooley v*

5–093

---

[370] See para.5–048.

[371] As in the case of the claimant in *Chadwick v British Transport Commission* [1967] 1 W.L.R. 912; cf. *Gregg v Ashbrae Ltd* [2006] NICA 17; [2006] N.I. 300. Claims by officers who worked within the pens seem to have been settled on the basis that they were at personal risk of physical injury: [1999] 2 A.C. 455 at 466.

[372] *White v CC South Yorkshire* [1999] 2 A.C. 455 at 510 per Lord Hoffmann.

[373] Strictly speaking, the police are not employees, but they are owed the same duty as those who are.

[374] See para.5–096.

[375] Thus in *Keen v Tayside Contracts* [2003] Scot CS 55; 2003 S.L.T. 500 the claim failed where the pursuer, a road worker, was required to remain at the scene while four burned bodies were removed from a crash. Cf. *Harrhy v Thames Trains Ltd* [2003] EWHC 2286 (QB).

[376] That, however, is more likely if the exposure is frequent (*Hartman v South Essex Mental Health etc. NHS Trust* [2005] EWCA Civ 6; [2005] I.R.L.R. 293) or prolonged (cf. *Harrhy v Thames Trains Ltd* [2003] EWHC 2120 (QB)). In *French v CC Sussex* [2006] EWCA Civ 312 officers became subject to criminal charges (dismissed) and disciplinary proceedings (largely not pursued) after a shooting incident which, they alleged, had been brought about by management failures. It was alleged that these events caused the officers to suffer mental injury. The claims were struck out. The Court said that "[t]he appellants' case involves postulating a duty of care on the part of employers towards their employees not to cause or permit an untoward event to occur that could foreseeably lead to

Cammell Laird & Co Ltd[377] the claimant, a crane operator, suffered shock when, by the negligence of his employers, the rope snapped and the load fell into the hold where the operator's colleagues were working.[378] Lord Oliver in *Alcock* regarded this as a case where the negligent act of the defendant had put the claimant in the position of thinking that he had been the involuntary instrument of death or injury to another and for that reason felt that it might not be subject to the *Alcock* restrictions.[379] In *Frost* Lord Hoffmann also said that there might be reason for regarding such cases as outside the *Alcock* control mechanisms for secondary victims.[380]

v. Claimant Shocked by Defendant's Exposure of Himself to Danger

5–094   In *Greatorex v Greatorex*[381] the defendant was seriously injured in a road accident due to his own fault. The claimant, a fire officer and the defendant's father, attended at the scene and contended that he had suffered post-traumatic stress disorder from seeing the defendant's injuries. The defendant was uninsured, so the claim was in reality one against the Motor Insurers' Bureau. The claimant, given the rather extraordinary circumstances, fulfilled the *Alcock* requirements for a secondary victim, but Cazalet J dismissed the claim on the ground that the defendant, as the primary victim, did not owe a duty of care to others not to inflict shock upon them by the self-infliction of his injuries. Given that the "relationship" requirement in *Alcock* would confine such claims to cases between close family members, to admit a duty of care would open up the possibility of undesirable litigation arising from domestic accidents or deliberate self-harm.[382] Furthermore, a duty to take care of oneself so as not to shock others would, it was said, impinge upon the defendant's right of self-determination.[383] Most people would probably be surprised if, on such facts, the general body of motorists, via the Motor Insurers' Bureau, were made to bear the cost of the injury inflicted by the defendant on his father. Nevertheless, the result may not be entirely just where another defendant is involved. If the accident is caused by the combined fault of the defendant (D1) and another person (D2), D1's own personal injury claim against D2 would be reduced for contributory negligence,

---

proceedings in which the employees' conduct would be in issue. It would not be appropriate for a lower court to make such an extension to the law of negligence and we see no prospect that the House of Lords would be minded to do so": at [34].

[377] [1951] 1 Lloyd's Rep. 271.

[378] In fact none of them was injured.

[379] [1992] 1 A.C. 310 at 408. See also *W v Essex CC* [2000] 2 W.L.R. 601 at 607.

[380] [1999] 2 A.C. 455 at 508.

[381] [2000] 1 W.L.R. 1970.

[382] This does not explain why there is no bar on a claim where one family member injures another, nor where member A endangers member B in the presence of member C.

[383] This reasoning cannot explain why, if D negligently gets himself into danger and C is physically injured trying to rescue him, D may be liable to C: *Harrison v British Railways Board* [1981] 3 All E.R. 679.

whereas D2 would be liable in full to the shock claimant and, because D1 would not be liable to the claimant, D2 would be unable to recover any contribution from him.[384]

vi. Other Situations

The primary/secondary victim distinction is not exhaustive. The view is sometimes taken that in all psychiatric trauma cases claimants must be placed in one or other of the primary/secondary victim categories, but the distinction was created around the case where there is sudden danger to the claimant or a third party and there are situations of liability (or possible liability) which bear no resemblance to that. These situations are considered here.

5–095

Prolonged exposure to a stressful situation. Most psychiatric injury cases arise from accidents caused by the defendant's negligence that threaten injury to the claimant or, more usually, which injure or threaten injury to a third party. However, claims in other situations are possible. Liability has, for example, been imposed for mental trauma caused by long drawn out exposure to stress,[385] usually at work. Plainly here there is no requirement that the injury must be a response to a sudden event. In these cases there are no special control mechanisms. Rather, the issue is simply whether the employer has fulfilled the general duty (which is a matter of contract as well as tort) which he owes not to injure his workers.[386] The employer must take account of the workers' individual weaknesses where these ought to be known to the employer[387] so one cannot apply the test of "persons of normal fortitude" which is used in respect of secondary victims of accidents, with whom the defendant will have had no prior connection. But the duty is still one of reasonable care and an employer is usually entitled to assume that the employee can withstand the normal pressures of the job unless he knows of some particular problem or vulnerability.[388] It has also been said that the employer will not incur liability if, having done what is reasonable[389] to reduce the risk, he declines to dismiss an employee who is willing to continue.[390] However, there may no longer be any absolute rule to this effect.[391]

5–096

---

[384] Of course, in a motor vehicle case all liabilities would end up with insurers collectively whichever line one adopts.

[385] *Hatton v Sutherland* [2002] EWCA Civ 76; [2002] I.C.R. 613; *Walker v Northumberland CC* [1995] I.C.R. 702; *Cross v Highlands and Islands Enterprise* [2001] I.R.L.R. 336.

[386] *Hatton v Sutherland* [2002] EWCA Civ 76; [2002] I.C.R. 613 at [22].

[387] See para.6–024.

[388] *Hatton v Sutherland* [2002] EWCA Civ 76; [2002] I.C.R. 613 at [29]. And what must be foreseeable is psychiatric injury, not just anger or resentment: *Fraser v State Hospitals Board for Scotland* 2001 S.L.T. 1051.

[389] In the light of the terms of the contract, which is an essential part of the picture, though the relationship of the contract and the tort duty has not been explored much in the cases: *Barber v Somerset CC* [2004] UKHL 13; [2004] 1 W.L.R. 1089 at [35] per Lord Rodger.

[390] *Hatton* [2002] EWCA Civ 76; [2002] I.C.R. 613 at [43].

[391] See *Coxall v Goodyear Great Britain Ltd* [2002] EWCA Civ 1010; [2003] 1 W.L.R. 536 and para.9–025.

5–097   **Prior relationship.** Similar issues may arise in other relationships, for example that of a school and pupil.[392] In *Leach v CC Gloucestershire*[393] the claimant had agreed to act as the "responsible adult" required under the Police and Criminal Evidence Act 1984 where the police interview a person who may be mentally disordered, and she claimed that she suffered psychiatric injury and a stroke as a result of her involvement and that the police ought to have been aware that she was susceptible to this. The majority of the Court of Appeal struck out the claim on the basis that if the police owed a duty to safeguard the claimant's mental well-being that might impede their investigation of the offence; however, that aspect of her claim which was based on failure to offer counselling was allowed to go forward because that was offered to police officers in the case and would not have interfered with the investigative process.[394]

Another case which does not fit easily into the tidy categories created in the accident cases is *W v Essex CC*[395] in which the House of Lords refused to strike out a claim based on parents' reaction to the discovery that they had taken into their home a foster child who had a history of abusing other children and had taken the opportunity to abuse their children. It was not a case of witnessing a sudden event threatening their children, nor were the parents in any danger; but the case had some affinity with those where claimants had felt guilt at thinking themselves responsible for an accident[396] and on the pleaded facts the defendants had knowingly sent a child with a history of abuse even though the parents had made it clear that they would not take such a child.

Damages have been recovered for psychiatric illness where a spouse's children were kidnapped as a result of the negligence of a solicitor engaged in the matrimonial proceedings,[397] where organs were removed from deceased children without the parents' consent[398] and where the claimant was falsely informed of the death of her child soon after birth.[399] The Court of Appeal has declined to strike out a claim where the alleged negligence of the defendants caused a loss of liberty.[400]

5–098   **Psychiatric injury resulting from damage to property.** Claims may arise where psychiatric trauma is caused by damage to property. In *Attia v British Gas Plc*[401] the Court of Appeal declined to strike out a claim for psychiatric illness arising from the defendant's negligent destruction of the claimant's house by fire. In *Attia* the claimant witnessed the fire. What would have happened if she had been abroad, had been told of it on the telephone and suffered the same trauma? It

---

[392] *Bradford-Smart v West Sussex CC* [2002] EWCA Civ 7 (bullying).

[393] [1999] 1 W.L.R. 1421.

[394] In *Swinney v CC Northumbria* [1997] Q.B. 464 the claimants claimed that they were suffering from psychiatric illnesses because they had been threatened with violence and arson after some confidential information furnished by the first claimant to the police had been stolen from a police vehicle broken into by criminals. The claim was allowed to proceed. The court did not pay any particular attention to the fact that the claims were for damages for psychiatric illness.

[395] [2001] 2 A.C. 592.

[396] See para.5–093.

[397] *Al-Kandari v JR Brown & Co* [1988] Q.B. 665.

[398] *Organ Retention Group Litigation, Re*, [2004] EWHC 644 (QB); [2005] Q.B. 506.

[399] *Allin v City & Hackney HA* (1996) 7 Med. L.R. 91 (but the duty issue was conceded).

[400] *McLoughlin v Grovers* [2001] EWCA Civ 1743; [2002] Q.B. 1312.

[401] [1988] Q.B. 304.

would be strange if she could recover when a person told of the death of his child cannot recover under the *Alcock* principles. Yet a person may recover damages for mental distress falling well short of psychiatric illness in certain types of claim for breach of a contract, e.g. to provide a holiday[402] or damages for inconvenience consequent on a negligent survey,[403] where peace of mind is an important element in the obligation undertaken, so it would be hard to support a principle which automatically rejected the claim of a householder whose home and possessions were destroyed before his eyes.[404] The same could perhaps be said of one who suffered shock by hearing of the destruction of his home. In *Yearworth v North Bristol NHS Trust*[405] some of the claimants claimed to have suffered psychiatric trauma from hearing of the destruction of sperm samples which they had deposited for storage before treatment which affected their fertility. Others suffered a lesser degree of mental distress. The Court of Appeal found it unnecessary to decide the fate of their claims in tort because there was a bailment which, although non-contractual, involved a specific promise to the claimants and should therefore be treated as akin to a claim in contract for this purpose. Accordingly, all the claimants would be able to recover if they showed that their loss was foreseeable.

---

[402] *Jarvis v Swans Tours Ltd* [1973] 1 Q.B. 233.

[403] *Farley v Skinner* [2001] UKHL 49; [2002] 2 A.C. 732

[404] It is difficult to know how to classify the strange case of *Owens v Liverpool Corp* [1939] 1 K.B. 394, where mourners recovered damages when they witnessed a collision involving the hearse, the overturning of the coffin and the threat that the contents might fall out. It seems unrealistic to treat it as a case of a threat to property (there is no property in a corpse). It does not fall within *Alcock* since no "third person" was endangered, yet one can imagine that such an event would be traumatic for the widow. Lord Oliver in *Alcock* doubted whether the case could any longer be relied on.

[405] [2009] EWCA Civ 37; [2009] 3 W.L.R. 118.

CHAPTER 6

NEGLIGENCE: BREACH OF DUTY

1.   INTRODUCTION

The defendant will breach his duty of care if he acts negligently. A defendant   6–001
will only be liable in the tort of negligence if he breaches his duty of care, that is
to say, acts negligently. The test for deciding whether there has been a breach of
duty is laid down in the oft-cited dictum of Alderson B in *Blyth v Birmingham
Waterworks Co.* Alderson B said: "Negligence is the omission to do something
which a reasonable man, guided upon those considerations which ordinarily
regulate the conduct of human affairs, would do, or doing something which a
prudent and reasonable man would not do."[1] Put differently, a defendant will be
in breach of his duty of care if he takes less care than the reasonable person
would have taken. The concept of the reasonable person, which is one of the most
important and ubiquitous constructs in the entire law of torts, has already been
mentioned briefly.[2] This chapter develops that account. The focus is firmly on the
reasonable person in the context of the tort of negligence. However, what is said
here is to a large extent equally applicable to the many other contexts within tort
law in which the reasonable person features.

An objective enquiry. A critical point to bear in mind throughout the analysis,   6–002
and one that is hence worth stressing at the outset, is that because the reasonable
person is invoked, the breach element poses an objective enquiry as to the
adequacy of the defendant's conduct. The reasonable person sets an impersonal
standard that eliminates the idiosyncrasies of the defendant.[3] The defendant is
judged not against the benchmark of what could reasonably have been expected
of him, but against the yardstick of the reasonable person.

Incompetent defendants. The fact that the standard of care is determined   6–003
objectively means that defendants who are incapable of achieving the standard of
the reasonable person may incur liability in negligence. Whether or not this rule

---

[1] (1856) 11 Ex. 781 at 784.
[2] See para.3–009.
[3] See para.6–009.

[143]

is just is one of the most disputed points in the whole of the law of torts.[4] On the one hand, it seems grossly unfair to hold a defendant liable for failing to take care that he was incapable of taking (although this unfairness might be mitigated to a degree on account of the fact that most defendants are insured). On the other hand, it is usually a matter of luck from the perspective of the claimant whether he was injured by a negligent but capable defendant or by a negligent but incapable defendant, and is it fair to the claimant to deny recovery where he has the "misfortune" of being injured by an incapable defendant?

6–004 **Especially capable defendants.** What is the position in relation to defendants who are exceptionally capable[5] and are able to easily exceed the standard of the reasonable person? Are they permitted to "live down" to the standard of the reasonable person? Or are they held to, for example, the standard of care that could reasonably be expected of them given their ability?[6] The position is unclear, although traces of authority suggest that provided the standard of the reasonable person is met, it is irrelevant that the defendant was capable of exceeding that standard but failed to do so.[7] This solution has the significant advantage of simplicity. It means that the same standard—that of the reasonable person—applies irrespective of the abilities of the defendant.

6–005 **The process of determining whether the defendant breached his duty of care.** The process of determining whether there has been a breach of duty involves three steps. These steps are often not neatly separated from each other, but it is essential to distinguish between them if one is to understand properly this area of the law. First, it is necessary to ascertain the qualities of the reasonable person. This is a question of law. Secondly, it must be asked how much care the reasonable person, given the qualities attributed to him, would have taken in the circumstances. The factors that are permissible to take into account in this regard are prescribed by the law, but the amount of care that the reasonable person would have taken given those factors is a question of fact.[8] Thirdly, it must be determined whether the defendant took less care of the claimant's interests than the reasonable person would have taken. This is a question of fact. If the defendant took less care than the reasonable person would have taken, the defendant will be found to have acted negligently, and the breach element of the tort of negligence will be satisfied. This chapter investigates these three steps. In the vast majority of cases in which the breach element is in issue only the third step is in dispute.

---

[4] Honoré (1988) 104 L.Q.R. 530; Weinrib, *The Idea of Private Law* (1995), Ch.6; Cane, *Responsibility in Law and Morality* (2002), Ch.3; Goudkamp (2004) 28 M.U.L.R. 343; Goldberg and Zipursky (2007) 92 Cornell L. Rev. 1123.

[5] As was the case in *Heydon v NRMA Ltd* (2000) 51 N.S.W.L.R. 1; *R. v Banister* [2009] EWCA Crim 1571 (noted in Goudkamp [2010] C.L.J. 8).

[6] The issue is explored in Goudkamp (2004) 12 Tort L. Rev. 111.

[7] *Rust v Needham* (1974) 9 S.A.S.R. 510 at 523; *Heydon v NRMA Ltd* (2000) 51 N.S.W.L.R. 1 at 53, 117, 236.

[8] "What is reasonable care in a particular circumstance is a jury question": *Wooldridge v Sumner* [1962] 2 All E.R. 978 at 988 per Diplock LJ.

2. THE QUALITIES OF THE REASONABLE PERSON

The general characteristics of the reasonable person. The reasonable person **6–006** does not suffer from defects in his constitution, but neither is he an individual of exceptional ability or skill. Thus, the reasonable person does not have the courage of Achilles, the wisdom of Ulysses or the strength of Hercules. Nor does he have "the prophetic vision of a clairvoyant".[9] The reasonable person is not a perfect citizen or a "paragon of circumspection"[10] and therefore will not anticipate folly in all its forms. However, he never puts out of consideration the teachings of experience and so will guard against the negligence of others when experience shows such negligence to be common.[11] While the reasonable person is not all-seeing and all-knowing and can therefore make reasonable mistakes, he is not the average person. This is principally because he always acts reasonably. In reality, no individual is infallible and even the most careful person will, on a few occasions, fail to take reasonable care. In the limited sense that the legal personification of due care never takes less than reasonable care he does not resemble any human being.

The reasonable person is attributed with such knowledge of the world as would **6–007** have been reasonable to have at the time of the alleged breach of duty. Thus, if an accident occurred five years before the trial, the reasonable person would have had reasonable knowledge about the world according to the standards that prevailed at the time of the accident rather than according to the standards that existed at the time of the trial. In *Roe v Minister of Health*[12] the claimant was, in 1947, a patient in a hospital. An anaesthetist administered a spinal anaesthetic to the claimant in preparation for a minor operation. The anaesthetic was contained in a glass ampoule which had been kept in a solution of phenol. Unfortunately, some of the phenol had made its way through an "invisible crack" into the ampoule. The phenol thus contaminated the anaesthetic, with the result being that the claimant became permanently paralysed from the waist down. The anaesthetist was aware of the consequences of injecting phenol, and he therefore subjected the ampoule to a visual examination before administering the anaesthetic, but he was not aware of the possibility of invisible cracks. Had he been aware of this possibility, the danger to the claimant could have been eliminated by adding a colouring agent to the phenol so that contamination of the anaesthetic could have been observed. It was held that he was not negligent in failing to take this step because the risk of invisible cracks had not been drawn to the attention of the profession until 1951. Morris LJ said: "[C]are has to be exercised to ensure that conduct in 1947 is only judged in the light of knowledge which then was or ought reasonably to have been possessed. In this connexion the then-existing state of medical literature must be had in mind".[13]

---

[9] *Hawkins v Coulsdon & Purley UDC* [1954] 1 Q.B. 319 at 341 per Romer LJ.
[10] *AC Billings & Sons Ltd v Riden* [1958] A.C. 240 at 255 per Lord Reid. For a brilliant caricature of "this excellent but odious creature" see Herbert, *Uncommon Law* (1935), pp.1–5.
[11] *London Passenger Transport Board v Upson* [1949] A.C. 155 at 173, 176; *Lang v London Transport Executive* [1959] 1 W.L.R. 1168 at 1175.
[12] [1954] 2 Q.B. 66.
[13] [1954] 2 Q.B. 66 at 92.

6–008   **The reasonable person is placed in the position of the defendant.** The reasonable person is placed into the shoes of the defendant at the time of the alleged breach of duty. Thus, if the defendant is a motorist, it is asked how much care the reasonable motorist would have taken, and if the defendant is a golfer, the question becomes how much care would the reasonable golfer have taken. This principle can have important consequences. It means that a footballer is not expected to take as much care for another player's safety as if he were going on a leisurely walk with the latter in the countryside.[14] Similarly, if the defendant is undertaking some activity in a domestic context he will not be held to the standards that would be expected in a business setting.[15] Thus, a householder who does some repair work in his house is not required to show the skill which might be required of a professional carpenter—he need only do his work with the skill of a reasonably competent householder doing the work in question.[16] This principle also dictates that a jeweller who pierces ears is held to the hygiene standards of the reasonable jeweller, rather than those of the reasonable surgeon.[17]

6–009   **The reasonable person is generally not attributed with the shortcomings of the defendant.** Generally speaking, the reasonable person is not attributed with the defendant's shortcomings.[18] Accordingly, no allowance is made in determining the qualities of the reasonable person for the fact that the defendant was, for example, blind, deaf, intoxicated, dim-witted[19] or insane.[20] Nor is any account normally taken of the fact that the defendant is a beginner or inexperienced. The leading authority on this point is *Nettleship v Weston*, in which the Court of Appeal held that the defendant learner driver should be judged by reference to the standard of the reasonable experienced driver,[21] even where the claimant was her instructor.[22] The Court was heavily influenced by the presence of compulsory insurance, but the holding is consistent with the general rule that the standard of the reasonable person eliminates the personal attributes of the defendant.

6–010   **Exceptionally, the courts take the defendant's limitations into account.** Occasionally, the courts take account of the defendant's subjective qualities. An example of a case in which this happened is *Goldman v Hargrave* where, in dealing with the liability of the defendant for failing to extinguish a fire started on his land by natural causes, the Privy Council held that the standard was what it was reasonable to expect of him in the individual circumstances. The Privy Council's advice was that "[l]ess must be expected of the infirm than of the able-bodied . . . [and the defendant] should not be liable unless it is clearly proved that he could, and reasonably in his individual circumstances should, have done

---

[14] *Condon v Basi* [1985] 1 W.L.R. 866.
[15] *Surtees v Kingston on Thames BC* [1991] 2 F.L.R. 559.
[16] *Wells v Cooper* [1958] 2 Q.B. 265.
[17] *Phillips v William Whiteley Ltd* [1938] 1 All E.R. 566
[18] For discussion of this rule, and departures from it, see Seavey (1927) 41 Harv. L. Rev. 1.
[19] *Vaughan v Menlove* (1837) 3 Bing N.C. 468; 132 E.R. 490.
[20] Goudkamp (2012) 31 O.J.L.S. 727.
[21] [1971] 2 Q.B. 691.
[22] Cf. *Vowles v Evans* [2003] EWCA Civ 318; [2003] 1 W.L.R. 1607 at [28].

more".[23] This, however, was a case in which the defendant was making no unusual use of his land and had a risk thrust upon him by no fault of his own. It seems, therefore, that this approach would not be employed where the danger arose from the defendant's activity, even where the activity is a public service operating with limited resources.[24] Generally speaking, if the defendant embarks on an activity he must ensure that he has the skill and resources to complete it without exposing others to unreasonable risks.

The professional post occupied by the defendant. The objective standard appears to make no allowance for the fact that everyone must, to some extent, learn by practical experience on the job. Novices must achieve the same benchmark as everyone else.[25] The potential for unfairness that this rule is liable to produce was pressed upon the Court of Appeal in *Wilsher v Essex Area Health Authority*.[26] In this case, one of the defendants was a junior doctor of limited experience. It was put to the court that what should be expected of an individual doctor was what was reasonably required of a person of his qualifications and experience. The majority rejected this argument on the ground that it would entail that "the standard of care which the patient is entitled to demand [would] vary according to the chance of recruitment and rostering".[27] Rather, the standard was to be set by reference to the post held by the defendant in the unit in which he operated.[28] A junior member of the team could not be expected to show the skill of a consultant, but subject to that no allowance would be made for the inexperience of the individual any more than for his domestic circumstances or his financial worries, either of which might equally contribute to an error. This principle means that a "general practitioner" (whether in medicine, law, the valuation of pictures or any other trade or profession) will not be held to the standard of a specialist, but he should possess a sense of when it is necessary to take appropriate specialist advice.[29] It also follows that a specialist will be held to the higher standard of those practising within that specialism. *Wilsher* can be interpreted both as affirming the rule that no account will be taken of the fact that the defendant is a beginner,[30] and the rule that the reasonable person is placed in the position of the defendant.[31]

6–011

Account is taken of the conditions with which the defendant was faced. The principle that the reasonable person is placed in the position of the defendant

6–012

---

[23] [1967] 1 A.C. 645 at 663, see para.15–047.

[24] *PQ v Australian Red Cross Society* [1992] V.R. 19 (where charity required to test blood for HIV); cf. *Knight v Home Office* [1990] 3 All E.R. 237 (claimant's husband committed suicide in prison hospital).

[25] See para.6–009.

[26] [1987] Q.B. 730. The case was reversed by the House of Lords but not on this point: [1988] A.C. 1074.

[27] [1987] Q.B. 730 at 750 per Mustill LJ.

[28] It has been held that a barrister "must conduct himself in his professional work with the competence (care and skill) of a barrister of ordinary skill who is competent to handle that type of and weight of work and a breach of that duty occurs when the error is one which no reasonably competent member of the profession possessing those skills should have made": *McFaddens v Platford* [2009] EWHC 126 (TCC) at [49].

[29] *Luxmore-May v Messenger May Baverstock* [1990] 1 W.L.R. 1009.

[30] See para.6–009.

[31] See para.6–008.

means that account must be taken of the pressures of the situation in which the defendant found himself. For example, if the defendant was confronted with an emergency,[32] challenging conditions, the need to make a decision on the spur of the moment[33] or a novel problem,[34] it will be asked how the reasonable person would manage if placed in such a predicament.

6–013 **Childhood.** It is a well-established principle that if the defendant is a child, the adequacy of his conduct will be judged against the standard set by a reasonable child of the same age.[35] The reason for this rule has never been made sufficiently clear. Why should the fact that the defendant is a child be taken into account, but not other qualities? One possible answer to this question is that age is not truly idiosyncratic: everyone begins their life as a child. It is unclear whether allowances are made for the defendant's age when the defendant is elderly. There is a lack of case law on this point. An exception to the rule that the defendant's tender age is attributed to the reasonable person is where the defendant, although he is a child, was engaged in an adult activity at the time of the alleged wrongdoing. In this situation, the defendant's age is ignored.[36] For example, if a 10-year-old defendant takes his parents' car he will be held to the standard of the reasonable adult motorist.[37]

6–014 **Sudden incapacitation of the defendant.** If the defendant is suddenly incapacitated through no fault of his own (suppose that he suffered from a spontaneous blackout[38]) the defendant will not be liable in negligence for any damage that he inflicts. There are several ways of explaining this result. One way in which it can be accounted for is on the ground that the defendant did as well in the circumstances as the reasonable person who suffered from the same condition would have done.[39] This attributes the condition from which the defendant suffered to the reasonable person. However, this solution sits uncomfortably with the principle that the reasonable person eliminates the subjective qualities of the defendant. Furthermore, the notion of the reasonable incapacitated person is arguably contradictory. Another way of accounting for this outcome is to say that a defendant who is suddenly incapacitated is not acting, and that in the absence of an act (or, exceptionally, a failure to act where there is a duty to act), no one can incur liability in tort.[40] This line of reasoning shifts the issue of sudden incapacitation out of the breach element. It is treated instead as negating a separate element—an "act element"—of the action in negligence. Such treatment

---

[32] *Greene v Sookdeo* [2009] UKPC 31.

[33] *Smoldon v Whitworth* [1997] P.I.Q.R. P133.

[34] *A v Tameside and Glossop HA* (1996) 35 B.M.L.R. 79 (how to inform patients that they had been treated by HIV positive members of staff).

[35] *Mullin v Richards* [1998] 1 W.L.R. 1304; *Blake v Galloway* [2004] EWCA Civ 814; [2004] 1 WLR 284; *Orchard v Lee* [2009] EWCA Civ 295; [2009] P.I.Q.R. P16.

[36] An infant defendant is required to meet the standard set by the reasonable adult where he is engaged in a "dangerous activity that is characteristically undertaken by adults": Restatement (Third) of Torts, § 10(c).

[37] *Tucker v Tucker* [1956] S.A.S.R. 297.

[38] See, e.g. *Robinson v Glover* [1952] N.Z.L.R. 669; *Dessaint v Carriere* [1958] O.W.N. 481; [1958] 17 D.L.R. (2d) 222; *Jones v Dennison* [1971] R.T.R. 174.

[39] This analysis was adopted in *Mansfield v Weetabix Ltd* [1998] 1 W.L.R. 1263.

[40] See Goudkamp, *Tort Law Defences* (2013), pp.48–49.

would require the conventional list of the elements of negligence[41] to be revised. An act element would need to be added to it.

The doctrine of prior fault. The question of whether conditions that result in the **6–015** defendant being suddenly incapacitated should be attributed to the reasonable person rarely arises in practice. This is because the issue can usually be sidestepped by virtue of the doctrine of prior fault. This doctrine, when it applies, fixes liability on the defendant not in respect of what happened at the time of the injury but at some earlier point. Suppose that D carelessly fails to take his heart medication and, while driving, suffers from a heart attack that the medication would have prevented. In driving without having taken his medication, D breached his duty of care.[42] Liability can be straightforwardly pinned on D for this carelessness and the issue of whether to attribute D's heart condition to the reasonable person can be bypassed.

Skills that the defendant holds himself out as possessing. Where a defendant **6–016** represents, expressly or by implication, that he possesses particular skills, the reasonable person will be attributed with those skills, regardless of whether the defendant actually has the skills concerned. Thus, where a brewing company owned a ship it was held that the board of directors of the company must exercise the same degree of care and skill in the management of the ship as would any other ship owner: "The law must apply a standard which is not relaxed to cater for their factual ignorance of all activities outside brewing: having become owners of ships, they must behave as reasonable shipowners."[43]

The reasonable person is imputed with special knowledge possessed by the **6–017** **defendant.** Usually, the reasonable person will only possess such knowledge of the world as ordinary, competent people would possess. However, if the defendant enjoys knowledge regarding the risk of injury that materialised that is above and beyond that which most similarly situated people would possess such knowledge will be attributed to the reasonable person.[44] This rule is, essentially, an exception to the principle that it is permissible for defendants who are able to take an exceptional level of care to live down to the standard of the reasonable person.[45]

General practice and new developments. The reasonable person takes account **6–018** of the general practice in the particular field in question. He also keeps his knowledge up-to-date.[46] However, the reasonable person is not necessarily an avid reader of scientific and technical periodicals,[47] and he may not learn of new knowledge until it becomes fairly widespread.[48] Even once the reasonable person acquires new knowledge, he may not put it into effect immediately. The fact that

---

[41] See para.5–002.
[42] *C (A child) v Burcombe*[2003] C.L.Y. 3030. See also *Kay v Butterworth* (1945) 110 J.P. 75.
[43] *The Lady Gwendolen* [1965] P. 294 at 350 per Winn LJ.
[44] *Baker v Quantum Clothing Group Ltd* [2011] UKSC 17; [2011] I.C.R. 523 at [104].
[45] This rule is discussed at para.6–004.
[46] *Stokes v GKN (Bolts and Nuts) Ltd* [1968] 1 W.L.R. 1776 at 1783.
[47] *Thompson v Smiths Shiprepairers (North Shields) Ltd* [1984] Q.B. 405.
[48] *N v UK Medical Research Council* [1996] 7 Med. L.R. 309 (failure to undertake thorough reappraisal of human growth hormone programme after the discovery of Creutzfeldt-Jakob disease risk); *Bowman v Harland & Wolff Plc* [1992] I.R.L.R. 349 (vibration white finger).

the defendant failed to comply or has complied with a general practice may be evidence for or against a finding of negligence. The use that can be made of such evidence is addressed later.[49]

3. HOW MUCH CARE WOULD THE REASONABLE PERSON HAVE TAKEN?

6–019   **A single standard of care.** According to conventional wisdom, there is only a single standard of care in the English law of torts, namely, that of the reasonable person. Of course, what taking reasonable care involves will vary with the facts of each case. But the test is usually thought to be the same in all cases. Defendants are not required to achieve more highly than the standard of the reasonable person, nor are they permitted to sink beneath it. For example, it would be possible for tort law to require gross negligence to be established on the part of a defendant in order to make out a breach of a duty of care, but this is not what tort law does. There are no degrees of negligence.[50] Theorists have questioned whether this traditional understanding is entirely accurate[51] and whether the standard of care should not be varied in certain circumstances.[52] It is not denied that there may be advantages in varying the standard of care on occasion, but the current single-standard approach has the merit of simplicity.

6–020   **The risk that materialised must have been reasonably foreseeable.** The first question to consider in asking how much care the reasonable person would have taken is whether the risk of injury that materialised was reasonably foreseeable.[53] This is of critical importance, since the reasonable person will take no precautions at all in respect of risks of injury that are not reasonably foreseeable. He will simply dismiss the existence of such dangers. Accordingly, unless the claimant can establish that the risk that materialised was reasonably foreseeable, he will be unable to establish that the defendant fell short of the standard of the reasonable person in respect of it.

6–021   **When is a risk of injury reasonably foreseeable?** Several points need to be made about the approach of the courts in determining whether a risk is reasonably foreseeable. First, the rule that the risk that materialised must be reasonably foreseeable is of limited practical significance. It is rare for a court to conclude that a risk is not reasonably foreseeable. It is commonplace for courts to hold that quite unusual risks are reasonably foreseeable.[54] Only exceptionally rare and far-fetched risks are likely to qualify as not reasonably foreseeable.[55] Cases in

---

[49] See para.6–033.
[50] See para.3–010.
[51] The *Bolam* principle (see para.6–034) is arguably an exception to it.
[52] Nolan (2013) 72 C.L.J. 651.
[53] Foreseeability is also important in relation to the duty of care (see para.5–027) and remoteness of damage (see para.7–033).
[54] For a high degree of prescience, see *Versic v Connors* (1969) 90 W.N. (N.S.W.) 33 (risk of drowning in a gutter as a result of a motor vehicle accident was reasonably foreseeable); *Bohlen v Perdue* [1976] 1 W.W.R. 364 (risk of injury to children who stuck their arm out of bus window where sufficiently sharp turns were made was reasonably foreseeable); *Chappel v Hart*(1998) 195 C.L.R. 232 (risk so rare that it was not mentioned in the medical textbooks was reasonably foreseeable).
[55] See Goudkamp (2008) 124 L.Q.R. 37.

which the claimant failed because the risk of injury was not reasonably foreseeable are few and far between.[56] Nevertheless, the risk must be one that is "not only imaginable, but that there is some reasonable prospect or expectation that it will arise".[57] Secondly, this is an area where different judges are likely to reach different conclusions. The question of whether a risk is reasonably foreseeable is not always susceptible of only one possible answer. "What to one judge may seem far-fetched may seem to another both natural and probable."[58] Thirdly, what is in question at this stage is the foreseeability of a risk, not the probability of it occurring. Quite improbable risks can be reasonably foreseeable. Conversely, there may be situations where risks that are not reasonably foreseeable are likely to occur. Fourthly, it is not necessary for the precise risk of injury that materialised to be reasonably foreseeable. All that is needed is for the general risk that eventuated to be reasonably foreseeable. This last point is borne out by *Alexis v Newham LBC*.[59] The claimant in this case was a school teacher. Two unsupervised pupils poured cleaning fluid into the claimant's water bottle, and the claimant was injured when she drank its contents. The court held that the requirement of reasonable foreseeability was satisfied. It was enough to foresee that unsupervised pupils might, if they were allowed to get up to mischief, create a situation where there was a danger to teaching staff. It did not matter that the precise danger was not reasonably foreseeable.[60]

The negligence calculus. If the risk of injury that materialised is reasonably foreseeable, the next question to address is how the reasonable person would have responded to it. This enquiry is sometimes referred to as the "negligence calculus". It involves weighing four factors: (1) the size of the risk; (2) the gravity of the risk (i.e. how serious would the likely harm be if the risk materialised); (3) the utility of the defendant's conduct; and (4) the cost of taking precautions. Describing this exercise as a calculus can be criticised on the ground that it suggests that it involves a mechanical or scientific process.[61] It is certainly true that the process involves the application of common sense and that there is no formula that can be applied to determine automatically the outcome in particular cases.

6–022

It is important to note several facts about the requirement to take reasonable care. First, reasonable care can involve doing nothing in respect of a particular risk. The reasonable person will advert to risks that are reasonably foreseeable but, very often, he will do nothing in an attempt to ameliorate the danger that they present, because that is what acting reasonably with respect to those risks entails.

---

[56] A rare case in which it was held that the risk was unforeseeable is *Tacagni v Penwith DC* [2013] EWCA Civ 702.

[57] *Fullowka v Royal Oak Ventures Inc* [2008] NWTCA 4; [2008] 7 W.W.R. 411 at [53].

[58] *Glasgow Corp v Muir* [1943] A.C. 448 at 457 per Lord Macmillan.

[59] [2009] EWHC 1323 (QB).

[60] [2009] EWHC 1323 (QB) at [99]–[100].

[61] "Reference to 'calculus', 'a certain way of performing mathematical investigations and resolutions', may wrongly be understood as requiring no more than a comparison between what it would have cost to avoid the particular injury that happened and the consequences of that injury": *New South Wales v Fahy* [2007] HCA 20; (2007) 81 A.L.J.R. 1021 at [57] (footnote omitted); "What is involved ... is not a calculation; it is a judgment": *Mulligan v Coffs Harbour City Council* [2005] HCA 63; (2005) 223 C.L.R. 486 at [2].

For instance, it is reasonably foreseeable that a person who enters an office may stumble and hit his head on the desk, but that does not mean that taking reasonable care involves eliminating desks from all offices or encasing them in bubble wrap. The reasonable thing to do in respect of this particular risk is nothing at all. As Gleeson CJ put it in the Australian case of *New South Wales v Fahy*: "There have been occasions when judges appear to have forgotten that the response of prudent and reasonable people to many of life's hazards is to do nothing."[62] A second point that is sometimes overlooked is that taking reasonable care may involve discontinuing the activity in question, rather than merely taking additional precautions in the course of the activity concerned.[63] Thirdly, taking reasonable care with respect to a given risk will often involve doing nothing more than warning of its existence.

6–023   **The magnitude of the risk.** This factor refers to the probability of the risk of injury occurring. The lower the likelihood that the risk would materialise, the more likely it is that the reasonable person would ignore it and vice versa. "The law in all cases exacts a degree of care commensurate with the risk."[64] In *Bolton v Stone*[65] the claimant was standing on the highway in a road adjoining a cricket ground when she was struck by a ball which a batsman had hit out of the ground. Such an event was reasonably foreseeable and, indeed, balls had to the defendant's knowledge occasionally been hit out of the ground before. Nevertheless, the House of Lords considered that the likelihood of injury to a person in the claimant's position was so slight that the cricket club was not negligent in allowing cricket to be played without having taken additional precautions. The House took into account several factors including the distance from the pitch to the edge of the ground, the presence of a 7 foot fence and the upward slope of the ground in the direction in which the ball was struck. In *Hilder v Associated Portland Cement Manufacturers Ltd*[66] the claimant's husband was riding his motorcycle along a road outside a piece of open land, occupied by the defendants, where children were permitted to play football, when a ball was kicked into the road and caused him to have an accident. The conditions were such that the likelihood of injury to passers-by was much greater than in *Bolton v Stone*, and accordingly the defendants were held liable for having permitted football to be played on their land without having taken any additional precautions.

6–024   **The gravity of the risk.** The relevance of the seriousness of the risk is illustrated by the decision of the House of Lords in *Paris v Stepney BC*.[67] The claimant, a one-eyed man, was employed by the defendants. The conditions in which he worked involved some risk of eye injury. The likelihood of injury was regarded

---

[62] *New South Wales v Fahy* [2007] HCA 20 at [6]. "[A]n ordinarily careful man does not take precautions against every foreseeable risk": *Bolton v Stone* [1951] A.C. 850 at 863 per Lord Oaksey.
[63] *Bolton v Stone* [1951] A.C. 850 at 867.
[64] *Read v J. Lyons & Co Ltd* [1974] A.C. 156 at 173 per Lord Macmillan. "As the danger increases, so must the precautions increase": *Lloyds Bank Ltd v Ry Executive* [1952] 1 All E.R. 1248 at 1253 per Denning LJ.
[65] [1951] A.C. 850. Cf. *Miller v Jackson* [1977] Q.B. 966, on somewhat similar facts.
[66] [1961] 1 W.L.R. 1434.
[67] [1951] A.C. 367.

as insufficient to require the defendants to provide goggles to a normal two-eyed workman. However, the House of Lords held that in the case of the claimant goggles should have been provided. This was because the risk to which he was exposed was total blindness, whereas the risk to a two-eyed man was a lesser one, namely, the loss of one eye. In assessing the gravity of the risk it is important to notice that the duty of care is owed to the claimant himself and therefore if he suffers from some disability that increases the gravity of the risk to him that disability must be taken into account so long as it is, or should be, known to the defendant.[68] If it is unknown and could not reasonably have been known then it is irrelevant.[69]

The utility of the defendant's conduct. Account must be taken of the benefits of the defendant's conduct that gave rise to the risk. As Asquith LJ said: "[I]f all the trains in this country were restricted to a speed of 5 miles an hour, there would be fewer accidents, but our national life would be intolerably slowed down. The purpose to be served, if sufficiently important, justifies the assumption of abnormal risk."[70] In *Watt v Hertfordshire CC*,[71] the claimant, a fireman, was injured by the movement of a heavy jack when travelling with it in a lorry that was not specially equipped to carry it. A woman had been trapped under a vehicle and the jack was urgently required to save her life. It was held that the fire authorities had not been negligent bearing in mind that the jack was needed in order to save a life.[72] While rescuers are treated sympathetically because of the value of their conduct,[73] the mere fact that a defendant is a rescuer does not mean that he cannot fall short of reasonable care.[74] Emergency services have no special exemption from liability in the tort of negligence.[75]   **6–025**

The cost of taking precautions. In determining how the reasonable person would have acted, it is necessary to take account of how practicable it would have   **6–026**

---

[68] *Haley v London Electricity Board* [1965] A.C. 778; *Baxter v Woolcombers* (1963) 107 S.J. 553 (claimant's low intelligence relevant to standard of care due to him); *Morrell v Owen, Times,* December 14, 1993 (coach of disabled athletes); *Walker v Northumberland CC* [1995] I.C.R. 702; *Hatton v Sutherland* [2002] EWCA Civ 76; [2002] I.C.R. 613 (susceptibility to stress).
[69] *Bourhill v Young* [1943] A.C. 92 at 109–110.
[70] *Daborn Bath Tramways* [1946] 2 All E.R. 333 at 336 (left-hand drive ambulance during emergency period of war not negligent in turning right without giving a signal). See also *Brisco v Secretary of State for Scotland* 1997 S.C. 14 (small risk of injury justified in training of prison officers). Cf. *Quinn v Scott* [1965] 1 W.L.R. 1004 (National Trust negligent in not felling dangerous tree near highway as safety of public must take precedence over preservation of the amenities).
[71] [1954] 1 W.L.R. 835.
[72] The outcome would have been different if the jack had been carried in the course of a commercial enterprise. "The commercial end to make profit is very different from the human end to save life or limb": [1954] 1 W.L.R. 835 at 838 per Denning LJ.
[73] *Marshall v Osmond* [1983] Q.B. 1034 (no liability by police for injury caused to suspect); *Scutts v MPC* [2001] EWCA Civ 715 (police responding to emergency); *Robinson v Chief Constable of West Yorkshire Police* [2014] EWCA Civ 15 (police not negligent in knocking down pedestrian while arresting drug dealer); *Craggy v CC Cleveland* [2009] EWCA Civ 1128 (collision between emergency vehicles).
[74] See, e.g. *Ward v LCC* [1938] 2 All E.R. 341; *Wardell-Yerburgh v Surrey CC* [1973] R.T.R. 462; *Rigby v CC Northamptonshire* [1985] 1 W.L.R. 1242; *Purdue v Devon Fire and Rescue Service* [2002] EWCA Civ 1538.
[75] Even though they may be exempt from criminal liability for, e.g. exceeding the speed limit. See *Gaynor v Allen* [1959] 2 Q.B. 403; *Griffin v Mersey Regional Ambulance* [1998] P.I.Q.R. P34.

been to eliminate or reduce the risk. As Lord Reid explained in *Morris v West Hartlepool Steam Navigation Co*, "the difficulty and expense and any other disadvantage of taking the precaution" must be factored into the standard of care.[76] In *Latimer v AEC*[77] a factory floor became slippery after a flood. The occupiers of the factory went to considerable lengths to get rid of the effects of the flood, but the claimant was nevertheless injured and contended that the occupiers should have closed the factory. The House of Lords held that the reasonable person would not have taken this precaution.[78] The greater the risk, the less receptive a court is likely to be to a defence based simply upon the cost, in terms of money, of the required precautions[79] and there are likely be activities that are so dangerous that they must be abandoned altogether.

Costs other than financial costs must be considered. This includes the inconvenience that the precautions might cause[80] and the possibility that taking precautions might create new risks.[81] Also relevant is the extent to which taking precautions would interfere with autonomy.[82] Tea and coffee are only palatable when they are made with hot water; people generally want them to be served hot and a person who caters for that is not negligent merely because there is some risk of scalding.[83] If the law goes too far in setting the standard of care required the legitimate activities of people in general will be curtailed. The point is made with great force by the House of Lords in *Tomlinson v Congleton BC*.[84] The claimant had been catastrophically injured when he dived into a lake on land occupied by the defendant. The House rejected the argument that the defendant should have taken effective steps to keep people away from the water. Lord Hoffmann said:[85]

> "I think that there is an important question of freedom at stake. It is unjust that the harmless recreation of responsible parents and children with buckets and spades on the beaches should be prohibited in order to comply with what is thought to be a legal duty to safeguard irresponsible visitors against dangers which are perfectly obvious. The fact that such people take no notice of warnings cannot create a duty to take other steps to protect them . . . A duty to protect against obvious risks or self-inflicted harm exists only in cases in which there is no genuine and informed choice, as in the case of employees whose work requires them to take the risk, or some lack of capacity, such as the inability of children to recognise danger . . . or the despair of prisoners which may lead them to inflict injury on themselves . . .

---

[76] [1956] A.C. 552 at 574.

[77] [1953] A.C. 643. Cf. *Bolton* [1951] A.C. 850 at 867 per Lord Reid: "I think that it would be right to take into account not only how remote is the chance that a person might be struck but also how serious the consequences are likely to be if a person is struck; but I do not think that it would be right to take into account the difficulty of remedial measures."

[78] In *Gough v Upshire Primary School* [2002] E.L.R. 169 the fact that a child might slide down a banister was perfectly foreseeable, but that did not require alteration of the staircase.

[79] See, e.g. *Morris v Luton Corp* [1946] 1 All E.R. 1 at 4 per Lord Greene MR (the report of this case at [1946] K.B. 116 is incomplete); *Christmas v General Cleaning Contractors* [1952] 1 K.B. 141 at 149 per Denning LJ (affirmed [1953] A.C. 180).

[80] *Yorkshire Traction Co Ltd v Searby* [2003] EWCA Civ 1856.

[81] *Morris v West Hartlepool Steam Navigation Co Ltd* [1956] A.C. 552

[82] This is a relevant consideration pursuant to s.1 of the Compensation Act 2006. Section 1 is discussed in para.1–052.

[83] *Bogle v McDonald's Restaurants Ltd* [2002] EWHC 490 (QB).

[84] [2003] UKHL 47; [2004] 1 A.C. 46.

[85] [2003] UKHL 47; [2004] 1 A.C. 46 at [46]. See also *Keown v Coventry Healthcare NHS Trust* [2006] EWCA Civ 39; [2006] 1 W.L.R. 953 at [17].

It is of course understandable that organisations like the Royal Society for the Prevention of Accidents should favour policies which require people to be prevented from taking risks. Their function is to prevent accidents and that is one way of doing so. But they do not have to consider the cost, not only in money but also in deprivation of liberty, which such restrictions entail. The courts will naturally respect the technical expertise of such organisations in drawing attention to what can be done to prevent accidents. But the balance between risk on the one hand and individual autonomy on the other is not a matter of expert opinion. It is a judgment which the courts must make and which in England reflects the individualist values of the common law."

A cost/benefit analysis? The foregoing factors have sometimes been thought to create, or to call for, a cost/benefit analysis of the breach of duty element. Especially in the United States, it has been argued that the breach element can be explained entirely in economic terms.[86] The idea is that the negligence calculus can be interpreted as imposing liability where the burden of taking precautions is less than the damage suffered by the materialisation of the risk in question bearing in mind the probability of that risk occurring. It is clear, however, that English courts and, indeed, Commonwealth courts generally, have not reduced the breach of duty element to an economic question. McHugh JA summed up the position in Commonwealth jurisdictions as follows: "Negligence is not an economic cost/benefit equation. Immeasurable 'soft' values such as community concepts of justice, health, life and freedom of conduct have to be taken into account."[87]

6–027

Relaxation of the standard of care where the defendant is a child. It has been explained earlier that where the defendant is a child, the reasonable person will be imputed with the defendant's age.[88] This can have important implications since the reasonable child does not take as much care as the reasonable adult. As a result, the fact that the defendant is a child operates to the defendant's advantage. The defendant is held to a lower standard of care than that to which he would be held were he an adult. This principle often exerts a powerful effect on the outcomes of cases where the defendant is, say, 10 years old. Cases in which defendants of such tender years have been held liable are rare. Conversely, the standard of care will hardly be reduced at all where the defendant is just shy of reaching the age of majority. Although infancy is not a defence to liability in tort,[89] and defendants of all ages are in principle subject to the law of torts, if the defendant so young that he is incapable of taking any precautions or exercising any care, liability cannot arise. This is because it is impossible for a defendant to sink below such a standard.[90]

6–028

Hindsight bias. Before leaving the issue of the standard of care it is worth emphasising that it is easy to be wise after the event. This must be kept in mind when asking what the reasonable person in the defendant's position would have done. The defendant should not be judged with the benefit of hindsight.[91] It is

6–029

---

[86] See, e.g. Posner, *Economic Analysis of Law*, 7th edn (2007), Ch.6. Cf. Wright (2003) 4 Theoretical Inq. L. 1; Zipursky (2007) 48 Wm. & Mary L. Rev. 1999.
[87] *Western Suburbs Hospital v Currie* (1987) 9 N.S.W.L.R. 511 at 523.
[88] See para.6–013.
[89] See para.25–022.
[90] For further discussion see Goudkamp, *Tort Law Defences* (2013), pp.50 51.
[91] *Marks and Spencer Plc v Palmer* [2001] EWCA Civ 1528 at [27].

important to remember that the risk that materialised is just one of many that might have occurred and which consequently may have made calls on the reasonable person's attention. Accordingly, the court must resist the temptation to fixate on the risk that eventuated. The reasonable person acts reasonably and that involves turning one's mind to the full range of reasonably foreseeable risks. It might be reasonable to take no or minimal precautions in relation to the risk that resulted in injury to the claimant risk in order to address more pressing risks.

4. PROVING THAT THE DEFENDANT FELL BELOW THE STANDARD OF THE REASONABLE PERSON

6–030   **Introduction.** The final step in establishing a breach of a duty of care is proving that the defendant took less care of the claimant's interests than the reasonable person would have taken. This is not the place to discuss the relevant principles of procedure and evidence in any detail. Those must be sought in works in those fields. However, some brief observations will be made.

6–031   **Determination of whether the defendant acted reasonably is a question of fact.** The question of whether the defendant took less care than the reasonable person would have taken is a question of fact. Each case must be decided according to its own individual circumstances, and the facts in two cases will never be identical.[92] Thus, strictly speaking decisions on the issue of whether the defendant fell short of the objective standard of care have no precedential value.[93] So a decision in one case that the reasonable occupier would have installed a sign to warn of the risk presented by submerged rocks does not mean that all occupiers must install such signs where the danger posed by such rocks exists. Different judges confronted with similar conduct are at liberty to reach different conclusions as to whether the conduct concerned is reasonable. On the other hand, situations tend to repeat themselves and it is permissible to look to other decisions for guidance.

6–032   **Burden and standard of proof.** The claimant bears the onus of establishing that the defendant fell below the standard of the reasonable person. This rule is subject to a few exceptions, which are discussed below. The standard of proof required in this regard is the normal civil standard, that is to say, the balance of probabilities.

6–033   **General practice.** The mere fact that the defendant complied with the general practice in a given line of work does not necessarily mean that he took reasonable care. "Neglect of duty does not cease by repetition to be neglect of duty"[94] and it is for the courts, not a particular industry, to determine whether conduct complies with the standard of the reasonable person. As Lord Mance explained in *Baker v Quantum Clothing Group Ltd*: "Respectable general practice is no more than a factor, having more or less weight according to the circumstances, which may . . .

---

[92] "[N]o one case is exactly like another": *Baker v E Longurst & Sons Ltd* [1933] 2 K.B. 461 at 468 per Lord Wright.
[93] *Qualcast (Wolverhampton) Ltd v Haynes* [1959] A.C. 743; *Foskett v Mistry* [1984] R.T.R. 1.
[94] *Bank of Montreal v Dominion Guarantee and Casualty Co Ltd* [1930] A.C. 659 at 666 per Lord Tomlin.

guide the court [when determining whether the defendant complied with the standard of the reasonable person]."[95] Thus, the courts have sometimes held that following a general practice amounts to negligence.[96] That said, if it is shown that the defendant complied with widely accepted professional standards the court is likely to find in the defendant's favour:[97]

"[W]hen the court finds a clearly established practice . . . the practice weighs heavily in the scale on the side of the defendant and the burden of establishing negligence, which the plaintiff has to discharge, is a heavy one."[98] Where the defendant has not complied with the general practice that is not of itself negligence for, "otherwise all inducement to progress . . . would then be destroyed.[99]

But non-compliance with a general practice may raise an inference of negligence.[100]

The Bolam principle. It has just been observed that the mere fact that the defendant complied with the general practice in a particular industry will not establish that the defendant met the standard of the reasonable person. There is an important exception to this rule, which has become known as the *Bolam* principle.[101] The rule applies where the defendant is a professional (although the courts have given little guidance as to what counts as a profession for this purpose). Typically, it is relevant in context of medical professionals, but it is clear that it is not confined to that setting. When the principle is applicable, the defendant will have discharged his duty of care provided that what he did was supported by a responsible body of opinion within his profession.[102] This means that if there are, for instance, two views in a profession as to what should be done in a given situation, and both views are endorsed by a responsible body of opinion, no breach of duty will have been committed regardless of which view the defendant followed. The *Bolam* principle is inapplicable where the body of opinion with which the defendant complied is illogical.[103] The rationale for the *Bolam* principle is that it permits the courts to deal with cases where there is no consensus within the relevant profession as to what practice is proper. The idea is

6–034

---

[95] *Baker v Quantum Clothing Group Ltd* [2011] UKSC 17; [2011] I.C.R. 523 at [82].
[96] *Lloyd's Bank Ltd v Savory* [1933] A.C. 201; *Markland v Manchester Corp* [1934] 1 K.B. 566; *Barkway v South Wales Transport Co Ltd* [1950] A.C. 185; *Paris v Stepney BC* [1951] A.C. 367; *General Cleaning Contractors v Christmas* [1953] A.C. 180; *Morris v West Hartlepool Steam Navigation Co Ltd* [1956] A.C. 552; *Cavanagh v Ulster Weaving Co Ltd* [1960] A.C. 145; *MacDonald v Scottish Stamping & Engineering Co* 1972 S.L.T. (Notes) 73; *Edward Wong Finance Co Ltd v Johnson Stokes & Master* [1984] A.C. 296; *Organ Retention Group Litigation, Re* [2004] EWHC 644; [2005] Q.B. 506.
[97] *Wright v Cheshire CC* [1952] 2 All E.R. 789; *Rich v LCC* [1953] 1 W.L.R. 895; *Simmons v Pennington & Sons* [1955] 1 W.L.R. 183; *Brown v Rolls-Royce Ltd* [1960] 1 W.L.R. 210; *Gray v Stead* [1999] 2 Lloyd's Rep. 559; *Baker v Quantum Clothing Group Ltd* [2011] UKSC 17; [2011] I.C.R. 523.
[98] *Morris v West Hartlepool Steam Navigation Co Ltd* [1956] A.C. 552 at 579 per Lord Cohen.
[99] *Hunter v Hanley* 1955 S.C. 200 at 206 per Lord Clyde.
[100] *Lloyd Cheyham & Co Ltd v Littlejohn & Co* [1987] B.C.L.C. 303.
[101] *Bolam v Friern Hospital Management Committee* [1957] 1 W.L.R. 582.
[102] It is not necessary that the defendant has made a conscious choice between the two schools: *Adams v Rhymney Valley DC* [2000] Lloyd's Rep. P.N. 777.
[103] *Bolitho v City and Hackney HA* [1998] A.C. 232 at 243 ("incapable of withstanding logical analysis"). For careful analysis of this exception see Mulheron (2010) 69 C.L.J. 609.

that it is too difficult for the courts to resolve disputes about technical matters between professional people. On the other hand, the *Bolam* principle is objectionable because it involves an abdication by the courts of their responsibility to determine the appropriate standard of care, and permits professionals to determine what counts as reasonable care.

6–035   **Statutory standards.** Modern life is controlled by an endless array of regulatory provisions. These provisions touch on virtually every conceivable subject, including road transport, construction and industrial activities. It is relatively unusual for such rules to specify the consequences of a breach thereof for the purposes of the law of torts.[104] However, breach of such rules may be evidence of negligence on the part of the defendant. This is said expressly in, for example, the case of the Highway Code. Legislation provides that a failure to observe the Code may be relied upon to establish (or to negate) any tortious liability.[105] Failure to comply with the criminal law is normally good evidence of negligence, but it is not possible to lay down any hard and fast rule. For example, there are circumstances in which it would not be negligent to exceed the speed limit. Equally, it is not difficult to imagine a case in which statutory requirements are met but the court finds negligence. With regard to the latter type of case, however, a distinction must be drawn between activities like driving, where there must be room for varying standards to meet varying circumstances, and matters such as the legally permissible level of toxic materials in products. For example, if statutory regulations lay down the amount of an ingredient which may be incorporated in petrol, it is not negligent to incorporate this amount even in the face of evidence that this amount is harmful.[106]

6–036   **Criminal convictions.** In many cases (especially road accident cases) there may have been criminal proceedings that resulted in the conviction of the defendant. Section 11 of the Civil Evidence Act 1968 provides that a conviction can be used as evidence in civil proceedings, and that if a person has been convicted of an offence, then he shall be taken to have committed that offence unless he proves to the contrary. Accordingly, a conviction of dangerous driving in respect of the incident in which the claimant was injured is likely to be compelling evidence that the defendant fell short of the standard of the reasonable person.[107] Of course the defendant may, if he can, show that he did not in fact commit the offence[108] or that for some reason his conduct did not amount to civil negligence; and the criminal conviction may not determine issues in the civil case (for example, causation of damage) because they were simply not relevant in the earlier proceedings.

---

[104] See Ch.8

[105] Road Traffic Act 1988 s.38(7). See further Ch.8.

[106] See *Albery and Budden v BP Oil* [1980] J.P.L. 586.

[107] An acquittal is of no evidential relevance to civil liability since the criminal standard of proof is higher.

[108] This does not infringe the rule against collateral attacks on issues decided in criminal proceedings: *McCauley v Hope* [1999] P.I.Q.R. P185; *J v Oyston, The Times*, December 11, 1998. Care must be taken to distinguish s.11 from s.13, which makes proof of a conviction *conclusive* evidence of guilt for the purposes of defamation: see para.13–050.

Res ipsa loquitur. It is open to the court to infer negligence from the 6–037
circumstances in which the accident occurred. This has traditionally been
described by the phrase res ipsa loquitur—the thing speaks for itself. Morris LJ
commented upon this phrase as follows:[109]

> "[T]his convenient and succinct formula possesses no magic qualities: nor has it any added
> virtue, other than that of brevity, merely because it is expressed in Latin. When used on behalf
> of a plaintiff it is generally a short way of saying: 'I submit that the facts and circumstances
> which I have proved establish a prima facie case of negligence against the defendant' . . .
> There are certain happenings that do not normally occur in the absence of negligence, and
> upon proof of these a court will probably hold that there is a case to answer."

In the past, there was a tendency to elevate the phrase res ipsa loquitur to a
special rule of the law of negligence. The older cases should therefore be read
cautiously and are of limited value. One had disputes as to whether res ipsa
loquitur "could" apply to complex matters like surgery or the operation of an
aircraft,[110] but to modern eyes these controversies are misplaced, because the
question of drawing inferences from particular facts cannot be subject to rules of
law and it is not possible to identify in advance the categories of fact situations to
which res ipsa loquitur will apply. It would be impossible to argue convincingly
that if a patient dies during surgery or a child is born with brain damage that
necessarily establishes a prima facie case of negligence against the doctors or the
theatre staff. On the other hand, if the procedure is simple and regarded as
unattended by serious risk, an adverse outcome may well justify an inference of
negligence. Even in such a case, however, the claimant will probably[111] need to
lay a foundation with expert evidence about the procedure, whereas a court is not
likely to require expert evidence before it concludes that a car veering across the
carriageway suggests negligence on the part of the driver.[112] It has been said that
in medical negligence cases the essential function of res ipsa loquitur is not so
much to prove the claimant's case as to enable him, when he is not in possession
of all the material facts "to be able to plead an allegation of negligence in an
acceptable form and to force the defendant to respond to it at the peril of having
a finding of negligence made against the defendant if the defendant does not
make an adequate response".[113]

Rebutting an inference of negligence. If an inference of negligence is drawn the 6–038
claimant will win unless the defendant offers an explanation consistent with due
care.[114] In most cases where the claim gets as far as trial, however, the defendant
will have something to say in response and the question arises of what he has to

---

[109] *Roe v Minister of Health* [1954] 2 Q.B. 66 at 87.

[110] It was held that in suitable circumstances res ipsa loquitur could be applied to air crashes in
George v Eagle Air Services [2009] UKPC 21; [2009] 1 W.L.R. 2133.

[111] Cf. *Ludlow v Swindon Health Authority* [1989] 1 Med. L.R. 104.

[112] In the case of a head-on collision in the middle of the road there may be no pointer one way or the
other as to whose fault it was and the correct inference will often be that both drivers were to blame:
Bray v Palmer [1961] 1 W.L.R. 1455; *Baker v Market Harborough Co-operative Society* [1953] 1
W.L.R. 1472.

[113] *Ratcliffe v Plymouth and Torbay HA* [1998] P.I.Q.R. P 170 at 189 per Hobhouse LJ.

[114] "The issue will be decided in the claimant's favour unless the defendants by their evidence
provide some answer which is adequate to displace the prima facie inference": *Henderson v Henry E
Jenkins & Sons* [1970] A.C. 282 at 310 per Lord Pearson.

do to rebut the prima facie case. At one time there was support for the view that once res ipsa loquitur applied the burden of proof shifted to the defendant. This is inconsistent with the current view of res ipsa loquitur. It is clear that there is no shift in the formal burden of proof.[115] Accordingly, at the end of the day, the court must ask itself what the effect is of the rebutting evidence upon the cogency of the initial inference of negligence.

---

[115] *Ng v Lee* [1988] R.T.R. 296.

CHAPTER 7

NEGLIGENCE: CAUSATION AND REMOTENESS (SCOPE OF LIABILITY)

The claimant must show a causal link on the usual civil standard of a balance of probabilities between the loss he has suffered and the defendant's wrong. He must also show that the loss in respect of which he claims is not too "remote", i.e. that it is within the range of that for which it is just to make the defendant responsible (though this element, too, is to some extent expressed in the language of "causation"). These issues arise in connection with other torts, too, but most of the case law involves claims for negligence, so they are dealt with here, though it will be necessary to consider them again at various later points.

7–001

1. TERMINOLOGY AND CLASSIFICATION

Even if the claimant proves every other element in tortious liability he will lose the action or, in the case of torts actionable per se, normally fail to recover more than nominal damages,[1] if what the defendant did is not treated as a legal cause of his loss. This issue is logically distinct from and anterior to the question of measure of damages which will be dealt with at a later stage.[2] Thus, in one of the

7–002

---

[1] The recovery of exemplary damages cannot be ruled out: para.23–012.
[2] See *The Argentino* (1881) 13 P.D. 101 at 196.

leading cases, the issue was whether the defendants were liable for fire damage to a wharf which arose from a rather unusual chain of events after the defendants spilled oil into a harbour.[3] If they had been liable (in fact they were not) the prima facie measure of damages would have been the cost of repairing the wharf plus consequential losses like loss of business. It should, however, be acknowledged that the line between "causation/remoteness" and "measure" is not always easy to draw,[4] for measure of damages is not merely a matter of mathematical calculation.[5]

7–003   **"Causation in fact".** In the first part of this chapter, we are concerned with the initial question of whether the defendant's acts (or conduct) should be excluded from the events which contributed to the occurrence of the claimant's loss. If it is so excluded, that is the end of the case, for if there is found to be no connection between the defendant's act and the loss there is no reason for a private law system of liability to operate with regard to him. It is conceivable that in another society or another time or in a different context it might be regarded as a good reason for saying that D must pay for damage suffered by C, that D was rich and C was poor, or that D was head of C's clan; or we might, as to some extent we do, via social security, decide that society as a whole should pay for C's loss. However, to our way of thinking the necessary bedrock[6] of tort liability as a general rule is at least a causal connection between D's act and C's loss,[7] and if what D did is found to have made no contribution to the situation in which C now finds himself the connection is absent, whatever other legal sanctions (such as criminal law penalties and professional discipline) may be directed at D's *behaviour.*

7–004   **"Causation in law".** If we conclude that D's act or omission was *a* cause of C's loss, we move on to consider whether it was a sufficiently legally effective cause among the complex of other causes (and there may be many) to justify imposing liability on the defendant. Suppose D leaves a loaded shotgun in an unlocked cupboard, X steals it and uses it to murder C (D knowing nothing of X's murderous intentions). D's breach of duty in failing to lock up the gun was a cause of C's death in the sense used above because had the gun not been available X would not have used it to kill C (though he might of course have done so at another time with another weapon). However, a court is quite likely to say that if X is an adult of sound mind, then X, not D, is responsible for C's death and it

---

[3] *The Wagon Mound* [1961] A.C. 388, para.7–032.

[4] Furthermore, "measure of damages" is sometimes used by judges when causation/remoteness is meant. See, e.g. *The Wagon Mound (No.2)* [1967] 1 A.C. 617 at 638 per Lord Reid.

[5] For example, if the claimant has contributed to the occurrence of his loss his damages may be reduced (or even extinguished). In previous editions, reduction on the basis of contributory negligence was discussed in this chapter, given the link with questions of causation. In the present edition, it is discussed as part of the law of remedies in Ch.23.

[6] Any other view would be irrational: *Kuwait Airways Corp v Iraqi Airways Co (Nos 4 and 5)* [2002] UKHL 19; [2002] 2 A.C. 883 at [127] per Lord Hoffmann.

[7] *Sindell v Abbot Laboratories* 607 P. 2d 924 (1980), where a Californian court imposed a "market share proportion" liability upon manufacturers of a generic drug when the claimant could not show which manufacturer produced the batch in question may be regarded either as extreme modification of private law principles to cope with damage done by one of a group, or as an ad hoc, judicially created and industry based compensation system.

may do so by speaking in terms of X's act being "the cause" or of X's act having "broken the chain of causation"[8] between D's negligence and C's death.[9] On the other hand, if a little child had taken the gun in our example and shot C while playing with it, we would probably readily agree that C's death was well within the risk created by D's negligence in leaving the cupboard unlocked, and that D ought to be responsible, even though what D did was just as much an "historical" or "mechanical" cause in one case as in the other. So if we are going to distinguish between the two cases and still speak in the language of causation we are now using a different concept and despite a tendency even at this stage to use mechanical metaphors about chains and links, the issue is much more obviously[10] one of fairness and of legal policy, about setting limits to the responsibility which D bears for his negligence.[11]

Terminological difficulty. None of what has just been stated is controversial, but the problem lies in expressing it in the shorthand way we need for easy reference. To describe the first stage above as "causation in fact" may give the false impression that the process of determining cause is akin to using a litmus paper to establish acidity. Admittedly, the "but-for" test of causation which is considered below comes somewhere near that but it involves a hypothetical inquiry into what would have happened if the defendant had not been at fault and the answers to hypothetical questions can never be entirely certain; furthermore, there are cases in which it produces a result which offends our intuitive "common sense" or sense of justice and we abandon it.[12]

7–005

The real difficulties of terminology arise, however, at the second stage. Traditionally, English lawyers would probably have used the phrase "remoteness of damage" to describe this (though some would have continued to speak in terms of causation; hence "causation in law" or "legal causation") and their American counterparts would have said that not only must the defendant's act have been a cause in fact of the damage, it must have been a "proximate cause".[13] So in the

---

[8] Lord Bingham has said that it is "perhaps equally accurate to say that the . . . independent act forms no part of a chain of causation beginning with the tortfeasor's breach of duty": *Corr v IBC Vehicles Ltd* [2008] UKHL 13; [2008] A.C. 884 at [15].

[9] See also Lord Hoffmann's illustration of the theft of a car radio in *Environment Agency v Empress Car Co (Abertillery) Ltd* [1999] 2 A.C. 22 at 29, where he points out that the meaning of "cause", like that of most words, depends on the context in which it is used. While at the trial of the thief we would unhesitatingly say that his act caused the loss of the radio, the owner's spouse might also properly say, by way of complaint, that the owner's negligence in leaving it in the car had caused its loss. This is not to say, of course, that a negligent defendant can never be liable in tort for wilful harm inflicted by another: para.7–054.

[10] The usual distinction between "factual" and "legal" causation is criticised by Hoffmann 121 L.Q.R. 592. It is of course true that the requirements of the first are set by law as much as the second and sometimes we depart from "historical mechanics" but it is still the case that there are major practical differences between the issues considered in sections 2 and 3 of this chapter.

[11] "A value judgment ('*ought* to be held liable')": *Kuwait Airways Corp v Iraqi Airways Co (Nos 4 and 5)* [2002] UKHL 19; [2002] 2 A.C. 883 at [70] per Lord Nicholls; *Corr v IBC Vehicles Ltd* [2008] UKHL 13; [2008] A.C. 884 at [15].

[12] See e.g. para.7–008.

[13] "The law has to set a limit to the causally connected losses for which a defendant is to be held responsible. In the ordinary language of lawyers, losses outside the limit may bear one of several labels. They may be described as too remote because the wrongful conduct was not a substantial or

wharf fire case we have referred to[14] we would say that the fire was "too remote" because it was unforeseeable and they would have said (assuming that they would have reached the same conclusion, for these things are not governed by precise, scientific laws) that the spilling of the oil on the water was not the "proximate cause" of the fire (for the same reason). To the layman, however, neither expression would seem very apt to describe the process of reasoning. The oil was dumped just across the bay from the site of the fire and while, admittedly, a couple of days passed before it ignited, the decision did not turn on this but upon the fact that the fire was unforeseeable. Some would say that "proximate cause" is even worse because it is liable to produce confusion with the first stage and to give the erroneous impression that the defendant's act has to be the factor closest in time to the damage. This has led the American Law Institute in the *Third Restatement of Torts* to abandon "proximate cause" in favour of "scope of liability",[15] though the fact that old habits die hard has compelled it to use "proximate cause" in parentheses after the new expression.

7–006   **"Scope of liability".** There is no doubt that "scope of liability" is a better expression than either remoteness or proximate cause because it immediately conveys the idea that we are concerned with setting limits to the defendant's responsibility after the first stage has been passed. It also accords very well with those cases where it has been held that the nature of the duty undertaken by the defendant limits the range of the consequences for which he is liable.[16] However, it may not quite accord with our natural way of thinking about some aspects of this area. Although it is perfectly clear that we accept that a loss may have more than one cause, there is something (perhaps the fact that the causation inquiry is, after all, concerned with attributing responsibility) that makes us link causation and responsibility and makes us look for the legally relevant cause. To adapt a well-known example, if I set fire to a piece of paper and we ask what was the cause of the paper being burned, everyone would say, "He set fire to it". Not even a combustion engineer would also refer to the presence of oxygen in the air as a cause, though that is just as necessary a condition of the paper being burned as my striking the match. To go back again to X and the shotgun (though that is not such a clear-cut case) our notions of individual responsibility would lead us to say that X caused the claimant's death, not D or (which amounts to the same thing) that what X did overwhelms D's fault and renders it part of the history. To say that D's conduct was a cause in fact of the death but that wilful interventions by a third party to exploit a danger produced by D's conduct are not within the scope of D's potential liability produces the same result but perhaps looks "over-scientific" compared with using the language of "responsibility-causation".

---

proximate cause, or because the loss was the product of an intervening cause": *Kuwait Airways Corp v Iraqi Airways Co (Nos 4 and 5)* [2002] UKHL 19; [2002] 2 A.C. 883 at [70] per Lord Nicholls.

[14] See para.7–002.

[15] *Restatement of Torts 3d: Liability for Physical and Emotional Harm* (2011), Ch.6. See also the *Principles of European Tort Law: Text and Commentary* (2005), which uses the same expression, though under the section heading of "Causation".

[16] See para.7–059.

2.   CAUSATION IN FACT

The "but for" test. As a first—but not, it must be emphasised, conclusive—step   7–007
it must be decided whether the defendant's breach of duty was, as a matter of fact,
a cause of the damage. Although the question of factual causation has exercised
philosophers and more than one approach is possible,[17] for the practical purposes
of the law that most generally mentioned by the courts is the so-called "but-for"
test, or in Latin, causa (or conditio) sine qua non.[18] If the result would not have
happened but for a certain event then that event is a cause; contrariwise, if it
would have happened anyway, the event is not a cause.[19] Of course this test will
produce a multitude of causes which are not legally effective from the point of
view of allocating responsibility,[20] but it is only intended to act as a preliminary
filter to eliminate the irrelevant.

The application of the "but for" test is neatly illustrated by *Barnett v Chelsea
and Kensington Hospital Management Committee.*[21] The claimant's husband, a
night watchman, called early in the morning at the defendants' hospital and
complained of vomiting after drinking tea. He was told to go home and consult
his own doctor later, which amounted to a breach of the hospital's duty of care.
Later that day the claimant's husband died of arsenical poisoning and the
coroner's verdict was of murder by persons unknown. The hospital's breach of
duty was held not to be a cause of the death because, even if the deceased had
been examined and treated with proper care, the probability was that the deceased
would have died anyway. The claimant's claim therefore failed.[22]

Despite the seemingly mechanical nature of the but-for approach, care must be
taken to make the correct inquiry in the light of the nature of the tort in question.
Thus the tort of conversion[23] protects a person's rights in his goods and any
person who wrongfully takes them is treated as under a continuing duty to restore
them or their value. If, therefore, D converts C's goods it is irrelevant that if he
had not done so it is inevitable that they would have been converted instead by
X.[24]

---

[17]   Hart and Honoré, *Causation in the Law*, 2nd edn (1985), Pt I; Honoré in Owen (ed.), *Philosophical Foundations of Tort Law* (1995).

[18]   i.e. "a cause without which [the event would] not [have happened]". A legally effective cause is known as a *causa causans*.

[19]   *Cork v Kirby Maclean Ltd* [1952] 2 All E.R. 402 at 406.

[20]   *Rahman v Arearose Ltd* [2001] Q.B. 351 at 367.

[21]   [1969] 1 Q.B. 428. See also *Deloitte Haskins & Sells v National Mutual Life Nominees Ltd* [1993] A.C. 774; *Chittock v Woodbridge School* [2002] EWCA Civ 915; [2003] P.I.Q.R. P6.

[22]   See also *McWilliams v Sir William Arrol & Co Ltd* [1962] 1 W.L.R. 295, (death by falling; breach of employer's duty to provide safety harness; evidence showed that deceased would not have used it); cf. *Chubb Fire Ltd v Vicar of Spalding* [2010] EWCA Civ 981; [2010] 2 C.L.C. 277 (insufficient evidence that church would not have installed "messy" type of fire extinguisher if given appropriate warning).

[23]   Ch.18.

[24]   *Kuwait Airways Corp v Iraqi Airways Co (Nos 4 and 5)* [2002] UKHL 19; [2002] 2 A.C. 883.

A. Multiple Causation

7–008 **Cumulative torts.** Although the but-for test is a useful rule of thumb,[25] it leads to absurd results where there is more than one sufficient cause of C's damage, as where A and B at the same moment inflict fatal injuries upon C.[26] In such a case, there is no doubt that, however we justify it,[27] each wrongdoer is liable in full for the loss, subject to the right of contribution against the other (a matter which does not concern the claimant).[28]

7–009 **Cumulative causes: material contribution to the claimant's injury.** Where the claimant's injury is produced by a combination of the defendant's conduct and some innocent cause, factual causation will be established if the defendant's conduct made a "material contribution" to the injury. Thus, the defendant was held liable in a case where the claimant contracted a lung condition from the combination of dust which the defendants had created in breach of safety regulations and other dust which was an inevitable accompaniment of the activity.[29] The same approach underlies the law where the claimant is partly to blame for his own loss, save that in such a situation the damages are reduced in proportion to his share of the blame.[30] What is required is a finding that the defendant's conduct made a material[31] contribution *to the injury*, not to the *risk* of the injury (though, in exceptional circumstances, even that may be sufficient).[32] Where the injury caused is divisible the defendant may be liable to the claimant only for that part of the harm that he has been proved to have caused[33] and this is discussed in Ch.22. It has been said that the test of material contribution only

---

[25] *Smith New Court Securities Ltd v Scrimgeour Vickers (Asset Management) Ltd ('SAAMCO')* [1997] A.C. 254 at 285 per Lord Steyn ("does not always" yield the right answer); *Kuwait Airways Corp v Iraqi Airways Co (Nos 4 and 5)* [2002] UKHL 19; [2002] 2 A.C. 883 at [83], per Lord Nicholls ("not always a reliable guide").

[26] On one view of the facts *Roberts v J.W. Ward & Son* (1981) 126 S.J. 120 involved two errors by the defendants which were both fatal to the claimant's contract but only one of which was negligent. The CA said that in this event the defendants would not be allowed to set up their innocent error to escape the consequences of their negligence. Nor can a defendant say that his breach of duty A was not a cause of the claimant's injury because anyway he would have committed breach of duty B which would have had the same effect: *Bolitho v City and Hackney HA* [1997] A.C. 232 at 240; cf. *Beart v Prison Service* [2005] EWCA Civ 467; [2005] I.C.R. 1206; *Wright v Cambridge Medical Group* [2011] EWCA Civ 669; [2012] 3 W.L.R. 1124 at [56]–[58]; *Robbins v Bexley LBC* [2013] EWCA Civ 1233; [2014] B.L.R. 11.

[27] See Wright (1985) 73 Cal. L.Rev 1735 and (2001) 53 Vanderbilt L.R. 1071; Honoré in Owen (ed.) *Philosophical Foundations of Tort Law* (1995); Stapleton in Cane and Gardner (eds), *Relating to Responsibility* (2001).

[28] See Ch.22.

[29] *Bonnington Castings Ltd v Wardlaw* [1956] A.C. 613.

[30] See para.23–036. So if C contracts cancer and this was produced both by a toxic agent for which D is responsible and by C's smoking, C's damages are to be reduced but if the second agent is one for which C is not responsible he recovers in full: *Badger v MoD* [2005] EWHC 2941 (QB); [2006] 3 All ER 173.

[31] "More than negligible": *Bailey v MoD* [2008] EWCA Civ 883; [2009] 1 W.L.R. 1052 at [46].

[32] See para.7–015.

[33] See e.g. *Holtby v Brigham & Cowan (Hull) Ltd*[2000] 3 All ER 421. The disease in *Bonnington Castings Ltd v Wardlaw* [1956] A.C. 613 was divisible, but no submission for an apportionment of liability was put to the court.

applies where the disease or condition is divisible,[34] but even if that is correct[35] there are cases in which the injury for which the claim is made is indivisible and in them the claimant recovers in full from the defendant. In *Bailey v MoD*[36] the *condition* was the weakened state of the claimant which was the result of a combination of the defendant's negligent post-operative care and a naturally occurring ailment but her claim, which succeeded in full, was for the brain damage she suffered when she inhaled her vomit as a result of her weakness.[37]

A distinction must be drawn between the case of cumulative torts and that where a tort combines with some factor for which no one is to blame. Where A and B both fatally wound C, the law treats both as having caused C's death because otherwise it would reach the absurd result that neither did.[38] However, it seems that where A's conduct combines with a natural force which would in itself have been sufficient to cause all the damage, A is not liable.[39] The real benefit to the claimant of the test of material contribution to injury seems therefore to lie in those cases where the injury is indivisible (or is divisible but the evidence does not enable the courts to determine any apportionment) and the court is not satisfied that the tort or the natural force alone would have been sufficient to cause the injury; a finding of material contribution will be sufficient for the claimant to recover in full. It is perhaps only in such cases that it is true to speak of the but-for test having been "modified",[40] or to describe "material contribution" as an "exception" to the but-for test.[41]

Successive events. It may be that the claimant is affected by two successive   **7–010** events or the act of the defendant precludes the operation of some other cause which would otherwise have taken effect. If D injures or kills C then it is of course obvious that C would have one day died anyway and the law therefore limits the damages recoverable by C or his dependants by reference to C's pre-accident life expectancy. Likewise, if D tortiously kills a person who is very old or who is suffering from a terminal disease he is undoubtedly liable for the

---

[34] *Ministry of Defence v AB* [2010] EWCA Civ 1317; [2011] 117 B.M.L.R. 101 at [150].

[35] By the very nature of the material contribution test (based on an accumulation of causes) the "condition" must be divisible (the totality of the exposure in cases like *Bonnington* or the weakened state of the claimant in *Bailey* (see below)), but if disease is just one type of injury for which a claim may be made, it may not be entirely correct to say that the disease (injury) must be divisible.

[36] [2008] EWCA Civ 883; [2009] 1 W.L.R. 1052.

[37] *Dickins v O2 Plc* [2008] EWCA Civ 1144; [2009] I.R.L.R. 58 at [53] per Sedley LJ: "While the law does not expect tortfeasors to pay for damage that they have not caused, it regards them as having caused damage to which they have materially contributed." See also *Badger v* MoD [2005] EWHC 2941 (QB); [2006] 3 All ER 173; *Leigh v London Ambulance Service NHS Trust* [2014] EWHC 286 (QB).

[38] See para.7–008.

[39] "If the evidence demonstrates on a balance of probabilities that the injury would have occurred as a result of the non-tortious cause or causes in any event, the claimant will have failed to establish that the tortious cause contributed": *Bailey v MoD* [2008] EWCA Civ 883; [2009] 1 W.L.R. 1052 at [46] per Waller LJ.

[40] *Bailey v MoD* [2008] EWCA Civ 883; [2009] 1 W.L.R. 1052 at [46] per Waller LJ; cf. *Mugweni v NHS London* [2012] EWCA Civ 20 at [44].

[41] In *Sienkiewicz v Greif (UK) Ltd* [2011] UKSC 10; [2011] 2 A.C. 229, Lord Phillips (at [17]) referred to "material contribution" as an "important exception" to the but-for test; Lord Brown (at [176]) had "difficulty" in seeing it as a "true exception", but he seems only to have been addressing those cases where the injury is divisible.

death, but the damages will be much lower than they would be in the case of a young, healthy victim.[42] So also if D injures C and, before C's action comes to a trial, C dies from some wholly unrelated cause, the damages payable by D will be limited to those representing the loss incurred before the death.[43] In other cases it may not be so easy to determine whether the later event obliterates the causative effect of the defendant's act.

7–011 **Baker v Willoughby.** In *Baker v Willoughby*,[44] as a result of the defendant's negligence, the claimant suffered an injury to his left leg. Before the trial, however, the claimant was the victim of an armed robbery in the course of which he suffered gunshot wounds to his left leg of such severity that the leg had to be amputated. The defendant argued that his liability was limited to the loss suffered before the robbery: all loss suffered thereafter was said to have merged in and flowed from the robbery.[45] This argument was rejected by the House of Lords because it would have produced a manifest injustice. Even if the robbers had been successfully sued to judgment,[46] they would only have been liable to the claimant for depriving him of an already damaged leg[47] and the claimant would therefore have been left uncompensated in the period after the robbery for the "difference" between a sound leg and a damaged one. The defendant's argument was said to contain a fallacy in its assertion that the first injury to the leg was obliterated by the subsequent amputation because, as Lord Reid put it,[48] a person:

> "[I]s not compensated for the physical injury: he is compensated for the loss which he suffers as a result of the injury. His loss is not in having a stiff leg: it is his inability to lead a full life, his inability to enjoy those amenities which depend on freedom of movement and his inability to earn as much as he used to earn or could have earned if there had been no accident. In this case the second injury did not diminish any of these. So why should it be regarded as having obliterated or superseded them?"

---

[42] *Smith v Cawdle Fen Commissioners* [1938] 4 All E.R. 64 at 71.

[43] A well-known conundrum is the following: D injures C in a road accident while C is on the way to the airport, crippling him for life. The aircraft on which C was booked crashes, killing all on board. We cannot, without a degree of fiction, escape by saying that C might not have taken the flight, but there is a reluctance to accept that D escapes liability for losses after the notional death.

[44] [1970] A.C. 467.

[45] Note that in a purely factual sense the accident was a cause of the injury in the robbery since the claimant changed his job as a result of the accident, but it could not possibly be contended that the defendant was liable in law for the shooting: *Carslogie SS Co Ltd v Royal Norwegian Government* [1952] A.C. 292, para.7–049.

[46] The speeches do not disclose whether the claimant made any claim under the Criminal Injuries Compensation Scheme.

[47] *Performance Cars Ltd v Abraham* [1962] 1 Q.B. 33; *Baker v Willoughby* [1970] A.C. 467 at 495. An argument that the robbers would in theory be liable for the whole of the claimant's loss because they had reduced the value of his right of action against the defendant was rejected: at 496. However, an award of this nature was made in the fatal accident case of *Singh v Aitken* [1998] P.I.Q.R. Q37, though *Baker v Willoughby* is not mentioned in the judgment; cf. *Fox v British Airways* [2013] EWCA Civ 972; [2013] ICR 1257; *Haxton v Philips Electronics UK Ltd* [2014] EWCA Civ 4; [2014] P.I.Q.R. P11 (husband killed by mesothelioma allowing dependency claim in favour of wife, but wife then also killed by mesothelioma; held wife had a claim against the employer for the diminution of her dependency claim caused by her shortened life expectancy).

[48] *Baker v Willoughby* [1970] A.C. 467 at 492.

In other words, the claimant's loss after the removal of the leg was regarded as having two concurrent causes, though it is clear that if the robbers had shot him dead the defendant's liability would not have extended beyond that point.[49]

Jobling v Associated Dairies Ltd. The decision in *Baker v Willoughby* received a hard knock in *Jobling v Associated Dairies Ltd*.[50] The claimant suffered a back injury due to the defendants' negligence. Three years later, and before trial, the claimant was diagnosed as suffering from a condition (myelopathy), unrelated to, and arising after, the accident,[51] which of itself rendered him totally unfit for work. The defendants naturally contended that the onset of the myelopathy terminated the period in respect of which they were liable for the effects of the back injury; in reply, the claimant argued that the case should be governed by *Baker v Willoughby*. The House of Lords unanimously found for the defendants. The myelopathy was one of the "vicissitudes of life" in respect of which the courts regularly made discounts in the assessment of damages for future loss of earnings[52] and it followed that it must be taken into account in full when it had actually occurred before the trial:[53]

> "When the supervening illness or injury which is the independent cause of the loss of earning capacity has manifested itself before trial, the event has demonstrated that, even if the plaintiff had never sustained the tortious injury, his earnings would now be reduced or extinguished. To hold the tortfeasor, in this situation, liable to pay damages for a notional continuing loss of earnings attributable to the tortious injury, is to put the plaintiff in a better position than he would be in if he had never suffered the tortious injury."

This approach is inconsistent with the theory of the concurrent effect of consecutive causes advanced in *Baker v Willoughby* and that case can no longer be regarded as a general authority on causation.[54] How far it is an authority on successive *tortious* injuries is less clear. Lord Russell was prepared to suggest that it might have been correctly decided on the basis that a subsequent tortious injury was not to be regarded as within the "vicissitudes" principle, and hence should not be regarded as removing the effects of the first injury,[55] and Lord Keith, though not for the same reasons, drew a distinction between tortious and non-tortious injuries.[56] However, Lord Bridge, while recognising the force of the argument that the claimant should not be under-compensated by reason of the

7–012

---

[49] The robbers would (in theory) have been liable to his dependants under the Fatal Accidents Act, but the damages would take account of any reduction in earning capacity attributable to the accident (subject to the argument rehearsed in fn.47. If the claimant had died of natural causes before the trial the liability of neither the defendant nor the robbers would have extended beyond that point.

[50] [1982] A.C. 794.

[51] The claimant conceded that if the myelopathy had been existing but dormant at the time of the accident it would have to be taken into account in assessing damages.

[52] See Ch.23. If the case had come on quickly or been settled without anyone knowing about the impending illness then recovery for the injury would of course have been much more substantial and the matter could not have been reopened. See also *Dudarec v Andrews* [2006] EWCA Civ 256; [2006] 1 W.L.R. 3002; *Whitehead v Searle* [2008] EWCA Civ 285; [2009] 1 W.L.R. 549.

[53] [1982] A.C. 794 at 820 per Lord Bridge.

[54] [1982] A.C. 794 at 802, 809, 815, 821. However, in *Rahman v Arearose Ltd* [2001] Q.B. 351 at 367 Laws LJ saw "no inconsistency whatever between the two cases", though the matter was not pursued.

[55] [1982] A.C. 794 at 810. See also *Penner v Mitchell* [1978] 4 W.W.R. 328.

[56] [1982] A.C. 794 at 815.

chance that he is the victim of two torts rather than one, pointed out that the distinction between tortious and non-tortious causes was implicitly rejected in *Baker*.[57] It would be a fiction to say that a second tortious injury was necessarily more unlikely than an illness: in the case of a police officer, for example, it might be a good deal more likely.[58]

7–013   **Linked successive events.** The illness in *Jobling* was not produced by the initial injury. If it had been the defendant might have been liable for it. So in *Corr v IBC Vehicles Ltd*[59] the defendants were liable for the suicide of the victim of an accident brought about by depression induced by the initial injury suffered in the accident. Equally if he had failed in his suicide attempt and had suffered further injuries the defendant would have been liable to him for those. However, the mere fact that an event which causes the claimant loss is linked to a tort does not mean that the claimant can recover damages for that loss. In *Gray v Thames Trains*[60] the defendants were not liable for the detention of the claimant following a conviction for an offence of manslaughter even though the claimant would not have committed the manslaughter but for the fact that they tortiously inflicted upon the claimant a psychiatric injury. That was because of two related principles of public policy: first, that to award the claimant damages would risk stultifying the operation of the criminal law and, secondly, that the defendant's act is not to be regarded in law as the cause of an act for which the claimant is criminally responsible.[61]

---

[57] [1982] A.C. 794 at 819. Lord Edmund Davies seemed to agree with Lord Bridge, for he said that he could "formulate no convincing juristic or logical principles supportive of the decision" in *Baker*. Lord Wilberforce in *Jobling* paid a good deal of attention to the fact that compensation is not merely a matter of tort damages and that the claimant's position with regard to other sources of money may determine whether he is under-or over-compensated. With respect, however, this is the general problem of offsets and deductions of collateral benefits (see Ch.23) and raises no more issues in multiple causation cases than in those where the issue of causation is clear.

[58] It is hard to see the justification for dissecting the "accident" side of life's vicissitudes but not the "illness" side. In *Heil v Rankin* [2001] P.I.Q.R. Q16 (not to be confused with the case of the same name [2001] Q.B. 272 on damages for non-pecuniary loss, para.23–066) the CA held that the claimant's damages were to be reduced to take account of the fact that some other incident [should "incident" be replaced with "tort"?] might have occurred which would have triggered an aggravation of the claimant's low grade PTSD and rendered him incapable of continuing in the police service. *Baker v Willoughby* was explained as a case where it was necessary to ignore the *occurrence* of the second tort to prevent the claimant being caught between the two propositions that: (a) the first tortfeasor could argue that the damage inflicted by him was now to be attributed to another cause; and (b) the second tortfeasor could argue that he took the devalued claimant as he found him. That was necessary to avoid under-compensation, whereas in *Heil* to ignore the risk of future disabling tortious conduct would lead to over-compensation. These matters are clearly to be decided on the basis of pragmatism rather than logic but from an intuitive point of view it looks odd to ignore what we know has happened and take into account what might have happened.

[59] *Corr v IBC Vehicles Ltd* [2008] UKHL 13; [2008] A.C. 884, para.7–057.

[60] *Gray v Thames Trains* [2009] UKHL 33; [2009] 1 A.C. 1339.

[61] See para.26–062.

B. Proof, Uncertainty and Causation

i. What Happened?

In the cases we have considered so far we have essentially been concerned with
what the outcome for the claimant would have been had it not been for the
defendant's conduct in question but there may, of course, be a preliminary
question of whether what the defendant did had any impact on the claimant at
all,[62] as in the classic case of the two hunters who fire simultaneously in the
claimant's direction and one bullet hits him but it cannot be shown which did so.
According to traditional principles the claimant fails since he cannot prove on a
balance of probabilities that either of the hunters shot him,[63] but the law is not as
simple as that.

7–014

The Fairchild exception. The problem of proof of causation has arisen most
frequently in disease cases, particularly those arising from asbestos. In some
cases it has been possible to establish liability on the basis that the defendant's
breach of duty made a material contribution to the disease in question,[64] e.g. in
claims for asbestosis caused by exposure to asbestos dust where only part of the
exposure was the consequence of the defendant's breach.[65] But in others it has
not been possible to prove even this; in particular in claims in respect of
mesothelioma, a form of cancer. In *Fairchild v Glenhaven Funeral Services Ltd*[66]
the claimant worked for differing periods for several employers,[67] each of whom
negligently exposed him to asbestos dust. He contracted a mesothelioma as a
result of this exposure.[68] The claimant was unable to prove, on the balance of
probabilities, that exposure during any one period of employment was the cause
and nor could he prove that each period of exposure had materially contributed to
the onset of the cancer.[69] Such was the state of scientific knowledge about the

7–015

---

[62] Causation may, of course, be "proved" as a matter of inference: *Levicom International Holdings
BV v Linklaters* [2010] EWCA Civ 494; [2010] P.N.L.R. 29 (solicitors advised C that it had a strong
case to litigate rather than settle and C litigated; normal inference was that the advice was causative).
See also: *Drake v Harbour* [2008] EWCA Civ 25; 121 Con L.R. 18; *Vaile v Havering LBC* [2011]
EWCA Civ 246; [2011] E.L.R. 274; cf. *Saunders v Chief Constable of Sussex* [2012] EWCA Civ
1197.

[63] *Cook v Lewis* [1951] S.C.R. 830. But the Supreme Court of Canada held the opposite on the basis
that where two defendants have committed acts of negligence in circumstances that deprive the
claimant of the ability to prove which of them caused his damage, the burden is cast upon each of the
defendants to exculpate himself, and if both fail to discharge this burden, then both are liable.

[64] See para.7–009.

[65] See, e.g. *Holtby v Brigham & Cowan (Hull) Ltd* [2000] 3 All ER 421; discussed at para.22–004.

[66] [2002] UKHL 22; [2003] 1 A.C. 32.

[67] This feature of the case is commonly encountered because there is usually a very long period
between the exposure to asbestos and the development of the first malignant cell; typically, at least 30
years.

[68] There was said to be no doubt about this since the disease is very rare and those occupationally
exposed have a 1,000 times greater incidence than the general population; but contraction of the
disease as a result of non-occupational environmental exposure cannot be ruled out, as is evident from
Sienkiewicz v Greif (UK) Ltd [2011] UKSC 10; [2011] 2 AC 229; para.7–019.

[69] It seems that the day when this might be possible is getting closer, if not already here: see
para.7–022.

aetiology of mesothelioma that it was impossible[70] to know whether any particular inhalation of asbestos played any or no part in its development, and on that basis it appeared that none of the employers could be held liable.[71] Nevertheless, the House of Lords held that the claimant could recover on the basis that, as Lord Nicholls put it: "Any other outcome would be deeply offensive to instinctive notions of what justice requires and fairness demands."[72] The real difficulty, as he went on to acknowledge, was to determine the precise basis for this exceptional departure from the normal requirement of proof on the question of causation.

7–016 **Material increase in risk.** The starting point for the House of Lords was its earlier decision in *McGhee v NCB*,[73] where the pursuer developed dermatitis and alleged that it had been caused by the defenders' failure to provide washing facilities at the workplace. The defenders admitted negligence in failing to provide these facilities but medical knowledge about the causes of dermatitis was such that it was not possible to say that had washing facilities been provided the pursuer would have escaped the disease; nor was it a case of cumulative causes where the breach of duty had made a material contribution. All that could be said was that the defenders' failure had materially increased the risk of dermatitis. On these facts the House held that the pursuer was entitled to succeed in the absence of proof by the defenders that their breach of duty was not causative and there seems little doubt that the decision was motivated as much by policy as by logic. As Lord Wilberforce candidly said:[74]

> "[I]f one asks which of the parties, the workman or the employers, should suffer from this inherent evidential difficulty, the answer as a matter of policy or justice should be that it is the creator of the risk who, ex hypothesi, must be taken to have foreseen the possibility of damage, who should bear its consequences."

A subsequent interpretation of *McGhee* by the House of Lords[75] which viewed it as merely a "robust and pragmatic" decision that it was legitimate to infer from the primary facts that the defenders' breach of duty had probably made some contribution to the development of the disease was rejected by the House of Lords in *Fairchild*. Instead, it was taken to stand for the proposition that proof of a material[76] increase in a risk could be sufficient to satisfy the causal

---

[70] The impossibility of drawing any conclusions even on the basis of the balance of probability, or material contribution (the "rock of uncertainty" ([2003] 1 A.C. 32 at [7] per Lord Bingham) is a pre-requisite for the application of the *Fairchild* exception. In *Hull v Sanderson* [2008] EWCA Civ 1211; [2009] P.I.Q.R. P7 the Court of Appeal found that this pre-requisite had not been met and the judge should not have fallen back on the *Fairchild* exception as a way of avoiding making the necessary findings of fact to reach a decision on causation.

[71] So held the Court of Appeal: [2002] 1 W.L.R. 1052.

[72] *Fairchild v Glenhaven Funeral Services Ltd* [2002] UKHL 22; [2003] 1 A.C. 32 at [36].

[73] [1973] 1 W.L.R. 1.

[74] *McGhee v NCB* [1973] 1 W.L.R. 1 at 6.

[75] *Wilsher v Essex Area Health Authority* [1988] A.C. 1074 at 1090 per Lord Bridge.

[76] Defined as "more than de minimis": *Sienkiewicz v Greif (UK) Ltd* [2011] UKSC 10; [2011] 2 AC 229 at [176] (in *Greif* the increase in risk attributable to the defendant's breach of duty was 18 per cent (from 24 cases per million, to 28.39 cases per million) which was regarded as sufficient by the Supreme Court); cf. *Cox v Rolls Royce Industrial Power* [2007] EWCA Civ 1189 (sufficient that C

requirements for liability:[77] "[I]n the particular circumstances, a breach of duty which materially increased the risk [of the disease] should be treated *as if* it had materially contributed to the disease."[78]

Fairchild exception applies to a combination of tortious and non-tortious   **7–017**
causes. Any prospect that the *Fairchild* exception was confined to cases where all potential causes of the defendant's injury are tortious was effectively eliminated by the approval of *McGhee* where this factor was not present.[79] This was confirmed by the subsequent decision of the House of Lords in *Barker v Corus (UK) Ltd*[80] in which *Fairchild* was applied to a case where the claimant had been exposed to asbestos dust as a result of breach of duty by the defendant employer (and other employers) and due to his own negligence during a period of self-employment. As Lord Hoffmann put it:[81]

> "The purpose of the *Fairchild* exception is to provide a cause of action against a defendant who has materially increased the risk that the claimant will suffer damage and may have caused that damage, but cannot be proved to have done so because it is impossible to show, on a balance of probability, that some other exposure to the same risk may not have caused it instead. For this purpose, it should be irrelevant whether the other exposure was tortious or non-tortious, by natural causes or human agency or by the claimant himself. These distinctions may be relevant to whether and to whom responsibility can also be attributed, but from the point of view of satisfying the requirement of a sufficient causal link between the defendant's conduct and the claimant's injury, they should not matter."

Of course if the *Fairchild* exception is extended so that it applies to cases where some of the exposure is non-tortious we have to accept that the injustice which prompted the decision in *Fairchild* to some extent "loses its edge".[82] This is because it can no longer be said that: "This harm *must* have been caused by defendant A or defendant B, even though we cannot determine which it was."

The Barker experiment: apportionment of liability. The *Fairchild* appeals   **7–018**
were conducted on the basis that if the defendants before the court were liable at all, each was liable for all the damage suffered by the claimant in accordance with

---

had only been exposed to asbestos by D for one year out of 24). A claim failed in *Garner v Salford CC* [2013] EWHC 1573 because the evidence that the dust created by D contained *any asbestos at all* was minimal.
[77] And only the causal requirements: *Williams v University of Birmingham* [2011] EWCA Civ 1242; [2012] P.I.Q.R. P4 (nothing to suggest that the breach of duty test had been altered in mesothelioma cases so that a claimant only had to demonstrate that the defendant failed to take reasonable steps to ensure that the claimant or victim was not exposed to a material increase in the risk of mesothelioma; the duty was to take reasonable care to ensure that a person was not exposed to a foreseeable risk of asbestos related injury).
[78] *Fairchild v Glenhaven Funeral Services Ltd* [2002] UKHL 22; [2003] 1 A.C. 32 at [65] per Lord Hoffmann.
[79] Though in *Fairchild* the defendant was as much responsible for the potential non-tortious cause (unavoidable brick dust) as he was for the potential tortious cause in *Fairchild* (lack of showers) which is consistent with one of the conditions laid down by Lord Bingham that "any cause of C's mesothelioma other than the inhalation of asbestos dust *at work* can be effectively discounted": [2002] UKHL 22; [2003] 1 A.C. 32 at [2] (emphasis added).
[80] [2006] UKHL 20; [2006] 2 A.C. 572.
[81] *Barker v Corus (UK) Ltd* [2006] UKHL 20; [2006] 2 A.C. 572 at [17]. See also Lord Rodger (at [97]).
[82] *Barker v Corus (UK) Ltd* [2006] UKHL 20; [2006] 2 A.C. 572 at [117] per Lord Walker.

the normal rule about contributing causes of indivisible injuries (joint and several liability).[83] Each defendant is, of course, entitled to seek contribution from any other persons liable[84] but under the normal rule the claimant is entitled to enforce the whole judgment against any one of them. In *Barker v Corus (UK)* the House of Lords was invited to depart from the normal rule and impose "proportionate" liability, that is to say liability based in amount on the extent to which the defendant increased the risk of the harm. This invitation was accepted by the majority, essentially on the basis of taking the *Fairchild* exception to what might be seen as its logical conclusion, i.e. the claimant had failed to prove causation of the disease itself but succeeded on the different basis that he had shown that the defendant was responsible for a material increase in the risk of his succumbing to the disease.

Lord Rodger dissented and regarded the approach of the majority as amounting to a rewriting of *Fairchild* (and *McGhee*). In his view *Fairchild* decided that, by showing that the defendant had materially increased the risk of the disease, the claimant had done enough for the court to deem that causation of the disease had been proved, or at least that the defendant's breach of duty had made a material contribution, and the normal rule should apply. Lord Rodger's view has since prevailed. First, in cases of mesothelioma induced by exposure to asbestos where the defendant is found liable on the basis of the *Fairchild* exception, the normal rule of joint and several liability applies as a result of s.3 of the Compensation Act 2006.[85] Secondly, any possibility that the majority in *Barker* might have created a new tort of increased risk (which would only be available in claims other than for mesothelioma as a result of s.3 of the 2006 Act) appears to have been denied by the decision of the majority of the Supreme Court in *BAI (Run Off) Ltd v Durham (Employers' Liability Insurance "Trigger" Litigation)*.[86]

The issue in the *Trigger Litigation* case was the enforceability of employers' liability insurance policies in circumstances where cover was provided at the time of exposure but not at the later onset of mesothelioma. The Court of Appeal had held that for policies where the insured risk was disease or injury "contracted" it was enough that the policy was in force at the time of exposure, but for policies where the insured risk was disease or injury "sustained",[87] the policy must have been in force at the time the tumour developed.[88] In the Supreme Court a majority held that a claim could be made in both instances if the policy was in force at the time of the exposure for which the employer was held liable in accordance with the *Fairchild* exception. Lord Phillips dissented on the more fundamental basis that, under the *Fairchild* exception, the employer is only made liable for *increasing the risk* of mesothelioma and this form of liability could not satisfy

---

[83] See para.22–001.

[84] See para.22–005.

[85] This amounted to a swift reversal of the decision in *Barker* by Parliament and with retrospective effect, so as to apply to cases which had not come to judgment or been settled. On facts like *Barker*, where there was self-exposure, a reduction may still be made for contributory negligence.

[86] [2012] UKSC 14; [2012] 1 W.L.R. 867.

[87] Cf. "occurring": *Bolton MBC v MMI Ltd* [2006] EWCA Civ 50; [2006] 1 W.L.R. 1492, where public liability insurance was in issue.

[88] *Durham v BAI (Run Off) Ltd* [2010] EWCA Civ 1096; [2011] 1 All E.R. 605.

either the concept of injury or of causation for the purposes of the insurance policies under consideration (whether defined in terms of injury sustained, or injury contracted). The majority disagreed pointing out that, even after *Barker*, the employer is only liable if mesothelioma develops and the liability of the employer is *for mesothelioma*, albeit it was to be apportioned until this aspect of the decision was reversed by s.3 of the 2006 Act. A subsequent decision of the Court of Appeal[89] has confirmed that it is the dissenting approach of Lord Rodger in *Barker* which has prevailed and where the test of material increase in risk is applied, the claimant is deemed to have proved that the defendant's breach of duty caused the injury in question, or at least made a material contribution to it.

Fairchild exception applies to "single exposure" cases. What remains of *Barker* confirms that the *Fairchild* exception applies in cases of multiple potential tortious and non-tortious causes.[90] In *Sienkiewicz v Greif (UK) Ltd*[91] it was argued that, nonetheless, the exception should not apply in so-called "single exposure" cases, i.e. where the claimant was the victim of environmental exposure which carried the risk of contracting mesothelioma, but was also exposed to an increase in risk due to the breach of duty of just one negligent defendant.[92] Instead, in such cases it was appropriate to apply a test of "the doubling of risk".[93] The scope for application of that test in other types of case is considered below,[94] but it was rejected by the Supreme Court for mesothelioma claims on two grounds. First, the unreliability, or inadequacy, of the data currently available on the incidence of the risk of mesothelioma from exposure to asbestos.[95] Secondly, that cases of "single exposure" raised exactly the same issue of the impossibility of proof of causation and therefore the same policy justification for the application of the *Fairchild* exception.[96]

7–019

---

[89] *International Energy Group Ltd v Zurich Insurance PLC UK Branch* [2013] EWCA Civ 39; [2013] 3 All E.R. 395. At first instance ([2012] EWHC 69 Comm; [2012] Lloyd's Rep. I.R. 594) Cooke J had applied *Barker* in a case of mesothelioma because the appeal was from Guernsey, where s.3 of the Compensation Act 2006 did not apply. He held that, as a result, an insurer was only liable to the insured employer for a sum which represented the 6 years out of 27 that the employee had worked for the employer. The view taken by the Court of Appeal was that it was bound by the approach of the majority of the Supreme Court in *The "Trigger" Litigation* which was consistent with Lord Rodger's dissenting speech in *Barker*. As a result, the *Fairchild* exception is one where material increase in risk is adopted for reasons of legal policy as a "weaker cause or relationship" for the imposition of responsibility, and D is made liable for *the injury*.

[90] See para.7–017.

[91] [2011] UKSC 10; [2011] 2 A.C. 229; Stapleton (2012) 128 L.Q.R. 221.

[92] In reality, this is just another form of multiple exposure: the non-tortious environmental exposure *and* the tortious exposure due to D's breach of duty.

[93] In the *Greif* appeal (the Supreme Court also heard a conjoined appeal in *Knowsley MBC v Willmore*), the trial judge had found that the background risk from the claimant's environmental exposure was 24 cases per million and D's breach of duty had increased that risk to 28.39 cases per million; an increase in risk of 18 per cent and therefore well below the 100 per cent required.

[94] See para.7–023.

[95] [2011] UKSC 10; [2011] 2 AC 229 at [97]–[105], [204]–[206]. Such unreliable data still have to be employed faute de mieux to deal with claims of contribution between joint tortfeasors: [106].

[96] [2011] UKSC 10; [2011] 2 AC 229 at [160]: "The claimant comes up against the same rock of uncertainty. In that respect single exposure cases are no different from multiple defendant cases and the same approach should be applied", per Lord Rodger.

7–020   **Is the Fairchild exception limited to cases of "single agency"?** Thus far, the principal requirements for the application of the *Fairchild* exception are that the claimant must have contracted the disease in question[97] and it must be impossible to prove on the balance of probability that the defendant's breach of duty caused the disease, or made a material contribution to it. An earlier case which appeared to meet those requirements, and in which the claim failed, was nonetheless approved in *Fairchild* and *Barker.* In *Wilsher v Essex Area Health Authority*[98] the claimant was born prematurely and succumbed to retrolental fibroplasia (RLF), a retinal condition causing serious damage to his sight. A possible cause, or contributing cause, of this was an excess of oxygen caused by a mistaken placing of a catheter. The conflicting expert evidence at the trial identified a number of other possible causes which were not attributable to the fault of the defendants and the failure of the trial judge to decide whether the mistake was more likely as a cause than these others meant that there had to be a retrial on the causation issue. It was argued that the claimant could succeed on the basis of the increased risk of RLF due to the excess of oxygen, but the decision in *McGhee* was distinguished on the unsatisfactory basis, since acknowledged,[99] that it was no more than a "robust and pragmatic" application of the balance of probability test. It now seems that a case like *Wilsher* is distinguished on the basis that there were several different agents operating in entirely different ways, while the *Fairchild* exception is confined to "single agent" cases,[100] or to multiple agents which operate "in substantially the same way".[101] The distinction is not a principled one[102] and appears to have been adopted on the pragmatic basis that it places *a* limit on the *Fairchild* exception.[103] If, as is suggested below,[104] the *Fairchild* exception is to be confined to mesothelioma claims in any event, the single agent limitation may have been rendered redundant.[105]

---

[97] The development of pleural plaques caused by exposure to asbestos is not actionable because the plaques themselves do not constitute the injury necessary to complete the cause of action in negligence (*quaere* the prospect of a claim for breach of the employer's contractual duty of care) and nor can a claim be brought based on the risk of later development of actionable disease such as asbestosis or mesothelioma. If the claimant does go on to contract mesothelioma the *Fairchild* exception may come to his assistance and the claimant may be able to sue before then if he foreseeably suffers a psychiatric disorder from fear of the risk: *Rothwell v Chemical and Insulating Co Ltd* [2007] UKHL 39; [2008] A.C. 281, para.5–087. Pleural plaques should be distinguished from pleural thickening, for which a claim may be made: *Sir Robert Lloyd & Co Ltd v Hoey* [2011] EWCA Civ 1060.

[98] [1988] A.C. 1074.

[99] See para.7–016.

[100] *Fairchild v Glenhaven Funeral Services Ltd* [2002] UKHL 22; [2003] 1 A.C. 32 at [22] per Lord Bingham; *Barker v Corus (UK) Ltd* [2006] UKHL 20; [2006] 2 A.C. 572 at [64] per Lord Scott and at [114] per Lord Walker.

[101] *Fairchild v Glenhaven Funeral Services Ltd* [2002] UKHL 22; [2003] 1 A.C. 32 at [71] per Lord Rodger; *Barker v Corus (UK) Ltd* [2006] UKHL 20; [2006] 2 A.C. 572 at [24] per Lord Hoffmann.

[102] We have this on the authority of Lord Hoffmann in *Fairchild* (at [72]), but in *Barker* (at [23]) he recanted and said that he was wrong. One suspects he was right in his initial view.

[103] See Peel [2006] L.M.C.L.Q. 289.

[104] See para.7–021.

[105] It is noticeable that the single agent limitation is either not mentioned at all (*Jones v Sec. of State for Energy & Climate Change* [2012] EWHC 2936 (QB)) or only in passing (*Sienkiewicz v Greif (UK) Ltd* [2011] UKSC 10; [2011] 2 A.C. 229) in the cases in which it is suggested that the Fairchild exception is confined to mesothelioma claims. In *Greif* Lord Phillips (at [45]) appears sceptical about

Is the Fairchild exception confined to mesothelioma claims? In *Sienkiewicz v*   7–021
Greif Lord Brown lamented the state of the law, describing the position reached
after that decision as "unsatisfactory" and the path by which it was reached as
"quixotic".[106] It is no doubt for this reason that he refers to mesothelioma claims
as "in a category all their own",[107] and "save only for mesothelioma cases,
claimants should henceforth expect little flexibility from the courts in their
approach to causation".[108] Similarly, in a subsequent case primarily concerned
with limitation periods, Lord Phillips endorsed as "plainly correct" the view of
the Court of Appeal that there was no foreseeable possibility that the Supreme
Court would extend the *Fairchild* exception.[109] Such comments have led to the
observation that there is no "appetite in the appellate courts for extending the
Fairchild exception to cases involving diseases other than mesothelioma".[110]
There is an obvious temptation to place this most pragmatic of limitations on the
Fairchild exception, but one obstacle is the decision in *McGhee* which was not a
mesothelioma case. Furthermore, it cannot be ruled out that the same evidential
difficulties[111] might be present in future cases in different contexts and that this
will lead the courts to embark on a further policy based departure from the
normal requirements of proof of causation.

Advances in medical science. The *Fairchild* exception was introduced to deal   7–022
with the evidential difficulty faced by claimants in the proof of causation. Such
difficulty was due to the state of scientific knowledge at the time, but the science
has moved on. The "single fibre" theory which featured prominently in *Fairchild*
has been discredited[112] and it also seems that one can rule out inhalation of
asbestos occurring between 5 to 10 years prior to diagnosability.[113] More recently,
there has been the suggestion that the understanding of the carcinogenesis of
mesothelioma has reached the point at which it is possible to conclude that the
claimant's exposures to asbestos have a cumulative effect; on that basis, cases
like *Fairchild* might now be decided on the basis of the test of material
contribution.[114] If this is the position which has been reached, or indeed if this is

---

the single agent limitation and Lord Brown (at [187]) had "difficulty even in recognising the
distinction between these categories", i.e. between "single agent" cases and "multiple agent" cases.

[106] [2011] UKSC 10; [2011] 2 A.C. 229 at [174].

[107] [2011] UKSC 10; [2011] 2 A.C. 229 at [186].

[108] [2011] UKSC 10; [2011] 2 A.C. 229 at [187].

[109] *AB v Ministry of Defence* [2012] UKSC 9; [2013] 1 A.C. 78 at [157]; see para.26–098.

[110] *Jones v Sec of State for Energy & Climate Change* [2012] EWHC 2936 (QB) at [6.18].

[111] A wider embrace of the test of doubling of risk (see para.7–023) may reduce this possibility, but
cannot eliminate the prospect of a case, like *Sienkiewicz v Greif*, where the data are considered to be
too unreliable.

[112] *Sienkiewicz v Greif (UK) Ltd* [2011] UKSC 10; [2011] 2 AC 229 at [102].

[113] *BAI (Run Off) Ltd v Durham (Employers' Liability Insurance "Trigger" Litigation)* [2012] UKSC
14; [2012] 1 W.L.R. 867 at [5] ("10 years or so"); *Sienkiewicz* [2011] UKSC 10; [2011] 2 AC 229 at
[19] ("...at least 5 years. During this period, further exposure to asbestos fibres will have no
causative effect").

[114] This *appears to be* the view of one of the experts who appeared in *Fairchild* in the later case of
Jones v Sec of State for Energy & Climate Change [2012] EWHC 2936 (QB) at [8.21]: "Dr Rudd said
that, if he were asked the same questions now as he had been asked in *Fairchild*, he would say that it
was probable that the asbestos fibres from each source had contributed to the carcinogenic process."

the position which is one day reached,[115] the significance of such a development for the law of negligence is open to debate. It may be thought to vindicate the decision in *Fairchild* to equate material increase in the risk of injury with material contribution to injury. On the other hand, given the uncertainty surrounding the *Fairchild* exception and the quixotic process it unleashed,[116] it may be that the law should have been left unaltered while the state of scientific knowledge was left to develop, notwithstanding the policy based impulse for alteration.[117]

7–023 **Doubling of risk.** The test which the Supreme Court was invited to apply in *Sienkiewicz v Greif (UK) Ltd* as proof of causation was the "doubling of risk". It is a test based on epidemiological evidence and can be best illustrated by an example used by Lord Mackay in *McGhee* and adopted by a number of the Supreme Court Justices in *Greif*: if epidemiological evidence showed that of 100 men working in the same conditions as the claimant 30 would develop dermatitis even though they had showered after their shift, but the evidence also indicated that, if the men did not shower, 70 would develop dermatitis, the introduction of the defendant's breach of duty in failing to provide showers would have more than doubled the risk. Should this suffice to prove that, on the balance of probability, the defendant's breach caused the dermatitis? As noted above, the test of doubling of risk was rejected for cases of mesothelioma because of the unreliability of the data available, but what of other cases?[118] Lord Rodger was most sceptical on the basis that the only "fact" that will have been proved in the example above is that *in most cases* the dermatitis would have been related to the lack of showers.[119] What the test lacks is the personal element which would allow the court to determine whether the claimant was one of the 30 who would have contracted dermatitis in any event, or whether he was one of the additional 40.[120] But as Lord Rodger acknowledged, "in the absence of any evidence that the claimant is atypical, it is more probable than not that his dermatitis was caused by lack of showers",[121] and, as Lord Phillips noted: "the law of causation does not deal in certainties; it deals in probabilities".[122] It has subsequently been said that

---

[115] *Sienkiewicz v Greif (UK) Ltd* [2011] UKSC 10; [2011] 2 A.C. 229 at [142] per Lord Rodger: "If the day ever dawns when medical science can identify which fibre or fibres led to the malignant mutation and the source from which that fibre or fibres came, then the problem which gave rise to the exception will have ceased to exist."

[116] See text to fn.106.

[117] See the further reflections of Lord Hoffmann, writing extra-judicially, in Goldberg (ed.), *Perspectives on Causation* (2011).

[118] In the Court of Appeal ([2009] EWCA Civ 1211; [2010] E.L.R. 227 at [23]) Smith LJ endorsed it for non-mesothelioma cases.

[119] *Sienkiewicz v Greif (UK) Ltd* [2011] UKSC 10; [2011] 2 A.C. 229 at [156]; cf. Lord Kerr (at [204]); Gold (1986) 96 Yale L.J. 376 at 382–384; *Merrell Dow Pharmaceuticals Inc v Havenr* 953 SW 2d 706 (1997).

[120] In *Herskovits v Group Health Cooperative of Pugent Sound* 664 P 2d 474 (1983) Brachtenbach J regarded it as an essential and minimal requirement that there be evidence connecting the relevant statistical information to the facts of the case; cf. *Amaca Pty Ltd v Ellis* [2010] HCA 5; (2010) 263 A.L.R. 576 at [70].

[121] *Sienkiewicz v Greif (UK) Ltd* [2011] UKSC 10; [2011] 2 A.C. 229 at [156].

[122] For an illustration that the balance of *probability* is no more than that and does not require it to be proved, in the strict scientific sense, that *x* was the cause of *y*, see: *Wood v Ministry of Defence* [2011] EWCA Civ 792 (judge entitled to conclude that C's exposure to organic solvents probably caused his neurological condition given the unrebutted expert evidence of a probable link).

a majority in *Sienkiewicz*[123] "considered that the test can be used in appropriate circumstances although there was obvious concern about over-reliance on epidemiological evidence alone",[124] and on that basis it has been applied to resolve claims for lung cancer, bladder cancer and skin cancer caused by other types of carcinogens.[125]

ii.   What Would Have Happened?

A question of damages. As we have seen, the "but-for" test involves a hypothetical inquiry into what the situation would have been had it not been for the defendant's conduct in question. This is not really a matter of historical fact like "when did the accident occur?" or "how fast was the defendant going?"; but the basic approach is to treat it in the same way for purposes of proof. The burden of proving that the harm would not have occurred had it not been for the defendant's conduct rests, as a general rule, upon the claimant.[126] If he succeeds in showing this on a balance of probabilities then the hypothetical non-occurrence of the harm is treated as being conclusively established even though there may be a substantial chance that it would have happened just the same; and the claimant recovers all the damages flowing from the wrong, not a proportion of them discounted by that chance. We must contrast with this the issue of what may happen in the future, or what would have happened in the future had it not been for the defendant's wrong, both of which have obvious relevance to the quantification of the claimant's damages.[127] Here the balance of probabilities is irrelevant and: "[T]he court must make an estimate as to what are the chances that a particular thing will or would have happened and reflect those chances, whether they are more or less than even, in the amount of damages which it awards."[128]

7–024

In such cases, where proof "is necessarily unattainable, it would be unfair to treat as certain a prediction which has a 51 per cent probability of occurring, but to ignore altogether a prediction which has a 49 per cent probability of occurring".[129]

Thus, damages are generally discounted to reflect the "vicissitudes of life" but if there is evidence that the claimant was in some way at greater risk of loss in the future from some other cause (for example if he has a weak heart or is in insecure

---

[123] In addition to the more receptive approach of Lord Phillips, see also: *Sienkiewicz v Greif (UK) Ltd* [2011] UKSC 10; [2011] 2 A.C. 229 at [191] per Lord Mance; at [222] per Lord Dyson.

[124] *Jones v Secretary of State for Energy & Climate Change* [2012] EWHC 2936 (QB) (test cases for those who contracted cancers and respiratory diseases after working in the phurnacite industry).

[125] *Jones v Secretary of State for Energy & Climate Change* [2012] EWHC 2936 (QB); cf. *Novartis Grimsby Ltd v Cookson* [2007] EWCA Civ 1261; *Shortell v BICAL Construction Ltd* Unreported May 16, 2008.

[126] "There is no inherent uncertainty about what caused something to happen in the past or about whether something which happened in the past will cause something to happen in the future. Everything is determined by causality. What we lack is knowledge and the law deals with lack of knowledge by the concept of the burden of proof": *Gregg v Scott* [2005] UKHL 2; [2005] 2 A.C. 176 at [79] per Lord Hoffmann.

[127] *Smithurst v Sealant Construction Services Ltd* [2011] EWCA Civ 1277; [2012] Med L.R. 258 at [10].

[128] *Mallet v McMonagle* [1970] A.C. 166 at 176 per Lord Diplock.

[129] *Malec v JC Hutton Pty Ltd* (1990) 92 A.L.R. 545 at 549.

employment) the discount may be greater. Equally, the damages may in a suitable case be increased to allow for contingencies—for example it has been commonplace in cases of head injury to award something for the risk that epilepsy may develop.[130]

iii.   Loss of a Chance

7–025 **Hotson v East Berkshire Health Authority.** An attempt to apply the same approach to causation as is applied to the quantification of damages (i.e. assessment of the chance rather than all-or-nothing balance of probabilities) was rejected by the House of Lords in *Hotson v East Berkshire Health Authority*.[131] The defendants negligently failed to diagnose the claimant's condition after a fall and there developed a serious disability of the hip joint. On the facts there was, statistically, a 75 per cent risk that this disability would have developed even if the claimant had been treated properly[132] but the trial judge (and the Court of Appeal) held that he was entitled to damages representing 25 per cent of his full loss. This was reversed by the House of Lords: the judge's findings of fact amounted to a conclusion that on the balance of probability the disability would have occurred anyway and that the fall was therefore to be treated as the cause of the loss. On this basis there was no foundation for awarding damages for loss of the chance of recovery.[133] As we have seen, had the claimant shown on a slight balance of probability that he would have been cured if given proper treatment, then he would have recovered his damages in full.

7–026 **Gregg v Scott.** The issue was revisited in *Gregg v Scott*.[134] There was a negligent delay in the diagnosis of the claimant's cancer and when treatment began he had (in similar statistical terms to those in *Hotson*) only a 25 per cent chance of recovery, whereas if it had been diagnosed promptly his chance would have been 42 per cent. Even on the latter assumption it was still more likely than not that he would not have survived with prompt treatment. The majority of the House of Lords rejected his claim that the delay in treatment had caused the damage of

---

[130] Though since the Administration of Justice Act 1982 such a case would probably be more suitable for the award of provisional damages: para.23–094. Periodical payments awards can help with the "what will happen" problem but not the "what would have happened" one: para.23–095.

[131] [1987] A.C. 750. On this case and its ramifications, see Stapleton (1988) 104 L.Q.R. 389.

[132] To say that the claimant had such a chance is a considerable over-simplification. It seems to have represented a conclusion that of a sample of 100 people with a similar injury 25 would have recovered with prompt treatment, but the precise degree of blood vessel damage suffered by C before he entered the hospital was not known, nor will the figure be known for any of the sample. Some of the 100 would inevitably have suffered the disability whatever was done and the claimant might have been one of those. The point is made by Lord Mackay in *Hotson*. In principle one must look at the chances of this individual claimant rather than the statistical group (*Wardlaw v Farrar* [2003] EWCA Civ 1719; [2004] P.I.Q.R. P19) but how far one can dissociate the two in practice must be debatable; cf. para.7–023.

[133] If C is killed by D and it is shown that C had a weak heart, C's dependants will recover damages but they will be less than if C had been fit. Yet the question is a hypothetical one of the same general nature as that in *Hotson*: what would have happened to the victim but for D's wrong? The only difference appears to be that in *Hotson* the claimant is unable to show any loss at all, whereas in our example his difficulty will lie in being able to show how long the loss would have lasted.

[134] [2005] UKHL 2; [2005] 2 A.C. 176.

which he complained, i.e. the 17 per cent reduction in his chance of recovery. The case was different from *Hotson* in that the immediate spread of the cancer would probably not have occurred had there been prompt diagnosis[135] but the basis of the claim was that the claimant had been deprived of the chance of a *cure*. It also differed from *Hotson* in the fact that in that case the outcome was predetermined by the (unknown) amount of blood vessel damage which had been caused by the fall (so that, strictly speaking, the question of loss of a chance was never before the court) whereas now the developments which reduced his life expectancy were subsequent to the negligence. Nevertheless, for Lord Hoffmann and Baroness Hale the claim was an attempt to reformulate the basis of the law in terms of lost chances rather than causal outcomes and they consequently rejected it. According to Lord Hoffmann: "In effect, the appellant submits that the exceptional rule in *Fairchild*'s case should be generalised and damages awarded in all cases in which the defendant may have caused an injury and has increased the likelihood of the injury being suffered."[136]

Fairchild itself did not apply because there was no impossibility of proof; rather, on the balance of probability test, the claim simply failed.[137] If the adverse outcome has occurred (which it had not in *Gregg*) and it is impossible to prove what the chances are that it could have been avoided but for the negligence of the defendant, the requirements for the *Fairchild* exception appear to have been met. Such cases of clinical negligence might then be explained on the basis of the single agent limitation,[138] though not others,[139] but it now seems that the *Fairchild* exception may be confined to cases of mesothelioma in any event.[140]

Among the minority, Lord Nicholls would have allowed recovery based upon the loss of a chance in those cases of medical negligence relating to the treatment of an existing illness[141] where there was significant uncertainty about the outcome at the time of the negligence.[142] However, as we have seen in connection with *Fairchild*, it is difficult for the common law to create and maintain special pockets of causation rules for particular types of litigation.[143] Although Lord Hope agreed with Lord Nicholls, the emphasis in his speech seems to have been on the view that this was really a case of a proved physical injury (the enlargement of the tumour) which simply had to be *quantified*.[144] Lord Phillips,

---

[135] [2005] UKHL 2; [2005] 2 A.C. 176 at [70].

[136] [2005] UKHL 2; [2005] 2 A.C. 176 at [85].

[137] Cf. *Hussain v Bradford Teaching Hospital NHS Foundation Trust* [2011] EWHC 2914; [2013] Med L.R. 353.

[138] For example, *Wilsher v Essex Area Health Authority*[1988] A.C. 1074, see para.7–020.

[139] For example, *Hotson*: see Peel [2006] L.M.C.L.Q. 289.

[140] See para.7–021.

[141] And not, therefore, to the *Fairchild* situation: [2005] UKHL 2; [2005] 2 A.C. 176 at [51].

[142] He would also, therefore, exclude the *Hotson* situation: at [38]. Quaere how realistic this is. To say that there was "no uncertainty" in that case is only true in so far as we assume that the "but-for/balance of probabilities" approach gives us the correct answer but we know that there is a one in four chance that it is incorrect. Cf. Porat and Stein, *Tort Liability under Uncertainty* (2001) who would award the *Hotson* claimant 25 per cent of his loss on the basis that the defendants' negligence in not examining him has deprived him of the chance of showing that they were responsible for his physical condition.

[143] *Gregg v Scott* [2005] UKHL 2; [2005] 2 A.C. 176 at [172] per Lord Phillips.

[144] *Gregg v Scott* [2005] UKHL 2; [2005] 2 A.C. 176 at [118]. Lord Nicholls thought this approach was only "superficially attractive": at [58].

who agreed in rejecting the claim, emphasised the difficulty of deciding cases about individual claimants on the basis of statistical evidence based on groups.[145] He contemplated that the law might allow a "chance-based" claim where the adverse outcome which due care might have averted had actually occurred,[146] but subsequent case law suggests that there is no appetite for the introduction of such a claim in cases of clinical negligence.[147]

Baroness Hale acknowledged that the defendant could be liable for other types of loss which it could be proved were caused by the defendant's negligence such as any "*extra* pain, suffering, loss of amenity, financial loss and loss of expectation of life which may have resulted from the delay".[148] Based on this, in a later case an award was made for loss of median life expectancy of three years, but since (as in *Gregg*) the claimant had not yet died, there is some force in the submission of counsel for the defendant that it was "too early to say what difference has been made in the Claimant's case".[149]

7–027   **Assessment.** The general question of loss of a chance has been widely debated in other jurisdictions and systems.[150] The American case law is divided[151] with some courts denying such recovery, others allowing it on the basis of the value of the chance lost and yet others going so far as to allow the jury to give damages on the basis that the loss *would* have occurred. The last seems to give the claimant the best of all possible worlds. Indeed, even if one adopts the second position it seems logical that one could no longer maintain the position of the claimant who can show causation on a balance of probabilities and who now recovers damages in full. Hence if the House of Lords had taken the opposite line in *Hotson* many currently successful claimants would receive less.[152] Although the effect of the loss of a chance approach would mean that fewer cases would fail altogether, it does not follow that the global liability bill would be any greater, for the reduction in the claims which now succeed in full might offset (or even exceed)

---

[145] See para.7–023. Although the case had been treated below in terms of loss of the chance of a "cure" the medical definition of this was survival for 10 years. The trial took place five years after the negligence and the claimant was still alive at the time of the appeal decision, a little over 10 years after the negligence.

[146] *Gregg v Scott* [2005] UKHL 2; [2005] 2 A.C. 176 at [188]. The fact that the claimant had not died did not feature prominently in the reasoning of the other judges in the majority (Lord Hoffmann and Baroness Hale), but has been stressed in later cases as a further basis for distinguishing *Gregg v Scott* from *Fairchild*: see *Barker v Corus UK Ltd* [2006] UKHL 20; [2006] 2 A.C. 572 at [48] per Lord Hoffmann.

[147] *Wright v Cambridge Medical Group* [2011] EWCA Civ 669; [2012] 3 W.L.R. 1124 at [84], [96].

[148] *Gregg v Scott* [2005] UKHL 2; [2005] 2 A.C. 176 at [206]–[207].

[149] *JD v Mather* [2012] EWHC 3063 (QB); [2013] Med L.R. 291; cf. *Oliver v Williams* [2013] EWHC 600 (QB); [2013] Med L.R. 344.

[150] After making some progress in Australia the doctrine appears to have been blocked for the time being in *Tabet v Gett* [2010] HCA 12; (2010) 240 C.L.R. 537. While the Supreme Court of Canada rejected loss of a chance in *Laferrière v Lawson* [1991] 1 S.C.R. 541, the decision in *Resurfice Corp v Hanke* [2007] SCC 7; [2007] 1 S.C.R. 333 contains passages which can be read as supporting liability in a limited class of cases based on increase in risk but it does not seem to have made any difference in the typical "loss of a chance of a better medical outcome" situation: *Bohun v Segal* [2007] BCCA 23; 289 D.L.R. (4th) 614.

[151] See Dobbs, *Torts* (2000), para.178.

[152] The claimant in *Gregg v Scott* accepted that any change to a "chance-based" system would have to "cut both ways": [2005] UKHL 2; [2005] 2 A.C. 176 at [225].

the amount payable to claimants like *Hotson*. Since under the present law there is no reason for a judge to put any figure on the probability of causation, whether or not it passes the point of balance, there is no way of accumulating the data from which we could know what the effect would be. In any event, it would certainly make the negotiation and adjudication of claims a great deal more complicated and would result in more *claims* if not any increase in the global liability bill. "Almost any claim for loss of an outcome could be reformulated as a claim for loss of a chance of that outcome"[153] and despite the fact that it is difficult to counter the argument that to make the success or failure of a case turn on whether a risk is, say, 45 per cent or 55 per cent is "irrational and indefensible",[154] it seems right to say that the effects of such a shift would be incalculable,[155] crude as the present system may appear to be.

Successful "loss of chance" claims. There have been cases in which the claimant has recovered damages for "loss of a chance" and these were little considered in the House of Lords in *Hotson*. Some of them are cases of contract[156] but it now appears that the explanation of them does not rest on the distinction between contract and tort and that it would be going too far to say that loss of a chance is wholly outside the scope of tort law. Damages for loss of a chance appear to be recoverable where the claimant's loss depends upon what action would have been taken by a third party.[157] In *Allied Maples Group Ltd v Simmons & Simmons*[158] the facts assumed for the purpose of a preliminary issue were that the defendants had been negligent in advising the claimants about potential liabilities resulting from a purchase. The Court of Appeal held that in order to establish liability on the part of the defendants it was not necessary for the claimants to show that if they had been properly advised they would have succeeded in persuading the seller to grant them protection or indemnity against these liabilities; merely that there was a substantial, rather than merely speculative, chance of success, the damages then being discounted to allow for the chance.[159] The same approach would have been taken even if it was more likely than not that the protection would have been obtained,[160] until it becomes a "near certainty"[161] when the chance that it would not have been obtained can be ignored. As it has been

7–028

---

[153] *Gregg v Scott* [2005] UKHL 2; [2005] 2 A.C. 176 at [224] per Baroness Hale.

[154] *Gregg v Scott* [2005] UKHL 2; [2005] 2 A.C. 176 at [3] per Lord Nicholls.

[155] The potential impact on the NHS is prominent in the reasoning of Lord Hoffmann: *Gregg v Scott* [2005] UKHL 2; [2005] 2 A.C. 176 at [90].

[156] Such as *Chaplin v Hicks* [1911] 2 K.B. 786.

[157] It is not clear why it was necessary to rely on this in *Doyle v Wallace* [1998] P.I.Q.R. Q146, since that was a pure case of quantification. Nor does it apply where C's ship would probably have earned profits and there is evidence of the market: *The Vicky I* [2008] EWCA Civ 101; [2008] 1 Lloyd's Rep 45.

[158] [1995] 1 W.L.R. 1602.

[159] It would, however, be necessary for the claimants to prove on a balance of probabilities that they would have taken steps to persuade the group. The principle in *Allied Maples* does not apply if the issue is what the claimant would have done if properly advised.

[160] Thus in *Kitchen v Royal Air Force Association* [1958] 1 W.L.R. 563 the claimant recovered two-thirds of the damages she would have received if successful in the action which had never been pursued because of the defendants' negligence.

[161] *Allied Maples v Simmons & Simmons* [1995] 1 W.L.R. at 1614; *Charles v Hugh James Jones & Jenkins* [2000] 1 W.L.R. 1278.

succinctly put in the context of loss of opportunity to pursue a case: "[T]he court has to decide whether [the claimant] lost something of value, in the sense that the prospects were better than negligible. If the answer to that is 'yes', then it has to put a figure on what [the claimant] has lost."[162]

Examples of other situations where this approach will be adopted are failure by a solicitor to proceed with a claim within the limitation period[163] and an inaccurate reference which deprives the claimant of an opportunity of employment.[164] In view of the common assumption that personal well-being deserves a higher level of protection than property or money, it may be asked why we are more ready to admit a claim based on loss of a chance in these cases where the claim is for financial loss.[165]

3. REMOTENESS OF DAMAGE (SCOPE OF LIABILITY)

7–029 No defendant is responsible ad infinitum for all the consequences of his wrongful conduct, however remote in time and however indirect the process of causation, for otherwise human activity would be unreasonably hampered. The law must draw a line somewhere, some consequences must be abstracted as relevant, not on grounds of pure logic, but simply for practical reasons.[166] Nor is the law of tort (or even the private law of obligations) unique in this way: a social security or "no fault" compensation scheme has, for the same practical reason, to find a formula which will limit the reach of compensation.[167] The dominant (though by no means conclusive or all-embracing) question in the determination of the scope of the defendant's liability is whether the harm in respect of which he is sued was a foreseeable consequence of his negligent act.

---

[162] *Dixon v Clement Jones Solicitors* [2004] EWCA Civ 1005; [2005] P.N.L.R. 6 at [53] per Carnwath LJ.

[163] *Kitchen v Royal Air Forces Association* [1958] 1 W.L.R. 563; *Pearson v Sanders Witherspoon* [2000] Lloyd's Rep. 151.

[164] This was the view of Lord Lowry in *Spring v Guardian Assurance Plc* [1995] 2 A.C. 296 at 327. See also *Davies v Taylor* [1974] A.C. 207, where although the House of Lords dismissed the claim on the ground that the chance was merely speculative, it accepted that for the purposes of establishing her claim under the Fatal Accidents Act the claimant did not have to prove that a reconciliation with her deceased husband was more probable than not.

[165] Consider *Gouldsmith v Mid-Staffordshire etc NHS Trust* [2007] EWCA Civ 397 [2007] L.S. Law Medical 363. D was negligent in failing to refer C for specialist treatment and C lost fingers. The evidence was that "most" specialists would have operated and the fingers would have been saved. The majority of the CA treated this as amounting to evidence that on a balance of probabilities the surgery would have been carried out and the claimant therefore succeeded, but Maurice Kay LJ dissented on the basis that there was no evidence of to whom the claimant would have been referred and that the evidence clearly implied that a respectable body of specialists would not have operated. He suggested that the case was essentially one of loss of a chance but this was not a route pursued by either party and has since been discouraged: *Wright v Cambridge Medical Group* [2011] EWCA Civ 669; [2012] 3 W.L.R. 1124.

[166] *Liesbosch Dredger v Edison SS* [1933] A.C. 449 at 460 per Lord Wright.

[167] A Frenchman, in celebrating the restoration of Alsace to France in 1919, fired a revolver which burst and injured him. His claim that his injuries were due to the outbreak of war in 1914 was rejected by the Metz Pensions Board as too remote: *The Times*, February 6, 1933.

A.   The Wagon Mound Test

Two competing views. In the 100 years or so until the middle of the 20th century   **7–030**
two competing views of the test for remoteness were current in the law.
According to the first, consequences are too remote if a reasonable man would
not have foreseen them[168]; according to the second, if a reasonable man would
have foreseen any damage to the claimant as likely to result from his act, then he
is liable for the direct consequences of it suffered by the claimant, whether a
reasonable man would have foreseen them or not.

Re Polemis. In 1921, in the case known as *Re Polemis*,[169] the Court of Appeal   **7–031**
apparently settled English law in favour of the second rule. A chartered vessel
was unloading in Casablanca when stevedores, who were servants of the
charterers, negligently let a plank drop into the hold. Part of the cargo was a
quantity of benzine in tins, which had leaked, and a rush of flames at once
followed, totally destroying the ship. The Court of Appeal held that the charterers
were responsible for all the direct consequences of the stevedores' negligence,
even though they could not reasonably have been anticipated. None of the
members of the Court except Scrutton LJ defined "direct" consequences. He said
that damage is indirect if it is, "due to the operation of independent causes having
no connection with the negligent act, except that they could not avoid its
results".[170] It is important to note that in *Re Polemis* it was foreseeable that the
ship would suffer some damage from the dropping of the plank and the initial
breach of duty was therefore established. The case was no authority on the
"unforeseeable claimant",[171] despite some passages which might suggest the
contrary.

The Wagon Mound. In *The Wagon Mound*[172] the Privy Council, through   **7–032**
Viscount Simonds, expressed its unqualified disapproval of *Re Polemis* and
refused to follow it. The defendants were charterers by demise[173] of *The Wagon
Mound*, an oil-burning vessel which was moored at the C. Oil Co's wharf in
Sydney Harbour for the purpose of taking on fuel oil. Owing to the carelessness
of the defendants' servants a large quantity of fuel oil was spilt on to the water,
and after a few hours this had spread to the claimants' wharf about 600ft away
where another ship, the *Corrimal*, was under repair. Welding operations were
being carried out on the *Corrimal*, but when a manager on the claimants' wharf
became aware of the presence of the oil he stopped the welding operations and
inquired of the claimants whether they might safely be continued. The result of
this inquiry, coupled with his own belief as to the non-inflammability of fuel oil
in the open, led him to give instructions for the welding operations to continue,

---

[168] First propounded by Pollock CB in *Rigby v Hewitt* (1859) 5 Ex. 240 at 243; *Greenland v Chaplin*
(1850) 5 Ex. 243 at 248.
[169] [1921] 3 K.B. 560.
[170] *Re Polemis* [1921] 3 K.B. 560 at 577.
[171] See para.5–007.
[172] [1961] A.C. 388.
[173] That is, they were in full possession of it with their own crew.

though with all precautions to prevent inflammable material from falling into the oil. Two days later the oil caught fire and extensive damage was done to the claimants' wharf.

The two key findings of fact were: (1) It was unforeseeable that fuel oil spread on water and would catch fire;[174] and (2) some foreseeable damage was caused to the claimants' wharf from the spillage of the oil as the oil had got on to the slipways and interfered with their use. The case was dealt with, therefore, on the footing that there was a breach of duty and direct damage of which the breach was a factual cause, but that the damage caused by fire was unforeseeable. The Privy Council, reversing the decision below in favour of the claimants, held that *Re Polemis* should no longer be regarded as good law and the defendants were not liable for the fire damage: "It is the foresight of the reasonable man which alone can determine responsibility. The *Polemis* rule by substituting 'direct' for 'reasonably foreseeable' consequence leads to a conclusion equally illogical and unjust."[175]

7–033 **Scope of the Wagon Mound test.** Notwithstanding the fact that *The Wagon Mound* was a decision of the Privy Council, the technical point of precedent was side-stepped or ignored and it was immediately accepted as stating the law in England. However, whether this made very much difference to the results of cases is debatable in view of subsequent decisions.[176]

The essence of *The Wagon Mound* is that in proceedings in negligence foreseeability is relevant not only for the purpose of asking whether a duty of care is owed and whether the defendant breached that duty but also in relation to remoteness of damage, and the Privy Council clearly attached importance to the supposed illogicality of using different tests at different stages of the inquiry in any given case. It might have been thought from this that the effect of *The Wagon Mound* was restricted to actions for negligence. In *The Wagon Mound (No.2)*,[177] however, the Privy Council held that foreseeability is the test for remoteness of damage in cases of nuisance also,[178] and, though they pointed out that liability in many cases of nuisance depends on fault and thus on foreseeability, they stated that the same test must apply even where this is not so.[179]

7–034 **The competing rules compared.** It will be seen below that *The Wagon Mound* has made little difference to the law in terms of practical result, and, indeed, Viscount Simonds indicated that this would probably be so in *The Wagon Mound*

---

[174] In *Overseas Tankship (UK) Ltd v Miller Steamship Co Pty Ltd (The Wagon Mound) (No.2)* [1967] A.C 617, an action by the owners of the *Corrimal* for damage caused to their ship by the same fire, the Privy Council, on somewhat different evidence, held that the damage was foreseeable: see para.7–042.

[175] *The Wagon Mound* [1961] A.C. 388 at 424.

[176] See paras7–037—7–042.

[177] [1967] 1 A.C. 617.

[178] See para.15–031.

[179] Although not couched in terms of remoteness of damage, it has since been held that the test of liability under the rule in *Rylands v Fletcher* is whether the damage done was to be anticipated from the escaped thing: see para.16–035.

itself.[180] However, it undoubtedly produced a change of principle and much has been written on its merits as compared with those of *Re Polemis*. Only two points can be considered here.

Simplicity. The Privy Council laid much stress upon the difficulties of the directness test, but it is difficult to see how the foreseeability test is any easier. Not only does the change from the one to the other raise the question of the meaning of the "kind" of damage which must have been foreseeable but it "gets rid of the difficulties of determining causal connection by substituting the difficulty of determining the range and extent of foresight of the hypothetical reasonable man".[181] The fact is that the issue of remoteness of damage is not susceptible to short cuts. As Prosser put it:[182]

> "There is no substitute for dealing with the particular facts, and considering all the factors that bear on them, interlocked as they must be. Theories . . . have not improved at all on the old words 'proximate' and 'remote' with the idea they convey of some reasonable connection between the original negligence and its consequences, between the harm threatened and the harm done."

7–035

Fairness. According to the Privy Council the test of directness works unfairly:[183]

7–036

> "It does not seem consonant with current ideas of justice or morality that for an act of negligence, however slight or venial, which results in some trivial foreseeable damage the actor should be liable for all consequences however unforeseeable and however grave, so long as they can be said to be 'direct'."

It is no doubt hard on a negligent defendant that he should be held liable for unexpectedly large damages, but it is not clear that the final outcome is any fairer if the claimant is left without redress for damage which he has suffered through no fault of his own. Bearing in mind that negligence involves the creation of an unreasonable risk of causing some foreseeable damage to the claimant it might be thought that even though "justice" may be impossible of achievement where unforeseeable damage occurs,[184] greater injustice is produced by *The Wagon Mound* than by *Re Polemis*.

B.   Application of Foreseeability

Precision unnecessary as to the extent of damage or the manner of its infliction. The test of foreseeability involves the assessment of facts against a legal standard and, because all the facts of the particular case have to be brought into account, it is generally undesirable to engage in extensive citation of authority.[185] Nevertheless, the student will want to be given some idea of how in practice judges approach these matters. The test was from the beginning heavily

7–037

---

[180] *The Wagon Mound* [1961] A.C. 388 at 422.
[181] Walker 1961 S.L.T. 37.
[182] Prosser (1953) 52 Michigan L. Rev 1 at 32.
[183] *The Wagon Mound* [1961] A.C. 388 at 422.
[184] Prosser (1953) 52 Michigan L. Rev 1 at 17.
[185] *Jolley v Sutton LBC* [2000] 1 W.L.R. 1082.

qualified by the fact that neither the precise extent of the damage nor the precise manner of its infliction need be foreseeable. As Lord Denning MR put it:[186]

"It is not necessary that the precise concatenation of circumstances should be envisaged. If the consequence was one which was within the general range which any reasonable person might foresee (and was not of an entirely different kind which no one would anticipate) then it is within the rule that a person who has been guilty of negligence is liable for the consequences."

In *Hughes v Lord Advocate*[187] employees of the Post Office opened a manhole in the street and in the evening negligently left the open manhole covered by a canvas shelter, unattended and surrounded by warning paraffin lamps. The claimant, a boy aged eight, took one of the lamps into the shelter and was playing with it there when he stumbled over and it fell into the manhole. A violent explosion followed and the claimant himself fell into the hole, sustaining terrible injuries from the burns. It was quite unpredictable that a lamp might explode, but the Post Office men were in breach of duty leaving the manhole unattended because they should have appreciated that boys might take a lamp into the shelter and that, if the lamp fell and broke, they might suffer serious injury from burning. So the lamp, a known source of danger, caused injury through a particular sequence of events which may not have been envisaged, but the defendants were nevertheless held liable.

Similarly, in *Jolley v Sutton LBC*[188] the defendants had failed to take steps to remove an old, abandoned boat from their land to which the public had easy access. The obvious risk (indeed the defendants conceded the point) was that a child might suffer injury from climbing on the boat and falling through the rotten planking; in fact the claimant and a friend embarked on a futile project to restore the boat and, while the claimant was working underneath it, it fell on him, breaking his back. The House of Lords restored the decision for the claimant by the trial judge, who it held had been entitled to conclude that the accident which occurred was within the range of what was foreseeable, given the ingenuity of children, "in finding unexpected ways of doing mischief to themselves and others".[189]

It is also clear from the decisions in *Hughes* and *Jolley* that if the accident occurs in a foreseeable way, as broadly defined, the defendant will be liable even though the damage is also much greater in extent than might have been anticipated.[190]

---

[186] *Stewart v West African Terminals Ltd* [1964] 2 Lloyd's Rep. 371 at 375; *Bradford v Robinson Rentals Ltd* [1967] 1 W.L.R. 337 at 344–345 per Rees J.

[187] [1963] A.C. 837. Cf. *Doughty v Turner Manufacturing Co Ltd* [1964] 1 Q.B. 518; *Hadlow v Peterborough City Council* [2011] EWCA Civ 1329.

[188] [2000] 1 W.L.R. 1082.

[189] *Jolley v Sutton LBC* [2000] 1 W.L.R. 1082 at 1093 per Lord Hoffmann; and see *Jebson v MoD* [2000] 1 W.L.R. 2055 (drunken person).

[190] One of the few clear examples of this is *Vacwell Engineering v BDH Chemicals* [1971] 1 Q.B. 88 (minor explosion foreseeable; huge explosion took place because claimants put a number of ampoules in the same sink). See also *Bradford v Robinson Rentals Ltd* [1967] 1 W.L.R. 337 (exposure causing frostbite). Where the loss is economic, this is in practical terms indistinguishable from the principle discussed in para.7–039.

The egg-shell skull principle. *The Wagon Mound* did not displace the principle **7–038** that the defendant must take his victim as he finds him.[191] It has for long been the law that if a person is: "[N]egligently run over or otherwise negligently injured in his body, it is no answer to the sufferer's claim for damages that he would have suffered less injury . . . [192] if he had not had an unusually thin skull or an unusually weak heart."[193]

This principle is as applicable to "nervous shock" as to any other sort of personal injury[194] and applies where the foreseeable danger is of physical trauma but the claimant is shocked, because of his susceptible personality, into mental illness, even though no physical injury has in fact occurred.[195] It has also been applied where the immediate cause of the loss is voluntary conduct by the claimant to which his personality may have predisposed him but which would not have occurred but for his injury,[196] but the conduct in question in the case was the commission of a crime and in such a case the claim would now be barred by public policy.[197] The claimant's weakness cuts both ways, however: his damages are likely to be less than those of a "normal" person suffering the same overall injury in order to reflect the greater risk to which he was exposed by the normal vicissitudes of life.[198]

Since the egg-shell skull principle seems to be based either on the great difficulty that would arise if the court had to determine in detail what were the foreseeable physical consequences of an injury or on the view that all sorts of individually unlikely consequences are foreseeable in a general way,[199] the same (or a similar) principle operates when the claimant's injury is exacerbated by a

---

[191] *Smith v Leech Brain & Co Ltd* [1962] 2 Q.B. 405; *Warren v Scruttons* [1962] 1 Lloyd's Rep. 497; *Lines v Harland and Wolff* [1966] 1 Lloyd's Rep. 400; *Boon v Thomas Hubback* [1967] 1 Lloyd's Rep. 281; *Wieland v Cyril Lord Carpets Ltd* [1969] 3 All E.R. 100.

[192] The missing words are "or no injury at all". Kennedy J went too far here, for there must be a breach of duty owed to the claimant and if no damage at all could have been foreseen to a person of normal sensitivity and the claimant's abnormal sensitivity was unknown to the defendant, then he is not liable: *Bourhill v Young* [1943] A.C. 92 at 109; *Cook v Swinfen* [1967] 1 W.L.R. 457.

[193] *Dulieu v White* [1901] 2 K.B. 669 at 679 per Kennedy J. On the burden of proof of whether the greater injury was caused by the susceptibility, see *Shorey v PT Ltd* [2003] HCA 87; 197 A.L.R. 410.

[194] Does it apply to property damage? In *The Sivand* [1998] 2 Lloyd's Rep. 97 the unusual ground conditions at the claimants' harbour meant that unexpected delay and expense was incurred in effecting repairs to damage to moorings caused by the defendants' vessel. The defendants were liable for this and, although he regarded the problem as foreseeable, Pill LJ said at 100 that the, "liability of the defendants is founded on one aspect of the principle that a tortfeasor takes his victim as he finds him"; but note that in the context of nuisance we tend to say that a landowner cannot increase the liabilities of a neighbour by putting his property to unusually sensitive use: see para.15–016.

[195] *Page v Smith* [1996] A.C. 155, para.5–085; contra Lord Goff dissenting in *Frost v CC South Yorkshire* [1999] A.C. 455 at 476.

[196] *Meah v McCreamer* [1985] 1 All E.R. 367, though the point is only referred to in subsequent proceedings: *Meah v McCreamer (No.2)* [1986] 1 All E.R. 943.

[197] *Clunis v Camden and Islington HA* [1998] Q.B. 978 and para.26–064. Indeed the claim in *Meah v McCreamer (No.2)* was dismissed on this basis.

[198] Apparently known in Canada as the "crumbling skull" doctrine: *Athey v Leonati* (1996) 140 D.L.R. (4th) 235. The damages in *Page v Smith* [1996] A.C. 155 were reduced by some 40 per cent on account of this.

[199] See *The Sivand* [1998] 2 Lloyd's Rep. 97.

combination of his abnormality and some external force which foreseeably and naturally intervenes after the accident, for example medical treatment to which he is allergic.[200]

It has sometimes been said that the "egg-shell skull" rule is simply an example of the principle that the precise extent of the damage need not have been foreseeable,[201] though that would involve saying that the law regarded personal injury as indivisible and that damage from cancer triggered by a burn[202] was damage of the same kind as the burn.[203] At any rate, the principles are obviously closely related.

7–039   **Pecuniary amount of the damage.** If the defendant injures a high income earner or a piece of property with a high intrinsic value (such as an antique vase) he cannot argue that he had no reason to expect the amount of the loss to be so great.[204] The law is not, however, so clearly committed to this stand where the loss claimed is not "intrinsic" but arises from the fact that the damage to the claimant's goods renders him unable to earn profits with them.[205] Support can be found in the cases for the view that foreseeability is irrelevant,[206] but the better view is that where the loss is not "intrinsic" the defendant's liability is limited to "ordinary" or "foreseeable" losses.[207] The recoverability of such loss cannot be pre-determined by prior contractual arrangements made between the claimant and third parties who are affected by the damage done to the claimant's property.[208]

7–040   **The same "kind" of damage.** *The Wagon Mound* contains the requirement that the foreseeable damage must be of the same "kind" as the damage which actually occurred. In point of fact even under *Re Polemis* it was probably necessary to distinguish between three very broad "kinds" of damage, namely injury to the

---

[200] *Robinson v Post Office* [1974] 1 W.L.R. 1176. As to whether negligent treatment amounts to a novus actus interveniens, see para.7–053.

[201] The suggestion seems to be made by Lord Wright in *Liesbosch Dredger v Edison SS* [1933] A.C. 449 at 461 and by Lord Parker CJ in *Smith v Leech Brain & Co Ltd* [1962] 2 Q.B. 405 at 415.

[202] As in *Smith v Leech Brain* [1962] 2 Q.B. 405 at 415.

[203] Though this may be the implication of *Page v Smith* [1996] A.C. 155, below and para.5–085: *Margereson v JW Roberts Ltd* [1996] P.I.Q.R. P154 (on appeal [1996] P.I.Q.R. P358).

[204] The point is perhaps so obvious that the only express authority for it appears to be the celebrated dictum of Scrutton LJ in *The Arpad* [1934] P. 189 at 202, though that case had nothing to do with negligence and the judgment was a dissenting one.

[205] The case of a claimant who is disabled from performing particular contracts (e.g. a musician) is perhaps analogous: see *The Arpad* [1934] P. 189 at 221 per Greer LJ.

[206] *The Star of India* (1876) 1 P.D. 466; *Liesbosch Dredger v SS Edison* [1933] A.C. 449 at 463–464 ("The measure of damages is the value of the ship to her owner as a going concern at the time and place of the loss. In assessing that value regard must naturally be had to her pending engagements, either profitable or the reverse"). This case is, of course, best known on the different point relating to the claimant's impecuniosity, para.7–043.

[207] *The Argentino* (1899) 14 App. Cas. 519 at 523; *The Arpad* [1934] P. 189; *The Daressa* [1971] 1 Lloyd's Rep. 60.

[208] *Conarken Group Ltd v Network Rail Infrastructure Ltd* [2011] EWCA Civ 644; 136 Con L.R. 1 (where the negligence of D caused damage to the rail network operated by C, C's losses included the sums it was contractually required to pay to train operating companies (T). Whether C was entitled to recover those sums from D was to be determined by ordinary principles of remoteness and mitigation, i.e. it did not follow automatically from C's obligation under contract to pay T. However, the losses in question were reasonably foreseeable and the sums payable under the C-T contracts were reasonable. They were therefore recoverable).

person, damage to property and pure financial loss, but *The Wagon Mound* certainly demands a more elaborate classification of "kinds" of damage than that: in the case itself damage to the claimants' wharf was foreseeable and damage to the claimants' wharf occurred. It follows that, in the Privy Council's judgment, a distinction must be taken between damage by fouling, which was foreseeable, and damage by fire, which occurred. The difficulty is to know how narrowly the kind of damage in question in any given case must be defined. In *Tremain v Pike*[209] the rat population on the defendant's farm was allowed to become unduly large and the claimant, a herdsman on the farm, contracted leptospirosis, otherwise known as Weil's disease, in consequence. Even on the assumption that the defendants had been negligent in failing to control the rat population,[210] Payne J held that the claimant could not succeed. Weil's disease is extremely rare and is caused by contact with rat's urine, and in Payne J's opinion it was therefore both unforeseeable and "entirely different in kind" from such foreseeable consequences as the effect of a rat bite or food poisoning from contaminated food. The claimant could not simply say that rat-induced disease was foreseeable and rat-induced disease occurred.[211]

Wide meaning of "foreseeable". *Tremain v Pike* requires a rather high degree of precision in classifying kinds of damage, but there do not seem to be very many personal injury[212] cases since *The Wagon Mound* where the claim has failed on the basis of remoteness.[213] The House of Lords, in emphasising the difference between the rules of remoteness in contract and tort has given to the word "foreseeable" a meaning which is very far removed from "probable" or "likely". The rule in tort imposes a much wider liability than that in contract: "[T]he defendant [in tort] will be liable for any type of damage which is reasonably foreseeable as liable to happen, *even in the most unusual case*, unless the risk is so small that a reasonable man would in the whole circumstances feel justified in neglecting it."[214]

7–041

However, "reasonable foreseeability must imply *some* understanding of the chain of events which is putatively foreseen; otherwise we are looking not at foresight, but divination".[215]

Foreseeability a relative concept. In *The Wagon Mound* the Privy Council accepted and based its reasoning on the trial judge's finding that the defendants

7–042

---

[209] [1969] 1 W.L.R. 1556; cf. *Bradford v Robinson Rentals Ltd* [1967] 1 W.L.R. 337; *Malcolm v Broadhurst* [1970] 3 All E.R. 508.

[210] The defendant's negligence in this respect was not actually made out.

[211] Cf. the opinion of Edmund Davies LJ in *Draper v Hodder* [1972] 2 Q.B. 556 that the foreseeable risk of the infant claimant being injured by being bowled over by the dogs would justify the imposition of liability where the dogs attacked him.

[212] A "broad brush" approach is also discernible with regard to property damage: see *The Carnival* [1994] 2 Lloyd's Rep. 14.

[213] Though see *Pratley v Surrey CC* [2003] EWCA Civ 1067; [2004] I.C.R. 159 (employer aware of risk of injury to health from over-work but not of the sudden collapse which occurred as a result of disappointment at non-implementation of palliative measures; not enough to categorise the risk as "risk of psychiatric illness").

[214] *C Czarnikow Ltd v Koufos* [1969] 1 A.C. 350 at 385 per Lord Reid (emphasis added). See also at 411, 422.

[215] *Arscott v The Coal Authority* [2004] EWCA Civ 892; [2005] Env L.R. 6 at [58] (a nuisance case).

did not know and could not reasonably be expected to have known that furnace oil was capable of being set afire when spread on water. In *The Wagon Mound (No.2)*, however, somewhat different evidence was presented[216] and in the Privy Council the trial judge's finding to similar effect, not being a primary finding of fact but an inference from other findings, was rejected. There was, it was held, a real risk of fire such as would have been appreciated by a properly qualified and alert chief engineer and this, given the fact that there was no justification for discharging oil into Sydney Harbour in any case, was sufficient to fix liability on the defendants. In other words, the mere fact that the damage suffered was unlikely to occur does not relieve the defendant of liability if his conduct was unreasonable—a proposition very little different from that contained in *Re Polemis* itself. On the facts of that case, notwithstanding the arbitrator's finding that the spark which caused the explosion was not reasonably foreseeable, there was, surely, a "real risk" that the vapour in the hold might be accidentally ignited and there was, of course, no justification for dropping the plank into the hold.

C. Claimant's Lack of Means

7–043 **The Liesbosch decision: no liability for loss due to claimant's lack of means.** In *Liesbosch Dredger v Edison SS*[217] the House of Lords held that where the claimant, whose dredger had been sunk and who could not afford to purchase a substitute, incurred extra expense in hiring one in order to complete his contracts he could not recover that extra expense, which was an extraneous matter and too remote. The then leading case of *Re Polemis* was distinguished on the ground that it was concerned with the, "immediate physical consequences of the negligent act".[218] It was never very clear why a distinction was drawn between the claimant's physical weakness, in which context the defendant took his victim as he found him, and his financial weakness.[219] Indeed, from a different point of view the defendant *did* take the claimant's financial position as he found it, for the claimant was always entitled to base his claim for lost earnings upon his pre-accident income, not some sort of national average.

7–044 **Lagden v O'Connor: no bar to recovery of loss due to claimant's lack of means.** For a good many years the decision in the *Liesbosch* case was criticised and frequently distinguished and the House of Lords finally departed from it in *Lagden v O'Connor*.[220] The claimant's car was damaged by the defendant's negligence. On normal principles the claimant was entitled to the costs of repairs and the hire of a substitute vehicle while those were done.[221] However, being unable to afford the outlay on the hire of a car in the ordinary way, the claimant had contracted with a credit hire company, on terms that the company would take

---

[216] See Lord Reid's explanation of this [1967] 1 A.C. 617 at 640–641, and Dias [1967] C.L.J. 63–65.
[217] [1933] A.C. 448.
[218] [1933] A.C. 448 at 461.
[219] The rule may have had some connection with the former rule that damages are not recoverable for non-payment of money, but this is no longer the law: *Sempra Metals Ltd v Commissioners of Inland Revenue* [2007] UKHL 34; [2008] 1 A.C. 561.
[220] *Lagden v O'Connor* [2003] UKHL 64; [2004] 1 A.C. 1067.
[221] *Bee v Jenson* [2007] EWCA Civ 923; [2007] 4 All E.R. 791.

over the prosecution of his claim, he would receive a hire car on credit while his was repaired and the charges would be paid out of the damages recovered from the defendant. Due to the cost of handling the claim and the element of risk the charge for hire was about 30 per cent more than the standard "spot rate" for car hire in that area. The House of Lords unanimously held that there should no longer be any hard and fast rule that additional losses attributable to the claimant's impecuniosity were irrecoverable. However, the House was divided on whether the particular claim should succeed. For the majority this was a case where the defendant had failed to show that the claimant had behaved unreasonably in using the credit hire company. His financial position was such that he had no choice but to do so if he wished to obtain a car. That would not necessarily be so in other cases where the claimant had greater resources. The effect therefore is that a rule which was mechanical and "efficient" in terms of the disposition of claims is replaced with a test that is somewhat open-ended and therefore more likely to be productive of dispute. While the majority recognised this risk, they thought it exaggerated because it would be in the interests of motor insurers to keep down the costs of small claims.

A question of remoteness, or of mitigation? In *Lagden v O'Connor* the majority of opinions were couched, as was *The Liesbosch*, mainly in terms of remoteness but the placing of the burden on the defendant to show that the claimant had a realistic choice between taking an ordinary hire car and using credit hire matches the approach to mitigation,[222] and subsequent decisions have regarded it as a question of mitigation.[223]   **7–045**

D.   Further Principles

Remoteness not simply a question of foreseeability. The account already given of *The Wagon Mound* test should not mislead one into thinking that foreseeability is all there is to the law of remoteness: the task of determining the scope of the defendant's responsibility has many strands to it. The starting point is that a defendant "is not liable for a consequence of a kind which is not reasonably foreseeable; it does not follow that he is liable for all damage that was reasonably foreseeable".[224]   **7–046**

As was stated at the beginning of this chapter remoteness is an aspect of causation in a broader sense than that of simply "but-for" and frequently the courts will speak in the language of causation because although the defendant's act is a cause in the "but-for" sense some subsequent act or event is regarded as eclipsing it. Sometimes policy comes to the surface and a loss is dismissed as too remote simply because the court does not think it reasonable or desirable to

---

[222] The claimant must show that the damage is not too remote; the defendant must show that the claimant failed to take reasonable steps in mitigation: *Geest Plc v Lansiquot* [2002] UKPC 48; [2002] 1 W.L.R. 3111.

[223] For Lord Walker in *Lagden* (at [101]) it was not a question of mitigation at all in that the hire was not incurred in mitigating some greater loss. See also Lord Hobhouse in *Dimond v Lovell* [2002] 1 A.C. 384 at 406. See Ch.23.

[224] *British Steel Plc v Simmons* [2004] UKHL 20; [2004] I.C.R. 585 at [67] per Lord Rodger.

impose it on the defendant. Thus in *Pritchard v JH Cobden Ltd*,[225] it was held that where the claimant's marriage broke up as a result of his injuries, orders for financial provision made against him by the divorce court could not be the subject of a claim against the tortfeasor: quite apart from the point that redistribution of assets on divorce could not be regarded as a "loss", acceptance of such claims would risk confusion in the judicial process and be open to abuse. There are also a number of commonly recurring situations in which principles have developed which are qualifications of foreseeability and which we must consider in more detail.

i.   Intended Consequences and Intentional Wrongdoers

7–047   Intended consequences are never too remote. "The intention to injure the plaintiff . . . disposes of any question of remoteness of damage."[226] However, the liability of an intentional wrongdoer is not limited to the intended consequences and it will extend at least to such results as are foreseeable. *Scott v Shepherd*[227] may be regarded as a classical instance of this. D throws a squib into a crowd. A, in alarm, throws it away and B does likewise. The squib ends its journey by falling upon C, exploding and putting out his eye. D certainly intended to scare somebody or other. With equal certainty he did not, in common parlance, "intend" to hurt C, much less to destroy his eye, but he was nevertheless held liable to C. The law insists that fools and mischievous persons must answer for consequences which common sense would unhesitatingly attribute to their wrongdoing.[228] Indeed, the intentional wrongdoer's liability may extend beyond the foreseeable because intentional torts have not necessarily been affected by *The Wagon Mound*. A fraudster is liable for unforeseeable consequences[229] and an intentional departure from the terms of a bailment may make the bailee subject to the liability of an insurer.

ii.   Intervening Acts or Events.

7–048   Here it is common to return to the language of causation, but whether regarded as a question of "legal causation", or of remoteness, has been said "does not matter".[230] Everyone agrees that a consequence is too remote if it follows a "break in the chain of causation" or is due to a *nova causa interveniens*.[231] This means that although the defendant's breach of duty is a cause of the claimant's damage in the sense that it satisfies the "but-for" test of causation in fact, nevertheless in the eyes of the law some other intervening event is regarded as the sole effective cause of that damage. Three classes of case fall to be considered, namely: (1) where a natural event occurs independently of the act of any human

---

[225] [1988] Fam. 22.
[226] *Quinn v Leatham* [1901] A.C. 495 at 537 per Lord Lindley.
[227] (1773) 2 W.Bl. 892.
[228] See para.3–002.
[229] See para.12–019.
[230] *Chubb Fire Ltd v Vicar of Spalding* [2010] EWCA Civ 981; [2010] 2 C.L.C. 277 at [63] per Aikens LJ.
[231] If a human act is involved novus actus is often substituted.

being; (2) where the event consists of the act or omission of a third party; and (3) where the event consists of the act or omission of the claimant himself. It should not be thought, however, that in any of these cases the law will be particularly astute to attribute the claimant's damage to a single cause. There is no objection to a finding that the separate torts of two independent actors were both causes of the damage, and where this is so the claimant may recover in full from either of them.[232] Nor is there any objection to a finding that the defendant's breach of duty and the claimant's own fault were both causes of the claimant's damage. On the contrary, such a finding is a condition precedent to the operation of the law of contributory negligence.[233]

Intervening natural event. It is, of course, impossible for anything to happen in   **7–049**
the physical world without the operation of natural forces, but sometimes the claimant suffers damage as the immediate result of a natural event which occurs independently of the defendant's breach of duty but which would have caused the claimant no damage if the breach of duty had not occurred. In such a case, if the breach of duty has neither increased the likelihood that the claimant will suffer damage nor rendered him more susceptible to damage, it will not be treated as a cause of the damage. Thus, in *Carslogie Steamship Co Ltd v Royal Norwegian Government*[234] the claimant's ship was damaged in a collision for which the defendant's ship was wholly responsible. After temporary repairs which restored the ship to a seaworthy condition she set out on a voyage to the United States, a voyage which she would not have made had the collision not occurred. During her crossing of the Atlantic she suffered extensive damage due to heavy weather, and on her arrival in the United States the collision damage was permanently repaired at the same time that the heavy weather damage was dealt with. It was held in the House of Lords that the claimants were not even entitled to damages for the loss of the use of the ship while the collision damage was being repaired because that time was used also for the repair of the heavy weather damage. There was no question of the defendants being liable for the heavy weather damage itself—that damage "was not in any sense a consequence of the collision, and must be treated as a supervening event occurring in the course of a normal voyage".[235]

It was true that with the benefit of hindsight it was possible to say that if the collision had not taken place the storm damage also would not have taken place because the vessel would not have been there at that time, but no reasonable man would have said that such damage was within the likely or foreseeable risk created by the defendant's negligence.[236]

---

[232] See para.7–008. For contribution between tortfeasors, see, Ch.22.

[233] See para.23–036.

[234] [1952] A.C. 292.

[235] *Carslogie Steamship Co Ltd v Royal Norwegian Government* [1952] 1 All E.R. 20 per Viscount Jowitt. Not all of his Lordship's speech is reported in the Law Reports. It seems that if the supervening event had been detention caused by an outbreak of war, the defendants would have been liable: *Monarch SS Co v Karlshamns Oljifabriker* [1949] A.C. 196.

[236] Distinguish the situation where the vessel is rendered less able to ride out the storm because of the damage inflicted on it by the defendant. Cf. the cases on "scope of duty" discussed below: para.7–058.

7–050   **Intervening act of a third party.** If the defendant's breach of duty has done no more than provide the occasion for an entirely independent act by a third party and that act is the immediate cause of the claimant's damage, then it will amount to a nova causa interveniens and the defendant will not be liable.[237] This, however, may not be the case if the act of the third party was not truly independent.[238] In *The Oropesa*[239] a collision occurred between the ship of that name and another ship, the *Manchester Regiment*, for which both ships were to blame. The *Manchester Regiment* was severely damaged and her master decided to cross to the *Oropesa* in one of the ship's boats to discuss salvage arrangements with the master of the *Oropesa*. The boat overturned in heavy seas before reaching the *Oropesa* and nine of the men on board, one of whom was the claimant's son, were drowned. The question was whether his death was caused by the negligence of those in control of the *Oropesa*,[240] or whether the action of the master of the *Manchester Regiment* in taking to the boat constituted a nova causa interveniens. It was held that that action could not be severed from the circumstances affecting the two ships, that the "hand of the casualty lay heavily" upon the *Manchester Regiment*, and so that it was caused by and flowed from the collision.[241] According to Lord Wright: "To break the chain of causation it must be shown that there is something which I will call ultroneous,[242] something unwarrantable, a new cause which disturbs the sequence of events, something which can be described as either unreasonable or extraneous or extrinsic."[243]

7–051   **The intervening act of a third party need not be tortious.** In *The Oropesa*, the action of the master of the *Manchester Regiment* was not itself tortious: he was not guilty of a breach of duty to the deceased in ordering him into the boat, but that fact is not itself decisive one way or another. A wholly unpredictable but non-tortious intervention may break the chain of causation in one case while in another even deliberate tortious conduct may not do so, though as a general proposition it is probably correct to say that the further along the scale from innocent mistake to wilful wrongdoing the third party's conduct moves the more likely it is to terminate the defendant's liability.[244] The matter is what in former

---

[237] *Weld-Blundell v Stephens* [1920] A.C. 956; *Harnett v Bond* [1925] A.C. 669; *SS Singleton Abbey v SS Paludina* [1927] A.C. 16.

[238] This appears to be the best explanation of the difficult case of *Wright v Cambridge Medical Group* [2011] EWCA Civ 669; [2012] 3 W.L.R. 1124 in which the defendant medical practice negligently delayed C's referral to hospital, but the hospital then treated C negligently. The resolution of the claim was not assisted by the fact that no claim had been brought against the hospital, either by C or by the medical practice (by way of contribution) so that key issues had to be resolved on the basis of hypothesis rather than any finding of fact.

[239] [1943] P. 32.

[240] It is irrelevant to this question that the negligence of the *Manchester Regiment* leading to the collision may also have been a cause of the death.

[241] *The Oropesa* [1943] P. 32 at 37 per Lord Wright.

[242] "So Lord Wright found it necessary to go outside the dictionary, or at least to explore its furthest corners, in order to identify the kind of circumstances in which the defendant might cease to be liable for what could otherwise be regarded as the consequences of his act": *The Sivand* [1998] 2 Lloyd's Rep. 97 at 102 per Evans LJ.

[243] *The Oropesa* [1943] P. 32 at 39.

[244] *Knightley v Johns* [1982] 1 W.L.R. 349 at 365.

times would have been regarded as a jury question.[245] It calls for "common sense rather than logic"[246] and a "robust and sensible approach".[247]

Illustrations. The student is only likely to get a "feel" for the current application of the law by reading cases,[248] but some multiple collision cases, on each side of the line, may be used for illustration. In *Rouse v Squires*[249] D1, driving negligently, jack-knifed his lorry across a motorway; a following car collided with the lorry, and some minutes later D2's lorry, also being driven negligently, collided with the other vehicles, killing C, who was assisting at the scene. The Court of Appeal, reversing the trial judge, held that D1's negligence was an operative cause of C's death,[250] for if:[251]

7–052

> "[A] driver so negligently manages his vehicle as to cause it to obstruct the highway and constitute a danger to other road users, including those who are driving too fast or not keeping a proper lookout, but not those who deliberately or recklessly drive into the obstruction, then the first driver's negligence may be held to have contributed to the causation of an accident of which the immediate cause was the negligent driving of the vehicle which because of the presence of the obstruction collides with it."

In contrast, in *Wright v Lodge*[252] D1's vehicle broke down and she negligently failed to take steps to remove it from the highway. D1 was liable to her passenger C1, who was injured when D2's lorry struck the car, but not to C2 and C3, who were injured by colliding with the lorry in the opposite carriageway, where it had come to rest after the collision. The effective cause of the lorry being in the other carriageway was the reckless manner in which D2 had been driving when he collided with the car.[253] The chain of causation was broken by intervening events though there was no recklessness in *Knightley v Johns*.[254] D1's negligent driving caused the blocking of a busy tunnel. After a good deal of confusion as to the location of the accident, D2, a police inspector, took charge but did not immediately close the tunnel as he should have done. He then ordered C, a constable, to drive back against the traffic for that purpose. While doing so C was struck and injured by D3, who was driving too fast into the tunnel. The Court of

---

[245] *Wright v Lodge* [1993] 4 All E.R. 299 at 307.

[246] *Knightley v* [1982] 1 W.L.R. 349 at 367.

[247] *Lamb v Camden LBC* [1981] Q.B. 625 at 647.

[248] "[W]here there are successive tortfeasors, the contention that the causative potency of the negligence of the first is destroyed by the subsequent negligence of the second depends very much on the facts of the particular case": *Wright v Cambridge Medical Group* [2011] EWCA Civ 669; [2012] 3 W.L.R. 1124 at [32] per Lord Neuberger MR.

[249] [1973] Q.B. 889; *Lloyds Bank Ltd v Budd* [1982] R.T.R. 80.

[250] For which D1 was held 25 per cent to blame under the Law Reform (Married Women and Tortfeasors) Act 1935.

[251] *Rouse v Squires* [1973] Q.B. 889 at 898 per Cairns LJ.

[252] [1993] 4 All E.R. 299.

[253] D2 was of course liable to C2 and C3 (and to C1). The issue was whether D2 could claim contribution from D1. D1's share in the liability to C1 was only 10 per cent. It will be observed that both of these cases could equally well be analysed in terms of duty of care to the particular claimant, indeed *Wright v Lodge* has some affinities with *Palsgraf v Long Island Railroad* (para.5–007).

[254] [1982] 1 W.L.R. 349.

Appeal set aside a judgment for C against D1.[255] While it might be natural, probable and foreseeable that the police would come to deal with the accident in the tunnel and that there might be risk-taking[256] and even errors on their part, there had in fact been so many errors before the claimant was ordered to ride back down the tunnel[257] that the subsequent collision with D3 was too remote a consequence of D1's original negligence.

7–053   **Negligent medical treatment.** It is not too difficult to say that if C is knocked down and injured by D1 and a few moments later is struck and further injured by D2, also driving negligently, D1 may bear some responsibility for the further injury. It is perhaps less intuitive to conclude that D1 might be liable for the consequences of negligent medical treatment of the injury directly inflicted by him, but he usually will be unless the treatment is completely inappropriate.[258] Generally, of course, the matter will be one of contribution between the two defendants in respect of the second injury.[259]

7–054   **Intervening wilful wrongdoing.** Most difficulty arises in the case of acts of a third party which are wilfully wrong towards the claimant, for it is especially here that the straightforward and literal application of the test of reasonable foreseeability (at least as it has been applied to personal injury cases) leads to an unacceptably wide-ranging liability: "In general . . . even though A is in fault, he is not responsible for injury to C which B, a stranger to him, deliberately chooses to do. Though A may have given the occasion for B's mischievous activity, B then becomes a new and independent cause."[260]

Much of the case law in this area analyses the problem in terms of the existence of a duty of care to prevent wilful injury by a third party and the problem has already been considered in that context.[261] It has been suggested that "the question of the existence of duty and that of whether damage brought about by the act of a third party is too remote are simply two facets of the same problem".[262]

---

[255] However, D2 and D3 were liable to C. In many cases, provided all defendants are claim-worthy, these issues will essentially be related to contribution among defendants and will be of no direct concern to the claimant.

[256] Taking risks to save others from danger does not normally break the chain of causation: see para.26–022.

[257] See in particular [1982] 1 W.L.R. 349 at 365–366.

[258] *Webb v Barclays Bank Plc* [2001] EWCA Civ 1141; [2002] P.I.Q.R. P8, following *Mahony v Kruschich (Demolitions) Pty* (1985) 59 A.L.R. 722. In *Prendergast v Sam & Dee Ltd, The Times,* March 14, 1989, D1, a doctor, wrote an unclear prescription; D2, a pharmacist misread it, though he should have been put on inquiry. D2's act did not break the chain of causation and the relative responsibility was assessed as 75 per cent to D2. Cf. *Horton v Evans* [2006] EWHC 2808 (QB); [2007] P.N.L.R. 17 (pharmacist liable for failing to question prescription, doctor prescribing repeat prescription not at fault).

[259] Cf. the difficult case of *Rahman v Arearose Ltd* [2001] Q.B. 351, where it was conceded that the medical treatment was the sole cause of the loss of the eye; and see the divisions in the Court of Appeal in the equally difficult case of *Wright v Cambridge Medical Group* [2011] EWCA Civ 669; [2012] 3 W.L.R. 1124.

[260] *Weld-Blundell v Stephens* [1920] A.C. 956 at 986 per Lord Sumner.

[261] See para.5–044.

[262] *Perl v Camden LBC* [1984] Q.B. 342 per Oliver LJ.

However, where the defendant has caused some initial injury to the claimant before the intervention of the third party the cases have continued to look at the question as one of remoteness. Not surprisingly, however, there is the same reluctance to find the defendant liable for the wilful wrongdoing of others. It has been said that the conduct of the third party must be something very likely to happen if it is not to break the chain of causation[263] but if anything, this formulation, whether it is to be regarded as a separate test to be applied after that of reasonable foreseeability,[264] or as representing what the hypothetical reasonable man would contemplate[265] probably understates the burden on the claimant and "there may be circumstances in which the court would require a degree of likelihood amounting almost to inevitability before it fixes the defendant with responsibility for the act of a third party over whom he had and can have no control".[266]

In *Lamb v Camden LBC*[267] the defendants' negligence caused the claimant's house to be damaged and become unoccupied but they were not liable for the further damage done by the depredations of squatters, notwithstanding a finding by the Official Referee that squatting was "foreseeable". On the other hand, in *Ward v Cannock Chase DC* on rather similar facts, but where the defendants had been guilty of wilful delay in effecting repairs and where the risk of vandal damage was rather higher, they were found liable for the further loss.[268] The consequence of all of this may be, of course, that precisely the same physical act may or may not break the chain of causation depending on the mental state of the actor: further negligence may be within the risk created by the defendant when wilful conduct may not.[269] So also, the intervening deliberate act of a child may not break the chain when that of an adult would.

Where defendant is under a duty to guard against intervener's wrongdoing. 7–055
The above principles apply where there are no special circumstances imposing upon the defendant a duty to take care to guard against the wrongdoing of the third party. If such a duty exists, it would be nonsensical to classify the damage as too remote merely because it was wilfully inflicted. A driver who knocks down a pedestrian would not be liable for theft of the pedestrian's wallet while he was lying injured, but a bailee, who is under a duty (normally, but not necessarily, arising from a contract) to safeguard his bailor's goods, is just as much liable where, by his default, they are stolen by a burglar as he is where they are destroyed in a fire.[270] In *Stansbie v Troman*[271] a decorator was at work in a house

---

[263] *Home Office v Dorset Yacht Co Ltd* [1970] A.C. 1004 per Lord Reid. Note, however, that the majority of the House of Lords regarded this case as about duty, not causation.

[264] *Lamb v Camden LBC* [1981] Q.B. 625 at 647 per Watkins LJ.

[265] *Lamb v Camden LBC* [1981] Q.B 625 at 644, 647 per Oliver LJ. Lord Mackay in *Smith v Littlewoods Organisation Ltd* [1987] A.C. 241, would appear to agree, despite the remark at 263E.

[266] *Lamb v Camden LBC* [1981] Q.B. 625 at 647 per Oliver LJ. Cf. *Alexis v Newham LBC* [2009] EWHC 1323 (QB); [2009] I.C.R. 1517 (prank by school child; but no breach).

[267] [1981] Q.B. 625.

[268] *Ward v Cannock Chase DC* [1986] Ch. 546. But the defendants were not liable for theft of the claimant's goods, perhaps because he could have taken steps himself to secure those.

[269] *Environment Agency v Empress Car Co Ltd* [1999] 2 A.C. 22 at 30. See also *Philco Radio and Television Corp of Great Britain v J Spurling Ltd* [1949] 2 All E.R. 882.

[270] In *Lockspeiser Aircraft Ltd v Brooklands Aircraft Co Ltd*, *The Times*, March 7, 1990, the intruder started a fire which destroyed the goods.

and left it for two hours to get wallpaper. He was alone and had been told by the householder to close the front door whenever he left the house. Instead of doing so he left the door unlocked and during his absence a thief entered the house and stole a diamond bracelet and some clothes. The Court of Appeal held that the decorator was liable for the loss.[272] Similarly, in *Haynes v Harwood*[273] the defendants were held liable when the claimant was injured by their horses which had been left unattended in the street and caused to bolt by a mischievous boy. It was negligent to leave the horses unattended precisely because children might interfere.[274]

7–056   **Intervening act of the claimant.** Where it is the claimant's own act or omission which, in combination with the defendant's breach of duty, has brought about his damage, then the problem is generally seen as one of contributory negligence.[275] Before there can be any question of contributory negligence, however, it is necessary that both the claimant's lack of care and the defendant's breach of duty shall be found to have been causes of the claimant's damage and in some cases, especially those in which the claimant seeks to recover for damage suffered in a second accident, the defendant has been exonerated on the ground that the claimant's conduct amounted to a nova causa interveniens. In *McKew v Holland & Hannen & Cubitts (Scotland) Ltd*[276] the pursuer suffered an injury in an accident for which the defenders were liable and as a result his left leg occasionally gave way under him. Some days after this accident he went to inspect a flat which was approached by a steep stair between two walls and without a handrail. On leaving the flat he started to descend the stair holding his young daughter by the hand and going ahead of his wife and brother-in-law who had accompanied him. Suddenly he lost control of his left leg, threw his daughter back in order to save her, and tried to jump so as to land in an upright position instead of falling down the stairs. As a result he sustained a severe fracture of his ankle. The House of Lords agreed that the pursuer's act of jumping in the emergency in which he found himself did not break the chain of causation, but that it had been broken by his conduct in placing himself unnecessarily in a position where he might be confronted by just such an emergency, when he could have descended the stair slowly and carefully by himself or sought the assistance of his wife or brother-in-law.

The basis of the decision of the House of Lords in this case was that the pursuer's conduct amounted to a nova causa interveniens because, even though it

---

[271] [1948] 2 K.B. 48, criticised by Lord Denning MR in *Lamb v Camden LBC* [1981] Q.B. 625 at 638 but approved by Lord Goff in *Smith v Littlewoods Organisation Ltd* [1987] A.C. 241 at 272. The defendant was not a bailee.

[272] Even in these cases the loss must be within the ambit of the duty. Would the defendant have been liable for malicious damage? For the seizure of the house by squatters?

[273] [1935] 1 K.B. 147.

[274] *Haynes v Harwood* [1935] 1 K.B. 147 at 153 per Greer LJ. Would the defendant have been liable if an adult had caused the horses to bolt? Cf. *Topp v London Country Bus* [1993] 1 W.L.R. 976, where the matter was considered in terms of duty.

[275] See Ch.23.

[276] [1969] 3 All E.R. 1621 (H.L.Sc.); *The San Onofre* [1922] P. 243; cf. *Wieland v Cyril Lord Carpets Ltd* [1969] 3 All E.R. 1006; *Dalling v R J Heale & Co Ltd* [2011] EWCA Civ 365.

may have been foreseeable, it was unreasonable in the circumstances.[277] If he had no reasonable alternative to acting as he did his conduct would not have broken the chain of causation.[278] The threshold of unreasonableness set by *McKew* is a high one, though there is no basis for saying that it must involve deliberate or reckless risk-taking.[279] The rationale of nova causa interveniens is fairness between the parties[280] and the court should be slow to stigmatise the claimant's behaviour as unreasonable merely because he does not take the course which is cheapest for the defendant. In *Emeh v Kensington and Chelsea and Westminster Health Authority*[281] the defendants negligently performed a sterilisation operation on the claimant and she became pregnant again, though she did not discover this until 20 weeks into the pregnancy. The Court of Appeal rejected the argument that her refusal to have an abortion broke the chain of causation between the negligence and the child's birth.[282] As Slade LJ put it:[283]

> "[S]ave in the most exceptional circumstances, I cannot think it right that the court should ever declare it unreasonable for a woman to decline to have an abortion, in a case where there is no evidence that there were any medical or psychiatric grounds for terminating the particular pregnancy."

Intervening wilful conduct of the claimant. We have seen that the wilful conduct of a third party is more likely to break the chain of causation than negligence on his part but that the defendant may be liable in respect of wilful acts the guarding against which is the very foundation of his duty. There is a close analogy in the case of wilful conduct by the claimant. In *Reeves v Metropolitan Police Commissioner*[284] the claimant committed suicide while in police custody. The case was fought on the basis that he was sane at the time. A majority of the House of Lords held that since the defendants owed the claimant a duty of care to prevent him inflicting harm on himself[285] it would make no sense at the next step to go on to hold that his suicide broke the chain of causation.[286] There was, however, a reduction of damages for contributory negligence.[287]

7–057

---

[277] [1969] 3 All E.R. 1621 at 1623 per Lord Reid.

[278] A rescuer will not be regarded as acting unreasonably because he takes a risk, para.26–022.

[279] *Spencer v Wincanton Holdings Ltd* [2009] EWCA Civ 1404; [2010] P.I.Q.R. P8 at [45] per Aikens LJ: "[The] line between a set of facts which results in a finding of contributory negligence and a set of facts which results in a finding that the 'unreasonable conduct' of the claimant constitutes a novus actus interveniens is not, in my view, capable of precise definition". Cf. *Smith v Youth Justice Board* [2010] EWCA Civ 99.

[280] *Corr v IBC Vehicles Ltd* [2008] UKHL 13; [2008] A.C. 884 at [15].

[281] [1985] Q.B. 1012.

[282] This was at a time when the courts allowed damages for the cost of upbringing of an unwanted child in such cases, but see now para.25–021.

[283] *Emeh v Kensington and Chelsea and Westminster Health Authority* [1985] Q.B. 1012 at 1024. See also *The Calliope* [1970] P. 172 (maritime collision caused by negligence of claimant and defendant; claimant vessel sustaining further damage in turning because of Chief Officer's negligence; manoeuvre difficult but not unreasonable and did not break chain of causation; defendant liable for further damage, subject to further apportionment for contributory negligence: see para.23–036).

[284] [2000] 1 A.C. 360.

[285] The duty was conceded: see para.5–047.

[286] Nor was volenti applicable (para.26–018) or the claim against public policy (para.26–062).

[287] See para.23–036.

Another possibility is that the defendant injures the claimant and the latter, because of depression brought about by the accident, commits suicide. Can the defendant be liable for his death? An affirmative answer was given by the House of Lords in *Corr v IBC Vehicles Ltd*[288] even though the deceased was not insane in the legal sense. Whether or not suicide could be regarded as "reasonably foreseeable" at the time of the initial injury the defendant had to take his victim as he found him, his psychological weaknesses as well as physical ones.[289]

iii.   Scope of Duty

7–058   It has been emphasised that in deciding the scope of the defendant's liability for the consequences of his wrong it is necessary to consider the nature of the loss against which the legal rule in question is designed to keep the claimant harmless:

> "One cannot separate questions of liability from questions of causation. They are inextricably connected. One is never simply liable; one is always liable *for* something and the rules which determine what one is liable for are as much part of the substantive law as the rules which determine which acts give rise to liability."[290]

> "Damage is of the essence of a cause of action for negligence, and the critical question in a particular case is a composite one, that is whether the scope of the duty of care[291] in the circumstances of the case is such as to embrace damage of the kind which the claimant claims to have suffered."[292]

The point is more obvious in the tort of breach of statutory duty, so that, for example, a claim in respect of the loss of unpenned livestock from a ship in a storm failed because the purpose of the statute requiring penning was to prevent the spread of disease;[293] but the same principle is applicable at common law and liability is generally limited to those consequences, factually caused by the defendant and not otherwise too remote, which are attributable to that which makes the act complained of wrongful. It is "the scope of the tort which determines the extent of the remedy to which the injured party is entitled".[294]

7–059   **SAAMCO.** The cases on scope of duty with which we are concerned in this part have generally involved a contract between the parties, but in the professional

---

[288] [2008] UKHL 13; [2008] A.C. 884. A similar answer had been given in *Pigney v Pointer's Transport Services* [1957] 1 W.L.R. 1121, even though suicide was then a crime.

[289] There is some difference of opinion as to which it was because some members of the court did not wish to rely on the controversial decision in *Page v Smith* (para.5–085). However, it is not clear this concern was well founded. Page was not physically injured in the accident, Corr was and very severely.

[290] *Kuwait Airways Corp v Iraq Airways Co* [2002] UKHL 19; [2002] 2 A.C. 883 at [128] per Lord Hoffmann.

[291] This language is open to criticism because the "scope of the duty of care" is to prevent the damaging event (see Hoffmann (2005) 121 L.Q.R. 592) but the point is clear enough.

[292] *Calvert v William Hill Ltd* [2008] EWCA Civ 1427; [2009] Ch 330 at [54] per May P. See the extraordinary case of *Bhamra v Dubb* [2010] EWCA Civ 13.

[293] *Gorris v Scott* (1874) L.R. 9 Exch. 125, para.8–017. This has obvious affinities with the notion of the "protective purpose of the norm" which is found in Austrian and German law. See van Gerven, Lever and Larouche, *Tort Law and Scope of Protection: Cases, Materials and Text (Casebooks for the Common Law of Europe)* (1998), Ch.4.1.1.

[294] *Platform Home Loans Ltd v Oyston Shipways Ltd* [2000] 2 A.C. 190 at 209 per Lord Hobhouse.

negligence context contract and tort are interchangeable.[295] In *Banque Bruxelles Lambert SA v Eagle Star Insurance Co Ltd* (or *SAAMCO*)[296] the issue in a number of consolidated appeals was whether a valuer who had negligently overvalued a property on which a lender advanced money on mortgage was liable for all of the losses suffered by the lender under the loan, including loss due to a precipitous fall in the property market. The lender would not have entered into the transaction if he had known the true valuation and it could hardly be denied that falls in markets are foreseeable as a general rule.[297] Nevertheless, the House of Lords held that the valuer's liability was more limited. In the case of "information" provided to enable the claimant to decide on a course of action, liability for negligence[298] is determined not by asking what position the claimant would have been in if the correct information had been given (the claimant would not have entered into the transaction), but by asking what was the consequence of the information actually provided being inaccurate (the claimant entered into the transaction with less security than he had been looking for). It was avoiding this false basis for the transaction which fell within the scope of the valuer's duty, not the risks associated with entering the transaction as a whole.[299] So, suppose property is valued at £500,000 when a true valuation would have been £400,000. When, on default, the property is sold, it realises only £300,000 because of a general fall in the market. The lender's loss is £200,000 but the valuer's liability is only £100,000 because the balance represents the risk which the claimant would have taken on himself even if the transaction had been sound.[300]

---

[295] See *Rubenstein v HSBC Bank Plc* [2012] EWCA Civ 1184; [2013] P.N.L.R. 9 (no distinction drawn between claims in tort and in contract against D. D held liable for loss of capital in an investment made by C when it had been part of D's duty not to recommend an investment subject to the risk of loss of capital and such loss was consequently not too remote even if the consequence of unpredictable events).

[296] *Banque Bruxelles Lambert SA v Eagle Star Insurance Co Ltd* [1997] A.C. 191 (reported in [1996] 3 All E.R. 365 sub nom. *South Australia Asset Managment Corp v York Montague Ltd*). See also *Nykredit Mortgage Bank Plc v Edward Erdman Group Ltd (No.2)* [1997] 1 W.L.R. 1627; Cf. *Kenny & Good Pty Ltd v MGICA (1992) Ltd* (1999) 163 A.L.R. 611; Peel in Burrows and Peel (eds), *Commercial Remedies Current Issues and Problems* (2003), Ch.7.

[297] In *John Grimes Partnership Ltd v Gubbins* [2013] EWCA Civ 37; 146 Con L.R. 26 an engineer (D) failed, in breach of contract, to do the work required of him by the agreed date with the result that a development was delayed during which time it declined in market value. Such loss was easily foreseen at the time of the contract and there was nothing to suggest that this was not a type of loss for which D assumed responsibility; he was therefore held liable.

[298] The position is different if the defendant is guilty of fraud, for then he is liable for all losses flowing from the fraudulently induced transaction: *Smith New Court Securities Ltd v Scrimgeour Vickers (Asset Management) Ltd* [1997] A.C. 254 at 283. Indeed, he is liable even for unforeseeable consequences.

[299] Cf. *Caparo v Dickman* [1990] 2 A.C. 605, para.5–032, where the purpose of the rule infringed went to whether a duty was owed to the claimant.

[300] *Nykredit Mortgage Bank Plc v Edward Erdman Group Ltd (No.2)* [1997] 1 W.L.R. 1627 at 1631 per Lord Nicholls. Cf. *Haugesund Kommune v Depfa ACS Bank*[2011] EWCA Civ 33; 134 Con L.R. 51 (D advised C that Norwegian municipalities had capacity to enter into swaps with C, but also advised that any claim against the municipalities could not be enforced. D's advice about capacity was negligent and wrong. C had a claim in restitution against the municipalities which was only part satisfied. C could not recover the balance from D. C's loss flowed either from the impecuniosity of the municipalities or the inability to pursue a claim: the credit risk was for C and did not fall within the scope of D's duty; the enforcement risk fell within the scope of a duty which had not been breached (since D had advised correctly about the enforcement risk)). See also *Capita Alternative Fund*

7–060   **"Information", or "advice"?** *SAAMCO* was concerned with an obligation to provide information on the basis of which the claimant could take a decision. The position is said to be different where the defendant undertakes to "advise" generally upon the wisdom of entering into a transaction, for he will then be liable for all the foreseeable consequences of it.[301] In *Aneco Reinsurance Underwriting Ltd v Johnson & Higgins Ltd*[302] the defendant brokers, acting on behalf of the claimant reinsurers, negligently failed to disclose certain facts on a proposal for further reinsurance (or retrocession) of a US $10 million portion of a risk to be carried by the claimants. This meant that the retrocessionaires, who would have refused cover had they known the full facts, lawfully repudiated the claim. The claimants lost US $35 million on the risk as a whole. The majority of the House of Lords held that the brokers were liable for the full amount. Had the brokers carried out their duty properly they would have become aware that cover was not obtainable in the market on commercially sensible terms and the claimants would therefore have declined the main risk and suffered no loss at all. In the view of the majority the duty of the brokers was not merely to seek to obtain valid cover of US $10 million and report on having done so, but to advise on the market's estimation of the risk. For Lord Millett, dissenting, it was not enough that the brokers might have volunteered their estimation of the state of the market; the relevant question was whether such an estimation was within the scope of the duty they had undertaken and he thought that it was not.

7–061   **Limits of the distinction between "information" and "advice".** The courts have not found it easy to discern the true basis of the *SAAMCO* principle and, in particular, to draw the distinction between "information" and "advice".[303] It is not wholly obvious why responsibility for risks like market forces should be imposed on the defendant even where his function is to advise the claimant as to the wisdom of a transaction, at least where those risks are as apparent to the claimant as to the defendant. In *SAAMCO* Lord Hoffmann gave an example[304] of a doctor negligently informing a mountaineer about the fitness of his knee. If the mountaineer were to be injured on an expedition because his knee gave way, the doctor might be liable; but if the mountaineer were injured by a foreseeable risk of mountaineering unconnected with his knee (for example, being hit by a rock fall) the doctor would not be liable for that. That conclusion is plainly correct. One might say that the rock fall is a mere coincidence (like the victim of a road accident being injured in another road accident while in the ambulance on the way to hospital) or (which amounts to the same thing) that it is not within the risk created by the doctor's negligence. However, suppose the doctor is consulted by a

---

Services Ltd v Drivers Jonas [2011] EWHC 2336 (Comm); 139 Con L.R. 125; *Torre Asset Funding Ltd v Royal Bank of Scotland Plc* [2013] EWHC 2670 (Ch).

[301] *Banque Bruxelles Lambert SA v Eagle Star Insurance Co Ltd* [1997] A.C. 191 at 214.

[302] [2001] UKHL 51; [2002] 1 Lloyd's Rep. 157.

[303] The cases are numerous, but in addition to those already cited in this part, see e.g. *Bristol and West Building Society v Fancy & Jackson* [1997] 4 All E.R. 582 (Ch); *Harrison v Bloom Camillin* [2000] 1 Lloyd's Rep PN 89 (Ch); *Intervention Board for Agricultural Produce v Leidig* [2000] Lloyd's Rep PN 144 (CA); *Portman Building Society v Bevan Ashford* [2000] 1 E.G.L.R. 81; *Crosse & Crosse v Lloyds Bank plc* [2001] EWCA Civ 366; *Petersen v Rivlin* [2002] EWCA Civ 194, [2002] Lloyd's Rep PN 386; *Gabriel v Little*[2013] EWCA Civ 1513.

[304] *SAAMCO* [1997] A.C. at 213.

patient with a history of heart trouble and the doctor negligently advises him that the best way to improve his fitness is to take up again the climbing activities of his youth. It is not difficult to say that the doctor could be liable if the patient suffers a heart attack, but is he now to be responsible for death in the rock fall? That is just as much a coincidence as in the other case. The answer lies in what the doctor's duty is, that is to say to advise the mountaineer about his health, not his physical safety. The scope of his duty is, ultimately, a question of construction and "information" or "advice" should probably be seen as little more than labels to be applied once that construction exercise is complete; or, perhaps better still, simply abandoned as unhelpful.[305]

Chester v Afshar. This approach may also be taken to assess the difficult case of **7–062** *Chester v Afshar*.[306] A doctor owes a patient a duty to inform him of certain risks attached to treatment[307] and it is clear that if he breaches this duty and the patient can show that he would not have consented to the treatment but for this breach then the doctor is liable for adverse effects relating to the failure to warn, even though the treatment has been carried out with all due care and skill.[308] In *Chester v Afshar*[309] the defendant negligently failed to warn the claimant of a 1 or 2 per cent unavoidable risk of paralysis in surgery on her spinal column and this eventuated. Had the claimant been properly warned the operation would not have taken place when it did since the claimant would have sought another medical opinion. The claimant may or may not have submitted to the surgery at a later date. A majority of the House of Lords held that the claimant was entitled to recover damages. The decision may be explained as a simple, straightforward application of the standard combination of "but-for" causation and proof on a balance of probabilities.[310] There was a finding of fact that if she had been informed she would not have had the surgery on that day, the adverse outcome was exactly within the risk about which the defendant had failed to warn her and even if it could have been positively shown that she would have had it on another day a random risk of 1 or 2 per cent would have come nowhere near establishing that the adverse outcome would have been suffered on the later occasion:[311] if I win on a particular number at the casino on Monday that does not make it likely that I would win on the same number on the following Tuesday.[312] Nevertheless, even the majority of the House who found in the claimant's favour felt compelled to say that they were modifying the standard principles of causation, albeit in a "narrow and modest"[313] way, in order to vindicate the claimant's autonomy and

---

[305] I am indebited for part of this analysis to the suggestions made by my doctoral research student, Niranjan Venkatesan.

[306] [2004] UKHL 41; [2005] 1 A.C. 345. See also *Chappel v Hart* (1998) 195 CLR 232 and *Elbourne v Gibbs* [2006] NSWCA 127.

[307] See para.26–012.

[308] *Chatterton v Gerson* [1981] Q.B. 432.

[309] [2004] UKHL 41; [2005] 1 A.C. 345. See also *Chappel v Hart* (1998) 195 CLR 232; *Elbourne v Gibbs* [2006] NSWCA 127; *Wallace v Kam* [2013] HCA 19.

[310] As the CA had held: [2002] EWCA Civ 724; [2003] Q.B. 356 at [40]. And see *Wallace v Kam* [2013] HCA 19 at [20].

[311] See para.7–007.

[312] Cf. Lord Hoffmann's use of the roulette analogy to the opposite effect: *Chester v Afshar* [2004] UKHL 41; [2005] 1 A.C. 345 at [31].

[313] *Chester v Afshar* [2004] UKHL 41; [2005] 1 A.C. 345 at [24] per Lord Steyn.

to recognise her freedom to make an informed choice over the treatment she was to receive.[314] But if this amounts to a finding that, in circumstances where the claimant would have gone ahead at some point, the scope of duty of the doctor is only to ensure that the claimant makes an informed choice, there is much force in the suggestion of Lord Hoffmann, in the minority, that the appropriate award was a solatium to reflect the loss of autonomy, not damages for the paralysis.[315]

---

[314] Cf. *Wallace v Kam* [2013] HCA 19 at [36]: "[T]he policy that underlies requiring the exercise of reasonable care and skill in the giving of [the] warning is neither to protect [the] right to choose nor to protect the patient from exposure to all unacceptable risks. The underlying policy is rather to protect the patient from the occurrence of physical injury the risk of which is unacceptable to the patient. It is appropriate that the scope of liability for breach of the duty reflect that underlying policy."

[315] Cf. *Rees v Darlington Memorial Hospital NHS Trust* [2003] UKHL 52; [2004] 1 A.C. 309 (para.25–021) where, in a different context, the award of a fixed, conventional sum was regarded as the proper way to deal with the violation of the right to autonomy.

CHAPTER 8

BREACH OF STATUTORY DUTY[1] AND MISFEASANCE IN A PUBLIC OFFICE

1. BREACH OF STATUTORY DUTY

A. Nature of the Action

This chapter is not concerned with statutes which have as their principal objective the imposition of tort liability,[2] nor with the circumstances in which the courts may pay regard to a statutory requirement or standard in deciding whether the defendant's conduct amounts to negligence.[3] What it is concerned with, is when a court will conclude that a statute which is primarily regulatory or criminal in its purpose should be treated as giving rise to a civil action for damages at the suit of a person who is injured as a result of non-compliance with it. Fundamentally, the question is one of interpretation of the particular statute, but enough case law has accumulated around the subject to require treatment in a book on torts.

8–001

A tort independent of negligence. Before looking at the approach of the courts to this question of interpretation, something should be said about the nature of the action for breach of statutory duty. In purely numerical terms, the most important area of operation of the tort of breach of statutory duty has been that concerned with work injuries[4] and there is, of course, no doubt that an employer owes his employee a duty of care for the purposes of the tort of negligence.[5] The English view is that liability for breach of statutory duty is a wholly separate tort superimposed on this, but this is not the approach of all common law countries. In

8–002

---

[1] Stanton, Skidmore and Harris, *Statutory Torts* (2003); Williams (1960) 23 M.L.R. 233; Buckley (1984) 100 L.Q.R. 204; Stanton (2004) 120 L.Q.R. 324; Foster (2011) 33 Syd. L.R. 67.

[2] For example, the Occupiers' Liability Act 1957 (Ch.10) and the Consumer Protection Act 1987 Pt I (Ch.11).

[3] See para.6–035.

[4] Much of the statute law in this area has undergone radical amendment (para.9–007) but the proposition in the text remains true. *Quaere* the effect hereafter of the change made to the Health and Safety at Work etc. Act 1974 s.47(2): see para.8–005.

[5] See Ch.9.

the majority of jurisdictions in the United States, in accident cases, breach of a statute is "negligence per se" and this is tantamount to saying that the statute "concretises" the common law duty by putting beyond controversy the question whether reasonable care in the circumstances required that a particular precaution be taken. Other American states adopt the view that the statutory standard is compelling evidence of what reasonable care demands but in the last resort does not bind the court, a view taken since 1983 in Canada.[6] There are attractions in these views where a common law duty already exists, for they relieve the court of the task of searching for a legislative intention on civil liability, but where there is no common law duty it would amount to rejecting statutes as a source of civil liability, a view which is inconsistent with English law as it stands. In any event, even where there is a common law duty, the overwhelming weight of authority is to the effect that the action for breach of statutory duty is a separate tort. As Lord Wright put it in *LPTB v Upson*:[7]

> "A claim for damages for breach of a statutory duty intended to protect a person in the position of the particular plaintiff is a specific common law right which is not to be confused in essence with a claim for negligence . . . I have desired before I deal specifically with the regulations to make it clear how in my judgment they should be approached, and also to make it clear that a claim for their breach may stand or fall independently of negligence. There is always a danger if the claim is not sufficiently specific that the due consideration of the claim for breach of statutory duty may be prejudiced if it is confused with the claim in negligence."

Thus, where the statute imposes strict liability it is possible for the defendant to be acquitted of negligence but still held liable for breach of the statute; contrariwise, the defendant may have fulfilled his statutory duty but is still nevertheless liable for negligence because the statute is not inconsistent with a common law duty broader in extent.

8–003 **Relationship with negligence.** In the industrial safety cases it would have been impossible to deny a general common law duty of care to workers, but in the modern law many claims for breach of statutory duty have been advanced on the basis of legislation concerned with child protection, education and other matters of social welfare. They have generally failed because the nature of the legislation did not support the inference of a Parliamentary intention to confer a civil right of action.[8] It may also be the case that the statutory framework is inconsistent with a common law duty of care, in which case there is no liability at all, but subject to this there is no reason why the common law of negligence should not operate.[9] It is wrong to assume that because a statute in the area in question does not give rise to civil liability it therefore excludes a common law duty: the two questions are entirely separate.[10] Any common law duty must be sought in the principles of the

---

[6] *R v Saskatchewan Wheat Pool* (1983) 1 S.C.R. 205.
[7] [1949] A.C. 155 at 168–169.
[8] See para.8–007.
[9] *X (Minors) v Bedfordshire CC* [1995] 2 A.C. 633 at 765; *Barrett v Enfield LBC* [2001] 2 A.C. 550; *Phelps v Hillingdon LBC* [2001] 2 A.C. 619. An obvious example is road accidents: road traffic legislation hardly ever gives rise to an action for breach of statutory duty but road accidents are a major source of negligence cases.
[10] *Gorringe v Calderdale MBC* [2004] UKHL 15; [2004] 1 W.L.R. 1057 at [3].

law of negligence, not in the non-actionable statute.[11] Equally, just because breach of a statute is actionable does not give rise to a co-existent common law duty of care.[12]

B. Existence of Liability

Establishing the intention of Parliament. Whether a private right of action in tort is available to someone who is injured by the breach of a statutory duty depends upon the intention of Parliament in imposing the duty in question. When Parliament has clearly stated its intention one way or the other no difficulty arises,[13] but all too often this is not the case. Until the 19th century the view seems to have been taken that whenever a statutory duty is created, any person who can show that he has sustained harm from its non-performance can bring an action against the person on whom the duty is imposed.[14] During the first half of that century, however, a different view began to be taken, and in *Atkinson v Newcastle Waterworks Co*[15] the Court of Appeal's doubts about the old rule were so strong as to amount to disapproval of it. With the vast increase in legislative activity, the old rule was perceived to carry the risk of liability wider than the legislature could have contemplated, particularly in relation to public authorities. Since that time, therefore, the claimant has generally been required to point to some indication in the statute that it was intended to give rise to a civil action. If there is no such indication, the claimant is thrown back on such common law right of action as he may have.

Although, as we have seen, a common law duty of care may coexist with a statutory duty (whether or not the latter gives rise to a civil action) there is no common law tort of "careless performance of a statutory duty". Either there is a duty of care under the common law which has been breached, or breach of the statute gives rise to liability in its own right, or both; but if there is no common law duty and the statute only operates in the public law sphere then the fact that the duty under the statute is carried out carelessly does not avail the claimant seeking damages.[16]

8–004

---

[11] *Gorringe v Calderdale MBC* [2004] UKHL 15; [2004] 1 W.L.R. 1057 at [32]; *Neil Martin Ltd v Revenue and Customs Comrs* [2007] EWCA Civ 1041; [2007] S.T.C. 1802.

[12] *Green v Royal Bank of Scotland Plc* [2013] EWCA Civ 1197; [2014] P.N.L.R. 6.

[13] See, e.g. Health and Safety at Work etc Act 1974 s.47 (recently reformed: see para.8–005); Building Act 1984 s.38 (actionable); Copyright Designs and Patents Act 1988 s.103 (actionable); Financial Services and Markets Act 2000 ss.71, 150 (actionable); Railways Act 2005 s.44 (not actionable). The European Convention on Human Rights, via the Human Rights Act 1998, gives rise to the possibility of an award of damages. However, there is no *right* to damages and one would not describe such a claim as one for breach of statutory duty, nor even for tort.

[14] *Anon* (1704) 6 Mod. 26 per Holt CJ Com.Dig.tit. "Action upon Statute," F; *Ashby v White* (1703) 2 Ld.Raym. 938; *Couch v Steel* (1854) 3 E. & B. 402.

[15] (1877) 2 Ex.D. 441.

[16] *X (Minors) v Bedfordshire CC* [1995] 2 A.C. 633.

On the question whether the statute gives rise to a civil right of action: "[T]he only rule which in all circumstances is valid is that the answer must depend on a consideration of the whole Act and the circumstances, including the pre-existing law, in which it was enacted."[17]

Where the civil right of action is alleged to arise from subordinate legislation an intention to confer such a right (or at least authority to confer it) must be found in the enabling legislation.[18] Unfortunately, statutes all too rarely contain very much in the way of a clear indication on legislative intent and various presumptions have been developed by the courts.[19]

8–005   **Health and safety at work: a change of intention.** Before such presumptions are considered, a recent change in Parliament's express intention should be acknowledged. It has already been noted that, in purely numerical terms, the most important area of operation of the tort of breach of statutory duty is that concerned with work injuries. In this area, there was previously an express indication of civil liability as a result of s.47(2) of the Health and Safety at Work etc. Act 1974 which stated that breach of a duty imposed by health and safety regulations shall, so far as it causes damage, "be actionable except in so far as the regulations provide[20] otherwise".[21] However, this has been reversed for any breach of such regulations committed after October 1, 2013 which henceforward is regarded as "not actionable" unless otherwise provided.[22] The statement in the explanatory notes to the reforming legislation that "it will only be possible to claim for compensation in relation to breaches of affected health and safety legislation where it can be proved that the duty holder . . . has been negligent" presumes that no amendments will be made to the regulations in question so that they might expressly provide for civil liability.[23] It remains to be seen what effect,

---

[17] *Cutler v Wandsworth Stadium Ltd* [1949] A.C. 398 at 407 per Lord Simonds, see also at 412 per Lord Normand; *Ministry of Housing and Local Government v Sharp* [1970] 2 Q.B. 223 at 272 per Salmon LJ.

[18] *R v Deputy Governor of Parkhurst Prison Ex p. Hague* [1992] 1 A.C. 58 per Lord Jauncey. See also *Olotu v Home Office* [1997] 1 W.L.R. 328 at 339; *The Maraghetha Maria* [2002] EWCA Civ 509; [2002] 2 Lloyd's Rep. 293.

[19] See paras 8–006–8–013.

[20] Meaning "expressly provide": *"Wembridge Claimants" v Winter* [2013] EWHC 2331 (QB) at [188].

[21] Under s.47(1) breach of the duties set out in ss.2–8 of the 1974 Act itself are not actionable and this is not affected by the latest reform.

[22] Enterprise & Regulatory Reform Act 2013 (ERRA) s.69(3), (10); SI 2013/2227 art.2(f). The reform followed two reports on health and safety legislation (by Lord Young of Graffham, in 2010, and by Professor Löfstedt, in 2011). The author of the latter felt it necessary to state publicly that the approach taken in s.47(2) is "more far-reaching" than anticipated in his recommendations (Progress Report, January 2013, para.30); his principal recommendation was to remove any element of strict liability.

[23] The principal regulations affected are: Personal Protective Equipment at Work Regulations 1992 (SI 1992/2996); Manual Handling Operations Regulations 1992 (SI 1992/2793); Workplace (Health, Safety and Welfare) Regulations 1992 (SI 1992/3004); Provision and Use of Work Equipment Regulations 1998 (SI 1998/2306); Lifting Operations and Lifting Equipment Regulations 1998 (SI 1998/2307); Management of Health and Safety at Work Regulations 1999 (SI 1999/3242); Control of Substances Hazardous to Health Regulations 2002 (SI 2002/2677); Work at Height Regulations 2005 (SI 2005/735). For limited exceptions to the principle of non-actionability which have been introduced, see: Health and Safety at Work etc. Act 1974 (Civil Liability) (Exceptions) Regulations 2013 (SI 2013/1667).

if any, this change may have on claims in negligence by those injured at work,[24] but one inevitable result is that, even in cases where the statutory duty is an absolute one,[25] there will no longer be a claim without proof of fault by the duty holder.

The protection of a class. It has been said that an indication that the intention of Parliament was to provide a civil action is that the statute was passed for the protection of a limited class of the public, rather than for the benefit of the public as a whole. This was criticised many years ago by Atkin LJ on the ground that "it would be strange if a less important duty, which is owed to a section of the public, may be enforced by action, while a more important duty owed to the public at large cannot".[26] Furthermore, the concept of a "class of persons" lacks clear definition:[27] road users are not treated as a class of persons for this purpose since traffic legislation has generally not been interpreted so as to give rise to a civil action, but workers have been, the opposite conclusion having been consistently reached under industrial safety legislation.[28] Nevertheless, this factor has been repeated in more modern statements of the law.[29] Perhaps it is more helpful to put the matter negatively: it is not so much that the identifiability of a protected class is a particularly powerful pointer towards liability, as that, where there is no such class, it is inherently unlikely that Parliament would have intended a duty, sounding in damages, to the public as a whole in the absence of plain words.[30] This has some affinity with the "floodgates" argument that we encounter so frequently in the context of negligence.[31]

In *Atkinson v Newcastle Waterworks Co*[32] an Act requiring a water company to keep pipes, to which fire plugs were fixed, charged with a certain pressure of water, was construed as in the nature of a bargain between the company and Parliament for the supply of water to the city rather than as creating a duty actionable by householders. The court regarded it as startling that the water company should virtually become insurers of the safety from fire, so far as water can produce that safety, of all the houses in the district. A modern example is the refusal by the Court of Appeal to find that the duty owed by a fire authority to take reasonable measures to ensure an adequate supply of water for fire-fighting

8–006

---

[24] See further, para.9–007.

[25] See para.8–019.

[26] *Phillips v Britannia Hygienic Laundry Co Ltd* [1923] 2 K.B. 832 at 841. The oddness of such a conclusion is illustrated by *Cullen v CC Royal Ulster Constabulary* [2003] UKHL 39; [2003] 1 W.L.R. 1763, where the majority held that there was no action for breach of a duty which went to, "a quasi-constitutional right of fundamental importance in a free society": at [67]. But *quaere* the effect of the decision in *Cadder v HM Advocate* [2010] UKSC 43; [2010] 1 W.L.R. 2601.

[27] It seems the class must be definable by reference to their type or status or in some analogous way. "Victims of this offence" is not enough: *Issa v Hackney LBC* [1997] 1 W.L.R. 956.

[28] But see now para.8–005.

[29] *X (Minors) v Bedfordshire CC* [1995] 2 A.C. 633 at 731; *O'Rourke v Camden LBC* [1998] A.C. 188 at 194; *Ali v Bradford City MDC* [2010] EWCA Civ 1282; [2012] 1 W.L.R. 161 at [33].

[30] Thus in *Mid Kent Holdings Plc v General Utilities Plc* [1997] 1 W.L.R. 14, a literal interpretation of the Fair Trading Act 1973 s.93A, would have led to the extraordinary result of allowing any of the whole population to bring proceedings to enforce an undertaking to the Minister.

[31] Also with the "special damage" requirement in public nuisance: para.15–006.

[32] (1877) 2 Ex.D. 441.

gave rise to civil liability.[33] In any event, the mere fact that the statute intends to confer some benefit upon an identified group of persons is not conclusive. In one case it was contended that bookmakers were a class of persons intended to be benefited by a provision in the Betting and Lotteries Act 1934 requiring the owner of a dog track to provide space for them. The action failed, for the purpose of the statute was not the conferring of private rights but the regulation of dog racing.[34] Ultimately, the question of the existence or nonexistence of an identifiable class does not provide an easy substitute for the fundamental question of what purpose the legislature intended to achieve by the particular legislation, taken as a whole.[35]

8–007 **Nature of the legislation.** Closely related to the "class" issue is the nature of the legislation. While a private law duty may more readily be inferred from legislation prescribing safety standards,[36] it is unlikely to be found in legislation on "social welfare", especially when that confers a wide discretion upon the body responsible for administering it. The proper remedy for maladministration is judicial review, not an action for damages. Thus, the House of Lords has rejected claims based upon child protection legislation,[37] the duty to provide sufficient and appropriate education under the Education Acts[38] and the duty to house homeless persons under the housing legislation.[39] As Lord Hoffmann put it in relation to the last issue:[40]

> "[T]he Act is a scheme of social welfare, intended to confer benefits at the public expense on grounds of public policy. Public money is spent on housing the homeless not merely for the benefit of people who find themselves homeless but on grounds of general public interest: because, for example, proper housing means that people will be less likely to suffer illness, turn to crime or require the attention of other social services. The expenditure interacts with expenditure on other public services such as education, the National Health Service and even the police. It is not simply a private matter between the claimant and the housing authority."

In the child protection case it will be recalled that the House of Lords had rejected a common law duty of care because of the delicate nature of the local authority's function in investigating allegations of child abuse[41] and it was not, therefore, surprising that a private law action under the statute (which would not necessarily even have required proof of negligence) was also rejected. However, the

---

[33] *Capital & Counties Plc v Hampshire CC* [1997] Q.B. 1004. See also para.5–046.

[34] *Cutler v Wandsworth Stadium Ltd* [1949] A.C. 398.

[35] *R. v Deputy Governor of Brixton Prison Ex p. Hague* [1992] 1 A.C. 58 at 171; *Morrison Sports Ltd v Scottish Power* [2010] UKSC 37; [2010] 1 W.L.R. 1934.

[36] *Roe v Sheffield CC* [2003] EWCA Civ 1; [2004] Q.B. 653. Cf. *The Maraghetha Maria* [2002] EWCA Civ 509; [2002] 2 Lloyd's Rep 293 (safety of trawlers; designed to protect crew but indications that this was to be enforced by administrative means); similarly *Morrison Sports Ltd v Scottish Power* [2010] UKSC 37; [2010] 1 W.L.R. 1934 (safety of electricity supply).

[37] *X (Minors) v Bedfordshire CC* [1995] 2 A.C. 633.

[38] *Phelps v Hillingdon LBC* [2001] 2 A.C. 619.

[39] *O'Rourke v Camden LBC* [1998] A.C. 188. See now the Housing Act 1996. Such duties may not involve individual civil rights so as to attract art.6(1) of the European Convention on Human Rights: *Ali v Birmingham CC* [2010] UKSC 8; [2010] 2 W.L.R. 471.

[40] *O'Rourke v Camden LBC* [1998] A.C. at 193.

[41] See para.5–072.

European Court of Human Rights has subsequently held[42] that the failure to intervene constituted a breach of art.3 of the Convention (torture or inhuman or degrading treatment) and that the failure of domestic law to afford a remedy for this was a violation of art.13. The consequence seems to be that now in such a case there is a common law duty of care (at least to the child who is not adequately protected)[43] or damages may be awarded by an English court (since the Human Rights Act 1998) for breach of the Convention, but there seems to be no direct impact on the actionability of the breach of statutory duty.

Remedy provided by the statute. A potential factor in deciding whether there is a civil action is the nature of the remedy, if any, provided by the statute.[44] If the statute provides no remedy for its breach and there is an intention to protect a limited class,[45] that may be an indication that Parliament intended a civil action, "since otherwise there is no method of securing the protection the statute was intended to confer".[46] In the great majority of cases, however, some machinery or sanction, whether administrative or criminal, will be contained in the statute and it has been said that "where an Act creates an obligation, and enforces the performance in a specified manner, we take it to be a general rule that performance cannot be enforced in any other manner".[47]

8–008

Where the statute provides its own administrative machinery for redress (for example, by appeal to the Minister) the court is likely to adopt this approach.[48] It now seems that on the parallel issue of whether there is a common law duty of care attaching to the performance of a statutory function, the court must take into account how far, if at all, the availability of an alternative remedy enables the claimant to gain financial redress,[49] but there is no indication that the principles applicable to breach of statutory duty are affected. The existence of the general remedy of judicial review may be an indication that no private law action for damages is available, though it is not conclusive.[50]

Criminal penalties. Statutes which are silent on civil liability frequently impose criminal penalties. In principle the starting point is said to be the same as in the

8–009

---

[42] *Z v UK* (2001) 34 E.H.R.R. 3. See para.5–073.

[43] See para.5–073.

[44] *Hall v Cable and Wireless Plc* [2009] EWHC 1793 (Comm); [2010] 1 B.C.L.C. 95 (no action for breach of the listing rules under s.74 of the Financial Services and Markets Act 2000 given the scheme of remedies provided by the statute).

[45] This element is important: in practice the most likely case in which a statute will not provide a sanction is where it imposes a general duty owed to the public.

[46] *X (Minors) v Bedfordshire CC* [1995] 2 A.C. 633 at 731; *Doe d Murray v Bridges* (1831) 1 B. & Ad. 847 at 859; cf. *Poulton's Trustee v Ministry of Justice* [2010] EWCA Civ 392; [2011] Ch. 1.

[47] *Doe d Murray v Bridges* (1831) 1 B. & Ad. 847 at 859.

[48] *Wyatt v Hillingdon LBC* (1978) 76 L.G.R. 727; *Scally v Southern Health and Social Services Board* [1992] 1 A.C. 294; *X (Minors) v Bedfordshire CC* [1995] 2 A.C. 633.

[49] *Phelps v Hillingdon LBC* [2001] 2 A.C. 619 at 672.

[50] *Calveley v CC Merseyside Police* [1989] A.C. 1228. The possibility of judicial review of a complaints procedure was regarded as pointing away from a civil action because it reduced the possibility of damage being suffered by the person being investigated. So also in *Cullen v CC Royal Ulster Constabulary* [2003] UKHL 39; [2003] 1 W.L.R. 1763 the majority relied on the availability of judicial review to deny a claim for damages for being refused access to a lawyer; the minority adverted to the "formidable practical problems" in applying for judicial review when access to a lawyer is refused.

case of administrative remedies, that is to say the criminal penalty is presumed to be the sole means of enforcement but it has to be pointed out that in the area where breach of statutory duty has been of most importance (safety at work) the express provisions of the legislation in question were, for over a century and almost without exception, based solely on criminal penalties.[51]

8–010   **Wording or structure of the statute.** Sometimes an indication of an intention on civil liability may be found in the wording or structure of the statute. In *Keating v Elvan Reinforced Concrete Ltd*[52] the fact that the Public Utilities Street Works Act 1950 contained provisions creating civil liabilities in favour of public authorities was regarded as a reason for holding that it gave no right of action to individuals. On this basis the decision in *Groves v Wimborne*[53] is rather surprising. The statute made the occupier of a factory who did not properly fence dangerous machinery liable to a fine of £100 and it provided that the whole or any part of the fine might be applied, if the Secretary of State should so determine, for the benefit of the person injured by the occupier's neglect. A boy employed in the factory of the defendant was caught by an unfenced cog wheel and his arm had to be amputated. The Court of Appeal held that he was entitled to recover damages for breach of the statute in a civil action. The court reasoned that there was no certainty that any part of the fine would be awarded to the victim[54] and, even if it were awarded, its upper limit of £100, it was said, made it incredible that Parliament would have regarded that as a sufficient and exclusive compensation for mutilation or death.[55] Nevertheless, since Parliament had expressly adverted to the matter of compensation and the law of negligence applied as between employer and employee,[56] there was some force in the argument that no civil claim was intended. Nevertheless, *Groves v Wimborne* was the progenitor of hundreds of reported cases (and no doubt thousands of others) giving a civil remedy for breach of industrial safety legislation.

A common form of words in statutes creating offences is that "nothing in this Act shall be taken to prejudice any liability or remedy to which a person guilty of an offence thereunder may be subject in civil proceedings",[57] but such words do not create civil liability, they merely preserve whatever liability (for example, for negligence or trespass) may exist apart from the statute.[58] It has also been said, though the point is far from decisive, that it is easier to spell out a civil right of action if Parliament has expressly stated that something is unlawful and then

---

[51] Thus the Factories Act 1961 and its predecessors contained no mention of civil liability. See now the position under the Health and Safety at Work etc. Act 1974: paras 8–005 and 9–007.

[52] *Keating v Elvan Reinforced Concrete Ltd* [1968] 1 W.L.R. 722.

[53] *Groves v Wimborne* [1898] 2 Q.B. 402.

[54] Cf. *Richardson v Pitt-Stanley* [1995] Q.B. 123, where there was no such power to divert the penalty and where its potential quantum militated against the victim's chances of recovery of damages in an action for negligence.

[55] But the remedy provided by the statute need not be "complete" in order to infer the intention that no action is available: *Francis v Southwark LBC* [2011] EWCA Civ 1418; [2012] H.L.R. 16.

[56] Though then restricted by the doctrine of "common employment": para.9–003.

[57] See e.g. Protection from Eviction Act 1977, s.1(5).

[58] *McCall v Abelesz* [1976] Q.B. 585.

provided a penalty, rather than merely saying, "it is an offence to do such-and-such",[59] but this seems a very tenuous basis upon which to decide this issue.[60]

Type of injury. The fact that the loss likely to be suffered as a result of the breach of statutory duty is of a type not recoverable (or recoverable only on a restricted basis) under the general law of tort is, it seems, a factor pointing away from the implication of a civil right of action. In *Pickering v Liverpool Daily Post and Echo Newspapers Plc*[61] the statutory provision related to the publication of information about an application to a Mental Health Review Tribunal. This gave rise to no civil right of action because although the publication might be said to be against the applicant's interest in the sense that it involved the disclosure of information he would prefer not to have ventilated in public, that was not then[62] any form of damage known to the civil law. The court will more readily imply a civil action where the damage inflicted by the breach is physical harm, rather than economic loss, reflecting the common law's more restrictive approach to the latter.[63] However, this is not a universal rule,[64] for in *Monk v Warbey*[65] the court imposed civil liability upon the owner of a vehicle who allowed an uninsured driver (who was destitute of means) to use it, and thereby committed an offence under s.35 of the Road Traffic Act 1930.[66] The owner, who had no reason to doubt the driver's competence, had not in any legally relevant sense caused the

8–011

---

[59] *Rickless v United Artists Corp* [1988] Q.B. 40 at 51 (civil action found nonetheless); *Richardson v Pitt-Stanley* [1995] Q.B. 123 (action rejected).

[60] See the dissent of Sir John Megaw in *Richardson v Pitt-Stanley* [1995] Q.B. 123.

[61] [1991] 2 A.C. 370; and see *Cullen v CC Royal Ulster Constabulary* [2003] UKHL 39; [2003] 1 W.L.R. 1763 (no damage at all, not even substantial distress; it is not clear what the position would have been if there had been damage of a type generally recognised by the common law).

[62] Nowadays there might of course be claims under the law of misuse of private information or under the data protection legislation: see Ch.13.

[63] *Richardson v Pitt-Stanley* [1995] Q.B. 123.

[64] That there may be liability for breach of statutory duty causing economic loss is expressly accepted by Lord Bridge in *Pickering v Liverpool Daily Post and Echo Newspapers Plc* [1991] 2 A.C. 370 at 420.

[65] [1935] 1 K.B. 75. *Richardson v Pitt-Stanley* [1995] Q.B. 123 involved a rather similar situation, failure to comply with the Employers' Liability (Compulsory Insurance) Act 1969. However, the majority of the CA rejected a civil claim against the directors (the company was in insolvent liquidation) for breach of statutory duty. The reason was that to allow an action for breach of statutory duty against it would add nothing to the (worthless) claims against it for breach of the Factories Act 1961 and negligence, and without an action lying against the company there could be none against the directors.

[66] See now the Road Traffic Act 1988 s.143(1)(b).

claimant to be *injured*,[67] but he had caused the claimant to be in a position whereby his claim against the driver was worthless.[68]

8–012   **Other "adequate" remedies in law.** An indication that a civil action does not arise from the statute may be the fact that the common law and other statute law already contain adequate remedies to enforce private rights in the area in question. Thus in *McCall v Abelesz*[69] the Court of Appeal, in denying that the crime of harassment of tenants in s.30 of the Rent Act 1965[70] gave rise to civil liability, laid stress upon the fact that many acts of harassment by a landlord must inevitably involve trespass or breach of contract. That, of course, leaves the question of what is "adequate". Atkin LJ in *Phillips v Britannia Hygienic Laundry Co*,[71] in rejecting the contention that regulations governing the construction and use of motor vehicles gave rise to civil liability, spoke of highway accidents being "already well provided for" by the common law, but that is a view that would not necessarily command widespread assent today. In any event, the fact that the general law of tort and the law of contract are applicable to the relationship between employer and employee has not prevented the courts from holding that an action lies for breach of industrial safety legislation. More convincing (though once again industrial accident cases may have to be treated as an exception) is the view that the courts, in the absence of clear words, will tend to lean against a civilly actionable statutory duty which would contradict the general pattern of liability in a particular area of activity, but will tend to find one which will support or supplement it. This would explain why the courts have consistently[72] rejected road traffic legislation as a direct source of civil liability, for the effect would have been to introduce isolated pockets of strict liability into an area generally governed by negligence. At the same time, however, it would support the decision in *Monk v Warbey* because that case made it more likely that a victim of actionable negligence would recover.[73]

---

[67] But the claim is still one for damages for personal injuries for limitation purposes: *Norman v Ali* [2000] R.T.R. 107. A permits B to drive A's car while uninsured. There is an accident caused by the combined fault of B, and C driving another vehicle (the proportions of fault being 25 per cent and 75 per cent) in which A is injured. A sues C and recovers in full. C's counterclaim against A under *Monk v Warbey* will fail because the Act requires insurance only against personal injury and property damage and C's counterclaim is economic loss: *Bretton v Hancock* [2005] EWCA Civ 404; [2005] R.T.R. 22 (s.143(1)(a) rather than (b) was in issue but the point is the same).

[68] It has been held that the court must look at the realities of the matter, and it is not necessary to show that the driver can never pay: *Martin v Dean* [1971] 2 Q.B. 208; but in *Norman v Ali* [2000] R.T.R. 107 the court left open how far it was necessary to establish impecuniosity.

[69] [1976] Q.B. 585.

[70] Replaced by the Housing Act 1988 Pt I Ch.IV, which does give rise to civil liability. See also the more general statutory crime and tort of harassment under the Protection from Harassment Act 1997, para.4–034.

[71] [1923] 2 K.B. 832.

[72] *Phillips v Britannia Hygienic Laundry Co*[1923] 2 K.B. 832; *Clark v Brims* [1947] K.B. 497; *Coote v Stone* [1971] 1 W.L.R. 279; *Exel Logistics Ltd v Curran* [2004] EWCA Civ 1249. A rare exception is *LPTB v Upson* [1949] A.C. 155 (breach of the Pedestrian Crossing Regulations). See also *Roe v Sheffield CC* [2003] EWCA Civ 1; [2004] Q.B. 653, though that related to the condition of the highway rather than the manner of using it.

[73] *Richardson v Pitt-Stanley* [1995] Q.B. 123 certainly does not support the policy of *Monk v Warbey*, but the decision is based more on the wording of the statute than on policy.

Again, in *Issa v Hackney LBC*[74] an attempt to bring a civil action on the basis of the "statutory nuisance" provisions of the Public Health Act 1936[75] was rejected. In the normal case of activities on land A causing disturbance to the occupiers of land B, the common law of nuisance would give an adequate remedy for harm suffered if that was still necessary after the operation of the statutory enforcement procedures and the exercise of the court's power to make a compensation order; but on the facts, the statute was being used in an attempt to outflank established principles governing the responsibility of a landlord for the upkeep of premises. Those principles were seriously deficient because of legislative inaction,[76] but the solution was to be sought in direct legislative amendment, not by the side-wind of straining the law of breach of statutory duty.

Public rights and special damage. In *Lonrho Ltd v Shell Petroleum Co Ltd (No.2)*[77] Lord Diplock, having referred to the cases on statutes for the protection of particular classes of persons, such as those dealing with industrial safety, said that there was a further exception to the general rule (that a statute was to be enforced only by the means prescribed in it) namely:[78]   **8–013**

> "[W]here the statute creates a public right (i.e. a right to be enjoyed by all those of Her Majesty's subjects who wish to avail themselves of it) and a particular member of the public suffers what Brett J in *Benjamin v Storr*[79] described as 'particular, direct and substantial' damage 'other and different from that which was common to all the rest of the public'."

Benjamin v Storr was in fact a case on whether an individual can bring an action for damages in respect of a public nuisance.[80] The principal authority relied on by Lord Diplock in the context of statutory duty was not an action for damages but concerned the question whether a member of the public could, without the assistance of the Attorney General, seek an injunction to restrain an interference with public rights.[81] However, it was said in *Lonrho* that a, "mere prohibition on members of the public generally from doing what it would otherwise be lawful for them to do is not enough" to create a public right for this purpose. It will not therefore be enough for the claimant to point to the commission of a crime and say that he has been damaged by it and he cannot escape by this route from the fundamental question of whether the statute is intended to give rise to a civil action.[82]

Assessment. The law on inferring civil actions from statutory duties is not very satisfactory. The drastic reduction in the availability of a civil action in the one   **8–014**

---

[74] [1997] 1 W.L.R. 956.
[75] See now Pt III of the Environmental Protection Act 1990, para.15–002.
[76] As is devastatingly demonstrated in the judgment of Brooke LJ.
[77] [1982] A.C. 173.
[78] [1982] A.C. 173 at 185.
[79] *Benjamin v Storr* (1874) L.R. 9 C.P. 400 at 407.
[80] See para.15–006. However, the connection is obvious. Public nuisance, like breach of statutory duty, is an example of civil liability arising out of what is primarily a crime, though in this case a common law crime.
[81] *Boyce v Paddington BC* [1903] 1 Ch. 109.
[82] *Mid Kent Holdings Plc v General Utilities Plc* [1997] 1 W.L.R. 14 (whether the claim is for damages, an injunction or a declaration).

area where it has hitherto consistently been available, i.e. industrial safety,[83] may revive the suggestion that it should be abolished altogether.[84] As it is, Lord Denning MR commented with perhaps a little pardonable exaggeration that the legislature "has left the courts with a guess-work puzzle. The dividing line between the pro-cases and the contra-cases is so blurred and so ill-defined that you might as well toss a coin to decide it".[85]

As Lord du Parcq pointed out[86] the draftsmen of Acts of Parliament are aware of the principles—and lack of principles—applied by the courts to fill the gaps left in legislation, and it can be argued, therefore, that the silence of a statute on the question of civil remedies for its breach is a deliberate invitation to the courts to decide the question for themselves. Certainly it should not be assumed that where the statute is silent this is because its promoters have not adverted to the point—much more likely that it would be politically inconvenient to attempt to answer the question one way or the other. If this is so, then the pretence of seeking for the non-existent intention of Parliament should be abandoned.[87] Not only does it involve an unnecessary fiction, but it may lead to decisions being made on the basis of insignificant details of phraseology instead of matters of substance. If the question whether a person injured by breach of statutory duty is to have a right of action for damages is in truth a question to be decided by the courts, then it should be acknowledged as such and some useful principles of law developed, if that is possible.[88] It is, however, debatable whether a clear overall presumption might help.[89] At least it can be said that there are numerous decisions on particular statutes so that in many cases it is already settled that a right of action does or does not exist.[90] Even where a right of action has been held to exist, however, it is not enough for the claimant simply to prove breach of the statute. There are other elements in the tort which we must now consider. We may, however, note that where the statute creates a criminal offence the victim may choose to seek a compensation order from the criminal court, a procedure which is not dependent upon the establishing of a civil right of action. Though applicable to all criminal offences outside the road traffic field, this mechanism

---

[83] See para.8–005.

[84] The suggestion by the Law Commission that the action for breach of statutory duty should be abolished "in most contexts" (Administrative Redress: Public Bodies and the Citizen (2008), Law Com. No.187, para.4–105) was abandoned, along with the recommendation of an entirely new remedy, in its later report (Law Com No. 232 (2010)). But if Parliament does *expressly* indicate that an action for damages may be brought, what can the courts do other than to give effect to it?

[85] *Ex p. Islands Records* [1978] Ch. 122 at 134–135. See also Schiemann J in *R. v Knowsley MBC Ex p. Maguire* (1992) 90 L.G.R. 653.

[86] *Cutler v Wandsworth Stadium Ltd* [1949] A.C. 398 at 411; *Solomons v R. Gertzenstein Ltd* [1954] 2 Q.B. 243 at 267 per Romer LJ.

[87] Williams (1960) 23 M.L.R. 233.

[88] For a case decided by reference to principle and policy rather than the supposed intention of Parliament, see *Hargreaves v Bretherton* [1959] 1 Q.B. 45 (no action in tort for perjury).

[89] The Law Commission suggested a general presumption in favour of actionability: Law Com. No.21 (1969). But recent moves have been in the opposite direction: see para.8–005.

[90] Williams (1960) 23 M.L.R. 233 concluded that, as a very broad and oversimplified conclusion, legislation concerning industrial safety gave rise to civil liability while other legislation did not, but even in this area there is now a presumption of non-actionability: see para.8–005. It is also the case that many statutory duties are less than absolute: para.9–012.

has so far been of limited importance in the type of case considered in this chapter but its role in compensating losses may increase.[91]

C. European Legislation

The general reluctance to find an actionable breach of statutory duty in cases brought against public authorities reflects the general principle that an ultra vires act does not of itself give rise to a claim for damages—there must be some tort,[92] breach of contract or other actionable wrong. However, one has to take account of the interaction of English private law remedies with European law, a matter of which only a bare outline can be attempted here. The House of Lords in *Garden Cottage Foods Ltd v Milk Marketing Board*[93] held that directly applicable provisions of the Treaty of Rome might give rise to a civil action for damages in an English court.[94] The Court of Appeal in *Bourgoin SA v Ministry of Agriculture, Fisheries and Food*[95] later held that this was not the case where the legislation in question imposed obligations only on the state and not on private persons but since then another element has entered the picture, for the European Court of Justice in *Francovich v Italy*[96] held that a Member State may be liable to make good damage suffered by individuals as a result of the state's failure to implement a Directive and the Court spoke in rather broader terms of a principle of Community Law "according to which a Member State is obliged to make good the damage to individuals . . . by a breach of Community law for which it is responsible". This is apt to cover direct breaches of the Treaty provisions as well as failure to implement Directives. The subsequent case law indicates that the following conditions must be satisfied to give rise to such a liability: (1) the law infringed must be intended to confer rights on individuals; (2) (in cases where the state has any element of discretion) the breach by the Member State must be sufficiently serious;[97] and (3) there must be a direct causal link between the breach and the damage sustained by the claimant.[98]

8–015

This is plainly wider than the common law notion of breach of statutory duty, most obviously in that it allows an action where the legislation itself is in breach of Community law. However, the first requirement is not wholly dissimilar from the underlying question in claims for breach of statutory duty, for Community law may be intended to confer benefits on a particular group without granting them rights enforceable by action in municipal courts. Thus, in *Three Rivers DC v Bank of England (No.3)*[99] the House of Lords held that the 1977 Banking

---

[91] For the powers of the criminal court, see para.4–006.
[92] As to misfeasance in a public office, see para.8–024.
[93] [1984] A.C. 130.
[94] Article 86 (now art.82) abuse of a dominant market position.
[95] [1986] Q.B. 716.
[96] (C–6/90) [1995] I.C.R. 722.
[97] See *Test Claimants in the FII Group Litigation v Revenue and Customs Commissioners* [2010] EWCA Civ 103; [2010] S.T.C. 1251; revsd. in part [2012] UKSC 19; [2012] 2 A.C. 337; *AB v Home Office* [2012] EWHC 226 (QB); [2012] 4 All E.R. 276.
[98] See the summary in *R. v Secretary of State Ex p. Factortame Ltd (No.5)* [2000] 1 A.C. 524 at 538.
[99] [2001] UKHL 16; [2003] 2 A.C. 1.

Directive[100] was intended as a measure to harmonise the regulation of banking but did not create a right to damages for depositors who suffered loss by reason of the failure of supervisory mechanisms. There has been some dispute as to the nature of the state's liability under this head for the purposes of English law, but in *R. v Secretary of State Ex p. Factortame Ltd (No.7)*,[101] where the issue arose in the context of limitation of actions, it was held that it was in the nature of a breach of statutory duty and therefore an action in tort.[102]

D. Elements of the Tort

8–016 **Duty must be owed to the claimant.** Some statutory duties are so expressed as to limit the classes of person for whose benefit they exist, and where this is so it is a question of the construction of the statutory provision in question whether the claimant is a member of the protected class. If he is not, then his action for breach of statutory duty cannot succeed. In *Hartley v Mayoh & Co*,[103] for example, a fireman was electrocuted while fighting a fire at the defendants' factory. His widow relied, inter alia, upon a breach by the defendants of their obligations under certain statutory regulations, but these existed only for the protection of "persons employed", and firemen did not come within this description. The claim for breach of statutory duty therefore failed. In *West Wiltshire DC v Garland*[104] it was held that the statutory duty of a district auditor gave rise to a civil cause of action in the local authority, the accounts of which were audited by him, but there was no duty to an individual officer of the authority.

8–017 **Injury must be of the kind which the statute is intended to prevent.** If the object of the statute was to prevent mischief of a particular kind, one who suffers from its non-observance loss of a different kind cannot twist its remedy into an action for his own recoupment. In *Gorris v Scott*[105] the defendant, a shipowner, was under a statutory duty to provide pens for cattle on his ship in order to lessen the risk of murrain among them. The claimant's sheep were swept overboard in consequence of lack of such pens. The defendant was held not liable, because it was not part of the purpose of the statute to protect cattle against perils of the sea.[106] The modern tendency is, however, not to apply this decision too strictly, and it has been said that if the claimant's damage is of the kind that the statute was designed to prevent, then it does not matter that it occurred in a way not

---

[100] Directive 77/80.

[101] [2001] 1 W.L.R. 942.

[102] The inadequacy of the implementation may not be apparent to the claimant until his claim has been adjudicated but the limitation period runs from the date of the injury: see *Spencer v Secretary of State for Work and Pensions* [2008] EWCA Civ 750; [2009] Q.B. 358.

[103] [1954] 1 Q.B. 383.

[104] [1995] Ch. 297.

[105] (1874) L.R. 9 Exch. 125; *Larrimore v American National Insurance Co* 89 P.2d 340 (1939).

[106] The claimants relied on the statutory obligation and on nothing else, e.g. a claim in negligence. Yet even in a case of negligence, the defendant's liability may be limited by an approach similar to that in *Gorris v Scott*: see *Banque Bruxelles Lambert SA v Eagle Star Insurance Co Ltd* [1997] A.C. 191 in which Lord Hoffmann draws an analogy with *Gorris v Scott*, para.7–059.

contemplated by the statute.[107] On the other hand the House of Lords held that a workman who was injured by a dangerous part of machinery which flew out of a machine and hit him could not base a claim on the statutory obligation that dangerous parts of machinery "shall be securely fenced".[108] The object of this provision, it was said, was, "to keep the worker out, not to keep the machine or its product in".[109] It was only if he came into contact with the dangerous part of the machine, therefore, that the workman could rely upon breach of the obligation to fence, and an injury caused in a different way was not covered.[110]

Scope of the statutory duty. Many statutes and statutory regulations have strictly defined spheres of application, and outside their proper sphere they are irrelevant.[111] For example, many actions for injury caused by acts or omissions which would have amounted to breaches of the Factories Act had they occurred in a factory failed on the ground that the place where they in fact occurred was not a factory as defined.[112] The modification of much safety legislation so that it applies to workplaces in general reduces the likelihood of such cases[113] but the general point remains valid.[114] In *Chipchase v British Titan Products Co*,[115] a workman was injured when he fell from a platform 9in wide and 6ft above the ground. Statutory regulations then required that "every working platform from which a person is liable to fall more than six feet and six inches shall be . . . at least 34 inches wide" and it was argued that the case was so nearly within the regulations that the court ought to take them into account. The argument was rejected and the defendants were held not liable either for breach of statutory duty, for there was none, or for negligence at common law.

8–018

Standard of conduct. The measure of the defendant's obligation in every case must be found in the statute itself and no single standard of conduct exists.[116] In some cases the statute imposes an unqualified obligation, i.e. an absolute duty that a certain state of affairs shall exist, and in such cases the nonexistence of that state of affairs constitutes the breach.[117] Historically, the best-known example

8–019

---

[107] *Donaghey v Boulton & Paul Ltd* [1968] A.C. 1 at 26 per Lord Reid. Note the similarity to the development at common law subsequent to *The Wagon Mound*, para.7–037.

[108] Factories Act 1961 s.14; *Close v Steel Co of Wales Ltd* [1962] A.C. 367; *Sparrow v Fairey Aviation Co Ltd* [1964] A.C. 1019.

[109] *Nicholls v F Austin (Leyton) Ltd* [1946] A.C. 493 at 505 per Lord Simonds. See also *Fytche v Wincanton Logistics Plc* [2004] UKHL 31; [2004] I.C.R. 975 (steel toe-capped boot; purpose of regulations to protect from impact injury, not wet and cold).

[110] Cf. *Young v Charles Church (Southern) Ltd* (1997) 39 B.M.L.R. 146 (regulation designed to prevent electrocution covered nervous shock at seeing workmate electrocuted).

[111] In addition to the cases discussed herein, see para.9–013.

[112] An example is *Longhurst v Guildford, etc. Water Board* [1963] A.C. 265.

[113] See para.9–013.

[114] See, e.g. *Kmiecic v Isaacs* [2011] EWCA Civ 451; [2011] I.C.R. 1269 where the occupier of premises was not liable for the injury suffered by a building contractor's employee because, under the relevant regulations, she did not control the way the construction work was carried out (the building contractor was potentially liable, but he was uninsured); contrast *Tafa v Matsim Properties Ltd* [2011] EWHC 1302 (QB) and *Ceva Logistics Ltd v Lynch* [2011] EWCA Civ 188; [2011] I.C.R. 746 (under different regulations, statutory duty owed to contractor's employee by owner and operator of a warehouse).

[115] [1956] 1 Q.B. 545.

[116] See further, para.9–010.

[117] *Galashiels Gas Co v Millar* [1949] A.C. 275.

was the provision of s.14 of the Factories Act 1961 requiring that "every dangerous part of any machinery ... shall be securely fenced".[118] This has been replaced by more complex regulations which create a less than absolute obligation but there continue to be examples in industrial safety legislation of duties to secure a result, not merely to take care to do so. In such cases, the "result" which must be achieved will itself be open to interpretation, e.g. whether personal protective equipment is "suitable",[119] or whether a workplace is "safe".[120] Sometimes a duty is imposed "so far as is reasonably practicable", which has some similarity to the standard of common law negligence, though it is by no means identical and the burden is on the defendant to show that the requirement in question was not reasonably practicable.[121] Duties to secure something "so far as practicable" or to "take such steps as may be necessary" are more onerous but still not absolute.[122] There is no substitute for an analysis of the particular provision in its context.[123]

8–020   **Causation: conduct of the claimant.** In an action for breach of statutory duty, as in an action for common law negligence, the claimant bears the burden of proving the causal connection between the breach of duty and the damage.[124] There is, however, one rather special kind of case, peculiar to actions for breach of statutory duty, which must be mentioned, namely that in which the act or omission of the claimant himself has the legal result that both claimant and defendant are in breach of the same duty.

In *Ginty v Belmont Building Supplies Ltd*[125] the claimant was an experienced workman in the employment of the defendants, who were roofing contractors. Statutory regulations binding upon both parties required that crawling boards should be used for work done on fragile roofs and, although boards had been provided by the defendants, the claimant neglected to use them and fell through a roof in consequence. In law both claimant and defendants were in breach of their statutory duties, but Pearson J held that the claimant's claim failed altogether

---

[118] See, e.g. *John Summers & Sons Ltd v Frost* [1955] A.C. 740.

[119] See *Threlfall v Hull City Council* [2010] EWCA Civ 1147; [2011] I.C.R. 209; *Chief Constable of Hampshire v Taylor* [2013] EWCA Civ 496; [2013] I.C.R. 1150 ("suitability" of gloves under the Personal Protective Equipment at Work Regulations 1992). See also *Hide v Steeplechase Co (Cheltenham) Ltd* [2013] EWCA Civ 545; [2014] 1 All E.R. 405, discussed in para.9–011.

[120] See *Baker v Quantum Clothing Group Ltd* [2011] UKSC 17; [2011] 1 W.L.R. 1003 (safety (in the context of noise) held to be a "relative" concept to be judged by reference to the knowledge and standards of the time): see para.9–011.

[121] See para.9–012.

[122] See para.9–012.

[123] In the case of the industrial safety legislation which has provided the examples referred to in this paragraph, it should be noted that there may no longer be a civil action for breach of the relevant duty: see para.8–005.

[124] *Bonnington Castings Ltd v Wardlaw* [1956] A.C. 613; *McWilliams v Sir William Arrol & Co Ltd* [1962] 1 W.L.R. 295. These cases concern "factual causation"; factors which go to "legal causation" such as acts of a third party, may be relevant (*Horton v Taplin Contracts Ltd* [2002] EWCA Civ 1604; [2003] I.C.R. 179) but everything finally depends on the words of the statute.

[125] [1959] 1 All E.R. 414.

because the defendants' breach consisted of and was coextensive with his own wrongful act.[126] In other words, there was no wrongful act but the claimant's own, and:[127]

> "[I]t would be absurd if, notwithstanding the employer having done all he could reasonably be expected to do to ensure compliance, a workman, who deliberately disobeyed his employer's orders and thereby put the employer in breach of a regulation, could claim damages for injury caused to him solely by his own wrongdoing."

Although the result reached in *Ginty* has been judicially described as "obvious",[128] the scope of the decision is restricted. If the claimant establishes the defendant's breach of duty and that he suffered injury as a result, he establishes a prima facie case against the defendant. The defendant will escape liability only if he can rebut that prima facie case by proof that the only act or default of anyone which caused the breach was that of the claimant himself.[129] It follows that where some fault is to be attributed to the defendant, as where an employer calls upon a worker to do a job beyond his proper competence,[130] fails to provide adequate instructions or supervision,[131] is responsible for some independent fault,[132] or encourages him in his own breach of statutory duty,[133] then the claimant is entitled to recover some damages, even though they may be substantially reduced on account of his contributory negligence.

Volenti non fit injuria.[134] It was long thought that the defence of volenti non fit injuria was not available in actions for breach of statutory duty and perhaps this is still generally so, though the law needs to be clarified. It is obviously open to Parliament to create a statutory duty and to provide that the defence does not apply; but where, as is often the case, the actionable duty is conjured up by a process of construction somewhat akin to divination it is not easy to see why there should be any hard and fast rule. In 1964 the House of Lords held that the defence was available where a worker engaged with a colleague in flagrant breach of safety rules and sued the employer on the basis that there was a breach

8–021

---

[126] [1959] 1 All E.R. 414 at 424.

[127] *Boyle v Kodak Ltd* [1969] 1 W.L.R. 661 at 665–666 per Lord Reid. "To say 'You are liable to me for my own wrongdoing' is neither good morals nor good law": at 673 per Lord Diplock.

[128] *Donaghey v Boulton & Paul Ltd* [1968] A.C. 1 at 24 per Lord Reid. See also *Brumder v Motornet Service and Repairs Ltd* [2013] EWCA Civ 195; [2013] 1 W.L.R. 2783 where the claimant was director and sole shareholder of the employer company.

[129] *Boyle v Kodak Ltd* [1969] 1 W.L.R. 661 at 672–673 per Lord Diplock.

[130] *Byers v Head Wrightson & Co Ltd* [1961] 1 W.L.R. 961; *Ross v Associated Portland Cement Manufacturers Ltd* [1964] 1 W.L.R. 768; *Bhatt v Fontain Motors Ltd* [2010] EWCA Civ 863; [2010] P.I.Q.R. P17.

[131] *Jenner v Allen West & Co Ltd* [1959] 1 W.L.R. 554; *Ross v Associated Portland Cement Manufacturers Ltd* [1964] 1 W.L.R. 768; *Boyle v Kodak Ltd* [1969] 1 W.L.R. 661; *Sharp v Top Flight Scaffolding Ltd* [2013] EWHC 479 (QB).

[132] *McMath v Rimmer Bros (Liverpool) Ltd* [1962] 1 W.L.R. 1; *Leach v Standard Telephones & Cables Ltd* [1966] 1 W.L.R. 1392; *Donaghey v Boulton & Paul Ltd* [1968] A.C. 1; *Keaney v British Railways Board* [1968] 1 W.L.R. 879. It appears that the fault for which the employer is responsible need not be such as to suffice as an independent ground of action.

[133] *Barcock v Brighton Corp* [1949] 1 K.B. 339; *Laszczyk v National Coal Board* [1954] 1 W.L.R. 1426.

[134] See para.26–018.

of statutory duty only via vicarious liability for the other worker's acts.[135] That was not a case where the employer was in breach of a duty directly imposed on *him*, and the case is consistent with a position whereby in that event the defence is still inapplicable.[136] It is certainly true that the courts are much less willing than they once were to accept, even at common law, that a worker has voluntarily run a known risk without access to a claim for damages and that there are often other routes (for example causation) to denying liability.[137] However, a blanket rule of exclusion based on the public policy of recognising the will of Parliament is in the nature of a fiction.

8–022   **Contributory negligence.** Before the Law Reform (Contributory Negligence) Act 1945 the contributory negligence of the claimant was a complete defence to an action for breach of statutory duty[138] and now, therefore, it is a reason for reducing the damages which he may recover. This matter is considered below.[139]

8–023   **Delegation of the duty to the claimant.** It is clear that in the ordinary way it is no defence for a person subjected to a statutory duty to claim that he has delegated the duty or its performance to another person.[140] In some cases, however, it seems to have been thought that delegation may be a defence where performance of the tasks necessary to secure compliance with the statutory obligation has been delegated to the claimant himself.[141] Nevertheless, although some specific requirements for the defence of delegation were laid down,[142] in no case did the claimant clearly fail in his action on the express ground that the defendant's statutory duty had been delegated to him[143] and the doctrine has now

---

[135] *Imperial Chemical Industries Ltd v Shatwell* [1965] A.C. 656.

[136] However, the dicta on the point are not perhaps entirely consistent: compare Lord Reid at 674 referring to, "an employer who is himself at fault in persistently refusing to comply with a statutory rule"; Lord Pearce at 687, seeming to accept a general rule of non-applicability of the defence; Lord Donovan at 693, referring to unequal bargaining strength.

[137] There is no defence of "fireground immunity" in relation to fire officers and police officers injured at the scene of a fire: *"Wembridge Claimants" v Winter* [2013] EWHC 2331 (QB) (claims for breach of statutory duty and in negligence), but some regulations simply may not apply: eg the obligation on employers to ensure that work at height is carried out only when the weather conditions do not jeopardise health or safety (Working at Height Regulations 2005) is expressly dis-applied "where members of the police, fire, ambulance or other emergency service are acting in an emergency" (reg. 4(4)).

[138] *Caswell v Powell Duffryn Associated Colleries* [1940] A.C. 152.

[139] See para.26–036.

[140] *Gray v Pullen* (1864) 5 B. & S. 970; *Whitby v Burt, Boulton & Hayward Ltd* [1947] K.B. 918. See para.21–050.

[141] See, e.g. *Vincent v Southern Ry* [1927] A.C. 430; *Smith v Baveystock & Co* [1945] 1 All E.R. 531.

[142] See, e.g. *Beale v E Gomme Ltd* (1949) 65 T.L.R. 543; *Manwaring v Billington* [1952] 2 All E.R. 747.

[143] However, the judgments of Lord Goddard in *Smith v Baveystock & Co* [1945] 1 All E.R. 531 at 533–534 and Hilbery J in *Barcock v Brighton Corp* [1949] 1 K.B. 339, could be taken as supporting this view.

fallen into disrepute. In *Ginty v Belmont Building Supplies Ltd*,[144] in a passage subsequently approved by the Court of Appeal,[145] Pearson J doubted its soundness:[146]

> "There has been a number of cases . . . in which it has been considered whether or not the employer delegated to the employee the performance of the statutory duty. In my view, the law which is applicable here is clear and comprehensible if one does not confuse it by seeking to investigate this very difficult and complicated question whether or not there was a delegation. In my view, the important and fundamental question in a case like this is not whether there was a delegation, but simply the usual question: Whose fault was it? . . . If the answer to that question is that in substance and reality the accident was solely due to the fault of the plaintiff, so that he was the sole author of his own wrong, he is disentitled to recover."

It is submitted, therefore, that there is no special defence of delegation of a statutory duty and, indeed, that any other view would conflict with the general principle that no duty can be delegated.[147]

2. MISFEASANCE IN A PUBLIC OFFICE

Nature of the action. This is a convenient point at which to outline the tort of misfeasance in a public office.[148] It is not based upon breach of statutory duty, but a claim for it is not infrequently coupled with a claim for breach of statutory duty in an action against a public authority. The tort is traceable back to the 17th century,[149] and was described in modern times by the Privy Council as "well-established" in *Dunlop v Woollahra Municipal Council*.[150] The law was comprehensively reviewed by the House of Lords in *Three Rivers DC v Bank of England (No.3)*.[151] The purpose of the tort is to give compensation to those who have suffered loss as a result of improper abuse of public power,[152] it being based

8–024

---

[144] [1959] 1 All E.R. 414 at 423–424.
[145] *McMath v Rimmer Bros (Liverpool) Ltd* [1962] 1 W.L.R. 1 at 6. See also *Jenner v Allen West & Co Ltd* [1959] 1 W.L.R. 554.
[146] *Ginty v Belmont Building Supplies Ltd* [1959] 1 All E.R. 414 at 423-424 per Pearson LJ. See also *Ross v Associated Portland Cement Manufacturers Ltd* [1964] 1 W.L.R. 768 at 777 per Lord Reid ("Fault is not necessarily equivalent in this context to blameworthiness. The question really is whose conduct caused the accident").
[147] *Ross v Associated Portland Cement Manufacturers Ltd* [1964] 1 W.L.R. 768 at 776 per Lord Reid.
[148] There is a comparable common law crime of misbehaviour in a public office: *R. v Bowden* [1996] 1 W.L.R. 98. In s.9(5) of the Anti-Social Behaviour Act 2003 the tort is called "misfeasance in public duty".
[149] *Turner v Sterling* (1671) 2 Vent. 25.
[150] [1982] A.C. 158. See also *David v Abdul Cader* [1963] 1 W.L.R. 834.
[151] [2001] UKHL 16; [2003] 2 A.C. 1. This is an amalgam of two hearings, the first (judgment given on May 18, 2000—[2003] 2 A.C. at 187) examining the law and the second applying it to the application to amend the particulars of claim (judgment given on March 22, 2001—[2003] 2 A.C. at 237). The second has the now usual paragraph numbers, the first does not.
[152] Since *Kuddus v CC Leicestershire Constabulary* [2001] UKHL 29; [2002] 2 A.C. 222 exemplary damages may be available for this tort: para.23–016. On damages see also para.8–030. It is capable of applying to personal injury: *Akenzua v Secretary of State for the Home Dept* [2002] EWCA Civ 1470; [2003] 1 W.L.R. 741.

on the principle that such power may be exercised only for the public good and not for ulterior and improper purposes.[153]

8–025 **Elements of liability.** The tort of misfeasance in a public office applies to an unlawful (that is to say, unauthorised) act[154] by a person holding a public office (which includes a public body such as a local authority,[155] a government department[156] or the Bank of England)[157] provided it is done with the requisite mental element. Where a claim is brought against a public body or institution it will be necessary to show that the mental element was possessed by an identifiable human agent.[158] Although the mental element is restricted to intention or "recklessness" the tort has a considerable reach, for there is no requirement that the conduct should be actionable in damages in its own right:[159] it covers non-actionable breach of statutory duty and a decision which is taken contrary to the requirements of natural justice.

8–026 **The mental element.** The mental element relates both to the validity of the act and its effect upon the claimant. As to the first, the officer must act in bad faith, that is to say he must either be aware that his act is unlawful or be consciously indifferent as to its lawfulness—mere negligence is not enough. As to the effect on the claimant, there are two situations. The first is what has been called "targeted malice", that is to say, the case where the defendant acts with the *purpose* of causing harm to the claimant.[160] An example of this category is *Roncarelli v Duplessis*[161] (though the case was actually decided under the civil law of Quebec) where the defendant, Prime Minister and Attorney General of

---

[153] *Three Rivers DC v Bank of England (No.3)* at [2003] 2 A.C. 190 per Lord Steyn, citing Nourse LJ in *Jones v Swansea CC* [1990] 1 W.L.R. 54 at 85. See the analogy with the tort of malicious prosecution drawn by Lord Sumption in *Crawford Adjusters v Sagicor General Insurance Ltd* [2013] UKPC 17; [2013] 3 W.L.R. 927: para.20–021.

[154] In principle the tort is equally applicable to an omission by a public officer, provided there is a decision not to act (see *Three Rivers* at [2003] 2 A.C. 228 per Lord Hutton, at 230 per Lord Hobhouse) or at least the ignoring of obvious risks (*Three Rivers* at 254); but liability for mere inadvertence or oversight is precluded by the mental element of bad faith.

[155] *Jones v Swansea CC* [1990] 1 W.L.R. 1453.

[156] *Bourgoin SA v Ministry of Agriculture, Fisheries and Food* [1986] Q.B. 716. Including vicarious liability for an individual officer: *Racz v Home Office* [1994] 2 A.C. 45.

[157] The *Three Rivers* case; but not the governing body of Lloyd's: *Society of Lloyd's v Henderson* [2007] EWCA Civ 930; [2008] 1 W.L.R. 2255. The tort is also applicable to the police (*Darker v CC W Midlands Police* [2001] 1 A.C. 435; *Kuddus v CC Leicestershire Constabulary* [2001] UKHL 29; [2002] 2 A.C. 222; *L v Reading BC* [2001] EWCA Civ 346; [2001] 1 W.L.R. 1575) and the Crown Prosecution Service (*Elguzouli-Daf v MPC* [1995] Q.B. 335), but it has been held that it does not apply to an independent prosecutor or lawyer representing the government: *Cannon v Tahche* (2002) 5 V.R. 317; *Leerdam v Noori* [2009] NSWCA 90; (2009) 255 A.L.R 553.

[158] *Chagos Islanders v Attorney General* [2004] EWCA Civ 997; *Southwark LBC v Dennett* [2007] EWCA Civ 1091; [2008] L.G.R. 94.

[159] One category of case, the unnecessary release of embarrassing information, may now be directly actionable under the Human Rights Act 1998 or at common law.

[160] As Lord Millett (who, however, did not agree with the "two limb" analysis of the tort) points out in *Three Rivers* [2003] 2 A.C. 1 at 235 the claimant in this case does not have to show independently that the official exceeded his power, for, "his deliberate use of the power of his office to injure the plaintiff takes his conduct outside the power". The tort is, "an exception to 'the general rule that, if conduct is presumptively unlawful, a good motive will not exonerate the defendant, and that, if conduct is lawful apart from motive, a bad motive will not make him liable'": Lord Steyn at 190.

[161] (1959) 16 D.L.R. (2d) 689.

Quebec, deprived the claimant of his restaurant licence as an act of revenge for standing bail for members of the Jehovah's Witnesses sect, against whose activities there had been a campaign. Alternatively, the defendant will be liable if he is aware that his act will probably (or in the ordinary course of things)[162] cause damage of the type in fact suffered by the claimant[163] or he is consciously indifferent to that risk.[164] So, turning a blind eye to either invalidity or consequences will do, but not failure to appreciate the risk of those matters. This:[165]

> "[R]epresents a satisfactory balance between the two competing policy considerations, namely enlisting tort law to combat executive and administrative abuse of power and not allowing public officers, who must always act for the public good, to be assailed by unmeritorious actions."

Relationship with negligence. In some circumstances the public officer may be exposed to an action for negligence[166] but the tort of misfeasance is wider: for example, a claim against the police for negligence in allowing a murderer to remain at large would be likely to fail on the grounds that there was insufficient proximity between them and the next, unidentifiable victim and for the policy reason of a fear of "defensive policing", but if they procured his release for some corrupt purpose a claim for misfeasance would not be defeated on that ground.[167] Judicial review is, of course, available on the basis of the invalidity of the act in question and without reference to fault, but there is no claim for damages unless there is a tort or some other wrong.[168]

8–027

The *Three Rivers* litigation arose out of allegations that the Bank of England had acted wrongfully in granting a banking licence to the Bank of Credit and Commerce International (or failing to revoke the existing licence), thereby causing loss to over 6,000 depositors, in circumstances where any liability in negligence was precluded.[169] The amended particulars of claim were held sufficiently to set out the elements of the tort and the majority of the House of

---

[162] The former expression is used by Lord Steyn ([2003] 2 A.C. 1 at 191) and Lord Hutton (at 228), the latter by Lord Hobhouse (at 230) who adds a requirement that the loss must be such as to arise "directly". Cf. Lord Millett at 236: "I do not think that it is sufficient that he should foresee that it will probably do so. The principle in play is that a man is presumed to intend the natural and probable consequences of his actions . . . it should be calculated (in the sense of likely) in the ordinary course of events to cause injury. But the inference cannot be drawn unless the official did foresee the consequences." In the second decision Lord Hope refers to awareness of "a serious risk of loss" (at 247).

[163] *Three Rivers* [2003] 2 A.C. 1 at 196 per Lord Steyn. Compare the narrower test which now seems to apply in the economic torts—the defendant must intend to harm the claimant as an end in itself or as a means to some other end: Ch.19.

[164] See *Muuse v Secretary of State for the Home Dept* [2010] EWCA Civ 453 at [56].

[165] *Three Rivers* [2003] 2 A.C. 1 at 196.

[166] See para.5–065.

[167] *Akenzua v Secretary of State for the Home Dept* [2002] EWCA Civ 1470; [2003] 1 W.L.R. 741. In *Carter v CC Cumbria* [2008] EWHC 1072 (QB); [2008] Po L.R. 66 at [66] Tugendhat J cautioned against the tort of misfeasance being used to circumvent the defendant's "immunity" in negligence.

[168] See generally Law Commission, *Administrative Redress: Public Bodies and the Citizen*, CP No.187 (2008); Report No.232 (2010) and para.5–065.

[169] Section 1(4) of the Banking Act 1987. Another argument based on European law failed: para.8–015.

Lords held that the question of whether the pleaded particulars could be established was a question which could not be determined on the pleadings but required the case to go to trial.[170]

8–028 **Standing to sue.** The claimant must obviously have sufficient legal standing to sue,[171] so that if, for example, the defendant were alleged to have improperly refused the claimant's vote in an election (at a time when this was remediable by an action for damages) the claimant must necessarily show that he had the right to vote[172]—there must be some damage which, "completes the special connection between him and the official's act".[173] But normally it will not be necessary to show that the claimant has some legal "right" peculiar to him and it is enough that the defendant causes him injury with the requisite state of mind.[174] Thus in a case like *Roncarelli v Duplessis* it would not matter that the claimant had no absolute right to a licence.

8–029 **Misfeasance must be in the public office.** A malicious act done by the defendant solely in his private capacity falls outside this tort, but if the officer acts out of motives of personal profit or spite those are plain examples of the abuse of power which underlies the tort. In the case of a public body the tort is not confined to things done in the direct exercise of functions which can only be carried on by a public body, so that a local authority would be liable in this way if, for example, it acted maliciously in refusing consent to a change of use of premises of which it was landlord, even though the source of its power to refuse was contract, not statute: "It is not the nature or origin of the power which matters. Whatever its nature or origin, the power may be exercised only for the public good. It is the office on which everything depends."[175]

Where a local authority passes a resolution with the object of damaging the claimant the authority is liable for the tort where, "a majority of the councillors present, having voted for the resolution, did so with the object of damaging the plaintiff".[176] It is clear that one member may be "infected" with the malice of another where he knows of it and merely follows the party whip, but such a case is likely to raise extremely difficult evidential issues.[177]

8–030 **The requirement of damage.** Historically, misfeasance in a public office is an action on the case, for which the general rule is that there is no cause of action unless the claimant has suffered damage. Usually this will be economic

---

[170] The claim collapsed in November 2005.

[171] *Three Rivers* [2003] 2 A.C. 1 at 193.

[172] The subject-matter of some of the older cases. However, this situation is now entirely governed by the Representation of the People Act 1985.

[173] *Three Rivers* [2003] 2 A.C. 1 at 231 per Lord Hobhouse.

[174] See *Three Rivers* [2003] 2 A.C. 1 at 230.

[175] *Jones v Swansea CC* [1989] 3 All E.R. 162 at 186 per Nourse LJ. The decision was reversed by the HL, [1990] 1 W.L.R. 1453, but on the facts. Lord Lowry (at 1458), with whom the other members of the House concurred, said that he was, "inclined to agree" with the trial judge and the Court of Appeal on the question of the nature of the power exercised. So also Lord Steyn in *Three Rivers* [2003] 2 A.C. 1 at 191.

[176] *Jones v Swansea CC* [1990] 1 W.L.R. 1453 at 1458 per Lord Lowry.

[177] No individual councillor was sued in *Jones*. Cf. *Barnard v Restormel BC* [1998] 3 P.L.R. 27 (allegation merely that other committee members deceived).

damage,[178] but the tort is capable of extending to personal injury[179] or loss of liberty.[180] However, in *Watkins v Home Office* the House of Lords rejected an attempt to make it actionable per se in the case of infringement of rights of a "constitutional" nature: it would be, "entirely novel to treat the character of the right invaded as determinative . . . of whether material damage need be proved".[181] In *Watkins* prison officers had interfered with the claimant's correspondence in contravention of the Prison Rules. At that time the Human Rights Act 1998 was not in force, but for the future that is where redress for such conduct should be sought.

Reform? Claims for misfeasance in public office have been brought frequently in recent years but they have rarely succeeded, probably because of the difficulty of proving the requisite state of mind in the public officials involved. The Law Commission provisionally proposed that the tort be abolished as part of a wider project on claims for damages against public bodies where there would be a new liability for "serious fault" when the claim involved a "truly public" function.[182] These proposals will not, however, be taken forward.[183]

8–031

---

[178] As an action on the case it should not cover "mere" loss of reputation without proof of financial loss though such damages have been awarded in Canada: *Uni-Jet Industrial Pipe Ltd v Canada (Attorney General)* (2001) 198 D.L.R. (4th) 577. In *Odhavji Estate v Woodhouse* [2003] S.C.C. 69; [2003] 3 S.C.R. 263 at [32] it is said that the loss must be such as is "compensable in tort law" and *Uni-Jet* is referred to without disapproval. On the other hand, if some material loss is established damages should be available for worry and distress.

[179] *Akenzua v Secretary of State for the Home Dept* [2002] EWCA Civ 1470; [2003] 1 W.L.R. 741.

[180] *Karagozlu v MPC* [2006] EWCA Civ 1691; [2007] 1 W.L.R. 1881.

[181] *Watkins v Home Office* [2006] UKHL 17; [2006] 2 A.C. 395 at [25] per Lord Bingham; *Hussain v CC West Mercia* [2008] EWCA Civ 1205.

[182] *Administrative Redress: Public Bodies and the Citizen*, Law Com. CP No.187 (2008).

[183] Law Com. Report No.232 (2010).

CHAPTER 9

EMPLOYERS' LIABILITY

1. INTRODUCTION

Statutory compensation for injury at work. Since 1948, when the National
Insurance (Industrial Injuries) Act 1946[1] came into force, there has been in
operation a national insurance system under which benefits are payable to the
victims of industrial accidents and to sufferers from certain prescribed industrial
diseases. Both employer and worker make national insurance contributions and,
generally speaking, any person employed under a contract of service or
apprenticeship is entitled to the benefits provided by the Act. Since 1948 the
scheme of benefits provided for industrial injuries has to some extent been
assimilated with the general social security system, but disablement benefit
remains special to this area. This is paid when as a result of an accident, the
claimant suffers disablement amounting to at least a 14 per cent loss of physical
or mental faculty.[2] Benefit is payable in respect of personal injury by accident,
"arising out of and in the course of insurable employment". An accident arising in
the course of the employment is deemed in the absence of evidence to the
contrary, to have arisen out of that employment.[3] If the employee was, at the time
of the accident, disobeying any statutory or other regulations applicable to his
employment, or disobeying his employer's order, the accident is nevertheless
deemed to arise out of and in the course of the employment, provided: (1) the
accident would be deemed so to have arisen if there had been no disobedience;
and (2) the act was done for the purpose of, and in connection with, the
employer's trade or business.[4] The employee is insured against injuries sustained
while travelling to and from work in transport provided by his employer[5] or while
acting in an emergency (actual or supposed) on his employer's premises, for
instance, averting damage by fire. The legislation is administered on behalf of the

9–001

---

[1] The principal Act is now the Social Security (Contributions and Benefits) Act 1992.
[2] Social Security (Contributions and Benefits) Act 1992 s.103(1).
[3] Social Security (Contributions and Benefits) Act 1992 s.94(3).
[4] Social Security (Contributions and Benefits) Act 1992 s.98.
[5] Social Security (Contributions and Benefits) Act 1992 s.99.

Dept for Work and Pensions and not by the ordinary courts. Claims under the Act are not a matter for the employer, they are made against the State, and their validity depends in no way upon proof of the fault or breach of duty of the employer.

9–002 **Relationship with other claims against employers.** The Act of 1946 replaced the Workmen's Compensation Acts, the first of which was enacted in 1897, and these Acts too, though in a different way, provided compensation to an injured worker without requiring him to prove the fault or breach of duty of his employer. It has thus been possible since 1897 for an injured worker to receive some compensation independently of the ordinary law governing the civil liability of his employer. Under the law now in force the worker is entitled to retain his benefits under the scheme and also to bring an action for damages against his employer.[6] There has thus always been a strong incentive for a worker whose case offers reasonable prospects of success to bring an action against his employer, and those prospects were considerably enhanced by the abolition of the rule that contributory negligence is a complete defence[7] and of the doctrine of common employment.[8] Actions by workers against their employers are, in fact, amongst the most numerous to be dealt with by the courts. In earlier times cases nearly always concerned physical injury by accident; nowadays a much greater proportion of claims against employers arise from illness and disease. Many cases now concern mental illness caused by stress[9] and this presents formidable problems of risk assessment for employers and of adjudication for the courts.

9–003 **Liability of the employer in negligence: the doctrine of common employment.** The recorded history of employers' liability does not start until 1837, and then it began by denying the worker a remedy. *Priestley v Fowler*,[10] decided in that year, is generally regarded as the fons et origo of the doctrine of common employment, which held that the employer was not liable to his employee for injury caused by the negligence of another employee, but the case really went further than that. It came close to denying that an employer might be liable to his workmen on any grounds,[11] and there can be no doubt that the judges of the first half of the 19th century viewed with alarm the possibility of widespread liability for industrial accidents.[12] Nevertheless, by 1858, if not earlier, common employment was recognised to be an exception to the ordinary principle that an employer is liable for the tort of his servant done in the course of the servant's

---

[6] However, since 1990 there has existed a "clawback" system whereby certain benefits payable in the first five years are deductible from damages with a concomitant obligation on the defendant to reimburse the Secretary of State: para.23–091. There is no such deduction in fatal accident cases in respect of benefits payable on death.

[7] Law Reform (Contributory Negligence) Act 1945, para.23–053.

[8] See para.9–003.

[9] See para.5–095.

[10] (1837) 3 M. & W. 1; *Farwell v Boston and Worcester Railroad Corp* (1842) 4 Metcalf 49.

[11] "The mere relation of the master and the servant can never imply an obligation on the part of the master to take more care of the servant than he may reasonably be expected to do of himself": per Lord Abinger CB at 6.

[12] Striking instances are the judgments of Pollock CB in *Vose v Lancs & Yorks Ry* (1858) 27 L.J. Ex. 249 and of Bramwell B in *Dynen v Leach* (1857) 26 L.J.(N.S.) Ex. 221.

employment.[13] It was said to rest upon the theory that the contract of service contained an implied term to the effect that the servant agreed to run the risks naturally incident to the employment, including the risk of negligence on the part of his fellow employees, but it did not follow that he agreed to take the risk of negligence on the part of the employer himself. If the employer had been negligent the worker's claim was still defeated if he had been guilty of contributory negligence, or even if he merely knew of the danger,[14] but something of a general principle had emerged. If the worker was injured by the employer's own negligence he could recover, but if he was injured by the negligence of a fellow employee he could not.[15]

The advent of the employer's non-delegable duty of care. During the second half of the 19th century judicial opinion veered in favour of the worker, and efforts began to be made to limit the scope of common employment. The doctrine was not finally abolished, however, until 1948[16] and, though much restricted in scope before that date,[17] the harshness of the law was chiefly modified by the evasion of common employment through the development of the rule that an employer was liable for an injury to his worker caused by his own negligence or breach of statutory duty.[18] So far as the latter is concerned, no particular difficulty existed: if a duty is placed directly upon the employer by statute, then he does not discharge that duty by entrusting its performance to another.[19] Nonetheless, how can an employer be personally negligent unless he actually takes a hand in the work himself, a physical impossibility where the employer is not a human individual but, as was increasingly the case during the 19th century and is now the general rule, a company with independent legal personality? Such an employer could only act through its servants, and if they were negligent the doctrine of common employment applied and relieved the employer of liability.

9–004

The answer to this difficulty was found in the concept of duties personal to the employer, for the careful performance of which the employer remained responsible even though the tasks necessary to discharge the duties were entrusted to a servant.[20] "It is quite clear", said Lord Herschell:[21]

> "[T]hat the contract between employer and employed involves on the part of the former the duty of taking reasonable care to provide proper appliances, and to maintain them in a proper condition, and so to carry on his operations as not to subject those employed by him to unnecessary risk. Whatever the dangers of the employment which the employed undertakes, amongst them is certainly not to be numbered the risk of the employer's negligence and the creation or enhancement of danger thereby engendered."

---

[13] Ch.21.

[14] In *Smith v Baker & Sons* [1891] A.C. 325 the House of Lords finally held that mere knowledge did not defeat the workman's claim: para.26–021.

[15] The negligent employee was, of course, liable, but he was seldom worth suing.

[16] Law Reform (Personal Injuries) Act 1948 s.1(1). Contracting out of the Act is forbidden: s.1(3).

[17] See, e.g. *Radcliffe v Ribble Motor Services* [1939] A.C. 215; *Graham v Glasgow Corp* [1947] A.C. 368; *Lancaster v LPTB* [1948] 2 All E.R. 796 HL.

[18] It was settled in *Groves v Wimborne* [1898] 2 Q.B. 402 that common employment afforded no defence in an action brought against the employer for breach of his statutory duty.

[19] See para.8–023.

[20] On the scope of non-delegable duties generally, see Ch.21.

[21] *Smith v Baker* [1891] A.C. 325 at 362.

9–005   **The employer's threefold duty of care.** In the famous case of *Wilsons and Clyde Coal Co Ltd v English*,[22] Lord Wright redefined the employer's duty as threefold, "the provision of a competent staff of men, adequate material, and a proper system and effective supervision". The duty is not absolute, for it is fulfilled by the exercise of due care and skill. "But it is not fulfilled by entrusting its fulfilment to employees, even though selected with due care and skill."[23] Before the abolition of common employment, therefore, it was important to maintain carefully the distinction between a breach of the employer's personal duty, for which he was liable, and the mere negligence of a fellow employee, for which he was not.[24]

9–006   **The present position.** With the abolition of the doctrine of common employment in 1948,[25] the employer became liable as much for the negligence of a fellow servant of the claimant acting in the course of his employment as for breach of his personal duty, and it thus became unnecessary always to distinguish between the two kinds of wrongdoing. Nevertheless the concept of the employer's personal non-delegable duty was not destroyed, and the employer is today liable either vicariously or for breach of his personal duty.[26] Additionally, there are numerous and detailed statutory duties which are imposed directly upon employers and these have, at least previously,[27] had the effect of increasing his overall liability for injury suffered by his workers. Vicarious liability is the subject of a separate chapter and here we shall consider the employer's personal duty to his employees, but in view of the mass of statutory duties in existence, to consider the common law alone would give a false picture of the present law of employer's liability. We shall also, therefore, consider first some of the more significant of these duties and their effect upon employer's liability as a whole.

2.   STATUTE LAW[28]

9–007   The Health and Safety at Work, etc. Act 1974 was passed as a result of the report of a Royal Commission which recommended a thorough review of the then existing patchwork of industrial safety legislation.[29] The Act contains a generalised duty upon employers to ensure, so far as is reasonably practicable, the health, safety and welfare at work of all employees. This duty is in some respects reminiscent of the employer's common law duty of care towards his workers, but the duty is supported only by penal sanctions and does not give rise to any civil liability.[30] However, the Act also gave power to repeal existing statutes governing safety and replace them with regulations which would

---

[22] [1938] A.C. 57.

[23] [1938] A.C. 57 at 78 per Lord Wright.

[24] *Winter v Cardiff RDC* [1950] 1 All E.R. 819 at 822–823 per Lord Oaksey.

[25] Law Reform (Personal Injuries) Act 1948 s.1(1).

[26] See *Staveley Iron & Chemical Co v Jones* [1956] A.C. 627.

[27] See the significant reform referred to in para.9–008.

[28] Liability for breach of statutory duty generally is dealt with in Ch.8.

[29] Cmnd.5034.

[30] 1974 Act s.47(1).

continue to give rise to civil liability unless they provided otherwise.[31] This process made comparatively slow progress until the arrival on the scene of European Community legislation. As a result of a series of EC Directives, implemented by a number of important Regulations, there was a radical reform of the statutory law in this area. It would be entirely out of place in a book of this kind to attempt to consider these provisions in detail but they are (or have been)[32] an important source of civil liability and without some sketch it is not possible to see the general common law in its wider context.

Reform: no civil liability for breach of the regulations. While it is still relevant   9–008
to sketch out the operation of the regulations which govern the workplace, it must be stressed at the outset that they will, or may, no longer lead to the civil liability of the employer based on breach of the regulations alone. This is the result of an amendment to the operative provision of the 1974 Act, which came into force on October 1, 2013, the effect of which is that the breach of any provision after that date shall *not be actionable* unless the regulations themselves so provide.[33] The intention of the present Government appears to be that the regulations shall not so provide.[34] One consequence of this reversal in the presumption of actionability is that the question of the precise relationship between breach of the regulations and any liability of the employer in negligence will become more significant.[35]

The Regulations. The Management of Health and Safety at Work Regulations   9–009
1999[36] are, from an administrative point of view, the central element in the scheme and implement the so-called "framework" EC Directive[37] in so far as the general provisions of the Health and Safety at Work, etc. Act do not already incorporate the principles of the Directive into English law. Perhaps the most significant feature of these Regulations is the duty of every employer to make a "suitable and sufficient assessment" of the risks to the health and safety of workers and of other persons likely to be affected. These Regulations, unlike the others, did not at first generally give rise to civil liability and a later provision for liability[38] has now been reversed,[39] as a result of the reform referred to above.[40] Broadly speaking, the scheme was to replace the old system of legislating separately for each type of trade by a unified set of regulations governing particular aspects of employment, so that, for example, the Workplace (Health, Safety and Welfare) Regulations[41] deal with ventilation, cleanliness and working facilities in offices and shops as well as in factories.[42]

---

[31] 1974 Act s.47(2), but see now para.9–008.
[32] See para.9–008.
[33] See s.47(2) as amended by Enterprise and Regulatory Reform Act 2013 (ERRA) s.69(3), (10).
[34] See para.8–005 and the further reform referred to in fn.39 below.
[35] See para.9–015.
[36] SI 1999/3242 (replacing SI 1992/2051).
[37] Directive 89/391.
[38] SI 2003/2457.
[39] SI 2013/1667 reg.3
[40] See para.9–008.
[41] SI 1992/3004. Other regulations include: Personal Protective Equipment at Work Regulations 1992 (SI 1992/2966); Manual Handling Operations Regulations 1992 (SI 1992/2793); Workplace (Health, Safety and Welfare) Regulations 1992 (SI 1992/3004); Provision and Use of Work Equipment

9–010   **The nature of the obligations imposed.** As was previously the case, the regulations impose a mixture of unqualified, or absolute, obligations and obligations which are qualified in some way. Broadly speaking, such obligations may be divided as follows: (1) to ensure a result; (2) to do what is practicable to ensure a result; and (3) to do what is reasonably practicable to ensure a result. A further distinction to be borne in mind is that while the burden is on the employee to prove that the employer has not ensured a particular result, the burden of proving that this was not practicable, or reasonably practicable, rests on the employer.[43] The decisions of the courts on the interpretation of the obligations imposed by the regulations and the earlier provisions regulating health and safety at work are not easy to reconcile. The only general proposition that can be stated with any confidence is that it is a question of the proper construction of the regulation in each case.

9–011   **The obligation to ensure a result.** Where the obligation is an unqualified one to ensure a result, it may be regarded as absolute. One of the best known provisions of the old law was s.14 of the Factories Act 1961, which required that every dangerous part of machinery should be securely fenced and which was construed as imposing an absolute duty in the sense that difficulty or even impossibility of complying and at the same time leaving the machine in a usable condition afforded no defence.[44] But in relation to other results, the concept of reasonable foreseeability which is relevant to a claim in negligence may be imported, even without the qualification of practicality or reasonable practicality. This is one of the issues on which it is not easy to reconcile the decisions of the courts. For example, in *Hide v Steeplechase Co (Cheltenham) Ltd*[45] the relevant obligation under the Provision and Use of Work Equipment Regulations 1998 was to ensure that work equipment was "suitable".[46] This was defined in the Regulations to mean "suitable in any respect which it is reasonably foreseeable will affect the health or safety of any person".[47] The Court of Appeal overturned the finding of the judge that this imported the common law test of "reasonably foreseeable" in negligence. It referred only to the limited defences available under the Directives which are implemented by the Regulations, under which the burden is on the defendant to prove either: (a) occurrences due to unforeseeable circumstances

---

Regulations 1998 (SI 1998/2306); Lifting Operations and Lifting Equipment Regulations 1998 (SI 1998/2307); Control of Substances Hazardous to Health Regulations 2002 (SI 2002/2677); Work at Height Regulations 2005 (SI 2005/735).

[42] However, the coverage is not universal: e.g. SI 1992/3004 does not apply to ships, building sites or mines and quarries.

[43] *Nimmo v Alexander Cowan & Sons Ltd* [1968] AC 107; *Egan v Central Manchester etc NHS Trust* [2008] EWCA Civ 1424; [2009] I.C.R. 585. After all the evidence has been produced the initial burden of proof is rarely of importance: *Dorman Long (Steel) Ltd v Bell* [1964] 1 W.L.R. 333 at 335 per Lord Reid; *Jenkins v Allied Ironfounders Ltd* [1970] 1 W.L.R. 304 at 312 per Lord Guest.

[44] *John Summers & Sons Ltd v Frost* [1955] A.C. 740.

[45] [2013] EWCA Civ 545; [2014] 1 All E.R. 405 (not strictly a case of employer liability; the claim was brought by a jockey injured by colliding with a railing post against the owners and operators of the racecourse on the basis of their "control" of the work equipment, i.e. the rail); cf. *Willock v Corus UK Ltd* [2013] EWCA Civ 519; [2013] P.I.Q.R. P21.

[46] See also *Robb v Salamis (M & I) Ltd* [2006] UKHL 56; [2007] I.C.R. 175 (in determining suitability the employer has to bear in mind that workers may be inattentive).

[47] Regulation 4(4)(a).

beyond his control; or (b) occurrences due to exceptional events, the consequences of which were unavoidable despite the exercise of all due care.[48] By contrast, in *Baker v Quantum Clothing Group Ltd*,[49] where claims for hearing loss were made by those who had worked in the knitting industry, the issue was whether the workplace was "safe" within the meaning of s.29 of the Factories Act 1961.[50] A majority of the Supreme Court held that while safety must be determined objectively, it is a relative and not an absolute concept; foreseeability of the risk of hearing loss was therefore relevant and it had to be judged by the level of knowledge and standards prevailing at the time.[51]

The obligation to do what is "practicable" or "reasonably practicable". It **9–012** seems likely that an obligation to do what is "practicable" to ensure a result is intended to be more onerous than an obligation to do what is "reasonably practicable" to ensure a result.[52] Beyond that, the case law on their meaning is, again, not easy to reconcile.[53] In *Baker v Quantum*, the obligation to make the workplace "safe" was in fact one to do so "so far as is reasonably practicable" and Lord Mance expressed the view that "the criteria relevant to reasonable practicability must on any view very largely reflect the criteria relevant to satisfaction of the common law duty to take care".[54] This was, however, said in circumstances where the correctness of the approach taken by the Court of Appeal did not arise for consideration given the finding that the workplace had not been found to be unsafe in any event.[55] The Court of Appeal had followed an earlier decision in which it was suggested that the test of whether steps were not reasonably practicable required there to be "gross disproportion" between the risk of injury[56] and the steps necessary to avoid it, or for the risk to be "insignificant" in relation to the cost.[57] Whatever the meaning given to reasonably practicable, one difference between the statutory requirement and common law negligence is

---

[48] Directive 89/391 art.5(4).

[49] [2011] UKSC 17; [2011] 1 W.L.R. 1003.

[50] It was the provisions of the 1961 Act which were in force at the time of the relevant exposure to noise.

[51] Overruling *Larner v British Steel Plc* [1993] I.C.R. 551. Lord Kerr and Lord Clarke dissented, but agreed with the majority that the test of safety is not confined to some structural or permanent feature of the workplace; it can extend to operations constantly and regularly carried on in it. According to Lord Clarke, s.29 of the 1961 Act is "a results provision" (at [204]). It does not create an absolute liability because of the defence that the employer took all reasonably practical steps (see para.9–012), but it is only that defence which involves consideration of what risks are reasonably foreseeable (at [213]).

[52] "Likelihood or foresight of injury does not come into the matter. Nor is it of any relevance to consider whether [the measures to be taken] would be sensible (as opposed to impractical) . . . This is a sea-change from the old concepts of common law negligence": *Blair v Chief Constable of Sussex Police* [2012] EWCA Civ 633; [2012] I.C.R. D33 at [14] per Longmore LJ.

[53] See, e.g. *Sanderson v National Coal Board* [1961] 2 Q.B. 244; *Brown v National Coal Board* [1962] A.C. 574; *Jayne v National Coal Board* [1963] 2 All E.R. 220.

[54] *Baker v Quantum Clothing Group Ltd* [2011] UKSC 17; [2011] 1 W.L.R. 1003.

[55] On the basis of the test referred to in para.9–011.

[56] i.e. both "the gravity of the harm which might occur as well as the likelihood of its occurrence": *Mann v Northern Electric Distribution Ltd* [2010] EWCA Civ 141 at [12] (risk of steps taken to enter sub-station not foreseeable).

[57] [2009] EWCA Civ 499 at [82]-[87] per Smith LJ, citing *Edwards v National Coal Board* [1949] 1 All E.R. 743 at 747 per Asquith LJ. See also: *Austin Rover Group Ltd v HM's Inspector of Factories* [1990] 1 A.C. 619 at 626–627.

that, as noted above, it is for the employer to prove that he has done what was reasonably practicable. Once the employee has proved that a result has not been achieved, he is not required to aver what measures the defendant should have taken to comply with the regulation.

9–013   **Scope of the obligations imposed.** In some cases any civil liability of the employer has turned not on the nature and meaning of the obligation imposed, but on whether the relevant obligation is owed at all. For example, under the Provision and Use of Work Equipment Regulations 1998 "work equipment" means, "any machinery, appliance, apparatus, tool or installation for use at work (whether exclusively or not)" and the requirements of the Regulations apply to, "such equipment provided for use or used by an employee at his work". The Regulations present formidable problems in determining how far they extend beyond the "direct sphere of [the employer's] undertaking or control"[58] since they plainly do not require that the equipment should have been provided by the employer or even specifically approved by him.[59] In *Smith v Northamptonshire CC*[60] the claimant was injured when a ramp at the house from which she was collecting a person confined to a wheelchair collapsed. Her employers knew of the ramp, indeed they had inspected it properly and that had revealed no defect. A majority of the House of Lords held that there had been no breach of the Regulations. There had to be "some specific nexus (beyond the mere fact of use) . . . between the equipment and the employer's undertaking"[61]; the equipment had to be:[62]

> "[I]ncorporated into and adopted as part of the employer's business or other undertaking, whether as a result of being provided by the employer for use in it or as a result of being provided by anyone else and being used by the employee in it with the employer's consent and endorsement."

The position where the employer's business is to deal with equipment submitted for repair by third parties is unclear.[63] In *"Wembridge Claimants" v Winter*[64] the court also felt some difficulty in applying the concept of control of the "workplace" in the context of the scene of a fire.

---

[58] *Smith v Northamptonshire CC* [2009] UKHL 27; [2009] I.C.R. 734 at [64].
[59] Cf. the wording of para.3(1) of the underlying Directive.
[60] [2009] UKHL 27; [2009] I.C.R. 734.
[61] [2009] UKHL 27; [2009] I.C.R. 734 at [63] per Lord Mance.
[62] [2009] UKHL 27; [2009] I.C.R. 734 at [65] per Lord Mance. Cf. Lord Hope, who thought that control was enough; but Lord Mance thought it unrealistic to say there was control of the ramp. See also *Spencer-Franks v Kellogg Brown and Root* [2008] UKHL 46; [2008] I.C.R. 863; *PRP Architects v Reid* [2006] EWCA Civ 1119; [2007] ICR 78; *Couzens v T McGee & Co Ltd* [2009] EWCA Civ 95; *Mason v Satelcom* [2008] EWCA Civ 494; [2008] I.C.R. 971.
[63] In *Spencer-Franks v Kellogg Brown and Root* [2008] UKHL 46; [2008] I.C.R. 863 Lord Hoffmann at [26] doubted whether the Regulations would make an employer liable for defects in equipment submitted by a third party for repair but thought that, since the Regulations extended the scope of the liability to persons having "control" of the equipment, the third party might be liable. It seems extraordinary that a person taking his car to a garage for repair could incur liability without fault for a vehicle about which he has no expertise to a mechanic with whom he has no relationship whatever.
[64] [2013] EWHC 2331 (QB).

The compensatory role of the Regulations. The old legislation was always 9–014
primarily regulatory in its nature, that is to say it provided an administrative
mechanism, backed by the enforcement powers of bodies like the Factory
Inspectorate and the Health and Safety Executive, and, if necessary, by criminal
prosecution,[65] to promote safety by preventing accidents and disease. That
remains true under the present regime.[66] There has always therefore been a
tension between the regulatory and compensatory roles. The Regulations were
never designed as a code of compensation under the civil law. That is merely their
incidental effect as a result of the long tradition in this country of treating
industrial safety legislation as giving rise to a civil cause of action. Indeed, the
background European legislation comes from a legal tradition in which
compensation for work injury is exclusively or predominantly dealt with under
various forms of workers' compensation schemes. Rather than a coherent system
of employer's civil liability, English law has consisted of a patchwork of statutory
duties overlaying general common law liability for negligence. There do seem to
have been differences of approach to the balance of these elements of liability,
one seeking to reconcile them with the common law approach, the other
emphasising compensation.

In *Fytche v Wincanton Logistics Plc*[67] the claimant was a tanker driver who
had been issued with steel-toed boots by his employers because there was a risk
of heavy things falling on his feet. During freezing weather in which the claimant
had had to dig to extricate his tanker, some water got into one of the boots
through a tiny hole and he suffered mild frostbite to a toe. The employers were
not negligent in failing to provide weatherproof boots because as a rule he would
not be exposed to freezing conditions: a travelling salesman might conceivably
get stuck in a snowdrift but no one would suggest that his employers should
provide equipment to guard against that risk. However, because the boots had
been provided as a precaution against the risk of falling objects they were safety
equipment under the Personal Protective Equipment at Work Regulations[68] and
had to be, "maintained . . . in an efficient state, in efficient working order and in
good repair". So, it was argued, the tiny hole meant that they were not in this state
and this had caused his injury, leading to liability. The majority of the House of
Lords regarded such a result as "very strange and arbitrary"[69] and they rejected it:
the equipment only had to be efficient and in good repair in respect of the risk
against which it was provided. For the minority, however, this involved reading a
restriction into the legislation which was not there.[70]

The new liability regime. Questions about how expansively the Regulations 9–015
should be interpreted will continue to be just as relevant so far as any penal

---

[65] The regulations themselves say nothing about criminal penalties, those are to be found in the 1974
Act s.33. See the remarks of Ormrod LJ in *Mirza v Ford Motor Co Ltd* [1981] I.C.R. 757 at 761, on
the tension between the penal purposes and the compensatory effect of the Factories Act 1961.
[66] The various regulations, "are there primarily to promote a culture of good practice with a view to
preventing injury": *Smith*[2009] UKHL 27; [2009] I.C.R. 734 at [4] per Lord Hope.
[67] [2004] UKHL 31; [2004] I.C.R. 975.
[68] SI 1992/2966.
[69] [2004] UKHL 31; [2004] I.C.R. 975 at [7] per Lord Hoffmann.
[70] See to similar effect the division of opinion in the Supreme Court in *Baker v Quantum Clothing
Group Ltd* [2011] UKSC 17; [2011] 1 W.L.R. 1003; para.9–011.

sanctions are concerned, but in terms of civil liability they have become less significant in light of the change from a presumption of actionability to a presumption of non-actionability.[71] What significance, if any, remains will depend on their relevance to the claims in negligence to which employees will henceforward be confined. It has always been possible to rely on statutory infringements as evidence of common law negligence,[72] but where all that has been established is infringement of an absolute obligation that, in and of itself, will not suffice for a successful claim in negligence.[73] It is in relation to such cases of strict liability that the change in the law will be felt most keenly.[74] In some cases, however, the regulations (and their associated Codes of Practice)[75] may come very close in practice to being treated as the standard measure of what is required under the common law,[76] albeit the burden of proof will remain on the employee throughout.[77] In practice, at least in cases other than those involving breach of an absolute obligation, this shift in the burden of proof may prove to be the most significant effect of the change in the law.[78]

9–016   **Compatibility with EU law.** The various regulations have been made to implement EC Directives in pursuance of this country's treaty obligations. As in

---

[71] See para.9–008.

[72] See *Lochgelly Iron and Coal Co Ltd v M'Mullan* [1934] A.C. 1; *Franklin v Gramophone Co Ltd* [1948] 1 K.B. 542; *National Coal Board v England* [1954] A.C. 403.

[73] Unless the approach is taken of regarding it as negligence per se in cases where there is already a common law duty of care: para.8–002.

[74] For example, see *Stark v Post Office* [2000] I.C.R. 1013 where a postman was injured because the brakes on his bicycle failed. The fault could not reasonably have been detected, but the employer was liable under the applicable regulations (Provision and Use of Work Equipment Regulations 1992) on the basis of the failure to ensure the bicycle was in "good condition" and "properly maintained"; cf. *Ball v Street* [2005] EWCA Civ 76. The shift away from strict liability may be welcomed by some: "the relative inflexibility of the regulations seem to me to be less apt to do justice than the suppleness of the common law": *"Wembridge Claimants" v Winter* [2013] EWHC 2331 (QB) at [197] per Irwin J.

[75] Though not a code of practice, the statutory duty to conduct a risk assessment may begin to play an even bigger role in negligence claims. In *Threefall v Hull City Council* [2010] EWCA Civ 1147; [2011] I.C.R. 209 Smith LJ (at [35]) observed that: "Such a requirement (whether statutory or not) has to a large extent taken the place of the old common law requirement that an employer had to consider (and take action against) those risks which could reasonably be foreseen. The modern requirement is that he should take positive thought for the risks arising from his operations"; and see *Uren v Corporate Leisure (UK) Ltd* [2011] EWCA Civ 66; [2013] EWHC 353 (QB); cf. *Blair-Ford v CRS Adventures Ltd* [2012] EWHC 2360 (QB) at [46].

[76] The Manual Handling Operations Regulations 1992 (SI 1992/2793) may provide an example because the Regulations themselves are (necessarily, given their subject-matter) rather less precise than the others. On the application of these Regulations see *O'Neill v DSG Retail Ltd* [2002] EWCA Civ 1139; [2003] I.C.R. 222. See also the extent to which the negligence concept of reasonably foreseeable may be imported into the result which must be ensured (para.9–011) and the meaning given to "reasonably practicable" (para.9–012).

[77] Cf. the position under the regulations themselves where the burden is on the employer to show that it was not "reasonably practicable" to ensure a particular result: para.9–012.

[78] *Galashiels Gas Co v Millar* [1949] A.C. 275, 282 per Lord Morton: "[The] sub-section must have been so worded in order to relieve the injured workman from the burden of proving that there was some particular step which the employers could have taken and did not take. This would often be a difficult matter, more especially if the cause of the failure of the mechanism to operate could not be ascertained. The statute renders the task of the injured workman easier by saying 'You need only prove that the mechanism failed work efficiently and that this failure caused the accident'."

any such case there must be a possibility of conflict between the local legislation and the Directives, even allowing for the clear principle that the local legislation is to be construed so far as is reasonably possible so as to give effect to the Directive. This is a complex question which should be pursued elsewhere but there is a possibility[79] that a claimant damnified by failure to implement one of the Directives may have an action against the Crown.[80] Such a claim might now be made on the basis of the change to a presumption of non-actionability, but since the penal sanctions remain this may not be viewed as a failure to implement.[81]

3. COMMON LAW

The utility of the employer's personal duty. Since, as we have seen,[82] the employer is now liable to his employee for an injury caused by a fellow employee, it might be thought that there is no longer value in retaining the concept of the employer's personal duty. The enormous majority of workers are in the service of corporate employers who are in reality not capable of negligence, or anything else, so why not treat every case as one of vicarious liability? One answer to this may be that habits of thought acquired under the rule of common employment have survived its abolition, but in fact the concept of the personal duty continues to serve a useful purpose. In many cases it is obviously much more convenient to say that a given state of affairs or a given event proves a breach by the employer of his personal duty than to say that some employee must somehow have been negligent for that state of affairs to exist or for that event to come about. If a worker is injured because no one has taken the trouble to provide him with an obviously necessary safety device, it is sufficient and in general satisfactory to say that the employer has not fulfilled his duty, even if the employer is a company. It is unnecessarily complicated to say that someone whose duty it was to provide the device in question, or someone whose duty it was to see that there was someone else to consider what safety devices were required and to provide them, must have been negligent and therefore that the employer is liable. Again, in many cases the only person involved in the sequence of events leading up to the accident is the claimant himself and yet his employer is liable, for example because the claimant should not have been left alone to do the job. In terms of vicarious liability this would have to be explained by saying

9–017

---

[79] Before the Management of Health and Safety at Work Regulations became civilly actionable, unsuccessful attempts were made to argue that they could be directly relied on in *Cross v Highlands and Islands Enterprises* [2001] I.R.L.R. 336, OH and *Millward v Oxfordshire CC* [2004] EWHC 455 (QB). Note, however, that in the latter case liability was imposed at common law in respect of failure to undertake and implement an adequate risk assessment.

[80] *Francovich v Italy* [1995] I.C.R. 722, para.8–015. See *Spencer v Sec. of State for Work and Pensions* [2008] EWCA Civ 750; [2009] Q.B. 358 where the claim was time-barred in any event.

[81] But it may also be noted that, as part of the same reforms, inspections by the Health and Safety Executive are to be reduced.

[82] See para.9–006.

that some other employee had somehow failed in his duty of organising the work. It is simpler, and no less accurate, to say that the employer himself was in breach of his duty.[83]

It is not only for its convenience, however, that the continued use of the employer's personal duty is justified. True vicarious liability exists only where a servant has committed a tort in the course of his employment,[84] but the employer's liability is not so restricted, so that there are cases in which the worker's injury is attributable to the negligence of an independent contractor and yet the employer is liable for breach of his personal duty to the worker.[85] Moreover, though employer's liability is most commonly dealt with as a matter of tort, it is also a matter of contract,[86] and the worker's contract of service is made with his employer, not with his fellow employees. Duties which exist by virtue of express or implied terms in the contract of employment must, therefore, be duties owed by the employer himself.

A.   The Employer's Duty

9–018   **One general duty.** We have already noted Lord Wright's threefold division of the employer's duty—"the provision of a competent staff of men, adequate material and a proper system and effective supervision"[87]—and, making due allowance for its being expressed in terms contemplating industrial work, it is convenient to adhere approximately to this in the exposition of the law which follows. In truth, however, there is but one duty, a duty to take reasonable care so to carry on operations as not to subject the persons employed to unnecessary risk.[88] According to Slade J:[89]

> "In case there is any doubt about the meaning of 'unnecessary' I would . . . take the duty as being a duty not to subject the employee to any risk which the employer can reasonably foresee, or, to put it slightly lower, not to subject the employee to any risk which the employer can reasonably foresee and which he can guard against by any measure, the convenience and expense of which are not entirely disproportionate to the risk involved."

The majority of the reported cases concern accidents, but that is only because in earlier times there was less awareness of the risks to health (as opposed to safety) presented by employment. The development of knowledge about matters like the effects of asbestos,[90] noise,[91] vibration[92] and the effects of repetitive

---

[83] *McCafferty v Metropolitan Police Receiver* [1977] 1 W.L.R. 1073 is a good example of this approach.

[84] See Ch.21.

[85] See para.9–030.

[86] *Matthews v Kuwait Bechtel Corp* [1959] 2 Q.B. 57; *Reid v Rush & Tompkins* [1989] 3 All E.R. 228; *Johnstone v Bloomsbury HA* [1992] Q.B. 333; *Scally v Southern Health & Social Services Board* [1992] 1 A.C. 294 and see para.1–004.

[87] *Wilsons and Clyde Coal Co v English* [1938] A.C. 57 at 78, para.9–005.

[88] i.e. risk of injury: it is not the employer's duty to insure his employee nor to advise him to insure himself (*Reid v Rush & Tompkins* [1989] 3 All E.R. 228) nor, in the absence of some specific assumption of responsibility, to take steps to safeguard the employee's economic well-being: *Crossley v Faithful & Gould Holdings Ltd* [2004] EWCA Civ 293; [2004] I.C.R. 1615.

[89] *Harris v Brights Asphalt Contractors* [1953] 1 Q.B. 617 at 626.

[90] See, e.g. *Jameson v C.E.G.B.* [2000] 1 A.C. 455.

manual movements,[93] coupled with a relaxation of the former strict provisions on limitation of actions,[94] has produced litigation in recent years, sometimes on a very large scale indeed. Furthermore, it is now recognised that the employer's duty may extend to the effect of working conditions[95] on the mental health of his employees.[96]

In many respects, therefore, the duty is similar to the duty of care in the tort of negligence generally, but expressed in terms appropriate to the relationship of employer and employee.[97] As we shall see, the duty of the employer cannot, as can an ordinary duty of care, always be discharged by the employment of an independent contractor,[98] but it is nevertheless a duty of care, not an absolute duty,[99] and it is for the claimant to prove its breach. If a worker cannot prove negligence, whether by direct evidence or with the aid of res ipsa loquitur, an action based upon breach of the employer's personal duty must fail.[100]

Scope of the employer's duty of care. The employer's duty of care concerns not only the actual work of his employees, but also all such acts as are normally and reasonably incidental to a day's work,[101] and the mere fact that an employee disobeys an order does not necessarily deprive him of the protection of his employer's duty, though he may, of course, be guilty of contributory negligence.[102] The special duty we are now considering arises only when the relationship of employer and employee exists[103] and so an independent contractor employed to do work in a factory, or a visitor, cannot rely upon it. Such a person will, however, generally be owed some other duty of care.[104]

9–019

Emergency services and armed forces. The same general duty will be owed in relationships which are not, strictly speaking, within the category of contracts of employment but which are closely analogous, such as that between a police

9–020

---

[91] See, e.g. *Thompson v Smith's Shiprepairers (North Shields) Ltd* [1984] Q.B. 405; *Baker v Quantum Clothing Group Ltd* [2011] UKSC 17; [2011] 1 W.L.R. 1003.

[92] See, e.g. *Bowman v Harland & Wolff* [1992] I.R.L.R. 349.

[93] See, e.g. *Pickford v ICI Plc* [1998] 1 W.L.R. 1189.

[94] See Ch.26.

[95] i.e. long-term conditions, not merely in respect of "nervous shock" caused by being threatened by an accident.

[96] *Hatton v Sutherland* [2002] EWCA Civ 76; [2002] I.C.R. 613. See para.5–096.

[97] The special relationship of employer and worker may impose positive duties of assistance or protection: thus an employer may be obliged to provide medical assistance in cases of illness or injury in no way attributable to him (*Kasapis v Laimos* [1959] 2 Lloyd's Rep. 378) or to warn his workers to be medically examined if he learns that past working conditions, which were then regarded as proper, have caused a danger of disease (*Wright v Dunlop Rubber Co* (1971) 11 K.I.R. 311).

[98] See para.9–029.

[99] *Winter v Cardiff RDC* [1950] 1 All E.R. 819 at 823 per Lord MacDermott; *Davie v New Merton Board Mills* [1959] A.C. 604.

[100] Where difficulty of proof is the result of the defendant's breach, the claimant's evidence will be judged benevolently: *Keefe v Isle of Man Steam Packet Co Ltd* [2010] EWCA Civ 683 (employer failed to take noise measurements in the workplace).

[101] *Davidson v Handley Page Ltd* [1945] 1 All E.R. 235.

[102] *Rands v McNeil* [1955] 1 Q.B. 253 (but no breach of duty on the facts).

[103] The importance of safety may lead the court to emphasise the substance rather than the form of the relationship: *Lane v Shire Roofing (Oxford) Ltd* [1995] I.R.L.R. 493; see *Mullaney v CC West Midlands* [2001] EWCA Civ 700 (police—"quasi-employment"); and see para.9–020.

[104] For example, under the Occupiers' Liability Act 1957.

officer and a chief constable.[105] In the case of the emergency services generally, whether the relationship is strictly one of employment or analogous thereto, the operational requirements of the job may mean that the employee accepts the risks which are inherent in the nature of the work, but the duty owed by the employer remains the same:[106]

> "The starting point is that an Ambulance Service owes the same duty of care towards its employees as does any other employer. There is no special rule in English law qualifying the obligations of others towards firefighters, or presumably police officers, ambulance technicians and others whose occupations in the public service are inherently dangerous... Such public servants accept the risks which are inherent in their work, but not the risks which the exercise of reasonable care on the part of those who owe them a duty of care could avoid."

While, therefore, "there is no established 'battle immunity' in relation to decisions taken in the heat of the moment by those in charge in the emergency services",[107] those circumstances will be relevant in determining whether there was any breach of duty, e.g. "it is incumbent on the Courts... to make every allowance for the difficulty of exercising command and making swift decisions on a fireground".[108] In relation to the armed forces, however, a "battle immunity" or "combat immunity" may mean that it is not appropriate to impose a duty of care, but such immunity, which applies in "the conduct of an active military operation or act of war", is narrowly construed.[109]

9–021   **Competent staff.** The duty to take reasonable care to provide a competent staff is still extant, but it is of comparatively little importance since the abolition of common employment. If, however, an employer engages a person with insufficient experience or training for a particular job and as a result a worker is injured, it may well be that there is a breach of this branch of the employer's duty.[110] In one situation of a slightly different kind, however, this branch of the employer's liability retains its importance. If one employee is injured by the violent horseplay of another, or is actually assaulted by him, the employer may not be liable vicariously on the basis that the horseplay or the attack will not have been done in the course of the employment.[111] It may be, however, that the employer should have known of his employee's playful or vicious propensities

---

[105] *Mullaney v CC West Midlands* [2001] EWCA Civ 700; *Waters v MPC* [2000] 1 W.L.R. 1607.
[106] *Sussex Ambulance NHS Trust v King* [2002] EWCA Civ 953, per Hale LJ, cited as "an authoritative exposition of the relevant principles" concerning the duties owed by employers to their staff in the context of the delivery of emergency services: *Smith v The Ministry of Defence* [2013] UKSC 41; [2014] A.C. 52 at [171] per Lord Carnwath. Cf. *Burn v Ministry of Justice* [2012] EWHC 876 (QB).
[107] *"Wembridge Claimants" v Winter* [2013] EWHC 2331 (QB) at [225].
[108] *"Wembridge Claimants" v Winter* [2013] EWHC 2331 (QB) at [225].
[109] *Smith v The Ministry of Defence* [2013] UKSC 41; [2014] A.C. 52; see para.5–034.
[110] See *Butler v Fife Coal Co* [1912] A.C. 149.
[111] *O'Reilly v National Rail and Tramway Appliances Ltd* [1966] 1 All E.R. 499. But see *Weddall v Barchester Healthcare Ltd* [2012] EWCA Civ 25; [2012] I.R.L.R. 307 (employer vicariously liable for assault by junior employee on senior employee when reacting to instructions).

and have taken steps to prevent them from resulting in injury to another. In that case he may be liable for breach of his personal duty.[112]

Adequate plant and equipment. The employer must take reasonable care to provide his workers with the necessary plant and equipment,[113] and is therefore liable if an accident is caused through the absence of some item of equipment which was obviously necessary or which a reasonable employer would recognise to be needed.[114] He must also take reasonable care to maintain the plant and equipment in proper condition, and the more complex and dangerous that machinery the more frequent must be the inspection.[115] What is required in each case, however, is reasonable care according to the circumstances, and in some cases it may be legitimate to rely upon the worker himself to rectify simple defects in the plant he is using.[116] The duty extends to the installation of necessary safety devices on dangerous machinery[117] and the provision of protective equipment when required,[118] but the employer does not warrant the safety of plant and equipment. At common law, therefore, he is not liable if an accident is caused by some latent defect in equipment which could not have been discovered by the exercise of reasonable care on the part of the persons for whose negligence he is answerable.[119] By the Employer's Liability (Defective Equipment) Act 1969,[120] however, if an employee is injured in the course of his employment in consequence of a defect in equipment provided by his employer and the defect is due to the fault of a third party, whether identified or not, then the injury is deemed to be also attributable to the negligence of the employer. Today, therefore, if a worker can show, for example, that a tool he was using was defective in such a way that there must, on a balance of probabilities, have been negligence or other fault in its manufacture, and that his injury was caused by that

9–022

---

[112] *Hudson v Ridge Manufacturing Co* [1957] 2 Q.B. 348. Cf. *Smith v Crossley Bros* (1951) 95 S.J. 655; *Coddington v International Harvester Co of Great Britain Ltd* (1969) 6 K.I.R. 146. The principle may extend to victimisation or bullying where there is sufficient injury: *Waters v MPC* [2000] 1 W.L.R. 1607.

[113] While a defendant who engages a contractor is generally entitled to look to the contractor to safeguard the latter's employees, he may owe the employees a duty if he in some way assumes some responsibility, for example by providing some unsuitable piece of equipment: *McGarvey v Eve NCI Ltd* [2002] EWCA Civ 374.

[114] *Williams v Birmingham Battery and Metal Co* [1892] 2 Q.B. 338; *Lovell v Blundells & Crompton & Co* [1944] 1 K.B. 502; *Ross v Associated Portland Cement Manufacturers Ltd* [1964] 1 W.L.R. 768. It is not always necessary, however, for the employer to adopt the latest improvements: *Toronto Power Co v Paskwan* [1915] A.C. 734 per Sir Arthur Channell. See also *O'Connor v BTC* [1958] 1 W.L.R. 346.

[115] For example, *Murphy v Phillips* (1876) 35 L.T. 477; *Baxter v St Helena Hospital Management Committee, The Times*, February 14, 1972. Even inspection may not always be sufficient: *Barkway v S Wales Transport Co* [1950] A.C. 185; *Pearce v Round Oak Steel Works Ltd* [1969] 1 W.L.R. 595.

[116] *Bristol Aeroplane Co v Franklin* [1948] W.N. 341; *Richardson v Stephenson Clarke Ltd* [1969] 1 W.L.R. 1695.

[117] *Jones v Richards* [1955] 1 W.L.R. 444; *Lovelidge v Anselm Odling & Sons Ltd* [1967] 2 Q.B. 351.

[118] *Qualcast Ltd v Haynes* [1959] A.C. 743 per Lord Denning; but see *Brown v Rolls-Royce* [1960] 1 W.L.R. 210. See also *McGhee v NCB* [1973] 1 W.L.R. 1 (washing facilities).

[119] *Davie v New Merton Board Mills* [1959] A.C. 604; contrast the position under statute in *Stark v Post Office* [2000] I.C.R. 1013, above fn.74.

[120] "Equipment" has been held to include a 90,000-ton ship: *Coltman v Bibby Tankers Ltd* [1988] A.C. 276. The word extends to material which is used in the employment and is not confined to tools with which that material is processed: *Knowles v Liverpool CC* [1993] 1 W.L.R. 1428.

defect, then the employer as well as the manufacturer will be liable to him, whether or not the employer was in any way to blame.[121] The principal advantage of this from the worker's point of view is that he is relieved of any need to identify and sue the manufacturer of defective equipment provided by his employer. Since the coming into force of the Consumer Protection Act 1987,[122] the manufacturer is subject to a stricter liability not dependent on proof of negligence. Since "fault" is defined in the 1969 Act as, "negligence, breach of statutory duty or other act or omission which gives rise to liability in tort"[123] it seems that in such a case the employer may be liable even if there is no real fault on anyone's part. Since there is no longer any civil liability for breach of the statutory regulations which regulate work equipment,[124] the prospect of such "no fault" claims under the 1969 Act may have renewed significance.

9–023 **Safe place of work.** Though not expressly mentioned by Lord Wright in *Wilsons and Clyde Coal Co v English*,[125] it is clear that the employer's duty of care extends to the place of work[126] and in some cases may even also apply to the means of access to the place of work.[127] No particular difficulty exists where the place of work is in the occupation or control of the employer, but it must be recalled that the duty is one of reasonable care only and thus the employer is not obliged to take unreasonable precautions even against foreseeable risks.[128] At one time, however, it was thought that because an employer had no control over premises in the occupation of a third party he could owe no duty in respect of those premises, but it is now clear that this is wrong.[129] The duty of care remains, but what is required for its performance may well be different where the place of work is not under the employer's control.[130]

---

[121] *Clarkson v Jackson, The Times*, November 21, 1984. The employer is entitled to raise the defence of contributory negligence against the worker and may seek to recover indemnity or contribution from the person to whose fault the defect is attributable. He cannot, however, contract out of the liability imposed by the Act.

[122] See para.11–015 (strict liability of manufacturer).

[123] 1969 Act s.1(3).

[124] The Provision and Use of Work Equipment Regulations 1998: see para.9–008. The Regulations would not cover the case where the complaint is that there has been a failure to provide necessary equipment.

[125] [1938] A.C. 57.

[126] For example, *Cole v De Trafford (No.2)* [1918] 2 K.B. 535 per Scrutton LJ; *Davidson v Handley Page* [1945] 1 All E.R. 235 at 236 per Lord Greene MR. At the lowest, the employer's duty to his employee in respect of premises occupied by the employer must be the common duty of care under the Occupiers' Liability Act 1957, but probably it is stricter than that. Most workplaces are now likely to be covered by the Workplace (Health, Safety and Welfare) Regulations 1992 (SI 1992/3004), but there is no longer any civil liability for breach of the regulations alone: see para.9–008.

[127] *Ashdown v Samuel Williams & Sons* [1957] 1 Q.B. 409 at 430–432 per Parker LJ; *Smith v National Coal Board* [1967] 1 W.L.R. 871. The employer can be subject to no duty of maintenance so far as the means of access consists of a public highway, but if the employee has to cross private property, whether the employer's own or that of a third party, the duty should exist.

[128] *Latimer v AEC* [1953] A.C. 643; *Thomas v Bristol Aeroplane Co* [1954] 1 W.L.R. 694. Nor is he liable for a defect which would not have been revealed by inspection: *O'Reilly v National Rail and Tramway Appliances Ltd* [1966] 1 All E.R. 499.

[129] *Wilson v Tyneside Window Cleaning Co* [1958] 2 Q.B. 110; *Smith v Austin Lifts* [1959] 1 W.L.R. 100; *Clay v AJ Crump & Sons Ltd* [1964] 1 Q.B. 533.

[130] *Wilson v Tyneside Window Cleaning Co* [1958] 2 Q.B. 110 at 121–122 per Pearce LJ; *Kilbride v Scottish & Newcastle Breweries* 1986 S.L.T. 642.

Even if the employer is not responsible for defects in someone else's premises under this heading, he may be under a duty to give advice, instructions or orders about commonly encountered hazards (a matter which would fall under the next heading). Thus it has been held that in modern conditions[131] the employer of a window cleaner should place an embargo on cleaning upper floor windows by standing on the sill unless there are anchorage points for a safety harness.[132]

Safe system of working. This, the most frequently invoked branch of the employer's duty, is also the most difficult to define, but it includes:[133]

9–024

" . . . [T]he physical lay-out of the job—the setting of the stage, so to speak—the sequence in which the work is to be carried out, the provision in proper cases of warnings and notices and the issue of special instructions. A system may be adequate for the whole course of the job or it may have to be modified or improved to meet the circumstances which arise; such modifications or improvements . . . equally fall under the head of system."

The employer's duty in respect of the system of working is most evident where the work is of regular or routine nature, but its application is not limited to such cases. The concept is a flexible one, which can be applied as much to a police operation as to work in a factory.[134] Even where a single act of a particular kind is to be performed, the employer may have an obligation to organise the work, for example if it is of a complicated or unusual kind or if a large number of people are involved.[135] In each case it is a question of fact whether a reasonable employer would have left it to his workers to decide for themselves how the job should be done.[136]

In devising a system of working the employer must take into account the fact that workers are often heedless of their own safety,[137] and this has two consequences. First, the system should so far as possible minimise the danger of a worker's own foreseeable carelessness. Secondly, the employer must also exercise reasonable care to see that his system of working is complied with by those for whose safety it is instituted and that the necessary safety precautions are observed.[138] Lord Denning said in one case,[139] however, (and others have

---

[131] Cf. *General Cleaning Contractors Ltd v Christmas* [1953] A.C. 180, where the HL was not prepared to go so far.

[132] *King v Smith* [1995] I.C.R. 339.

[133] *Speed v Thomas Swift & Co* [1943] K.B. 557 at 563–564 per Lord Greene MR.

[134] *Mullaney v CC West Midlands* [2001] EWCA Civ 700; *French v Sussex CC* [2006] EWCA Civ 312 (claim failed on other grounds).

[135] *Winter v Cardiff RDC* [1950] W.N. 193 at 200 per Lord Reid; *Boyle v Kodak Ltd* [1969] 1 W.L.R. 661. The fact that an untrained young man with indifferent English is a member of a team may call for special precautions by the employer: *Hawkins v Ian Ross (Castings) Ltd* [1970] 1 All E.R. 180 at 186.

[136] Since the abolition of common employment the employer is liable vicariously for the negligence of the person in charge of the operation, but this cannot assist the claimant if he was himself in charge or if no worker was guilty of negligence.

[137] *General Cleaning Contractors v Christmas* [1953] A.C. 180 at 189–190 per Lord Oaksey; *Smith v National Coal Board* [1967] 1 W.L.R. 871 at 873 per Lord Reid; *Kerry v Carter* [1969] 1 W.L.R. 1372.

[138] *General Cleaning Contractors v Christmas* [1953] A.C. 180. Cf. *Woods v Durable Suites* [1953] 1 W.L.R. 857; *Bux v Slough Metals Ltd* [1973] 1 W.L.R. 1358; *Birch v Ministry of Defence* [2013] EWCA Civ 676 (M.O.D. liable for allowing soldier to drive when unqualified to so).

[139] *Qualcast (Wolverhampton) Ltd v Haynes* [1959] A.C. 743 at 760.

agreed)[140] that this is not a proposition of law but a proposition of good sense, so that proof that a worker was never actually instructed to wear necessary protective clothing is not of itself proof of negligence. The employer's personal duty is not confined to devising a safe system, but also extends to its implementation, so that the employer is liable even if the system itself is safe but A fails to follow it and causes injury to B.[141] It is clear that the duty to provide a safe system of work includes the duty to conduct an appropriate risk assessment.[142]

B.   Standard of Care

9–025   **Common practice.**[143] As has been emphasised in the foregoing paragraphs and has been constantly reiterated by the courts, the employer's duty is a duty of care only and there are limits to the protection which the employer must provide, even against foreseeable risk to his employee:[144]

> "He must weigh up the risk in terms of the likelihood of injury occurring and the potential consequences if it does; and he must balance against this the probable effectiveness of the precautions that can be taken to meet it and the expense and inconvenience they involve. If he is found to have fallen below the standard to be properly expected of a reasonable and prudent employer in these respects, he is negligent."

The common practice of other employers is relevant in determining whether the defendant employer has fallen below the standard of care, but is not determinative,[145] e.g. it is not sufficient to follow common practice if "in the light of common sense or newer knowledge it is clearly bad",[146] or if a risk which was previously "acceptable" is, at the time of injury, no longer "acceptable".[147] In determining the latter a distinction may be drawn between the "average

---

[140] *Smith v Austin Lifts* [1959] 1 W.L.R. 100 at 105 per Viscount Simonds. In *Smith v Scot Bowyers* [1986] I.R.L.R. 315 it was held to be enough to inform workers about the availability of replacement boots; it was not necessary to inspect boots in use from time to time.

[141] *McDermid v Nash Dredging and Reclamation Co Ltd* [1987] A.C. 906; *Chandler v Cape Plc* [2012] EWCA Civ 525; [2012] 1 W.L.R. 3111.

[142] See, e.g. *Vaile v Havering LBC* [2011] EWCA Civ 246; [2011] E.L.R. 274. The source of the duty to conduct the assessment may be statutory.

[143] See, generally, para.6–033.

[144] *Stokes v Guest, Keene and Nettlefold (Bolts and Nuts) Ltd* [1968] 1 W.L.R. 1776 at 1783 per Swanwick J. See, e.g. *Latimer v AEC* [1953] A.C. 643; *Coates v Jaguar Cars Ltd* [2004] EWCA Civ 337; and *Mitchell v United Co-operatives Ltd* [2012] EWCA Civ 348 (not negligent not to have fitted security screens or install a security guard in a shop to deter robbery)

[145] *Morris v West Hartlepool Steam Navigation Co Ltd*[1956] A.C. 552.

[146] *Stokes v Guest, Keene and Nettlefold (Bolts and Nuts) Ltd* [1968] 1 W.L.R. 1776 at 1783 per Swanwick J.

[147] *Thompson v Smiths Shiprepairers (North Shields) Ltd*[1984] QB 405 at 415–416 per Mustill J; *Williams v University of Birmingham* [2011] EWCA Civ 1242; [2012] E.L.R. 47.

employer" and larger employers with additional resources who should have formed the view at an earlier stage that a risk was no longer acceptable.[148] The same is true of any code of practice:[149]

"[T]o follow a relevant code of practice or regulatory instrument will often afford a defence to a claim in negligence. But there are circumstances where it does not do so. For example, it may be shown that the code of practice or regulatory instrument is compromised because the standards that it requires have been lowered as a result of heavy lobbying by interested parties; or because it covers a field in which apathy and fatalism has prevailed amongst workers, trade unions, employers and legislators ... or because the instrument has failed to keep abreast of the latest technology and scientific understanding."

The employee's individual circumstances. It is important to notice that although the employer's duty springs from the relationship of employment, the duty is owed individually to each worker, so that circumstances concerning the particular worker which are known or which ought to be known to the employer will affect the precautions which the employer must take in order to fulfil his duty. Thus in *Paris v Stepney BC*[150] the claimant had only one eye and it was therefore held that he should have been provided with goggles even though the risk involved in his work was not so great as to require the provision of goggles to a normal two-eyed man doing a similar job. Conversely[151]This point is particularly important in the context of mental harm caused by stress.[152]

9–026

Protecting the employee from himself.[153] In *Withers v Perry Chain Co*[154] the claimant had previously contracted dermatitis from contact with grease in the course of her work and was therefore given by her employers the driest work they had available. This work she accepted without protest but nevertheless she again contracted dermatitis and sued her employers on the ground that, knowing that she was susceptible to dermatitis, they should not have permitted her to do work carrying a risk of causing that disease. Her action was dismissed by the Court of

9–027

---

[148] *Baker v Quantum Clothing Group Ltd* [2011] UKSC 17; [2011] 1 W.L.R. 1003 (the "larger employers" should have departed from the applicable code of practice on noise levels five years earlier than the "average employers". Lord Mance dissented, on this issue, on the basis that it made employers liable not "for not ploughing a lone furrow" (see *Thompson v Smiths Shiprepairers (North Shields) Ltd* [1984] QB 405 at 415–416 per Mustill J) but "for ploughing a lone furrow but not doing so deeply enough" (at [25])).

[149] *Baker v Quantum Clothing Group Ltd* [2011] UKSC 17; [2011] 1 W.L.R. 1003 at [101] per Lord Dyson.

[150] [1951] A.C. 367. Cf. *Hatton v Sutherland* [2002] EWCA Civ 76; [2002] I.C.R. 613 (stress; employer's legitimate expectations about capacity): para.5–096.

[151] *Qualcast (Wolverhampton) Ltd v Haynes* [1959] A.C. 743 at 754 per Lord Radcliffe. But the employer cannot necessarily accept at face value the servant's assertion of previous experience: "[A]n experienced man dealing with a familiar and obvious risk may not reasonably need the same attention or the same precaution as an inexperienced man who is likely to be more receptive of advice or admonition." *Tasci v Pekalp of London Ltd* [2000] I.C.R. 633.

[152] *Hatton v Sutherland* [2002] EWCA Civ 76; [2002] I.C.R. 613. See para.5–096.

[153] The issue here is whether the employer fulfils the standard of care by leaving the decision whether to run the risk of injury to the employee. Whether the employer's breach was the cause of the injury when it is based on the conduct of the claimant (see, e.g. *Ginty v Belmont Building Supplies Ltd* [1959] 1 All E.R. 414) is dealt with in para.8–020.

[154] [1961] 1 W.L.R. 1314.

Appeal because the employers had done everything they reasonably could have done to protect the claimant short of refusing to employ her at all:[155]

> "In my opinion there is no legal duty on an employer to prevent an adult employee from doing work which he or she is willing to do. If there is a slight risk . . . it is for the employee to weigh it against the desirability, or perhaps the necessity, of employment. The relationship of master and servant is not that of a schoolmaster and pupil[156] . . . It cannot be said that an employer is bound to dismiss an employee rather than allow her to run a small risk."

There is a tension here between the stance of the common law in giving primacy to the worker's personal autonomy and the expanding responsibility of employers. While what is said in *Withers* is probably still the starting point, there is no absolute rule that an employer may expose a willing worker to *any* risk by continuing to employ him: it has been said that to employ someone known to suffer from vertigo as a "spiderman" would be a plain breach of the employer's duty.[157] That is not necessarily good news from the worker's point of view, for it follows that dismissal may be fair for the purposes of employment protection or discrimination legislation.[158] In the case of stress, even where the risk to health is substantial, it has been said that it is for the employee to decide whether or not to carry on: it should not be for the law to say that the employer must sack a worker to protect his mental health.[159]

9–028   **Volenti non fit injuria.** The general defence of voluntary assumption of risk is rarely available in cases of employers' liability because the courts are unwilling to infer an agreement by the worker to run the risk of his employer's negligence merely because he remains in unsafe employment.[160] However, in *Johnstone v Bloomsbury Health Authority*,[161] where the claimant was contractually committed to work up to an average of 88 hours a week if the employer so required, it was contended that the express term of the contract limited or overrode the employer's duty of care not to injure his health. On a striking-out application, this was accepted in principle by Browne-Wilkinson VC and Leggatt LJ[162] but the majority of the court (Stuart-Smith LJ and Browne-Wilkinson VC) held that the contractual right to call for long hours was, on the proper construction of the contract of employment, limited to calling for work that was compatible with the employer's duty of care. Such a case will also raise issues under the Unfair Contract Terms Act 1977.[163]

---

[155] [1961] 1 W.L.R. 1314 at 1320 per Devlin LJ.

[156] See, e.g. *Rozario v Post Office* [1997] P.I.Q.R. P15 (simple lifting task).

[157] *Coxall v Goodyear Great Britain Ltd* [2002] EWCA Civ 1010; [2003] 1 W.L.R. 536 at [26].

[158] *Lane Group Plc v Farmiloe* [2004] P.I.Q.R. 22. Cf. *Canterbury CC v Howletts* [1997] I.C.R. 925 (duty under the Health and Safety at Work etc. Act 1974 s.2, to ensure safety to employees was duty to do what could be done in the context of the job and did not prohibit work—entering tiger's cage—which could not be done without danger; but on the civil liability in such a situation, see the Animals Act 1971 s.6(5), para.17–008).

[159] *Hatton v Sutherland* [2002] EWCA Civ 76; [2002] I.C.R. 613 at [43](12); but see *Barber v Somerset CC* [2004] UKHL 13; [2004] 1 W.L.R 1089 at [30] per Lord Rodger.

[160] See para.26–021.

[161] [1992] Q.B. 333.

[162] In fact, Stuart-Smith LJ also accepted that what he called an "express term of *volenti non fit injuria*" would exclude the employer's duty.

[163] See para.26–017.

C. Nature of the Duty

A non-delegable duty of care. It might be supposed that an employer who 9–029
entrusts some task to a third party (not a servant), whose competence he has taken
reasonable care to ascertain, has thereby discharged his own duty of reasonable
care. To state the law in this way, however, would be to deny the ratio decidendi
of *Wilsons and Clyde Coal Co v English*[164] that the employer's duty is personal
and is not discharged simply by the appointment of a competent person to carry
out the necessary tasks.[165] In that case the defendant employers were held liable
in respect of an injury sustained by a miner because the system of working was
not reasonably safe. The system had been devised by the manager of the mine, a
fellow servant of the claimant, to whom the employers were obliged by statute to
leave the matter, but yet, despite the existence of common employment and
despite the fact that the employers personally had done everything they possibly
could, they were held to be in breach of their duty to the claimant. Their duty
was: "[T]he employer's personal duty, whether he performs or can perform it
himself, or whether he does not perform it or cannot perform it save by servants
or agents. A failure to perform such a duty is the employer's personal
negligence."[166] The employer's liability, therefore, not being a vicarious liability,
was not defeated by the doctrine of common employment.

Liability for independent contractors. Although the non-delegable nature of the 9–030
employer's personal duty was developed to avoid the now defunct doctrine of
common employment, its practical effect goes beyond cases formerly covered by
that doctrine because it involves the proposition that the employer's duty is not so
much a duty to take care but a duty that care be taken and therefore the employer
may be liable for damage caused by independent contractors. A person can only
be vicariously liable for the torts of his employees committed in the course of
employment, but a duty that care will be taken is not fulfilled if there is fault on
the part of anyone to whom the employer entrusts its performance.[167] This view
of the law is confirmed by *McDermid v Nash Dredging and Reclamation Co
Ltd*.[168] The defendants were a wholly owned subsidiary of S, a Dutch company,
and their function was to employ British staff engaged in S's dredging work in
Sweden. While the claimant, an employee of the defendants, was aboard a tug
owned by S he was seriously injured as a result of the negligence of the skipper
(an employee of S) in putting the engines astern without warning to the claimant.

---

[164] [1938] A.C. 57, para.9–005.
[165] In *Uren v Corporate Leisure UK Ltd* [2011] EWCA Civ 66, the Court of Appeal inclined to the
view that the duty to conduct a risk assessment under reg.3(1) of the Management of Health and
Safety at Work Regulations 1999 (which may be relevant to a claim in negligence: see para.9–024)
was itself non-delegable.
[166] *Wilsons and Clyde Coal v English* [1938] A.C. 57 at 83–84 per Lord Wright. See also per Lord
Thankerton at 64–65, per Lord Macmillan at 75, per Lord Maugham at 87–88.
[167] Non-delegable duties are not confined to defendants who stand in the position of employer of the
claimant. Employment has been explained as one example of a wider test based on an antecedent
relationship; in particular one where the defendant assumes responsibility for those who are in a
"vulnerable position": *Woodland v Essex CC* [2013] UKSC 66; [2013] 3 W.L.R.1227, para.21–048.
[168] *McDermid v Nash Dredging and Reclamation Co Ltd* [1987] A.C. 906; cf. *Hopps v Mott
Macdonald Ltd* [2009] EWHC 1881 (QB).

The defendants were liable because they had delegated the performance of their duty to take care for the claimant's safety to S and its employees on the tug and could not escape liability when that duty was not fulfilled.[169] Given the close connection between the defendants and S the decision is not surprising,[170] for if the law were otherwise the claimant's rights would be at risk from the chances of corporate organisation.[171]

One Court of Appeal decision in which liability was not imposed upon the employer for injury suffered by an employee working in Saudi Arabia distinguished *Nash* on the basis that it was confined to cases where there was some sort of "joint venture"[172] but this seems an unsatisfactory distinction and the principle of *Nash* has been applied at first instance[173] and by the Court of Appeal[174] to cases where the employer was a "labour only" contractor and in one of which[175] the injury took place abroad.[176] However, it has been said that the "suggestion that the homebased employers have any responsibility for the daily events of a site in [another country] has an air of unreality"[177] and it may be that the question of how far the employer has control of the distant site is a critical factor in such cases.[178] Where no actual fault is attributable to the employer, that may justify awarding him a complete indemnity in contribution proceedings against the person at fault.[179]

9–031   **The need for delegation.** The employer's non-delegable duty of care does not mean that he is liable whenever his employee is injured at work as a result of the negligence of a third party: the employer is only responsible if it can be fairly said that he has delegated the performance of his duty of care to the third party. Thus, if a lorry driver delivering goods to a factory were negligently to run down a worker, the worker's employer would not be liable—the negligence of the lorry driver (and the vicarious responsibility of his employer) does not negative the exercise of care in the employer's personal duty for it is unrelated to any aspect of that duty, and the employer has delegated nothing to him.[180] Similarly, although

---

[169] It was not regarded as important whether the case was one of failing to devise a safe system of work or failing to operate a safe system.

[170] The tug was skippered turn and turn about by an employee of S and an employee of the defendants. Had the accident occurred on the next shift there could have been no disputing the defendants' liability.

[171] Where the claimant has a contract with one member of a group it may be that on the facts other members of the group have assumed responsibility for his safety: *Newton-Sealey v Armor Group Services Ltd* [2008] EWHC 233 (QB); cf. *Chandler v Cape* [2012] EWCA Civ 525; [2012] 1 W.L.R. 3111; cf. *Thompson v Renwick Group Plc* [2014] EWCA Civ 635.

[172] *Cook v Square D Ltd* [1992] I.C.R. 262.

[173] *Johnson v Coventry Churchill International Ltd* [1992] 3 All E.R. 15.

[174] *Morris v Breaveglen Ltd* [1993] I.R.L.R. 350.

[175] *Johnson v Coventry Churchill International Ltd* [1992] 3 All E.R. 15.

[176] Cf. *A v MoD* [2004] EWCA Civ 641; [2005] Q.B. 183, para.21–048.

[177] *Cook v Square D Ltd* [1992] I.C.R. 262 at 271. However, it was accepted that in some cases it might be incumbent on the employer of someone working abroad to inspect the site and satisfy himself that the occupiers were conscious of safety obligations.

[178] See *DIB Group Pty Ltd v Cole* [2009] NSWCA 210, in which the use of the concept of non-delegable duty is criticised.

[179] *Nelhams v Sandells Maintenance Ltd, The Times*, June 15, 1995.

[180] This is an example of the "collateral negligence" of the independent contractor which is discussed generally at para.21–051.

the effect of the case has been reversed by the Employer's Liability (Defective Equipment) Act 1969,[181] the underlying ratio of *Davie v New Merton Board Mills*,[182] denying the liability of the employer for a latent defect in a tool, was that the employer had discharged rather than delegated his duty by buying from a reputable supplier. If, on the other hand, a gas fitter negligently installs a gas appliance at the employer's premises with the result that a worker is injured by an explosion, it is submitted that the employer's personal duty with regard to the safety of the place of work has not been fulfilled and he is liable, whether or not the worker is entitled to rely on the Act of 1969.[183]

---

[181] See para.9–022.

[182] *Davie v New Merton Board Mills* [1959] A.C. 604.

[183] In *Knowles v Liverpool CC* [1993] 1 W.L.R. 1428 *Davie* is given a broad interpretation so as to include material with which the employee is working. However, this is done for the purpose of justifying an equally wide meaning of "equipment" in the 1969 Act. It is accepted in *Coltman v Bibby Tankers Ltd* [1988] A.C. 276 that the Act does not extend to the factory premises themselves.

CHAPTER 10

LIABILITY FOR LAND AND STRUCTURES

1. INTRODUCTION

The greater part of this chapter concerns the liability of an occupier of premises **10–001**
for damage done to visitors on the premises[1] and the main source of the law is the
Occupiers' Liability Act 1957. Where things done on the premises affect other
premises, that is the province of the law of nuisance, which is dealt with in Ch.15.
"Liability for premises", though it would be a neat antithesis to the "liability for
products" in the next chapter would not, however, be an exact description, for the
rules now to be discussed are not limited to immovable property like open land,
houses, railway stations and bridges, but have been extended to movable
structures like ships, gangways and scaffolding. Little of consequence flows from
a degree of indeterminacy about the meaning of "premises" because the duty
under the Act is for most purposes identical to the ordinary duty in negligence

---

[1] i.e. persons who have entered the premises. It is conceivable that an occupier may "assume
responsibility" at common law in respect of the safety of the approach to the premises, which may be
the explanation of *Dodkins v West Ham Utd* [2000] C.L.Y. 4226 Cty Ct (season ticket holder fell on
broken manhole cover outside gate to ground).

and the courts are in any event quite ready to accept that the law of negligence can operate concurrently with the statutory liability.[2] Henceforth we shall use the expression "premises" because that does cover the vast majority of cases.

2. LIABILITY OF OCCUPIERS TO VISITORS[3]

10–002 **Common Law before the Occupiers' Liability Act 1957.** At common law the duties of an occupier were cast in a descending scale to four different kinds of persons and a brief account is necessary to gain a full understanding of the Act. The highest degree of care was owed by the occupier to one who entered in pursuance of a contract with him (for example a guest in a hotel): in that case there was an implied warranty that the premises were as safe as reasonable care and skill could make them. A lower duty was owed to the "invitee", that is to say, a person who (without any contract) entered on business of interest both to himself and the occupier (for example a customer coming into a shop to view the wares): he was entitled to expect that the occupier should prevent damage from unusual danger, of which he knew or ought to have known.[4] Lower still was the duty to the "licensee", a person who entered with the occupier's express or implied permission but without any community of interest with the occupier: the occupier's duty towards him was to warn him of any concealed danger or trap of which he actually knew. Finally, there was the trespasser, to whom under the original common law there was owed only a duty to abstain from deliberate or reckless injury.[5] With regard to lawful visitors the tripartite classification into contractual entrants, invitees and licensees did not provide a complete picture of the law for the courts sometimes showed themselves willing to confine these categories to cases arising from the static condition of the premises, and to treat accidents arising from an activity on the premises as governed by the general law of negligence. As Denning LJ graphically put it:[6]

> "If a landowner is driving his car down his private drive and meets someone lawfully walking upon it, then he is under a duty to take reasonable care so as not to injure the walker and his duty is the same, no matter whether it is his gardener coming up with his plants, a tradesman delivering his goods, a friend coming to tea, or a flag seller seeking a charitable gift."

The law was widely thought to be unsatisfactory and to have ossified in the form in which it was stated in *Indermaur v Dames*[7] at a time when the general law of negligence was undeveloped. It was, therefore, referred to the Law Reform Committee in 1952 and as a result of the Committee's Report[8] the Occupiers' Liability Act 1957 was passed.

---

[2] See para.10–003.
[3] North, *Occupiers' Liability* (1971).
[4] *Indermaur v Dames* (1866) L.R. 1 C.P. 274; affirmed (1867) L.R. 2 C.P. 311.
[5] *Robert Addie & Sons (Collieries) Ltd v Dumbreck* [1929] A.C. 358.
[6] *Slater v Clay Cross Co Ltd* [1956] 2 Q.B. 264 at 269.
[7] (1866) L.R. 1 C.P. 274; affirmed (1867) L.R. 2 C.P. 311.
[8] (1954) Cmnd. 9305.

A. Scope of the Occupiers' Liability Act 1957

A single duty of care. The Act abolished the common law distinction between   **10–003**
invitees and licensees and substituted for it a single common duty of care owed
by the occupier to his "visitors". The definition of "occupier" remains the same as
at common law, and "visitors" are those persons who would at common law have
been treated as either invitees or licensees.[9] The law therefore continues to treat
contractual entrants as a separate category, but this is now of less significance
than formerly: if there is an express provision in the contract warranting the
safety of the premises, that will govern the case,[10] but if, as is usual, the contract
is silent on the matter, the Act provides that there shall be implied into the
contract a term that the occupier owes the entrant the common duty of care.[11]
There may, of course, be obligations under a contract which are wholly outside
the scope of the law of occupiers' liability: if, for example, a lease requires the
landlord to maintain a lift, failure to do so, so that it becomes inoperative, would
be a breach of contract but it would not be a breach of the common duty of care,[12]
except in the unlikely event that there was no other reasonably safe access to
accommodation in the building.

Do "activity duties" fall outside the Act? We have just seen how the courts   **10–004**
utilised the concept of the "activity duty" to blur the distinction between invitees
and licensees at common law and it may be asked whether this concept has
survived the Act. On the one hand, it is enacted that the rules provided by the
Occupiers' Liability Act: "[S]hall have effect, in place of the rules of the common
law, to regulate the duty which an occupier of premises owes to visitors in respect
of dangers due to the state of the premises or to things done or omitted to be done
on them."[13]

   On the other hand, it is also enacted that those rules, "shall regulate the nature
of the duty imposed by law in consequence of a person's occupation or control of
premises",[14] and the "activity duty" does not seem to be aptly described in this
way. It arises, generally speaking, by the application of the ordinary principles of
negligence and applies equally to occupiers and non-occupiers.[15] It seems that the
first provision is not to be read literally as covering all conduct of an occupier on
his own premises so that, for example, the Act was regarded as irrelevant when
the defendant failed to warn his children against playing with lighted candles,[16]

---

[9] 1957 Act s.1(2).
[10] In the majority of personal injury cases an express provision can now only be effective if it favours
the entrant: a term reducing the occupier's duty below the common duty of care will usually be
unenforceable under the Unfair Contract Terms Act 1977 s.2, para.10–025.
[11] 1957 Act s.5(1). *Maguire v Sefton MBC* [2006] EWCA Civ 316; [2006] 1 W.L.R. 2550. A
contractual entrant may frame his claim in the alternative as a non-contractual visitor: *Sole v WJ Hallt*
[1973] Q.B. 574.
[12] *Berryman v Hounslow LBC, The Times*, December 18, 1996.
[13] 1957 Act s.1(1).
[14] 1957 Act s.1(2).
[15] *Riden v Billings & Sons* [1957] 1 Q.B. 46 at 56 per Denning LJ, affirmed [1958] A.C. 240; *Ogwo
v Taylor* [1988] A.C. 431 at 434 per Dillon LJ, affirmed at 441.
[16] *Jauffar v Akhbar, The Times*, February 10, 1984.

and in *Ogwo v Taylor*[17] a claim arising out of the defendant's negligence in setting fire to his house was decided on the basis of common law negligence.[18] Defects in the premises which were not created by the occupier but which he has failed to remedy must be within the Act and the Act alone if there is no other relationship between him and the claimant,[19] for it is then only his role as occupier that puts the defendant under any duty to make the premises safe. The intermediate case is where the defendant by some positive act creates a danger affecting the condition of the premises and here the matter is probably covered both by the Act and by the law of negligence.

The issue is not very often likely to be of very much practical significance for there will typically be little if any difference between the duty of care in negligence and the common duty of care as applied to current activities. From a pleading point of view the answer would seem to be to plead the Act and negligence as alternatives[20] wherever there is any doubt.[21] The Act may also overlap with other statutory liabilities: for example, it is quite possible to hold that the occupier/employer is not negligent in a claim by a worker for an injury caused by the state of the premises but that he is liable on the basis of some stricter liability in employment safety regulations.[22]

10–005   **Premises.** As before, the occupier's duties apply not only to land and buildings but also to fixed and movable structures,[23] and they govern his liability in respect of damage to property as well as injury to the person, including the property of persons not themselves visitors.[24] The Act also made certain alterations in the liability of a landlord to the visitors of his tenants though these have now been replaced by further legislation.[25]

---

[17] [1988] A.C. 431. The case was in fact pleaded in the alternative under both heads: see the decision of the Court of Appeal at 434.

[18] See also *Fowles v Bedfordshire CC, The Times*, May 22, 1995; *Revill v Newberry* [1996] Q.B. 567 (Occupiers' Liability Act 1984).

[19] If there is (e.g. employer and employee), the claimant may rely upon both the Act and any duty incidental to that relationship; but where A is carrying out operations at B's property and the conduct of those causes injury to C, any liability of B for failing to protect C is governed by the general law rather than the Act: *Fairchild v Glenhaven Funeral Services Ltd* [2001] EWCA Civ 1881; [2002] 1 W.L.R. 1052.

[20] *Grimes v Hawkins* [2011] EWHC 2004 (QB) at [64] ("conventionally adopted").

[21] In *Everett v Comojo (UK) Ltd* [2011] EWCA Civ 13; [2012] 1 W.L.R. 150 (liability of nightclub when one guest assaulted another) the claim was pleaded in ordinary negligence, but the duty of care was determined by reference to the common duty of care which the defendant owed as occupier: see Smith LJ at [33]; cf. *Glaister v Appleby in Westmorland Town Council* [2009] EWCA Civ 1325; [2010] P.I.Q.R. P6 at [47] per Toulson LJ where ensuring safety from the activities of third parties is seen as an aspect of the common duty of care itself.

[22] See, e.g. *Irvine v MPC* [2004] EWHC 1536 (QB); [2005] P.I.Q.R. P11. But civil liability for breach of such regulations is now severely curtailed: see para.8–005.

[23] 1957 Act s.1(3)(a). *Bunker v Charles Brand & Son Ltd* [1969] 2 Q.B. 480; *Hollingworth v Southern Ferries* [1977] 2 Lloyd's Rep. 70; *Furmedge v Chester-le-Street D.C.* [2011] EWHC 1226 (QB) (inflatable art installation). Cf. *Wheeler v Copas* [1981] 3 All E.R. 405.

[24] 1957 Act s.1(3)(b). See further para.10–033.

[25] See para.10–061.

B. Occupier

A test of "control". The duty under the Act is imposed upon the "occupier," but   **10–006**
that is a word which may vary considerably in its meaning according to the
context in which it is used. Its meaning in the context of landlord and tenant
legislation, for example, is not necessarily the same as in the context of the
Occupiers' Liability Act.[26] Here the essential question is "who has control of the
premises?" The word occupier is simply a convenient one to denote a person who
has a sufficient degree of control over premises to put him under a duty of care
towards those who come lawfully upon the premises.[27] An owner in possession
is, no doubt, an "occupier";[28] an owner who has let the premises to another and
parted with possession is not;[29] but an absentee owner may "occupy" through his
servant and remain subject to the duty[30] and he may also be subject to it though
he has contracted to allow a third party to have the use of the premises.[31] On the
other hand, it is not necessary that an "occupier" should have any estate in land[32]
or even exclusive occupation.[33] The foundation of occupier's liability is
occupational control,[34] i.e. control associated with and arising from presence in
and use of or activity in the premises.[35] Whether this exists is a question of
degree: a builder undertaking a large development would be an occupier of the
site, but a decorator painting a house would not.[36] Such occupational control may
perfectly well be shared between two or more people, but where this is so, though
each is under the same common duty of care, it does not follow that what that
duty requires of each of them is necessarily itself the same.[37]

---

[26] *Graysim Holdings Ltd v P&O Property Holdings Ltd* [1996] A.C. 329.

[27] *Wheat v Lacon & Co Ltd* [1966] A.C. 552 at 577 per Lord Denning.

[28] In *Harvey v Plymouth CC* Unreported November 13, 2009 QBD the defendants admitted that they
were occupiers even though they were not conscious they owned the land (appeal allowed ([2010]
EWCA Civ 860; [2010] N.P.C. 89 on the basis that the claimant was not a visitor).

[29] A landlord may, nevertheless, be liable if the conditions of the Defective Premises Act 1972 s.4, are
fulfilled. See para.10–061.

[30] *Wheat v Lacon & Co Ltd* [1966] A.C. 552; *Stone v Taffe* [1974] 1 W.L.R. 1575.

[31] *Wheat v Lacon & Co Ltd* [1966] A.C. 552; *Fisher v CHT Ltd (No.2)* [1966] 2 Q.B. 475. See also
Greene v Chelsea BC [1954] 2 Q.B. 127, where requisitioning authorities were held to occupy
requisitioned houses which were being lived in by persons they had placed in them; cf. *Kearney v Eric
Waller Ltd* [1967] 1 Q.B. 29.

[32] *Humphreys v Dreamland (Margate) Ltd* (1930) 144 L.T. 529.

[33] *Hartwell v Grayson Rollo and Clover Docks Ltd* [1947] K.B. 901; *Donovan v Cammell Laird &
Co* [1949] 2 All E.R. 82. A local authority which has made a compulsory purchase order and served a
notice of entry becomes an occupier when the former owner vacates the premises, and it is
unnecessary that there should be any actual or symbolic taking of possession: *Harris v Birkenhead
Corp* [1976] 1 W.L.R. 279.

[34] " . . . an appreciation of danger within the structure if proper care was not shown" (*Furmedge v
Chester-le-Street DC* [2011] EWHC 1226 (QB) at [152] may seem more appropriate to a claim in
ordinary negligence, but "the boundary between what might be termed 'pure' occupation (arising
from the mere fact of a degree of physical control over the premises) and a broader duty of care in
negligence is somewhat blurred" (at [150]).

[35] *Wheat v Lacon & Co Ltd* [1966] A.C. 552 at 589 per Lord Pearson.

[36] *Page v Read* (1984) N.L.J. 723.

[37] *Wheat v Lacon & Co Ltd* [1966] A.C. 552 at 581, 585–586, 587.

C.   Visitors

10–007   **A single category.** The common duty of care is owed by the occupier to his "visitors" and they are those persons who would at common law have been treated as invitees or licensees.[38] For all practical purposes, therefore, the distinction between invitees and licensees was abolished.[39] A visitor is generally a person to whom the occupier has given express or implied permission to enter and the principal category opposed to visitor is that of trespasser, whose rights are governed not by the Act of 1957 but by the Occupiers' Liability Act 1984.[40]

10–008   **An extended category.** The Act of 1957 extends the concept of visitor to include persons who enter the premises for any purpose in the exercise of a right conferred by law, for they are to be treated as permitted by the occupier to be there for that purpose, whether they in fact have his permission or not.[41] The occupier therefore owes the common duty of care to firemen attending a fire, to policemen executing a search warrant and to members of the public entering recreation grounds under rights guaranteed by law.

10–009   **Rights of way.** It has been held that despite the wide wording of the Act, a person using a public[42] or private[43] right of way is not a visitor for the purposes of the Act. The user of a private right of way is now owed a duty under the Occupiers' Liability Act 1984,[44] but that aside, the owner of the highway[45] or servient tenement has no obligation to the user to maintain its safety, as opposed to not creating dangers on it. While it is true that public rights of way pass over so many different types of property and in such varying circumstances that any blanket duty of care would be impracticable[46] the present state of the law may lead to results which the public might consider arbitrary. For example, the owners of shopping malls commonly take steps to ensure that the public do not acquire rights of way through them, but if such a right is acquired by user,[47] or by express dedication, entrants to the property, who may know nothing of this, will lose the protection of the Occupiers' Liability Act which they formerly had, whereas if they were outside on the pavement they would be likely to have the protection of the highway authority's duty of care under the Highways Act 1980.[48] Persons exercising access rights under the National Parks and Access to the Countryside

---

[38] 1957 Act s.1(2).

[39] Payne (1958) 21 M.L.R. 359 at 360. Lord Browne-Wilkinson in *McGeown v Northern Ireland Housing Executive* [1995] 1 A.C. 233 attempted to revive the distinction in relation to public rights of way, but see *Campbell v Northern Ireland Housing Executive* [1996] 1 B.N.I.L. 99.

[40] See para.10–034.

[41] 1957 Act s.2(6).

[42] *Greenhalgh v British Railways Board* [1969] 2 Q.B. 286.

[43] *Holden v White* [1982] 2 Q.B. 679.

[44] See para.10–044.

[45] *McGeown v Northern Ireland Housing Executive* [1995] 1 A.C. 233. A highway authority may have a duty to maintain a highway under the Highways Act 1980: para.15–073.

[46] Lord Keith in *McGeown*'s case at [1995] 1 A.C. 243.

[47] As in *Cumbernauld and Kilsyth DC v Dollar Land (Cumbernauld) Ltd* 1993 S.L.T. 1318.

[48] See Lord Browne-Wilkinson *McGeown v Northern Ireland Housing Executive* [1995] 1 A.C. 233. See generally Barker and Parry (1995) 15 L.S. 335.

Act 1949 or the Countryside and Rights of Way Act 2000 are not visitors[49] but a duty is owed to them under the Act of 1984.[50]

Implied permission. Where there is no express permission, it is a question of fact **10–010** in each case whether the occupier has impliedly given permission to a person to enter upon his premises, and the onus of proving an implied permission rests upon the person who claims that it existed.[51] The simplest example of implied permission is also the commonest in practice. Any person who enters the occupier's premises for the purpose of communicating with him[52] will be treated as having the occupier's tacit permission unless he knows or ought to know that he has been forbidden to enter,[53] for example by a notice.[54] The occupier may, of course, withdraw this licence by refusing to speak or deal with the entrant, but if he does so the entrant has a reasonable time in which to leave the premises before he becomes a trespasser.[55]

Other cases depend very much upon their particular facts and it is difficult to state any general rule. This much, however, is clear in principle: the facts must support the implication from the occupier's conduct that he has permitted entry,[56] not merely tolerated it, for knowledge is not tantamount to consent and failure to turn one's premises into a fortress does not confer a licence on anyone who may seek to take advantage of one's inaction.[57] This said, it must be admitted that in some cases the courts have gone to surprising lengths in implying licences in the teeth of the facts.[58] In many cases the court has been astute to find an implied licence because of the severity of the law relating to liability to trespassers.[59] The trespasser's position has now been improved,[60] and it is likely that implied permission will be rather less readily found, but the courts will still have to

---

[49] 1957 Act s.1(4), as substituted by s.13 of the Countryside and Rights of Way Act 2000.

[50] See para.10–044.

[51] *Edwards v Ry Executive* [1952] A.C. 737.

[52] Not necessarily in connection with business of the occupier: *Brunner v Williams* [1975] Crim.L.R. 250.

[53] *Robson v Hallett* [1967] 2 Q.B. 393. Cf. *Dunster v Abbott* [1954] 1 W.L.R. 58 at 59–60 per Denning LJ and *Great Central Ry v Bates* [1921] 3 K.B. 578.

[54] For example, "no canvassers, hawkers or circulars". Quaere as to the effect of "Private" or "Keep Out" in such cases: cf. *Christian v Johanesson* [1956] N.Z.L.R. 664 at 666.

[55] *Robson v Hallett* [1967] 2 Q.B. 393; *Kay v Hibbert* [1977] Crim.L.R. 226. Dismissive words may sometimes be abuse rather than revocation of the licence: *Snook v Mannion* [1982] Crim. L.R. 601.

[56] *Edwards v Ry Executive* [1952] A.C. 737; *Phipps v Rochester Corp* [1955] 1 Q.B. 450 at 455; *Faulkner v Willetts* [1982] R.T.R. 159. It is what may properly be inferred that counts, not the occupier's actual intention. Where O licenses A to enter his land to do work, A may have ostensible authority to invite B to enter as a sub-contractor even though the contract between O and A forbids this: *Ferguson v Welsh* [1987] 1 W.L.R. 1553.

[57] *Edwards v Ry Executive* [1952] A.C. 737 at 746 per Lord Goddard CJ ("Repeated trespass itself confers no licence").

[58] See, e.g. *Lowery v Walker* [1911] A.C. 10 and *Cooke v Midland GW Ry of Ireland* [1909] A.C. 229. More easily supportable are the decisions in: *Oldham v Sheffield Corp* (1927) 136 L.T. 681; *Coleshill v Manchester Corp* [1928] 1 K.B. 776; *Purkis v Walthamstow BC* (1934) 151 L.T. 30; *Phipps v Rochester Corp* [1955] 1 Q.B. 450.

[59] *British Railways Board v Herrington* [1972] A.C. 877 at 933 per Lord Diplock.

[60] See para.10–034.

grapple with the problem of the implied licence, for the duty owed to a trespasser is by no means identical with that owed to a visitor under the Occupiers' Liability Act 1957.

10–011   **Exceeding permission.** The duty owed to a visitor does not extend to anyone who is injured by going where he is expressly or impliedly warned by the occupier not to go, as where a person falls over a cliff by getting on the wrong side of railings erected by the proprietor who has also put up a notice of the danger of going near the cliff[61] or where a tradesman's boy deliberately chooses to go into a pitch dark part of the premises not included in the invitation and falls downstairs there.[62] Further, the duty does not protect a visitor who goes to a part of the premises where no one would reasonably expect him to go.[63] A person who has two pieces of land and invites the public to come on one of them, can, if he chooses, limit the invitation to that one of the two pieces but if the other piece is contiguous to the first piece, he may be held to have invited the public to come to both pieces.[64]

Again the claimant cannot succeed if, although rightly on the structure, he makes a use of it alien to the invitation.[65] So, where a stevedore in loading a ship was injured by making use of the hatch covers for loading, although he knew that a statutory regulation forbade this practice in his own interests, it was held that he had no remedy.[66] In fact, in all these cases the claimant ceases to be a visitor and becomes a mere trespasser.[67] Where, however, the negligence of the occupier causes the visitor to take an involuntary step outside the area in which he is permitted to be, he does not thereby cease to be a visitor to whom a duty of care is owed,[68] and the position is probably the same even if the involuntary step is not caused by the occupier's negligence.[69] A person may equally exceed his licence by staying on premises after the occupier's permission has expired but the limitation of time must be clearly brought home to him. Thus, a person on licensed premises who remained there when drinks were being consumed long

---

[61] *Anderson v Coutts* (1894) 58 J.P. 369.

[62] *Lewis v Ronald* (1909) 101 L.T. 534 distinguished in *Prole v Allen* [1950] 1 All E.R. 476.

[63] *Mersey Docks and Harbour Board v Procter* [1923] A.C. 253, where there was a great difference of opinion as to the application of this principle to the facts; *Lee v Luper* [1936] 3 All E.R. 817; *Gould v McAuliffe* [1941] 2 All E.R. 527.

[64] *Pearson v Coleman Bros* [1948] 2 K.B. 359 at 375 per Lord Greene MR.

[65] "When you invite a person into your house to use the staircase you do not invite him to slide down the bannisters": Scrutton LJ in *The Calgarth* [1927] P. 93 at 110 (a hypothetical example now made real: *Geary v JD Wetherspoon Plc*[2011] EWHC 1506 (QB); [2011] N.P.C. 60). In any case, the common duty of care only applies where the visitor is using the premises for the purpose for which he is invited or permitted to be there: s.2(2), below and *Keown v Coventry Healthcare NHS Trust* [2006] EWCA Civ 39; [2006] 1 W.L.R. 953; *Harvey v Plymouth CC* [2010] EWCA Civ 860; [2010] N.P.C. 89 at [22].

[66] *Hillen v ICI (Alkali) Ltd* [1936] A.C. 65.

[67] *Hillen v ICI (Alkali) Ltd* [1936] A.C. 65 at 69–70 per Lord Atkin.

[68] *Braithwaite v S Durham Steel Co* [1958] 1 W.L.R. 986.

[69] See the difference of opinion in the High Court of Australia in *Public Transport Commission (NSW) v Perry* (1977) 137 C.L.R. 107. Quaere as to the claimant whose initial entry is involuntary. He cannot be sued for trespass, but that does not necessarily make him a visitor.

after closing time was held to continue to be a visitor in the absence of evidence that he knew of instructions from the brewers to their manager forbidding this practice.[70]

Young children. The above principles have been applied with some degree of allowance for the proclivities of young children. The common duty of care, like the common law before it, requires that the occupier must be prepared for children to be less careful than adults[71] but the special characteristics of children may be relevant also to the question of whether they enjoy the status of visitor. In *Glasgow Corp v Taylor*[72] it was alleged that a child aged seven had died from eating poisonous berries which he had picked from a shrub in some public gardens under the control of the corporation. The berries looked like cherries or large blackcurrants and were of a very tempting appearance to children. They thus constituted an "allurement" to the child. The corporation was aware of their poisonous nature, but nevertheless the shrub was not properly fenced from the public nor was any warning given of its deadly character. It was held that these facts disclosed a good cause of action. Certainly the child had no right to take the berries nor even to approach the bush, and an adult doing the same thing might well have become a trespasser, but since the object was an "allurement" the very fact of its being left there constituted a breach of the occupier's duty. That, however, was a case where entry into the general area was permitted:[73] it does not follow that the same would have applied if the park had been private,[74] nor if the danger had been obvious. Very young children, however, may be incapable of appreciating even the most obvious danger. In determining whether the occupier has fulfilled his duty to them there must be taken into account his reasonable expectations of the habits of prudent parents in relation to their children. This is dealt with below.[75] It must, however, be said that since the Occupiers' Liability Act 1984 there is likely to be very little practical difference between the duties owed to a very young child who is a trespasser and one who is a lawful visitor.

10–012

D. Common Duty of Care

The common duty of care, owed to all visitors and also where the duty of the occupier depends upon a term to be implied in a contract, is defined as: "[A] duty to take such care as in all the circumstances of the case is reasonable to see that the visitor will be reasonably safe in using the premises for the purposes for which he is invited or permitted to be there."[76]

10–013

---

[70] *Stone v Taffe* [1974] 1 W.L.R. 1575. The manager, as agent of the brewers, had authority to invite the claimant on to the premises in the first place.

[71] 1957 Act s.2(3)(a). See para.10–016.

[72] [1922] 1 A.C. 44.

[73] See also *Jolley v Sutton LBC* [2000] 1 W.L.R. 1083.

[74] *Edwards v Ry Executive* [1952] A.C. 737.

[75] See para.10–017.

[76] 1957 Act s.2(2).

The question whether the occupier has fulfilled his duty to the visitor is thus dependent upon the facts of the case,[77] and, though the purpose of the visit may be a relevant circumstance, it can no longer be conclusive as it so often was before when it governed the status of the entrant.[78] All the circumstances must be taken into account.[79] If, for example, the owner of an inn permits the resident manager to accept paying guests, both are "occupiers" in relation to such guests, but while the owner may be liable for injury caused to them by a structural defect such as the collapse of a staircase, the manager alone would be liable for injury caused by a defect in his own furnishings, such as a dangerous hole in the carpet of the living room.[80] Where appropriate, the standard of care to be observed is subject to the *Bolam* test,[81] i.e. it is sufficient if the occupier has acted in accordance with a practice accepted as proper by a responsible body of opinion in the particular field.[82]

10–014 **"Dangers due to the state of the premises".** The Act itself gives some guidance on the application of the common duty of care but we have been forcefully reminded that this must be set in the context of the "threshold" question of the scope of the 1957 Act. Whatever the precise relationship between the Act and general negligence law with regard to activities on the premises[83] the heart of the Act is liability for "dangers due to the state of the premises".[84]

In *Tomlinson v Congleton BC*[85] the claimant was injured when he dived from a standing position into the shallow water of a lake occupied by the defendants in a country park. Because swimming was forbidden by notices it was held by the majority of the House of Lords that he was a trespasser,[86] but the same words appear in the Occupiers' Liability Act 1984 dealing with trespassers. It is clear therefore that the same decision in favour of the defendants would have been reached even if he had been a lawful visitor[87] and the case is as relevant to the Act of 1957 as it is to the later Act. The risk, such as it was, was obvious to any sensible person.[88] There was no concealed hazard or trap and the lake presented

---

[77] The similarity of the duty to the common law duty of care is demonstrated in *Simms v Leigh Rugby Football Club Ltd* [1969] 2 All E.R. 923. On the relevance of any risk assessment, or the failure to conduct one, see: *Bowen v National Trust* [2011] EWHC 1992 (QB); *Hufton v Somerset CC* [2011] EWCA Civ 789; [2011] E.L.R. 482; *Furmedge v Chester-le-Street DC* [2011] EWHC 1226 (QB).

[78] Where premises are hired for a purpose about which the hirer knows more than the occupier, the latter may be entitled to leave it to the hirer's judgment whether the premises are suitable: *Wheeler v St Mary's Hall, The Times*, October 10, 1989

[79] Including the era when the building was constructed: *Hogg v Historic Buildings and Monuments Commission* [1988] 3 C.L. 285 Cty Ct.

[80] *Wheat v Lacon & Co Ltd* [1966] A.C. 552 at 585–586 per Lord Morris, at 587 per Lord Pearce.

[81] See para.6–034.

[82] *Bowen v National Trust* [2011] EWHC 1992 (QB) (tree inspectors).

[83] See para.10–004.

[84] 1957 Act s.1(1).

[85] [2003] UKHL 47; [2004] 1 A.C. 46.

[86] See para.10–040.

[87] See at [1] (Lord Nicholls agreeing with Lord Hoffmann), [50], [67], [92] (Lord Scott who thought that the claimant was not a trespasser).

[88] Even a commercial operator of a climbing wall is not obliged to point out to users that matting does not provide security in the event of a fall or to train him before allowing access: *Poppleton v Portsmouth Youth Activities Committee* [2008] EWCA Civ 646; [2009] P.I.Q.R. P1. As to children, who may lack powers of discernment, see para.10–016.

no dangers other than those (in particular drowning) inherent in any substantial body of water. In the view of the majority of the House of Lords the injury could not fairly be said to have been due to the state of the premises.[89]

It would be a misuse of language on facts like those in *Tomlinson* to describe obvious natural features like cliffs, trees, rivers and lakes as "the state of the premises", otherwise any premises would be dangerous to those prepared to encounter risks.[90] Nor is there liability in respect of some artificial thing like a building which is in good repair if the claimant chooses to use it in order to carry out some hazardous activity.[91] That does not of course mean that the occupier cannot be liable in respect of a natural feature: one could not rent out a hotel room with a balcony overlooking a cliff without incorporating an adequate guard rail. The underlying idea, vague as it may be, seems to be: "Was there something wrong with the premises, given the purposes for which visitors were invited[92]?" No one could deny that there would be something wrong with the hotel room; but it could hardly be said that there was something wrong with Beachy Head. Many cases of this type might be dealt with by saying that it was not reasonable to require the occupier to take protective steps,[93] or the claimant voluntarily assumed the risk or that his own fault was so great as to be the sole effective cause of his loss; but that is not necessary if the analysis is that the Act is simply not engaged.[94]

The particular visitor. The Act provides[95] that the relevant circumstances in applying the common duty of care include the degree of care and of want of care that may be looked for in the particular visitor:

10–015

    "[S]o that (for example)[96] in proper cases:
    (a)   an occupier must be prepared for children to be less careful than adults and

---

[89] At [1], [28] and [69]. Lord Scott does not address the state of the premises issue directly but he agreed with Lord Hoffmann, save as to whether the claimant was a trespasser. Contra, Lord Hutton at [53].

[90] Nor can it be said that failure to remove the natural condition which may be a temptation to some is a "thing omitted to be done thereon". "The trouble with the island of the Sirens was not the state of the premises. It was that the Sirens held mariners spellbound until they died of hunger. The beach, give or take a fringe of human bones, was an ordinary Mediterranean beach. If Odysseus had gone ashore and accidentally drowned himself having a swim, Penelope would have had no action against the Sirens for luring him there with their songs. Likewise in this case, the water was perfectly safe for all normal activities": Lord Hoffmann at [28].

[91] *Keown v Coventry Healthcare NHS Trust* [2006] EWCA Civ 39; [2006] 1 W.L.R. 953 (another trespasser case; climbing up underside of fire escape); *Grimes v Hawkins* [2011] EWHC 2004 (QB) (a visitor case; diving into a private swimming pool).

[92] The last phrase is important. The murky condition of natural waters presents an obvious hazard. A municipal swimming pool with water so murky one could not see the bottom might be a different matter.

[93] *Grimes v Hawkins* [2011] EWHC 2004 (QB). But, of course, the circumstances may be such that the occupier owes a duty to protect even against obvious risks or has assumed such responsibility: *Risk v Rose Bruford College* [2013] EWHC 3869; [2014] E.L.R. 157 at [79] (where such submissions failed on the facts).

[94] One might say that this case provided the classic example of the overlap of the duty and breach issues: para.5–004.

[95] Section 2(3).

[96] The two categories which follow are therefore not exhaustive and the court must also take account of the degree of care that could reasonably be expected of an "ordinary visitor": *Tacagni v Cornwall*

(b)   an occupier may expect that a person, in the exercise of his calling, will appreciate and guard against any special risks ordinarily incident to it, so far as the occupier leaves him free to do so."

10–016   **Children.** We have seen above that one cannot say there is a danger due to the state of the premises simply because a visitor may choose to take obviously hazardous risks, but children may lack the awareness of danger which can be expected of an adult: an ordinary, well-maintained staircase may present a hazard to a toddler. Even where children are involved it is not right to take no account of someone's choice to ignore a danger simply because he is a child[97] but even where there is no capacity for discernment at all it would be unrealistic to expect that all land must be made safe enough for unaccompanied toddlers. A person who owns a mountain in the vicinity of a town is not obliged to fence it off in case small children come there.[98] What Lord M'Laren said a hundred years ago about the Scots common law remains true under the Occupiers' Liability Act:[99]

> "In a town, as well as in the country, there are physical features which may be productive of injury to careless persons or to young children against which it is impossible to guard by protective measures. The situation of a town on the banks of a river is a familiar feature; and whether the stream be sluggish like the Clyde at Glasgow, or swift and variable like the Ness at Inverness, or the Tay at Perth, there is always danger to the individual who may be so unfortunate as to fall into the stream. But in none of these places has it been found necessary to fence the river to prevent children or careless persons from falling into the water. Now, as the common law is just the formal statement of the results and conclusions of the common sense of mankind, I come without difficulty to the conclusion that precautions which have been rejected by common sense as unnecessary and inconvenient are not required by the law."

This simply reflects the fact that the law of occupiers' liability is not an insurance scheme to compensate people for any misfortune which may occur on another's land.[100]

10–017   **Parental responsibility.** The reason for saying that there is no relevant danger due to the state of the premises in such cases no doubt reflects the fact that society expects parents to take care of their children. That is the basis of the decision in *Phipps v Rochester Corp.*[101] The claimant, a boy aged five, was out blackberrying with his sister, aged seven, and they walked across a large open space which formed part of a housing estate being developed by the defendants. The defendants had dug a long deep trench in the middle of the open space, a danger which was quite obvious to an adult. The claimant fell in and broke his leg. On the facts it was held that a prudent parent would not have allowed two

---

CC [2013] EWCA Civ 702. In some cases the occupier may be required to take account of the risk of wrongful conduct by other visitors: *Cunningham v Reading FC, The Independent,* March 20, 1991 (hooligans using lumps of rubble as weapons).

[97] *Keown v Coventry Healthcare NHS Trust* [2006] EWCA Civ 39; [2006] 1 W.L.R. 953 (a trespasser case, but the same must apply to visitors).

[98] *Simkiss v Rhondda BC* (1983) 81 L.G.R. 460.

[99] *Stevenson v Glasgow Corp* 1908 SC 1034 at 1039.

[100] That it is a duty of care only has led to expressions of regret when judges have been required, as a result, to dismiss claims brought by children who have been killed or injured: *Bowen v National Trust* [2011] EWHC 1992 (QB) at [43]; *Hufton v Somerset CC* [2011] EWCA Civ 789; [2011] E.L.R. 482 at [39].

[101] [1955] 1 Q.B. 450.

small children to go alone on the open space in question or, at least, he would have satisfied himself that the place held no dangers for the children. The defendants were entitled to assume that parents would behave in this way and therefore, although the claimant was a licensee, the defendants were not in breach of their duty to him. Devlin J's judgment squarely placed the primary responsibility for the safety of small children upon their parents.

The occupier will have discharged his duty if the place is reasonably safe for a child who is accompanied by the sort of guardian whom the occupier is in all the circumstances entitled to expect him to have with him. If the child is in fact accompanied by a guardian, then the question will be whether the occupier ought to have foreseen that the source of the child's injury would be a danger to the child, bearing in mind the guardian's responsibility for the child's safety. There seems no reason, at least in theory, why the child's injury should not in an appropriate case be attributed both to the occupier's breach of his common duty of care and to the negligence of the guardian. In such a case the occupier would be liable in full to the child, but presumably could recover contribution from the guardian.[102] However, it is not the case that either one or both of the occupier and the parents must be liable: if a danger to a small child is obvious to accompanying parents the occupier will have discharged his duty, but as far as the parents are concerned a child may be "gone in an instant".[103]

Injury to contractors. Paragraph (b) above clearly preserves such decisions as **10–018** *Bates v Parker*,[104] to the general effect that: "[W]here a householder employs an independent contractor to do work, be it of cleaning or repairing, on his premises, the contractor must satisfy himself as to the safety or condition of that part of the premises on which he is to work."[105]

In *Roles v Nathan*[106] two chimney sweeps were killed by carbon monoxide gas while attempting to seal up a "sweep hole" in the chimney of a coke-fired boiler, the boiler being alight at the time, but the occupier was not held liable for their deaths, partly at least on the ground that paragraph (b) applied.[107] As Lord Denning MR said: "When a householder calls in a specialist to deal with a defective installation on his premises, he can reasonably expect the specialist to appreciate and guard against the dangers arising from the defect."[108]

Nonetheless, the result might no doubt have been different if, for example, the stairs leading to the cellar where the boiler was had given way,[109] for that would not have been a special risk ordinarily incidental to the calling of a sweep. In any case, it is important to note that the fact that the claimant is an expert is only a factor to be taken into account in determining whether there has been a breach of

---

[102] Civil Liability (Contribution) Act 1978, para.22–009.

[103] *Marsden v Bourne Leisure Ltd* [2009] EWCA Civ 671; [2009] N.P.C. 93 at [17].

[104] [1953] 2 Q.B. 231; *Christmas v General Cleaning Contractors* [1952] 1 K.B. 141, affirmed [1953] A.C. 180; *Roles v Nathan* [1963] 1 W.L.R. 1117 at 1123 per Lord Denning MR.

[105] *Bates v Parker* [1953] 2 Q.B. 231 at 235 per Lord Goddard CJ.

[106] [1963] 1 W.L.R. 1117.

[107] [1963] 1 W.L.R. 1117 at 1123–1125 per Lord Denning MR.

[108] [1963] 1 W.L.R. 1117 at 1123; *Clare v Whittaker & Son (London) Ltd* [1976] I.C.R. 1; *Kealey v Heard* [1983] 1 W.L.R. 573.

[109] *Roles v Nathan* [1963] 1 W.L.R. 1117; *Bird v King Line* [1970] 2 Lloyd's Rep. 349; *Eden v West & Co* [2002] EWCA Civ 991; [2003] P.I.Q.R. Q2.

duty: his calling is not in itself a defence. Thus an occupier who negligently starts a fire may be liable to a fireman injured by even an ordinary risk of fighting it if that risk is one which remains even when all proper skill is used.[110] Furthermore, the fact that there is someone else whose duty it is to safeguard the visitor, for example his employer, does not of itself insulate the occupier from liability, though the occupier may be able to seek contribution from the other.[111]

10–019 **Warnings.** Under the Act: "Where damage is caused to a visitor by a danger of which he had been warned by the occupier, the warning is not to be treated without more as absolving the occupier from liability, unless in all the circumstances it was enough to enable the visitor to be reasonably safe."[112]

In most cases, probably, a warning of the danger will be sufficient to enable the visitor to be reasonably safe and so amount to a discharge by the occupier of his duty of care, but if, for some reason, the warning is not sufficient then the occupier remains liable.[113] There are, after all, some situations in which a reasonable person incurs a known risk and the question now, therefore, is whether such a situation existed on the particular facts of the case. It is clear too, since a warning of the danger is not necessarily sufficient to constitute performance of the occupier's duty, that the decision in *London Graving Dock Co v Horton*[114] is no longer good law.[115] In that case, the House of Lords held that an invitee could not succeed if he had full knowledge of the nature and extent of the danger. Now, however, as in cases where he has actually received a warning, the question is whether a visitor with knowledge of the danger reasonably incurred it.[116]

10–020 **Injury caused by contractors.** The Act also states that:[117]

"where damage is caused to a visitor by a danger due to the faulty execution of any work of construction, maintenance or repair[118] by an independent contractor[119] employed by the occupier, the occupier is not to be treated without more as answerable for the danger if in all

---

[110] *Ogwo v Taylor* [1988] A.C. 431; *Salmon v Seafarers Restaurant Ltd* [1983] 1 W.L.R. 1264. As to the position of "rescuers" generally, see para.26–022, but where there is no negligence by the defendant in starting the fire, then he will only be liable for failing to call attention to unusual risks in the premises: *Bermingham v Sher Bros* (1980) 124 S.J. 117 (cf. *"Wembridge Claimants" v Winter* [2013] EWHC 2331 (QB) where the occupiers incurred criminal liability on the basis of misleading information as to the fireworks stored in a container). Strictly, perhaps, only the second type of case falls within the Act, the other involving the common law, but if the claimant pleads both the Act and the common law nothing turns on the point.

[111] *Intruder Detection etc Ltd v Fulton* [2008] EWCA Civ 1009.

[112] Section 2(4)(a). The warning may be given by the occupier's agent: *Roles v Nathan* [1963] 1 W.L.R. 1117.

[113] See the different opinions expressed in the Court of Appeal about the warning given in *Roles v Nathan* [1963] 1 W.L.R. 1117.

[114] [1951] A.C. 737.

[115] *Roles* [1963] 1 W.L.R. 1117 at 1124 per Lord Denning MR.

[116] *Bunker v Charles Brandt & Son Ltd* [1969] 2 Q.B. 480 at 489 per O'Connor J. For contributory negligence in relation to the occupier's liability, see para.10–023.

[117] Section 2(4)(b).

[118] A broad, purposive interpretation is required which will embrace demolition: *Ferguson v Welsh* [1987] 1 W.L.R. 1553.

[119] The burden of proving that the danger was due to the fault of an independent contractor rests with the occupier: *Christmas v Blue Star Line* [1961] 1 Lloyd's Rep. 94; *AMF International Ltd v Magnet Bowling Ltd* [1968] 1 W.L.R. 1028 at 1042–1043

the circumstances he had acted reasonably in entrusting the work to an[120] independent contractor and had taken such steps (if any) as he reasonably ought in order to satisfy himself that the contractor was competent[121] and that the work had been properly done."

This is designed to afford some protection for the occupier who has engaged an independent contractor who has done the work in a faulty manner and was intended to reverse the decision of the House of Lords in *Thompson v Cremin*[122] in so far as that laid down that an invitor was responsible for the shortcomings of his contractor. The paragraph therefore makes the law under the Act accord with the general law, under which, as a rule, there is no vicarious liability for independent contractors.[123]

The operation of the paragraph is illustrated by two cases from the period before the Act. In *Haseldine v Daw*[124] H was going to visit a tenant in a block of flats belonging to D and was injured when the lift fell to the bottom of its shaft as a result of the negligence of a firm of engineers employed by D to repair the lift. It was held that D, having employed a competent firm of engineers to make periodical inspections of the lift, to adjust it and report on it, had discharged the duty owed to H, whether H was an invitee or licensee.[125] In *Woodward v Mayor of Hastings*,[126] on the other hand, a pupil at a school for which the defendants were responsible fell and was injured on an icy step which had been negligently left in a dangerous condition by a cleaner. Even assuming that the cleaner was an independent contractor, it was held that the defendants were liable and *Haseldine v Daw* was distinguished. Technical knowledge was required in the maintenance and repair of a lift, but such considerations were not relevant in *Woodward*'s case: "The craft of the charwoman may have its mysteries, but there is no esoteric quality in the nature of the work which the cleaning of a snow-covered step demands."[127]

Ensuring the competence of the contractor and the competence of the work. 10–021
Where an independent contractor has been employed, therefore, the question today is whether the occupier himself has done all that reasonable care requires of him. He must take reasonable steps to satisfy himself that the contractor he employs is competent, and, if the character of the work permits, he must take similar steps to see that the work has been properly done. In fact, where the work is especially complex, as with the construction of a large building or a ship, he may even have to cause the independent contractor's work to be supervised by a

---

[120] Surely "the"?
[121] On the content of this duty see para.10–021.
[122] *Thompson v Cremin* [1953] 2 All E.R. 1181.
[123] *AMF International Ltd v Magnet Bowling Ltd* [1968] 1 W.L.R. 1028. See para.21–043.
[124] [1941] 2 K.B. 343.
[125] *Haseldine v Daw* [1941] 2 K.B. 343 at 356 per Scott LJ. See also per Goddard LJ at 374.
[126] [1954] K.B. 174.
[127] *Woodward v Mayor of Hastings* [1954] K.B. 174 at 813 per du Parcq LJ. See also *Alexander v Freshwater Properties Ltd* [2012] EWCA Civ 1048 (landlord liable for failing to ensure repair to front door had been done properly: "It was not suggested that the builder was not a competent contractor or that the landlord had failed to satisfy himself properly of that fact, but that is not an answer if there has been negligence on the part of the landlord himself", at [19] per Moore-Bick LJ).

properly instructed architect or other professional person.[128] There are many cases in which the technical nature of the work to be done will require the occupier to employ an independent contractor and he will be negligent if he attempts to do it himself. This does not mean, however, that a householder must not himself undertake some ordinary domestic repair such as the fixing of a new door handle. Provided that he does the work with the care and skill of a reasonably competent carpenter he has fulfilled his duty.[129]

One justification for a general rule of non-liability for independent contractors is that the contractor (who is of course personally liable) is more likely to be claim-worthy than an individual servant of the occupier. That prompts the question, "Is the occupier therefore obliged to investigate the liability insurance position of the contractor?" Some statements in *Gwilliam v West Hertfordshire NHS Trust*[130] might be taken as supporting that but in *Payling v T Naylor (Trading as Mainstreet)*[131] the court rejected any such general, free-standing duty. The claimant suffered injury by the fault of a doorman when he was ejected from a club. The doorman was the servant of W, who carried no liability insurance and could not satisfy a judgment. The occupier of the club was held not liable because W had been licensed by the local authority to carry out such activities and that knowledge was sufficient to give the occupier reasonable cause to be satisfied as to his competence. Not only would the contrary rule be difficult to reconcile with the wording of the statute, which refers to "competence" rather than "suitability", it would also, it is submitted, be rather impracticable—consider, for example, the position of the householder who engages a contractor to do a job around the house or garden.[132] It has been said that:[133]

> "[I]f D had no duty to protect C against the *physical* consequences of an accident caused by the negligence of T, I would not regard it as just and reasonable to impose on D the more remote duty to protect C against the *economic* consequences of C being unable to enforce a judgment against T."

Where an occupier engages a contractor to do work on his premises and the claimant suffers injury not from the condition in which the contractor leaves the premises but from the manner in which the operation is carried out,[134] any

---

[128] *AMF International Ltd v Magnet Bowling Ltd* [1968] 1 W.L.R. 1028 at 1044, 1045–1047 per Mocatta J; *Kealey v Heard* [1983] 1 All E.R. 973. Mocatta J also held that the negligence of the architect or other supervisor would not itself involve the occupier in liability for otherwise, in technical cases, the common duty of care would become equivalent to the obligation of an insurer.

[129] *Wells v Cooper* [1958] 2 Q.B. 265.

[130] [2002] EWCA Civ 1041; [2002] Q.B. 443.

[131] [2004] EWCA Civ 560; [2004] P.I.Q.R. P36.

[132] It is also submitted that the fact that the employer of the contractor is required to carry liability insurance should not lead to the contrary conclusion. To take an example outside the area of occupiers' liability, the owner of a vehicle is required to have liability insurance in respect of its use and that would have to cover, inter alia, accidents caused by defects in the vehicle; but that should not mean that the owner should have to inquire into the garage's liability insurance cover when he took the car to be serviced.

[133] *Glaister v Appleby in Westmorland Town Council* [2009] EWCA Civ 1325; [2010] P.I.Q.R. P6 at [63] per Toulson LJ.

[134] For example, removing asbestos lagging without taking the recognised precautions.

liability arises under the general law and not under the Act.[135] However, there may be circumstances where the occupier is required to intervene where he has failed to take care in selecting a competent contractor[136] or if it is obvious that the contractor is using an unsafe system of work.

E. Personal Responsibility: *Tomlinson*'s Case

It must be emphasised that the provisions dealt with in the preceding paragraphs are no more than explanations or illustrations of the fundamental rule, which is that the occupier must do what is reasonable in the circumstances of the case and that standard, as in any other case of negligence, will be arrived at by the court's weighing the relative risks and burdens.[137] The burdens are not only those that would be directly imposed on the particular occupier if he were required to take the action contended for by the claimant, they include the restrictions on the freedom of the majority of people which will be imposed[138] if what is required of the occupier is set at a level which will prevent the foolhardy encountering obvious risks.[139] This is the basis of *Tomlinson v Congleton BC*[140] and even though that case was, strictly, concerned with the question of whether there was a danger within the meaning of the Act rather than breach of the occupier's duty, the point is the same. As Lord Hobhouse said:[141]

10–022

> "It is not, and should never be, the policy of the law to require the protection of the foolhardy or reckless few to deprive, or interfere with, the enjoyment by the remainder of society of the liberties and amenities to which they are rightly entitled. Does the law require that all trees be cut down because some youths may climb them and fall? Does the law require the coastline and other beauty spots to be lined with warning notices? Does the law require that attractive waterside picnic spots be destroyed because of a few foolhardy individuals who choose to ignore warning notices and indulge in activities dangerous only to themselves? The answer to

---

[135] "It would not ordinarily be reasonable to expect an occupier of premises having engaged a contractor whom he has reasonable grounds for regarding as competent, to supervise the contractor's activities in order to ensure that he was discharging his duty to his employees to observe a safe system of work": *Ferguson v Welsh* [1987] 1 W.L.R. 1553 at 1560. See also *Fairchild v Glenhaven Funeral Services Ltd* [2001] EWCA Civ 1881; [2002] 1 W.L.R. 1052.

[136] *Bottomley v Todmorden Cricket Club* [2003] EWCA Civ 1575; [2004] P.I.Q.R. P18.

[137] See, e.g. *Lewis v Six Continents Plc* [2005] EWCA Civ 1805 (no need to make upper storey hotel window unopenable). See also *Neindorf v Junkovic* [2005] HCA 75; 222 A.L.R. 631 at [8].

[138] See *Hampstead Heath Winter Swimming Club v London Corp* [2005] EWHC 713 (Admin); [2005] 1 W.L.R. 2930, where an attempt was made by the defendants to ban unsupervised swimming on Hampstead Heath on the ground of risk to the participants.

[139] Indeed, even where the risk is not obvious and the claimant is not foolhardy there is a danger of inhibiting ordinary activities if the standard of care is set too high: *Cole v Davis-Gilbert* [2007] EWCA Civ 396.

[140] [2003] UKHL 47; [2004] 1 A.C. 46, para.10–014. See also: *Donoghue v Folkestone Properties Ltd* [2003] EWCA Civ 231; [2003] Q.B. 1008; *Darby v National Trust* [2001] EWCA Civ 189; [2001] P.I.Q.R. P27.

[141] At [81]. See also Lord Hoffmann at [46]. See also *Mulligan v Coffs Harbour CC* [2005] HCA 63; 223 C.L.R. 486 ("…defendants have rights and interests too. A tendency to see cases through the eyes of plaintiffs only is to be avoided", at [80] per Callinan and Heydon JJ). The sentiment expressed by Lord Hobhouse and Lord Hoffmann is now enshrined in the Compensation Act 2006 s.1, but it does "not add anything to the common law position": *Uren v Corporate Leisure UK Ltd* [2011] EWCA Civ 66; [2011] I.C.R. D11 at [13] (the case was remitted where Foskett J ([2013] EWHC 353 (QB)) drew as much, if not more so, on the speeches in *Tomlinson* than on s.1 of the 2006 Act).

all these questions is, of course, no. But this is the road down which your Lordships, like other courts before, have been invited to travel and which the councils in the present case found so inviting. In truth, the arguments for the claimant have involved an attack upon the liberties of the citizen which should not be countenanced. They attack the liberty of the individual to engage in dangerous, but otherwise harmless, pastimes at his own risk and the liberty of citizens as a whole fully to enjoy the variety and quality of the landscape of this country. The pursuit of an unrestrained culture of blame and compensation has many evil consequences and one is certainly the interference with the liberty of the citizen."

F. Contributory Negligence

10–023   In view of some doubts which existed as to whether the scheme of the Law Reform Contributory Negligence Act 1945 applied where an invitee was guilty of lack of care for his own safety it is perhaps surprising that the Occupiers' Liability Act does not expressly incorporate the Act of 1945. However, the point is probably implicit and judges have in numerous cases applied the 1945 Act without hesitation to reduce damages.[142] Where the claimant's fault is extreme it may, of course, amount to the sole legal cause of his loss.[143]

G. Volenti non fit injuria

10–024   The defence of *volenti non fit injuria* is available under the Act,[144] as it was previously. The Unfair Contract Terms Act 1977 which now regulates the power of the occupier to exclude liability[145] provides that a person's agreement to or awareness of an exempting condition or notice, "is not of itself to be taken as indicating his voluntary acceptance of the risk".[146]

H. Exclusion of Liability

10–025   **Exclusion of liability by contract or notice.** Under s.2(1) of the Act the common duty of care is owed by the occupier "except in so far as he is free to and does extend, restrict, modify or exclude his duty . . . by agreement or otherwise".[147] No contract is necessary for this purpose, for s.2(1) gives statutory force to the decision of the Court of Appeal, shortly before the Act, in *Ashdown v Samuel Williams & Sons*.[148] The claimant was a licensee on land belonging to the defendants when she was knocked down and injured by railway trucks which were being negligently shunted along a railway line on the land. Various notices had been posted by the defendants to the effect that every person on the land was there at his own risk and should have no claim against the defendants for any

---

[142] See, e.g. *Woolins v British Celanese Ltd* (1966) 1 K.I.R. 438; *Stone v Taffe* [1974] 1 W.L.R. 1575.
[143] See, e.g. *Brayshaw v Leeds CC* [1984] 2 C.L. 234.
[144] Section 2(5) ("indistinguishable from the common law defence": *Geary v JD Wetherspoon Plc* [2011] EWHC 1506 (QB); [2011] N.P.C. 60 at [36]).
[145] See para.10–027.
[146] UCTA s.2(3).
[147] We are not concerned here with the question of whether the occupier has *discharged* his duty, e.g. by the use of an appropriate warning: see para.10–019.
[148] [1957] 1 Q.B. 409; *White v Blackmore* [1972] 2 Q.B. 651. The decision in both cases would now go the other way because of the Unfair Contract Terms Act 1977: see para.10–027.

injury whatsoever, and it was found as a fact that they had taken reasonable steps to bring the conditions contained in the notices to the claimant's attention. It was held, therefore, that the claimant could not recover.[149] Despite criticism that the absence of a contract should have been fatal to the defence,[150] the decision seems to accord with general principle. If I can exclude you from my property altogether, why can I not permit you to enter upon any terms that I like to make? The result might, indeed, be construed as a contract whereby you give up what would otherwise be your legal rights in return for my allowing you to enter, but this construction is not essential to the validity of the conditions.[151]

As with any purported exclusion of liability any term to this effect must have been validly incorporated in the contract and in the case of a non-contractual notice reasonable steps must have been taken to bring it to the attention of the visitor, though he need not actually be aware of it.[152] In both cases the wording will be construed *contra proferentem*, i.e. in favour of the visitor in the event of any ambiguity.[153]

Common law limits on the power to exclude liability. The occupier may only   **10–026**
exclude the common duty of care "in so far as he is free to" do so. The principal restrictions are now provided by statute,[154] but clearly the Act does not enlarge the power to exclude which existed at common law. It is submitted, for example, that there could be no exclusion of liability to a person entering in exercise of a right conferred by law and the same may be true of those who do not enter as of right, but have no "free choice" in the matter.[155]

Unfair Contract Terms Act 1977. The power of the occupier to exclude or   **10–027**
restrict his liability (or duty)[156] to a visitor may now be subject to the controls set out in the Unfair Contract Terms Act 1977. This Act, despite its short title, extends much further than the control of contractual exemption clauses. Section 2 provides that:

> "(1)   A person cannot by reference to any contract term or to a notice[157] exclude or restrict his liability for death or personal injury resulting from negligence;
>
> (2)   in the case of other loss or damage, a person cannot so exclude or restrict his liability for negligence except in so far as the term or notice satisfies the requirement of reasonableness.[158]"

---

[149] The case was concerned not with the static condition of the land on which the claimant was a licensee but with the current activities of the occupier. Clearly, therefore, the power to exclude liability is not restricted to the static condition of the structure even if it is less easy to justify the existence of that power with regard to current activities: Odgers [1957] C.L.J. 39 at 54.

[150] See Gower (1956) 19 M.L.R. 536.

[151] It was rejected by Lord Greene MR in *Wilkie v LPTB* [1947] 1 All E.R. 258 at 260. Cf. *Gore v Van Der Lann* [1967] 2 Q.B. 31; Odgers 86 L.Q.R. 69.

[152] *Ashdown v Samuel Williams & Sons* [1957] 1 Q.B. 409 at 425.

[153] *Ashdown v Samuel Williams & Sons* [1957] 1 Q.B. 409 at 429–430.

[154] See para.10–027.

[155] *Burnett v British Waterways Board* [1973] 1 W.L.R. 700.

[156] See s.13(1) of the 1977 Act.

[157] Defined in s.14, e.g. a sign at the entry to the premises.

[158] See s.11.

10–028   **"Business liability".** The definition of "negligence" under the 1977 Act expressly includes the breach of the common duty of care imposed by the Occupiers' Liability Act 1957[159] but the prohibitions on exclusion of liability apply only where the duty arises from things done in the course of a business or from the occupation of premises used for the business purposes of the occupier.[160] A business probably requires at least some degree of regularity, so that an isolated transaction whereby access to land was granted for payment would probably not fall within the ban, but the Act contains an extended definition which makes the concept cover some activities which would not ordinarily be thought of as a business.[161] Activities in aid of charity are an obvious example which would present the court with difficult questions of degree.[162] Since the owner of a farm or a commercial forest is clearly occupying his land in the course of a business, the effect of the Act as originally formulated was to cause restriction of public access and it was amended by s.2 of the Occupiers' Liability Act 1984, as a result of which s.1(3) of the 1977 Act now provides that:

> "[T]he liability of an occupier of premises for breach of an obligation or duty towards a person obtaining access to the premises for recreational or educational purposes, being liability for loss or damage suffered by reason of the dangerous state of the premises, is not a business liability of the occupier unless granting that person such access for the purposes concerned falls within the business of the occupier."

Hence, if a farmer has on his land a ruinous castle he may allow access on condition that he is not liable for death or personal injury caused by the state of the premises,[163] but the ancient monuments body English Heritage may not impose such a condition because admission for recreation or education is (probably) its business within the meaning of the Act. The liberty to exclude liability is, however, confined to damage suffered by reason of the dangerous state of the premises, so that if the visitor is knocked down by the farmer's tractor the exclusion, no matter how widely drawn, is ineffective.

I.   Effect of Contract on Occupier's Liability to Third Parties

10–029   **Occupier's Liability Act 1957 s.3.** It was the opinion of the Law Reform Committee[164] that where a person contracts with the occupier for the use of premises on the footing that he is to be entitled to permit third persons to use them, the duty owed by the occupier to those third persons is the same as that

---

[159] The Act does not prevent exclusion of a stricter duty: s.1(1)(b). By virtue of s.1(4) it is immaterial whether liability "arises directly or vicariously". This would probably cover any situations where the occupier is liable for the negligence of an independent contractor.

[160] Section 1(3).

[161] By s.14 "'business' includes a profession and the activities of any government department or local or public authority".

[162] See, e.g. *White v Blackmore* [1972] 2 Q.B. 651.

[163] If the farmer charges the public even a small sum for admission there is likely to be a business occupation.

[164] On the authority of *Fosbroke-Hobbes v Airwork Ltd* [1937] 1 All E.R. 108. (1954), Cmd. 9305, para.55. See, too, para.79.

owed to the other party to the contract. This could lead to a person being deprived of his rights by a contract to which he was not a party and of whose provisions he was unaware. It is therefore provided by the Act that:[165]

> "[W]here an occupier of premises is bound by contract to permit persons who are strangers to the contract[166] to enter or use the premises, the duty of care which he owes to them as his visitors cannot be restricted or excluded by that contract, but (subject to any provision of the contract to the contrary) shall include the duty to perform his obligations under the contract, whether undertaken for their protection or not, in so far as those obligations go beyond the obligations otherwise involved in that duty."

Furthermore, where a tenancy, including a statutory tenancy which does not in law amount to a tenancy, requires either the landlord or the tenant to permit persons to enter premises of which he is the occupier, the section applies as if the tenancy were a contract between the landlord and the tenant.[167]

Effect of the section. This section has a twofold effect. The occupier cannot by contract reduce his obligations to visitors who are strangers to the contract to a level below that imposed by the common duty of care.[168] If, however, the contract requires him to take some precaution not required in the circumstances by that duty, the visitor shall have the benefit of that precaution. If, for example, A contracts with B to allow B and C to use his premises and the contract provides that the premises shall be lit during the hours of darkness, C has a right of action against A for injury due to A's failure to light the premises, whether or not such a failure would amount to a breach of the common duty of care. It is provided, however, that the section shall not have the effect, unless the contract so provides, of making an occupier who has taken all reasonable care liable for dangers due to the faulty execution of any work of construction, maintenance or repair or other like operation by persons other than himself, his servants or persons acting under his direction and control.[169]   **10–030**

Contracts (Rights of Third Parties) Act 1999. There will now be cases where the visitor may be able to rely on the general provisions of the Contracts (Rights of Third Parties) Act 1999 in order to enforce a term in the contract between the occupier and another under which the visitor is allowed entry and which imposes a higher duty than the common duty of care.[170] Like the Occupiers' Liability Act,   **10–031**

---

[165] Section 3(1).

[166] Defined in s.3(3).

[167] 1957 Act s.3(4).

[168] It may be that as far as personal injuries are concerned much the same effect is achieved by the Unfair Contract Terms Act 1977 s.2(1). According to Law Com. No.69, p.133 "contract term" bears, "its natural meaning of any term in any contract (and is not limited to the terms in a contract between the instant parties)". However, the provisions of the Occupiers' Liability Act are more favourable to the claimant since: (1) they are not confined to business occupation; and (2) they extend to all types of loss or damage whereas the Unfair Contract Terms Act prohibition is a qualified one with regard to property damage.

[169] 1957 Act s.3(2). The wording of this subsection differs from that of s.2(4)(b) (see para.10–020), but the effect of the two subsections is probably the same and if s.2(4)(b) includes demolition (*Ferguson v Welsh* [1987] 1 W.L.R. 1153) so should s.3(2).

[170] However, the 1999 Act would not apply if the obligation to admit the third party was an implied one, because the third party would not then be expressly identified in the contract: s.1(3).

this right is subject to the contrary agreement of the contracting parties.[171] However, in practice the 1957 Act may continue to be relied on, if only because it is unnecessary to establish that the term in question "purported to confer a benefit"[172] on the third party.

10–032   **Effect of a non-contractual notice.** It was formerly an open question whether the occupier, though unable to restrict his duty to third parties by a provision in the contract itself, could do so by publishing a notice as in *Ashdown v Samuel Williams & Sons*.[173] Where the occupation is of a business nature it is now clear that such a notice is caught by the Unfair Contract Terms Act[174] and in other situations it is submitted that the case is one where the occupier is not "free to" restrict or exclude his duty of care, for the alternative view would tend to defeat the object of s.3 of the Occupiers' Liability Act.[175]

J.   Damage to Property

10–033   The 1957 Act provides[176] that the rules which it enacts shall apply:

> " . . . [I]n like manner and to the like extent as the principles applicable at common law to an occupier of premises and his invitees or licensees would apply to regulate . . . the obligations of a person occupying or having control over any premises or structure in respect of damage to property, including the property of persons who are not themselves his visitors."

Clearly, therefore, where property lawfully on the premises is damaged by a structural defect of the premises,[177] whether it actually belongs to a visitor or not, the question in each case is whether the occupier has discharged the common duty of care. Where there has been a bailment, however, as where goods are deposited in a warehouse, the liability of the warehouse-keeper will not depend upon the common duty of care but upon his duty under the bailment or special contract. The rules contained in the Occupiers' Liability Act replace only the principles of the common law formerly applicable between the occupier and his invitee or licensee. They do not affect the relationship of bailor and bailee.[178] Where there is no bailment, the common law rule was that there was no duty on the occupier to protect the goods of his visitors from theft by a third party[179] and

---

[171] Contracts (Rights of Third Parties) Act 1999 s.1(2).

[172] 1999 Act s.1((1)(b).

[173] [1957] 1 Q.B. 409, para.10–025.

[174] See para.10–028.

[175] Cf. *Clerk & Lindsell on Torts*, 20th edn (2013), para.12–55. It must be admitted, however, that the Law Reform Committee seem to have been concerned only with the position of a person affected by an exempting term unknown to him: (1954), Cmnd. 9305, para.55.

[176] Section 1(3)(b).

[177] For example, if, with your permission, I leave my car in the drive outside your house and a tile falls off the roof and damages it: *AMF International Ltd v Magnet Bowling Ltd* [1968] 1 W.L.R. 1028. Damages may be recovered not only in respect of actual damage to the property but also in respect of consequential financial loss: at 1049–1051 per Mocatta J.

[178] Cf. *Fairline Shipping Corp v Adamson* [1975] Q.B. 180.

[179] *Tinsley v Dudley* [1951] 2 K.B. 18. See also *Ashby v Tolhurst* [1937] 2 K.B. 242; *Deyong v Shenburn* [1946] K.B. 227; *Edwards v West Herts Group Hospital Management Committee* [1957] 1 W.L.R. 418.

the Act has not changed this. A mere licence to put goods on land (as in the case of most car parks) does not make the occupier a bailee.[180]

3. LIABILITY TO TRESPASSERS AND OTHER NON-VISITORS

The common law. The duty of an occupier to a trespasser was unaffected by the Occupiers' Liability Act 1957. The original common law rule was that the occupier was only liable to a trespasser in respect of some wilful act, "done with deliberate intention of doing harm . . . or at least some act done with reckless disregard of the presence of the trespasser",[181] but the law underwent substantial alteration and development by the House of Lords in 1972 in *British Railways Board v Herrington*.[182] As a result of that case the occupier owed to the trespasser a "duty of common humanity" which, generally speaking, was lower than the common duty of care but substantially higher than the original duty. *Herrington*'s case was applied by the Court of Appeal on a number of occasions without undue difficulty[183] but on a reference to the Law Commission that body decided that no sufficiently clear principle emerged from the case and recommended legislative action. After a long delay, this was done by the Occupiers' Liability Act 1984.[184]

10–034

Scope of the 1984 Act. Though in this section we shall continue to speak of trespassers, for that is the commonest case, the Act in fact covers a rather wider field, for it applies to liability to persons other than the occupier's visitors. It applies, for example, to persons exercising private rights of way,[185] and persons exercising access rights under National Parks legislation[186] but not to persons using a public right of way,[187] whose rights, if any, must be sought in the highways legislation.[188]

10–035

When duty is owed. Section 1(3) provides that a duty is owed to the trespasser in relation to the risk of their suffering injury by reason of any danger due to the state of the premises or things done or omitted to be done thereon[189] if:

10–036

"(a)   [The occupier] is aware of the danger or has reasonable grounds to believe that it exists;

(b)   he knows or has reasonable grounds to believe that the [trespasser] is in the vicinity of the danger concerned or that he may come into the vicinity of the danger . . . and

(c)   the risk is one against which, in all the circumstances of the case, he may reasonably be expected to offer the other some protection."

---

[180] *Tinsley v Dudley* [1951] 2 K.B. 18; *John C. Dogherty v Drogheda Harbour Commissioners* [1993] 1 I.R. 315.

[181] *Robert Addie & Sons (Collieries) Ltd v Dumbreck* [1929] A.C. 358 at 365.

[182] [1972] A.C. 877.

[183] See, e.g. *Pannett v P. McGuinness & Co Ltd* [1972] 2 Q.B. 599; *Harris v Birkenhead Corp* [1976] 2 W.L.R. 279.

[184] Law Com. No.75.

[185] *Vodden v Gayton* [2001] P.I.Q.R. P4 (owners of servient tenement across which fenced track ran occupiers of the track; no breach of duty on facts).

[186] See para.10–009. As to persons exercising rights under the Countryside and Rights of Way Act 2000, see below.

[187] Section 1(7).

[188] See para.15–082.

[189] See s.1(1)(a).

The expression "has reasonable grounds to believe" in paras (a) and (b) requires actual knowledge of facts which would lead a reasonable person to be aware of the danger or the presence of the trespasser[190] and simple ignorance, though blameworthy, is not enough, though it would be under the 1957 Act.[191]

10–037 **The content of the duty.** The duty is to take such care as is reasonable in all the circumstances to see that the entrant does not suffer injury[192] on the premises by reason of the danger concerned[193] and it may, in appropriate circumstances, be discharged by taking such steps as are reasonable to give warning of the danger concerned or to discourage persons from incurring the risk.[194]

10–038 **An objective standard.** On the face of it, the standard appears to be objective and not conditioned by the occupier's own resources, which was not true of the duty of common humanity,[195] but in *Ratcliffe v McConnell*[196] the Court of Appeal treated the Act as largely a restatement of what Lord Diplock had said in *Herrington*, citing a passage which had referred to the occupier's resources. The nature or character *of the trespass* is a matter which is very relevant in determining what the occupier may reasonably be expected to do: the very same precautions which should be taken for the benefit of a lawful visitor may in some cases be required to protect young trespassing children, but it would be wholly unacceptable that they should be required for the benefit of a burglar or entrant intent on criminal damage.

10–039 **Warnings.** Furthermore, while the giving of a prominent warning will not necessarily in all cases discharge the occupier's duty[197] it is more likely to do so than with regard to lawful visitors. The latter may have no choice but to encounter the risk and the warning must therefore in itself make them reasonably safe; the trespasser who continues to intrude after passing a prominent warning notice has himself to blame for any injury he may suffer.

---

[190] *Swain v Puri* [1996] P.I.Q.R. P442. See also *Rhind v Astbury Water Park Ltd* [2004] EWCA Civ 756; [2004] N.P.C. 95. The question is whether the occupier has reason to expect the trespasser at that time: *Donoghue v Folkestone Properties Ltd* [2003] EWCA Civ 231; [2003] Q.B. 1008.

[191] Consciously closing one's eyes to an obvious risk should suffice. However, it is suggested in *Young v Kent CC* [2005] EWHC 1342 (QB) that in the case of premises like a school a risk assessment exercise is necessary even with regard to dangers to trespassers. The actual decision is called into question in *Keown v Coventry Healthcare NHS Trust* [2006] EWCA Civ 39; [2006] 1 W.L.R. 953.

[192] 1984 Act s.1(9).

[193] 1984 Act s.1(4).

[194] 1984 Act s.1(5). In some cases there may be specific, statutory provisions aimed at preventing access: *Mann v Northern Electric Distribution Ltd* [2010] EWCA Civ 141.

[195] *Herrington* [1972] A.C. 877 at 899, 920–921, 942. It might be argued that the occupier's resources are to be taken into account as part of "all the circumstances of the case", but the same words appear in s.2(2) of the 1957 Act and it has not been suggested that the occupier's "personal equation" forms part of the standard of care owed to visitors.

[196] [1999] 1 W.L.R. 670 at 680.

[197] For example, where the likely trespassers are young children; but the principle that the occupier must be entitled to look to parents to take principal responsibility for the safety of their children must apply here, too: para.10–017.

Obvious risks. Even where no effective warning is given, an adult trespasser (or even a child with sufficient understanding[198]) who takes a risk which should be obvious to him cannot complain that the occupier did not take more rigorous steps to discourage his folly.[199] The leading case of *Tomlinson v Congleton BC*[200] has been considered above in the context of the 1957 Act. In fact the majority of the House of Lords considered that the claimant was a trespasser in the lake and if the occupier was not liable under the 1957 Act then a fortiori this was true under the 1984 Act. The latter uses the same formula as the former in relation to defining its scope and some members of the House were of the view that the injury suffered could not even be said to be, "due to the state of the premises or things done or omitted to be done thereon".[201] In such a case it is unnecessary to rely on volenti non fit injuria as an answer to the claim, though the defence is expressly preserved.[202]

"Activity duties". Although the 1984 Act is in terms as ambiguous as that of 1957 on the relationship between the "occupancy" and "activity" duties, it has been said that it is confined to the liability of "an occupier as occupier".[203] On this basis it does not therefore apply to a case where the occupier negligently[204] shoots a trespasser.[205] However, both the wording of the statute and history show that it must apply to some activities carried out on the land—some of the leading cases on the common law involved activities, such as operating winding gear[206] or running trains.[207] These cases are perhaps distinguishable from that of the shooting since the pursuit of the activity was the very reason for the occupation of the land.[208] Where the common law is applicable it should, as a matter of precedent, be that stated by the House of Lords in *Herrington*'s case[209]—in summary, the occupier was not obliged to institute checks for the presence of trespassers or dangers but a duty arose if on the facts of which he knew there was a likelihood of serious harm to the trespasser sufficient to make it inhumane to fail to take steps against it. Putting aside the point that *Herrington*'s case made some allowance for the ability and resources of the individual occupier and that the Act may not do that,[210] this is very similar indeed to the approach of the Act and in *Revill v Newberry*[211] Neill LJ suggested that the Act might provide useful

10–040

10–041

---

[198] *Keown v Coventry Healthcare NHS Trust* [2006] EWCA Civ 39; [2006] 1 W.L.R. 953.
[199] *Ratcliffe v McConnell* [1999] 1 W.L.R. 670.
[200] [2003] UKHL 47; [2004] 1 A.C. 46, para.10–014; and see *Donoghue v Folkestone Properties Ltd* [2003] EWCA Civ 231; [2003] Q.B. 1008.
[201] See para.10–014.
[202] 1984 Act s.1(6).
[203] *Revill v Newberry* [1996] Q.B. 567 per Neill LJ.
[204] If the injury is inflicted deliberately or recklessly the question will not be one of occupiers' liability but of what force may be used in the defence of property.
[205] *Revill v Newberry* [1996] Q.B. 567.
[206] *Robert Addie and Sons (Collieries) Ltd v Dumbreck* [1929] A.C. 358.
[207] *Videan v British Transport Commission* [1963] 2 Q.B. 650; *Herrington* [1972] A.C. 877.
[208] Consider the case of the trespasser shot on a grouse moor by its owner. In *Revill* [1966] Q.B. 567 Neill LJ admitted that if the case were framed as the negligent organisation of a shooting party by the owner of the estate, it would plainly fall within the 1984 Act.
[209] [1972] A.C. 877.
[210] See para.10–038.
[211] [1996] Q.B. 567.

guidance on the nature of the duty owed at common law. If this is so, then where the precautions required do not involve significant effort or expenditure there will be little, if any, practical difference between the Act and the common law.[212]

10–042 **Property damage.** The Act is plainly inapplicable to damage to the property of the trespasser. If therefore, C trespasses on D's property and he suffers injury when his car falls down a disused and concealed mine shaft, he may well be able to recover damages for his personal injuries but not for the loss of his car. However, the Act seems to leave the common law untouched on this point.[213] There can be little doubt that where an occupier is in breach of his duty of common humanity at common law his liability would extend beyond the personal injuries suffered by the trespasser to, say, the destruction of his clothing and it has been said, obiter, that there can be liability even where no personal injury is involved—on the facts where the claimant's bees were foraging across land sprayed by the defendant with a poisonous chemical.[214] It is not, however, easy to apply the concept of "common humanity" to a situation where there is no personal injury or even no threat of personal injury.

10–043 **Claims against non-occupiers.** One more situation appears to be governed by the common law. Suppose the defendant is not the occupier but the occupier's contractor or guest, a situation to which the 1984 Act is plainly inapplicable. There was authority that, as between the trespasser and the non-occupier, trespassory status as such[215] was irrelevant,[216] but the balance of the dicta in *Herrington's* case pointed towards the removal of any sharp distinction between occupiers and others in this respect,[217] and in *Revill v Newberry* it was assumed that a non-occupier would be in the same position as the occupier.

10–044 **Other non-visitors.** Those who enter premises in the exercise of private rights of way are not visitors, but are owed the more limited duty of care under the 1984 Act.[218] As for public rights of way, the Countryside and Rights of Way Act 2000 introduced a general right of public access to open land for recreational purposes. Persons exercising this right, like those taking advantage of the access agreements under the more limited National Parks and Access to the Countryside

---

[212] So it seems that the common law is to be looked at to interpret the Act (*Ratcliffe v McConnell* [1999] 1 W.L.R. 670, para.10–038) and the Act is to be looked at to decide the common law.
[213] Section 1(1) provides that the Act is to replace the rules of the common law in respect of personal injury. S.1(8), preventing recovery in respect of "loss of or damage to property", applies only to breaches of duty under s.1.
[214] *Tutton v AD Walter Ltd* [1986] Q.B. 61. The judge's decision, however, was that the categories of "visitor" and "trespasser" were inapt terms to be applied to the bees and the ordinary law of negligence applied.
[215] On the facts, a trespasser might of course be unforeseeable when a lawful visitor would not.
[216] *Buckland v Guildford Gas Light and Coke Co* [1949] 1 K.B. 410; *Davis v St Mary's Demolition and Excavation Co Ltd* [1954] 1 W.L.R. 592; *Creed v McGeogh & Sons Ltd* [1955] 1 W.L.R. 1005.
[217] *Herrington* [1972] A.C. 877 at 914 per Lord Wilberforce and at 929 per Lord Pearson. Cf. Lord Diplock at 943.
[218] *Vodden v Gayton* [2001] P.I.Q.R. P4.

Act 1949, are not visitors of the occupier[219] but they are owed a duty under the 1984 Act. However, the occupier's duty to them is specifically excluded in respect of:[220]

> "(a) [A] risk resulting from the existence of any natural feature of the landscape, or any river, stream, ditch or pond whether or not a natural feature, or (b) a risk of [the entrant] suffering injury when passing over, under or through any wall, fence or gate, except by proper use of the gate or of a stile."

This restriction does not apply to dangers arising from anything done by the occupier with the intention of creating the risk, or reckless as to whether the risk is created.[221] At first sight these provisions are curious, for their purpose appears to be to impose a more restricted liability than that to trespassers.[222] The answer may be that their purpose was to head off any argument that, the duty under the 1984 Act being a flexible one, it should embrace such hazards in relation to the lawful entrant exercising his statutory "right to roam". However, in the light of *Tomlinson*'s case[223] in 2003 it is not very likely that these matters would attract liability under either the 1957 or 1984 Acts. It is also provided that in determining the duty owed to an entrant under the Act of 2000 regard is to be had to the fact that the existence of that right ought not to place an undue burden (whether financial or otherwise) on the occupier, and to the importance of maintaining the character of the countryside.[224]

Exclusion of liability. Both the 1984 Act and the Unfair Contract Terms Act 1977 are silent when it comes to the power of the occupier to exclude his liability to a trespasser. As a consequence, the law in this respect cannot be stated with any certainty. The omission from the 1984 Act of any express reference to a power to exclude liability appears to have been deliberate[225] and it is the case that the law's original level of duty to trespassers (not to injure them deliberately or recklessly) represented a minimum standard of conduct which could not be excluded. However, the duty owed to trespassers is now much higher and, if non-excludable, the trespasser would be treated more favourably than the visitor (where there is undoubtedly a power to exclude liability).[226] On balance, therefore, it is submitted that the occupier does have the power to exclude liability, through an appropriate term or notice,[227] in the case of a trespasser.[228] The same premise, i.e. that the regime for the exclusion of liability should be the

10–045

---

[219] Occupiers' Liability Act 1984 s.1(4)(a) (as substituted by s.13(1) of the Countryside and Rights of Way Act 2000).

[220] Occupiers' Liability Act 1984 s.1(6A) (as inserted by s.13(2) of the Countryside and Rights of Way Act 2000). See also s.306 of the Marine and Coastal Access Act 2009.

[221] Section 1(6C).

[222] Which the entrants will become if they abuse their privilege: Countryside and Rights of Way Act 2000 s.2.

[223] See para.10–014.

[224] Occupiers' Liability Act 1984 s.1A (as inserted by s.13(3) of the Countryside and Rights of Way Act 2000). Regard to be had also to Codes of Conduct to be issued under that Act.

[225] It had been allowed for in the draft bill put forward by the Law Commission (Law Com No.75), but was dropped in Parliament.

[226] See para.10–025.

[227] More likely notice, but a contract prohibiting entry from part only of the premises might also contain exclusions of liability in respect of any prohibited entry.

same for both trespassers and visitors, leads to the conclusion that any exercise of the power should be subject to the Unfair Contract Terms Act 1977, where applicable.[229] But while claims arising under the 1957 Act are caught by the 1977 Act, there is no reference to claims arising under the 1984 Act.[230] If there is a power to exclude liability, it should, it is submitted, be subject to the controls in the 1977 Act but that would appear to require its amendment. Until such amendment, this may be a further reason why the occupier should have no power to exclude liability in the first place.

4. LIABILITY OF VENDORS AND LESSORS

10–046   We are concerned here with the situation where a vendor or lessor creates a danger or defect in his premises and then sells or lets them to another who (or whose successor) suffers damage from that danger or defect. The common law was at first solicitous to the vendor or lessor then, in the 1970s, it swung sharply in favour of the purchaser or tenant but at the price of getting into a quite extraordinary state of complexity and uncertainty. At this stage a complicating strand in the story was the imposition of liability on local authorities for faulty exercise of their statutory functions of approval and inspection; indeed, since the builder had commonly gone into liquidation by the time the problem became apparent, local authorities usually ended up with the bill. One of the main characteristics of the cases in this period was to blur the distinction between contract and tort. From 1988 there was a sharp reaction, culminating in the decision in *Murphy v Brentwood DC*[231] and scores of cases in the middle period must now be regarded as wrongly decided.

A. Vendor[232]

i. Claims in Contract

10–047   There is, of course, a contract between vendor and purchaser of land but the implied contractual obligations as to quality are very much less extensive than they are in contracts for the sale of goods even if the vendor is a builder or developer, and hence "in the business" of selling houses. The basic rule is caveat emptor though this may be displaced by express terms in the contract or misrepresentations. In one situation, however, there is a limited implied obligation, namely, when there is a contract for the sale of a house to be built or

---

[228] Previous editions suggested a power to exclude liability for all injury except that inflicted wilfully or recklessly. For a limited version of this proposition, see s.1(6)(C) of the 1984 Act: para.10–044.

[229] i.e. in relation to "business liability": see para.10–028.

[230] See the definition of "negligence" for the purposes of the 1977 Act in s.1(1): para.10–028.

[231] [1991] 1 A.C. 398.

[232] Since we are also concerned with the position of successors to the property, this part is not confined to claims against the immediate vendor, but extends to claims against those who may have been responsible for creating the defect or danger, such as the builder or the local authority responsible for inspection.

completed by the vendor.[233] There is then a threefold implied warranty: that the builder will do his work in a good and workmanlike manner,[234] that he will supply good and proper materials and that it will be reasonably fit for human habitation.[235] This warranty avails only the first purchaser from the builder and the limitation period (six years) will start to run when the defective work is done, not when it comes to the purchaser's notice. The latter rule is, however, somewhat mitigated by the fact that if the builder knowingly covers up defective work this will constitute concealment of the cause of action so that time will not run until the purchaser discovers, or could with reasonable diligence have discovered, the defect.[236] In practical terms, the NHBC insurance scheme, which is considered below, is a good deal more important than the implied contractual warranties. While the law of contract may be of limited importance in the context of dwellings it may have a larger role to play in respect of defects in commercial buildings and in such cases recovery by, or for the benefit of, a subsequent transferee may be possible, either by the transferee if the original contracting party's claim is assigned to him[237] or by the contracting party for the benefit of the transferee.[238]

ii. Liability in Tort

As for the law of tort, the original position was that if the builder was not himself **10–048** the vendor he was liable for injury caused by negligent work, but if he was also vendor he enjoyed an immunity from suit once the property had been transferred. The rule, which may have been based on an unwillingness to allow contractual and tortious duties to exist concurrently, was established before *Donoghue v Stevenson* and survived that decision.[239] This immunity has now disappeared from the common law and in any event was firmly buried from January 1, 1974 by s.3 of the Defective Premises Act 1972 which provides that:

> "[W]here work of construction, repair, maintenance or demolition or any other work[240] is done on or in relation to premises any duty of care owed because of the doing of the work, to persons who might reasonably be expected to be affected by defects in the state of the premises created by the doing of the work shall not be abated by the subsequent disposal of the premises."

---

[233] Thus there is no implied warranty if the house is already completed before sale.

[234] The Supply of Goods and Services Act 1982 s.13, seems to apply but not to add anything of substance.

[235] *Hancock v BW Brazier (Anerley) Ltd* [1966] 1 W.L.R. 1317.

[236] Limitation Act 1980 s.32(1)(b); *King v Victor Parsons & Co* [1973] 1 W.L.R. 29.

[237] *Darlington BC v Wiltshier Northern* [1995] 1 W.L.R. 68.

[238] See *Linden Gardens Trust Ltd v Lenesta Sludge Disposal* [1994] 1 A.C. 85 and *Alfred McAlpine Construction Ltd v Panatown Ltd* [2001] 1 A.C. 518. As the latter case shows, the builder may give some direct undertaking to the third party. In some cases, the Contracts (Rights of Third Parties) Act 1999 may also be applicable.

[239] *Otto v Bolton* [1936] 2 K.B. 46. Winfield 52 L.Q.R. 313 suggested that if no one had ever sued in tort for injury arising from a ruinous house until after *Donoghue v Stevenson* the "jerry-builder" would then have been held to be the "neighbour" of the injured person.

[240] To be construed *ejusdem generis*?

10–049   **No liability for mere defect in quality.** The question which has given rise to difficulty in tort is for what type of loss is the builder liable? Personal injuries caused by structural defects in premises, though not unknown,[241] are rare in comparison with complaints that the premises are inadequately built and are deteriorating, perhaps with a long-term threat of collapse. It was to just such cases that the courts in the 1970s extended the liability of the builder, even though a house which threatens to collapse (or even one which does collapse, causing no injury to person or other property) is surely analogous to a manufactured article which is fragile and inferior in quality, matters which have traditionally been looked on as the province of contract rather than tort. In other words, the loss, though having physical symptoms in the form of, for example, cracks in walls, is in its nature economic. Orthodoxy was restored by the House of Lords in *Murphy v Brentwood DC*.[242] The case concerned only the liability of a local authority in connection with the approval of the plans of a house[243] but the reasoning is inescapably applicable to the builder's liability for defective premises—indeed much of the discussion is couched directly in terms of the builder's liability.[244] It is now clear that in the absence of a special relationship of proximity such as existed in *Junior Books v Veitchi*[245] (and which, it appears, does not normally exist between the builder and even the first purchaser of a standard house)[246] there is no liability in tort for defects in quality in the building. In fact, even the previous case law had not gone so far as to impose such liability in all cases[247] but had done so only where the defect in the premises presented an imminent danger to the health or safety of the persons occupying it.[248]

---

[241] See, e.g. *Otto v Bolton* [1936] 2 K.B. 46; *Sharpe v ET Sweeting & Son Ltd* [1963] 1 W.L.R. 665.

[242] [1991] 1 A.C. 398. Cooke 107 L.Q.R. 46; Howarth (1991) 50 C.L.J. 58; Markesinis and Deakin (1992) 55 M.L.R. 619; Wallace 107 L.Q.R. 228.

[243] The plans had been prepared by apparently competent consulting engineers, but since the authority was under no duty in respect of the loss in question the HL did not find it necessary to consider how far the authority was entitled to rely on the engineers.

[244] *DoE v Thomas Bates & Son Ltd* [1991] A.C. 499, decided on the same day, is a direct authority applying *Murphy* to a builder.

[245] [1983] 1 A.C. 520. See para.5–065.

[246] It is not entirely clear why this should be so with regard to the first purchaser. If even in the absence of a contract there may be a special relationship of proximity sufficiently akin to contract to attract liability for economic loss (*Junior Books*), should there not be such liability where there is a contract? In *Bryan v Maloney* (1995) 182 C.L.R. 609, the majority point out that this appears to be the classic instance of assumption of responsibility and actual reliance. Nevertheless, in *Lancashire and Cheshire Association of Baptist Churches Inc v Howard & Seddon Partnership* [1993] 3 All E.R. 467 liability in tort was denied even though there would seem to have been a clear contractual duty (the right of action for which was assumed to be statute-barred for the purpose of the proceedings). The decision in *Robinson v PE Jones* [2011] EWCA Civ 9; [2012] Q.B. 44 can be explained on the basis that the terms of the contract negated the assumption of responsibility but the Court of Appeal went further to deny that the contract could be the source of any such assumption in cases "beyond the realm of professional retainers" (at [76] per Jackson LJ).

[247] At least after *Anns v Merton LBC* [1978] A.C. 728.

[248] *Anns v Merton LBC* [1978] A.C. 728 at 760. The logic of this requirement lies in the fact that the local authority's duty of care (with which the cases were primarily concerned) originated in its functions under the public health legislation. Though the measure of damages is not much discussed in the case law, it seems that liability would only have been in such an amount as was necessary to avert the danger.

Essentially, the basis of this approach was that because, if the defect had not been discovered and someone had been injured, the defendant would have been liable for that injury on the principle of *Donoghue v Stevenson*, therefore it would be absurd to deny liability for the cost of preventing that injury arising.[249] However, this reasoning is now held to be fallacious because once, it is said, the defect becomes apparent (which is, ex hypothesi, the first point at which any claim can be made) it no longer presents a danger:[250]

"The injury will not now ever occur unless the claimant causes it to do so by courting a danger of which he is aware and his expenditure [in removing the danger] is incurred not in preventing an otherwise inevitable injury but in order to enable him to continue to use the property."

The argument that the loss is in truth economic and that the "averting of danger" does not change its nature is logically compelling, though it raises severe difficulties for an owner who simply cannot afford to abandon his house. The justification that if the claimant does not abandon the property and suffers injury he is the author of his own loss may, however, mislead if it is divorced from the underlying nature of his complaint. Suppose, for example, that the claimant owns property which is initially sound and the defendant by negligence causes it damage which renders it dangerous. It may well be that if the claimant chooses to remain in the property (unrepaired because he cannot immediately afford to repair it) rather than move into temporary accommodation, he is the author of his own loss if the property collapses on him,[251] but no one would suggest that he was therefore precluded from recovering the cost of repairs from the defendant. In such a case he had something which was perfect and which was rendered imperfect by what the defendant did. In *Murphy* the essence of the complaint was that the property was imperfect from the beginning. It was not "damaged"; it was simply worth less than he paid for it.

Personal injury caused by a known defect. The argument that if the house   10–050
owner remained and suffered injury he would be the author of his own loss was advanced in a slightly different context in *Targett v Torfaen BC*[252] where the claimant was a weekly tenant of a council house and was aware of the defect and the danger presented by it, but had failed to persuade the council to repair it. The Court of Appeal, in finding for the claimant, distinguished *Murphy* on the ground that the House of Lords was there concerned with the nature of the loss and could not be taken to have intended to lay down any absolute rule to the effect that a claimant suffering personal injury from a defective building was automatically barred by his knowledge of the defect.[253] So to hold would be absurdly

---

[249] See Lord Oliver in *Murphy v Brentwood DC* [1991] 1 A.C. 398 at 488. In *Dutton v Bognor Regis UDC* [1972] 1 Q.B. 373 at 396 (overruled in *Murphy*) Lord Denning MR described any attempted distinction between the two cases as "impossible".

[250] *Murphy v Brentwood DC* [1991] 1 A.C. 398 at 488 per Lord Oliver. See also *DoE v Thomas Bates & Son Ltd* [1991] 1 A.C. 499 (building safe if used below design loading).

[251] The case is more obvious with continued use of a chattel, e.g. an unroadworthy car.

[252] [1992] 3 All E.R. 27.

[253] The CA pointed out that its own decision in *Rimmer v Liverpool CC* [1985] Q.B. 1, which was inconsistent with this view, had not been referred to in *Murphy*.

unrealistic[254] for many householders and the question should rather be determined by asking whether in all the circumstances it was reasonable, in the light of the danger, to remain in the house.[255]

10–051   **Damage to "other property".** *Murphy v Brentwood* in no way casts doubt upon the proposition that if a negligently constructed building causes damage to other property, whether of the claimant or a third party, the defendant is liable for that.[256] So if the claimant's house collapses he can, at least on the assumption that he was unaware of imminent danger, recover damages for loss of the contents. However, a certain amount of obscurity still remains on the question of what is "other property". In *D&F Estates Ltd v Church Commissioners*[257] (which had anticipated many of the issues in *Murphy*) Lord Bridge had, to use his words in *Murphy*:[258]

> "[M]ooted the possibility that in complex structures or complex chattels one part of a structure or chattel might, when it caused damage to another part of the same structure or chattel, be regarded in the law of tort as having caused damage to 'other property' for the purpose of the application of *Donoghue v Stevenson* principles."

This theory of the complex structure was not embraced with any enthusiasm in the *D&F Estates* case, rather it was offered as a possible explanation of the line of cases centring on *Anns v Merton*, which the House of Lords was at that stage unwilling to overrule without further argument. It is clear as a result of *Murphy* that these cases cannot be supported in this way. When a single builder builds a house from the foundations upwards he is creating a single, integrated unit and it is completely unrealistic to argue that the foundations (the usual source of problems) are one piece of property and, when they fail, they cause damage to "other" property—the walls, floors, etc. of the house.[259] However, some difficult and perhaps arbitrary lines will still have to be drawn. If, for example, something ancillary to the building (say, the central heating boiler) malfunctions and sets the building on fire then the manufacturer of the boiler (or the negligent installer) would be liable for the damage to the building. Lords Keith and Bridge would be willing to extend this to the electrical system of the building[260] and Lord Jauncey would even go so far as to bring within this principle a case where a separate contractor had negligently installed the steel frame on which the structure of the building depended.[261]

---

254 *Targett v Torfaen BC* [1992] 3 All E.R. 27 at 37 per Nicholls VC.

255 Both *Targett* and *Rimmer* concern lettings but no distinction can be drawn between tenants and purchasers. If anything, the former are likely to be in a better position to find alternative accommodation than the latter.

256 Illustrated by *Bellefield Computer Services v E Turner & Sons* [2000] B.L.R. 97 and [2002] EWCA Civ 1823; [2003] Lloyd's Rep. P.N. 53.

257 [1989] A.C. 177.

258 *Murphy v Brentwood DC* [1991] 1 A.C. 398 at 476.

259 *Broster v Galliard Docklands Ltd* [2011] EWHC 1722 (TCC); [2011] B.L.R. 569 (no distinction between roof and rest of the building). The position was held to be different where the defendants inserted underpinning (itself defective) to cure an existing defect: *Jacobs v Morton & Partners* (1996) 72 B.L.R. 92.

260 *Murphy v Brentwood DC* [1991] 1 A.C 398 at 470–478.

261 *Murphy v Brentwood DC* [1991] 1 A.C. 398 at 497; cf. *Linklaters Business Services v Sir Robert McAlpine Ltd* [2010] EWHC 2931 (TCC); [2010] Con L.R. 211 at [115]–[119]. The suggestions in

Exceptional recovery of "pre-emptive repairs" to the defective property?   10–052
Even where no physical damage has been done there remains the possibility that
the cost of "pre-emptive repairs" may be recoverable in one situation. Lord
Bridge suggested[262] that:

> "[I]f a building stands so close to the boundary of the building owner's land that after discovery
> of the dangerous defect it remains a potential source of injury to persons or property on
> neighbouring land or on the highway, the building owner ought, in principle, to be entitled to
> recover in tort from the negligent builder the cost of obviating the danger."

His Lordship did not set out the reasoning behind this possible exception, but it
could perhaps be justified on the basis that the building would constitute a
nuisance in respect of which the adjoining landowner[263] would be able to obtain
an injunction requiring repair or demolition.[264] Alternatively, it may represent a
rather broader principle whereby the claimant may recover the cost of removing a
danger which threatens others[265] (for example members of his family, visitors and
even trespassers) and for which the defendant is responsible. If this is confined to
the cost of demolition where that is less than the cost of repairs it does not
represent too serious a derogation from the reasoning upon which *Murphy* is
based.

The position in other jurisdictions. While *Murphy v Brentwood* certainly   10–053
clarified the law, it has been the subject of widespread criticism and three major
Commonwealth courts have declined to accept it. In *Winnipeg Condominium
Corp v Bird Construction Co*[266] the Supreme Court of Canada held that a remote
purchaser might recover in negligence against a builder the cost of remedying
dangerous defects in the building. In *Bryan v Maloney*[267] the majority of the High
Court of Australia held that such a purchaser might recover in respect of defects
in quality which rendered a house less valuable even though they presented no
danger.[268] In the New Zealand case of *Invercargill CC v Hamlin*,[269] as in *Murphy*
itself, the liability of the builder was not directly in issue because he had gone out

---

The Orjula [1995] 2 Lloyd's Rep. 395 and *Payne v John Setchell Ltd* [2002] P.N.L.R. 146 that
Murphy "disapproves" the complex structure theory is, with respect, something of an over-
simplification.

[262] *Murphy v Brentwood DC* [1991] A.C. 398 at 475.

[263] Or the local authority under the "statutory nuisance" procedure: para.15–006.

[264] Though the builder may be said to have created the nuisance, no injunction could be obtained
against him because he is not in occupation. Though the building owner's loss is still "economic", it
seems just that the builder should have to pay the cost, imposed on the house owner by law, of
averting the threatened collapse.

[265] See *The Orjula* [1995] 2 Lloyd's Rep. 395, where Mance J held it arguable that it could apply to
the cost of decontamination work on a cargo ordered by harbour authorities.

[266] (1995) 121 D.L.R. (4th) 193 (thereby reviving the reasoning in the dissent in *Rivtow Marine v
Washington Iron Works* (1973) 40 D.L.R. (3d) 530).

[267] (1995) 182 C.L.R. 609. See, however, the criticism by Clarke JA of the assumptions upon which
this case is based in *Woolahra MC v Sved* (1996) 40 N.S.W.L.R. 101 (in which the majority found an
absence of reliance on the facts); *Fangrove Pty Ltd v Tod Group Holdings Pty Ltd* [1999] 2 Qd. R.
236.

[268] Brennan J, dissenting, would have imposed liability, in line with the *Winnipeg* case, if the
expenditure had been to remove a danger. Cf. *Woolcock St Investments Pty Ltd v CDG Pty Ltd* [2004]
HCA 16; 216 C.L.R. 515 (no duty because no duty in circumstances to initial purchaser).

[269] [1994] 3 N.Z.L.R. 513.

of business, but the New Zealand Court of Appeal rejected the whole line of English development leading up to *Murphy* by imposing liability upon the local authority for negligence in inspection during construction.[270] The decision was upheld by the Privy Council[271] on the bases that: (1) New Zealand courts were entitled to develop their version of the common law in accordance with local policy considerations and community expectations, of which they were the best judge;[272] and (2) there were differences in the statutory backgrounds, in particular the existence in England of the Defective Premises Act 1972, which had been an important factor lying behind the decision in *Murphy*.

10–054 **Claims against local authorities.** As we have seen, *Murphy v Brentwood*, like most of the earlier building cases, was a claim against the local authority. The House of Lords in *Murphy* agreed with the reasoning in *Anns v Merton* in so far as it had held that any liability of the local authority could not be more extensive than that of the builder, who is, after all, primarily responsible. If the duty of the local authority is co-extensive with that of the builder then the authority would be liable in the comparatively rare case where there is personal injury or damage to other property. However, the House of Lords did not have to decide whether the local authority's liability extended even this far and the decision should not therefore be taken as approval of *Anns* even to this very limited extent.[273] This issue is part of the wider question of how far statutory functions which do not attract an action for breach of statutory duty can nevertheless be the basis of a common law duty of care.[274]

10–055 **Claims against the house owner for defective work.** Finally, what of the house owner himself? If he does work on his house in a negligent manner and this injures a subsequent owner then there would be liability in negligence.[275] If, however, he has not created the danger by his own action but knew or ought to have known about it at the time of sale it is unlikely that any liability would be imposed upon him. It is true that such a liability has been imposed upon a trader

---

[270] The position is different with commercial buildings: *Te Mata Properties Ltd v Hastings DC* [2008] NZCA 446; [2009] 1 N.Z.L.R. 460; *Queenstown Lakes DC v Charterhall Trustees Ltd* [2009] NZCA 374.

[271] *Invercargill City Council v Hamlin* [1996] A.C. 624.

[272] A fortiori this is the case for Canadian and Australian courts, since there was no appeal from those jurisdictions. Lord Lloyd referred to the majority view in the High Court of Australia in *Bryan v Maloney* as "a possible and indeed respectable view".

[273] Lord Bridge said [1991] 1 A.C. 398 at 479: "I am content for present purposes to assume, though I am by no means satisfied that the assumption is correct, that where the local authority . . . have in fact approved the defective plans or inspected the defective foundations and negligently failed to discover the defect, their potential liability in tort is co-extensive with that of the builder."

[274] See para.5–067.

[275] *Hone v Benson* (1978) 248 E.G. 1013; Defective Premises Act 1972 s.3. For mere defects of quality there is of course no liability because of *Murphy v Brentwood*.

disposing of goods[276] but such a great departure from the principle of caveat emptor would, in the case of realty, be open only to the House of Lords[277] or the legislature.[278]

iii.   Statute

Defective Premises Act 1972. A recurrent theme of the speeches in *Murphy v Brentwood* is the need for the courts not to trespass upon ground already covered by parliamentary action. Some years before the decision in *Dutton v Bognor Regis Urban DC* started the short-lived revolution in the common law the issue of liability for defective premises was referred to the Law Commission and the result was the Defective Premises Act 1972, which was passed more or less contemporaneously with *Dutton's* case and which came into force on January 1, 1974.[279] It cannot be pretended that the development of the law in this area provides a model in law reform techniques.[280] The common law developments had the effect of making the Act something of a dead letter but *Murphy v Brentwood* has now restored it to primacy. The provisions of the Act cannot be excluded or restricted by any agreement.[281]

10–056

The duty owed. Section 1 of the Act imposes upon persons who undertake work[282] for, or in connection with, the provision[283] of a dwelling[284] a statutory duty to see that the work taken on is done[285] in a workmanlike or professional manner, with proper materials and so that as regards that work the dwelling will be fit for habitation when completed. This is a single composite duty.[286] It is in some ways stricter than a duty of care. It corresponds closely with the implied warranty at common law in a contract for the construction of a house[287] and in

10–057

---

[276] *Andrews v Hopkinson* [1957] 1 Q.B. 229 (dealer selling goods to a finance company to be let by it to the claimant on hire-purchase terms).

[277] See *Rimmer v Liverpool CC* [1985] Q.B. 1 (a landlord-tenant case).

[278] It may be of some significance that the Defective Premises Bill, cl.3, would have made the "mere" vendor liable in respect of defects of which he knew, but this was rejected by Parliament.

[279] See Law Com. No.40 (1970).

[280] *Sparham-Souter v Town and Country Developments (Essex) Ltd* [1976] Q.B. 858 at 876 per Roskill LJ: "[I]n the [early 1970s] law reform was being pursued through two different channels—the Law Commission and Parliament on the one hand, and the courts on the other—without either apparently appreciating what developments the other was seeking to make."

[281] Section 6(3).

[282] Or arrange the work in question "in the course of a business" (s.1(4)(a)): see *Zennstrom v Fagot* [2013] EWHC 288 (TCC); 147 Con L.R. 162.

[283] This does not include work of rectification (*Jacobs v Morton & Partners* (1996) 72 B.L.R. 92) or improvement (*Jenson v Faux* [2011] EWCA Civ 423; [2011] 1 W.L.R. 3038) to an existing building.

[284] Industrial and commercial premises are therefore outside the scope of this section. Such premises are also outside the scope of the NHBC scheme referred to in para.10–058.

[285] The Act applies as much to failing to do necessary work as to doing work badly: *Andrews v Schooling* [1991] 1 W.L.R. 783.

[286] *Alexander v Mercouris* [1979] 1 W.L.R. 1270; *Harrison v Shepherd Homes Ltd* [2011] EWHC 1811 (TCC); [2011] 27 Con L.J. 709; *Bole v Huntsbuild Ltd* [2009] EWCA Civ 1146; 127 Con. L.R. 154.

[287] See para.10–047.

that context it has been held that the warranty in relation to materials is strict.[288] The range of persons on whom the duty is imposed therefore goes beyond the builder himself and includes the architect[289] and surveyor and any sub-contractors involved,[290] though the manufacturer of standard components is not covered.[291] The duty is owed not only to the persons ordering the work but also to every person who then or later acquires an interest (whether legal or equitable) in the dwelling. The duty is therefore a statutory hybrid, having characteristics of both contract and tort: on the one hand, it covers mere defects of quality (provided they make the house unfit for human habitation) without any necessity for imminent danger of personal injury; on the other hand it may pass along a chain of purchasers notwithstanding the lack of privity between them and the builder.

10–058 **Scope of the Act.** For many years the operation of the Act was very substantially restricted because it has no application to houses protected by an "approved scheme".[292] In practice this was the scheme operated by the National House-Building Council (NHBC), which covers the great majority of newly-constructed dwelling-houses. The NHBC scheme, though by no means unlimited, generally provides superior cover in comparison with the Act because claims for major structural defects may be made for up to 10 years and, although the primary responsibility for defects in the initial period lies upon the builder, his liability is underwritten by the scheme. However, the NHBC no longer submits the scheme for approval and the Act now has a much wider field of operation.

The protection offered by the Act is still very much less favourable to the claimant than the common law cases struck down by *Murphy v Brentwood* because the six-year limitation period begins to run when the dwelling is completed[293] whereas at common law time might start to run at a later date, when some physical symptoms appeared (though they might not then necessarily be observable by the owner). Indeed, Parliament by the Latent Damage Act 1986 sought to improve the claimant's position still further by providing, in actions for negligence, an alternative limitation period of three years running from the time when the claimant could reasonably have known about the damage (subject to a "long-stop" of 15 years from the last act of negligence) and specifically providing

---

[288] *Hancock v BW Brazier (Anerley) Ltd* [1966] 1 W.L.R. 1317; see also Supply of Goods and Services Act 1982 s.4

[289] *Payne v John Setchell Ltd* [2002] P.N.L.R. 146 (structural engineer).

[290] See also s.2(4) (developers), but note the important provisions of s.1(2), (3), which will generally relieve a person of liability if he does the work properly in accordance with instructions given by another. This would appear to cover not only the builder on whom the client imposes detailed specifications, but also the sub-contractor who receives instructions from the builder. However, "a person shall not be treated . . . as having given instructions for the doing of work merely because he has agreed to the work being done in a specified manner".

[291] He may, however, be liable under the Consumer Protection Act 1987 Pt I (para.11–023) and if he were negligent he might be in breach of a common law duty. A builder held liable under s.1 might anyway seek a contractual indemnity from him. A local authority exercising powers of inspection probably cannot be said to, "take on work for or in connection with the provision of a dwelling"; but cf. the doubts of Lord Denning MR and Roskill LJ in *Sparham-Souter v Town and Country Developments (Essex) Ltd* [1976] Q.B. 858 at 870, 877.

[292] See s.2.

[293] Section 1(5).

for the case where the property was acquired by a subsequent purchaser.[294] The 1986 Act is not confined to building cases but they were undoubtedly the prime cause of its enactment and *Murphy v Brentwood* removed most of them from its ambit by declaring that there is simply no cause of action in the first place.[295]

Building Regulations. Finally, there are the Building Regulations,[296] which impose detailed obligations on builders. In *Anns v Merton* Lord Wilberforce thought that the builder might be liable for breach of statutory duty by reason of non-compliance with building byelaws, the then equivalent of the building regulations,[297] though this was doubted even before *Murphy v Brentwood*.[298] It seems inconceivable that Lord Wilberforce's view can represent the law after *Murphy*, especially bearing in mind that there has existed since 1974 a statutory provision creating just such a cause of action but which has never been brought into force.[299]

10–059

B. Lessor

Common law. A lease is a contract as well as an estate in land, but at common law the range of implied terms relating to the fitness of the premises is very limited. There is an implied warranty in the letting of furnished premises that they are fit for occupation at the commencement of the tenancy[300] and the House of Lords has held that in the case of a "high rise" block, obligations may be implied with regard to the maintenance of such necessary things as stairs and lifts.[301] These obligations sound in contract and hence avail only the tenant, unless the Contracts (Rights of Third Parties) Act 1999 applies.[302] As for tort, the lessor's position was equated with that of the vendor and he was immune from liability for negligence in respect of defects created by him before the demise.[303] This immunity has now died along with that of the vendor,[304] subject to the point that the range of damage recoverable is restricted by *Murphy v Brentwood*.

10–060

---

[294] See para.26–093.

[295] Where there is damage to other property or personal injury time will run under the general law of limitation from the date when that injury or damage occurs.

[296] Now SI 2010/2214.

[297] [1978] A.C. 728 at 759. Cf. *Solomons v R. Gertzenstein Ltd* [1954] 2 Q.B. 243 (London Building Acts).

[298] [1991] 1 A.C. 398. See also *Worlock v SAWS* (1982) 26 E.G. 774; *Perry v Tendring DC* (1984) 30 Build. L.R. 118.

[299] Building Act 1984 s.38 (formerly Health and Safety at Work, etc. Act 1974 s.71). Is there another example of a provision which has lain dormant for 30 years? If it were brought into force it is very arguable that the definition of "damage" would lead to the same result as under *Murphy*.

[300] *Collins v Hopkins* [1923] 2 K.B. 617.

[301] *Liverpool CC v Irwin* [1977] A.C. 239. As to licences for occupation of business premises, see *Wettern Electric Ltd v Welsh Development Agency* [1983] Q.B. 796.

[302] Which will require that the contract: (a) purports to confer a benefit on the third party; and (b) sufficiently "identifies" him.

[303] *Robbins v Jones* (1863) 15 C.B.(N.S.) 221 ("Fraud apart, there is no law against letting a tumbledown house": at 240 per Erle CJ).

[304] *Anns v Merton LBC* [1978] A.C. 728 was a case of a long lease, but where the landlord did not create the defect, only the House of Lords can impose a duty: *Rimmer v Liverpool CC* [1985] Q.B. 1; *McNerny v Lambeth BC* [1989] 19 E.G. 77; *Boldack v East Lindsey DC* (1999) 31 H.L.R. 41.

10–061 **Statute.** Sections 1 and 3 of the Defective Premises Act, which have been discussed above in relation to vendors, apply equally to lessors.[305] Statute, however, also imposes certain non-excludable obligations during the currency of the lease. By s.8 of the Landlord and Tenant Act 1985 there is implied into contracts for the letting of a house at a very low rent an undertaking by the landlord that it is, and will be kept, fit for human habitation, but the rent limits are so low that the section is never in practice applicable.[306] By s.11 of the same Act[307] there is imposed upon the landlord in relation to leases for less than seven years an obligation to carry out certain repairs to the structure and to installations for sanitation and the supply of water, gas and electricity. Though primarily designed to allow the tenant to compel the landlord to do repairs, these provisions would also avail the tenant if, for example, he suffered personal injury as a result of the landlord's breach of obligation, but being contractual covenants their breach gave rise to no liability towards the tenant's family or visitors. This was first changed by s.4 of the Occupiers' Liability Act 1957, which imposed on the landlord a tortious duty of care in respect of dangers arising from default in his repairing obligations under the lease.[308] This was replaced and carried very much further by s.4 of the Defective Premises Act 1972.[309] Where premises are let under a tenancy which puts on the landlord an obligation to the tenant for the maintenance or repair of the premises, the landlord owes to all persons who might reasonably be expected to be affected by defects in the state of the premises a duty to take such care as is reasonable in all the circumstances to see that they are reasonably safe from personal injury or damage to their property caused by a defect within the maintenance or repairing obligation.[310]

The duty of care is not limited by requirements of notice which might be relevant to the contractual obligation.[311] Most significant of all, a landlord who has a power, express or implied, to enter and repair is to be treated for the purposes of the section (but no other[312]) as if he were under an obligation to the tenant to repair.[313] The obvious beneficiaries of s.4 are the tenant's family and visitors, but other persons who might reasonably be expected to be affected

---

[305] See para.10–056.

[306] *Quick v Taff-Ely BC* [1986] Q.B. 809 at 817.

[307] Extended by the Housing Act 1988 s.116, to cover parts of the building and installations outside the demised premises.

[308] Whether those obligations arose from express covenants in the lease or from the equivalent statutory obligations existing before the Landlord and Tenant Act 1985. Care should be taken to note that we are now concerned with dangers arising on the premises which the landlord has demised. If he retains part in his own occupation (e.g. staircases and lifts in a block of flats), he is liable for that *qua* occupier under the general provisions of the Occupiers' Liability Act.

[309] Described as "somewhat tortuous provisions": *Hannon v Hillingdon Homes Ltd* [2012] EWHC 1437 (QB).

[310] "Safety" is narrower than "fitness for habitation": Law Com. No.238, s.5.28. Nor is the landlord required to make safe an existing "design" defect: *Alker v Collingwood Housing Association* [2007] EWCA Civ 343; [2007] 1 W.L.R. 2230.

[311] *Sykes v Harry* [2001] EWCA Civ 167; [2001] Q.B. 1014.

[312] Thus the tenant could not compel such a landlord to repair under the Landlord and Tenant Act 1985 s.17.

[313] Section 4(4). *Smith v Bradford Metropolitan Council* (1982) 44 P.&C.R. 171; *Barrett v Lounova Ltd* [1989] 1 All E.R. 351. Such a power is said to exist in the case of small houses let on periodic tenancies (*Mint v Good* [1951] 1 K.B. 517, para.15–055).

include trespassers,[314] neighbours and passers-by[315] and even the tenant himself, notwithstanding the existence of a contractual obligation to him.[316] The tenant, however, is not owed any duty in respect of a defect arising from, or continuing because of, a failure to carry out an obligation expressly imposed on the tenant by the tenancy.[317]

---

[314] Cf. the position of the tenant-occupier himself: para.10–034.

[315] In other words the section creates liability in nuisance, though it probably adds nothing to the common law in this respect: para.15–055.

[316] *Sykes v Harry* [2001] EWCA Civ 167; [2001] Q.B. 1014.

[317] Section 4(4).

CHAPTER 11

LIABILITY FOR DEFECTIVE PRODUCTS[1]

This chapter is primarily concerned with the liability in tort of manufacturers **11–001** (and certain other transferors) of defective products but since transfers of products normally take place pursuant to a contract, a realistic picture of the incidence of liability can only be obtained by bearing the relevant contractual principles in mind. Where a claimant is injured by a product transferred to him under a contract of sale[2] he may rely, subject to any valid exemption clause,[3]

---

[1] Miller, *Product Liability and Safety Encyclopaedia*; Miller and Goldberg, *Products Liability*, 2nd edn (2004); Stapleton, *Product Liability* (1994); Grubb and Howells, *The Law of Product Liability* (2000); Whittaker, *Liability for Products* (2005).

[2] The duties of the creditor under a contract of hire-purchase are for practical purposes the same as those of a seller: see the Supply of Goods (Implied Terms) Act 1973, as amended by the Consumer Credit Act 1974. Under the Supply of Goods and Services Act 1982 similar terms are implied into other contracts for the transfer of goods (e.g. exchange) and hire of goods.

[3] If the purchaser is a "consumer" the clause will be void under the Unfair Contract Terms Act 1977, s.6(2). Otherwise it will be subject to a test of reasonableness: s.6(3).

upon the seller's implied undertakings as to compliance with description, satisfactory quality, fitness for purpose and compliance with sample under the Sale of Goods Act 1979. These undertakings give rise to absolute obligations, i.e. the seller is liable if the goods do not come up to the standard required by the Act even though he has taken all possible care that they should do so and is in no way to blame for the defect.[4] Though the purpose of these undertakings when they were being developed at common law was probably to allow the buyer a remedy for the financial loss he suffered in acquiring goods of inferior quality, it has been accepted for many years that they also allow recovery for consequential damage to other property and, most significantly, for personal injuries.[5]

The existence of this strict liability in the seller (often, in modern conditions, a much larger organisation than the manufacturer) means that as far as the purchaser is concerned his right of action in tort, dependent on proof of negligence, is often of academic interest and may only be utilised where the seller is insolvent or cannot, for some other reason, be successfully sued.[6] Where a contractual action is successfully pursued then, in theory, the implied terms in the chain of contracts between manufacturer and retailer will lead to the manufacturer bearing the ultimate responsibility, but in practice this chain may be broken by the insolvency of a "middleman" or by some valid exemption clause. The contractual liability outlined above is of no assistance to persons injured by the product who have not acquired any interests in it by contract—members of the purchaser's family,[7] passers-by[8] or donees from the buyer[9] and they will not generally be assisted by the Contracts (Rights of Third Parties) Act 1999.[10] It is this class of "ultimate consumers" who are most likely to seek to rely on tort.

1. LIABILITY AT COMMON LAW

11–002   **The origin of the ordinary claim in negeligence.** Before *Donoghue v Stevenson*[11] was decided in 1932, it was doubtful whether the transferor of a product owed any duty to the ultimate transferee (in the absence of a contractual

---

[4] He may, of course, have an indemnity under the contract of sale between him and his supplier, and so on up the chain to the manufacturer.

[5] *Godley v Perry* [1960] 1 W.L.R. 9; *Grant v Australian Knitting Mills Ltd* [1936] A.C. 85.

[6] There is nothing to prevent the claimant suing both seller (in contract) and manufacturer (in tort): *Grant v Australian Knitting Mills Ltd* [1936] A.C. 85. Furthermore, in the present state of the law there is nothing to prevent the claimant suing the seller in tort which he may do for the important advantage of a later starting point for the limitation period: *Nitrigin Eireann Teoranta v Inco Alloys Ltd* [1992] 1 All E.R. 854.

[7] *Evans v Triplex Safety Glass Co* [1936] 1 All E.R. 283.

[8] *Stennett v Hancock* [1939] 2 All E.R. 578.

[9] *Donoghue v Stevenson* [1932] A.C. 562; *Fisher v Harrods* [1966] 1 Lloyd's Rep. 500.

[10] Because a third party seeking to enforce a term in a contract to which he is not a party must show: (a) that the contract purported to confer a benefit on him; and (b) that he was identified by name, class or description in the contract. Nor will the Act generally be of assistance to the buyer from the retailer seeking to establish a contractual right against the manufacturer. However, art.6 Directive 1999/44 required that manufacturers' guarantees should be legally enforceable and the Sale and Supply of Goods to Consumers Regulations 2002 SI 3045/2002 made them so. They probably were already (as a collateral contract) where the buyer knew he would get one before he entered into the sale contract with the retailer.

[11] [1932] A.C. 562.

relationship between them) unless it belonged to the class of "dangerous chattels"[12] or was actually known to the transferor to be dangerous. The classification of products into those which are dangerous and those which are not is, however, an unsatisfactory one and Scrutton LJ confessed that he did not understand the difference: "[B]etween a thing dangerous in itself, as poison, and a thing not dangerous as a class, but by negligent construction dangerous as a particular thing. The latter, if anything, seems to me the more dangerous of the two; it is a wolf in sheep's clothing instead of an obvious wolf."[13] *Donoghue v Stevenson* finally established, by a majority of three to two, that apart from contract and without reference to any special rule about dangerous chattels, there are circumstances in which a person owes a duty of care in respect of products. Lord Atkin laid down the following principle[14] for both Scots and English law:[15]

> "A manufacturer of products, which he sells in such a form as to show that he intends them to reach the ultimate consumer in the form in which they left him with no reasonable possibility of intermediate examination and with the knowledge that the absence of reasonable care in the preparation or putting up of the products will result in an injury to the consumer's life or property, owes a duty to the consumer to take that reasonable care."

The category of dangerous chattels lingered on for some years but had expired by the 1950s. Now, apart from statute, there is no liability in tort for damage caused by products unless there is negligence and there is no class of product in respect of which there is no liability for negligence. There is simply the ordinary rule that the greater the risk the greater the precautions that must be taken to obviate it.[16] It is true that the law expects a great deal more care in the handling of a pound of dynamite than a pound of butter, but that is the result of the general law of negligence, not of the application of a special rule of law concerning dangerous things.

Effect of the Consumer Protection Act 1987. Liability under *Donoghue v Stevenson* stands completely untouched by the enactment of the principle of strict liability in the Consumer Protection Act 1987[17] but in practice claimants will be much more likely to rely upon the latter than upon the former and the existence of the Act may be a reason for not extending the common law liability.[18] However, recourse to the common law will remain necessary in some cases, for example where the loss takes the form of damage to property not intended for private use[19] or where the special limitation period under the Act has expired.[20]

11–003

---

[12] The "privity of contract fallacy" held that because the manufacturer (A) had a contract with the retailer (B) he could not owe a tort duty to the consumer (C).

[13] *Hodge v Anglo-American Oil Co* (1922) 12 Ll. L. Rep. 183 at 187.

[14] This is sometimes known as the "narrow rule" in *Donoghue v Stevenson*. The "wide rule" about the duty of care in general has been considered, para.5–015.

[15] [1932] A.C. at 599.

[16] *Read v J Lyons & Co* [1947] A.C. 156 at 172–173 per Lord Macmillan, at 180–181 per Lord Simonds.

[17] See para.11–015.

[18] Simon Brown LJ in *Hayes v Leo Scaffolding Ltd* Unreported December 3, 1996 CA.

[19] See para.11–024.

[20] See para.11–042.

A. Persons Liable

11–004   **Manufacturers, repairers, assemblers etc.** The principle laid down in *Donoghue v Stevenson* has been extended from manufacturers to include repairers,[21] fitters, erectors,[22] and assemblers.[23] Where a manufacturer of a finished article (such as a motor car) buys in components from another he is under a duty to consider their suitability and cannot rely blindly on the other to produce a good design.[24] The manufacturer's duty extends to taking steps (for example, warnings) concerning dangers which are discovered only after the product has gone into circulation.[25]

11–005   **Suppliers.** A mere distributor or supplier has not actively created the danger in the same way as a manufacturer but he, too, may be under a duty to make inquiries or carry out an inspection of the product and if it is dangerous for some reason of which he should have known, his failure to warn of it will then amount to negligence.[26] In *Andrews v Hopkinson*,[27] by arrangement with the claimant the defendant sold a second-hand car to a finance company and the company hired the car to the claimant under a hire-purchase agreement. The car was some 18 years old, and the defendant, who was a dealer in second-hand cars, had taken no steps to see that it was in a roadworthy condition although the car had been in his possession for a week. In fact the car had a defective steering mechanism which caused the claimant to have an accident a week after he took delivery of the car. Evidence showed that in an old car the danger spot is the steering mechanism and that the defect in question could have been discovered by a competent mechanic if the car had been jacked up. McNair J held that the defendant was liable and said:[28]

> "Having regard to the extreme peril involved in allowing an old car with a defective steering mechanism to be used on the road, I have no hesitation in holding that the defendant was guilty of negligence in failing to make the necessary examination, or at least in failing to warn the plaintiff that no such examination had been carried out."[29]

---

[21] *Stennett v Hancock* [1939] 2 All E.R. 578; *Haseldine v Daw* [1941] 2 K.B. 343.

[22] *Brown v Cotterill* (1934) 51 T.L.R. 21.

[23] *Howard v Furness-Houlder Argentine Lines Ltd* [1936] 2 All E.R. 296.

[24] *Winward v T.VR. Engineering* [1986] B.T.L.C. 366.

[25] *E Hobbs v Baxenden Chemical Co* [1992] 1 Lloyd's Rep. 54; *Hamble Fisheries Ltd v Gardner* [1999] 2 Lloyd's Rep. 1. See also *Carroll v Fearon* [1998] P.I.Q.R. P416.

[26] In the case of a gratuitous transfer, it is true that older authorities held that, unless the product was in the class of dangerous things, the transferor was liable only for wilful or reckless conduct, i.e. when he actually knew of the danger: *Gautret v Egerton* (1867) L.R. 2 C.P. 371 at 375; *Coughlin v Gillison* [1899] 1 Q.B. 145. The validity of these cases is now very doubtful (see *Griffiths v Arch Engineering Co Ltd* [1968] 3 All E.R. 217 at 220; Marsh (1950) 66 L.Q.R. 39) and it is submitted that in the modern law the gratuitous nature of the transfer is simply a factor to be taken into account in assessing what is reasonable care by the transferor. Cf. *Chaudhury v Prabhakar* [1989] 1 W.L.R. 29 (gratuitous agent inspecting property liable to principal, though the existence of a duty of care was conceded).

[27] [1957] 1 Q.B. 229. See also *White v John Warwick & Co* [1953] 1 W.L.R. 1285; *Griffiths v Arch Engineering Co Ltd* [1968] 3 All E.R. 217.

[28] *Andrews v Hopkinson* [1957] 1 Q.B. 229 at 237. Cf. *Rees v Saville* [1983] R.T.R. 332 (duty of private purchaser; MOT certificate).

[29] He was also prepared to hold the dealer liable on a collateral contract with the claimant.

Similarly, suppliers may be liable if they carelessly represent the goods to be harmless[30] without having made any adequate tests,[31] but it should not be thought that these cases impose a general duty on suppliers to subject all their goods to an exhaustive examination. The duty to examine will only arise if in all the circumstances they could reasonably be expected to carry out an examination. A second-hand car dealer may be expected to discover a patent defect in the steering mechanism of one of his cars, and a manufacturer and supplier of chemicals must take reasonable care to discover and give warning of industrial hazards arising out of the chemicals he supplies,[32] but a retail grocer, for example, cannot be expected to institute inspections to discover whether his tinned food is contaminated. He may be obliged to satisfy himself as to the reputation of his supplier[33] and he must certainly follow proper practices in keeping his wares but otherwise, unless the contamination was caused by his negligence or he actually knew of it, his only liability is to the actual purchaser under the contract of sale. If a third party becomes ill on eating the contaminated food, his remedy, if any, is against the manufacturer.

The effect of warnings. Given the potential liability for negligence of a supplier **11–006** of goods (particularly second-hand goods) for failing to trace defects is there any way in which he can protect himself other than by carrying out an adequate inspection? It is clear that any exclusion clause in the contract of sale or otherwise will generally be unenforceable under the Unfair Contract Terms Act 1977,[34] but a suitable warning of possible defects may be regarded not as an attempt to exclude liability but as a discharge of the duty of care. In this respect, *Hurley v Dyke*,[35] a claim arising before the Act, suggests that the supplier will be treated fairly leniently. The defendant, a garage owner, sold an old three-wheeler car by auction on terms that it was sold, "as seen and with all its faults and without warranty". It was then resold by the purchaser to one Clay and eight days later it crashed because of corrosion in the chassis, injuring the claimant passenger. It was conceded before the House of Lords that the defendant's duty would be satisfied by giving adequate warning to his purchaser and that if the defendant knew only that the car might be dangerous but had no knowledge of the specific defect the "all faults" terms on which it was sold would provide such a warning. The House seems to have thought these concessions rightly made and, no specific knowledge having been established, the claimant's claim failed. No concluded opinion was expressed on what the position would have been if the defendant had had knowledge of the defect but two judges said that it should not be assumed that on such facts he would be in breach of duty.[36]

---

[30] Those who test and certify goods may incur liability for negligence: *N v Medical Research Council* (1997) 7 Med. L.R. 309; *Perrett v Collins* [1998] 2 Lloyd's Rep. 255.

[31] *Watson v Buckley, Osborne, Garrett & Co* [1940] 1 All E.R. 174 (distributors of a dangerous hair dye held liable because they advertised it as positively harmless and requiring no tests); *Devilez v Boots Pure Drug Co* [1962] C.L.Y. 2015; *Goodchild v Vaclight* [1965] C.L.Y. 2669.

[32] *Vacwell Engineering Co Ltd v B.D.H. Chemicals Ltd* [1971] 1 Q.B. 88.

[33] *Fisher v Harrods* [1966] C.L.Y. 8148.

[34] See para.26–017.

[35] [1979] R.T.R. 265.

[36] Viscount Dilhorne and Lord Scarman. In such circumstances, or in the circumstances which actually obtained in *Hurley v Dyke*, the warning given may fall within the Unfair Contract Terms Act

B. Extension of Subject Matter

11–007 Liability in negligence has been extended from articles of food and drink and has been applied to, inter alia, kiosks,[37] tombstones,[38] hair dye,[39] industrial chemicals,[40] lifts,[41] motor cars[42] and pants.[43] Likewise the term "consumer" includes the ultimate user of the article[44] or anyone who is within physical proximity to it.[45] The significance of *Donoghue v Stevenson* in the context of liability for defective buildings has already been considered.[46] The duty of reasonable care extends not only to the manufacture, erection or repair of the product itself but also to any container,[47] package or pipe[48] in which it is distributed, and to the labels, directions or instructions for use that accompany it.[49] It may also extend to the information provided in a book, or map.[50]

C. Burden of Proof

11–008 The duty owed is that of reasonable care[51] and the burden of proving negligence is on the claimant. Although in *Donoghue v Stevenson*[52] itself Lord Macmillan said that in a case such as that[53] there was no justification for applying res ipsa loquitur,[54] the practice of the courts is to draw inferences of negligence in suitable product liability cases as much as in any other.[55] The question in each case is whether the claimant has given sufficient evidence to justify the inference of negligence against the defendant and he is not necessarily required to specify

---

1977 on the basis that rather than amounting to a discharge of the duty, it amounts to a notice which excludes or restricts "the relevant obligation or duty" (s.13(1)).

[37] *Paine v Colne Valley Electricity Supply Co* [1938] 4 All E.R. 803.

[38] *Brown v Cotterill* [1934] 51 T.L.R. 21.

[39] *Watson v Buckley* [1940] 1 Al E.R. 174.

[40] *Vacwell Engineering Co Ltd v BDH Chemicals Ltd* [1971] 1 Q.B. 88.

[41] *Haseldine v Daw* [1941] 2 K.B. 343.

[42] *Herschtal v Stewart & Ardern* [1940] 1 K.B. 155; *Andrews v Hopkinson* [1957] 1 Q.B. 229.

[43] *Grant v Australian Knitting Mills* [1936] A.C. 85.

[44] *Grant v Australian Knitting Mills* [1936] A.C. 85; *Griffiths v Arch Engineering Co Ltd* [1968] 3 All E.R. 217.

[45] *Brown v Cotterill* [1934] 51 T.L.R. 21 (child injured by falling tombstone); *Stennett v Hancock* [1939] 2 All E.R. 578 (pedestrian hit by flange of lorry wheel). In *Lambert v Lewis* [1978] 1 Lloyd's Rep. 610 manufacturers were held liable for a design defect in a vehicle coupling which caused a trailer to come adrift and injure the claimant. This was not challenged on appeal: [1982] A.C. 225.

[46] Ch.10.

[47] *Donoghue v Stevenson* [1932] A.C. 585.

[48] *Barnes v Irwell Valley Water Board* [1938] 2 All E.R. 650.

[49] *Watson v Buckley* [1940] 1 All E.R. 174; *Holmes v Ashford* [1950] 2 All E.R. 76; *Vacwell Engineering Co Ltd v BDH Chemicals Ltd* [1971] 1 Q.B. 88; *Thompson v Johnson & Johnson* [1991] 2 VR. 449.

[50] *Munro v Sturrock* [2012] CSIH 35.

[51] A manufacturer is not liable on the ground only that an independent contractor employed by him had been negligent: *Taylor v Rover Co Ltd* [1966] 1 W.L.R. 1491.

[52] *Donoghue v Stevenson* [1932] A.C. 585 at 622.

[53] Decomposed snail found in a bottle of ginger beer (allegedly).

[54] See para.6–037.

[55] *Carroll v Fearon* [1998] P.I.Q.R. P416; *Divya v Toyo Tire & Rubber Co Ltd* [2011] EWHC 1993 (QB).

what the defendant did wrong.[56] Indeed, any other rule would stultify the principle of *Donoghue v Stevenson*, for normally it will be impossible for a claimant to bring evidence of particular negligent acts or omissions occurring in the defendant's manufacturing processes.

In *Mason v Williams & Williams Ltd*[57] the claimant was injured while using a cold chisel manufactured by the defendants and which was too hard for its purpose. Finnemore J held that since the claimant had established that nothing had happened to the chisel after it left the defendants' factory which could have caused the excessive hardness, the defendants' negligence was established. It is suggested that the claimant will generally discharge his burden of proof by showing that the article was defective and that, on a balance of probabilities, the defect arose in the course of manufacture by the defendant. In many cases in practice this comes very close to the imposition of a strict liability, for even if the defendant gives evidence that the quality control system in his factory complies with approved practice, there is still the possibility—indeed it perhaps becomes stronger by this very evidence—that one of his servants was careless and prevented that system operating correctly, in which case he remains liable, though vicariously rather than for breach of his personal duty.[58]

D. Possibility of Alternative Cause

In *Grant v Australian Knitting Mills Ltd*,[59] the Judicial Committee held that the **11–009** defendants were liable to the ultimate purchaser of some pants which they had manufactured and which contained a chemical that gave the claimant a skin disease when he wore them. It was argued for the defendants that as they dispatched the pants in paper packets of six sets there was greater possibility of intermediate tampering with the goods before they reached the user than there was with the sealed bottle in *Donoghue*'s case, but the court held that: "[T]he decision in that case did not depend on the bottle being stoppered and sealed; the essential point in this regard was that the article should reach the consumer or user subject to the same defect as it had when it left the manufacturer."[60]

Mere possibility of interference did not affect their liability. There must, however, be sufficient evidence that the defect existed when the article left the manufacturer's hands and that it was not caused later. In *Evans v Triplex Safety Glass Co Ltd*,[61] the claimant bought a motor car fitted with a "Triplex Toughened Safety Glass" windscreen of the defendants' manufacture. A year later, when the car was being used, the windscreen suddenly and for no apparent reason broke

---

[56] *Grant v Australian Knitting Mills* [1936] A.C. 85 at 101 per Lord Wright: "The appellant is not required to lay his finger on the exact person in all the chain who was responsible, or to specify what he did wrong. Negligence is found as a matter of inference from the existence of the defects taken in conjunction with all the known circumstances".

[57] [1955] 1 W.L.R. 549.

[58] See *Grant v Australian Knitting Mills* [1936] A.C. 85 at 101; *Daniels v White & Sons* [1938] 4 All E.R. 258 is hard to reconcile with *Grant*'s case and MacKenna J refused to follow it in *Hill v J Crowe (Cases)* [1978] 1 All E.R. 812.

[59] [1936] A.C. 85.

[60] [1936] A.C. 85 at 106–107.

[61] [1936] 1 All E.R. 283. Cf. *Mason v Williams & Williams Ltd* [1955] 1 W.L.R. 549.

into many fragments and injured the occupants of the car. The defendants were held not liable for the following reasons: (1) the lapse of time between the purchase and the accident; (2) the possibility that the glass may have been strained when screwed into its frame; (3) the opportunity of intermediate examination by the intermediate seller; and (4) the breaking of the glass may have been caused by something other than a defect in manufacture. By contrast, in *Carroll v Fearon*,[62] although the tyre, the bursting of which caused the accident, was seven years old and three-quarters worn, there was evidence of a manufacturing defect and the action against the manufacturer succeeded.

The use of the article by the claimant for a purpose materially different from that for which the maker designed it or which he might reasonably be taken to have contemplated will also defeat a claim, but use for a different but similar purpose does not ipso facto absolve him from liability. The question here is one of fact and degree,[63] and it is suggested that the right thing to ask is whether the cause of the claimant's injury was the defect in the article or the claimant's own misuse of it.[64]

E.   Intermediate Examination

11–010   As originally formulated by Lord Atkin the principle in *Donoghue v Stevenson* applies where there is, "no reasonable possibility of intermediate examination". These words have been the subject of much analysis, "almost as if they formed part of a statute"[65] but the better view is that they do not constitute an independent requirement which the claimant must satisfy but rather are to be taken into account in determining whether the injury to the claimant was foreseeable.[66] Even a probability of an intermediate examination will not exonerate the defendant unless it gives him reason to expect that it will reveal the defect and that this will result in the elimination of the defect or at least the claimant's being warned of it in such a way as to make him safe.[67]

In *Griffiths v Arch Engineering Co Ltd*[68] the claimant borrowed from the first defendants a portable grinding tool which had been lent to them by its owners, the second defendants. The tool was in a dangerous condition because an incorrect part had been fitted to it at some time by a servant of the second defendants, and the claimant was injured in consequence. Although the first defendants had an opportunity of examining the tool, the second defendants had no reason to suppose that an examination would actually be carried out and they

---

[62] *Carroll v Fearon* [1998] P.I.Q.R. P416.

[63] *Davie v New Merton Board Mills Ltd* [1957] 2 Q.B. 368 at 378–379 per Ashworth J. The manufacturers' liability was not in issue on appeal: [1959] A.C. 604.

[64] If both are causes, then damages should be reduced under the Law Reform (Contributory Negligence) Act 1945, as in *Griffiths v Arch Engineering Co Ltd* [1968] 3 All E.R. 217.

[65] *M/S Aswan Engineering Establishment Co v Lupdine Ltd* [1987] 1 W.L.R. 1 at 22 per Lloyd LJ.

[66] *M/S Aswan Engineering Establishment Co v Lupdine Ltd* [1987] 1 W.L.R. 1 at 23.

[67] *McIlveen v Charlesworth Developments* [1982] N.I. 216 at 221; *Pearson Education Ltd v Charter Partnership Ltd* [2007] EWCA Civ 130; [2007] B.L.R 324. It may not be so much a matter of intermediate examination as of intermediate treatment.

[68] [1968] 3 All E.R. 217; *Lambert v Lewis* [1978] 1 Lloyd's Rep. 610 (point not involved on appeal [1982] A.C. 225). Cf. *Taylor v Rover Co Ltd* [1966] 1 W.L.R. 1491.

were liable to the claimant. The fact that the first defendants were also liable to the claimant meant not that the second defendants had a defence to the claimant's claim but that the case was one for ultimate apportionment of liability between the defendants.[69] On the other hand, in *Kubach v Hollands*[70] a manufacturer sold a chemical to an intermediary with an express warning that it had to be tested before use. The intermediary was liable for the resulting injury, but the manufacturer was not and it would be difficult to do business on any other basis.[71] Prescription drugs will commonly have untoward side-effects upon a minority of users and a manufacturer will normally fulfil his duty under *Donoghue v Stevenson* by giving adequate warning to the prescribing physician (who is far more likely than is the patient to be able to understand the warning):[72] if the physician fails to heed the warning his default may properly be regarded as the sole cause of injury to the patient.[73]

F. Nature of the Loss

General rule: no liability for the defect itself. Liability under *Donoghue v Stevenson* clearly covers personal injury and damage to other property: if, for example, a defectively wired heater causes a fire which burns down the consumer's house he could sue for the value of the house. It does not, however, normally cover the financial loss caused by the failure of a product to fulfil the function for which it was acquired.[74] Such loss is properly claimable only in an action by the buyer against the seller under the Sale of Goods Act. In other words, *Donoghue v Stevenson* is about dangerous products, not merely defective ones and a modern Mrs Donoghue could not sue Stevenson if her bottle of "ginger beer" contained pure water. These matters have already been discussed in the context of the duty of care and economic loss[75] and the related area of defective premises.[76] In so far as *Junior Books v Veitchi Co Ltd*[77] remains an authority on economic loss it may no doubt be applicable to chattels where the requisite special and unusual relationship subsists between the parties,[78] but that will not

11–011

---

[69] See para.22–007. If the claimant himself neglects an opportunity of examination it may be a case for reduction of damages under the Law Reform (Contributory Negligence) Act 1945. If his default is so extreme as to break the chain of causation there may be a complete defence: *Nitrigin Eireann Teoranta v Inco Alloys Ltd* [1992] 1 All E.R. 854 at 862.

[70] [1937] 3 All E.R. 970.

[71] Similarly, one may well sell an unroadworthy vehicle for scrap and if it is then used on the road that will be the purchaser's responsibility. See also *Hurley v Dyke*, para.11–006.

[72] *Hollis v Dow Corning* (1996) 129 D.L.R. (4th) 609 (breast implants).

[73] But what if there is no warning? In *Hollis v Dow Corning* the Supreme Court of Canada held that in such a case the manufacturer cannot escape liability by giving evidence tending to show that the doctor would not have passed the information on. That would leave the claimant in the position of failing against the doctor (who is not negligent because he received no warning) and against the manufacturer. Cf. *Walker Estate v York Finch General Hospital* [2001] SCC 23; [2001] 1 S.C.R. 647.

[74] *Finesse Group Ltd v Bryson Products* [2013] EWHC 3273 (TCC).

[75] See para.5–064.

[76] See para.10–049.

[77] [1983] 1 A.C. 520.

[78] See para.5–064.

normally be so between manufacturer and ultimate consumer, even if the manufacturer is aware of the destination of his product.[79]

11–012 **Damage to other property: "complex products".** The undoubted proposition that *Donoghue v Stevenson* applies where the product causes damage to other property of the claimant causes some difficulty where failure of a component in a complex product causes damage to the product itself.[80] This is essentially the same issue as that of the "complex structure" which has been discussed earlier in connection with *Murphy v Brentwood DC*.[81] It is clear that if the negligently manufactured component is a replacement or added[82] part the manufacturer is liable for damage to the rest of the article[83] whether or not he was the manufacturer of the article in its original state.[84] The discussion of complex structures in *Murphy v Brentwood* is somewhat inconclusive but members of the House of Lords did not rule out the possibility that sub-contractors constructing or installing elements of a building which then caused damage to the building as a whole might be liable for this damage. The problem in the case of chattels may be considerably more complex: in the case of a motor vehicle, for example, there may be hundreds of component parts by dozens of different manufacturers and the "manufacturer" of the vehicle may in reality be no more than a designer and assembler.

On the basis of what is said in *Murphy v Brentwood* we may, at one end of the spectrum, fairly safely say that if an engine component made by the assembler of the vehicle fails and causes damage to the rest of the engine[85] a claim for damage to "other property" caused by the failure of the component would be hopeless. The same is almost certainly true even if the failed component is manufactured by B and installed into the engine by the manufacturer of the car, A. At the other end of the spectrum is the case in which a car radio negligently manufactured by B and installed in a car assembled by A causes a fire which destroys the car. B may be liable to the owner for that,[86] since the radio is "accessory to the car", but

---

[79] See *Simaan General Contracting Co v Pilkington Glass Ltd (No.2)* [1988] Q.B. 758.

[80] See Tettenborn [2000] L.M.C.L.Q. 333.

[81] See para.10–051.

[82] For the case where the part is a component of a new product produced by the claimant, see *Bacardi-Martini Beverages Ltd v Thomas Hardy Packaging Ltd* [2002] EWCA Civ 549; [2002] 2 Lloyd's Rep. 379; cf. *Omega Proteins Ltd v Aspen Insurance UK Ltd* [2010] EWHC 2280 (Comm); [2010] 2 C.L.C. 370.

[83] For example a replacement tyre on a car which bursts and causes a crash damaging the car. In *Andrew Weir Shipping Ltd v Wartsila UK Ltd* [2004] EWHC 1284 (Comm); [2004] 2 Lloyd's Rep. 377 (fire starting in ship's engine) there was no dispute that there was physical damage, the contest being whether the defendants were under a duty to warn the owners of the risk. However, the question of assumption of responsibility or "special relationship" may be relevant both to the existence of liability for economic loss and to the existence of a duty to speak: at [59].

[84] The defendants in *Nitrigin Eireann Teoranta v Inco Alloys Ltd* [1992] 1 All E.R. 854 were manufacturers of the original and replacement material, though the case concerned only limitation.

[85] Cf. the facts of *Bernstein v Pamson Motors (Golders Green) Ltd* [1987] 2 All E.R. 220 where: (1) the action was against the seller; and (2) the problem arose from the process of assembly rather than a failure of a component. However, the fact that the damage was repaired under the manufacturer's warranty shows why the issue is of limited practical importance in the case of vehicles.

[86] Not for the value of the radio itself: *Aloe Coal Co v Clark Equipment Co* 816, F. 2d 110, cited with approval by Lord Keith in *Murphy v Brentwood DC* [1991] 1 A.C. 398 at 469.

not perhaps where the failed component is a tyre manufactured by B and fitted (not as replacement) to a car assembled by A.[87]

The question of liability for defects in packaging was considered in *M/S Aswan Engineering Establishment Co v Lupdine Ltd*.[88] The claimants lost a quantity of waterproofing compound when the pails in which it was contained collapsed because of the high temperatures to which they were exposed in Kuwait. An action against the manufacturer of the pails failed[89] on the ground that the circumstances in which the damage occurred were outside the range of what was reasonably foreseeable, but Lloyd LJ[90] expressed the provisional view that had that not been the case the loss of the compound would have been damage to the property of the claimants for which the manufacturer would have been liable.[91] Nicholls LJ, on the other hand, inclined to the view that *Donoghue v Stevenson* should not extend to making a container manufacturer liable for loss of contents,[92] not so much because the contents are not in strict legal analysis "other property of the claimant" but because such a liability would be unreasonable.

Difficult lines have to be drawn here but as the law now stands we must guard against the natural assumption that because the defect manifests itself in some external, physical form or by sudden catastrophe it is necessarily "damage to property" for the purposes of tort:[93]

> "Even when the harm to the product itself occurs through an abrupt, accident-like event, the resulting loss due to repair costs, decreased value and lost profits is essentially the failure of the purchaser to receive the benefits of its bargain—traditionally the core concern of contract law."

Pre-emptive repairs. A further possibility is that a dangerous defect is discovered in a product before it has the opportunity to cause harm and is then repaired. There was once some support for the view that the claimant in such a case could recover the costs of repair but this approach was flatly rejected in the *D&F Estates* case.[94] This was reaffirmed in *Murphy v Brentwood DC*[95] where it is said that where the property is used with knowledge of the danger the user is likely to be treated as the author of his own loss. This causes some difficulty in the case of defects in buildings but less in the case of chattels.[96]

11–013

---

[87] Yet a car radio, while easily detachable, can only be used in a car; and tyres can be removed and put on another car.

[88] [1987] 1 W.L.R. 1.

[89] An action in contract against other defendants who had sold the compound and pails to the claimants also failed.

[90] With whose judgment Fox LJ agreed.

[91] Cf. *Linklaters Business Services v Sir Robert McAlpine Ltd* [2010] EWHC 2931 (TCC); [2010] Con L.R. 211 at [115]–[119] (Akenhead J regarding the insulation fitted to pipes and the pipes themselves as one "thing" for the purposes of tort).

[92] Mance J in *The Orjula* [1995] 2 Lloyd's Rep. 395 thought that the view of Nicholls LJ gained some support from *Murphy v Brentwood DC* [1991] 1 A.C. 398.

[93] *East River Steamship Corp v Transamerica Delaval Inc* 476 U.S. 858 (1986) (referred to approvingly by the House of Lords in *D&F Estates Ltd v Church Commissioners* [1989] A.C. 117 and *Murphy v Brentwood DC* [1991] 1 A.C. 398).

[94] *D&F Estates Ltd v Church Commissioning* [1989] A.C. 117 at 177 per Lord Bridge.

[95] [1991] 1 A.C. 398.

[96] See para.10–049.

11–014   **Assessment.** The post-*Junior Books* cases are part of a general pattern of restriction on the reach of negligence law and represent an attempt to keep separate the spheres of tort and contract law. In none of them, however, is there very much discussion of the practical impact of placing upon the manufacturer a liability for defects of quality and performance and it must be borne in mind that if the claimant is a purchaser of the article and the usual chain of contractual indemnities functions fully it is the manufacturer, as the originator of the defect, who carries responsibility, even if he is not negligent. Certainly, the creation of a direct liability from manufacturer to consumer might raise formidable difficulties. For example, how would a standard of "defectiveness of quality" be set, since that is something which must be related to the terms of the contract (in particular, the price) between the manufacturer and the intermediary (the seller or some more remote person in the distribution chain)? Further, what would be the effect of exclusions or limitations of liability in the contract between the manufacturer and the intermediary?[97] Perhaps these problems would be far from insuperable in the context of standard form transactions with little room for bargaining and judicial control of exemption clauses.

2.   LIABILITY UNDER THE CONSUMER PROTECTION ACT 1987

11–015   **The trend towards strict liability.** Looked at against the background of the general law of tort the level of protection given to victims of dangerous goods by *Donoghue v Stevenson* may be thought not unreasonable, though it may be hard to justify the strict liability in respect of death or personal injury[98] which the purchaser acquires by virtue of his contract of sale. Such a view is, however, out of accord with the spirit of a time in which consumer interest has become one of the most important pressures for law reform. In the United States, liability for negligence was overtaken by judicial reform in favour of the consumer. The first step was liability for express warranty, shorn of the restriction of privity of contract and based on advertising claims,[99] but this was soon overtaken by the idea of the implied warranty of safety.[100] The culmination was *Greenman v Yuba Power Products Inc*[101] in which the court abandoned the idea of warranty and imposed a straightforward strict liability in tort. Various arguments have been advanced in favour of these developments[102] but the most commonly occurring ones are that the manufacturer, as creator of the risk, should bear its consequences;[103] that he is in the best position to insure that risk and to cover the

---

[97] For example, in *Junior Books v Veitchi* Lord Fraser thought that the claimant in tort could be in no better position than the purchaser from the manufacturer: [1983] 1 A.C. 520 at 534.

[98] As opposed to the liability for financial loss caused by the failure of the goods to function.

[99] *Baxter v Ford Motor Co* 12 P. 2d 409 (1932). This has obvious affinities with the collateral contract.

[100] *Henningsen v Bloomfield Motors* 161 A 2d 69 (1960).

[101] *Greenman v Yuba Power Products Inc* (1963) 27 Cal. Rptr. 697.

[102] See, e.g. *Liability for Defective Products* (1977) Law Com. No.82, para.38.

[103] This argument proves too much—it would suggest strict liability for any injury caused in the production and distribution process, e.g. an accident to a worker in the factory or a crash caused by

cost of that insurance in his price;[104] that strict liability is even more of an incentive than fault to the taking of adequate precautions; and that strict tort liability only achieves in one action what the law of contract achieves in many cases by the chain of indemnities stretching back from the consumer-purchaser to the manufacturer.

Developments in the EU. In numerical terms the problem of injuries caused by product defects is small when compared with those attributable to other risks[105] and the difficulty of establishing a case under the law of negligence can be exaggerated,[106] but there was a powerful tide in favour of change in the 1970s, prompted in part by the Thalidomide tragedy and given impetus by pressure for harmonisation of laws within Europe. The adoption by the Council of the EEC of a Directive on liability for defective products meant that the United Kingdom was required, by virtue of its treaty obligations, to legislate to implement the Directive and this was done by Pt I of the Consumer Protection Act 1987.[107] The Act came into force on March 1, 1988.[108]   **11–016**

Strict liability under the Act? The 1987 Act is too complicated to summarise accurately in one sentence and it is necessary to look at particular provisions in some detail, but very broadly its effect is to make the producer of a product (and certain others dealing with it) liable in damages for personal injury and some property damage caused by a defect in the product, without the necessity for the claimant to show fault, though certain defences may be raised by the producer. Liability is by no means absolute; how far it is properly described as "strict" is debatable but judgment on that must be suspended until the Act has been looked at more closely.   **11–017**

Relationship with other bases of liability. Article 13 of the Directive provided that it should not: "[A]ffect any rights which an injured person may have according to the rules of contractual or non-contractual liability or a special liability system existing at the moment when" the Directive was notified. It was widely thought that this meant that the Directive merely set a minimum standard and left it open to the local law to impose a stricter or more extensive liability. However, the European Court of Justice has ruled that this is incorrect in the light   **11–018**

---

the driving of a delivery van. Liability under the Consumer Protection Act 1987 is confined to injuries caused by a defect *in the product*, which is by no means the same thing as injuries caused *by the product*.

[104] A sufficiently bad claims record should raise his premium costs to such a level that he is driven off the market.

[105] On the basis of its personal injury survey the Pearson Commission in 1978 estimated that between 30,000 and 40,000 injuries per year (about 1 per cent of all injuries) might be attributable to defective products other than drugs and that the risk of death was lower than for other categories of risk: *Civil Liability And Compensation For Personal Injury* (1978), Cmnd.7054, Vol.1, para.1201. The 1987 Act hardly figured in case law for 12 years but there have been some important decisions since 2000.

[106] See para.11–008.

[107] Miller, *Product Liability and Safety Encyclopaedia*, Division III, (1991); Fairest, *Guide to the Consumer Protection Act, 1987* (1988); Howells, *Comparative Product Liability* (1993). For a highly critical account of the changes produced by the Directive, see Stapleton (1986) 6 O.J.L.S. 392 and Stapleton, *Product Liability* (1994).

[108] The Act applies if the product was supplied to any person by the producer on or after that date. It has no effect beyond the United Kingdom, the European Union or the European Economic Area: *Allen v Depuy International Ltd* [2014] EWHC 753 (QB).

of the fact that divergences in liability law may distort competition and "maximal" rather "minimal" harmonisation is imposed.[109] Hence, the French transposition of the Directive, which put the liability of the supplier on the same level as the manufacturer (whereas under the Directive the supplier is liable only if the manufacturer is unidentified) was struck down.[110] However, art.13 allows the imposition of liability on some other ground such as fault or warranty[111] so in English law the general liability for negligence and breach of contract operate in parallel with the Directive regime.

A. Who is Liable?

11–019 **Producers.** Subject to a point discussed below, the Act does not impose liability on persons who merely supply goods, though it must again be emphasised that the supplier usually has a contractual liability which is more onerous than that imposed by the Act, albeit only to his immediate purchaser. The three principal categories of persons liable under the Act are listed in s.2(2) and the first is the producer of the product,[112] who is further defined in s.1(2) as:

> "(a)   the person who manufactured it;
> (b)   in the case of a substance which has not been manufactured but has been won or abstracted, the person who won or abstracted it;
> (c)   in the case of a product which has not been manufactured, won or abstracted but essential characteristics of which are attributable to an industrial or other process having been carried out (for example, in relation to agricultural produce), the person who carried out that process."

The first class within s.1(2) is self-explanatory, but it is important to note that if a product causes damage as a result of failure of a component part (for example, an aircraft which crashes because of a defective altimeter) then both the manufacturer of the component part and the final manufacturer/assembler are treated as producers and are liable under the Act.[113] Their liability is joint and several,[114] that is to say, each is liable in full to the claimant, though as between themselves the liability may be apportioned under the contribution legislation[115] and there may, of course, be contractual rights of indemnity. Paragraph (b) covers minerals and raw materials (oil, coal, cement). Paragraph (c), which covers things not falling within either of the two previous categories,[116] will raise some awkward questions of degree as to what is an "essential characteristic": the

---

[109] *Gonzalez Sanchez v Medicina Asturiana SA* [2002] E.C.R. I–3901.
[110] *Commission v France* [2002] E.C.R. I–3827.
[111] *Commission v France* [2002] E.C.R. I–3827 at [31].
[112] Section 2(2)(a).
[113] This is the effect of the definition of "product" in s.1(2), though this very important point could, perhaps, have been stated more clearly.
[114] Section 2(5).
[115] Ch.22.
[116] If X extracts oil and Y refines it into petroleum, X falls within paragraph (b). Does Y fall within paragraph (a) or paragraph (c)? If (c), it is presumably irrelevant that it has been abstracted in another form.

packing of vegetable crops does not, presumably, bring this paragraph into play but the processing and freezing of poultry probably do.[117]

Holding out as producer. The second category in s.2(2) is the "own brander" or, as the Act puts it "any person who by putting his name on the product or using a trade mark or other distinguishing mark in relation to the product, has held himself out to be the producer of the product". This provision may be of narrower effect than it has often been assumed to be, for it is not enough to put your name on the goods; you must do so in such a way as to hold yourself out as the producer. Does anyone really believe that, for example, Marks & Spencer Plc actually makes the products marketed under the "St Michael" brand? The matter is, of course, fundamentally a question of fact but labelling which clearly states that the product is made for and not by the store will presumably exclude s.2(2).[118]

11–020

Importers into Europe. Vast quantities of consumer goods are imported from abroad and the third category set out in s.2(2)(c) goes some way towards relieving the claimant from the problems of suing a foreign producer. It imposes liability upon the person who has imported the product into a Member State, from a place outside the Member States but only if the importation is in order, in the course of his business, to supply it to another.[119] Hence, if A, a Belgian company, imports goods into Belgium from China and then sells them to B, who imports them into the United Kingdom, where they are sold to C, A (but not B) is liable under this head.

11–021

Suppliers. This part opened by saying that the mere supply of goods to another did not of itself attract the operation of the Act, but under s.2(3) a supplier[120] who receives a request from the injured person to identify the producer (or other person liable under s.2(2)) is liable under the Act if he does not within a reasonable time either comply with the request or identify his supplier. The idea is to enable the claimant to trace "anonymous" goods back along the chain of distribution to a producer or importer who carries primary liability under the Act and anyone who breaks this chain[121] by his inability to identify his supplier is made liable as if he were the producer. Since in this way a wholesaler who is contractually remote from the claimant and who is in no way at fault with regard to the goods may incur heavy damages without hope of recourse, the importance of adequate record keeping can hardly be overemphasised.

11–022

---

[117] A cup of coffee is served in a restaurant. Is the restaurant a producer under para.(a) or para.(c)? It must be one or the other but in *Bogle v McDonalds Restaurants Ltd* [2002] EWHC 490 (QB) the defendants seem to have conceded it was (a).

[118] A similar issue may arise over franchised outlets but in *Bogle v McDonalds Restaurants Ltd* [2002] EWHC 490 (QB) the defendants accepted responsibility for franchisees.

[119] An airline which brings an American airliner to England to use it here is not liable under this paragraph: s.46(9).

[120] "Supply" is defined in s.46(1) and extends a good deal more widely than supply under a sale. But a finance company is not a supplier for the purposes of this Act; the "effective supplier" (e.g. the garage in a car hire-purchase transaction) is: s.46(2).

[121] The request may be made to any supplier, not merely the one who directly supplied the goods to the claimant.

B. Products

11–023   A product is any goods or electricity[122] and "goods" is further defined as including, "substances,[123] growing crops[124] and things comprised in land by virtue of being attached to it and any ship, aircraft or vehicle".[125] Components of a building are, therefore, covered, so that a manufacturer of defective steel joists would be liable for injury caused by the collapse of a block of flats but it is thought that the building as a whole is not "goods" and that a builder is not therefore responsible under the Act for shoddy workmanship,[126] though the law of negligence and the Defective Premises Act 1972 of course apply to these cases. It seems that information is not within the Act even though it is incorporated in tangible form in a book[127] but the same may not be true of computerised information, where the line between "software" and "hardware" may be difficult to draw sensibly. If an airliner crashes because a component in an automatic landing device fails above a certain temperature there is clearly a defective product within the Act. Can the position really be any different if it is programmed so that it simply does not operate in certain, foreseeable conditions or if it gives the pilot a misleading indication?[128] It has been said that while software as such is not "goods" within the Sale of Goods Act, a disk containing a programme is, and when that is sold[129] the statutory implied terms apply to the software as well as the disk itself.[130] Misleading instructions for use of a product are clearly not to be equated with "pure" information, for they may themselves render an otherwise perfect product defective.[131]

C. Damage

11–024   The Act applies to death or personal injury but the position with regard to property damage is more restricted. First, there is no liability in respect of loss of or damage to the product itself or the whole or any part of any product which has

---

[122] Section 1(2).

[123] It was conceded in *A v National Blood Authority* [2001] 3 All E.R. 289 that blood and blood products for transfusion were within the Act.

[124] Until 2000 the producer of primary agricultural produce and game (the farmer or fisherman) was exempt from liability under the 1985 Directive if he supplied them before they had undergone an industrial process. This exemption was removed by the Consumer Protection Act 1987 (Product Liability) (Modification) Order 2000 (SI 2000/2771), implementing Directive 1999/34. While there is no doubt as to the legislative intention, it must be observed that the farmer does not fall easily into any of the definitions of producer in s.1(2). With a little strain he could be described as the "producer of . . . raw material" under art.3(1) of the 1985 Directive.

[125] Section 45(1).

[126] Even if this view is wrong, the same result will be reached in cases where the builder sells the house as a result of the combined effect of ss.4(1)(b), 46(3), 46(4).

[127] This was certainly the Government's intention, though two remarkably opaque sub-clauses in the Bill which were designed to make this clear were removed. Cf. Whittaker 105 L.Q.R. 125.

[128] It must, however, be confessed that the distinction between this and the book which contains misleading information is not easy to discern, still less to state. Cf. *Brocklesby v US* 767 F. 2d 1288 (C9,1985).

[129] Or hired: Supply of Goods and Services Act 1982.

[130] *St Albans DC v ICL* [1996] 4 All E.R. 481 at 493.

[131] See s.3(2)(a).

been supplied with the product in question comprised in it.[132] If, therefore, my car radio catches fire as a result of faulty components and burns out the car, neither the car assembler nor the radio manufacturer is strictly liable,[133] but if the same thing were to happen with a replacement radio liability would be imposed on the manufacturer of that. Secondly, no liability arises unless the damages (apart from interest) would be at least £275.[134] Thirdly, the Act is inapplicable unless the property is of a description ordinarily intended for private use and is mainly so intended by the claimant.[135] The Act would, therefore, have no application to the *Muirhead* and *Aswan* cases.[136]

D.   Defect

This is the core of the Act, the proposition that the damage must be caused wholly   **11–025**
or partly by a defect in the product.[137] Defect is defined in s.3 as being present where, "the safety of the product is not such as persons generally are entitled to expect".[138] Section 3 goes on to provide that all the circumstances are to be taken into account in determining whether the product is as safe as persons generally are entitled to expect, specifically drawing attention to the following:

"(a)   [T]he manner in which, and the purposes for which, the product has been marketed, its get-up, the use of any mark in relation to the product and any instructions for, or warnings with respect to, doing or refraining from doing anything in relation to the product;
(b)   what might reasonably be expected to be done with or in relation to the product and
(c)   the time when the product was supplied by its producer to another; and nothing . . . shall require a defect to be inferred from the fact alone that the safety of a product which is supplied after that time is greater than the safety of the product in question."

i.   Non-standard Products

It is crucial to note that the standard is what persons generally are entitled to   **11–026**
expect, a standard to be set by the court and which may be lower than what they do expect: public expectations may be unreasonably high, especially in a litigation-conscious society. On the other hand, the standard may be *higher* than what they do expect: the public may be stoically aware that some examples of a particular product will turn out to be defective, but this does not necessarily mean that they are not entitled to expect them to be perfect.[139] American product

---

[132] Section 5(2).
[133] Compare the rather uncertain position at common law: para.11–012.
[134] Section 5(4). It seems that the Directive, art.9(2), from which this curious limit stems, is mandatory.
[135] Section 5(3).
[136] See paras 5–064 and 11–012.
[137] Although the burden of proof is on the claimant, it is possible that the existence of the defect and its causal relationship may be established merely by inference: *Ide v ATB Sales Ltd* [2008] EWCA Civ 424; [2008] P.I.Q.R. P13.
[138] It is further provided that, "safety, in relation to a product, shall include safety with respect to products comprised in the product and safety in the context of risks of damage to property, as well as in the context of risks of death or personal injury".
[139] *A v National Blood Authority* [2001] 3 All E.R. 289.

liability law has generally drawn a distinction between the "production or manufacturing defect" (the case where, despite quality controls, the production line turns out a sub-standard article) and the "design defect" (the case where the danger is inherent even in standard products of that type).[140] In *A v National Blood Authority*[141] Burton J rejected this categorisation as alien to the structure of the Product Liability Directive and the Act. Nevertheless there are differences between the two situations of the product which is dangerous only because it is non-standard and the product every example of which carries a risk.

In the case of the non-standard product (that is to say, one which is not in the condition in which the manufacturer intended it to be distributed to the public) the claimant will succeed by showing the non-standard nature of the article and that that made it dangerous and caused his damage. Although in many cases the mere existence of the defect would provide powerful indirect evidence of negligence[142] the claimant is no longer required to rely on this and will succeed even if there is no fault. In the *A v National Blood Authority* case the claims arose from hepatitis C infections from blood products at a time when no reasonable and effective methods of screening for the virus were available—indeed, in the case of the earlier claims the products had been administered before the virus had even been identified. In concluding that the products were defective within the meaning of the Act, Burton J held that the focus was upon the individual item which caused the damage and that the cost and practicability of eliminating the "rogue product" were not elements in the "circumstances of the case" in determining what the user was entitled to expect in the way of safety. Even if (which was not the case) the public had been generally aware of the risk of untraced infected samples of blood, the individual user was entitled to expect that his bag of blood was infection-free and was not to be taken to be participating in a form of Russian roulette.[143]

ii. Standard Products

11–027 **Liability turns on a "value judgment".** Turning to inherent dangers in standard products, some of them will not work effectively unless there is an element of risk to everyone in their design—carving knives which cut meat well are also more efficient at lopping off users' fingers. In other cases, the product— medicines, for example—will be harmless and even beneficial to most but will present a danger to a minority. Yet other products could be made safer only by the expenditure of amounts of money which would be incompatible with the price range in the market at which the product is aimed—if all cars were required to be fitted with ABS brakes and four-wheel drive there would be no cheap cars available to the public. The relationship of the Act with the law of negligence in

---

[140] A distinction maintained by Restatement, Torts, Product Liability 3d §2.

[141] *A v National Blood Authority* [2001] 3 All E.R. 289.

[142] See, e.g. *Mason v Williams & Williams Ltd* [1955] 1 W.L.R. 549: para.11–008.

[143] *A v National Blood Authority* [2001] 3 All E.R. 289 at [65]. Cf. *Richardson v LRC* [2000] P.I.Q.R. P164. In *Pollard v Tesco Stores Ltd* [2006] EWCA Civ 393 where a child-resistant cap did not quite conform to its design standards, it was held that the public could reasonably expect such a cap to be difficult to open but not to be compliant with design standards (about which they would know nothing).

these cases has not been fully explored but it must surely be that the court is required to come to a judgment on whether the risks associated with the product in its present form are outweighed by the benefits that it brings, otherwise there would be liability for injuries caused by products rather than for injuries caused by defects in products, which would be neither socially acceptable nor within the scope of the Directive. While scientific evidence is no doubt relevant and often helpful there is no escaping the fact that in the last resort the judgment is a "value" one: there is no scientific formula which will tell us whether the risk of allowing cars to be made without advanced safety systems is greater or less than the benefits obtained by having cheaper cars. "Benefit" should not be taken too narrowly for this purpose because it may include elements that are completely unquantifiable. The dangers of alcohol are well known but in our society it is a generally accepted source of pleasure and even if some may think that the (very roughly quantifiable) cost still outweighs the (wholly unquantifiable) benefit, it is important that we respect people's right to self-determination, so even if alcohol could be said to be defective in any sense of the word, it is not so within the meaning of the Act. The necessity of adopting a cost-benefit approach was candidly admitted by the DTI explanatory note on the Directive, which commented, in relation to drugs:[144]

> "The more active the medicine, and the greater its beneficial potential, the more extensive its effects are likely to be, and therefore the greater the chances of an adverse effect. A medicine used to treat a life threatening condition is likely to be much more powerful than a medicine used in the treatment of a less serious condition, and the safety that one is reasonably entitled to expect of such a medicine may therefore be correspondingly lower."

Comparison with negligence. The ultimate question for the common law of negligence in such cases would be, "was it reasonable to market this design in the light of the risks and benefits?" Under the Act (where the safety of the product rather than the conduct of the defendant is the point of focus) we have to modify the question so that it becomes "can the public legitimately expect a greater degree of safety from the product?", but there is clearly a substantial overlap between the two. However, it has been denied that the two issues are identical and in *Iman Abouzaid v Mothercare (UK) Ltd*[145] the claim under the Act succeeded even though the common law claim failed because the risk was not one, which, at the time of distribution, the manufacturer could reasonably have been expected to have in contemplation as a serious one—though how, precisely, the court is to determine legitimate public expectations in such cases remains unclear.[146] Furthermore, in the *National Blood Authority* case Burton J regarded the question of what the defendant could have done to reduce or eliminate the danger as just as irrelevant in this type of case as in that of the non-standard product. Referring to

11–028

---

[144] A different view is taken in *A v National Blood Authority* [2001] 3 All E.R. 289, that there is no weighing of risks and benefits but rather that the general knowledge of the inherent danger is a factor in the standards persons are entitled to expect. The distinction is probably only significant where the inherent danger comes to light after the product has been used for some time.

[145] Unreported December 21, 2000 CA (design of pushchair strap).

[146] Pill LJ contented himself with saying, at [27], "members of the public were entitled to expect better from the appellants".

the fact that s.3(2) requires that a product is not to be considered defective for the sole reason that a better product is subsequently put into circulation, he continued:[147]

> "In the comparative process, the claimant may point to a product which is safer, but which the producer shows to be produced five years later. Particularly if no other contemporary product had these features, this is likely to be capable of being established, and insofar as such product has improved safety features which have only evolved later in time, they should be ignored, as a result of [section 3(2)].[148] The claimant might however want to allege that the later safety features *could* have been developed earlier by the producer. That would obviously amount to the *claimant* running the evidence of 'should have done', to which the producer would no doubt respond 'could not have done'. This would however once again go to the issue of *avoidability*, which I have concluded to be outside the ambit of [section 3], and so once again if the claimant really wanted to do so he could run the point, but only in negligence."

However, it is unclear how the court is to determine legitimate expectation without taking into account how, if at all, the product could have been improved.

11–029 **Time element.** The proposition in s.3(2) that the safety of a product is to be judged by reference to standards prevailing when it was put into circulation (so that a 2002 car is not defective merely because subsequent models are produced with more advanced safety features) seems to be an inevitable concomitant of the concept of "defect"[149] and if the rule were otherwise there might be a positive disincentive to an industry to introduce safety improvements. The "product" in question for this purpose is, of course, the individual item which causes the damage, not the product "line" or design—one cannot go on forever producing cars to 2002 standards when everyone else's safety standards have improved— but except in cases where legislative requirements are imposed (for example, as to the fitting of safety belts) it may be very difficult for the court to decide at what point a development becomes necessary to satisfy the requirement of safety, as opposed to being merely desirable. Again, too, we have the problem, if the *National Blood Authority* case is correct, of the apparent exclusion of what the manufacturer should have done from the "defect" issue.

iii. Warnings and Instructions

11–030 A standard product may be perfectly safe if used properly but unsafe if used in an improper way or for an improper purpose. To take from the demonology of American product liability law the (apocryphal) case of the claimant who attempted to dry her dog in a microwave oven, the oven would not for that reason be defective. However, where a risk is not obvious to the user, the product may be

---

[147] *A v National Blood Authority* [2001] 3 All E.R. 289 at [72].

[148] Throughout his judgment Burton J refers to the Directive rather than the Act.

[149] Stapleton, *Product Liability* (1994) (writing from the standpoint that the Act is a misguided and ineffective compensation measure which sticks much too closely to common law concepts, a proposition perhaps now less easy to defend than when it was put forward) argues that reformers are illogical in readily accepting this proposition while at the same time rejecting (as many of them do) the "development risks" defence now enshrined in s.4(1)(e): "It is odd that risks discovered after circulation should be taken into account to show that a product was defective all along, but the development of better products after circulation should not be taken into account to demonstrate that the benefits of the product were all along less than supposed."

defective because it is not accompanied by adequate warnings or instructions. The standard here would seem to be similar to that for negligence but circumstances of danger are so infinitely various that very little can be said in general about instructions and labelling[150] beyond the general proposition that the manufacturer should err on the side of caution.[151]

E.   The Development Risks Defence

The defence. By s.4(1)(e) it is a defence for the defendant to prove that: "[T]he   **11–031** state of scientific and technical knowledge at the relevant time[152] was not such that a producer of products of the same description as the product in question might be expected to have discovered the defect if it had existed in his products while they were under his control."

This defence proved highly controversial during the passage of the Act but the Government insisted on its inclusion. The first point is that the Directive merely allows the inclusion of such a defence[153] and the policy among Member States has not been uniform: Germany, for example, allows such a defence generally, but not for pharmaceuticals. Secondly, the terms of s.4(1)(e) do not accord completely with art.7(e) of the Directive, which provides: "[T]hat the state of scientific and technical knowledge at the time when [the producer] put the product into circulation was not such as to enable the existence of the defect to be discovered..."

While the Directive speaks in terms of scientific possibility, the references in s.4(1)(e) to comparable producers and what might have been expected comes closer to a traditional negligence formula. A challenge to s.4(1(e) by the European Commission was rejected by the European Court of Justice[154] on the grounds that the provision did not plainly and irremediably fail to comply with art.7(e) and that the English court would have to interpret it in the light of the Directive. The Court said that art.7(e) was not directed at the state of knowledge in the industrial sector on which the producer is operating but at the state of knowledge in general; on the other hand it was implicit in art.7(e) that the knowledge in question must be accessible.[155]

---

[150] See *Worsley v Tambrands Ltd* Unreported December 3, 1999 QBD. These matters are obviously intimately connected with foreseeable use. By way of example—(1) most perfume is highly inflammable, but should a manufacturer have to give warning of this? Yes, according to an American court in *Moran v Faberge* 332 A. (2d) 11 (1975)—claimant dowsing candle in perfume.

[151] There is no blanket rule that the manufacturer may safely ignore a danger which is "obvious", for the product may foreseeably get into the hands of children or other incompetents and if a simple design change will reduce the danger to them, the law may require it: see Miller, *Product Liability and Safety Encyclopaedia*, Division III. But warnings of obvious dangers may detract from safety by diminishing the significance of warnings about non-obvious risks.

[152] The time of the supply by the producer: s.4(2).

[153] See generally, Newdick [1988] C.L.J. 455 and (1992) 20 Anglo-American L.R. 309.

[154] *European Commission v United Kingdom* [1997] All E.R. (EC) 481.

[155] Advocate General Tesauro in his opinion had given the example of an article published only in Chinese in Manchuria. In *A v National Blood Authority* [2001] 3 All E.R. 289 at [49] Burton J regarded as a more realistic example results which had not been published and were held within the research department of a company.

11–032 **The relevant knowledge.** Although as a matter of language both s.4(1)(e) and art.7(e) of the Directive could be read as allowing the defence to operate where there is no known method of discovering the defect in an individual product (the non-standard product), this is not so: the defence only applies if there is no knowledge of the existence of the risk in a generic sense, and once this knowledge has been acquired, the manufacturer produces at his own risk, even if it is impossible to identify the individual, non-standard products in which that risk is present.[156] Hence, "development risks defence" is better shorthand than "state of the art defence".[157]

11–033 **Assessment.** The argument in favour of s.4(1)(e), at least in so far as it applies to unknown design risks, is succinctly put in the DTI Consultative Document on the Directive:

> "Manufacturers . . . have argued that it would be wrong in principle, and disastrous in practice, for businesses to be held liable for defects that they could not possibly have foreseen. They believe that the absence of this defence would raise costs and inhibit innovation, especially in high risk industries. Many useful new products, which might entail a development risk, would not be put on the market, and consumers as well as businesses might lose out."

On the other hand, there is no such defence in contract law,[158] and it has been suggested that another thalidomide-type tragedy might slip through the liability net under the Act, for which reason both the Law Commission and the Pearson Commission rejected any exemption for development risks.[159]

F. Other Defences

11–034 Section 4 contains other defences which, like s.4(1)(e), are defences in the proper sense of that term, i.e. matters which must be raised and proved by the defendant. To the common law mind some of them are matters which might more naturally be regarded as casting a burden on the claimant but the Act is a consumer protection measure and the allocation of the burden is deliberate. Section 4 will, therefore, come into play if we postulate that the claimant has proved, directly or by getting the court to draw inferences, that he has suffered damage which is attributable to a defect in an article for which the defendant is responsible under the Act, as producer or otherwise.

11–035 **Requirements imposed by law.** It is a defence to show that the defect "is attributable to compliance with any requirement imposed by or under any enactment or with any Community obligation".[160] For example, suppose that the law required all wine to contain sulphur dioxide. Suppose also that the ingredient

---

[156] *A v National Blood Authority* [2001] 3 All E.R. 289.

[157] The decision of the German Supreme Court in *NJW* 1995, 1262 can be read as holding that the defence can never apply to non-standard products. However, Burton J, in the *National Blood Authority* case thought that this would not be so if the very possibility of the existence of the non-standard product were unknown.

[158] *Henry Kendall & Sons v William Lillico & Sons Ltd* [1969] 2 A.C. 31; *Ashington Piggeries Ltd v Christopher Hill Ltd* [1972] A.C. 441.

[159] See Law Com. No.82, para.105; Cmnd. 7054, Vol.1, para.1259.

[160] Section 4(1)(a).

was then found to be harmful. The producer would have a defence without reference to the "development risks" defence of s.4(1)(e). This defence does not mean that compliance with minimum legal standards automatically provides a defence. For example, suppose that the hypothetical wine law forbids the addition of ingredients A, B and C and the producer complies, but he adds ingredient X, widely thought to be beneficial, but then discovered to be harmful. Subject to s.4(1)(e), the producer is liable. Perhaps a more likely state of affairs is one where an ingredient is expressly permitted by law (as opposed to required) even though it is believed, or even known, to carry some risk of injury. Section 4(1)(a) would seem not to provide a defence, though it might be very difficult to establish a case of negligence in such circumstances.[161]

No supply. It is a defence to show that the defendant "did not at any time supply the product to another".[162] Being a supplier does not involve liability under the Act unless the "tracing" provision of s.2(3) comes into play.[163] But even a producer is not liable if he has not supplied the article to another. "Supply" is widely defined to include hiring out or lending but it does not cover merely putting goods in someone's hands for him to use, so if D produces a machine for internal use in the factory and it has a defect which injures workman C the Act does not apply.[164]   **11–036**

"Non-commercial" supply. It is a defence to show that any supply by the defendant was otherwise than in the course of his business and that section 2(2)[165] either does not apply to him or only does so by virtue of things done "otherwise than with a view to profit".[166] Hence, a person donating a home-made pie to a church fete escapes liability, but if he sold it he would be liable if the cooking made him a "producer" within s.1(2)(c). A private seller of second-hand goods would escape the "tracing" liability under s.2(3)[167] because s.2(2) does not apply to him.   **11–037**

No defect at the relevant time. It is a defence to show that the defect did not exist in the product at the "relevant time",[168] i.e. when the defendant put it into circulation.[169] The producer is not liable for defects which have arisen from interference, misuse or fair wear and tear but once the claimant has shown that the product was defective in the s.3 sense and has caused damage it is up to the producer to raise and prove such matters. Of course he may do so by indirect evidence (for example, by showing that a weakness in the wall of a burst tyre is reasonably consistent only with impact damage in use) but where the court is left in doubt the claimant should win. It should be noted that where the defect does   **11–038**

---

[161] Cf. *Albery and Budden v BP Oil* [1980] J.P.L. 586 a claim in negligence, para.6–035.
[162] Section 4(1)(b).
[163] See para.11–022.
[164] Section 46. Miller, op. cit., points out that for the same reason the Act would have no application to an incident like the Bhopal disaster; but see *Veedfald v Arhus Amtskommune* [2001] E.C.R. I–3569.
[165] Which defines who is liable under s.2(1): see paras 11–019–11–022.
[166] Section 4(1)(c).
[167] See para.11–022.
[168] Section 4(1)(d).
[169] This is the position for defendants falling within s.2(2). There are, however, special provisions as to the relevant time in relation to electricity and to s.2(3) defendants.

exist when the product leaves the hands of the producer, the possibility or probability of intermediate examination does not insulate him from liability.[170]

11–039   **"Subsequent products".** Section 4(1)(f) provides that it shall be a defence show:

"that the defect
(i) constituted a defect in a product ('the subsequent product') in which the product in question had been comprised and
(ii) was wholly attributable to the design of the subsequent product or to compliance by the producer of the product in question with instructions given by the producer of the subsequent product."

A Co orders a consignment of standard tyres from B Co and fits them to a high-speed sports car model for which they are wholly unsuitable. The car is therefore "defective". If, as this paragraph seems to assume, the tyre is also thereby defective as a result, B Co. has a defence to an action by an injured consumer. Where the component producer knows or ought to know that the final assembler intends, through inexperience, to make an unsuitable use of the component then an action in negligence might lie against the component producer at the suit of an injured consumer,[171] quite apart from any liability in contract to the assembler. The position is less clear where the assembler is aware of the danger and presses on regardless but it is submitted that the component manufacturer must be entitled, after due warning to the assembler, to act on assurances by the latter and is not obliged to investigate compliance with those assurances.

G.   Contributory Negligence

11–040   The Consumer Protection Act applies the Law Reform (Contributory Negligence) Act 1945[172] by providing that when damage is caused partly by a defect in a product and partly by the fault of the person suffering the damage then the defect is to be treated as if it were the fault of every person liable for it under the Act.[173] In "deeming" fault to exist in the producer the Act recognises the difficulty of balancing blameworthy against non-blameworthy conduct, though it does not really solve the problem. However, there is plenty of experience under acts and regulations on industrial safety of applying apportionment of liability to strict liability situations and the courts should have no difficulty with this. Where the claimant's fault is extreme then it may amount to the sole cause in law and

---

[170] Cf. the common law, para.11–010. In *Hayes v Leo Scaffolding Ltd* Unreported December 3, 1996 CA, where the employers of the claimant had submitted to judgment in respect of a fall caused by a defective plank, their claim for contribution against the producer of the plank failed because, in the court's view, the likelihood of intermediate examination insulated the producer from liability to the claimant and therefore the producer was not a person "liable to" the claimant for the purposes of the Civil Liability (Contribution) Act 1978. However, the employers did not rely upon the Consumer Protection Act, which, in the words of Simon Brown LJ: "on the face of it, would have provided them with a well-nigh impregnable argument."
[171] Whether the Act also applies in this situation would not seem to matter.
[172] See para.23–036.
[173] Section 6(4). Various other Acts are also applied by s.6, e.g. the Fatal Accidents Act 1976 and the Congenital Disabilities (Civil Liability) Act 1976.

deprive him of damages altogether; in many cases, exactly the same result may be reached by concluding that the claimant's use of the product is so unusual that it is not defective, even if it has caused damage.

H.   Exclusion of Liability

Section 7 enacts a simple rule invalidating any limitation or exclusion of liability, "by any contract term, by any notice or by any other provision", no matter what the nature of the damage.[174] Of course, care must be taken to distinguish substance from form: "manufacturers will not be responsible unless this product is earthed" is not an exclusion of liability but a warning which goes to the safety of the product under s.3.   **11–041**

I.   Limitation

This is dealt with in Ch.26. At this stage, however, it is worth noting the "cut-off" provision whereby any liability is extinguished 10 years after the product has been put into circulation, thus smothering to some extent the risk of mass disaster litigation arising from defects which come to light only after many years.[175] This does not, however, affect the common law of negligence.   **11–042**

3.   CONCLUSION

From a theoretical point of view, the Consumer Protection Act is one of the most important developments in English tort law. However, liability is by no means absolute: the Act has affinities with the common law in some respects and it is still difficult to tell, especially in relation to development risks, how far it has effected any change in practice. One matter of great controversy is the cost of implementation. There is no doubt that in the United States strict product liability judgments became a serious burden on some sectors of manufacturing industry[176] but the cause of this may have lain as much in American practice on the use of juries, contingency fees and other matters as in strict liability.[177] One estimate was that the implementation of the Directive would lead to an increase of no more than 25 per cent in liability insurance premiums, which means, on average, an increase in unit costs of the order of 0.02 per cent,[178] though there might be huge variations from one trade to another. However, the European Commission in   **11–043**

---

[174] Contrast s.2 of the Unfair Contract Terms Act 1977 (para.26–017), which makes exclusion of liability for property damage caused by negligence subject to a reasonableness test.

[175] For example, asbestosis. On when a product is put into circulation, see *O'Byrne v Sanofi Pasteur MSD Ltd* [2006] 1 W.L.R. 1606 ECJ and *O'Byrne v Aventis Pasteur SA* [2010] UKSC 23; [2010] 1 W.L.R. 1412.

[176] There has been widespread state legislation in an effort to stem the tide: reduced limitation periods and "caps" on non-pecuniary loss damages have been popular devices.

[177] There has been a similar crisis (or perceived crisis) in medical malpractice, which remains governed by the law of negligence.

[178] See North (1978) 128 New L.J. 315 at 318 (based on the Law Commission/Pearson proposals, i.e. with no development risks defence).

its review of the operation of the Directive was wholly unable to make any assessment of the cost of strict liability in Europe after 13 years.[179] In any event, greater "litigation consciousness" could wholly falsify early estimates.[180]

It should also be noted that there is a further, modest element of strict liability in the consumer protection field. Since 1961 the Secretary of State has had power to make regulations imposing safety requirements for classes of goods and to make orders prohibiting the supply of goods which are not safe.[181] This power is now contained in Pt II of the Consumer Protection Act 1987 (s.11) and contravention of the regulations is actionable[182] (as a breach of statutory duty) by any person affected thereby.[183] Part II is, however, primarily concerned with the enforcement of safety by criminal sanctions.

---

[179] COM/2000/0893 at p.8. Apart from the fact that no uniform statistics are kept, many cases will be based on negligence and contract law as well as on strict tort liability.

[180] Curiously, the UK has had a very low rate of cases arising from the Directive, even though there is a common view in Europe that the English legal system has a more "American" culture than others. Of course, many claims may have been settled out of court.

[181] Originally in the Consumer Protection Act 1961, succeeded by the Consumer Safety Act 1978. See also General Product Safety Regulations 2005 (SI 2005/1803).

[182] Except in so far as safety regulations provide otherwise.

[183] Section 41.

CHAPTER 12

LIABILITY FOR STATEMENTS

1. INTRODUCTION

The title of this chapter raises the difficulty of arranging a general account of tort **12–001** law, for a good deal of the law about liability for damage done by statements will be found elsewhere in this book. Statements may cause harm even if true, as where they involve invasions of a person's privacy or breach of his confidences. Liability for untrue statements has a wider canvas. First, a statement may injure a person's reputation, if defamatory and published to a third party; secondly, it may cause direct injury by shock to the person to whom it is addressed; third, it may cause him to act in reliance on it and suffer loss as a result; or, fourth, it may cause him loss because it is addressed to other persons who, in reliance on it, act (perhaps perfectly lawfully) to his detriment. The first is covered by the tort of defamation, the subject of a separate chapter, which also looks at privacy and

[321]

confidence.[1] The second is the liability under *Wilkinson v Downton*, which has been considered in connection with intentional wrongs to the person.[2] This chapter is concerned with the third category and part of the fourth; only part of the fourth, because that category includes malicious falsehood, which is considered with defamation because it often overlaps with it.

Even on this basis the arrangement is still to a certain extent arbitrary. Deceit typically involves deliberate interference with economic interests in a business or contractual context and could be placed in the chapter on the economic torts.[3] "Negligent misstatement" is certainly not a tort in its own right (though deceit is) and liability is often (though not wholly)[4] based upon a broader concept of assumption of responsibility, which we have examined in the context of the duty of care in negligence[5]: if a professional person undertakes a task in respect of which he owes a duty to the claimant he is liable whether he performs that task incompetently or negligently advises the claimant on the action he should take. Nevertheless, "statement" cases throw up enough commonly recurring features (legitimacy of reliance and the range of persons to whom a duty is owed) to justify some further, separate treatment.

2. DECEIT

12–002   Since *Pasley v Freeman*[6] in 1789, it has been the rule that A is liable in tort to B if he knowingly or recklessly (i.e. not caring whether it is true or false) makes a false statement to B with intent that it shall be acted upon by B, who does act upon it and thereby suffers damage. This is the tort of deceit (or "fraud"), and for liability in deceit the defendant must have been dishonest, i.e. he must have made the statement with knowledge of its falsity or at least reckless whether it is true or false.[7]

12–003   **The effect of the introduction of liability for negligent mis-statement.** It was for long thought that there could be no liability in tort for a false statement honestly made, however negligent its maker may have been and, however disastrous its consequences: a careless person is not a dishonest one. Eventually however, the House of Lords held that there may in certain circumstances be a duty of care upon the maker of a statement,[8] and thus that a person may be liable for a false statement honestly but negligently made. Such liability cannot be brought under the tort of deceit—it is liability for negligence and not for fraud—but its existence has a profound bearing on liability for statements as a whole. If there may be liability in negligence it may be of little more than academic interest that absence of fraudulent intent is fatal to a claim founded on

---

[1] Ch.13.

[2] *Wilkinson v Downton* [1897] 2 Q.B. 57, para.4–031.

[3] Ch.19.

[4] *Caparo v Dickman* [1990] 2 A.C. 605, para.5–026.

[5] See para.5–039.

[6] (1789) 3 T.R. 51.

[7] *Derry v Peek* (1889) 14 App.Cas. 337.

[8] *Hedley Byrne & Co Ltd v Heller & Partners Ltd* [1964] A.C. 465. See, too, the Misrepresentation Act 1967 s.2.

deceit. Nevertheless, the tort has not been abolished and the claimant may have good reason for seeking to establish a case of deceit (for example, there is no need to establish a duty based on a special relationship,[9] it may enable him to avoid a disclaimer which would otherwise be valid,[10] his claim cannot be met by an allegation of contributory negligence[11] and the rules on damages will be more favourable to him).[12] However, a case based on deceit should not be advanced without clear instructions and credible material to support it;[13] it must be unequivocally pleaded[14] and put to the defendant;[15] and it must be distinctly proved,[16] for fraud is inherently less likely than negligence.[17] Summary judgment is now in principle available in a case of deceit[18] but is rather unlikely in practice.

Summary requirements.[19] The requirements for the common law action of deceit may be summarised as follows:[20] (1) there must be a representation of fact made by words or conduct;[21] (2) the representation must be made with knowledge that it is or may be false, or at least made in the absence of any genuine belief that it is true;[22] (3) the representation must be made with the intention that it should be acted upon by the claimant, or by a class of persons which includes the claimant, in the manner which resulted in damage to him;[23] (4) it must be proved that the claimant has acted upon the false statement;[24] (5) it must be proved that the claimant suffered damage by so doing.[25]

12–004

---

[9] *Noel v Poland* [2001] B.C.L.C 645 at [48].

[10] It should be noted that "fraud" is sometimes used in equity in a broader sense than the common law tort of deceit: see *Armitage v Nurse* [1998] Ch. 241.

[11] See para.23–058.

[12] See para.12–019. Oddly, however, the effect of *Royscott Trust v Rogerson* [1991] 2 Q.B. 297 is to apply the deceit rule on damages to the statutory cause of action under the Misrepresentation Act 1967 s.2(1): see further. *Treitel: The Law of Contract*, 13th edn (2011), para.9–066.

[13] Though not necessarily admissible evidence at the pleading stage: *Medcalf v Weatherill* [2002] UKHL 27; [2003] 1 A.C. 120.

[14] *Armitage v Nurse* [1998] Ch. 241 at 257.

[15] *Haringey LBC v Hines* [2010] EWCA Civ 1111; [2011] H.L.R. 6 at [39].

[16] *Hornal v Neuberger Products Ltd* [1957] 1 Q.B. 247.

[17] *H (Minors), Re* [1996] A.C. 563 at 586, but on principle it would not seem necessary for the claimant to establish damage to the same elevated standard: *GE Commercial Finance Ltd v Gee* [2005] EWHC 2056 (QB); [2006] 1 Lloyd's Rep. 367 at [122].

[18] CPR r.24.3; *Cheshire Building Society v Dunlop Haywards (DHL) Ltd* [2008] EWHC 51 (Comm); [2008] P.N.L.R. 19.

[19] See *ECO3 Capital Ltd v Ludsin Overseas Ltd* [2013] EWCA Civ 413 at [77] per Jackson LJ, where requirements (4) and (5) are collapsed into one.

[20] A principal may recover damages for "fraud" in respect of a transaction into which his agent is bribed (*Mahesan v Malaysia Government Officers' Co-operative Housing Society* [1979] A.C. 374) although there will not usually be any representation to the principal. This has been described as, "not . . . deceit, but a special form of fraud": *Petrotrade Inc v Smith* [2001] 1 Lloyd's Rep. 486 at 490.

[21] See para.12–010.

[22] See para.12–013.

[23] See para.12–014.

[24] See para.12–015. The most likely act of the claimant in reliance on a fraudulent misrepresentation is to enter into a contract with the misrepresentor. For detailed consideration of fraud, and misrepresentation in general, in this context, see *Treitel: The Law of Contract* (2011), Ch.9.

[25] See para.12–018.

A. A False Statement of Fact

12–005   **An objective test.** For liability in deceit, there must be a representation of fact, or possibly of law.[26] It need not be the representation of the defendant himself, as for example where he knowingly participates in a scheme to defraud and the representations in question are made by another party to the scheme.[27] The representation may be made by words, or by conduct[28] and it follows from the latter that it may be implied as well as express. In determining whether and what representation has been made, the courts adopt an objective test:[29]

> "In determining whether there has been an express representation, and to what effect, the court has to consider what a reasonable person would have understood from the words used in the context in which they were used. In determining what, if any, implied representation has been made, the court has to perform a similar task, except that it has to consider what a reasonable person would have inferred was being implicitly represented by the representor's words and conduct in their context."

12–006   **Promises and other statements of intention.** It is commonly said that mere promises are not statements of fact, but this is misleading, for every promise involves a statement of present intention as to future conduct: "There must be a misstatement of an existing fact: but the state of a man's mind is as much a fact as the state of his digestion."[30] If, then, I make a promise believing that I shall fulfil it, the reason that I am not liable for deceit if I do not fulfil it is not that my promise was not a statement of fact but that the statement of fact involved in the promise was true. If at the time I made it I had no intention of fulfilling my promise, I may be liable for deceit. So in *Edgington v Fitzmaurice*[31] directors of a company were held liable for deceit in procuring the public to subscribe for debentures by falsely stating in a prospectus that the loan secured by the debentures was for the purpose of completing buildings of the company, purchasing horses and vans and developing the trade of the company; in fact the directors intended to use it for paying off pressing liabilities.

12–007   **Statements of opinion.** A statement of opinion frequently carries within itself a statement of fact. A person who says "I believe X to be honest" is making a statement of fact as to his state of mind, and if it is untrue there is no reason why, if the other requirements of the tort are met, he should not be held liable for deceit. Often also an expression of opinion carries the implication that the person expressing it has reasonable grounds for it, and where this is not the case he may

---

[26] See para.12–008.
[27] *Dadourian Group International Inc v Simms* [2009] EWCA Civ 169; [2009] 1 Lloyd's Rep. 601 at [72]–[94].
[28] I.e. "active" conduct. There is no representation from mere silence unless there is a prior duty to speak: see para.12–011.
[29] *IFE Fund SA v Goldman Sachs International* [2006] EWHC 2887 (QB); [2007] 1 Lloyd's Rep. 264 at [50] per Toulson J.
[30] *Edgington v Fitzmaurice* (1885) 29 Ch. D. 459 at 483 per Bowen LJ; *Clydesdale Bank Ltd v Paton* [1896] A.C. 381 at 394 per Lord Herschell: cf. at 397 per Lord Davey.
[31] (1885) 29 Ch.D. 459; cf. *East v Maurer* [1991] 1 W.L.R. 461.

be guilty of a misstatement of fact.[32] On the other hand, there must be some latitude for "sales talk" and a seller's imprecise commendations of his wares do not give rise to liability merely because even the seller might, on careful reflection, think them exaggerated.

Statements of law. As a matter of general principle a misstatement of law ought   **12–008**
to be a sufficient misstatement of fact for the purposes of deceit.[33] A great many statements which we should not hesitate to describe as statements of fact involve inferences from legal rules and the distinction between law and fact is by no means as precise as might at first appear. So, in *West London Commercial Bank Ltd v Kitson*,[34] where directors of a company, knowing that the private Act of Parliament which incorporated the company gave them no legal power to accept bills of exchange, nevertheless represented to the claimant that they had such authority there was held to have been deceit:[35]

> "Suppose I were to say I have a private Act of Parliament which gives me power to do so and so. Is not that an assertion that I have such an Act of Parliament? It appears to me to be as much a representation of a matter of fact as if I had said I have a particular bound copy of 'Johnson's Dictionary'."

Even if the representation is of a pure proposition of law and not a deduction from a rule of law it is not easy to see what argument can be produced the other way. To urge that everyone is presumed to know the law is to carry into the law of deceit a distinction between law and fact which, artificial enough in any event, was never invented for the purpose of shielding swindlers.[36]

Half-truths. While the general rule is that there must be a statement or   **12–009**
representation by words or conduct, this does not mean that there must be a direct lie; it is sufficient that there is "such a partial and fragmentary statement of fact, as that the withholding of that which is not stated makes that which is stated absolutely false".[37] For example, where a husband whose income is £80,000 a year is under agreement to pay half to his wife and writes to her saying, "I send £30,000, half my income"—that would be a lie. It makes no difference if he sends her £30,000 and says nothing, for it would be an implied statement that it is half his income and he is guilty of deceit.[38]

---

[32] *Brown v Raphael* [1958] Ch. 636, a case of innocent misrepresentation in contract: see further *Treitel: The Law of Contract* (2011), para.9–008.

[33] Direct authority for this propositon is lacking but see the cases discussed in fn.36. A deliberate false statement of law is sufficient for the crime of fraud under s.2(3) of the Fraud Act 2006.

[34] (1884) 13 Q.B.D. 360.

[35] (1884) 13 Q.B.D. 360 at 363 per Bowen LJ.

[36] Furthermore, money may now be recovered for mistake of law as well as fact (*Kleinwort Benson v Lincoln CC* [1999] 2 A.C. 349, a decision of which it has been said it "now permeates the law of contract": *Brennan v Bolt Burdon* [2004] EWCA Civ 1017; [2005] Q.B. 303 at [10]) and it has been held that a statement of law can fall within the Misrepresentation Act 1967 (*Pankhania v Hackney LBC* [2002] EWIIC 2441 (Ch)).

[37] *Peek v Gurney* (1873) L.R. 6 H.L. 377 at 392 per Lord Chelmsford ("Half the truth will sometimes amount to a real falsehood"), at 403 per Lord Cairns; *Smith New Court Securities Ltd v Scrimgeour Vickers (Asset Management) Ltd* [1997] A.C. 254 at 274 per Lord Steyn ("A cocktail of truth, falsity and evasion is a more powerful instrument of deception than undiluted falsehood"). See also *Briess v Woolley* [1955] A.C. 333.

[38] *Legh v Legh* (1930) 143 L.T. 151 at 152 per MacKinnon LJ.

12–010 **Conduct.** A representation may be implied from conduct, e.g. a customer's conduct in sitting down in a restaurant amounts to a representation that he is able to pay for his meal.[39] If the defendant deliberately acts in a manner calculated to deceive the claimant and the other elements of the tort are present, the defendant is as much liable for deceit as if he had expressly made a false statement of fact.[40] Deliberate concealment, too, amounts to deceit,[41] but subject to what is said below[42] mere silence, however morally wrong, will not support an action for deceit.[43]

12–011 **Mere silence.** Silence will not normally support an action for deceit in the absence of any conduct which carries with it an implied representation. Sometimes, however, a person is under a legal duty to disclose facts[44] and Lord Blackburn said that in such a case if he deliberately held his tongue with the intention of inducing the other party to act on the belief that he did not speak because he had nothing to say, that would be fraud.[45]

12–012 **Continuing representations.** Related to the above is the situation where D makes a true statement to C and then discovers, before C acts upon it, that it has become false.[46] Does the law permit D to remain silent or does it compel him to correct C's false impression under pain of an action of deceit? It is submitted that the latter answer is in general correct. The tort of deceit is not complete when the representation is made. It only becomes complete when the misrepresentation— not having been corrected in the meantime—is acted upon by the representee.[47] The proper question in any case, therefore, is whether the statement was false when it was acted upon, not when it was made, and so a person whose true statement becomes false to his knowledge before it is acted upon should be liable in deceit if he does not correct it.[48]

---

[39] See *DPP v Ray* [1974] AC 370 at 379D per Lord Reid (cited by Longmore LJ in refusing to strike out claims based on the implied representations alleged to have been made by banks simply by proposing transactions on the basis of the manipulated LIBOR rate of interest: *Graiseley Properties Ltd v Barclays Bank Plc* [2013] EWCA Civ 1372).

[40] *Ward v Hobbs* (1878) 4 App. Cas. 13 at 16 per Lord O'Hagan; *Bradford Building Society v Borders* [1942] 1 All E.R. 205 at 211 per Lord Maugham; *Advanced Industrial Technology Corp Ltd v Bond Street Jewellers Ltd* [2006] EWCA Civ 923.

[41] *Gordon v Selico* (1984) 275 E.G. 899.

[42] See paras 12–011—12–012.

[43] *Bradford Building Society v Borders* [1942] 1 All E.R. 205 at 211 per Lord Maugham.

[44] For established categories where there is a duty of disclosure, see *Treitel: The Law of Contract* (2011), paras 9–130—9–151. Beyond them, the precise scope of any "duty to speak" is far from certain: see *Graiseley Properties Ltd v Barclays Bank Plc* [2013] EWCA Civ 1372 at [26].

[45] *Brownlie v Campbell* (1880) 5 App. Cas. 925 at 950; *Conlon v Simms* [2006] EWCA Civ 1749; [2008] 1 W.L.R. 484 at [130].

[46] In *Cramaso LLP v Ogilvie Grant* [2014] UKSC 9; [2014] 2 W.L.R. 317 (a case of negligent misrepresentation) the representation was initially made by D to C1, but continued until it was later relied upon by C2, a limited liability partnership incorporated by C1 for the purpose of entering into the contract.

[47] *Briess v Woolley* [1954] A.C. 333 at 353 per Lord Tucker, at 349 per Lord Reid; *Diamond v Bank of London & Montreal* [1979] Q.B. 333 (service out of jurisdiction); *Lindsay v O'Loughnane* [2010] EWHC 529 (QB); [2012] B.C.C. 153.

[48] See *Incledon v Watson* (1862) 2 F. & F. 841; *With v O'Flanagan* [1936] Ch. 575 at 584 per Lord Wright; *Bradford Building Society v Borders* [1941] 2 All E.R. 205 at 220; cf. *Arkwright v Newbold* (1881) 17 Ch.D. 301 at 325, 329.

Closely akin to this is another problem. Suppose that D's statement was false from the very beginning, but that when he made it he honestly believed it to be true and then discovers later and before C has acted upon it that it is false. Must he acquaint C with this? Here equity has a decided answer, whereas the common law is short of any direct decision. In *Reynell v Sprye*[49] a deed was cancelled by the Court of Chancery because D had not communicated the falsity of his belief. As to the wider liability to an action of deceit, it might be inferred from a dictum of Lord Blackburn that it exists.[50]

However we treat the question, there is no substantial difference between the two problems just put,[51] so that D is guilty of deceit in both of them if he withholds from C the further information. This certainly ought to be the law where there is plenty of time to retract the statement and where the result of not doing so is certain to result in widespread loss or damage (as in the case of a company prospectus) or in physical danger or serious business loss to even one person; but it must not be taken too far. As we have seen, a false statement of present intention is a sufficient misrepresentation of fact to support an action of deceit, and the difference between a false statement of intention and a breach of a promise is that in the latter case the promisor believes what he says about his intention. The subsequent breach of promise shows, however, that at some time his intention must have changed, but it does not follow that his failure to inform the promisee of his change of intention is fraudulent. Suppose that C has booked (but not paid for) a seat on D's coach at 9.00, and that D tells him correctly that he intends to start the journey at 11.00. Suppose that D, finding it more convenient to start at 10.30, starts then without informing C of his change of plans, because it would take nearly half an hour to find C. Here, D has certainly committed a breach of contract, but it is wrong to style his silence as to the changed circumstances deceit, even though it is admittedly intentional. It is really no more than a churlish indifference to a breach of contract. On the other hand where D induced C to embark on the development of a shopping centre by representing that it proposed to restrict the "tenant mix" at a nearby development by X and then made a secret agreement with X to relax that, D was liable in deceit for loss suffered by C when, a few months later, C irrevocably committed itself to the work. In fact, there were further, positive misrepresentations of D's intention after the secret agreement, but it seems that the result would have been the same if D had kept silent. Certainly it seems realistic in this situation to treat D as making a continuing representation up to the time when C acts in reliance.[52]

One more possible case of silence raises no difficulty. If D knowingly makes a false statement to C, but before C acts upon it subsequent events have turned the statement into a true one, this is not deceit. Thus, in *Ship v Crosskill*,[53] a false

---

[49] (1852) 1 De G.M. & G. 660 at 708–709.

[50] *Brownlie v Campbell* (1880) 5 App. Cas. 925 at 950. It was not necessary to decide the point in *Henry Ansbacher & Co Ltd v Brinks Stern, The Times*, June 26, 1997.

[51] Except that in the latter case the statement was false from the moment it was made, while in the former it was not. Since it is impossible for a person to make a false statement of his intention while believing it to be true, it would appear that the qualification stated below has no application to the solution of the second problem put.

[52] *Slough Estates Plc v Welwyn Hatfield DC* [1996] 2 P.L.R. 50.

[53] (1870) L.R. 10 Eq. 73.

allegation in a prospectus, that applications for more than half the capital of the company had been subscribed, had become true before the claimant made his application for shares, and it was held that there was no misrepresentation for which relief could be given to him. "If false when made but true when acted upon there is no misrepresentation."[54]

B.   The Fraudulent State of Mind

12–013   **Derry v Peek.** The representation must be made with knowledge that it is or may be false, or at least made in the absence of any genuine belief that it is true This rule is the result of the decision in *Derry v Peek*,[55] where the House of Lords made it clear that blundering but honest belief in a representation cannot be deceit. In Lord Herschell's classic formulation:[56]

> "[F]raud is proved when it is shewn that a false representation has been made (1) knowingly,[57] or (2) without belief in its truth, or (3) recklessly,[58] careless whether it be true or false. Although I have treated the second and third as distinct cases, I think the third is but an instance of the second, for one who makes a statement under such circumstances can have no real belief in the truth of what he states. To prevent a false statement being fraudulent, there must, I think, always be an honest belief in its truth."

The facts of *Derry v Peek* were that the directors of a tramway company issued a prospectus in which they stated that they had parliamentary powers to use steam in propelling their trams. In fact the grant of such powers was subject to the consent of the Board of Trade. The directors honestly but mistakenly believed the giving of this consent to be a merely formal matter; it was, however, refused. The company was wound up in consequence and the claimant, who had bought shares in it on the faith of the prospectus, instituted an action for deceit against the directors. The House of Lords, reversing the decision of the Court of Appeal, gave judgment for the defendants, holding that a false statement made carelessly and without reasonable ground for believing it to be true could not be fraud, though it might furnish evidence of it. A careless person is not a deceitful one and no amount of argument will prove he is one. However, dishonesty[59] in the criminal law sense is not necessary,[60] so the defendant is not excused by a belief that such a misrepresentation is common practice or will facilitate the

---

[54] *Briess v Woolley* [1954] A.C. 333 at 353 per Lord Tucker.

[55] (1889) 14 App. Cas. 337.

[56] *Derry v Peek* (1889) 14 App. Cas. 337 at 374.

[57] *Armstrong v Strain* [1951] 1 T.L.R. 856 at 871 per Devlin J ("A man may be said to know a fact when once he has been told it and pigeonholed it somewhere in his brain where it is more or less accessible in case of need. In another sense of the word a man knows a fact only when he is fully conscious of it. For an action of deceit there must be knowledge in the narrower sense and conscious knowledge of falsity must always amount to wickedness and dishonesty").

[58] For recklessness, see *Angus v Clifford* [1891] 2 Ch. 449 at 471 per Bowen LJ; *Derry v Peek* (1889) 14 App. Cas. 337 at 371 per Lord Herschell. "Recklessness" in the third situation has therefore been described as a species of dishonest knowledge: *AIC Ltd v ITS Testing Services (UK) Ltd* [2006] EWCA Civ 1601; [2007] 1 Lloyd's Rep 555 at [257].

[59] However, the word "dishonest" is frequently used in the civil cases. It should be understood as simply meaning knowledge or recklessness as to untruth.

[60] *Society of Lloyd's v Jaffray* [2002] EWCA Civ 1101 at [66].

transaction.[61] It must be noted that Lord Herschell's formulation of the law as requiring an honest belief in the truth of the statement was made in the context of a statement by promoters, who had a completely free choice as to what they said. It has been suggested that it does not necessarily follow that an employee is personally guilty of deceit where he makes a statement on the instruction of a senior officer and has some uncertainty as to its accuracy.[62]

C.   The Protected Claimant

The statement must be made with intent that the claimant shall act upon it. So long as that is satisfied, it need not be made to him either literally,[63] or in particular. In *Langridge v Levy*,[64] the seller of a defective gun which he had falsely and knowingly warranted to be sound, was held liable to the claimant who was injured by its bursting, although it was the claimant's father to whom the gun had been sold, but who had acquainted the seller with the fact that he intended his sons to use it. The claimant need not be individually identifiable[65] but if the statement is made to a limited class of persons, no one outside that class can sue upon it. Thus a company prospectus was at common law ordinarily confined in its scope to the original shareholders. For false statements in it they could sue, but purchasers of the shares from them could not do so;[66] but circumstances might quite possibly make the prospectus fraudulent with respect even to them, as where it was supplemented by further lying statements intended to make persons who were not original allottees of the shares buy them in the market.[67] The intent need not be to cause damage to the claimant: it is enough that the claimant was intended to act on it and did act on it in the manner contemplated. The defendant is liable whether he actually intended damage to ensue or not.[68]

12–014

---

[61] *Standard Chartered Bank v Pakistan National Shipping Corp* [2000] 1 Lloyd's Rep. 218 (on appeal on other issues, [2002] UKHL 43, [2003] 1 A.C. 959); *Brown Jenkinson & Co Ltd v Percy Dalton (London) Ltd* [1957] 2 Q.B. 621.

[62] *GE Commercial Finance Ltd v Gee* [2005] EWHC 2056 (QB); [2006] 1 Lloyd's Rep 337. However, if there is the requisite state of mind the fact that a person purports to speak on behalf of a company does not insulate him from personal liability: para.25–033.

[63] It has been held that a fraudulent misrepresentation may be made to a machine acting on behalf of the claimant, rather than to an individual, if the machine was set up to process certain information in a particular way in which it would not process information about the material transaction if the correct information were given: *Renault UK v Fleetpro Technical Services Ltd* [2007] EWHC 2541 (QB).

[64] (1837) 2 M. & W. 519 4 M. & W. 337.

[65] *Abu Dhabi Investment Co v H. Clarkson & Co* [2008] EWCA Civ 699.

[66] *Peek v Gurney* (1873) L.R. 6 H.L. 377. But the statutory remedy under the Financial Services and Markets Act 2000 s.90, is not so limited. As to the position in common law negligence, see para.12–036.

[67] *Andrews v Mockford* [1896] 1 Q.B. 372.

[68] *Polhill v Walter* (1832) 3 B. & Ad, 114; *Edgington v Fitzmaurice* (1885) 29 Ch.D. 459 at 482; *Brown Jenkinson & Co Ltd v Percy Dalton (London) Ltd* [1957] 2 Q.B. 621.

D. Reliance

12–015 The claimant must have been induced by the false representation of the defendant to act as he did, which, in the vast majority of cases,[69] is to have entered into a transaction.[70] It is rare for a person to enter upon a transaction solely on the basis of one factor and it is no bar to a claim for damages for deceit that the claimant was influenced by other things beside the defendant's misrepresentation.[71] Nor need the misrepresentation be even the decisive factor, so long as it has a real or substantial effect on the claimant's decision.[72] It is wrong to ask what the claimant would have done if he had known the truth:[73] if he proves that he was induced by the lie he has made out his case on liability.[74]

12–016 **Opportunity to discover the truth.** If the claimant does rely on the defendant's statement it is no defence that he acted incautiously and failed to take those steps to verify its truth which a prudent person would have taken[75] and since 1945 the Law Reform (Contributory Negligence) Act has no application to cases of deceit.[76] In *Central Ry of Venezuela v Kisch*[77] directors of a company made deceitful statements in a prospectus and were held liable to a shareholder defrauded thereby, although the prospectus stated that certain documents could be inspected at the company's office and, if the shareholder had taken the trouble to do so, he would have discovered the fraud.[78]

12–017 **Ambiguous statements.** In the case of an ambiguous statement the claimant must prove: (1) the sense in which he understood the statement; (2) that in that sense it was false; and (3) that the defendant intended him to understand it in that sense or deliberately made use of the ambiguity with the express purpose of deceiving him.[79] It does not follow because the defendant uses ambiguous language that he is conscious of the way in which the claimant will understand it. Unless the defendant: "[I]s conscious that it will be understood in a different

---

[69] But not all: *Parabola Investments Ltd v Browallia Cal Ltd* [2009] EWHC 901 (Comm) (the claimant abstained "from doing something bearing on his material interests" when he continued with financially disastrous trading because of the defendant's misrepresentations as to performance; (affirmed, without reference to this point: [2010] EWCA Civ 486; [2011] Q.B. 477).

[70] *Downs v Chappell* [1997] 1 W.L.R. 426.

[71] *Edgington v Fitzmaurice* (1885) 29 Ch.D. 459.

[72] *JEB Fasteners Ltd v Marks Bloom & Co* [1983] 1 All E.R. 583 at 589 per Stephenson LJ.

[73] In the sense that one should not allow the fraudster to say "you would still have acted in the same way", but there is no reason why the claimant should not be allowed to prove that he would have acted differently as cogent evidence of inducement: *Parabola Investments Ltd v Browallia Cal Ltd* [2009] EWHC 901 (Comm) (affirmed, without reference to this point: [2010] EWCA Civ 486; [2011] Q.B. 477).

[74] *Downs v Chappell* [1997] 1 W.L.R. 426; *Smith v Kay* (1859) 7 H.L. Cas. 750 at 759.

[75] In an extreme case a submission of this sort and the evidence in support of it may point to the conclusion that the claimant was not, in fact, misled.

[76] *Standard Chartered Bank v Pakistan National Shipping Corp (Nos 2 and 4)* [2002] UKHL 43; [2003] 1 A.C. 959. See para.23–058.

[77] (1867) L.R. 2 H.L. 99.

[78] So too, *Dobell v Stevens* (1825) 3 B. & C. 623; *Mellor v Partridge* [2013] EWCA Civ 477 at [20].

[79] *Smith v Chadwick* (1884) 9 App. Cas. 187 at 201 per Lord Blackburn; *Arkwright v Newbold* (1881) 17 Ch. D. 301 at 324 per Cotton LJ; *AIC Ltd v ITS Testing Services (UK) Ltd* [2006] EWCA Civ 1601; [2007] 1 Lloyd's Rep 555 at [253].

manner from that in which he is honestly though blunderingly using it, he is not fraudulent. An honest blunder in the use of language is not dishonest."[80]

An ambiguous statement must therefore be taken in the sense in which the defendant intended it to be understood, and however reasonable a claimant may be in attaching the untrue meaning to the statement, there is no deceit unless the defendant intended his words to be taken in that sense.[81]

In *Smith v Chadwick*,[82] the prospectus of a company alleged that, "the present value of the turnover or output of the entire works is over £1,000,000 sterling per annum". Did this mean that the works had actually turned out in one year produce worth more than a million, or at that rate per year? If so, it was untrue. Or did it mean only that the works were capable of turning out that amount of produce? If so, it was true. The claimant failed to prove that he had interpreted the words in the sense in which they were false, so he lost his action. On the question of the actual meaning of the statement, the court was evenly divided, but there is no doubt that if an allegation is deliberately put forth in an ambiguous form with the design of catching the claimant on that meaning of it which makes it false, it is fraudulent and indeed is aggravated by a shabby attempt to get the benefit of a fraud without incurring the responsibility.[83]

E. Damage

Nature of the damage. Damage is the gist of the action for deceit. The damage which the claimant must prove that he has suffered in consequence of acting upon the statement will usually be financial but it may consist of personal injury[84] or mental distress[85] or damage to property; and it has also been held that loss of possession of a regulated tenancy under the Rent Acts, even without actual financial loss, will suffice.[86]

12–018

Recoverable loss. In principle the claimant is entitled, so far as money can do it, to be put into the position in which he would have been if the fraudulent statement had not been made and the defendant must make reparation for all the actual losses which flow from his deceit. Although the fraudulent statement will usually have induced the claimant to enter a contract, the damages recoverable in deceit differ from the damages recoverable for breach of contract in that the

12–019

---

[80] *Angus v Clifford* [1891] 2 Ch. 449 at 472 per Bowen LJ; *Smith v Chadwick* (1892) 20 Ch.D. 27 at 79 per Lindley LJ; *Gross v Lewis Hillman Ltd* [1970] Ch. 445.

[81] *Akerhielm v De Mare* [1959] A.C. 789 at 805 per Lord Jenkins. The meaning placed by the defendant on the representation may be so far removed from the sense in which it would be understood by any reasonable person as to make it impossible to hold that the defendant honestly understood the representation to bear the meaning claimed by him and honestly believed it in that sense to be true: *Henry Ansbacher & Co Ltd v Brinks Stern, The Times*, June 26, 1997.

[82] (1884) 9 App. Cas. 187.

[83] *Smith v Chadwick* (1884) 9 App. Cas. 187 at 201 per Lord Blackburn.

[84] *Langridge v Levy* (1837) 2 M. & W. 519 (1838) 4 M. & W. 337; *Burrows v Rhodes* [1899] 1 Q.B. 816. See also *Allan v Ellis & Co* [1990] 11 E.G. 78 (misdescription in survey causative of claimant's subsequent fall); *Banks v Cox* [2002] EWHC 2166 (Ch) (depression).

[85] *Shelley v Paddock* [1979] Q.B. 120, affirmed [1980] Q.B. 348; *Saunders v Edwards* [1987] 1 W.L.R. 1116, *A v B* [2007] EWHC 1246 (QB); [2007] 2 F.L.R. 1051. In *F. v Wirral MBC* [1991] Fam. 69 it is suggested that deceit leading to loss of parental "rights" could be actionable.

[86] *Mafo v Adams* [1979] 1 Q.B. 548.

claimant cannot recover the gains he would have made from that transaction (his expectation loss). In an action for deceit he gets his money back, not the profit, if any, he would have earned from investing it. However, in some cases he may recover for the loss of opportunity to lay out his money in other, more profitable ways which he is unable to pursue as a result of the tort, including other contracts.[87] A decision that he may even recover on the basis of what his deal *with the defendant* would have been had the latter told him the truth seems almost to elide the difference between the two measures of damages.[88]

12–020 **Time of assessment.** Where the claimant has been induced to buy property by a fraudulent representation the normal assessment of damages is the difference between the price he paid and the real value of the property as at the time of acquisition,[89] but this is only a method of giving effect to the overriding principle of compensation.[90] Thus, if a fraud does not come to light for some time the claimant is not necessarily barred from recovering his full loss because the property might have been disposed of at its "false" value immediately after the sale.[91]

In *Smith New Court Securities Ltd v Scrimgeour Vickers (Asset Management) Ltd*[92] C was induced to bid 82p a share for a parcel of 28 million-odd Ferranti shares by a fraudulent misrepresentation that there were other buyers in the market. At that time the shares had a market value of 78p. Unknown to D, Ferranti had itself been defrauded on a massive scale by one G, and when this came out the shares fell in value to 44p. The House of Lords restored the trial judge's decision that C was entitled to damages based on the difference between 82p and 44p and did not have to give credit for the "value" of the shares at the time of purchase.[93] The shares in *Smith New Court* were "fatally flawed" or "pregnant with loss"[94] at the time of acquisition. If D induced C to buy a racehorse by representing that it had a good record as a winner and then it died as

---

[87] *East v Maurer* [1991] 1 W.L.R. 461; *4 Eng Ltd v Harper* [2008] EWHC 915; [2009] Ch. 91. The claimant does not need to identify a specific alternative transaction: *Parabola Investments Ltd v Browallia Cal Ltd* [2009] EWHC 901 (Comm), affirmed [2010] EWCA Civ 486; [2011] Q.B. 477. It would seem to follow that damages should be reduced if the defendant can prove that the claimant would have invested in another *loss making* transaction, but this point is not free from doubt: *Yam Seng Pte Ltd v International Trade Corp Ltd* [2013] EWHC 111 (QB); [2013] 1 Lloyd's Rep 526, where the contrary position is described as "impossible to defend" (at [217]).

[88] *Clef Aquitaine SARL v Laporte Materials (Barrow) Ltd* [2001] Q.B. 488.

[89] Or at the time at which the claimant was irrevocably committed to the purchase, which may be earlier, e.g. exchange of contracts: *Butler-Creagh v Hersham* [2011] EWHC 2525 (QB).

[90] *Smith New Court Securities Ltd v Scrimgeour Vickers (Asset Management) Ltd* [1997] A.C. 254 at 284.

[91] *Peek v Derry* (1887) 37 Ch. D. 541 at 591 (reversed on a different point (1889) 14 App. Cas. 337). For an extreme application of this in a case of negligent misrepresentation, see *Naughton v O'Callaghan* [1990] 3 All E.R. 991, though quaere whether it is consistent with *Banque Bruxelles Lambert SA v Eagle Star Insurance Co Ltd* [1997] A.C. 191.

[92] [1997] A.C. 254.

[93] Note that if C had been able to rescind the contract he would have recovered the price in exchange for the shares and the quantum of loss would have been irrelevant. A claim to rescind seems to have been abandoned because the shares had been sold, but Lord Browne-Wilkinson was of the tentative opinion that C might have rescinded by tendering an equivalent quantity of other Ferranti shares.

[94] *Smith New Court Securities Ltd v Scrimgeour Vickers (Asset Management) Ltd* [1997] A.C. 254 at 267 per Lord Browne-Wilkinson.

a result of some latent disease it already had, C would be able to recover all he had paid for it.[95] The case would have been different if the slump in value had been caused by a subsequent fraud, for then the fraud practised by D would have been a cause of C's loss only in the sine qua non sense, not an effective cause: it would have been like a case where a person buys a horse for 200 per cent of its true value as the result of a fraudulent misrepresentation about its record and then it *later* catches a disease (wholly unrelated to the fraud) from which it dies.[96] It may be, however, that the fraudster bears the risk of subsequent general falls in the market where, by the nature of the transaction, the claimant will be "locked into" the property[97] or where it is acquired with the intention of retaining it. In *Banque Bruxelles Lambert SA v Eagle Star Insurance Co Ltd*[98] the House of Lords held that a negligent valuer did not bear this risk because his liability was confined to the consequences of the information which he gave being wrong, but the position in a case of fraud, where the law looks to the consequences of the transaction, was left open.[99]

Mitigation and remoteness. The claimant must, of course, give credit for any 12–021 benefit he may have received from the transaction into which he entered as a result of the deceit, provided it may fairly be said to be causally related to the transaction.[100] He is also required to mitigate his loss once he is aware of the fraud and he can reasonably act upon it. Indeed, this is the basis for the "normal" assessment of loss by reference to the date of acquisition,[101] referred to above.[102] Subject to this the claimant may also[103] recover consequential loss which is directly caused by the fraud, for example liabilities reasonably incurred in seeking to run a business[104] or damage to other property caused by a fraudulently

---

[95] Cockburn CJ's example in *Twycross v Grant* (1877) 2 C.P.D. 469 at 544–545. See also *MAN Nutzfahrzeuge AG v Freightliner Ltd* [2005] EWHC 2347 (Comm) at [242] ("bad apple" financial controller within acquired company, on appeal on other issues [2007] EWCA Civ 910; [2008] P.N.L.R. 6).
[96] The other example in *Twycross v Grant*, approved by Lord Steyn in *Smith New Court*. Both he and Cockburn CJ plainly thought that D would be liable for the difference between the price paid and the "true" value, but should D be liable at all in such a case? Has the supervening event prevented his fraud having damaging effect? The view that D is liable for the difference between the price paid and the true value can of course be defended by reference to a mechanical rule based on assessment of damages at the time of the sale but such a rule is rejected in *Smith New Court. Naughton v O'Callaghan* [1990] 3 All E.R. 991 is a difficult case. The horse "as was" would have been worth, at the time of sale, a very large proportion of the price paid. Its value fell sharply because it turned out not to be a winner; but there was no evidence that it would have been a winner "as represented".
[97] As where he lends money on an over-valued security.
[98] [1997] A.C. 191, para.7–059.
[99] In *Downs v Chappell* [1997] 1 W.L.R. 426, Hobhouse LJ in a case of fraud applied what seems to be essentially the negligence principle and Lord Steyn (and perhaps Lord Browne-Wilkinson) in *Smith New Court* said that this was wrong. May J in *Slough Estates Plc v Welwyn Hatfield DC* [1996] 2 P.L.R. 50 imposed liability in deceit for losses attributable to a general fall in the market.
[100] Cf. *Hussey v Eels* [1990] 2 Q.B. 227 (not a case of fraud).
[101] *Smith New Court Securities Ltd v Scrimgeour Vickers (Asset Management) Ltd* [1997] A.C. 254 per Lord Browne-Wilkinson.
[102] See para.12–020.
[103] As to exemplary damages, see para.23–012.
[104] *Doyle v Olby (Ironmongers) Ltd* [1969] 2 Q.B. 158; *Downs v Chappell* [1997] 1 W.L.R. 426. In *Hornal v Neuberger Products Ltd* [1957] 1 Q.B. 247, the claimant was induced to buy a lathe by a

concealed danger.[105] As an intentional wrongdoer the fraudster is not entitled to the benefit of the reasonable foreseeability test of remoteness commonly applicable in tort,[106] but has to pay for all actual loss directly flowing from the transaction he induced.[107]

F.   Excluding Liability[108]

12–022   A person guilty of deceit will remain liable whatever he may have said by way of disclaimer,[109] though the same does not necessarily apply to a clause excluding liability for the fraud of his agent.[110]

3.   LIABILITY FOR NEGLIGENT MISSTATEMENT

12–023   **The introduction of liability in negligence.** *Derry v Peek* settled that liability for deceit is liability for fraudulent and not for careless statements, but for many years the case was treated as authority for more than that, for the House of Lords was taken to have held that there could be no tortious liability for a misstatement unless it was fraudulent.[111] In 1914 the House itself, in *Nocton v Lord Ashburton*,[112] pointed out that *Derry v Peek* had not ruled out every form of liability (independent of statute) but that for fraud. Not only would there be liability in contract but it could exist in equity as well, where there was a fiduciary relationship, for advice which was not "dishonest" in the common law sense. Fifty years later, in *Hedley Byrne & Co Ltd v Heller & Partners Ltd*,[113] the House was able to rely on *Nocton v Lord Ashburton* as showing that *Derry v Peek* governed only liability for deceit so that they were not precluded from holding that a tortious duty of care in making statements might exist. In the period between these cases it was also recognised that there could be liability for

---

fraudulent representation that it was fit for immediate use. Although it was worth what he paid for it, he was put to seven weeks delay in preparing it for use and recovered damages for this delay.

[105] See, e.g. *Mullett v Mason* (1866) L.R. 1 C.P. 559; *Nicholls v Taylor* [1939] V.L.R. 119.

[106] See para.7–037.

[107] *Doyle v Olby (Ironmongers) Ltd* [1969] 2 Q.B. 158; *Smith New Court Securities Ltd v Scrimgeour Vickers (Asset Management) Ltd* [1997] A.C. 254.

[108] The Statute of Frauds Amendment Act 1828 which may provide a defence to a claim in deceit is considered below in terms of its application to both deceit and negligence: see para.12–054.

[109] *HIH Casualty and General Insurance Ltd v Chase Manhattan Bank* [2003] UKHL 6; [2003] 2 Lloyd's Rep. 61.

[110] This was the view of the CA in *HIH Casualty and General Insurance Ltd v Chase Manhattan Bank* [2001] EWCA Civ 1250; [2001] 2 Lloyd's Rep. 483. However, the HL did not have to decide the point since the clause did not cover such a situation. It is probably "extraordinarily unlikely" that parties to a contract will agree such a term, "with sufficient clarity to raise squarely the question of whether it should be lawful to do so": Lord Hoffmann [2003] UKHL 6; [2003] 2 Lloyd's Rep. 61 at [81]. Cf. *Frans Maas (UK) Ltd v Samsung Electronics (UK) Ltd* [2004] EWHC 1502 (Comm); [2004] 2 Lloyd's Rep. 251 (wilful wrongdoing of servants in performance of contract).

[111] However, the year after *Derry v Peek*, Parliament imposed liability for false statements in prospectuses by the Directors Liability Act 1890. See now Financial Services and Markets Act 2000 ss.90, 90A.

[112] [1914] A.C. 932.

[113] [1964] A.C. 465.

physical damage caused by a misleading statement.[114] Many cases which are primarily thought of in terms of acts also contain elements of misstatement: no harm would have come to the pursuer in *Donoghue v Stevenson*, for example, if there had been no implied representation that the ginger beer was fit for human consumption. Indeed, in some cases the distinction between word and deed is for all practical purposes non-existent. Quite apart from contract, a doctor is as much liable for negligently advising his patient to take a certain drug as he is for negligently injecting the drug himself. However, in *Hedley Byrne* the loss was unquestionably pecuniary or economic.

Hedley Byrne v Heller. The facts of *Hedley Byrne* were that the claimants, who were advertising agents, were anxious to know whether they could safely give credit to a company, Easipower, on whose behalf they had entered into various advertising contracts, and they therefore sought bankers' references about Easipower. For this purpose the claimants' bankers approached the defendants, who were Easipower's bankers, and on two occasions the defendants gave favourable references. These were passed on to the claimants by their bankers and, although the defendants did not know who the claimants were and had in fact marked their communications to the claimants' bankers "Confidential. For your private use . . . ", they did know the inquiry was made in connection with an advertising contract. They must also have known that the references were to be passed on to a customer.[115] In reliance on these references the claimants incurred expenditure on Easipower's behalf and, when Easipower went into liquidation, they suffered substantial loss. This loss they sought to recover from the defendants in an action based upon the defendants' alleged negligence in giving favourable references concerning Easipower. **12–024**

At first instance McNair J held that the defendants owed no duty to the claimants, and this decision was affirmed in the Court of Appeal[116] both on the ground that the case was covered by authority and also on the ground that it would not be reasonable to impose upon a banker an obligation to exercise care when informing a third party of the credit-worthiness of his client. In the House of Lords the decision in favour of the defendants was affirmed, but none of their Lordships based his decision on a general rule of non-liability for negligent misstatement. On the contrary, Lords Reid, Devlin and Pearce held that, assuming the defendants to have been negligent, the only reason for exonerating them was that the references had been given "without responsibility".[117] Lord Hodson and, perhaps, Lord Morris considered that even without this denial of responsibility there was no duty of care on the facts, but nevertheless agreed that a duty of care in making statements was a legal possibility.

---

[114] See, e.g. *Watson v Buckley, Osborne, Garrett & Co Ltd* [1940] 1 All E.R. 174. See also *Clayton v Woodman & Son (Builders) Ltd* [1962] 2 Q.B. 533 (reversed on the facts [1962] 1 W.L.R. 585) and *The Apollo* [1891] A.C. 499.

[115] [1964] A.C. 465 at 482, 503.

[116] *Hedley Byrne & Co Ltd v Heller & Partners Ltd* [1962] 1 Q.B. 396.

[117] See para.12–044.

A. A Special Relationship

12–025   We have seen that *Hedley Byrne* has been regarded as the progenitor of the principle of "assumption of responsibility", which has now been extended beyond liability for statements.[118] In that broader context the decision has really become part of the background to the House of Lords cases in the 1990s concerning services to be performed for the claimant or a third party.[119] However, we are now concerned with *Hedley Byrne* in the particular context of statements and advice and it should not be assumed that all cases based upon assumption of responsibility have common characteristics: for example, in the situations dealt with in this section it is always necessary that the claimant should have relied on the statement, whereas reliance is not always necessary in the broader context.[120]

It is clear from *Hedley Byrne* that for a duty of care to arise in respect of speech or writing, something more is required than in the straightforward case of physical damage caused by an act where, generally speaking, foreseeability of harm will be sufficient. This is very largely because a statement is likely to cause economic loss rather than physical harm and the risk of crushing liability is exacerbated by the fact that information is likely to be disseminated among a large number of persons even if it was originally addressed only to a small group. In some activities, for example auditing or financial advice, the potential liability is so great that it is beyond the capacity of the insurance market.[121] Their Lordships in *Hedley Byrne* were in general agreement that *Donoghue v Stevenson* had little, if any, direct bearing on the problem of negligent misstatement and that a duty of care would exist in relation to statements only if there is a "special relationship" between the parties, a relationship of close "proximity". Indeed, Lord Devlin spoke in terms of a relationship "equivalent to contract"[122] and in a later case where liability was imposed on a valuer engaged by a mortgagee for loss incurred by the mortgagor as a result of a negligent report, the relationship between the valuer and mortgagor was described as "akin to contract".[123] While expressly disclaiming any intention to lay down conditions which were either conclusive or exclusive, Lord Oliver in *Caparo Plc v Dickman*[124] described the necessary relationship as typically having four characteristics:

> "(1) the advice is required for a purpose, whether particularly specified or generally described, which is made known, either actually or inferentially, to the adviser at the time when the advice is given; (2) the adviser knows, either actually or inferentially, that his advice will be communicated to the advisee, either specifically or as a member of an ascertained class, in order that it should be used by the advisee for that purpose; (3) it is known, either actually or

---

[118] See para.5–049.

[119] See para.5–051.

[120] See para.5–054.

[121] See para.5–032.

[122] *Hedley Byrne & Co Ltd v Heller & Partners Ltd* [1964] A.C. 465 at 530.

[123] *Smith v Eric S. Bush* [1990] 1 A.C. 831 at 846 per Lord Templeman. However, the situation here was different: the recipient had paid for the advice but he had paid a third party, who was the direct recipient.

[124] [1990] 2 A.C. 605 at 638.

inferentially, that the advice so communicated is likely to be acted upon by the advisee for that purpose without independent inquiry[125]; and (4) it is so acted upon by the advisee to his detriment."

B. Professional Advisers

There is a view that liability is further restricted to professional advisers or those claiming equivalent skills. This is based on the majority view in the Privy Council in *Mutual Life and Citizens' Assurance Co Ltd v Evatt*.[126] The claimant, a policyholder in the defendant company, sought advice from it as to the financial soundness of another company, "Palmer", with which it was closely associated. The information he was given was incorrect and he lost his money. It was held by the majority that the omission from the claimant's declaration of any allegation that the defendant was in the business of supplying information or advice or had claimed to possess the necessary skill to do so was fatal. However, the minority took a broader approach:[127]

12–026

> "[O]ne must assume a reasonable man who has that degree of knowledge and skill which facts known to the inquirer (including statements made by the adviser) entitled him to expect of the adviser, and then inquire whether a reasonable man could have given the advice which was in fact given if he had exercised reasonable care."

This approach has recommended itself to judges at first instance[128] and in the Court of Appeal,[129] though strictly perhaps it has not been necessary for them to choose between the majority and minority views in *Evatt*'s case.[130] The issue was also really irrelevant when the House of Lords considered *Hedley Byrne* in *Smith v Eric S Bush*[131] and in *Caparo Industries Plc v Dickman*.[132] In fact, the extent of the practical difference between the two camps very much depends upon the way in which the court interprets the majority test in *Evatt* and its qualifications.[133] Thus, it seems clear that the expression "business or profession" is not meant to confine liability to those engaged in private enterprise or the pursuit of profit, but may extend to a public authority supplying information and in *Spring v Guardian*

---

[125] See *Patchett v Swimming Pool and Allied Trades Association Ltd* [2009] EWCA Civ 717; [2010] 2 All E.R. (Comm) 138 (trade association website; advice to seek further information). Cf. *HSBC Bank Plc v So* [2009] EWCA Civ 296; [2009] 1 C.L.C. 503 (no reason to investigate matter where other party had made unqualified statement about matter within its own knowledge).

[126] [1971] A.C. 793.

[127] [1971] A.C. 793 at 812 per Lords Reid and Morris.

[128] *Argy Trading Development Co Ltd v Lapid Developments Ltd* [1977] 1 W.L.R. 444.

[129] *Esso Petroleum Co Ltd v Mardon* [1976] Q.B. 801 at 827; *Howard Marine and Dredging Co Ltd v A Ogden (Excavations) Ltd* [1978] Q.B. 574.

[130] See the differing views expressed in *Shaddock v Parramatta CC* (1981) 36 A.L.R. 385 about the extent to which the facts could be covered by the *Evatt* formula.

[131] [1990] 1 A.C. 831.

[132] [1990] 2 A.C. 605.

[133] Namely, that a duty may arise if the defendant holds himself out as possessing a skill equivalent to that of a "professional" or if he has a financial interest in the transaction. The former case in particular seems capable of almost infinite expansion.

Assurance Plc,[134] where the claim arose from an incorrect reference, Lord Goff, having referred to the criticisms of *Evatt*, said that in any event it did not stand in the way of a decision in favour of the claimant, for the skill of preparing a reference in respect of an employee falls as much within the expertise of an employer as the skill of preparing a bank reference fell within the expertise of the bank.

C. Voluntariness

12–027   There is a clear thread running through *Hedley Byrne* that the duty arises from an "undertaking", express or implied, to use due care, a voluntary assumption of responsibility, but it is plain that these expressions should not be understood as requiring any actual or subjective acceptance of legal liability by the defendant. In *Smith v Eric S Bush*, Lord Griffiths said that: "[T]he phrase 'assumption of responsibility' can only have any real meaning if it is understood as referring to the circumstances in which the law will deem the maker of the statement to have assumed responsibility to the person who acts upon the advice."[135]Indeed, where a surveyor carried out a valuation of an ordinary dwelling house on the instructions of a building society he thereby "assumed responsibility" to the intending purchaser who, as he knew, would rely upon his skill, even though in fact he attempted (unsuccessfully) to exclude his liability.[136] The test is an objective one applied to the context and what passes between the claimant and the defendant:[137]

> "Because the question of whether a defendant has assumed responsibility is a legal inference to be drawn from his conduct against the background of all the circumstances of the case, it is by no means a simple question of fact. Questions of fairness and policy will enter into the decision."[138]

The assumption of responsibility is certainly voluntary in the sense that at common law the defendant can normally displace the duty by disclaimer, but this escape route is often barred by the Unfair Contract Terms Act 1977.[139]

---

[134] [1995] 2 A.C. 296. Note that this case does not represent a straightforward *Hedley Byrne* situation since the statement was made by D to X about C: see para.12–050. See also *Lennon v MPC* [2004] EWCA Civ 130; [2004] 1 W.L.R. 2594.

[135] *Smith v Eric S Bush* [1990] 1 A.C. 831 at 862. See also *Phelps v Hillingdon LBC* [2001] 2 A.C. 619 at 654 per Lord Slynn ("It is not so much that responsibility is assumed as that it is recognised or imposed by the law").

[136] *Smith v Eric S Bush* [1990] 1 A.C. 831. Note that the building society does not assume responsibility for the accuracy of the report of an independent valuer: its duty is to take care in selecting the valuer. Cf. *Harris v Wyre Forest DC* [1990] 1 A.C. 831 (appeal heard with *Smith v Bush*) where the valuer was a servant of the lender and the lender was vicariously liable for his negligence.

[137] *Williams v Natural Life Health Foods Ltd* [1998] 1 W.L.R. 830 at 835; *Electra Private Equity Partners v K.P.M.G. Peat Marwick* [2001] B.C.L.C. 589.

[138] Lord Hoffmann in *Customs and Excise Commrs v Barclays Bank Plc* [2006] UKHL 28; [2007] 1 A.C. 181 at [36].

[139] See para.12–045.

D. Public Officers and Bodies

We have already seen that a certification or inspection authority may incur liability for personal injury to a member of the public even without any direct communication or reliance.[140] Even where there is a direct statement, however, matters are not so simple with regard to economic loss, even though a public authority has no "immunity".[141] For example, a person who alleges that an inspection authority has told him to spend more than was necessary on safety precautions may have difficulty in establishing a duty of care because such a duty might encourage untoward cautiousness in the performance of the statutory function.[142] In one of the early American cases liability was imposed upon a public weigher whose negligent notification caused a purchaser of goods to pay too much for them[143] and Lord Oliver in *Caparo* implied that the result would be the same here. A local land registry was held liable when its answer to an inquiry caused an incumbrancer to lose his rights.[144] Although this was not a "standard" statement case in that the loss was suffered by a third party rather than the recipient of the statement, it does show that voluntary assumption of responsibility cannot, even in an attenuated sense, be the universal solvent—it was the defendant's statutory function to respond to search requests.

12–028

It will be recalled that a local authority owes no duty of care to prospective owners of houses in respect of statutory inspections during construction.[145] In principle, however, it has been said that a clear, subsequent assertion, in response to an inquiry, that an inspection had proved satisfactory could attract liability under *Hedley Byrne*.[146] Persons undertaking development of land must, perforce, rely on planning authorities to perform their functions and may make inquiries before embarking on the project. It has been held that "the ordinary process of giving routine advice to an applicant for planning permission and answering such questions as he or she may raise, especially when the applicant is one known to have her own professional advisers" does not give rise to any duty of care.[147]

---

[140] See para.5–031.

[141] So in *Gooden v Northamptonshire CC* [2001] EWCA Civ 1744; [2002] P.N.L.R. 18 it was accepted that a local authority could owe a duty in answering search enquiries.

[142] *Harris v Evans* [1998] 1 W.L.R. 1285. In fact the case involved not advice but the making of a prohibition notice, which brought into play the statutory appeal process. In *Welton v North Cornwall DC* [1997] 1 W.L.R. 570, where the defendants' environmental health officer imposed wholly excessive hygiene requirements upon the claimants' guest house, the claim was described as "well within" *Hedley Byrne* and "incontrovertible". The court in *Harris* was able to distinguish *Welton* because there the "advice" was directly given to the claimant, whereas in *Harris* the officer caused the local authority to impose the prohibition notice, but it clearly had doubts about *Welton*.

[143] *Glanzer v Shepherd* 135 N.E. 275 (1922).

[144] *Ministry of Housing and Local Government v Sharp* [1970] 2 Q.B. 223.

[145] See para.10–049.

[146] *King v North Cornwall DC* [1995] N.P.C. 21.

[147] *Haddow v Secretary of State for the Environment* [2000] Env L.R. 212; *Tidman v Reading BC* [1994] E.G.C.S. 180; *Fashion Brokers Ltd v Clarke Hayes* [2000] Lloyd's Rep. P.N. 398.

E.   *Hedley Byrne* and Contract Relations

12–029   **Concurrent liability.** Negligent misstatement very often takes place in the context of a contract. It was established in *Henderson v Merrett Syndicates Ltd*[148] that a duty of care in tort could coexist with a contractual obligation where there had been an assumption of responsibility in relation to the provision of services and the same is true in relation to a statement.[149] Where there is a contract between the parties there is no reason in principle why there should not be a tort duty of care, during the currency of the contract, which involves a matter outside the scope of the contract,[150] but the fact that the proposed duty is inconsistent with the terms of the contact is, of course, reason for rejecting it.[151]

12–030   **Section 2(1) of the Misrepresentation Act 1967.** In relation to the negotiations leading to a contract the importance of *Hedley Byrne* was very much diminished by s.2(1) of the Misrepresentation Act 1967. This provides that where a person has entered into a contract after a misrepresentation has been made to him by another party to the contract then, if the representor would have been liable in damages if the representation had been made fraudulently, he shall be so liable unless he proves that he had reasonable grounds to believe that the statement was true.[152] This is more favourable to the claimant than *Hedley Byrne* because there can be no argument about duty and the defendant bears the burden of proving that he had reasonable grounds to believe in the truth of his statement.[153] However, there may still be cases where no contract is concluded (but the claimant has still suffered loss) or where it is sought to impose liability upon an agent.[154]

12–031   **Duty owed to non-contracting parties.** The fact that D, in relation to the statement which causes damage to C, is performing a task under contract for X does not mean that D may not owe a duty of care to C—this is, after all, the "statement" equivalent of *Donoghue v Stevenson*.[155] A valuer engaged to value an ordinary dwelling on behalf of the mortgagee owes a duty of care to the mortgagor (purchaser) to whom he knows the report will be shown[156] and where accountants or financial advisers provide information to persons contemplating a

---

[148] [1995] 2 A.C. 145.

[149] *Esso Petroleum Co Ltd v Mardon* [1976] Q.B. 801; *Howard Marine and Dredging Co Ltd v A. Ogden & Son (Excavations) Ltd* [1978] Q.B. 574; *Hagen v ICI* [2002] I.R.L.R. 31.

[150] *Holt v Payne Skillington* (1995) 49 Con L.R. 99 (where, however, there was no sufficient pleaded case).

[151] *J Nunes Diamonds Ltd v Dominion Electric Co* (1972) 26 D.L.R. (3d) 699. Though not a *Hedley Byrne* case, *Tai Hing Cotton Mill Ltd v Liu Chong Hing Bank Ltd* [1986] A.C. 80 is another example of the principle.

[152] Since the liability created by s.2(1) is, ex hypothesi, non-contractual (a misrepresentation is not a term) the measure of damages is tortious, not contractual, but it was some time before the case law settled to this view in *Royscott Trust v Rogerson* [1991] 2 Q.B. 297. The application in that case of the deceit rule of remoteness is regrettable.

[153] See also Bridge LJ in *Howard Marine and Dredging*[1978] Q.B. 574 who points out that, quite apart from the burden of proof, the "fault" required under the Act is not necessarily the same as common law negligence.

[154] See para.12–032.

[155] See *White v Jones* [1995] 2 A.C. 207.

[156] *Smith v Eric S. Bush* [1990] A.C. 831.

transaction with their client they may owe a duty to those persons.[157] However, the nature of the contractual arrangements between the various parties[158] or the nature of the transaction may lead to the conclusion that no special relationship arises. Thus, the valuer for the mortgagee may not owe a duty to the purchaser where the sale involves a commercial[159] or industrial property or an expensive residential property[160] and the same will apply where for other reasons it is legitimate to expect that the claimant will undertake his own inquiries.[161] Although it has been said that once a case falls "within the *Hedley Byrne* principle, there should be no need to embark upon any further inquiry whether it is fair, just and reasonable to impose liability for economic loss",[162] cases of this type sometimes show an inclination to test the issue of duty against the *Caparo* tripartite factors, even if assumption of responsibility is the starting point.[163]

F. Agents

Personal liability of the agent. The statement may be made by the agent of one party to a transaction, in the sense of representing that party in the matter. The principal will incur liability for what the agent says if that is within the scope of his authority and, depending on the terms of any contract between them, the principal will in turn have recourse against the agent. The agent may also incur personal liability in tort to the recipient of the statement[164] and this will be relevant, for example, if the principal is insolvent. In *Williams v Natural Life Health Foods Ltd*[165] the House of Lords held that a director of a company did not owe a duty of care to its customers merely because he worked on the fulfilment of the contract which they made with the company—there must be something in his conduct to justify a finding of assumption of personal responsibility. However, it was never doubted in earlier cases that a valuer was (in theory) personally liable

12–032

---

[157] See the dissenting judgment of Denning LJ (which was approved in *Hedley Byrne*) in *Candler v Crane Christmas & Co* [1951] 2 K.B. 164; *Morgan Crucible v Hill Samuel Bank Ltd* [1991] Ch. 295; *Electra Private Equity Partners v K.P.M.G. Peat Marwick* [2001] B.C.L.C. 589.

[158] As in *Pacific Associates Inc v Baxter* [1990] 1 Q.B. 993 and *Galliford Try Infrastructure Ltd v Mott MacDonald Ltd* [2008] EWHC 1570 (TCC); 120 Con L.R. 1. But there is certainly no rule that the fact that the parties have arranged their relationships so that there is no direct contractual link precludes a duty of care: *Henderson v Merrett Syndicates Ltd* [1995] 2 A.C. 181; *Riyad Bank v Ahli United Bank (UK)* [2006] EWCA Civ 780; [2006] 2 Lloyd's Rep 292.

[159] No duty was found to be owed where the mortgagor was purchasing a residential house as part of a buy-to-let scheme: *Scullion v Bank of Scotland Plc* [2011] EWCA Civ 693; [2011] 1 W.L.R. 3212.

[160] *Smith v Eric S. Bush* [1990] A.C. 831; cf. *McCullagh v Lane Fox & Partners Ltd* [1996] 1 E.G.L.R. 35.

[161] *James McNaughton Paper Group Ltd v Hicks Anderson & Co* [1991] 2 Q.B. 295 (draft accounts requested as quickly as possible for use in negotiation; buyers aware of poor state of client's affairs).

[162] Lord Goff in *Henderson v Merrett Syndicates Ltd* [1995] 2 A.C. 145 at 181.

[163] *Electra Private Equity Partners v KPMG Peat Marwick* [2001] B.C.L.C. 589; *Bank of Credit and Commerce International (Overseas) Ltd v Price Waterhouse (No.2)* [1998] P.N.L.R. 564. However, if the assumption of responsibility is clear such questions may tend to answer themselves: *Customs and Excise Commrs v Barclays Bank* [2006] UKHL 28; [2007] 1 A.C. 181 at [85].

[164] The agent will generally not be party to any contract with the recipient. Nor will the agent incur a personal liability under the Misrepresentation Act 1967 s.2(1): *Resolute Maritime v Nippon Karji Kyokai* [1983] 1 W.L.R. 857.

[165] [1998] 1 W.L.R. 830. See para.25–033.

to the house buyer whose intended house he surveyed and in *Merrett v Babb*[166] the Court of Appeal held that this was so, notwithstanding *Williams*,[167] even though the house buyer had never had any communication with him and his employer was insolvent and uninsured.

On the other hand, in *Gran Gelato Ltd v Richcliff (Group) Ltd*[168] (which was not referred to in *Merrett v Babb*) Nicholls VC declined to impose a duty of care upon the vendor's solicitor in answering inquiries before contract because the vendor's liability for the acts of his agent done on his behalf was a reasonable and sufficient legal protection for the purchaser, even though that liability would become worthless in the event of the vendor's insolvency. This seems difficult to reconcile with *Merrett v Babb*. What was being done in *Gran Gelato* was not concerned with an adversarial matter, where there is no doubt that one should deny a duty of care in the agent to the third party,[169] but on the other hand it cannot be described as a merely ministerial act. Perhaps the case represents a general rule only for solicitors who are doing no more than representing their clients in conveyancing transactions[170] or transactions of a similar nature. Certainly it does not rule out the possibility that even in such a transaction there may be facts to support a direct assumption of responsibility;[171] and in *Dean v Allin & Watts*[172] the Court of Appeal held that a solicitor acting for a borrower on a loan transaction owed a duty of care to the lender to create the effective security which was fundamental to the transaction and which the borrower was willing to grant to the lender.

G. Failure to Speak

12–033   Failure to speak raises the same issues as omissions generally in the law of negligence and misrepresentation. There is no general duty to volunteer information for the protection of others, even between contracting parties,[173] and even where there is a duty to disclose, that primarily relates to the avoidance of the contract, though it seems that in a suitable case there may be damages for

---

[166] [2001] EWCA Civ 214; [2001] Q.B. 1174. See also *McCullagh v Lane Fox & Partners Ltd* [1996] 1 E.G.L.R. 35.

[167] Which May LJ at [45] regarded as turning on the fact that it involved a director.

[168] [1992] Ch. 560.

[169] See the position of lawyers in connection with litigation, para.5–077. See also *Huxford v Stoy Hayward, The Times*, January 11, 1989 (person advising on appointment of receiver; no duty to company's guarantors).

[170] The view of Hobhouse LJ in *McCullagh v Lane Fox & Partners Ltd* [1996] 1 E.G.L.R. 35. See also Lord Goff in *White v Jones* [1995] 2 A.C. 207 at 256, though the point was not in issue there.

[171] See the approval of *Allied Finance and Investments Ltd v Haddow* [1983] N.Z.L.R. 22 in *Gran Gelato Ltd v Richcliff (Group) Ltd* [1992] Ch. 560 at 571.

[172] [2001] EWCA Civ 758; [2001] 2 Lloyd's Rep 249; cited with approval by Lord Bingham in *Customs and Excise Commrs v Barclays Bank Plc* [2006] UKHL 28; [2007] 1 A.C. 181 at [22].

[173] The relationship between banker and customer is not fiduciary and in the absence of some positive assumption of responsibility the bank does not owe a duty to advise the customer on the wisdom of a transaction in respect of which he seeks a loan: *Williams & Glyns Bank Ltd v Barnes* [1981] Com. L.R. 205; *Murphy v HSBC Plc* [2004] EWHC 467 (Ch). In other contexts, the existence and scope of any "duty to speak" is uncertain: *ING Bank N.V. v Ros Roca SA* [2011] EWCA Civ 353 and [2012] 1 W.L.R. 472 at [90]–[96]; cf. *Graiseley Properties Ltd v Barclays Bank Plc* [2013] EWCA Civ 1372 at [26].

deceit.[174] However, everything turns on the responsibility which the defendant has assumed towards the claimant: if, as is clear, D may be liable for an omission if he has undertaken the management of C's affairs,[175] there is no reason why he should not be equally liable if he fails to perform an undertaking to warn C of hazards or problems.[176] If a statement is made in circumstances where there is a duty of care which at the time is fulfilled (because the statement is true or the maker has reasonable cause to believe it to be true) then, by analogy with the law on rescission for misrepresentation and fraud there should be a duty to take steps to bring a change of circumstances to the notice of the recipient where this occurs before he acts upon it.[177] The defendant may, however, make it clear that he is not undertaking to inform of any future developments.[178]

H.   Advice Informally Given

No duty on "social occasions". It is universally agreed that no duty arises in respect of advice requested and given on a purely social occasion, for it is then neither reasonably foreseeable to the defendant that the claimant will rely upon it nor reasonable for the claimant to do so. The boundaries of this type of case, where the informality of the transaction leads to a denial of duty, cannot be drawn with precision.[179] In *Chaudhry v Prabhakar*[180] liability was imposed upon a friend making an assessment of a used car for the claimant. The friend had some knowledge about cars and the task undertaken was related to a specific purchase but the existence of a duty was conceded and one judge doubted the correctness of that concession. In *Howard Marine and Dredging Co Ltd v A Ogden (Excavations) Ltd*[181] the defendant answered an inquiry as to the carrying capacity of barges on the basis of his (accurate) recollection of the Lloyd's Register figure, which was incorrect, and without checking the barge's papers. The actual decision went on s.2(1) of the Misrepresentation Act 1967 but as far as the common law was concerned, two members of the court were of the view that, given the impromptu, "off the cuff" circumstances of the response, the defendant's only duty was to give an honest answer.[182]

12–034

---

[174] See para.12–011.

[175] *Henderson v Merrett Syndicates* [1995] 2 A.C. 145 at 181.

[176] *Holt v Payne Skillington* (1995) 49 Con. L.R. 99 (no duty on facts). Cf. *Van Oppen v Bedford School* [1989] 1 All E.R. 273 and *Reid v Rush & Tompkins Group Plc* [1990] 1 W.L.R. 212 where, despite an existing relationship, there was no implied undertaking to advise about insurance and *Tai Hing Cotton Mill Ltd v Liu Chong Hing Bank Ltd* [1986] A.C. 80 (no duty to check bank statements to check against fraud). In *Hamble Fisheries Ltd v L Gardiner & Sons Ltd* [1999] 2 Lloyd's Rep. 1 there was no relationship at all, simply the fact that C owned an engine made by D's predecessor.

[177] Cf. *McCullagh v Lane Fox & Partners Ltd* [1996] 1 E.G.L.R. 35.

[178] *IFE Fund SA v Goldman Sachs International* [2007] EWCA Civ 811; [2007] 2 Lloyds Rep 449.

[179] If an investment adviser were officiously to seek out someone at a party and suggest the purchase of particular shares, the "social occasion" factor might not help him; in context, is it a "social occasion" at all?

[180] [1989] 1 W.L.R. 29.

[181] [1978] Q.B. 574.

[182] See also *Titan Steel Wheels Ltd v Royal Bank of Scotland Plc* [2010] EWHC 211 (Comm); [2010] 2 Lloyd's Rep. 92 (mere sales conversation). There was a difference of opinion in *Hedley Byrne* as to the outcome of the case in the absence of the disclaimer.

12–035   **Standard of care.** The fear of imposing an unreasonably onerous duty in respect of responses to comparatively informal inquiries may, in the alternative, be met by manipulation of the standard of care required. If it is unreasonable to expect a banker answering a query about a customer to spend time and trouble in searching records and so on, then a duty to take such care as is reasonable in all the circumstances of the case does not require him to do so. The duty of care is not a duty to take every possible care still less is it a duty to be right. Similarly, a surveyor conducting a valuation for mortgage purposes is not expected to go to the lengths required in an expensive structural survey; but if his inspection reveals grounds for suspicion he must take reasonable steps to follow the trail, even though he is working to a standard fee-he must "take the rough with the smooth" or decline to proceed.[183]

I.   The Protected Claimant

12–036   **A test of purpose.** It is clearly not necessary that the defendant should know the identity of the claimant, for in *Hedley Byrne* itself the inquiry was made and the response received via an intermediary bank[184] but the inquiry was clearly on behalf of a particular individual or company. What is the position where information is foreseeably relied on by a larger group of persons? Most of the cases have concerned accountants and auditors and all the earlier decisions must be read in the light of *Caparo Industries Plc v Dickman*,[185] which concerned the statutory audit of the accounts of a public company, which, it was alleged, was performed negligently and gave a misleading impression of the company's financial position and upon which the claimants relied to make a successful bid to acquire the company's shareholding. The House of Lords held that the claim failed. While it was perfectly true that it was foreseeable that the accounts of a public company (which are public documents) might be relied upon by a vast range of persons in an almost infinite variety of dealings with the company, the liability of the auditors had to be considered against the background of the statutory purpose of the audit and this was to enable shareholders to exercise their rights in the management of the company; it was not to provide information to investors, least of all predators. Accordingly, a duty of care was owed neither to persons investing in the company for the first time in reliance on the accounts, nor to existing shareholders who acquired further shares.[186] The auditors are, of course, liable to the company (which engages them on the basis of a contract) for

---

[183] *Roberts v J Hampson & Co* [1990] 1 W.L.R. 94; *Eric S Bush* [1990] 2 A.C. 831. Cf. *Cross v Davis Martin & Mortimer* [1989] 10 E.G. 110.

[184] Lord Reid (at 482) and Lord Morris (at 493) regarded it as sufficient that it was obvious that the inquiry was being made by someone thinking of doing business with Easipower, but the later cases suggest that some more specific knowledge of the nature of the transaction is necessary.

[185] [1990] 2 A.C. 605. See also the decisions of the High Court of Australia in *Esanda Finance Corp Ltd v Peat Marwick Hungerfords* (1997) 188 C.L.R. 241 and the Supreme Court of Canada in *Hercules Management Ltd v Ernst & Young* (1997) 146 D.L.R. (4th) 577.

[186] On the policy factors, see para.5–032. The HL did not decide whether shareholders who, in reliance on an under-valuation, sold existing holdings could sue, but since the basis of the decision is that any duty is owed to the shareholders as a whole it is thought the answer should be "No".

losses caused by a negligent audit, (for example failure to expose an employee who has been defrauding the company).[187]

Given the decision in *Caparo*, it is inevitable that there is no duty on the part of the auditors to the creditors of the company even though they are far fewer in number than potential investors and are easily identified,[188] for the purpose of the audit is not to provide information for them. However, this situation presents legal issues of some difficulty and complexity. Suppose that X is sole beneficial owner of the company and has sole managerial control of it (the so-called "one man company"). X uses the company as a vehicle to defraud C, something which the auditors of the company fail to detect. In accordance with the normal principles of attribution this fraud by X, the "directing mind", would be regarded as also the fraud of the company.[189] The company is therefore liable to C but is probably by now insolvent. Can the liquidator (acting as the company) sue the auditors for the damages for which the company is liable to C? The majority of the House of Lords in *Stone & Rolls Ltd v Moore Stephens*[190] held that he cannot, largely because they viewed it as a de facto reversal of the effect of *Caparo*. The decision is expressly limited to the situation where there is no person involved in the management and ownership of the company other than those implicated in the fraud, the position where there is an "innocent constituency"[191] being left for a future case.

To be contrasted with *Caparo* is the "auditing" situation in *Law Society v KPMG Peat Marwick*.[192] The defendants supplied to a firm of solicitors, DF, a report required by the Solicitors Act 1974 to the effect that the firm had complied with the professional accounting rules and, as the defendants knew, this report was to be sent to the Law Society. It was subsequently discovered that two partners in DF had taken large amounts of clients' money and this led to payments of £8.5 million out of the compensation fund administered by the Law Society. On a preliminary issue based on an allegation that the report was insufficiently qualified, the Court of Appeal held that the defendants owed a duty of care to the Society: although the report was obtained and paid for by DF, the whole purpose of the reporting system was to allow the Law Society to intervene in the running of a firm in order to protect the compensation fund.[193]

Statements made for more than one purpose. It is clear from the cases already considered that the purpose of a statement is not necessarily equivalent to the reliance which may foreseeably be placed on it. Thus, a marine surveyor or   **12–037**

---

[187] However, ss.534 to 538 of the Companies Act 2006 now allows auditors to enter into a fair and reasonable agreement for limitation of liability with the audited company.

[188] *Al Saudi Banque v Clarke Pixley* [1990] Ch. 313, approved in *Caparo*.

[189] See para.25–031.

[190] [2009] UKHL 39; [2009] 3 W.L.R. 455.

[191] *Stone & Rolls Ltd v Moore Stephens* [2009] UKHL 39; [2009] 3 W.L.R. 455 at [22] per Lord Mance. His Lordship's powerful dissent is based on the claimed inconsistency of the majority view with some elementary principles of company law and denies that recovery by the company would be inconsistent with *Caparo* because the loss of the company and the creditors are not the same, though there may be an overlap.

[192] [2000] 1 W.L.R. 1921. A claim by a person who provides a bond to the audited firm for the fulfilment of its duties to the regulatory body would be, "at or near the margin of existing decisions": *Independents' Advantage Insurance Co Ltd v Cook* [2003] EWCA Civ 1103; [2004] P.N.L.R. 3.

[193] Cf. *Royal Bank of Scotland v Bannerman Johnstone Maclay* [2005] CSIH 39; [2005] P.N.L.R. 43.

certifier does not owe a duty to a potential purchaser of the vessel surveyed,[194] even if he is aware that it may be sold.[195] However, the purpose test is not easy to apply, for it may often be arguable that there is a further, superadded purpose beyond the primary purpose for which the information is given and *Caparo*, it will be recalled, turned on the court's interpretation of the statutory scheme underlying the audit. A clear example of a secondary purpose giving rise to a duty of care is *Smith v Eric S Bush*,[196] where the immediate purpose of the valuation was to enable the mortgagees to decide whether the property valued provided adequate security for the loan. The knowledge that the report would probably be passed on to the mortgagor, who would use it to confirm his decision to buy the house, was sufficient to impose on the valuer a duty of care to him. This was so even though the report contained a notice that it was given without any assumption of responsibility to the purchaser, this being held unreasonable under the Unfair Contract Terms Act 1977.[197] The pointers towards a finding in favour of the claimant were, however, very strong in this case: the sum at stake was modest because the house was at the lower end of the market and liability in such cases would not place an unmanageable burden on valuers; it was virtually certain that the purchaser would have no form of independent advice;[198] and the purchaser was in effect paying the valuer's fee because he was reimbursing the mortgagees in respect of it.[199] Even here, however, a line is drawn at the purchaser in pursuance of whose application the report is prepared—the duty does not extend to subsequent purchasers of the house.[200]

A narrow view of the purpose of the statement was taken in *Al Nakib Investments (Jersey) Ltd v Longcroft*.[201] Directors issued a prospectus inviting shareholders of CT to subscribe for shares in CT and in M (a new company). While it was conceded that a duty was owed to shareholders who accepted the invitation, that part of the statement of claim which related to "after-market" purchases[202] was struck out, for the purpose of the prospectus was to invite participation in the rights issue, not market dealings in the shares.[203] Nonetheless, market practices (and hence reasonable expectations) may change and it may be that *Al Nakib* represents too narrow a view in modern conditions. In *Possfund*

---

[194] *Reeman v DoT* [1997] 2 Lloyd's Rep. 648.

[195] *Mariola Marine Corp v Lloyd's Register of Shipping* [1990] 1 Lloyd's Rep. 547. See also *Marc Rich & Co AG v Bishop Rock Marine Co Ltd* [1996] A.C. 211, para.5−031.

[196] [1990] 1 A.C. 831, para.12−031.

[197] See para.12−044.

[198] No duty was found to be owed where the claimant was purchasing a residential house as part of a buy-to-let scheme, in part because it was reasonable for the valuer to expect that the purchaser would commission his own report because of the need to verify other matters such as rental prospects: *Scullion v Bank of Scotland Plc* [2011] EWCA Civ 693; [2011] 1 W.L.R. 3212.

[199] Compare the audit situation, where the claimant is relying on something paid for by someone else. In *Preston v Torfaen BC* (1993) Con. L.R. 48 a surveyor engaged to do a site survey for a housing development was held not to owe a duty to the purchasers of houses.

[200] *Smith v Eric S Bush* [1990] 1 A.C. 831 at 865.

[201] [1990] 1 W.L.R. 1390.

[202] i.e. purchases in the market from persons to whom shares had been allotted in the issue.

[203] The result is the same as in the deceit case of *Peek v Gurney* (1873) L.R. 6 H.L. 377. See also Denning LJ in *Candler v Crane Christmas* [1951] 2 K.B. 164 at 183: "for the guidance of the very person in the very transaction in question."

Custodian Trustee Ltd v Diamond[204] the claimants proposed to produce expert evidence that the current perception of the function of a prospectus in the unlisted securities market was that it was intended to influence after-market purchases as well as applications for allotment and Lightman J accordingly held that the issue of liability was arguable and could only be determined at trial.[205] Another example of a refusal to strike out is *Morgan Crucible Co Plc v Hill Samuel Bank Ltd*[206] where the claimants were bidders for FCE and the defendants had issued profit forecasts in circulars to shareholders in FCE advising them to reject the bid.[207] Although this was the primary or immediate purpose of the circulars it would be unrealistic in the normal take-over situation to deny that the circulars were also intended to persuade the bidders to increase the amount of their bid and this was, arguably, another purpose of the circulars.

Purpose distinguished from knowledge of reliance. If the reliance by the claimant takes place outside the relevant purpose, the defendant's knowledge of the reliance is irrelevant: it would have made no difference in *Caparo* if at the time of the audit a partner in the defendant firm had been aware, as a result of a conversation in the pub, that his next-door neighbour was interested in acquiring Fidelity shares. At the opposite extreme, a bidder for a company may extract from the auditors a warranty that the accounts are an accurate view of the company's financial health, in which case there can be no possible defence to a claim if they are not. However, something less may do, as where the defendant is aware of the claimant's interest in the transaction and supplies information relating to it directly to the claimant[208] or expressly or impliedly confirms information he has supplied before for another purpose. In principle a duty may arise even where an auditor simply repeats what he has said in his audit report, provided it can be said that in the circumstances the defendant can be taken to have assumed responsibility to an identified person, which may be possible where he is aware that that person contemplates a transaction with the client and makes no qualification or disclaimer.[209]

12–038

Ultimately a fact specific enquiry. While concepts such as purpose, or mere knowledge may be employed to determine the outcome, every case will require detailed examination of the facts to see if the provider of the information can fairly be said to have behaved in such a way as to indicate that he is assuming responsibility to the particular person relying on it. In *Precis (521) Plc v William M Mercer Ltd*[210] the defendant actuaries prepared a valuation report on the pension fund of the SG company and this turned out to have seriously underestimated the deficit of the fund. Later the claimants made a successful

12–039

---

[204] [1996] 1 W.L.R. 1351.
[205] For the somewhat complicated statutory background to this case see [1996] 1 W.L.R. 1351 at 1359. See now Financial Services and Markets Act 2000 ss.90, 90A.
[206] [1991] Ch. 295.
[207] The claim was brought against: (1) the directors of FCE, who had issued the circulars; (2) a merchant bank, FCE's advisers; and (3) FCE's auditors. The claims against (2) and (3) were allowed to go to trial, even though they were at one step removed from those against the directors.
[208] See the dissenting judgment of Denning LJ in *Candler v Crane Christmas* [1951] 2 K.B. 164.
[209] *Andrew v Kounis Freeman* [1999] 2 B.C.L.C. 641; cf. *Peach Publishing Ltd v Slater & Co* [1998] P.N.L.R. 364 See also *Galoo Ltd v Bright Grahame Murray* [1994] 1 W.L.R. 1360.
[210] [2005] EWCA Civ 114; [2005] P.N.L.R. 28.

offer for SG and sued the defendants when they discovered the size of the deficit. The defendants were held not liable. They had prepared the valuation for the information of SG (it expressly declared that its purpose was to enable SG to review its contribution rate) and even though they had provided a copy of the valuation for SG to pass to the claimants that could just as well have been done by SG, in which case there would have been no shadow of a claim. There was no direct contact between the claimants and the defendants and the knowledge that there was some sort of "corporate transaction" on foot between SG and the claimants was not enough to justify treating them as having assumed any responsibility to the claimants.[211] In *MAN Nutzfahrzeuge AG v Freightliner Ltd* auditors might have been under a duty to the purchaser of a company in respect of losses arising from statements in the accounts used in the share-purchase agreement but they could not foresee what was the true cause of the loss, namely fraudulent statements about the accounts made (on behalf of the parent company) during the negotiations by the company's financial controller; and even if they had been able to foresee that, to:[212]

> "[H]old that the auditors assumed responsibility for the use which a dishonest employee of the audited company might make of the accounts in the context of the parent company's negotiations for the sale of the company would . . . be to impose on them a liability greater than they could reasonably have thought they were undertaking."

12–040　**Not necessary to have fully identified the claimant.** D may be instructed to prepare a report by X in circumstances in which a duty of care is clearly owed (probably by contract) to X, but the report may also be relied on by C. If it is clear that X is acting with, or on behalf of, others, the fact that C is not identified by name should not prevent a duty of care being owed to him[213] but if D has no reason to know of C's involvement it may be that C cannot sue: D is entitled to know who his client is,[214] even if, where C is merely a joint purchaser or lender, D's liability is not then increased beyond what he could have expected.[215] It is true that there may be a duty to each member of an ascertained class, but that begins from the assumption that the defendant has reason to know there *is* a class. When this condition is fulfilled is a question of fact, so probably not a great deal by way of general application can be said. However, it has been held (not surprisingly) that where a person acting on behalf of a vendor of property engages an architect to certify the progress of conversion work (being done by the vendor) the architect should contemplate that the certificate may be shown to

---

[211] The claimants had chosen to ignore legal advice to obtain their own actuarial assessment, which was at least contributory negligence. Furthermore, SG had supplied the valuation report on the basis that neither SG nor its advisers had any responsibility for its accuracy and the defendants had "accepted" the benefit of this for the purposes of the Contracts (Rights of Third Parties) Act 1999.

[212] *MAN Nutzfahrzeuge AG v Freightliner Ltd* [2007] EWCA Civ 910; [2008] P.N.L.R. 6 at [56].

[213] This was, after all, essentially the position in *Hedley Byrne*.

[214] The point was left undecided in *Omega Trust Co Ltd v Wright Son & Pepper* (1997) 75 P. & C.R. 57 since the case turned on the disclaimer, but Henry LJ's judgment seems sympathetic to this submission.

[215] In *Smith v Carter* 1995 S.L.T. 295 the point is made that it is not uncommon for one person to instruct a report as the undisclosed agent of others whose interest in a property transaction might not be fully known at the early stages.

the purchaser, though it does not follow that he necessarily assumes responsibility to the purchaser if the latter takes the decisive step of completing the purchase.[216]

Reliance on statement for a transaction different in nature to that **12–041** **contemplated.** Even if the adviser has a particular person in mind as likely to rely on his statement he will not be liable if the reliance takes place in the context of a transaction different from that which the adviser contemplated. However, it is thought that the law should not require too literal a congruence between the transaction contemplated and that which in fact takes place, so long as this does not increase the liability to which the adviser would be exposed. Where, for example, a valuer provides a report knowing that it will be shown to a particular intending purchaser of a property it ought not to matter that, say, the recipient eventually takes a long lease rather than buying the freehold.[217] Even if the transaction is exactly what was contemplated, one must also bear in mind that the defendant only owes a duty of care in respect of a type of damage arising from it which he ought to have in contemplation, so that if, for example, a local authority receives from a potential purchaser an inquiry about the maintenance obligations governing a way fronting a property, it does not follow that if its answer is incorrect it is responsible for losses which are attributable to the impact on the development value of the site.[218]

J.   Physical Damage

Liability for physical damage is plainly much wider than for economic loss.   **12–042** Nevertheless, some intriguing questions remain to be explored by the courts on the extent of liability for physical damage caused by negligent misstatements. Cases like *Caparo* effectively block liability for economic loss caused by generally published information. However, in *Candler v Crane Christmas & Co* Denning LJ gave his opinion that a marine hydrographer would not be liable for omitting a reef and causing the wreck of an ocean liner.[219] Though the matter has not been much discussed here, cases in other jurisdictions seem not to have adopted a blanket rejection of liability in all cases arising from generally

---

[216] *Machin v Adams* (1997) 59 Con. L.R. 14. The majority held that there was no duty, but why, precisely, is not clear.

[217] In *JEB Fasteners Ltd v Marks, Bloom & Co* [1981] 3 All E.R. 289 it was held that a duty was owed by accountants to a person whom they believed might be approached by the company for financial support even though in fact he effected a takeover rather than making a loan. The claim failed for lack of causative reliance (on appeal [1983] 1 All E.R. 583). It was said in *Caparo* that the case might have been correctly decided on its facts and it seems that the accountants had in fact been aware of developments right up to the acquisition.

[218] *Gooden v Northamptonshire CC* [2001] EWCA Civ 1744; [2002] P.N.L.R. 18 (where there was a difference of opinion on what the authority ought to have foreseen).

[219] *Candler v Crane Christmas & Co* [1951] 2 K.B. 164 at 182. Lord Brown appears to have agreed in *Sutradhar v National Environmental Research Council* [2006] UKHL 33; [2006] 4 All E.R. 490.

published material[220] and it would seem unreasonable to deny liability where, say, a handbook on edible mushrooms[221] or a book on DIY electrics gave dangerously misleading instructions.

K. Immunities

12–043   As with any other head of negligence, there may be reasons of public policy which prevent a duty of care arising. *Hedley Byrne* has not affected the immunity from suit of a judge[222] but there is no reason for extending that immunity to a person appointed as a valuer[223] or to an architect granting certificates of completion of work under a building contract[224] and the immunity which expert witnesses had previously enjoyed in relation to their participation in legal proceedings has been removed.[225] Although there was some doubt about the position of an arbitrator at common law, s.29 of the Arbitration Act 1996 provides that an arbitrator "is not liable for anything done or omitted to be done in the discharge or purported discharge of his functions as arbitrator unless the act or omission is shown to have been in bad faith".

L.   Excluding Liability

12–044   It must not be overlooked that, in the result, judgment in *Hedley Byrne* went to the defendants and this, at least in the opinion of the majority, was because they had supplied the information "without responsibility". In effect, therefore, the liability created by the House of Lords would exist only if the defendant has been too careless of his own interests or too proud to protect himself by such a declaration or was unable for some reason (such as professional conduct rules) to do so. However, this situation was radically altered by the Unfair Contract Terms Act 1977.[226]

12–045   **Unfair Contract Terms Act 1977.** By s.2(2) of the Act, a person cannot by means of any contract term or notice restrict his liability for loss or damage other than personal injury[227] caused by negligence in the course of a business[228] unless he shows that the term or notice is reasonable. Section1(1)(b) defines "negligence" as including the breach of any common law duty to take reasonable

---

[220] In the *Willemstad* (1976) 136 C.L.R. 529 producers of a navigation plotting chart were held liable at first instance. There was no appeal on the issue of duty by these defendants. In *Brocklesby v US* 767 F.2d 1288 (C9, 1985) the publisher of an inaccurate instrument approach chart for aircraft was held liable on strict product liability and negligence theories.

[221] See the decision of a French court on such facts cited by Whittaker 105 L.Q.R. 125. On instructions accompanying products, see para.11–006.

[222] See para.25–008.

[223] *Arenson v Casson Beckman Rutley & Co* [1977] A.C. 405.

[224] *Sutcliffe v Thackrah* [1974] A.C. 727.

[225] *Jones v Kaney* [2011] UKSC 13; [2011] 2 A.C. 398.

[226] The Unfair Terms in Consumer Contracts Regulations 1999 apply only to a "tèrm in a contract". They might be relevant where liability was being asserted concurrently in contract and tort.

[227] Such loss or damage is typical of claims for negligent statements. Liability for death and personal injury cannot be excluded: s.2(1).

[228] Section 1(3).

care or exercise reasonable skill. It may be objected that this is not apt to catch a statement given "without responsibility"[229] since the defendant is then making it clear that he does not undertake a duty in the first place but this objection is met by the provision in s.13 that s.2 also prevents, "excluding or restricting liability by reference to terms and notices which exclude or restrict the relevant obligation or duty".[230] However, there is a distinction between such a case and one where there cannot fairly be said to be any assumption of responsibility at all and this is said to be a matter of substance rather than form.[231]

The test of reasonableness. Of course, even where the case falls under the Act the disclaimer may still be effective if it is reasonable in all the circumstances and the inquirer may not be able to expect the same standard of care in response to a gratuitous inquiry as he could expect if paying for the service. Furthermore, while it will generally be unreasonable for a surveyor conducting a valuation for the purchase of a dwelling on mortgage to disclaim liability,[232] the more "commercial" the transaction becomes the more likely it is that a disclaimer or limit of liability will be found reasonable. Thus in a valuation of commercial property a clause which has the effect of restricting the duty to the client and excluding liability to any unknown participants is valid,[233] as is a disclaimer by an estate agent made to a prospective purchaser of property at the upper end of the housing market.[234] **12–046**

Interpretation of the disclaimer. Clear language should be used to disclaim liability.[235] For example, it is submitted that the letters "E. & O.E." (errors and omissions excepted) which are printed on some documents should not necessarily be regarded as sufficient in themselves to exclude a duty of care. However, a disclaimer should not be treated to that sort of strained interpretation which once (though no longer) was applied to contractual exclusion clauses: subject always to s.2 of the Unfair Contract Terms Act, the ultimate question is not whether the defendant has excluded his liability but whether it is legitimate for the recipient **12–047**

---

[229] Or as now seems more common, statements made against the background of an acknowledgement by the recipient that "no representations" are being made, or the recipient "has not relied" on any representations made.

[230] See *Smith v Eric S Bush* [1990] 1 A.C. 831; but cf. Nourse LJ in *First National Commercial Bank v Loxleys* [1997] P.N.L.R. 211.

[231] *IFE Fund SA v Goldman Sachs International* [2007] EWCA Civ 811; [2007] 2 Lloyds Rep 449. See also the approach of Christopher Clarke J in *Raiffeisen Zentralbank Osterreich AG v Royal Bank of Scotland Plc* [2010] EWHC 1392 (Comm); [2011] 1 Lloyd's Rep 123 of asking whether the clause attempts to "re-write history", i.e. where representations clearly have been made and have been relied upon (dealing mainly with the application of s.3 of the Misrepresentation Act 1967 which applies the same test of reasonableness to pre-contractual misrepresentations which induce the representee to contract with the representor); cf. *Springwell Navigation Corporation v JP Morgan Chase Bank* [2010] EWCA Civ 1221; [2010] 2 C.L.C. 705.

[232] *Smith v Eric S Bush* [1990] 1 A.C. 831.

[233] *Omega Trust Co Ltd v Wright Son & Pepper* [1997] 75 P. & C.R. 57.

[234] *McCullagh v Lane Fox & Partners Ltd* [1996] 1 E.G.L.R. 35; and see *Bank of Scotland v Fuller Peiser* 2002 S.L.T. 574 (survey commissioned by purchaser of hotel; disclaimer reasonable against lending bank).

[235] In the context of liability for pre-contractual misrepresentation, see the comments of Rix LJ in *Axa Sun Life Services Plc v Campbell Martin Ltd* [2011] EWCA Civ 133; [2011] 2 Lloyd's Rep. 1 at [92].

of the advice to regard the defendant as having assumed responsibility for his statement.[236] Given that the liability is non-contractual and that reliance by the claimant is an essential element of it,[237] it is thought that it should be sufficient that the defendant makes it known that he disclaims responsibility before the claimant acts on the information or advice and he need not necessarily do so when the statement is made.[238] However, an acknowledgement that "no representation" is made at all may be more likely to be regarded as falling outside the statutory controls if it is made before any words or conduct of the defendant from which a representation might otherwise have been implied.[239]

M. Reliance and Contributory Negligence

12–048   **Reliance by the claimant must be a cause of the loss.** Although reliance by the claimant is not necessary in all cases based upon assumption of responsibility,[240] it is plainly required where the damage arises from a statement by the defendant to the claimant and this reliance must be a cause of the loss.[241] Although here, as in the case of deceit, the law allows for mixed motives, if the claimant, though aware of the defendant's statement, did not believe it[242] or was uninfluenced by it, there is no liability.

12–049   **Contributory negligence.** As to contributory negligence, Woolf J in *JEB Fasteners v Marks, Bloom & Co*[243] (where the issue did not in fact arise) commented that in the case of negligent auditing of accounts: "[I]f it is reasonable to rely on the accounts, it is difficult to envisage circumstances where as a matter of fact it would be negligent to do so without taking further steps to protect yourself from the consequences of relying on the auditor's certificate."

However, perhaps because of the modern emphasis on assumption of responsibility as the basis of liability, the case law shows that there are situations in which the claimant's failure to look after his own interests justifies a reduction in damages[244] (though it has been said that only in a "very special case" would the court be justified in reducing the damages of a claimant who has done what

---

[236] See the judgment of Hobhouse LJ in *McCullagh v Lane Fox & Partners Ltd* [1996] 1 E.G.L.R. 35.

[237] See para.12–048.

[238] This is perhaps supported by *McCullagh v Lane Fox & Partners Ltd* [1996] 1 E.G.L.R. 35 though the point there was different, there being no duty at the time the statement was made and the disclaimer being made before it became known that the statement would be acted on without verification.

[239] *Raiffeisen Zentralbank Osterreich AG v Royal Bank of Scotland Plc* [2010] EWHC 1392 (Comm); [2011] 1 Lloyd's Rep 123 (dealing with s.3 of the Misrepresentation Act 1967).

[240] See para.5–054.

[241] So also where there is a statement about C to X, X must act in reliance on it in relation to C: *Spring v Guardian Assurance* [1995] 2 A.C. 296, para.12–050.

[242] *Rushmer v Smith* [2009] EWHC 94 (QB).

[243] [1981] 3 All E.R. 289 at 297.

[244] See *Platform Home Loans Ltd v Oyston Shipways Ltd* [2000] 2 A.C. 190 (imprudent to make large loan on "non-status" basis; however, the issue was the impact on contributory negligence of *Banque Bruxelles Lambert SA v Eagle Star Insurance Co Ltd* [1997] A.C. 191, para.7–059); *Precis (521) Plc v William M. Mercer Ltd* [2005] EWCA Civ 114; [2005] P.N.L.R. 28 (where, however, there was held to be no duty); *Webb Resolutions Ltd v E Surv Ltd* [2012] EWHC 3653 (TCC); [2013] P.N.L.R. 15; *Blemain Finance Ltd v E Surv Ltd* [2012] EWHC 3654 (TCC).

the defendant intended him to do by way of reliance on the misrepresentation[245]). If the fault alleged against the claimant was subsequent to the point at which he had irrevocably committed himself to a transaction in reliance on the defendant's advice,[246] that might be a case of failure to mitigate rather than contributory negligence properly so called.[247]

N.   Injury to Persons Not Relying on the Statement

The nature of the claim. Reliance on a statement made by D to X may cause X to act in a manner detrimental to C, but in respect of which C has no redress against X. The question then arises whether D is liable to C. Putting aside the case where the statement is defamatory of C there is no doubt that D incurs liability where the statement was made with "malice" and causes damage[248] to C, as where D knowingly published a false story that C had ceased to trade.[249] This is the tort of malicious falsehood, which is outlined at a later point.[250] It is also possible that D may incur liability to C for damage caused by lies to X under the head of unlawful interference with trade;[251] but neither of these wrongs is committed by mere negligence. That there may, however, be liability for negligence in some such situations is established by the decision of the House of Lords in *Spring v Guardian Assurance Plc*.[252]

12–050

Spring v Guardian Assurance Plc. The claimant had been employed by A and had been a "company representative" of G, selling G's policies. He was dismissed by G when G took over A. The claimant then went into business and sought to gain authority to sell SA's policies. In accordance with the rules of the regulatory body under the Financial Services Act 1986, SA sought a reference on the claimant and this was very uncomplimentary, asserting inter alia that the claimant was, "of little or no integrity and could not be regarded as honest".[253] SA thereupon declined to authorise the claimant to sell its policies. The trial judge held that while the claimant had certainly been guilty of incompetence he had not been dishonest and that the sources in G who had supplied information to the compiler of the reference had failed to exercise reasonable care, although they were not malicious.[254] There was some dispute as to whether the claimant's status

12–051

---

[245] *Gran Gelato Ltd v Richcliff (Group) Ltd* [1992] Ch. 560. Contributory negligence is inapplicable to a claim for deceit: para.23–058.

[246] For example, C buys a house on D's negligently conducted survey but C then negligently fails to notice warning signs so that the damage is greater than it would otherwise have been.

[247] *Webb Resolutions Ltd v E.Surv Ltd* [2012] EWHC 3653 (TCC); [2013] P.N.L.R. 15 at [144]–[146].

[248] Damage is now sometimes presumed.

[249] *Ratcliffe v Evans* [1892] 2 Q.B. 525.

[250] See para.13–131.

[251] See para.19–019.

[252] [1995] 2 A.C. 296.

[253] [1995] 2 A.C. 296 at 306.

[254] The above is a somewhat simplified account, since the reference was in fact compiled by an employee of GRE, the parent company of G, on the basis of information supplied by other employees of GRE and an employee of A (which was itself two associated companies) but this was treated as the responsibility of G. Lord Goff did not think GRE were under any duty of care to the claimant but the other members of the majority treated all four companies as one unit.

was that of employee or independent contractor but nothing was thought to turn upon that and for convenience the judgments were largely couched in terms of the former status.[255]

The words were plainly defamatory but the provision of a reference at the request of a prospective employer is the classic occasion of qualified privilege[256] and the finding of lack of malice was therefore fatal to the claimant's libel claim, as it was to the alternative claim for malicious falsehood. However, a majority of the House of Lords held that if causation of loss could be established[257] the claimant had a cause of action in negligence. The argument (which had convinced the Court of Appeal) that the imposition of liability for negligence would subvert the protection which the law of defamation had deliberately cast around referees was rejected by the House of Lords because there were significant differences between the two heads of liability: on the one hand, negligence required proof of fault and damage; on the other, an inaccurate statement might be damaging without being defamatory, in that it reflected on a person's suitability for employment without being defamatory of him. It was, of course, accepted that the introduction into this area of liability for negligence would significantly affect for the worse the position of the referee, but this was said to be a necessary change in the law in view of developments in the relationship between employer and employee:[258]

> "There would be no purpose in extending the tort of negligence to protect the subject of an inaccurate reference if he was already adequately protected by the law of defamation . . . The result of [the requirement of malice in such cases] is that an action for defamation provides a wholly inadequate remedy for an employee who is caused damage by a reference which due to negligence is inaccurate. This is because it places a wholly disproportionate burden on the employee. Malice is extremely difficult to establish . . . If the law provides a remedy for references which are inaccurate due to carelessness this would be beneficial. It would encourage the adoption of appropriate standards when preparing references."

12–052 **Scope of the duty.** The duty of the referee extends to not making misleading (as opposed to simply untrue) statements[259] but does not extend to an obligation to write a "full" reference.[260] The majority of the judges in *Spring* were of the view that there would be a parallel liability based on the (terminated) contract between the former employer and the claimant.[261] As far as the tort liability is concerned, there is some difference in the reasoning employed: Lord Goff's speech rests primarily upon the principle of assumption of responsibility, but the other members of the minority base their reasoning upon the general tripartite approach

---

[255] See, e.g. [1995] 2 A.C. 296 at 340 and at 341.

[256] See para.13–061.

[257] For which purpose the case had to be remitted to the Court of Appeal.

[258] *Spring v Guardian Assurance Plc* [1995] 2 A.C. 296 at 346 per Lord Woolf. Similar reasoning applies to malicious falsehood, which is wider than defamation in that the statement need not be defamatory, but it still requires malice.

[259] *Bartholomew v Hackney LBC* [1999] I.R.L.R. 246.

[260] *Kidd v Axa Equity and Law* [2000] I.R.L.R. 301.

[261] There is some discussion in the case of whether there could be a duty on the employer to provide a reference (as opposed to taking care when he does provide one).

to the duty of care in *Caparo v Dickman*.[262] Looked at as a case of assumption of responsibility, the decision may be said to stand between *Hedley Byrne*[263] and the fullest extension of the principle in *White v Jones*.[264] In the latter case there was no reliance at all by the claimants. In *Spring* the direct reliance on the statement was by the new employer who rejected the claimant but there is commonly an element of reliance by the claimant, who will have asked for the reference or will at least know that it is likely to be given. It seems, however, that there would be liability in such a case even if the claimant is entirely unaware that the reference is being written.[265]

Other relationships. It is clear from the case that because a former employer is liable to the subject of a reference it by no means follows that the same applies to a reference written by a social acquaintance.[266] The speeches concentrate very heavily upon the "reference situation" and emphasise the close degree of proximity between the parties. It therefore seems most unlikely that the law will be developed so as to create liability for damaging but non-malicious and non-defamatory statements which are published generally (for example that a company has ceased to trade or that its sales are lower than in fact they are).[267] However, there are obvious relationships which are as "proximate" as those of referee and subject. Consider, for example, the case of a doctor who is commissioned by an insurer to report on the health of a proposer or by an employer on the health of a prospective employee. Both cases seem very similar to the case of a reference, save that they are carried out under contract with a person other than the claimant.[268] However, in *X v Bedfordshire CC*,[269] Lord Browne-Wilkinson, in rejecting the argument that a social worker and psychiatrist investigating a case of suspected child abuse owed a duty of care to the child said:[270]

12–053

> "The social workers and the psychiatrists were retained by the local authority to advise the local authority, not the plaintiffs. The subject matter of the advice and activities of the professionals is the child . . . But the fact that the carrying out of the retainer involves contact with and relationship with the child cannot alter the extent of the duty owed by the professionals under the retainer from the local authority. The Court of Appeal[271] drew a correct analogy with the doctor instructed by an insurance company to examine an applicant for life insurance. The doctor does not, by examining the applicant, come under any general duty of medical care to

---

[262] See para.5–026; cf. *McKie v Swindon College*[2011] EWHC 469 (QB); [2011] I.R.L.R. 575 (not a reference case; unfounded email about former employee led to his dismissal).

[263] This was also, of course, a case about a reference but it involved liability to the recipient, not to the subject.

[264] [1995] 2 A.C. 207; see para.5–054.

[265] Cf. *Wade v State of Victoria* [1999] 1 V.R. 121. However, *Spring* may not be the law in Australia: *Cornwall v Rowan* [2004] SASC 384; 90 S.A.S.R. 269.

[266] *Spring v Guardian Assurance Plc* [1995] 2 A.C. 296 at 319, 336, 345.

[267] *Smeaton v Equifax Plc* [2013] EWCA Civ 108; [2013] 2 All E.R. 959 (no duty of care owed by credit reference agency for misleading credit report which prevented C from raising a business loan).

[268] Even this is not necessarily true: a family doctor may receive an inquiry from an insurer which is to be answered briefly on the basis of the patient's records.

[269] [1995] 2 A.C. 633 at 752–753. See para.5–072.

[270] This view is supported by Denning LJ in *Candler v Crane Christmas* [1951] 2 K.B. 164. Staughton LJ in the CA had said the same would be true of a police surgeon called to examine a suspected drunken motorist: *X v Bedfordshire CC* [1995] 2 A.C. at 673–674.

[271] See *X v Bedfordshire CC* [1995] 2 A.C. 633 at 651.

the applicant. He is under a duty not to damage the applicant in the course of the examination: but beyond that his duties are owed to the insurance company and not to the applicant."

Since then it has been held that a doctor employed by a company owed no duty of care to a prospective employee in reporting on his health.[272] However, it may be unsafe to conclude that there is necessarily a simple rule of non-liability in all these cases. First, matters have moved on somewhat in the context of child abuse investigations and it is now held that there may be a duty of care to the child, though still not to the parents.[273] Secondly, the denial of duty in *X v Bedfordshire* rested primarily upon the view that a duty of care would cut across and interfere with the statutory framework of child care, a matter which is hardly relevant to the case of the insurance company or the employer's doctor.[274] Thirdly, it has since been held in *Phelps v Hillingdon LBC*[275] that where an educational psychologist was asked to assess a child in circumstances where it was clear that others would act on the assessment, a duty of care was owed to the child despite the fact that the psychologist had been engaged to report to the education authority. "The duty to the pupil would march hand in hand with the professional's responsibilities to his own employer."[276] It is hard to see why the same could not be said of the insurer's or employer's doctor.[277]

O.   Lord Tenterden's Act

12–054   By the Statute of Frauds 1677 promises that are guarantees to answer for another's debts must be in writing and signed by the party to be charged or his agent in order to make them actionable. The Statute of Frauds Amendment Act 1828 (commonly called Lord Tenterden's Act) s.6 was passed (providing, in effect, that a false representation as to credit cannot be sued upon unless it is

---

[272] *Kapfunde v Abbey National* [1999] I.C.R. 1. Of course even if one took the alternative view the purpose of the examination has to be borne in mind. It is one thing to say that the doctor should be liable for causing the claimant to lose his job; it is another to say that he should be liable for failing to warn of abnormalities, at least so long as they are not life-threatening. See *R. v Croydon HA* (1997) 40 B.M.L.R. 40.

[273] *D v East Berkshire Community NHS Trust* [2003] EWCA Civ 1151; [2004] Q.B. 558 and [2005] UKHL 23; [2005] 2 A.C. 373, para.5–073.

[274] The statutory context appears nonetheless to have been the principal basis upon which C's claim failed in *Desmond v Chief Constable of Nottinghamshire* [2011] EWCA Civ 3; [2011] 1 F.L.R. 1361 (no duty of care owed by chief constable to C in responding to a request for an enhanced criminal record certificate under the Police Act 1997 Pt V even though the misleading information provided prevented C's employment as a teacher. The statutory purpose of the certificate was to provide a degree of protection to vulnerable young people generally and the court noted that C had other remedies available to him, including under the 1997 Act and for breach of the Data Protection Act 1998); cf. *Smeaton v Equifax Plc* [2013] EWCA Civ 108; [2013] 2 All E.R. 959, where the court again noted the availability of a claim under the Data Protection Act 1998).

[275] [2001] 2 A.C. 619.

[276] *Phelps v Hillingdon LBC* [2001] 2 A.C. 619 at 666 per Lord Nicholls.

[277] In *Farah v British Airways, The Times*, January 26, 2000, the CA, referring to *Spring*, declined to strike out a claim alleging that a Home Office immigration liaison officer negligently and wrongly advised an airline that the claimants did not have the required documentation to obtain access to this country, with the result that they lost their flights.

made in writing and signed by the party to be charged)[278] to prevent the Statute being evaded by utilising the comparatively new action of deceit. The section clearly covers fraudulent representations as to a person's credit[279] but it does not apply to an action between contracting parties in respect of advice negligently given.[280] The section was not considered in *Hedley Byrne* and rightly so, for it has no more place in actions for tortious negligence than it has in actions founded upon contract.[281] Nevertheless it is strange that what would be a defence in an action for fraud should not be one in an action for negligence.[282] It would be even stranger if a defendant against whom negligence is alleged could affirmatively set up his own fraudulent intent and plead the statute. Presumably, however, such a plea could be struck out on the general ground that no one should be allowed to take advantage of his own wrongful act.[283]

---

[278] See *Contex Drouzhba Ltd v Wiseman* [2006] EWCA Civ 1201; [2008] 1 B.C.L.C. 631; *Lindsay v O'Loughnane* [2010] EWHC 529 (QB); [2012] B.C.C. 153.

[279] Given a narrow construction: *Lindsay v O'Loughnane* [2010] EWHC 529 (QB); [2012] B.C.C. 153; *Roder UK Ltd v West* [2011] EWCA Civ 1126; [2012] Q.B. 752.

[280] *Banbury v Bank of Montreal* [1918] A.C. 626.

[281] *WB Anderson & Sons Ltd v Rhodes (Liverpool) Ltd* [1967] 2 All E.R. 850.

[282] It does apply to the Misrepresentation Act 1967 s.2(1), because of the form of that provision: *UBAF Ltd v European Banking Corp* [1984] Q.B. 713.

[283] Cf. *Alghussein v Eton College* [1988] 1 W.L.R. 587.

CHAPTER 13

DEFAMATION, PRIVACY AND RELATED MATTERS

1. DEFAMATION

A. Elements of the Action

13–001   The elements of defamation are: (1) a defamatory statement; (2) that refers to the claimant; (3) that is published (that is, is communicated to at least one person other than the claimant); (4) that causes damage to the claimant; and (5) the defendant is a type of person who can bring proceedings in defamation. These elements must be proved by the claimant. It should be noted at the outset that a distinction is drawn between two forms of defamation: libel and slander. The distinction will be explored in detail later, but for the moment it suffices to say that libel is defamation in permanent form whereas slander is defamation in non-permanent form. Damage is presumed in the case of libel and in relation to certain types of slander.

i. A Defamatory Statement

13–002   **General tests.** A comprehensive definition of a defamatory statement has eluded courts and commentators. It has been said that a statement is defamatory if it tends to bring a person into "hatred, contempt or ridicule".[1] Another frequently quoted test is that the words must tend to lower the claimant in the estimation of right-thinking members of society generally.[2] But to these definitions it is necessary to at least add that words may be defamatory if they tend to cause the claimant to be shunned or avoided, for it is unquestionably defamatory to impute insanity or insolvency to a person, although, far from exciting hatred, contempt or ridicule, it would rouse only pity or sympathy in the minds of reasonable people, who may nevertheless be inclined to shun his society.[3] A statement, in order to be defamatory, must tend to give rise to the feelings mentioned above, though there is no necessity that they actually do so. For example, if D defames C to C's best friend who does not believe a word of it C has still been defamed.[4]

13–003   **The issue of whether a statement is defamatory is determined objectively.** The question is whether the statement induces the relevant feelings in the mind of

---

[1] *Parmiter v Coupland* (1840) 6 M. & W. 105.

[2] *Sim v Stretch* (1936) 52 T.L.R. 669 per Lord Atkin.

[3] Consider *Youssoupoff v Metro-Goldwyn-Mayer Pictures Ltd* (1934) 50 T.L.R. 581 in which it was held that an imputation that the claimant had been raped was defamatory of the claimant.

[4] *Hough v London Express Newspaper* [1940] 2 K.B. 507 at 515. In *Morgan v Odhams Press Ltd* [1971] 1 W.L.R. 1239 at 1246 Lord Reid referred to this as a proposition so obvious that no one had had the hardihood to dispute it. However, in modern practice such a claim must be at risk of being struck out as an abuse of process: see para.26–077. It is also unlikely to satisfy the "serious harm" requirement: see para.13–004.

the reasonable person, here transformed into the reasonable reader or viewer or listener. This rules out on the one hand those persons who are so cynical that they would think none the worse of a person whatever was imputed to him, and on the other hand those who are so censorious as to regard even trivial accusations as lowering a person's reputation. The way in which the claimant or defendant would regard the statement is also irrelevant for the purposes of determining whether it is defamatory. The reasonable person is the "right-thinking member of society generally"[5] and in reality of course he is the personification of the judge's view of the state of public feelings and opinion. The reasonable person is a layman not a lawyer and the judge must therefore try to put himself in the position of someone who may be guilty of a certain amount[6] of loose thinking and who may not reflect fully and carefully upon a newspaper story or a television programme.

Serious harm requirement. By virtue of s.1(1) of the Defamation Act 2013, a **13–004** "statement is not defamatory unless its publication has caused or is likely to cause serious harm to the reputation of the claimant". Section 1(2) provides that in the case of a body that trades for profit, this requirement will not be satisfied unless the statement "has caused or is likely to cause the body serious financial loss". Section 1 is aimed at preventing trivial claims from being commenced. It is doubtful that this provision accomplishes anything. Two commentators predict that "it is likely that section 1 will make only the most marginal of differences to the existing law".[7] The courts already had at their disposal a variety of mechanisms for ensuring that trivial claims do not proceed, especially the defence of abuse of process.[8] Section 1 probably also addresses a largely imaginary problem. Claimants simply do not have much incentive to bring trivial claims because they will likely yield, if successful, trivial damages. A further powerful disincentive not to sue is the risk of being met by an adverse costs order.

Changing public views. Plainly, public views on topics change over time. In the **13–005** reign of Charles II it was defamatory to accuse someone of being a Roman Catholic or a witch but neither would be defamatory now. At a particular point opinion may be in the process of change. Fifty years ago to say that a man was a homosexual would have been regarded as a very serious defamation. Whether or not the courts would regard such a statement as defamatory today is unclear.[9]

The issue of truth is irrelevant for the purposes of determining whether a **13–006** **statement is defamatory.** Truth is normally a complete defence to an action for defamation. This is discussed below.[10] But the issue of whether a statement is true

---

[5] *Sim v Stretch* (1936) 52 T.L.R. 669.
[6] Lord Devlin's view in *Lewis v Daily Telegraph* [1964] A.C. 234 at 277 was that the "layman reads in an implication much more freely; and unfortunately, as the law of defamation has to take into account, is especially prone to do so when it is derogatory". This view has been described as perhaps rather patronising to the modern way of thinking: *Armstrong v Times Newspapers* [2005] EWHC 2816 (QB) at [31].
[7] Mullis and Scott (2014) 77 M.L.R. 87 at 105.
[8] See para.26–077.
[9] See *Quilty v Windsor* [1999] S.L.T. 346 and *John Fairfax Publications Pty Ltd v Rivkin* [2003] HCA 50; 201 A.L.R. 77 at [140].
[10] See para.13–040.

is separate from the question of whether the statement is defamatory, which looks solely to the effect of the statement upon the claimant's reputation. "The fact that words are false . . . is not germane to the question whether they are defamatory."[11] Thus, the statement "C is a thief" is defamatory of C even if D can show that C is a thief, but if he can show that, it is not, ordinarily, actionable.

13–007   **Statements that disparage a person professionally.** A statement that disparages a person in his reputation in relation to his office, profession, calling, trade or business may be defamatory—for example, conduct that breaches widely recognised canons of business ethics[12] and fraudulent or dishonest conduct.[13] The fact that an imputation in a business or employment context cannot be said to reflect on the claimant's character does not necessarily prevent it from being defamatory. However, a statement that does not reflect on the claimant's reputation at least in a broad sense is not defamatory. Thus, it is not defamatory to say that a trader has ceased to trade,[14] though there may be some difficult borderline cases.[15]

13–008   **The meaning of the statement is determined objectively.** There may be a dispute about what the words used in the statement in question mean. What the defendant intended them to mean is irrelevant in this regard.[16] Here, again, the test is the meaning that would be conveyed to the reasonable person. The reasonable person is neither unusually suspicious[17] nor unusually naive and he does not always interpret the meaning of words as would a lawyer. He "is not inhibited by knowledge of the rules of construction".[18] However, the reasonable person is fair-minded and will be taken, at least in the case of an article in a popular newspaper, to have read the piece as a whole. The allegedly defamatory statement will, in order words, be read in context. Thus, where pictures in an article might have given the impression that the claimants had participated in the making of a pornographic video game, it was held that the defendants were not liable because the attached article made it plain that they had not and it was irrelevant that many readers of the newspaper might just have seen the "bane" in the photographs and not the "antidote" in the text.[19]

---

[11] *Daniels v British Broadcasting Corporation*[2010] EWHC 3057 (QB) at [46].

[12] *Clark v Express Newspapers* [2004] EWHC 481 (QB) (politician "ratted" on manifesto promise).

[13] See, e.g. *Turner v MGM Pictures Ltd* [1950] 2 All E.R. 449; *Angell v H.H. Bushell & Co Ltd* [1968] 1 Q.B. 813; *Drummond-Jackson v BMA* [1970] 1 W.L.R. 688.

[14] *Ratcliffe v Evans* [1892] 2 Q.B. 524.

[15] See *Sungravure Pty Ltd v Middle East Airlines* (1978) 5 A.L.R. 147 (not defamatory at common law to say that an airline, without any fault on its part, was peculiarly susceptible to hijacking); *Dawson Bloodstock Agency v Mirror Newspapers* [1979] 2 N.S.W.L.R. 733 (not defamatory to say stud farm had closed because of virus).

[16] "Trite law": *Berkoff v Burchill* [1996] 4 All E.R. 1008 at 1018.

[17] In *Bennison v Hulton, The Times*, April 13, 1926 Scrutton LJ said that "suspicious people might get a defamatory meaning out of 'chop and tomato sauce'".

[18] *Lewis v Daily Telegraph Ltd* [1964] A.C. 234 at 258 per Lord Reid.

[19] *Charleston v News Group Newspapers Ltd* [1995] 2 A.C. 65. *Charleston* is strongly criticised by Kirby J in *Chakravarti v Advertiser Newspaper* [1998] HCA 37; (1998) 193 C.L.R. 519 at [134]. He said that "it ignores the realities of the way in which ordinary people receive, and are intended to receive, communications of this kind. It ignores changes in media technology and presentation".

The statement must be defamatory in the eyes of persons generally rather than in the eyes of a particular group of persons. It is not enough in order for a statement to be defamatory that the words would tend only to disparage the claimant in the eyes of a particular class or group of persons; they must have that effect in the eyes of persons "generally". In practice this is not quite so restrictive as it seems because in many cases where a claimant is charged with offending against the tenets of a group to which he belongs there may be an implication of disloyalty or hypocrisy, which is actionable in its own right, even though ordinary people are indifferent to the direct charge against him.[20] To say of a person that he takes alcohol in moderation is not defamatory; but to say it of a temperance crusader may very well be.[21] To say of someone that he has put in motion the proper machinery for suppressing crime, in that he has reported certain acts, wrongful in law, to the police, is not defamatory, for the law cannot admit that a reasonable person would think less of the claimant for that (even though in practice where the crime was a minor one real people might well do so).[22]

13–009

The role of the judge and jury. Since the Defamation Act 2013, defamation cases are heard without a jury unless the court orders otherwise.[23] It is predicted that the court will rarely order a jury trial. However, in light of the possibility that a jury might still be used in defamation proceedings a few words will be said about the respective roles of the judge and jury in relation to the issues of: (1) whether a statement is defamatory; and (2) what the statement in question means. Some of what is said in this regard is relevant even where the trial is by judge alone.

13–010

Where a jury is used, the judge acts as a gatekeeper on the issue of whether the statement is defamatory. He must first rule that the words are capable as a matter of law of being defamatory—that is, could a reasonable jury come to the conclusion that the statement satisfies the legal criteria for being defamatory? Thus, a statement that the claimant had influenza last month would be withdrawn from the jury for that in no way impugns his character or reputation; on the other hand, a statement that he has a sexually transmitted disease is plainly capable of being defamatory. In *Lewis v Daily Telegraph Ltd*[24] it was held that the ordinary sensible person would not think that whenever there is a police inquiry there is guilt. If the words are obviously defamatory, the judge, although he cannot directly tell the jury that they are so, may nevertheless indicate to them that no other conclusion is reasonably open.

Similar principles apply in relation to the issue of the meaning of the statement in question. It is for the judge to decide what the words are capable of meaning. His task is to "evaluate the words complained of and to delimit the range of meanings of which the words are reasonably capable",[25] excluding meanings that are "fanciful, absurd or factitious".[26] It is then for the jury to decide which of the meanings that the words are capable of bearing they do in fact bear. The verdict

---

[20] *Leetham v Rank* (1912) 57 Sol. Jo. 111; *Myroft v Sleight* (1921) 90 L.J.K.B. 883.

[21] Compare *Peck v Tribune Co* 214 U.S. 185 (1909).

[22] *Byrne v Deane* [1937] 1 K.B. 818.

[23] Section 11(1). See further para.13–112.

[24] [1964] A.C. 234.

[25] *Mapp v News Group Newspapers Limited* [1998] Q.B. 520 at 526.

[26] *Jeynes v News Magazines Ltd* [2008] EWCA Civ 130 at [20].

of the jury must pertain to what they have found is *the* meaning of the words. In other words, they must give the words a single meaning.[27] If the case is tried by judge alone he must decide what the words mean, not what they are capable of meaning.

13–011 **Statements that are defamatory by implication.** A statement may be defamatory by implication: just as it is defamatory of C to say that he murdered X, it is defamatory of C to say that justice miscarried when C was acquitted of murdering X.[28] As Lord Morris put it in *Jones v Skelton*: "The ordinary and natural meaning [of words] may . . . include any implication or inference which a reasonable reader guided not by any special but only by general knowledge, and not fettered by any strict legal rules of construction would draw from the words."[29] Juxtaposition of material about the claimant with other material may make an otherwise innocent statement defamatory. A famous instance is *Monson v Tussauds Ltd*.[30] The defendants, who kept a waxwork exhibition, placed an effigy of the claimant, with a gun, in a room adjoining the "Chamber of Horrors". The claimant had been tried for murder in Scotland and released on a verdict of "Not Proven" and a representation of the scene of the alleged murder was displayed in the Chamber of Horrors. The Court of Appeal considered that the exhibition was capable of being found by a jury to be defamatory. On the other hand, the mere fact that an article about the claimant appeared in a newspaper where numerous articles attacking dishonest businessmen had appeared on other occasions was held incapable of carrying a defamatory imputation.[31] If reliance is placed upon juxtaposition it must be shown that a reasonable person, seeing the two objects together, would draw from their relative positions an inference defamatory of the claimant.

13–012 **Innuendo.** In ordinary English any implied or allusive meanings are called "innuendoes" but the technical legal meaning is narrower.[32] An innuendo in the legal sense arises only when the defamatory nature of the statement depends upon facts or circumstances which are not part of general knowledge but which are known to the persons to whom the statement is published. So to state that the claimant is "no Mother Theresa" might imply to the ordinary reader that she was wanting in kindness or charity because people generally know about Mother Theresa; but to say of a surgeon that he had carried out 10 private operations last week would convey nothing defamatory at all except to people who know that he is contracted full time to the National Health Service, in which case it might carry the implication that he was "moonlighting". Each innuendo is a separate cause of action[33] and the claimant must identify the persons with knowledge of the special

---

[27] As far as the jury is concerned, the words have a single, "right" meaning: *Slim v Daily Telegraph* [1968] 2 Q.B. 157 at 174. The same "single meaning" rule does not apply to malicious falsehood: *Ajinomoto Sweeteners Europe SAS v Asda Stores Ltd* [2010] EWCA Civ 609; [2011] Q.B. 497.
[28] See, e.g. Lord Reid and Lord Devlin in *Lewis v Daily Telegraph* [1964] A.C. 234 at 258 and 280 respectively.
[29] [1963] 1 W.L.R. 1362 at 1370–1371.
[30] [1894] 1 Q.B. 671.
[31] *Wheeler v Somerfield* [1966] 2 Q.B. 94.
[32] Lord Devlin in *Lewis v Daily Telegraph* [1964] A.C. 234 at 279 doubted the value of the technical distinction.
[33] *Grubb v Bristol United Press Ltd* [1963] 1 Q.B. 309 at 327.

facts to whom he alleges the words were published and prove their knowledge[34] and publication to them. So if it is stated that the claimant was seen entering a particular house that is a brothel, but the nature of the house is not specified, the words are defamatory only insofar as it is proved that they were published to persons who knew the character of the house.[35] If the claimant fails to establish the supporting facts for the innuendo he may, of course, still fall back on the ordinary meaning of the words if those are defamatory. The line between the true and the popular innuendo may be very difficult to draw because it turns on the general knowledge possessed by ordinary people and this changes from time to time.[36] Nowadays most people know what the Mafia is and so words alleging that a company is controlled by the Mafia are defamatory in their ordinary meaning,[37] but, "cony catcher" is unlikely to convey much to people today, though once upon a time it was a common word for a swindler; and a knowledge of Biblical allusions and characters is probably far less common than would have been assumed by Victorian judges.

Mere vulgar abuse. It is commonly said that mere vulgar spoken abuse is not defamation[38] but this needs some explanation. Spoken words that are prima facie defamatory are not actionable if it is clear that they were uttered merely as general vituperation *and* were so understood by those who heard them,[39] and the same applies to words spoken in jest.[40] The burden is on the defendant to show that his listeners understood the words in a non-defamatory sense.[41] This makes the manner and context in which the words were spoken very important—for example, whether they are used deliberately in cold blood or bawled out at the height of a violent quarrel. It is generally said that written words cannot be protected as abuse because the defendant had time for reflection before he wrote and his readers may know nothing of any dispute or other circumstances which caused him to write as he did—no doubt this is generally true but it is hard to see why there should be any absolute rule and it is submitted that the same should be true where a jest is expressed in writing or in a cartoon.

13–013

---

[34] At the time of the publication: *Grappelli v Derek Block (Holdings) Ltd* [1981] 1 W.L.R. 822. The issue of whether a statement is defamatory must be determined as at the time of publication.

[35] Lord Devlin's example in *Lewis v Daily Telegraph* [1964] A.C. 234 at 278. See also *Cassidy v Daily Mirror* [1929] 2 K.B. 331. It seems that in principle a defendant may contend that words which are defamatory in their ordinary sense are not so because of special knowledge possessed by the persons to whom they were published, but he will have to show that all the persons to whom the words were published knew those facts, which might be very difficult and impossible in the case of a generally circulated libel: *Hankinson v Bilby* (1847) 16 M. & W. 422.

[36] It was suggested in *Lennon v Scottish Daily Record and Sunday Mail Ltd* [2004] EWHC 359 (QB); [2004] E.M.L.R. 18 that the ordinary reader must now be credited with having achieved a level of education which was not widely accessible to earlier generations.

[37] Even "Mafia" may be used in a non-defamatory, metaphorical sense meaning a close-knit group: *Brooks v Lind, The Times*, March 26, 1997.

[38] "For mere general abuse spoken no action lies": Mansfield CJ in *Thorley v Kerry* (1812) 4 Taunt. 355 at 365. See also *Parkins v Scott* (1862) 1 H. & C. 153 at 158, 159; *Trimingham v Associated Newspapers* [2012] EWHC 1296 (QB); [2012] 4 All E.R. 717 at [69]. Abuse may of course be a crime. It might also give rise to an action for harassment: see paras 4–034, 4–040.

[39] For entertaining cases on abuse see *Rambo v Cohen* 587 N.E. 2d 147 (Ind. 1992) and *Ralston v Fomich* [1994] 2 W.W.R. 284 (variations on the theme of "son of a bitch").

[40] *Donoghue v Hayes* (1831) Hayes (Ir. Ex.) R. 265.

[41] *Penfold v Westcote* (1806) 2 B. & P. (N.R.) 335.

ii.   Reference to the Claimant

13–014   **The claimant need not be named.** The tort of defamation is not committed unless the defamatory statement refers to the claimant. If the claimant is mentioned by name there is usually no difficulty in establishing the requirement of reference to the claimant, but the claimant need not be named, for the issue is whether the statement may be understood by reasonable people as referring to the claimant. For example, the claimant may be referred to by a nickname or by initials[42] or by his job or by reference to some allegorical or historical character or by a word picture. In *I'Anson v Stuart*[43] a newspaper paragraph stated: "This diabolical character, like Polyphemus the man-eater, has but one eye, and is well-known to all persons acquainted with the name of a certain noble circumnavigator." It was clear that the claimant was the person referred to on his giving proof that he had one eye and bore a name similar to that of Anson, the famous admiral.

13–015   **A statement may refer to more than one person.** A reference to A may by implication also amount to a reference to B, so that, for example, a derogatory statement about the conduct of a company may impute wrongdoing or incompetence to its directors or officers.[44]

13–016   **The claimant may rely on innuendo to show that the reference requirement is satisfied.** In many cases there is at least some "peg or pointer" in the article itself that points to the claimant but this is not necessary. In *Morgan v Odhams Press Ltd*[45] a newspaper article alleged that a girl had been kidnapped by a dog-doping gang. At the relevant time the girl had been staying at the claimant's flat and the claimant produced six witnesses who swore that they understood from the article that he was connected with the gang. A majority of the House of Lords held that these facts constituted sufficient material to leave to the jury. The test of whether the words "refer to the claimant" in this situation is whether a hypothetical, sensible reader, having knowledge of the special circumstances, would believe that the claimant was referred to. In such a case of course it is essential that the claimant shows that the material was published to persons who knew the special facts. Where, on the other hand, the article identifies the claimant on its face, so that no true innuendo is necessary, it seems that the claimant does not need to show that anyone who read it knew him and therefore was actually put in mind of him. Provided there is evidence that the words were published to others, the question is whether ordinary, sensible readers, knowing of the claimant, would be of opinion that the words referred to him (though evidence that people actually did so may of course inflate the damages). Thus, in

---

[42] See *Heller v Bianco* 244 P. (2d) 757 (Cal. 1952) (Christian name and telephone number on toilet wall).

[43] (1787) 1 T.R. 748.

[44] *Aspro Travel Ltd v Owners Abroad Group* [1996] 1 W.L.R. 132. For the reverse case of imputations about officers reflecting on the company, see *Jameel v Times Newspapers Ltd* [2004] EWCA Civ 983; [2004] E.M.L.R. 31.

[45] [1971] 1 W.L.R. 1239.

Shevill v Presse Alliance SA[46] the court refused to strike out a claim by a claimant in Yorkshire in respect of an issue of *France Soir*, of which perhaps 10 copies had been sold in Yorkshire and 230 in England and Wales.

Circumstances in which recourse may be made to subsequent publications for identification purposes. Where a defamatory publication does not sufficiently identify the claimant, he may rely for identification purposes on a subsequent publication by the same defendant,[47] or on a forthcoming publication by another to which the defendant draws attention.[48] It has been said that were the law otherwise, it would be open to a newspaper to publish a virulent libel without identifying the person defamed but adding a statement that the victim would be identified in a week's time.[49]

13–017

The defendant's intention is irrelevant. As in the case in relation to the requirement that the statement be defamatory, the ultimate question with respect to the requirement of reference to the claimant is not what the defendant intended but what the words can reasonably be understood as conveying. Therefore, the reference requirement may be satisfied even if the defendant intended to write about a fictitious character. In *Hulton & Co v Jones*[50] H were newspaper proprietors who published a humorous account of a motor festival at Dieppe in which imputations were cast on the morals of one Artemus Jones, a churchwarden at Peckham. This person was intended to be, and was believed by the writer of the article and the editor of the paper to be, purely fictitious. In fact there was a barrister named Artemus Jones, who was not a churchwarden, did not live at Peckham and had taken no part in the Dieppe motor festival. He sued H for libel and friends of his swore that they believed the article referred to him. In affirming a verdict for the claimant the House of Lords held that there was evidence upon which the jury could have come to the conclusion that reasonable people would believe the claimant was referred to and that it was immaterial that the defendants did not intend to defame him.[51] It logically follows from *Hulton* that if D intends to refer to X, about whom the statement is true, and reasonable people might take it as referring to C, then D has defamed C, and this was accepted by the Court of Appeal in *Newstead v London Express*,[52] where a report of the conviction of "Harold Newstead, thirty year old Camberwell man" for bigamy was held to be actionable by another Harold Newstead in Camberwell of about the same age.

13–018

The fact that it is irrelevant whether the defendant was at fault in referring to the claimant is likely to be challenged under art.10 of the European Convention on Human Rights. A sign of this appeared in *O'Shea v MGN Ltd*[53] where the

---

[46] [1992] 1 W.L.R. 1. A minimal publication may lead the court to strike out the claim as an abuse of process: see para.26–077. The serious harm requirement may also be unsatisfied: see para.13–004.

[47] *Hayward v Thompson* [1982] Q.B. 47.

[48] *Baltinos v Foreign Language Publications Ltd* (1986) 6 N.S.W.L.R. 85.

[49] *Hayward v Thompson* [1982] Q.B. 47 at 72 per Sir Stanley Rees.

[50] [1910] A.C. 20.

[51] Mere coincidence of name is not of course necessarily enough to lead to this conclusion. The jury may have been influenced by the fact that the claimant had once worked for the newspaper, although his counsel accepted that they had forgotten about him.

[52] [1940] 1 K.B. 377.

[53] [2001] E.M.L.R. 40.

defendants published an advertisement for pornographic internet services that contained a photograph of a woman, E, who was alleged to be the "spit and image" of the claimant. Morland J held that the reference requirement was satisfied according to the law as articulated by *Hulton* and *Newstead*. However, he concluded that such a result would be incompatible with art.10 and the claim was dismissed as having no reasonable prospect of success. Morland J wrote:[54]

> "It would impose an impossible burden on a publisher if he were required to check if the true picture of someone resembled someone else who because of the context of the picture was defamed. Examples are legion—unlawful violence in street protest demonstrations, looting, hooliganism at football matches, people apparently leaving or entering Court with criminal defendants and investigative journalism into drug dealing, corruption, child abuse and prostitution."

13–019   **References to a group of persons.** The question whether an individual can sue in respect of words that are directed against a group, or body, or class of persons generally was considered by the House of Lords in *Knuppfer v London Express Newspaper Ltd*,[55] and the law may be summarised as follows: (1) the crucial question is whether the words were published "of the claimant" in the sense that he can be said to be personally pointed at; (2) normally, where the defamatory statement is directed at a class of persons, no individual belonging to the class is entitled to say that the words were published of him;[56] (3) words that appear to apply to a class may be actionable if there is something in them, or in the circumstances in which they were published, that indicates a particular claimant or claimants;[57] (4) in practice the smaller the group upon which the attack is directed the more likely it is that the claimant will be able to make out a case; and (5) where the charge is very specific and levelled against an entire group it is possible that the reference requirement would be satisfied in relation to each member of the group, irrespective of the size of the group.[58] A conundrum arises where a charge is made in terms like "one of these people stole my watch". It might be argued that the statement does not impute the wrongdoing to any individual, but it is not clear that this is the law[59] and the statement would seem to impute suspicion, which is itself defamatory, though to a lesser degree.[60]

iii.   Publication

13–020   **Generally.** The tort of defamation is not committed unless the statement concerned is communicated to at least one person other than the claimant. This is the requirement of publication. Simply making a statement to the claimant alone

---

[54] [2001] E.M.L.R. 40 at [43].

[55] [1944] A.C. 116.

[56] "[I]f a man wrote that all lawyers were thieves, no particular lawyer could sue him unless there was something to point to the particular individual": *Eastwood v Holmes* (1858) 1 F. & F. 347 at 349 per Willes J.

[57] *Le Fanu v Malcolmson* (1848) 11 H.L.C. 637.

[58] *Knuppfer v London Express Newspaper Ltd* [1944] A.C. 116 at 124.

[59] *Farrington v Leigh*, The Times, December 10, 1987.

[60] *Lewis v Daily Telegraph* [1964] A.C. 234.

will not satisfy it because the tort of defamation is concerned with protecting reputation rather than one's opinion of oneself.

Any statement is capable of being a publication. Publication in the commercial sense, as in a book or newspaper or broadcast is not necessary, although these are of course likely to attract larger damages. A statement made by any means whatsoever is in principle capable of satisfying the publication requirement.

13–021

The statement need not be published to more than a single person. It is still the law that publication to one person will suffice but nowadays this must be read in the light of the court's power to strike out the claim as an abuse of process[61] and the "serious harm" requirement.[62]

13–022

Each publication gives rise to a separate cause of action subject to statutory exceptions. At common law, each time a defamatory statement is published a separate cause of action arises.[63] This rule is highly significant since every time a statement was republished a new limitation period commenced. An exception to this rule has been created by s.8 of the Defamation Act 2013. Section 8 applies when D publishes a statement "to the public" and subsequently republishes the statement or a statement that is substantially the same, whether or not to the public. When s.8 applies, new limitation periods will not be triggered by the republication. Section 8 was enacted principally to deal with the perceived problem of online archives. At common law, each time a website is accessed and material downloaded, the material in question is treated as republished and the republication triggers a fresh limitation period. The fear, consequently, was that website operators would purge archived material or not establish archives in the first place due to a fear of incurring liability in defamation indefinitely. It is important to note that s.8(6)(a) provides that s.8 does not affect the court's discretion to extend the limitation period under s.32A of the Limitation Act 1980.[64] This discretion may significantly reduce the importance of s.8.

13–023

Statements made to and by one's assistant. The handing back by a printer or typist to the author of a defamatory document processed by them on the author's instructions is not a publication by them,[65] but there is, of course, publication to the printer or typist when the author hands or sends the document to them. Unless a defence applies, it follows that if a manager of a company in the course of his duties dictates to a secretary a memorandum defamatory of a fellow employee, not only has the manager committed libel but the company is also vicariously liable.[66]

13–024

Communications between spouses. Communication of defamatory matter by a husband to his wife or vice versa is not a publication: what passes between them is protected on the ground that any other rule "might lead to disastrous results to social life".[67] This rule probably emerged as a result of the doctrine of unity

13–025

---

[61] See para.26–077.
[62] See para.13–004.
[63] *Duke of Brunswick v Harmer* (1849) 14 Q.B. 185.
[64] See para.26–101.
[65] *Eglantine Inn Ltd v Smith* [1948] N.I. 29.
[66] *Riddick v Thames Board Mills Ltd* [1977] Q.B. 881.
[67] *Wennhak v Morgan* (1888) 20 Q.B.D. 635 at 639.

(which is now largely a relic of a bygone age)—namely, the idea that husband and wife were one person in the eyes of the law. This supported the rule that communications between spouses could not satisfy the publication requirement on the logic that a person could not publish a statement to himself. In modern conditions a broader rule based on "domestic relations", however hard to define, might be more apt. Communication by a third party to one spouse of matter defamatory of the other is a publication.

13–026 **For the publication requirement to be satisfied the statement must be one that can be understood by the recipient.** The statement must be intelligible to the recipient of it.[68] There is no publication if it is in a foreign language that the recipient does not understand or if he is too deaf to hear it or too blind to read it, although in the case of books, newspapers or broadcasts it will of course be inferred that it was intelligible to the majority of recipients. Similarly in the case of postcards there is a presumption that these are published on being sent through the post without proof that anyone did in fact read them. This is based on the practical impossibility of proving that anyone did read them; in theory the presumption is rebuttable but it very difficult to conceive, if the postcard is written in English, how such rebutting evidence could be given.

13–027 **Passive role in facilitating the transmission of information.** Persons who merely play a passive role in transferring information do not publish the statements transmitted. Thus, a telephone company or internet service provider does not publish information that they transmit.[69]

13–028 **Responsibility for publication by a third party.** If X publishes a statement and D has knowledge of the publication and the means to remove or withdraw the publication (where it is not merely transitory material), D may be taken to have published the statement from the point in time at which D acquired knowledge of the publication. This principle is nicely illustrated by *Byrne v Deane*.[70] In this case T published a statement regarding C on a notice board at D's golf club where it remained for several days. D had control of the notice board and it was held that D published it because it failed to remove it. In *Tamiz v Google Inc*[71] Google hosted a blogging service. It was held that once Google became aware that a blog created by a third-party was defamatory it was arguable that it became a publisher of the material on the blog.

13–029 **The statement must be published intentionally or negligently.** Unless the statement is communicated intentionally or negligently, the publication requirement will not be satisfied. A defendant will publish a statement negligently if he should have foreseen that it would be read by someone. For example, the publication requirement will not be established if D locked in a safe a defamatory note which was then read by a burglar who broke into it. However, the position is likely to be otherwise if D sends a letter to C containing defamatory imputations about C (which would not be actionable if read by C) and it is opened in the

---

[68] *Daniels v British Broadcasting Corporation* [2010] EWHC 3057 (QB) at [46].
[69] *Bunt v Tilley* [2006] EWHC 407; [2007] 1 W.L.R. 124; *Metropolitan International Schools Ltd v DesignTechnica Corp* [2009] EWHC 1765 (QB); [2009] E.M.L.R. 27.
[70] [1937] 1 K.B. 818.
[71] [2013] EWCA Civ 68; [2013] 1 W.L.R. 2151.

ordinary course of business by an employee of C.[72] If the defendant leaves his correspondence about for people to read, or if he inadvertently puts a letter in the wrong envelope or if he speaks too loudly so that he is overheard he will have published the material.[73] In *Huth v Huth* it was held that there was no publication where a letter addressed to C was opened by C's inquisitive butler, even though it was unsealed on the ground that it was not part of the butler's duties to open C's mail.[74]

Secondary publishers. The common law spreads the net of liability very wide. In the case of an article in a newspaper, for example, not only is the author treated as a publisher, but so is the editor, the printer, the proprietor of the newspaper,[75] indeed anyone who participated in the publication.[76] However, those concerned with the mere mechanical distribution of material—newsagents, libraries, booksellers—may be entitled to the defence of innocent dissemination. That defence is discussed later.[77] There is a further defence available to secondary publishers where it is not reasonably practical to sue the primary publisher. That defence is also discussed below.[78]

13–030

iv. Damage

Introduction. The tort of defamation requires proof that the defamatory statement caused the claimant to suffer damage, but damage is presumed in the case of libel and in certain types of slander. When the presumption of damage applies it is irrebuttable.[79]

13–031

The distinction between libel and slander. Historically, it was thought that the distinction between libel and slander was that between written (which were libel) and spoken words (which were slander). Today, the general view is that libellous statements are statements in permanent form whereas slanderous statements are statements in non-permanent form. Examples of libel are a piece of writing, printed material, or other mark or sign exposed to view, or a picture, waxwork, statue or effigy. On the other hand, defamation in the sign language of the deaf and dumb, and mimicry and gesticulation generally (e.g. holding up an empty purse to indicate that the claimant has been robbed by the defendant[80]) would be slander, because the movements are more transient. However, some arbitrary lines have to be drawn: it is thought that chalk marks on a wall would be libel even though they may be quickly washed away by the rain. Far more important in

13–032

---

[72] *Pullman v Hill* [1891] 1 Q.B. 524. Consider also *Theaker v Richardson* [1962] 1 W.L.R. 151.
[73] *Pullman v Hill* [1891] 1 Q.B. 524 at 527.
[74] [1915] 3 K.B. 32.
[75] In modern conditions newspapers are of course always operated as companies.
[76] Hence there may be many separate publications before it is issued to the public, though it is that which will in practice be sued on. Technically there is a separate publication to each reader. In practice the edition will be sued on as a whole but the issue of separate publications may be significant if a true innuendo is relied on. Now that many newspapers publish internet editions, we have another example of separate publication.
[77] See para.13–084.
[78] See para.13–090.
[79] *Jameel (Yousef) v Dow Jones & Co Inc* [2005] EWCA Civ 75; [2005] Q.B. 946.
[80] *Cook v Cox* (1814) 3 M. & S. 110 at 114.

practice are the statutory provisions whereby broadcasting, both radio and television,[81] and theatrical performances,[82] are libel. The Court of Appeal in *Youssoupoff v Metro-Goldwyn-Mayer Pictures Ltd* held that the showing of defamatory matter embodied in a film with a soundtrack was libel. Obviously, if a defamatory oral utterance is communicated to a person it is a slander which is published and if a written statement is shown it is libel, but an oral statement by A may be written down by D and shown by D to B. In that case D publishes a libel. No doubt A's original uttering of the words to D was slander, but the communication to B is not by word of mouth. Conversely, if A writes to D something defamatory of C and D reads it aloud to B, that ought logically to be slander, but the balance of authority is the other way.[83] If D dictates a defamatory letter to a typist D publishes a slander in doing so, but when the typist reads or hands it back to D it seems that there is no publication at all by him.[84]

13–033   **Consequences of the distinction.** The distinction between libel and slander used to have greater importance in the past than it does today because libel, but not slander, used to be a common law crime as well as a tort. The crime of libel was abolished by s.73(b) of the Coroners and Justice Act 2009. Now that there is no longer a crime of defamatory libel the consequence of the distinction between libel and slander is that libel is always actionable per se (damage is presumed), whereas in most cases of slander "special damage" must be shown.

"Special damage" is a phrase that has been rightly criticised as either meaningless or misleading and "actual" damage has been suggested as a more accurate expression.[85] It involves loss of money or of some temporal or material advantage estimable in money. The mere loss of society of one's friends, even ostracism, is insufficient. Hence, while loss of your friend's hospitality is special damage, exclusion from the religious congregation to which you belong is not, for a dinner has a temporal and material value, while spiritual communion has none in this connection.[86] In contrast, in cases of libel (and in those cases of slander where proof of damage is not needed) the claimant can recover damages for the injury to his reputation without adducing any evidence that it has in fact been harmed, for the law presumes that some damage will arise in the ordinary course of things.

The special damage must not be too remote a consequence of the slander. It was once held that if D slandered C so that C was wrongfully dismissed from employment by X, D was not liable to C because the damage was not the "legal and natural consequence" of the words spoken: X's wrongful act was regarded as breaking the chain of causation.[87] It is not the law now that this is necessarily so. In *Lynch v Knight* Lord Wensleydale said:[88]

---

[81] Broadcasting Act 1990 s.166.
[82] Theatres Act 1968 s.4.
[83] *Forrester v Tyrrell* (1893) 9 T.L.R. 257; *Robinson v Chambers* [1946] N.I. 148. Cf. *Osborne v Boulter* [1930] 2 K.B. 226.
[84] See para.13–024.
[85] Bowen LJ in *Ratcliffe v Evans* [1892] 2 Q.B. 524. For other meanings of the phrase, see Jolowicz [1960] C.L.J. 214.
[86] *Roberts v Roberts* (1864) 5 B. & S. 384; *Davies v Solomon* (1871) L.R. 7 Q.B. 112.
[87] *Vicars v Wilcocks* (1806) 8 East 1.
[88] (1861) 9 H.L.C. 597 at 600.

"To make the words actionable by reason of special damage, the consequence must be such as, taking human nature as it is, with its infirmities and having regard to the relationship of the parties concerned, might fairly and reasonably have been anticipated and feared would follow from the speaking of the words."

In other words, if D slanders C, the chain of causation may possibly be broken by the unlawful act of X, but it does not follow that it must necessarily be severed thereby.[89] Illness arising from worry induced by the slander is too remote.[90]

The significance of the fact that libel is actionable per se is limited. A defendant who is libelled but is unable to establish that he suffered damage will be unable to recover more than nominal damages. He is also unlikely to be able to establish the serious harm requirement[91] and his case is also vulnerable to being struck out as an abuse of process.[92]

Cases of slander actionable per se. There are two cases in which slander is actionable without proof of special damage.[93] These may have originated in the idea that the nature of the allegation made damage so likely that it should be presumed. The first case is where the statement is the effect that the claimant is guilty of a criminal offence punishable with imprisonment.[94] There must be a direct imputation of the offence, not merely of suspicion of it,[95] and the offence must be punishable by imprisonment in the first instance[96] and not merely because, for example, a fine imposed on conviction has not been paid.[97] Technical language need not be used[98] but if the words as a whole in their context do not impute a crime punishable by imprisonment they do not fall within the rule.[99] It now seems to be established that the basis of this exception is the probability of social ostracism of the claimant and not his jeopardy of imprisonment,[100] though such ostracism may of course arise in the case of conduct not punishable by imprisonment.

The second exception is much more important in practical terms. It is actionable per se to impute to any person unfitness, dishonesty or incompetence in any office,[101] profession, calling trade or business[102] carried on by him at the time when the slander was published. At common law its scope was severely

13–034

---

[89] See also *Bowen v Hall* (1881) 6 Q.B.D. 333.

[90] *Allsop v Allsop* (1865) 5 H. & N. 534.

[91] See para.13–004.

[92] See para.26–077.

[93] There were previously four cases, but two of these were abolished by the Defamation Act 2013 s.14.

[94] A company cannot be imprisoned but in *D&L Caterers v D'Ajou* [1945] K.B. 210 Stable J thought that an imputation of a crime to a company which would be punishable by imprisonment in the case of a natural person was actionable per se. The Court of Appeal left the point open.

[95] *Simmons v Mitchell* (1880) 6 App. Cas. 156.

[96] *Hellwig v Mitchell* [1910] 1 K.B. 609.

[97] *Ormiston v G.W. Ry* [1917] 1 K.B. 598.

[98] *Webb v Beavan* (1883) 11 Q.B.D. 609.

[99] *Jackson v Adams* (1835) 2 Bing. N.C. 402.

[100] *Gray v Jones* (1939) 160 L.T. 361.

[101] A distinction used to be drawn between offices of profit and offices of honour but this is no longer the case: *Maccaba v Liechtenstein* [2004] EWHC 1580 (QB).

[102] The exception was held not to apply to performance of a duty imposed on citizens in war time: *Cleghorn v Sadler* [1945] K.B. 325 (fire watching).

restricted by the rule that the slander must be spoken of the claimant in the way of his office so that it was not, for example, slander actionable per se to say of a schoolmaster that he had committed adultery with one of the school cleaners.[103] Now, however, it is provided by s.2 of the Defamation Act 1952:

> "In an action for slander in respect of words calculated to disparage the claimant in any office, profession, calling, trade or business held or carried on by him at the time of publication, it shall not be necessary to allege or prove special damage, whether or not the words are spoken of the claimant in the way of his office, profession, calling, trade or business."

Though there is no decisive authority, "calculated to" probably means "likely to". What will satisfy this test is of course going to turn on the nature of the office and the nature of the charge: a charge of uncharitable behaviour against a clergyman may be more likely to be damaging than the same charge against an ordinary person, and to say of a judge that he could not stay awake on the bench would be actionable per se, though to say that he had committed adultery would not be.

13–035   **The distinction between libel and slander is anachronistic.** The distinction between libel and slander has few friends and many jurisdictions have abolished it.[104] The distinction appears to have arisen for historical reasons which are to some extent obscure, though it was firmly set in the law by the end of the 18th century.[105] Even then it was subject to criticism and its abolition was advocated by a Select Committee of the House of Lords in 1843 and rationalisations such as that libel has a greater potentiality for harm or is more likely to be premeditated do not alter the fact that, as Sir James Mansfield CJ said long ago: "[A]n assertion made in a public place, as upon the Royal Exchange, concerning a merchant in London, may be much more extensively diffused than a few printed papers dispersed or a private letter."[106] Had it not been for the intervention of the legislature in the case of broadcasting the distinction would probably have come under greater pressure. The Faulks Committee recommended in 1975[107] that the distinction should be abolished and fears that this might lead to a flood of petty actions for spoken words appear not to be borne out by the experience in other parts of the world.

13–036   **Republication.** If D slanders C and the case is not within one of the categories of slander that are actionable per se C will have no action against D unless he can establish that he suffered special damage. However, C will have an action against D if D's statement is republished by X, such republication causes special damage and the republication was foreseeable by a reasonable person in D's position.[108] (C will, of course, also be able to sue X.) Republication will usually be

---

[103] *Jones v Jones* [1916] 2 A.C. 481; *Hopwood v Muirson* [1945] K.B. 313 ("the slander was upon the solicitor as a man; not upon the man as a solicitor").

[104] New Zealand, the Australian states and most Canadian provinces. Ireland moved to this position by s.6 of the Defamation Act 2009. The distinction does not exist in Scots law, though the expressions "libel" and "slander" are in common use there.

[105] *Thorley v Kerry* (1812) 4 Taunt. 355. For detail, see Holdsworth (1924) 40 L.Q.R. 302; Holdsworth (1925) 41 L.Q.R. 13; Kaye (1975) 91 L.Q.R. 524.

[106] *Thorley v Kerry* (1812) 4 Taunt. 355 at 364.

[107] Cmnd. 5909, Ch.2.

[108] *McManus v Beckham* [2002] EWCA Civ 939; [2002] 1 W.L.R. 2982 at [44]; *Slipper v BBC* [1991] 2 Q.B. 283 at 301.

foreseeable where, for example, D speaks at a press conference.[109] The starting position, however, is that D is not liable for the republication by another person by virtue of the general principle that the voluntary act of another will break the chain of causation.[110]

v.   Standing to Sue

Any living human being may be the claimant in a defamation action.[111] There is no doubt that a trading corporation may sue for defamation in respect of words affecting its trading reputation or property[112] and the same is probably true of non-trading corporations insofar as they raise funds and own property. However, a governmental body (whether a local authority or an organ of central government) cannot sue even if the statement in no way concerns its "governing" reputation.[113] The reason for this rule is that in a democratic society it is important that people be free to criticise the government. The principle has been applied to a political party[114] and it is probably not necessary that the "governmental body" should be popularly elected, but it remains to be seen whether it will be applied, for example, to public utility suppliers, which in legal form are now generally ordinary trading companies, although regulated in their activities. On the other hand, an attack on a governmental body may be defamatory of individual members or officers. There is no restriction on an individual who manages a governmental body suing in respect of a statement that is defamatory of him in relation to his work for the governmental body.[115]

13–037

vi.   Not Elements

It is important to reflect upon matters that are not elements of the action in defamation. Falsity is not an element, although truth is a defence. That defence is discussed below.[116] Malice is not an element either. It is perfectly possible to succeed in an action in defamation without showing that the defendant was acting out of spite, for example. However, malice is relevant to certain defences, and, significantly, the claimant will often endeavour to prove that the defendant published the statement concerned maliciously in the hope that doing so will increase their recovery.[117] The fact that the defendant published the statement maliciously may, for example, open the door to an award of aggravated damages.

13–038

---

[109] *Sims v Wran* [1984] 1 N.S.W.L.R. 317.

[110] *Ward v Weeks* (1830) 7 Bing. N.C. 211; *Weld-Blundell v Stephens* [1920] A.C. 956.

[111] One cannot be liable for defaming the dead: see para.24–004.

[112] *Metropolitan Saloon Omnibus Co v Hawkins* (1859) 4 H. & N. 87; *South Hetton Coal Co v North Eastern News Association Ltd* [1894] 1 Q.B. 133.

[113] *Derbyshire CC v Times Newspapers Ltd* [1993] A.C. 534 (management of local authority pension fund).

[114] *Goldsmith v Boyruhl* [1998] Q.B. 459.

[115] *McLaughlin v London Borough of Lambeth* [2010] EWHC 2726 (QB) at [46].

[116] See para.13–039.

[117] For discussion, see *Adelson v Anderson* [2011] EWHC 2497 (QB) at [81].

B.   Defences

13–039   It is extraordinarily easy for the elements of the tort of defamation to be satisfied. The fact that the tort is so easily committed means that defences to liability in defamation are particularly important. Defences play a very major role in delimiting liability.

i.   Truth

13–040   **Generally.** Falsity of the statement in question is not an element of the action in defamation. However, truth is a defence. This defence used to be known by the label "justification". However, that label has been banished and the defence has been put on a statutory footing in s.2 of the Defamation Act 2013.

13–041   **The defendant's motive is irrelevant.** This defence is concerned simply with whether the statement was true. The motive of the defendant is utterly irrelevant in relation to the question of whether the defence applies. It is immaterial, therefore, that the defendant published the statement out of ill-will or spite, provided that the statement is true. It is not that the law has any special relish for the indiscriminate infliction of truth on other people, but defamation is an injury to a person's reputation, and if people think the worse of him when they hear the truth about him that merely shows that his reputation has been reduced to its proper level.

13–042   **It is irrelevant whether the statement is in the public interest.** In order to clinch the defence, the defendant does not need to show that his statement was in the public interest. If one introduces a condition that the publication must relate to a matter of public interest one is in effect creating a form of liability for invasion of privacy.[118]

13–043   **Failure to succeed on the defence of truth can increase damages.** Truth may be a dangerous plea if it fails since the court may regard the defendant's conduct as wanton and return a verdict for heavier damages.

13–044   **The statement must be substantially true.** The defendant need not show that the statement is precisely true in every particular: what matters is whether it is substantially true[119] and it has been said that journalists "need to be permitted a degree of exaggeration even in the context of factual assertions".[120] Subject to that, it is a general principle that the defence must be as broad as the charge, and must cover the precise charge.

13–045   **Repetition rule.** Suppose that X publishes a defamatory statement and that D republishes that statement. D cannot avoid liability by showing that it is true that X published the defamatory statement. He must show that the facts asserted in the

---

[118] See para.13–143.
[119] Defamation Act 2013 s.2(1).
[120] *Turcu v News Group Newspapers Ltd* [2005] EWHC 799 (QB) at [108].

statement are themselves true. In other words, D must prove that the content of the statement was true, not merely that it was made.[121] This is commonly known as the "repetition rule".

Distinct charges. If the defamatory statement contains distinct charges and the defendant can only show that one or some of them are substantially true, the defence of truth will not fail provided that the imputations that are not proved to be substantially true do not seriously harm the claimant's reputation.[122] To give a simple example: if D were to allege of C (1) that he had participated in genocide during a war, and (2) while so serving had made certain dishonest expenses claims, proving that (1) is true would entitle the court to deliver a verdict for D on the whole article even if there was no evidence at all that (2) is true. However, this rule only applies where the claimant sues in respect of two or more distinct charges. If the claimant chooses to sue only in respect of one charge (and the initiative is his) the defendant cannot adduce evidence of truth relating to the other charge or charges.[123] "It is no defence to a charge that 'You called me A' to say 'Yes, but I also called you B on the same occasion and that was true'."[124]   13–046

Common sting. As has just been discussed, it is for the claimant to decide in respect of which statements he will bring proceedings, and the defendant cannot plead that a different statement that he made was true. However, despite this general rule, where several defamatory allegations have a common sting the defendant is entitled to show that the sting is true even though it amounts to a charge of more general wrongdoing in respect of which the claimant has not sued.[125] In *Williams v Reason*[126] the allegation was that the claimant had written a book for money and had thereby compromised his amateur status as a Rugby Union player. The defendants obtained leave to allege that the claimant had taken money for wearing the boots of a named manufacturer, for the sting of the libel was "shamateurism", not merely the writing of the book. However, in *Bookbinder v Tebbit*,[127] where a local politician was accused of squandering public money by overprinting stationery in support of "nuclear free zones", the defendant was not allowed to introduce several other alleged instances of irresponsibility with public money. Had the charge been made in the context of a broader political attack on maladministration the position might have been different but on the facts to accept the defendant's contention would be tantamount to saying that a particular charge of wrongdoing necessarily included a general charge of that sort of wrongdoing, thereby considerably widening the field in the defendant's favour.   13–047

The defendant's pleadings. The defendant must make clear the defamatory meaning that he seeks to justify.[128] This is not quite the same as requiring him to specify what the words do mean: he may give notice in his defence of his   13–048

---

[121] *Shah v Standard Chartered Bank* [1999] Q.B. 240.
[122] Defamation Act 2013 s.2(3).
[123] *Polly Peck (Holdings) Plc v Trelford* [1986] Q.B. 1000; *Bookbinder v Tebbit* [1989] 1 W.L.R. 640; *McKeith v News Group Newspapers Ltd* [2005] EWHC 1162 (QB).
[124] *Cruise v Express Newspapers Plc* [1999] Q.B. 931 at 954.
[125] *Khashoggi v I.P.C. Magazines Ltd* [1986] 1 W.L.R. 1412.
[126] [1988] 1 W.L.R. 96.
[127] [1989] 1 W.L.R. 640.
[128] *Lucas-Box v News Group Newspapers Ltd* [1986] 1 W.L.R. 147.

preparedness to justify two or three different meanings and he is not obliged to pick out one of those as his exclusive defence.

13–049   **Burden of proof.** The burden is on the defendant to demonstrate that the statement in question is true. The fact that the burden of proof is allocated to the defendant in respect of the issue of truth is often expressed by saying that it is assumed that defamatory statements are false. Although the burden of proof rests on the defendant, it is routine for claimants to seek to establish that the statement about which they complain is false. The reason why this is done is that unless it is shown that the statement is false they are unlikely to be awarded a remedy, and especially not substantial damages.[129]

13–050   **Standard of proof.** The standard of proof is the balance of probabilities but the seriousness of the defendant's allegation may be taken into account in determining whether he has discharged that burden.[130] Where the defamatory allegation was that the claimant had committed a criminal offence, the common law rule was that his criminal conviction was not even prima facie evidence of guilt for the purpose of the defamation proceedings, and this meant that the defendant had to prove the guilt of the claimant all over again if the defence of justification was to succeed.[131] However, it is provided by s.13 of the Civil Evidence Act 1968 that in an action for libel or slander in which the question whether the claimant committed a criminal offence is relevant, proof that he stands convicted of the offence is conclusive evidence that he did commit it.

13–051   **Rehabilitation of Offenders Act 1974.** The only qualification to the proposition that truth is a complete defence is to be found in the Rehabilitation of Offenders Act 1974. The Act seeks to rehabilitate convicted offenders by restricting or forbidding the disclosure of "spent convictions". Speaking very broadly, spent conventions are convictions that are sufficiently old. The Act permits defendants to adduce evidence of spent convictions to establish the defence of truth provided that the defendant did not publish the defamatory statement in question maliciously.[132] Malice here means that the publication is made with some spiteful, irrelevant or improper motive.[133]

ii.   Absolute Privilege

13–052   **Generally.** In certain situations, it is thought to be so important that people can speak freely that the law confers complete protection from liability in defamation, including in respect of false statements. The logic is that unless total protection is given, people might be fearful of speaking in case what they say turns out to be untrue and they are consequently unable to avoid liability on the basis of the defence of truth. When the law of defamation confers such protection it gives

---

[129]   For discussion see *Adelson v Anderson* [2011] EWHC 2497 (QB) at [76]–[78].
[130]   *Laurence v Chester Chronicle, The Times*, February 8, 1986.
[131]   This he did not always succeed in doing: *Hinds v Sparks* [1964] Crim. L.R. 717; *Goody v Odhams Press Ltd* [1967] 1 Q.B. 333.
[132]   Section 8(5).
[133]   *Herbage v Pressdram Ltd* [1984] 1 W.L.R. 1160.

what is known as "absolute privilege". The term privilege is apt to be misleading. For the moment it prevails, but in the future it might be replaced by "immunity".

Falsity and malice are irrelevant to absolute privilege. Absolute privilege **13–053** covers cases in which complete freedom of communication is regarded as being of such paramount importance that actions for defamation cannot be entertained at all: a person defamed on an occasion of absolute privilege has no legal redress via the law of defamation, however outrageous the untrue statement which has been made about him and however malicious the motive of the maker of it.

Contrast with qualified privilege. Absolute privilege contrasts with qualified **13–054** privilege. Qualified privilege is discussed in detail below,[134] although it is necessary to mention it briefly here since reference is made to it on several occasions in the dicussion here of absolute priviledge. Qualified privilege differs from absolute privilege principally in that it is lost if the defendant published the defamatory statement concerned maliciously.

The choice between absolute privilege and qualified privilege. The law **13–055** recognises absolute privilege in some situations and qualified privilege on other occasions. The choice between them depends on how important it is thought that persons be free to speak. The law confers absolute privilege when it is seen as absolutely critical that people be free to speak, including if they are motivated by malice. Qualified privilege obtains in situations where it is still important that people feel free to speak, but it is not as important that they be free to speak, as is the case in respect of situations where absolute privilege is conferred.

Statements made in Parliament. The Bill of Rights 1688 provides: "[T]he **13–056** freedom of speech and debates or proceedings in Parliament ought not to be impeached or questioned in any court or place out of Parliament."[135] This provision confers absolute privilege on statements made in the chamber of either House of Parliament.[136] The purpose of this head of privilege is to ensure that Parliament is not restricted in its functions by the law of defamation. If a member of either House repeats outside the House what he said inside it, the second statement is not protected,[137] although this rule is subject to an exception where the following three conditions are met:[138] (1) it is in the public interest that the member repeat or refer to his earlier utterance in Parliament; (2) there is such a close connection between the Parliamentary and extra-Parliamentary utterances that it was reasonably foreseeable that there may be an obligation, expectation or promise to speak outside of Parliament; and (3) the purpose of speaking on both

---

[134] See para.13–061.

[135] The Bill of Rights was declared law by 2 W. & M., c.1 (1689). For an unsuccessful challenge under the European Convention on Human Rights, see *A v UK* (2003) E.H.R.R. 51.

[136] What is a "proceeding in Parliament" is not wholly clear. See, for example, *Re Parliamentary Privilege Act 1770* [1958] A.C. 331, on a letter written by an MP to a Minister. Section 13(5) of the Defamation Act 1996 makes it clear that the privilege extends to, inter alia, giving evidence before either House or a committee and the presentation or submission of a document to either House or a committee. See also *Hamilton v Al Fayed* [2001] A.C. 395 (proceedings before the Parliamentary Commissioner for Standards).

[137] Even if he repeats it by reference rather than *in extenso*: *Buchanan v Jennings* [2004] UKPC 36; [2005] 1 A.C. 115.

[138] *Church of Scientology v Johnson-Smith* [1972] 1 Q.B. 522.

occasions is the same or very closely related.[139] It has been held that the claimant may not use statements in Parliament as evidence of malice in respect of statements made outside it.

The Bill of Rights 1688 may have the effect of blocking a libel action *by* a member of either House of Parliament if a significant element of the defendant's case turns on what happened in Parliament. One of the functions of the Bill of Rights 1688 is to prevent the courts from inquiring into the proprietary of Parliamentary proceedings. The restrictions imposed on the courts in this regard (which cannot be discussed here) means that the only just course is to stay the defamation action in such circumstances, since the defendant would otherwise be deprived of material that may be critical to making a proper defence.[140] However, to ensure that the Bill of Rights 1688 does not prevent members of either House from invoking the law of defamation by s.13 of the Defamation Act 1996 a member of either House may waive the restrictions that prevent proceedings in Parliament from being questioned in the courts.[141]

13–057   **Reports, papers, votes and proceedings ordered to be published by either House of Parliament.** These are the subject of absolute privilege under s.1 of the Parliamentary Papers Act 1840.[142] Extracts from or abstracts of Parliamentary papers and reports of Parliamentary proceedings (e.g. in the press) enjoy qualified privilege.[143]

13–058   **Judicial proceedings.** Anything said, whether orally or in documentary form, in judicial proceedings[144] is absolutely privileged. It does not matter how false or malicious the statement may be. Neither does it matter who makes it—the judge,[145] the jury, the parties, the advocates,[146] or the witnesses.[147] The function of this head of privilege is to ensure that the administration of justice is not frustrated. Justice could not be done if, for example, judges could not write freely in their opinions, and if witnesses could give evidence unconstrained by the threat that, if they defame someone, they might be sued.

The absolute privilege applies not only to proceedings before an ordinary court of law but also whenever there is an authorised inquiry which, although not before a court of justice, is before a tribunal that has similar attributes[148]—for

---

[139] *Makudi v Baron Triesman of Tottenham* [2014] EWCA Civ 179; [2014] 3 All E.R. 36 at [21]–[28].

[140] *Prebble v Television New Zealand* [1995] 1 A.C. 321.

[141] *Hamilton v Al Fayed* [2001] A.C. 395. This does not affect the immunity in respect of what was said in the House: s.13(4).

[142] Passed as a result of *Stockdale v Hansard* (1839) 9 A. & E. 1.

[143] See para.13–072.

[144] The judgment and the reasons for it are part of the proceedings, so neither the judge nor court officials who disseminate the judgment need rely on the reporting privilege (see para.12–044).

[145] *Glick v Hinchcliffe* (1967) 111 S.J. 927 is a modern example. The privilege appears to be broader than the general immunity of judges for acts done in the execution of their office (see para.24–008) in that no distinction is drawn between the various steps in the judicial hierarchy.

[146] *Munster v Lamb* (1883) 11 Q.B.D. 588 at 603–604. This is unaffected by the removal of the immunity from suit for negligence enjoyed by advocates in relation to the conduct of a case in court: see para.5–077.

[147] *Seaman v Netherclift* (1876) 2 C.P.D. 53.

[148] *Royal Aquarium Society Ltd v Parkinson* [1892] 1 Q.B. 431 at 442. For a more recent statement of the law, see *Trapp v Mackie* [1979] 1 W.L.R. 377.

example, an employment tribunal,[149] a military court of inquiry[150] or the Disciplinary Committee of the Law Society.[151] However, an industrial concilia- tion procedure,[152] a social security adjudication,[153] and an investigation by the Commission of the European Union into breaches of the competition provisions of the Treaty[154] have been held not to possess these attributes. In any case it is essential that the tribunal be one "recognised by law".[155]

The absolute privilege is not confined to what is said in the presence of the court or tribunal but extends to statements made in preparation for judicial proceedings. In *Watson v McEwan*, where privilege was held to apply to what was said by a witness to a solicitor taking a proof of his evidence, Lord Halsbury said that:[156]

> "[I]f the law were otherwise . . . the object for which the privilege exists is gone, because then no witness could be called; no one would know whether what he was going to say was relevant to the question in debate between the parties. A witness would only have to say: 'I shall not tell you anything; I may have an action brought against me tomorrow if I do; therefore I shall not give you any information at all'."

In *Evans v London Hospital Medical College*[157] Drake J said that absolute privilege covered any "statement or conduct . . . that can fairly be said to be part of the process of investigating a crime or a possible crime with a view to a prosecution or a possible prosecution in respect of the matter being investigated". This was approved by the House of Lords in *Taylor v Director of the Serious Fraud Office*.[158] Where people answer police questions it may be unclear whether they will be called to give evidence or whether any crime has been committed at all, but it is necessary, in order to ensure that they speak freely, that they should know where they stand when they answer. Similarly, it is necessary for the investigating officers to share information among themselves. This immunity from suit is not confined to defamation—it would extend, for example, to malicious falsehood—but it does not extend to malicious prosecution,[159] nor does it apply to a claim (e.g. for conspiracy to injure or misfeasance in a public office) involving the fabrication of a case or the "planting" of evidence[160] and it is unlikely that a case will be struck out where such allegations are made.[161]

---

[149] *Wilson v Westney* [2001] EWCA Civ 839.

[150] *Dawkins v Lord Rokeby* (1873) L.R. 8 Q.B. 255, affirmed (1875) L.R. 7 H.L. 744. *Heath v MPC* [2004] EWCA Civ 943 (police disciplinary tribunal).

[151] *Addis v Crocker* [1961] 1 Q.B. 11. That the Committee sits in private makes no difference provided that its functions are similar to those of a court of justice: *Marrinan v Vibart* [1963] 1 Q.B. 234, affirmed [1963] 1 Q.B. 528 (barrister). Compare an organisation or company's internal disciplinary committee: *Gregory v Portsmouth CC* [2000] 1 A.C. 419.

[152] *Tadd v Eastwood* [1985] I.C.R. 132.

[153] *Purdew v Serres-Smith, The Times*, September 9, 1992.

[154] *Hasselblad (GB) Ltd Orbinson* [1985] Q.B. 475.

[155] *Trapp v Mackie* [1979] 1 W.L.R. 377 at 379. See also *Gregory v Portsmouth CC* [2000] 1 A.C. 41

[156] [1905] A.C. 480 at 487; *Beresford v White* (1914) 30 T.L.R. 591.

[157] [1981] 1 W.L.R. 184.

[158] [1999] 2 A.C. 177.

[159] *Darker v CC West Midlands* [2001] 1 A.C. 435.

[160] *Darker v CC West Midlands* [2001] 1 A.C. 435.

[161] *L v Reading BC* [2001] 1 W.L.R. 1575.

Traditionally, a mere complaint[162] or the voluntary giving of information[163] attracted only qualified privilege for they were not regarded as a "step in judicial or quasi-judicial proceedings". Now, however, this head of absolute privilege has been extended to those who make a complaint to the police.[164] It is debatable whether this is a desirable development. Of course, the previous law may have deterred the making of some honest complaints, but the burden of proving malice to defeat qualified privilege is a heavy one. A person's life may be ruined by a false accusation of crime but now any claim against the complainant will be automatically struck out. Perhaps not all whose good name has been maliciously traduced would agree that they should be satisfied with the fact that the Crown Prosecution Service has decided not to prosecute them. If a prosecution does take place and there is an acquittal it is possible in theory to sue the complainant for malicious prosecution but there may be great difficulty in showing that he is a "prosecutor" for this purpose.[165]

It is important to distinguish privilege for the purposes of the law of defamation from legal professional privilege. Legal professional privilege is a right to refuse to disclose information. There are two quite separate varieties of legal professional privilege. First, there is what is known as litigation privilege. Litigation privilege applies to communications between solicitors, their clients and third-parties (such as experts) made for the dominant purpose of pending or contemplated litigation. Secondly, there is legal advice privilege. Legal advice privilege confers a right to keep private communications between lawyers and their clients made for the purpose of obtaining advice in relation to one's legal rights and obligations. Legal professional privilege is totally separate in origin from privilege in the law of defamation. However, both types can apply to the same communication. A communication between a client and his lawyer might be subject to legal professional privilege and be privileged for the purposes of the law of defamation. The Court of Appeal in *More v Weaver*[166] was of the view that any professional communication between solicitor and client was protected by absolute privilege in the defamation sense. The House of Lords in *Minter v Priest*[167] found it unnecessary to decide whether any such privilege should be absolute or qualified and left the matter open. In *Waple v Surrey CC*[168] the Court of Appeal was of the view that, at least in non-contentious matters, communications between a solicitor and his client would be adequately protected from liability in defamation by qualified privilege.

13–059   **Communications between certain officers of State.** *In Chatterton v Secretary of State for India*[169] the Court of Appeal held that an action for libel based on a letter from the defendant Secretary of State to the Under-Secretary of State concerning the claimant's removal to the list of half pay officers was rightly dismissed, on the ground that to allow any judicial inquiry into such matters

---

[162] See *Lincoln v Daniels* [1962] 1 Q.B. 237, especially the judgment of Devlin LJ.
[163] *Hasselblad (GB) Ltd Orbinson* [1985] Q.B. 475.
[164] *Westcott v Westcott* [2008] EWCA Civ 818; [2009] Q.B. 407.
[165] See para.20–006.
[166] [1928] 2 K.B. 520.
[167] [1930] A.C. 558.
[168] [1998] 1 W.L.R. 860.
[169] [1895] 2 Q.B. 189.

would tend to deprive officers of State of their freedom of action "in matters concerning the public weal". The decision in *Isaacs & Sons Ltd v Cook*[170] shows that the fact that a report relates to commercial matters does not preclude it from falling within this principle. The extent of this head of absolute privilege is, however, somewhat uncertain, though there is certainly no blanket immunity for communications between civil servants. It has been suggested that it does not extend to officials below the rank of Minister,[171] and in *Merricks v Nott-Bower*[172] the Court of Appeal refused to strike out a claim for libel based on a report regarding two police officers written by a Deputy Commissioner of the Metropolitan Police to the Commissioner. The position is equally uncertain in relation to military affairs. In *Dawkins v Lord Paulet*[173] it was held that a report concerning a lieutenant-colonel made by a major-general to the adjutant-general of the Army was covered by absolute privilege, but in *Dawkins v Lord Rokeby*[174] the Exchequer Chamber regarded the matter as open for consideration by the House of Lords.

The argument generally advanced for absolute rather than qualified privilege is to the effect that a person will perform his duties better by being released from the fear of being sued than by being given an easily substantiated defence if he is sued. Absolute privilege should be reserved for those cases alone in which complete freedom of communication is so important that it is right to deprive the citizen of his remedy for all defamatory statements made about him including even those made maliciously. No one could claim that this is true of all communications between all servants of the Crown. It is submitted, therefore, that the caution of the Court of Appeal in *Merricks v Nott-Bower* was fully justified and that care should be taken not to extend absolute privilege further than can be shown to be really necessary.

Reports of court proceedings. By s.14 of the Defamation Act 1996 (which replaced a very similar provision in the Law of Libel amendment Act 1888) absolute privilege is accorded to fair and accurate contemporaneous reports of court[175] proceedings in public in the United Kingdom or of certain supranational tribunals.[176] In practice the requirement of contemporaneity probably restricts this privilege to reports in the news media. "Contemporaneous" probably means at the first reasonable opportunity after the event (which will vary with the frequency of the journal or broadcast involved) but if publication is restricted by law[177] time will not begin to run until that restriction is removed. It is not necessary that the report should be verbatim,[178] nor that it should await the

13–060

---

[170] [1925] 2 K.B. 391.
[171] Henn-Collins J in *Szalatnay-Stacho v Fink* [1946] 1 All E.R. 303. The Court of Appeal made no reference to this point: [1947] K.B. 1.
[172] [1965] 1 Q.B. 57; *Richards v Naum* [1967] 1 Q.B. 620.
[173] (1869) L.R. 5 Q.B. 94.
[174] (1873) L.R. 8 Q.B. 255. On appeal the decision was on the basis of witness immunity: (1875) L.R. 7 HL 744.
[175] This "includes any tribunal or body exercising the judicial power of the State": s.14(3).
[176] The European Court of Justice or any court attached to it, the European Court of Human Rights and certain international criminal tribunals: s.14(3)
[177] See, e.g. *Contempt of Court Act 1981* s.4.
[178] *McDougall v Knight* (1886) 17 Q.B.D. 636 at 642.

outcome of a trial lasting several days,[179] and a report in the press cannot be judged by the standards of a law report.[180] Nonetheless, it should be impartial and should not give the evidence for one side and suppress that of the other.[181] The basis of the privilege is that the reporter is merely the eyes and ears of the public, who have the right to attend and therefore it is said that it is confined to what passes in open court,[182] and does not extend to the publication of the contents of documents such as pleadings and affidavits, which are not brought up in court.[183] However, this may need reconsideration in view of changes in the way litigation is conducted and the provision in rules of court for public access to documents.

iii.   Qualified Privilege at Common Law

13–061   **Generally.** Like absolute privilege, qualified privilege also protects the maker of an untrue defamatory statement from liability. However, unlike absolute privilege, qualified privilege is lost if the maker of the statement acted maliciously. If, therefore, the claimant can establish malice, the defence will not apply and (assuming that no other defence is enlivened) the claimant will be able to recover damages. It falls to the claimant to prove malice.[184] Heads of qualified privilege are provided for both by the common law and by statute. This section deals with qualified privilege at common law.

13–062   **Two tests.** The common law confers qualified privilege upon statements made by D to X about C: (1) which D is under a legal, moral or social duty to communicate to X and which X has a corresponding interest in receiving (the "duty/interest test"); or (2) where X has an interest to be protected and D has a corresponding interest or has a duty to protect the interest of X (the "common interest test"). The situation was put as follows by Parke B in *Toogood v Spyring*:[185]

> "In general, an action lies for the ... publication of statements which are false in fact, and injurious to the character of another ... unless it is fairly made by a person in the discharge of some public or private duty whether legal or moral, or in the conduct of his own affairs, in matters where his interest is concerned. In such cases the occasion ... affords a qualified defence depending on the absence of actual malice."

It is impossible to classify the cases precisely according to the two tests and there is a good deal of overlap between them, so that where the Bar Council issued a circular on the propriety of accepting instructions from the claimants it was said that it mattered: "not at all whether the . . . Bar Council are properly to

---

[179] *Kimber v Press Association Ltd* [1893] 1 Q.B. 65 at 71.

[180] *Hope v Leng Ltd* (1907) 23 T.L.R. 243.

[181] *Wright v Outram* (1890) 17 R. 596.

[182] On irrelevant matters such as interruptions, see *Hope v Leng Ltd* (1907) 23 T.L.R. 243 and *Farmer v Hyde* [1937] 1 K.B. 728.

[183] This was common ground in *Stern v Piper* [1997] Q.B. 123.

[184] *Adam v Ward* [1917] A.C. 309.

[185] (1834) 1 C.M. & R. 181 at 193.

be regarded as owing a duty to the Bar to rule on questions of professional conduct such as arose here, or as sharing with the Bar a common interest in maintaining professional standards."[186]

Both tests involve reciprocity and, normally, some relationship between the defendant and the recipient of the statement. Regardless of which test is in play, there must "reciprocity" and a prior relationship between the defendant and the recipient. "Reciprocity" means that, in the case of the duty/interest test, the duty corresponds to the interest and, in the case of the common interest test, the interests of both parties are aligned with each other. As Lord Atkinson put it in *Adam v Ward*: "A privileged occasion is . . . an occasion where the person who makes a communication has an interest, or a duty, legal, social or moral, to make it to the person to whom it is made, and the person to whom it is so made has a corresponding interest or duty to receive it. This reciprocity is essential."[187] A good illustration of these principles is *Watt v Longsdon*.[188] B was a manager of a company. He wrote a letter to D, a director of the company, alleging gross charges of immorality, drunkenness and dishonesty on the part of C, who ran the company abroad. D wrote a reply to B in which he stated his own suspicions of C's immorality and asked B to get confirmation of B's allegations in order that D might communicate them to C's wife whom D stated to be an old friend of his. Then, without waiting for any corroboration of B's statement, D showed B's letter to S, the chairman of the board of directors and largest shareholder in the company and also to C's wife. All the allegations against C were false. C sued D for libel in respect of: (1) his reply to B; (2) in communicating B's letter to S; and (3) in communicating B's letter to C's wife. D pleaded qualified privilege. The Court of Appeal had little difficulty in holding that: (1) D's letter to B was privileged, because both B and D had a common interest in the affairs of the company, and that entitled them to discuss the behaviour of C as another employee of the company and to collect further information for the chairman of the company; and (2) D's communication of B's letter to S was privileged, because a duty to make it arose both from the fact of employment in the same company and from the possibility that S might be asked by C for an employment reference. But the court held that: (3) the communication of the letter to C's wife was not privileged. No doubt she had the strongest possible interest in hearing a statement about C's moral conduct; no doubt also there may be occasions on which a friend of the wife is under a duty, or has a corresponding interest, in informing her of statements about her husband.[189] However, here D had no sufficient interest or duty to pass the letter to C's wife, for the information came from a very doubtful source and he had never consulted C nor obtained any confirmation of the outrageous accusations.

What is a duty? The question of whether there is a duty to communicate the facts concerned is one of law. It is easy enough to answer where there is a legal

13–063

13–064

---

[186] *Kearns v General Council of the Bar* [2003] EWCA Civ 331; [2003] 1 W.L.R. 1357 at [39].
[187] [1917] A.C. 309 at 334.
[188] [1930] 1 K.B. 130.
[189] [1930] 1 K.B. 130 at 149 per Scrutton LJ.

duty but in this context "duty" embraces "moral" or "social" duties that could not be enforced by legal means. Lindley LJ said in *Stuart v Bell*:[190]

> "[E]ach judge must decide [the question of moral or social duty] as best he can for himself. I take moral or social duty to mean a duty recognised by English people of ordinary intelligence and moral principle, but at the same time not a duty enforceable by legal proceedings, whether civil or criminal."

Scrutton LJ in *Watt v Longsdon*[191] referred to the difficulties in this area when he asked: "Is the judge merely to give his own view of moral and social duty, although he thinks that a considerable portion of the community hold a different opinion? Or is he to endeavour to ascertain what view the great mass of right-minded men would take?" The classic example of a moral or social duty is that under which former employers are under to give a reference in respect of a former employee. A distinction has been drawn between a statement that is made in answer to an inquiry and one that is merely volunteered. Where there has been a request for information that may show that a duty exists. One is a poor citizen if one stays silent when one sees the safety or property of another person imperilled and it has therefore been held that "when a person has reason to believe that a crime has been committed it is his duty and his right to inform the police".[192]

13–065 **What is an interest?** In most of the reported cases the interest is a business or financial one, such as where a complaint is made about the quality of work done,[193] where an employer informs workers about the reason for the dismissal of a fellow worker,[194] where an insurance company writes to policyholders about an agent,[195] where a creditor informs an auctioneer holding funds from a sale of a suspected act of bankruptcy by the seller,[196] and where information is given to hoteliers about the imminent collapse of a travel firm so as to minimise claims on a travel insurance fund.[197] But any legitimate interest worthy of protection by the law will suffice. "So long as the interest is of so tangible a nature that for the common convenience and welfare of society it is expedient to protect it, it will come within the rule."[198] So it was held that a complaint to the Home Secretary that a magistrate had incited breaches of the peace,[199] to a bishop that a clergyman had got into a fight with a schoolmaster[200] and a statement by an invigilator to examinees that one of their number had cheated[201] were privileged.

---

[190] [1891] 2 Q.B. 341 at 350.
[191] [1930] 1 K.B. 130 at 144.
[192] *Croucher v Inglis* (1889) 16 R. 774 at 778. If a person reports a crime against himself he may be regarded as acting in protection of an interest, though nowadays this situation attracts absolute privilege: see para.13–058.
[193] *Toogood v Spyring* (1834) 1 C.M. & R. 181.
[194] *Hunt v GN Ry* [1891] 2 Q.B. 189.
[195] *Nevill v Fine Art and General Insurance Co* [1897] A.C. 68.
[196] *Baker v Carrick* [1894] 1 Q.B. 838; *Boston v W.S. Bagshaw & Sons* [1966] 1 W.L.R. 1126.
[197] *Aspro Travel v Owners Abroad Group* [1996] 1 W.L.R. 132 (interest arguable).
[198] *Howe v Lees* (1910) 11 C.L.R. 361 at 377. Not a "matter of gossip or curiosity": at 398.
[199] *Harrison v Bush* (1855) E. & B. 355.
[200] *James v Boston* (1846) 2 C. & K. 4.
[201] *Bridgman v Stockdale* [1953] 1 W.L.R. 704.

Reality of duty or interest. The question is whether the law recognises a duty or   **13–066**
interest, not whether the defendant believes there is one. For example, if a
defendant submits a compliant with a body that he mistakenly believes has
jurisdiction to receive the complaint will not be privileged.[202] However, it might
be enough to attract the protection of qualified privilege that the reasonable
person would believe that there is a duty or interest. If a person receives a request
for a reference from someone who represents that he is a prospective employer
but in fact is a nosy busybody, it would be odd if the giver of the reference would
lose the protection of qualified privilege because the recipient has no legitimate
interest. However, the defendant can only rely on matters which were known to
him at the time when he published the statement for the purposes of establishing
a duty.[203]

In deciding whether there is a sufficient common interest in respect of a
communication it may be important to consider the stage which has been reached
in the matter upon which the statement is made. In *De Buse v McCarthy*[204] a
committee of the council had been charged to inquire into the loss of petrol from
depots and the report of the committee was placed in public libraries in the
borough as part of the agenda papers for the meeting of the council at which it
was to be considered. The Court of Appeal held that at that stage, the report being
still a matter of internal administration upon which no decision or resolution had
been made, the council had neither a duty nor an interest in making the contents
known to the body of ratepayers. Although it was not necessary to decide the
matter, the court accepted that the position might have been different once the
council had come to a decision on the matter.

Relevance. A statement made on a privileged occasion may contain material   **13–067**
which is unrelated to the purpose for which the law grants the privilege. One
view is that this goes only to malice[205] but the judgments in *Adam v Ward*[206] are
to the effect that the inclusion of irrelevant material may take the case outside the
protection of privilege altogether. Either way, a statement that contains material
that is not logically connected to the privilege occasion will not be protected by
privilege. For example, if A were to make an inquiry to D about C's
creditworthiness and D were to give a reply on this subject and added the
imputation that C was a paedophile the latter imputation would not be privileged.
In *Warren v Warren*[207] D wrote a letter to the manager of property in which D and
C were jointly interested that was principally about C's conduct in relation to the
property but which also contained charges against C in relation to his conduct
towards his family. It was held that the latter were not privileged.

---

[202] *Hebditch v MacIlwaine* [1894] 2 Q.B. 54; *Blagg v Stuart* (1846) 10 C.B. 899. Cf. *Beach v Freeson*
[1972] 1 Q.B. 14 (Lord Chancellor having no formal disciplinary powers over solicitors but having an
interest in receiving complaints in view of his position in the legal system).
[203] *G.K.R. Karate (UK) Ltd v Yorkshire Post Newspapers Ltd* [2000] 1 W.L.R. 2571; *Loutchansky v
Times Newspapers Ltd* [2001] EWCA Civ 536; [2002] Q.B. 321.
[204] [1942] 1 K.B. 156.
[205] *Horrocks v Lowe* [1975] A.C. 135 at 151 per Lord Diplock.
[206] [1917] A.C. 309 at 318, 339, 340, 348.
[207] (1834) 1 C.M. & R. 250.

It seems that the test of relevance is applied leniently. In *Watts v Times Newspapers*[208] the defendant solicitors negotiated, on behalf of their client, an apology in the newspaper for a libel which had arisen from a confusion of identity between their client and C.[209] The apology contained a defamatory reference to C, upon which the defendant solicitors insisted. This reference went beyond the bounds of what was objectively necessary as an apology to the client but was still protected by privilege, for the content of the apology was not "unconnected with the theme" and did not include "entirely irrelevant and extraneous material".[210]

13–068 **Range of publication.** The requirement of reciprocity[211] means that a publication that reaches uninterested persons and is therefore wider than is reasonably necessary to serve the interest underlying the protection may take the case outside the protection of privilege.[212] A simple example is *Williamson v Freer*[213] where a communication which would have been privileged if sent by sealed letter was not so protected when sent by telegram. Another illustration is *Clift v Slough Borough Council*.[214] In this case a council placed the claimant on a register of violent persons and published that register to 66 council employees and also to "partner organisations" that provided services on behalf of the council, such as environmental management services. It was held that such publication was wider than necessary. While the council was under a duty to protect its employees, not all of its employees had contact with members of the public in their work, and publishing the register in the indiscriminate way that it did deprived the council of the foundation of the claim to qualified privilege.

"[I]f a business communication is privileged . . . the privilege covers all the incidents of the transmission and treatment of that communication which are in accordance with the reasonable and usual course of business."[215] Suppose that D decides to write a letter to X and that publishing the letter to X would be privileged. If D dictates the letter to his secretary the publication to the secretary is likely to be privileged too.[216] Such a privilege may be regarded as ancillary to that which protects the communication to X.[217] In some cases, of course, there may be an independent, "original" privilege between the sender of the letter and the secretary based upon a common interest. In *Bryanston Finance Ltd v de Vries* it was said that "[t]he businessman has an interest in dictating the letter to [the secretary] – so as to get it written – and [the secretary] has an interest or duty to

---

[208] [1997] Q.B. 650.

[209] On the position of a solicitor speaking in defence of his client's interests, see also *Regan v Taylor* [2000] E.M.L.R. 549.

[210] The newspaper failed on the issue of privilege for its position had to be judged independently of that of the solicitors' client.

[211] See para.13–063.

[212] See e.g. *Brady v Norman* [2008] EWHC 2481(QB) (union journal with circulation of 18,000; about 130 subscribers not connected with union).

[213] (1884) L.R. 9 C.P. 393. See also *De Buse v McCarthy* [1942] 1 K.B. 156.

[214] [2010] EWCA Civ 1484; [2011] 1 W.L.R. 1774.

[215] *Edmondson v Birch & Co* [1907] 1 K.B. 371 at 382.

[216] *Boxsius v Goblet Frères* [1894] 1 Q.B. 842; *Lawless v Anglo-Egyptian Co* (1869) L.R. 4 Q.B. 262 (company circular delivery to printer).

[217] *Bryanston Finance Ltd v de Vries* [1975] Q.B. 703 at 727, 736.

take it down – so as to type it out for him to sign".[218] A further possibility is that D sends a letter to C that is defamatory of C himself[219] and in the usual course of business first dictates the letter to a typist. The "ancillary privilege" explanation will hardly serve here for the only publication apart from that to the typist is to C and that needs no privilege for it is not tortious.[220] Nonetheless, the Court of Appeal in *Osborne v Thomas Boulter & Sons*[221] assumed that there was some sort of privilege in such a situation.

The foregoing issues have been important because the classical qualified privilege at common law has, by virtue of the requirement of reciprocity, tended to be confined to communications of a private nature and not those directed at the public. However, there are sometimes situations where a much wider range of communication is necessary and justifiable: the issue of a circular to all members of the Bar was held to be a privileged occasion[222] and it was held arguable that the same was true of the publication of material on a website directed at British Jews and warning them about terrorism—it: "could hardly be suggested that the Board [of Deputies] should address their information by individual letters to each and every Jew in the country".[223] In such cases the fact that the communication is likely to come to the attention of "uninterested" persons is irrelevant.

Miscellaneous heads of qualified privilege at common law. It has been seen that qualified privilege principally arose (or was denied) at common law pursuant to the duty/interest test or the common interest test. However, there are several miscellaneous heads of qualified privilege recognised by the common law. These are of minimal practical importance, partly because of the creation of statutory forms of qualified privilege.[224] These miscellaneous heads of privilege are as follows. First, the common law gives the protection of qualified privilege to fair and accurate reports of public judicial proceedings. As far as *contemporaneous* reports of court proceedings an absolute privilege exists under s.14 of the Defamation Act 1996.[225] Fair and accurate reports, contemporaneous or not, of proceedings in public before a court anywhere in the world are also protected by a qualified privilege under para.2 of Sch.1 of the Act. The common law qualified privilege seems to be effectively redundant. Secondly, the common law affords qualified privilege to fair and accurate reports of Parliamentary proceedings.[226] Now, under para.5 of Sch.1 to the Defamation Act 1996 there is privilege for fair and accurate reports of proceedings in public of a legislature anywhere in the world, so that the common law privilege seems to have been largely eclipsed.

13–069

---

[218] [1975] Q.B. 703 at 719–720.

[219] If the intended publication is to a third party but this never in fact takes place (e.g. because it is restrained by injunction) it is, "the use which the author . . . intends to make of it, . . . that attracts whatever ancillary privilege there may be": *Bryanston Finance Ltd v de Vries* [1975] Q.B. 703 at 729 per Diplock LJ.

[220] See para.13–020.

[221] [1930] 2 K.B. 226.

[222] *Kearns v General Council of the Bar* [2003] EWCA Civ 331; [2003] 1 W.L.R. 1357.

[223] *Hewitt v Grunwald* [2004] EWHC 2959 (QB) at [74].

[224] See para.13–071.

[225] See para.13–060.

[226] *Wason v Walter* (1868) L.R. 4 Q.B. 73. The publication of extracts from Parliamentary papers etc. is privileged under s.3 of the Parliamentary Papers Act 1840, provided the defendant proves he published bona fide and without malice (this burden of proof is unique).

Thirdly, the publication of a fair and accurate copy of or extract from a statutory register open to public inspection (e.g. the register of county court judgments) enjoys qualified privilege at common law.[227] Once again, the matter is also covered by the Defamation Act 1996.[228] Fourthly, statements made in self-defence (and, sometimes in defence of others) are covered by qualified privilege. For example, it was held that a statement by a bishop justifying conduct of his that had been attacked in public[229] and a reply by a daughter to a statement in the press about her father were privileged.[230] The basic rule here is that the defendant "is entitled to protect his reputation by a proportionate response".[231] It seems that this head of qualified privilege is governed by similar principles to those that control the defence of self-defence for the purposes of the tort of trespass to the person. In contrast to the previous miscellaneous forms of qualified privilege, this miscellaneous species of qualified privilege has not been superseded by legislation, although it is rarely invoked.

13–070 **Malice.** Malice defeats qualified privilege both at common law and under statute. Malice means use of the privileged occasion for some improper purpose. It was described as follows by Brett LJ in *Clarke v Molyneux*:[232]

> "If the occasion is privileged it is so for some reason, and the defendant is only entitled to the protection of the privilege if he uses the occasion for this reason. He is not entitled to the protection if he uses the occasion not for the reason which makes the occasion privileged but for an indirect or wrong motive."

Of course people often act with mixed motives and to constitute malice in law the improper purpose must be the dominant one: D does not lose the protection of qualified privilege if D receives information that a person D dislikes has committed a crime and D takes pleasure in reporting it to the police. "It is only where [D's] desire to comply with the relevant duty or to protect the relevant interest plays no significant part in his motives for publishing what he believes to be true that . . . malice can properly be found."[233]

Although a desire to injure the claimant is malice, such a desire is not needed in order for malice to exist. Malice will be present where the defendant's motive is to advance his own interests or to injure some third person. The central issue is whether the defendant used the privileged occasion for an improper purpose. Lack of belief in the truth of what is said is generally conclusive evidence of malice, except where the defendant is obliged to pass on defamatory statements made by another, such as where he receives a complaint or is under a duty to protect the interests of a third party.[234] Mere carelessness in arriving at a belief, or even belief produced by unreasoning prejudice is not malice: "[D]espite the imperfection of the mental process by which the belief is arrived at it may still be

---

[227] *Searles v Scarlett* [1892] 2 Q.B. 56.
[228] Sch.1, para.5.
[229] *Laughton v Bishop of Sodor and Man* (1872) L.R. 4 P.C. 495.
[230] *Bowen-Rowlands v Argus Press, The Times*, March 26, 1926.
[231] *Hamilton v Clifford* [2004] EWHC 1542 at [65].
[232] (1877) 3 Q.B.D. 237 at 246.
[233] *Horrocks v Lowe* [1975] A.C. 135 at 151.
[234] See, e.g. *Stuart v Bell* [1891] 2 Q.B. 341.

'honest'. The law demands no more."[235] Even an honest belief will not, however, protect the defendant if he uses the occasion for some purpose other than that for which the privilege is accorded by law.

Evidence of malice may be found in the publication itself. The use of gratuitous language may lead to an inference of malice,[236] but the law does not weigh words with a jeweller's scales and it does not follow that merely because the words are excessive there is therefore malice.[237] "Malice is not established by forensic imagination, however, eloquently and subtly expressed."[238] Malice may also be inferred from the relations between the parties before or after publication or from the conduct of the defendant in the course of the proceedings themselves, as, for example, where the defendant persisted in a plea of truth while nevertheless making no attempt to prove it.[239] The mere pleading of truth is not of itself evidence of malice even though the plea ultimately fails: on the contrary, it may point more to honesty than to malice.[240] There may also be evidence of malice in the mode of publication.

Malice is "individual". Thus, when a defamatory communication is made by several persons (e.g. partners or a committee) on an occasion of qualified privilege, only those against whom malice is proved are liable.[241] However, it was for a long time thought that where a defamatory communication was published by an agent (e.g. a clerk or a printer), the agent was liable if the principal was actuated by malice, for the agent's privilege was "ancillary" to or "derivative" from that of the principal and the malice of the principal therefore destroyed the protection of the agent.[242] However, in *Egger v Viscount Chelmsford*[243] the Court of Appeal declared this to be wrong. The malice of an agent may make the innocent principal liable in some cases on the ordinary principles of vicarious liability, but the malice of the principal cannot do the same for the innocent agent: it is *respondeat superior*, not *respondeat inferior*. It may be argued that there are difficulties in a derivative privilege standing alone in this way and that the Court of Appeal in effect created a new head of privilege—namely, publication by an agent in circumstances in which the principal has a prima facie privilege to make the defamatory communication, but the decision accords well with commonsense (it would be absurd to hold a typist liable because the employer was malicious).[244]

---

[235] *Horrocks v Lowe* [1975] A.C. 135 at 150.

[236] *Adam v Ward* [1917] A.C. 309 at 327, 330, 335.

[237] *Nevill v Fine Arts and General Insurance Co* [1895] 2 Q.B. 156 at 170.

[238] *Broadway Approvals Ltd v Odhams Press Ltd (No.2)* [1965] 1 W.L.R. 805 at 815 per Sellers LJ.

[239] *Simpson v Robinson* (1848) 12 Q.B. 511.

[240] *Broadway Approvals Ltd v Odhams Press Ltd (No.2)* [1965] 1 W.L.R. 805 at 825.

[241] *Longdon-Griffiths v Smith* [1951] 1 K.B. 295; *Meekings v Henson* [1964] 1 Q.B. 472.

[242] *Smith v Streatfield* [1913] 3 K.B. 764.

[243] [1965] 1 Q.B. 248. See also *Richardson v Schwarzenegger* [2004] EWHC 2422 (QB).

[244] Even though the typist could recover a full indemnity under the Civil Liability (Contribution) Act 1978: see Ch.20. In some of these cases the agent might have an alternative defence under s.1 of the Defamation Act 1996 (see para.13–084) but that is narrower than privilege since negligence is in issue.

iv. Qualified Privilege under Statute

13–071 **Generally.** Various heads of qualified privilege are created by statute. The most important provisions are in Sch.1 of the Defamation Act 1996. This Act confers a qualified privilege on "fair and accurate reports" of a wide range of proceedings. The privilege is not limited to publications in the news media although it is confined to reports of what others have said on public occasions or in statements that are of an "official" or "quasi-official" nature. Thus, it does not cover the newspaper's own conclusions from its inquiries or "reports" that are heavily editorialised with comment.[245] The reports and other statements of proceedings that are privileged are divided into two categories: the first (Pt.I) comprising those which are privileged "without explanation or contradiction"; and the second (Pt.II) those which are privileged "subject to explanation or contradiction". As regards matters in the second category, the defence of qualified privilege is lost if[246] the defendant has been requested by the claimant to publish in a suitable manner a reasonable letter or statement by way of explanation or contradiction, and has refused or neglected to do so. In other words, in some cases, the defendant must accord the claimant a "right of reply" if he wishes to rely on the defence. The idea behind this two-category system is that it is more important that reports of matters in the first category be published, all other things being equal, than matters in the second category. Fairness and accuracy are approached in a manner similar to that under the statutory and common law privileges for reports of judicial proceedings[247]—that is to say, the report need not be verbatim (indeed it may be a very brief summary[248]) and need only be substantially accurate. The law should take care not to impose too high a duty upon the press and to transform "investigative journalism from a virtue to a necessity".[249] Protection is not given to the publication of any matter which is not of "public interest" and the publication of which is not for the "public benefit",[250] nor to the publication of matter which is prohibited by law.[251] Another head of statutory qualified privilege is found in s.6 of the Defamation Act 2013. It concerns academic research.

13–072 **Statements privileged without explanation or contradiction.** Part I of Sch.1 provides that a fair and accurate report of the following matters benefit from qualified privilege "without explanation or contradiction": (1) proceedings in public of a legislature anywhere in the world; (2) proceedings in public before a court anywhere in the world; (3) proceedings in public of a person appointed to hold a public inquiry by a government or legislature anywhere in the world;[252] (4) proceedings in public anywhere in the world of an international organisation or

---

[245] *Henry v BBC* [2005] EWHC 2787 (QB).

[246] See Defamation Act 1996 s.15(2).

[247] See paras 13–060, 13–069.

[248] *Tsikata v Newspaper Publishing* [1997] 1 All E.R. 655 (decided under previous legislation).

[249] *Tsikata v Newspaper Publishing* [1997] 1 All E.R. 655 at 671.

[250] Defamation Act 1996 s.15(3). These are, at least in theory, distinct requirements: *Kelly v O'Malley* (1889) 6 T.L.R. 62; *Crossley v Newsquest (Midlands South) Ltd* [2008] EWHC 3054 (QB).

[251] Section 15(4).

[252] The fact that there are doubts about the correctness of the conclusions does not remove the privilege: *Tsikata v Newspaper Publishing* [1997] 1 All E.R. 655.

an international conference; (5) a copy or an extract from any register or other document required by law to be open to public inspection; (6) a notice or advertisement published by or on the authority of a court, or of a judge or officer of a court, anywhere in the world; (7) a copy of or extract from matter published by or on the authority of a government or legislature anywhere in the world; and (8) a copy of or extract from matter published anywhere in the world by an international organisation or an international conference.

Statements privileged subject to explanation or contradiction. Part II of Sch.1 **13–073** is lengthy and unnecessarily convoluted. It will be described leaving out most of the detail. It provides that fair and accurate reports of the following matters will enjoy qualified privilege provided that the defendant does not refuse or neglect to publish in a suitable manner a reasonable letter or statement by way of explanation or contradiction if requested to do so by the claimant:

(1)   a notice or other matter issued[253] for the information of the public by or on behalf of:
    (a)   a legislature anywhere in the world;
    (b)   an authority anywhere in the world performing governmental functions; or
    (c)   an international organisation or international conference;
(2)   a copy of or extract from a document made available by a court anywhere in the world for the discussion of a matter of public interest;
(3)   proceedings at any public meeting or sitting in the United Kingdom of a local authority, before a justice of the peace acting otherwise than as a court, a commission, tribunal, committee or person appointed for the purposes of any inquiry, and before any tribunal, board, committee or body constituted by or under any statutory provision;
(4)   proceedings at a press conference held anywhere in the world for the discussion of a matter of public interest;
(5)   proceedings at any "public meeting"[254] held anywhere in the world;[255]
(6)   proceedings at a general meeting of a listed company and copies and extracts from any document circulated to members of a public company in the United Kingdom;
(7)   any finding or decision of a very large range of diverse associations; and
(8)   proceedings of a scientific conference held anywhere in the world.

Section 6 of the Defamation Act 2013. Section 6 of the Defamation Act 2013 **13–074** provides that statements in scientific or academic journals enjoy qualified privilege. This privilege obtains only if the journal concerned is peer-reviewed. This provision does not protect academic speech generally. It would not, for

---

[253] That is, volunteered rather than extracted by questioning: *Blackshaw v Lord* [1984] Q.B. 1.

[254] A "public meeting" means "a meeting bona fide and lawfully held for a lawful purpose and in the furtherance or discussion of a matter of public interest, whether admission to the meeting is general or restricted": para.12(2).

[255] A public meeting does not require any participation or opportunity for participation by those attending it: *McCartan Turkington Breen v Times Newspapers Ltd* [2001] 2 A.C. 227.

example, apply when an academic writes an opinion piece in a newspaper or in a book, even if the book is peer-reviewed.[256]

13–075 **Malice**. As with common law qualified privilege, malice will defeat statutory qualified privilege. Malice has been discussed above.[257]

v. Publication on a Matter of Public Interest

13–076 **Generally.** Section 4 of the Defamation Act 2013 provides for a defence on a matter of public interest. The defence has two elements: (1) the statement in question must have been a statement on a matter of "public interest"; and (2) the defendant must have reasonably believed that publishing the statement was in the public interest. Presumably, the onus of proof rests on the defendant. The defendant will only need this defence where the statement that he has published is false. Section 4(2) instructs the court to consider all of the circumstances of the case in determining whether the defence is enlivened. Pursuant to s.4(4), the court must, in deciding whether the defendant reasonably believed that publishing the statement was in the public interest, make such allowance for the editorial judgement as it considers appropriate. This provision suggests that the courts should apply the test of reasonableness leniently. It is important to note that the s.4 defence is not confined to particular people (it applies potentially to everyone), to particular types of publications or to publications in particular formats.

13–077 **Purpose.** The purpose of this defence is to ensure that people are not unduly fearful of publishing statements on matters of public interest which they think are true simply because the statement might turn out to be false. Provided that publishers act sufficiently carefully—they must reasonably believe that publishing the statement was in the public interest—they will be protected from liability in defamation even if it transpires that what they say is false. The defence involves a trade-off. It opts for increased statements on matters of public interest that look, at the time of publication, that they are likely to be true. The downside is that more people will have untrue defamatory things said about them for which they will be left without redress.

13–078 **The Reynolds defence.** The defence in s.4 replaces what was known as the *Reynolds* defence. The House of Lords in *Reynolds v Times Newspapers Ltd*[258] created a new defence—a new form of qualified privilege—for the general communication of matters of public concern.[259] It was not confined to publications by the news media but they were in almost all cases the persons

---

[256] Numerous ambiguities and puzzles in s.6 are explored in Mullis and Scott (2014) 77 M.L.R. 87 at 98–99.

[257] See para.13–070.

[258] [2001] 2 A.C. 127.

[259] The House of Lords and then the Supreme Court elaborated upon the application of the *Reynolds* defence in *Jameel (Mohamed) v Wall Street Journal Europe Sprl* [2006] UKHL 44; [2007] 1 A.C. 359 and *Flood v Times Newspapers Ltd* [2012] UKSC 11; [2012] 2 A.C. 273.

relying on it.[260] The defence had two elements: (1) the defendant must have acted responsibly in publishing the statement; and (2) the statement must have been on a matter of public interest. The issue of whether the defendant acted maliciously was incorporated within the first element, on the logic that a defendant who acts maliciously does not act responsibility.[261]

The House of Lords created the *Reynolds* defence primarily because of concerns about the compatibility of the pre-existing law of defamation with art.10 of the European Convention on Human Rights (the Human Rights Act 1998 was not in force when *Reynolds* was decided, but the House was aware that the Convention rights were imminently to be incorporated into domestic law). The difficulty was caused mainly by the fact that traditional qualified privilege did not apply to publications to the world generally because of the requirement of reciprocity.[262] Except in unusual situations, the media could not take advantage of common law qualified privilege.

Has the law been changed in any significant way? It is not clear whether the   13–079
defence in s.4 is a very different creature from the *Reynolds* defence. Arguably, the main aim of s.4 is not so much to change the law but to make it clear that the *Reynolds* defence is fundamentally different from traditional qualified privilege (some judges had conflated the *Reynolds* defence with qualified privilege at common law despite their different tests). There had been calls prior to the enactment of the Defamation Act 2013 that the *Reynolds* defence "might more appropriately be called the *Reynolds* public interest defence rather than privilege".[263] The requirement of reasonable belief in the s.4 defence looks very similar, if it is not identical, to the requirement in the *Reynolds* defence that the publisher act responsibly. However, the situation is not entirely certain and it is inevitable, therefore, that significant argument will break out as to whether the principles governing the *Reynolds* defence apply also to s.4. What is clear is that some or all of the rules that controlled the *Reynolds* defence will continue to be relevant. Accordingly, it is necessary to describe how the *Reynolds* defence worked.

The Reynolds factors. Lord Nicholls, with whom Lord Cooke and Lord   13–080
Hobhouse explicitly agreed, delivered the leading speech in *Reynolds*. He set out a non-exhaustive list of circumstances which would be relevant to the question of whether the defendant acted responsibly. Lord Nicholls wrote:[264]

> "1.   The seriousness of the allegation. The more serious the charge, the more the public is misinformed and the individual harmed, if the allegation is not true.
>
> 2.   The nature of the information, and the extent to which the subject-matter is a matter of public concern.

---

[260] "*Reynolds* privilege is not reserved for the media, but it is the media who are most likely to take advantage of it": *Flood v Times Newspapers Ltd* [2012] UKSC 11; [2012] 2 A.C. 273 at [44] per Lord Phillips P.
[261] *Jameel (Mohamed) v Wall Street Journal Europe Sprl* [2006] UKHL; [2007] 1 A.C. 359 at [46] per Lord Hoffmann.
[262] See para.13-063.
[263] *Jameel (Mohamed) v Wall Street Journal Europe Sprl* [2006] UKHL; [2007] 1 A.C. 359 at [46].
[264] [2001] 2 A.C. 127 at 205.

3.   The source of the information. Some informants have no direct knowledge of the events. Some have their own axes to grind, or are being paid for their stories.
4.   The steps taken to verify the information.
5.   The status of the information. The allegation may have already been the subject of an investigation which commands respect.
6.   The urgency of the matter. News is often a perishable commodity.
7.   Whether comment was sought from the claimant. He may have information others do not possess or have not disclosed. An approach to the claimant will not always be necessary.
8.   Whether the article contained the gist of the claimant's side of the story.
9.   The tone of the article. A newspaper can raise queries or call for an investigation. It need not adopt allegations as statements of fact.
10.   The circumstances of the publication, including the timing.
The list is not exhaustive. The weight to be given to these and any other relevant factors will vary from case to case. Any disputes of primary facts will be a matter for the jury, if there is one. The decision on whether, having regard to the admitted or proved facts, the publication was subject to qualified privilege is a matter for the judge. This is the established practice and seems sound. A balancing operation is better carried out by a judge in a reasoned judgment than by a jury. Over time, a valuable corpus of case law will be built up."

As mentioned above, it is highly likely that some or all of these considerations will be relevant to determining whether the requirement of reasonable belief in the defence in s.4 is satisfied. However, the extent to which the law regarding the *Reynolds* defence will apply to the s.4 defence is something that must await judicial determination.

13–081   **Public interest.** In order for the defence in s.4 to apply, the statement in question must be a statement on a matter of "public interest". This hurdle is so low as to be virtually non-existent. Lord Nicholls in *Reynolds* said that the "court should be slow to conclude that a publication was not in the public interest and, therefore, the public had no right to know, especially when the information is in the field of political discussion".[265] There is no reason to think that the matter is any different under s.4.

13–082   **Fact and comment.** One change in the law wrought by s.4(5) is that the s.4 defence is capable of applying to both statements of fact and to comments. The *Reynolds* defence applied only to statements of fact.[266] The result of this provision is that the s.4 defence can apply to defamatory comments to which the defence of honest comment[267] does not.

13–083   **Reportage.** As we have seen, the "repetition rule"[268] says that if D repeats a statement made by X then D is treated as publishing the imputations in it even if D makes it clear that he is only repeating what X said. Since *Reynolds* was decided, however, there has been some modification of this. In *Al-Fagih v H.H. Saudi Research & Marketing (UK) Ltd*[269] the *Reynolds* defence was held to apply to the publication in a newspaper circulating among Saudi residents in England of developments in a feud in a group seeking political change in Saudi Arabia. This was so even though it was obvious that an informant had an axe to grind and

---

[265] [2001] 2 A.C. 127 at 205.
[266] *Reynolds v Times Newspapers Ltd* [2001] 2 A.C. 127 at 201, 237–238.
[267] See para.13–093.
[268] See para.13-045.
[269] [2001] EWCA Civ 1634; [2002] E.M.L.R. 13.

there were no steps taken to verify the story. The court held that the defendants had in no way adopted or endorsed the allegation: this was a report of a stage in an ongoing political dispute of legitimate interest to the readership and the failure of the defendants to take steps to verify the allegation did not in such a case exclude the report's being protected by the *Reynolds* defence. The court said that there:[270]

> "will be circumstances where, as here, . . . both sides to a political dispute are being fully, fairly and disinterestedly reported in their respective allegations and responses. In this situation . . . the public is entitled to be informed of such a dispute without having to wait for the publisher, following an attempt at verification, to commit himself to one side or the other."

This rule is known as the doctrine of reportage. In *Roberts v Gable* the Court of Appeal offered the following guidance as to when the doctrine will apply:[271]

> "To qualify as reportage the report, judging the thrust of it as a whole, must have the effect of reporting, not the truth of the statements, but the fact that they were made . . . If upon a proper construction of the thrust of the article the defamatory material is attributed to another and is not being put forward as true, then a responsible journalist would not need to take steps to verify its accuracy. He is absolved from that responsibility because he is simply reporting in a neutral fashion the fact that it has been said without adopting the truth."

What remains unclear is how far this is confined to the reporting of a dispute. It has been said that "the reportage doctrine . . . cannot logically be confined to the reporting of reciprocal allegations. A unilateral libel, reported disinterestedly, will be equally protected";[272] but if we travel far down this road it will change the balance between claimants and the media quite dramatically. It has subsequently been said that the doctrine has no application to ordinary investigative journalism.[273]

Just as the reportage doctrine (rightly or wrongly) was seen as part of the *Reynolds* defence,[274] the Defamation Act 2013 has absorbed it within the s.4 defence. Section 4(3) provides that if the statement in question "was, or formed part of, an accurate and impartial account of a dispute to which the claimant was a party", the court must in determining whether the reasonable belief requirement is satisfied "disregard any omission of the defendant to take steps to verify the truth of the imputation conveyed by it". The case law that preceded the enactment of the Defamation Act 2013 suggests that the reportage doctrine will apply relatively rarely.[275]

---

[270] [2001] EWCA Civ 1634; [2002] E.M.L.R. 13 at [52].

[271] [2007] EWCA Civ 721; [2008] Q.B. 502 at [61].

[272] [2007] EWCA Civ 721; [2008] Q.B. 502 at [91].

[273] *Charman v Orion Publishing Ltd* [2007] EWCA Civ 972; [2008] 1 All E.R. 750 at [49].

[274] In *Flood v Times Newspapers Ltd* [2012] UKSC 11; [2012] 2 A.C. 273 at [35] Lord Phillips P said that reportage is "a special example of *Reynolds* privilege". He warned against "putting reportage in a special box of its own". This is doubtful. The test that governs the reportage doctrine is quite different from that which controlled the *Reynolds* defence.

[275] See the comments of Lord Phillips P in *Flood v Times Newspapers Ltd* [2012] UKSC 11; [2012] 2 A.C. 273 at [77].

vi.   Innocent Dissemination

13–084   **Generally.** Under s.1 of the Defamation Act 1996, it is a defence for the defendant to show that (1) he was not the author,[276] editor or publisher of the statement, (2) that he took reasonable care in relation to the publication and that he did not know, and had no reason to believe, that what he did caused or contributed to the publication of a defamatory statement. These are cumulative requirements.

13–085   **Meaning of "publisher".** For the purpose of s.1 of the Defamation Act 1996, a "publisher" is defined as a "commercial publisher".[277] A "commercial publisher" is in turn defined as "a person whose business is issuing material to the public". It was held in *Tamiz v Google Inc*[278] that Google was not a "publisher" of material on a blogging service that it hosted since it did not "issue" to the public information on the service.

13–086   **Determining whether a person took reasonable care or had reason to believe that he was contributing to the publication.** In determining whether a person took reasonable care or had reason to believe that he was contributing to the publication of a defamatory statement, the court is to have regard to the extent of his responsibility for the content of or the decision to publish the statement, the nature and circumstances of the publication, and the previous conduct or character of the author, editor or publisher.[279] Obvious examples of questions which may arise in litigation are: at what point does a publication acquire a "reputation for libel" and what steps does a distributor have to take to check new issues? What steps should a radio company running a live phone-in programme take to "vet" potential contributions? And should the broadcaster in such a case utilise a delay mechanism on transmission? In the case of material which is not of a transitory nature the distributor who receives notice of its defamatory nature will of course be liable for further publications if he fails to withdraw it.[280]

13–087   **The Electronic Commerce (EC Directive) Regulations.** Internet service providers have further protection under the Electronic Commerce (EC Directive) Regulations.[281] One acting as a mere conduit (e.g. for the transmission of email or access to the site where the information sought is stored) is simply not liable in damages at all. One who hosts information (e.g. stores on its servers web pages produced by others) is not liable in damages if he is not aware of facts from which it is apparent to him that the information is "unlawful" and acts expeditiously to remove it when he acquires such knowledge. Though not identical with the 1996 Act, this is at least similar to it.

---

[276] "Author" is defined as the originator of the statement: s.1(2).

[277] That is, whose business is issuing material to the public or a section of the public: s.1(2)

[278] [2013] EWCA Civ 68; [2013] 1 W.L.R. 2151 at [40].

[279] See s.1(5). For consideration, see *Tamiz v Google Inc* [2013] EWCA Civ 68; [2013] 1 W.L.R. 2151 at [41]–[43].

[280] *Godfrey v Demon Internet Ltd* [2001] Q.B. 201. Though he must have a reasonable opportunity to make inquiry into the complaint.

[281] SI 2002/2013. Strangely described in the Directive and Regulations as "information society service providers". See *Bunt v Tilley* [2006] EWHC 407; [2007] 1 W.L.R. 1243; *Davison v Habeeb* [2011] EWHC 3031 (QB).

Internet search engines. This complex web of domestic and European   **13–088** legislation has not proved easy to apply to internet publications. Take, for example, a search engine that leads the user to a defamatory publication originated by another. Does the search engine operator publish the communication to which it leads? Does it make any difference if the "snippet" which the operator shows itself contains defamatory words? Does the search engine operator provide its service "for remuneration" (a requirement of the Regulations) when it obtains its funds from advertising rather than direct charges to users? How is the concept of reasonable care to be applied when the information collected by the search engine is obtained by web-crawling "robots" that simply look for particular words and the ability of the search engine operator to "close off" offending sites without at the same time blocking thousands of innocuous ones is very limited? English courts have so far shown an inclination instead to deal with these problems via the common law concept of publication.[282] Eady J in *Bunt v Tilley*[283] was prepared to hold that any service provider playing only a passive role in facilitating internet transactions was not a "publisher" at common law and in *Metropolitan International Schools Ltd v DesignTechnica Corp*[284] the same approach was applied to a search engine.

Does the defence in s.1 of the Defamation Act 1996 go far enough? While the   **13–089** defence in s.1 of the Defamation Act 1996 gives a distributor a degree of protection, the fact that he is presumptively liable may lead him to refuse to distribute a journal, with or without the threat of legal proceedings. In *Goldsmith v Pressdram*[285] the claimant, considering himself defamed by *Private Eye*, brought a criminal prosecution (as was then possible) against the magazine in respect of one article and a civil action in respect of two others but he also sued 37 distributors of the magazine. Many settled by an undertaking not to distribute *Private Eye* again, but some sought an order that the actions against them be stayed as an abuse of the process. The majority of the Court of Appeal dismissed this application because, whilst it was undoubtedly an abuse of process to pursue by legal action a collateral advantage which the law would not allow, the claimant believed that the magazine was carrying on a defamatory campaign against him and the terms of the settlements were thus directly related to the grievances which had caused him to sue. His purpose was not to shut down *Private Eye* (though the proceedings might, conceivably, have had that effect[286]) but to protect his reputation

vii. Secondary Publishers

It was noted earlier that, essentially, everyone who is involved in the distribution   **13–090** of a defamatory statement is regarded as a publisher and is consequently

---

[282] See para.13–020.
[283] [2006] EWHC 407 (QB); [2007] 1 W.L.R. 1243.
[284] [2009] EWHC 1765 (QB); [2009] E.M.L.R. 27. Email carriers must fall within the "passive role" concept.
[285] [1977] Q.B. 83.
[286] The dispute between Sir James Goldsmith and *Private Eye* was eventually compromised.

potentially liable in defamation.[287] However, secondary publishers may be entitled to the defence created by s.10 of the Defamation Act 2013. Section 10 provides that the court does not have jurisdiction to hear an action for defamation brought against a person who is not the "author, editor or publisher" of the statement unless it is not reasonably practicable for the "author, editor or publisher" to be sued.

viii.   Website Operators

13–091   **Generally.** One of the main reasons for the enactment of the Defamation Act 2013 was to bolster the protection afforded to website operators. There was a concern that website operators were removing information posted by other persons out of a concern that, if they failed to do so, they might be liable in defamation as secondary publishers of the information. This worry is addressed in s.5 of the Act. It provides "the operator of a website" (a term that is not defined[288]) with a defence in respect of statements posted on its website. The defence applies when the following requirements are met. First, the operator must not have been the person who posted the statement on the website. Secondly, the defence will be excluded if the claimant proves the following matters: the person who posted the statement cannot be identified; the claimant gave the operator notice of the statement; and the operator failed to respond to the notice in accordance with any regulations. Thirdly, the defence is lost if the operator acted maliciously, but the mere fact that the operator moderates statements posted on its website does not strip the operator of the defence. Where the defence in s.5 applies, a website operator may leave the defamatory statement on its website unless the court orders its removal.[289]

13–092   **The regulations.** The only regulations that have been made to date under s.5 of the Defamation Act 2013 are the Defamation (Operator of Websites) Regulations 2013. These Regulations are verbose and complex. Describing them at the highest level of generality, they provide as follows. First, the claimant must in his notice describe the meaning that he attributes to the statement about which he complains and identify the aspects of it that are factually inaccurate or are opinions not supported by fact. Secondly, where the operator can contact the poster, the operator must notify within 48 hours the poster of the fact that a complaint has been made and the poster must, if he does not consent to the statement being removed, provide the operator with his full correspondence details. Thirdly, if the operator cannot contact the poster, the operator must remove the statement with 48 hours. Fourthly, if the poster fails to respond within five days, the operator must remove the statement within 48 hours. Fifthly, if the poster responds but does not consent to the removal of the statement and to his contact details being passed to the claimant the operator must remove the statement within 48 hours. Because of the highly cumbersome nature of the regulations, it is suspected that few website operators will make use of the

---

[287] See para.13–121.
[288] Difficulties that the failure to define this term are bound to cause are discussed in Mullis and Scott (2014) 77 M.L.R. 87 at 100–101.
[289] See para.13–128.

defence in s.5. Other defences that might be particularly useful to website operators include the defence of innocent dissemination[290] and the defence granted to secondary publishers.[291]

ix. Honest Opinion

Generally. The common law provided for a defence which was originally known as fair comment. It was rebranded in *Joseph v Spiller* as "honest comment"[292] and then replaced with the defence of "honest opinion" by s.3 of the Defamation Act 2013. The defence in s.3 is similar in many ways to the common law defence that it ousted, and it is apparent that some of the common law principles will inform the operation of s.3. Exactly how much of the common law has survived is debatable. The basic function of the defence is to ensure that people are free to express their opinions, which is an important aspect of a democratic society. "The basis of our public life is that the crank, the enthusiast, may say what he honestly thinks."[293]   **13–093**

Elements of the defence. The defence has three elements. First, the statement in question must be a statement of opinion (as opposed to a statement of fact). Secondly, the statement must indicate, in general or specific terms, the basis of the opinion. Thirdly, it must be shown that an honest person could have held the opinion based on any fact that existed at the time that the statement was published or anything asserted to be a fact in a privileged statement. Pursuant to s.3(5), the defence will be lost if the claimant proves that the defendant did not hold the opinion. In a case where the statement was republished by someone other than the author, the defence will be lost if the person who republished the statement knew or ought to have known that the author did not hold the opinion.   **13–094**

Public interest not an element. In a break from the position at common law, it is not necessary in order for the defence of honest opinion to apply that the statement be on a matter of public interest.   **13–095**

Defence not restricted to certain types of person. The defence of honest opinion is potentially available to everyone. It is not restricted to certain individuals. Nor is it limited to publications made in a particular format or way.   **13–096**

Statement of opinion. The honest opinion defence applies only to statements of opinion. Unfortunately, the borderline between fact and opinion is difficult to draw, which is why a critic should take pains to keep his facts and his opinions on them separate from each other, for if it is not reasonably clear that the matter purports to be an opinion, he cannot succeed on the honest opinion defence,[294] and will be forced to rely on another defence, such as truth or privilege. Every statement must be taken on its merits. The very same words may be one or the other according to the context.   **13–097**

---

[290] See para.13–084.
[291] See para.13-090.
[292] [2010] UKSC 53; [2011] 1 A.C. 852 at [117]
[293] *Silkin v Beaverbrook Newspapers Ltd* [1958] 1 W.L.R. 743 at 747.
[294] *Hunt v Star Newspaper Co Ltd* [1908] 2 K.B. 309 at 320; *London Artists Ltd v Littler* [1969] 2 Q.B. 375 at 395.

To describe the line "A Mr. Wilkinson, a clergyman",[295] as the worst in English poetry is obviously an opinion, for verification of it as exact is impossible. Comments upon a person's competence are treated as opinion. In *Dakhyl v Labouchere*[296] the claimant described himself as "a specialist for the treatment of deafness, ear, nose, and throat diseases". The defendant described him as a "quack of the rankest species". The House of Lords held that the common law predecessor to s.3 should be left to the jury. In *British Chiropractic Association v Singh*[297] the defendant, a science writer, wrote an article in the *The Guardian* about chiropractors. He said that the British Chiropractic Association claims that their members can treat various conditions "even though there is not a jot of evidence" that their treatments are effective. The Court of Appeal concluded that this was an opinion on the ground that it constituted a "value judgment".[298] It is doubtful that this is correct. In reality, it seems that the court reached this conclusion partly because if they had held that the statement was one of fact, courts would, in cases such as this, be required to decide whether the statement was true, which would see them resolving scientific disputes.

Although concerned with "evaluation", the defence of honest opinion may embrace certain inferences or deductions or conclusions of fact drawn from other facts stated or referred to. Thus, in *Branson v Bower*[299] a statement that the claimant's motive for his actions was revenge fell within the scope of the defence. However, the defence will not apply to statements of fact which are verifiable in the ordinary way, such as the statement that there are reasonable grounds to suspect that the claimant is guilty of committing an offence.[300]

13–098 **The statement must indicate, in general or specific terms, the basis of the opinion.** This element of the defence of honest opinion in s.3 tracks the decision of the Supreme Court in *Joseph v Spiller*.[301] In that case, the court indicated that the common law ancestor to s.3 required the defendant to identify in his statement "at least the general nature of the facts that have led him to make the criticism".[302] The following example was supplied:[303]

> "If [the defendant] states that a barrister is 'a disgrace to his profession' he should make it clear whether this is because he does not deal honestly with the court, or does not read his papers thoroughly, or refuses to accept legally aided work, or is constantly late for court, or wears dirty collars and bands."

That which qualifies as a sufficient reference to the facts upon which the opinion purports to be made is something upon which no hard and fast rule can be laid down. Certainly it is not necessary that the defendant should set out verbatim in his statement all of the facts upon which he expresses his opinion. The question

---

[295] A parody of Wordsworth in Benson's *Life of Fitzgerald*.
[296] [1908] 2 K.B. 325n.
[297] [2010] EWCA Civ 350; [2011] 1 W.L.R. 133.
[298] [2010] EWCA Civ 350; [2011] 1 W.L.R. 133 at [26].
[299] [2001] EWCA Civ 791.
[300] *Hamilton v Clifford* [2004] EWCA Civ 1407.
[301] [2010] UKSC 53; [2011] 1 A.C. 852.
[302] [2010] UKSC 53; [2011] 1 A.C. 852 at [103].
[303] [2010] UKSC 53; [2011] 1 A.C. 852 at [103].

is whether there is a sufficient substratum of facts indicated in the words that are the subject matter of the action to show that an opinion is being expressed.

The substratum of facts or subject matter may be indicated impliedly in the circumstances of the publication, even by their general notoriety. In *Kemsley v Foot*[304] the claimant newspaper owner sued the defendant, which had published a newspaper article under the heading "Lower than Kemsley". The article was violently critical of the conduct of a newspaper not owned by the claimant and contained no reference to the claimant other than in the heading. The House of Lords found for the defendant as in the circumstances the conduct of the Kemsley press in its publications was sufficiently indicated as the fact on which the opinion was expressed. However, in determining whether a statement is capable of being comment the court may not voyage beyond what is said expressly or by implication in the defendant's words.

In *Telnikoff v Matusevitch*[305] it was held that where a defendant writes a letter to a newspaper refuting an article published in it, then, in deciding whether statements in the letter were protected as opinion, the court is confined to the letter itself because the readers of the letter may include a substantial number of people who have not read the article. The court denied that this meant that the whole of the material about which an opinion is expressed would have to be repeated in the letter containing the opinion (a situation obviously unacceptable to any newspaper editor) as long as some form of words was used that made it plain that the letter was an opinion and nothing else.

The factual basis of the opinion is true or privileged. For an opinion to be   **13–099** protected by the defence of honest opinion, it must be such that an honest person could have held the opinion on the basis of any true fact or privileged fact that existed at the time that the statement was published. Thus, opinions that are based on facts that are neither true nor privileged are not protected. Several points should be noted about this requirement. First, facts that emerge after the statement was published cannot be considered in asking whether this requirement is satisfied.[306] Secondly, it does not seem that it is necessary that the defendant knew about the facts when he published the statement in question. Thirdly, it is unclear that the opinion can be based on all privileged statements or on only certain types of privileged statements. Section 3(4) suggests that the first interpretation is correct. However, s.3(7) says that for the purposes of the defence "privileged statements" are: (1) statements protected under the public interest defence in s.4;[307] (2) statements covered by the qualified privilege enjoyed by academic publications;[308] (3) the absolute privilege that covers reports of court proceedings;[309] and (4) the heads of qualified privilege provided for by the Defamation Act 1996.[310] Section 3(7) leans in favour of the second interpretation. It is fairly clear that the first interpretation was intended by Parliament, and that

---

[304] [1952] A.C. 345.
[305] [1992] 2 A.C. 343.
[306] *Cohen v Daily Telegraph Ltd* [1968] 1 W.L.R. 916.
[307] See para.13–076.
[308] See para.13–074.
[309] See para.13–060.
[310] See para.13–071.

Parliament has chosen its words badly. Thus, the defence of honest opinion may protect opinions regarding untrue statements of fact made by a witness in court that is absolutely privileged.

The foregoing rules do not apply where the defendant bases his opinion on a statement of another person. Where this is the case, pursuant to s.3(6), the defence will be lost only if the claimant shows that the defendant knew or ought to have known that the original author did not hold the opinion. This subsection is defectively drafted. Suppose that C publishes a statement that there are men on the planet Mars and D criticises this allegation as unfounded. This criticism would seem to be an opinion yet C knows that D does not hold the opinion that he expressed and so the defence of honest opinion will not be available. It is very doubtful that the law should withhold the defence of honest opinion in this situation.

13–100   **The opinion does not need to be reasonable.** There is no requirement that the opinion be reasonable. It is not necessary that the court should accept the opinion as correct.

13–101   **The defence will be lost if the defendant did not hold the opinion.** As mentioned above, the defence will be lost if the claimant establishes that the defendant did not hold the opinion. It does not matter that the defendant held the opinion maliciously. The sole question here is whether, subjectively, the defendant believed the opinion that he expressed. The unreasonableness of the defendant's belief would seem to be irrelevant save insofar that the more unreasonable it is the more likely it may be that the defendant did not believe the opinion in question.

x.   Apology and Payment into Court

13–102   Under s.2 of the Libel Act 1843, a newspaper that publishes a libel without malice and without gross negligence may plead in defence the publication of a full apology and payment of money into court. This has fallen into complete disuse because it is more advantageous for the defendant to make a "Pt 36 offer" under the general provisions applicable to all actions for damages.[311]

xi.   Offer of Amends

13–103   **Generally.** Sections 2–4 of the Defamation Act 1996 provide for a defence of offer of amends. It requires the defendant to admit that he was wrong (or partly wrong). If the defendant is unwilling to do this he must take his chances on another defence. An offer under the statute must be[312] to make a suitable correction and a sufficient apology, to publish those in a manner that is reasonable and practicable in the circumstances and to pay to the claimant[313] such compensation (if any), and such costs, as may be agreed or determined to be

---

[311] CPR Pt. 36. See para.1–042.

[312] It must be in writing and be expressed to be under the Act: s.2(3).

[313] Strictly, in the words of the statute, "person aggrieved" since no proceedings may have been started when the offer is made.

payable.[314] An offer may only be made before service of a defence,[315] although once a defence has been served the defendant may still of course offer to settle the dispute under the general law.

Situation where the offer is accepted. If the offer is accepted the claimant may not bring an action for defamation or continue one that he has started against the defendant. This is so even if the parties have not agreed the details of what should be done under the offer. If so, there is no question of the court being able to compel the defendant to do anything in particular by way of correction, apology or publication—in the absence of agreement that is a matter for the defendant to decide. If, however, the parties have also failed to agree on the amount of the compensation to be paid, that is something which will be settled by the court "on the same principles as damages in defamation proceedings"[316] and account may be taken in setting the figure of the suitability and sufficiency of what the defendant has done by way of correction and apology.[317] An early and unqualified offer of amends followed by an agreed apology will attract a "discount" on the damages. The discount has been said to be approximately 50 per cent,[318] although this might be regarded as the top of scale.[319]   **13–104**

Situation where the offer is not accepted. If the offer is not accepted the action will proceed but the defendant may use the making of the offer as a defence to the action unless the claimant is able to show[320] that the defendant knew at the time of publication or had reason to believe that the statement referred to the claimant (or was likely to be understood as referring to him) and was both false and defamatory of him.[321] "Had reason to believe" is not to be equated with "failed to take reasonable care"—it is equivalent to the recklessness or conscious indifference as to truth which constitutes malice for the purpose of qualified privilege.[322]   **13–105**

Qualified offer of amends. Since defamatory words are often capable of more than one interpretation, it is open to the defendant to make a qualified offer in relation to a specific defamatory meaning that he accepts that the words bear. So if the allegation against a company director is that his conduct has caused his company to get into difficulties the defendant might concede that this imputed incompetence and make an offer in respect of that meaning. The claimant, however, might contend that the words in their context carried the implication that he had been dishonest. If the offer of amends in respect of the lesser meaning is not accepted then it will be for the court at the trial to determine what the words do mean. If, though untrue, they bear only the lesser meaning and the claimant is unable to show that the defendant had reason to believe them to be untrue the   **13–106**

---

[314] Section 2(4).
[315] Section 2(5).
[316] Section 3(6).
[317] *Nail v News Group Newspapers Ltd* [2004] EWCA Civ 1708; [2005] 1 All E.R. 1040 at [19].
[318] *Nail v News Group Newspapers Ltd* [2004] EWCA Civ 1708; [2005] E.M.L.R. 12.
[319] *Cairns v Modi* [2012] EWCA Civ 1382; [2013] 1 W.L.R. 1015 at [50].
[320] The burden is on the claimant: s.4(3).
[321] Section 4(3).
[322] *Milne v Express Newspapers* [2004] EWCA Civ 664; [2004] E.M.L.R. 24.

defence based upon the offer of amends will succeed; if the court considers that the words were to be understood in the more serious sense, the claimant will win.

13–107 **Defence is mutually exclusive of other defences.** The defendant cannot rely on an offer by way of defence in combination with any other defence,[323] although this is subject to an exception where the defendant makes a qualified offer of amends.[324]

13–108 **Offer of amends cannot be accepted after a reasonable time.** The provisions of the Defamation Act 1996 merely speak of the consequences of the offer being accepted or not accepted: it contains no concept of the offer being refused. However, the claimant cannot simply sit on the offer and pursue his case, accepting it at the last moment if things go badly, thereby pulling the plug on the statutory defence at the price perhaps of suffering some adverse consequence on costs. Although the matter is not strictly contractual,[325] a claimant cannot accept an offer after a reasonable time.[326]

13–109 **Rationale.** The purpose of the offer of amends procedure is to encourage settlement. A claimant accepting an offer has his reputation vindicated and obtains compensation without the worry and expense of trial. A defendant who is willing to make an offer gets to put the claimant to the difficult burden of proof of malice if it is not accepted. The fact that an offer of amends has been made will have a significant deflationary effect on the amount of compensation that is payable if proceedings are needed to determine that issue.

xii.   Consent

13–110 Consent is a defence to liability in defamation, but it is very rarely engaged. In *Chapman v Lord Ellesmere*[327] the claimant, a horse trainer, complained about a report regarding doping allegations that had been published by the stewards of a horse racing club of which he was a member. It was held that the claimant had consented to the publication of this report as he had agreed to be governed by the club's rules (which permitted the stewards to publish the report in question) when he joined the club.

xiii.   Apology is Not a Defence

13–111 It is open to the defendant to a claim for defamation, as in the case of any other tort, to settle out of court. This may involve an apology, which may be incorporated in a statement in open court (approved by the judge).[328] However, generally speaking, an apology is not, as such, a defence, though it may of course

---

[323] Section 4(4). But even if not relied on by way of defence the offer may be relied on in mitigation of damages: s.4(5).

[324] The defendant may rely on any other defence in respect of a meaning to which a qualified offer does not relate: s.4(4).

[325] *Warren v Random House Group Ltd* [2008] EWCA Civ 834; [2009] Q.B. 600.

[326] *Tesco Stores Ltd v Guardian News & Media Ltd* [2009] E.M.L.R. 5.

[327] [1932] 2 K.B. 431.

[328] CPR PD 53, para.6.1. This will come to the attention of the press and will be protected by absolute privilege: *Barnet v Crozier* [1987] 1 W.L.R. 272.

reduce the damages if the claimant wins.[329] An apology need not be an abject one, but it should at least withdraw completely the imputation and express regret for having made it. To say that someone has manners not fit for a pig and then to retract that by saying that his manners are fit for a pig would merely aggravate the damages.

C. Procedure in Defamation

The demise of the jury. The law of defamation has for much of its history been subjected to severe criticism. Few commentators have had kind words to say about it. Many of the attacks on the tort have been made in the public arena, and successive governments have changed the law with a view to making it more difficult to sue for defamation. An important change effected by the Defamation Act 2013, mentioned above,[330] is effectively to eliminate juries in defamation cases. Section 11 of the Act provides that defamation cases will be tried without a jury unless the court orders otherwise.[331] This change will, in practice, ensure that juries are no longer used in this setting, thereby removing what was virtually the last refuge of the jury in tort law. This shift in the law was prompted primarily by a belief that the use of juries lay behind many of the problems from which the law of defamation was perceived to suffer. Juries had in several cases made very large awards even though no measurable financial loss was suffered. This created the image that the law of defamation was a bonanza for claimants. The Court of Appeal had sought to combat this issue[332] but evidently its efforts were thought to be insufficient by Parliament. There was also a feeling that juries drove up the cost of defamation actions on the grounds that it was slower to try a case before a jury than a judge sitting alone.

13–112

Summary judgment. The court may give judgment for the claimant and grant him summary relief if it appears that there is no defence that has a realistic prospect of success and there is no other reason why the claim should be tried.[333] Summary relief is a declaration that the statement was false and defamatory, an order that the defendant publish a suitable correction and apology, and damages not exceeding £10,000.[334] This provision may mislead on a superficial reading of it for the court cannot in fact dictate the terms of any correction and apology: if the defendant is intransigent the court can only compel him to publish a summary of the court's judgment.[335] For the claimant who desires a cheaper and speedier vindication of his reputation than is offered by a full trial this provides a "fast

13–113

---

[329] See para.13–121.
[330] See para.13–010.
[331] Section 11(1).
[332] See, e.g. the measures implemented in *John v Mirror Group Newspapers Ltd* [1997] Q.B. 586 aimed at limiting damages awards by juries.
[333] Defamation Act 1996 s.8(3).
[334] Defamation Act 1996 s.9(1).
[335] Defamation Act 1996 s.9(2), which contemplates that the content and venue will normally be agreed by the parties.

track" route,[336] but it should not be looked on solely in this light for the court may force this solution on the claimant and deny him a trial if it is satisfied that the summary relief "will adequately compensate him for the wrong he has suffered".[337] It is therefore clearly contemplated that there is a distinction between "minor" and "serious" libels, the former being suitable for summary disposition even if the claimant wishes to go to trial. The judicial declaration of falsity under the summary procedure goes some way to meeting that element of libel damages which are concerned with vindicating the claimant's reputation[338] so that the procedure may extend further up the scale than libels which are "worth" £10,000 in damages terms.[339]

13–114 **Costs.** From the point of view of claimants, the bonanza image was never the whole story, and if the law of defamation has presented a harsh face to media defendants it can present an even harsher one to claimants, for costs in defamation cases can be very high[340] and legal aid has never been available. Most defamation defendants are media corporations and most claimants are individuals and under the traditional system of funding litigation whereby clients paid their lawyers by the hour the cards were necessarily stacked in favour of the former. The picture changed to some extent under the system of conditional fees.[341] Provided that the claimant can find lawyers willing to conduct his claim on a no-win/no-fee basis he avoids the risk of having to pay his own legal costs if he loses. As a result of recent reforms to the costs system, success fees are no longer recoverable from the losing party, nor are ATE insurance premiums.[342]

As discussed above, to protect claimants from having to pay the defendant's costs if their claim is unsuccessful, costs protection has been implemented in the personal injury context.[343] The idea behind this protection is that people should not be deterred from bringing meritorious claims by a fear that, if their claim fails for some reason, they will be met with a large costs bill. The Government has accepted that similar costs protection is needed in the defamation (and privacy) context, and is currently considering the shape that this protection should take. The Government has suggested that the protection will be means tested. It should be noted that conferring one party with costs protection necessarily means that the other party will be exposed to the risk of being left out of pocket in terms of their costs should they succeed in the proceeding.

From the perspective of defendants, the high costs in defamation cases can have a "chilling effect" on free speech. One concern here is that defendants will refrain from publishing statements even though they might not incur liability if they went ahead and published because of the fear that they might lose and have

---

[336] A defendant wishing to take advantage of the summary relevant procedure may legitimately waive a triable defence: *Milne v Telegraph Group Ltd* [2001] E.M.L.R. 30. The origin of the summary procedure is a Bill drafted by Lord Hoffmann in 1989.

[337] Defamation Act 1996 s.8(3)

[338] See para.13–116.

[339] *Mawdsley v Guardian Newspapers Ltd* [2002] EWHC 1780 (QB).

[340] It has been suggested that even an award of £30,000 damages against a solvent defendant might leave a claimant out of pocket on irrecoverable costs: *Clarke v Bain* [2008] EWHC 2636 (QB) at [54].

[341] See para.1–031.

[342] See para.1–033.

[343] See para.1–033

to pay significant costs. To mitigate this problem, the Government has indicated that it will introduce costs protection for defendants, and this too will be means tested. The present system also has the potential to "chill" speech because defendants that win are presented with the risk of being unable to recover their costs where the claimant is impecunious and decides not to secure ATE insurance. The irrecoverable costs of defending the action may be so significant that it is not worth publishing a given statement even if publishing the statement would probably not attract liability.

Very occasionally the libel claimant has ample means and the defendant is impecunious, as was the case in *Steel v UK*,[344] where the McDonald's Corp had obtained judgment for £76,000 against the unwaged defendants (which there was not the remotest hope of enforcing). The European Court of Human Rights held that the absence of legal aid for the defendants contravened art.6 of the European Convention on Human Rights.

Actions involving persons not domiciled in the United Kingdom or a Member State. There is a concern that English defamation law, because it has traditionally provided the right to reputation with robust protection, has resulted in proceedings being commenced in Britain rather than elsewhere in circumstances where the case has little connection with Britain. This concern has been heightened by publications on the internet. Internet publications accessed within Britain will be treated as published in Britain. This means that if D, who is domiciled in another jurisdiction, writes something defamatory about C, who is also located in that jurisdiction, but the statement is accessed by X in Britain, D will in principle be liable for defamation in Britain. The main device that the courts have at their disposal to prevent proceedings from being brought by claimants based overseas where there is minimal publication within Britain is the defence of abuse of process.[345] The courts have not been reluctant in recent years to strike out as abusive proceedings where the defamatory statement has only been published to a handful of people in Britain. Furthermore, the courts have the power to stay proceedings on the basis of *forum non conveniens* where Britain is not an appropriate jurisdiction in which to hear the case. However, the legislature did not think that the mechanisms developed by the courts to deal with "libel tourism" were sufficient and enacted s.9 of the Defamation Act 2013. This section denies jurisdiction to British courts in a case where the defendant is based outside of the United Kingdom and the rest of the European Union unless the court is of the view that England "is clearly the most appropriate place in which to bring an action in respect of the statement".[346] This development seems to have been motivated at least in part by demands from stakeholders in the United States for increased protection for defendants based there from liability in defamation. Congress in 2010 enacted legislation (the Securing and Protecting our Enduring and Established Constitutional Heritage Act 2010, which is also known as the "SPEECH Act") that prevented courts in the United States from enforcing foreign defamation judgments unless a remedy for defamation could have been obtained had the proceedings been commenced in the United States. Additional legislation

13–115

---

[344] [2005] E.M.L.R. 15
[345] See para.26–077.
[346] Section 9(2).

has been enacted by some state legislatures. It is debatable whether s.9 really adds anything to the existing measures to prevent forum shopping.

D. Remedies

i. Damages

13–116 **Generally.** A claimant who succeeds in establishing liability in defamation is entitled to compensatory damages to compensate him for the wrong committed by the defendant. The leading case in this regard is *John v MGN Ltd*.[347] Sir Thomas Bingham MR, giving the judgment of the Court of Appeal, wrote:[348]

> "The successful plaintiff in a defamation action is entitled to recover, as general compensatory damages, such sum as will compensate him for the wrong he has suffered. That sum must compensate him for the damage to his reputation; vindicate his good name; and take account of the distress, hurt and humiliation which the defamatory publication has caused."

In *Cairns v Modi* the Court of Appeal said that these three purposes of awarding compensatory damages—repairing damage to the claimant reputation, vindicating his name, and compensating him for the distress caused—are relevant in every case, "but the emphasis to be placed on each will vary from case to case".[349]

The mere fact that a judge delivered a reasoned judgment in which he explained his conclusions for finding in the claimant's favour will not be its own vindication and will not render it unnecessary to award damages vindicating the claimant's name.[350] While a judgment will sometimes provide sufficient vindication, the issue of whether it does so is one of fact.[351] A judgment alone is unlikely to serve as sufficient vindication where the defamatory statement was disseminated widely and a substantial award is necessary to convince interested bystanders of the claimant's good name.

The trial judge has significant leeway in terms of deciding the sum that should be awarded, although he should not award more than is necessary to compensate the claimant for the injury done to him, and the damages should consequently be proportionate to the injury.[352]

13–117 **Gravity of the libel.** A central factor to consider in calculating damages is the gravity of the defamatory statement. This refers to how closely "it touches the plaintiff's personal integrity, professional reputation, honour, courage, loyalty and the core attributes of his personality".[353] The closer the connection between the defamatory statement and the claimant's "core attributes" the greater the damages will be, all other things being equal. An example of a statement that will strike at

---

[347] [1997] Q.B. 586.
[348] [1997] Q.B. 586 at 607.
[349] [2012] EWCA Civ 1382; [2013] 1 W.L.R. at [22].
[350] *Cairns v Modi* [2012] EWCA Civ 1382; [2013] 1 W.L.R. at [30]–[31].
[351] *Cairns v Modi* [2012] EWCA Civ 1382; [2013] 1 W.L.R. at [32].
[352] *Cairns v Modi* [2012] EWCA Civ 1382; [2013] 1 W.L.R. at [34]–[35].
[353] *John v MGN Ltd* [1997] Q.B. 586 at 607.

the core of the claimant's character is where the claimant is a professional cricketer and the statement alleges that he is guilty of match-fixing.[354]

Extent of the publication. Another important factor to consider is the extent of the publication. The more widely it is published the greater the award that will be called for.[355] As the Court of Appeal explained in *Cairns v Modi*:[356]

13–118

> "[I]t is virtually self-evident that in most cases publication of a defamatory statement to one person will cause infinitely less damage than publication to the world at large, and that publication on a single occasion is likely to cause less damage than repeated publication and consequent publicity on social media."

It is important to bear in mind in this connection that publication of a defamatory statement will rarely end with the person to whom it is originally published.[357] This "percolation phenomenon" is likely to be particularly significant in the modern world where communications systems enable stories to be spread widely virtually instantaneously.[358] Thus, damages may be sought not only for the original publication but also in respect of loss that flows from that publication, provided that it is reasonably foreseeable.[359]

It may be important to consider not only the extent of the publication but also the number of people who realised that the publication referred to the claimant. In one of the appeals in *Cairns v Modi*[360] the claimant, who was alleged to be a paedophile due to an error by the defendant newspaper, remained anonymous throughout the proceedings, and only a handful of people, such as the claimant's relatives, understood that the article was referring to the claimant. Once this factor was taken into account, the Court of Appeal felt that damages should be reduced by a third.

Relationship of the claimant to the publishees. It is relevant to consider the nature of the relationship between the claimant and the persons to whom the defamatory statement was published. For example, publication to persons with whom the claimant is in a business relationship might call for a greater award of damages than publication to persons with whom the claimant is unlikely to enter such a relationship.[361]

13–119

Unsuccessful reliance on plea of truth. A defendant who unsuccessfully invokes the defence of truth is likely to be met with a heavier award than would have been the case had he accepted that the statement was false.[362]

13–120

Retraction and apology. A defendant who withdraws a defamatory statement and apologises, especially if he does so promptly, will reduce the damage caused

13–121

---

[354] *Cairns v Modi* [2012] EWHC 756 (QB) at [121] (not doubted on appeal in [2012] EWCA Civ 1382; [2013] 1 W.L.R. 1015).
[355] *John v MGN Ltd* [1997] Q.B. 586 at 607.
[356] [2012] EWCA Civ 1382; [2013] 1 W.L.R. at [24].
[357] *Slipper v British Broadcasting Corpn* [1991] 1 Q.B. 283 at 300.
[358] *Cairns v Modi* [2012] EWCA Civ 1382; [2013] 1 W.L.R. 1015 at [26]–[27].
[359] *McManus v Beckham* [2002] EWCA Civ 939; [2002] 1 W.L.R. 2982.
[360] [2012] EWCA Civ 1382; [2013] 1 W.L.R. 1015 at [46] [49].
[361] *Cooper v Turrell* [2011] EWHC 3269 (QB) at [96]–[97].
[362] *John v MGN Ltd* [1997] Q.B. 586 at 607–608.

to the claimant and will consequently be liable for a smaller sum.[363] The more effective the apology, the greater the reduction.

13–122   **Evidence of general bad reputation.** The defendant may adduce evidence of general bad reputation on the issue of damages. The idea here is that the law should prevent the recovery of substantial damages by a person whose reputation is unworthy of protection. However, the defendant is not permitted to adduce evidence of specific acts of misconduct[364] for it would be oppressive to allow the defendant (perhaps a newspaper with large financial resources) to lengthen a trial with detailed evidence of the claimant's past conduct. Despite this restriction, the defendant is entitled to rely in mitigation of damages on any evidence which has been properly before the court and this may include evidence of specific acts of misconduct advanced under an unsuccessful plea of truth.[365] However, the court will not countenance the pleading of such specific acts under the guise of a plea of truth with the sole purpose of mitigation of damages.[366] It is the restriction on evidence which may be given in mitigation of damages which lies at the heart of most of the fencing on the defence of truth.

The rule that evidence of specific misconduct is generally inadmissible in mitigation of damages does not prevent the admission into evidence of matters that relate to the background context which is directly relevant to the publication. In *Burstein v Times Newspapers Ltd*[367] the defendant could not prove that it was true that the claimant had organised bands of hecklers to wreck musical performances. However, the defendant could give evidence of an incident in which the claimant had booed after one performance. This principle applies equally to the situation where the claimant has accepted the defendant's offer of amends under the Defamation Act 1996[368] and the court has to assess compensation because the amount of this has not been agreed[369]—indeed, it is particularly important that it should apply in such a case because the defendant will have had no opportunity to raise the claimant's conduct under a plea of truth or honest opinion. It is inevitable that cases will arise where it is difficult to decide whether the evidence relates to the "directly relevant background context" and it should be applied with some caution.

13–123   **Maximum allowable compensatory damages.** In an effort to bring greater consistency to damages awards, the courts have placed a "ceiling" on allowable damages, leaving aside exemplary damages and damages for financial loss. The ceiling is the prevailing maximum level of damages for pain and suffering and loss of amenity in personal injury cases. The Court of Appeal in *Cairns v Modi* indicated that the relevant sum would be in the region of £275,000.[370]

---

[363] Libel Act 1843 s.1; *John v MGN Ltd* [1997] Q.B. 586 at 607–608.
[364] *Plato Films v Speidel* [1961] A.C. 1090. The restriction on such evidence is commonly known as the rule in *Scott v Sampson* (1882) 8 Q.B.D. 491.
[365] *Pamplin v Express Newspapers Ltd (Note)* [1988] 1 W.L.R. 116.
[366] *Atkinson v Fitzwalter* [1987] 1 W.L.R. 201; *Prager v Times Newspapers Ltd* [1988] 1 W.L.R. 77.
[367] [2001] 1 W.L.R. 579.
[368] See para.13–104.
[369] *Turner v News Group Newspapers Ltd* [2006] EWCA Civ 540; [2006] 1 W.L.R. 3469.
[370] [2012] EWCA Civ 1382; [2013] 1 W.L.R. 1015 at [25].

Corporations. Corporations that establish that they have been defamed are entitled to substantial damages.[371] Generally speaking, the principles that determine the award of damages to a corporation are the same as those that govern awards to persons. However, corporations, since they have no feelings, are not entitled to damages for distress, hurt and humiliation.[372]

13–124

Aggravated and exemplary damages. An award of damages for defamation may include aggravated or exemplary damages. These are considered below.[373]

13–125

ii.   Injunctive Relief

The availability of injunctive relief is discussed elsewhere in this book.[374]

13–126

iii.   Publication of Summary of the Court's Judgment

Under s.12 of the Defamation Act 2013, the court has the power to order the defendant to publish a summary of its judgment. If the parties cannot agree on the time, manner, form and place of the summary's publication, the court is to settle those matters. The court cannot exercise this power when it disposes summarily of a claim.[375]

13–127

iv.   Removal of Statements

Section 13 of the Defamation Act 2013 empowers the court to order the operator of a website on which a defamatory statement is posted to remove the statement. The court can also order any person who is not the "author, editor or publisher" of the defamatory statement to stop "distributing, selling or exhibiting material contained in the statement".

13–128

v.   Remedies that are Not Available

The court has no power to order the defendant to publish a correction or to issue a retraction or to give the claimant a right of reply. Nor can it compel the defendant to apologise.

13–129

vi.   Is the Focus on Damages Satisfactory?

It is arguable that the virtually exclusive emphasis on the law on damages as a remedy militates against what a claimant will (or should, according to some conventional wisdom) regard as the major purpose of his claim—that is, the vindication of his good name. The recovery of damages, whether by judgment or settlement, will not necessarily achieve this end unless the fact of recovery is widely publicised. Furthermore, the defences available in a defamation action,

13–130

---

[371] *Cooper v Turrell* [2011] EWHC 3269 (QB) at [95].
[372] *Cooper v Turrell* [2011] EWHC 3269 (QB) at [99].
[373] See paras 23–012, 23–024.
[374] See para.21–122.
[375] See para.13–113.

while they are undoubtedly necessary to protect freedom of speech, may have the effect that the issue of the truth of the allegations is wholly or partly suppressed and a wholly unfounded and very damaging accusation may still lead to a verdict for the defendant. Even where the claimant's reputation is vindicated it will only be after protracted litigation, the expense of which is at least in part produced by the necessity to hold the balance between the protection of reputation and free speech. On the face of it, therefore, there is much attraction in a system for media defamation whereby there would be a speedy procedure for requiring a correction of a defamatory statement or the publication of a counter-statement by the complainant. It must also be borne in mind that a person aggrieved by inaccurate statements may complain to the Press Complaints Commission (a self-regulatory body for the press) or to the Broadcasting Standards Commission (a statutory body) which do not award compensation but which may require the offending newspaper or broadcaster to publish a summary of any adjudication. However, there are some difficulties with such remedies if they are made the exclusive or even the primary form of redress. From the claimant's point of view "mud sticks"[376] and the possibility of being required to publish an apology and correction would not be a very powerful deterrent against the dissemination of the careless or even reckless falsehoods which are undoubtedly from time-to-time published by the media.[377] As for the defendant, it would be a new and perhaps dangerous step to impose upon a newspaper a legal requirement (which presumably would have to be backed by criminal sanctions) to publish a statement "extolling the complainant's non-existent virtue".[378] In any event, forced publication might not convince the reader that the smoke really had no underlying fire.

2. MALICIOUS FALSEHOOD[379]

13–131 **Introduction.** A false statement may be damaging even though it is not defamatory. It may be relied on by others to their detriment, in which case it may be actionable as deceit if made knowingly or recklessly[380] or, if there is a "special relationship", as negligence.[381] But a false, non-defamatory statement may also cause damage by influencing the way in which other persons behave towards the claimant. For example, a newspaper may publish incorrectly that a trader has closed his business, with the result being that potential customers do not approach him; or a manufacturer may circulate false information that because of technological development his product is now twice as effective as the claimant's and thereby take business away from him; alternatively, the manufacturer may represent that his goods are in fact the goods of the claimant, which enjoy a good reputation. None of these representations is, on the face of it, defamatory, for they

---

[376] See the remarks in the Supreme Court of Canada in *Hill v Church of Scientology* (1995) 126 D.L.R. (4th) 129 at 176.
[377] See, e.g. *John v Mirror Group Newspapers* [1997] Q.B. 586.
[378] The phrase is the Faulks Committee's (Cmnd. 5909, 1975).
[379] Injurious falsehood is an alternative name.
[380] See para.12–002.
[381] See para.12–051.

do not impute anything derogatory, indeed in the third case the position is quite the reverse. The third case is covered by the tort of passing off, which is dealt with elsewhere in this book,[382] but the other two may constitute malicious falsehood, which overlaps considerably with defamation. This area of the law shows clearly that we have a law of separate torts: there is no general right to sue in respect of untruths or even to restrain the circulation of untruths.[383]

Elements of the action. The tort of malicious falsehood has the following elements: (1) the making of false statement; (2) maliciously; (3) to some person other than the claimant; and (4) damage is suffered by the claimant as a result of the making of the statement. It is for the claimant to prove that the statement is false. There is no presumption in his favour.[384] If the statement is true, no liability can arise in malicious falsehood. It is not, therefore, malicious falsehood for a businessperson to utter true but damaging remarks about a competitor.   **13–132**

A.   The Making of a False Statement to some Person other than the Claimant

Statements. The statement may be oral or written, and even conduct conveying a false impression will be sufficient.[385]   **13–133**

Actionable statements often affect the claimant's trade or business but this is not required. The statement usually affects the claimant's trade or business. So, in the leading case of *Ratcliffe v Evans*[386] an action succeeded in respect of a statement by a newspaper that the claimant had ceased to trade. However, it does not matter that it affects the claimant in other ways. In one of the earliest cases the false statement was that the claimant was already married, whereby she lost a proposed marriage.[387] In an American case the defendant gave false information that the claimant was not a citizen, subjecting him to deportation proceedings.[388] In *Kaye v Robertson*[389] the tort was established where a newspaper published what was falsely claimed to be an interview to which a television personality had consented, thereby depriving him of the chance to sell his story as an "exclusive".   **13–134**

The statement must relate to the claimant or his property. The tort does not extend to statements that have no connection with the claimant or his property: it is not malicious falsehood (though it may be another tort) if A tells B lies in order to obtain B's property and thereby deprives C of the opportunity to bid for it.[390]   **13–135**

---

[382] See para.19–072.

[383] *Kingdom of Spain v Christie, Manson & Woods Ltd* [1986] 1 W.L.R. 1120.

[384] Cf. the position in defamation: see para.13-049.

[385] *Wilts United Dairies v Robinson & Sons* [1958] R.P.C. 94.

[386] [1892] 2 Q.B. 524.

[387] *Sheperd v Wakeman* (1662) 1 Sid. 79.

[388] *Al Raschid v News Syndicate Co* 191 N.E. 713 (1934). The deportation proceedings were not "judicial proceedings" for the purposes of the tort of malicious prosecution.

[389] [1991] F.S.R. 52.

[390] *Lonrho Plc v Fayed* [1988] 3 All E.R. 464 (though no claim for malicious falsehood appears to have been made). On appeal on another point [1992] 1 A.C. 448.

13–136 **Statement by D about the purported superiority of his goods to C's.** A statement by a trader that his goods are superior to those of a rival (mere "puffing"), even if it is false and known to be so and causes damage is not actionable, for courts of law cannot be converted into agencies for trying the relative merits of rival productions.[391] However, this is only the case with respect to those imprecise commendations that are a common part of advertising and to which a reasonable person does not attach much importance. Accordingly, if a defendant chooses to frame his comparison in the form of scientific tests or other statements of ascertainable fact, he will be liable if they are proved untrue.[392]

13–137 **The single meaning rule in defamation does not apply in malicious falsehood.** In defamation, the words about which the claimant complains must be given a single meaning.[393] This rule does not apply in malicious falsehood.[394] Thus, it does not matter for the purposes of malicious falsehood if the false meaning of the words relied upon by the claimant is not the only meaning that they might be capable of bearing. The court is not forced to adopt a meaning that is reasonably open that is not false.

13–138 **Each publication gives rise to a separate cause of action.** Each publication of the statement complained of generates a fresh cause of action and, consequently, a fresh limitation period. The changes to the law in this connection in relation to defamation[395] do not apply to malicious falsehood.

B. Malice

13–139 Malice exists if the defendant knows that the statement is false or if he makes the statement not caring whether it is true or false, but negligence is not enough to establish malice.[396] "Honest belief", said Scrutton LJ, "in an unfounded claim is not malice, but the nature of the unfounded claim may be evidence that there is not an honest belief in it. It may be so unfounded that the particular fact that it is put forward may be evidence that it is not honestly believed".[397] However, even if the defendant does believe the untrue statement there will still be malice if he is actuated by some indirect, dishonest or improper motive, which seems here to mean the purpose of injuring the claimant rather than defending his own interests or pushing his own business.[398]

---

[391] *White v Mellin* [1895] A.C. 154 at 164; *Hubbuck & Sons Ltd Wilkinson* [1899] 1 Q.B. 86.

[392] *De Beers Products Ltd v International General Electric Co of New York* [1975] 1 W.L.R. 972. Even imprecise assertions of superiority may be actionable if they denigrate the claimant's wares in a manner that a reasonable person would take seriously: *White v Mellin* [1895] A.C. 154 at 171; *Alcott v Miller's Karri etc. Ltd* (1904) 91 L.T. 722.

[393] See para.13–010.

[394] *Ajinomoto Sweeteners Europe SAS v Asda Stores Ltd* [2010] EWCA 609; [2011] Q.B. 497.

[395] See para.13–024.

[396] *Shapiro v La Morta* (1923) 40 T.L.R. 39 and 201.

[397] *Greers Ltd v Pearman & Corder Ltd* (1922) 39 R.P.C. 406 at 417.

[398] *Dunlop v Maison Talbot* (1904) 20 T.L.R. 579.

C. Damage

Except in cases falling within s.3(1) of the Defamation Act 1952 proof of special **13–140** (that is, actual, pecuniary) damage is required[399] but this is satisfied by proof of a general loss of business where the falsehood is in its very nature intended, or is reasonably likely, to produce and actually does produce in the ordinary course of things, such loss.[400] By s.3(1) of the Defamation Act 1952 it is no longer necessary to allege or prove special damage if: (1) the words complained of are published in writing or other permanent form; or (2) the words are calculated to cause pecuniary damage to the claimant in respect of any office, profession, calling, trade or business carried on by him at the time of the publication. The words "calculated to cause pecuniary damages" mean "more likely than not to cause pecuniary damage".[401]

Distress and injury to feelings do not amount to special damage for the purpose of malicious falsehood. However, where special damage is established (or where s.3 of the Defamation Act 1952 applies) the claimant may recover aggravated damages for injury to feelings as in an action for defamation. The award may take account of the conduct of the defendant during the litigation, for example, in trying to blacken the claimant's name.[402]

D. Varieties of the Tort

Particular varieties of malicious falsehood have acquired names of their own: **13–141** slander of goods (where the defendant disparages the claimant's goods); and slander of title (where he questions the claimant's ownership of property). These are not separate torts and have nothing to do with "slander" in the defamation sense. It would be better if the expressions were dropped.

E. Defences

Generally speaking, the rules concerning absolute privilege in the law of **13–142** defamation apply also to malicious falsehood. Thus, if a judge disparages C's business in the course of court proceedings C will not be able to recover damages from the judge. Qualified privilege is not a defence to malicious falsehood. Because malice is one of the elements of the action in malicious falsehood, where the action is constituted, the defence will be necessarily excluded since it is forfeited if the defendants acted maliciously. The defence of abuse of process is available. It might be triggered where, for example, the claim is for trivial loss.

---

[399] *White v Mellin* [1895] A.C. 154; *Royal Baking Powder Co v Wright & Co* (1900) 18 R.P.C. 95 at 99.
[400] *Ratcliffe v Evans* [1892] 2 Q.B. 524 at 533. Cf. *Joyce v Sengupta* [1993] 1 W.L.R. 337 at 347.
[401] *Tesla Motors Ltd v British Broadcasting Corporation* [2011] EWHC 2760 (QB) at [7].
[402] *Khodaparast v Shad* [2000] 1 W.L.R. 618.

3. PRIVACY

13–143   **Introduction.** English law does not recognise any direct action for the invasion of privacy.[403] However, the technically correct proposition that there is no tort of invasion of privacy would be seriously misleading if not substantially qualified. The protection of privacy is a value recognised by the law and the interest of privacy is protected in several ways. First, there is indirect protection afforded by torts like trespass and nuisance. Secondly, protection is provided by various statutory provisions, most particularly those relating to data protection and the behaviour of public authorities under the Human Rights Act 1998. Thirdly, recent years have seen the substantial development of the old law of breach of confidence resulting in an offshoot that is sometimes called the tort of misuse of private information.

A.   The Indirect Impact of Other Torts

13–144   **Defamation.** It is perhaps an oversimplification to say that the law of defamation is not concerned with the invasion of privacy: the distress which is felt by the victim of a libel may be as much due to the torrent of intrusive publicity that descends upon him as to the affront he feels at having untrue things said about him. However, the protection given to privacy by the law of defamation is limited. This is partly because truth is a complete defence to liability in defamation.[404] If a defendant publishes private information he will not incur liability in defamation provided that it is true. Even where the statement is untrue there is no liability in defamation unless the statement in question can properly be said to reflect on the reputation of the person about whom it is made. Thus it is not difficult to conceive of statements about, say, a person's health which would be distressing but not defamatory of him.

13–145   **Trespass to land and nuisance.** Where there is a trespass to land it is quite likely that one of the claimant's grievances will be the invasion of his privacy and in a suitable case there is no reason why damages for trespass should not reflect that.[405] However, the law of trespass operates only in favour of the person who is the occupier of the premises entered and that has been affirmed to be also the case for the law of nuisance.[406] Further, neither tort is apt to deal with modern means of electronic and optical surveillance, which may be carried on from a great distance. There is no trespass in watching or listening from outside and it is difficult to see how the law of nuisance could be stretched to cover an "interference" of which the occupier was wholly unaware at the time.

---

[403] *Wainwright v Home Office* [2003] UKHL 53; [2004] 2 A.C. 406. The law in the United States took a different course at the end of the 19th century, largely as a result of a famous article: Warren and Brandeis (1890) 4 Harv L.R. 193. But, like the law of defamation there, has been affected by the constitutional protection afforded to freedom of speech by the First Amendment.

[404] The clear exception, but of limited scope, is the Rehabilitation of Offenders Act 1974 (see para.13–051), but while that may prevent the dragging up of old convictions it is no use if what is revealed is a crime for which the claimant was never convicted.

[405] *Morris v Beardmore* [1981] A.C. 446 at 464.

[406] *Hunter v Canary Wharf* [1997] A.C. 655.

Copyright. Another actionable form of interference with proprietary rights that **13–146** may indirectly involve a court in protecting privacy is breach of copyright. In *Williams v Settle*[407] the claimant's father-in-law had been murdered in circumstances that attracted publicity. The defendant, who had taken the photographs at the claimant's wedding two years previously, sold one for publication in the national press. The copyright in the photographs was the claimant's and therefore the court was able to award him heavy damages for the defendant's "scandalous conduct" which was "in total disregard not only of the legal rights of the claimant regarding copyright but of his feelings and his sense of family dignity and pride".[408] Under current copyright law the rights in such a photograph would probably be in the photographer but, ironically, this is one instance in which the law does address the issue of privacy head on, for under s.85 of the Copyright, Designs and Patents Act 1988, breach of which is actionable as a breach of statutory duty, a person who for private and domestic purposes commissions the making of a photograph or film has the right to prevent the issue of copies to the public.

B.   The Human Rights Act 1998 and the Data Protection Act 1998

The right to private and family life in art.8 and its protection generally. **13–147** There is no doubt that the "development" of the law of confidence into a law of misuse of private information[409] has been influenced by the presence of the European Convention on Human Rights but the effect of the Human Rights Act 1998 is also to some extent to create a free-standing right of privacy in English law. Article 8 of the Convention provides:

> "1.   Everyone has the right to respect for his private and family life, his home and his correspondence.
>
> 2.   There shall be no interference by a public authority with the exercise of this right except such as is in accordance with the law and is necessary in a democratic society in the interests of national security, public safety or the economic well-being of the country, for the prevention of disorder or crime, for the protection of health or morals, or for the protection of the rights and freedoms of others."

Section 6 of the Human Rights Act 1998 makes it unlawful for a public authority to act in a way which is incompatible with a Convention right and a breach of s.6 gives rise to such remedy as the court considers just and appropriate, including damages if the court considers them necessary to afford just satisfaction.[410] Accordingly, bodies like the police, central and local government departments and statutory regulatory bodies that contravene art.8 in their dealings with a citizen are now exposed to a claim for damages in the English courts, whether or not there is a parallel common law liability based on misuse of private information, and in their case there may fairly be said to be a wrong of "invasion of privacy", although a warning has been sounded against the assumption that

---

[407] [1960] 1 W.L.R. 1072.
[408] Compare *Bradley v Wingnut Films* [1994] E.M.L.R. 195 (use of C's family gravestone in "comedy horror" film disclosed no cause of action).
[409] See para.13–151.
[410] Section 8.

this would extend to cases where an intrusion which the victim in fact found offensive was the result of sloppiness rather than malice. It is one thing to wander carelessly into the wrong hotel bedroom and another to hide in the wardrobe to take photographs.[411]

13–148   **Article 8 provides protection in circumstances where the common law does not.** The giving effect of art.8 in domestic law in this way may create rights of action that would have been wholly beyond the reach of the common law or they may in practical terms negate the effect of a rule of the common law. Thus, a common law claim for nuisance or trespass by a non-occupier will fail but the art.8 right applies to "everyone". However, a newspaper is clearly not a public authority and is not therefore directly subjected to s.6. Equally, the current view is that the substantive articles of the Convention do not require the common law to be automatically modified so long as they can be given effect by the mechanisms in the Act[412] and *Wainwright v Home Office*[413] is consistent with this in rejecting any "high level" right of privacy.

13–149   Article 8 may require the State to implement measures to protect private and family life from being interfered with by private individuals. While the Convention itself is directed at conduct by the State and is not a code of private law, it may, on an international plane, require the State to take adequate steps to protect the relevant rights from interference by private persons. As the European Court of Human Rights has said in relation to art.8:[414]

> "The essential object of Article 8 is to protect the individual against arbitrary interference by public authorities. There may, however, be positive obligations inherent in an effective 'respect' for family life. Those obligations may involve the adoption of measures designed to secure respect for family life, even in the sphere of relations between individuals, including both the provision of a regulatory framework of adjudicatory and enforcement machinery protecting individual's rights and the implementation, where appropriate, of specific steps."

13–150   **Data Protection Act 1998.** It is not possible here to give any extended account of the amazingly complex Data Protection Act 1998, most of which is of a regulatory nature but which has very significant civil liability consequences. Although it is by no means confined to privacy, the protection of that right has been described as its "central mission".[415] Unlike its previous legislation it is not confined to computerised data but extends to sophisticated manual filing systems which enable information to be readily accessed.[416] Section 13 provides for compensation for damage (and in certain cases for distress) suffered as a result of contravention of the Act. The "data protection principles" which must be complied with by the data controller include that the data must be processed fairly and lawfully, that they be obtained only for the means which the data controller specified, that they be not excessive or retained for longer than is necessary and that they be accurate. There is a very wide-ranging exemption from

---

[411] *Wainwright v Home Office* [2003] UKHL 53; [2004] 2 A.C. 406 at [51] per Lord Hoffmann.
[412] See para.2–010.
[413] [2003] UKHL 53; [2004] 2 A.C. 406
[414] *Glaser v UK* (2001) 33 E.H.R.R. 1 at [63].
[415] *Johnson v Medical Defence Union* [2007] EWCA Civ 262 at [1].
[416] *Durant v Financial Services Authority* [2003] EWCA Civ 1746; [2004] F.S.R. 28.

many requirements of the Act for processing for publication of journalistic material where the data controller reasonably believes that publication would be in the public interest and that compliance with the relevant requirements would be impracticable.[417]

C. Misuse of Private Information

Evolution of the action. The action for misuse of private information derives from the equitable action for breach of confidence. Although the foundational case regarding breach of confidence[418] may fairly be said to have been, in modern terms, one concerned with "privacy", the primary focus of the law of confidence was for many years on commercial (and then governmental) secrets. Even where it was applied to personal information[419] it was typically conceived of in terms of information having been imparted in a relationship that expressly or impliedly created an obligation of confidence. However, it became accepted that an obligation of confidence might arise from wrongful taking of confidential material or from accidentally coming across an obviously confidential document.[420] Thus was born (after a quite short gestation period) a cause of action that has now come to be described as "misuse of private information". As Lord Nicholls put it in the landmark decision in *Campbell v MGN Ltd*:[421]

    13–151

> "This cause of action has now firmly shaken off the limiting constraint of the need for an initial confidential relationship. In doing so it has changed its nature . . . Now the law imposes a 'duty of confidence' whenever a person receives information he knows or ought to know is fairly and reasonably to be regarded as confidential. Even this formulation is awkward. The continuing use of the phrase 'duty of confidence' and the description of the information as 'confidential' is not altogether comfortable. Information about an individual's private life would not, in ordinary usage, be called 'confidential'. The more natural description today is that such information is private. The essence of the tort is better encapsulated now as misuse of private information."

In a later case Lord Nicholls said that we now have, "two distinct causes of action, protecting two different interests: privacy and secret ('confidential') information".[422]

The decision in Campbell v MGN Ltd. The leading case in relation to the action for misuse of private information is that in *Campbell*. The claimant, a famous model, publicly denied having a drug addiction. She was later photographed by the defendant newspaper leaving a Narcotics Anonymous meeting. The defendant printed these photographs in its newspaper and details of the meetings that she attended. The claimant accepted that the defendant was entitled to report the bare fact that she suffered from an addiction to drugs and

    13–152

---

[417] See *Campbell v MGN Ltd* [2002] EWCA Civ 1373; [2003] Q.B. 633 (no appeal to the House of Lords on this aspect).
[418] *Prince Albert v Strange* (1849) 1 De G. & Sm. 652 (catalogue of etchings by Queen Victoria and Prince Albert).
[419] As in *Argyll v Argyll* [1967] Ch. 302 and *Stephens v Avery* [1988] Ch. 449 (sexual behaviour).
[420] *Att Gen v Guardian Newspapers Ltd (No.2)* [1990] A.C. 109 at 281.
[421] [2004] UKHL 22; [2004] 2 A.C. 457 at [14].
[422] *Douglas v Hello! Ltd (No.3)* [2007] UKHL 21; [2008] 1 A.C. 1 at [255].

was receiving treatment, but contended that the publication of the photographs and details of the meetings was actionable. A majority of the House of Lords found for the claimant. The majority held that the photographs and details of the meetings were private information and that the defendant, in publishing them, did more than was necessary to lend credibility to its story that the claimant had misled the public.

13–153   **Elements of the action.** The action for misuse of private information consists of the following elements:[423] (1) the defendant must have disclosed private information; and (2) the defendant's interest in publishing the information must be less important than the claimant's interest in the information remaining private.

13–154   **Private information.** It is difficult to define private information without a degree of circularity: it is information that the "holder" does not intend to be imparted to the public[424] and in respect of which he has a reasonable expectation of privacy. The determination of whether information is private information needs to be made based on all of the circumstances of the case including:[425]

> "the attributes of the claimant, the nature of the activity in which the claimant was engaged, the place at which it was happening, the nature and purpose of the intrusion, the absence of consent and whether it was known or could be inferred, the effect on the claimant and the circumstances in which and the purposes for which the information came into the hands of the publisher."

Information about a person's sexual life[426] or health[427] or financial affairs or (at least where disclosure might expose him to some danger) his address or whereabouts[428] qualifies. It has been said that information stored on a person's mobile phone will generally be regarded as private information.[429] It should not be assumed that the information must relate to something discreditable or embarrassing to the claimant: for example, it has been suggested that a donor to charity might restrain the disclosure of his gifts.[430]

Information that is already in the public domain is not private information but this should not be taken too literally—something may still be private even though it could be traced by extensive and determined research and it has been suggested that publication of improperly obtained photographs could be restrained even though they had been widely circulated.[431] Nor does the fact that certain aspects of the information are public knowledge prevent other aspects of it being private

---

[423] *McKennitt v Ash* [2006] EWCA Civ 1714; [2008] Q.B. 73 at [11].

[424] *Douglas v Hello! Ltd (No.3)* [2005] EWCA Civ 595; [2006] Q.B. 125 at [83].

[425] *Murray v Express Newspapers plc* [2008] EWCA Civ 446; [2009] Ch. 481 at [36].

[426] *Stephens v Avery* [1988] Ch. 449; *Mosley v News Group Newspapers Ltd* [2008] EWHC 1777 (QB); *AMP v Persons Unknown* [2011] EWHC 3454 (TCC); *Ferdinand v MGN Ltd* [2011] EWHC 2454 (QB).

[427] *W v Egdell* [1990] Ch. 359; *Campbell v MGN Ltd* [2004] UKHL 22; [2004] 2 A.C. 457.

[428] *Venables v News Group Newspapers Ltd* [2001] Fam. 430; *Mills v News Group Newspapers Ltd* [2001] E.M.L.R. 41.

[429] *AMP v Persons Unknown* [2011] EWHC 3454 (TCC).

[430] *Att Gen v Guardian Newspapers Ltd (No.2)* [1990] 1 A.C. 109 at 256.

[431] *Douglas v Hello! Ltd (No.3)* [2005] EWCA Civ 595; [2006] Q.B. 125 at [105].

and secret. So, in *Douglas v Hello! Ltd (No.3)*,[432] the upcoming glamorous wedding of the claimants had received widespread coverage in the tabloid press but that did not mean that they were not entitled to control the taking and use of photographs at the event. The fact that a person is a public figure who speaks out on controversial matters does not deprive him of his right to confidentiality over his thoughts on those matters committed to a private journal, even if that has been circulated among associates,[433] still less to his right of privacy in matters unrelated to his public activities.[434] In contrast, a person who ran a "blog" containing criticisms, made from an insider's point of view, of the management of police services or a journalist who wrote under a pseudonym had no reasonable expectation that their identities might not be revealed when discovered by investigation.[435]

Justified disclosure. There are circumstances in which the disclosure of private **13–155** information is justified. Disclosure will be justified when the defendant's interest in publishing the information outweighs the claimant's interest in the information remaining private. Essentially, this issue involves balancing the claimant's art.8 right to privacy with the defendant's art.10 right to freedom of expression. In *Re S (a Child)* Lord Steyn offered the following guidance as to how this balancing exercise should proceed. He isolated four propositions:[436]

> "First, neither article has *as such* precedence over the other. Secondly, where the values under the two articles are in conflict, an intense focus on the comparative importance of the specific rights being claimed in the individual case is necessary. Thirdly, the justifications for interfering with or restricting each right must be taken into account. Finally, the proportionality test must be applied to each. For convenience I will call this the ultimate balancing test. This is how I will approach the present case."

Mosley v News Group Newspapers Ltd[437] illustrates the balancing exercise. In this case the defendant newspaper published photographs of the claimant, who played a leading role in the organisation of motor racing, engaging in sado-masochistic activities. The photographs had been clandestinely taken by one of the women who had been involved in the activities. She used a camera which had been supplied by the newspaper. The newspaper contended that the activities had a "Nazi" or "death camp" theme to them. Had this been true, the defendant might have been justified in disclosing those activities because would have cast doubt on the suitability of the claimant for the organisational role that he was discharging. However, since this theme was not established the disclosure was not justified. It was insufficient that many people might regard his behaviour as immoral. It is:[438]

---

[432] [2007] UKHL 21; [2008] A.C. 1.
[433] *Prince of Wales v Associated Newspapers Ltd* [2006] EWCA Civ 1776; [2008] Ch. 57.
[434] Even well-known people are entitled to some private life: *X v Persons Unknown* [2006] EWHC 2783 (QB); [2007] E.M.L.R. 10.
[435] *Author of a Blog v Times Newspapers Ltd* [2009] EWHC 1359 (QB); *Mahmood v Galloway* [2006] EWHC 1286; [2006] E.M.L.R. 26.
[436] *In re S (A Child) (Identification: Restrictions on Publication)* [2004] UKHL 47; [2005] 1 A.C. 593 at [17] (emphasis in original).
[437] [2008] EWHC 1777 (QB).
[438] [2008] EWHC 1777 (QB) at [127].

"not for the state or for the media to expose sexual conduct which does not involve any significant breach of the criminal law. That is so whether the motive for such intrusion is merely prurience or a moral crusade. It is not for journalists to undermine human rights, or for judges to refuse to enforce them, merely on grounds of taste or moral disapproval."

Disclosure may be justified where it is necessary to correct a false image that the claimant had projected to the public.[439] The claimant in *Campbell* accepted that the defendant newspaper was entitled to publish information that corrected the false image that she had cultivated. Her action succeeded only because the newspaper had gone too far in publishing a photograph and details of her attendance at the drug counselling meetings.

13–156   **Photographs taken in public places.** *Campbell v MGN Ltd* raises a more general issue about photographs taken in public places. Some legal systems give a person, as part of the general "right of personality", the right to control the use of their "image". Hence, while a person may not object to the publication of a photograph in which he is merely an incidental "face in a crowd" he may object if he is the subject of the photograph, even if it is innocuous and entirely non-derogatory.[440] The general thrust of the decision in *Campbell* is against any such right in English law but this may be difficult to reconcile[441] with the decision of the European Court of Human Rights in *von Hannover v Germany*,[442] where it was held that the denial by German law of a remedy to the daughter of the Prince of Monaco in respect of continual publication of innocuous photographs of her taken in public places amounted to a contravention of art.8 of the Convention. The majority judgment in this case certainly reveals a "high minded" attitude to the activities of the media which is very much at odds with our traditions of tabloid journalism.

After *von Hannover* the issue arose here in *Murray v Express Newspapers Ltd*[443] where it was held to be arguable for the purpose of a striking out application that the right to privacy of the claimant, the young son of a famous author, had been infringed by publication in the press of innocuous photographs of him taken in the street.[444] However, the following points should be noted. First, the claimant was a very young child; the court did not go so far as to say that it would necessarily have been wrongful to publish a photograph of his famous mother taken in such circumstances. Secondly, it was not a case of a single photograph taken by random chance but was the product of sustained "paparazzo" interest in the mother.

13–157   **Damages.** Compensatory damages are assessed according to general principles. The purpose of awarding such damages is to acknowledge the wrong committed by the defendant and to repair the injury to feelings, the embarrassment and

---

[439] *Campbell v MGN Ltd* [2004] UKHL 22; [2004] 2 A.C. 457; *Ferdinand v MGN Ltd* [2011] EWHC 2454 (QB) at [65].
[440] See, e.g. *Aubry v Editions Vice-Versa Inc* [1998] 1 S.C.R. 591, under the Civil Code of Québec.
[441] *McKennitt v Ash* [2006] EWCA Civ 1714; [2008] Q.B. 73 at [39].
[442] (2005) 40 E.H.R.R. 1.
[443] [2008] EWCA Civ 446; [2009] Ch. 481.
[444] It still seems to be the law that in the mere *taking* of a photograph is not actionable but its improper use may be.

distress caused. The award in *Mosley v News Group Newspapers Ltd*[445] was £60,000. Since it is difficult to think of more damaging revelations than which occurred in this case the disclosure of which would not be justified as being in the public interest, this must be near the maximum. Exemplary damages are not available.[446]

Injunctive relief. A court may grant an injunction to restrain the wrongful disclosure of personal information, understandably so, since once it is out in the open the harm is done and the award of damages may be a poor consolation prize. Here the law on misuse of private information differs radically from that applicable in defamation cases. It is practically impossible to obtain an interim injunction against defamation if the defendant asserts that he will raise one of the standard defences like truth or privilege.[447] Interim relief is discussed in a later chapter.[448] The fact that it is easier to obtain an interim injunction against misuse of private information than against defamation raises an interesting point. Private information may be defamatory. If faced with threatened disclosure may a claimant say "I deny that what you are about to say is true but whether it is true or not makes no difference because publication would invade my privacy" and proceed for an injunction on the basis of misuse of private information? Indeed, can he go further and, even when the information has been disclosed, sue for damages for misuse of private information rather than defamation and deprive the defendant of the opportunity to prove that what he said was true? Of course it might require a certain hardihood to do that because many people would no doubt conclude that the unwillingness of the claimant to sue for defamation showed that it *was* true; furthermore, a court assessing damages for misuse of private information would surely have to proceed on the basis that the allegation was true and award lower damages. The point has not been squarely decided but the Court of Appeal said in *McKennett v Ash* that the "question in a case of misuse of private information is whether the information is private not whether it is true or false. The truth or falsity of the information is an irrelevant inquiry in deciding whether the information is entitled to be protected".[449] However, in the same case the court said that:[450]

> "[I]f it could be shown that a claim in [misuse of private information] was brought where the nub of the case was a complaint of the falsity of the allegations, and that that was done in order to avoid the rules of the tort of defamation, then objections could be raised in terms of abuse of process. That might be so at the interlocutory stage in an attempt to avoid the rule [about interim injunctions in defamation cases]."

Despite what the court said in this regard it is doubtful whether the defence of abuse of process should be available here. No reasons were given by the court as to why the claimant should not be able to exercise his right to choose which action to bring. It is a familiar feature of the common law that a single act will

13–158

---

[445] [2008] EWHC 1777 (QB).

[446] *Mosley v News Group Newspapers Ltd* [2008] EWHC 1777 (QB).

[447] *Bonnard v Perryman* [1891] 2 Ch. 269.

[448] See para.23–127.

[449] [2006] EWCA Civ 1714; [2008] Q.B. 73 at [86]. See also at [80].

[450] [2006] EWCA Civ 1714; [2008] Q.B. 73 at [79].

generate liability in one action but not in another. This is ordinarily thought to be entirely unproblematic. The difficulty with the court's suggestion regarding abuse of process is that it intimates that where it would be defamatory to publish the private information the case should be seen as a defamation case and subject to the restrictions on liability recognised by the law of defamation. However, more is needed than a mere assertion that the case should be analysed only as one in defamation.

13–159   **Costs.** The costs arrangements in relation to defamation actions, which are discussed above,[451] apply also to privacy actions.

---

[451] See para.13–114.

CHAPTER 14

TRESPASS TO LAND

1. TRESPASS DEFINED

Trespass to land is the name given to that form of trespass which is constituted by unjustifiable interference with the possession of land. Contrary to popular belief trespass is not criminal in the absence of some special statute which makes it so.[1] Since the decision in *Fowler v Lanning*,[2] it may be asked whether tortious liability for trespass to land, like that for trespass to the person, requires proof of intention or at least negligence on the part of the defendant. We must, however, be careful to define what that intention or negligence goes to, for it is clear law that an entry upon another's land is tortious whether or not the entrant knows that he is trespassing.[3] Thus it is no defence that the only reason for his entry was that he had lost his way or even that he genuinely but erroneously believed that the land was his. It follows that the great majority of trespasses to land are, for legal purposes, self-evidently intentional—I intend to enter upon your land if I consciously place myself upon what proves to be your land, even though I neither knew nor could reasonably have known that it was not mine.

14–001

---

[1] There are a number of exceptions to the basic rule: see, e.g. Criminal Law Act 1977 ss.6–9, as modified by the Criminal Justice and Public Order Act 1994; Criminal Justice and Public Order Act 1994 ss.61, 68; Serious Organised Crime and Police Act 2005 s.128.

[2] [1959] 1 Q.B. 426. See para.4–004.

[3] *Conway v George Wimpey & Co Ltd* [1951] 2 K.B. 266 at 273–274; *Jolliffe v Willmett & Co* [1971] 1 All E.R. 478.

14–002 **Liability for involuntary entry.** We are left with those cases where the defendant's entry was involuntary, whether caused by his fault or not. Where he is thrown or pushed on to the land he is not liable for trespass simply because there is no act on his part.[4] As for other situations it is clear that where land adjoining the highway is unintentionally entered, as a result, for example, of a motor accident, the claimant must prove negligence, a proposition established long before *Fowler v Lanning*.[5] In *League against Cruel Sports v Scott*,[6] Park J had to deal with trespass by hounds in pursuit of a stag and he concluded that the law was that the master of the pack was liable if he intended the hounds to enter the claimant's land or if, knowing that there was a real risk that they would enter, their entry was caused by his failure to exercise proper control of them.[7] The burden of proof of either condition is upon the claimant.[8]

14–003 **A tort actionable per se.** Trespass is actionable per se, i.e. whether or not the claimant has suffered any damage.[9] This rule may seem harsh but in earlier times trespass was so likely to lead to a breach of the peace that even trivial deviations on to another person's land were reckoned unlawful. Whether or not there is now greater respect for the law, the theoretical severity of the rules as to land trespass is rarely exploited in practice. An action will not normally be brought for trespass without damage unless the claimant wishes to deter persistent trespassing or there are disputes over boundaries or rights of way.[10]

2. POSSESSION

14–004 **A contextual meaning.** Trespass to land, like the tort of trespass to goods which is considered in a later chapter, consists of interference with possession, and it is necessary to say something here of this concept.[11] Our law has, however, not worked out a consistent theory of possession, and its meaning turns upon the context in which it is used.[12]

14–005 **Physical presence or de facto control.** Mere physical presence on the land or the use[13] or de facto control of it does not necessarily amount to possession sufficient to bring an action of trespass. It is, for example, generally said that a lodger in

---

[4] *Smith v Stone* (1647) Style 65.

[5] See, e.g. *River Wear Commissioners v Adason* (1877) 2 App. Cas. 743.

[6] [1986] Q.B. 240.

[7] Despite the reference to "knowing", this is a negligence standard, though it is not the tort of negligence since no damage is required.

[8] Cf. *Fowler v Lanning* [1959] 1 Q.B. 426, para.4–004.

[9] *Entick v Carrington* (1765) 2 Wils. K.B. 275 at 291, per curiam Blackstone, Comm. iii, 209–210.

[10] In the modern law an action for a declaration might be used to settle disputed rights.

[11] See further Wonnacott, *Possession of Land* (2006); Pollock and Wright, *Essay on Possession in the Common Law*; Harris in *Oxford Essays in Jurisprudence*, p.69.

[12] *Towers & Co Ltd v Gray* [1961] 2 Q.B. 351 at 361 per Lord Parker CJ; *Greenmanor Ltd v Pilford* [2012] EWCA Civ 756 at [27]

[13] A person who has been granted a right to grow crops in another's land has sufficient possession to sue for trespass to land in respect of damage to them: *Monsanto Plc v Tilly* [2000] Env L.R. 313.

another's house does not have possession,[14] nor does a servant occupying a room in his employer's house,[15] since possession lies in another, i.e. the owner of the house, or the employer.

Possession under a lease. On the other hand, a lessor of land gives up possession   **14–006** to his tenant so that the tenant alone can bring trespass during the currency of the lease—even against the lessor unless, of course, the lessor's entry was effected in accordance with the provisions of the lease.[16] Most of the cases on the distinction between a tenant and a licensee (who does not have possession) have arisen in the context of security of tenure under the Rent Acts, but it is clear that the matter is to be determined by the substance of the agreement between the parties rather than by the label which they have chosen to attach to their relationship[17] and the hallmark of a tenancy is the right in the tenant to "exclusive possession".[18] It is, however, possible that in modern conditions there may be rare cases in which a person has sufficient possession to bring trespass against a third party even though he is not a tenant.[19] The lessor cannot bring proceedings for a wrongful entry during the currency of the lease except in so far as it has caused permanent damage to the land, leading to a reduction in the value of his reversion, such as would result from the cutting of trees or the pulling down of buildings.[20]

Relevance of a legal interest in the land. It is not necessary that the claimant   **14–007** should have some lawful estate or interest in the land so that there is no doubt, for example, that a squatter occupying the land without any claim of right may have sufficient possession to bring trespass[21] and, generally speaking, a stranger who enters the land without the squatter's consent cannot rely in his defence upon another person's superior right (the *jus tertii*) unless he can prove that he acted

---

[14] *Allan v Liverpool Overseers* (1874) L.R. 9 Q.B. 180 at 191–192 per Blackburn J, adopted by Davies LJ in *Appah v Parncliffe Investments Ltd* [1964] 1 W.L.R. 1064 at 1069–1970. But see *Mehta v Royal Bank of Scotland* [1999] 3 E.G.L.R. 153, below fn.19.

[15] *White v Bayley* (1861) 10 C.B. (N.S.) 227.

[16] *Lane v Dixon* (1847) 3 C.B. 776. *Aliter* if there was only an oral contract for a lease, unenforceable by virtue of the Law of Property Act 1925 s.40: *Delaney v TP Smith Ltd* [1946] K.B. 393, but a tenant in occupation under an unenforceable contract can certainly bring trespass against a stranger: at 397 per Tucker LJ.

[17] *Street v Mountford* [1985] A.C. 809; *Antoniades v Villers* [1990] A.C. 417; *Aslan v Murphy* [1990] 1 W.L.R. 766.

[18] That is to say, the right to exclude the landlord during the currency of the term except in so far as a right of entry is reserved for a limited purpose, e.g. to repair. See *Radaich v Smith* (1959) 101 C.L.R. 209 at 222 per Windeyer J, adopted in *Street v Mountford* [1985] A.C. 809.

[19] See *Clerk and Lindsell on Torts*, 20th edn (2013), para.19–21. *Mehta v Royal Bank of Scotland* [1999] 3 E.G.L.R. 153 seems to be an example (very long term occupancy of hotel room).

[20] *Ward v Macaulay* (1791) 4 T.R. 489; *Mayfair Property Co v Johnson* [1894] 1 Ch. 508; *Jones v Llanrwst UDC* [1911] 1 Ch. 393.

[21] There is no reason why this proposition should be affected by the upheavals in the law of acquisition of title to registered land by adverse possession. The ECHR has held that the law of adverse possession relating to registered land before the Land Registration Act 2002 contravenes art.1 of the First Protocol to the Convention: *JA Pye (Oxford) Ltd v UK* (2006) 43 E.H.R.R. 3. Under the 2002 Act there is an entirely new regime which requires the squatter to give formal notice of his wish to apply to be registered as the proprietor after 10 years adverse possession: see *Baxter v Mannion* [2011] EWCA Civ 120; [2011] 1 W.L.R. 1594; *Swan Housing Association Ltd v Gill* [2012] EWHC 3129 (QB); [2013] 1 W.L.R. 1253.

with that person's authority.[22] This is not to say that legal title is irrelevant, for where the facts leave it uncertain which of several competing claimants has possession it is in him who can prove title, i.e. who can prove that he has the right to possess.[23] More generally, "in the absence of evidence to the contrary, the owner of land with the paper title is deemed to be in possession of the land".[24]

What will amount to possession varies according to the nature of the property, so that possession of a flat with a front door which can be locked is obviously different from possession of part of an unfenced moor or hillside.[25] Possession once acquired is not, however, determined by sending the defendant a letter demanding delivery-up of the land.[26] Some estate or interest in the land may also lead the court to find possession in the claimant in other circumstances. For example, it is probably still the law that a spouse who is merely occupying a matrimonial home along with the other spouse does not have possession so as to maintain trespass,[27] but a spouse who has a share in the ownership (as would normally be the case today) would certainly have it.

14–008 **Continuous physical control not necessary.** Possession may obviously extend to things which are beyond a person's immediate physical control. I do not lose possession of my house and its contents when I leave them to go to the office or even to go away on holiday.

14–009 **Immediate right to possess: trespass by relation.** The immediate right to possess, sometimes also known as constructive possession,[28] signifies the lawful right to retain possession when one has it or to acquire it when one has not. Without possession it is not sufficient to support an action of trespass[29] but, owing to the willingness of the courts to extend the superior protection afforded by the older law to possession as distinct from ownership, it has for long been the law that once a person entitled to immediate possession actually enters upon the land and so acquires possession, he is deemed to have been in possession from the moment that his right to it accrued.[30] This fiction, known as trespass by relation, has the result that he can sue for acts of trespass committed while he was actually out of possession and it also provides the foundation for the claim in respect of "mesne profits", that is, the claim for the damage suffered by a person as a result of having been kept out of the possession of his land.[31]

---

[22] *Chambers v Donaldson* (1809) 11 East 65; *Nicholls v Ely Beet Sugar Factory* [1931] 2 Ch. 84. As to the jus tertii in relation to trespass to goods, see para.18–033.

[23] *Jones v Chapman* (1849) 2 Exch. 803 at 821 per Maule J.

[24] *Powell v McFarlane* (1977) 38 P & C.R. 452 at 470 per Slade J; *Star Energy Weald Basin Ltd v Bocardo SA* [2010] UKSC 35; [2011] 1 A.C. 380, at [30] (where the claimant, as owner of the surface, had done nothing to reduce the subsoil to its actual possession).

[25] *Simpson v Fergus* (1999) 79 P. & C.R. 398; *Ocean Estates Ltd v Pinder* [1969] 2 A.C. 19.

[26] *Mount Carmel Investments Ltd v Peter Thurlow Ltd* [1988] 1 W.L.R. 1078.

[27] *Hunter v Canary Wharf Ltd* [1997] A.C. 655, para.15–034 (a case of nuisance but, it is thought, still in point).

[28] For an explanation of this term, see *Alicia Hosiery Ltd v Brown Shipley & Co Ltd* [1970] 1 Q.B. 195 at 207 per Donaldson J.

[29] It is, however, sufficient for an action of conversion and is explained more fully in connection with that tort, para.18–027.

[30] See *Dunlop v Macedo* (1891) 8 T.L.R. 43.

[31] The action for mesne profits is explained in para.14–034.

3. INTERFERENCE

Must be direct and immediate. Interference with the possession of land **14–010** sufficient to amount to trespass may occur in many ways. The most obvious example is unauthorised walking upon it or going into the buildings upon it, but it is equally trespass if I throw things on to your land[32] or allow my cattle to stray on to it from my land, and even if I do no more than place my ladder against your wall.[33] If you have given me permission to enter your land and I act in excess of the permission or remain on your land after it has expired, then, again, I am a trespasser.[34] The one restriction is that for trespass the injury must be direct and immediate. If it is indirect or consequential, there may well be a remedy (usually for nuisance or for negligence), but whatever it is it will not be trespass. If I plant a tree on your land, that is trespass, but if the roots or branches of a tree on my land project into or over your land, that is a nuisance.[35]

A. Trespass on Highway

It is obvious that a person who uses a highway for the purpose of travelling from **14–011** one place to another commits no trespass against anyone, but at one time it was held that the right of user of the highway was confined to use for passage and matters incidental thereto, like resting. Otherwise there was a trespass against the owner of the subsoil.[36] However, in *Director of Public Prosecutions v Jones*[37] (where the civil law issue arose in the context of a charge of taking part in a trespassory assembly under the Public Order Act 1986) the majority of the House of Lords held that it was not a trespass to participate in a peaceful assembly on the highway so long as it was reasonable and caused no obstruction. Lord Irvine LC went so far as to say that any reasonable use of the highway, not involving nuisance or obstruction, was lawful. However, he did not seem to regard as wrongly decided earlier cases in which it had been held to be trespass to use the highway to disrupt shooting[38] or to gain information about racehorse trials[39] on

---

[32] For a modern, power-assisted example, see *Rigby v CC Northamptonshire* [1985] 1 W.L.R. 1242. Discharging water into the flowing watercourse of another is trespass: *British Waterways Board v Severn Trent Water Ltd* [2001] EWCA Civ 276; [2001] 1 W.L.R. 613 at [38].

[33] *Westripp v Baldock* [1938] 2 All E.R. 779 affirmed [1939] 1 All E.R. 279; *Home Brewery Co Ltd v William Davis & Co (Leicester) Ltd* [1987] Q.B. 339.

[34] *Hillen v ICI (Alkali) Ltd* [1936] A.C. 65; *Canadian Pacific Ry v Gaud* [1949] 2 K.B. 239 at 249 per Cohen LJ, at 254–255 per Singleton LJ; but a lessee holding over after the termination of his lease is no trespasser, for trespass can only be committed against the person in present possession of the land: *Hey v Moorhouse* (1839) 6 Bing. N.C. 52. Cf. *Minister of Health v Bellotti* [1944] K.B. 298 (licensee holding over after termination of licence and after lapse of reasonable time, becomes a trespasser).

[35] *Smith v Giddy* [1904] 2 K.B. 448, 451; *Davey v Harrow Corp* [1958] 1 Q.B. 60.

[36] At common law this is the person whose land abuts upon the highway. Cf. *Tithe Redemption Commission v Runcorn UDC* [1954] Ch. 383, and Highways Act 1980 ss.263–265. Where the top surface is vested in a highway authority, there would seem no reason why that authority could not bring proceedings for trespass: see the comment of Collins LJ in *DPP v Jones* [1998] Q.B. 563 on the view of Lord Denning MR in *Hubbard v Pitt* [1976] Q.B. 142.

[37] [1999] A.C. 240.

[38] *Harrison v Duke of Rutland* [1893] 1 Q.B. 142.

[39] *Hickman v Maisey* [1900] 1 Q.B. 752.

land crossed by the highway. As in all cases of trespass, however, only the person having possession can complain of it and, accordingly, the fact that a person on the highway is a trespasser upon it does not relieve lawful users of the highway of any duty of care they may owe to him in accordance with the ordinary law of negligence.[40]

B. Trespass to Subsoil

14–012 Any intrusion upon the subsoil is just as much a trespass as entry upon the surface, and subsoil and surface may be possessed by different persons. If A is in possession of the surface and B of the subsoil, and I walk upon the land, that is a trespass against A, but not against B. If I dig holes vertically in the land, that is a trespass against both A and B. If I bore a tunnel from my land into B's subsoil, that is a trespass against B only.[41] Even if the landowner has been deprived of ownership of minerals by statute (as is the case here with oil) intrusions beneath the surface, such as pipelines, in order to obtain them still amount to trespass, though in such a case the quantum of damages may be limited.[42]

C. Interference with Airspace

14–013 Despite earlier doubts[43] it is now clear that invasion of the air space above a person's land can amount to trespass. In *Kelsen v Imperial Tobacco Co*[44] McNair J held that an advertising sign erected by the defendants on their own property, which projected into the airspace above the claimant's shop, created a trespass.[45] The issue arises not infrequently as a result of the operation of tower cranes on building sites, which swing over adjoining land. There is no doubt that this amounts to trespass[46] and the claimant will normally be entitled to an injunction[47] even though this state of the law allows him to take a "dog in the manger" attitude[48] and force the defendant to pay him a sum in excess of any damage he has suffered.[49]

---

[40] *Farrugia v GW Ry* [1947] 2 All E.R. 565.

[41] *Cox v Glue* (1848) 5 C.B. 533.

[42] *Star Energy Weald Basin Ltd* v *Bocardo SA* [2010] UKSC 35; [2011] 1 A.C. 380: "There must obviously be some stopping point, as one reaches the point at which physical features such as pressure and temperature render the concept of the strata belonging to anybody so absurd as to be not worth arguing about", per Lord Hope (at [27]) ("stopping point" not reached at a depth of 2900 feet).

[43] *Pickering v Rudd* (1815) 4 Camp. 219 at 220–221 per Lord Ellenborough.

[44] [1957] 2 Q.B. 334.

[45] See also *Stadium Capital Holdings v St Marylebone Properties Company Plc* [2010] EWCA Civ 952.

[46] *Woollerton & Wilson Ltd v Richard Costain Ltd* [1970] 1 W.L.R. 411; *Anchor Brewhouse Developments v Berkley House (Docklands Developments)* (1987) 284 E.G. 625.

[47] In the *Woollerton & Wilson* case the injunction was suspended for long enough to allow the defendant to complete the works but this cannot be supported: *Jaggard v Sawyer* [1995] 1 W.L.R. 269.

[48] *Anchor Brewhouse Developments v Berkley House (Docklands Developments)* (1987) 284 E.G. 625 at 633.

[49] Entry on neighbouring land to effect repairs may now be justified: para.14–026.

Extent of the landowner's rights. Although an intrusion into air space at a   **14–014**
relatively low height constitutes trespass,[50] it is now settled that the landowner's
rights in airspace extend only to such height as is necessary for the ordinary use
and enjoyment of the land and structures on it,[51] so that the flight of an aircraft
"several hundred feet" above a house is not a trespass at common law;[52] but if an
aircraft, or anything from it, falls upon the land or comes into contact with a
structure on it, that might be a trespass, no matter the height from which it fell.[53]

Quite apart from the position at common law, it is provided by statute that civil
aircraft which fly at a reasonable height (having regard to wind, weather and all
the circumstances of the case) do not commit trespass.[54] A landowner is not,
however, without protection from persistent aerial surveillance from a height
outside his zone of user, for such conduct may constitute a nuisance.[55] The Civil
Aviation Act also provides that if material loss or damage[56] is caused to any
person or property by, or by a person in, or an article or person falling from an
aircraft while in flight, taking off[57] or landing, then, unless the loss or damage
was caused or contributed to by the negligence of the person by whom it was
suffered, damages are recoverable without proof of negligence or intention or
other cause of action as if the loss or damage had been caused by the wilful act,
neglect, or default of the owner of the aircraft.[58]

D.   Continuing Trespass

Trespass, whether by way of personal entry or by placing things on the claimant's   **14–015**
land, may be "continuing" and give rise to actions from day-to-day so long as it
lasts. In *Holmes v Wilson*,[59] highway authorities supported a road by wrongfully
building buttresses on the claimant's land, and they paid full compensation in an
action for trespass. They were nevertheless held liable in a further action for
trespass, because they had not removed the buttresses. Nor does a transfer of the
land by the injured party prevent the transferee from suing the defendant for
continuing trespass.[60]

---

[50] *Liaquat v Majid* [2005] EWHC 1305 (QB); 26 E.G. 130 (CS) (75cm projection 4.5m above
ground).
[51] *Didow v Alberta Power* [1988] 5 W.W.R. 606 (power lines 50 feet up within zone of user).
[52] *Bernstein v Skyviews & General Ltd* [1978] Q.B. 479.
[53] Unless the contact were without negligence. In view of the Civil Aviation Act 1982 s.76(2), the
matter is largely academic in relation to civil aircraft: see below.
[54] Civil Aviation Act 1982 s.76(1). It is conceivable that s.76 confers a wider exemption than the
common law and might, in certain circumstances, justify an entry even into the zone of normal user.
[55] Or harassment under the Protection from Harassment Act 1997.
[56] Which includes psychiatric trauma, subject to the usual control mechanisms applicable to a claim
for negligence in respect of such harm: *Glen v Korean Airlines Co Ltd* [2003] EWHC 643 (QB);
[2003] Q.B. 1386.
[57] This expression appears to be confined to the period after the pilot has come to the take-off
position: *Blankley v Godley* [1952] 1 All E.R. 436n.
[58] Section 76(2).
[59] (1839) 10 A. & E. 50.
[60] *Hudson v Nicholson* (1839) 5 M. & W. 437 followed in *Konskier v Goodman Ltd* [1928] 1 K.B.
421.

14–016 **Trespass by omission.** At one time it may have been the law that trespass did not lie for omission to remove something from the land which was lawfully there to begin with,[61] although if the thing did damage to the land after it ought to have been removed an action on the case would lie. However, more modern authority imposes liability for trespass[62] and there is a close analogy with the situation where a visitor's stay exceeds the duration of his licence. However, there is no trespass if the defendant merely omits to restore land to the same condition (apart from removing anything which he has put on it) in which he found it, for example if he fails to fill up a pit which he has dug on his neighbour's land. He is, of course, liable in trespass for the original digging (but not for continuing trespass in allowing it to remain there) and, no doubt, for negligence if anyone falls into the pit.[63]

4. DEFENCES

A. Licence

14–017 For the purposes of trespass, the best definition of licence is that given by Sir Frederick Pollock. A licence is "that consent which, without passing any interest in the property to which it relates, merely prevents the acts for which consent is given from being wrongful".[64] In the law of real property it is important to distinguish a licence from interests in land like leases, easements or profits à prendre, existing at law. These confer rights in rem, i.e. rights which avail against persons generally, including, of course, the lessor or grantor himself, whereas a licence normally gives only a right in personam against the licensor; but the distinction seems to have little importance so far as defences to trespass are concerned. A person is not a trespasser if he is on land with the permission, express or implied,[65] of the possessor, and that is all that matters for present purposes.[66] Whether that permission is given is a matter for the possessor, even if the public generally have free access to the property (such as a shopping mall) and whether he has a good reason for exclusion or not.[67] Where a landowner refuses to allow access to such premises to demonstrate or collect signatures for a petition the provisions of the European Convention on Human Rights on freedom

---

[61] *Shapcott v Mugford* (1696) 1 Ld. Raym. 187 at 188: trespass *vi et armis* does not apply to non-feasance.

[62] *Konskier v Goodman Ltd* [1928] 1 K.B. 421. Cf. *Penarth Dock Co v Pounds* [1963] 1 Lloyd's Rep. 359 (breach of contract).

[63] *Clegg v Dearden* (1848) 12 Q.B. 576 at 601; but a tenant who removes fixtures and does not make good may be liable for waste. This is a tort, but not one of much importance, since the landlord will normally rely on covenants in the lease: *Mancetter Developments Ltd v Garmanson Ltd* [1986] Q.B. 1212.

[64] *Pollock's Law of Torts*, 15th edn (1951), p.284. It necessarily follows that the acts of the licensee must not exceed the terms of the licence: *Seeff v Ho* [2011] EWCA Civ 186.

[65] See *Robson v Hallett* [1967] 2 Q.B. 939 at 950–951 per Lord Parker CJ; at 953–954 per Diplock LJ.

[66] *Armstrong v Sheppard and Short Ltd* [1959] 2 Q.B. 384 at 399 per Lord Evershed MR.

[67] Exclusion might of course amount to a statutory wrong under anti-discrimination legislation.

of expression or association are not brought into play, at least where there is some
other means of bringing the subject to public attention.[68]

Revocable licences. A bare licence, i.e. one granted otherwise than for valuable   **14–018**
consideration, may be revoked at any time,[69] and so may many contractual
licences, even though revocation may involve the licensor in liability for breach
of contract.[70] After revocation the licensee becomes a trespasser, but he must be
allowed a reasonable time in which to leave and to remove his goods.[71]

Irrevocable licences. Some contractual licences are, however, irrevocable   **14–019**
because revocation in breach of contract would be prevented by the grant of an
equitable remedy to the licensee. A licence coupled with an interest is irrevocable
because, although the licence itself—the bare permission to enter—is only a right
in personam, it confers a right in rem to something when you have entered:[72]

> "A licence to hunt in a man's park and carry away the deer killed to his own use to cut down a
> tree in a man's ground, and to carry it away the next day to his own use, are licences as to the
> acts of hunting and cutting down the tree, but as to the carrying away of the deer killed and the
> tree cut down, they are grants."

Until the tree or deer is carried away the licence is irrevocable.[73]

Uncertain cases. A contractual licence may also be irrevocable even if it is not   **14–020**
coupled with an interest, but the circumstances in which this will be so are not
finally settled. It seems, however, that the following conclusion is warranted by
the cases.[74] Whether a contractual licence is revocable is a question of
construction of the contract in the light of relevant and admissible circumstances.[75] It will be irrevocable if such is the intention of the parties, and it may
be inferred from the terms of the contract, the character of the transaction, and the
attendant circumstances that the licence is intended to endure for a definite or
ascertainable period. Where it is granted for a limited period and for a definite

---

[68] *Appleby v UK* (2003) 37 E.H.R.R. 38.
[69] On a licence granted by one co-occupier and revoked by another, see *Robson-Paul v Farrugia*
(1969) 20 CCR 820.
[70] *Thompson v Park* [1944] K.B. 408. Cf. *Kerrison v Smith* [1897] 2 Q.B. 445; *King v David Allen &
Sons Ltd* [1916] 2 A.C. 54. In *Stokes v Brent LBC* [2009] EWHC 1426 (QB) C was unable to
challenge the revocation of the licence granted to her by the Council on the basis of a violation of art.8
of the ECHR.
[71] *Cornish v Stubbs* (1870) L.R. 5 C.P. 334; *Canadian Pacific Ry v The King* [1931] A.C. 414;
Minister of Health v Bellotti [1944] K.B. 289; *Robson v Hallett* [1967] 2 Q.B. 939.
[72] *Thomas v Sorrell* (1672) Vaughan 330 at 351 per Vaughan CJ.
[73] *Wood v Leadbitter* (1845) 13 M. & W. 838 at 844–845; *Jones & Sons Ltd v Tankerville* [1909] 2
Ch. 440 at 442 per Parker J. Cf. *Frank Warr & Co Ltd v LCC* [1904] 1 K.B. 713; *Clore v Theatrical
Properties Ltd* [1936] 3 All E.R. 483.
[74] See especially *Hurst v Picture Theatres Ltd* [1915] 1 K.B. 1; *Winter Garden Theatre (London) Ltd
v Millennium Productions Ltd* [1948] A.C. 173; *Bendall v McWhirter* [1952] 2 Q.B. 466; *Hounslow v
Twickenham Garden Developments Ltd* [1971] Ch. 233. Cf. *Wood v Leadbitter* (1845) 13 M. & W.
838.
[75] *Winter Garden Theatre (London) Ltd v Millennium Productions Ltd* [1946] 1 All E.R. 678 at 680
per Lord Greene MR; *Re Spenborough UDC's Agreement* [1968] Ch. 139. Cf. *Winter Garden case*
[1948] A.C. 173 at 193, per Lord Porter; Wade 64 L.Q.R. 57 at 69.

purpose, it will be irrevocable until the accomplishment of the purpose.[76] If the licensee is prepared to observe the terms of the contract the licensor may be restrained by injunction from revoking the licence[77] and even where there is no opportunity to seek such a remedy (for example, where the claimant is ejected from the cinema) the equitable right which the licensee has destroys the defence of "trespasser" which the licensor would otherwise plead to an action for assault.[78]

14–021 **Executed licence.** If a licence has been executed, it cannot be revoked in the sense that the licensee can be compelled to undo what he has lawfully done. If I allow you to post bills on my hoarding, I can cancel my permission, but I cannot force you to remove bills that you have already stuck there. So in *Liggins v Inge*[79] where an oral licence had been given to lower a riverbank and make a weir above the licensor's mill, it was held that the licensor could not sue the licensee for continuing the weir which the latter had erected; but the rule that an executed licence is irrevocable applies only where the licence can be construed as authorising the doing of exactly what has been done. It does not apply where there has been mere acquiescence in something which was never authorised before it was done.[80] Nor does it apply if its application would amount to the creation of an easement in favour of the licensee. An easement cannot be granted by parol and therefore, after the licence has been revoked, the claimant is prima facie entitled to an injunction restraining the continuation of the trespass.[81]

14–022 **Public law restrictions.** The power of a public body to revoke a licence to enter its premises may be restricted by the requirements of public law, for example by requiring it to hear the licensee first,[82] but there is no basis for restricting the power of revocation of occupiers of shopping malls, public utility showrooms or the like on the ground that they are "quasi-public" places.[83]

---

[76] *Winter Garden Theatre (London) Ltd v Millennium Productions Ltd* [1948] A.C. 173 per Lord Porter; at 189 per Lord Simon.

[77] *Winter Garden Theatre (London) Ltd v Millennium Productions Ltd* [1946] 1 All E.R. 678 at 685 per Lord Greene MR; *Bendall v McWhirter* [1952] 2 Q.B. 466 at 478–483 per Denning LJ. In a proper case, revocation of the licence may be restrained even though performance has not yet commenced: *Verrall v Great Yarmouth BC* [1981] Q.B. 202.

[78] Wade 64 L.Q.R. 57, 76; *Errington v Errington* [1952] 1 K.B. 290 at 297–299 and *Bendall v McWhirter* [1952] 2 Q.B. 466 at 479–483 per Denning LJ. *Bendall v McWhirter* was overruled by *National Provincial Bank Ltd v Ainsworth* [1965] A.C. 1175 but, it is submitted, without affecting the statements in the text.

[79] (1831) 3 Bing. 683; 131 E.R. 263; *Davies v Marshall* (1861) 10 C.B.(N.S.) 697. See Wade 64 L.Q.R. 57, pp.68–69.

[80] *Canadian Pacific Ry v The King* [1931] A.C. 414 at 428–429 per Lord Russell.

[81] *Armstrong v Sheppard & Short Ltd* [1959] 2 Q.B. 384. The right to an injunction is not unqualified and an injunction may be refused on the ground that the injury is trivial.

[82] *Wandsworth LBC v A* [2000] 1 W.L.R. 1246 (parent's licence to enter child's school).

[83] *CIN Properties Ltd v Rawlins* [1995] E.G.L.R. 30; *Porter v MPC* Unreported October 20, 1999 CA.

B. Justification by Law

Acts which would otherwise be trespasses, whether to land, goods or the person, are frequently prevented from being so by the existence of some justification provided by the law. The majority of such justifications are provided by statute.   **14–023**

Entry by law officers. Most important are the innumerable instances in which officers of the law are authorised to enter land, to take goods or to arrest or restrain a person, but these belong more to public than to private law and only one or two illustrations can be given here. The police have no general common law power to enter private premises without consent or warrant but their most important statutory powers are those conferred by the Police and Criminal Evidence Act 1984. Under s.17[84] a constable may enter[85] and search premises (if need be, by force) for the purpose of arresting a person for an indictable offence and for various other purposes (including those of saving life or limb or preventing serious damage to the property)[86] and under s.18 there is power to enter premises after an arrest for an indictable offence and search for evidence of that offence or connected or similar offences.[87] However, when a constable is lawfully on the premises (for example, with the consent of the occupier or, it seems, pursuant to a lawful entry under s.18) he may seize anything which he reasonably believes to be evidence of any offence provided he has reasonable grounds to believe it would otherwise be concealed, destroyed, etc. A police officer also has a power of entry to premises to prevent a breach of the peace.[88]   **14–024**

Entry by private persons in furtherance of the law. Nor is it only officers of the law who may be thus empowered. A private person may in certain circumstances arrest a criminal, and it is no trespass if he breaks into the house of another person in order to prevent him from murdering his wife,[89] or probably from committing other serious offences.[90]   **14–025**

Entry under statute: other examples. In addition to the powers granted to law officers, other forms of entry may be authorised by statute and so not amount to trespass. For example, a person entering land in pursuance of arrangements made for the public to have access to open country is not a trespasser so long as he does no damage and complies with the specified restrictions.[91] Under the Access to Neighbouring Land Act 1992 the court may make an order allowing access to land for the purpose of carrying out works which are reasonably necessary for the preservation of adjoining land and which cannot be carried out, or would be   **14–026**

---

[84] For search warrants, see ss.8–16.
[85] The officer must, unless the circumstances make it impracticable or undesirable, give the occupier the reason for exercising the power of entry: *O'Loughlin v CC Essex* [1998] 1 W.L.R. 364. For emergency powers of entry of fire officers see s.44 of the Fire and Rescue Services Act 2004.
[86] For the power to enter in pursuit of persons "unlawfully at large" see the Prisoners (Return to Custody) Act 1995.
[87] Only premises occupied by the arrested person: *Khan v MPC* [2008] EWCA Civ 723; [2008] Po L.R. 112 (arrestee giving false address). See also s.32, as amended.
[88] *Thomas v Sawkins* [1935] 2 K.B. 249.
[89] *Handcock v Baker* (1800) 2 Bos. & P. 260.
[90] *Handcock v Baker* (1800) 2 Bos. 6 P. 260 at 265, per Chambre J. Such cases would now fall under the Criminal Law Act 1967 s.3.
[91] Countryside and Rights of Way Act 2000 s.2.

substantially more difficult to carry out, without entry upon the land. It is not, however, to make the order if it would cause unreasonable interference with the enjoyment of the land sought to be entered or unreasonable hardship. The Act does not permit entry for development or improvement as such but does permit entry for the purpose of work of, "alteration, adjustment or improvement [or] demolition if merely incidental to the work necessary for preservation".[92] More generally, the scope of the entry authorised by the statute concerned is a question of its proper construction.[93]

14–027 **Abuse of authority: trespass ab initio.** Where an entry upon land or other prima facie trespass is justified by the authority of the law itself, then, according to an ancient doctrine of the common law, if the actor abuses his authority he becomes a trespasser ab initio and his act is reckoned as unlawful from the very beginning, however innocent his conduct may have been up to the moment of the abuse.[94] The doctrine applies only if the authority is that of the law,[95] not that of the other party concerned,[96] and the abuse must be by a positive act, not a mere omission.[97] The explanations of these restrictions on the doctrine are historical,[98] but they show that its purpose, derived from its origin in the law of distress, was to provide protection against abuses of authority. Seen in this light it would seem to be unduly optimistic to suppose that the doctrine has outlived its usefulness,[99] even given the modern limitation that partial abuse of an authority does not render everything done under it unlawful. For example, in *Elias v Pasmore*[100] police had lawfully entered the claimant's premises in order to arrest a man, and while there they seized a number of documents, some of them unlawfully. It was held that this did not render their original entry a trespass. However, in *Chic Fashions (West Wales) Ltd v Jones*[101] though no point involving trespass ab initio was in fact in issue, the three members of the Court of Appeal criticised the doctrine as offending against the principle that subsequent events cannot render unlawful an act which was lawful when it was done. This principle is, in general, a sound one, but it should not be over-stressed. Not only may subsequent events illuminate the intent with which an act was originally done and thus assist in

---

[92] See s.1(5). See also the Party Wall, etc., Act 1996.

[93] *British Waterways Board v Severn Trent Water Ltd* [2001] EWCA Civ 276; [2001] 1 W.L.R. 613 (the power to lay a pipe did not extend to an implied power to discharge its contents). See also *Star Energy Weald Basin Ltd v Bocardo SA* [2010] UKSC 35; [2011] 1 A.C. 380, on the construction of s.10(3) of the Petroleum (Production) Act 1934 (re-enacted as s.9(2) of the Petroleum Act 1998). Cf. the defence of statutory authority in nuisance: para.15–063.

[94] *Six Carpenters' Case* (1610) 8 Co. Rep. 146a.

[95] Where entry takes place by virtue of an access order under the Access to Neighbouring Land Act 1992 the doctrine is excluded by s.3(6) of the Act.

[96] *Delta Holdings Ltd v Magrum* (1975) 59 D.L.R. (3d) 126.

[97] *Delta Holdings Ltd v Magrum* (1975) 59 D.L.R. (3d) 126.

[98] Holdsworth, *H.E.L.*, vii, pp.499–501.

[99] Pace the Court of Appeal in *Chic Fashions (West Wales) Ltd v Jones* [1968] 2 Q.B. 299.

[100] [1934] 2 K.B. 164; *Harvey v Pocock* (1843) 11 M. & W. 740; *Canadian Pacific Wine Co Ltd v Tuley* [1921] 2 A.C. 417.

[101] [1968] 2 Q.B. 299.

determining its lawfulness or unlawfulness,[102] but there are, and should continue to be, cases in which, in effect, the law withholds judgment on the lawfulness of an act for a time and allows it to depend upon subsequent events.[103] The doctrine of trespass ab initio enables this to be done in the important area of the protection of one's person, goods and land against abuse of official power.[104]

5.   REMEDIES

The action for trespass, besides being used to remedy trespass as a pure tort, has also some varieties which are employed for the recovery of land and the profits thereof.

14–028

A.   Re-entry

The remedies for trespass as a pure tort[105] need no special mention except the right of re-entry. The person entitled to possession can enter or re-enter the premises, but the Criminal Law Act 1977 makes it an offence punishable with imprisonment for anyone (other than a displaced residential occupier) to use or threaten violence for the purposes of securing entry to any premises occupied by another.[106] This replaces earlier criminal legislation in a series of Forcible Entry Acts, beginning in 1381. However, in *Hemmings v Stoke Poges Golf Club*[107] the Court of Appeal held that whatever might be his criminal liability under the Statutes of Forcible Entry, a landowner was not civilly liable if he used no more force than necessary to remove the other party and his property. It is submitted that the law remains the same under the Criminal Law Act[108] and it has been said in the Supreme Court that "self-help is a remedy still available, in principle, to a landowner against trespassers (other than former residential tenants)",[109] even if the risk of criminal liability has curtailed its utility against an uncooperative trespasser.[110]

14–029

---

[102] This was one of the explanations of the doctrine of trespass ab initio itself given by Coke: 8 Co. Rep. 146b. Winfield ridiculed it (see the 8th edn of this book, p.346) but even though it contains an element of fiction, it is submitted that it does have some merit.

[103] *Southam v Smout* [1964] 1 Q.B. 308 provides one example, and there are others also. The power of a private person to arrest on reasonable suspicion of an offence exists only if the offence suspected has actually been committed (Police and Criminal Evidence Act 1984 s.24A), and this cannot be known until further investigations have been carried out.

[104] Lord Denning MR, a member of the court in *Chic Fashions*, subsequently referred to the doctrine with approval in *Cinnamond v British Airports Authority* [1980] 1 W.L.R. 582.

[105] As to damages in respect of land, see para.23-117.

[106] The proposition in the text is a bare summary of a complex provision (the 1977 Act was amended by the Criminal Justice and Public Order Act 1994).

[107] [1920] 1 K.B. 720, where the earlier authorities are considered.

[108] See *Clerk and Lindsell on Torts*, 20th edn (2013), para.30–13. This was the view of Clarke LJ in *Ropaigealach v Barclays Bank Plc* [2000] 1 Q.B. 263.

[109] *Secretary of State for Environment etc v Meier* [2009] UKSC 11; [2009] 1 W.L.R. 2780 at [66] per Lord Neuberger.

[110] *Malik v Fassenfelt* [2013] EWCA Civ 798; [2013] 28 E.G. 84 (CS) at [25].

B. Action for the Recovery of Land

14–030   **Origin and development.** By the action of ejectment, or, as it now should be called, the action for the recovery of land, a person dispossessed of land can recover it specifically. The story of this remedy is an old one and neatly exemplifies the use of fictions in the development of a legal system. It was originally a species of the action for trespass to land, and was invented for the benefit of the leaseholder, to whom the remedies of the freeholder were denied because he had mere "possession" of the land and not that blessed and superior "seisin" which gave the freeholder very adequate, if excessively dilatory, protection in the shape of the real actions. Then, by a notable paradox, the action of ejectment was seen to be so quick and efficient compared to the ponderous progress of the real actions that the freeholder adopted it by a series of fictions. If, for example, Smith, a freeholder, were seeking to recover the land from Brown, he was allowed to pretend that he had leased the land to John Doe, an imaginary person, and that John Doe had been ejected by another non-existent person, Richard Roe (the "casual ejector"). Then Smith began his action with Doe as the nominal claimant against Roe as the nominal defendant, but he first served on Brown a notice signed by "your loving friend, Roe", in which Roe informed Brown that Roe claimed no interest in the land and advised Brown to defend the action. The fictitious parties then disappeared and the stage was cleared for the proceedings between Smith and Brown. The title of the action was "John Doe on the Demise [i.e. lease] of Smith v Brown", or, more briefly, "Doe d. Smith v Brown". It was useless for Brown to protest against these fictions: he was not allowed to defend the action unless he acquiesced in them.[111] The remarkable result was that the question of ownership of land was fought under the guise of an action of trespass.

14–031   **Summary procedure now available.** These fictions have been long abolished,[112] and an action for the recovery of land differs in no formal respect from any other action. A special summary procedure has, however, been devised to enable a claimant to obtain an order for possession against persons in occupation of his land if they entered or remained there without his licence or consent, whether or not he is able to identify all, or even any, of those persons.[113]

---

[111] Sometimes the fictitious names were more descriptive: e.g. *Fairclaim v Shamtitle* (1762) 3 Burr. 1290.

[112] By the Common Law Procedure Act 1852. For the history of the matter, see Holdsworth, *HEL*, iii, pp.213–217 vii, pp.4–23. The best account is in Maitland, *Equity: A Course of Lectures*, pp.352–355 reprinted separately as *Forms of Action*, pp.56–59.

[113] CPR Pt 55, replacing the former RSC Ord.113 and CCR Ord.24. The court's jurisdiction extends to making an order for possession of the whole premises, not just that part presently under adverse occupation provided an intention to decamp can be inferred: *University of Essex v Djemal* [1980] 1 W.L.R. 1301. Where the defendants are in occupation of land A it is possible to grant an injunction restraining them from going on to other, separate land B to which the claimant fears they may decamp, but the special procedure for possession is not available in such a case. The reason is that a possession order would require the defendants to do what they cannot then do, surrender possession of land B: *Secretary of State for Environment etc v Meier* [2009] UKSC 11; [2009] 1 W.L.R. 2780. On the potential application of the Human Rights Act see *Malik v Fassenfelt* [2013] EWCA Civ 798; [2013] 28 E.G. 84 (CS).

Requirements to be met. What is it that a person seeking to recover land under **14-032** the modern procedure must show?[114] He succeeds if he shows that he has a "better title" than the defendant, as where he is a purchaser from an owner who has been excluded by the defendant. However, nothing approaching a paper title is necessary. Although it was said that for ejectment it was insufficient to set up the mere de facto possession which, as we have seen, will usually enable the claimant to sue for trespass as a tort,[115] this distinction is now very tenuous in view of *Asher v Whitlock*,[116] where it was held that if A takes possession of wasteland without any other title than such seizure, he could get possession against B who subsequently enters on the land.[117] When, therefore, it is said that A's former possession raises only a presumption of title it must be confessed that this presumption is not easily upset.[118] Indeed, it may now be that the law goes further and allows the claimant to succeed in a claim for possession where he would fail in an action of pure trespass. In *Manchester Airport Plc v Dutton*[119] the airport needed to lop and fell trees in Arthur's Wood in order to build a new runway. To stop this, the wood was occupied by protestors and the owner then granted the airport a licence to "enter and occupy" the site. An order for possession against the protestors was upheld by the majority of the Court of Appeal. For Laws LJ, modern proceedings for the recovery of land were no longer subject to the requirements of ejectment so the fact that that remedy had not concerned itself with the position of the licensee out of occupation was not decisive: "[A] licensee not in occupation may claim possession against a trespasser if that is a necessary remedy to vindicate and give effect to such rights of occupation as by contract with his licensor he enjoys."[120]

Although the airport would not have been able to sue for damages for trespass, nevertheless, for the purpose of gaining possession it had a "superior right" to that of the defendants. However, the same court has subsequently declined to extend this decision to a situation where the licence was to enter and carry out work on the land but not to occupy it.[121]

The defence of jus tertii. The modern cases on recovery of land have not **14-033** addressed another question, which has been controversial: if the claimant relies on his title to the land, how far may the defendant defeat his claim by showing a superior right in a third party? In an ordinary action of trespass the defendant cannot as a general rule set up the defence of *jus tertii*,[122] but is this rule applicable to the defendant to an action for the recovery of land? If the claimant must prove his title,[123] it would seem to be a corollary that if the evidence, whether it appear from the claimant's own case or be produced by the defendant,

---

[114] An action to rectify the land register is not an action for the recovery of land within the meaning of the Limitation Act 1980, s.15: *Parshall v Bryans* [2013] EWCA Civ 240; [2013] Ch. 568 at [59].

[115] *Harper v Charlesworth* (1825) 4 B. & C. 574 at 589 per Bayley J at 592–594 per Holroyd J.

[116] (1865) L.R. 1 Q.B. 1. See, too, *Doe d. Hughes v Dyeball* (1829) Moo. & M. 346.

[117] Approved by the Judicial Committee in *Perry v Clissold* [1907] A.C. 73 at 79.

[118] *Whale v Hitchcock* (1876) 34 L.T. 136.

[119] [2000] Q.B. 133.

[120] [2000] Q.B. 133 at 150.

[121] *Countryside Residential (North Thames) Ltd v Tugwell* [2000] 34 E.G. 87.

[122] See para.14-007.

[123] For example, where he is someone who has purchased or inherited the property.

shows that some third person is entitled to the land, the claimant ought not to succeed: in other words, the defendant ought to be allowed to plead *jus tertii*. The position is, however, not necessarily the same where the claimant relies on prior possession of the land. Although the title of the third party (the lord of the manor) was not directly in issue in *Asher v Whitlock*[124] the reasoning seems inconsistent with the view that the defendant could have raised that title and in *Perry v Clissold*[125] Lord Macnaghten thought that the earlier case of *Doe d. Carter v Barnard*[126] could not stand with *Asher v Whitlock*. Although the matter has been greatly debated[127] and is perhaps not finally settled, the better view seems to be that the *jus tertii* cannot be raised in this case.[128]

Whether or not *jus tertii* is in general a defence in such cases, it cannot be relied upon where the defendant has acquired possession from the claimant himself or from one through whom the claimant claims. The rule that a tenant is estopped from denying his landlord's title is well known, but a licensee is similarly estopped from denying the title of his licensor,[129] and indeed this rule of estoppel extends to anyone who is sued in ejectment by one from whom he derived his interest.[130]

C. Damages

14–034   **Mesne profits.** The action for mesne profits is another species of the action for trespass and lies for the damage which the claimant has suffered through having been out of possession of his land. By Blackstone's time nothing but a shilling or some trivial sum was usually recoverable in the action of ejectment because it had been "licked into the form of a real action"[131] and its chief purpose had become the trial of the title to land.[132] If the claimant was successful, he got possession of the land but no compensation for having been kept out of it. The action for mesne profits enables the claimant to claim a reasonable rent for the possession of the property by the defendant[133] up to the time when possession is surrendered[134] and damages for any deterioration, as well as the reasonable costs

---

[124] (1865) L.R. 1 Q.B. 1.

[125] [1907] A.C. 73 at 79.

[126] (1849) 13 Q.B. 945.

[127] For full discussion of the question, see: Wiren (1925) 41 L.Q.R. 139; Hargreaves 56 L.Q.R. 376; Holdsworth 56 L.Q.R. 479.

[128] See *Mayor of London v Hall* [2010] EWCA Civ 817; [2011] 1 W.L.R. 504, where, however, there was an implied statutory right to obtain possession. Winfield was firmly of the contrary view: see earlier editions of this book.

[129] *Doe d. Johnson v Baytup* (1835) 3 Ad. & E. 188. A general denial in a pleading by a tenant does not amount to a sufficient denial of the landlord's title to cause a forfeiture of the lease: *Warner v Sampson* [1959] 1 Q.B. 297.

[130] Lopes LJ in *Dalton v Fitzgerald* [1897] 2 Ch. 86 at 93.

[131] *Goodtitle v Tombs* (1770) 3 Wils. K.B. 118 at 120 per Wilmot CJ.

[132] Blackstone, Comm, ii, p.205.

[133] It does not matter that the claimant cannot show that he could have let the property while he was out of possession, nor that the defendant has not profited from the property: *Inverugie Investments Ltd v Hackett* [1995] 1 W.L.R. 713.

[134] *Jones v Merton L.B.C.* [2008] EWCA Civ 660; [2009] 1 W.L.R. 1269 (tenant found to have surrendered possession before landlord became aware of surrender)

of getting possession.[135] It remains a matter of debate whether the sum payable by way of a reasonable rent represents a compensatory measure of damages (based on the claimant's gain) or a restitutionary measure (based on the defendant's benefit),[136] but the method adopted is to calculate the sum which the parties would have agreed by way of a rent or a licence fee on a hypothetical basis as a willing seller and buyer at the time of the trespass.[137] Such a hypothetical calculation must take account of the context, so that where the defendant trespassed on the substrata below the claimant's land in drilling for oil damages were assessed by reference to the principles governing compulsory purchase in recognition of the defendant's statutory entitlement[138] to enforce the right to drill.[139]

The claimant in an action for the recovery of land may join with it a claim for mesne profits, and if he does so it is unnecessary for him to have entered the land before he sues.[140] If he prefers he can still bring the action for mesne profits separately but in that event he must first enter, for the action is one of trespass, trespass is a wrong to possession, and until he enters he has not got it. Once he has entered, however, then by the fiction of trespass by relation[141] the claimant is deemed to have been in possession during the whole period for which he claims the mesne profits.

---

[135] In *Ramzan v Brookwide Ltd* [2011] EWCA Civ 985; [2012] 1 All E.R. 903 where the trespass took the form of the appropriation of a store room which had also provided access to a fire escape, the claimant was required to elect between alternative heads of loss: the loss of profits from his inability any longer to use an adjoining room as a restaurant *or* mesne profits since he could not both use the room himself and let it out.

[136] Or whether this even matters: *Inverugie Investments Ltd v Hackett* [1995] 1 W.L.R. 713, at 718. See also *MoD v Ashman* (1993) 66 P. & C.R. 195 at 201 where Hoffmann LJ would leave it to the election of the claimant; cf. *Penarth Dock Engineering Co Ltd v Pounds* [1963] 1 Lloyd's Rep. 359. In *Stadium Capital Holdings v St Marylebone Properties Company Plc* [2010] EWCA Civ 952 the trial judge was held to have erred in awarding damages equivalent to the total revenue generated by the defendant in the employment of advertising hoardings which trespassed on the airspace above the claimant's land, but the CA remitted the question of damages without indicating which of the possible bases for assessment should have been adopted.

[137] *Eaton Mansions (Westminster) Ltd v Stinger Compania De Inversion SA* [2013] EWCA Civ 1308; [2014] 1 P & C.R. 5, in which the CA held that the parties were only to be taken to be negotiating for a licence period equivalent to the actual duration of the trespass which had occurred. This is debatable if what is being compensated is the loss suffered by the claimant in not being able to bargain for a fee at the time of the trespass; *at that time* the parties would not have known anything about the subsequent disposal of the underlease by the defendant which brought his trespass to an end so that the parties would have been negotiating for a permanent irrevocable licence and not the temporary licence which was the basis of the damages awarded. This may suggest that the measure of damages is thought of as restitutionary, "the damages awarded should be compensation for the loss suffered *in the sense of what the tortfeasor has gained from his trespass*", per Patten LJ at [24] (emphasis added); cf. *Jones v Ruth* [2011] EWCA Civ 804; [2012] 1 W.L.R. 1495 at [37]; *Enfield LBC v Outdoor Plus Ltd* [2012] EWCA Civ 608; [2012] 2 E.G.L.R. 105.

[138] Under the Mines (Working Facilities and Support) Act 1966.

[139] *Star Energy Weald Basin Ltd v Bocardo SA* [2010] UKSC 35; [2011] 1 A.C. 380.

[140] If the claimant's title to the land has been extinguished by adverse possession, so is his claim for mesne profits: *Mount Carmel Investment Ltd v Peter Thurlow Ltd* [1988] 1 W.L.R. 1078.

[141] See para.14–009.

14–035 **Aggravated and exemplary damages.** Aggravated damages may be awarded in cases of trespass where the defendant's conduct has been high-handed, insulting or oppressive.[142] Similarly, where the requisite conditions are met,[143] the court may award exemplary damages.[144]

---

[142] *Horsford v Bird* [2006] UKPC 3; [2006] 1 E.G.L.R. 175; *Eaton Mansions (Westminster) Ltd v Stinger Compania De Inversion SA* [2013] EWCA Civ 1308; [2014] 1 P & C.R. 5 at [26] (not awarded in the case of a company). For aggravated damages generally, see paras 23–024—23–029.

[143] See paras 23–012—23–023.

[144] *Eaton Mansions (Westminster) Ltd v Stinger Compania De Inversion SA* [2012] EWHC 3354 (Ch); [2012] 49 EG 66 (CS) at [75]–[77] (appeal dismissed but without any appeal against the judge's decision not to award exemplary damages: [2013] EWCA Civ 1308; [2014] 1 P & C.R. 5).

CHAPTER 15

NUISANCE[1]

---

[1] Buckley, *Law of Nuisance*, 2nd edn (1996).

1. INTRODUCTION

15–001 In modern parlance, nuisance is that branch of the law of tort most closely concerned with "protection of the environment". Thus nuisance actions have concerned pollution by oil[2] or noxious fumes,[3] interference with leisure activities,[4] offensive smells from premises used for keeping animals[5] or noise from industrial installations.[6] Three important qualifications must be made, however, to this broad generalisation. First, there are areas of nuisance, such as obstruction of the highway or of access thereto,[7] which have no "environmental" flavour. Secondly, the prevailing stance of nuisance liability is that of protection of private rights in the enjoyment of land,[8] so that control of injurious activity for the benefit of the whole community is incidental.[9] Thirdly, the common law of nuisance has been supplemented and to a large extent replaced by an array of statutory powers designed to control environmental damage.

15–002 **Statutory protection of the environment.** A full account of the statutory powers in question would be beyond the scope of a book on tort[10] but a very brief sketch of the principal provisions may help the reader to put the common law in context. The main statute is the Environmental Protection Act 1990, which consolidated and restated much previous law as well as introducing a new administrative system for pollution control. Under Pt III of this Act[11] various matters[12] are "statutory nuisances". A local authority which is satisfied that such a nuisance exists is under a duty to serve an abatement notice requiring the nuisance to be terminated and failure, without reasonable excuse, to comply with the notice is a

---

[2] *Esso Petroleum Co Ltd v Southport Corp* [1956] A.C. 218.

[3] *St Helen's Smelting Co v Tipping* (1865) 11 H.L.C. 642.

[4] *Bridlington Relay v Yorkshire Electricity Board* [1965] Ch. 436.

[5] *Rapier v London Tramways Co* [1893] 2 Ch. 588.

[6] *Halsey v Esso Petroleum Co Ltd* [1961] 1 W.L.R. 683.

[7] See para.15–073.

[8] *Hunter v Canary Wharf Ltd* [1997] A.C. 655, para.15–034. There is, however, a strong public law element in the shape of the power of public authorities to bring proceedings for an injunction to restrain a public nuisance: see para.15–006.

[9] For an economic analysis see Ogus and Richardson (1977) 36 C.L.J. 284; Campbell (2000) 63 M.L.R. 197.

[10] See *Encyclopedia of Environmental Health Law and Practice*; *Garner's Environmental Law.*

[11] As amended, particularly by the Noise and Statutory Nuisance Act 1993 and the Environment Act 1995. For earlier provisions see the Public Health Act 1936 Pt II. Much of the case law on that Act remains relevant.

[12] Section 79, e.g. premises in a state prejudicial to health or constituting a nuisance; similar states of affairs in relation to smoke, fumes, dust, noise or accumulations or deposits. If the complaint is that the premises constitute a nuisance there must be a nuisance in the common law sense, i.e. the matter has to affect neighbouring land: *National Coal Board v Neath BC* [1976] 2 All E.R. 478; but this is not necessary if, e.g. the premises are in a state prejudicial to health, though even then the statute is concerned with the condition of the premises, not the layout or facilities: *Birmingham CC v Oakley* [2001] 1 All E.R. 385.

criminal offence.[13] Part II of the Act contains wide-ranging powers to control the deposit of waste and contravention of these provisions causing damage may give rise to civil liability.[14] The statutory nuisance provisions do not, as such, give rise to civil liability,[15] though conviction of the criminal offence would entitle the criminal court in a straightforward case to make a compensation order under the Powers of Criminal Courts (Sentencing) Act 2000. However, the principal remedy sought by most victims of nuisance is an order to prevent its continuance and a complaint to the local authority under the 1990 Act will often be a considerably cheaper and more expeditious way of getting redress than a common law action for an injunction. Indeed, even if the local authority declines to take proceedings in the matter it is possible under s.82 for summary proceedings to be brought by a "person aggrieved."

The residuary role of the common law. The common law is, therefore, something of a residuary category where, for one reason or another, the statutory provisions are inapt or the victim considers there are advantages in a civil action.[16] The traditional "neighbour dispute nuisance" may also now fall under the Protection from Harassment Act 1997,[17] which contains civil as well criminal sanctions.[18] Civil actions for nuisance certainly continue to be brought[19] and it would be wrong to think that the role of the common law is insignificant[20] but the reader should be aware that some of the older cases in this chapter might now be dealt with by other means.

15–003

European law. As is so often the case nowadays, there is a European dimension. In 2004 the European Union adopted a Directive on Environmental Liability.[21] It rests on the principle that "the polluter must pay" but the "liability" imposed in respect of the cost of preventive and remedial action rests on an administrative mechanism rather than the private law of tort. Indeed, it does not apply to "cases of personal injury, to damage to private property or to any economic loss and does not affect any right regarding these types of damages".[22]

15–004

---

[13] If the local authority considers that summary proceedings would afford an inadequate remedy it may proceed in the High Court: s.81(5).

[14] See para.16–007.

[15] *Issa v Hackney LBC* [1997] 1 W.L.R. 956.

[16] Possible reasons include: (1) an injunction may be more effective than a criminal fine (even though there are "topping up" provisions where the nuisance continues) see, e.g. *City of London Corp v Bovis Construction Ltd* [1992] 3 All E.R. 697; (2) the nuisance may fall outside the matters listed in s.79; (3) where damage has been suffered the case may be too complex for a compensation order; (4) under s.80(7) it is in some cases a defence to a prosecution that the "best practicable means" have been used to prevent it. This may be more favourable to the defendant in some cases than the common law (but see *Wivenhoe Port v Colchester BC* [1985] J.P.L. 175).

[17] See para.4–034.

[18] See e.g. *Fowler v Jones* Unreported June 10, 2002 Hayward's Heath CC.

[19] Sometimes on a large scale. In *Hunter v Canary Wharf Ltd* [1997] A.C. 655 there were 690 claimants.

[20] For example, there were substantial settlements in 1993 of civil claims arising from alleged dioxin pollution in Derbyshire where regulatory action had not been taken.

[21] Directive 2004/35/EC.

[22] Recital 14.

Article 8(1) of the European Convention on Human Rights requires respect for "private and family life, [and the] home"[23] and there are signs that this may have a significant impact in the context of nuisance law, forming (as we have seen in other contexts) a parallel or alternative system of redress, at least where a public authority is involved.[24]

2. PUBLIC AND PRIVATE NUISANCE

A. Public Nuisance

15–005 **Primarily a crime.** Nuisances are divided into public and private, although it is quite possible for the same conduct to amount to both. A public nuisance is a crime, while a private nuisance is only a tort. A public or common nuisance is one which materially affects the reasonable comfort and convenience of life of a class of the public who come within the sphere or neighbourhood of its operation; the question whether the number of persons affected is sufficient to constitute a class is one of fact in every case, and it is sufficient to show that a representative cross-section of that class has been so affected for an injunction to issue.[25] This definition is vague and it has been rightly said that nuisance, "covers a multitude of sins, great and small".[26] Public nuisances at common law include such diverse activities as carrying on an offensive trade, keeping a disorderly house, selling food unfit for human consumption, obstructing public highways, and throwing fireworks about in the street. In many cases such conduct will now be covered by a specific statutory offence and where this is so a criminal prosecution should normally be brought for that rather than at common law.[27] Subject to this, however, the common law of public nuisance meets the requirement of certainty prescribed by the European Convention on Human Rights.[28]

15–006 **Civil liability for special or particular damage.**[29] So long as the public only or some section of it is injured no civil action can be brought by a private individual for public nuisance. Where a public highway is obstructed, I cannot sue the obstructor for nuisance if I can prove no damage beyond being delayed on several occasions in passing along it and being obliged either to pursue my journey by a devious route or to remove the obstruction, for these are inconveniences common to everyone else.[30] The reason normally given for the rule is that it prevents multiplicity of actions, for if one were allowed to sue, a thousand might do so and

---

[23] In addition, art.1 of the First Protocol provides that everyone, "is entitled to the peaceful enjoyment of his possessions".

[24] See para.15–066.

[25] *Attorney General v PYA Quarries Ltd* [1957] 2 Q.B. 169 at 184 per Romer LJ (quarrying blasting, stones and splinters projected from quarry, dust, noise and vibration). Provided it affects the public it does not matter that only a small number of people in fact use the facility: *Jan de Nul (UK) Ltd v Axa Royal Belge* [2000] 2 Lloyd's Rep. 700 (on appeal, [2002] EWCA Civ 209; [2002] 1 Lloyd's Rep. 583).

[26] *Southport Corp v Esso Petroleum Co Ltd* [1954] 2 Q.B. 182 at 196 per Denning LJ.

[27] *R. v Rimmington* [2005] UKHL 63; [2006] 1 A.C. 459.

[28] *R. v Rimmington* [2005] UKHL 63; [2006] 1 A.C. 459.

[29] Kodilinye (1986) 6 L.S. 182.

[30] *Winterbottom v Lord Derby* (1867) L.R. 2 Ex. 316 at 321–322.

this would lead to harsh results.[31] If, for instance, a public body obstructed a highway temporarily for the purpose of draining, paving or lighting it and it was then discovered that owing to some technical error they had no authority to do so, they would be sufficiently punished by a criminal prosecution.[32] If, for some reason, a criminal prosecution is an inadequate sanction, the Attorney General may, on the information of a member of the public, bring a civil action for an injunction (known as a "relator" action), but if he refuses to do so the courts are not at liberty to inquire into the propriety of his actions or to grant declarations at the suit of the individual instead of injunctions.[33] By statute, a local authority may bring proceedings for an injunction where they "consider it expedient for the promotion or protection of the interests of the inhabitants of their area".[34] The provision has been called in aid in support of the criminal law,[35] though it has been said that the relationship between it and the "classic public nuisance case" requires further consideration.[36]

Where, however, any private person is injured in some way peculiar to himself, that is, if he can show that he has suffered some particular or special loss over and above the ordinary inconvenience suffered by the public at large, then he can sue in tort, for example if he falls into a trench unlawfully opened in a street and breaks his leg. Particular damage[37] is not limited to special damage in the sense of pecuniary loss actually incurred, for example in an action for negligence. It may consist of proved general damage, such as inconvenience and delay, provided it is substantial, direct and not consequential and is appreciably different in nature or extent to that in fact suffered by the general public, although in another sense it is "general" and not "special" to him.[38] "Direct" here means damage other or different from the damage caused to the rest of the public. It is narrower than when "direct" is used in determining whether damage is too remote.[39] The distinction between public and private nuisance and the meaning of particular damage is illustrated by *Tate & Lyle Industries Ltd v GLC*.[40] Ferry terminals constructed by the defendants in the Thames caused silting which obstructed large vessels' access to the claimants' jetty and the claimants had to spend large sums in dredging operations. Their claim in private nuisance was dismissed because the jetty itself was unaffected and they had no private rights of property in the river bed, but the silting had caused interference with the public

---

[31] However, this is not entirely easy to square with the undoubted proposition that the same thing may be both a public nuisance and a private nuisance to persons whose property interests are affected. See *Sutherland v Canada* [2002] BCCA 416; 215 D.L.R. 4th 1.

[32] *Winterbottom v Lord Derby* (1867) L.R. 2 Ex. 316.

[33] *Gouriet v Union of Post Office Workers* [1978] A.C. 435 (not a case of public nuisance).

[34] Local Government Act 1972 s.222.

[35] It was used in the "Sunday trading" cases (see, e.g. *Kirklees MBC v Wickes Building Supplies Ltd* [1993] A.C. 227).

[36] *Birmingham CC v Shafi* [2008] EWCA Civ 1186; [2009] 1 W.L.R. 1961 at [42].

[37] *Rose v Groves* (1843) 5 Man. & G. 613 at 616.

[38] *Walsh v Ervin* [1952] V.L.R. 361 at 368–369 per Sholl J reviewing the English authorities; *Jan de Nul (UK) Ltd v NV Royal Belge* [2000] 2 Lloyd's Rep. 700. Particular damage includes injury to claimant's person, loss of custom, depreciation in the actual value of the property by reducing or cutting off the approach to it; *Boyd v GN Ry* (1895) 2 I.R. 555 (doctor held up at level crossing for 20 minutes, recovered).

[39] *Overseas Tankship (UK) Ltd v The Miller Steamship Co Pty* [1967] 1 A.C. 617 at 636.

[40] [1983] 2 A.C. 509.

right of navigation which the claimants enjoyed along with all other river users and the expenditure incurred by the claimants was damage sufficient to entitle them to bring an action for public nuisance.[41]

15–007 **Comparison with private nuisance.** In truth, beyond the fact that both involve "unreasonable" behaviour and both may arise from the same facts, public and private nuisance have little in common. Private nuisance is firmly rooted in the protection of landholding rights, whereas public nuisance represents a rather unsuccessful attempt to link the criminal law with compensation for damage. It is questionable whether in a modern system of law there should be any connection between liability for interference with the enjoyment of land and for damage done by a crime (often obstruction of the highway) affecting the public as a whole. At any rate, the rules relating to them are not identical. It has now been reaffirmed that to sue in private nuisance one must have an interest in land but no such interest is necessary in public nuisance. On the other hand, while a private nuisance claimant must generally show some damage,[42] the person who sues for public nuisance must show damage going beyond that suffered by the public as a whole. Although it has long been assumed—and now held[43]—that damages for personal injury may be recovered in public nuisance,[44] this is not now the case in the private variety.[45] The same state of affairs may, of course, constitute both torts, a private nuisance in so far as A suffers interference with the enjoyment of land and a public nuisance in so far as B suffers some special damage.[46]

B. Private Nuisance

15–008 Private nuisance may be described as unlawful interference with a person's use or enjoyment of land, or some right over, or in connection with it.[47] It has been said[48] that the tort takes three forms: encroachment on a neighbour's land;[49] direct physical injury to the land; or interference with the enjoyment of the land. The varieties of the third form are almost infinite but it is still a tort against rights of property and therefore lies only at the suit of a person with a sufficient interest in the land.[50] Generally, the essence of a nuisance is a state of affairs that is either

---

[41] See also *Jan de Nul (UK) Ltd v Axa Royal Belge* [2002] EWCA Civ 209; [2002] 1 Lloyd's Rep. 583; *Rose v Miles* (1815) 4 M. & S. 101; *News Group Newspapers Ltd v SOGAT'82* [1986] I.R.L.R. 337 (cost of "bussing-in" employees because of picketing). Note that in these cases the loss is "economic" but though that may be a bar to a claim for negligence it is not to one for public nuisance. Cf. the position where the claim relates to failure to repair the highway: para.15–082.

[42] This is not as onerous a requirement as might appear: para.15–056.

[43] *Claimants in Corby Group Litigation v Corby BC* [2008] EWCA Civ 463; [2009] 2 W.L.R. 609.

[44] See the doubts of Lord Goff in *Hunter v Canary Wharf Ltd* [1997] A.C. 655 at 692.

[45] See para.15–037.

[46] *Colour Quest Ltd v Total Downstream UK Plc* [2009] EWHC 540 (Comm); [2009] 2 Lloyd's Rep 1. Indeed, the same person may have a claim for both.

[47] Adopted by Scott LJ in *Read v Lyons & Co Ltd* [1945] K.B. 216 at 236; by Lord Goddard CJ in *Howard v Walker* [1947] 2 All E.R. 197 at 199; by Evershed J in *Newcastle-under-Lyme Corp v Wolstanton Ltd* [1947] Ch. 92 at 107; and by Windeyer J in *Hargrave v Goldman* (1963) 37 A.L.J.R. 277 at 283, affirmed [1967] 1 A.C. 645.

[48] *Hunter v Canary Wharf Ltd* [1997] A.C. 655 at 695 per Lord Lloyd.

[49] For example, by spreading roots or overhanging branches.

[50] See para.15–034.

continuous or recurrent, a condition or activity which unduly interferes with the use or enjoyment of land. It is not necessary that there be any *physical* emanation from the defendant's premises. Noises and smells can be nuisances, but so, it seems, can be otherwise offensive businesses.[51] The mere presence of a building is not, however, a nuisance.[52] Not every slight annoyance is actionable. Stenches, smoke, the escape of effluent and a multitude of different things may amount to a nuisance in fact but whether they constitute an actionable nuisance will depend on a variety of considerations, especially the character of the defendant's conduct, and a balancing of conflicting interests.

In fact the whole of the law of private nuisance represents an attempt to preserve a balance between two conflicting interests, that of one occupier in using his land as he thinks fit, and that of his neighbour in the quiet enjoyment of his land.[53] Everyone must endure some degree of noise, smell, etc. from his neighbour, otherwise modern life would be impossible and such a privilege of interfering with the comfort of a neighbour is reciprocal. It is repeatedly said in nuisance cases that the rule is *sic utere tuo ut alienum non laedas*,[54] but the maxim is unhelpful and misleading. If it means that no person is ever allowed to use his property so as to injure another, it is palpably false.[55] If it means that a person in using his property may injure his neighbour, but not if he does so unlawfully, it is not worth stating, as it leaves unanswered the critical question of when the interference becomes unlawful.[56] In fact, the law repeatedly recognises that a person may use his own land so as to injure another without committing a nuisance. It is only if such use is unreasonable that it becomes unlawful.

C. Nuisance to Servitudes

We have so far been considering private nuisance as the interference with a person's use or enjoyment of land, and we have seen that in determining liability, the nature and quality of the defendant's conduct is a factor of great importance. In addition to this situation, however, the tort of nuisance provides a remedy for the infringement of a servitude,[57] such as the obstruction of a right of way or the

15–009

---

[51] *Thompson-Schwab v Costaki* [1956] 1 W.L.R. 335 (prostitution); *Laws v Florinplace Ltd* [1981] 1 All E.R. 659 (sex shop, interlocutory injunction, triable issue of nuisance independently of risk of undesirable activities by customers). In *Hunter v Canary Wharf Ltd* [1997] A.C. 655, Lord Goff seems to approve *Thompson-Schwab*. No doubt it is generally true that nuisance involves some "emanation" from the defendant's land to the claimant's land but (a) this must sometimes be taken rather metaphorically and (b) there are exceptions, e.g. where works on the defendant's land cause a watercourse on the claimant's land to flood: *Bybrook Barn Centre Ltd and others v Kent CC* [2001] B.L.R. 55.

[52] *Hunter v Canary Wharf Ltd* [1997] A.C. 655, para.15–020.

[53] "A balance has to be maintained between the right of the occupier to do what he likes with his own, and the right of his neighbour not to be interfered with": *Sedleigh-Denfield v O'Callaghan* [1940] A.C. 880 at 903 per Lord Wright.

[54] Use your own property in such a way as not to harm that of others.

[55] *Bamford v Turnley* (1862) 3 B. & S. 66 at 79, 83–84 per Bramwell B.

[56] The maxim was described by Erle J as an "ancient and solemn imposter": *Bonomi v Backhouse* (1858) E.B. & E. 622 at 643.

[57] i.e. easements, profits à prendre and natural rights.

blocking of an acquired right to light. In *Colls v Home and Colonial Stores Ltd*,[58] Lord Macnaghten regarded the action for interference with an easement as sui generis, the function of the action being to remedy the infringement of a right, not to compensate for the commission of a wrong, so that the nature of the defendant's conduct would be a less relevant consideration than in other cases of nuisance. However, while this may be true of a simple case of obstruction of a right of way, servitude rights may be as qualified as the general right to enjoyment.[59]

3.   REASONABLENESS

15–010   **A balancing exercise.** The central issue of the whole law of nuisance is the question of reasonableness of the defendant's conduct, "according to the ordinary usages of mankind living in . . . a particular society".[60] It is vital to grasp at the outset that reasonableness is being used here in a sense rather different from that in the law of negligence. It is a comparatively simple proposition that you are liable for negligence if you drive a car carelessly against a pedestrian in the street and it would be ridiculous to say that there are some circumstances in which you may do so and others in which you may not. In other words, our attention is concentrated on the relative issue of the characterisation of the defendant's conduct as foreseeably likely to injure and once we have determined this in the claimant's favour we immediately progress to legal liability, treating the claimant's right to personal security as absolute. Nuisance, however, generally approaches the issue from the other end and we cannot make such a proposition as that you may not make a noise which irritates your neighbour, for common sense tells one that such a rule would be totally unworkable. Some intrusion by noise (or smells or dust, etc.) is the inevitable price of living in an organised society in proximity to one's neighbours, indeed: "[T]he very nuisance the one complains of, as the ordinary use of his neighbour's land, he himself will create in the ordinary use of his own and the reciprocal nuisances are of a comparatively trifling character."[61]

Accordingly, the protection of such interests must be approached with an attempt to balance the competing rights of neighbours, a process of compromise, a, "rule of give and take, of live and let live".[62] It is to this issue that we are directing our attention when we talk of the "reasonableness" of the defendant's conduct rather than to whether he took reasonable care in the negligence sense. "Reasonableness" signifies what is legally right between the parties taking account of all the circumstances of the case. The difference between the two approaches is in some ways more apparent than real and is perhaps the product of

---

[58] [1904] A.C. 179.

[59] For example the right at common law of a riparian owner to take a reasonable amount of water for agricultural and domestic purposes; but the right to take water is now subject to extensive statutory control.

[60] *Sedleigh-Denfield v O'Callaghan* [1940] A.C. 880 at 903 per Lord Wright.

[61] *Bamford v Turnley* (1862) 3 B. & S. 62 at 83 per Bramwell B; *Kennaway v Thompson* [1981] Q.B. 88 at 94.

[62] *Bamford v Turnley* (1862) 3 B. & S. 62 at 83; *Cambridge Water Co v Eastern Counties Leather Plc* [1994] 2 A.C. 264 at 299.

the fact that the majority of nuisance actions involve deliberate interference by the defendant,[63] but for practical purposes there is still a good deal of truth in the statement that knocking a person down carelessly is a tort simpliciter while making a noise that irritates him is only a tort *sub modo*. This is far short of saying that care is irrelevant to liability for nuisance: lack of care may lead to liability, for it is not reasonable to expect the claimant to put up with interference which could be reduced by the adoption of reasonable proper measures;[64] but if two neighbours live in adjoining properties with sound insulation which does not meet modern construction standards neither is liable for the inevitable noise which is produced by their ordinary activities of living, each acting with reasonable consideration[65] for the other.[66] On the other hand, if after balancing the competing interests of the parties, the court considers that the interference is excessive by any standards then the fact that the defendant has taken all reasonable care and reduced it to a minimum provides no defence—the irreducible minimum is itself the nuisance.[67]

A question of fact. No precise or universal formula is possible to determine **15–011** reasonableness in the above sense. Whether an act constitutes a nuisance cannot be determined merely by an abstract consideration of the act itself, but by reference to all the circumstances of the particular case, the time and place of its commission, the seriousness of the harm, the manner of committing it, whether it is done maliciously or in the reasonable exercise of rights and the effect of its commission, that is whether it is transitory or permanent, occasional or continuous; so that it is a question of fact whether or not a nuisance has been committed.[68] Certain of these factors will now be discussed in greater detail.

A. The Type of Harm and the Character of the Locality

The distinction between "material injury" and personal discomfort. In the **15–012** leading case of *St Helen's Smelting Co v Tipping*[69] where trees on the claimant's estate were injured by fumes from a copper smelter, the House of Lords drew a distinction between matters producing "sensible injury to the value of property"

---

[63] All the circumstances of the case, including the utility of the defendant's activity must be taken into account in determining whether his conduct is so unreasonable as to amount to a nuisance (see below) but such matters may be equally relevant to determine whether his conduct constitutes legal negligence. Indeed, where there is physical damage but no deliberate interference by the defendant one can discern a strong tendency to run nuisance and negligence together: *Bolton v Stone* [1951] A.C. 850; *Goldman v Hargrave* [1967] 1 A.C. 645.

[64] *Southwark LBC v Mills* [2001] 1 A.C. 1 at 16. Compare *Leeman v Montagu* [1936] 2 All E.R. 1677 (750 cockerels crowing between 2.00 and 7.00, no attempt to rearrange farm, held a nuisance) with *Moy v Stoop* (1909) 25 T.L.R. 262 (crying children in day nursery, no lack of care, no nuisance); and see the cases on malicious activity, para.15–026. It has been said that once the interference is of sufficient magnitude to be a nuisance the burden then shifts to the defendant to show that he took all proper steps: *Hiscox Syndicates Ltd v The Pinnacle Ltd* [2008] EWHC 145 (Ch); [2008] 5 E.G. 166 (CS).

[65] Cf. *Ball v Ray* (1873) LR 8 Ch. App. 467.

[66] *Southwark LBC v Mills* [2001] 1 A.C. 1.

[67] *Rapier v London Tramways Co* [1893] 2 Ch. 588.

[68] *Bamford v Turnley* (1862) 3 B. & S. 66 at 79 per Pollock CB.

[69] *St Helen's Smelting Co v Tipping* (1865) 11 H.L.C. 642.

or "material injury"[70] on the one hand and those causing personal discomfort on the other. In assessing whether the latter constitute an actionable nuisance it is necessary to take into account the character of the locality, so that interference which may not be permissible in one area may be in another; as it was once put, "What would be a nuisance in Belgrave Square would not necessarily be so in Bermondsey",[71] though it must at once be added that even the inhabitants of Bermondsey are entitled to a measure of legal protection. In these cases there must be something over and above the everyday inconveniences which are inevitable in that locality. "The law does not regard trifling inconveniences; everything is to be looked at from a reasonable point of view";[72] but in the other type of case these considerations are said not to apply: property damage must not be inflicted wherever the defendant is carrying on his activity. The distinction is not free from difficulty and its consequences do not seem to have been fully investigated by the courts,[73] but it has been reiterated on a number of occasions.[74]

15–013   **Character of the locality: relevance of the defendant's own activity.** In *Coventry v Lawrence*[75] the Supreme Court was required to consider whether a nuisance was committed as a result of the noise generated by the defendants' motoring events: speedway and stock car racing (held in a stadium) and moto-cross (held on a track at the rear of the stadium). One issue was the extent to which the defendants' own activities could be taken into account in determining the character of the locality. According to Lord Neuberger they were to be taken into account, but not to the extent that they constituted a nuisance to the claimant, i.e. the court could take into account that motoring events were held and that they generated noise, but not noise at the level which constituted a nuisance.[76] The circularity involved in this proposition was not lost on Lord Neuberger but he considered it preferable to either of the alternatives—namely, to ignore the defendants' activities altogether or to take them into account without modification (as the Court of Appeal had done)[77] which would mean that there could rarely be a successful claim for nuisance.[78] As for the circularity involved,

---

[70] *St Helen's Smelting Co v Tipping* (1865) 11 H.L.C. 642 at 651.

[71] *Sturges v Bridgman* (1879) 11 Ch.D. 852 at 865 per Thesiger LJ; *Polsue and Alfieri v Rushmer* [1907] A.C. 121; *Andreae v Selfridge & Co* [1938] Ch. 1.

[72] *St Helen's Smelting Co v Tipping* (1865) 11 H.L.C. at 653.

[73] It seems fairly clear from Lord Westbury's speech that he did have in mind physical damage (including visible deterioration). Noises or smells primarily cause only personal discomfort but they may seriously reduce the selling value of the property affected by them and injure a business (e.g. a hotel) carried on therein. If this is not "injury to property" it may be asked whether the distinction is justified. In *Hunter v Canary Wharf Ltd* [1997] A.C. 655 at 706 Lord Hoffmann emphasises that even in the case of nuisances of the "personal discomfort" variety the damages are awarded for the effect on the amenity value of the land.

[74] See e.g. *Halsey v Esso Petroleum Co* [1961] 1 W.L.R. 683; *Miller v Jackson* [1977] Q.B. 966 at 986.

[75] [2014] UKSC 13; [2014] 2 W.L.R. 433.

[76] [2014] UKSC 13; [2014] 2 W.L.R. 433 at [65]. It follows from this approach that "if the activities couldn't be carried out without creating a nuisance, then they would have to be entirely discounted when assessing the character of the neighbourhood": at [74].

[77] [2012] EWCA Civ 26; [2012] 1 W.L.R. 2127.

[78] The Supreme Court reinstated the injunction which had been granted at first instance, but suggested that the defendant might exercise the permission to apply contained in the judge's order and seek an order for damages instead, for the reasons considered below: para.15–071.

while this gave "cause for concern", the court would be required to go through an "iterative process" when assessing the character of the locality and what noise within it constituted a nuisance.[79] Lord Carnwath noted that in earlier cases involving noise[80] the courts did not find it necessary to undertake an "interative process". Rather, they proceeded "on the basis that a change in the intensity or character of an existing activity may result in a nuisance, no less than the introduction of a new activity". Whether it did so was a matter for the judge to determine "as an issue of fact or degree".[81]

Character of the locality: relevance of planning permission. It may be that in the course of time Belgrave Square declines and Bermondsey goes up in the world. Nowadays, a major factor in such changes in the character of the locality will be the planning process, but in *Coventry v Lawrence* the Supreme Court criticised the Court of Appeal and a number of earlier cases for overstating the significance of the grant of permission for the defendant's activities.[82] According to Lord Neuberger, the granting of permission is "normally of no assistance to the defendant in a claim brought by a neighbour who contends that the activity causes a nuisance to her land in the form of noise or other loss of amenity".[83] He acknowledged that there will be "occasions" when the *terms* of a planning permission could be of relevance,[84] but Lord Carnwath went a little further (and a little closer to the earlier authorities) when he accepted that, in "exceptional cases", planning permission cannot sensibly be ignored when assessing the character of the locality.[85] Such cases are those in which the project is exceptional in scale and where the permission is the "result of a considered policy decision by the competent authority leading to a fundamental change in the pattern of uses" in

15–014

---

[79] [2014] UKSC 13; [2014] 2 W.L.R. 433 at [65]

[80] *Kennaway v Thompson* [1981] Q.B. 88; *Watson v Croft Promo Sport Ltd* [2009] EWCA Civ 15; [2009] 3 All E.R. 249.

[81] *Coventry v Lawrence* [2014] UKSC 13; [2014] 2 W.L.R. 433 at [190]. Lord Mance noted the two approaches (at 164]) but made no comment of his own. Neither Lord Sumption, nor Lord Clarke, made any comment on this aspect of Lord Neuberger's speech, but agreed with his reasons for allowing the appeal.

[82] *Gillingham BC v Medway (Chatham) Dock Co Ltd* [1993] Q.B. 343; *Watson v Croft Promo Sport Ltd* [2009] EWCA Civ 15; [2009] 3 All E.R. 249; *Hirose Electrical UK Ltd v Peak Ingredients Ltd* [2011] EWCA Civ 987; [2011] Env L.R. 34. See also the earlier criticism of Peter Gibson LJ in *Wheeler v JJ Saunders* [1996] Ch. 19 and Pill LJ in *Hunter v Canary Wharf* [1997] A.C. 655; cf. Lee [2011] J.E.P.L. 986. In the *Gillingham* case (no public nuisance in the serious disturbance caused by the "round the clock" operation of a commercial dock following the grant of planning permission in 1983) it was the local authority which had granted the permission which also sought the injunction (under the Local Government Act 1971 s.222 (see para.15–006)). It had power to revoke the permission, to impose conditions or to make traffic schemes to reduce the disturbance, but to take these steps might have involved it in paying statutory compensation to the defendants. In view of the authority's continuing powers and certain assurances about access which had been given to the defendants in 1983 Buckley J would in any event have exercised his discretion to refuse an injunction and in *Coventry v Lawrence* both Lord Neuberger ([2014] UKSC 13 at [99]) and Lord Carnwath (at [203]) commented that this alternative basis for the decision was probably right.

[83] *Coventry v Lawrence* [2014] UKSC 13; [2014] 2 W.L.R. 433 at [94].

[84] *Coventry v Lawrence* [2014] UKSC 13; [2014] 2 W.L.R. 433 at [96].

[85] Lord Mance agreed with Lord Neuberger (at [165]–[166]); Lord Sumption held that the grant of permission would "at best" provide some evidence of the reasonableness of the particular use of the land in question (at [156]); Lord Clarke held that it is "capable of being relevant" but the facts of cases are so varied "that it is difficult to lay down hard and fast rules" (at [169]).

the locality,[86] as opposed to a single grant, such as permission to expand a pig farm.[87] It should be emphasised that, at this stage, we are concerned with the question of *liability* for nuisance. When it comes to the question of the appropriate *remedy* if a nuisance has been established, the Justices in *Coventry v Lawrence* were agreed that the grant of planning permission is of potentially greater significance. This is dealt with below.[88]

B.   Utility of the Defendant's Conduct

15–015   Since nuisance is the law of give and take the court is inevitably concerned to some extent with the utility or general benefit to the community of the defendant's activity. Thus we must all put up with the rattle of early morning milk deliveries, though probably not with the same amount of noise made by drunken neighbours.[89] This approach, however, will only justify an injurious activity up to a certain point, and that point is reached when serious damage is being done to the claimant's enjoyment of his property or to his livelihood. In such a case the court will not accept the argument that the claimant should put up with the harm because it is beneficial to the community as a whole, for that would amount to requiring him to carry the burden alone of an activity from which many others benefit. Even in such cases, however, the "public interest" in the continuation of the defendant's activity may be taken into account when it comes to determining the appropriate remedy.[90]

C.   Abnormal Sensitivity

15–016   In considering what is reasonable the law does not take account of abnormal sensitivity in either persons or property. If the only reason why a person complains of fumes is that he has an unusually sensitive nose or that he owns an exotic flower, he cannot expect any sympathy from the courts.

15–017   **Sensitive persons.** In *Heath v Mayor of Brighton*[91] the incumbent and trustees of a Brighton church sought an injunction to restrain noise from the defendants' electrical power station. There was no proof of diminution of the congregation or of any personal annoyance to anyone except the incumbent and he was not prevented from preaching or conducting his services, nor was the noise such as to distract the attention of ordinary healthy persons attending the church. An

---

[86] Such as in the *Gillingham* case above; cf. the reference by Staughton LJ in *Wheeler v JJ Saunders Ltd* [1996] Ch. 19, 30 to "a strategic planning decision affected by considerations of public interest"; and see the observations of Lord Cooke in *Hunter v Canary Wharf Ltd* [1997] A.C. 655 at 722.

[87] *Wheeler v JJ Saunders* [1996] Ch. 19; cf. *Watson v Croft Promo Sport Ltd* [2009] EWCA Civ 15; [2009] 3 All E.R. 249. In *Barr v Biffa Waste Services Ltd* [2012] EWCA Civ 312; [2013] Q.B. 455 a change in the character of the locality was not found to have occurred as a result of the grant of a permit pursuant to planning permission previously given (the permit for the tipping of pre-treated waste was granted not by the planning authority, but by the Environment Agency).

[88] See para.15–071.

[89] This is demonstrated most clearly where the activity is actuated by malice, for malicious conduct can have no utility: see para.15–026.

[90] See para.15–071.

[91] (1908) 98 L.T. 718.

injunction was not granted. It seems that no regard should be had to the special needs of invalids, or to special occupational needs, for there is no redress for damage due solely to the exceptionally delicate nature of the operations carried on by an injured party.[92]

Sensitive property. *Robinson v Kilvert*[93] illustrates the point with regard to sensitive property. The defendant began to manufacture paper boxes in the cellar of a house the upper part of which was in the occupation of the claimant. The defendant's business required hot and dry air and he heated the cellar accordingly. This raised the temperature on the claimant's floor and dried and diminished the value of brown paper which the claimant warehoused there but it did not inconvenience the claimant's workmen nor would it have injured paper generally. It was held that the defendant was not liable for nuisance. A person who carries on an exceptionally delicate trade cannot complain because it is injured by his neighbour doing something lawful on his property, if it is something which would not injure anything but an exceptionally delicate trade.[94] You cannot increase the liabilities of your neighbour by applying your property to special uses, whether for business or pleasure;[95] but once the nuisance is established, the remedies by way of damages or an injunction will extend to delicate and sensitive operations such as the growing of orchids.[96]

15–018

An unnecessary principle? It has been suggested that it is difficult to see any further life in the principle about abnormal sensitivity because of the current general approach to reasonableness in nuisance.[97] With respect, that does not seem correct: to say that C cannot restrict the freedom of action of his neighbour by putting his property to a very sensitive use is part and parcel of the idea of reasonableness. Of course, that is not to say that the law's response to what were once regarded as abnormally sensitive activities may not change over time: for example, the use of sensitive electronic equipment is now part of everyday life and there are detailed regulatory controls designed to minimise interference.[98]

15–019

D. Limits to Protection

Protected interests. Nowadays it is probably unlikely that many people would regard as "unduly sensitive" a claimant who complained that his view was ruined or his sitting room darkened or smoke caused to blow back down his chimney by the erection of neighbouring premises. Nevertheless it is well established that

15–020

---

[92] *Bloodworth v Cormack* [1949] N.Z.L.R. 1058 at 1064; cf. *Stretch v Romford Football Club* (1971) 115 S.J. 741.

[93] *Robinson v Kilvert* (1889) 41 Ch. D. 88; *Whycer v Urry* [1955] C.L.Y. 1939 (CA held practice of ophthalmic optician in a business area too specially delicate for protection).

[94] There may be no evidence that migration of GM organisms from one property to another will cause any damage in the sense of making the non-GM crop unfit for consumption, but the loss of accredited "non-GM" status may be commercially damaging. How far is the non-GM activity "sensitive"? How far is it unreasonable to carry on GM farming in the vicinity? For various aspects of the problem see *Hoffmann v Monsanto Canada Inc* [2005] SKQB 225.

[95] *Eastern and SA Telegraph Co v Cape Town Tramways* [1902] A.C. 381 at 383.

[96] *McKinnon Industries Ltd v Walker* [1951] 3 D.L.R. 577 at 581 per Lord Simonds.

[97] *Network Rail Infrastructure Ltd v Morris* [2004] EWCA Civ 172 at [35] per Buxton LJ.

[98] *Network Rail Infrastructure Ltd v Morris* [2004] EWCA Civ 172 at [18].

there is no natural right to a view[99] or to light or to the free passage of air[100] though the last two at least may be acquired by prescription[101] and may of course be conferred by grant. The cases on the absence of a right to a view or light provided the basis of the decision in *Hunter v Canary Wharf Ltd*[102] in which the House of Lords held that the defendants were not liable in nuisance for constructing a 250m high stainless steel-clad tower which interfered with the claimants' television reception: if a landowner has a right, at common law, to build on his land in such a way as to block sunlight from reaching the claimant's land, the same must apply to a structure which blocks television signals.[103] It does not, however, necessarily follow that the same is true of some activity (for example, the generation of electricity) on the defendant's land which interferes with television signals. In *Bridlington Relay Ltd v Yorkshire Electricity Board*[104] Buckley J in the 1960s doubted whether interference with such a purely recreational amenity was an actionable nuisance,[105] but the overall result of *Hunter v Canary Wharf* is to leave the matter open[106] and it is thought that in principle receiving television should now be a "protected interest": television is watched by virtually the entire population for both recreational and educational purposes and the "ordinary usages of mankind" must be judged by contemporary standards.

15–021   **Non-physical damage.** We have seen that the law of negligence protects only against physical damage caused by the interruption of utility supplies.[107] Plainly the law of nuisance has no general requirement of "physical damage" otherwise it would not be possible to complain of noise and smells.[108] However, it has been held that the rule on utility supplies cannot be evaded by framing the claim in nuisance. If D damages the X Co's gas main supplying C then, in the absence of physical damage, C's rights are confined to those, if any, which C has under his supply agreement with X.[109]

---

[99] *Dalton v Angus* (1881) 6 App. Cas. 740 at 824.

[100] *Bryant v Lefever* (1879) 4 C.P.D. 172; *Belfast CC v Irish Football Association Ltd* [1988] N.I. 290.

[101] See further *Clerk & Lindsell on Torts*, 20th edn (2013), paras 20–147, 20–153.

[102] [1997] A.C. 655.

[103] Especially bearing in mind that the direction of these signals may change and the defendant has no control over that.

[104] [1965] Ch. 436.

[105] The interference was only on one channel and was contributed to by the special nature of the claimants' relay services. The actual reason for the refusal of the injunction was that the defendants proposed to correct the matter.

[106] Lords Goff and Cooke ([1997] A.C. 655 at 684 and 719) seem favourable. Lord Hoffmann leaves the issue open (at 708). Lord Lloyd inclines against; *Kidner* [1989] Conv 279.

[107] See para.5–061.

[108] For an intermediate case see the claim of Hampshire Wildlife Trust in *Jan de Nul (UK) Ltd v Axa Royal Belge* [2002] EWCA Civ 209; [2002] 1 Lloyd's Rep. 583 (interference with land by deposit of silt; claimants commissioned survey which showed that no serious damage done; cost of survey recoverable).

[109] *Anglian Water Services Ltd v Crawshaw Robbins Ltd* [2001] B.L.R. 173. If, however, this is treated as resting on the proposition that it is not a nuisance to prevent something coming onto the claimant's land it presents difficulties about saying that interference with television reception caused

Right to support of land. The only natural right to support of one's land by one's neighbour's is for the land in its natural state and a right to support of the land with buildings on it must be acquired by grant or prescription.[110] This cannot be evaded by framing a claim for damages as one for negligence, as is shown by the cases on the closely analogous issue of support by underground water. In *Langbrook Properties Ltd v Surrey CC*[111] and *Stephens v Anglia Water Authority*[112] pumping out of underground water led to withdrawal of support and collapse of the claimants' properties. Since the House of Lords had confirmed in *Bradford (Mayor of) v Pickles*[113] that there was no interest at common law in percolating or underground water until appropriation[114] it was said to be an inevitable logical consequence that the claim should fail even:[115]

> "[I]f the defendant's activities . . . resulted in subsidence of buildings or even personal injury. As the law stands the right of the landowner to abstract subterranean water flowing in undefined channels appears . . . to be exercisable regardless of the consequences, whether physical or pecuniary, to his neighbours."

E.   Temporary Injury

Temporary injury and injunctions. Where the claimant seeks an injunction to restrain a nuisance, it will not be issued, except in extreme cases, if the nuisance is temporary and occasional only. The reason for this is that an injunction is a remedy depending on the discretion of the court and it will not be issued where damages would be an adequate remedy.[116] In *Swaine v GN Ry*,[117] for example, manure heaps which were ordinarily inoffensive were occasionally rendered offensive by a delay in their removal and also by the presence of dead cats and dogs. The Court of Chancery declined to grant an injunction, leaving the claimant to his common law action for damages. An instance of the exceptional circumstances in which the court did grant an injunction was pile-driving carried on by night for building purposes for to do it at that time was unreasonable.[118]

Temporary injury and damages. Where the claim is for damages, as distinct from an injunction, the duration of the alleged nuisance is one of the relevant factors in determining whether the defendant has acted unreasonably and is

15–022

15–023

15–024

---

by an activity can be a nuisance. See also *Colour Quest Ltd v Total Downstream UK Plc* [2009] EWHC 640 (Comm); [2009] 2 Lloyd's Rep. 1 at [467] and *Shell UK Ltd v Total UK Ltd* [2010] EWCA Civ 180; [2010] 3 W.L.R. 1192 at [151].

[110] See *Dalton v Angus* (1881) 6 App. Cas. 740.

[111] [1970] 1 W.L.R. 161.

[112] [1987] 1 W.L.R. 1381.

[113] [1895] A.C. 587.

[114] In the sense that no one can complain of appropriation by another, but it is tortious to pollute an underground stratum from which neighbours draw water: *Ballard v Tomlinson* (1885) 29 Ch. D. 115; *Cambridge Water Co Ltd v Eastern Counties Leather Plc* [1994] 2 A.C. 264.

[115] *Prenn v Simmonds* [1971] 1 W.L.R. 1381 at 1387.

[116] See para.15–069.

[117] (1864) 4 De G.J. & S. 211 at 215–216.

[118] *De Keyser's Royal Hotel Ltd v Spicer Bros Ltd* (1914) 30 T.L.R. 257.

liable.[119] All other circumstances must be taken into account and they may on the one hand make a temporary annoyance a nuisance or, on the other, render it lawful. A person who pulls down his house for the purpose of building another no doubt causes considerable inconvenience to his neighbours and it may well be that he will take some months in the process but if he uses all reasonable skill and care to avoid annoyance, that is not a nuisance, for life could scarcely be carried on if it were.[120] On the other hand, blocking up a highway for no more than a month may well be a nuisance because circumstances will usually make the resulting damage so much more serious.[121] When it is said therefore that the injury must be, "of a substantial character not fleeting or evanescent",[122] what is signified is that the temporary nature of the injury may be evidence, but certainly not conclusive evidence, that it is too trivial to be considered as a nuisance.[123]

15–025   **A "continuing state of affairs".** It is often said that a continuing state of affairs is normally necessary in nuisance. The meaning of this was put by Thesiger J in *SCM (UK) Ltd v WJ Whittal & Son Ltd* as follows:[124]

> "[W]hile there is no doubt that a single isolated escape may cause the damage that entitles a claimant to sue for nuisance, yet it must be proved that the nuisance arose from the condition of the defendant's land or premises or property or activities thereon that constituted a nuisance."

The frequency of the escape on to the claimant's land (or, in the case of public nuisance, on to the highway)[125] and the gravity of the harm likely to be caused, are important factors in determining whether a dangerous state of affairs existed on the defendant's land.[126] On the other hand, it has been said that the "position is that on appropriate facts there can be liability in private nuisance for a single or isolated escape as opposed to a state of affairs where there is both unreasonable or negligent user of land and foreseeability of escape".[127] What makes the point of limited importance is that where the defendant's activity falls within the rule in *Rylands v Fletcher* (itself very closely related to nuisance) there is no difficulty in

---

[119] Per Pollock CB in *Bamford v Turnley* (1862) 3 B. & S. 66 at 79 31 L.J.Q.B. 286 at 292 (a dissenting judgment, but certainly not on this point).

[120] Vaughan Williams J in *Harrison v Southwark and Vauxhall Water Co* [1891] 2 Ch. 409 at 413–414; *Clift v Welsh Office* [1999] 1 W.L.R. 796. Cf. *Andreae v Selfridge & Co Ltd* [1938] Ch. 1 at 6 per Sir Wilfrid Greene MR.

[121] *Iveson v Moore* (1699) 1 Ld.Raym. 486.

[122] Brett J in *Benjamin v Storr* (1874) L.R. 9 C.P. 400 at 407.

[123] See *Crown River Cruises v Kimbolton Fireworks* [1996] 2 Lloyd's Rep. 533 (15–20 minutes firework display with falling debris a nuisance).

[124] [1970] 1 W.L.R. 1017 at 1031. The learned judge continued: "I am satisfied that one negligent act that causes physical damage to an electric cable does not thereby constitute a nuisance." Nuisance was not considered on appeal by the Court of Appeal: [1971] 1 Q.B. 337.

[125] Compare the facts of *Stone v Bolton* [1950] 1 K.B. 201 (the element of nuisance was not discussed in the House of Lords [1951] A.C.850) with those of *Miller v Jackson* [1977] Q.B. 966.

[126] See also *Castle v St Augustine's Links* (1922) 38 T.L.R. 615; *Spicer v Smee* [1946] 1 All E.R. 489; *Hilder v Associated Portland Cement Manufacturers Ltd* [1961] 1 W.L.R. 1434.

[127] *Colour Quest Ltd v Total Downstream UK Plc* [2009] EWHC 640 (Comm); [2009] 2 Lloyd's Rep. 1 at [421].

saying that an isolated escape is actionable without reference to a "state of affairs"; indeed the rule has been said to be merely a special sub-rule of nuisance applicable to certain isolated escapes.[128]

F.   Malice

Is malice material in nuisance? If A's legitimate use of his own property causes   **15–026**
to B annoyance which does not amount to a nuisance, will the fact that A's acts are done solely for the purpose of annoying B convert them into a nuisance? In *Christie v Davey*,[129] the defendant, exasperated by a considerable number of music lessons given by the claimant,[130] a teacher of music whose residence was separated from that of the defendant only by a party-wall, interrupted the claimant's lessons by knocking on the party-wall, beating on trays, whistling and shrieking. North J issued an injunction because the defendant had acted deliberately and maliciously for the purpose of annoying the claimant. The learned judge added: "If what has taken place had occurred between two sets of persons both perfectly innocent, I should have taken an entirely different view of the case."[131] Two years later, however, the House of Lords in *Bradford (Mayor of) v Pickles*[132] asserted that a bad motive cannot make wrongful an act otherwise legal, and they reaffirmed this principle in *Allen v Flood*[133] but in neither decision was any reference made to *Christie v Davey*.

In *Hollywood Silver Fox Farm Ltd v Emmett*,[134] Macnaghten J followed *Christie v Davey*. The defendant deliberately caused guns to be fired on his own land near the boundary of the claimant's land in order to scare the claimant's silver foxes during breeding time. The vixens of these animals are extremely nervous during breeding time and much damage was done in consequence of the defendant's act, which was motivated by pure spite. Macnaghten J considered that the intention of the defendant is relevant in determining liability in nuisance and granted an injunction and awarded damages to the claimant.

Assessment. It is submitted that the decisions in *Christie v Davey* and *Hollywood*   **15–027**
Silver Fox Farm Ltd v Emmett represent the better view. The courts, in judging what constitutes a nuisance, take into consideration the purpose of the defendant's activity,[135] and acts otherwise justified on the ground of reciprocity, if done wantonly and maliciously with the object of injuring a neighbour are devoid of any social utility and cannot be regarded as "reasonable". The element of unreasonableness in nuisance as a tort had been recognised long before *Bradford (Mayor of) v Pickles* and that decision did not affect the principle of nuisances of this type, i.e. those in which the law recognises that a certain amount of

---

[128] See para.16–003.
[129] [1893] 1 Ch. 316; *Palmar v Loder* [1962] C.L.Y. 2233.
[130] Would this now be an "ordinary use" of a terraced house? *Southwark LBC v Mills* [2001] 1 A.C. 1.
[131] *Christie v Davy* [1893] 1 Ch. 316 at 326–327.
[132] [1895] A.C. 587.
[133] [1898] A.C. 1.
[134] [1936] 2 K.B. 468 at 475.
[135] *Harrison v Southwark and Vauxhall Water Co* [1891] 2 Ch. 409 at 414 per Vaughan Williams LJ; *Bamford v Turnley* (1862) 31 L.J.Q.B. 286 at 294 per Bramwell B; *Grant v Fynney* (1872) L.R. 8 Ch.App. 8 at 12 per Lord Selborne LC.

discomfort is inevitable in life owing to the activities of one's neighbours, but also expects that neighbours by their mutual forbearance will lessen this discomfort as much as they are reasonably able. The law of private nuisance gives to each party a qualified privilege of causing harm to the other. When the activity of one party is motivated principally by malice, his privilege is at an end and he is liable for the damage he has caused.

In both *Christie v Davey* and *Hollywood Silver Fox Farm Ltd v Emmett* the defendant interfered with a legally protected interest of the claimant and the issue was whether, in doing so, he had acted unreasonably. If, however, the defendant's activity has not infringed any such right or interest, the claimant has no cause of action[136] and the defendant's motive is irrelevant. This was in fact the position in *Bradford (Mayor of) v Pickles* itself, where the defendant deliberately drained his land so as to diminish the water supply reaching the land of the claimants. His purpose was to coerce the claimants into purchasing his land. It had previously been established that no interest in percolating waters exists until appropriation,[137] and as no interest or right could therefore have been infringed, the motive of the defendant was not material.[138] In other words, *Christie v Davey* and the *Hollywood Silver Fox Farm* case represent the normal rule, most rights of enjoyment and use of land being relative, and *Bradford (Mayor of) v Pickles* turns on the peculiarity of the law governing percolating water.[139] However, it is not easy to support the view of Lord Cooke in *Hunter v Canary Wharf Ltd*[140] that the construction of a building with the purpose of interfering with a neighbour's television reception[141] would be actionable. The decision in that case rested on the analogy of the absence of a right to a view and that would appear to be as much a "no right" situation as that involving percolating water.

4. STANDARD OF LIABILITY IN PRIVATE NUISANCE[142]

15–028 The question of the extent to which fault (in the sense of negligence) is necessary to establish liability in damages for nuisance has given rise to great difficulty. There are many judicial statements of various vintages asserting that liability in nuisance is "strict" but there are very few cases in which the meaning of that

---

[136] See para.15–020.

[137] *Acton v Blundell* (1843) 12 M. & W. 324; *Broadbent v Ramsbotham* (1856) 11 Exch. 602; *Chasemore v Richards* (1859) 7 H.L.C. 349.

[138] See Fridman (1954) 40 Va.L.R. 583.

[139] In the case of water flowing in a defined channel a riparian owner can take water only for use on the adjoining land. Water supplies, whether percolating or channelled, are now generally subject to licensing control by regional water authorities under statute.

[140] [1997] A.C. 655 at 721.

[141] Perhaps a somewhat unlikely scenario, given modern planning controls.

[142] This section is concerned only with private nuisance. As we have seen above, public nuisance is really a quite different tort but the position on that is even more obscure. The parties in *Claimants in Corby Group Litigation v Corby BC* [2008] EWCA Civ 463; [2009] 2 W.L.R. 609 took the preliminary issue of whether it covered personal injuries to the CA. In fact the claimants were able to establish fault and public nuisance figures hardly at all in the decision on liability, Aikenhead J contenting himself with saying that, "strictly speaking, negligence or breach of a statutory duty is not essential in public nuisance although, if there is negligence or a breach of statutory duty which causes life or health to be endangered, there will be a public nuisance": [2009] EWHC 1944 (TCC) at [688].

expression has really been explored. It is impossible to reconcile everything that has ever been said on this subject but it is submitted that the current law may be summarised in the following propositions.

Remedy by way of an injunction. Where the claimant seeks an injunction to restrain a nuisance the purpose of the remedy is to protect him from future damage. As the Law Commission has pointed out:[143]

> "[C]onsideration of the strictness of the duty is then out of place—all that the court is concerned with is the question, 'Should the defendant be told to stop this interference with the claimant's rights?' Whether or not the defendant knew of the noise or smell or the like when it first began to annoy the plaintiff does not matter; he becomes aware of it at the latest when the plaintiff brings his claim before the court."

In such a case, as we have seen in the previous section, the court is concerned with balancing the respective rights of the two parties and determining the permissible extent of an interference which, since the defendant ex hypothesi knows about it, is deliberate. If the stench of my pig farm fouls your air, I am liable because I have knowingly created an intolerable situation for you—and if it is intolerable to you by ordinary, sensible standards it is meaningless to ask whether I was negligent in creating the smell. Accordingly, great care must be taken in transferring statements in injunction cases to the different context of claims for damages for past loss.[144]

Creation of a nuisance distinguished from continuing a nuisance. When it comes to a claim for damages we must draw a distinction between the creation or adoption of a nuisance by the defendant and the continuance of a nuisance[145] created by a third party or an act of nature. An occupier "continues" a nuisance, for the initial creation of which he is not responsible, if, once he knows or ought to know of its existence, he fails to take reasonable precautions to abate it and it is clear that he is not liable in damages if these conditions are not satisfied.[146] Here there is a "sort of condominium" with the law of negligence.[147]

Innocently created nuisance: previously unknown risks. Even where the defendant has created the situation which interferes with the claimant's land,

15–029

15–030

15–031

---

[143] Law Commission, Report No.32, *Civil Liability for Dangerous Things and Activities*, p.25.

[144] *Cambridge Water Co v Eastern Counties Leather Plc*[1994] 2 A.C. 264 at 300; e.g. *Rapier v London Tramways Co* [1893] 2 Ch. 588 at 560 per Lindley LJ: "If I am sued for nuisance, and the nuisance is proved, it is no defence on my part to say, and to prove, that I have taken all reasonable care to prevent it." In its context, this statement means no more than that if the activity is unreasonably injurious when carried on with all care, it should not be carried on at all; but see how in *Transco Plc v Stockport MBC* [2003] UKHL 61; [2004] 2 A.C. 1 at [97] Lord Walker cites the passage in support of the proposition that, "negligence (in the sense of a demonstrable failure to take reasonable care) has traditionally been regarded as irrelevant".

[145] *Sedleigh-Denfield v O'Callaghan* [1940] A.C. 880 at 904–908 per Lord Wright and at 913 per Lord Romer.

[146] This situation is discussed further, para.15–045. The burden of proof would appear to lie upon the claimant (*Sedleigh-Denfield v O'Callaghan* [1940] A.C. 880 at 887, 899, 908) and it is significant that in *Goldman v Hargrave* [1967] 1 A.C. 645 the Privy Council thought it unnecessary to decide whether the cause of action lay in nuisance or negligence. See also *Smith v Littlewoods Organisation Ltd* [1987] A.C. 241 at 274 per Lord Goff.

[147] Lord Walker in *Transco Plc v Stockport MBC* [2003] UKHL 61; [2004] 2 A.C. 1 at [96].

there is no liability in damages where the possibility of interference of the type which occurs could not reasonably have been foreseen by a person in the defendant's position when he did the acts which are called in question. This has some significance in cases of what has been called "historic pollution", that is to say, contamination by activities which were thought harmless when they were carried on but which are shown, in the light of subsequent advances in knowledge, to be hazardous. In *Cambridge Water Co v Eastern Counties Leather Plc*[148] the defendants had for some years used PCE (an organochlorine) in their trade in tanning. Continual small spillages had gradually built up a pool of PCE under the land and contaminated the aquifer from which the claimants drew their supply of water, forcing them to find another source at a cost of nearly £1 million. PCE evaporates quickly in the air but is not readily soluble in water. When the contamination was taking place it was not foreseeable to a skilled person that quantities of the chemical would accumulate in the aquifer nor, even if this could have been foreseen, was it foreseeable that there would be any significant damage to the claimants' water.[149] The only known hazard of PCE at that time was that someone might be overcome by fumes in the case of a large spillage. A unanimous House of Lords held that the defendants were not liable in damages for the contamination. Strictly speaking, because of the way the litigation had gone below, nuisance was not a live issue but it would be nonsense to dismiss as mere dicta the view of a unanimous House of Lords, especially where it gains force from being delivered in one speech.[150]

Where the defendant has thus innocently created the danger its source may remain on his land after the point at which its nature becomes known. Examples are the PCE in the *Cambridge Water* case, which had formed in pools at the base of the aquifer, or chemical contamination of the soil or removal of spoil which unexpectedly turns out to increase the risk of flooding. In such a case liability in damages will not be imposed for a state of affairs which has passed beyond the control of the defendant. Indeed, Lord Goff said that:[151] "[I]n such circumstances, I do not consider that [the defendant] should be under any greater liability than that imposed for negligence. At best, if the case is regarded as one of nuisance, it should be treated no differently from, for example, the case of the landslip in *Leakey v National Trust*[152]."

In other words, the defendant is expected to do what is reasonable in the circumstances and the duty to remove the danger is not an absolute one, for he is in morally no different a position from the occupier whose land suffers an immediately recognisable nuisance from the act of trespassers or of nature.[153]

---

[148] [1994] 2 A.C. 264.

[149] Indeed, at no point was it contended that the contaminated water was dangerous to health. The problem arose because EC requirements set very low levels for PCE in water.

[150] That of Lord Goff. See also *Savage v Fairclough* [2000] Env L.R. 183.

[151] *Cambridge Water Co v Eastern Counties Leather Plc* [1994] 2 A.C. 264 at 307.

[152] [1980] Q.B. 485 (a case of a natural hazard not created by the defendant).

[153] *Anthony v The Coal Authority* [2005] EWHC (QB) 1654; [2006] Env L.R. 17 (where failure to take steps to prevent foreseeable spontaneous combustion of a spoil tip was actionable; but the defendants would not have been held liable for combustion as a result of fires lit by trespassers). Cf. *Arscott v The Coal Authority* [2004] EWCA Civ 892; [2005] Env L.R. 6, where an increased risk of flooding was not foreseeable when infilling works were done.

Liability for known risks. In *Cambridge Water* the risk was unknown at the   **15–032**
relevant time. However, what is the position where the defendant is carrying on
an activity which presents a known, albeit remote, risk to neighbours but which is
carried on with all reasonable care,[154] notwithstanding which some catastrophe
occurs for which the defendant is not to blame? It is clearly stated in *Cambridge
Water* that where the defendant (or someone for whom he is responsible) has
created the nuisance.[155]

However, in the later case of *Transco Plc v Stockport MBC*[156] the House of
Lords accepted that the rule in *Rylands v Fletcher* was a sub-species of the tort of
nuisance (as indeed had been said in *Cambridge Water*) concerned with liability
for exceptional risks created by the use of land.[157] That rule undoubtedly involves
some element of "strict" liability, though it is far from absolute, and the House
was concerned at the same time to preserve it and to draw its boundaries fairly
narrowly. Nonetheless, if the sub-species represents a special rule of strict
liability for foreseeable risks it is difficult to see how the general species itself
can also involve strict liability; if it did there would be no point in worrying about
the precise definition of the sub-species.[158] Nor does it help to appeal to the idea
of "unreasonable user". If the defendant is carrying on his activity with all due
precautions and it is not sufficiently fraught with risk to attract the rule in *Rylands
v Fletcher*, how can it be said to be unreasonable?

Assessment. It does therefore seem difficult to support the proposition that in the   **15–033**
modern law nuisance involves any general rule of strict liability for damage done.

---

[154] Liability for tree root damage depends upon the defendant having means of knowledge of the risk:
Delaware Mansions Ltd v Westminster CC [2001] UKHL 55; [2002] 1 A.C. 321. The principles of
factual causation are the same as in negligence, i.e. it is enough to show that the defendant's roots
made a material contribution to the damage: *Loftus-Brigham v Ealing LBC* [2003] EWCA Civ 1490;
103 Con L.R. 102.

[155] *Cambridge Water Co v Eastern Counties Leather Plc* [1994] 2 A.C. 264 at 269. But even in this
situation remoteness of damage is based on foreseeability: "[I]t is still the law that the fact that [he]
has taken all reasonable care will not of itself exonerate him from liability, the relevant control
mechanism being found within the principle of reasonable user."*The Wagon Mound (No.2)*,
para.7–033.

[156] [2003] UKHL 61; [2004] 2 A.C. 1. See Ch.16.

[157] Whether this is entirely reconcilable with the view taken in *Cambridge Water* is another matter.
The whole thrust of that case is that *Rylands v Fletcher* is not a category of liability for
ultra-hazardous activities and the emphasis is upon its applicability to "isolated escapes". While
"exceptional risk" may not be precisely the same thing as "ultra-hazardous" it looks rather similar.
The speech of Lord Hobhouse comes closer than the others to equating *Rylands v Fletcher* with the
general rule in private nuisance (see at [55]–[57]) and at [64] he refers to a "recognizable" rather than
an "exceptional" risk, but despite his criticisms of the use of expressions like "ordinary" and
"reasonable" at the end of the day he goes along with the conclusion that a standard water system in
a block of flats does not attract the rule.

[158] The occurrence of an interference with the claimant's land, the risk of which was remote, will
often amount to an "isolated escape", but as has been seen in para.15–025 it is difficult to say that
nuisance has no application at all in such cases. Is it the law that liability for an isolated escape is strict
if the use of the defendant's land involved exceptional risk (*Rylands v Fletcher*), but that otherwise
negligence must be proved (even if the claim can be brought in nuisance): see *Northumbrian Water
Ltd v Sir Robert McAlpine Ltd* [2014] EWCA Civ 685.

That is not necessarily to say that this is not a desirable rule.[159] If nuisance involves "give and take", "live and let live" it might also be said that it involves reciprocity between benefits and burdens. If D undertakes construction work to improve his property and despite the exercise of all possible care by him damage is caused to the property of his neighbour, C, why should D be able to gain the benefit of improvement at the expense of C? A very long time ago Bramwell B put such an argument in the context of inevitable damage done by public works such as the construction of railways and the contention that they were for the public benefit:[160]

> "It is for the public benefit that there should be railways, but it would not be unless the gain of having the railway was sufficient to compensate the loss occasioned by the use of the land required for its site; and accordingly no one thinks that it would be right to take an individual's land without compensation to make a railway. It is for the public benefit that trains should run, but not unless they pay their expenses. If one of those expenses is the burning down of a wood of such value that the railway owners would not run the train and burn down the wood if it were their own, neither is it for the public benefit if the wood is not their own. If, though the wood were their own, they would still find it compensated them to run trains at the cost of burning the wood, then they obviously ought to compensate the owner of the wood, not being themselves."

In modern economic jargon Bramwell B was saying that the costs of an enterprise ought to be "internalised".[161] Before he spoke, the legislature in the Lands Clauses Consolidation Act 1845, the ancestor of the modern compulsory purchase legislation, had recognised the right to compensation for compulsory taking and for "injurious affection"; and the Railway Fires Acts[162] imposed limited strict liability in his example of the burnt wood some time later. However, such provisions have not been by any means universal[163] and a shift to this broad approach would involve the rewriting of much of our law.

5. WHO CAN SUE?

A. Private Nuisance

15–034   **Those with an interest in land.** "He alone has a lawful claim [for private nuisance] who has suffered an invasion of some proprietary or other interest in land."[164] This proposition was reaffirmed by the House of Lords in *Hunter v Canary Wharf Ltd*.[165] As far as encroachment on or damage to the land is

---

[159] An intermediate position is suggested in *Hamilton v Papakura DC* [2000] 1 N.Z.L.R. 265 at [74], that liability is prima facie strict subject to a defence of reasonable care in the ordinary use of land. The PC did not deal with this point: [2002] UKPC 9; [2002] 3 N.Z.L.R. 308.

[160] *Bamford v Turnley* (1862) 3 B. & S. 66. The case involved the burning of bricks.

[161] *Transco Plc v Stockport MBC* [2003] UKHL 61; [2004] 2 A.C. 1 at [29] per Lord Hoffmann. For a full discussion see Oliphant, in Koziol and Steininger (eds), *European Tort Law 2004*.

[162] See para.16–038.

[163] See para.15–063.

[164] *Read v J Lyons & Co Ltd* [1947] A.C. 156 at 183 per Lord Simonds.

[165] [1997] A.C. 655 (Lord Cooke's dissent on this point relies in part on art.8 of the European Convention on Human Rights); *Jan de Nul (UK) Ltd v Axa Royal Belge* [2000] 2 Lloyd's Rep. 700 at 719, on appeal [2002] EWCA Civ 209; [2002] 1 Lloyd's Rep. 583 (contractual mooring rights

concerned the proposition is self-evident, but it is equally applicable to nuisances like smells and noise which affect the enjoyment of the land, for what is being remedied by the law is not the personal discomfort of the persons on the land but the diminution in the value of the land. Of course in such cases there may not have been any effect on the capital value of the land, but what may be called the "amenity value" of the land is diminished so long as the nuisance continues.[166] It follows that even in such cases a claim may only be brought by a person with sufficient interest in the land (whom for the moment we shall call the occupier) and not by members of the occupier's family,[167] guests, lodgers or employees. In the majority of cases, where the object of the complaint is to obtain an injunction to put an end to the nuisance, this causes no hardship and a contrary rule might be productive of practical difficulties. If the occupier sues, then the other persons using the premises will benefit from the grant of the injunction; if the others were allowed to sue it would mean that a person on adjoining land who wished to come to an arrangement with the occupier whereby the latter would license some temporary nuisance (for example during repairs or improvements) could not safely rely on it.

Qualifying interests. As to the precise nature of the interest required, the "owner occupier" can obviously sue.[168] So can a tenant or a person who has de facto exclusive possession.[169] The owner of an incorporeal hereditament such as an easement or profit can sue for disturbance of his right.[170] A reversioner can bring an action in nuisance if he can show that there is a likelihood that permanent injury will be caused to the property and his right is then coexistent with that of the occupier.[171] A permanent injury is one which will continue indefinitely unless something is done to remove it,[172] for example a building which infringes the right to ancient lights,[173] vibrations causing structural damage,[174] or keeping

15–035

---

insufficient; alternative claim for public nuisance); cf. *Crown River Cruises v Kimbolton Fireworks* [1996] 2 Lloyd's Rep. 533 (exclusive occupation of mooring).

[166] The assessment of diminution in amenity may have to be via expert evidence on a notional rental value. This may be a somewhat artificial exercise but no doubt evidence of the actual impact on persons living in the premises will be relevant: *Dobson v Thames Water* [2009] EWCA Civ 28; [2009] 3 All E.R. 319 at [33], where it is also said that if the premises were empty the damages would be nominal.

[167] Cf. *Khorasandjian v Bush* [1993] Q.B. 727 (overruled in *Hunter*, a situation now within the Protection from Harassment Act 1997).

[168] Where there is a continuing nuisance (e.g. intrusion of tree roots) an owner may recover damages for remedial work even though some of the damage may have been done before he acquired the property: *Delaware Mansions Ltd v Westminster CC* [2001] UKHL 55; [2002] 1 A.C. 321.

[169] *Hunter v Canary Wharf Ltd* [1997] A.C. 655 at 688; *Foster v Warblington UDC* [1906] 1 K.B. 648; *Pemberton v Southwark LBC* [2000] 1 W.L.R. 1672 (where the court relied in part upon art.8 of the European Convention on Human Rights); *Transco Plc v Stockport MBC* [2003] UKHL 61; [2004] 2 A.C. 1 at [92]; *Tinsel Time Ltd v Roberts* [2011] EWHC 1199 (TCC); [2011] B.L.R. 515 (licensee with exclusive possession).

[170] *Nicholls v Ely Beet Sugar Factory Ltd* [1936] 1 Ch. 343 (destruction of fish by pollution); *Weston v Lawrence Weaver Ltd* [1961] 1 Q.B. 402 (physical damage to an easement of way without interference with right of passage not actionable).

[171] The damages will have to be divided according to the relative interests of reversioner and occupier: *Hunter v Canary Wharf Ltd* [1997] A.C. 655 at 707.

[172] *Jones v Llanrwst UDC* [1911] 1 Ch. 393 at 404 per Parker J.

[173] *Jesser v Gifford* (1767) 4 Burr. 2141.

locked a gate across a path over which the reversioner has a right of way;[175] but the emission of noise or fumes or other invasions of a temporary nature, even if they cause the tenants to leave, or reduce the letting value, will not suffice.[176]

15–036   **Effect on the assessment of damages.** Given the premise above about damages for "interference with enjoyment" being granted for what is essentially injury to the property it follows that where damages are sought, their quantum is in no way affected by whether the property is inhabited by one person or by a family of 12 and that only the occupier has title to sue. Nor will the damages be any larger if there is more than one person who qualifies as "occupier":[177]

> "The damages for nuisance recoverable by the . . . occupier may be affected by the size, commodiousness and value of his property but cannot be increased merely because more people are in occupation and therefore suffer greater collective discomfort. If more than one person has an interest in the property, the damages will have to be divided among them . . . But the damages cannot be increased by the fact that the interests in the land are divided; still less according to the number of persons residing on the premises."

15–037   **No claim for personal injury.** Although *Hunter v Canary Wharf Ltd* does not perhaps decide the point as a matter of precedent, the reasoning in the case irresistibly suggests that even the occupier of the land may not frame a claim for personal injuries as one for private nuisance.[178]

15–038   **Article 8 ECHR.** Since *Hunter v Canary Wharf Ltd* English courts have become able to give direct effect to the European Convention on Human Rights and art.8 provides that, "*everyone* has the right to respect for his private and family life [and] his home". It is plain that a situation which would give rise to common law liability for nuisance may also constitute an infringement of art.8 and where the defendant is a public authority there is a direct right of action which is not on the face of it constrained by the land-holding qualification set by the common law. However, where an occupier has been awarded damages at common law it is most improbable that any additional sum would be awarded to him for violation of the Convention right; in the case of non-occupying members of his family, who cannot recover at common law, it will be necessary, in determining whether "just satisfaction" requires an award of damages to them, to consider how far the

---

[174] *Colwell v St Pancras BC* [1904] Ch. 707.

[175] *Kidgill v Moor* (1850) 9 C.B. 364.

[176] *Simpson v Savage* (1856) 1 C.B.(N.S.) 347; *Cooper v Crabtree* (1882) 20 Ch.D. 589. But see the suggestion of a broader approach in *John Smith & Co (Edinburgh) Ltd v Hill* [2010] EWHC 1016 (Ch); [2010] 2 B.C.L.C. 566.

[177] *Hunter v Canary Wharf Ltd* [1997] A.C. 655 at 706 per Lord Hoffmann.

[178] There are statements to this effect by Lord Lloyd [1997] A.C. 655 at 696 and Lord Hoffmann at 706 (but cf. *Ribee v Norrie* [2001] P.I.Q.R. P128, para.16–015). As to public nuisance see para.15–007. Logically the same might be argued to apply to damage to personal property owned by the occupier but where this is combined with damage to land or buildings that might cause practical complications. Lord Hoffmann thought the occupier could recover damages for chattels or livestock as consequential loss (at 706) but that personal injury was not a consequential loss. See also *Crown River Cruises v Kimbolton Fireworks* [1996] 2 Lloyd's Rep. 533. This assumes of course that even damages for physical injury to the land are recoverable: cf. *Hunter v Canary Wharf Ltd* [1997] A.C. 655 at 692.

process of assessing the occupier's damages for diminution in amenity have in fact taken account of the impact of the nuisance on the family.[179]

B. Public Nuisance

As we have seen, if a public nuisance has been committed, any person who has suffered special damage can sue in respect of it. It may, for instance, be the occupier of adjacent property and it may be a user of the highway.[180]   **15–039**

6.   WHO CAN BE SUED?

A.   Creator of the Nuisance

Not necessary that the nuisance should have been created by the use of the   **15–040**
defendant's land. In *Hussain v Lancaster CC*[181] persons engaged in a campaign of racial harassment against the claimants, who were shopkeepers. Various acts of trespass and intimidation were committed which were no doubt torts in their own right. However, the Court of Appeal said that there was no nuisance because the acts did not involve the wrongdoers' use of their land, even though it affected the claimants' enjoyment of theirs.[182] With respect, this seems an unnecessary restriction: to say that nuisance is a tort to the claimant's land does not require the additional proposition that it must involve the defendant's use of his land. Suppose, for example, that D, in pursuit of a vendetta against C, repeatedly disturbs C in his remote farmhouse by parking outside, shining his car headlights through the windows and playing his music system at full volume. That is not a public nuisance because it does not affect a "class" of people. Is there any reason why it should not be a private nuisance?[183] Of course, such conduct might now be a tort under the Protection from Harassment Act 1997[184] but it is surprising that it was not a nuisance before the Act. Furthermore, the issue in *Hussain* was not the liability in tort of the wrongdoers, but whether their landlord could be held responsible for their actions. A perfectly adequate basis for the negative answer would have been that the relationship of landlord and tenant between the defendant and the wrongdoers had no connexion with what was going on at the claimants' shop.[185]

The approach in *Hussain* would insulate from liability persons like independent contractors who may create a nuisance affecting the land of C while

---

[179] *Dobson v Thames Water* [2009] EWCA Civ 28; [2009] 3 All E.R. 319. If such a separate award is made it does not call for a reduction in the occupier's common law damages: at [44], disapproving *Dennis v MoD* [2003] EWHC 793 (QB); [2003] Env L.R. 34 on this point.
[180] For example, *Holling v Yorkshire Traction Co Ltd* [1948] 2 All E.R. 662; *Dollman v Hillman Ltd* [1941] 1 All E.R. 355; *Hilder v Associated Portland Cement Manufacturers* [1961] 1 W.L.R. 1434.
[181] [2000] Q.B. 1.
[182] *Hussain v Lancaster CC* [2000] Q.B. 1 at 23.
[183] In *Hussain v Lancaster CC* [2000] Q.B. 1 at 24 significance is attached to the fact that in *Page Motors Ltd v Epsom and Ewell BC* (1982) 80 L.G.R. 337 the wrongdoers had been "occupying" the council's land for some years.
[184] See para.4–034. This was not in force at the time of *Hussain v Lancaster CC* [2000] Q.B. 1.
[185] See Evans LJ in *Lippiatt v South Gloucestershire Council* [2000] Q.B. 51 at 61.

working on the land of B but have no possession of the latter. In a later decision the Court of Appeal held that a local authority which had undertaken as the agent of the highway authority to maintain trees was liable for a "nuisance of omission" in allowing encroachment by roots, whether or not it was occupier of the land in which the trees stood and said that there was no authority "for the proposition that a person cannot be liable in nuisance unless he is in occupation of the land or has some legal interest in it".[186] In other cases it has simply been assumed that the creator of the nuisance is liable even though he has no interest in any relevant land.[187]

B. Occupier

15–041   The occupier of the premises where the nuisance exists is in general liable during the period of his occupancy.[188] This is simple enough where he himself created the nuisance, but further questions arise where it originated: (1) with someone else lawfully on the premises; or (2) with a trespasser or as a result of an act of nature; or (3) with someone from whom the occupier acquired the property. In such cases:[189]

> "[T]he basis for the liability of an occupier for a nuisance on his land is not his occupation as such. Rather, it is that, by virtue of his occupation, an occupier usually has it in his power to take the measures that are necessary to prevent or eliminate the nuisance. He has sufficient control over the hazard which constitutes the nuisance for it to be reasonable to make him liable for the foreseeable consequences of his failure to exercise that control so as to remove the hazard."

i.   Nuisance Created by Persons Lawfully on Premises

15–042   **Servants.** If a nuisance is caused by the servant of the occupier the latter is liable according to the ordinary rules of vicarious liability.

15–043   **Independent contractors.** As a general rule, a principal cannot be held liable for the acts or defaults of an independent contractor employed by him, but there are certain exceptions to this rule. In some cases, for instance, the principal is said to be under a "non-delegable" duty to see that care is taken and if, in fact, damage is caused to a third party by the activity of the contractor, the principal will be liable, because he himself is thereby in breach of his duty of care.[190]

---

[186] *LE Jones (Insurance Brokers) Ltd v Portsmouth CC* [2002] EWCA Civ 1723; [2003] 1 W.L.R. 427. It is true that *Transco Plc v Stockport MBC* [2003] UKHL 61; [2004] 2 A.C. 1 is replete with statements like, "interference by one occupier of land with the right in or enjoyment of land by another occupier of land" (at [9]) but: (a) this may simply reflect what is the position in the vast majority of cases; and (b) nothing turned on the defendant's status since it plainly was an occupier. Cf. *Dwr Cymru Cyfyngedig (Welsh Water) v Barratt Homes Ltd* [2013] EWCA Civ 233; [2013] 1 W.L.R. 3486: "nuisance does not require a use by the defendant of its land", at [57] per Lloyd Jones LJ.

[187] *Fennell v Robson Excavations Pty Ltd* [1977] 2 N.S.W.L.R. 486 is most directly in point and reviews the authorities. See also *Southport Corp v Esso Petroleum Ltd* [1954] 2 Q.B. 182 at 204; [1956] A.C. 218 at 225; *Rosewell v Prior* (1701) 12 Mod. 635 at 639.

[188] *Sedleigh-Denfield v O'Callaghan* [1940] A.C. 880.

[189] *LE Jones (Insurance Brokers)* [2002] EWCA Civ 1723; [2003] 1 W.L.R. 427 at [11].

[190] See para.21–049.

Whether or not there is still any special rule that a person who engages in any activity which involves an exceptional danger is under such a non-delegable duty of care[191] there certainly seem to be nuisance cases where the idea of the non-delegable duty has been applied. Thus, in *Bower v Peate*[192] the defendant employed a contractor to do construction work on his land in the course of which the contractor undermined the support for the claimant's adjoining house. The defendant was held liable. In *Matania v National Provincial Bank*[193] the occupier of the first floor of a building was liable to the occupier of the higher floors for a nuisance by dust and noise created by his independent contractor. In both cases the nature of the work was such that there was a special danger of a nuisance being caused by it. On the other hand, it may be that it is the general rule in nuisance that the occupier is liable for his contractor's negligence.[194]

A principal whose contractor interferes with or creates a danger on the highway may be liable to anyone who in consequence suffers special damage. In *Hole v Sittingbourne Ry*,[195] for instance, a railway company had authority to build a bridge across a navigable river provided that they did not impede navigation. The contractors whom they employed constructed it so imperfectly that it would not open to let boats through. The company were held liable to a user of the highway.

Licensees. There is little authority on the position where the nuisance is created by a person who is licensed to be on the premises for his own purposes rather than to do work for the occupier.[196] It seems that the occupier is not liable unless he had knowledge, or means of knowledge, of the nuisance and failed to take steps to control the licensee.[197] **15–044**

ii. Nuisance Created by a Trespasser or Resulting from an Act of Nature

Liability for "adopting" or "continuing" the nuisance. An occupier is not liable for a state of affairs either created by a trespasser or resulting from an act of **15–045**

---

[191] *Honeywill & Stein Ltd v Larkin Bros (London's Commercial Photographers) Ltd* [1934] 1 K.B. 191; see para.21–046.

[192] (1876) 1 Q.B.D. 321; *Dalton v Angus* (1881) 6 App. Cas. 740.

[193] [1936] 2 All E.R. 633; *Duncan's Hotel (Glasgow) Ltd v J&A Ferguson Ltd* 1972 S.L.T. (Notes) 84.

[194] This (rather than any general "primary" rule of strict liability in nuisance) is the way that *Spicer v Smee* [1946] 1 All E.R. 489 seems to be explained in *Johnson v BJW Property Developments Ltd* [2002] EWHC 1131 (TCC); [2002] 3 All E.R. 574.

[195] (1861) 6 H. & N. 488; *Gray v Pullen* (1864) 5 B. & S. 970.

[196] In *Pusey v Somerset CC* [2012] EWCA Civ 988 it was submitted that a claim that a highway authority had failed properly to exercise its powers in relation to the use of a lay-by by highway users was not justiciable in private law. This was said to raise "important issues of public interest" but it was unnecessary to resolve them as the use in question was found not to amount to an actionable nuisance in any event.

[197] *White v Jamieson* (1874) L.R. 18 Eq. 303, which contains statements which might be regarded as placing a more onerous liability on the occupier, was in fact an action for an injunction. In *Lippiatt v South Gloucestershire Council* [2000] Q.B. 51 (below) it was regarded as of no importance whether the wrongdoers were licensees or trespassers but it was made plain that there was no question of any liability for acts of which the council had no knowledge: at 56. See also *Winch v Mid Bedfordshire DC* Unreported July 22, 2002 QB.

nature unless either he adopts the nuisance by using the state of affairs for his own purposes or he "continues" the nuisance. An occupier continues a nuisance if once he has actual or constructive knowledge of its existence he fails to take reasonably prompt and efficient steps to abate it. He cannot of course be liable unless he is in a position to take effective steps to abate the nuisance.[198]

15–046   **Trespassers.** This principle was enunciated by the House of Lords in relation to a nuisance created by a trespasser in the leading case of *Sedleigh-Denfield v O'Callaghan*.[199] The defendant occupied land on which there was a ditch. A trespasser laid a pipe in it with a grating designed to keep out leaves, but placed in such an ill-chosen position that it caused a blockage of the pipe when a heavy rainstorm occurred, and in consequence the claimant's adjacent land was flooded. The storm occurred nearly three years after the erection of the grating and during that period the defendant's servant who was responsible for clearing the ditch ought to have realised the risk of flooding presented by the obstruction. The defendant was held liable in nuisance. The House of Lords refused to draw any distinction in this connection between public and private nuisance. The principle of *Sedleigh-Denfield* is not confined to cases where the trespasser interferes with the state of the land itself: a local authority was held liable for failing to take steps to remove from its land gypsies whose objectionable behaviour damaged the claimants' business next door.[200] Indeed, a landowner has been held liable where the wrongdoers used his land as a base from which they made damaging forays on to the *claimant's* land.[201]

15–047   **Acts of nature.** Although it had been held even before *Sedleigh-Denfield v O'Callaghan* that an occupier can be liable for continuing a nuisance created by a third party,[202] until quite recent times it was considered that he was never under a duty to abate a natural nuisance.[203] This rule of immunity was however decisively rejected by the Judicial Committee in the important case of *Goldman v Hargrave*,[204] where the defendant was held liable for his failure to take adequate steps to extinguish a fire in a redgum tree on his land which had been struck by lightning, the fire having spread to his neighbour's property. Lord Wilberforce rejected the traditional policy of regarding occupation of land as a source of privilege and immunity: "It is only in comparatively recent times that the law has recognised an occupier's duty as one of a more positive character than merely to abstain from creating, or adding to, a source of danger or annoyance."[205]

---

[198] *Smeaton v Ilford Corp* [1954] Ch. 450 at 462; *Goldman v Hargrave* [1967] 1 A.C. 645.

[199] [1940] A.C. 880; *Leanse v Egerton* [1943] K.B. 323.

[200] *Page Motors Ltd v Epsom and Ewell BC* (1982) 80 L.G.R. 337.

[201] *Lippiatt v South Gloucestershire Council* [2000] Q.B. 51. Something more, however, is required than a mere foreseeable possibility that intruders may gain access to the land and cause damage to the neighbouring owner: *Smith v Littlewoods Organisation Ltd* [1987] A.C. 241, para.5–045.

[202] For example, *Barker v Herbert* [1911] 2 K.B. 633.

[203] *Giles v Walker* (1890) 24 Q.B.D. 656; *Pontardawe UDC v Moore-Gwyn* [1929] 1 Ch. 656; *Neath R.D.C. v Williams* [1951] 1 K.B. 115. The rule of immunity did not extend to public nuisance: *Noble v Harrison* [1926] 2 K.B. 332.

[204] [1967] 1 A.C. 645.

[205] [1967] 1 A.C. 645 at 657.

The principle of *Goldman v Hargrave* was formally accepted as part of English law by the Court of Appeal in *Leakey v National Trust*,[206] which involved damage done by movement of the land itself on to adjoining land below it. As regards such nuisances of omission, therefore, it is no longer relevant whether the state of affairs was originally created by a third party or by nature.[207] Once the occupier becomes aware of the nuisance and fails to remedy it within a reasonable time, he may be liable for any damage it may cause, either to his neighbour[208] or the user of the highway.[209]

A subjective standard of care. In determining the standard of care required the court cannot disregard the fact that the occupier is confronted with a nuisance not of his own creation, and because of this the court is entitled to consider the occupier's individual circumstances. As Lord Wilberforce said in a passage of great clarity:[210]   **15–048**

> "The law must take account of the fact that the occupier on whom the duty is cast has, *ex hypothesi*, had this hazard thrust upon him through no seeking or fault of his own. His interest, and his resources, whether physical or material, may be of a very modest character either in relation to the magnitude of the hazard, or as compared with those of his threatened neighbour. A rule which required of him in such unsought circumstances in his neighbour's interest a physical effort of which he is not capable, or an excessive expenditure of money, would be unenforceable or unjust. One may say in general terms that the existence of a duty must be based upon knowledge of the hazard, ability to foresee the consequences of not checking or removing it, and the ability to abate it . . . The standard ought to be to require of the occupier what is reasonable to expect of him in his individual circumstances."

This partly subjective test is an exception to the general rule in negligence[211] and is carefully limited by Lord Wilberforce to cases where the defendant was not himself responsible for the creation of the source of danger.[212] In these cases it is

---

[206] [1980] Q.B. 485. Shaw LJ agreed that *Goldman* represented English Law, but expressed substantial misgivings. See also the use made of this principle in the *Cambridge Water* case, para.15–031.

[207] It is therefore no longer the law that a higher occupier owes no duty in any circumstances to prevent the natural, unconcentrated flow of water from his land to lower land: *Green v Somerleyton* [2003] EWCA Civ 198; [2004] 1 P & C.R. 520.

[208] As a result of this principle the rule that the owner of a servient tenement subject to an easement of support owes no duty to incur expenditure has been outflanked: *Holbeck Hall Hotel Ltd v Scarborough BC* [2000] Q.B. 836 at 856; *Rees v Skerrett* [2001] EWCA Civ 760; [2001] 1 W.L.R. 1541.

[209] "The basis of the occupier's liability lies not in the use of his land; in the absence of 'adoption' there is no such use; but in the neglect of action in the face of something which may damage his neighbour": *Goldman v Hargrave* [1967] 1 A.C. 645 at 661.

[210] *Goldman v Hargrave* [1967] 1 A.C. 645 at 663.

[211] See para.6–002; but in applying this test, "I do not think that, except perhaps in a most unusual case, there would be any question of discovery as to means of the plaintiff or the defendant, or evidence as to their respective resources. The question of reasonableness . . . would fall to be decided on a broad basis, in which on some occasions, there might be included an element of obvious discrepancy of financial resources": *Leakey v National Trust* [1980] Q.B. 485 at 527 per Megaw LJ.

[212] It seems that where there is a public nuisance the ordinary, objective standard applies: *Wandsworth LBC v Railtrack Plc* [2001] EWCA Civ 1236; *The Times*, August 2, 2001, applying *Attorney General v Tod Heatley* [1897] 1 Ch. 560.

immaterial whether the cause of action is termed "nuisance" or "negligence": the duty of the defendant is a general duty of care to his neighbours and the standard imposed on him is the same.[213]

15–049   **Scope of liability.** The magnitude of the hazards which may be involved in cases of this type is illustrated by *Holbeck Hall Hotel Ltd v Scarborough BC*.[214] The lower part of the South Cliff at Scarborough was vested in the council and the cliff became unstable, leading to the collapse of the claimants' hotel at the top. The Court of Appeal held that *Leakey's* case was in principle applicable[215] but although the problem had been apparent in a general way for years and there had been progressive landslides, which might continue and foreseeably affect the grounds of the hotel, on the facts it was found that the council did not have reason to be aware of the likelihood of a comparatively sudden, catastrophic collapse such as took place and it was held not liable. Despite the general rule that when a defendant could foresee some injury to the claimant he was liable for all damage of that type,[216] it would not be fair, just and reasonable to impose such an onerous requirement in respect of the "measured duty of care" which arose in these cases. This approach rendered it unnecessary to consider other issues which may arise in future, similar cases. For example, what are the implications of the fact that the defect in the soil may be present in both the upper and lower properties?[217] Or that the claimant has considerably more at stake than the defendant, even though the latter may have the greater resources?[218] Should they not at least share the burden? But if that is the law the basis of the allocation is far from clear.[219] Furthermore, if the problem is caused not by an isolated event like a lightning strike, why should the defendant (whose own property may also be under threat) owe *any* duty to put his hand in his pocket to protect the claimant?[220] Although obiter, the Court of Appeal contemplated that it might not necessarily have been incumbent on someone in Scarborough's position to carry out extensive and expensive remedial work to prevent the damage which they ought to have foreseen and that the scope of the duty might have been limited to warning of the risk and sharing information.[221]

This approach in the *Holbeck Hall* case was applied in *Lambert v Barratt Homes Ltd*[222] where the work of a developer on land sold by D, the local

---

[213] See para.15–030.

[214] *Holbeck Hall Hotel Ltd v Scarborough BC* [2000] Q.B. 836.

[215] *Leakey* was a case of the collapse of the upper property on to the lower. *Holbeck* [2000] Q.B. 836 involved the collapse of the lower property damaging the upper.

[216] See para.7–040.

[217] Counsel for the hotel argued that if both did nothing each would be liable in full for damage to the other's land. Stuart Smith LJ was inclined to the view that neither would be liable: *Holbeck Hall Hotel Ltd v Scarborough BC* [2000] Q.B. 836 at 863.

[218] As was the case in *Holbeck Hall Hotel Ltd v Scarborough BC* [2000] Q.B. 836.

[219] In *Holbeck Hall Hotel Ltd v Scarborough BC* [2000] Q.B. 836 the trial judge (who had come to a different conclusion on liability) would have awarded damages subject to a deduction for what the hotel *would* have contributed to the cost of remedial works.

[220] Parts of the east coast of England are subject to rapid and continuous erosion. Suppose D has a field half a mile wide on the edge of the sea and this is eaten away by the waves, which then begin to erode C's land. It seems bizarre to suggest that D can be under any liability to C.

[221] *Holbeck Hall Hotel Ltd v Scarborough BC* [2000] Q.B. 836 at 863.

[222] [2010] EWCA Civ 681; [2010] B.L.R. 527.

authority, led to water collecting on land which had been retained by D and which occasionally flooded C's neighbouring property. A number of factors, including the liability of the developer to C, led the court to confine D's duty of care to one to co-operate in a solution which involved the construction of suitable drainage and a catch pit on their retained land, e.g. by allowing access and the necessary consents, but not to carry out and pay for the work itself. By contrast, the same approach in *Vernon Knight Associates v Cornwall Council*[223] resulted in the liability of a highway authority for its failure to prevent damage to neighbouring property caused by flooding at a previously identified "hotspot" on one of the roads for which it was responsible.

Public utilities. The development of the law in this line of cases was thought to mean that a public authority engaged in drainage or sewerage could no longer necessarily rely on a principle that it escapes liability if its facilities were adequate when installed and have failed to keep pace with increased demand. However, such activities are carried out under statutory schemes and the position is not the same as it is between two adjoining landowners. In *Marcic v Thames Water Utilities Ltd*[224] (where the claimant's property was repeatedly flooded as a result of overloading of the sewerage system, to which owners of new property had the right of connexion) the statutory scheme in question placed the decision on what expenditure to require to increase sewerage provision in the hands of the industry regulator. The regulator set limits on what the sewerage undertakers could charge for their services and was better able than the courts to take account of the various competing interests.[225] The House of Lords held that to expose the defendants to liability for nuisance would cut across this structure.[226] This statutory scheme was compatible with the rights of the claimant under the European Convention on Human Rights to respect for his private and family life and home and to the peaceful enjoyment of his possessions. It was open to persons aggrieved by flooding to complain to the regulator, who had power to issue enforcement notices against the sewerage undertaker and his decision in response would be open to judicial review.[227] However, since the claimant had never approached the regulator there was no decision of his which could be challenged in this way or under the Human Rights Act 1998.

15–050

---

[223] [2013] EWCA Civ 950; [2014] Env. L.R. 6, where the approach required of the court was referred to as a "multi-factorial assessment": at [50].

[224] [2003] UKHL 66; [2004] 2 A.C. 42.

[225] Between the trial and the decision of the HL, remedial work was done to the claimant's property and nine other houses at a cost of £731,000. The estimated cost of remedial work for the defendants' whole area, without taking account of new house building, was £1 billion: [2004] 2 A.C. 42 at [23].

[226] Cf. *Dwr Cymru Cyfyngedig (Welsh Water) v Barratt Homes Ltd* [2013] EWCA Civ 23; [2013] 1 W.L.R. 3486 (no cause of action in nuisance for wrongfully refusing connection to the public sewers under s.106 of the Water Industry Act 1991; not because such liability would be inconsistent with the statutory scheme, but rather because there could be no claim for breach of statutory duty (see *Bowden v South West Water Services Limited* (unreported, 17 December 1997): "If failure to perform a statutory duty does not give rise to a private right to sue for damages for breach it is difficult to see how it can provide the essential basis for a cause of action for damages in nuisance": at [38] per Lloyd Jones LJ); Arden LJ dubitante on the question of liability for breach of statutory duty.

[227] Cf. *Andrews v Reading BC* [2005] EWHC 256 (QB).

iii. Nuisance Created by Predecessor in Title

15–051 Where the nuisance existed before the occupier acquired the property he will be liable if it can be proved that he knew, or ought reasonably to have known, of its existence but not otherwise.[228] In *St Anne's Well Brewery Co v Roberts*,[229] C owned an ancient inn, one side of which was bounded by the old city wall of Exeter. D owned part of the wall. On either side of C's kitchen fireplace, recesses had at some time unknown been formed by excavations in the wall. Part of the wall belonging to D collapsed and demolished the inn. C sued D, who was held not liable because he neither knew of the defect nor could have discovered it by reasonable diligence. It is arguable that the special standard of care discussed in *Goldman v Hargrave* should apply also to this situation. If the predecessor in title created the nuisance he may remain liable for injury done by it after he disposes of the land.[230] If, however, he did not create it his liability ceases upon disposal. The duty to remedy a nuisance created by another or by natural causes is part of the price of the occupation of land but there is no reason why it should continue after that occupation has ceased.[231]

C. Landlord

15–052 Since the basic liability for nuisance rests upon the occupier of the land it might be thought that a landlord's liability ceased upon letting the land, except where he created the nuisance by some positive act. However, the law has gone a long way towards displacing this general rule, without of course affecting the liability of the tenant as occupier.

15–053 **Nuisance authorised by landlord.** The landlord is liable if he has expressly or impliedly authorised his tenant to create the nuisance. Where D let a field to B for working it as a lime quarry and B's acts in blasting the limestone and letting kiln smoke escape constituted a nuisance to C, D was held liable, for B's method of working the quarry was the usual way of getting lime and D was taken to have authorised it;[232] and a local authority was liable when it let land for go-karting and a nuisance was a natural and necessary consequence of that activity.[233] Here the liability of the landlord is not different from that of any principal who authorises his agent to commit a tort. The tenant, of course, is also liable, indeed if the tenant is not liable because his actions are not a nuisance then neither is the

---

[228] *Montana Hotels v Fasson Pty* (1986) 69 A.L.R. 258 (a Privy Council decision where the defendant was lessee of a newly completed building with a latent defect).

[229] (1929) 140 L.T. 1. Followed in *Wilkins v Leighton* [1932] 2 Ch. 106. Cf. *Hall v Duke of Norfolk* [1900] 2 Ch. 493.

[230] *Roswell v Prior* (1701) 12 Mod. 635.

[231] This is the position of the vendor/lessor with regard to injuries occurring on the premises: *Rimmer v Liverpool CC* [1985] Q.B. 1: para.10–055.

[232] *Harris v James* (1876) 45 L.J.Q.B. 545; *Pwllbach Colliery Co v Woodman* [1915] A.C. 634 at 639 per Lord Loreburn ("But permission to carry on a business is quite a different thing from permission to carry it on in such a manner as to create a nuisance, unless it is impossible in a practical sense to carry it on without committing a nuisance").

[233] *Tetley v Chitty* [1986] 1 All E.R. 663.

landlord liable.[234] A local authority which let a house to a "problem" family was not liable to be enjoined in respect of nuisance created by the family even though the authority could have terminated the lease for breaches of covenant:[235] the authority had not expressly authorised the nuisance and it was caused solely by the acts of the tenants, not by any condition of the premises themselves.[236] A person does not authorise another to do an act merely because he has furnished him with the means of doing it or because he has sufficient control to stop him.[237]

Landlord knew or ought to have known[238] of the nuisance before the letting.   15–054
At one time it was the law that even if he was aware of the nuisance at the time of the letting the landlord escaped liability if he had taken from the tenant a covenant to repair[239] but this was finally rejected by the Court of Appeal in *Brew Bros Ltd v Snax (Ross) Ltd.*[240] As Sachs LJ remarked, there is no reason why liability to a third party should be:[241]

> "[S]huffled off merely by signing a document which as between owner and tenant casts on the latter the burden of executing remedial work. The duty of the owner is to ensure that the nuisance causes no injury—not merely to get someone else's promise to take the requisite steps to abate it."

The tenant is of course liable in this situation, but that is because of his occupation, not because of his covenant[242] and any additional obligation he may have undertaken by that covenant cannot affect his liability to third parties.[243]

Landlord has covenanted to repair or has the right to enter and repair.   15–055
Liability in this situation extends to nuisances which arise after the tenancy has commenced. The first point to make is that the landlord will be liable to persons outside the premises as well as to visitors on them if he is in breach of s.4 of the Defective Premises Act 1972, which has already been considered in connection with occupiers' liability.[244] The duty under that section is owed to, "all persons who might reasonably be expected to be affected by defects in the state of the

---

[234] *Southwark LBC v Mills* [2001] 1 A.C. 1.
[235] "Social landlords" (e.g. local authorities) have extensive powers against anti-social behaviour causing nuisance or annoyance, including application for an injunction, under Pt 2 of the Anti-Social Behaviour Act 2003.
[236] *Smith v Scott* [1973] Ch. 314; *Hussain v Lancaster CC* [2000] Q.B. 1. Article 8 of the European Convention on Human Rights was unsuccessfully relied on in this context in *Mowan v Wandsworth LBC* [2001] L.G.R. 228, CA, albeit on facts before the Human Rights Act 1998 came into force.
[237] See *CBS Songs Ltd v Amstrad Consumer Electronics Plc* [1988] A.C. 1013 (not a nuisance case).
[238] *Gandy v Jubber* (1865) 5 B. & S. 485 9 B & S. 15; *Wilchick v Marks* [1934] 2 K.B. 56 at 67–68; *Brew Bros Ltd v Snax (Ross) Ltd* [1970] 1 Q.B. 612 at 638, 644; *Mistry v Thakor* [2005] EWCA Civ 953 at [44] ("There appears to be no authority on the case where an owner, who is responsible for property which is in a dangerous condition, has in effect delegated his management of the property to an apparently competent surveyor as an independent contractor, but who in the particular case discharges his duty incompetently and in breach of his duty to his client").
[239] *Pretty v Bickmore* (1873) L.R. 8 C.P. 401.
[240] [1970] 1 Q.B. 612.
[241] [1970] 1 Q.B. 612 at 638–639.
[242] *Montana Hotels v Fasson Pty* (1986) 69 A.L.R. 258.
[243] Except in the unlikely event that the Contracts (Rights of third Parties) Act 1999 applies. The covenant may, of course, entitle the landlord to be indemnified if sued.
[244] See para.10–061.

premises" and is a duty to: "take such care as is reasonable in all the circumstances to see that they are reasonably safe from personal injury or from damage to their property" caused by the defects. Though this largely covers the liability which already existed at common law, the latter continues to exist concurrently. It was extended from the case where the landlord had covenanted to do repairs[245] to that where he had reserved a right to enter and repair (without any obligation to do so) and then to the situation where the right was implied, as it would be, for example, in the case of a weekly tenancy.[246] The Landlord and Tenant Act 1985 provides that in any lease of a dwelling house for a term of less than seven years or any lease which is terminable by the lessor in less than seven years, there is an implied covenant by the lessor to keep in repair the structure and exterior and certain installations.[247] Any provision seeking to place these liabilities on the tenant is ineffective.

If the landlord has undertaken to repair or has the right to enter and repair his liability does not affect that of the tenant, who is liable as occupier.[248] Where the landlord has covenanted to repair the tenant will, of course, be able to obtain an indemnity if sued.

7. DAMAGE

15–056 **Public nuisance.** It has long been settled that the claimant must prove damage in a claim for public nuisance.[249]

15–057 **Private nuisance.** In the case of private nuisance, however, although it is said that damage must be proved, the law will often presume it. In *Fay v Prentice*[250] a cornice of the defendant's house projected over the claimant's garden so that rainwater dripped from it on the garden, and it was held that the law would infer injury to the claimant without proof of it. This inference appears to apply to any nuisance where the damage is so likely to occur that it would be superfluous to demand evidence that it has occurred. The inference cannot be made if the discomfort is purely personal, for personal sensitivity to smells, smoke and the like varies considerably and it is only fair that evidence of substantial annoyance should be required. However, such evidence will suffice and it is not necessary that the claimant should show any loss of trade or diminution in the capital value of the property.[251] Where no damage has yet occurred but it is imminent, a quia timet injunction may be granted.[252]

---

[245] *Payne v Rogers* (1794) 2 H.Bl. 350.

[246] *Mint v Good* [1951] 1 K.B. 517.

[247] Section 11, as extended by the Housing Act 1988 s.116.

[248] *St Anne's Well Brewery Co v Roberts* (1929) 140 L.T. 1; *Heap v Ind Coope & Allsopp Ltd* [1940] 2 K.B. 476 at 482; but the tenant may not be sued, as in *Heap's* case and *Mint v Good*, perhaps because he is uninsured and a man of straw, which is the rationale for imposing liability on the landlord.

[249] See para.15−006.

[250] (1845) 1 C.B. 828.

[251] See *Hunter v Canary Wharf Ltd*, para.15−034. As to what constitutes damage where the property is physically affected by the activity, see para.5−058.

[252] See para.23−131.

Nuisance to servitudes. No present damage need be proved where the nuisance **15–058** is to an easement or profit à prendre, at any rate where the claim is for damages as distinct from a mandatory injunction.[253] As a series of such acts or the continuation of one particular act is evidence of acquiescence by the claimant in the annoyance, if no remedy were available in these circumstances for merely presumed damage the claimant would be barred by prescription after 20 years from suing at all.[254] If damage were not presumed, it might be difficult to establish that any one act had caused it. In these cases, however, although no present damage need be proved, probability that substantial damage will ensue must be shown otherwise the law would be redressing merely fanciful claims.[255] In *Nicholls v Ely Beet Sugar Factory Ltd*,[256] large quantities of refuse and effluent were alleged to have been discharged from the defendants' beet sugar factory into the river in which the claimant owned two several and exclusive fisheries. The Court of Appeal held that there was no need for him to prove pecuniary loss, the injury being one actionable per se, although he lost his action on the ground that he had failed to show that the defendant had caused the injury.

8. DEFENCES AND NON-DEFENCES

A. Non-defences

Coming to nuisance. It is usually said that it is no defence to prove that the **15–059** claimant came to the nuisance or that the place is a convenient one for committing it. What this means is that, if the annoyance is unreasonable in that particular district, then the claimant can recover even if it has been going on long before he came there. In *Bliss v Hall*,[257] the defendant had set up a tallow-chandlery which emitted: "divers noisome, noxious, and offensive vapours, fumes, smells and stenches" to the discomfort of the claimant, who had taken a house near it. It was held to be no defence that the business had been in existence for three years before the claimant's arrival, for he, "came to the house . . . with all the rights which the common law affords, and one of them is a right to wholesome air".[258]

However, the principle that coming to the nuisance is no defence has to be qualified by another principle. As we have seen,[259] where the claim does not

[253] There substantial damage must be proved, at any rate in infringement of light: *Colls v Home and Colonial Stores* [1904] A.C. 179. The decision might, however, be interpreted rather as defining the limits of the right of light than as laying down any rule with respect to the necessity of proving damage. It is arguable that what the HL actually decided was that the right exists only with respect to a particular amount of light.

[254] Cf. Kelly CB in *Harrop v Hirst* (1868) L.R. 4 Ex. 43 at 45, 46–47; Lord Wright MR in *Nicholls v Ely Beet Sugar Factory Ltd* [1936] Ch. 343 at 349–350.

[255] *Kensit v GE Ry* (1884) 27 Ch. D. 122.

[256] [1936] Ch. 343. See also *Pride of Derby and Derby Angling Association Ltd v British Celanese Ltd* [1953] Ch. 149.

[257] (1838) 4 Bing. N.C. 183 (followed, with some reluctance, by the majority of the Court of Appeal in *Miller v Jackson* [1977] Q.B. 966).

[258] *Bliss v Hall* (1838) 4 Bing. N.C. 183 at 186 per Tindal CJ. So too, *Elliotson v Feetham* (1835) 2 Bing. N.C. 134.

[259] See para.15–012.

relate to "material injury" to property the nature of the locality is an important element in deciding if there is a nuisance at all. If you choose to make your home in the heart of a manufacturing district, you can expect no more freedom from the discomfort usually associated with such a place than any other resident.[260] Furthermore, it may be a defence for a defendant to contend that, as it is only because the claimant has changed the use of, or built on, her land that the defendant's pre-existing activity is claimed to have become a nuisance.[261]

15–060 **Usefulness.** The mere fact that a process or business is useful to persons generally, while not irrelevant in determining whether a nuisance has been committed,[262] is no defence once a nuisance has been proved. One who keeps a pigsty, a tannery, a limekiln or an iron foundry is pursuing a laudable occupation and possibly one of great benefit to the public, yet that by itself will not excuse him. In *Adams v Ursell*[263] a fried-fish shop was held to be a nuisance in the residential part of a street where it was carried on. It was argued unsuccessfully that an injunction would cause great hardship to the defendant and to the poor people who were his customers. The defendant could engage in his business in an area where it would not constitute a nuisance and indeed the injunction granted did not extend to the whole street. Nor does the need to maintain an airforce for national defence excuse serious and continual noise caused by low flying, though that is a case where damages rather than an injunction is likely to be the proper remedy.[264]

15–061 **Nuisance due to many.** It is no defence that the nuisance was created by independent acts of different persons, although the act of any one of them was not per se unlawful; for example where 100 people independently leave 100 wheelbarrows in a place and the obstruction consists in the accumulation of these vehicles and not in the presence of any one of them.[265] It may appear paradoxical that a defendant is held liable although his act alone would not be a tort, but the explanation lies in the fact that the standard of what is reasonable is governed by the surrounding circumstances, including the conduct of the others.

15–062 **Jus tertii.** In *Nicholls v Ely Beet Sugar Factory*,[266] Farwell J held that the defendant to an action for pollution of a private fishery could not plead *jus tertii* as a defence, i.e. that some third party had a better title to the land than the claimant, but the learned judge left it open whether this applied to nuisance in general. It is true that at common law *jus tertii* might be pleaded in certain actions for conversion of goods but it was irrelevant where the action was based upon possession, for example trespass.[267] Now that it is established that possession or

---

[260] A tenant takes the building as it is in respect of the effects of ordinary use by other tenants (*Southwark LBC v Mills* [2001] 1 A.C. 1) or defects present at the commencement of the lease (*Jackson v JH Watson Property Investment Ltd* [2008] EWHC 14 (Ch); [2008] Env L.R. 30).

[261] *Coventry v Lawrence* [2014] UKSC 13; [2014] 2 W.L.R. 433 at [58] per Lord Neuberger.

[262] See para.15−015.

[263] [1913] 1 Ch. 269.

[264] *Dennis v MoD* [2003] EWHC 793 (QB); [2003] Env L.R. 34.

[265] *Thorpe v Brumfitt* (1873) L.R. 8 Ch.App. 650 at 656; *Lambton v Mellish* [1894] 3 Ch. 163.

[266] [1931] 2 Ch. 84.

[267] The position has now been substantially altered by the Torts (Interference with Goods) Act 1977 (para.18−034) but this has no application to land.

occupation of the land is necessary to entitle the claimant to sue for nuisance it is clear that *jus tertii* does not afford a defence.[268]

B. Defences

i. Conduct Permitted by Statute[269]

Defence depends on the proper construction of the statute. Many alleged nuisances are caused by public authorities acting under statutory powers and the defence of legislative authority is thus particularly important in this area.[270] Everything of course depends on the construction of the particular statute in question and one must therefore be wary of laying down definite propositions.[271]

15–063

Activity carried out must be intra vires. Since we are dealing with statutory powers the primary question where what is complained of is damage arising from the exercise of the powers (as opposed to some "collateral" damage)[272] must be whether that exercise is intra vires the statute.[273] If it is, the claimant who suffers damage is left without redress unless the statute makes some provision for compensation.[274]

15–064

Test for intra vires. Work causing substantial interference with neighbouring property will not normally be intra vires the statute unless that interference is the "inevitable" consequence of the work, i.e. unless it must arise even though the work is carried on with reasonable care and with approved techniques. The burden of showing inevitability is on the defendant.[275] Where the statute contains a "nuisance clause",[276] then if the authority is merely permissive there may be liability even for the inevitable consequences of the works, but this is not so if the undertaker is under a statutory duty to carry them out.[277] A more rational

15–065

---

[268] *Hunter v Canary Wharf Ltd* [1997] A.C. 655 at 688, 703.

[269] As to planning permission, see para.15–014.

[270] For a modern (and comprehensive) example, see the Railways Act 1993 s.122.

[271] The cases draw no clear distinction between liability in nuisance and liability under *Rylands v Fletcher*: but in the light of the *Cambridge Water* case (para.16–003) this may be justifiable.

[272] For example, careless driving of a lorry on the way to the construction site or an industrial accident at the site.

[273] See the speech of Lord Diplock in *Home Office v Dorset Yacht Co Ltd* [1970] A.C. 1004 at 1064–1071.

[274] A major general compensation provision is that for "injurious affection" in s.10 of the Compulsory Purchase Act 1965, which is the successor of Victorian legislation dating back to the construction of railways. It is reviewed in *Wildtree Hotels Ltd v Harrow LBC* [2001] 2 A.C. 1. It covers damage which is: (a) caused by the construction of the works; (b) caused by the lawful exercise of the statutory power; and (c) is such as would have been actionable at common law in the absence of statutory authority. Work carried on without reasonable regard for people living in the area will be outside the scope of the statutory power and therefore in such a case the claimant must rely on the law of nuisance.

[275] *Manchester Corp v Farnworth* [1930] A.C. 171. In *Allen v Gulf Oil Refining Ltd* [1981] A.C. 1001 at 1017, Lord Edmund Davies said this issue was to be determined without regard to expense.

[276] For example: "Nothing in this Act shall exonerate the undertakers from any indictment, action, or other proceedings for nuisance in the event of any nuisance being caused by them."

[277] See the summary in *Dept of Transport v NW Water Authority* [1983] 3 W.L.R. 105 and in the HL [1984] A.C. 336. It might be argued that even without a nuisance clause the granting of merely

distinction is probably between statutes which require works to be done in a particular place and those which give the undertaker a wide discretion in this respect. In the former case, there is no liability provided that the work is undertaken with reasonable care;[278] in the latter, the undertaker may be liable if he chooses to carry out the works in a place where they cause a nuisance to neighbours when he could have carried them out elsewhere without such consequences.[279]

Another type of case is where a power is given to effect a variety of works as and when the undertaker deems it necessary or expedient to do so (for example the powers given to land drainage authorities). While no hard and fast line can be drawn between this and the previous situation it is obvious that if powers of this sort are read subject to an implied limitation that they are not to be exercised so as to cause any avoidable infringement of private rights the object of the legislation will be largely frustrated.[280] Accordingly, the court is not, under the guise of imposing liability for nuisance, to substitute its own discretion for that granted to the statutory undertaker by Parliament.[281]

15–066 **Human rights.** All of the above must now be read subject to the European Convention on Human Rights and the Human Rights Act 1998. Article 8 of the Convention requires respect for private and family life and the home and breach of that requirement by a public authority is, under the 1998 Act, directly actionable in damages. Although under the common law the protection of private rights was a value that influenced the court in the interpretation of statutory authority, it was subsidiary to the meaning of the words. However, s.3 of the Human Rights Act 1998 requires legislation to be read and given effect in a way which is compatible with the Convention rights "so far as it is possible to do so", which goes beyond merely relying on the rights to resolve an ambiguity in the statute.[282] If the words of the statute are clear by this standard the court may not strike it down but may make a declaration of incompatibility.

However, the right of appeal to the Court in Strasbourg remains after the 1998 Act and that body is not hampered by any vestiges of Parliamentary supremacy, as illustrated by *Hatton v United Kingdom*.[283] Section 76(1) of the Civil Aviation

---

permissive powers showed an intention not to take away any private rights, particularly since we are here commonly dealing with private Acts, to which the *contra proferentem* approach may fairly be applied, but this would be inconsistent with the authorities. Similarly, the absence of a provision for compensation in the Act is no more than a weak indication of an intention to preserve private rights: *Allen v Gulf Oil Refining Ltd* [1981] A.C. 1001 at 1016.

[278] *Manchester Corp v Farnworth* [1930] A.C. 171; *Allen v Gulf Oil Refining Ltd* [1981] A.C. 1001.

[279] *Metropolitan Asylum District v Hill* (1881) 6 App.Cas. 193; but if Parliament had specified the site there would have been no liability: *Allen v Gulf Oil Refining Ltd* [1981] A.C. 1001 at 1014.

[280] *Marriage v East Norfolk Rivers Catchment Board* [1950] 1 K.B. 284 at 308 per Jenkins LJ.

[281] See also *Buley v British Railways Board* [1975] C.L.Y. 2458. Jenkins LJ in *Marriage v East Norfolk Rivers Catchment Board* [1950] 1 K.B. 284 speaks of liability in nuisance remaining: (1) where the board's exercise of its discretion is capricious; or (2) where an act of negligence in the course of carrying out the work produces some unintended consequence. Note that in *Marriage's* case the statute contained provision for compensation for persons suffering damage by the exercise of the statutory powers.

[282] *R v A (No.2)* [2001] UKHL 25; [2002] 1 A.C. 45 at [44]. For a tort example, see *Cachia v Faluyi* [2001] EWCA Civ 998; [2002] 1 All E.R. 192.

[283] (2003) 37 E.H.R.R. 28.

Act 1982 states that, provided the relevant regulations made under the Act have been observed, no action shall lie for nuisance: "[B]y reason only of the flight of an aircraft over any property at a height above the ground which, having regard to wind, weather and all the circumstances of the case, is reasonable, or the ordinary incidents of such flight."

In *Hatton* the applicants were residents in the vicinity of Heathrow who complained of night flights and the majority of the European Court of Human Rights held that the 1993 Scheme produced by the Minister for the restriction of such flights failed to give adequate protection to the applicants' rights under art.8. Subsequently the Grand Chamber overturned this decision by a majority of 12 votes to 5 on the ground that in preparing the Scheme the Government had not exceeded the margin of appreciation allowed it by the Convention. That decision turned on the particular facts and it does not follow that another claim for aircraft noise would necessarily fail. The claim was not of course an action for nuisance against the airlines or the airport and any such claim would have been doomed to failure by the 1982 Act but that is not determinative where art.8 is in issue. The underlying question was one of the proper balance between the rights of enjoyment of property and the economic well-being of the country (including the role of Heathrow as a major European entry point). That has traditionally been regarded as a political issue, but it has now become also a legal one (at least in the sense that it may be decided by a court).[284]

ii. Other Defences

Prescription. Twenty years' continuance will, by prescription, legalise a private nuisance[285] but not a public one. The period will not commence to run until the nuisance is known by the claimant to exist.[286] The secret discharge of pollution upon his premises cannot be a root of prejudice to his rights until he knows of, or suspects, it.[287] This qualification is of special importance where the nuisance has been in existence before the claimant came to it. In *Sturges v Bridgman*[288] a confectioner had for more than 20 years used large pestles and mortars in the back of his premises which abutted on the garden of a physician, and the noise and vibration were not felt to be a nuisance during that period. In other words there had been no actionable interference with the physician's enjoyment of his own property. Then, however, the physician built a consulting room at the end of

15–067

---

[284] See the dissenting judgment of Sir Brian Kerr in the initial proceedings in *Hatton*.

[285] The right to commit a private nuisance may be acquired by prescription as an easement in cases where such right is capable of being an easement, e.g. a right to discharge rainwater from your eaves on to your neighbour's land. To acquire a right by prescription there must be certainty and uniformity, "for the measurement and determination of the user by which the extent of the prescriptive rights is acquired": per Eve J in *Hulley v Silversprings Bleaching Co* [1922] 2 Ch. 281.

[286] This, plus the requirement that this state of affairs must endure for 20 years make it difficult to acquire the right to commit what would otherwise amount to nuisance by noise, but there is no reason in principle why prescription should not be available in such a case: *Coventry v Lawrence* [2014] UKSC 13; [2014] 2 W.L.R. 433 at [36]–[46] per Lord Neuberger (who also noted that the nuisance need not continue entirely uninterrupted (two year gap not fatal): at [142]–[143]); cf. *Waterfield v Goodwin* (1957) 105 L.J. 332; *Dennis v MoD* [2003] EWHC 793 (QB); [2003] Env L.R. 34

[287] *Liverpool Corp v Coghill & Son Ltd* [1918] 1 Ch. 307.

[288] (1879) 11 Ch.D. 852.

his garden and, for the first time, found that the noise and vibration materially interfered with the pursuit of his practice.[289] He was granted an injunction against the confectioner, whose claim to a prescriptive right failed because the interference had not been an actionable nuisance during the whole preceding period of 20 years.

15–068   **Consent and contributory negligence.** Other valid defences are: consent of the claimant,[290] and contributory negligence subject to the provisions of the Law Reform (Contributory Negligence) Act 1945.[291]

9.   REMEDY

15–069   **Injunction, or damages?** The only effective remedy for a nuisance already committed by the defendant is an award of damages. The normal remedy for any further commission is an injunction, but the circumstances in which the court should be willing to award damages in lieu of an injunction,[292] or in combination with an injunction which may order less than a complete cessation of the defendant's activity was fundamentally re-assessed by the Supreme Court in *Coventry v Lawrence.*[293] The Court was unanimous in its view that the courts should be more flexible than they had been,[294] but with varying degrees of emphasis as to how far that flexibility should be taken.[295]

15–070   **An "unfettered discretion"?** According to Lord Neuberger, the court's power to award damages in lieu of an injunction should not, as a matter of principle, be fettered but while firm guidance was "likely to do more harm than good" it was nonetheless necessary to provide as much guidance as possible as to the relevant factors in the interest of predictability.[296] The prima face position is that an injunction should be granted, so the legal burden is on the defendant to show why

---

[289] See *Bliss v Hall* (1838) 4 Bing. N.C. 183.

[290] *Kiddle v City Business Properties Ltd* [1942] 1 K.B. 269.

[291] *Trevett v Lee* [1955] 1 W.L.R. 113 at 122; *Gilson v Kerrier RDC* [1976] 1 W.L.R. 904.

[292] Now under s.50 of the Senior Courts Act 1981.

[293] [2014] UKSC 13; [2014] 2 W.L.R. 433. The facts and circumstances of the case (nuisance by noise) are considered above: para.15–013.

[294] For observations that damages were only to be awarded in an exceptional case, see dicta in the following: *Slack v Leeds Industrial Co-operative Society Ltd* [1924] 2 Ch 475; *Miller v Jackson* [1977] Q.B. 966 (Lord Denning dissenting); *Kennaway v Thompson* [1981] Q.B. 88; *Regan v Paul Properties DPF No 1 Ltd* [2006] EWCA Civ 1391; [2007] Ch. 135; *Watson v Croft Promo Sport Ltd* [2009] EWCA Civ 15; [2009] 3 All E.R. 249. For dicta adopting a more "open-minded approach, taking into account the conduct of the parties" (Lord Neubgerger in *Coventry v Lawrence* at [117]), see: *Colls v Home & Colonial Storel Ltd*[1904] A.C. 179; *Kine v Jolly* [1905] 1 Ch. 480; *Fishenden v Higgs & Hill Ltd* (1935) 153 L.T. 128.

[295] Since this represented a departure from previous decisions, the defendants had not raised the point that the judge should have awarded damages at trial and they were criticised for not having at least reserved their position. They were refused permission to raise it in the Supreme Court, but it was held that they should be free to raise the argument before the trial judge on the reinstatement of his order for an injunction under the provision therein giving the parties permission to apply: [2014] UKSC 13; [2014] 2 W.L.R. 433 at [151].

[296] *Coventry v Lawrence* [2014] UKSC 13; [2014] 2 W.L.R. 433 at [120]–[121].

it should not.[297] While in each case the outcome should depend on all the evidence and arguments, Lord Neuberger suggested a continued role for the tests which had been laid down by A.L. Smith LJ in *Shelfer v City of London Electric Lighting Co*, namely:[298]

> "(1) If the injury to the plaintiff's legal rights is small, (2) And is one which is capable of being estimated in money, (3) And is one which can be adequately compensated by a small money payment, (4) And the case is one in which it would be oppressive to the defendant to grant an injunction – then damages in substitution for an injunction may be given."

Lord Neuberger stressed that the application of these tests only offer some guidance as to how the courts might exercise their discretion.[299] While it would normally be right to refuse an injunction if the tests were satisfied, in the absence of additional relevant circumstances pointing the other way, the fact that these tests are not all satisfied does not mean that an injunction should be granted.[300]

Public interest. The most important development in *Coventry v Lawrence* was the extent to which the Supreme Court was willing to take into account the public interest in the continuation of the defendant's activity when determining whether to grant an injunction. It is also here where the Court regarded any grant of planning permission as potentially significant, having greatly restricted its relevance to the question of liability.[301] If there is any such public interest, it should be regarded as a relevant factor in all cases and not, as had previously been held, only where the damage done to the claimant was minimal:[302] **15–071**

> "... the court may well be impressed by a defendant's argument that an injunction would involve a loss to the public or a waste of resources on account of what may be a single claimant, or that the financial implications of an injunction for the defendant would be disproportionate to the damage done to the claimant if she was left to her claim in damages. In many such cases, particularly where an injunction would in practice stop the defendant from pursuing the activities, an injunction may well not be the appropriate remedy."[303]

---

[297] In the absence of submissions (for the reasons explained in fn.295 above) Lord Clarke preferred to reserve this question: at [170].

[298] *Shelfer v City of London Electric Lighting Co* [1895] 1 Ch. 287 at 322–323.

[299] How much reliance is likely to be placed on these tests in future is debatable. Lord Sumption (at [161]) described the *decision* in *Shelfer* as "out of date, and it is unfortunate that it has been followed so recently and so slavishly"; Lord Clarke (at [171]) concurred.

[300] *Coventry v Lawrence* [2014] UKSC 13; [2014] 2 W.L.R. 433 at [124].

[301] See para.15–014.

[302] Lord Neuberger and Lord Carnwath are particularly critical of *Watson v Croft Promo Sport Ltd* [2009] EWCA Civ 15; [2009] 3 All E.R. 249 in this respect.

[303] *Coventry v Lawrence* [2014] UKSC 13; [2014] 2 W.L.R. 433 at [126] per Lord Neuberger. A decision which may be easier to explain in the light of this development is *Dennis v Ministry of Defence* [2003] EWHC 793 (QB); [2003] Env L.R. 34 where the court refused a declaration against the defendants in relation to the flying of Harrier jets in view of the needs of national defence and the enormous inconvenience and cost of relocating the airfields in question, though a total of £950,000 in damages was awarded. The claimants pursued a declaration in order to avoid the niceties of the grant of injunctions against the Crown. It is not clear from the transcript how the proposed declaration was framed. It could not have been that the flying constituted a nuisance because that was the basis of the court's decision to award damages. A declaration in the form that the defendants should cease or moderate their activities would have been an injunction in all but name.

This is a significant departure from an earlier view that to award damages in lieu of an injunction would amount to expropriation without the sanction of Parliament.[304] As for the grant of planning permission, Lord Neuberger regarded it as a factor which would have "real force in cases where it was clear that the planning authority had been reasonably and fairly influenced by the public benefit of the activity, and where the activity cannot be carried out without causing the nuisance complained of".[305] Lord Sumption suggested that, in future, it may be appropriate to go further: "it may well be that an injunction should as a matter of principle be granted in a case where a use of land to which objection is taken requires and has received planning permission".[306]

15–072 **Measure of damages.** A greater willingness of the courts to award damages in lieu of an injunction inevitably throws a sharper focus on the basis for assessing such damages. According to Lord Neuberger in *Coventry v Lawrence*:[307]

> "It seems to me at least arguable that, where a claimant has a *prima facie* right to an injunction to restrain a nuisance, and the court decides to award damages instead, those damages should not always be limited to the value of the consequent reduction in the value of the claimant's property. While double counting must be avoided, the damages might well, at least where it was appropriate, also include the loss of the claimant's ability to enforce her rights, which may often be assessed by reference to the benefit to the defendant of not suffering an injunction."

In assessing the "benefit to the defendant", Lord Neuberger suggested that the courts might begin to adopt a similar approach to that taken in cases of trespass of determining the "licence fee" which a willing claimant might reasonably have demanded for the continuation of the nuisance.[308] Lord Carnwath was reluctant to open up this possibility without fuller argument. He noted that cases relating to a clearly defined interference with a specific property right could not readily be transferred to claims for nuisance such as in *Coventry v Lawrence* relating to interference with the enjoyment of land. Such an approach would also be a "radical departure" from the normal basis for assessment regarded by Parliament as appropriate in relation to injury done by activities carried out under statutory authority.[309]

---

[304] *Shelfer v City of London Electric Co* [1895] 1 Ch. 287; *Elliott v Islington LBC* [1991] 10 E.G. 145; *Watson v Croft Promo Sport Ltd* [2009] EWCA Civ 15; [2009] 3 All E.R. 249. Indeed, in *Bellew v Cement Co* [1948] Ir. R. 61. the court enjoined a nuisance even though the order would have the effect of closing for three months the only cement factory in Ireland at a time when building was an urgent public necessity. In *Miller v Jackson* [1977] Q.B. 966 Lord Denning MR, dissenting, had held that public interest must prevail over private rights of property whether the issue was the existence of a legal nuisance or the grant of an injunction, but the Court of Appeal had rejected this: *Kennaway v Thompson* [1981] Q.B. 88.

[305] *Coventry v Lawrence* [2014] UKSC 13; [2014] 2 W.L.R. 433 at [125].

[306] *Coventry v Lawrence* [2014] UKSC 13; [2014] 2 W.L.R. 433 at [161]. Lord Mance (at [167]–[168]) thought this put the significance of planning permission and public benefit "too high" and agreed with Lord Carnwath (at [246]–[247]) that the grant of permission could not give rise to a presumption that there should be no injunction. Lord Clarke (at [169]) noted only that the grant of permission may be "particularly relevant" to the remedy to be granted.

[307] [2014] UKSC 13; [2014] 2 W.L.R. 433 at [128].

[308] See para.14–034.

[309] *Coventry v Lawrence* [2014] UKSC 13; [2014] 2 W.L.R. 433 at [248]. Lord Clarke preferred to leave this question "open" (at [172]) but also noted that there may be scope for the award of general damages, citing the contract case of *Farley v Skinner* [2002] 2 A.C. 732.

10.   HIGHWAYS[310]

"Nuisance may be defined, with reference to highways, as any wrongful act or omission upon or near a highway, whereby the public are prevented from freely, safely, and conveniently passing along the highway."[311] In considering the general law of public nuisance we have to some extent considered its application to highways. We must now discuss some of the applicable rules in greater detail and also certain other matters which have not yet been mentioned.

15–073

A.   Actionable Obstructions

Not every obstacle on the highway constitutes an actionable nuisance, for the highway would be scarcely usable if it were. The law requires of users of the highway a certain amount of "give and take" and each person is deemed to assume the normal risks of passage along the highway by way of inconvenience and even danger.[312] It is only when the defendant does something which in the circumstances is unreasonable that it becomes actionable. For this reason, the repair of the water, gas and electric mains which run under the street, of the surface of the street itself, and the building and alteration of the houses bordering on it, all constitute lawful occasions, either under statutory powers or by the common law, for temporary interference with its free passage and its amenities; and if shops and houses are to get any supplies, vehicles and persons must pause on the highway to deliver them. A temporary obstruction, provided it is reasonable in amount and duration, is permissible.[313] Whether it is so is a question of fact varying with the circumstances of each particular case. Nor is every permanent obstruction a nuisance.[314]

15–074

Accidents. Continuing obstructions are one thing, highway accidents are another. In a number of cases the courts have been faced with accidents arising from the parking or stopping of vehicles on the highway. If the vehicle is left[315] in such a position that it is a foreseeable source of danger to other road users then there may be liability in nuisance but the defendant's conduct would anyway amount to negligence.[316] It has been said, however, that, quite apart from foreseeability of

15–075

---

[310] *Encyclopedia of Highway Law and Practice.* Navigable waters are analogous to highways on land. As to ferries see *Gravesham BC v British Rail* [1978] Ch. 379.

[311] *Jacobs v LCC* [1950] A.C. 361 at 375 per Lord Simonds.

[312] *Fletcher v Rylands* (1866) L.R. 1 Ex. 265 at 286 per Blackburn J. See also the comments of the same judge in *River Wear Commissioners v Adamson* (1877) 2 App.Cas. 743 at 767.

[313] *Harper v Haden & Sons Ltd* [1933] Ch. 298 at 304.

[314] *Attorney General v Wilcox* [1938] Ch. 934.

[315] It is important to distinguish between one who deliberately parks a vehicle and one who stops temporarily, e.g. to deal with an emergency: *Dymond v Pearce* [1972] 1 Q.B. 496 at 504 per Edmund Davies LJ. Thus, if the driver, on finding his lights are out, stops the vehicle, this is not of itself a nuisance, though it may be so if he leaves it on the highway for an unreasonable time or without giving warning of its presence there or if the vehicle became unlit because of some fault on his part: *Maitland v Raisbeck* [1944] K.B. 689, explaining and distinguishing *Ware v Garston Haulage Co Ltd* [1944] K.B. 30.

[316] This is not to say that it makes no difference that the liability is founded on nuisance, for, a "nuisance situation" being shown, it may be that the burden of proof of lack of fault is on the

danger, the defendant will be liable in nuisance if he so leaves his vehicle as to constitute an obstruction of the highway even though it does not constitute a risk to other road users.[317] Whether or not this view represents the law, it may be doubted whether the distinction drawn between nuisance and negligence in relation to a stationary vehicle on the highway has any justification in the modern law. As Professor Newark pointed out,[318] such cases are more conveniently dealt with in negligence.[319] It is only because the factual situation became common before the development of the law of negligence that it was incorporated into public nuisance. Whether or not the framing of a claim in nuisance gives the claimant any advantage, the duplication of action and the difficulty of drawing a line between nuisance on the highway and negligence give rise to confusion.

B. Access To and From Highway

15–076 **Impeding access to the highway.** It is clear that the right of passage along the highway is a public right[320] and that interference with it is remediable by an action for public, not private, nuisance. As we have seen,[321] this means that the claimant can only sue if he has suffered damage over and above that suffered by the rest of the public. However, the owner of property adjoining the highway has a common law right of access to the highway[322] which is a private right remediable by an action of private nuisance, so that anything which prevents his access (as opposed to making it less convenient for his purposes)[323] enables the recovery of at least nominal damages.[324] The private right of access is subject to the public right of passage, which is the higher right,[325] but the right of passage of the public is also subject to the private right of access to the highway and is liable to be temporarily interrupted by the adjoining owner.[326] The conflict of these two rights is resolved on the ordinary principle that a reasonable exercise of both must be allowed.[327]

---

defendant: *Southport Corp v Esso Petroleum Co Ltd* [1954] 2 Q.B. 182 at 197 per Denning LJ. It has been held that the statutory obligations in relation to the lighting of vehicles do not give rise to civil liability: *Clarke v Brims* [1947] K.B. 497.

[317] *Dymond v Pearce* [1972] 1 Q.B. 496; but see the contrary view of Edmund Davies LJ at 503.

[318] Newark 65 L.Q.R. 480 at 485. See also Pritchard [1964] C.L.J. 234 at 237.

[319] In fact, many cases involving a dangerous obstruction of the highway are not pleaded in nuisance at all: e.g. *Tart v GW Chitty & Co Ltd* [1933] 2 K.B. 453; *Baker v E Longhurst & Sons Ltd* [1933] 2 K.B. 461 (though horse and cart were moving); *Tidy v Battman* [1934] 1 K.B. 319; *Moore v Maxwells of Emsworth Ltd* [1968] 1 W.L.R. 1077.

[320] *Boyce v Paddington BC* [1903] 1 Ch. 109 at 114 per Buckley J.

[321] See para.15–006.

[322] The right is now heavily qualified by statute.

[323] See *Attorney General v Thames Conservators* (1862) 1 H. & M. 1; *Tate & Lyle Ltd v GLC* [1983] A.C. 509 (siltation prevented large vessels approaching claimants' jetty; interference with public right of navigation rather than with private right).

[324] *Walsh v Ervin* [1952] V.L.R. 361. Cf. *Chaplin v Westminster Corp* [1901] 2 Ch. 329 (transfer of goods across pavement into adjoining premises an aspect of public right of passage).

[325] *Vanderpant v Mayfair Hotel Co* [1930] 1 Ch. 138 at 152–154 per Luxmoore J.

[326] *Marshall v Blackpool Corp* [1935] A.C. 16 at 22 per Lord Atkin; *Farrell v John Mowlem & Co Ltd* [1954] 1 Lloyd's Rep. 437 at 439, 440 per Devlin J; *Trevett v Lee* [1955] 1 W.L.R. 113.

[327] The public right now extends to holding a reasonable assembly: *DPP v Jones* [1999] A.C. 240, para.14–011.

Impeding access to business premises. In some cases the gist of the claimant's   **15–077**
complaint has been not so much that his access to and from the highway has been
impeded but that the obstruction has prevented other people coming on to his
premises and doing business with him. It seems that such a state of affairs is both
a private and a public nuisance, though as far as the latter is concerned the loss of
trade will amount to special damage.[328] Picketing in pursuance of a trade dispute
is, in certain circumstances, made lawful by statute[329] but otherwise it is certainly
capable of amounting to a nuisance if it involves violence or intimidation[330] and
perhaps even if it is carried on so as to exert pressure to regulate and control
access to and from the claimant's premises.[331] Such conduct may also now fall
within the Protection from Harassment Act 1997.[332]

Queues. Problems have also arisen with queues. A queue as such is not unlawful   **15–078**
even if its occupation of the pavement makes foot passengers deviate or access to
shops difficult. It is only when it is unreasonable that the proprietors of the
establishment which causes it are liable for nuisance, for example where the
queue was at times five deep, extended far beyond the theatre itself and remained
there for very considerable portions of time, it was held to be a nuisance to the
claimants, whose premises were adjacent to the theatre.[333] The defendant is not
liable if, although the queue was one of prospective customers at his shop, he was
not responsible for it because other circumstances (for example shortage of
supplies in consequence of war) were the primary cause of it nor will he be liable
unless the claimant can prove damage.[334] However, the defendant is liable if the
obstruction by means of the queue is due to an unusual method of conducting
business.[335]

C.   Damage on the Highway from Premises Adjoining the Highway

Projection over the highway. This area deserves special mention because the   **15–079**
authorities are not of the clearest. The mere fact that something (for example a
tree, a clock, a sign, an awning or a corbel) projects over the highway from land
or a building adjacent to it does not per se constitute an actionable nuisance. This

---

[328] *Wilkes v Hungerford Market Co* (1835) 2 Bing. N.C. 281; *Lyons, Sons & Co v Gulliver* [1914] 1
Ch. 631; *Blundy, Clark & Co v L & NE Ry* [1931] 2 K.B. 342 at 352, 362; cf. at 372; *Harper v Haden
& Sons Ltd* [1933] Ch. 298 at 306–307. There is, "long standing and consistent authority in support of
the proposition that a claimant can recover damages in public nuisance where access to or from his
premises is obstructed so as to occasion a loss of trade attributable to obstruction of his customers' use
of the highway and liberty of access": *Colour Quest Ltd v Total Downstream UK Plc* [2009] EWHC
640 (Comm); [2009] 2 Lloyd's Rep. 1 at [459].
[329] See para.19–067.
[330] *Messenger Newspapers Group Ltd v N.G.A.* (1982) [1984] I.R.L.R. 397; *News Group Newspapers
Ltd v S.O.G.A.T. '82* [1986] I.R.L.R. 337; but cf. the view in *Hussain v Lancaster CC* [2000] Q.B. 1
that there can be no private nuisance unless the defendant is making use of his land: para.15–040.
[331] *Mersey Dock & Harbour Co v Verrinder* [1982] I.R.L.R. 152; *Hubbard v Pitt* [1976] Q.B. 142.
[332] See para.4–034.
[333] *Lyons, Sons & Co v Gulliver* [1914] 1 Ch. 631.
[334] *Dwyer v Mansfield* [1946] K.B. 437.
[335] *Fabbri v Morris* [1947] 1 All E.R. 315. See also *Chartered Trust Plc v Davies* [1997] 2 E.G.L.R.
83, which did not involve the highway but where the trader's method of doing business caused
inconvenience to others.

must be so, for no conceivable damage is done to anyone and there is scarcely a garden or a building on the edge of the highway which would not have to be altered if the law were otherwise.[336] The rule is different where the projection is over private property because the rights of the proprietor of it are much wider than the limited right of the user of a highway.[337]

15–080 **Collapse of projections on the highway: natural things.** If damage is done owing to the collapse of the projection on the highway or by some other mischief traceable to it, the occupier of the premises on which it stood is liable if he knew of the defect or ought, on investigation, to have known of it. At any rate that is the rule with respect to a thing that is naturally on the premises, for example a tree. In *Noble v Harrison*,[338] a branch of a beech tree growing on X's land overhung the highway and in fine weather suddenly broke and fell upon Y's vehicle passing along the highway. Neither X nor his servants knew that the branch was dangerous and the fracture was due to a latent defect undiscoverable by any reasonably careful inspection,[339] and for this reason Y's action against X in nuisance failed.

15–081 **Collapse of projections on the highway: artificial things.** With respect to artificial things which fall and do damage it might be argued that there was no reason to treat the occupier's liability differently from that in the case of trees and some of the earlier judicial statements seem to take that view.[340] However, in *Wringe v Cohen*[341] the Court of Appeal stated the law in the following terms:[342]

> "If, owing to want of repair, premises on a highway become dangerous and, therefore, a nuisance and a passer-by or an adjoining owner suffers damage by their collapse, the occupier, or owner if he has undertaken the duty of repair, is answerable whether he knew or ought to have known of the danger or not."

The unforeseeable act of a trespasser is a good defence and the Court of Appeal also held that the defendant would escape liability should the damage result from, "a secret and unobservable operation of nature, such as subsidence under or near the foundations of the premises". "Stylistically" this looks different from the law of negligence because it states a rule of liability subject to exceptions and in that respect echoes the special Roman law rule about buildings which can still be traced into modern civil law systems. However, as Professor Friedmann pointed out, these exceptions seem to deprive the rule itself of much of its significance:

---

[336] *Noble v Harrison* [1926] 2 K.B. 332 at 337.

[337] *Noble v Harrison* [1926] 2 K.B. 332 at 340 and *Lemmon v Webb* [1895] A.C. 1; but the context of these statements concerns the right of the neighbour to abate the nuisance by lopping the branches. There is less reason to think that the occupier is liable in damages for a collapse unless he has knowledge or means of knowledge of the defect. As to liability for encroachment by tree roots, see para,15–032 and for trespass by oversailing structures, see para.14–013.

[338] [1926] 2 K.B. 332; *Caminer v London and Northern Investment Trust Ltd* [1951] A.C. 88; *Cunliffe v Bankes* [1945] 1 All E.R. 459; *Shirvell v Hackwood Estates Co Ltd* [1938] 2 K.B. 577; *British Road Services v Slater* [1964] 1 W.L.R. 498.

[339] Cf. *Quinn v Scott* [1965] 1 W.L.R. 1004 (means of knowledge of disease).

[340] Blackburn J in *Tarry v Ashton* (1876) 1 Q.B.D. 314; Wright J in *Noble v Harrison* [1926] 2 K.B. 332 at 343–344.

[341] [1940] 1 K.B. 229.

[342] *Wringe v Cohen* [1940] 1 K.B. 229 at 233.

"It can hardly be imagined that any damage caused neither by the act of a third person nor by a latent defect could be due to anything but knowledge or negligence of the occupier."[343]

In effect, it would seem that *Wringe v Cohen* sets a standard somewhere between strict liability and ordinary fault liability. The claimant need only show that the defendant had control over the defective premises and that the injury resulted from their dangerous condition.[344] This gives rise to a presumption that the defendant has failed in his duty of inspection and repair, which can only be rebutted by proof that the accident was inevitable, i.e. it was not, nor could have been, avoided by reasonable inspection. As Denning LJ said in *Mint v Good*,[345] the defendant "is liable when structures fall into dangerous disrepair, because there must be some fault on the part of someone or other for that to happen". From a substantive point of view, *Wringe v Cohen* differs from ordinary liability in negligence because the occupier is liable for the default of his independent contractor.[346]

D.   Condition of the Highway

Development of the law. At common law a highway authority could not be liable   **15–082** for injury suffered by a user of the highway and resulting from the authority's failure to discharge its duty to keep the highway in repair. The remedy for breach of the duty was proceedings on indictment. This civil law immunity did not extend to misfeasance on the highway nor to acts of repair improperly performed. The distinction between misfeasance and non-feasance and the rule of immunity were criticised and eventually the latter was abrogated by s.1 of the Highways (Miscellaneous Provisions) Act 1961 which came into force on August 3, 1964. The law is now to be found in the Highways Act 1980.

Highways Act 1980. Under s.41(1) of the Highways Act 1980: "The authority   **15–083** who are for the time being the highway authority for a highway maintainable at the public expense[347] are under a duty . . . to maintain the highway."[348]

---

[343] Friedmann (1940) 3 M.L.R. 305, 309. In other cases attempts have been made to distinguish between inactivity causing the nuisance and the mere continuance of an inherited nuisance: *Cushing v Peter Walker & Sons Ltd* [1941] 2 All E.R. 693 at 699 per Hallett J; *Mint v Good* [1951] 1 K.B. 517 at 524 per Somervell LJ. It is suggested that this is not a valid distinction. The failure of the occupier to discover and remedy an inherited nuisance is equally the cause of the damage. It results just as much from the occupier's breach of his duty to inspect and repair as does, e.g. the negligent failure to discover a defective gable-end.

[344] The evidence must show that the damage has occurred as a result of the want of repair of some structure for which the defendant was responsible: *Cartwright v McLaine & Long Pty Ltd* (1979) 24 A.L.R. 97.

[345] [1951] 1 K.B. 517 at 526.

[346] *Tarry v Ashton* (1876) 1 Q.B.D. 314. It has been suggested (*Mint v Good* [1951] 1 K.B. 517 at 526) that this more onerous liability may be justified by a desire to protect users of the public highway, but one of the oddities of *Wringe v Cohen* is that the premises fell, not on to the highway, but on to adjoining premises.

[347] See *Gulliksen v Pembrokeshire CC* [2002] EWCA Civ 968; [2003] 1 Q.B. 123.

[348] This provision does not cover a complaint of failure to *improve* the highway, e.g. by painting or erecting traffic signs or removing obstructions in the line of sight, nor will there be any such liability at common law: *Gorringe v Calderdale MBC* [2004] UKHL 15; [2004] 1 W.L.R. 1057; *Stovin v Wise*

In any action against a highway authority for damage resulting from its failure to maintain it is provided by s.58(1) of the Act that it is a defence (without prejudice to any other defence such as voluntary acceptance of risk and contributory negligence) to prove that the authority had taken such care as in all the circumstances was reasonably required to secure that the part of the highway to which the action relates was not dangerous for traffic. For the purpose of such a defence the court is in particular to have regard to: (a) the character of the highway, and the traffic which was reasonably to be expected to use it; (b) the standard of maintenance appropriate for a highway of that character and used by such traffic; (c) the state of repair in which a reasonable person would have expected to find the highway; (d) whether the highway authority knew, or could reasonably have been expected to know, that the condition of the part of the highway to which the action relates was likely to cause danger to users of the highway; and (e) where the highway authority could not reasonably have been expected to repair that part of the highway before the cause of action arose, what warning notice of its condition had been displayed.[349]

15–084   **Liability confined to personal injury or property damage.** The Act applies whether the claimant is suing in nuisance, negligence or for breach of a statutory duty.[350] It is clear from the wording of the statute that it avails only road users who suffer personal injury or property damage and that it does not give an action to an adjoining owner whose business is ruined because the condition of the highway means that vehicles cannot get to his premises, even though such loss would amount to special damage for the purposes of public nuisance if the highway were obstructed or damaged by misfeasance.[351] The only remedy in such a case is an application to the Crown Court for an order for repair.[352]

15–085   **Application.** The approach to the statutory liability created by the Act was summed up by Steyn LJ in *Mills v Barnsley BC*:[353]

> "In order for a plaintiff to succeed against a highway authority . . . the plaintiff must prove that: (a) the highway was in such a condition that it was dangerous to traffic or pedestrians in the sense that, in the ordinary course of human affairs, danger may reasonably have been anticipated from its continued use by the public (b) the dangerous condition was created by the failure to maintain or repair the highway and (c) the injury or damage resulted from such a failure. Only if the plaintiff proves these *facta probanda* does it become necessary to turn to the highway authority's reliance on the special defence under section 58(1) of the 1980 Act."

[1996] A.C. 923; *Valentine v Transport for London* [2010] EWCA Civ 1358; [2011] B.L.R. 89, para.5–071. Cf. *Bird v Pearce* [1979] R.T.R. 369 (obliterating existing markings; see the remarks on this case in *Gorringe*); *Yetkin v Newham LBC* [2010] EWCA Civ 776; [2011] Q.B. 827 (planting shrubs and bushes so as to create a new source of danger).

[349] Highways Act 1980 s.58(2). See *Wilkinson v City of York Council* [2011] EWCA Civ 207.

[350] A claim under the Act may involve concurrent issues against other undertakers, e.g. tramway operators: *Roe v Sheffield CC* [2003] EWCA Civ 1; [2004] Q.B. 653.

[351] *Wentworth v Wilts CC* [1993] Q.B. 654.

[352] In *Wentworth v Wilts CC* Beldam LJ suggests that there might be cases where non-repair might create a liability for public nuisance ([1993] Q.B. 654 at 673) but it is difficult to see how this could be so since the common law gave complete immunity for non-feasance and that immunity is only abolished so far as the statute provides.

[353] [1992] 1 P.I.Q.R. P291 at 292.

It was held that the duty under the Act was to keep the fabric of the highway in suitable condition for ordinary traffic at all seasons of the year but that it did not extend to a duty to remove ice or snow, because that would not have fallen within the duty of the inhabitants at large, enforceable by indictment, before the 1961 Act.[354] This was despite the fact that s.58 would allow the authority, in a particular case, to show that it had taken reasonable steps to remove the hazard, so that although the basic duty may be "absolute" the liability is not in fact so. However, s.41(1A) of the Act now provides that the highway authority is under a duty to ensure, so far as is reasonably practicable, that safe passage is not endangered by snow or ice.[355]

Condition of pavements. With regard to the condition of the highway, there is an inevitable risk in travelling along the highway of unevenness in the pavement, and a highway is not to be criticised by the standards of a bowling green.[356] In *Littler v Liverpool Corp*[357] Cumming-Bruce LJ stated that the criterion to be applied in assessing whether any particular length of pavement is dangerous is that of reasonable foreseeability of danger:[358]   **15–086**

> "A length of pavement is only dangerous if, in the ordinary course of human affairs, danger may reasonably be anticipated from its common use by the public . . . It is a mistake to isolate and emphasise a particular difference in levels between flagstones unless that difference is such that a reasonable person who noticed and considered it would regard it as presenting a real source of danger."

Vehicular traffic. In relation to danger to vehicular traffic, it has been held that the highway authority must provide not merely for model drivers, but for the normal run of drivers to be found on the roads and that includes those who make the mistakes which experience and common sense teach us are likely to occur.[359] However, the duty is significantly less stringent than to repair every defect in the highway which might foreseeably cause harm.[360]   **15–087**

Nature of the defence under s.58. Where the statutory defence under s.58 comes into play it is not in all respects equivalent to a plea of "no negligence" at common law. It is provided that it shall not be relevant to prove that the highway authority had arranged for a competent person to carry out or supervise the maintenance of the part of the highway to which the action relates unless it is also proved that the authority had given him proper instructions with regard to the maintenance of the highway and that he carried out the instructions[361]—in other   **15–088**

---

[354] *Goodes v E Sussex CC* [2000] 1 W.L.R. 1356. Despite this case the Act does cover failure to keep drains clear: *Mitchell v Department for Transport* [2006] EWCA Civ 1089; [2006] 1 W.L.R. 3356.
[355] Inserted by s.111 of the Railways and Transport Safety Act 2003. It is not clear what is the relationship between s.41(1A) and the statutory defence under s.58. In the industrial safety context, "reasonably practicable" has generally been held to require the defendant to show what steps could have been taken and that those were not reasonably practicable: para.9–012.
[356] [1968] 2 All E.R. 343 at 345; *Ford v Liverpool Corp* (1973) 117 S.J. 167.
[357] *Littler v Liverpool Corp* [1968] 2 All E.R. 343.
[358] A tilting manhole cover is plainly a danger: *Atkins v Ealing LBC* [2006] EWHC 2515 (QB); [2006] N.P.C. 111.
[359] *Rider v Rider* [1973] Q.B. 505; *Tarrant v Rowlands* [1979] R.T.R. 144.
[360] *Jones v Rhondda Cynon Taff CBC* [2008] EWCA Civ 1497; [2009] R.T.R. 151 at [12].
[361] Section 58(2).

words the authority is liable for the negligence of its contractors. It has also been said that proof that the accident would have happened even if due care had been taken would not be a defence.[362]

15–089   **Cellar coverings.** A frontager must take reasonable care to keep safe gratings or flagstones covering a cellar under the street.[363]

---

[362] *Griffiths v Liverpool Corp* [1967] 1 Q.B. 374 at 391, 395. However, Diplock LJ said at 391 that it: "may be that if the highway authority could show that no amount of reasonable care on its part could have prevented the danger the common law defence of inevitable accident would be available to it."

[363] See *Scott v Green & Sons* [1969] 1 W.L.R. 301, relying on what is now the Highways Act 1980 s.180(6).

CHAPTER 16

THE RULE IN RYLANDS V FLETCHER

1. THE RULE IN RYLANDS V FLETCHER

The rule in *Rylands v Fletcher*[1] had its origins in nuisance but for most of the **16–001** 20th century was probably regarded by the majority of lawyers as having developed into a distinct principle. Now it seems to have returned to what are regarded as its roots: it is a "sub-species of nuisance"[2]; but on balance it still merits some separate treatment. Liability under the rule is strict in the sense that it relieves the claimant of the burden of showing fault; however, it is far from absolute since there are a number of wide-ranging defences.

---

[1] (1865) 3 H. & C. 774 (Court of Exchequer); (1866) L.R. 1 Ex. 265 (Court of Exchequer Chamber); (1868) L.R. 3 H.L. 330 (House of Lords). See generally: Simpson (1984) 13 J. Leg. Stud. 209; *Civil Liability for Dangerous Things and Activities* (1970) Law Com. No.32; *Report of the Royal Commission on Civil Liability and Compensation for Personal Injury* (1978), Cmnd. 7054, Vol.1, Ch.31.

[2] *Transco Plc v Stockport MBC* [2003] UKHL 61; [2004] 2 A.C. 1 at [9] per Lord Bingham.

A. Genesis and Nature of the Principle

16–002   **The case.** The facts in *Rylands v Fletcther* were as follows. B, a mill owner, employed independent contractors, who were apparently competent, to construct a reservoir on his land to provide water for his mill. In the course of the work the contractors came upon some old shafts and passages on B's land. They communicated with the mines of A, a neighbour of B, although no one suspected this, for the shafts appeared to be filled with earth. The contractors did not block them up, and when the reservoir was filled the water from it burst through the old shafts and flooded A's mines. It was found as a fact that B had not been negligent, although the contractors had been. A sued B and the House of Lords held B liable. The decision of the House affirmed that of the Court of Exchequer Chamber, the judgment of which, delivered by Blackburn J, has become a classical exposition of doctrine:[3]

> "We think that the true rule of law is, that the person who for his own purposes brings on his lands and collects and keeps there anything likely to do mischief if it escapes, must keep it in at his peril, and, if he does not do so, is prima facie answerable for all the damage which is the natural consequence of its escape."

This may be regarded as the "rule in *Rylands v Fletcher*", but what follows is equally important:

> "He can excuse himself by showing that the escape was owing to the plaintiff's default or perhaps that the escape was the consequence of vis major, or the act of God but as nothing of this sort exists here, it is unnecessary to inquire what excuse would be sufficient. The general rule, as above stated, seems on principle just. The person whose grass or corn is eaten down by the escaping cattle of his neighbour, or whose mine is flooded by the water from his neighbour's reservoir, or whose cellar is invaded by the filth of his neighbour's privy, or whose habitation is made unhealthy by the fumes and noisome vapours of his neighbour's alkali works, is damnified without any fault of his own and it seems but reasonable and just that the neighbour, who has brought something on his own property which was not naturally there, harmless to others so long as it is confined to his own property, but which he knows to be mischievous if it gets on his neighbour's, should be obliged to make good the damage which ensues if he does not succeed in confining it to his own property. But for his act in bringing it there no mischief could have accrued, and it seems but just that he should at his peril keep it there so that no mischief may accrue, or answer for the natural and anticipated consequences. And upon authority, this we think is established to be the law whether the things so brought be beasts, or water, or filth, or stenches."

In the House of Lords Lord Cairns LC rested his decision on the ground that the defendant had made a "non-natural use" of his land, though he regarded the judgment of Blackburn J as reaching the same result and said he entirely concurred in it.[4] Though Blackburn J did not use this expression in his statement of the law, he had clearly intended the rule to apply only to things collected by the defendant as opposed to things naturally on the land and it may be that Lord Cairns meant nothing more by non-natural use. However, the subsequent case law has given a rather different interpretation to it and it has been regarded as

---

[3] *Rylands v Fletcher* (1866) L.R. 1 Ex. 265 at 279–280.
[4] *Rylands v Fletcher* (1868) L.R. 3 H.L. 330 at 338–340.

additional to the requirements set out by Blackburn J.[5] In other words, the rule in *Rylands v Fletcher* must be sought in the judgments of both the Exchequer Chamber and the House of Lords.

A new principle or an application of nuisance to isolated escapes? The earlier cases from which Blackburn J drew his statement of the law, concerned cattle trespass (animals having to some extent travelled in a compartment of their own for purposes of tort law),[6] overflowing privies and noisome fumes from alkali works and the last two are clear instances of nuisance. Nevertheless, it was Winfield's view (and probably that of most of the profession) that the case should not be regarded as merely an application of the law of nuisance but as laying down a new principle governing a rather ill-defined category of "exceptional" or "unusual" risks. English courts displayed an ambivalent attitude towards the rule but in the United States it made a contribution (after an initially hostile reception) towards the creation of a category of liability for damage caused by ultra-hazardous or abnormally dangerous activities which present an unavoidable risk even when due care is taken.[7] This was justified on the basis that persons carrying them on should bear all the risks associated with them and not merely those arising from negligence. However, there was another view, advanced by Professor Newark,[8] to the effect that all *Rylands v Fletcher* did was to apply a general rule of strict liability in nuisance to situations where there was a claim for damages for an isolated escape rather than the more usual ongoing state of affairs. Nevertheless, the strictness of the liability was brought into sharper focus because in the normal situation of a trickle from a watercourse or pollution from a factory the interference will be apparent for some time: "[I]t is the single escape which raises the question of whether or not it was reasonably foreseeable and, if not, whether the defendant should nevertheless be liable."[9]

The continuing connection of the rule with nuisance was demonstrated by the decision of the House of Lords in *Read v J Lyons & Co*[10] to the effect that there must be an "escape", that is to say that it was only applicable to damage occurring outside the place in which the dangerous thing was kept,[11] and by doubts expressed in the case as to the applicability of the rule to personal injuries. In *Cambridge Water Co v Eastern Counties Leather Plc*[12] the House of Lords firmly accepted Professor Newark's view of the origin of the rule.[13] However, it also accepted that in a number of respects the law had moved on since 1868. The judgment emphasises the close connection between the rule and the law of nuisance and at one point it is said that: "[I]t would . . . lead to a more coherent

16–003

---

[5] See para.16–016.
[6] *Read v J Lyons & Co* [1947] A.C. 156 per Lord Simonds.
[7] See *Restatement* 3d §20 (Tentative Draft No.1, 2001).
[8] 65 L.Q.R. 480.
[9] *Transco Plc v Stockport MBC* [2003] UKHL 61; [2004] 2 A.C. 1 at [27] per Lord Hoffmann.
[10] [1947] A.C. 156.
[11] *Transco Plc v Stockport MBC* [2003] UKHL 61; [2004] 2 A.C. 1 at [9].
[12] [1994] 2 A.C. 264. For the facts, see para.15–031.
[13] Cf. Oliphant in Koziol and Steininger (eds), *European Tort Law 2004*, p.81, who supports the view that the case was more than a special application of the law of nuisance and points out that the modern position whereby fault liability is the norm and strict liability the exception would not have been so familiar to mid-nineteenth-century eyes. See also Lord Hobhouse in *Transco Plc v Stockport MBC* [2003] UKHL 61; [2004] 2 A.C. 1 at [57].

body of common law principles if the rule were to be regarded as essentially an extension of the law of nuisance to isolated escapes from land."[14]

16–004   **Current relevance of the rule.** The rule in *Rylands v Fletcher* has comparatively rarely been the basis of a successful claim in the English courts since 1900[15] and it has been said that "it is hard to escape the conclusion that the intellectual effort devoted to the rule by judges and writers over many years has brought forth a mouse".[16] This has been largely because of the defences of act of a third party and statutory authority and, above all, the very restrictive attitude taken by many twentieth century cases to the concept of non-natural use. The tendency was to say that common large scale activities, especially services such as the supply of gas or water, do not constitute a non-natural use of land even though their potential for causing damage is very great. Moreover, in determining whether there is a non-natural use, the courts had regard to the benefit accruing to the public from the activity and this was an important element in the rejection of the rule in some of the leading cases.[17]

The *Cambridge Water* case was, strictly, concerned only with the issue of whether the risk presented by the defendant's activity must be a foreseeable one to attract the rule but the case went beyond this and gives some indication of the likely future role of *Rylands v Fletcher* in the law. It is indicated that non-natural use should perhaps be given a rather broader meaning than had been the case,[18] and this may guard the rule against further atrophy. However, while the rule is an example of strict liability for abnormal risk, it does not now represent a general rule of strict liability for ultra-hazardous activities and the House of Lords declined to convert it to that purpose. It is a rule applicable between adjoining landowners which requires an escape from one property into another and, even where that has taken place, it is inapplicable to personal injuries. The last point looks odd to the modern way of thinking which tends to place bodily integrity at the top of the tree of protected interests; but it makes sense on the assumption that the rule is an offshoot of the law of private nuisance, which was (and still is) concerned only with the protection of the enjoyment of land.

16–005   **No general strict liability for exceptional risk.** The English common law contains a good deal less in the way of strict liability for physical damage than most other European legal systems.[19] In the *Cambridge Water* case the House of Lords did not disagree with the proposition that strict liability might be economically or morally or socially justifiable but it inclined to the view that:[20]

---

[14] *Cambridge Water Co v Eastern Counties Leather Plc* [1994] 2 A.C. 264 at 306.

[15] See *Civil Liability for Dangerous Things and Activities* (1970) Law Com. No.32, p.7.

[16] *Transco Plc v Stockport MBC* [2003] UKHL 61; [2004] 2 A.C. 1 at [39] per Lord Hoffmann. However, the assertion, that no claimant had successfully relied on *Rylands v Fletcher* since the Second World War is incorrect: see *LMS International Ltd v Styrene Packaging Ltd* [2005] EWHC 2065 (TCC); [2006] T.C.L.R. 6 at [26].

[17] *Read v J Lyons & Co Ltd* [1947] A.C. 156; *Dunne v NW Gas Board* [1964] 2 Q.B. 806.

[18] See para.16–016.

[19] See van Gerven, Lever and Larouche, *Tort Law, Common Law of Europe Casebooks* (2000), Ch.7; Koziol and Koch (eds), *Unification of Tort Law: Strict Liability* (2002). See also Reid (1999) 48 I.C.L.Q. 731.

[20] *Cambridge Water Co v Eastern Counties Leather Plc* [1994] 2 A.C. 264 at 305. Reference is also made to likely European action on environmental pollution, as to which see para.15–004.

> "[A]s a general rule, it is more appropriate for strict liability in respect of operations of high risk to be imposed by Parliament than by the courts. If such liability is imposed by statute, the relevant activities can be identified, and those concerned can know where they stand. Furthermore, statute can where appropriate lay down precise criteria establishing the incidence and scope of such liability."

Thus, for example, statutory water undertakers are strictly liable by statute[21] for damage (including personal injury) caused by escapes of water from mains but the strict liability does not avail other statutory undertakers, such as gas and electricity suppliers or highway authorities, who presumably have a greater capacity to absorb such risks than members of the public, by loss insurance or otherwise. The approach of the House of Lords in the *Cambridge Water* case bears some resemblance to that of the Pearson Commission,[22] though the terms of reference of that body meant that its recommendations were confined to death and personal injury. The Commission proposed a parent statute which would have empowered a Minister to list dangerous things or activities as giving rise to strict liability, the listing being done on the advice of an advisory committee. The Commission's preference, on the ground of certainty, was for the abolition of the rule in *Rylands v Fletcher* rather than its retention as a "back-up".[23]

Assessment. These approaches are open to the objection that they would leave without redress (except in so far as it was provided by the law of nuisance) any persons suffering injury from an activity which was not the subject of legislation, whether because of commercial or political pressure on the government of the day or because of simple inaction or lack of foresight: if there is a regime of strict liability for injury caused by a burst water main, why should the victim of a gas explosion be in any different position? Furthermore, civil liability arising from a particular statute, even where directly imposed, tends (at least in our system) to be an adjunct to a criminal/regulatory regime and the statutory requirements may be framed with criminal penalties or administrative controls in mind, allowing defences which are not necessarily appropriate to civil liability based on the idea of risk.[24] The absence of a "general clause" on strict liability in the civil law may unduly hamper the courts in fairly allocating responsibility. Any overlap or potential clash with a specific legislative scheme could easily be avoided, the argument continues, by a provision in the scheme excluding other forms of liability from the particular area: an example is to be found in the current statutory regime for nuclear accidents.[25] Nevertheless, the introduction of such a general clause would present formidable problems of uncertainty in its relationship with the fault regime.[26]

16–006

---

[21] Water Industry Act 1991 s.209, replacing the Water Act 1981 s.6.

[22] Cmnd.7054 (1978), Vol.1, Ch.31.

[23] The majority of the High Court of Australia in *Burnie Port Authority v General Jones Pty Ltd* (1994) 120 A.L.R. 42, cast *Rylands v Fletcher* out from the Australian common law on the ground that adequate protection was afforded by the "non-delegable duty" under developed negligence law: para.21–049.

[24] See, e.g. industrial safety legislation (Ch.8), though here there has been a radical contraction of strict liability.

[25] See para.16–007.

[26] It might be argued that American experience has not borne this out, but American courts seemed to have practised a self-denying ordinance over strict liability for dangerous activities.

16–007 **Strict liability under modern legislation.** We saw, when considering nuisance, how that branch of the common law has been supplemented (indeed, in some respects almost obliterated) by detailed statutory provisions governing pollution of the environment. Most of this legislation is of a "regulatory" nature and does not give rise to liability in damages.[27] The reader should be aware, however, that recent years have seen the enactment of a number of important statutory forms of liability in particular areas of exceptional risk which go a long way towards avoiding the likelihood of protracted litigation inherent in the ill-defined nature of the rules of strict liability at common law.[28] Full accounts of these Acts must be sought elsewhere.

16–008 **The present law.** Given the various shifts in the fortunes of *Rylands v Fletcher* over the years earlier cases must be approached with more than usual caution, but with this in mind, we may attempt to state the present law.

B. Summary Requirements

16–009 While it will be necessary to consider each of them in a little more detail, it is helpful to begin with a recent statement of the principles to be derived from the authorities, particularly some of the more recent authorities. It has been said that the proper approach is this:[29]

> "(1) The defendant must be the owner or occupier of land.[30]
> (2) He must bring or keep or collect an exceptionally dangerous or mischievous thing on his land.[31]
> (3) He must have recognised or ought reasonably to have recognised, judged by the standards appropriate at the relevant place and time, that there is an exceptionally high risk of danger or mischief if that thing should escape, however unlikely an escape may have been thought to be.[32]
> (4) His use of his land must, having regard to all the circumstances of time and place, be extraordinary and unusual.[33]
> (5) The thing must escape from his property into or onto the property of another.[34]
> (6) The escape must cause damage of a relevant kind to the rights and enjoyment of the claimant's land.[35]
> (7) Damages for death or personal injury are not recoverable.[36]
> (8) It is not necessary to establish the defendant's negligence but an Act of God or the act of a stranger will provide a defence.[37]"

---

[27] See para.15–002.
[28] See, e.g. Nuclear Installations Act 1965, Environmental Protection Act 1990 Pt II. See also Gas Act 1965 s.14, which imposes virtually absolute liability for damage caused by gas in underground storage and the Water Industry Act 1991 s.209, imposing strict liability for burst mains.
[29] *Stannard v Gore* [2012] EWCA Civ 1248; [2014] Q.B. 1 at [22] per Ward LJ. The principal significance of this case lies in the application of these principles to damage caused by the spread of fire: see para.16–037.
[30] See para.16–013.
[31] See paras 16–010–16–011.
[32] See paras 16–011, 16–035.
[33] See paras 16–016–16–020.
[34] See para.16–012.
[35] See para.16–014.
[36] See para.16–015.
[37] See paras 16–024, 16–030.

C. Dangerous Things

Rylands v Fletcher has been applied (or said to apply, because the cases **16–010** sometimes turned on other points) to a remarkable variety of things: fire;[38] gas;[39] blasting and munitions;[40] electricity;[41] oil and petrol;[42] noxious fumes;[43] colliery spoil;[44] rusty wire from a decayed fence;[45] vibrations;[46] poisonous vegetation;[47] a flag pole;[48] a "chair-o-plane" in a fairground;[49] and even (in a case of very questionable validity) noxious persons.[50] However, there seems little point in seeking to identify the precise characteristics of a *"Rylands v Fletcher* object". What matters is the scale of the risk presented by the defendant's activity: a box of matches or a glass of water do not fall within the rule, a million boxes of matches in a store or a reservoir may do so. The requirement that the thing must be likely to do mischief if it escapes cannot therefore be viewed in isolation from the further requirement of non-natural user, which encapsulates the element of exceptional risk which underlies the rule.[51]

The Cambridge Water case. The House of Lords in the *Cambridge Water*[52] case **16–011** held, by analogy with their decision on nuisance[53] that the rule was inapplicable unless it could be foreseen that damage of the relevant type would occur as the result of an escape. Accordingly, if the possibility of the damage which occurs is scientifically unknown at the time when the escape takes place there is no liability. It is clear that the defendant is liable notwithstanding that he has exercised all due care to prevent the escape occurring[54] for the liability is not based on negligence. Nor does the escape have to be likely: the issue is whether

---

[38] See para.16–036.

[39] *Batchellor v Tunbridge Wells Gas Co* (1901) 84 L.T. 765.

[40] *Miles v Forest Rock Co* (1918) 34 T.L.R. 500; *Rainham Chemical Works Ltd v Belvedere Fish Guano Co Ltd* [1921] 2 A.C. 465.

[41] *National Telephone Co v Baker* [1893] 2 Ch. 186; *Eastern and South African Telegraph Co Ltd v Cape Town Tramways Companies Ltd* [1902] A.C. 381; *Hillier v Air Ministry* [1962] C.L.Y. 2084 (cows electrocuted by an escape of electricity from high-voltage cables laid under claimant's field).

[42] *Smith v GW Ry* (1926) 135 L.T. 112; *Colour Quest Ltd v Total Downstream UK Plc* [2009] EWHC 540 (Comm); [2009] 1 Lloyds Rep 1.

[43] *West v Bristol Tramways Co* [1908] 2 K.B. 14 (in so far as the case applied the rule to a risk which was not foreseeable it cannot stand with the *Cambridge Water* case).

[44] *Attorney General v Cory Bros Ltd* [1921] 1 A.C. 521.

[45] *Firth v Bowling Iron Co* (1878) 3 C.P.D. 254.

[46] *Hoare & Co v McAlpine* [1923] 1 Ch. 167; cf. *Dodd Properties Ltd v Canterbury CC* [1979] 2 All E.R. 118 at 122.

[47] *Crowhurst v Amersham Burial Board* (1878) 4 Ex. D. 5; *Ponting v Noakes* [1894] 2 Q.B. 281.

[48] *Shiffman v Order of St John* [1936] 1 All E.R. 557 (obiter, it was decided on the ground of negligence).

[49] *Hale v Jennings Bros* [1938] 1 All E.R. 579.

[50] *Attorney General v Corke* [1933] Ch. 89 but cf. *Smith v Scott* [1973] Ch. 314, where it is suggested that this case could at least equally well have been decided on the basis that the landowner was in possession of the property and was himself liable for nuisances created by his licensees. Liability in nuisance was imposed in similar circumstances in *Lippiatt v South Gloucestershire Council* [2000] Q.B. 51; para.15–040.

[51] *Transco Plc v Stockport MBC* [2003] UKHL 61; [2004] 2 A.C. 1 at [10], [103].

[52] *Cambridge Water Co v Eastern Countries Leather Plc* [1994] 2 A.C. 264.

[53] See para.15–031.

[54] *Cambridge Water Co v Eastern Countries Leather Plc* [1994] 2 A.C. 264 at 302.

damage is likely if the escape occurs, but perhaps it goes a little too far to say that the risk of escape need not be *foreseeable*. In *Cambridge Water*,[55] the damage which occurred was rather unusual in that the pollution of the claimants' water supply did not render it harmful to health but it was technically unwholesome under regulations made to comply with an EC Directive and could not lawfully be supplied as drinking water. Nevertheless the "harmful" qualities of the chemical as potentially polluting a water supply must have been known in the sense that even before the regulations came into effect it is unlikely that the owners of the borehole would have cheerfully stood by while someone injected the borehole with it. The critical point, which was determinative of the case, was that no one ever contemplated as a possibility that the spilled chemical would get into the aquifer[56] or, even if it did, that it would be found in detectable quantities downstream at the claimants' borehole. That is different from a situation where, for example, a defendant stores quantities of a chemical known to be highly toxic in containers made to the very best standards of quality and safety. In the *Cambridge Water* case the idea of an escape from the defendants' land would simply never have occurred to anyone; in the other case the possibility would be recognised (which is why the precautions are taken) even if it would be regarded as far-fetched.

D. Escape

16–012   The requirement of escape, which demonstrates the connection of the rule with nuisance, was firmly set in the law by the House of Lords' decision in *Read v J Lyons & Co Ltd*.[57] The claimant was employed by the Ministry of Supply as an inspector of munitions in the defendants' munitions factory and, in the course of her employment there, was injured by the explosion of a shell that was being manufactured. It was admitted that high explosive shells were dangerous. The defendants were held not liable. There was no allegation of negligence on their part and *Rylands v Fletcher* was inapplicable because there had been no "escape" of the thing that inflicted the injury. "Escape" was defined as, "escape from a place where the defendant has occupation or control over land to a place which is outside his occupation or control".[58] Viscount Simon stated that *Rylands v Fletcher* is conditioned by two elements which he called: (1) "the condition of 'escape' from the land of something likely to do mischief if it escapes"; and (2) "the condition of 'non-natural' use of the land".[59] However, the House of Lords

---

[55] For the facts, see para.15–031.

[56] See also *Dempsey v Waterford Corp* [2008] IEHC 55.

[57] [1947] A.C. 156; *Transco Plc v Stockport MBC* [2003] UKHL 61; [2004] 2 A.C. 1 at [9], [34], [77].

[58] Viscount Simon [1947] A.C. 156 at 168 and at 177 per Lord Porter: "Escape from the place in which the dangerous object has been maintained by the defendant to some place not subject to his control."

[59] [1947] A.C. 156 at 173 per Lord Macmillan: "Escape . . . and non-natural use of the land, whatever precisely that may mean."

emphasised that the absence of an "escape" was the basis of their decision. The rule is probably inapplicable to a deliberate release of the thing, the cause of action in that situation being trespass.[60]

E. Land

Defendant need not have an interest in the land from which the escape emanates. The rule is not confined to the case where the defendant is the freeholder of the land on which the dangerous thing is accumulated: the defendant in *Rylands v Fletcher* itself appears to have had only a licence from the landowner to construct the reservoir. Similarly, the rule has been applied in cases where the defendant has a franchise or statutory right, for example to lay pipes to carry gas[61] or cables for electricity.[62] Indeed, there are statements to the effect that anyone who collects the dangerous thing and has control of it at the time of the escape would be liable,[63] even when it is being carried on the highway and escapes therefrom.[64] A landowner who is not in occupation of the land when the thing escapes is probably liable if he has authorised the accumulation.[65]

16–013

The claimant must have an interest in land. As to the status of the claimant, the position is governed by the fact that the rule is an offshoot or variety of private nuisance and in *Hunter v Canary Wharf Ltd*[66] the House of Lords held that an interest in land or de facto exclusive possession of it was a necessary qualification to bring a claim in nuisance.[67] A number of earlier cases applying *Rylands v Fletcher* should probably therefore be regarded as wrongly decided on this basis alone.[68]

16–014

---

[60] *Rigby v CC Northamptonshire* [1985] 1 W.L.R. 1242 (firing of CS gas canister). Doubted, unless the thing is aimed at the claimant, in *Crown River Cruises v Kimbolton Fireworks* [1996] 2 Lloyd's Rep. 533. See also *Smeaton v Ilford Corp* [1954] Ch. 450 at 462.

[61] *Northwestern Utilities Ltd v London Guarantee Ltd* [1936] A.C. 108 at 118; cf. *Read v J Lyons & Co Ltd* [1947] A.C. 156 at 183.

[62] *Charing Cross Electricity Supply Co v Hydraulic Power Co* [1914] 3 K.B. 772; but if C has an easement to have e.g. a gas main in D's land and there is an escape from one part of D's land to the part where the easement is located there is no "escape" for the purposes of the rule: *Transco Plc v Stockport MBC* [2003] UKHL 61; [2004] 2 A.C. 1 at [80] (though only Lord Scott decided the case on this basis).

[63] *Rainham Chemical Works v Belvedere Fish Guano Co* [1921] 2 A.C. 465 at 479.

[64] *Powell v Fall* (1880) 5 Q.B.D. 597; *Rigby v CC Northamptonshire* [1985] 1 W.L.R. 1242. See also *Crown River Cruises v Kimbolton Fireworks* [1995] 2 Lloyd's Rep. 533. But as to whether under the general law of nuisance the defendant needs to be the occupier of land from which the invasion comes see para.15–040.

[65] See *Rainham Chemical Works* [1921] 2 A.C. 465 at 476, 489.

[66] [1997] A.C. 655, para.034.

[67] *McKenna v British Aluminium Ltd* [2002] Env L.R. 30.

[68] For example, *Shiffman v Order of St John* [1936] 1 All E.R. 557; *Miles v Forest Rock Granite Co Ltd* (1918) 34 T.L.R. 500. Some of them might, however, be regarded as cases of public nuisance. In *Weller v Foot and Mouth Disease Research Institute* [1966] 1 Q.B. 569, Widgery J held that the claimants, cattle auctioneers who suffered loss when sales of cattle were stopped during an outbreak of foot and mouth, could not sue under the rule because they had no interest in any land to which the virus escaped. However, it would have been sufficient to arrive at this result to apply the general principle that A cannot sue for financial loss which arises because of physical damage to the property of B.

F. Personal Injury

16–015 Cases which have held[69] or assumed[70] that *Rylands v Fletcher* is applicable to personal injuries may have ignored the requirement of landholding status, but it is possible that an adjoining occupier might suffer personal injury,[71] in which case the question of the applicability of the rule to personal injuries has to be directly addressed. Again the relationship with nuisance is decisive and the strong indications in *Hunter v Canary Wharf* that such losses fall outside the scope of that tort[72] indicated that the same result would be reached under *Rylands v Fletcher,*[73] a proposition decisively accepted by the House of Lords in the *Transco* case.[74]

G. Non-natural User[75]

16–016 **Origin of the requirement.** We have already noted that Blackburn J in the Court of Exchequer Chamber made no mention of the requirement of non-natural user. He did, however, make it plain that the principle he stated applied only to things which the defendant collected for his own purposes. Hence he cannot be liable under the rule merely for permitting a spontaneous accumulation (for example, of water, vegetation or birds) on his land,[76] or even for inducing a spontaneous accumulation as an undesired by-product of the normal working of the land.[77] However, as a practical matter these principles have been much reduced in importance by the recognition that an occupier may owe a duty of care to abate a nuisance arising naturally on his land.[78]

It may well be that Lord Cairns in the House of Lords in *Rylands v Fletcher* did not intend to add anything to Blackburn J's requirement that the defendant should have accumulated the dangerous thing by positive action but it is recognised in *Cambridge Water Co v Eastern Counties Leather Plc*[79] that the law

---

[69] See previous note.

[70] *Perry v Kendricks Transport* [1956] 1 W.L.R. 85.

[71] As happened in *Hale v Jennings Bros* [1938] 1 All E.R. 579 (tenant of fairground stall) and *Benning v Wong* (1969) 122 C.L.R. 249.

[72] See para.15–037.

[73] However, the relationship also calls into question Lord Goff's doubts in *Hunter* as to whether nuisance covers damage to the property as opposed to interference with enjoyment of it ([1997] A.C. 655 at 692). If that is the law of nuisance and *Rylands v Fletcher* follows the same principle, the rule in the case would in effect disappear.

[74] *Transco Plc v Stockport MBC* [2003] UKHL 61; [2004] 2 A.C. 1 at [9], [35], [52]; but this makes it difficult to accept the assertion in *Transco* that the background to *Rylands v Fletcher* was public concern about disasters causing widespread loss of life such as the Bradfield reservoir burst in 1864: at [28].

[75] Williams [1973] C.L.J. 310.

[76] *Giles v Walker* (1890) 24 Q.B.D. 656 (thistledown); *Pontardawe RDC v Moore-Gwyn* [1929] 1 Ch. 656 (falls of rocks); *Seligman v Docker* [1949] Ch. 53.

[77] *Wilson v Waddell* (1876) 2 App. Cas. 95; *Smith v Kenrick* (1849) 7 C.B. 515. *Giles v Walker* (1890) 24 Q.B.D. 656 is in fact such a case, since the thistle crop had been produced for unexplained reasons by the defendant's ploughing of some forest land.

[78] However, they remain relevant where there is a sudden disaster against which the occupier cannot take steps: *Ellison v MoD* (1997) 81 B.L.R. 101 (flood produced by works at airfield).

[79] [1994] 2 A.C. 264 at 308.

has developed so as to give the expression a meaning which excludes from the rule deliberate accumulations which are brought about by "ordinary" uses of the land.

Definition. The most frequently quoted "definition" is that given by Lord   **16–017** Moulton, speaking for the Privy Council in *Rickards v Lothian*: "It must be some special use bringing with it increased danger to others and must not merely be the ordinary use of the land or such a use as is proper for the general benefit of the community."[80] It would be hopeless to contend that all of the case law on this issue is reconcilable and the *Cambridge Water* case may require that we reconsider some of the earlier cases. However, the following propositions seem to represent the present state of the law.

Changing circumstances. Lord Porter said in *Read v J Lyons & Co Ltd*[81] that in   **16–018** deciding the question of non-natural user: "[A]ll the circumstances of time and practice of mankind must be taken into consideration so that what may be regarded as dangerous or non-natural may vary according to the circumstances."

For this reason what may seem extraordinary to one generation may seem ordinary to its successor. At the time of the First World War the Court of Appeal held that keeping a motor car in a garage with petrol in a tank was a non-natural use of land,[82] a decision which may well have been dubious even at that time but, it is submitted, would be inconceivable today notwithstanding the doctrine of precedent.[83]

Common or domestic use. Notwithstanding the refusal to develop *Rylands v*   **16–019** *Fletcher* into a general principle of strict liability for ultra-hazardous activities, the effect of the case law seems to go some way along this road in its particular nuisance-related context by excluding from the scope of the rule minor or common or domestic uses of things which have some potential for danger. So the following have been regarded as natural or ordinary uses of land: water installations in a house or office;[84] the main water supply to a block of flats;[85] a fire in a domestic grate;[86] electric wiring;[87] gas pipes in a house or shop;[88] erecting or pulling down houses or walls;[89] burning stubble in the normal course of agriculture;[90] the ordinary working of mines or minerals;[91] the possession of

---

[80] *Rickards v Lothian* [1913] A.C. 263 at 279–280. See *Read v J Lyons & Co Ltd* [1947] A.C. 156 at 169; *Cambridge Water Co v Eastern Counties Leather Plc* [1994] 2 A.C. 264 at 308.
[81] [1947] A.C. 156 at 176.
[82] *Musgrove v Pandelis* [1919] 2 K.B. 43.
[83] See *Transco Plc v Stockport MBC* [2003] UKHL 61; [2004] 2 A.C. 1 at [107] (even though in *Perry v Kendricks Transport Ltd* [1956] 1 W.L.R. 85 at 92 (coach left on parking ground after emptying tank) Parker LJ considered *Musgrove v Pandelis* was binding on the CA).
[84] *Rickards v Lothian* [1913] A.C. 263.
[85] *Transco Plc v Stockport MBC* [2003] UKHL 61; [2004] 2 A.C. 1.
[86] *Sochacki v Sas* [1947] 1 All E.R. 344.
[87] *Collingwood v Home and Colonial Stores Ltd* [1936] 3 All E.R. 200.
[88] *Miller v Addie & Sons (Collieries) Ltd* 1934 S.C. 150.
[89] *Thomas and Evans Ltd v Mid-Rhondda Co-operative Society* [1941] 1 K.B. 381.
[90] *Perkins v Glyn* [1976] R.T.R. ix (note).
[91] *Rouse v Gravelworks Ltd* [1940] 1 K.B. 489.

trees whether planted or self-sown;[92] or generating steam on a ship.[93] These are commonplace risks with which people must put up unless there is fault. There has, however, been a greater willingness to apply the rule to the bulk storage or transmission of water[94] or gas or electricity,[95] or to the bulk storage of chemicals,[96] or combustible materials,[97] though the defence of statutory authority has in many cases prevented a decision in the claimant's favour.

16–020 **The relevance of public benefit.** Blackburn J's reference to the defendant collecting the dangerous thing "for his own purposes" does not mean that he must be seeking to profit from the activity; indeed, in one case the phrase was said not to be a sufficient reason to refuse to apply the rule to a local authority which was required by statute to receive sewage into its sewers.[98] However, there has sometimes been a marked tendency to say that a use is natural where it leads to a public benefit, whether by way of the provision of public services[99] or by manufacturing,[100] a course which requires the court either to make very difficult value judgments or to deprive the rule of all practical effect. In *Rainham Chemical Works Ltd v Belvedere Fish Guano Co Ltd*[101] it was assumed without argument that the manufacture of military explosives during the First World War was a non-natural use but on similar facts in the Second World War in *Read v J Lyons & Co Ltd* Viscount Simon and Lord Macmillan suggested that this might not be so because of the urgent public necessity for munitions in time of war.[102] That seems a utilitarian extension too far[103] and the House of Lords in the *Cambridge Water* case said that the rule would not be excluded merely because the activity was one which provided employment and was therefore worthy of encouragement. Furthermore, it was said that the storage of substantial quantities of chemicals on industrial premises should be regarded as "an almost classic case of non-natural use" and this would be so even if the use was common or ordinary

---

[92] *Noble v Harrison* [1926] 2 K.B. 332. Cf. *Crowhurst v Amersham Burial Board* (1878) 4 Ex.D. 5 (poisonous yew tree).

[93] *Howard v Furness Ltd* [1936] 2 All E.R. 781; *Miller Steamship Co Pty Ltd v Overseas Tankship (UK) Ltd* [1963] 1 Lloyd's Rep. 402 at 426.

[94] *Rylands v Fletcher* itself; cf. *Transco Plc v Stockport MBC* [2003] UKHL 61; [2004] 2 A.C. 1.

[95] *Charing Cross Electricity Supply Co v Hydraulic Power Co* [1914] 3 K.B. 772; *Northwestern Utilities v London Guarantee and Accident Co* [1936] A.C. 108.

[96] *Cambridge Water Co v Eastern Counties Leather Plc* [1994] 2 A.C. 264.

[97] *Mason v Levy Auto Parts of England Ltd* [1967] 2 Q.B. 530; *Hobbs (Farms) Ltd v Baxenden Chemical Co Ltd* [1992] 1 Lloyd's Rep. 54; *LMS International Ltd v Styrene Packaging and Insulation Ltd* [2005] EWHC 2065 (TCC); *Colour Quest Ltd v Total Downstream UK Plc* [2009] EWHC 540 (Comm); [2009] 1 Lloyds Rep 1.

[98] *Smeaton v Ilford Corp* [1954] 1 Ch. 459 at 469, 472.

[99] In *Dunne v NW Gas Board* [1964] 2 Q.B. 806 the CA was reluctant to hold a nationalised industry liable in the absence of fault and see the differing views on local authorities expressed by Lord Evershed MR and Denning LJ in *Pride of Derby and Derby Angling Association Ltd v British Celanese Ltd* [1953] Ch. 149.

[100] *British Celanese Ltd v AH Hunt Ltd* [1969] 1 W.L.R. 959 at 963–964: "The manufacturing of electrical and electronic components in the year 1964 ... cannot be adjudged to be a special use ... The metal foil was there for use in the manufacture of goods of a common type which at all material times were needed for the general benefit of the community."

[101] [1921] 2 A.C. 465.

[102] [1947] A.C. 156 at 169, 174

[103] *Transco Plc v Stockport MBC* [2003] UKHL 61; [2004] 2 A.C. 1 at [105].

in the industry in question.[104] One cannot say that these storage activities are unreasonable in the nuisance sense for they may be very necessary, but they do impose an "exceptional risk", as those living in the vicinity of such twentieth century disasters as Rainham and Flixborough would no doubt agree.[105] Despite the fact that the *Cambridge Water* case shows a clear intention to prevent *Rylands v Fletcher* becoming a growing point in the general design of the common law, this aspect of the case may lead to a modest revival of the rule.

H. Defences

In *Rylands v Fletcher* possible defences to the rule were no more than outlined and we must look to later decisions for their development. It will be seen that with some of them it is now probably misleading to think of them as independent defences.

16–021

i. Consent of the Claimant

Where the claimant has expressly or impliedly consented to the presence of the source of danger and there has been no negligence on the part of the defendant, the defendant is not liable.[106] The exception merely illustrates the general defence, volenti non fit injuria. The main application of the principle of implied consent is found in cases where different floors in the same building are occupied by different persons and the tenant of a lower floor suffers damage as the result of water escaping from an upper floor, though it has to be said that the cases which have discussed this defence have tended to involve perfectly ordinary domestic fittings which would to modern eyes be a natural use of land.[107] In a block of premises each tenant can normally be regarded as consenting to the presence of water on the premises if the supply is of the usual character, but not if it is of quite an unusual kind, or defective or dangerous, unless he actually knows of that. The defendant is liable if the escape was due to his negligence.[108]

16–022

---

[104] *Cambridge Water Co v Eastern Counties Leather Plc* [1994] 2 A.C. 264 at 309. In *Colour Quest Ltd v Total Downstream UK Plc* [2009] EWHC 540 (Comm); [2009] 1 Lloyds Rep 1 (the Buncefield oil depot explosion in 2005) the defendants conceded liability under *Rylands v Fletcher*, subject to the defence of consent by those within the perimeter of the area,

[105] See *Transco Plc v Stockport MBC* [2003] UKHL 61; [2004] 2 A.C. 1 at [104].

[106] *Gill v Edouin* (1894) 71 L.T. 762, 72 L.T. 579; *Attorney General v Cory Bros Ltd* [1921] 1 A.C. 521 at 538, 543, 550. *Ross v Fedden* (1872) L.R. 7 Q.B. 661 and *Kiddle v City Business Properties Ltd* [1942] 1 K.B. 269 are cases of this type.

[107] Cf. *Western Engraving Co v Film Laboratories Ltd* [1936] 1 All E.R. 106. In *Transco Plc v Stockport MBC* [2003] UKHL 61; [2004] 2 A.C. 1 at [61] Lord Hobhouse equates the cases in this category with the basic "live and let live" approach of ordinary nuisance law.

[108] *Prosser v Levy* [1955] 1 W.L.R. 1224 at 1233, CA; *Colour Quest Ltd v Total Downstream UK Plc* [2009] EWHC 540 (Comm); [2009] 1 Lloyds Rep 1 (reviewing previous cases and taking the view that where there is negligence the *Rylands v Fletcher* claim remains and is not simply merged into the tort of negligence).

ii. Common Benefit

16–023 Where the source of the danger is maintained for the common benefit of the claimant and the defendant, the defendant is not liable for its escape. This is akin to the defence of consent of the claimant, and Bramwell B in *Carstairs v Taylor*[109] treated it as the same thing. In *Peters v Prince of Wales Theatre (Birmingham) Ltd*,[110] the Court of Appeal regarded "common benefit" as no more than an element (although an important element) in showing consent. In other judicial dicta the exception has been regarded as an independent one.[111] One passage in the *Cambridge Water* case[112] suggests that the rule may be inapplicable to the provision of services to a defined area such as a business park or an industrial estate, but this statement is made in the context of non-natural use. The view that there is a defence of common benefit among consumers of a generally supplied service like gas or electricity seems inconsistent with that case.[113] On balance, common benefit seems redundant (and indeed misleading) as an independent defence.

iii. Act of Stranger

16–024 **Unforeseeable act of a stranger.** If the escape was caused by the unforeseeable act of a stranger, the rule does not apply. In *Box v Jubb*[114] the defendant's reservoir overflowed partly because of the acts of a neighbouring reservoir owner and the defendant escaped liability. The claimant also failed in his claim in *Rickards v Lothian*[115] where some third person deliberately blocked up the waste pipe of a lavatory basin in the defendant's premises, thereby flooding the claimant's premises. It has been suggested that the defence is limited to the "mischievous, deliberate and conscious act of a stranger",[116] and therefore excludes his negligent acts. However, as Jenkins LJ pointed out in *Perry v Kendricks Transport Ltd*[117] the basis of the defence is the absence of any control by the defendant over the acts of a stranger on his land and therefore the nature of the stranger's conduct is irrelevant.

16–025 **Foreseeable act of a stranger: liability in negligence.** The onus is on the defendant to show that the escape was due to the unforeseeable act of a stranger without any negligence on his own part. If, on the other hand, the act of the stranger could reasonably have been anticipated or its consequences prevented,

---

[109] *Carstairs v Taylor* (1871) L.R. 6 Ex. 217. So too, *Northwestern Utilities Ltd v London Guarantee Co Ltd* [1936] A.C. 108 at 120 and *Gilson v Kerrier RDC* [1976] 1 W.L.R. 904.

[110] [1943] 1 K.B. 73 at 78.

[111] *Gill v Edouin* (1894) 72 L.T. 579; *Anderson v Oppenheimer* (1880) L.R. 5 Q.B.D. 602.

[112] *Cambridge Water Co v Eastern Counties Leather Plc* [1994] 2 A.C. 264 at 308.

[113] Cf. *Dunne v NW Gas Board* [1964] Q.B. 806 at 832.

[114] (1879) 4 Ex.D. 76

[115] [1913] A.C. 263.

[116] [1956] 1 W.L.R. 85 at 87 per Singleton LJ. Similarly in *Prosser v Levy* [1955] 1 W.L.R. 1224 by the same judge.

[117] *Perry v Kendricks Transport Ltd* [1956] 1 W.L.R. 85 at 90. Similarly per Parker LJ in *Smith v Great Western Ry* (1926) 42 T.L.R. 391 the negligent act of a third party (failing to ascertain a defect in an oil tank) was held to be a good defence, but this case was not brought to the attention of the court in *Prosser v Levy*.

the defendant will still be liable. In *Northwestern Utilities Ltd v London Guarantee and Accident Co Ltd*,[118] a hotel belonging to and insured by the claimants was destroyed in a fire caused by the escape and ignition of natural gas. The gas had percolated into the hotel basement from a fractured welded joint in an intermediate pressure main situated below street level and belonging to the defendants, a public utility company. The fracture was caused during the construction of a storm sewer, involving underground work beneath the defendants' mains, by a third party. The Privy Council accepted that the defences of act of God and act of third party prevent a claimant from succeeding in a claim based on the rule in *Rylands v Fletcher* but held the defendants liable for negligence. The risk involved in the defendants' operations was so great that a high degree of care was expected of them. They knew of the construction of the sewer, and they ought to have appreciated the possibility of damage to their mains and taken appropriate action to prevent or rectify it.

It is evident from the *Northwestern Utilities* case that once the defendant proves the act of a stranger, the point is reached when a claim based on the rule in *Rylands v Fletcher* for practical purposes merges into a claim in negligence, so that if there is no fault the claimant will not succeed. By means of the defence of act of a stranger the basis of the liability is shifted from the creation of a risk to responsibility for culpable failure to control the risk. The rule in *Rylands v Fletcher* thus ceases to be available at the very moment when the claimant needs it. One can compare liability under the rule with the liability at common law for dangerous animals which was stricter.[119] It seems that the act of a stranger was not a valid defence in the case of the animal, because it was within the risk that must be accepted by anyone who knowingly chooses to keep a dangerous animal.

Employees and independent contractors. It is clear that a trespasser is a "stranger" for this purpose.[120] For the defaults of his servants in the course of their employment, the occupier is of course liable; he is also liable for the negligence of an independent contractor[121] unless it is entirely collateral.[122] In the closely related context of liability for fire it has been held that the occupier is liable for the fault of his licensees or guests unless the act is wholly alien to the invitation[123] and this seems to be the general rule.

16–026

Predecessor in title. In connection with this exception to the rule in *Rylands v Fletcher*, we must consider whether the rule applies to a danger created on the premises by the occupier's predecessor in title. It may be inferred from the decision in the *Northwestern Utilities* case[124] that if the occupier knew, or might with reasonable care have ascertained, that the danger existed, he is liable for its escape. If, however, this condition is not satisfied, it is submitted that he ought

16–027

---

[118] [1936] A.C. 108.
[119] The new statutory liability is similarly strict, para.17–017.
[120] *Mandraj v Texaco Trinidad Inc* (1969) 15 W.I.R. 251.
[121] *Balfour v Barty-King* [1957] 1 Q.B. 496 at 505–506 (CA) per Lord Goddard CJ (the defendant has control of his independent contractor in that he chooses him, invites him to his premises to do work, can order him to leave at any moment, although it is left to the contractor how the work is to be done).
[122] See para.21–051.
[123] See para.16–036.
[124] Indeed, from *Goldman v Hargrave* [1967] 1 A.C. 465 and associated cases: para.15–047.

not to be liable. There is no direct decision on the point, but the rule itself seems to make it essential that the defendant should "bring on his lands" the danger.[125]

iv.   Statutory Authority

16–028   **A question of the proper construction of the statute.** The rule in *Rylands v Fletcher* may be excluded by statute. Whether it is so or not is a question of construction of the particular statute concerned. In *Green v Chelsea Waterworks Co*,[126] for instance, a main belonging to a waterworks company, which was authorised by Parliament to lay the main, burst without any negligence on the part of the company and the claimant's premises were flooded; the company was held not liable. On the other hand, in *Charing Cross Electricity Co v Hydraulic Power Co*[127] where the facts were similar, the defendants were held to have no exemption upon the interpretation of their statute. The distinction between the cases is that the Hydraulic Power Co were empowered by statute to supply water for industrial purposes, that is, they had permissive power but not a mandatory authority, and they were under no obligation to keep their mains charged with water at high pressure, or at all. The Chelsea Waterworks Co were authorised by statute to lay mains and were under a statutory duty to maintain a continuous supply of water; it was an inevitable consequence that damage would be caused by occasional bursts and so by necessary implication the statute exempted them from liability where there was no "negligence".[128] Where a statutory authority is under a mandatory obligation to supply a service, whether with a savings or nuisance clause (that nothing shall exonerate it from proceedings for nuisance) or whether without such a clause, the authority is under no liability for anything expressly required by statute to be done, or reasonably incidental to that requirement, if it was done without negligence.[129] Where the statutory authority is merely permissive, with no clause imposing liability for nuisance, the authority is not liable for doing what the statute authorises, provided it is not negligent; but it is liable when there is a clause imposing liability for nuisance, even if it is not negligent.[130] As to the escape of water from reservoirs, even express statutory authority for their construction will not by itself exonerate their undertakers since the Reservoirs (Safety Provisions) Act 1930, now replaced by the Reservoirs Act

---

[125] See also *Whitmores Ltd v Stanford* [1909] 1 Ch. 427 at 438.

[126] (1894) 70 L.T. 547 applied by the House of Lords in *Longhurst v Metropolitan Water Board* [1948] 2 All E.R. 834. Note, however, that since April 1, 1982 statutory water undertakers are strictly liable for damage (including personal injury) caused by an escape of water from a communication pipe or main under what is now the Water Industry Act 1991 s.209. This strict liability does not avail other statutory undertakers such as gas and electricity suppliers or highway authorities.

[127] [1914] 3 K.B. 772. Where there is negligence of the sort occurring in *Northwestern Utilities Ltd v London Guarantee Co Ltd* [1936] A.C. 108, statutory authority will be no defence.

[128] *Smeaton v Ilford Corp* [1954] Ch. 450 at 475–477. "Negligence" in this connection is not a very appropriate word for it means, "adopting a method which in fact results in damage to a third person, except in a case where there is no other way of performing the statutory duty": per Farwell J in *Provender Millers (Winchester) Ltd v Southampton CC* [1940] Ch. 131 at 140.

[129] *Department of Transport v NW Water Authority* [1984] A.C. 336.

[130] *Dunne v North Western Gas Board* [1964] 2 Q.B. 806 at 833–837.

1975.[131] The Dolgarrog Dam disaster of 1925 led to the passing of this legislation. A reservoir 1,400 feet above sea level and holding 200 million gallons of water burst and caused great devastation and loss of life.

Burden of proof? One important question in this area awaits a final answer: if, on its proper construction, the statutory authority exempts the undertaker from *Rylands v Fletcher* liability and imposes only an obligation to use due care, upon whom does the burden of proof lie? A bare majority of the High Court of Australia[132] held that the burden lies upon the claimant to prove lack of such care but the contrary arguments of the minority seem more convincing in principle and allow for the grave difficulties facing a claimant with the task of proving negligence against the supplier of a public utility such as gas or electricity.

16–029

v. Act of God

Extraordinary acts of nature. Where the escape is caused directly by natural causes without human intervention in, "circumstances which no human foresight can provide against and of which human prudence is not bound to recognise the possibility",[133] the defence of act of God applies. This was recognised by Blackburn J in *Rylands v Fletcher*[134] itself and was applied in *Nichols v Marsland*.[135] In this case the defendant for many years had been in possession of some artificial ornamental lakes formed by damming up a natural stream. An extraordinary rainfall, "greater and more violent than any within the memory of witnesses" broke down the artificial embankments and the rush of escaping water carried away four bridges in respect of which damage the claimant sued. Judgment was given for the defendant; the jury had found that she was not negligent and the court held that she ought not to be liable for an extraordinary act of nature which she could not reasonably anticipate.

16–030

A restricted approach. Whether a particular occurrence amounts to an act of God is a question of fact, but the tendency of the courts nowadays is to restrict the ambit of the defence, not because strict liability is thought to be desirable but because increased knowledge limits the unpredictable. In *Greenock Corp v Caledonian Ry*,[136] the House of Lords criticised the application of the defence in *Nichols v Marsland*, and four of their lordships cast doubt on the finding of facts by the jury in that case.[137] The defendants constructed a concrete paddling pool

16–031

---

[131] Section 28, Sch.2. However, things may not now be so simple. The wording is: "Where damage or injury is caused by the escape of water from a reservoir constructed . . . under statutory powers . . . the fact that the reservoir was so constructed shall not exonerate the persons for the time being having the management and control of the reservoir from any indictment, action or other proceedings to which they would otherwise have been liable." In other words, the question seems to turn on what their liability is at common law. At the time of the legislation it would have been widely thought that *Rylands v Fletcher* covered personal injuries, but now this is not so: para.16–015.

[132] *Benning v Wong* (1969) 122 C.L.R. 249.

[133] *Tennent v Earl of Glasgow* (1864) 2 M. (HL) 22 at 26–27 per Lord Westbury, approved by the House of Lords in *Greenock Corp v Caledonian Ry* [1917] A.C. 556.

[134] (1866) L.R. 1 Ex. 265 at 280.

[135] (1876) 2 Ex.D. 1.

[136] [1917] A.C. 556.

[137] [1917] A.C. 556 at 573–574, 575, 580–581.

for children in the bed of the stream and to do so they had to alter the course of the stream and obstruct the natural flow of the water. Owing to a rainfall of extraordinary violence, the stream overflowed at the pond, and a great volume of water, which would normally have been carried off by the stream, poured down a public street into the town and caused damage to the claimants' property. The House of Lords held that the rainfall was not an act of God and that the defendants were liable. It was their duty "so to work as to make proprietors or occupiers on a lower level as secure against injury as they would have been had nature not been interfered with".[138] Similar considerations apply to an extraordinary high wind[139] and an extraordinary high tide.[140] Lightning,[141] earthquakes, cloudbursts and tornadoes may be acts of God but there seems to be no English decision in which they have been involved.

16–032 **Criticism.** In law, then, the essence of an act of God is not so much a phenomenon which is sometimes attributed to a positive intervention of the forces of nature, but a process of nature not due to the act of man[142] and it is this negative side which deserves emphasis. The criterion is not whether or not the event could reasonably be anticipated, but whether or not human foresight and prudence could reasonably recognise the possibility of such an event. Even in such limited form, however, this defence, like the defence of act of a stranger, shifts the basis of the tort from responsibility for the creation of a risk to culpable failure to control that risk. This has been criticised on the ground that an accidental escape caused by the forces of nature is within the risk that must be accepted by the defendant when he accumulates the substance on his land.[143] As Scrutton LJ put it in his strong dissenting judgment in *Attorney General v Cory Bros*, "the fact that an artificial danger escaped through natural causes was no excuse to the person who brought an artificial danger there".[144] Nevertheless, the defence, though rarely or never applied in practice, seems to be rooted in the law and brings the rule in *Rylands v Fletcher* closer to the tort of negligence.[145]

vi. Default of the Claimant

16–033 If the damage is caused solely by the act or default of the claimant himself, he has no remedy. In *Rylands v Fletcher* itself, this was noticed as a defence.[146] If a

---

[138] [1917] A.C. 556 at 579 per Lord Shaw.

[139] *Cushing v Walker & Sons* [1941] 2 All E.R. 693 at 695 per Hallett J.

[140] *Greenwood Tileries Ltd v Clapson* [1937] 1 All E.R. 765 at 772 per Branson J.

[141] *Nichols v Marsland* (1875) L.R. 10 Ex. 255 at 260, dictum of Bramwell B.

[142] "Something in opposition to the act of man": Lord Mansfield in *Forward v Pittard* (1785) 1 T.R. 27 at 33.

[143] Particularly, Goodhart (1951) 4 C.L.P. 177; 72 L.Q.R. 184.

[144] *Attorney General v Cory Bros* (1919) 35 T.L.R. 570 at 574 (fall of refuse in Rhondda Valley probably caused by the saturation of its inferior strata by an extraordinary rainfall). Also *Dixon v Metropolitan Board of Works* (1881) 7 Q.B.D. 418 per Lord Coleridge CJ.

[145] See Buxton (1966) 8 U. Malaya L.R. 7: the decision in *Nichols v Marsland*, "leaves very few cases where a defendant could be held liable who had not in fact been negligent". See also Street (1965) I.C.L.Q. 862, 870; *Transco Plc v Stockport MBC* [2003] UKHL 61; [2004] 2 A.C. 1 at [39].

[146] (1868) L.R. 3 H.L. 330 at 340. If the rule applies to a deliberate discharge of the thing (which is unlikely) necessity is as much a defence as in trespass: *Rigby v CC Northamptonshire* [1985] 1 W.L.R. 1242.

person knows that there is a danger of his mine being flooded by his neighbour's operations on adjacent land, and courts the danger by doing some act which renders the flooding probable, he cannot complain.[147] So, too, in *Ponting v Noakes*,[148] the claimant's horse reached over the defendant's boundary, nibbled some poisonous tree there and died accordingly, and it was held that the claimant could recover nothing, for the damage was due to the horse's own intrusion and, alternatively, there had been no escape of the vegetation.[149] Where the claimant is contributorily negligent, the apportionment provisions of the Law Reform (Contributory Negligence) Act 1945 will apply.[150]

Abnormal sensitivity of the claimant's property. If the injury due to the escape of the noxious thing would not have occurred but for the unusual sensitiveness of the claimant's property, there is some conflict of authority whether this can be regarded as default of the claimant. In *Eastern SA Telegraph Co Ltd v Cape Town Tramways Companies Ltd*,[151] an escape of electricity stored and used by the defendants in working their tramcars, interfered with the sending of messages by the claimants through their submarine cable. The claimants failed to recover as no tangible injury had been done to their property—no apparatus had been damaged. The defendants' operations were not destructive of telegraphic communication generally, but only affected instruments unnecessarily so constructed as to be affected by minute currents of the escaping electricity. With regard to such instruments it was said, "A man cannot increase the liabilities of his neighbour by applying his own property to special uses, whether for business or pleasure." However, in *Hoare Co v McAlpine*,[152] where vibrations from pile-driving caused structural damage to a large hotel on adjoining land, Astbury J held it to be a bad plea that the vibrations had this effect only because the hotel was so old as to be abnormally unstable but he found also that the evidence did not establish that it was in such a condition. Thus the question remains an open one, and it can hardly be said that the hotel proprietor had put his property to any special or unusually sensitive use.

16–034

I.   Remoteness of Damage

The defendant under *Rylands v Fletcher* cannot be liable ad infinitum and in Blackburn J's formulation of the rule he, "is prima facie answerable for all the damage which is the natural consequence of its escape". The Privy Council in *The Wagon Mound (No.1)*[153] stated that their Lordships had not found it necessary to consider the rule in *Rylands v Fletcher* in relation to remoteness of

16–035

---

[147] *Lomax v Stott* (1870) 39 L.J. Ch. 834; *Dunn v Birmingham Canal Co* (1872) L.R. 7 Q.B. 244.

[148] *Ponting v Noakes* [1894] 2 Q.B. 281; cf. *Cheater v Cater* [1918] 1 K.B. 247.

[149] Had it been grown there expressly for the purpose of alluring cattle to their destruction, the defendant would have been liable, not on the grounds of *Rylands v Fletcher*, but because he would have been in the position of one who deliberately sets traps baited with flesh in order to attract and catch dogs which are otherwise not trespassing at all: *Townsend v Wathen* (1808) 9 East 277.

[150] See Ch.23.

[151] [1902] A.C. 381 at 393; *Western Silver Fox Ranch Ltd v Ross and Cromarty CC* 1940 S.C. 601 at 604–606 (breeding silver foxes not a non-natural use of land).

[152] *Hoare Co v McAlpine* [1923] 1 Ch. 167.

[153] *The Wagon Mound (No.1)* [1961] A.C. 388 at 427.

damage but the *Cambridge Water* case, though it does not speak in terms of remoteness of damage, has the effect that reasonable foreseeability is the test.[154] There is no very compelling reason, indeed, why foreseeability should not be utilised as the test of remoteness in cases where it is irrelevant to the initial determination of liability: "granted that an escape takes place, albeit unforeseeably, what would a reasonable man regard as the foreseeable consequences of such an escape?"[155]

It will also be recollected that so many qualifications have been placed upon the decision in *The Wagon Mound (No.1)* that the concept of foreseeability is now applied in a very broad and liberal manner[156] and there is unlikely to be much practical difference between an inquiry whether a consequence is foreseeable or natural. The natural or foreseeable consequences of a dam bursting are, inter alia, the inundation of subjacent land, damage to buildings, roads and personal injury (though the last is, as we have seen, irrecoverable under this rule for different reasons). If the water flows into the shaft of an adjoining mine, with the result that the mine cannot be worked for six months, the mine owner may recover damages, but the miners who lose their wages during that period have no remedy,[157] not because the loss is "unnatural" or "unforeseeable" but because, (1) they have no sufficient interest in the mine, or (2), which in effect amounts to the same thing, it is a loss of a type for which the law restricts recovery.[158] Even if the escaping water flows into a carbide factory and thereby generates gas which causes a tremendous explosion it is unlikely that much will be achieved by seeking to draw distinctions between what is natural and foreseeable. As in all such cases the issue is finally one of legal policy.

2. FIRE

A. Common Law

16–036 Winfield traced the history of the earlier forms of action available as remedies for damage caused by the spread of fire.[159] The usual remedy was the special action of trespass on the case for negligently allowing one's fire to escape in contravention of the general custom of the realm which we first hear of in *Beaulieu v Finglam*.[160] The allegation in the action for fire that the defendant *tam negligenter ac improvide* "kept his fire that it escaped", referred to negligence in

---

[154] See para.15–031.

[155] See para.7–032. *The Wagon Mound (No.2)* [1967] 1 A.C. 617 seems to support this view.

[156] See para.7–037.

[157] *Cattle v Stockton Waterworks Co* (1875) L.R. 10 Q.B. 453 at 457; *Pride v Institute for Animal Health* [2009] EWHC 685 (QB); [2009] N.P.C. 56.

[158] See *Shell UK Ltd v Total UK Ltd* [2010] EWCA Civ 180; [2011] Q.B. 86 at [151].

[159] Winfield 42 L.Q.R. 46, or *Select Essays*, pp.25–28 and (1931) 4 C.L.J. 203–206; Newark (1945) 6 N.I.L.Q. 134–141; Ogus [1969] C.L.J. 104.

[160] (1401) Y.B. Pashc. 2 Hen. 4, f. 18, pl. 6, translated in Fifoot, *History and Sources of the Common Law: Tort and Contract*(New York: Greenwood Press, 1970), p.166.

its older sense—one mode of committing a tort. Centuries later remedies became available under the rule in *Rylands v Fletcher*,[161] in nuisance,[162] and in negligence.[163]

Exactly what "negligenter" meant can only be conjectured, for the old authorities are confused, but it certainly excluded liability where the fire spread or occurred (1) by the act of a stranger[164] over whom he had no control, such as a trespasser,[165] and (2) by the act of nature. He is responsible for the default of his servant,[166] his guest[167] or one entering his house with his leave[168] and for his independent contractor,[169] unless the act done is wholly alien to the permission to enter. The second exception was established in *Tuberville v Stamp*[170] where it was held that liability extended to a fire originating in a field as much as to one beginning in a house, but if the defendant kindles it at a proper time and place and the violence of the wind carry it to his neighbour's land, that is fit to be given in evidence. The common law liability still remains in all cases which are not covered by statutory provision.

Strict liability? Although it is repeatedly said that at common law a person must keep his fire "at his peril", research shows that we cannot be sure that at any period in the history of the common law he was absolutely liable for the escape of his fire.[171] He is liable for damage done by his fire if it has been caused wilfully,[172] or by his negligence, or by the escape without negligence of a fire which has been brought into existence by some non-natural user of the land. In some cases, the latter type of liability could not strictly speaking be brought within the rule in *Rylands v Fletcher* in that the thing accumulated on the land did not itself escape. It was suggested that the rule had to be adapted so that the criterion of liability is: "Did the defendants . . . bring to their land things likely to

16–037

---

[161] *Jones v Festiniog Ry* (1866) L.R. 1 Ex. 265, fire included in "things likely to do mischief if they escape" and thus within *Rylands v Fletcher*; *Powell v Fall* (1880) 5 Q.B.D. 597; *Musgrove v Pandelis* [1919] 2 K.B. 43; *Job Edwards Ltd v Birmingham Navigations* [1924] 1 K.B. 341 at 351–352; *Balfour v Barty-King* [1957] 1 Q.B. 496 at 505 CA (Lord Goddard CJ deals with the history of the action on the case from its origin to modern times).

[162] *Spicer v Smee* [1946] 1 All E.R. 489.

[163] Bankes LJ in *Musgrove v Pandelis* [1919] 2 K.B. 43 at 46 per Scrutton LJ; *Job Edwards Ltd v Birmingham Navigations* [1924] 1 K.B. 341 at 361.

[164] *Balfour v Barty-King* [1957] 1 Q.B. 496 at 504; *Tuberville v Stamp* (1697) 1 Ld. Raym. 264; *H.N. Emanuel Ltd v GLC* [1971] 2 All E.R. 835

[165] Unless the occupier has knowledge of the fire and fails to take steps to extinguish it within a reasonable time.

[166] A servant acting outside the course of his employment is a stranger: *McKenzie v McLeod* (1834) 10 Bing. 385.

[167] *Crogate v Morris* (1617) 1 Brownl. 197; *Iverson v Purser* (1990) 73 D.L.R. (4th) 33.

[168] *Ribee v Norrie* [2001] P.I.Q.R. P128.

[169] *Balfour v Barty-King* [1957] 1 Q.B. 496 (defendant was held liable for a fire caused by an independent contractor whom he employed to thaw frozen pipes in an attic which contained large quantities of combustible material. Contractor used blowlamp and caused a fire which spread and destroyed plaintiff's adjoining house); *HN Emanuel Ltd v GLC* [1971] 2 All E.R. 835; *Johnson v BJW Property Developments Ltd* [2002] EWHC 1131 (TCC); [2002] 3 All E.R. 574; *Spicer v Smee* [1946] 1 All E.R. 489 (as explained in *Johnson*).

[170] (1697) 1 Ld. Raym. 264.

[171] Winfield 42 L.Q.R. 46–50 or *Select Essays*, pp.26–29

[172] If the damage is intentional it is a trespass or assault, e.g. deliberately throwing a lighted match on a haystack or a lighted firework in a person's face.

catch fire, and keep them there in such conditions that if they did ignite the fire would be likely to spread to the claimant's land?"[173]

However, in *Stannard v Gore*[174] the Court of Appeal held that such an extension of the rule could no longer stand following the emphasis in *Transco Plc v Stockport MBC*[175] on, first, the need to re-state the principles of liability with certainty and, second, the requirement within those re-stated principles that it is the dangerous "thing" which has been brought on to the land which must have escaped.[176] On this basis, the defendant can only be liable for a fire which he deliberately or negligently started on his land, or perhaps where fire is an "essential part" of the dangerous thing.[177] In *Stannard v Gore* itself the defendant ran a business fitting tyres and stored large quantities of them on his land. A fire which started in the electrical wiring of his workshop, without fault on the defendant's part, became hot enough to ignite the tyres and the more intense fire which resulted spread to and damaged the claimant's neighbouring property. The Court found that the defendant's use of his land was not non-natural and the quantity of tyres and the method of storing them did not amount to a dangerous thing in that they were 'likely to catch fire', but even if those requirements had been met, it was the fire which 'escaped' and not the tyres.

B. Statute[178]

16–038

Fires beginning accidentally on the defendant's land. The common law liability has been modified in respect of fires spreading from the defendant's land by the Fires Prevention (Metropolis) Act 1774,[179] which provides that no action shall be maintainable against anyone in whose building or on whose estate[180] a fire shall accidentally begin. This section of the Act is of general application and

---

[173] *Mason v Levy Auto Parts of England Ltd* [1967] 2 Q.B. 530 at 542 per MacKenna J. If the damage is to persons or goods on the property on which the fire starts the only liability is for negligence: *Johnson v B.J.W. Property Developments Ltd* [2002] EWHC 1131 (TCC); [2002] 3 All E.R. 574 at [32].

[174] [2012] EWCA Civ 1248; [2014] Q.B. 1.

[175] [2003] UKHL 61; [2004] 2 A.C. 1.

[176] In *Stannard v Gore* Lewison LJ was of the view that McKenna J would have welcomed this rejection of his suggested adaptation on the basis that he was forced into it by the decision in *Musgrove v Pandelis* [1919] 2 K.B. 43 (see below) which could be explained as a case of negligence, but not under the rule in *Rylands v Fletcher*.

[177] See e.g. Ward LJ's explanation in *Stannard v Gore* (at [36]) of *Jones v Festiniog Ry* (1866) L.R. 1 Ex. 265 as a readily understandable example of the rule in *Rylands v Fletcher*: "The dangerous thing which the defendant railway company brought onto their land was a steam engine which depended for its locomotion on the burning of coal, particles of which would be belched forth from its maw onto the haystack adjoining the railway line. Although the engine itself remained on the defendant's land the sparks, *which were an essential part of the machine*, escaped and the danger posed by such an escape was high and it was foreseeable" (emphasis added).

[178] The only statute considered herein is the Fires Prevention (Metropolis) Act 1774. For consideration of the now practically obsolete Railway Fires Acts 1905 and 1923, see the 13th edn of this work.

[179] Section 86.

[180] Estate applies to land not built upon.

is not limited to London.[181] In *Filliter v Phippard*[182] the word "accidentally" was interpreted restrictively so as to cover only, "a fire produced by mere chance or incapable of being traced to any cause".[183] In other words a fire caused by negligence[184] or due to a nuisance[185] will give rise to a cause of action.

The immunity of a defendant under the statute is illustrated by *Collingwood v Home and Colonial Stores Ltd.*[186] A fire broke out on the defendants' premises and spread to those of the claimant. It originated in the defective condition of the electrical wiring on the defendants' premises, but as there was no negligence on their part they were held not liable. Nor was the rule in *Rylands v Fletcher* applicable, for the installation of electric wiring, whether for domestic or trade purposes, was a reasonable and ordinary use of premises.[187] If it had been, the Act of 1774 does not provide a defence and the defendant will be liable.[188]

However, the statute does not confer protection on one who was not at fault so far as the origin of the fire is concerned but who was negligent in letting it spread. In *Musgrove v Pandelis*,[189] the claimant occupied rooms over a garage and let part of the garage to the defendant who kept a car there. The defendant's servant, who had little skill as a chauffeur, started the engine of the car and without any fault on his part the petrol in the carburettor caught fire. If he had acted like any chauffeur of reasonable competence he could have stopped the fire by turning off the tap connecting the petrol tank with the carburettor. He did not do so and the fire spread and damaged the claimant's property. The defendant was held liable, for the fire which did the damage was not that which broke out in the carburettor but that which spread to the car and this second or continuing fire did not

---

[181] *Filliter v Phippard* (1847) 11 Q.B. 347 at 355. The High Court has said that it is obsolete in Australia: *Burnie Port Authority v General Jones Pty Ltd* (1994) 120 A.L.R. 42 at 50. It was repealed in New Zealand by s.365 of the Law of Property Act 2007, seemingly on the ground that any common law liability stricter than that for negligence had been absorbed into *Rylands v Fletcher*.

[182] (1847) 11 Q.B. 347.

[183] (1847) 11 Q.B. 347 at 357 per Denman CJ.

[184] For example, *Mulholland and Tedd v Baker Ltd* [1939] 3 All E.R. 253 at 255 per Asquith J (paper lit and inserted in drainpipe to smoke out a rat, fire spread to packing case and exploded drum of paraffin. Liable in negligence and under the rule in *Rylands v Fletcher*).

[185] For example, *Spicer v Smee* [1946] 1 All E.R. 489 at 495 per Atkinson J (defective electric wiring negligently installed by contractor caused fire, owner liable in nuisance or negligence; see the comments on this case in *Johnson v B.J.W. Property Development Ltd* [2002] EWHC 1131 (TCC); [2002] 3 All E.R. 574 at [51]).

[186] (1936) 155 L.T. 550.

[187] Cf. *Stannard v Gore* [2012] EWCA Civ 1248; [2014] Q.B. 1. Even if the fire is lit intentionally, providing it is lit properly, there is no liability if it spreads without negligence and causes damage, for example a spark jumps out of an ordinary household fire and causes it to spread: *Sochacki v Sas* [1947] 1 All E.R. 344. It would be different, of course, if the fire were made too large for the grate.

[188] *Mason v Levy Auto Parts of England Ltd* [1967] 2 Q.B. 530 at 540–541. MacKenna J after reviewing the authorities felt bound to follow them but did so reluctantly: "In holding that an exemption given to accidental fires, 'any law usage or custom to the contrary notwithstanding,' does not include fires for which liability might be imposed on the principle of *Rylands v Fletcher*, the Court of Appeal (in *Musgrove v Pandelis*) went very far." In *Stannard v Gore* [2012] EWCA Civ 1248; [2014] Q.B. 1 Lewison LJ concluded that section 86 of the Fires Prevention (Metropolis) Act 1774 defeated any liability in *Rylands v Fletcher* but this view was not shared by the other members of the court: cf. Etherton LJ at [71].

[189] [1919] 2 K.B. 43.

"accidentally" begin.[190] The same principle applies where the fire originated as a consequence of an act of nature so that in *Goldman v Hargrave*,[191] the statute provided no defence: the fire in the tree caused by the lightning strike was not the defendant's fault, but that which spread after his inadequate attempts to extinguish it was. The burden of proving such negligence is on the claimant: it is not for the defendant to prove that the fire was accidental.[192]

---

[190] See also *Sturge v Hackett* [1962] 1 W.L.R. 1257.

[191] [1967] 1 A.C. 645. See para.15–047.

[192] *Mason v Levy Auto Parts of England Ltd* [1967] 2 Q.B. 530 at 538.

ANIMALS[1]

At common law a person might be liable for damage caused by an animal on one **17–001**
or more of three distinct grounds, namely ordinary liability in tort, liability under
the strict *scienter* rule[2] and liability for cattle trespass. The law was substantially
modified with regard to two of these matters by the Animals Act 1971[3] but its
structure is still in large measure the same and it is convenient to retain the
common law headings for the purposes of exposition.[4]

1. ORDINARY LIABILITY IN TORT

There are many possible ways in which one may incur liability in tort through the **17–002**
instrumentality of an animal under one's control, but the fact that the agent
happens to be animate rather than inanimate is immaterial, for while the common
law, like other legal systems, developed special or additional rules of liability for
animals, it did not deny the applicability to them of general law.

Nuisance. A good example of this is nuisance, for you can be liable for nuisance **17–003**
through the agency of your animals, just as you can be for nuisance through the

---

[1] Williams, *Liability for Animals* (1939).
[2] This expression is properly confined to liability for animals which do not belong to a dangerous
species, but is commonly used in the wider sense used here.
[3] The Act came into force on October 1, 1971. The leading study of the modern law is North, *Civil
Liability for Animals* (2012) (previously, North, *Modern Law of Animals* (1972)). See too Law
Commission, *Civil Liability for Animals* (1967), Law Com. No.13. The Pearson Commission
recommended no change in the law: Cmnd.7054, Vol.1, Ch.30.
[4] For the previous law, see the 8th edn of this work, Ch.17, and Law Com. No.13 (1967).

agency of anything else you own. A person who keeps pigs too near his neighbour's house commits a nuisance, but that is not solely because they are pigs. He would commit a nuisance just as much if what he owned were a manure heap. There is no independent tort called "nuisance by pigs", or "nuisance by animals".[5] Indeed, nuisance may be the only appropriate remedy where there is no "escape" and where the animal is not dangerous, for example obstruction of the highway by large numbers of animals,[6] or stench from pigs[7] or the crowing of cockerels.[8] While at one time there was no liability for the escape of noxious animals on the defendant's land in the ordinary course of nature, such as rabbits, rats or birds,[9] and he only incurred liability for damage by them to neighbouring owners if it was caused by "extra-ordinary, non-natural or unreasonable action",[10] it seems that the modern law follows the principle that a landowner may be required to take steps against a situation which is not attributable to his actions.[11]

17–004   **Other torts.** Again, if a dog owner deliberately sets his dog on a peaceable citizen he is guilty of assault and battery in the ordinary way just as if he had flung a stone or hit him with a cudgel.[12] So, too, if a person teaches his parrot to slander anyone, that is neither more nor less the ordinary tort of defamation than if he prefers to say it with his own tongue rather than with the parrot's. Similarly, ordinary trespass can be committed by means of animals. Trespass by beasts so often takes the form of "cattle trespass" (with which we deal separately) that one does not meet with many ordinary actions for trespass in the reports. However an indirect example is *Paul v Summerhayes*[13] where fox hunters persisted in riding over the land of a farmer in spite of his protests and were held to have committed trespass.

17–005   **Negligence.**Liability for animals may also be based on the ordinary rules of negligence.[14] The action for negligence for harm done through animals was quite

---

[5] *Pitcher v Martin* [1937] 3 All E.R. 918 illustrates negligence and nuisance committed through the agency of a dog; *Farrer v Nelson* (1885) 15 Q.B.D. 258 nuisance through the agency of pheasants (distinguished in *Seligman v Docker* [1949] 1 Ch. 53).

[6] *Cunningham v Whelan* (1917) 52 Ir.L.T. 67.

[7] *Aldred's Case* (1610) 9 Co. 57b; *Wheeler v JJ Saunders Ltd* [1996] Ch. 19.

[8] *Leeman v Montagu* [1936] 2 All E.R. 1677. In *Clarkson v Bransford* (1987, Huddersfield County Court) the claimant recovered damages for nervous shock in nuisance and negligence in respect of the escape of the defendant's non-dangerous snakes from his house into hers. The defendant kept 24 snakes in the attic (Kemp & Kemp, *Quantum of Damages*, June 1987 issue).

[9] *Brady v Warren* [1900] 2 Ir. 636 (rabbits); *Seligman v Docker* [1949] 1 Ch. 53 (wild pheasant increasing in numbers owing to favourable weather conditions).

[10] *Farrer v Nelson* (1885) 15 Q.B.D. 258 at 260 (nuisance by unreasonable number of pheasants brought onto the land); *Peech v Best* [1931] 1 K.B. 1 at 14; *Seligman v Docker* [1949] 1 Ch. 53 at 61–63.

[11] *Wandsworth LBC v Railtrack Plc* [2001] EWCA Civ 1236; [2002] Q.B. 756.

[12] *Roberts v CC Kent* [2008] EWCA Civ 1588; [2009] Po L.R. 8 (where the action was justified under s.3 of the Criminal Law Act 1967).

[13] (1878) 4 Q.B.D. 9; *League against Cruel Sports v Scott* [1986] Q.B. 240.

[14] *Fardon v Harcourt-Rivington* (1932) 146 L.T. 391 at 392 per Lord Atkin; *Searle v Wallbank* [1947] A.C. 341 at 359–360.

distinct from both the cattle trespass rule and the scienter rule at common law[15] and now is distinct from the various forms of strict liability imposed by the Animals Act 1971.[16]

In one respect, however, the common law failed to extend the principles of negligence to cases involving animals. It was the rule for centuries that if animals (or at least, ordinary tame animals) strayed from adjacent land on to the highway neither the owner of the animals nor the occupier of the land was liable for any ensuing damage even though it could have been prevented by controlling the animal or by fencing.[17] This immunity was abolished by the Animals Act 1971,[18] so that where damage is caused by animals straying on the highway the question of liability is to be decided in accordance with the ordinary principles of negligence. It is provided, however, that if a person has a right to place animals on unfenced land, he is not to be regarded as in breach of a duty of care by reason only of his placing them there, so long as the land is in an area where fencing is not customary or is common land or a town or village green.[19] It is important to note that the Act does not require all landowners to fence against the highway: in moorland areas of Wales and the north of England this would be an intolerable burden and in such areas a motorist must be expected to be on the look-out for straying livestock. That is not to say that the burden imposed by s.8 is trivial: the Court of Appeal has held that the duty of care of the farmer extends to guarding against the carelessness of hikers lawfully on his land, and may require the provision of stiles, so enabling a stock gate to be secured.[20] Furthermore, there are situations in which the escape of animals attracts strict liability under s.2(2).[21]

2. LIABILITY FOR DANGEROUS ANIMALS

Animals Act 1971. At common law the keeper of an animal was strictly liable, independently of negligence, for damage done by the animal if: (1) the animal was *ferae naturae* (i.e. belonged to a dangerous species); or (2) the animal was *mansuetae naturae* (i.e. did not belong to a dangerous species) but he knew of its vicious characteristics. These forms of strict liability have been retained by the Animals Act 1971 and, though they have been subjected to considerable modification, some of the old learning may continue to be relevant. It is,

17–006

---

[15] See *Draper v Hodder* [1972] 2 Q.B. 556 (where a claim based upon *scienter* failed at the trial). Similarly, a claim might in some cases be founded upon the statutory variant of negligence created by the Occupier's Liability Act 1957.

[16] *Jones v Whippey* [2009] EWCA Civ 452; *Addis v Campbell* [2011] EWCA Civ 906.

[17] *Searle v Wallbank* [1947] A.C. 341. The immunity had no application where the animal was brought on to the highway and then got out of control: *Gomberg v Smith* [1963] 1 Q.B. 25.

[18] Section 8, which Lord Hailsham LC referred to as, "the only [section] which it is really worth enacting": *Hansard*, HL, Vol. 312, cols 887–888.

[19] Section 8(2). Like many "by reason only" exceptions, this subsection is a fertile source of difficulties. Even without it, the owner would not be liable by reason only of placing his animals there, for there would have to be sufficient traffic to create a serious danger. The subsection was applied in *Davies v Davies* [1975] Q.B. 172 but the case turned largely on the right of a commoner to license others to graze animals.

[20] *Wilson v Donaldson* [2004] EWCA Civ 972.

[21] See para.17 010.

however, important to remember that the only source of the law is now the words of the Act and these must always prevail.[22]

17–007   **No escape or attack necessary.** For the purpose of imposing liability animals are divided into two categories of dangerousness but with regard to both, the Act, unlike the common law,[23] contains no requirement that the animal must escape from control, nor that there must be any sort of attack.[24] If, therefore, an elephant slips or stumbles or a cow known to be prone to escape stands stock still in the road and is struck by a car,[25] the strict liability imposed by the Act will apply.

A.   Animals Belonging to a Dangerous Species

17–008   **Dangerous species.** Under section 2(1) of the Act, where any damage is caused by an animal which belongs to a dangerous species, any person who is a keeper of the animal is liable for the damage.[26] A dangerous species is defined as:[27] "[A] species[28] (a) which is not commonly domesticated in the British Islands and (b) whose fully grown animals normally have such characteristics that they are likely, unless restrained, to cause severe damage or that any damage they may cause is likely to be severe."

A number of points arise on this definition. First, it seems that as was the case at common law in classifying animals as *ferae naturae*, the question of whether an animal belongs to a dangerous species is one of law for the court. It is therefore to be expected that where an animal had been classified as *ferae naturae* at common law it will be regarded as belonging to a dangerous species under the Act (for example a lion,[29] an elephant[30] and at least certain types of monkeys).[31] In two respects, however, the definition is wider than at common law

---

[22] The Guard Dogs Act 1975 governs the keeping of guard dogs and the Dangerous Dogs Act 1991 controls the breeding and keeping of fighting dogs or other dogs appearing to the Secretary of State to have the same characteristics. The first does not impose civil liability (s.5(2)(a)). The second is silent on the point. No doubt certain contraventions of either Act would be almost conclusive evidence of negligence, e.g. the condition of muzzling in s.1(2)(d) of the 1991 Act.

[23] *Behrens v Bertram Mills Circus Ltd* [1957] 2 Q.B. 1; *Fitzgerald v AD and EH Cooke Bourne Farms Ltd* [1964] 1 Q.B. 249 at 270; Williams, *Liability for Animals* (1939), p.341.

[24] *Wallace v Newton* [1982] 1 W.L.R. 375. Cf. *Smith v Ainger, The Times*, June 5, 1990 (no abnormal characteristic).

[25] *McKenny v Foster* [2008] EWCA Civ 173 (though the claim failed for want of knowledge of the relevant characteristic). Compare *Jaundrill v Gillett, The Times*, January 30, 1996 and *Mirvahedy v Henley* [2003] UKHL 16; [2003] 2 A.C. 491 at [162]. There is an obvious tension with s.8 (para.17–005), which is based on negligence.

[26] Section 2(1). For the definition of "keeper", see para.17–009.

[27] Section 6(2).

[28] By s.11 "species" includes sub-species and variety: see further para.17–011.

[29] *Murphy v Zoological Society of London* [1962] C.L.Y. 68.

[30] *Behrens v Bertram Mills Circus Ltd* [1957] 2 Q.B. 1.

[31] Hale 1 P.C. 101. Cf. *Brooke v Cooke* (1961) 105 S.J. 684. As to other animals, see Williams, *Liability for Animals* (1939), pp.292–294. The Dangerous Wild Animals Act 1976 provides for a system of licensing of keepers of dangerous wild animals. Such animals are those listed in the Schedule to the Act and it is thought that such listing would be almost conclusive on the issue of whether the animal belonged to a dangerous species under the 1971 Act (none of the listed animals appears to be commonly domesticated here). Omission from the list should not, however, be

in that the Act: (1) renders a species dangerous if it poses a threat to property;[32] and (2) allows for a species to be considered dangerous if it is not commonly domesticated in Britain, even though it may be so domesticated overseas.[33]

Secondly it will remain the case that once a species has been judicially classified as dangerous, then, subject to the doctrine of precedent, there is no room for distinctions based upon the fact that some variants or individual animals within the species may not in fact be at all dangerous: in other words, the law continues to ignore "the world of difference between the wild elephant in the jungle and the trained elephant in the circus . . . [which] is in fact no more dangerous than a cow".[34] Furthermore, the Act clearly adopts as the test of danger either "the greater risk of harm" or "the risk of greater harm": an elephant may not in fact be very likely to get out of control and do damage, but if it does so, its bulk gives it a great capacity for harm.

Keeper. For the purposes of this form of liability a person is a "keeper" of the animal if:[35]   **17–009**

> "(a) [H]e owns the animal or has it in his possession or (b) he is the head of a household of which a member under the age of 16 owns the animal or has it in his possession and if at any time an animal ceases to be owned by or to be in the possession of a person, any person who immediately before that time was a keeper thereof . . . continues to be a keeper of the animal until another person becomes a keeper thereof . . . "

B.   Other Animals

Section 2(2) of the Act provides: **17–010**

> "Where damage is caused by an animal which does not belong to a dangerous species, a keeper[36] of the animal is liable for the damage if:
> (a) the damage is of a kind which the animal, unless restrained, was likely to cause or which, if caused by the animal, was likely to be severe; and
> (b) the likelihood of the damage or of its being severe was due to characteristics of the animal which are not normally found in animals of the same species or are not normally so found except at particular times or in particular circumstances; and
> (c) those characteristics were known to that keeper or were at any time known to a person who at that time had charge of the animal as that keeper's servant or, where that keeper

---

particularly persuasive that the animal is not dangerous under the 1971 Act; some species were omitted because it was not thought likely that any attempt would be made to keep them privately (HL Vol. 371 col.1180).

[32] The definition of "damage" in s.11 is not exhaustive, but does, it is submitted, include damage to property: see Law Com. No.13 (1967), para.15(iii).

[33] Thus a camel is dangerous under the Act, though not *ferae naturae* at common law: *Tutin v Chipperfield Promotions Ltd* (1980) 130 N.L.J. 807, not following *McQuaker v Goddard* [1940] 1 K.B. 687 (which probably applied the wrong test at common law, anyway).

[34] *Behrens v Bertram Mills Circus Ltd* [1957] 2 Q.B. 1 at 14. However, it is not clear to what extent the common law was prepared to distinguish among sub-species and the same problem will arise under the Act: see para.17–011.

[35] Section 6(3). It is provided, however, by s.6(4) that where an animal is taken into and kept in possession for the purpose of preventing it from causing damage or of restoring it to its owner, a person is not a keeper of it by virtue only of that possession.

[36] One keeper may be liable to another keeper: *Flack v Hudson* [2001] Q.B. 698 (owner liable to bailee/rider of horse who did not know of its characteristics).

is the head of a household, were known to another keeper of the animal who is a member of that household and under the age of sixteen."

The purpose of this rather complex subsection is to preserve a liability akin to the old rule of *scienter* liability for tame animals: while you are strictly liable in any case for damage done by your tiger you are only strictly liable for damage done by your dog or your horse if you have knowledge of some special dangerous characteristic.[37] This provision has come before the courts more frequently than other parts of the Act and has proved troublesome, as witnessed by the fact that it produces a regular stream of appellate decisions.[38]

17–011 **Range of animals covered.** The first problem is the range of animals to which s.2(2) applies. Common experience shows that, say, Rottweilers are a good deal fiercer than spaniels, but it has been stated in the Court of Appeal (though the point was not argued) in a case concerning a bull mastiff that the category is "dogs",[39] the generality of which could not possibly be said to belong to a dangerous species under s.2(1). However, the Act defines "species" as including "sub-species and variety"[40] and it has been held in the rather different context of determining what are "abnormal characteristics" under s.2(2)(b) that the proper comparators are other dogs of that breed.[41] However, even in the case of dogs of a breed commonly perceived to be fierce the argument that they are covered by s.2(1) would nearly always be defeated by the condition in that subsection requiring that such animals are not commonly[42] domesticated here.[43] Once it has been determined whether s.2(2) applies at all, it is necessary to consider each of the requirements in turn.

17–012 **Damage: s.2(2)(a).** Paragraph (a) follows the pattern of s.2(1) in adopting the likelihood (which means the foreseeable likelihood)[44] of damage or likelihood that any damage that may be caused will be severe. The second limb of this is not to be read as imposing any requirement that the likelihood that the damage will be severe must be related to any abnormality in the animal. Alsatians are powerful dogs and if a member of that breed does bite someone it is likely that

---

[37] The old *scienter* rule might be regarded as a primitive form of negligence under which the defendant was, subject to certain defences, irrebuttably presumed to be negligent in keeping the animal after he discovered its character. There is now no liability for negligence under the general law but there is no doubt that the defendant may be liable under s.2(2) even if he is not negligent (in the modern sense) on the occasion in question: *Curtis v Betts* [1990] 1 W.L.R. 459.

[38] "Unfortunately the language of section 2(2) is . . . opaque. In this instance the parliamentary draftsman's zeal for brevity has led to obscurity. Over the years section 2(2) has attracted much judicial obloquy": *Mirvahedy v Henley* [2003] UKHL 16; [2003] 2 A.C. 491 at [9]; "The drafting . . . is grotesque": *Turnbull v Warrener* [2012] EWCA Civ 412; [2012] P.I.Q.R. P16 at [4].

[39] *Curtis v Betts* [1990] 1 W.L.R. 459 at 462. A contrary contention was not pursued at the trial.

[40] Section 11.

[41] *Hunt v Wallis, The Times*, May 10, 1991. Indeed, this was in effect the approach to the same issue of the CA in *Curtis v Betts* [1990] 1 W.L.R. 459.

[42] Presumably, however, the test of whether a breed is commonly domesticated here would not be satisfied by showing that there were a tiny number here all kept as pets.

[43] If it be the case that there is a species (or sub-species or variety) which: (a) normally and in all circumstances has dangerous characteristics; and (b) is commonly domesticated here there would seem to be an illogical gap in the legislation since such animals fall under neither subsection.

[44] *Curtis v Betts* [1990] 1 W.L.R. 459 at 469.

the injury will be severe:[45] it is unnecessary to show that the particular Alsatian is unusually large or has unusually big teeth.[46] Paragraph (a) has given rise to comparatively little difficulty.[47] It seems plain that something is "likely" even though it does not reach the level of being "more likely than not" but it is not clear exactly how far down the scale of probability we can go: perhaps we can do no better than say that the damage (or, where relevant, its severity) is something which "might well happen"[48] or which is "reasonably to be expected".[49] One might break one's neck by falling downstairs after tripping over an escaped pet dormouse[50] but no one would suggest that a dormouse was likely to cause death or injury. On the other hand, it is probable that the requirement will be satisfied where, say, horses escape on to a busy oad.[51]

Abnormal characteristics: s.2(2)(b). Paragraph (b) has been the source of the problems under section 2(2).[52] The first limb deals with the straightforward case where the animal has "permanent" characteristics which depart from the norm of the species, for example a dog which has a propensity to attack humans in all situations and without discrimination as to persons; the second limb is a further, alternative, basis for a claim and imposes liability for damage caused by characteristics which may be normal to the species but only manifest themselves at particular times or in particular circumstances, for example a bitch being aggressive when she has pups[53] or a breed of dog having a tendency aggressively to defend its "territory".[54] In other words, "in such a case the animal's normal behaviour in abnormal circumstances is equated with a more vicious [animal's] abnormal behaviour in normal circumstances".[55]   **17–013**

Mirvahedy v Henley. In the leading case of *Mirvahedy v Henley*[56] horses owned by the defendants were terrified at night by persons unknown, broke down the fence and galloped onto a dual carriageway where one of them collided with the claimant's car and he suffered injury. Horses are not normally in a state of mindless panic but they will be when they are frightened and, for the majority of the House of Lords, their being frightened was "particular circumstances" for the purposes of the second limb of section 2(2)(b).[57] There is:[58]   **17–014**

---

[45] Note that the actual injury suffered does not have to be severe.

[46] *Curtis v Betts* [1990] 1 W.L.R. 459.

[47] But see the difference of opinion in the Court of Appeal in *Turnbull v Warrener* [2012] EWCA Civ 412; [2012] P.I.Q.R. P16.

[48] One of the interpretations offered by Neill LJ in *Smith v Ainger, The Times*, June 5, 1990.

[49] Lord Scott's preference in *Mirvahedy v Henley* [2003] UKHL 16; [2003] 2 A.C. 491 at [95]; but he thought this meant much the same as Neill LJ's suggestion. He did not accept Neill LJ's alternative of "such as might happen".

[50] Lord Scott's example in *Mirvahedy v Henley* [2003] UKHL 16; [2003] 2 A.C. 491 at [95].

[51] This was conceded in *Mirvahedy v Henley* and in *Jaundrill v Gillett, The Times*, January 30, 1996, though Lord Scott in *Mirvahedy* reserved his opinion.

[52] It is not in the same form as the Law Commission's original draft: see *Mirvahedy v Henley* [2003] UKHL 16; [2003] 2 A.C. 491 at [37].

[53] *Barnes v Lucille Ltd* (1907) 96 L.T. 680 (common law).

[54] *Curtis v Betts* [1990] 1 W.L.R. 459. See also *Cummings v Grainger* [1977] Q.B. 397.

[55] *Mirvahedy v Henley* [2003] UKHL 16; [2003] 2 A.C. 491 at [142] per Lord Walker.

[56] [2003] UKHL 16; [2003] 2 A.C. 491.

[57] Similarly, a horse which bucked when alarmed: *Goldsmith v Patchcott* [2012] EWCA Civ 183; [2012] P.I.Q.R. P11 (irrelevant that the bucking may have been more violent than anticipated), but the

"[A]n implicit assumption of fact in section 2(2) that domesticated animals are not normally dangerous. But the purpose of paragraph (b) is to make provision for those that are. It deals with two specific categories where that assumption of fact is falsified. The first is that of an animal which is possessed of a characteristic, not normally found in animals of the same species, which makes it dangerous. The second is an animal which, although belonging to a species which does not normally have dangerous characteristics, nevertheless has dangerous characteristics at particular times or in particular circumstances. The essence of these provisions is the falsification of the assumption, in the first because of the departure of the individual from the norm for its species, in the second because of the introduction of special factors."

The rival, unsuccessful interpretation, that the "second limb" is not an alternative basis of liability but merely explains the basic requirement of abnormality by recognising that in some circumstances even placid animals will react dangerously, is less consistent with the statutory wording but may be thought to reflect better policy, bearing in mind that the law of negligence is available as a fallback. Suppose, for example, that a road accident is caused by a panic-stricken deer which has escaped from a deer park. Despite the fact that there are deer parks, deer are presumably not commonly domesticated in this country, yet it would be impossible to say that deer in general satisfied the requirement of a dangerous species in s.6(2)(b). Yet, on the basis that the owner of this particular deer can hardly deny that he knows that deer may panic on the highway at night, we have:[59]

"[T]he paradoxical situation in which on the one hand deer are removed by section 6(2)(b) from being categorised as a 'dangerous species' but on the other hand an individual deer may impose strict liability on its keeper under section 2(2)(b) for damage caused by behaviour entirely normal for the species."

17–015   **Assessment.** As things stand, the owner of the animal is in danger of finding himself in a cleft stick: either the behaviour was abnormal by the general standards of the species or, even if it was normal in that sense, the behaviour was produced by the particular circumstances. Suppose, for example, that the claimant kicks a dog and the dog bites him. The owner can hardly be heard to deny that he knew that dogs are likely to bite when they are kicked, biting is a characteristic found in dogs in the particular circumstances of being kicked and therefore the requirements of paragraph (b) are fulfilled. Of course in such a case the owner would not be *liable*, for it is a defence to show that the damage was wholly due to the fault of the claimant[60] but it seems strange to treat the animal as "dangerous" in the first place.[61] It seems that once one attempts to bring in some cases where the ordinary or average animal[62] of the species would behave in that way, s.2(2) becomes very difficult to operate, even more so when it is held that "normally" in

---

rider is just as likely to be aware that this may happen so that there is a defence under s.5(2): see fn.76; and a horse which refused to respond to instructions given through a bitless bridle with which it was unfamiliar: *Turnbull v Warrener* [2012] EWCA Civ 412; [2012] P.I.Q.R. P16. Contrast *Freeman v Higher Park Farm* [2008] EWCA Civ 1185; [2009] P.I.Q.R. P6.

[58] *Mirvahedy v Henley* [2003] UKHL 16; [2003] 2 A.C. 491 at [71] per Lord Hobhouse.

[59] *Mirvahedy v Henley* [2003] UKHL 16; [2003] 2 A.C. 491 at [117] per Lord Scott.

[60] See para.17–017. *Nelms v CC Avon & Somerset* Unreported February 9, 1993 CA.

[61] See Lord Scott's example at [115] in *Mirvahedy* of the police horse attacked by a demonstrator and the horse's defensive kick connecting with someone other than the attacker.

[62] The "reasonable animal"?

s.2(2)(b) is to be read in the sense of "natural" or "conforming to type" even though on most occasions such animals would have reacted differently.[63] It would be better to abandon it and to make liability for domesticated animals turn on negligence in the keeper—or to have a simple, general rule of strict liability for damage done by animals.[64] The latter might be justified on the ground that, while no one would regard a horse or a dog as presenting the same risk as a tiger, yet they have "minds of their own" and are prone to behave unpredictably.[65]

Knowledge of the keeper: s.2(2)(c).[66] The strict liability under s.2(2) only arises **17–016**
if the characteristics of the animal were known to the keeper under paragraph (c). The requirement of knowledge is clearly of "actual" rather than of constructive knowledge,[67] though a person who ought to know of his animal's vicious characteristics may, of course, still be liable for negligence. Where the claim is based on the second limb of s.2(2)(b), the situation where the characteristic is common in the species in particular circumstances, it is sufficient that the keeper knows that animals of that type may react in the way which led to the damage, he does not need to have additional knowledge about the particular animal.[68] However, where the individual animal displays a common characteristic which would not normally be dangerous in such an exaggerated form as to make it so, the defendant will not be liable if he does not know of its propensity to do that.[69] In some cases the knowledge is imputed to the keeper by process of law under para.(c), but this does not mean that knowledge of a person not mentioned in that paragraph will be irrelevant: if, for example, the spouse of the keeper has knowledge of the animal's propensities it may be proper for the court to infer as a matter of fact that the keeper also knew of them.[70]

---

[63] *Welsh v Stokes* [2007] EWCA Civ 796; [2008] 1 W.L.R. 1224; cf. *Freeman v Higher Park Farm* [2008] EWCA Civ 1185; [2009] P.I.Q.R. P6.

[64] Such is French law: art.1385, Code Civil; but German law, while imposing strict liability for pets does not apply this to "working" animals.

[65] A consultation process by the Department for Environment Food and Rural Affairs in 2009 has not led to any concrete proposals for reform.

[66] The definition of "keeper" for this head of liability is the same as that for animals belonging to a dangerous species, i.e. the owner or the person in possession. See the appeal in *Hole v Ross-Skinner* [2003] EWCA Civ 774, which seems to have been pursued solely to absolve the possessor from negligence and allow him to seek contribution against the owner.

[67] *Chauhan v Paul* [1998] C.L.Y. 3990, CA. There is nothing in the Act to support the view that he must know, at the time of the incident, of the circumstances which bring the characteristic into play. The damage must be attributable to the characteristics referred to in paragraph (b): if the keeper knows that the animal becomes aggressive in certain conditions he is liable if a bite is inflicted in those conditions, but not for an unexpected attack in quite different conditions: *Curtis v Betts* [1990] 1 W.L.R. 459, but if a dog is prone to attack other dogs but not humans there may still be a likelihood of injury to a human being, namely the owner of the other dog: *Smith v Ainger, The Times*, June 5, 1990.

[68] *Welsh v Stokes* [2007] EWCA Civ 796; [2008] 1 W.L.R. 1224.

[69] *McKenny v Foster* [2008] EWCA Civ 173 (cow so distressed at being separated from her weaned calf that she was able to leap a six bar gate and a 12ft cattle grid).

[70] As in *Gladman v Johnson* (1867) 36 L.J.C.P. 153.

C.   Defences

17–017   **Conduct of the claimant.** Under s.5(1) it is a defence to an action brought under s.2 that the damage was wholly due to the fault of the person suffering it.[71] Where the claimant and the keeper are both at fault, s.5(1) cannot apply, but s.5(2) may do so.[72]

Under s.5(2) it is a defence that the person suffering damage voluntarily assumed the risk of it[73] (though a person employed as a servant by a keeper of the animal is not to be treated as accepting voluntarily risks incidental to his employment).[74] Although s.5(2) no doubt reflects the common law defence of volenti non fit injuria, it is to be interpreted according to the ordinary meaning of the words used.[75] The defence is engaged where the claimant has assumed the relevant *type* of risk. Thus, in *Goldsmith v Patchcott*[76] the claimant was aware of the risk that the horse she was riding would rear and buck if startled and s.5(2) applied even if the particularly violent bucking which occurred was not foreseen. Contributory negligence, is, of course, a partial defence.[77]

17–018   **Injury to trespassers.** There is special provision for injury to trespassers by dangerous animals. Section 5(3) provides that a person is not liable under s.2 for any damage by an animal kept on any premises or structure[78] to a person trespassing there, if it is proved either: (a) that the animal was not kept there for the protection[79] of persons or property; or (b) (if the animal was kept there for the protection of persons or property) that keeping it there for that purpose was not unreasonable. It would seem unreasonable to protect your premises with a lion or a cobra, but not, perhaps, with a fierce dog.[80] This subsection does not, of course, affect any liability for negligence which the defendant may incur qua occupier of the premises or keeper of the animal, but it is thought that the keeping of guard dogs is consistent with the occupier's duty to trespassers,[81] provided at least some warning of their presence is given.

---

[71] *Nelms v CC Avon & Somerset* Unreported February 9, 1993 CA, where the claimant kicked the dog. A person who ignores police warnings to come out and who is then bitten by a police dog brings his injury upon himself: *Dhesi v CC West Midlands, The Times*, May 9, 2000 CA.

[72] *Turnbull v Warrener* [2012] EWCA Civ 412; [2012] P.I.Q.R. P16. In some cases both defences may apply: *Smith v Harding*, Manchester County Court, 26 November 2013.

[73] The Unfair Contract Terms Act 1977 does not apply to the strict liability under the 1971 Act.

[74] Section 6(5). So if the lion tamer is eaten by the lion, his dependants can sue. Cf. *Canterbury CC v Howletts & Port Lympne* [1997] I.C.R. 925.

[75] *Freeman v Higher Park Farm* [2008] EWCA Civ 1185; [2009] P.I.Q.R. P6.

[76] [2012] EWCA Civ 183; [2012] P.I.Q.R. P11.

[77] Section 10.

[78] Not necessarily animals owned by or kept by the occupier.

[79] This probably does not have to be a dominant purpose. Thus the old lady who keeps a dog partly for companionship and partly for protection would fail on (a), though her conduct would certainly be reasonable under (b).

[80] So held in *Cummings v Grainger* [1977] Q.B. 397, "True it was a fierce dog. But why not? A gentle dog would be no good. The thieves would soon make friends with him": at 405 per Lord Denning MR. Since 1975 it is an offence to have a guard dog roaming about the premises unless under the control of a handler: Guard Dogs Act 1975. It has been suggested that contravention might make the keeping unreasonable under the 1971 Act: *Cummings v Grainger*.

[81] See para.10–037.

3. LIABILITY FOR STRAYING LIVESTOCK

Common law. At common law the possessor of "cattle"[82] was strictly liable, **17–019**
independently of *scienter*, for damage done by them when they trespassed on the
land of his neighbour.[83] Whatever may have been the original rationale of this
form of liability, it was certainly not the same as that of *scienter*, for agricultural
animals present no peculiar risk. However, the Law Commission recommended
the retention of strict liability for this type of harm on the ground that it provided
a simple method of allocating liability for what were usually comparatively small
damages.[84] The law was, however, in need of considerable modification and the
modern form of "cattle trespass" is found in s.4 of the Act.

Animals Act 1971 s.4. Section 4 of the Act provides: **17–020**

"(1)   Where livestock[85] belonging[86] to any person strays[87] on to land in the ownership or
occupation of another and—

(a)   damage is done by livestock to the land or to any property on it[88] which is in
the ownership or possession of the other person[89] or

(b)   any expenses[90] are reasonably incurred by that other person in keeping the
livestock while it cannot be restored to the person to whom it belongs or while
it is detained in pursuance of section 7 of [the] Act,[91] or in ascertaining to
whom it belongs;

the person to whom the livestock belongs is liable for the damage or expenses, except
as otherwise provided by [the] Act."

---

[82] "Cattle" or avers was a class virtually identical with livestock under the Act: see fn.85.

[83] See Williams, *Liability for Animals* (1939), pp.2, 3.

[84] Law Com. No.13 (1967), paras 62–63.

[85] Defined in s.11 as, "cattle, horses, asses, mules, hinnies, sheep, pigs, goats and poultry [which is
further defined as the domestic varieties of fowls, turkeys, geese, ducks, guinea-fowls, pigeons,
peacocks and quails] and also deer not in the wild state".

[86] By s.4(2) livestock belongs to the person in whose possession it is.

[87] The marginal note to s.4 refers to "trespassing", but the enacting words do not. "Stray" is probably
wide enough to cover the facts of *Ellis v Loftus Iron Co* [1874] L.R. 10 C.P. 10; *Wiseman v Booker*
(1878) 3 C.P.D. 184.

[88] Notwithstanding the general definition of "damage" in s.11, it is submitted that the words of this
paragraph make it clear beyond argument that damages are not recoverable for personal injuries under
this section and *Wormald v Cole* [1954] 1 Q.B. 614 is no longer law.

[89] The range of potential claimants and their claimable losses is, with regard to property, rather wider
than at common law.

[90] A local authority operating a pound for animals straying on its land may properly impose a
standard charge: *Morris v Blaenau Gwent DC* (1982) 80 L.G.R. 793

[91] See para.17–024.

A. Defences

17–021   **Conduct of the claimant.** The Act provides that there is no liability under this head for damage which is due wholly to the fault of the person suffering it[92] and that contributory negligence is a partial defence.[93] In this context default of the claimant is often closely bound up with fencing obligations and the Act therefore provides that damage:[94]

> " . . . [S]hall not be treated as due to the fault of the person suffering it by reason only that he could have prevented it by fencing but [the defendant] is not liable . . . where it is proved that the straying of the livestock on to the land would not have occurred but for a breach by any other person, being a person having an interest in the land, of a duty to fence."

17–022   **Lawful use of the highway.** One other common law defence is preserved by the Act: the defendant is not liable under this form of liability if his livestock strayed on to the claimant's property from the highway and its presence there was a lawful use[95] of the highway.[96] An example of this principle is the decision in *Tillet v Ward*.[97] D owned an ox which, while his servants were driving it with due care through a town, entered the shop of C, an ironmonger, through an open door. It took three-quarters of an hour to get it out and meanwhile it did some damage. D was held not liable to X, for this was one of the inevitable risks of driving cattle on the streets. It would have made no difference if the ironmonger's door had been shut instead of open, and the ox had pushed its way through, or had gone through a plate-glass window.[98]

B. Detention and Sale of Straying Livestock

17–023   **Common law.** The common law provided a form of self-help remedy to a person harmed by straying livestock by way of distress damage feasant.[99] The Law Commission concluded that some remedy of this type should be retained but considered that the old remedy was so hedged about with limitations (in particular, it provided no power of sale) and obscurities that it should be replaced.

---

[92] Section 5(1).

[93] Section 10.

[94] Section 5(6). The law relating to the obligation to fence is notoriously complex and the Law Commission thought it inappropriate to deal with it other than by providing a relatively simple rule: Law Com. No.13 (1967), fn.98. It should be noted that there is no requirement under s.5(6) that the duty in question be owed to the defendant.

[95] Hence, the defence is inapplicable if the animals had been allowed to stray on to the highway: *Matthews v Wicks, The Times*, May 25, 1987.

[96] Section 5(5). This does not, of course, remove any liability for negligence in such a case: *Gayler and Pope Ltd v Davies & Son Ltd* [1924] 2 K.B. 75.

[97] (1882) 10 Q.B.D. 17.

[98] *Gayler and Pope Ltd v Davies & Son Ltd* [1924] 2 K.B. 75. The driver of beasts which stray without his fault into property adjoining the highway is entitled to enter the property in order to get them out, and for that purpose he must be allowed such time as is reasonable in the circumstances: *Goodwin v Cheveley* (1895) 28 L.J. Ex. 298.

[99] See Williams, *Liability for Animals* (1939), Pt I.

Under s.7 of the Act the right of distress damage feasant is therefore abolished in relation to animals and is replaced by a new statutory right.[100]

Statutory right of detention. The occupier of land may detain any livestock which has strayed[101] on to his land and which is not then under the control of any person.[102] The right to detain the livestock ceases[103] at the end of a period of 48 hours (unless within that period the detainer gives notice of the detention to the police and if he knows the person to whom the livestock belongs, to that person[104]), or when the detainer is tendered sufficient money to satisfy any claim he may have for damage and expenses in respect of the straying livestock,[105] or if he has no such claim when the person to whom the livestock belongs claims it.[106] The detainer is liable for any damage caused to the livestock by failure to treat it with reasonable care and supply it with adequate food and water.[107]

17–024

Statutory right of sale. Where the livestock has been rightfully detained for not less than 14 days, the person detaining it may sell it at a market or by public auction, unless proceedings are then pending for the return of the livestock or for any claim for damages done by it or expenses incurred in detaining it.[108] Where the net proceeds of sale exceed the amount of any claim the detainer may have for damages and expenses, the excess is recoverable from him by the person who would be entitled to the livestock but for the sale.[109]

17–025

4.   REMOTENESS OF DAMAGE AND STRICT LIABILITY UNDER THE ACT

Common law. At common law both forms of *scienter* liability and cattle trespass had close affinities with *Rylands v Fletcher* and were probably governed by the remoteness principle applicable to that rule—was the consequence a "natural" one, a question of causation. There were, however, at least two exceptions to the generality of this principle. First, in the case of *scienter* liability for animals *mansuetae naturae*, the keeper was only liable if the animal caused some harm of the kind to be expected from its known vicious characteristics;[110] secondly, in the

17–026

---

[100] Section 7(1). The right is abolished for all animals and the new remedy applies only to livestock, for the definition of which see fn.85. The right of distress damage feasant remains in respect of other property: para.18-007.

[101] The word "strayed" may not be wide enough to encompass livestock which have been driven on to the land, though the condition that the animals must not be under the control of any person (see fn.102) suggests that the draftsman meant to include such a case.

[102] Section 7(2). The latter requirement was also a condition of the exercise of the common law right and is designed to prevent breaches of the peace.

[103] In the absence of a request for the return of the livestock, however, the detainer will not necessarily be liable for conversion.

[104] As to the person to whom livestock belongs, see fn.86.

[105] i.e. under s.4.

[106] Section 7(3).

[107] Section 7(6).

[108] Section 7(4).

[109] Section 7(5).

[110] See Williams, *Liability for Animals* (1939), p.301. If, however, the animal committed a "direct" wrong of the type to be expected, the keeper was probably liable for other losses stemming from that injury, e.g. a disease caught from the bite of a vicious dog: Williams, p.320.

case of cattle trespass, there was a rule that the damage had to be in accordance with the natural characteristics of the animals.[111]

17–027 **Animals Act 1971.** The Act contains no provisions relating to remoteness of damage and the position thereunder is to some extent speculative. The rule in *Rylands v Fletcher* was not considered in *The Wagon Mound (No.1)*, though as has been stated elsewhere in this book it is governed by the principles of foreseeability as developed since *The Wagon Mound*.[112] Those principles should also be applicable to the Animals Act. However, the form of s.2(2) means that with regard to liability for animals not belonging to dangerous species the position will be fundamentally the same as at common law, since the damage must be of a kind attributable to the characteristics known to the keeper.[113] As for animals belonging to a dangerous species, a camel has been held to be such because it may cause severe injury by kicking and biting, but strict liability was imposed for injuries suffered by falling off the camel because of its irregular gait.[114] Whether or not any special rule survives for trespassing cattle is not likely to be of any importance now that damages for personal injuries cannot be recovered under that head.[115]

5. PROTECTION OF LIVESTOCK AGAINST DOGS

17–028 **Liability for attacks on livestock.** Section 3 of the Animals Act re-enacted, with some modification, the form of strict liability formerly found in the Dogs Acts 1906 to 1928 and provides that where a dog causes damage by killing or injuring livestock,[116] any person who is a keeper[117] of the dog is liable for the damage.[118] The Act provides the following defences: that the damage was wholly due to the fault of the person suffering it[119] and that the livestock was killed or injured on land on which it had strayed and either the dog belonged to the occupier or its presence on the land was authorised by the occupier.[120] Contributory negligence is a partial defence.[121]

17–029 **Killing or injuring dogs to protect livestock.** It may, in certain circumstances, be lawful for a person to kill or injure an animal belonging to another if this is necessary for protection of his livestock or crops. The common law rule on this was laid down by the Court of Appeal in *Cresswell v Sirl*[122] but this rule has been

---

[111] *Wormald v Cole* [1954] 1 Q.B. 614.
[112] See para.16–035.
[113] See para.17–016.
[114] *Tutin v Chipperfield Promotions Ltd* (1980) 130 N.L.J. 807.
[115] See fn.88.
[116] "Livestock" for this purpose is slightly wider than under s.4, including pheasants, partridges and grouse in captivity: s.11.
[117] "Keeper" has the same meaning as in s.2: see para.17–009.
[118] Section 3.
[119] Section 5(1).
[120] Section 5(4).
[121] Section 10.
[122] *Cresswell v Sirl* [1948] 1 K.B. 241.

modified, so far as the protection of livestock against dogs is concerned,[123] by s.9 of the Animals Act. It is a defence[124] to an action for killing or injuring a dog to prove that the defendant acted for the protection of livestock and was a person entitled so to act and within 48 hours thereafter notice was given to the officer in charge of a police station.[125] A person is entitled to act for the protection of livestock if either the livestock or the land on which it is belongs[126] to him or to any person under whose express or implied authority he is acting[127] and he is deemed to be acting for their protection if and only if,[128] either the dog is worrying or is about to worry the livestock and there are not other reasonable means of ending or preventing the worrying or the dog has been worrying livestock, has not left the vicinity and is not under the control of any person and there are no practicable means of ascertaining to whom it belongs.[129]

---

[123] The rule in *Cresswell v Sirl* continues to govern in the case of animals other than dogs, e.g. pigeons damaging crops, as in *Hamps v Darby* [1948] 2 K.B. 311. See the 8th edn of this work, pp.761–762.

[124] Not the only defence. A defendant who fails to make out the statutory defence (e.g. because he has not informed the police) may presumably fall back on the common law.

[125] Section 9(1).

[126] For this purpose an animal belongs to a person if he owns it or has it in his possession and land belongs to the occupier thereof: s.9(5).

[127] Section 9(2)(a). If the livestock have strayed on to the land of another, there is no right under this section to shoot a dog which is lawfully on that land: s.9(2)(b).

[128] The two following conditions are satisfied by reasonable belief on the defendant's part: s.9(4).

[129] Section 9(3). This right to take punitive action in respect of an attack which is over is the major difference between s.9 and *Cresswell v Sirl* [1948] 1 K.B. 241.

CHAPTER 18

INTERFERENCE WITH GOODS

1. HISTORY

English law governing remedies for interference with goods is exceedingly **18–001** technical, partly because of the long survival and overlap of a number of different heads of liability and partly because the law, though tortious in form, is largely proprietary in function. The Torts (Interference with Goods) Act 1977 made some simplification by abolishing one head of liability but it is only a piecemeal attempt to deal with certain deficiencies in the common law and is in no way a code governing interference with goods.[1] Accordingly, the law must still be

---

[1] The Act is based upon the Report of the Law Reform Committee (1971) Cmnd.4774. See Bentley (1972) 35 M.L.R. 171. The Report proposed rather more thoroughgoing reforms than the Act in fact produces.

sought mainly in the decisions of the courts and it is impossible to give an intelligible account of the developed law without a brief historical sketch.

18–002   **Trespass.** The most obvious forms of interference, such as removing or damaging goods, were covered in early law by trespass *de bonis asportatis*, the forerunner of the modern "trespass to goods". Trespass was (and still is) essentially a wrong to possession[2] and the defendant need not have asserted any right to deal with the goods or indulged in any "appropriation" of them.[3]

18–003   **Detinue.** Trespass was obviously unsuitable to deal with the case where the owner had voluntarily put his goods into another's possession and the other refused to redeliver them, but this situation was covered by the remedy of detinue. In neither form of action could the claimant be sure of recovering his goods *in specie* since the judgment in trespass was for damages and in detinue gave the defendant the option of giving up the goods or paying damages, but it is unlikely that this was considered a defect and it should be noted that the remedy of specific restitution of chattels has remained unusual right up to modern times.[4] However, detinue was open to the very serious objection from the claimant's point of view that the defendant could insist on the method of trial known as wager of law, i.e. getting compurgators to swear that they believed him to be oathworthy, although they knew nothing of the facts of the case. This was the principal reason for the development whereby detinue was all but wiped out by the encroachment of trover.

18–004   **Trover.** Trover began as an action of trespass upon the case in which it was alleged that the defendant had converted the claimant's goods to his own use.[5] By the mid-16th century it had emerged as a distinct species of case involving four allegations.[6] It was alleged: (1) that the claimant was possessed of the goods; (2) that he accidentally lost them; (3) that the defendant found them;[7] (4) that the defendant converted them to his own use.[8] The losing and finding were soon treated as pure fictions and the defendant was not allowed to deny them.[9] The new remedy rapidly encroached upon the spheres of trespass and replevin, though the law never went quite so far as to say that touching or damaging or moving goods was conversion.

---

[2] See para.18–010.

[3] An alternative form of action for unlawful taking was replevin. This was originally a tenant's remedy for wrongful distress by his lord. By the 15th century it had become available for other forms of unlawful taking (Y.B. 19 Henry 6, 65 (Pasch. 5)) but in practice had tended to be used only for unlawful distress and is now all but displaced under Pt 3 of the Tribunals, Courts and Enforcement Act 2007; see para.18–006.

[4] See para.18–056.

[5] See Douglas (2009) 68 C.L.J. 198.

[6] Holdsworth, *History of English Law*, iii, pp.285–287, 350–351, 450, 581–584 vii, pp.403–513 viii, pp.466–468 ix, p.42; Milsom [1954] C.L.J. 105, 114; Simpson 75 L.Q.R. 364.

[7] This seems to have been borrowed from the earlier form of detinue sur trover which, unlike detinue sur bailment, "had no ancestry in debt, and no trace of contract": Milsom, *Historical Foundations of the Common Law*, p.327.

[8] Rastell, *Entries* (1596) 4b–5a.

[9] *Gumbleton v Grafton* (1600) Cro. Eliz. 781 (losing); *Isaack v Clark* (1614) 2 Bulstrode 306 (finding).

The difficulty in extending trover to cases covered by detinue was that conversion could only be committed by a positive act—misfeasance as opposed to nonfeasance. Detinue lay where a person was in possession of another's goods and refused to give them up but could it be said that such a mere refusal was a positive act? The line between misfeasance and nonfeasance is apt to be a fine one and the courts after some hesitation took advantage of this and held mere refusal to redeliver to be conversion.[10] Detinue, with its procedural disadvantages, wilted considerably under this treatment though it retained a place in the law because inability to redeliver as a result of loss or destruction of the goods was not regarded as conversion.[11]

The modern action for conversion. Nineteenth-century legislation swept away the fictions upon which trover was based and it became the modern action for conversion, though no change was made in the substance of the law. The abolition of the wager of law in 1833 caused some revival in detinue but in view of the expansion of conversion, detinue only really remained necessary where the defendant was unable to redeliver the goods. The process of simplification was carried a stage further by s.2 of the Torts (Interference with Goods) Act 1977 which abolished detinue and provided that conversion also covered the only case that was probably formerly the exclusive province of detinue—i.e. inability to redeliver goods as a result of their loss or destruction.[12] One still needs to look back at the common law of detinue to determine what constitutes the new form of conversion, and the action for conversion still has a considerable overlap with trespass to goods.[13] **18–005**

Replevin. Replevin is an ancient cause of action which is theoretically applicable to any trespassory taking[14] of goods but in practice is limited to taking by wrongful distress[15] and the modern procedure in the action was regulated by statute.[16] As a form of interim relief, replevin was largely overtaken by s.4 of the Torts (Interference with Goods) Act 1977 which added a new and more important form of interim relief, available in the county court and High Court, whereby goods the subject of present or future proceedings for wrongful interference may be ordered to be delivered up to the claimant, or a person appointed by the court, on such terms and conditions as may be specified. The procedure is particularly apt if there is a risk that the goods may be destroyed or disposed of before trial of **18–006**

---

[10] Holdsworth, *History of English Law*, vii, pp.405–415.

[11] *Owen v Lewyn* (1673) 1 Ventris 223.

[12] See para.18–025.

[13] The Law Reform recommended a new, all-embracing tort of "wrongful interference with chattels" ((1971) Cmnd.4774). The Act does use this terminology (see s.1) but only as a convenient label for the various reforms made by it on ancillary matters; it certainly does not merge the three torts of conversion, trespass and replevin (now all but displaced: para.18–006). Cf. the assertion in *HSBC Rail (UK) Ltd v Network Rail Infrastructure Ltd* [2005] EWCA Civ 1437; [2006] 1 W.L.R. 643 at [1] that there is a tort of wrongful interference with goods and that trespass and conversion are "now old-fashioned terms".

[14] Thus it does not lie against a carrier who detains them, for he did not obtain possession by trespass though he may be liable in conversion: *Galloway v Bird* (1827) 4 Bing. 299; *Mennie v Blake* (1856) 6 E. & B. 842.

[15] See fn.3.

[16] County Courts Act 1984 s.144 and Sch.1.

the action but it is not confined to such situations. An order was made under it in *Howard E Perry & Co Ltd v British Railways Board*[17] even though the goods were in no danger and the defendants recognised the claimants' title: the shortage of stock caused by industrial action was acute and damages would not adequately compensate the claimants for the injury to their business. The rules of replevin themselves have now been displaced by the Tribunals, Courts and Enforcement Act 2007 Pt 3.[18]

18–007   **Distress.** Distress is a common law remedy whereby a party in certain cases is entitled to enforce a right or obtain redress for a wrong in a summary manner, by seizing goods and retaining them as a pledge until satisfaction is obtained.[19] Illegal, irregular and excessive distress are actionable at the suit of the owner of the goods[20] but interference by him with a distress may in its turn be actionable as rescous or pound breach.[21] All of this old learning is replaced by Pt 3 of the Tribunals, Courts and Enforcement Act 2007. The common law power to distrain for rent is abolished[22] (though there will still be a limited form of non–court enforcement for commercial leases) and the various "writs of execution" such as *fi. fa.* are renamed "warrants of control". Schedule 12 initiates a new code of procedure to be followed by enforcement agents (known to most people as bailiffs).

2.   TRESPASS TO GOODS

18–008   **Direct interference required but not damage.** Trespass to goods is a wrongful physical interference with them.[23] It may take innumerable forms, such as scratching the panel of a vehicle,[24] removing a tyre from it[25] or the vehicle itself from a garage,[26] the cutting of nets and fish cages,[27] or, in the case of animals, beating[28] or killing[29] them. Putting out poison for an animal to take[30] is probably not trespass since the interference is not direct, a requirement of all true forms of trespass.[31] A defendant engaging in such conduct would, of course, be liable if injury to the animals ensued but his liability would be in what was classified before the abolition of the forms of action as case rather than trespass. Despite the fact that trespass is actionable per se, there is some authority to the effect that

---

[17] [1980] 1 W.L.R. 1375.

[18] Section 65(1).

[19] For distress damage feasant and the modern, statutory remedy replacing distress damage feasant in respect of straying livestock, see para.17–023 and para.18–018.

[20] *Clerk and Lindsell on Torts*, 14th edn, Ch.16 (distress is not treated separately in later editions).

[21] *Clerk and Lindsell on Torts*, 14th edn, Ch.16.

[22] Section 71.

[23] As to matters like unauthorised Internet access to computers (which may involve minute alterations to hard disk configuration) see *Clerk & Lindsell on Torts*, 20th edn (2013), para.17–131.

[24] Alderson B in *Fouldes v Willoughby* (1841) 8 M. & W. 538 at 549.

[25] *GWK Ltd v Dunlop Rubber Co Ltd* (1926) 42 T.L.R. 376 at 593.

[26] *Wilson v Lombank Ltd* [1963] 1 W.L.R. 1294.

[27] *Fish & Fish Ltd v Sea Shepherd UK* [2013] EWCA Civ 544; [2013] 1 W.L.R. 3700.

[28] *Slater v Swann* (1730) 2 Stra. 872.

[29] *Sheldrick v Abery* (1793) 1 Esp. 55.

[30] As opposed to forcing it down its throat.

[31] *Clerk and Lindsell on Torts*, 20th edn (2013), para.17–128.

trespass to goods requires proof of some damage or asportation[32] but the general view of textbook writers is to the contrary[33] and there must be many instances where, if mere touching of objects like waxworks or exhibits in a gallery or museum were not trespass, their possessor would be without remedy.[34]

Additional requirements for unintentional trespass. Where the touching of goods is not intentional the law may well be otherwise. Diplock LJ has said that actual damage is an essential ingredient in unintentional trespass to the person[35] (if that tort still exists) and if this is so there is no reason for distinguishing the case of trespass to goods. Certainly, the considerations of policy which point to making intentional meddling actionable even without damage have no application to unintended contacts.

18–009

Assuming that some damage has been caused, is negligence necessary for liability for unintentional trespass to goods? The answer is clearly yes[36] but the traditional view is that once a direct injury has been proved the defendant bears the burden of proving "inevitable accident"[37] as a defence. However, since the decision in *Fowler v Lanning*[38] which held that in an action for unintentional trespass to the person the claimant must prove negligence on the part of the defendant the same may be true of cases of trespass to goods, though the matter cannot be regarded as finally settled. A more extreme view, but one not without its attractions, is that in the modern law trespass to goods is confined to intentional interference and that negligent interference is remediable only by the tort of negligence.[39] Trespass, however, obviously remains appropriate where one takes another's goods in the mistaken belief that he is entitled to do so, for the act is intentional towards the goods.[40] In *Wilson v Lombank Ltd*[41] the claimant had "purchased" a car from a person who had no title to it and had sent it to a garage

---

[32] *Everitt v Martin* [1953] N.Z.L.R. 298; *Slater v Swann* (1730) 2 Stra. 872.

[33] *Clerk and Lindsell on Torts*, 20th edn (2013), para.17–128. See also *Leitch & Co Ltd v Leydon* [1931] A.C. 90 at 106 per Lord Blanesburgh.

[34] Perhaps even an intentional touching is not actionable if it is the sort of trivial interference to which people do not object, like moving a coat on a stand to get at one's own: see *White v Withers LLP* [2009] EWCA Civ 1122; [2009] 3 F.C.R. 435; cf. *Collins v Wilcock* [1984] 1 W.L.R. 1172.

[35] *Letang v Cooper* [1965] 1 Q.B. 232 at 244–245, para.4–004.

[36] *National Coal Board v Evans* [1951] 2 K.B. 861.

[37] See para.26–026.

[38] *Fowler v Lanning* [1959] 1 Q.B. 426, para.4–004.

[39] In *Letang v Cooper* [1965] 1 Q.B. 232 Lord Denning at 240 went so far as to say that negligence is the only cause of action for unintended injury to the person and presumably his Lordship would have said the same for unintended damage to goods, though there are clear authorities the other way on trespass to goods (e.g. Br. Abr. Trespass, 63 (AD 1373); *Covell v Laming* (1808) 1 Camp. 497). In truth, once it is conceded that the burden of proof of negligence lies on the claimant (a point on which the court in *Letang v Cooper* was unanimous) the traditional distinction between trespass and negligence loses almost all its significance and a classification like Lord Denning's, directed at the defendant's state of mind, is more satisfactory. However, some support for the view that there may still be an unintentional trespass to goods is found in the Torts (Interference with Goods) Act 1977. Section 1(1)(b) refers to "trespass to goods" but s.11(1), dealing with contributory negligence, refers only to "intentional trespass to goods".

[40] As in the case of excessive execution. Proof of malice is unnecessary: *Moore v Lambeth County Court Registrar (No.2)* [1970] 1 Q.B. 560.

[41] [1963] 1 W.L.R. 1294; *Colwell v Reeves* (1811) 2 Camp. 575.

for repair. The defendant, believing, wrongly, that the car was his, removed it from the garage. It was held that the defendant was liable in trespass.[42]

18–010   **Possession essential.** As trespass is an interference with possession, it follows that if the claimant were not in possession at the date of the alleged meddling, he cannot sue for trespass. He may be able to sue for conversion, but that is a different matter: "The distinction between the actions of trespass and trover is well settled: the former is founded on possession the latter on property."[43]

18–011   **Exceptions?** It is said that there are exceptions to this rule and that the following persons can sue for trespass although they had not possession: a trustee against any third person who commits a trespass to trust chattels in the hands of the beneficiary; an executor or administrator for trespasses committed to goods of the deceased after his death but before probate is granted to the executor or before the administrator takes out letters of administration; the owner of a franchise (for example a right to take wreck or treasure trove) against anyone who seizes the goods before he himself can take them.

However, it is questionable whether any of these exceptions is genuine. The language used in the authorities relating to the trustee is none too clear, but it indicates that the trustee has possession of chattels in the hands of the beneficiary, and not merely the right to possess them.[44] It does not follow from this that the beneficiary himself cannot sue, for if he holds the chattels he seems to have joint possession with the trustee. Again, the executor and administrator have long been regarded as having the deceased's possession continued in them; when they assume office their title relates back to his death. They have not merely the right to possess: they are in possession.[45] Similarly, in the case of the franchise, possession is deemed to be with the owner of the franchise.[46]

In a simple bailment determinable at will the bailor does not lose possession and may sue any wrongdoer other than his bailee[47] in trespass,[48] though the bailee may also have sufficient possession to bring trespass.[49]

---

[42] See para.18–035, as to the possible effect of the Torts (Interference with Goods) Act 1977 on this case.

[43] Lord Kenyon CJ in *Ward v Macauley* (1791) 4 T.R. 489 at 490; but in this case the claimant was a person who had let a furnished property to a tenant and had therefore surrendered even the right to possession. It has been said that it does not follow that D is not liable for trespass to C where X wrongfully takes C's goods and then passes them to D: *White v Withers LLP* [2009] EWCA Civ 1122; [2009] 3 F.C.R. 435 at [48]. If the goods are damaged or destroyed the owner out of possession will have an action formerly classified as case: *Mears v London & South Western Ry* (1862) 11 C.B. (N.S.) 850; *East West Corp v DKBS AF 1912 A/S* [2003] EWCA Civ 83; [2003] Q.B. 1509; *HSBC Rail (UK) Ltd v Network Rail Infrastructure Ltd* [2005] EWCA Civ 1437; [2006] 1 W.L.R. 643 (where, however, the claim failed, the owner having been indemnified under contract by the bailee). See Tettenborn, [1994] C.L.J. 326.

[44] *White v Morris* (1852) 11 C.B. 1015; *Barker v Furlong* [1891] 2 Ch. 172, a case of conversion, but Romer J approved *White v Morris*.

[45] *Tharpe v Stallwood* (1843) 5 M. & G. 760 at 770; Pollock & Wright, *Possession*, pp.146–147.

[46] *Bailiffs of Dunwich v Sterry* (1831) 1 B. & Ad. 831 (franchise of wreck; cask taken before franchisee could get it).

[47] If the act is licensed by the bailee it seems it is not trespass as against a bailor: Palmer, *Bailment*, 2nd edn (1991), p.206—the general chapter on the chattel torts is not included in the 3rd edn).

3. CONVERSION

Conversion at common law may be committed in so many different ways that any comprehensive definition is probably impossible[50] but the wrong is committed by dealing with the goods of a person which deprives him of the use or possession of them (though to "deprive" the owner does not necessarily require that the defendant should himself take the goods from him[51]). Thus it may be committed by wrongfully taking possession of goods, by wrongfully disposing of them, by wrongfully misusing them, by wrongfully destroying them or simply by wrongfully refusing to give them up when demanded. At common law there must be some deliberate act[52] depriving the claimant of his rights: if this element was lacking there was no conversion. Thus if a bailee negligently allowed goods in his charge to be destroyed the claimant's loss is just the same as if the bailee had wrongfully sold them to a third party but there was no conversion. Such conduct is now conversion by statute but this is merely for the draftsman's terminological convenience and has no effect on the concept of conversion at common law: for this reason, it must be kept separate in our analysis.

18–012

A. What may be Converted[53]

Any corporeal, movable property may be converted.[54] This includes money in the form of coins or notes, though once the taker has paid them to another they become currency and the payee and subsequent recipients cannot be sued for conversion by the original owner. There can be no conversion of a chose in action, so when invalidly appointed receivers dealt with a company's contracts they did not commit this tort.[55] Although the true value of cheques and other negotiable instruments or share certificates lies in their character as evidence of

18–013

---

[48] *Lotan v Cross* (1810) 2 Camp. 464; *Ancona v Rogers* (1876) L.R. 1 Ex. D. 285 at 292. The authorities are discussed in *Penfolds Wines Pty Ltd v Elliott* (1946) 74 C.L.R. 204 at 214–220, 226–236, 239–244; *USA v Dollfus Mieg et Cie* [1952] A.C. 582 at 605, 611–613; *Wilson v Lombank Ltd* [1963] 1 W.L.R. 1294.

[49] *Nicolls v Bastard* (1835) 2 C.M. & R. 659 at 660 per Parke B, *arguendo*.

[50] See *Kuwait Airways Corp v Iraqi Airways Co (Nos 4 and 5)* [2002] UKHL 19; [2002] 2 A.C. 883 at [39]; *Howard Perry & Co Ltd v BRB* [1980] 1 W.L.R. 1375 at 1380; *Hiort v London & North Western Ry Co* (1879) 4 Ex. D. 188 at 194.

[51] *Kuwait Airways Corp v Iraqi Airways Co (Nos 4 and 5)* [2002] UKHL 19; [2002] 2 A.C. 883 at [40].

[52] The defendant may still be liable even if he is motivated by some innocent mistake: para.18–041. However, innocently taking goods into one's custody (e.g. to transport them) is not conversion unless one is aware of the owner's rights: para.18–043.

[53] *Clerk and Lindsell on Torts*, 20th edn (2013), para.17–34.

[54] Hence not wild animals which have not been reduced into possession (they are not anyone's property) nor land. However, where material is wrongfully severed from land the owner may sue in conversion.

[55] *OBG Ltd v Allan* [2007] UKHL 21; [2008] 1 A.C.1 (though the HL was divided on both the feasibility and desirability of change). See also *Thunder Air Ltd v Hilmarsson* [2008] EWHC 355 (Ch) (electronic documents); cf. *Armstrong DLW GmbH v Winnington Networks Ltd* [2012] EWHC 10 (Ch); [2013] Ch. 156 (liability for knowing receipt of trust property or in restitution for misappropriation of carbon trading allowances).

non-corporeal rights, the owner may sue in conversion for their face value,[56] though not where a cheque has been materially altered, for then it ceases to be valid and becomes a worthless piece of paper.[57] There have been a number of cases about corpses and body parts, though generally in contexts other than conversion but where rights of ownership have been in issue. There is no property in a corpse[58] (as opposed to e.g. a preserved specimen[59] or skeleton prepared for anatomical purposes) but in suitable circumstances a person may have ownership of parts of or products obtained from his body.[60] Hence a tort claim may lie in respect of the destruction of sperm stored for potential future use or of a body part severed in an accident which had been capable of being reattached.[61]

B. What Constitutes Conversion at Common Law

i. Taking Possession

18–014   **A matter of degree.** Whether taking another's goods is conversion is a matter of degree. Generally it will constitute the tort but there will be no conversion where the interference is merely temporary and is unaccompanied by any intention to assert rights over the goods. Thus in *Fouldes v Willoughby*[62] it was not conversion (though no doubt it was trespass) to remove the claimant's horses from a ferry boat to the shore. If I snatch your hat from your head with intent to steal it or destroy it that is conversion as well as trespass, but if I throw it at another person that is trespass only.[63] It is sometimes said that this is because I am not questioning your title to it but a better explanation seems to be that it is because the interference is temporary and trivial[64] for it is clearly not necessary in cases of conversion that the defendant should assert ownership over the goods.

---

[56] *Morrison v London County and Westminster Bank* [1914] 3 K.B. 356; *Rugby Football Union v Viagogo Ltd* [2011] EWHC 764 (QB); [2011] N.P.C. 37 at [46] (rugby tickets).

[57] *Smith v Lloyd's TSB Group Plc* [2001] Q.B. 541.

[58] See *Clerk and Lindsell on Torts*, 20th edn (2013), para.17–41.

[59] See *R. v Kelly* [1999] Q.B. 621. In *Dobson v N Tyneside HA* [1997] 1 W.L.R. 596 it was held that conversion did not lie in respect of a brain which had been extracted and preserved for an inquest rather than research. The claim seems to have been linked to the claimants' action for medical negligence causing the death. The CA in *Yearworth v North Bristol NHS Trust* [2009] EWCA Civ 37; [2010] Q.B. 1 regarded *Dobson* as depending on the fact that the pathologist had never undertaken to preserve the brain. Where a post–mortem is lawfully carried out the removal of organs is lawful and the person who does that may have the initial right to possession of them. However, failure to explain the possibility of removal and retention of organs may give rise to a claim for negligence or, under art.8 of the European Convention on Human Rights: *Organ Retention Group Litigation, Re* [2004] EWHC 644 (QB); [2005] Q.B. 506.

[60] Wall (2011) 31 O.J.L.S. 783.

[61] *Yearworth v North Bristol NHS Trust* [2009] EWCA Civ 37; [2010] Q.B. 1 (sperm; this was despite the fact that legislation deprived the "owners" of the prime sign of ownership, to *direct* what should be done with the material. It would have been possible to decide the case on the basis that the skill used in preserving the sperm made it analogous to the cases on anatomical specimens but the CA did not wish to proceed on such a narrow basis).

[62] (1841) 8 M. & W. 540.

[63] *Price v Helyer* (1828) 4 Bing. 597.

[64] Cf. *The Playa Larga* [1983] 2 Lloyd's Rep. 171 (diversion of goods by seller at behest of third party conversion). To be conversion the conduct must be, "so extensive an encroachment on the rights

Taking for the purpose of acquiring a lien,[65] or even for temporary use[66] have been held to be conversion.[67] On the other hand, some of the cases talk in terms of "exercising dominion"[68] or of "denying the owner's right".[69] These expressions should not be taken too literally but if that is how the defendant's conduct would appear to an observer that is certainly a pointer towards its being conversion rather than trespass.[70]

Trespass or conversion: significance. Now that the claimant does not have to 18–015
choose the correct form of action the distinction between trespass and conversion is of course less important but it may still be significant on the question of remedy. There are essentially two points. First, if there is a conversion the claimant's damages are prima facie measurable by the value of the goods, in other words the judgment is a sort of forced sale. This may be thought a draconian remedy for a temporary deprivation and points towards keeping conversion within narrower bounds than trespass.[71] Yet if goods are destroyed while in the possession of a wrongdoer it would surely be wrong to allow him to escape by showing that it was not his fault, for that would be to treat him like a bailee. However, both problems can be solved without taking an artificial approach to what amounts to conversion. Where there is a temporary deprivation and the goods are returned to the claimant there is no doubt that this goes in reduction of the damages. If the claimant should refuse to take the goods back then the court has power to stay the action before judgment, if they are tendered undamaged.[72] As to the second situation, since the law imposes the liability of an insurer upon a person who came lawfully into the possession of another's goods but who deviates from the terms of his permission[73] it must inevitably do the same to a defendant who takes the goods wrongfully.

Third party recipients. Where A, without lawful authority, transfers B's goods 18–016
to C, the mere voluntary receipt of them by C is in general conversion, however

---

of the owner as to exclude him from use and possession of the goods": *Kuwait Airways Corp v Iraqi Airways Co (Nos 4 and 5)* [2002] UKHL 19; [2002] 2 A.C. 883 at [39]

[65] *Tear v Freebody* (1858) C.B. (N.S.) 228. Unlawful wheelclamping is plainly trespass (*Vine v Waltham Forest LBC* [2000] 1 W.L.R. 2383) but is it also conversion? In *Arthur v Anker* [1997] Q.B. 564 the cause of action was described as "tortious interference" with the car. See now Protection of Freedoms Act 2012, s.54 (criminal offence without lawful excuse to immobilise a vehicle on private land with a view to preventing its removal by the owner).

[66] For example, "joyriding": Rolle Abr. tit. *Action Sur Case*, p.5 (equine variety).

[67] It is no defence to an action for the taking of papers that they are admissible in evidence: *Imerman v Tchenguiz* [2010] EWCA Civ 908; [2011] Fam. 116 at [36]–[53], [116]–[117] (Lord Neuberger MR); cf. *White v Withers LLP* [2009] EWCA Civ 1122; [2009] 3 F.C.R. 435.

[68] *Hollins v Fowler* (1875) L.R. 7 H.L. 757 at 766, 782, 787, 790, 792; *Oakley v Lister* [1931] 1 K.B. 148 at 156.

[69] *Lancashire and Yorkshire Ry v MacNicholl* (1919) 88 L.J.K.B. 601 at 605; *Oakley v Lister* [1931] 1 K.B. 148 at 153.

[70] Is taking a document to read it and copy it conversion? See *White v Withers LLP* [2009] EWCA Civ 1122; [2009] 3 F.C.R. 435 at [53].

[71] Of course in another sense conversion is *wider* than trespass. I can commit conversion of goods without touching them or even seeing them, as where I sell them.

[72] *Fisher v Prince* (1762) 3 Burr. 1363; *Kuwait Airways Corp v Iraqi Airways Co (Nos 4 and 5)* [2001] 3 W.L.R. 1117 at 1235; on appeal [2002] UKHL 19; [2002] 2 A.C. 883.

[73] See, e.g. *Roberts v McDougall* (1887) 3 T.L.R. 666 and the well-known deviation cases about carriers and warehousemen; *Mitchell v Ealing LBC* [1979] Q.B.1; *Toor v Bassi* [1999] E.G.C.S. 9.

innocent C may be.[74] This is abundantly supported by decisions with respect to receipt of goods by a buyer[75] and a receipt of a cheque by a banker.[76] Some qualifications of this where the defendant acts bona fide are discussed below.[77] It was once held that receipt of goods by way of pledge did not amount to conversion even though the same receipt by way of purchase would have.[78] Whether or not this decision was ever good law it was reversed by the Torts (Interference with Goods) Act 1977.[79]

18–017   **Involuntary receipt of goods.** Involuntary receipt of goods is not conversion.[80] Such is the case of an innocent person into whose pocket a thief, in order to escape detection, inserts a purse which he has stolen from a third person. Even where the receiver knows that the thing belongs to someone else,[81] he incurs no liability by having it thrust upon him. Indeed, by legislation, where unsolicited goods are sent to a person with a view to his acquiring them he may be able to treat them as a gift to him.[82]

The recipient cannot, without his consent, be made a bailee in the strict sense of that term and mere negligence on his part with respect to the safe custody of the thing will not make him liable. So, in *Howard v Harris*,[83] where a playwright sent the manuscript of a play to a theatrical producer who had never asked for it and who lost it, the producer was held not liable. Similarly, the involuntary bailee does no wrong if he acts reasonably in trying to return the goods. In *Elvin and Powell Ltd v Plummer Roddis Ltd*,[84] X, a swindler, directed the claimants to supply the defendants with £350–worth of coats. X then forged a telegram to the

---

[74] "Certainly a man is guilty of a conversion who takes my property by assignment from another who has no authority to dispose of it for what is that but assisting that other in carrying his wrongful act into effect": Lord Ellenborough CJ in *McCombie v Davies* (1805) 6 East 538.

[75] *Wilkinson v King* (1809) 2 Camp. 335; *Farrant v Thompson* (1822) 5 B. & Ald. 826; *Dyer v Pearson* (1824) 3 B. & C. 38; *Hilbery v Hatton* (1864) 2 H. & C. 822.

[76] *Fine Art Society v Union Bank of London* (1886) 17 Q.B.D. 705; *Morison v London County & Westminster Bank* [1914] 3 K.B. 356 at 364; *Reckitt v Barnett* [1928] 2 K.B. 244 at 263; [1929] A.C. 726; *Lloyds Bank v Chartered Bank* [1929] 1 K.B. 40 at 69; *Orbit Mining & Trading Co Ltd v Westminster Bank Ltd* [1963] 1 Q.B. 794. Under the Cheques Act 1957 s.4, re-enacting and extending the Bills of Exchange Act 1882 s.82, the banker has a defence if he has acted in good faith and without negligence: *Middle Temple v Lloyd's Bank Plc* [1999] 1 All E.R. (Comm) 193 (effect of Cheques Act 1992); *Architects of Wine Ltd v Barclays Bank Plc* [2007] EWCA Civ 239; [2007] 2 Lloyd's Rep 471.

[77] See para.18–042.

[78] *Spackman v Foster* (1883) 11 Q.B.D. 99.

[79] Section 11(2). One must look to the substance of the transaction. If A deposits goods with B for B to sell and the contract provides that B has a lien and a residual right to sell to recover unpaid charges that is not a pledge: *Marcq v Christie Manson & Woods Ltd* [2003] EWCA Civ 731; [2004] Q.B. 286.

[80] See Burnett 76 L.Q.R. 364; Palmer, *Bailment*, 3rd edn (2009), Ch.13.

[81] According to the CA in *Marcq v Christie Manson & Woods Ltd* [2003] EWCA Civ 731; [2004] Q.B. 286 one cannot be a bailee without some knowledge of the existence of one's bailor but if one mistakenly destroys goods which are self-evidently someone else's one is negligent whether or not there is a bailment. Where one finds goods in property which one has acquired the nature of them will determine what inquiries one should make before concluding that they have been abandoned: *Robot Arenas Ltd v Waterfield* [2010] EWHC 115 (QB).

[82] Consumer Protection (Distance Selling) Regulations (SI 2000/2344).

[83] (1884) Cababe & Ellis 253; *Lethbridge v Phillips* (1819) 2 Starkie 544. Compare the view of Palmer, *Bailment*, 3rd edn (2009), para.13–013.

[84] (1933) 50 T.L.R. 158.

defendants: "Goods dispatched to your branch in error.—Sending van to collect. Elvin and Powell." Then a confederate of X called on the defendants, who delivered the coats to him under the impression that he was the claimants' agent. The confederate disappeared. The claimants sued the defendants for: (1) negligence as bailees; and (2) conversion. The jury negatived negligence and found that there was contributory negligence on the claimants' part, and Hawke J held that there was no conversion, for the defendants had acted reasonably.[85]

Contrast with this case *Hiort v Bott*,[86] where A mistakenly sent an invoice for barley to B (who had ordered none), which stated that B had bought the barley of A through G as broker and A also sent B a delivery order which made the barley deliverable to the order of A or of B. G then told B there had been a mistake and got B to endorse the delivery order to himself. G thereby got hold of the barley, disposed of it and absconded. Here B was held liable to A for conversion. Had he merely handed the delivery order to G for return to A, the decision might have been otherwise, but by endorsing it to G he had gone far beyond what was necessary to secure the return of it to A.

Wilful damage or destruction by involuntary recipient. The involuntary bailee **18–018** must not wilfully damage or destroy the thing.[87] The law has not, however, been fully explored here. It is simple enough with a small and imperishable article like a book or a fountain pen, but what of a parcel of fish or a piano which is delivered at my house in my absence? What I want to do is to get rid of them and I am certainly not bound to incur the expense of packing and returning them. If the sender is traceable, probably the most sensible thing to do is to notify him that the goods are at his risk and to request him to fetch them and if (as is likely with perishables) the goods become a nuisance, the recipient would surely be justified in abating the nuisance by destroying them, even without notice to the sender, if the emergency were so pressing as to leave him no time to give it.[88]

Detention of goods by involuntary recipient. A related question arises if the **18–019** involuntary bailee wishes to detain the goods as security for the payment of his expenses or for the inconvenience caused to him, a situation exemplified by the modern practice of wheel clamping. The ancient right of distress damage feasant applies only where the landowner has suffered actual damage, though this extends to inconvenience, as well as physical injury to the property.[89] The cost of

---

[85] So, too, *Batistoni v Dance* (1908) 52 S.J. 202.
[86] (1874) L.R. 9 Ex. 86. Note that the defendant was not, strictly, a bailee since he never had actual possession of the barley.
[87] "I am not bound to warehouse it, nor am I entitled to turn it into the street": Bramwell B, obiter, in *Hiort v Bott* (1874) L.R. 9 Ex. 86 at 90.
[88] The position is rather different when the goods came into the defendant's hands by reason of a genuine, voluntary bailment for then the bailee has a statutory power of sale of the goods if the bailor fails to collect them: see the Torts (Interference with Goods) Act 1977 ss.12, 13. The 1977 Act does not define "bailment" but it is thought that the provisions on sale would not extend to the "involuntary bailment": *Taylor v Diamond* [2012] EWHC 2900 (Ch) at [106].
[89] *Arthur v Anker* [1997] Q.B. 564.

clamping or of towing to another location is not "damage".[90] However, the display of a prominent notice warning of clamping may mean that the car owner consents to the risk.[91]

ii. Abusing Possession

18–020   **Numerous forms.** Abuse of possession which the defendant already has may take many forms, such as sale accompanied by delivery of the claimant's goods or their documents of title to another,[92] pawning them,[93] or otherwise disposing of them, even by innocently delivering them to a fraudster with forged delivery documents.[94] The use of a borrowed car for the transporting of uncustomed watches has been held a conversion of the car, for such conduct if discovered leads to the forfeiture of the car under the Customs and Excise legislation and its consequent loss to the owner.[95] In less extreme cases of unauthorised use by a bailee the question whether his act amounts to conversion probably depends upon the degree of departure from the terms of the bailment,[96] though it must be remembered that in any event the departure will expose the bailee to strict liability for damage or loss. However, at common law an omission on the part of the defendant (for example negligently allowing the goods to be stolen) would not make him liable for conversion[97] though if he were a bailee of the goods he might be liable in detinue in such circumstances.[98] Since this type of detinue is now by statute assimilated to conversion there may now be liability in conversion.[99]

18–021   **Disposition without transfer of possession.** A mere bargain and sale or other attempted disposition of goods by a person without a transfer of possession, i.e. delivery, is not a conversion: the act is void and does not change the property or

---

[90] *Arthur v Anker* [1997] Q.B. 564. The landowner may remove the car, but that may involve him in other trouble: *Lloyd v DPP* [1992] 1 All E.R. 982.

[91] *Arthur v Anker* [1997] Q.B. 564; *Vine v Waltham Forest LBC* [2000] 1 W.L.R. 2383. It seems from the latter case that it is not necessarily enough that the notices are sufficiently prominent to bring the matter to the attention of a reasonably alert entrant. See now Protection of Freedoms Act 2012 s.54 (criminal offence without lawful excuse to immobilise a vehicle on private land with a view to preventing its removal by the owner).

[92] *Hollins v Fowler* (1875) L.R. 7 H.L. 757.

[93] *Parker v Godin* (1728) 2 Stra. 813.

[94] *Motis Exports Ltd v Dampskibsselskabet AF 1912 A/S* [2000] 1 Lloyd's Rep. 211.

[95] *Moorgate Mercantile Co Ltd v Finch* [1962] 1 Q.B. 701. Cf. *BMW Financial Services (GB) Ltd v Bhagwanani* [2007] EWCA Civ 1230.

[96] Palmer, *Bailment*, 3rd edn (2009), para.21–07.

[97] *Ashby v Tolhurst* [1937] 2 K.B. 242; *Tinsley v Dudley* [1951] 2 K.B. 18. Both cases of theft of claimant's vehicle from defendant's car park. The decisions would, of course, have been different if the defendants had actually handed the vehicles over under a mistaken belief: *Hollins v J Davy Ltd* [1963] 1 Q.B. 844 (where, however, a contractual clause protected the defendants).

[98] It is important to note that there is no bailment where a vehicle is placed in an ordinary car park: *Chappell v National Car Parks, The Times*, May 22, 1987. The cases do not seem to have been affected by the Occupier's Liability act 1957: para.10–033; but cf. *Fairline Shipping Corp v Adamson* [1975] Q.B. 180.

[99] See para.18–025. Thus a carrier who negligently allows goods to be stolen may now be liable for conversion of the goods as well as negligent breach of bailment.

the possession.[100] However, in those cases where a person in possession of goods to which he has no title may confer a good title on someone else by selling, pledging, or otherwise disposing of the goods,[101] then, since the true owner is deprived of his title to the goods, such a disposition constitutes conversion whether or not the goods are actually delivered.[102]

Destruction or alteration. The destruction of goods amounts to conversion and so does the alteration of their nature. If I make an omelette of your eggs or a statue out of your block of marble, that is conversion.[103] However, the owner of the original material may wish to assert ownership in the product and that is a different question from that of whether the process wrongfully applied to the material constituted conversion. If the materials can still be identified in the new product, which is wholly or substantially composed of them[104] (leather turned into shoes,[105] skins turned into a fur coat)[106] the owner of the materials is owner of the product. Where the property of A is wrongfully mixed with that of B which is of substantially the same nature and quality and they cannot practicably be separated (grain in a bin, oil in a tank) the mixture is owned in common in proportion to the quantity contributed by each;[107] and it has been held that the same is true where the components are of different grades, so as to produce a commercially different mixture.[108]

18–022

iii.   Demand and Refusal

Merely keeping someone else's goods, while it may be a breach of contract,[109] is not a conversion of them for it does not necessarily show an intention to exclude the rights of the owner. In practice, proof of a demand by the claimant for the return of the goods met by a refusal of the defendant is the way in which a claimant will usually establish conversion.[110] Yet it is not the only way. In *Kuwait Airways Corp v Iraqi Airways Co (Nos 4 and 5)*[111] aircraft were seized by Iraqi forces in the invasion of Kuwait and transferred to the defendants, who were held to have converted them by resolving to register them in their name, using them to the limited extent possible in the circumstances and generally treating them as

18–023

---

[100] *Lancashire Waggon Co v Fitzhugh* (1861) 6 H. & N. 502.

[101] i.e. the exceptions to the rule *nemo dat quod non habet.*

[102] Though most of the exceptions require a delivery.

[103] The bottling of wine entrusted to a person in cask may be evidence of conversion even if none of the wine is drunk, but much will depend on the circumstances of the bottling. If done to preserve the wine from deterioration it is not conversion: see *Philpott v Kelley* (1835) 3 A. & E. 106.

[104] *Glencore International AG v Metro Trading International Inc* [2001] 1 Lloyd's Rep. 284 at 328.

[105] *Case of Leather* Y.B. 5 Hen.VII fol.15.

[106] *Jones v de Marchant* (1916) 28 D.L.R. 561, approved by Lord Millett in *Foskett v McKeown* [2001] 1 A.C. 102 at 132.

[107] *Indian Oil Corp Ltd v Greenstone Shipping SA* [1988] Q.B. 345.

[108] *Glencore International AG v Metro Trading International Inc* [2001] 1 Lloyd's Rep. 284.

[109] A bailee is not, in the absence of special contract, obliged to return the chattel to his bailor, he must merely allow the bailor to collect it: *Capital Finance Co Ltd v Bray* [1964] 1 W.L.R. 323.

[110] On the question of whether refusal may be inferred from mere inactivity in the face of a demand compare *R. (on the application of Atapattu) v Home Secretary* [2011] EWHC 1388 (Admin) with *Schwarzchild v Harrods Ltd* [2008] EWHC 521 (QB).

[111] *Kuwait Airways Corp v Iraqi Airways Co (Nos 4 and 5)* [2002] UKHL 19; [2002] 2 A.C. 883.

their own.[112] Where there is a demand, the refusal must be unconditional or, if it is conditional, the condition must be an unreasonable one. It is certainly not unreasonable to refuse to give up a banknote which you pick up in the street to the first stranger who alleges it to be his, if you tell him that you must make further inquiries or that he must produce evidence which will authenticate his claim.[113] Whether the length of time spent in making these inquiries and the mode in which they are made are reasonable or not may be nice questions.[114] Similarly, delivery in response to a demand need be immediate if it is necessary first to separate the claimant's goods from others to which he is not entitled.[115] However, the defendant cannot justify a refusal because compliance with the demand may have unpleasant consequences for him. In *Howard E Perry & Co Ltd v BRB*[116] it was held that the defendants' refusal to allow the claimants to enter their premises to collect goods which belonged to them could not be justified by their fear of intensified industrial action.

iv. Residual Forms of Conversion

18–024   Though most cases of conversion at common law fall within the categories of taking or abusing possession, or refusing to return the goods, such acts on the part of the defendant are not a necessary element in liability provided he has dealt with the goods in a way inconsistent with the claimant's rights, such as signing a delivery order for goods which are delivered under that order,[117] or an occupier refusing access to his premises to a lessor of goods brought onto the premises by the lessee.[118] It has even been held that refusing to hand over the registration book of the claimant's car amounts to conversion of the car since the absence of the book makes it difficult to deal with the car.[119] However, a mere denial of title without more is not conversion.[120]

Where the defendant is in possession of the claimant's goods there is no doubt that an unjustified refusal to return them generally constitutes conversion but it

---

[112] The initial seizure by the State of Iraq was not actionable in tort because of sovereign immunity: para.25–007. Under the law at the time of the events the usurpation by the defendants was actionable in an English court only if: (a) it was a tort in English law; and (b) civilly actionable under Iraqi law (see now Regulation (EC) 864/2007 on the law applicable to non–contractual obligations ('Rome II')). The decree of the Iraqi Government vesting the aircraft in the defendants was not recognised because it was a gross breach of international law.

[113] *Green v Dunn* (1811) 3 Camp. 215n.; *Alexander v Southey* (1821) 5 B. & Ald. 247; *Clayton v Le Roy* [1911] 2 K.B. 1031.

[114] For example, *Borroughes v Bayne* (1860) 5 H. & N. 296, where the court was not unanimous; *Pillott v Wilkinson* (1864) 3 H. & C. 345; *Spencer v S Franses Ltd* [2011] EWHC 1269.

[115] *Metall Market OOO v Vitorio Shipping Co Ltd* [2013] EWCA Civ 650; [2013] 1 C.L.C. 979.

[116] [1980] 1 W.L.R. 1875.

[117] *Hiort v Bott* (1874) L.R. 9 Ex. 86; *Van Oppen v Tredegars* (1921) 37 T.L.R. 504; *Douglas Valley Finance Co Ltd v S. Hughes (Hirers) Ltd* [1969] 1 Q.B. 738; see also *Ernest Scragg & Sons Ltd v Perseverance Banking and Trust Co Ltd* [1973] 2 Lloyd's Rep. 101.

[118] *London Trocadero Ltd v Family Leisure Holdings Ltd* [2012] EWCA Civ 1037 at [36]–[40] (the lessee was bankrupt).

[119] *Bryanston Leasings Ltd v Principality Finance Ltd* [1977] R.T.R. 45; see also *Douglas Valley Finance Co Ltd v S. Hughes (Hirers) Ltd* [1969] 1 Q.B. 738. In *Martin v Norbury*, July 21, 1999, CA, wrongfully registering a car with HPI, rendering it unsaleable, was held to be conversion.

[120] Torts (Interference with Goods) Act 1977 s.11(3).

has been held that where the claimant has possession there is no conversion if the defendant simply refuses to allow the claimant to remove them. In *England v Cowley*[121] M owed money to both the claimant and the defendant, her landlord. The claimant held a bill of sale over M's furniture and put a man into M's house to take charge of it. When the claimant then attempted to remove the furniture the defendant forbade him to do so and stationed a policeman at the gate to make sure he did not. The defendant was held not liable for conversion. Bramwell B said:[122]

> "In order to maintain trover, a plaintiff who is left in possession of the goods must prove that his dominion over his property has been interfered with, not in some particular way, but altogether that he has been entirely deprived of the use of it. It is not enough that a man should say that something shall not be done by the plaintiff he must say that nothing shall."

C. Conversion under the Torts (Interference with Goods) Act 1977

Apart from one or two minor matters[123] the 1977 Act did not interfere with the concept of conversion at common law. However, the Act abolished detinue,[124] which was wrongful retention of a chattel. In most cases of detinue there would be a concurrent liability in conversion based upon a demand and refusal to return[125] but as we have seen conversion required a positive act and had never lain where the defendant once had the claimant's goods but was unable to return them because they had been lost or negligently destroyed.[126] Accordingly, to deal with this situation, the Act provides[127] that an: "[A]ction lies in conversion for loss or destruction of goods which a bailee[128] has allowed to happen in breach of his duty to his bailor (that is to say it lies in a case which is not otherwise conversion, but would have been detinue before detinue was abolished)."[129]

18–025

D. Conversion and Co-owners

As between co-owners there is unity of possession, each is entitled to possession and use of the chattel, and the mere enjoyment in one way or another by one co–owner cannot amount to conversion against the other. The assertion of exclusive rights will, however, be actionable in tort. By s.10 of the Torts

18–026

---

[121] *England v Cowley* (1873) L.R. 8 Exch. 126; *Club Cruise etc BV v Department of Transport* [2008] EWHC 2794 (Comm); [2009] 1 Lloyd's Rep 201.

[122] *England v Cowley* (1873) L.R. 8 Exch. 126 at 128.

[123] Receipt by way of pledge (para.18–016) conversion by denial of title (para.18–024) co–ownership (para.18–026).

[124] Section 2(1).

[125] See para.18–004.

[126] See para.18–004. In cases where before the Act there was a concurrent liability in conversion and detinue the claimant might claim in detinue because this might enable him to get specific restitution. See now, s.3 of the Act.

[127] Section 2(2).

[128] Not, therefore, in a situation like that in *Ashby v Tolhurst* [1937] 2 K.B. 242, para.18–020.

[129] The claimant must, therefore, show a right to immediate possession since this was necessary for detinue at common law. As to the jus tertii, see para.18–033.

(Interference with Goods) Act 1977 co-ownership is no defence to an action in conversion[130] where one, without the authority of the other:[131]

> "(a)   [D]estroys the goods,[132] or disposes of the goods in a way giving a good title to the entire property in the goods[133] or otherwise does anything equivalent to the destruction of the other's interest in the goods,[134] or (b) purports to dispose of the goods in a way which would give a good title to the entire property in the goods if he was acting with the authority of all co–owners of the goods."

Paragraph (a) is by way of restatement of the common law;[135] paragraph (b) extends it so as to make the disposition conversion even if it does not confer a good title on the disponee.[136]

E.   Title of Claimant

18–027   **Possession or an immediate right to possess.** What kind of right to the goods must the claimant have in order that interference with it may amount to conversion? The answer is that he can maintain the action if at the time of the defendant's act he had: ownership and possession of the goods; or possession of them; or an immediate right to possess them, but without either ownership or actual possession.[137] Some of the older cases speak in terms that the claimant must have, "a right of property in the thing and a right of possession" and that unless both these rights concur the action will not lie[138] but the Court of Appeal has stated that an immediate right of possession, even if based on contract, is sufficient.[139] The fact that ownership is not necessary is demonstrated by the fact that it has never been doubted that a bailee (who has possession but not ownership) can sue.[140]

---

[130]   The same rules apply to trespass.

[131]   The position is different where co-ownership arises because the parties are buyers of portions of goods in bulk (e.g. oil in a tank) who have paid in full or in part. If there is delivery in full to one and then there is a shortfall as to the rest, the others are deemed to have authorised the first delivery, though they retain their contractual rights against the seller: Sale of Goods Act 1979 s.20B.

[132]   This does not, presumably, cover acts of the normal user which change the form of the property as in *Fennings v Grenville* (1808) 1 Taunt. 241 (cutting up and boiling down a whale).

[133]   For example, not a valid pledge under the Factors Act 1889, s.2, since that does not transfer the "entire property".

[134]   *Adventure Films Ltd v Tully, The Times*, October 14, 1982 (detention of television film).

[135]   On which see particularly *Baker v Barclays Bank Ltd* [1955] 1 W.L.R. 822.

[136]   In *Nyberg v Handelaar* [1892] 2 Q.B. 202 A and B were co-owners of a gold enamel box under an agreement that A was to have possession until it was sold. A entrusted it to B for a limited purpose but B pledged it to C. In A's successful action against C, Lopes LJ gave his opinion that A could have maintained conversion against B because of the agreement, but B's pledge would not now purport to dispose of the entire property.

[137]   *Rogers v Kennay* (1846) 9 Q.B. 594 at 596: "Any person having a right to the possession of goods may bring trover in respect of the conversion of them, and allege them to be his property: and lien, as an immediate right of possession, was held to constitute such a property": per Patteson J.

[138]   *Gordon v Harper* (1796) 7 T.R. 9 at 12; *Bloxam v Sanders* (1825) 9 B. & C. 941 at 950; *Owen v Knight* (1837) 4 Bing. N.C. 54 at 57; *Bradley v Copley* (1845) 1 C.B. 685.

[139]   *Iran v Barakat Galleries Ltd* [2007] EWCA Civ 1374; [2009] Q.B. 22, explaining *Jarvis v Williams* [1955] 1 W.L.R. 71.

[140]   *Burton v Hughes* (1842) 2 Bing. 173 at 175.

Examples of immediate right to possess. There is no need to enlarge upon   **18–028**
ownership and possession, or possession, for possession was analysed in Ch.14.
However, the immediate right to possess, must be briefly examined. A
reversionary owner out of possession certainly has not got it, for example in the
case of a landlord of premises let together with furniture to a tenant whose term is
still unexpired: if the furniture is wrongfully seized by the sheriff, it is the tenant
and not the landlord who can sue for conversion.[141] Again, an employee in
custody of his employer's goods has not possession of them, for it is
constructively in the employer;[142] but if the employer has made him a bailee of
them so as to vest him with exclusive possession, then, like any other bailee of
this sort, he has it; so, too, if goods are delivered to him to hand to his employer,
he has possession of them until he has done some act which transfers it to his
employer, for example a shop assistant has possession of money paid to him by a
customer until he puts it in the till. Up to that moment the employer has only the
right to possess.

These examples are tolerably plain, but it must depend to a large extent on the
facts of each case whether the law will attribute to a person the immediate right to
possess. A bailor had it against a mere bailee at pleasure[143] even if he never
himself had actual possession of the goods and only acquired title by virtue of an
illegal but completely executed contract of sale.[144] So, too, where furniture
dealers transferred furniture on hire-purchase to X with an express proviso that
the hiring was to terminate without any notice if the goods were taken in
execution for debt, they could sue the sheriff for conversion when he levied
execution on them.[145] The wrongful sale of goods subject to a hire-purchase
agreement will constitute a repudiation and hence vest a right to immediate
possession in the finance company even though the agreement does not expressly
provide for this.[146] However, in modern conditions legislation may restrict the
enforcement of the creditor's rights under a hire-purchase agreement.[147]

---

[141] *Gordon v Harper* (1796) 7 T.R. 9.

[142] See Holmes, *The Common Law* (2012), pp.227–228; Pollock and Wright, *Possession in the Common Law*, pp.58–60.

[143] *Manders v Williams* (1849) 4 Ex. 339 (brewers could maintain trover against a sheriff in respect of empty barrels in charge of publican). Distinguish *Bradley v Copley* (1845) 1 C.B. 685, where, upon the construction of a bill of sale, demand was held to be necessary to confer the immediate right to possess.

[144] *Belvoir Finance Co Ltd v Stapleton* [1971] 1 Q.B. 210 (claimant finance company buys car from dealer and lets it on HP to defendant's employer. Contracts of sale and HP both illegal. Defendant "sells" car on behalf of employer. Liable for conversion).

[145] *Jelks v Hayward* [1905] 2 K.B. 460, applied in *North General Wagon and Finance Co Ltd v Graham* [1950] 2 K.B. 7, CA; *Alexander v Ry Executive* [1951] 2 K.B. 882; distinguished in *Reliance Car Facilities Ltd v Roding Motors* [1952] 2 Q.B. 844, CA (hiring terminable on notice, but no notice given).

[146] *Union Transport Finance Ltd v British Car Auctions Ltd* [1978] 2 All E.R. 385. It may be necessary to identify the point in time when the conversion takes place since the right to possession must exist then. In *Smith v Bridgend CBC* [2001] UKHL 58; [2002] 1 A.C. 336 D's power of sale of C's plant was void as an unregistered floating charge. D contracted to sell the plant to X at a time when D had a contractual right to retain it to complete the works. This did not prevent the delivery of the plant to X when the works had been completed being a conversion.

[147] See, e.g. *Barclays Mercantile Business Finance Ltd v Sibec Developments Ltd* [1993] 2 All E.R. 195, where the restriction was regarded as only procedural. For hire–purchase transactions by individuals see the Consumer Credit Act 1974.

18–029   **Simple bailment.** In a simple bailment, i.e. one which does not exclude the bailor from possession, an action for conversion against a third person is maintainable by either bailor or bailee:[148] by the bailee because he is in possession, by the bailor because it is said that his title to the goods draws with it the right to possession, that the bailee is something like his servant and that the possession of the one is equivalent to that of the other.[149]

18–030   **Sale of goods.** A buyer of goods can sue the seller or a third party for conversion if he has ownership of the goods even though he has not yet got possession of them,[150] but he cannot sue the third party if ownership has passed to such third person by reason of exceptions to the rule *nemo dat quod non habet*, under ss.21–25 of the Sale of Goods Act 1979 or under the Factors Act 1889;[151] the seller, however, is liable for conversion to the original buyer.

18–031   **Temporary possession.** A person who is entitled to the temporary possession of a chattel and who delivers it back to the owner for a special purpose may, after that purpose is satisfied and during the existence of his temporary right, sue the owner for conversion of it;[152] a fortiori he can sue anyone else.

18–032   **Equitable interest.** A person who has a merely equitable right in property and who does not have possession,[153] does not have an immediate right to possession for the purposes of conversion, even though the legal owner is a mere nominee who has to transfer the property to the beneficiary on demand.[154] Though there may in some cases be little practical difference between them, the legal distinction between bailor and bailee on the one hand and beneficiary and trustee on the other hand, is fundamental.[155]

F.   Jus Tertii

18–033   **Common law.** Once a system of law accepts possession as a sufficient foundation for a claim for recovery of personal property it is faced with the question of how far the defendant should be allowed to raise the issue that a third party has a better right to the property than the claimant—the jus tertii. There are arguments either way. On the one hand, refusal to admit the jus tertii allows recovery by a claimant who may have himself wrongfully dispossessed the true owner and also exposes the wrongdoer to the risk of multiple liability. On the other hand, it may be argued that a person who has dispossessed another should

---

[148]   *Nicolls v Bastard* (1835) 2 C.M. & R. 659.

[149]   Williams, *Personal Property*, 18th edn, p.59; *Manders v Williams* (1849) 4 Ex. 339 at 344 per Parke B. As to the avoidance of double liability in such cases, see para.18–035.

[150]   For example, *North West Securities Ltd v Alexander Breckon Ltd* [1981] R.T.R. 518. Note that if the goods remain in the seller's possession subject to his lien for their unpaid price, the buyer cannot sue a wrongdoer for conversion: *Lord v Price* (1874) L.R. 9 Ex. 54.

[151]   See para.18–042.

[152]   *Roberts v Wyatt* (1810) 2 Taunt. 268.

[153]   Cf. *Healey v Healey* [1915] 1 K.B. 938, where the beneficiary had actual possession, which was disturbed by the trustee.

[154]   *MCC Proceeds Ltd v Lehman Bros* [1998] 4 All E.R. 675, rejecting a contrary view in *International Factors v Rodriguez* [1979] 1 Q.B. 351.

[155]   See further Tettenborn [1996] C.L.J. 36.

have no right to raise such issues concerning the relationship between the dispossessed and some other party having a claim over the goods, for there is a serious risk of abuse and of the interminable prolongation of actions. The common law compromised: if the claimant was in possession at the time of the conversion, the defendant could not set up the jus tertii,[156] unless he was acting under the authority of the true owner.[157] Where, however, the claimant was not in possession at the time of the conversion but relied on his right to possession, jus tertii could be pleaded by the defendant.[158] To this rule there was an exception where the defendant was the claimant's bailee, for the defendant was regarded as being estopped from denying the claimant's title unless evicted by title paramount or defending the action on behalf of the true owner.[159]

Fundamental change introduced by the 1977 Act. These rules were fundamentally changed by the Torts (Interference with Goods) Act 1977. Since then, in an action for "wrongful interference with goods"[160] the defendant is entitled to show, in accordance with Rules of Court,[161] that a third party has a better right than the claimant as respects all or any part of the interest claimed by the claimant or in right of which he sues.[162] The Rules require the claimant to identify any other person whom he knows to have a claim on the goods. The defendant may apply for directions as to whether any third person with a competing claim should be joined and if that person fails to appear on such a successful application the court may deprive him of any right of action against the defendant.[163]

18–034

Avoiding double liability. The general purpose of these provisions is to allow the court so far as possible to settle competing claims in one set of proceedings. Where all the claimants are before the court under s.8, then the relief granted is to be, "such as to avoid double liability of the wrongdoer",[164] which presumably means that the court is to apportion the damages representing the value of the chattel according to the respective interests of the claimants.[165] The Act is

18–035

---

[156] Assumed rather than decided in the famous case of *Armory v Delamirie* (1721) 1 Stra. 505 where a chimney–sweep's boy who had found a jewel recovered in conversion against a goldsmith who took it for valuation and refused to return it. The rule was the same for trespass where, of course, the claimant's possession was a pre-condition to his right to sue.

[157] See further the 10th edn of this work, pp.424–425. However, the fact that he had returned the property to the owner was not of itself a defence: *Wilson v Lombank Ltd* [1963] 1 W.L.R. 1294.

[158] *Leake v Loveday* (1842) 4 M. & G. 972. Cf. Atiyah (1955) 18 M.L.R. 97 and Jolly's reply, (1955) 18 M.L.R. 371.

[159] See *Clerk and Lindsell on Torts*, 20th edn (2013), para.17–81.

[160] Defined in s.1 as conversion, trespass, negligence so far as it results in damage to goods or to an interest in goods and "any other tort so far as it results in damage to goods or to an interest in goods". How far can the change in the law on jus tertii be evaded by framing the claim as breach of bailment or in contract? The courts may be able to block the former (cf. *American Express Co v British Airways Board* [1983] 1 W.L.R. 701) but the latter will be more difficult to deal with. See further Palmer (1978) 41 M.L.R. 629.

[161] CPR r.19.5A.

[162] Section 8(1). This provision applies even though the third party has disposed of the alleged interest before proceedings are begun: *De Franco v MPC, The Times*, May 8, 1987.

[163] See also s.9, which provides machinery to deal with concurrent claims in different courts.

[164] Section 7(2).

[165] As between finder and true owner, the interest of the finder would presumably be nil.

perhaps not so clear where only the claimant with a possessory title is before the court, for example, because the true owner does not appear or cannot be found. A literal interpretation of s.8 might suggest that the ability to plead the jus tertii provides the defendant with a defence,[166] but it seems clear that in such a case the provisions of s.7 preserve the common law rule that a claimant relying on a possessory interest may recover the full value of the thing converted.[167] In such a situation the true owner may have been divested of his claim against the wrongdoer under s.8(2)(d) but if not, he might still be entitled to sue by virtue of his title. Two provisions of the Act are aimed at this problem. By s.7(3): "[O]n satisfaction, in whole or in part, of any claim for an amount exceeding that recoverable if subsection (2) applied [i.e. where both claimants are parties], the claimant is liable to account over to the other person having a right to claim to such extent as will avoid double liability."[168]

And by s.7(4): "[W]here, as a result of enforcement of a double liability, any claimant is unjustly enriched to any extent, he shall be liable to reimburse the wrongdoer to that extent."

Thus, if A loses his goods, which are found by C and then converted by D, both C and A might bring successive claims against D. If C accounts to A under s.7(3), A must then reimburse D. If C does not so account, C is liable to reimburse D. A "double liability" would, however, still exist if both A and C were insolvent.[169]

18–036 **Double liability in cases of bailment.** A central difficulty in construing the provisions of the 1977 Act on jus tertii is the position where there is a bailment, which is presumably far and away the commonest source of a "possessory title". As we have seen, at common law the bailee could recover the full value of the goods on the basis of his possession. If he did so, he had to account to the bailor for the amount by which the damages exceeded his (the bailee's) interest.[170] In such a case the wrongdoer, having paid full damages to the bailee, had a complete

---

[166] Or at least reduce the claimant's damages to the value of his interest.

[167] *The Winkfield* [1902] P. 42 (a strong case since the bailee claimant would have been under no liability to the owners for loss of the goods); *Chabbra Corp Pte Ltd v Jag Shakti (owners)* [1986] A.C. 337. This was certainly the intention of the Law Reform Committee: Cmnd. 4774 (1971), para.75 and was the view taken in *Costello v CC Derbyshire* [2001] EWCA Civ 381; [2001] 1 W.L.R. 1437 at [15]. Some cases, e.g. *The Winkfield*, are claims for negligence but the position is the same.

[168] As to the bailee, see para.18–036.

[169] What is the effect of the Act upon *Wilson v Lombank Ltd* [1963] 1 W.L.R. 1294? C purchased a car from a person who had no title, the car in fact belonging to MC Co. While the car was at a garage after undergoing repairs, D's agents passed by and, mistakenly thinking it belonged to D, took it away. D discovered the truth and returned the car to MC Co. C sued D for trespass to goods and recovered the full value of the car (£470) because, in Hinchcliffe J's opinion, D could not set up the title of MC Co against C's possessory title. Since it is inconceivable that M.C. Co could have sued D for anything other than nominal damages it seems somewhat strained to talk of a "double liability" under s.7. Cf. *Clerk and Lindsell on Torts*, 20th edn (2013), para.17–86. Could this be a case where s.8(1) is to be taken at its face value?

[170] Among the many statements to this effect see *The Winkfield* [1902] P. 42 at 55; *Eastern Construction Co Ltd v National Trust* [1914] A.C. 197 at 210; *Hepburn v A. Tomlinson (Hauliers) Ltd* [1966] A.C. 451 at 467–468, 480.

answer to any action by the bailor.[171] Contrariwise, if the bailor sued first and recovered full value,[172] the bailee was equally barred.[173]

These principles might cast some doubt upon the reality of the risk of double liability which lies at the root of ss.7 and 8 of the 1977 Act but the Act might still provide a useful means of enabling the court to apportion the full range of loss which might arise from the conversion or destruction of goods and to avoid the risk that, say, the bailor might have difficulties in getting the bailee to account for part of the judgment sum.[174] Curiously, the common law principles have been applied in a modern case in which the Act is not even mentioned[175] and it is to be hoped that certain statements in the case will not present obstacles to the application of the Act's machinery.

Claim based on possession of stolen goods. It has been seen above that where the true owner of goods cannot be involved in the proceedings the common law rule that a mere possessory interest entitles the claimant to recover the full value of the goods against a wrongdoer still applies. Does this mean that if there is clear evidence that the goods were stolen by C from X (who has since disappeared) C may nevertheless recover from D, who converted them by taking them from C? In *Costello v CC Derbyshire*[176] the police seized a car in C's possession and refused to return it when their investigations were complete. The trial judge found that the car was stolen (though not by C) and that C was aware of that, though the person from whom it had been stolen remained unidentified. The Court of Appeal held that to refuse to return the car to C was conversion of it: his prior possession gave him a better claim to it than the defendants[177] and he was not required to

18–037

---

[171] *Nicolls v Bastard* (1835) 2 C.M. & R. 659 at 660; *The Winkfield* [1902] P. 42 at 61.

[172] It was held in *Chabbra Corp Pte Ltd v Jag Shakti (Owners)* [1986] A.C. 337 that a person with a mere right to possession might recover full value but this is controversial: Palmer, *Bailment*, 3rd end (2009), para.4–138

[173] *Nicolls v Bastard* (1835) 2 C.M. & R. 659 at 660; *O'Sullivan v Williams* [1992] 3 All E.R. 385, where there was a non–contractual bailment at will and the bailee therefore had no right to look to the bailor. Complications which might arise from the fact that the bailee might suffer loss of use damages which were not comprehended within the bailor's claim do not seem to have been fully explored in the cases: Palmer, *Bailment*, 3rd end (2009), para.4–099.

[174] See, e.g. Palmer, *Bailment*, 3rd edn (2009), para.4–138: "It is submitted that s.7(2) should be construed expansively to enable the court, in all cases where two or more claimants are parties, to divide the damages according to the value of their respective interests, whether this is strictly necessary to save the wrongdoer from a [double liability] or not."

[175] *O'Sullivan v Williams* [1992] 3 All E.R. 385. Perhaps this was because the claim arose from a (very unusual) vehicle collision and these were not then subject to the Rules made under the Act: RSC Ord.15 r.10(A).

[176] [2001] EWCA Civ 381; [2001] 1 W.L.R. 1437. See also *Webb v CC Merseyside* [2000] Q.B. 427 (even if it could be established on a balance of probabilities that money seized from claimant was the product of drug trafficking, that provided no basis for refusing to return it); *Gough v CC West Midlands* [2004] EWCA Civ 206; and *Jaroo v Attorney General of Trinidad and Tobago* [2002] UKPC 5; [2002] 1 A.C. 871 (where the claim was brought under a Constitutional guarantee of the right to enjoyment of property; cf. the First Protocol to the European Convention on Human Rights); *Ecclestone v Khyami* [2014] EWHC 29 (QB) at [125]–[129].

[177] There are powers under the Police and Criminal Evidence Act 1984 to retain property for the purposes of investigation or as evidence but the conditions for the exercise of these were not satisfied in these cases. The Police Property Act 1897 gives magistrates power to make orders for the disposition of property in the hands of the police but that does not override civil rights under the general law.

rely on any illegal transaction to establish that.[178] The only ground for refusing to treat him as entitled to the goods (apart from the case where the owner could be identified) would be that it was inherently unlawful to possess the goods, for example controlled drugs.[179] However, in cases like these consideration will have to be given to the enormously extensive powers of confiscation and forfeiture under the Proceeds of Crime Act 2002[180] and under s.329 it is an offence for a person to be in possession of property which constitutes a benefit from his criminal conduct.

G.   Finding[181]

18–038   **The finder has a limited title.** The popular saying that "finding is keeping" is a dangerous half–truth, which needs a good deal of expansion and qualification to make it square with the law. A finder of a chattel has such a title as will enable him to keep it against everyone,[182] with two exceptions.[183]

18–039   **No title as against the rightful owner.** Far from getting any title against the rightful owner, the finder, if he appropriates the chattel, not only commits the tort of conversion,[184] but is also guilty of the crime of theft unless he appropriates the chattel in the belief that the owner cannot be discovered by taking reasonable steps.[185]

18–040   **The relative rights of finder and occupier of the land.** The occupier[186] of the land on which the chattel[187] is found may in some cases have a title superior to that of the finder. The Court of Appeal in *Parker v British Airways Board*[188] took the opportunity to restate the law in a comprehensive manner and bring order to an area in which there were numerous conflicting precedents. The cases in which

---

[178] See *Tinsley v Milligan* [1994] 1 A.C. 340 and the general discussion of illegality at para.26–062.

[179] Cf. *Chief Constable of Merseyside v Owens* [2012] EWHC 1515 (Admin) (no entitlement to retain property only because the defendant reasonably suspects that the claimant may commit a crime with it).

[180] Various bodies (see the Serious Crime Act 2007) may take civil proceedings for the recovery by the State (on a civil standard of proof and involving assumptions against the defendant if he has a "criminal lifestyle") of the proceeds of criminal activity. See *Fletcher v Leicestershire Constabulary* [2013] EWHC 3357 (Admin); [2014] Lloyd's Rep. F.C. 60.

[181] Palmer, *Bailment*, 3rd edn (2009), Ch.26.

[182] Like the person in possession of stolen goods, the finder's claim is based upon his possession alone.

[183] While not an exception, a finder's right may be subject to the power to forfeit the proceeds of crime: *Fletcher v Leicestershire Constabulary* [2013] EWHC 3357 (Admin); [2014] Lloyd's Rep. F.C. 60.

[184] *Moffatt v Kazana* [1969] 2 Q.B. 152.

[185] Theft Act 1968 ss.1, 2(1)(c).

[186] Not a non–occupying owner: *Hannah v Peel* [1945] K.B. 509.

[187] Different rules apply where the property is "treasure", as to which, see the Treasure Act 1996, replacing the common law of treasure trove. The Crown's rights in treasure override those of the finder and the landowner, with a discretion in the Secretary of State to compensate either or both of them up to the value of the goods found. Treasure under the Act is a good deal wider than at common law.

[188] [1982] Q.B. 1004.

the occupier of the land has the superior title[189] are: (a) where the finder is a trespasser on the land;[190] (b) where the property is in or attached to the land, as in *Waverley BC v Fletcher*[191] where a medieval gold brooch was found embedded nine inches deep in the soil of a park; (c) where he is the occupier of premises on which the chattels (not attached to the premises) are found and, before the finding, "he has manifested an intention to exercise control over the [premises] and the things which may be upon it or in it".[192] The burden of proof of this rests upon the occupier, though in some cases the matter speaks for itself:[193]

> "If a bank manager saw fit to show me round a vault containing safe deposits and I found a gold bracelet on the floor, I should have no doubt that the bank had a better title than I, and the reason is the manifest intention to exercise a very high degree of control. At the other extreme is the park to which the public has unrestricted access during daylight hours. During those hours there is no manifest intention to exercise any such control. In between these extremes are the forecourts of petrol filling stations, unfenced front gardens of private houses, the public parts of shops and supermarkets as part of an almost infinite variety of land, premises and circumstances."

In *Parker*'s case itself the claimant found a gold bracelet on the floor of the executive lounge at Heathrow Airport and was held entitled to it as against the occupiers. The facts that they restricted entry to the lounge to certain classes of passengers and gave their staff instructions as to what to do with lost property were insufficient to manifest the intention to exercise the requisite degree of control.[194] It is, of course, open to the occupier to regulate the right to possession of lost property by contract with the entrant; it remains to be seen whether merely putting up notices at the entrance declaring that lost property is to vest in the occupier will be an effective manifestation of the intent to control required by *Parker*'s case.[195]

---

[189] It is assumed that the finder is not employed by the possessor of the land, for a servant (and perhaps agent) who finds in the course of his employment must account to his employer.

[190] Where the finder is not a trespasser but dishonestly intends to retain the property even against the true owner, the finder, "probably has some title, albeit a frail one, because of the need to avoid a free-for-all": *Parker v British Airways Board* [1982] Q.B. 1004 at 1010.

[191] *Waverley BC v Fletcher* [1996] Q.B. 334. See also *South Staffs Water Co v Sharman* [1896] 2 Q.B. 44. The case can also be explained on the ground that the finders were employed by the claimants: [1982] Q.B. 1004 at 1013.

[192] *South Staffs Water Co v Sharman* [1982] Q.B. 1004 at 1018 per Donaldson LJ.

[193] *South Staffs Water Co v Sharman* [1982] Q.B. 1004 at 1019.

[194] The much-battered case of *Bridges v Hawkesworth* (1851) 21 L.J.Q.B. 75, in which the occupier of a shop failed against the finder of banknotes on the floor of the shop, was approved in *Parker*'s case.

[195] Even if it is not, a finder who takes lost property in defiance of such a condition in his licence would seem to be a trespasser.

4.   STRICT LIABILITY AND CONVERSION

18–041   **Mistake no defence.** Mistake does not usually provide a defence,[196] for liability in conversion is strict:[197]

> "At common law one's duty to one's neighbour who is the owner . . . of any goods is to refrain from doing any voluntary act in relation to his goods which is a usurpation of his proprietary or possessory rights in them. Subject to some exceptions . . . it matters not that the doer of the act of usurpation did not know, and could not by the exercise of any reasonable care have known of his neighbour's interest in the goods. This duty is absolute; he acts at his peril."

The classic illustration is the position of the auctioneer, who is liable in conversion if he innocently effects the sale of another's goods[198] and of whom it has been said that conversion is one of "the risks of his profession".[199]

This rule was set solidly into law by the House of Lords in *Hollins v Fowler*.[200] B fraudulently obtained possession of cotton from Fowler. Hollins, a cotton broker who was ignorant of the fraud, bought it from B and resold it to another person, receiving only broker's commission. Hollins was held liable to Fowler for the conversion of the cotton. The justification for such a rule is not at all obvious, particularly when in the typical case the claimant will have handed his goods over to a rogue on some flimsy excuse while the defendant has acquired the goods not only in good faith but from some reputable dealer who has himself been deceived. One solution which has been suggested would be to apportion the loss between claimant and defendant in such a case[201] but this was rejected as impracticable by the Law Reform Committee.[202] An alternative approach would have been to apply the "ready-made" system of apportionment in the Law Reform (Contributory Negligence) Act 1945 to liability in conversion.[203] There was some authority for this but the matter is now governed by s.11(1) of the Torts (Interference with Goods) Act 1977 which firmly states that contributory negligence is no defence in proceedings founded on conversion, or on intentional trespass to goods.[204]

18–042   **Exceptions.** There are, however, exceptions to the rule that innocent mistake is no defence. The first group consists of what is sometimes known as the exceptions to the rule *nemo dat quod non habet*, whereby a bona fide purchaser

---

[196] Licence and the exercise of a right of distress are defences to an action for conversion but these have already been touched on in relation to trespass to land.

[197] *Marfani & Co Ltd v Midland Bank Ltd* [1968] 1 W.L.R. 956 at 971 per Diplock LJ. However, an innocent converter will be in a more favourable position with regard to limitation than one who knows the facts: para.26–096.

[198] *Consolidated Co v Curtis & Son* [1892] 1 Q.B. 495; *RH Willis & Sons v British Car Auctions Ltd* [1978] 1 W.L.R. 438, doubting *National Mercantile Bank Ltd v Rymill* (1881) 44 L.T. 767.

[199] *Sachs v Miklos* [1948] 2 K.B. 23 at 37.

[200] (1875) L.R. 7 H.L. 757.

[201] By Devlin LJ in *Ingram v Little* [1961] 1 Q.B. 31 at 73–74.

[202] Twelfth Report, *Transfer of Title to Chattels* (1966), Cmnd.2958.

[203] This would not have gone so far as Devlin LJ's proposal since the claimant's damages could only have been reduced if he was at fault.

[204] However, under s.47 of the Banking Act 1979 a "defence of contributory negligence" is available to a banker converting a cheque if the circumstances are such that he would be protected by s.4 of the Cheques Act 1957 if he were not negligent.

of goods from A commits no conversion but actually obtains a good title to them even though the goods really belonged to B and B never intended to allow A to sell them. B's remedy is against A alone. In such cases the law has sought to strike a compromise between the competing principles that ownership of property must be protected and that speedy commerce in goods should be facilitated. Details of this very large topic must be sought elsewhere[205] but the principal exceptions are briefly as follows: (1) Estoppel by representation or by negligent conduct;[206] (2) sale under a voidable title;[207] (3) disposition in the ordinary course of business by a mercantile agent in possession of the goods or documents of title with the owner's consent;[208] (4) second sale by seller in possession;[209] (5) sale by buyer in possession;[210] (6) private purchaser of vehicle subject to a hire–purchase agreement.[211]

No conversion in ministerial handling. We have seen above that a person   **18–043**
commits conversion if he sells the goods to another, whether on his own behalf or as an agent (e.g. an auctioneer), but the position is different where the defendant innocently interferes with the claimant's goods whether upon his own initiative or upon the instructions of another, when the defendant's act amounts to nothing more than transport or custody or redelivery of the goods.[212] So in *Marcq v Christie, Manson & Woods Ltd*[213] a painting was deposited by S with the defendant auctioneers for sale. Unknown to the auctioneers the painting had been stolen some years previously from M. It failed to sell at auction and was eventually returned by the defendants to S. A claim for conversion against the auctioneers in redelivering it failed and it was irrelevant that the terms of contract gave the auctioneers a lien for their charges against S. If, of course, M had demanded the painting from them their refusal by assertion of the lien against him *would* have been conversion. Similarly there is no liability if a railway company, acting upon A's directions, carries B's goods, honestly believing that A has B's authority to give such directions[214] or, of course, where a finder removes them to a place of safety.[215]

The test (artificial as it is) would protect all those persons in *Hollins v Fowler* who merely handled the cotton ministerially, such as a carrier who merely received and delivered the goods in the ordinary way[216] and it would not save the

---

[205] Benjamin, *Sale of Goods*, 8th edn (2010).
[206] Such a plea is extremely difficult to establish, no doubt because it would soon eat up all the other exceptions. Carelessness in allowing goods to be stolen or putting the goods in the hands of a third party will not found the estoppel. See *Moorgate Mercantile Co Ltd v Twitchings* [1977] A.C. 890.
[207] For example, *Lewis v Avery* [1972] 1 Q.B. 198.
[208] Factors Act 1889 s.2.
[209] Sale of Goods Act 1979 s.24.
[210] Sale of Goods Act 1979 s.25.
[211] Hire Purchase Act 1964 Pt III. See also Twelfth Report of the Law Reform Committee (1966), Cmnd.2958.
[212] *Hollins v Fowler* (1875) L.R. 7 H.L. 757 at 766–767.
[213] [2003] EWCA Civ 731; [2004] Q.B. 286. Hudson, 10 *Art, Antiquity & Law* 201.
[214] See (1875) L.R. 7 H.L. 757 at 767; cf. *The Pioneer Container* [1994] 2 A.C. 324 (bailee "assumes responsibility" only to person of whose interest he is aware).
[215] *Sorrell v Paget* [1950] 1 K.B. 252.
[216] In *Hollins v Fowler*, Blackburn J speaks of the delivery as merely "changing the custody" but it is hard to see why, as he suggests, it would be "very difficult, if not impossible" to fix the carrier with

person who has sold the cotton to another. A solicitor of an undischarged bankrupt who receives after-acquired property on behalf of his client and transfers it to another agent, even with knowledge that that agent has been instructed to sell, is not liable for conversion at the suit of the trustee in bankruptcy, for the solicitor's act can be described as ministerial within the test laid down by Blackburn J.[217] Unfortunately, as Blackburn J himself admitted, it is doubtful how far it goes. Does it protect the defendant if A wrongfully gives him B's wheat to grind into flour and he innocently does so? The learned judge thought not (and indeed a mere finder of lost wheat could not authorise the grinding of it), and yet he felt that it would be hard to hold the defendant liable. No doubt a finder of perishable commodities would be justified in taking any reasonable steps to preserve them pending the ascertainment of their owner; for example he would not commit conversion by making jam of strawberries if that were the only mode of preserving them, but cases like these might well be based on the general defence of necessity.[218]

5. REMEDIES FOR INTERFERENCE WITH GOODS

A. Retaking of Goods

18–044   **A self-help remedy.** Retaking of goods is a species of self-help. It may now be an oversimplification to say that if A's goods are wrongfully in B's possession there is no need for A to go to the expense of litigation to recover them.[219] No doubt there are still simple cases where this is so, as where A catches B immediately after he has seized A's property and retakes it.[220] It would be a hard rule (and an unrealistic one) which said that a citizen who seized a bag snatcher had to sue to recover his bag and committed an assault if he laid hands on the thief. In such a case there may anyway be the further justification of preventing crime or effecting an arrest. Beyond that simple case it is not easy to state the law with certainty. Perhaps there is also a right to retake the goods wherever the holder came into possession of them wrongfully (even by an innocent purchase from a thief conferring no title) but there is authority both ways on the situation where the taker initially consented to the possession of the holder but then withdrew it.[221] English criminal cases arising out of wheel clamping have shown a hostile attitude to self-help by the vehicle owner, though on the facts the vehicles were not lawfully on the property where the clamp was applied.[222] Even where the

---

knowledge that the goods had been sold to the consignee. Yet to impose liability on the carrier who had such knowledge would seem to be a wholly unreasonable burden. See *Samuel (No.2), Re* [1945] Ch. 408.

[217] *Samuel (No.2), Re* [1945] Ch. 408 at 411 per Lord Greene MR: "To involve conversion the act, looked at in isolation, must have the effect of depriving the true owner of his property."

[218] See para.26–042.

[219] Delay may mean destruction or carrying away of the goods by B, who may be quite incapable of paying damages: Blackstone, Comm., iii, 4.

[220] See, e.g. *Whatford v Carty, The Times*, October 29, 1960.

[221] The matter is reviewed at length in *Toyota Finance Australia Ltd v Dennis* [2002] NSWCA 605.

[222] *Lloyd v DPP* [1992] 1 All E.R. 982 ("no reasonable alternative"); *R. v Mitchell* [2003] EWCA Crim 2188. See also *Arthur v Anker* [1996] 1 W.L.R. 602.

owner is justified in using force it must be no more than is reasonably necessary and that varies with the facts of each case and the view of the court or jury after the event, so self-help is likely to be just as dangerous a remedy here as elsewhere in the law. Moreover, there are other qualifications of A's right to retake goods.[223]

Retaking and trespass. Further difficulty arises over the circumstances in which a person can enter premises to retrieve his goods without committing a trespass. There is no doubt that the person entitled to goods may enter and take them from the land of the first taker if the taker himself wrongfully put them there;[224] but it is by no means certain what the law is when the goods are on the premises of one who was not responsible for bringing them there and who has committed no tort with respect to them. The only case of any real assistance is *Anthony v Haney*,[225] but the dicta are obiter and, although of considerable weight, do not probe the question of recaption very deeply. Tindal CJ in that case gave as examples of permissible retaking by A from the land of an innocent person, C: (1) where the goods have come there by accident; (2) where they have been feloniously taken by B and A follows them to C's land; (3) where C refuses to deliver up the goods or to make any answer to A's demand for them.   **18–045**

Retaking goods accidentally on another's land. In this first category, the Chief Justice's examples were A's fruit falling upon C's land, or A's tree falling upon it by decay or being blown upon it by the wind. By "accident" it seems clear that "inevitable accident" was meant. Negligent or intentional placing of goods on the land of another is (technically at least) a tort, for example where a cricket ball is hit by any ordinary stroke out of the ground into another person's premises. Where, however, the entry of the goods was inevitable, not only is there no liability for trespass on the part of their owner, but the view that he can retake them seems to be right, even if there is no direct decision to that effect.   **18–046**

Following goods taken criminally on to another's land. The distinction between felonies and misdemeanours no longer exists[226] but there seems no reason why the rule, if it is a rule at all, should not apply wherever B's taking is criminal.[227]   **18–047**

Retaking goods when occupier refuses to deliver up the goods or answer a demand. Tindal CJ thought that where C refused to deliver up the goods or to answer A's demand "a jury might be induced to presume a conversion from such silence, or at any rate the owner might in such case enter and take his property subject to the payment of any damage he might commit",[228] though there are   **18–048**

---

[223] There are certain important statutory restrictions upon the retaking of goods, the best known of which are in the Consumer Credit Act 1974.

[224] *Patrick v Colerick* (1838) 3 M. & W. 483.

[225] (1832) 8 Bing. 186.

[226] Criminal Law Act 1967 s.1(1).

[227] There are practical difficulties here, too, for B's criminality might depend upon B's state of mind, of which A was ignorant: for example, B might have taken the property under a claim of right.

[228] *Anthony v Haney* (1832) 8 Bing. 186 at 192–193. The report in 1 L.J.C.P. 81 at 84 omits the passage about the right to enter, subject to payment of damages; the report in 1 Moo. & Sc. 300 at 308 omits any reference to the obligation to pay for the damage done. Since Tindal CJ had already dealt with accidental entry and wrongful appropriation it is not wholly clear what type of case he had in mind.

cases suggesting that mere refusal to allow collection would not be conversion.[229] As a matter of policy it may be argued that where the owner of goods was under no tortious liability for their appearance on the occupier's land, he ought to be able to retake them in any event, provided he does no injury to the premises or gives adequate security for making good any unavoidable injury. On the other hand, it may be urged that self-help ought to be strictly limited even against a wrongdoer and forbidden altogether against one who is not a wrongdoer, except that retaking might be permitted in circumstances of inevitable accident or of necessity (for example where the goods are perishable or are doing considerable damage to the land and it is impossible to communicate speedily enough with the occupier or his agent). It has been held that the owner of a swarm of bees has no right to follow it onto another person's land,[230] but this is of no general assistance for, once the bees get onto that land they become again ferae naturae[231] and the property of no one.

18–049 **The need for an explanation from the retaker.** The retaker, before he attempts to retake, must, if required to do so, explain to the occupier of the land or the person in possession of the goods the facts upon which his proposed action is based. A mere allegation that the goods are his, without any attempt to show how they came on the premises, will not do, for: "[T]o allow such a statement to be a justification for entering the soil of another, would be opening too wide a door to parties to attempt righting themselves without resorting to law, and would necessarily tend to breach of the peace."[232]

B. Judicial Remedies

18–050 **Damages the primary remedy.** It may be surprising in view of the proprietary nature of the tort, but in practice damages are, as in the case of other torts, the primary remedy. This is necessarily so where the defendant is no longer in possession because he has destroyed the goods or disposed of them or they have been returned, but even where the defendant is still in possession it is comparatively rare for him to be ordered specifically to return them, though he may be given the option of returning them or paying their value.

18–051 **Assessment of damages.** In most cases the judgment for damages will be for the value[233] of the goods at the time of the conversion[234] together with any consequential loss which is not too remote, or which the claimant failed to

---

[229] *British Economical Lamp Co Ltd v Empire Mile End Ltd* (1913) 29 T.L.R. 386. Maule J in *Wilde v Waters* (1855) 24 L.J.C.P 193 at 195 thought that if a former tenant of a house left a picture on a wall and the new tenant refused to admit him and merely said "I don't want your chattel, but I shall not give myself any trouble about it", that would not be conversion. This seems to be a sort of permanent legal stand-off, though since the former tenant undoubtedly remains the owner of the picture he must surely be able to obtain an order allowing collection. See also *Moffatt v Kazana* [1969] 2 Q.B. 152 at 156–157 and Palmer (1980) 9 Anglo-American L.R. 279.

[230] *Kearry v Pattinson* [1939] 1 K.B. 471.

[231] In the property law sense, not the sense of animals belonging to a dangerous species: para.17–008.

[232] Tindal CJ in *Anthony v Haney* (1832) 8 Bing. 186 at 191–192.

[233] For the value of documents such as negotiable instruments, see para.18–013. Exemplary damages may be awarded where the defendant calculates to make a profit exceeding compensatory damages: *Borders (UK) Ltd v MPC* [2005] EWCA Civ 197; [2005] Po L.R. 1 and para.23–015.

mitigate,[235] because that represents what the claimant has lost. Value is prima facie the market price of such goods, though where they cannot be obtained in the market the cost of replacement may be allowed where the claimant has replaced the goods or will do so.[236] If there is doubt as to the value of the chattel the claimant will get the benefit of it for, *omnia praesumuntur contra spoliatorem*,[237] though this cannot be pressed too far because it would negate the fundamental proposition that it is for the claimant to prove his loss.[238] However, damages for conversion are subject to the normal rule that they are assessed on the basis of what is necessary to give the claimant just compensation for his loss[239] and the test of the value of the goods will have to give way to that where the claimant's loss is smaller. Thus a finance company letting goods on hire-purchase is limited to recovering the amount owing under the agreement;[240] and a person who uses raw materials for processing rather than trading in them and who does not replace them during the period they are wrongfully detained cannot recover damages by reference to the fall in the market price during that period.[241]

Allowance for the value of returned goods. Where the goods (or an exact equivalent) are returned, one plainly cannot ignore the value of what the claimant receives. In *BBMB Finance (Hong Kong) Ltd v Eda Holdings Ltd*[242] D converted C's share certificates by selling the shares for HK $5.75 each. D later replaced these with equivalent shares at HK $2.40 each. On the basis that both these figures represented the market value of the shares at the relevant time, the Privy Council held that C was entitled to the value of the shares sold at the time of conversion, less the value of the replacements, though it has been suggested that in such cases the damages are "gain-based".[243]   **18–052**

Consequential loss. The recovery of consequential losses is illustrated in a very simple way by *Bodley v Reynolds*,[244] where a carpenter's tools were converted   **18–053**

---

[234] This is the general rule and reflects the claimant's duty to mitigate his loss, but the position would be different if the claimant were unaware of the conversion until later: *Sachs v Micklos* [1948] 2 K.B. 23; *BBMB Finance (Hong Kong) Ltd v Eda Holdings Ltd* [1990] 1 W.L.R. 409: but *Scheps v Fine Art Logistic Ltd* [2007] EWHC 541 (QB) simply allows the claimant to add on any subsequent notional rise in value to judgment as consequential loss.

[235] *Uzinterimpex JSC v Standard Bank Plc* [2008] EWCA Civ 819; [2008] 2 Lloyd's Rep. 456.

[236] *Hall v Barclay* [1937] 3 All E.R. 620; *Wilson v Robertsons (London) Ltd* [2006] EWCA Civ 1088; and see para.23–112 (damage and destruction).

[237] Everything is presumed against a wrongful taker; *Armory v Delamirie* (1721) 1 Stra. 505.

[238] *Zabihi v Janzemini* [2009] EWCA Civ 851; *Malhotra v Dhawan* [1997] Med.L.R. 319; *Colbeck v Diamanta (UK) Ltd* [2002] EWHC 616 (QB).

[239] *Kuwait Airways Corp v Iraqi Airways Co (Nos 4 and 5)* [2002] UKHL 19; [2002] 2 A.C. 883 at [67].

[240] *Wickham Holdings Ltd v Brooke House Motors Ltd* [1967] 1 W.L.R. 295. For the position of the claimant with a possessory interest, see para.18–035.

[241] *Brandeis Goldschmidt & Co Ltd v Western Transport Ltd* [1981] Q.B. 864.

[242] [1990] 1 W.L.R. 409, PC. See also *Solloway v McLaughlin* [1938] AC 247.

[243] *Kuwait Airways Corp v Iraqi Airways Co (Nos 4 and 5)* [2002] UKHL 19; [2002] 2 A.C. 883 at [88]; *Blue Sky One Ltd v Mahan Air* [2009] EWHC 3314 (Comm). However, it does not seem to be suggested that there should be an inquiry into the gain the defendant *actually* made (in *BBMB* for some obscure reason he seems never to have cashed the cheque for the converted shares) so this is arguably saying the same thing in a different way.

[244] (1846) 8 Q.B. 779. Cf. *Chubb Cash Ltd v John Crilley & Son* [1983] 1 W.L.R. 599 (market value recoverable, not higher sum claimant owed on the goods).

and he was thereby prevented from working: £10 above the value of the tools was awarded as special damage. Such loss may include personal inconvenience, such as loss of a hobby,[245] and the costs of seeking out the goods.[246] On a rather grander scale, when a fleet of airliners was converted during the Gulf War damages for consequential losses such as repairs, chartering substitutes and lost operating profits ran into hundreds of millions of US dollars.[247] Generally, however, loss incurred as a result of the claimant's inability to deliver the goods under a lucrative contract of sale is too remote unless the defendant is aware of the contract.[248]

C. Causation and Loss

18–054   **Not governed by the "but-for" test.** It is a general requirement of tort that the defendant must have caused the loss of which the claimant complains. However, damages for conversion are not governed by the application of the simple "but-for" test. Property may be successively converted by A and B and C and the claimant may sue all or any of them for the value of the goods. It has never been suggested that B or C might seek to reduce or extinguish the damages because A had already deprived the claimant of his goods or by showing that if A had not transferred them to B he would probably have transferred them to someone else:[249]

> "By definition, each person in a series of conversions wrongfully excludes the owner from possession of his goods. This is the basis on which each is liable to the owner. That is the nature of the tort of conversion. The wrongful acts of a previous possessor do not therefore diminish the plaintiff's claim in respect of the wrongful acts of a later possessor."

In *Kuwait Airways Corp v Iraqi Airways Co (Nos 4 and 5)*[250] the Iraqi Government seized 10 aircraft belonging to the claimants and the defendants subsequently converted them by incorporating them in their fleet pursuant to a decree which was not recognised by English law. Four were then destroyed on the ground by Allied bombing during the Gulf War, something which would probably have happened even if the defendants had not taken them over. Six were spirited away to Iran and eventually recovered by the claimants. As the law then stood,[251] the matters were only actionable in England if they: (a) amounted to a tort in English law; and (b) were civilly actionable under the law of Iraq. The claim failed in regard to the first four aircraft because in a case of destruction Iraqi law applied a "but-for" test, though the Court of Appeal (this matter was not considered in the House of Lords) thought there was liability in conversion in

---

[245] *Graham v Voigt* (1989) 89 A.C.T.R. 11.
[246] *Aziz v Lim* [2012] EWHC 915 (QB) (converted diamonds tracked to Geneva).
[247] *Kuwait Airways Corp v Iraqi Airways Co (Nos 4 and 5)* [2002] UKHL 19; [2002] 2 A.C. 883. Detention of a stallion turned out to be expensive in *Cash v CC Lancashire* [2008] EWHC 396 (Ch).
[248] *The Arpad* [1934] P. 189; *Saleslease Ltd v Davis* [1999] 1 W.L.R. 1664; *Checkprice (UK) Ltd (in administration) v Revenue & Customs Commissioners* [2010] EWHC 682 (Admin); [2010] S.T.C. 1153; cf. *France v Gaudet* (1871) L.R. 6 Q.B. 199, distinguished in *The Arpad*.
[249] *Kuwait Airways (Nos 4 and 5)* [2002] UKHL 19; [2002] 2 A.C. 883 at [82] per Lord Nicholls.
[250] [2002] UKHL 19; [2002] 2 A.C. 883.
[251] See para.18–023.

English law, unless perhaps it could be shown that the destruction was inevitable.[252] However, in the case of the other six the requirements of Iraqi law were no more stringent than those of the English law of conversion and accordingly it was no answer to the claim that if the defendants had not taken them the Iraqi Government would have retained them and probably flown them to Iran anyway.

Remoteness. The question may also arise, especially in relation to consequential losses, whether the damage suffered is too remote. In the *Kuwait Airways* case Lord Nicholls expressed the view that where the defendant converts the goods knowingly the test in deceit applies—was the loss the "direct and natural consequence" of the conversion?[253] Yet, where the conversion is innocent, although *liability* may be strict, the defendant is liable only for consequences which would be foreseeable on the basis of knowledge that the goods had been misappropriated.[254] On the facts, on any view the cost of hiring substitute aircraft and loss of business were to be expected; but when the claimants went into the market to buy replacement aircraft they did more than seek the most equivalent substitutes, they made significant changes in the structure of their fleet and although this was a commercially reasonable decision they were unable to recover the finance costs associated with it.[255]

18–055

D. Defendant Detaining Goods

The only remedy for conversion at common law was the purely personal one of damages. However, when the defendant was in possession of the goods and refused to deliver them up on demand his act was not only conversion but also detinue and the form of judgment in detinue might include an order for the delivery up of the goods.[256] Detinue has now been abolished but the remedies for

18–056

---

[252] See [2001] 3 W.L.R. 1251 at [606]. Suppose that a week after the conversion of an aircraft a design defect in the type was discovered and all such aircraft had to be scrapped. Is the defendant to be liable for their full market value at the date of the conversion?

[253] See para.12–021.

[254] *Kuwait Airways Corp v Iraqi Airways Co (Nos 4 and 5)* [2002] UKHL 19; [2002] 2 A.C. 883 at [100]–[104].

[255] See also *Sandeman Coprimar SA v Transitos y Transportes Integrales SL* [2003] EWCA Civ 113; [2003] Q.B. 1270 (loss of cartons; carrier unaware of consequent liability of consignor for customs duty).

[256] See the full discussion by Diplock LJ in *General and Finance Facilities Ltd v Cook Cars (Romford) Ltd* [1963] 1 W.L.R. 644 at 650–651. There were in fact three forms: (1) for the value of the chattel and damages for detention; (2) for the return of the chattel or recovery of its value as assessed and damages for detention; (3) for the return of the chattel and damages for detention.

conversion where goods are detained by the defendant[257] are now found in s.3 of the Torts (Interference with Goods) Act 1977, which is modelled on the common law remedies available for detinue.[258]

18–057   **Relief available under s.3 of the Torts (Interference with Goods) Act 1977.** The relief available under s.3 is in one of the following forms:[259] (1) an order for the delivery of the goods, and for payment of any consequential damages;[260] or (2) an order for delivery[261] of the goods, but giving the defendant the alternative of paying damages by reference to the value of the goods, together in either alternative[262] with payment of any consequential damages; or (3) damages.[263] Relief under (1) is at the discretion of the court, but the claimant may choose between (2) and (3).[264] If the claimant chooses damages the defendant cannot satisfy the judgment by returning the goods.[265]

It has traditionally been said (though there is nothing in s.3 to compel a court to take this line) that option (1), specific restitution, is apt only for rare articles or articles having a special value to the claimant and not for "ordinary articles of commerce".[266] Option (2) is said to be the commonest order in practice[267] but the value of the goods may have changed between wrong and the judgment and the statute contains no guidance as to the time at which the goods should be valued for the purpose of quantifying the damages which the defendant may choose to

---

[257] Except perhaps in the case of a "one man company", a director is not "in possession or control" of goods in the possession or control of the company: *Thunder Air Ltd v Hilmarsson* [2008] EWHC 355 (Ch); *Joiner v George* [2002] EWHC 90 (Ch); cf. *Mainline Private Hire Ltd v Nolan* [2011] EWCA Civ 189; [2011] C.T.L.C. 145 (possession of the defendant by way of possession of his bailee).

[258] *IBL Ltd v Coussens* [1991] 2 All E.R. 133 at 141. The section applies if the defendant ceases to be in possession between issue of proceedings and judgment: *Hillesden Securities Ltd v Ryjack Ltd* [1983] 1 W.L.R. 959.

[259] Section 3(2).

[260] See *Brandeis Goldschmidt Ltd v Western Transport Ltd* [1981] Q.B. 864, a case of detinue before the Act.

[261] At common law the form of judgment for detinue was that the claimant "do have delivery up" of the goods and while the defendant might have to facilitate their collection (*Metals & Ropes Co Ltd v Tattersall* [1966] 1 W.L.R. 1500) it was up to the claimant to go and get his goods. Quaere whether the rule is the same under the Act. Manchester (1977) 127 N.L.J. 1219 suggests that the court could order an actual redelivery by virtue of its power to impose conditions (s.3(6)) and it seems to be implied in *Howard E. Perry & Co Ltd v British Railways Board* [1980] 1 W.L.R. 1375, that a delivery could be ordered. Nonetheless, the wording of s.3(6) seems more apt for the imposition of conditions on the claimant.

[262] In *Tanks and Vessels Industries Ltd v Devon Cider Co Ltd* [2009] EWHC 1360 (Ch) consequential loss of use damages were only allowed if the defendant returned the goods, only interest being awarded if he chose to pay their value.

[263] i.e. assessed by reference to the value and the consequential loss. There is no reason to think the Act has changed the common law on consequential loss: *Trafigura Beheer BV v Mediterranean Shipping Co SA* [2007] EWCA Civ 794; [2007] 2 Lloyd's Rep 622 at [41].

[264] Section 3(3)(b).

[265] Section 3(5). Where there has been no fall in value it is thought that the court would still stay the action before judgment upon return of the goods: *Fisher v Prince* (1762) 3 Burr. 1363.

[266] See *Tanks and Vessels Industries Ltd v Devon Cider Co Ltd* [2009] EWHC 1360 (Ch); *Blue Sky One Ltd v Mahan Air* [2009] EWHC 3314 (Comm).

[267] If the defendant is in financial difficulties a judgment for damages alone is obviously unattractive to the claimant but this form of order if made for a specific date protects him: *Blue Sky One Ltd v Mahan Air* [2009] EWHC 3314 (Comm) at [323].

pay.[268] It was held in *IBL Ltd v Coussens* (which concerned cars which appreciated in value up to the time of trial) that it is inappropriate to lay down any hard and fast rule on this point and the value should be calculated by reference to such date as will fairly compensate the claimant for his loss if the defendant chooses to pay damages rather than return the goods,[269] though it has been said that the "general prima facie rule" is of assessment at the date of conversion.[270] There may be cases in which it will be found that the claimant could and should have replaced the converted goods at the time of the wrong or that he would have disposed of them at some later time, facts which would point towards taking the value at the time of the conversion or some intermediate time.[271] If, however, the claimant does not trade in the goods in question and acts reasonably[272] in seeking their return[273] it may be proper to take the value at the time of the trial.

E. Improvement of Goods

The problem of a converter improving goods is illustrated by *Munro v Willmott*.[274] The claimant was given a temporary licence to leave her car in the defendant's yard. After the car had been there for some years the defendant wished to convert the yard into a garage but was unable to communicate with the claimant. Accordingly, he "did up" the car (then worth £20) at a cost of £85 and then sold it for £100. In proceedings for conversion Lynskey J felt obliged to assess the value of the car at the date of judgment (£120) but he gave credit for the sum expended by the defendant, leaving £35 as the damages recoverable by the claimant.[275]

18–058

Torts (Interference with Goods) Act 1977, s.6. The matter is now governed by s.6 of the Torts (Interference with Goods) Act 1977 which provides that if the

18–059

---

[268] At common law it was said that in conversion the value was taken at the time of the conversion, in detinue at the time of the judgment.

[269] *IBL Ltd v Coussens* [1991] 2 All E.R. 133; *Trafigura Beheer BV v Mediterranean Shipping Co SA* [2007] EWHC 944 (Comm); [2007] 2 All E.R. (Com) 149 (affirmed on this point [2007] EWCA Civ 794; [2007] 2 Lloyd's Rep 622).

[270] *Kuwait Airways Corp v Iraqi Airways Co (Nos 4 and 5)* [2002] UKHL 19; [2002] 2 A.C. 883 at [67]; *BBMB Finance (Hong Kong) v Eda Holdings* [1990] 1 W.L.R. 409.

[271] In *Irving v Keen* Unreported March 3, 1995 CA, C was "incredibly lackadaisical" about getting his classic car back from D, a repairer, and settling the bill. D detained it for some years, during which it increased in value, but finally sold major parts of it and returned the remainder as scrap. Since there was no conversion until the sale of the parts, that was the earliest point at which damages could be set; cf. *Sachs v Micklos* [1948] 2 K.B. 23.

[272] Cf. *Radford v De Froberville* [1977] 1 W.L.R. 1262, another example of a general drift away from a general "breach date" rule.

[273] If the claimant replaces the goods and goes for damages only he obviously takes a risk in respect of the defendant's solvency when the matter comes to trial.

[274] *Munro v Willmott* [1949] 1 K.B. 295; *Reid v Fairbanks* (1853) 13 C.B. 692.

[275] It is submitted that the correct approach on the conversion count (there was an alternative count for detinue) would have been to assess the value at the date of conversion. On the basis of *Greenwood v Bennett* [1973] Q.B. 195 it seems that the defendant committed two acts of conversion (beginning work on the car and selling it) and that the claimant could rely on either. It has been held at first instance that where a series of acts of conversion constitute a continuous course of conduct the claimant can only claim the value at the beginning: *Highland Leasing v Paul Field* [1986] 2 C.L. 276; but cf. *The Saetta* [1994] 1 All E.R. 851 at 859.

improver acted in the mistaken but honest belief that he had a good title, an allowance is to be made for the extent to which the value of the goods, at the time at which it falls to be assessed, is attributable to the improvement.[276] The requirement of good faith would seem to make the law somewhat narrower than it was before.[277]

F. Effect of Judgment

18–060 Where damages for wrongful interference are assessed on the basis that the claimant is being compensated for the whole of his interest in the goods[278] (including a case where judgment is subject to a reduction for contributory negligence)[279] payment of the damages or of any settlement[280] in full extinguishes the claimant's title to that interest in the goods.[281] Until payment of the damages, however, the claimant retains his property in the goods and may exercise all his rights as owner even after judgment has been given in his favour. In *Ellis v John Stenning & Son*[282] A sold land to B, reserving to himself the right to cut and sell the uncut timber on the land. He then sold the timber to E. B wrongfully removed some of the timber and E obtained judgment against him for conversion but took no steps to enforce his judgment, because B was insolvent. B sold the timber to S. E then sued S for conversion of the timber. It was held that S was liable because, the judgment against B not having been satisfied, title to the timber remained with E.[283]

---

[276] Section 6(1).

[277] See, however, Palmer, *Bailment*, 3rd edn (2009), para.4–156, arguing that s.6 is in addition to rather than a replacement of the common law. It must also be pointed out that under s.12 of the 1977 Act the defendant in *Munro v Willmott* might now have a lawful power of sale though this does not help with the cost of improvement. The Act also provides for an allowance in favour of a defendant who is a bona fide purchaser of the car from the improver (who in this instance need not act bona fide), since though not an improver he will normally have paid a price reflecting the improved value (s.6(2)). See also s.6(3) (allowance in action for recovery of purchase price on total failure of consideration).

[278] For example, where the defendant's trespass or negligence has destroyed them or where they have been wrongfully disposed of. A judgment in respect of mere damage has no effect upon title.

[279] As where the defendant has negligently destroyed the goods. Contributory negligence is no defence to conversion or intentional trespass: para.18–041.

[280] See s.5(2). Where a claimant settles with one of two or more defendants the onus is upon him to establish that the settlement was not one which compensated him for the whole of his interest in the goods: *Macaulay v Screenkarn Ltd* [1987] F.S.R. 257.

[281] Section 5. This provision has no application, however, where the damages paid are limited to some lesser amount by virtue of any enactment or rule of law (e.g. under the Merchant Shipping Act 1995 or under the Carriage by Air Act 1961). The claimant's title is, therefore, presumably extinguished where there is a valid limitation of liability clause in a contract not governed by such statutory codes.

[282] [1932] 2 Ch. 81.

[283] E could not then enforce the judgment in full against both B and S: *Clerk and Lindsell on Torts*, 20th edn (2013), para.17–125.

CHAPTER 19

INTERFERENCE WITH CONTRACT OR BUSINESS[1]

---

[1] Carty, *An Analysis of the Economic Torts* (2000); Weir, *The Economic Torts*, (1997); Heydon, *Economic Torts*, 2nd edn; *Clerk and Lindsell on Torts*, 20th edn (2013), Ch.25.

D.   Remedies   **19–091**

1. INTRODUCTION

19–001   In this chapter we are concerned with a group of torts the function of which is to protect some of a person's intangible interests—those which may loosely be called his business interests—from unlawful interference. As we have already seen, the law has been less ready to protect these interests from negligently inflicted harm than it has been to protect persons and tangible property,[2] but we are now in the main[3] concerned only with liability for intended harm. It is not possible, however, to say simply that whenever one person intentionally causes harm to another that is a tort for, as we have also seen, the mere fact that my motive in performing an otherwise lawful act is to cause damage to another will not of itself make the act tortious.[4] This is so even if my motive is malevolence and it is a fortiori so if my motive is to advance my own interests even at the inevitable cost of harming my competitor's. There is more truth in the proposition that it is tortious intentionally to cause damage to a person's economic interests by an *unlawful* act, though even that would go a good deal too far as an unqualified statement.

19–002   **The principal heads of liability.** The law has developed around four situations which we must keep separate. First, it is a tort for the defendant D to induce or procure the breach of A's contract with the claimant C: that is a form of "accessory liability" for A's breach of contract and requires nothing independently unlawful on A's part.[5] Secondly, D may be liable to C if, with the intention of injuring C, he uses unlawful means against A in order to affect A's ability to deal with C.[6] Thirdly, D may be liable to C if, with the intention of injuring C, he uses unlawful means directly against C even if those unlawful means are not in themselves some other tort.[7] Fourthly, where two persons, D1 and D2 combine to injure C they may be liable for the tort of conspiracy. This tort has two forms: where unlawful means are used[8] or where the predominant purpose of the conspirators is to injure C (e.g. out of motives of revenge), in the latter case no unlawful means being required.[9]

19–003   **"Intention" and "unlawful".** Under all of these heads two difficulties have constantly recurred: the meaning of "intention" and that of "unlawful". A good deal of welcome clarity was brought to the first and second heads of liability by the decision of the House of Lords in *OBG Ltd v Allan*;[10] and to some extent to the fourth head by the further decision of their Lordships in *Revenue and*

---

[2] See the discussion of "economic loss" in para.5–059.
[3] Except in the case of passing off, though here, too, the harm is usually intended.
[4] See para.3–012.
[5] See paras 19–006—19–018.
[6] See paras 19–019—19–028.
[7] See paras 19–029—19–034.
[8] See paras 19–044—19–048.
[9] See paras 19–036—19–043.
[10] [2007] UKHL 21; [2008] 1 A.C.1.

Customs Commisioners v Total Network SL[11] (though in such a way as to produce a questionable distinction between this and the first two heads). The scope of the third head remains obscure. These cases substantially reinterpreted many of the earlier decisions and are the basis of the present structure of the law.

Trade disputes. A great many of the cases in this area of the law are concerned with industrial strife of one kind or another and where this is so the common law has been excluded or modified since 1906 by statutory immunities granted to persons acting in a "trade dispute". The scope of this immunity was subject to repeated change from the 1970s to the 1990s. Since the legislation assumes the existence of the common law background we must first endeavour to ascertain the general principles governing this area of tort and then see shortly how it is affected when there is a trade dispute.[12]

19–004

Competition law. The torts considered in this chapter may also come into question in cases of alleged unlawful competition between traders,[13] but in practice they are of limited significance because of the common law's refusal to adopt any principle of "fair competition" other than the prohibition of obviously unlawful acts like torts and breaches of contract. Any full study of "unfair competition" would have to take account of the legislation (now with a major European dimension) protecting intangible business property like trademarks and patents,[14] and of the statutory controls over restrictive trading agreements and monopolies. The last two for long had little or nothing to do with anything resembling the law of tort. However, one of the most significant sources of competition law is the Treaty on the Functioning of the European Union and the relevant provisions are directly applicable in England. Article 101 prohibits agreements which have the effect of restricting or distorting competition and art.102 prohibits the "abuse of a dominant [market] position". These provisions give rise to a civil right of action here for breach of statutory duty or something very like it and damages may therefore be obtained.[15] However, the Competition Act 1998 remodelled municipal competition law along the lines of the Treaty. The Act as enacted was silent on its private law consequences and if standing alone would perhaps not be of the type which gave rise by implication to a private law action, but it would be strange if there were different remedial consequences between two systems which were substantively very similar, and the Government thought that it would give rise to civil actions in the same way and to the same extent as the Treaty provisions do. Now, s.47A[16] makes express reference to claims for damages in connection with appeals to the Competition Appeal Tribunal. These are matters well outside the scope of a general book on tort law.

19–005

---

[11] [2008] UKHL 19; [2008] A.C. 1174. On these cases see Carty 124 L.Q.R. 641 and Deakin and Randall (2009) 72 M.L.R. 519.

[12] See paras 19–050—19–071.

[13] One of the "foundation" cases, *Mogul SS Co Ltd v McGregor Gow & Co* [1892] A.C. 25 arose from attempts by a cartel to monopolise the China tea trade.

[14] See specialist works, such as *Kerly's Law of Trade Marks and Trade Names*, 15th edn; *Terrel on the law of Patents*, 17th edn; *Copinger and Skone James on Copyright*, 16th edn. There is a substantial outline of these areas in *Clerk and Lindsell on Torts*, 20th edn (2013), Ch.25.

[15] See para.8–015.

[16] Inserted by the Enterprise Act 2002.

2. INDUCING OR PROCURING A BREACH OF CONTRACT

19–006   **Origins and summary: Lumley v Gye.** D commits a tort against C if, without lawful justification, he induces or procures A to break A's contract with C. The origin of this form of liability lies in the mid-19th century in *Lumley v Gye*.[17] The claimant's declaration alleged that he was owner of the Queen's Theatre, that he had contracted with Johanna Wagner,[18] a famous operatic singer, for her to perform exclusively in the theatre for a certain time and that the defendant, owner of a rival theatre, wishing himself to obtain Miss Wagner's services, "knowing the premises and maliciously intending to injure the plaintiff . . . enticed and persuaded [her] to refuse to perform". The claim succeeded on demurrer[19] on the basis, according to the majority of the court, that the action for enticement could be extended beyond the strict relation of master and servant to embrace other contracts for personal services, but support was also given in varying degrees to a broader view that a claimant might sue for the knowing violation of any contractual right.

19–007   **A form of "accessory liability".** In *Bowen v Hall*,[20] on rather similar facts, the Court of Appeal accepted the broader proposition and doubted whether *Lumley v Gye* could in fact be based upon the narrower ground of enticement. The rule that inducing or procuring another to break his contract could be actionable at the suit of the other contracting party who suffered damage thereby was only accepted in the face of strong dissent because it appeared to outflank privity of contract.[21] While it was argued in *Lumley v Gye* that the claimant ought to be satisfied with his action for breach of contract against the party induced, Crompton J said that the latter might be incapable of paying all the damages.[22] Of course, every contractor accepts the risk of insolvency in his co-contractor, but at least in the case of a contract for services he does not accept it in combination with the procurement of a breach by a third party. It has sometimes been said to rest on a property analogy[23] and commercial contractual relations had become valuable rights which could be regarded as entitled to at least some of the protection given by the law to property, but the requirements of knowledge and intent make this tort considerably more restrictive than conversion or trespass. The current view is that it is a form of "accessory" liability, that is to say the person who induces the breach incurs an additional liability in tort for the effects of the "primary" breach of contract.[24]

---

[17] (1853) 2 Bl. & Bl. 216.

[18] Students of contract will be familiar with *Lumley v Wagner* (1852) 1 De G.M. & G. 604, in which the claimant obtained an injunction against Miss Wagner.

[19] Lumley eventually lost, the trial jury finding that Gye believed that Wagner's contract was not binding: Waddams 117 L.Q.R. 431.

[20] (1881) 6 Q.B.D. 333.

[21] By Coleridge J in *Lumley v Gye* (1853) 2 Bl. & Bl. 216, and Lord Coleridge CJ in *Bowen v Hall* (1881) 6 Q.B.D. 333.

[22] *Lumley v Gye* (1853) 2 Bl. & Bl. 216 at 230; *OBG Ltd v Allan* [2007] UKHL 21; [2008] 1 A.C.1 at [32].

[23] See Bagshaw (1998) O.J.L.S. 729 and the discussion in *Zhu v Treasurer of NSW* [2004] HCA 56; 218 C.L.R.530 beginning at [123].

[24] *OBG v Allan* [2007] UKHL 21; [2008] 1 A.C. 1 at [3], [172], [320].

A. A Breach of Contract

Since this is a form of accessory liability it is necessary for D to be liable that **19–008**
there must have been a breach of contract by A against C.[25] Hence in *Allen v
Flood*[26] the defendant, an official of the boilermakers' trade union, told shipyard
owners that his members would not work unless Flood, a non-member who had
done ironwork, was discharged. Flood was dismissed but since he was engaged
by the day the owners committed no breach of contract and this tort was not
therefore committed by Allen.[27]

No liability for "interference" without any breach. At one time there was a **19–009**
view that there was a wider liability, even if no unlawful means were used, of
"interference" with the performance of a contract short of procuring a breach[28] at
least if the interference was "direct" (though it was never very clear what that
meant). That view is exploded by *OBG Ltd v Allan*.[29] No one suggests that,
without the use of unlawful means, it is a tort for D to persuade A not to contract
with C, for that is what competitors in business do every day (and are encouraged
to do). It cannot be different if there is an existing contract between A and C and
without unlawful means D persuades A to terminate it by proper notice. It would
be a strange law which said that if A could terminate his maintenance contract
with C on a month's notice, D could be liable for persuading A to do so and hand
the task to him. Whether a breach has been induced may, of course, turn on the
proper construction of the contract between A and C.[30]

Void and voidable contracts. If the contract between A and C is void for **19–010**
contravention of the law there can be no action for inducing breach of it.[31] If the
contract between A and C is voidable and D persuades A to exercise his right to
avoid the contract with C it is thought that this should plainly not be actionable by

[25] *OBG v Allan* [2007] UKHL 21 [2008] 1 A.C. 1 at [44]. The claimant may, of course, obtain a quia
timet injunction to restrain a threatened inducement. It has been said that the tort is capable of
extending to interference with a "secondary right to a remedy", but only where violation of the
secondary right is itself an actionable wrong: *Law Debenture Trust Ltd v Ural Caspian Oil Corp Ltd*
[1995] Ch. 152, where C failed because the transfer of shares from D1 to D2 meant that D2 had only
interfered with C's contingent right to obtain an order against D1 calling for the transfer of the shares
to C in circumstances where the transfer from D1 to D2 was not unlawful. In a memorable clash
between two of the most influential judges, Lord Bingham MR commented: "In concentrating on the
right, it seems to me that the judge (Hoffmann LJ, sitting as an additional judge of the Chancery
Division) did take his eye off the wrong."
[26] [1898] A.C. 1.
[27] Nor was there any unlawful means (see the next section) by a threat of breach of contract by the
boilermakers since they, too, were employed by the day.
[28] See, e.g. Lord Denning MR in *Torquay Hotel Co Ltd v Cousins* [1969] 2 Ch. 106 at 138.
[29] See, e.g. Lord Nicholls in *OBG* [2007] UKHL 21; [2008] 1 A.C. 1 at [185].
[30] In the *Torquay Hotel* case, which arose from the "blacking" by unions of fuel supplies to the hotel,
there was a force majeure clause in Esso's contract with the hotel. As Lord Nicholls points out in
OBG, if a contracting party chooses to succumb to persuasion not to perform, such a clause will not be
applicable and there will be a breach. Consider, however, a case where A's contract excuses
performance for inability to obtain supplies and D, in order to strike at C, corners the market and
refuses to supply A. There is no breach of contract induced, nor any unlawful means for the purposes
of the tort in the next section.
[31] *De Francesco v Barnum* (1890) 45 Ch. D. 430; *Joe Lee Ltd v Dalmeny* [1927] 1 Ch. 300; *Said v
Butt* [1920] 3 K.B. 497; *Associated British Ports Ltd v TGWU* [1989] 3 All E.R. 796 at 816.

C[32] and it has been held that D is equally not liable where he induces A not to perform the voidable contract without any formal avoidance.[33] If, on the other hand, it is C who has the right to avoid the contract there seems no reason why D should be allowed to set up its voidability in a claim by C.

B. Knowledge and Intention of the Defendant

19–011   **Knowledge of the contract and of its breach.** All are agreed that there is no liability under this tort for negligently interfering with a person's rights under contract (though the law of negligence may give limited protection in certain circumstances).[34] The tort presupposes knowledge of the contract but that does not mean knowledge of all its details. As Lord Denning MR said in *Emerald Construction Co Ltd v Lowthian*:[35]

> "Even if [the union officials] did not know the actual terms of the contract, but had the means of knowledge—which they deliberately disregarded—that would be enough. Like the man who turns a blind eye. So here, if the officers deliberately sought to get this contract terminated, heedless of its terms, regardless whether it was terminated by breach or not, they would do wrong. For it is unlawful for a third person to procure a breach of contract knowingly, or recklessly, indifferent whether it is a breach or not."

This state of mind of conscious indifference is not the same as negligence,[36] though of course the required state of mind may be inferred as a matter of evidence from circumstances which would have caused suspicion to a reasonable person. There is no general duty actively to inquire about contracts with others[37] and a supplier of services is not obliged to infer, from the fact that the services are obviously already being supplied by another, that there is a continuing contract, breach of which he must be careful not to induce.[38] In *Mainstream Properties Ltd v Young*, one of the three appeals reported as *OBG Ltd v Allan*,[39] the defendant had provided finance for a development venture by A and B, employees of the claimant development company. The risk that this was in conflict with their duties to the company was obvious and the defendant raised this issue with them but it was held that he was entitled to accept their assertion that the land had been offered to the company and it had declined.[40] At one time the view was taken that

---

[32] So assumed in *Greig v Insole* [1978] 1 W.L.R. 302.

[33] *Proform Sports Management Ltd v Proactive Sports Management Ltd* [2006] EWHC 22903 (Ch); [2007] 1 All E.R. 542.

[34] See para.5–057.

[35] [1966] 1 WLR 691 at 700; *Greig v Insole* [1978] 1 W.L.R. 302.

[36] *OBG v Allan* [2007] UKHL 21; [2008] 1 A.C. 1 at [41]; *Kallang Shipping SA Panama v Axa Assurances Senegal* [2008] EWHC 2761 (Comm); [2009] 1 Lloyd's Rep 124.

[37] *Leitch & Co v Leydon* [1931] A.C. 90.

[38] *Schindler Lifts Australia Pty Ltd v Debelak* (1989) 89 A.L.R. 275; *Unique Pub Properties Ltd v Beer Barrels and Minerals (Wales) Ltd* [2004] EWCA Civ 586; [2005] 1 All E.R. (Comm.) 181.

[39] [2007] UKHL 21; [2008] 1 A.C. 1.

[40] Perhaps to be seen as another case where, in accepting the defendant's evidence the court had "vindicated [his] honesty ... at the expense of his intelligence": *British Industrial Plastics Ltd v Ferguson* [1938] 4 All ER 504, 513; cf. *Led Technologies Pty Ltd v Roadvision Pty Ltd* [2012] FCA 3; (2012) 287 A.L.R. 1 at [54]. Contrast *Aerostar Maintenance International Ltd v Wilson* [2010] EWHC 2032 (Ch).

there would be liability if the defendant intended to bring about a situation where there would as a matter of law be a breach of contract even though he mistakenly believed there would not.[41] The contrary view is taken in clear terms in *OBG Ltd v Allan*: "It is not enough that you know that you are procuring an act which, as a matter of law or construction of the contract, is a breach. You must actually realize that it will have this effect. Nor does it matter that you ought reasonably to have done so."[42]

Intention to cause the breach of contract as an end or as a means to an end.   **19–012**
The defendant must intend to bring about a breach of the contract but that is not necessarily the same thing as saying that he must intend to cause damage to the claimant. In *South Wales Miners' Federation v Glamorgan Coal Co Ltd*[43] it did not help the union, when it induced breaches of employment contracts by calling a strike, to argue that its intention, "was, OPEC-like, to restrict production of coal and thereby raise its price"[44] thereby benefiting the coal owners as well as the workers. The meaning of intention does not give rise to much difficulty in this tort[45] (intentionally causing loss by unlawful means is a rather different matter)[46] since, given knowledge that your non-performance of your contract with C will be a breach of it, I can hardly persuade you not to perform it without intending to bring about a breach.[47] However, it certainly does not matter that I have no *desire* to injure C and am doing this simply in order to benefit myself: it is sufficient that A intended to bring about a breach as a means to an end, if not as an end in itself.[48]

C.   The Inducement

A question of intention and causation. There must be persuasion directed at[49] a   **19–013**
party to the contract. Doing something which has the inevitable consequence of causing that party to be in breach is not this tort, though it may lead to liability if unlawful means are used.[50] A distinction may be taken between persuasion and

---

[41] See, e.g. *Solihull MBC v National Union of Teachers* [1985] I.R.L.R. 211.
[42] [2007] UKHL 21; [2008] 1 A.C. 1 at [39] per Lord Hoffmann (see also Lord Nicholls at [202]); *Meretz Investments NV v ACP Ltd* [2007] EWCA Civ 1303; [2008] Ch. 244.
[43] [1905] AC 239.
[44] *OBG v Allan* [2007] UKHL 21; [2008] 1 A.C. 1 at [8] per Lord Hoffmann.
[45] In the case of a corporate defendant the claimant may have the evidential difficulty of identifying the individuals with the requisite knowledge and intent: *Porton Capital Technology Funds v 3M UK Holdings Ltd* [2011] EWHC 2895 (Comm) at [356].
[46] See para.19–026.
[47] cf. *Qantas Airways v Transport Workers Union of Australia* [2011] FCA 470; (2011) 280 A.L.R. 503 at [442]–[444]. Persuasion directed at a third party lawfully to decline to deal with A does not give rise to liability to C where this foreseeably brings about a breach of A's contract with C: *Middlebrook Mushrooms Ltd v TGWU* [1993] I.C.R. 612 (leafletting and picketing of supermarkets, persuasion directed at customers, exhorting them not to buy C's mushrooms sold in supermarket).
[48] "Mr Gye would very likely have preferred to be able to obtain Miss Wagner's services without her having to break her contract. But that did not matter": *OBG v Allan* [2007] UKHL 21; [2008] 1 A.C. 1 at [42] per Lord Hoffmann.
[49] There need be no individual contact between A and D: *Greig v Insole* [1978] 1 W.L.R. 302 (resolutions and press statement by cricket governing body).
[50] *Meretz Investments NV v ACP Ltd* [2007] EWCA Civ 1303; [2008] Ch 244.

mere advice, and advice in the sense of, "a mere statement of, or drawing of the attention of the party addressed, to the state of facts as they were",[51] is not actionable.[52] However, it has been said that advice which is intended to have persuasive effect is not distinguishable from inducement.[53] Further, "the fact that an inducement to break a contract is couched as an irresistible embargo rather than in terms of seduction does not make it any the less an inducement".[54]

It is submitted that the issue is really one of intention and causation.[55] If D's words were intended to cause and did cause A to break his contract with C, then they are actionable by C whatever their form. If so, bearing in mind that intention in this context is not the same as motive and that the tort may be committed without any ill will towards the claimant, it is likely to be a rare case in which D's words have had a causative effect on A's conduct and yet D escapes liability on the ground that they were only "advice".[56] If the inducement of A takes the form of wrongful threats against him there will be an overlap with the tort of intentionally causing damage by unlawful means (considered in the next section) this form being commonly known as intimidation.[57] It has been said that "even silence in certain circumstances can be persuasive in encouraging a breach of contract and can intend to do so".[58]

19–014   **Entering inconsistent contracts.** Liability under this head may arise from D's entering into a contract with A knowing that the contract is inconsistent with a prior contract of A's with C, as in *BMTA v Salvadori*[59] where D bought a car from A knowing that the sale constituted a breach by A of his contract with C that he would not sell the car within a year. However, while statements of principle are often couched in terms that merely knowingly entering into the transaction

---

[51] *DC Thomson & Co Ltd v Deakin* [1952] Ch. 646 at 686.

[52] A direction to do something which may be done lawfully or unlawfully cannot be said to induce wrongs committed by those who respond unlawfully, even if the person giving it harbours a secret desire that it be done unlawfully: *Sanders v Snell* (1998) 157 A.L.R. 491; and see *CBS Songs Ltd v Amstrad Consumer Electronics Plc* [1988] A.C. 1013 (provision of machines capable of being used for breach of copyright).

[53] *Camden Nominees Ltd v Forcey* [1940] Ch. 352 at 366; *DC Thomson & Co Ltd v Deakin* [1952] Ch. 646 at 686. Cf. the difficult case of *Stocznia Gdanska SA v Latvian Shipping Co* [2002] EWCA Civ 889; [2002] 2 Lloyd's Rep. 436, where the passage at [107] might be thought to question whether persuasion (as opposed to instruction) is sufficient. However, the case is best regarded as turning on the fact that the claim had been pleaded as one of instruction.

[54] *JT Stratford & Co Ltd v Lindley* [1965] A.C. 269 at 333 per Lord Pearce; *Greig v Insole* [1978] 1 W.L.R. 302.

[55] "[D]id the defendant's acts of encouragement, threat, persuasion and so forth have a sufficient causal connection with the breach by the contracting party to attract accessory liability?": *OBG v Allan* [2007] UKHL 21; [2008] 1 A.C. 1 at [36] per Lord Hoffmann.

[56] The defence of justification (para.19–016) might be relevant in a case of disinterested advice.

[57] Since the breach induced can constitute the necessary unlawful means, D and A may also be guilty of conspiracy by unlawful means: *Aerostar Maintenance International Ltd v Wilson* [2010] EWHC 2032 (Ch) at [171]–[172].

[58] *Lonmar Global Risks Ltd v West* [2010] EWHC 2878 (QB); [2011] I.R.L.R. 138 at [220]; cf. *Premier Model Management Ltd v Bruce* [2012] EWHC 3509 (QB) at [57] (silent receipt of information by D sent by A in breach of his contract with C, but there were also findings that D was not guilty of mere silence).

[59] [1949] Ch. 556.

amounts to the tort,[60] it is not wholly clear that this is so where the defendant merely accedes to an initiative of the contracting party.[61] Where the prior contract of A and C is specifically enforceable it would create an equitable interest in the subject matter in favour of C, which C could enforce against D even if D had only constructive notice of C's rights.[62] In many cases this would render consideration of D's tort liability in a case of actual knowledge otiose, but it seems possible to assert such a claim where there is some additional loss.[63]

Inducement by a servant. If my servant, acting bona fide within the scope of his authority, procures or causes me to break a contract which I have made with you, you cannot sue the servant for interference with the contract (despite the principle that the servant is generally liable as well as his employer) for he is my alter ego here, and I cannot be sued for inducing myself to break a contract, although I may be liable for breaking the contract. In *Said v Butt*[64] the claimant wished to get a ticket for X's theatre. He knew that X would not sell him one because they had quarrelled. He therefore persuaded a friend to procure him a ticket without disclosing his identity. When the claimant presented himself at the theatre, the defendant, who was X's manager of the theatre, detected the claimant and refused to admit him. He sued the defendant for procuring a breach of his contract with X. The action was dismissed because there was no contract, since the identity of the claimant was, in the circumstances, material to the formation of the alleged contract; and alternatively, even if there had been a valid contract, the principle stated above would prevent the action from lying.[65] If the servant does not act bona fide, he is liable on the ground that he has ceased to be his employer's alter ego.[66] It is true that even then he might still be acting in the course of his employment, but we must take it that this curious piece of metaphysics exempts the employer from vicarious liability for this particular tort.

19–015

D. Defence of Justification

An inexact definition. It is certain that justification is capable of being a defence to this tort, but what constitutes justification is incapable of exact definition.[67] It has been said that regard must be had to the nature of the contract broken, the position of the parties to the contract, the grounds for the breach, the means employed to procure it, the relation of the person procuring it to the person who

19–016

---

[60] *DC Thomson & Co Ltd v Deakin* [1952] Ch. 646 at 694; *Law Debenture Trust Ltd v Ural Caspian Oil Corp Ltd* [1993] 1 W.L.R. 138 at 151.

[61] *Batts Combe Quarry Ltd v Ford* [1943] Ch. 51.

[62] That is to say, unless D was a bona fide purchaser for value without notice.

[63] See *Pritchard v Briggs* [1980] Ch. 338, though on the facts the majority of the court rejected a claim for damages.

[64] [1920] 3 K.B. 497.

[65] Approved by Greer LJ in *Scammell Ltd v Hurley* [1929] 1 K.B. 419 at 443; cf. Scrutton and Sankey LJJ at 436, 449. This principle will protect company directors who vote to cause a breach of contract: *Crystalens Ltd v White* Unreported July 7, 2006 QBD; *O'Brien v Dawson* (1942) 66 C.L.R. 18. See also *Welsh Development Agency v Export Finance Co Ltd* [1992] BCLC 148, CA (receivers).

[66] *DC Thomson & Co Ltd v Deakin* [1952] Ch. 646 at 681 per Evershed MR.

[67] Cf. the more definite privileges in defamation. For the defence of statutory authority, see *Whittaker v Child Support Registrar* [2010] FCA 43; (2010) 264 A.L.R. 473.

breaks the contract, and the object of the person procuring the breach.[68] The advancement of one's own interests will not suffice, nor will that of the interests of one's own group[69] and the defendant cannot escape by showing that his motives are impersonal, disinterested and altruistic.[70] However, in *Brimelow v Casson*,[71] persuasion of theatre proprietors by a theatrical performers' protection society to break their contracts with a theatrical manager was justified on the grounds that the wage paid by the manager to chorus girls was so low that they were obliged to supplement it by resort to prostitution.[72] It has been suggested that pressure of a moral[73] obligation as justification is the basis of *Brimelow v Casson*, though the case has been said to stand alone[74] and there are conflicting dicta on moral obligation.[75] Presumably there is justification when a doctor urges[76] his patient to give up fixed-term employment because it is a danger to his health,[77] but what of the tutor who insists that his student give up a vacation job because it will interfere with his studies?[78]

19–017   **Inconsistent contracts.** The question of justification may also arise where D seeks to assert rights under a contract with A which is inconsistent with another contract between A and C. The question here is whether D has a right equal or superior to that of C and if he has he is justified in persuading A to break his contract with C. So if A enters into a contract on Monday to sell to D for £10,000 and then next day to sell the same property to C for £15,000, D, by persuading A to perform the first contract commits no wrong against C.[79] D will also be justified in reaching an accommodation with A rather than exercising his strict legal rights under the contract. In *Edwin Hill & Partners v First National Finance Corp*[80] a finance company which had a legal charge over A's property to secure a loan came to an arrangement with A whereby they would develop the property themselves rather than exercise their power of sale under the charge. A condition

---

[68] *Glamorgan Coal Co Ltd v S Wales Miners' Federation* [1903] 2 K.B. 545 at 574–575 per Romer LJ.

[69] *S Wales Miners' Federation v Glamorgan Coal Co Ltd* [1905] A.C. 239; *Camden Nominees Ltd v Forcey* [1940] Ch. 352; *Greig v Insole* [1978] 1 W.L.R. 302.

[70] *Greig v Insole* [1978] 1 W.L.R. 302; *Posluns v Toronto Stock Exchange* (1964) 46 D.L.R. (2d) 210 at 270 (affirmed (1968) 67 D.L.R. (2d) 165); *Slade & Stewart Ltd v Haynes* (1969) 5 D.L.R. (3d) 736.

[71] [1924] 1 Ch. 302.

[72] Cf. *Stott v Gamble* [1916] 2 K.B. 504 (banning of film under statutory powers).

[73] *Pritchard v Briggs* [1980] Ch. 338 at 416 per Goff LJ.

[74] *Camden Nominees Ltd v Forcey* [1940] Ch. 352 at 366 per Simmonds J; *Pritchard v Briggs* [1980] Ch. 338 at 416 per Goff LJ.; *Timeplan Education Group v NUT* [1996] I.R.L.R. 457 at 460.

[75] For example, *South Wales Miners' Federation v Glamorgan Coal Co Ltd* [1905] A.C. 239 at 245, 246, 249, 255; *Crofter Hand-Woven Harris Tweed Co v Veitch* [1942] A.C. 435 at 443, where the example is given of a man inducing his daughter not to marry a "scoundrel" (but engagement is no longer a contract).

[76] It is assumed that the advice is "persuasive" in the sense explained in para.19–013.

[77] Might not this give the patient lawful justification for withdrawing from the contract?

[78] The *Restatement* 2d., ss.770 and 772 treat as justification: (1) unrequested advice from a person charged with responsibility for the welfare of the other; and (2) all other honest advice if requested.

[79] *Smithies v National Association of Operative Plasterers* [1909] 1 K.B. 310 at 337.

[80] [1989] 1 W.L.R. 225; cf. *Meretz Investments NV v ACP Ltd* [2007] EWCA Civ 1303; [2008] Ch 244 at [142]; *Sar Petroleum Inc v Peace Hills Trust Co* [2010] NBCA 22; (2010) 318 D.L.R. (4th) 70 NBCA.

in this arrangement whereby the claimant was to be replaced as architect for the scheme did not constitute inducing breach of contract.[81]

E.   Inducing Breaches of Other Obligations

Although the principle of *Lumley v Gye* commonly appears under the heading of inducing breach of contract it has been regarded as a wider principle covering violation of legal rights.[82] It has been said that there is no need to call up the tort where the wrong procured is itself a tort against the claimant, for the procurer is then himself liable as a joint tortfeasor,[83] but the courts have recognised a cause of action for inducing breach of statutory duty where the statutory duty gives rise to a private right on behalf of the claimant[84] actionable by him in the courts.[85] There is no tort of inducing breach of trust because a person who procures such an act becomes himself, by the doctrines of equity, liable as a trustee and it is said that is sufficient to protect the beneficiary under the trust.[86] The tort liability probably extends to procuring breaches of equitable obligations such as that of confidence but the readiness of the courts to restrain the use of confidential information by the third party who acquires it makes the point of limited importance in most cases.[87] However, these issues are not discussed in *OBG Ltd v Allan* and Lord Nicholls said that he left "open the question of how far the *Lumley v Gye* principle applies equally to inducing a breach of other actionable obligations such as statutory duties or equitable or fiduciary obligations".[88]

19–018

3.   INTENTIONALLY CAUSING LOSS BY UNLAWFUL MEANS

A tort of "primary liability". This tort was the source of much confusion in the 20th century but its nature and its relationship with inducing breach of contract have been considerably clarified by *OBG Ltd v Allan*, at least in the case where it

19–019

---

[81] It appears that the claimant had succeeded in an action against A for breach of contract: (1984) 272 E.G. 63 at 179. It was common ground that if the claimants had appointed a receiver or sold the property a new architect could have been appointed. According to the High Court of Australia justification has to be found in a superior right of a proprietary nature and competing contractual rights, even if prior in time, will not do: *Zhu v Treasurer of NSW* [2004] HCA 56; 218 C.L.R. 530.

[82] "It is clear that the procurement of the violation of a right is a cause of action in all instances where the violation is an actionable wrong, as in violations of a right to property, whether real or personal, or to personal security...": *Lumley v Gye*(1853) 2 Bl. & Bl. 216, 232 per Erle J; cf. *Quinn v Leathem* [1901] A.C. 495 at 510 per Lord Macnaghten; *F v Wirral Metropolitan Council* [1991] Fam. 69 at 107.

[83] *CBS Songs Ltd v Amstrad Consumer Electronics Plc* [1988] A.C. 1013 at 1058; cf. *Belegging, etc. BV v Witten Industrial Diamonds Ltd* [1979] F.S.R. 59 at 66.

[84] *Meade v Haringey LBC* [1979] 1 W.L.R. 637; *Associated British Ports v TGWU* [1989] 3 All E.R. 822 (reversed on other grounds, at 822). See Ch.8.

[85] *Wilson v Housing Corp* [1997] I.R.L.R. 345 (no tort of inducing unfair dismissal).

[86] *Metall und Rohstoff AG v Donaldson Lufkin & Jenrette Inc* [1990] 1 Q.B. 391 (where it was sought to found the claim on tort in order to get service outside the jurisdiction). However, liability for "knowing assistance" in a breach of trust (as opposed to receipt of trust property) requires dishonesty: *Twinsectra Ltd v Yardley* [2002] UKHL 12; [2002] 2 A.C. 164; *Barlow Clowes International Ltd v Eurotrust International Ltd* [2005] UKPC 37; [2006] 1 W.L.R. 1476.

[87] See *Clerk and Lindsell on Torts*, 20th edn (2013), para.24–33.

[88] *Lumley v Gye* [2007] UKHL 21; [2008] 1 A.C. 1 at [189].

is deployed in a "three party situation". D commits a tort against C where, intending to cause loss to C, he uses unlawful means against A which affect A's liberty to deal with C. It is a good deal older than the liability under *Lumley v Gye* and an early example is to be found in *Tarleton v M'Gawley.*[89] D, master of the *Othello*, was trading on the coast of West Africa and when people (A) put off from the shore to trade with another vessel, the *Bannister*, belonging to C, D fired his guns at them, driving them away. C's action against D succeeded. The very short judgment is largely taken up with refuting the argument that C should fail because he had no licence from the local ruler but looked at in the light of *OBG Ltd v Allan* the wrongful act (assault or battery) directed at A and driving A away made D's conduct tortious against C even though C had no subsisting contract with A. In any event even if there had been a contract between A and C, A's retreat under artillery fire could hardly have been a breach of that contract: it was rather as if Johanna Wagner had been kidnapped by Gye rather than enticed away. This is a tort based on the primary liability of D for his wrongdoing and is in no sense, unlike *Lumley v Gye*, accessory to a liability of A. Both torts, it is true, have the common characteristic that they involve D's striking at C through acts directed at A,[90] but that does not make them the same. Of course the two torts may overlap: if A had had a contract with C and D's threats to A had not been serious enough to justify A's non-performance then D would no doubt have committed the *Lumley v Gye* tort and this one.

19–020   **Earlier confusion.** In earlier cases the relationship between the two torts became very confused. In *GWK Ltd v Dunlop Rubber Co Ltd*[91] C made tyres and had a contract with A, motor manufacturers, that all new cars would be fitted with tyres of C's manufacture and displayed with them at shows. D, a rival tyre company, surreptitiously removed the C tyres at the Glasgow motor show and substituted its own. D was held liable to C but on the basis that D had interfered without justification with the contractual relationship between A and C, thereby making it at least an offshoot, though not a direct application, of *Lumley v Gye*. In fact of course it was a simple case falling under the *Tarleton v M'Gawley* principle: D committed trespass to A's goods when it removed the tyres and used that as a means to inflict damage on C. Lord Hoffmann in *OBG Ltd v Allan* suggests that one reason for the confusion is that situations like *Tarleton* had been labelled "intimidation" because they commonly involved threats and this label did not easily fit the case where the unlawful means had been fully implemented.[92] If in *Tarleton* D had warned A that he would sink him if he approached C that would have been "intimidation"; if he had simply sunk A with his broadside before A could become aware of any threat it is inconceivable that the result of the case would have been different or even that it would have been a different tort against C. It is an irresistible inference from the existence of liability for intimidation that there is liability on the same basis where the threat is carried out.[93]

---

[89] (1793) 1 Peake NPC 270. See also *Garret v Taylor* (1620) Cro Jac 567.
[90] *OBG Ltd v Allan* [2007] UKHL 21; [2008] 1 A.C. 1 at [306].
[91] (1926) 42 T.L.R. 376.
[92] *OBG v Allan* [2007] UKHL 21; [2008] 1 A.C. 1 at [25].
[93] See *Rookes v Barnard* [1964] A.C. 1129 at 1168.

In the latter part of the 20th century we saw a process[94] whereby the *Lumley v Gye* tort was regarded as extending beyond simple inducement to: (a) "prevention" (the *GWK* situation); (b) "indirect" procurement of a breach (as where D persuaded X to break his contract with A so that A could not perform his contract with C);[95] or even (c) interference short of breach, though all these situations were generally regarded as requiring some independently unlawful means. Now, it seems, after *OBG Ltd v Allan*, we can dispense with these complexities: the *Lumley v Gye* tort is confined to the simple situation where D persuades A to break his contract with C and all the others fall into the "unlawful means" tort we are now considering. It is true that even before *OBG Ltd v Allan* it was recognised that some varieties of "interference with contract", where unlawful means were involved could be regarded as species of a wider "genus" tort of interference with business by unlawful means[96] but this recognition was befogged by the insistence on classifying the categories described above as offshoots or variants of the *Lumley v Gye* tort, even though it was impossible to bring that tort within the genus: it might be possible to describe persuading A to break his contract with C as an "unlawful act" but there was certainly no requirement of independently unlawful means. The persuasion "was only wrongful because the court in *Lumley v Gye* said that inducing a breach of contract was tortious. It is circular then to say that it was tortious because it involved a wrongful act".[97]

A. Unlawful Means

The restructuring of the law in *OBG Ltd v Allan* means that we now have two torts where before we had at least five: direct inducement of breach and causing loss by unlawful means (as we shall see below, we still need to treat conspiracy separately). Unlawful means are necessary for the second of these but not the first and *OBG Ltd v Allan* has brought some measure of clarity into the meaning of this concept. We are now concerned with the situation where, in our customary notation, D directs the unlawful means against A in order to strike at C.   **19–021**

Unlawful means confined to civil wrongs. One view has been that unlawful means embraces anything, "a defendant is not permitted to do, whether by the civil law or the criminal law" and this is supported by Lord Nicholls in *OBG Ltd v Allan*[98] but the majority view is narrower: it covers only acts or threats[99] of acts which are or would be civilly wrongful against and actionable by A (or would be actionable by him if he suffered loss).[100] It does not therefore include criminal   **19–022**

---

[94] The leading authority was *D.C. Thomson & Co Ltd v Deakin* [1952] Ch. 646.

[95] Exemplified by *JT Stratford & Son Ltd v Lindley* [1965] A.C. 269.

[96] *Merkur Island Shipping Corp v Laughton* [1983] 2 A.C. 581 at 610; *JT Stratford & Son Ltd v Lindley*[1965] A.C. 269 at 324, 329.

[97] *OBG v Allan* [2007] UKHL 21; [2008] 1 A.C. 1 at [18] per Lord Hoffmann.

[98] [2007] UKHL 21; [2008] 1 A.C. 1 at [162].

[99] i.e. the form of this wrong traditionally known as intimidation. Threats of unlawful means are probably commoner in practice than their actual implementation.

[100] *National Phonograph Co Ltd v Edison-Bell Consolidated Phonograph Co Ltd* [1908] 1 Ch 335 and *Lonrho Plc v Fayed* [1992] 1 A.C. 448 seem to be examples of this situation (fraudulently

breaches of statutory duty which do not give rise to a civil action[101] nor does it cover common law crimes, though many of them will be torts in their own right and "unlawful" under that head. However, even those who would extend the law beyond matters actionable in their own right would not go so far as to include all incidental infringements of the criminal law. The example often given is of a pizza delivery business which manages to gain a larger share of the market by constant infringement of the traffic regulations. For Lord Nicholls that would not amount to a tort actionable by its competitor because it would not be an, "offence committed against the rival company in any meaningful sense of that expression".[102] Perhaps the most significant point in practice is that the concept of unlawful means includes breaches, and threats of breaches, of contract, that being the means of coercion most commonly used.[103]

19–023   **Intimidation: threatened civil wrongs.** That a threat of a breach of contract was unlawful means was established in the narrower context of intimidation in the pre-*OBG* law in *Rookes v Barnard*.[104] C was employed by BOAC(A) in their design office and the three defendants (D) were officials of the AESD Union, two of them also being employees of BOAC. C had been but was no longer a member of the Union. In order to preserve 100 per cent union membership in the design office and notwithstanding the fact that a strike would have involved the men in breaches of their contracts of employment,[105] D notified A of the resolution passed by members of the union that if C was not dismissed, "a withdrawal of labour of all AESD Membership will take place". A yielded to this threat and lawfully terminated C's contract of employment. Owing to the provisions of the Trade Disputes Act 1906[106] C could not rely upon a simple conspiracy to injure but in the House of Lords it was held that he was entitled to succeed on the ground of intimidation. The House held, agreeing with the Court of Appeal,[107] that there was a tort of intimidation, but they also held, reversing the Court of Appeal, that the tort extended to threats by D to break his contract with A and was not confined to threats of tortious conduct.

19–024   **The privity of contract objection.** The criticism has been made (and this indeed was the opinion of the Court of Appeal in *Rookes v Barnard*) that if intimidation is extended to threats to break contracts "it would overturn or outflank some

---

inducing A to act to C's detriment). Lord Walker (with some hesitation), Baroness Hale and Lord Brown agreed with Lord Hoffmann in this respect.

[101] *OBG v Allan* [2007] UKHL 21; [2008] 1 A.C. 1 at [57] per Lord Hoffmann, supporting this aspect of *Lonrho Ltd v Shell Petroleum Co Ltd (No.2)* [1982] A.C. 173 (breach of sanctions order in Southern Rhodesian rebellion). Lord Walker in *Revenue and Customs Commisioners v Total Network SL* [2008] UKHL 19; [2008] A.C. 1174 at [95] is critical of the reasoning even though he concurred with Lord Hoffmann in *OBG*. However, *Revenue and Customs* involves the different tort of conspiracy.

[102] *OBG v Allan* [2007] UKHL 21; [2008] 1 A.C. 1 at [160].

[103] *Quaere* breach of a court order leading to contempt of court: *Acrow (Automation) Ltd v Rex Chainbelt Inc* [1971] 1 W.L.R. 1676; cf. *Chapman v Honig* [1963] 2 Q.B. 502.

[104] [1964] A.C. 1129. The general thrust of the speeches in *OBG v Allan* seems to be that *Rookes* is essentially about the tort of causing loss by unlawful means considered in *OBG*.

[105] An unusual feature of the case is that, as the defendants admitted, the men's contracts of employment contained an express undertaking that no strike would take place.

[106] Section 1. See para.19–055.

[107] [1963] 1 Q.B. 623.

elementary principles of contract law",[108] notably the doctrine of privity of contract, which holds that one who is not a party to a contract cannot found a claim upon it or sue for breach of it.

Two answers have been made to the privity of contract objection. First, it can be said not merely that C does not sue for breach of contract between D and A, but that his cause of action actually depends upon the contract not having been broken. It is only because A yields to D's threat that it might be broken that C suffers damage at all. If A does not yield and the contract is broken, then D's threat has not caused C to suffer loss;[109] and if it be objected that D may act first (against A) and explain why afterwards, whereupon A acts to C's detriment, the answer is that it is not D's act which has caused C's loss but the implied threat that it will be repeated.[110] Alternatively it may be said bluntly that in all cases of intimidation, whatever the nature of the threatened act, C's cause of action is wholly independent of A's. C founds not upon the wrong, if any, done to A but on the fact that D has set out to injure him by the use of an unlawful weapon:[111]

> "I can see no difference in principle between a threat to break a contract and a threat to commit a tort. If a third party could not sue for damage caused to him by the former I can see no reason why he should be entitled to sue for damages caused to him by the latter. A person is no more entitled to sue in respect of loss which he suffers by reason of a tort committed against someone else than he is entitled to sue in respect of loss which he suffers by reason of breach of a contract to which he is not a party. What he sues for in each case is loss caused to him by the use of an unlawful weapon against him—intimidation of another person by unlawful means."

The second approach does more than answer the privity of contract objection: it refutes its basic premise. The point is:[112]

> "[T]hat the 'weapon', i.e. the means, which the defendant used to inflict loss on the claimant, may be unlawful because it involves conduct wrongful towards a third party.[113] There is no reason in principle why such wrongful conduct should include torts and not breaches of contract. One might argue about whether it is expedient for the law to forbid the use of such acts as a means of causing loss, but the privity doctrine is a red herring."

If one asks why the law should draw the line at threats of breach of contract and not include within the tort some threats against A even though the acts threatened are not strictly unlawful, the answer can lie only in the structure of the law which

---

[108] [1963] 1 Q.B. 623 at 695 per Pearson LJ.

[109] This is the line of reasoning that seems to be preferred by Lords Evershed, Hodson and Devlin: *Rookes v Barnard* [1964] A.C. 1129 at 1187–1188, 1200–1201, 1207–1208.

[110] *Rookes v Barnard* [1964] A.C. 1129 at 1187–1188, 1208–1209. However, there may be cases where C suffers loss intended by D even though it cannot be said that A acts in response to any implied threat by D, as where D simply fails, in breach of contract, to deliver goods to A which he knows A has sold on to C (see Wedderburn (1964) 27 M.L.R. 257, 265). Such conduct would certainly not then have been actionable as intimidation but, provided the requisite intention to harm C by this means can be shown, it would seem to fall within the current broad tort of intentionally causing loss by unlawful means.

[111] *Rookes* [1964] A.C. 1129 at 1168 per Lord Reid. See also Lord Pearce at 1234–1235.

[112] Hoffmann 81 L.Q.R. 116, 125.

[113] "The wrong done to others reaches him": Lord Lindley in *Quinn v Leathem* [1901] A.C. 495 at 535.

has been accepted since *Allen v Flood*.[114] There is a legal "chasm"[115] between, for example, not entering into a contract and breach of an existing contract, which will not easily be bridged. Furthermore, the second approach extends further than intimidation by threats of breach of contract, which the Court was concerned with in *Rookes v Barnard*, but which we are now told is only a variant of the broader tort of causing loss by unlawful means. If, as now seems to be the case, the commission of a tort against A, and not merely the threat of a tort, in order to harm C may be a tort against C,[116] it is very difficult to see why a breach of contract (as opposed to the threat of a breach) with that purpose should not have the same effect[117]—though it is not clear that the court in *Rookes v Barnard* would have taken that view.[118]

19–025   **The unlawful means must hinder the third party's ability to deal with the claimant.** The majority in *OBG Ltd v Allan* impose a further requirement beyond the fact that there must be a wrong actionable or potentially actionable by A: the wrong (or the threat of it) must hinder A in his ability to deal with C.[119] In an earlier case approved on this basis by the majority,[120] C had an exclusive licence to exploit A's registered design and D sold articles alleged to infringe the design right. The relevant legislation gave A, but not C, the right to sue D and C's claim against D was said to have been rightly struck out for although C's sales may have been less than they would otherwise have been the performance of the contractual relations between A and C were unaffected.[121] As we have seen, Lord Nicholls took a broader view of unlawful means but he agreed with the result in the registered design case on the basis that a wider common law liability would be inconsistent with the statutory scheme of remedies.[122]

B.   Intention

19–026   **An intention to injure the claimant.** This tort requires that D strikes intentionally at C through A. So if Gye had kidnapped Johanna Wagner in order to damage Lumley's theatre she would no doubt have had a defence to any action for breach of contract by Lumley but Gye would (according to current thinking)

---

[114] [1898] A.C. 1.

[115] The word is Lord Herschell's: *Allen v Flood* [1898] A.C. 1 at 121.

[116] See para.19–019.

[117] See *Mennell v Stock* [2006] EWHC 2514 (QB).

[118] See *Allen v Flood* [1964] A.C. 1129 at 1187, 1200, 1208. As to cases where D acts directly against C, see para.19–029.

[119] Lord Walker (at [270]) is rather equivocal in his approval.

[120] *Oren v Red Box Toy Factory Ltd* [1999] FSR 785. See also *RCA Corporation v Pollard* [1983] Ch. 135.

[121] According to Lord Hoffmann this requirement would have been determinative in one of the appeals heard in *OBG Ltd v Allan* (*Douglas v Hello! Ltd*) had it been necessary to consider the claim for causing loss by unlawful means: D was a celebrity magazine which published photographs of A's wedding, where A had agreed to give C, another celebrity magazine, exclusive access. While A did cause loss to C (lower circulation) and intended it as a means to an end (A's own higher circulation) and did use unlawful means as against A (breach of confidence), those means did not interfere with A's freedom of action to deal with C. Such a claim was unnecessary because C had its own claim against D for breach of confidence; cf. *Indata Equipment Supplies Ltd v ACL Ltd* [1998] F.S.R. 248.

[122] *OBG v Allan* [2007] UKHL 21; [2008] 1 A.C. 1 at [157].

have been liable to Lumley for causing loss by unlawful means; if on the other hand, Gye had injured Johanna Wagner in a street accident so that she could not sing he would not be liable to Lumley, even though he knew the identity of the person he ran down and was aware of her contract with Lumley, because the latter's only claim would be for negligence and that does not generally cover "relational" economic loss.[123]

The mere fact that D's wrong is intentional towards A does not mean that he has the necessary intention to injure C. In *Millar v Bassey*[124] the facts which were required to be assumed to be provable for the purposes of a striking-out application were that D, a popular singer, entered into a contract with A, a recording company, to produce an album and C and others, the claimants, contracted with A to perform various services in connection with the album. D, in breach of contract, failed to turn up for rehearsals and then withdrew from the project. Since her services were irreplaceable, this inevitably caused A to be in breach of its contract with C. The House of Lords in *OBG Ltd v Allan* regarded the Court of Appeal's decision to allow the action to proceed as wrong. Although it may have been obvious to D that her action would prevent the performance of the A-C contract she did not intend to cause injury to C: "[A] defendant's foresight that his unlawful conduct may or will probably damage the claimant cannot be equated with intention for this purpose . . . Miss Bassey did not breach her recording contract with the intention of thereby injuring any of the plaintiffs."[125]

Intention to injure as an end, or as a means to an end. Although foresight of   **19–027**
probable harm is not sufficient, it is not necessary that an intention to injure the
claimant should be the sole purpose of the defendant:[126]

> "[T]he master of the *Othello* in *Tarleton v M'Gawley* may have had nothing against the other trader. If he had gone off to make his fortune in other waters, he would have wished him well. He simply wanted a monopoly of the local trade for himself. But he nevertheless intended to cause him loss."

So disinterested malice towards the claimant is not necessary: the defendant's purpose may be to advance his own interests by diverting business from the claimant to himself but in that case the claimant's loss and the defendant's gain are two sides of the same coin and in law he intends to injure the claimant.[127] On the other hand, a defendant is not liable where he believes that he is entitled to act as he does in protection of his own interests.[128]

---

[123] See para.5–061.
[124] [1994] E.M.L.R. 44.
[125] *OBG v Allan* [2007] UKHL 21; [2008] 1 A.C. 1 at [166] per Lord Nicholls. See also *Barretts & Baird (Wholesale) Ltd v Institution of Professional Civil Servants* [1987] IRLR 3.
[126] *OBG v Allan* [2007] UKHL 21; [2008] 1 A.C. 1 at [63] per Lord Hoffmann.
[127] *OBG v Allan* [2007] UKHL 21; [2008] 1 A.C. 1 at [167]; *Sorrell v Smith* [1900] A.C. 700 at 742.
[128] *Meretz Investments NV v ACP Ltd* [2007] EWCA Civ 1303; [2008] Ch 244. The proposition is made in the context of a claim for unlawful means conspiracy but it must equally apply to the unlawful means tort which may be committed by an individual This is, in effect, the defence of justification articulated as part of the requirement of intention; cf. *Sar Petroleum Inc v Peace Hills Trust Co* [2010] NBCA 22; (2010) 318 D.L.R. (4th) 70 NBCA at [73], but contrast *Johnson v BFI*

C. Trade or Business

19–028 **The tort is not necessarily confined to trade or business.** It has long been customary to call this tort interference with business (or trade) by unlawful means and *OBG Ltd v Allan* is replete with references to that or a similar formula.[129] This may simply be because the overwhelming majority of cases are likely to arise in a business context, but it is hard to see why the tort should be so confined.[130] If it is actionable to use unlawful means to drive away C's prospective customers[131] why should it not equally be actionable to use such means against a person who proposes to buy C's house but has not yet signed a contract to do so?[132]

D. "Two party" Cases

19–029 If there is no third party and D uses unlawful means to inflict harm directly on C, then in very many cases D will have committed one of the specific intentional torts dealt with in this book—deceit, conversion, assault and so on—and there seems little point in seeking for any generalised liability for causing loss by unlawful means; indeed, it might be thought positively confusing to erect such a parallel liability. Nonetheless, there may be cases in which C succumbs to the *threat* of unlawful action in which there is no completed, independent tort. In the past such cases have been discussed on the basis that "intimidation" amounted to a separate tort but after *OBG Ltd v Allan* it seems to be a variety (perhaps the most common variety) of causing loss by unlawful means. If, for example, D threatens C that he will do him grievous bodily harm unless he pays him money the threat may not be immediate enough to constitute an assault. Certainly C may recover his money by action because the transfer is voidable for duress,[133] but C may have suffered further damage as a result. If D tells lies to A in order to prevent C getting a licence, it seems that this is the tort of inflicting loss by unlawful means.[134] Why should it not be a tort for D to extract money from C by threatening to tell such lies to A in the future? *OBG Ltd v Allan* is not much help on these issues since the House of Lords did no more than barely mention the point and Lord Hoffmann warned that he did: "[N]ot intend to say anything about the question of whether a claimant who has been compelled by unlawful

---

Canada Inc[2010] MBCA 101; (2011) 326 D.L.R.(4th) 497 (Manitoba CA) at [55] where it is said that justification is "not usually regarded as a defence to this tort".

[129] For example, *OBG v Allan* [2007] UKHL 21; [2008] 1 A.C. 1 at [139], [141], [180], [247], [261].

[130] Lord Walker in *Revenue and Customs Commissioners v Total Network SL* [2008] UKHL 19; [2008] 1 A.C. 1174 at [100] seems to be of the view that it is so confined but conspiracy (see para.19–044) is not.

[131] *Tarleton v M'Gawley* (1793) Peake N.P. 270, para.19–019.

[132] Cf. Deakin and Randall (2009) 72 M.L.R. 519. Most cases of inducing a breach of contract will also occur in a business context, but it seems to be assumed that the tort could apply to a non-commercial property transaction (*Smith v Morrison* [1974] 1 W.L.R. 659) though the result may be affected by the statutory provisions on registration of land charges.

[133] See Treitel, *The Law of Contract*, 13th edn (2011), para.10–003.

[134] A reasonable inference from the facts of *Lonrho Plc v Fayed* [1992] 1 A.C. 448, approved in *OBG Ltd v Allan* [2007] UKHL 21; [2008] 1 A.C. 1.

intimidation to act to his own detriment, can sue for his loss. Such a case of 'two-party intimidation' raises altogether different issues."[135]

Threatened breach of contract. The Court of Appeal accepted two-party   **19–030**
intimidation as part of the law in a case where a young girl was kept in coercive
and exploitative conditions as a domestic servant.[136] However, Lord Reid warned
in *JT Stratford & Son Ltd v Lindley*:[137]

> "A case where a defendant presents to the claimant the alternative of doing what the defendant
> wants him to do or suffering loss which the defendant can cause him to incur is not necessarily
> *in pari casu* and may involve questions which cannot arise where there is intimidation of a
> third person."

The problems centre round the effect in the two-party situation of a threat of a
breach of contract, since it may be argued that the claimant should be confined to
his contractual remedies and he is also protected by the development of economic
duress.

Should the claimant be confined to his contractual remedies? In the two-party   **19–031**
situation there is normally a contractual remedy already available to C, while in
the three-party situation, if C cannot sue in tort, he cannot sue at all, because D's
threat of breach is made to A.[138] If C is threatened with a breach of contract by D
he may be able to treat the contract as repudiated and sue for anticipatory breach
or, of course, he may await the breach and then sue for damages. In fact, the
balance of advantage would seem to lie in holding that where D threatens C with
a breach of his contract with C, C should be restricted to his contractual remedies.
The law should not encourage C to yield to the threat but should seek to persuade
him to resist it.[139] In some cases he may be able to obtain an injunction to restrain
the breach and in any case he will be adequately compensated by his remedy in
damages for breach of contract as his damage can scarcely be other than
financial. If C is threatened with a tort it is, of course, equally true that he may
bring an action for damages if the tort is committed or bring an action for a quia
timet injunction first, but, especially where the threat is of violence, it is perhaps
less realistic to say that these legal remedies afford him adequate protection
against the consequences of resistance.[140] From the point of view of policy,
therefore, there is much to be said for the view that no independent tort is
committed when all that is threatened, in the two-party situation, is a breach of
contract.

The effect of the development of economic duress. Since threatened breaches   **19–032**
of contract were brought within the fold of unlawful means in *Rookes v Barnard*
there has been considerable development in the contractual context of the
doctrine of "economic duress", and in this context it is clear that not every threat

---

[135] [2007] UKHL 21; [2008] 1 A.C. 1 at [61].
[136] *Godwin v Uzoigwe* [1993] Fam. Law 65. See also *News Group Newspapers Ltd v S.O.G.A.T. '82*
[1986] I.R.L.R. 337 at 347, with reference to the seventh claimant.
[137] [1965] A.C. 269 at 325.
[138] Hoffmann (1965) 81 L.Q.R. 116 at 127–128.
[139] See the example given by Hoffmann (1965) 81 L.Q.R. 116.
[140] A point demonstrated clearly by *Godwin v Uzoigwe* [1993] Fam. Law 65.

to break a contract will amount to duress: the economic pressure on C must be "illegitimate" and constitute a significant cause inducing C to enter into the revised contract with D.[141] In *Pao On v Lau Yiu Long*[142] D threatened that unless C agreed to vary an existing contract between them by giving D a guarantee against loss, D would not fulfil his side of the agreement. D's action on the guarantee succeeded because, although C had acceded to the demand because of fears of delay in litigation and loss of public confidence, the pressure fell short of duress. Though intimidation was not discussed in the case it cannot be that C could have avoided the binding nature of the contract by the simple device of counter-claiming for damages for intimidation and it seems therefore that for the purposes of intimidation the claimant should be required to show unlawful coercion at least of such a degree as would enable him to avoid a contract.[143] If there are any cases in which the victim of unfair pressure may avoid a contract even though the threat is not of unlawful action,[144] there seems no possibility of any concurrent tort liability.[145]

19–033   **No tort claim where there has been an actual breach of contract.** It has been suggested above that in the three-party situation an actual breach of contract by D against A is as much unlawful means as a threatened breach in the context of D's liability in tort to C. Is it therefore the law that if D deliberately *breaks* his own contract with C that he is liable in tort as well as in contract? It is thought that the answer is plainly "No". The remedies provided to C by the law of contract are as effective, if not more so, than in the case where D threatens to break the contract; and there would be something very odd in turning every profit-motivated breach of contract into a tort.[146] English law is not unfriendly to concurrent liability[147] but this would be taking it a step too far.

---

[141] *Dimskal Shipping Co SA v I.T.W.F.* [1992] 2 A.C. 152 at 165 per Lord Goff. For discussion of the relationship between illegitimate pressure and causation, see Treitel, *The Law of Contract*, 13th edn (2011), para.10–006.

[142] [1980] A.C. 614.

[143] Another problem is that the right to avoid a contract for economic duress may be lost by affirmation: *North Ocean Shipping Co Ltd v Hyundai Construction Co Ltd* [1979] Q.B. 705. It is not easy to see on what basis the right to sue for intimidation could be similarly lost: cf. *Neibuhr v Gage* (1906) 108 N.W. 884.

[144] "Lawful act duress" was not ruled out by Steyn LJ in *CTN Cash & Carry Ltd v Gallaher Ltd* [1994] 4 All E.R. 714.

[145] In *Universe Tankships Inc of Monrovia v ITWF* [1983] A.C. 366 at 400, Lord Scarman, dissenting (but on another point) said: "It is, I think, already established law that economic pressure can in law amount to duress and that duress, if proved, not only renders voidable a transaction into which a person has entered under its compulsion but is actionable as a tort, if it causes damage or loss." Cf. Lord Diplock, at 385: "The use of economic duress to induce another person to part with property or money is not a tort *per se*; the form that the duress takes may, or may not, be tortious." In *Kolmar Group AG v Traxpo Enterprises Pvt Ltd* [2010] EWHC 113 (Comm); [2010] 2 Lloyd's Rep. 653 damages were awarded for the tort of intimidation, but the same sum was also awarded by way of restitution, either on the grounds of duress, or failure of consideration.

[146] The remedy of requiring the defendant to account for his profits from the breach to the claimant is very restricted and this is no accident: *Attorney General v Blake* [2001] 1 A.C. 268. Exemplary damages for profit-motivated torts go wider (para.23–015). The fact that it would suit the claimant to dress up his claim as tort rather than contract is not necessarily a reason for allowing him to do so.

[147] See para.1–008.

Protection from Harassment Act 1997. It should be noted that the Protection   19–034
from Harassment Act 1997 created a tort (and crime) of "harassment" by conduct
(which includes speech) on at least two occasions which a reasonable person
would think amounted to harassment.[148] While this is plainly wider than
two-party intimidation in that it is not confined to threats of wrongful acts and
allows damages for anxiety as well as financial loss, it would seem to overlap
with it to a considerable degree.

4. CONSPIRACY

Introduction. Though our early law knew a writ of conspiracy, this was   19–035
restricted to abuse of legal procedure and the action on the case in the nature of
conspiracy, which came into fashion in the reign of Elizabeth I, developed into
the modern tort of malicious prosecution. Conspiracy as a crime was developed
by the Star Chamber during the 17th century and, when taken over by the
common law courts, came to be regarded by them as not only a crime but also as
capable of giving rise to civil liability provided damage resulted to the claimant.
As a tort, however, it was little developed until the second half of the 19th
century[149] and the law remained obscure until the decision of the House of Lords
in *Crofter Hand-Woven Harris Tweed Co Ltd v Veitch*.[150] Conspiracy remains a
crime as well as a tort, but the scope of the crime has been curtailed by the
Criminal Law Act 1977 so that, broadly speaking, the only conspiracies which
are now indictable are those to commit a substantive criminal offence, to defraud
or to corrupt public morals or outrage public decency.[151] The Act, however, has
no effect on civil liability. In fact, even aside from the Act the tort and the crime
have cut loose from whatever common origin they had.[152] The tort of conspiracy
takes two forms according to whether or not unlawful means are used.

A.   Conspiracy to Injure or *Crofter* Conspiracy

The Crofter case. It was firmly established in *Crofter Hand-Woven Harris Tweed*   19–036
Co Ltd v Veitch[153] that if there is a combination of persons whose purpose is to
cause damage to the claimant, that purpose may render unlawful acts which
would otherwise be lawful and which would be lawful if committed by one
person even with the purpose of causing injury. The production of Harris Tweed
is an industry of the Isle of Lewis and other islands of the Outer Hebrides.
Originally the yarn for the cloth was hand-spun from wool by the crofters of
Lewis and was wholly produced in the Isle. By 1930, hand-spinning of wool had
become commercially impracticable and thenceforth many weavers in Lewis
imported yarn from the mainland. Five mill owners in Lewis nevertheless spun

---

[148] See para.4–034.
[149] It "is a modern invention altogether": *Midland Bank Trust Co Ltd v Green (No.3)* [1982] Ch. 529
at 539 per Lord Denning MR.
[150] [1942] A.C. 435.
[151] The last two may be offences even when committed by one person.
[152] *Midland Bank Trust Co Ltd v Green (No.3)* [1982] Ch. 529 at 541.
[153] [1942] A.C. 435.

yarn woven by the crofters. These mill owners alleged that cloth woven on Lewis from mainland yarn could be sold much more cheaply than cloth made from yarn spun in Lewis. It was therefore in their interest to get a minimum price fixed for the cloth. Of the workers in their mills 90 per cent belonged to the TGWU and the Lewis dockers were also members of it. The union, with the object of getting all mill workers to be members and of increasing wages, approached the mill owners, who replied that they could not raise the wages because of the competition of the crofters who wove imported yarn. The union officials then put an embargo on the importation of yarn by ordering Lewis dockers not to handle such yarn. They obeyed (without breaking any contract) and thus injured the trade of seven small producers of tweed who used imported yarn and who sued the officials for conspiracy.

It must be stressed at the outset, lest the importance of this form of liability be exaggerated, that the claimants lost their case because the predominant purpose of the embargo was to promote the interests of the union members rather than to injure the claimants,[154] but their Lordships made it clear that if the predominant purpose of a combination is to injure another in his trade or business[155] or in his other legitimate interests[156] then, if damage results, the tort of conspiracy exists. The *Crofter* principle was applied by the Court of Appeal in *Gulf Oil (Great Britain) Ltd v Page*[157] in granting an interlocutory injunction against a combination to publish a statement defamatory of the claimants even though the statement was admitted to be true and there would, therefore, have been an absolute defence to an action for libel; but this is confined to cases where the claimant suffers actual pecuniary loss: if the claim is for general loss of reputation or injured feelings the law of defamation cannot be sidestepped in this way.[158]

i. Purpose

19–037   **To cause damage to the claimant.** The object or purpose of the combination must be to cause damage to the claimant. The test is not what the defendants contemplated as a likely or even an inevitable consequence of their conduct; it is, "what is in truth the object in the minds of the combiners when they acted as they did?"[159] Malice in the sense of malevolence, spite or ill will is not essential for liability,[160] nor is it sufficient if merely superadded to a legitimate purpose; what is required is that the combiners should have acted in order that (not with the result that, even the foreseeably inevitable result that) the claimant should suffer damage. If they did not act in order that the claimant should suffer damage but to pursue their own advantage, they are not liable, however selfish their attitude and

---

[154] See also *Mogul SS Co Ltd v McGregor Gow* [1892] A.C. 25; *Sorrell v Smith* [1925] A.C. 700.

[155] This, so their Lordships held, had really been settled in *Quinn v Leathem* [1901] A.C. 495, notwithstanding earlier doubts about the meaning of that case.

[156] [1942] A.C. 435 at 446–447, 451, 462, 478.

[157] [1988] Ch. 327.

[158] *Lonrho Plc v Fayed (No.5)* [1993] 1 W.L.R. 1489. See also *Oyston v Blaker* [1996] 1 W.L.R. 1326.

[159] *Crofter Hand-Woven Harris Tweed Co Ltd v Veitch* [1942] A.C. 435 at 445 per Viscount Simon LC.

[160] *Crofter Hand-Woven Harris Tweed Co Ltd v Veitch* [1942] A.C. 435 at 450, 463, 469–471.

however inevitable the claimant's damage may have been.[161] Thus the principle applicable in the tort of causing loss by unlawful means[162] (or indeed the unlawful means variety of conspiracy) that a defendant who intends to advance his own interests by diverting business from the claimant to himself intends to injure the claimant because the claimant's loss and the defendant's gain are two sides of the same coin is inapplicable here. At common law an agreement between D1 and D2 to fix prices so that C is driven out of the market and his share passes to them is not an actionable wrong even though the agreement is invalid as in restraint of trade[163] (though it is likely to be so under the Competition Act 1998).[164] It is not, however, essential that the interest promoted be a material one. In *Scala Ballroom (Wolverhampton) Ltd v Ratcliffe*[165] the claimants refused to admit black people to their ballroom[166] but they did allow black musicians to play in the orchestra. The defendants were members of the Musicians' Union, a union with many black members, and they gave notice to the claimants that members of the union would not be permitted to play at the ballroom so long as the bar against black people was in operation. An injunction to restrain them from persuading their members not to play there was refused.

Malice not necessary but may be relevant. Although malevolence is not necessary, where that state of mind is what motivates the defendants they may be liable even though precisely the same acts would be lawful in pursuit of their interests. In *Huntley v Thornton*[167] damages were awarded against union officials whose object in keeping the claimant out of work was, as Harman J found, to uphold: "[T]heir own ruffled dignity . . . It had become a question of the district committee's prestige; they were determined to use any weapon ready to their hand to vindicate their authority, and grossly abused the quite frightening powers at their command."[168]   **19–038**

Predominant purpose. Of course even individuals rarely act from a single motive but in these cases the question must be asked what was the predominant purpose of the combination and if that is the pursuit of the defendant's interests their conduct is not actionable because they are also pleased by the claimant's loss.[169] The fact that the damage is disproportionate to the purpose sought to be   **19–039**

---

[161] As may be expected from this, successful actions for conspiracy are rare.

[162] See para.19–027.

[163] *Mogul SS Co Ltd v McGregor Gow & Co* [1892] A.C. 25.

[164] See para.19–005.

[165] [1958] 1 W.L.R. 1057.

[166] See now the Equality Act 2010.

[167] [1957] 1 W.L.R. 321; *Hutchinson v Aitchison* (1970) 9 K.I.R. 69.

[168] [1957] 1 W.L.R. 321 at 341 per Harman LJ. Such a case was foreshadowed by Lord Wright in the *Crofter* case, [1942] A.C. 435 at 445. The position was not perhaps so clear in *Quinn v Leathem* [1901] A.C. 495 but according to Lord Sumner in *Sorrell v Smith* [1925] A.C. 700 at 736 that case is to be explained on the basis that there was evidence from which the jury could find that the defendants' "real object was to punish Leathem for his conduct in harbouring non-unionists and was not simply to advance their own interests in the future by bringing those non-unionists into their fold". Cf. Lord Lindley in *Quinn v Leathem* at 536.

[169] *Crofter Hand-Woven Harris Tweed Co Ltd v Veitch* [1942] A.C. 435 at 471 per Lord Wright.

achieved does not itself render the conspiracy actionable[170] nor is the court concerned with the expediency or otherwise of the policy adopted by the combiners.[171]

19–040 **Common purpose.** There is no liability where the participants act in pursuance of different forms of self-interest.[172] If one participant has the object of causing injury to the claimant and the others do not there is no conspiracy because there is no common purpose to injure; but if the others are aware of the intention of the one bent on injury it may be that they are all liable.[173]

19–041 **Promoting the combiners' unlawful interest.** The *Crofter* case contains a number of statements to the effect that a combination to injure another without the use of unlawful means is not actionable where it is designed to pursue the "legitimate" or "lawful" interests of the defendants. Thus Viscount Simon said that if the:[174]

> "[P]redominant purpose is to damage another person and damage results, that is tortious conspiracy. If the predominant purpose is the lawful protection or promotion of any *lawful interest* of the combiners (no illegal means being employed), it is not a tortious conspiracy, even though it causes damage to another person."

Clearly therefore there is no actionable conspiracy where the defendants act to improve their share of the market at the claimant's expense[175] or to strengthen the position of a trade union or its members[176] or to maintain prices in the trade to the common benefit of members.[177]

However, what if the defendants' activity does not involve "trade" or "business" in any meaningful sense at all but is simply a scheme to cheat others of money? In *Revenue and Customs Commissioners v Total Network SL*[178] the defendants engineered a complex "carousel fraud" involving fictitious supplies of goods and based upon the facts that: (a) a trader in a chain who pays VAT on the supply of goods to him is entitled to reclaim it from the Revenue; and (b) that export transactions between EU countries are not subject to VAT. In its simplest form, A in country X contracts to sell goods to B in country Y. B then sells the goods (in country Y) to C, C paying VAT. B then ceases to trade and disappears without accounting to the Revenue for the tax. Before the Revenue discovers B's disappearance C then resells the goods to A in country X and reclaims the VAT he has paid. The whole scheme was criminal and in such a case it seems extraordinary to say that the parties are merely "advancing their interests" at the expense of the Revenue. Nevertheless in the case the Revenue abandoned a claim based upon conspiracy to injure, seemingly on the basis that causing damage to

---

[170] Though it may cast doubt upon the defendants' bona fides.
[171] *Crofter Hand-Woven Harris Tweed Co Ltd v Veitch* [1942] A.C. 435 at 447.
[172] Thus, in the *Crofter* case the interests of the mill owners and the trade unionists were by no means identical.
[173] *Crofter Hand-Woven Harris Tweed Co Ltd v Veitch* [1942] A.C. 435 at 495.
[174] *Crofter Hand-Woven Harris Tweed Co Ltd v Veitch* [1942] A.C. 435 at 445 (emphasis added); see also at 469.
[175] *Mogul SS Co Ltd v McGregor Gow & Co* [1892] A.C. 25.
[176] The *Crofter* case itself.
[177] *Ware and de Freville Ltd v Motor Trade Association* [1921] 3 K.B. 40.
[178] [2008] UKHL 19; [2008] 1 A.C. 1174.

the Revenue was not the primary aim of the carousel fraud[179] and instead advanced a case based solely on unlawful means conspiracy. That raised questions, which are explored below, about how far a criminal offence may be unlawful means for the purposes of that tort. However, as Lord Neuberger pointed out, on such facts:[180]

> "[T]here is little, if any, difference between the conspirators' intention to make money and their intention to deprive the commissioners of money: each is the obverse of the other. On that basis, it may well be that it could be said that the predominant purpose of Total and the other conspirators was indeed to inflict loss on the [Revenue] just as much as it was to profit the conspirators, and hence the claim in tort is made out in conspiracy to injure."

ii. Combination

For conspiracy there must be concerted action between two or more persons, which includes husband and wife.[181] It seems that there can be no conspiracy between an employer and his employees, at least where they merely go about their employer's business[182] and it is submitted that directors who resolve to cause their company to break its contract do not commit conspiracy by unlawful means against the other contracting party,[183] for they are identified with the company for this purpose;[184] if that were not so there would be an easy way to outflank the denial of liability for inducing breach of contract in such circumstances.[185] On the other hand, there might be circumstances where an employer would be vicariously liable for a conspiracy involving his servants provided the other requirements of that form of liability are met and there may be a conspiracy between a company and its directors, where the latter act so as to incur personal liability in circumstances where their knowledge may be imputed to the company.[186]

19–042

---

[179] [2008] UKHL 19; [2008] 1 A.C. 1174 at [226].

[180] [2008] UKHL 19; [2008] 1 A.C. 1174 at [228]. Lord Hope, too, thought at [44] that the, "case as a subspecies of unlawful means conspiracy [was] virtually indistinguishable from the tort of conspiracy to injure". Cf. para.19–037.

[181] *Midland Bank Trust Co Ltd v Green (No.3)* [1982] Ch. 529. This is a clear difference between the tort and the crime.

[182] *Clerk and Lindsell on Torts*, 20th edn (2013), para.24–93.

[183] See para.19–044.

[184] *Normart Management Ltd v West Redhill Redevelopment Co* (1998) 155 D.L.R. (4th) 627. See para.25–033; but in *De Jetley Marks v Greenwood* [1936] 1 All E.R. 863 at 871 Porter J thought that some of the directors could conspire before the meeting.

[185] See para.19–015.

[186] *Belmont Finance Corp Ltd v Williams Furniture Ltd (No.2)* [1980] 1 All E.R. 393; *Taylor v Smyth* [1991] I.R. 158. Cf. *Belmont Finance Corp Ltd v Williams Furniture Ltd* [1979] Ch. 250 (knowledge not to be imputed where company claimant). In *Barclay Pharmaceuticals Ltd v Waypharm LP* [2012] EWHC 306 (Comm) at [222] [229], these authorities were applied by Gloster J, "in the absence of full argument" to conclude that a civil conspiracy was possible between a corporate vehicle and its sole controller; cf. *Aerostar Maintenance International Ltd v Wilson* [2010] EWHC 2032 (Ch); *Concept Oil Services Ltd v En-Gen Group LLP* [2013] EWHC 1897 (Comm) at [53] per Flaux J ("there is no impediment to the liability of a director unless he is acting strictly and solely via the constitutional organs of the company concerned").

iii.   Damage

19–043   In contrast with the crime of conspiracy, an overt act causing damage is an essential element of liability in tort. If, therefore, the acts relied on are incapable of being made part of any cause of action—for example, evidence given by witnesses in a court of law—then the tort cannot be made out.[187] A sufficient element of damage is shown where expenses are necessarily incurred by the claimant in investigating and counteracting the machinations of the defendants.[188] Though the claimant is required to prove some actual pecuniary loss, once that is done damages are not limited to the amount so proved.[189]

B.   "Unlawful Means" Conspiracy

19–044   **Summary requirements.** This tort:[190]

> "[I]nvolves an arrangement between two or more parties, whereby they . . . agree that at least one of them will use 'unlawful means' against the claimant, and, although damage to the claimant need not be the predominant intention of any of the parties, the claimant must have suffered loss or damage as a result."

The requirement of causing damage is the same as under "*Crofter*" conspiracy, as essentially is the requirement of combination, though the latter may give rise to additional difficulty because of the requirement that the parties must agree not just to harm the claimant but to do so using unlawful means. The knowledge of an "accessory" conspirator may not be the same as that of the principal actor and it may be necessary to analyse the extent to which the accessory shared a common objective with the primary actor and the extent to which the achievement of that objective was to his knowledge to be achieved by unlawful means intended to injure the claimant, his liability being limited to that common extent.[191] Where the necessary combination has been proved there is no requirement that the particular defendant sued has to be the one who takes the

---

[187] *Marrinan v Vibart* [1963] 1 Q.B. 234, affirmed, at 528. Cf. *Darker v Chief Constable of West Midlands* [2001] 1 A.C. 435 and *Surzur Overseas Ltd v Koros* [1999] 2 Lloyd's Rep. 611.

[188] *BMTA v Salvadori* [1949] Ch. 556. Quaere when there is no other financial loss: *Lonrho Plc v Fayed (No.5)* [1993] 1 W.L.R. 1489. These and a number of other cases are examined in *R & V Versicherung AG v Risk Insurance and Reinsurance Solutions SA* [2006] EWHC 42 (Comm).

[189] *Lonrho Plc v Fayed (No.5)* [1993] 1 W.L.R. 1489. When actual pecuniary loss has been proved, damages are said to be at large, but not to the extent of allowing damages for loss of reputation. Loss of orders or loss of trade is actionable but not, "airy-fairy general reputation in the business or commercial community", nor a decline in the share value of a corporate claimant: [1993] 1 W.L.R. 1489 at 1496.

[190] Said to be "common ground" between the parties in *Revenue and Customs Commissioners v Total Network SL* [2008] UKHL 19; [2008] 1 A.C. 1174 at [213] per Lord Neuberger.

[191] *IS Innovative Software Ltd v Howes* [2004] EWCA Civ 275; *Bank of Tokyo-Mitsubishi UJF Ltd v Baskan Gida Sanayive Pazarlama AS* [2009] EWHC 1276 (Ch) at [847]; *The Dolphina* [2011] SGHC 273; [2012] 1 Lloyd's Rep. 304; cf. *Kuwait Oil Tanker Co SAK v Al Bader* [2000] 2 All E.R. Comm. 271.

unlawful action.[192] We need now to consider in a little more detail the mental element and the notion of unlawful means.

i. Intention

Predominant purpose to injure not necessary. After a period of uncertainty caused by *Lonrho Ltd v Shell Petroleum Ltd (No.2)*[193] the House of Lords in *Lonrho Plc v Fayed*[194] reaffirmed that this form of the tort, unlike the *Crofter* variety, does not require a predominant purpose to injure the claimant and *Revenue and Customs Commissioners v Total Network SL*[195] also proceeds on this basis. However, the tort still requires an intention to injure: it is not enough that the defendants combine to do an unlawful act which has the effect of causing damage to the claimant. The concept means the same as it does in the tort of intentional infliction of harm by unlawful means: if the damage to the claimant is not an end in itself it must at least be a necessary means to some other end and it is not enough that it is a foreseeable consequence of the unlawful means used.[196] The intentional harm tort (at least in its usual "three-party" form) involves unlawful conduct directed at a third party but with the intention of causing harm to the claimant by interfering with the business relationship between the third party and the claimant. Here, too, although there need be[197] no third party involved, the purpose of the combination must be to strike at the claimant. To take an example loosely based on *Lonrho Ltd v Shell Petroleum Ltd (No.2)*,[198] if D1 and D2 combine to evade legislation prohibiting trade with a country in which C has oil interests and the effect of this is to damage C's interests then even if the evasion of the legislation is unlawful means[199] they do not intend to harm C—that is simply a by-product, even if an inevitable one, of what they do. That is not to say that it will necessarily be easy to draw the line between this situation and the "means to an end" intention which does fall within the tort. If the correct analysis of the facts is that the conspirators wanted to get hold of the oil market for themselves in that country by destroying C's share,[200] that must be a classic

19–045

---

[192] *Kuwait Oil Tanker Co SAK v Al Bader* [2000] 2 All E.R. Comm. 271; *Barclay Pharmaceuticals Ltd v Waypharm LP* [2012] EWHC 306 (Comm) at [222].

[193] [1982] A.C. 173.

[194] [1992] 1 A.C. 448, overruling *Metall und Rohstoff v Donaldson Lufkin & Jenrette Inc* [1990] 1 Q.B. 391 and explaining *Lonrho Ltd v Shell Petroleum Ltd (No.2)* [1982] A.C. 173.

[195] [2008] UKHL 19; [2008] 1 A.C. 1174. See, e.g. at [40], [56], [82], [115], [213].

[196] *Bank of Tokyo-Mitsubishi UJF Ltd* [2009] EWHC 1276 (Ch) at [825]; *The Dolphina* [2011] SGHC 273; [2012] 1 Lloyd's Rep. 304 at [279].

[197] There may be a third party. If D threatens A that he will break his contract with A unless A ceases to trade with C that is inflicting harm on C by unlawful means. So also is it if D1 and D2 combine so to threaten A, but this time it is also unlawful means conspiracy.

[198] [1982] A.C. 173.

[199] See para.19–046.

[200] As far as can be judged from the CA transcript in *Lonrho v Shell*, that is not the way the points of claim in the arbitration were framed.

example of using illegal means to achieve some ulterior end. After all, in a conspiracy by D1 and D2 to defraud C, D1 and D2 plainly intend to deprive C of his property so that they can get it.[201]

ii. Unlawful means

19–046 **Not confined to civil wrongs.**[202] There has been an understandable desire in some quarters to give unity to the concept of unlawful means in the economic torts.[203] As we have seen above, the majority in *OBG Ltd v Allan* regarded the tort of intentionally causing loss by unlawful means as essentially one in which D strikes at C by using unlawful means directed against a third party (A)[204] and in that context unlawful means covers only acts or threats of acts which are or would be civilly wrongful against and actionable by A (or would be actionable by A if he suffered loss).[205] The equivalent proposition in a case of conspiracy where the unlawful means were not directed at a third party[206] would be that the means would have to be independently actionable by C.[207] However, the result of *Revenue and Customs Commissioners v Total Network SL*[208] is that in unlawful means conspiracy it also covers acts which are criminal but which would not be civilly actionable if done by one person.[209] Hence on the facts of that case the common law offence of cheating the Revenue, if established, would lead to liability in tort.[210] It would be difficult to say that this conclusion was very

---

[201] *Kuwait Oil Tanker Co SAK v Al Bader* [2000] 2 All E.R. Comm. 271. Indeed, as has been seen above para.19–041, Lord Neuberger in the *Revenue and Customs Commissioners* case regarded that as a predominant purpose to injure.

[202] Even if it is generally assumed that civil wrongs qualify as "unlawful means", reliance upon a civil wrong is not always free from difficulty: see the concern expressed by Morgan J in *Aerostar Maintenance International Ltd v Wilson* [2010] EWHC 2032 (Ch) (at [170]–[172]) in circumstances where D induced A to commit a breach of contract and a breach of fiduciary duty to C, the company of which A was a director, by diverting an opportunity from C to X, another company set up by A: conspiracy (between D, A, and X) based on the breach of fiduciary duty would result in the application of two different sets of principles (the equitable principles as to accessory liability and the principles of conspiracy to injure by unlawful means); similarly conspiracy based on the breach of contract leads to the overlap of conspiracy and the tort of inducing breach when the two do "not necessarily have the same ingredients". In *Concept Oil Services Ltd v En-Gen Group LLP* [2013] EWHC 1897 (Comm) the unlawful means was deceit but Flaux J saw no reason in principle why entering a transaction defrauding creditors within the meaning of s.423 of the Insolvency Act 1986 should not be sufficient unlawful means as well.

[203] The best discussion of the state of the law in the pre-*OBG/Revenue and Customs Commissioners* period is the judgment of Davis J in *Mbasogo v Logo Ltd* [2005] EWHC 2035 (QB).

[204] As to "two-party" cases see para.19–029.

[205] See para.19–022.

[206] As to which see fn.197.

[207] See *Powell v Boladz* [1998] Lloyd's Rep Med 116, overruled in *Revenue and Customs Commissioners v Total Network SL* [2008] UKHL 19; [2008] 1 A.C. 1174

[208] [2008] UKHL 19; [2008] 1 A.C. 1174.

[209] In *W H Newson Ltd v IMI Plc* [2013] EWCA Civ 1377; [2014] 1 All E.R. 1377 it was held that the remedy in damages made available by s.47A of the Competition Act 1998 permitted the claimant to bring a conspiracy claim provided that all the ingredients of the cause of action could be established by the infringement findings in the decision of the Commission (and such findings did not establish the necessary intent to injure).

[210] Lord Hope and Lord Neuberger, dissenting, were of the view that any claim in tort was barred by the existence of the statutory scheme for recovery in the Value Added Tax Act 1994.

closely reasoned. Indeed, as Lord Walker admits, the common assumption in many of the earlier dicta that a crime is unlawful means perhaps rests on a quasi-lay assumption that criminality is so obviously at the top of the tree of unlawfulness that its inclusion hardly needs justification,[211] and it is certainly true that a great deal more judicial effort has been devoted to breach of contract in the context of the economic torts than to crime. For Lord Scott, the imposition of tort liability is justified where the:[212]

> "[C]ircumstances [are] such as to make the conduct sufficiently reprehensible to justify imposing on those who have brought about the harm liability in damages for having done so. Bearing that in mind, the proposition that a combination of two or more people to carry out a scheme that is criminal in its nature and is intended to cause economic harm to some person does not, when carried out with that result, constitute a tort actionable by that person is, in my opinion, unacceptable. Such a proposition is not only inconsistent with the jurisprudence of tortious conspiracy, . . . but is inconsistent also with the historic role of the action on the case."

Comparison with the non-conspiracy tort. All this, however, does not explain why a conclusion which seems obvious in the context of conspiracy is rejected in the context of causing loss by unlawful means. One reason may be that if we confine unlawful means to civilly actionable conduct the tort of unlawful means conspiracy almost disappears because the conspirators will generally be joint tortfeasors anyway,[213] e.g. if D1 and D2 conspire to defraud C by making fraudulent misrepresentations to him they jointly commit deceit. The clear message of *Revenue and Customs Commissioners* is that unlawful means conspiracy is not merely a form of secondary liability; joint tortfeasance dressed up in other clothes.

19–047

The point has been made above that although the *Revenue and Customs Commissioners* case was presented only as one of unlawful means conspiracy, some members of the House of Lords had doubts whether it might not better have been regarded as a straightforward conspiracy to injure.[214] If it was not, that, for Lord Neuberger, was strong reason for including criminality within the scope of unlawful means:[215]

> "In my judgment, given the existence of [conspiracy to injure], it would be anomalous if an unlawful means conspiracy could not found a cause of action where, as here, the means 'merely' involved a crime, where the loss to the claimant was the obvious and inevitable, indeed in many ways the intended, result of the sole purpose of the conspiracy, and where the crime involved, cheating the revenue, has as its purpose the protection of the victim of the conspiracy."

---

[211] [2008] UKHL 19; [2008] 1 A.C. 1174 at [90]–[94].

[212] [2008] UKHL 19; [2008] 1 A.C. 1174 at [56].

[213] Counsel for the claimants contended that on the defendants' argument unlawful means conspiracy would become a "barren iteration of joint tortfeasance": at [66]; but even where the unlawful means involve a tort actionable directly by the claimant there is no doctrine that the conspiracy is "merged" in the substantive tort and it has been said that the conspiracy claim may express "the true nature and gravamen of the case": *Kuwait Oil Tanker Co SAK v Al Bader* [2000] 2 All E.R. Comm. 271 at [119] (where the conspiracy claim was significant for the then-applicable conflict of laws rules).

[214] See para.19–041.

[215] [2008] UKHL 19; [2008] 1 A.C. 1174 at [221].

19–048 **Incidental criminal wrongs.** It is not, however, in every case that the use of criminal means gives rise to unlawful means conspiracy. It is not enough that there is a crime somewhere in the story. We have already seen in the context of intentionally inflicting harm by unlawful means how even the minority who would have included crimes as unlawful means would not go so far as to say that the tort is committed by the infringement of road traffic rules by a pizza delivery company eager to take trade from its rivals because the crime is not directed at the rivals and is not in a real sense the instrumentality of the harm.[216] The same is true if the claim is framed as a conspiracy.[217] In the *Revenue and Customs Commissioners* case, in contrast, the claimants were the direct target of the offence of cheating and the offence existed, "in its very nature to protect the Revenue".[218] We have seen that the commission of a crime which is not a common law tort in its own right does not give rise to civil liability unless an intention to accord a civil action can be found in the legislation creating the offence.[219] That has been used as a reason for rejecting crime as unlawful means in the tort of intentionally causing harm by unlawful means.[220] It is unclear exactly how this principle stands in the context of unlawful means conspiracy, Lord Walker in *Revenue and Customs Commissioners* being content to say that:[221]

> "[T]he sort of considerations relevant to determining whether a breach of statutory duty is actionable in a civil suit . . . may well overlap, or even occasionally coincide with, the issue of unlawful means in the tort of conspiracy. But the range of possible breaches of statutory duty, and the range of possible conspiracies, are both so wide and varied that it would be unwise to attempt to lay down any general rule."

C. Place of Conspiracy in the Law

19–049 **The "magic of plurality".** *Crofter* conspiracy to injure is widely regarded as anomalous,[222] though it has attracted more controversy among academic writers than success in practical application.[223] The central issue has been why the "magic of plurality" should make something unlawful if it is not unlawful when done by one person alone. Numbers may, of course, bring increased power and in the *Crofter* case Viscount Maugham said that he had never felt any difficulty in

---

[216] See para.19–022.
[217] [2008] UKHL 19; [2008] 1 A.C. 1174 at [95].
[218] [2008] UKHL 19; [2008] 1 A.C. 1174 at [120] per Lord Mance.
[219] See Ch.8.
[220] *OBG v Allan* [2007] UKHL 21; [2008] 1 A.C. 1 at [57] per Lord Hoffmann. However, Lord Hoffmann relies on *Lonrho v Shell (No.2)* [1982] A.C. 173 for this and in the view of Lord Walker in *Revenue and Customs Commissioners* that case turned solely on the lack of intention to injure the claimants: [2008] UKHL 19; [2008] 1 A.C. 1174 at [95].
[221] [2008] UKHL 19; [2008] 1 A.C. 1174 at [96].
[222] *Lonrho Ltd v Shell Petroloeum Ltd (No.2)* [1982] A.C. 173 at 188; *Lonrho Plc v Fayed* [1992] 1 A.C. 448 at 463.
[223] *Lonrho Ltd v Shell Petroloeum Ltd (No.2)* [1982] A.C. 173 at 188.

seeing, "the great difference between the acts of one person and the acts in combination of two or of a multitude",[224] but, as Viscount Simon LC remarked in the same case:[225]

> "The view that the explanation is to be found in the increasing power of numbers to do damage beyond what one individual can do is open to the obvious answer that this depends on the personality and influence of the individual. In the play, Cyrano de Bergerac's single voice was more effective to drive the bad actor Montfleury off the stage than the protests of all the rest of the audience to restrain him. The action of a single tyrant may be more potent to inflict suffering on the continent of Europe than a combination of less powerful persons."

The argument from numbers continues to have some appeal in the criminal law but there are now few situations in which there may be an indictment for conspiracy in respect of acts which would not be criminal if done by one person. One day the law may (perhaps under the influence of the idea of abuse of rights) re-examine the place in our law of combination and of the "chasm" between lawful and unlawful acts which exists in the case of an individual, but at the moment there is no sign of a move towards a principle that the intentional infliction of harm without justification is actionable.[226]

5. TRADE DISPUTES

A general textbook on the law of tort is not the place for an extended discussion of the specialised law relating to trade disputes. Nevertheless these disputes have provided much of the "raw material" for the development of the law of economic torts and some of the leading cases can only be fully understood against the background of the legislative intervention since 1906, so some account is necessary. Unfortunately it cannot be as brief as one might like.

19–050

History. The Trade Disputes Act 1906, passed as a result of the *Taff Vale* case,[227] made trade unions immune from actions in tort and conferred protection on individuals, such as union officials, against liability for conspiracy to injure and inducing breach of contract where the acts were done in contemplation or furtherance of a trade dispute. The Trade Disputes Act 1965 extended this immunity to the tort of intimidation after *Rookes v Barnard*. After a brief and unsuccessful experiment by the Conservative Government of 1970–1974 with a new, statutory regime of civil remedies in trade disputes the Trade Union and Labour Relations Act 1974 restored the former position. After 1979 another Conservative Government passed a series of Acts which imposed liability on unions as well as individuals,[228] required ballots as a preliminary to industrial action and withdrew the immunity of unions and individuals in respect of action

19–051

---

[224] *Crofter Hand-Woven Harris Tweed Co Ltd v Veitch* [1942] A.C. 435 at 448.

[225] *Crofter Hand-Woven Harris Tweed Co Ltd v Veitch* [1942] A.C. 435 at 443. See also Lord Diplock's rather less colourful example of the street-corner grocers and a chain of supermarkets in single ownership in the *Lonrho v Shell* case: [1982] A.C. 173 at 189.

[226] Cf. *Bradford Corp v Pickles* [1895] A.C. 151 with *Tuttle v Buck* (1909) 119 N.W. 946.

[227] *Taff Vale Ry Co v Amalgamated Society of Ry Servants* [1901] A.C. 426.

[228] In fact the Trade Union and Labour Relations Act 1974 imposed liability on unions (where there was no trade dispute) for certain torts causing personal injury or breaches of duty connected with the union's property.

taken for certain purposes or directed at "secondary targets". The law is now consolidated in Pts II and V of the Trade Union and Labour Relations (Consolidation) Act 1992 (the 1992 Act) as amended.

A. Liability of Trade Unions

19–052   **Quasi-corporate status.** A trade union is not a body corporate[229] but the 1992 Act gives it certain attributes of a body corporate. It can make contracts and sue and be sued in its own name and, indeed, be prosecuted. Though the Act does not say so in so many words, it seems that where the claim does not concern a trade dispute the union's liability in tort is exactly the same as that of a natural person or corporate body[230] and its liability for the acts of individuals is to be determined by the general law of vicarious liability.

19–053   **Vicarious liability for the economic torts.** Where, however, the claim relates to one of the economic torts likely to be involved in a trade dispute[231] a different test of vicarious liability applies. The act of an individual or group is taken to have been done by the union if it is authorised or endorsed by it and it is taken to have done so if the act was done or was authorised or endorsed by any person empowered by the union rules so to act, by the executive or president or general secretary, or by any committee of the union or any official (whether employed by the union or not).[232] Furthermore, action by an official is deemed to be the action of the union for this purpose notwithstanding anything in the rules of the union.[233] These provisions represent a very considerable extension of union responsibility when compared with the legislation which first imposed liability on the union itself.[234] The only escape route for the union is to repudiate the actions under s.21 but this is not necessarily easy to do for not only must notice of the repudiation be given to the persons calling the action but the union must "do its best" to give written notice in prescribed form to every member of the union who the union has reason to believe is taking part, or might otherwise take part, in industrial action. Furthermore, any subsequent conduct by the executive, president or general secretary which is inconsistent with the repudiation renders it

---

[229] Trade Union and Labour Relations (Consolidation) Act 1992 s.10(1).

[230] There are restrictions on enforcement of judgments against certain property, no matter what the source of the claim: s.23.

[231] For the full statutory formula see s.20(1).

[232] Section 20(2). An act is taken to have been done, authorised or endorsed by an official if it was done, etc., "by, or by any member of, any group of persons of which he was at the material time a member, the purposes of which included organising or co-ordinating industrial action": s.20(3)(b). Read literally this would mean that the union was responsible where a works committee of which a shop steward was a member had been established to co-ordinate a "work to rule" but the committee had decided, against the vote of the shop steward, to call a strike.

[233] Section 20(4).

[234] The present law derives from the Employment Act 1990. Under the Employment Act 1982 the union was responsible only for the acts of employed officials and shop stewards were hardly ever union employees. Furthermore, action was not taken to have been authorised or endorsed if it was forbidden by union rules. See *Unofficial Action and the Law* (Cm.821). The rules in the 1992 Act apply to a union's responsibility for contempt by disobedience to an injunction as well as to the initial liability in tort.

ineffective.[235] The stringent requirements of effective repudiation may be expensive for a union but may also face it with "political" difficulties in making the unequivocal statement required.[236]

If the individual act is the union's responsibility under these provisions the union has the same protection against liability for acts done, "in contemplation or furtherance of a trade dispute"[237] as the individuals concerned, though this protection is withdrawn in a number of situations, including that where the action is not supported by a ballot,[238] a point of considerable importance given the width of the union's responsibility for action at local level which is not effectively repudiated in accordance with the Act.

Remedies. In practice the remedy sought in trade dispute cases has tended to be an injunction because it is far better from the employer's point of view to stop the strike than to seek compensation after the event. In addition, the fact that for many years liability was imposed only on individuals, probably of modest means,[239] made damages claims unattractive. Now that liability is directly imposed on the union, damages may become more attractive but the union's liability is limited on a scale geared to the size of the union and the maximum award of £250,000 is low in relation to the damage that may be suffered. The very large fines (on which there is no limit) imposed for contempt by disobedience to an injunction are probably a more powerful sanction. Where a union's liability arises in respect of personal injury caused by negligence, nuisance or breach of duty, or in respect of the ownership or occupation of property or under Pt I of the Consumer Protection Act 1987[240] there is no limit on damages.[241] There is no limit on the award of damages against an individual in any case.

19–054

B. Protection from Liability in Trade Disputes

Statutory immunity.[242] If the matter were left to the common law it would be virtually impossible to call a strike because the persons doing so would commit one or more of the torts of inducing breach of contract, intentional infliction of

19–055

---

[235] Section 21(5). See *Express and Star Newspapers v NGA* (1982) [1985] I.R.L.R. 455 ("nods, winks, turning of blind eyes and similar clandestine methods of approval").

[236] In particular, if the union repudiates the action it is "unofficial" and by s.237 the employer may dismiss any persons taking part in it. Of course, the basic rule of the common law is that a strike is a fundamental breach of contract justifying dismissal but under the 1992 Act as enacted where the action was official the employer could not dismiss "selectively". Now even non-selective dismissal is restricted where the action was supported by the requisite ballot: s.238A, inserted by the Employment Relations Act 1999. For a full account see *Clerk and Lindsell on Torts*, 20th edn (2013), para.24–133.

[237] See para.19–055.

[238] See para.19–066.

[239] There was, of course, nothing to prevent the union indemnifying its officials. Under s.15 of the 1992 Act it is unlawful for a union to indemnify an individual against penalties for a crime or a contempt, but this has no application to civil damages.

[240] The last seems an unlikely contingency.

[241] The restrictions on execution against certain types of property apply to all awards of damages.

[242] Although operating as an immunity, there is no requirement that s.219 should be construed strictly against those seeking to invoke it: *London & Birmingham Railway Ltd v ASLEF* [2011] EWCA Civ 226; [2011] I.C.R. 848; cf. *P v NASMUWT* [2003] UKHL 8; [2003] 2 A.C. 663 at [7] per Lord

harm by unlawful means and conspiracy. Since 1906, therefore, Parliament has granted a degree of protection (commonly called "immunity") to those engaged in trade disputes. The present law is contained in s.219(1) and (2) of the 1992 Act, which reads as follows:

> "(1) An act done by a person in contemplation or furtherance of a trade dispute is not actionable in tort on the ground only—
>   (a) that it induces another person to break a contract or interferes or induces another person to interfere with its performance, or
>   (b) that it consists in his threatening that a contract (whether one to which he is a party or not) will be broken or its performance interfered with, or that he will induce another person to break a contract or interfere with its performance.
> (2) An agreement or combination by two or more persons to do or procure the doing of an act in contemplation or furtherance of a trade dispute is not actionable in tort if the act is one which if done without any such agreement or combination would not be actionable in tort."

It will be observed that the law speaks in terms of rendering certain acts not actionable in tort rather than conferring a "right to strike".[243] Far from there being a right to strike it remains the general rule of contractual employment law that the withdrawal of labour will be a breach of contract, though there are now restrictions on the right to dismiss for it.[244]

i. Trade Disputes

19–056 **Definition of "trade dispute".** In order to gain the protection of s.219, the act done by the defendant must be, "in contemplation or furtherance of a trade dispute". This concept, the so-called "golden formula", is defined in great detail in s.244 but essentially it means a dispute[245] between workers[246] and their employer[247] and which relates wholly or mainly[248] to matters about the employment[249] of workers, such as terms and conditions of employment, engagement and dismissal, allocation of work, discipline, union membership or machinery for negotiation.[250] The central difficulty is to determine when the dispute "relates" to the relevant matters. To be protected the dispute must relate to current contracts of employment and not to potential contracts of employment

---

Bingham. There is also now a requirement, in the interpretation of the legislation, to observe the requirements of the Human Rights Act: *Balfour Beatty Engineering Services Ltd v Unite* [2012] EWHC 267 (QB); [2012] I.C.R. 822 at [8].

[243] See *Metrobus Ltd v UNITE* [2009] EWCA Civ 829; [2009] I.R.L.R. 851 at [118].

[244] See para.19–053.

[245] But by s.219(4) pressure which is so effective that the employer succumbs immediately to it is deemed to have been exerted in contemplation or furtherance of a dispute.

[246] Including former workers whose employment was terminated in connection with the dispute or whose dismissal was one of the circumstances giving rise to the dispute: s.244(5).

[247] An inter-union dispute is not, as such, within the protection but such a dispute is likely to involve an employer.

[248] Before 1982 the dispute had merely to be "connected with" the relevant matters and older cases should be read with this in mind.

[249] "Employment" in this context has a wider meaning than the technical one of master and servant because it includes, "any relationship whereby one person personally does work or performs services for another": s.219(5).

[250] For more detail see the Act.

with another person to whom the employer may at some time transfer the enterprise.[251] Subject to that: "[A] dispute about what workers are obliged to do or how the employer is obliged to remunerate them, at any level of generality or particularity, is about terms and conditions of employment."[252]

A dispute arising out of the validity of an order given by an employer can be a trade dispute; and it cannot be the law that protection is confined to disputes about the interpretation of existing terms, for strikes about pay scales or the frequency of rest breaks, for example, involve attempts to change the terms of the existing contracts.

Politically motivated strikes. Particular difficulty arises when it is contended that the strike is politically motivated. In *BBC v Hearn*[253] the defendants, in order to protest against apartheid, threatened to instruct the members of their union to commit breaches of contract in relation to a broadcast by satellite to South Africa of the 1977 Cup Final. In proceedings for an interlocutory injunction the Court of Appeal held that it was unlikely that it could be established at the trial that there was a trade dispute but it was suggested that the position might well have been different if, instead of simply threatening to "black" the broadcast, the defendants had gone to the BBC and said "we wish it to be established as part of our conditions of employment that we are not required to work on broadcasts to South Africa".[254] However, it has since been remarked in the House of Lords that a:[255]

19–057

> "[T]rade union cannot turn a dispute which in reality has no connection with terms and conditions of employment into a dispute connected with terms and conditions of employment by insisting that the employer inserts appropriate terms into the contracts of employment into which he enters."

These propositions are not logically inconsistent because the first does not assert that protection is to be given to what is in reality a political campaign merely dressed up as relating to employment and the second does not deny that a group of workers might demand that their contracts should contain provisions about matters on which they had strong beliefs. However, the dispute must be about what workers are employed to *do* and it has been suggested that even if the demand in *Hearn* had been couched in the above terms it would have made no difference because they would have been required to perform the same services whether or not the broadcast had been beamed to South Africa.[256] *Wandsworth LBC v NASMUWT*[257] concerned a boycott by a teaching union of testing under the national curriculum. The court held that on the evidence there was clearly a

---

[251] *UCL Hospitals NHS Trust v UNISON* [1999] I.C.R. 204. Some degree of protection for transferred workers is provided by the Transfer of Undertakings (Protection of Employment) Regulations 2006 (SI 2006/246), replacing earlier legislation.

[252] *P v NASMUWT* [2003] UKHL 8; [2003] 2 A.C. 663 at [28].

[253] [1977] 1 W.L.R. 1004.

[254] This was approved by Lord Diplock in *NWL Ltd v Woods* [1979] 1 W.L.R. 1294.

[255] Lord Cross in *Universe Tankships Inc of Monrovia v ITWF* [1983] 1 A.C. 366 at 392. However, that was an economic duress case in which there was no dispute between employer and workers and the union was an "interloper" waging a campaign against "flags of convenience".

[256] *P v NASMUWT* [2003] UKHL 8; [2003] 2 A.C. 663 at [31].

[257] [1994] I.C.R. 81.

trade dispute because the union's predominant concern was with the workload imposed by the tests, even though there was also objection to the methods of testing on educational grounds. However, by implication the result would have been different had the union said "our members believe that the methods proposed are bad methods and we believe we would be in breach of our professional duty to safeguard the welfare of children if we operated them".[258]

19–058   **Definition of "in furtherance of".** An act is "in furtherance of" a trade dispute when the doer genuinely believes that it will assist the cause in support of which it is done: the House of Lords has emphatically rejected the addition of any requirement that the act be "not too remote" or "reasonably likely to succeed".[259]

ii.   Inducing Breach of Contract and Causing Loss by Unlawful Means

19–059   **Effect of the development of the law.** The legislation was of course passed before the decisions in the *OBG* and *Revenue and Customs Commissioners* cases. If it were passed now it would undoubtedly be very differently drafted but we have to do the best we can to fit the present structure of the law into it. Calling a strike would be the *Lumley v Gye* tort at common law because it would involve inducing the workers to break their contracts of employment but it is clearly protected by the opening words of s.219(1)(a). It is now clear that there is no tort of "interference" with the performance of a contract[260] and any claim other than in respect of the direct procurement of breaches of the employment contracts is likely to be couched in terms of causing loss by unlawful means. Since the existence of this tort (even if not in precisely its present form) was recognized well before 1992 it is unfortunate that it was not dealt with directly in the statute but in *Hadmor Productions Ltd v Hamilton*[261] the House of Lords held that an act which was "not actionable" under an earlier equivalent of s.219(1) did not amount to unlawful means for the purposes of the tort of intimidation (hence the references to "threatening" in s.219(1)) and we now know that that tort may be only a variant of the general tort of causing loss by unlawful means. It seems therefore that there is immunity whether the strike caller is sued on the basis of: (a) an actual procurement of breaches of the contracts of employment; (b) threatening such breaches; or (c) causing loss by bringing about the non-performance of the employer's contract with a third party. So also the immunity extends to a claim based on causing loss by unlawful means brought by the third party against the strike-caller,[262] though in the normal case it would now seem

---

[258] In *Mercury Communications Ltd v Scott-Garner* [1984] Ch. 37, even though there was a potential threat to jobs of union members with BT because of the Government's policy of allowing Mercury to compete with BT, the court concluded that the action was mainly in support of an ideological campaign against the break-up of nationalised industries. Cf. *Westminster CC v Unison* [2001] EWCA Civ 443; [2001] I.C.R. 1046.

[259] *Express Newspapers Ltd v McShane* [1980] A.C. 672; *Duport Steels Ltd v Sirs* [1980] 1 W.L.R. 142.

[260] See para.19–009.

[261] [1983] 1 A.C. 191.

[262] *Hadmor Productions Ltd v Hamilton* [1983] 1 A.C. 191.

that the tort would not be committed at common law anyway since there would not be the requisite intention to harm the third party, even if that harm was an obviously likely consequence.[263]

Scope of the protection. The protection is conferred where the claim is on the ground *only* of the inducement or threat of breach: if therefore the defendant procures a strike by telling lies he is liable for deceit (and/or defamation).[264] Though the matter is not beyond doubt, it is probably the case that the defendant retains his immunity for the economic tort in question. That may be significant on the issue of damages (though damages are rarely sought in trade dispute cases) where the "other" tort is merely incidental (e.g. a trespass to land committed by a union official while persuading workers to strike) but where the other tort is the essential means of inflicting the harm this may make little difference.

19–060

iii. Conspiracy

Section 219(2) removes "conspiracy to injure" from the field of trade disputes because it involves a combination to do an act which would not be actionable in tort if done without any agreement or combination.[265] The scope of "unlawful means" conspiracy may also be restricted by this provision because of the requirement that the act should be one which would be actionable *in tort* if done by an individual. Thus an agreement to break a contract may not be actionable.[266] An agreement to induce a breach of contract might be thought to fall outside this provision because inducement is a tort if committed by one person, but this is not so if the inducement is protected by s.219(1) because the means are not then to be regarded as unlawful.[267] Despite the *Revenue and Customs Commissioners* case it also removes tort liability for conspiracy to commit a crime from this field.

19–061

C. Unprotected Acts

Action to enforce union membership. The protection of s.219 is withdrawn from industrial action in a number of situations. The first of them is action taken to enforce union membership.[268] The attempts to enforce the "closed shop" which were the source of many earlier trade dispute cases would now be exposed to legal liability.[269]

19–062

---

[263] See para.19–026, above.

[264] Nor was there any trade disputes issue in *Iqbal v Prison Officers Association* [2009] EWCA Civ 1310; [2010] I.N.L.R. 489, though the claim for false imprisonment caused by the action failed on the facts.

[265] The protection is really unnecessary: if the defendants are acting in contemplation or furtherance of a trade dispute they have a "legitimate purpose" at common law and they do not "intend to injure" the claimant: *Hadmor Productions Ltd v Hamilton* [1983] 1 A.C. 191 at 228.

[266] The point is of hardly any practical importance since collective agreements between employers and unions are rarely contracts.

[267] See para.19–059.

[268] See s.222.

[269] So there would again be liability on the facts of *Rookes v Barnard* [1964] A.C. 1129, even though the Trade Disputes Act 1965 brought intimidation within the protection of the trade disputes immunity.

19–063 **Action designed to impose union recognition requirements.** Sections 186 and 187 of the Act prevent commercial discrimination against a person (for example refusing to award him contracts or excluding him from tendering) on the ground that the work should be done by union labour. This is backed up by s.225(1), which withdraws trade dispute protection from action taken against an employer to induce him to contravene ss.186 and 187. In addition, by s.225(2), protection is withdrawn from action interfering with employment contracts which disrupts the supply of goods and services to the employer from a supplier and the reason for the action is the supplier's failure to accord recognition to a union.

19–064 **Action protesting dismissal for unofficial action.** By s.223 there is no protection for action taken because an employer has dismissed a worker for taking part in unofficial industrial action.

19–065 **"Secondary action".** Protection is withdrawn from "secondary action" (other than lawful picketing). Special provision was first made for secondary action by the exceedingly complex s.17 of the Employment Act 1980. This is replaced by s.224 of the 1992 Act,[270] which is a great deal simpler but also more restrictive of union activities. Secondary action is defined in s.224(2) as occurring when:

> "[A] person—
> (a) induces another to break a contract of employment or interferes or induces another to interfere with its performance, or
> (b) threatens that a contract of employment under which he or another is employed will be broken or its performance interfered with, or that he will induce another to break a contract of employment or to interfere with its performance,
> and the employer under the contract of employment is not the employer party to the dispute."

So protection is withdrawn when, say, there is a dispute with employer A and the union, to put pressure on A, calls out its members at employer B, a supplier of A.[271] A business may be an economic unit but have a corporate structure consisting of a number of companies under a holding company. In that event under the previous legislation the House of Lords held that one could not pierce the corporate veil and the companies were separate "employers" for this purpose.[272] The law seems to be the same under the 1992 Act which, indeed, provides that even if there are disputes with each of the companies within the group each one has to be treated as separate for this purpose.[273] The action must involve interference with contracts of employment:[274] if the action against A has

---

[270] Re-enacting the Employment Act 1990 s.4.

[271] It would seem that the protection is withdrawn whether the claimant is A or B. This was the case under the 1980 Act: *Merkur Island Shipping Corp v Laughton* [1983] 2 A.C. 570 at 609.

[272] *Dimbleby & Sons Ltd v NUJ* [1984] 1 W.L.R. 427.

[273] Section 224(4). The somewhat mysterious s.224(5) provides that: "primary action in relation to [one trade] dispute may not be relied on as secondary action in relation to another trade dispute." This seems to contemplate two trade disputes at employer A and employer B where, say, inducing breaches of contracts at A has the effect of interfering with the employment contracts at B, in which case B cannot complain of unlawful secondary action. This is the only purpose for which primary action is defined and it means action such as is described in s.224(2) directed against A. This seems to ignore the fact that the action against A might be something other than interference with A's contracts of employment.

[274] Given a somewhat extended meaning: see fn.249.

the effect of disrupting the commercial contract between A and B then even though B is in a sense a "secondary victim" of the action there is no secondary action for the purposes of the Act and the union is protected against action by B as well as by A.[275]

Action not supported by ballot. Protection is withdrawn from action which does not have the support of a majority in a ballot.[276] The voting paper must contain a question requiring the union member to state whether he is willing to take part in a strike or action short of a strike and contain a warning that what is proposed may be a breach of his contract of employment. Although there is provision for ignoring inconsequential errors,[277] the requirements on balloting must be strictly complied with.[278] A ballot ceases to be effective after four weeks but there are two qualifications to this. First, so long as the action has begun within the four-week period it may continue thereafter without further ballot;[279] secondly, where there has been an injunction restraining the action but subsequently that is discharged or set aside by the court, then the court may extend the period up to a maximum of 12 weeks from the date of the ballot.[280] The "action" referred to by s.226 is collective action, not the particular action by the person induced. Where, therefore, additional persons join the union after the ballot the immunity is not lost in respect of inducements of breaches of contract by them.[281]

19–066

D. Picketing

Picketing in various forms has shown itself to be one of the most effective forms of industrial action. At common law it may be unlawful as amounting to a trespass to the highway, or a public or private nuisance,[282] or as involving the inducement or procuring of a breach of contract. However, under s.220 of the 1992 Act it is lawful for a person in contemplation or furtherance of a trade dispute to attend at or near his own place of work,[283] "for the purpose of

19–067

---

[275] The core immunity provisions of s.219 are not confined to interference with contracts of employment. It might be of course that now there would be no tort against B at common law: para.19–026.

[276] Section 226. Further amendments to the balloting procedure were made by the Trade Union Reform and Employment Rights Act 1993, the Employment Relations Act 1999 and the Employment Relations Act 2004, inserting or substituting provisions in the 1992 Act. See s.226, 226A–C, 228, 228A, 231, 231A–B, 232A–B, 234, 234A.

[277] Section 232B; *British Airways Plc v Unite* [2010] EWCA Civ 669; [2010] I.C.R. 1316; *London & Birmingham Railway Ltd v ASLEF* [2011] EWCA Civ 226; [2011] I.C.R. 848; *RMT v Serco Ltd* [2011] EWCA Civ 226; [2011] I.R.L.R. 399.

[278] *NURMTW v Midland Mainline Ltd* [2001] EWCA Civ 1206; [2001] I.R.L.R. 813. Cf. *English, Welsh and Scottish Ry v NURMTW* [2004] EWCA Civ 1539.

[279] A further ballot is not necessary to reimpose industrial action which has been suspended during negotiations: *Monsanto Plc v TGWU* [1987] 1 W.L.R. 617; but if, as a matter of substance, the first action has ended and the union embarks on a new campaign then a fresh ballot is needed: *Post Office v Union of Communication Workers* [1990] 1 W.L.R. 981.

[280] Section 234.

[281] *London Underground Ltd v NURMTW* [1996] I.C.R. 170.

[282] See para.15–076.

[283] Or, where he is a union official, at or near the place of work of a member of the union whom he is accompanying and whom he represents. Where a person's employment was terminated because of a

peacefully obtaining or communicating information, or peacefully persuading any person to work or abstain from working". Immunity for acts done in the course of picketing (for example inducing breaches of contract) exists only if the picket is lawful under s.220.[284] Despite the general withdrawal of protection from secondary action interfering with a contract of employment, such action (for example persuading a supplier's lorry driver not to deliver) is protected when done in the course of lawful picketing,[285] but what used to be known as "secondary picketing", i.e. attendance at the premises of the employer's supplier or customer is not of course protected, given the fundamental requirements of s.220.

E.   Injunctions and Restraining Actions by Individuals

19–068   **Injunctions.** Where an employer is the victim of industrial action, his primary purpose in embarking on litigation is usually to obtain an injunction. Since an injunction may be granted on an interim basis pending trial (which may not take place for many months) and, in cases of great urgency, without notice to the other party, it is clear that there is a serious possibility of the union side being robbed of the initiative in an industrial dispute. Section 221 of the 1992 Act contains two provisions which go some way to meeting this point.

19–069   **Notice requirements.** Where an application for an injunction is made without notice and the defendant claims, or in the opinion of the court would be likely to claim, that he acted in contemplation or furtherance of a trade dispute, the court shall not grant the injunction unless satisfied that all reasonable steps have been taken to secure that notice of the application and an opportunity of being heard have been given to him.[286] This reduces the risk of the defendants in a "labour injunction" case being taken unawares but it contains nothing about how the court should proceed once the parties are before it.

19–070   **Interim injunctions.** Under the general law, according to *American Cyanamid Ltd v Ethicon Ltd*,[287] the claimant, in order to obtain an interim injunction, must show that there is a "serious question to be tried", something which is fairly easily established given the uncertainty of many issues about economic torts. What is now s.221(2) was enacted in 1976 in response to the *Cyanamid* case and provides that where an application is made for an interim injunction and the party against whom it is sought claims that he acted in contemplation or furtherance of a trade dispute, the court shall, in exercising its discretion whether or not to grant the injunction, have regard to the likelihood of that party's succeeding at the trial of the action in establishing a defence under ss.219 or 220. It is clear that it was intended to be more difficult to obtain an interim injunction in trade dispute cases than in others, but beyond this it is not easy to say what effect the provision has.

---

trade dispute or the termination is a cause of the trade dispute then he may attend his former place of work. Cf. *J&R Kenny Cleaning Services v TGWU, The Times*, June 15, 1989 (business transferred by former employer, no trade dispute).

[284] Section 219(3).
[285] Section 224(1), (3).
[286] Section 221(1).
[287] [1975] A.C. 396. See further para.23–127.

Under the *American Cyanamid* decision the court must ask itself whether the claimant has shown: (1) a serious question to be tried; and (2) a "balance of convenience" in his favour. It is unclear whether s.221(2) adds a third element or is subsumed in (2) or what practical difference it makes which view is taken.[288] It has been suggested that now that unions (and not merely officials) may in certain circumstances be liable in damages for unlawful industrial action it is more likely that the employer will pursue a claim to a full trial and there is less reason to refuse an interim injunction in trade dispute cases[289] but it has also been said that the "right to strike" is a valuable (indeed essential) element in the system of collective bargaining and that it "should not be rendered less valuable than parliament intended by too fanciful or ingenious a view of what might develop into a serious issue to be tried".[290]

Some strikes are likely to cause widespread inconvenience to the public or even economic damage to the nation as a whole and there are some judicial statements to the effect that the public interest in these cases may be a factor to be taken into account in the exercise of the judicial discretion, independently of the justice of the case between the parties.[291]

Restraining actions by individuals. The Trade Union Reform and Employment Rights Act 1993 introduced a novel and highly unusual restraint on industrial action which falls outside the trade dispute protection. An individual[292] who claims that a trade union[293] or other person has done or is likely to do an unlawful act[294] to induce any person to take part in industrial action and that the effect or likely effect of the action is to prevent or delay the supply of goods or services to the individual (or reduce their quality) may apply to the High Court for an order requiring him to desist from the inducement and to take steps to terminate the effect of any prior inducement.[295] There is no claim for damages. The effect of this is that a member of the public likely to be affected by industrial action may intervene even though he might be unable to show the requisite interest to found a claim at common law and even though he has no contractual claim to the delivery of the goods or services affected by the dispute.[296] If the claimant makes out the matters required by the section the court may make such order as it considers appropriate to require the defendant to desist, etc. but it appears that the court has no discretion simply to refuse relief.[297]

19–071

---

[288] For a detailed account see *Clerk and Lindsell on Torts*, 20th edn (2013), para.24–161.

[289] *Dimbleby & Sons Ltd v NUJ* [1984] 1 W.L.R. 427 at 431–432.

[290] *Barretts & Baird (Wholesale) Ltd v I.P.C.S.* [1987] I.R.L.R. 3 at 11 per Henry J; cf. *British Airways Plc v Unite* [2010] EWCA Civ 669; [2010] I.C.R. 1316 at [109].

[291] *Duport Steels Ltd v Sirs* [1980] 1 W.L.R. 142; *Associated British Ports v TGWU* [1989] 3 All E.R. 796 (reversed on appeal on other grounds [1989] 3 All E.R. 822).

[292] The term is not defined, but clearly excludes a corporation. There are said to have been instances of apparently private suits financed by pressure groups or parties to the dispute.

[293] The responsibility of the union under these provisions is in accord with s.20, see para.19–053.

[294] i.e. one which is actionable in tort.

[295] See s.235A of the 1992 Act as inserted by s.22 of the 1993 Act.

[296] See s.235A(3).

[297] This seems to be the effect of s.235A(4).

6. PASSING OFF[298]

19–072 **Introduction.** The tort of passing off is part of a much wider canvas of legal remedies controlling unfair competitive practices and we have already said that "unfair competition" would be beyond the scope of this book, so that such matters as copyrights, trade marks and patents must be sought elsewhere. However, a brief account of passing off may be justified since it is: (1) a tort; (2) is based entirely on the common law; and (3) may in some respects be capable of development.[299] The importance of the law of passing off was reduced by the Trade Marks Act 1994, particularly in so far as the Act allowed a trade mark to be registered in respect of a container or the "get-up" of the goods. Nevertheless, even where there appears to be a strong case of trade mark infringement it remains common to run a parallel claim for passing off and it will be the only remedy where the law of trade marks is inapplicable or the registration is invalid or, of course, where there has been no attempt at registration.[300]

19–073 **Summary requirements.** The action arose in the 19th century and depended upon the simple principle that a person is not to sell his goods or his services under the pretence that they are those of another.[301] It has three elements:[302] (a) a goodwill or reputation attached to and recognised by the public as distinctive of the claimant's goods or services; (b) a misrepresentation by the defendant leading the public, or a substantial number of members of the public, to believe that his goods or services are those of the claimant; (c) damage or likely damage.[303]

---

[298] See Carty, *An Analysis of the Economic Torts*, 2nd edn (2010), Ch.11; Wadlow, *Passing Off*, 4th edn.

[299] The other matters mentioned above depend almost entirely on statute. Other common law torts which may be relevant in this area include deceit and malicious falsehood.

[300] A trade mark is not to be registered in so far as its use is liable to be prevented by the law of passing off: Trade Marks Act 1994, s.5(4)(a). Similarly, passing off claims may be brought in parallel to claims for infringement of copyright. The gist of passing off is deceptive resemblance; but in the case of copyright, although there typically is resemblance, the gist of the complaint is that the defendant's work is derived from the claimant's: *Designers Guild Ltd v Russell Williams (Textiles) Ltd* [2001] 1 W.L.R. 2416.

[301] *Perry v Truefitt* (1842) 6 Beav 66 at 73 per Lord Langdale MR; *Spalding & Bros v AW Gamage Ltd* (1915) 84 L.J. Ch. 449 at 450 per Lord Parker.

[302] In *Erwen Warnink BV v J Townend & Sons (Hull) Ltd* [1979] A.C. 731 at 742 Lord Diplock referred to five elements: (a) a misrepresentation; (b) made by a trader in the course of trade; (c) to prospective customers of his or ultimate consumers of goods or services supplied by him; (d) which is calculated to injure the business or goodwill of another trader (in the sense that this is a reasonably foreseeable consequence); and (e) which causes or threatens actual damage to a business or goodwill of the trader by whom the action is brought. This formulation is quoted without criticism by Lord Jauncey in *Reckitt & Colman Products Ltd v Borden Inc* [1990] 1 W.L.R. 491 at 511, but Lord Oliver at 499 set out the more abbreviated three elements referred to in the text and this now seems to be the preferred formulation: see Nourse LJ in *Consorzio del Prosciutto di Parma v Marks & Spencer Plc* [1991] R.P.C. 351 at 368–369; *Woolley v Ultimate Products Ltd* [2012] EWCA Civ 1038 at [2].

[303] Damage may take the form of loss of sales or erosion of the distinctiveness of the trade name sought to be protected: *Erwen Warnink BV v J Townend & Sons (Hull) Ltd* [1979] AC 731 at 745 per Lord Diplock; *Chocosuisse v Cadbury Ltd* [1998] R.P.C. 117, 143 per Laddie J; *Woolley v Ultimate Products Ltd* [2012] EWCA Civ 1038 at [7]; an interim injunction may be granted on the basis of the latter before it has resulted in the former.

A. Varieties of Passing Off

"Simple" passing off.[304] The representation must be such as to cause confusion in the public mind between the claimant's goods or business and the defendant's goods or business: false statements disparaging the claimant's goods are actionable as malicious falsehood or libel and statements falsely exaggerating the worth of the defendant's wares are not, as such, actionable by a competitor even though he has suffered damage thereby.[305] Nor is passing off committed by using the claimant's name or trade mark in such a way that the public are not deceived about the provenance of the defendant's goods.[306] It is essential that the defendant should have made a representation[307] calculated to deceive,[308] though in the modern law no form of fraud or even negligence is essential to establish liability.[309] It is enough that the defendant "misrepresents his goods in such a way that it is a reasonably foreseeable consequence of the misrepresentation that the plaintiff's business or goodwill will be damaged".[310]

19–074

Trade marks. A common form of passing off involves copying or imitating the claimant's registered trade mark, in which case there has always been the possibility of claims both under the trade mark statute and at common law. A modern version of this activity against which passing off has been successfully invoked is registering Internet domain names as variations around the names of well-known companies and then offering the names to the companies at high prices with the express or implied threat of allowing them to be used for deception or as "blockers" to legitimate registration.[311]

19–075

Imitating the get-up of goods. An example of passing off by imitating the get-up of the claimant's goods (now also covered by the law of trade marks) is *Reckitt & Colman Products Ltd v Borden Inc.*[312] The claimants had for a good many years sold lemon juice ("Jif") in the United Kingdom in a "squeezy container" in the form of a small plastic lemon. They obtained an injunction against the

19–076

---

[304] The label employed by Briggs J in *Fage UK Ltd Chobani UK Ltd* [2013] EWHC 630 (Ch); [2013] F.S.R. 32 at [118], in contrast to "extended passing off": see para.19–080.
[305] See *BBC v Talksport Ltd* [2001] F.S.R. 6 (false claims that broadcasts were live; no interference with claimants' goodwill); *Schulke & Mayr UK Ltd v Alkapharm UK Ltd* [1999] F.S.R.161.
[306] *Arsenal Football Club Plc v Reed* [2001] R.P.C. 46. There were further proceedings in this case before the European Court of Justice and an appeal to the CA, but these concerned trade marks. At the end of his judgment ([2003] EWCA Civ 696; [2003] R.P.C. 39 at [70]) Aldous LJ said that he was not convinced that the reasoning below on passing off had been correct.
[307] Where there is no misrepresentation by the defendant it is not enough that, "people make assumptions, jump to unjustified conclusions, and put two and two together to make five": *HFC Bank Plc v Midland Bank Plc* [2000] F.S.R. 176. On the position of the producer of a new product in a market where there is a de facto monopoly see *British Sky Broadcasting Group Plc v Sky Home Services Ltd* [2006] EWHC 3165 (Ch); [2007] 3 All E.R. 1066.
[308] *Perkins v Shone* [2004] EWHC 2249 (Ch).
[309] The customer need not know or care about the identity of the manufacturer, provided the customer knows there is such a person and cares that the goods he buys are made by that person: *United Biscuits (UK) Ltd v Asda Stores Ltd* [1997] R.P.C. 513.
[310] *Reckitt & Colman Products Ltd v Borden Inc* [1990] 1 W.L.R. 491 at 511 per Lord Jauncey; "the essence of the action is not confusion, but misrepresentation": *Fine and Country Ltd v Okotoks Ltd* [2013] EWCA Civ 672 at [55] per Lewison LJ.
[311] *British Telecommunications Plc v One in a Million Ltd* [1999] 1 W.L.R. 903.
[312] [1990] 1 W.L.R. 491.

defendants' attempt to sell lemon juice in a similar but not identical container. The difference in the labelling of the products was such as to prevent any risk of confusion in the mind of a careful shopper but the evidence showed that most shoppers did not read labels with any care and that plastic lemons containing lemon juice had become strongly associated in the public mind with the claimants' product. It was no answer that the confusion would not have occurred if the shoppers had been, "more careful, more literate or more perspicacious. Customers have to be taken as they are found".[313] Certainly no person can, except under the patent legislation, claim a monopoly in selling a particular article and the law of passing off would not prevent other people selling plastic lemons; but the claimants' case was not that the defendants were selling plastic lemons but that they were selling lemon juice in a lemon shaped container which had become associated with the claimants.[314]

Though the dispute in this case concerned a container rather than the substance of what was sold, it seems that the law of passing off may protect part of the design or structure of the article itself and this is so even if it serves a utilitarian purpose.[315] This is not to say that as a matter of principle or theory the claimant can use the law of passing off to gain a monopoly in the shape of an article[316] for it is always open to the defendant sufficiently to differentiate his product, by labelling, colouring or otherwise, to avoid the risk of confusion: it is simply that it was very difficult and perhaps impossible to do this on the facts of *Reckitt & Colman*, where the goods were unlikely to be subjected to close inspection by purchasers,[317] without abandoning the key element of the plastic lemon.

19–077   **Descriptive words.** Had the claimants in *Reckitt & Colman* been for many years the sole producers of lemon juice in the country, selling it in bottles labelled "Lemon Juice" it is clear that they could not have restrained a competitor from entering the market and doing the same thing for no one is entitled to fence off

---

[313] *Reckitt & Colman Products Ltd v Borden Inc* [1990] 1 W.L.R. 491 at 508. See also *R Johnston & Co v Archibald Orr Ewing & Co* (1882) 7 App. Cas. 219 and *White Hudson & Co Ltd v Asian Organisation Ltd* [1964] 1 W.L.R. 1466 ("red paper cough sweets") in both of which the parties were trading in the Far East where customers might have a limited command of English and hence the effect of different labels or names might be limited. Actual confusion on the part of a member of the purchasing public need not be proved as a matter of law (*Lee Kar Choo v Lee Lian Choon* [1967] 1 A.C. 602) but proof that it has occurred will obviously assist the claimant's case, especially if substantial damages are claimed and not merely an injunction.

[314] There was nothing to prevent the defendants selling lemon juice in bottles (as they were doing) or in plastic carrots, but as a matter of marketing reality if not bottles it was lemons or nothing.

[315] *William Edge & Sons Ltd v William Niccolls & Sons Ltd* [1911] A.C. 693 (dye in cloth bags fitted with a stick which could be used for stirring); cf. *Numatic International Ltd v Qualtex UK Ltd* [2010] EWHC 1237 (Ch); [2010] R.P.C. 25 ("Henry" vacuum cleaner); and see Lord Jauncey's example in *Reckitt & Colman Products Ltd v Borden Inc* [1990] 1 W.L.R. 491 at 519.

[316] This is allowed on a limited and temporary basis by the Registered Designs Act 1949 and the Copyright Designs and Patents Act 1988 s.213.

[317] Cf. *Hodgkinson & Corby Ltd v Wards Mobility Services Ltd* [1994] 1 W.L.R. 1564 (only likely purchasers professionals, who would be unlikely to be deceived). In *Bostick Ltd v Sellotape GB Ltd* [1994] R.P.C. 556 the similarity was concealed by packaging. The only possible deception was therefore in relation to repeat orders (not shown on the facts).

and monopolise descriptive words of the English language.[318] However, long usage may have had the effect that the descriptive words have become distinctively attached to the claimant's goods[319] as opposed to merely saying what they are.[320] A leading case is *Reddaway v Banham*[321] where it was held that "camel hair belting", which originally signified nothing more than belting made of camel hair, had come to signify belting made by the claimants.[322]

Use of own name. As a general rule a person can freely use his own name, or one which he has acquired by reputation, although the use of it inflicts damage on someone else who has the same name.[323] This, however, is qualified to some extent by the law of passing off. In *Parker-Knoll Ltd v Parker-Knoll International Ltd*,[324] both parties were manufacturers of furniture, the claimants being a company well known in the United Kingdom and the defendant an American company which had only recently begun to trade in England. Notwithstanding that the defendant company did no more than use its own name on its furniture, the House of Lords, by a majority, granted an injunction to restrain it from continuing to do so without distinguishing its goods from those of the claimant. The claimant had established that its name had come to denote goods made by it alone and not goods made by anyone else possessing or adopting that name, and the use by the defendant of a similar name did, in the opinion of the majority, amount to the false representation that its goods were the claimant's goods.[325] The central question in each case is, therefore, whether the name or description given by the defendant to his goods is such as to create a likelihood that a substantial section of the purchasing public will be misled into

19–078

---

[318] *Marcus Publishing Plc v Hutton-Wild Communications Plc* [1990] R.P.C. 576 at 579. Note that the risk of confusion in the public's mind might be just as great where the claimant was an established de facto monopolist.

[319] Equally, though once so attached, they may become so public and in such universal use as to be again open to others to use: *Ford v Foster* (1872) L.R. 7 Ch. 611 at 628 per Mellish LJ; *Gramophone Co's Application* [1910] 2 Ch. 423; or the courts may accept that instances of "mere confusion" or deception are to be tolerated: *Phones 4U Ltd v Phone4U.co.uk Internet Ltd* [2006] EWCA Civ 244; [2007] R.P.C. 5.

[320] Thus "vacuum cleaner" was held to mean simply a cleaner working by suction and not necessarily one manufactured by the British Vacuum Cleaner Co: *British Vacuum Cleaner Co Ltd v New Vacuum Cleaner Co Ltd* [1907] 2 Ch. 312.

[321] [1896] A.C. 199.

[322] In 1931 it was held, upon the facts, that a Belgian manufacturer did not sufficiently distinguish his goods from the claimants' by describing them as "Lechat's camel hair belting": *Reddaway & Co Ltd v Hartley* (1930) 48 R.P.C. 283.

[323] *Brinsmead v Brinsmead* (1913) 30 R.P.C. 493; *Jay's Ltd v Jacobi* [1933] Ch. 411; but as to nicknames see *Biba Group v Biba Boutique* [1980] R.P.C. 413; *NAD Electronics Inc v NAD Computer Systems Ltd* [1999] F.S.R. 380. "A new company with a title of which the name 'A,' for instance, forms part has none of the natural rights that an individual born with the name 'A' would have": *Fine Cotton Spinners v Cash* (1907) 24 R.P.C. 533 at 538; *Asprey & Garrard Ltd v WRA (Guns) Ltd* [2001] EWCA Civ 1499 at [43]. In *Dent v Turpin* (1861) 2 J&H 139 Dent had two clock shops, one in the City, the other in the West End. He bequeathed one to each son—which resulted in two clock businesses each called Dent. "Neither could stop the other; each could stop a third party . . . from using 'Dent' for such a business": *Phones4U Ltd v Phone4u.co.uk Internet Ltd* [2006] EWCA Civ 244; [2007] R.P.C. 5 at [22].

[324] [1962] R.P.C. 265.

[325] Cf. *Habib Bank Ltd v Habib Bank A.G. Zurich* [1981] 1 W.L.R. 1265.

believing that his goods are the goods of the claimant.[326] That the defendant used his own name with no intention to deceive anybody does not mean that such likelihood has not been created,[327] but proof that the defendant did intend to deceive[328] will materially assist the claimant's case. As has often been pointed out, if it was the defendant's object to deceive people into thinking that his goods were the goods of the claimant, the court will not be reluctant to infer that he achieved his object.[329] Similarly, whatever tolerance is shown to the use of a person's own name will not be extended to altering it—"garnishing" it, as the expression is—so as to be likely to mislead; thus a firm of wine merchants, "Short's Ltd", obtained an injunction against one Short, who set up a similar business and styled it "Short's".[330]

19–079   **Address.** Imitation of an address[331] may be part of conduct amounting to a scheme of passing off, but there is no property in an address as such. In *Day v Brownrigg*[332] the house of X had been known for over 60 years as "Ashford Lodge", and his neighbour Y changed the name of his house (previously known as "Ashford Villa") to "Ashford Lodge". This caused much inconvenience and annoyance to X, who claimed an injunction to restrain Y from such alteration of the name. It was held on demurrer that he had no cause of action.[333] Perhaps the result would have been different if the defendant had had the purpose of deceiving others and thereby causing harm to the claimant in his profession.[334]

19–080   **Extended passing off.** The classic form of the tort involves A representing his goods to be those of B, but the basis of the liability is the wider one of injury to the claimant's goodwill ("the benefit and advantage of the good name, reputation and connection of a business . . . the attractive force which brings in custom")[335] by misrepresentation to customers. Goodwill may attach to the description of a product so that it is shared by all persons making that product and they have a cause of action against a defendant who falsely attributes that description to his own goods even though he does not represent them to be produced by anyone else. In *Erwen Warnink BV v Townend & Sons (Hull) Ltd*,[336] the claimants were the main producers of advocaat, a drink of Dutch origin compounded of eggs and

---

[326] *Parker-Knoll Ltd v Parker-Knoll International Ltd* [1962] R.P.C. 265 at 278–279, 285, 289–290.

[327] *Reed Executive Plc v Reed Business Information Ltd* [2004] EWCA Civ 159; [2004] R.P.C. 40 at [110].

[328] See James LJ's example, in *Massam v Thorley* (1880) 14 Ch. D. 748 at 757, of somebody finding a man named Bass and setting up a brewery at Burton as Bass & Co.

[329] *Brinsmead & Son Ltd v Brinsmead* (1913) 30 R.P.C. 493 at 507 per Buckley LJ; *Parker-Knoll Ltd v Parker-Knoll International Ltd* [1962] R.P.C. 265 at 290 per Lord Devlin.

[330] *Short's Ltd v Short* (1914) 31 R.P.C. 294; *Parker & Son (Reading) Ltd v Parker* [1965] R.P.C. 323.

[331] Or the acquisition of a similar telephone number: *Law Society v Griffiths* [1995] P.C.R. 16.

[332] (1878) 10 Ch.D. 294.

[333] Liability was also denied, but this time in a business context, in *Street v Union Bank of Spain and England* (1885) 30 Ch. D. 155.

[334] Cf. *National Phonograph Co v Edison Bell Consolidated Phonograph Co* [1908] 1 Ch. 335 (deception as unlawful means in tort).

[335] *IRC v Muller & Co's Margarine Ltd* [1901] A.C. 217 at 223–224 per Lord Macnaghten. In modern conditions it may be the reputation of the carefully nurtured brand name rather than the inherent quality of the product which is the basis of goodwill: *Chocosuisse v Cadbury Ltd* [1998] R.P.C. 117 (affirmed [1999] R.P.C. 826).

[336] [1979] A.C. 731.

spirits, enjoying substantial sales in England. The defendants manufactured a drink, properly known as "egg flip", made from sherry and eggs and marketed under the name of "Keelings Old English Advocaat". Due to it attracting a lower rate of duty than the spirit-based drink it could be sold more cheaply and captured an appreciable share of the English market for advocaat. On the basis of a finding of fact that advocaat was a distinct and recognisable species of beverage based on spirits,[337] the House of Lords held that the defendants were guilty of passing off.[338] In doing so they approved the decision in *J Bollinger v Costa Brava Wine Co Ltd*[339] (the Champagne case) and made it clear that the principle was not confined to goods produced in a particular locality.[340] Conversely, if the trade name is only descriptive of geographical origin, that is not sufficient for the necessary goodwill; it must connote "something more", "some drawing power in its own right".[341] To meet this requirement it is not necessary that the product has a cachet, i.e. it is of "superior quality", or a "premium product"[342] and, as with "simple passing off",[343] the perception of distinctiveness which will suffice need not be that of the public as a whole; some section, or significant section, of the public will suffice.[344] In these cases the common law has in effect produced something akin to the system of *appellation controlée* protection, though care must be taken not to give protection to merely descriptive words.[345]

---

[337] This is vital: to take an example of counsel for the defendants, the manufacturers of tomato chutney could not restrain someone from marketing "tomato chutney" containing mangoes simply because mangoes had not been used in tomato chutney before. "Tomato chutney" is as vague as "brown bread".

[338] "[the plaintiffs] were entitled to protection in respect of the goodwill built up by them in the product name even though the deception practised on the public was to pass off the defendant's product as genuine ADVOCAAT rather than to pass it off as ADVOCAAT produced by the plaintiff": *Diageo North America Inc v Intercontinental Brands (ICB) Ltd* [2010] EWCA Civ 920; [2011] 1 All E.R. 242 at [44] per Patten LJ. Cf. *Consorzio de Prosciutto di Parma v Marks & Spencer Plc* [1991] R.P.C. 351 (sliced and packaged Parma Ham still "Parma Ham" even though it could not be sold in that way in Italy and might be of lesser quality).

[339] [1960] Ch. 262; *Vine Products Ltd v Mackenzie & Co Ltd* [1969] R.P.C. 1 (sherry); *John Walker & Sons Ltd v Henry Ost & Co Ltd* [1970] 1 W.L.R. 917 (Scotch whisky). Cf. *Institut national etc. v Andres Wines Ltd* (1990) 71 D.L.R. (4th) 575 ("Canadian champagne" had built up a reputation as a different product).

[340] There would, of course, be nothing to prevent the defendants in *Warnink* from marketing an English-made egg and spirit drink as advocaat. In the Champagne case the defendants could only have joined the class enjoying the goodwill by setting up in Champagne as well as using Champagne grapes and the "champenoise" method. In *Taittinger SA v Allbey Ltd* [1993] F.S.R. 641 even the use of "elderflower champagne" was successfully prevented. See also *Matthew Gloag v Welsh Distillers* [1998] F.S.R. 718. Nowadays producers may apply for registration of a Protected Geographical Indication under EC Council Regulation 2081/92: *Northern Foods Plc v DEFRA and Melton Mowbray Pork Pie Association* [2005] EWHC 2971 (Admin); [2006] F.S.R. 29.

[341] *Fage UK Ltd Chobani UK Ltd* [2013] EWHC 630 (Ch); [2013] F.S.R. 32 at [124] ("greek yoghurt"); affd. [2014] EWCA Civ 5; [2014] F.S.R. 29.

[342] *Diageo North America Inc v Intercontinental Brands (ICB) Ltd* [2010] EWCA Civ 920; [2011] 1 All E.R. 242 (vodka), though so called premium products are "perhaps more likely" to acquire the distinctiveness required (at [51] per Patten LJ).

[343] See para.19–074.

[344] *Fage UK Ltd Chobani UK Ltd* [2014] EWCA Civ 5; [2014] F.S.R. 29; cf. *Marks & Spencer Plc v Interflora Inc* [2012] EWCA Civ; [2013] 2 All E.R 663 ("substantial proportion" of the public) (not a case of passing off).

[345] *Chocosuisse v Cadbury Ltd* [1999] R.P.C. 826 ("Swiss chocolate"); cf. *The Scotch Whisky Association v Glen Kella Distillers Ltd* [1997] E.T.M.R. 470 (whisky); *Diageo North America Inc v*

19–081   **Reverse passing off.** The broad principle underlying liability is also demon-strated by the fact that there can be a claim for what has been called "reverse (or inverse) passing off", that is to say a case where the defendant shows the customer the claimant's goods intending to fill the resulting contract with goods of his own manufacture.[346] It is obviously unfair for the defendant to increase his trade by claiming credit for the claimant's achievements.

19–082   **Initial confusion.** A misrepresentation by the defendant may have initially confused a customer into doing business with him, but such confusion may no longer be operative at the time when any business is concluded between them. Nonetheless, the initial confusion is sufficient for passing-off since even by then the damage is done to the claimant's goodwill.[347]

19–083   **No requirement of a "common field of activity".** As most of the cases did involve the defendant literally passing off his goods as the claimant's it is not surprising that the older decisions tended to speak in terms of a requirement for a common field of activity between the parties. However, this is now regarded as too narrow a view and the issue of common field of activity is a factor relevant in deciding whether there is a misrepresentation likely to deceive and whether damage is likely to result, rather than an independent requirement.[348] For example, in *Granada Group Ltd v Ford Motor Co Ltd*[349] the claimants, a major publishing and entertainment company failed (not surprisingly on the facts) to restrain the defendants from attaching the name "Granada" to a new car; and in *Fortnum & Mason Plc v Fortnam Ltd*[350] there was no serious risk of confusion between the activities of the claimants (a high class food store) and the defendants (importers and re-exporters of cheap, plastic goods).

19–084   **"Injurious association".** If, however, the public might think that there was some association between the activities of the parties the claimant is likely to succeed if, for example, the defendant is engaged in some activity which might harm the claimant's reputation even though they are in no sense competitors.[351] In this

---

Intercontinental Brands (ICB) Ltd, [2010] EWCA Civ 920; [2011] 1 All E.R. 242 at [76] ("I remain concerned that the extended form of passing off should not by dint of extensions upon extensions trespass beyond the legitimate area of protection of goodwill into an illegitimate area of anti-competitiveness", per Rix LJ).

[346] *Bristol Conservatories Ltd v Conservatories Custom Build Ltd* [1989] R.P.C. 380. But see *Woolley v Ultimate Products Ltd* [2012] EWCA Civ 1038 at [6] per Arden LJ.

[347] *Doosan Power Systems Ltd v Babcock International Group*[2013] EWHC 1364 (Ch); [2013] E.T.M.R. 40 at [178].

[348] *Harrods Ltd v Harrodian School* [1996] R.P.C. 697; *Nice and Safe Attitude v Flook (t/a Slaam! Clothing)* [1997] F.S.R. 14. Even where the parties are in the same line and there is similarity between their products the court may of course conclude that there is no real risk of the public being deceived: *Financial Times v Evening Standard* [1991] F.S.R. 7 (ES publishing business section on pink paper).

[349] [1972] F.S.R. 103; *Stringfellow v McCain Foods* [1984] R.P.C. 501.

[350] [1994] F.S.R. 438; *Box TV v Haymarket* (1997) 147 N.L.J. 601.

[351] See, e.g. *Annabel's (Berkeley Square) Ltd v G. Schock* [1972] F.S.R. 261 (night club and escort agency); *Harrod's Ltd v R. Harrod Ltd* (1923) 41 R.P.C. 74. See also *Hilton Press v White Eagle Youth Holiday Camp* (1951) 68 R.P.C. 126. Note, however, that in *Fortnum & Mason Plc v Fortnam Ltd* [1994] F.S.R. 438 Harman J remarked of the *Annabel's* case that, "it would be astonishing if there was not in the mind of the ordinary person a close connection between the provision of girls to go out dancing with a man and a place where men may dance with girls".

form the action is less "passing off" than "injurious association".[352] In *Associated Newspapers Plc v Insert Media Ltd*,[353] the defendants' practice of placing advertising inserts in the claimants' newspapers after they had been sold to newsagents was held to involve a representation that the defendants were associated with the claimants' business. There was a risk of damage to the goodwill of that business because while the claimants accepted only carefully vetted advertisements and took steps to protect readers against dishonest or insolvent advertisers, some members of the public might conclude that the claimants were responsible in the same way for the insert advertisers, over whom they had no control.[354] Though dishonesty is not a requirement of a successful claim for passing off, it is a relevant consideration in deciding whether the case has been established that the defendant intends to exploit the claimant's goodwill.[355]

"Misappropriation of business reputation". In the *Insert Media* case the defendants could at least be said to be risking damage to the claimants' goodwill in respect of their central activity as newspaper publishers. In modern conditions, sportsmen, performers, film makers and so on actively engage in turning their public images or their creations to profit by granting endorsements or licences to persons manufacturing goods. The trend of English cases was at first hostile to granting protection against "misappropriation of business reputation". This approach was reversed in *Irvine v Talksport Ltd*,[356] where a Formula 1 racing driver recovered damages for unauthorised advertisements which implied that he had given his endorsement to the defendants' sports radio station. Although many passing off cases arose from a claimant's fear that the sale of inferior goods under his name would damage his goodwill by associating him with those goods, the law was not confined to that situation. It was well known that in modern marketing conditions famous people made a substantial income from the endorsement of products and services and the law should vindicate their exclusive rights in their reputation or goodwill in that respect.[357]

19–085

"Character merchandising". The *Irvine* case is not intended to state the law for the situation where the defendant sells goods which exploit a demand produced by the artistic creation of the claimant—toys associated with film themes or

19–086

---

[352] Megarry J in *Unitex Ltd v Union Texturing Co Ltd* [1973] R.P.C. 119. See also *Taittinger SA v Allbey Ltd* [1993] F.S.R. 641 (insidious dilution of reputation of champagne); *Associated Newspapers Ltd v Express Newspapers* [2003] EWHC 1322; [2003] F.S.R. 51; and Carty 112 L.Q.R. 632.

[353] [1991] 1 W.L.R. 571. *Lego Systems A/S v Lego Lemelstrich* [1983] F.S.R. 155 seems to reduce the requirement of damage almost to vanishing point.

[354] However, it would not be enough that people might think the claimants were providing "sponsorship" for the defendants: *Harrods Ltd v Harrodian School* [1996] R.P.C. 697; cf. *Dawnay Day & Co Ltd v Cantor Fitzgerald International* [2000] R.P.C. 669 at 705.

[355] *Stringfellow v McCain Foods* [1984] R.P.C. 501 at 546; *Associated Newspapers Plc v Insert Media Ltd* [1991] 1 W.L.R. 571.

[356] [2002] EWHC 367 (Ch); [2003] 1 W.L.R. 2355. There was no appeal on the decision of law, though the CA clearly approved of it. It substantially increased the damages awarded: [2003] EWCA Civ 423; [2003] 2 All E.R. 881.

[357] As to whether there is a general right to control the use of one's image, see para.13–143.

cartoon characters,[358] for example, what is known as "character merchandising".[359] Since the artistic creator will commonly have authorised exploitation of this type or even be engaged in it, there is no reason of principle why the law of passing off should not apply. In *Mirage Studios v Counter-Feat Clothing*[360] Browne-Wilkinson VC granted an injunction[361] restraining unlicensed use of the "Teenage Mutant Ninja Turtle" image on clothing. Certainly the claimants were not in the clothing business but the financial significance in modern conditions of character merchandising meant that neither were they solely in the business of producing cartoon films. The public were now aware in a general way of the practice and the claimants would suffer damage in: (1) losing licensing fees; and (2) losing the ability to control the quality of products marketed with the "Turtle" image, with consequent damage to their goodwill with the public. However, it should certainly not be assumed that we have reached the stage where a celebrity has an exclusive right to exploit the valuable aspects of his own character[362] and in the case of the exploitation of fictional characters it has been suggested that it is difficult to prove confusion because the public may not generally care in these cases whether the product is "genuine" or not.[363]

B. Goodwill

19–087 **The need to establish the claimant's goodwill.** Mere confusion in the mind of the public is not enough to establish a case of passing off unless there is a risk of damage to the claimant's goodwill and it therefore follows that the tort is not committed if that goodwill has not been established. Hence, an action failed where the claimant planned to bring out a leisure magazine and had spent money promoting it but the defendant launched a scheme to publish a magazine with the same name;[364] and it seems that the result would have been the same even if the defendant's act had been a mere "spoiling" operation.[365] Goodwill cannot exist in a vacuum so if a business has been abandoned there is no longer any legally

---

[358] The law of copyright may be relevant with regard to cartoon characters (see *King Features v Kleeman* [1940] 1 Ch. 523—Popeye; *BBC Worldwide Ltd v Pally Screen Printing Ltd* [1998] F.S.R. 665—Teletubbies).

[359] Indeed, this might arise with regard to a real person. An advertiser might use the image of an actor in a film which had some association in the public mind with the type of product in question, but in such a way as not to imply any endorsement: cf. *Pacific Dunlop Ltd v Hogan* (1989) 87 A.L.R. 14.

[360] [1991] F.S.R. 145.

[361] It was interim but the claimants' case was regarded as more than merely arguable.

[362] *Elvis Presley Trade Mark* [1999] R.P.C. 567 CA.

[363] *BBC Worldwide Ltd v Pally Screen Printing Ltd* [1998] F.S.R. 665 at 674.

[364] *Marcus Publishing Plc v Hutton-Wild Communications Ltd* [1990] R.P.C. 576. However, there may be cases in which pre-launch publicity suffices to establish goodwill: *Labyrinth Media Ltd v Brave World Ltd* [1995] E.M.L.R. 38.

[365] *Marcus Publishing Plc v Hutton-Wild Communications Ltd* [1990] R.P.C. 576 at 580, 585. Cf. *Bradford Corp v Pickles* [1895] A.C. 587, para.3–012.

protected goodwill attached to it; but a temporary cessation of business is a different matter.[366] However, there may be damage to goodwill even though there is no evidence of diversion of sales.[367]

The "locality" of the goodwill. A matter of some significance in modern conditions of trade is the "locality" of the goodwill. There is no doubt that an action only lies if the claimant has goodwill here but whether or not that is so can be a difficult question of fact or inference.[368] It is not enough that the claimant has a reputation in the sense that he is known here (for example from advertising in publications which circulate here as well as abroad),[369] so that in *Bernardin & Cie v Pavilion Properties Ltd*[370] the proprietors of the "Crazy Horse Saloon" nightclub in Paris failed in an action against defendants who set up a similar establishment in London. On the other hand, while the claimant must have business with people here there is no necessity for him to have "a business" here in the sense of a physical presence or even direct sales relationships.[371] The requirement of having business here is not met simply on the basis of hits from within the jurisdiction on a website based abroad.[372]

19–088

C.   The Limits of Passing Off

No tort of "unfair competition". The law of passing off seems to be adaptable to changing trading practices and conditions and has had some notable extensions, particularly in the Champagne case and its successors and in the recognition of endorsement rights of "personalities"; but it has not generalised into a tort of "unfair competition".[373] Thus it is no tort for the defendant to exploit the claimant's advertising campaign so as to seize a share of the market which the claimant has created. In *Cadbury-Schweppes Pty Ltd v Pub Squash Co Pty Ltd*,[374] the claimants launched a lemon drink ("Solo") supported by an extensive advertising campaign evoking an idealised memory of soft drinks of the past. The

19–089

---

[366] *Pink v Sharwood & Co Ltd* (1913) 30 R.P.C. 725; *Star Industrial Co Ltd v Yap Kwee Kor* [1976] F.S.R. 256; cf. *Minimax GmbH & Co KG v Chubb Fire Ltd* [2008] EWHC 1960 (Pat).

[367] *Chelsea Man v Chelsea Girl* [1987] R.P.C. 189; *Phones4U Ltd v Phone4u.co.uk Internet Ltd* [2006] EWCA Civ 244; [2007] R.P.C. 5.

[368] There is an exhaustive review of the law throughout the Commonwealth by Lockhart J in *Conagra Inc v McCain Foods (Aust) Pty Ltd* (1992) 106 A.L.R. 465.

[369] *Athlete's Foot Marketing Associates Inc v Cobra Sports Inc* [1980] R.P.C. 43; *Anheuser-Busch Inc v Budejovicky Budvar N.P.* [1984] F.S.R. 413; *Jian Tools for Sales v Roderick Manhattan Group* [1995] F.S.R. 924.

[370] [1967] R.P.C. 581 (the claimants had in fact aimed advertising at England).

[371] *Hotel Cipriani Srl v Cipriani (Grosvenor Street) Ltd* [2010] EWCA Civ 110; [2010] R.P.C. 16. Thus in *SA etc. Panhard et Levassor v Panhard Levassor Motor Co Ltd* [1901] 2 Ch. 513 the claimants sold no cars in England but English people bought their cars in France and imported them. This was sufficient goodwill. See also *Tan-Ichi Co Ltd v Jancar Ltd* [1990] F.S.R. 151 (claimants operated Japanese restaurants; no establishments within the jurisdiction—Hong Kong—but goodwill in HK Japanese residents).

[372] *Plentyoffish Media Inc v Plenty More LLP* [2011] EWHC 2568 (Ch); [2012] R.P.C. 5; *Starbucks (HK) Ltd v British Sky Broadcasting Group Plc* [2012] EWHC 3074 (Ch); [2013] F.S.R. 29.

[373] *Diageo North America Inc v Intercontinental Brands (ICB) Ltd* [2010] EWCA Civ 920; [2011] 1 All E.R. 242 at [24]. *Pace* the suggestion of Aldous LJ in *Arsenal Football Club Plc v Reed* [2003] EWCA Civ 696; [2003] R.P.C. 39 at [70] that unfair competition would be a better name for it.

[374] [1981] 1 W.L.R. 193.

defendants then launched a lemon drink ("Pub Squash") with a get up and advertising theme closely related to that for "Solo". The dismissal of the claimants' claim for damages and an injunction on the ground of passing off was upheld by the Privy Council for the defendants had sufficiently distinguished their goods from those of the claimants to prevent any likely confusion in the public mind. The alternative claim of "unfair competition" was not even pursued before that court and the High Court of Australia subsequently delivered a categorical rejection of such a tort.[375]

We have seen that in *Associated Newspapers Group Plc v Insert Media Ltd* the newspaper publishers succeeded on the basis of passing off, but in earlier proceedings Hoffmann J rejected a cause of action alleging unfair competition by debasing or devaluing the claimants' goods without misrepresentation.[376] The balance of authority is similarly against a general liability where A appropriates B's valuable idea, design or information and exploits it without payment.[377] Nonetheless, there are modern examples of claims being held arguable which are extremely difficult to fit within traditional ideas of the tort so further development cannot be ruled out.

19–090   **Not confined to trade.** The setting of passing off is normally trade and it is possible for a relatively small trade to result in sufficient goodwill for a passing off case so long as it is more than trivial.[378] However, trade in the narrow sense is not essential, even if it is difficult to say precisely how far the law goes. A fundraising charity has succeeded in an action in respect of conduct which tended to appropriate its goodwill[379] and a religious organisation may also be able to sue.[380] An author may sue for a false representation that a book is his work[381] and a professional person or a professional association[382] may have a cause of action in respect of unauthorised use of their names in a manner likely to cause harm to their professional activities—for example, the use of a doctor's name to promote

---

[375] *Moorgate Tobacco Co Ltd v Phillip Morris Ltd* (1984) 56 A.L.R. 193; but see s.52 of the Australian Trade Practices Act 1974. An American doctrine of unfair competition enunciated in *International News Services v Associated Press* 248 US 215 (1918) has never gained ascendancy in the face of what are thought to be conflicting statutory rights.

[376] *Cadbury-Schweppes Pty Ltd v Pub Squash Co Pty Ltd* [1988] 1 W.L.R. 509.

[377] *Lever Bros v Bedingfield* (1896) 16 R.P.C. 3; *Victoria Park Racing Co v Taylor* (1937) 58 C.L.R. 479; *Conan Doyle v London Mystery Magazine Ltd* (1949) 66 R.P.C. 246. The law of copyright generally protects the form of a work, not the idea behind it, but the author of a work who does not have the copyright may have the right to be identified as the author under the Copyright, Designs and Patents Act 1988 s.77.

[378] *Knight v Beyond Properties Pty Ltd* [2007] EWHC 1251 (Ch); *Bocacina Ltd v Boca Cafes Ltd* [2013] EWHC 3090 (IPEC) at [23].

[379] *British Diabetic Association v Diabetic Society Ltd* [1995] 4 All E.R. 812.

[380] *Holy Apostolic etc. Church v Attorney General (NSW), ex rel. Elisha* (1989) 18 N.S.W.L.R. 291, approved in *British Diabetic Association v Diabetic Society Ltd* [1995] 4 All E.R. 812.

[381] *Lord Byron v Johnson* (1816) 2 Mer. 29; *Clark v Associated Newspapers Ltd* [1998] R.P.C. 261. See also Copyright, Designs and Patents Act 1988 s.84.

[382] *Society of Accountants and Auditors v Goodway* [1907] 1 Ch. 489; *Law Society v Society of Lawyers* [1996] F.S.R. 739.

a quack medicine or cure.[383] It has even been held that a political organisation may obtain an injunction to restrain a person standing at an election in its name.[384]

D. Remedies

The injunction is an important remedy in passing off cases and an interim **19–091** injunction may well determine the final outcome since the delay before trial may mean that the loser at the interim stage cannot resume production.[385] It may be made in qualified form, i.e. restraining the defendant from disposing of his goods without sufficiently distinguishing them from the claimant's.[386] In addition, damages may be granted in respect of losses to the claimant or, in the alternative, an account of profits made by the defendant from the passing off.[387] It has been held at first instance that damages may be recovered against an innocent defendant, though the alternative of an account of profits is not available in such a case.[388]

---

[383] See *Dockrell v Douglas* (1899) 80 L.T. 556 at 557, 558; *Walter v Ashton* [1902] 2 Ch. 282 at 293.

[384] *Burge v Haycock* [2001] EWCA Civ 900; [2002] R.P.C. 28.

[385] See, e.g. *Mirage Studios v Counter-Feat Clothing* [1991] F.S.R. 145, para.19–086. The *American Cyanamid* principles (para.23–128) are as applicable to passing off as to other torts: *County Sound v Ocean Sound* [1991] F.S.R. 367. However, s.12 of the Human Rights Act 1998 may be relevant: *Blandford Goldsmith & Co Ltd v Prime UK Properties Ltd* [2003] EWHC 326 (Ch).

[386] "It has been said many times that it is no part of the function of this court to examine imaginary cases of what the defendant could or could not do under this form of injunction. The best guide, if he is an honest man, is his own conscience and it is certainly not the business of this court to give him instructions or limits as to how near the wind he can sail": *Wright, Layman & Umney v Wright* (1949) 66 R.P.C. 149 at 152 per Lord Greene MR.

[387] There may be circumstances in which a person, e.g. a printer of labels, who facilitates a passing off without actual knowledge, may be liable for negligence, but such a case would be very unusual and a person who receives such orders in the ordinary course of trade is not to be expected to institute inquiries about the lawfulness of the intended use: *Paterson Zochonis & Co Ltd v Merfarken Packaging Ltd* [1986] 3 All E.R. 522.

[388] *Gillette UK Ltd v Eden West Ltd* [1994] R.P.C. 297.

CHAPTER 20

ABUSE OF LEGAL PROCEDURE

1. MALICIOUS PROSECUTION

History. The history of this tort[1] can be traced back to the writ of conspiracy   **20–001**
which was in existence as early as Edward I's reign. This fell into decay in the
16th century, partly because the writ of maintenance supplanted it. However, this
was probably confined to officious intermeddling in civil suits.[2] The gap was
filled by an action on the case which appeared in Elizabeth I's reign and
eventually became known as the action for malicious prosecution. It was put on a
firm footing in 1698 in *Saville v Roberts*.[3]

The majority of actions for malicious prosecution nowadays are probably
brought against the police, but the House of Lords has reaffirmed that a private
person who sets the law in motion may still incur liability.[4] However, the law was
largely shaped in an era when there was no formal, state system for investigation
and prosecution and care must be taken in applying broad principles established
under the old regime to present circumstances.

The need to balance competing principles. Liability for malicious prosecution   **20–002**
has always had to steer a path between two competing principles—on the one
hand the freedom of action that everyone should have to set the law in motion and
to bring criminals to justice and on the other hand the necessity to check lying
accusations against innocent people[5] and the burden which has to be undertaken
by the claimant in a case of malicious prosecution is a heavy one, so heavy that
no honest prosecutor is likely to be deterred from doing his duty.

---

[1] See Winfield, *History of Conspiracy and Abuse of Legal Procedure* and Winfield, *Present Law of Abuse of Legal Procedure*.
[2] Maintenance as a tort survived until 1967 but has now been abolished.
[3] *Saville v Roberts* 1 Ld. Raym. 374.
[4] *Martin v Watson* [1996] A.C. 74.
[5] *Glinski v McIver* [1962] A.C. 726 at 741, 753; *Gregory v Portsmouth CC* [2000] 1 A.C. 419 at 426.

20–003 **Relationship with other types of liability.** One reason for the complexity of the law in this area is that a number of other torts and principles come into play where the defendant is involved in the events leading up to a prosecution. First, the claimant may have been arrested on the basis of information given by the defendant. As we have seen, in modern conditions the exercise of discretion by the police officer carrying out the arrest[6] is likely to deprive the claimant of any claim against the defendant for false imprisonment.[7] Secondly, the information given by the defendant is likely to be defamatory, but not only will any evidence given by him in court be subject to absolute privilege, it has now been held that the same applies to a mere complaint to the police.[8] If, however, the defendant is a prosecutor the essence of the complaint is that he has abused the process of the court[9] and the fact that for other legal purposes he is immune from suit is irrelevant. The application of the law of negligence in this area would be inconsistent with the restrictions imposed by the law of malicious prosecution. There is no liability in negligence in respect of the conduct of a prosecution[10] nor the investigation of a charge made against the claimant.[11] There might be liability for misfeasance in a public office[12] but that requires a form of malice and this is not satisfied by negligence, however crass.[13]

20–004 **Only three kinds of damage?** The action for malicious prosecution being an action on the case it is essential for the claimant to prove damage, and in *Saville v Roberts*[14] Holt CJ classified damage for the purpose of this tort as of three kinds, any one of which might ground the action: malicious prosecution might damage a person's fame (i.e. his character),[15] or the safety of his person, or the security of his property by reason of his expense in repelling an unjust charge. A moral stigma will inevitably attach where the law visits an offence with

---

[6] Still more of a magistrate remanding the claimant in custody.

[7] See para.4–030.

[8] *Westcott v Westcott* [2008] EWCA Civ 818; [2009] E.M.L.R. 2. The same would apply to a claim for malicious falsehood. Even before this case it was held that the absolute privilege extended to preliminary statements or the preparation of reports outside court which can fairly be said to be part of the process of investigation. However, the immunity in respect of pre-trial matters does not extend to the fabrication of evidence to be used in court: *Darker v CC West Midlands* [2001] A.C. 435. In that case the claims were for conspiracy to injure and misfeasance in a public office. The claimants alleged that the defendants had conspired to cause them to be charged with offences which they knew or believed to be false, but there was no claim for malicious prosecution; cf. *Smart v Forensic Science Service Ltd* [2013] EWCA Civ 783; [2013] P.N.L.R. 32.

[9] *Martin v Watson* [1996] A.C. 74 at 88.

[10] *Elguzouli-Daf v MPC* [1995] Q.B. 335, para.5–080.

[11] *B v Reading BC* [2009] EWHC 998 (QB); [2009] 2 F.L.R. 1273. Mackay J thought that the decision of the CA in these proceedings at [2001] EWCA Civ 346; [2001] 1 W.L.R. 1575 could not stand with later developments.

[12] See para.8-024.

[13] Cf. *Hill v Hamilton-Wentworth Regional Police Services Board* [2007] SCC 41; [2007] 3 S.C.R. 129.

[14] (1698) 1 Ld. Raym. 374; 5 Mod. 394.

[15] Where the successful claimant is of bad character it may be proper to discount this first element to some extent, but this may be offset by the risk of heavier punishment to which his record exposes him if convicted: *Manley v MPC* [2006] EWCA Civ 879; [2006] Po L.R. 117. Bad character is not to be confused with an unconventional lifestyle: *Calix v Att-Gen. Of Trinidad & Tobago* [2013] UKPC 15; [2013] 1 W.L.R. 3283. Damages may be awarded for psychiatric harm: *Clifford v Chief Constable of Hertfordshire* [2011] EWHC 815 (QB).

imprisonment, but there are today innumerable offences which are punishable only by fine. In such cases the claimant can only rely upon damage to his fame if the offence with which he is charged is necessarily and naturally defamatory of him,[16] and in effect the question is the converse of the question of law which is involved in actions for defamation: Is the statement that the claimant was charged with the offence capable of a non-defamatory meaning?[17] Thus a charge of wrongly pulling the communication cord in a railway train does not necessarily affect the fair name of the accused and will not ground an action for malicious prosecution under Holt CJ's first head,[18] but it is otherwise where, for example, the claimant is charged with deliberately travelling on a train without having paid his fare.[19] On the other hand, unless the claimant was awarded the equivalent of the taxed costs which he has incurred in defending himself, the difference between the costs awarded in the criminal proceedings, if any, and the costs actually incurred is sufficient to ground the action under Holt CJ's third head.[20]

In *Crawford Adjusters v Sagicor General Insurance Ltd*[21] the Privy Council was principally concerned with the question of whether this tort should be extended to civil proceedings, but the majority who were in favour of this extension also considered that economic loss more generally should be recoverable for malicious prosecution of proceedings "whether criminal or civil"[22] (and for the tort of abuse of process)[23] and the minority do not appear to dissent on this point.[24]

Essentials of the tort. Assuming there is damage as explained above, the claimant must prove: (1) that the defendant prosecuted him; (2) that the prosecution ended in the claimant's favour; (3) that the prosecution lacked reasonable and probable cause; and (4) that the defendant acted maliciously.

20–005

A. Prosecution

Who qualifies as a "prosecutor"? A person who brings a private prosecution is obviously a prosecutor for this purpose and so is one who swears an information[25] or who is bound over to act as a prosecutor.[26] However, in *Martin v*

20–006

---

[16] *Berry v British Transport Commission* [1961] 1 Q.B. 149 at 166, following *Wiffen v Bailey and Romford UDC* [1915] 1 K.B. 600. This was not the original meaning intended by Holt CJ (*Berry v British Transport Commission* at 160–163 per Diplock J) and it has been criticised: *Berry v British Transport Commission* [1962] 1 Q.B. at 333 per Devlin LJ, at 335–336 per Danckwerts LJ.

[17] *Berry v British Transport Commission* [1961] 1 Q.B. 149 at 166 per Diplock J.

[18] *Berry v British Transport Commission* [1961] 1 Q.B. 149; *Wiffen v Bailey and Romford UDC* [1915] 1 K.B. 600.

[19] *Rayson v South London Transport Co* [1893] 2 Q.B. 304.

[20] *Berry v British Transport Commission* [1962] 1 Q.B. 306, where *Wiffen v Bailey and Romford UDC* [1915] 1 K.B. 600 was held not binding on this point. It is otherwise where costs incurred in a civil action are concerned: *Quartz Hill Consolidated Gold Mining Co v Eyre* (1883) 11 Q.B.D. 674.

[21] *Crawford Adjusters v Sagicor General Insurance Ltd* [2013] UKPC 17; [2013] 3 W.L.R. 927.

[22] [2013] UKPC 17; [2013] 3 W.L.R. 927 at [77], [90].

[23] See para.20–022.

[24] Lord Sumption (at [130]) referred to "all of the elements" of the tort being present save for the involvement of civil proceedings, but the "elements" referred to are the four essentials of the tort set out in the paragraphs which follow which simply presume that the necessary damage has been caused.

[25] *Watters v Pacific Delivery Service Ltd* (1963) 42 D.L.R. (2d) 661.

Watson[27] the House of Lords held that it is not necessary that the defendant should be the prosecutor in any technical sense: what matters is that he should in substance be the person responsible for the prosecution being brought. The defendant made various charges to the police that the claimant had indecently exposed himself to her and this led to a prosecution of the claimant at which no evidence was offered against him. Distinguishing the case of *Danby v Beardsley*[28] in which the defendant had been held not to be a prosecutor when he told the police that goods which he mistakenly believed to have been stolen from him had been found in the claimant's possession, on the ground that in that case there was no malice against the claimant, Lord Keith continued:[29]

> "Where an individual falsely and maliciously gives a police officer information indicating that some person is guilty of a criminal offence and states that he is willing to give evidence in court of the matters in question, it is properly to be inferred that he desires and intends that the person he names should be prosecuted. When the circumstances are such that the facts relating to the alleged offence can be within the knowledge only of the complainant,[30] as was the position here, then it becomes virtually impossible for the police officer to exercise any independent discretion or judgment, and if a prosecution is instituted by the police officer the proper view of the matter is that the prosecution has been procured by the complainant."

Martin v Watson was a strong case because the defendant conducted a campaign against the claimant by making repeated complaints which the police were reluctant to pursue. In contrast in *AH v AB*,[31] where the claimant's conviction for rape of the defendant had been set aside, the defendant had made no complaint to the police, the prosecution arising from a report to them several years after the event and originating with a person in whom the defendant had confided at the time, and it was only under pressure from the police that the defendant had given evidence in the criminal proceedings. She was not a prosecutor because it was impossible to say that she fulfilled the first requirement, which was that she should have "intended or desired" a prosecution.[32]

20–007   **Difficult cases.** The difficulties arise in cases lying between *Martin* and *AH*. Nowadays the decision to prosecute and the conduct of the proceedings are normally in the hands of the Crown Prosecution Service, which will exercise an independent discretion as to whether to proceed, taking account of the strength of the evidence and relevant guidelines.[33] In *AH* it is said that even a person who initiates the process of investigation and prosecution by making a false complaint[34] is not to be regarded as a prosecutor unless he does something to "manipulate" the prosecuting authorities into doing something they would not

---

[26] *Fitzjohn v Mackinder* (1861) 9 C.B. (N.S.) 505.

[27] [1996] A.C. 74.

[28] (1880) 43 L.T. 603.

[29] *Martin v Watson* [1996] A.C. 74 at 86.

[30] Liability for malicious prosecution is not necessarily confined to such cases: *Scott v Ministry of Justice* [2009] EWCA Civ 1215 at [38], [51].

[31] [2009] EWCA Civ 1092.

[32] *Mahon v Rahn (No.2)* [2000] 1 W.L.R. 2150.

[33] See Prosecution of Offences Act 1985, Criminal Justice Act 2003.

[34] Some passages in *Martin v Watson* may be thought to run together the issues of whether the defendant is a prosecutor and whether he is guilty of malice. According to *AH* the true position is that

otherwise have done[35] and that where the decision to prosecute is taken by the CPS it will be a rare case in which the complainant can be regarded as a prosecutor. No doubt this has merits in the case of a complainant but many prosecutions are brought mainly on the basis of police investigation and evidence, though the decision to prosecute is still made by the CPS. Is the same dispensation to apply to a police officer who concocts such a convincing false story that he does not need to take any further steps to influence the prosecution? If so the position of a falsely accused person would have been seriously weakened, but it is clear that review by the CPS does not insulate an officer from a finding that he was the prosecutor.[36] Very soon after *AH* a differently constituted Court of Appeal in *Scott v Ministry of Justice*[37] also held that where five prison officers had made clear and consistent statements accusing the claimant of assault on them there was an arguable case that they had procured the ensuing prosecution even though there had been no manipulation or overbearing by them of the responsible crown prosecutor's view.[38]

B. Favourable Termination of the Prosecution

Basis of termination not relevant. The claimant must show that the prosecution ended in his favour,[39] but so long as it did, it is of no moment how this came about, whether by a verdict of acquittal, or by discontinuance of the prosecution by leave of the court,[40] or by quashing of the indictment for a defect in it,[41] or because the proceedings were *coram non judice.*[42] The effect of a *nolle prosequi* (staying by the Attorney General of proceedings on an indictment) was left open to question in an old case which indicated that it was not a sufficient ending of the prosecution because it still left the accused liable to be indicted afresh on the same charge.[43] Yet, this seems inconsistent with the broad interpretation put upon "favourable termination of the prosecution" which signifies, not that the accused has been acquitted, but that he has not been convicted. The reason for the favourable termination requirement has been said to be the risk of diverse determinations by different courts on the same facts and between the same

20–008

---

knowledge of the falsity of the charge is relevant on the "prosecutor" issue in so far as it provides evidence of an intention to procure a prosecution. In the view of Moore-Bick LJ this makes the matter unsuitable to be dealt with as a preliminary issue.

[35] *AH v AB* [2009] EWCA Civ 1092 at [47], [58], [84].

[36] *Alford v Chief Constable of Cambridgeshire* [2009] EWCA Civ 100; [2009] Po L.R. 98; *Moulton v Chief Constable of West Midlands* [2010] EWCA Civ 524; *Clifford v Chief Constable of Hertfordshire* [2011] EWHC 815 (QB).

[37] [2009] EWCA Civ 1215.

[38] Longmore LJ remarked at [47] that the question of who is a prosecutor, "is in danger of becoming a little over-complicated".

[39] *Parker v Langly* (1713) 10 Mod. 145 and 209. The logical result is that the limitation period runs from the time of the acquittal, not the charge: *Dunlop v Customs and Excise, The Times*, March 17, 1998; *Baker v MPC*, June 24, 1996, QBD.

[40] *Watkins v Lee* (1839) 5 M. & W. 270.

[41] *Jones v Gwynn* (1712) 10 Mod. 148 at 214.

[42] *Attwood v Monger* (1653) Style 378. See also *Goddard v Smith* (1704) 1 Salk. 21 (non suit).

[43] *Goddard v Smith* (1704) 1 Salk. 21.

parties, but there is no inconsistency in the criminal court finding that C was not guilty and then the civil court finding that D had reasonable and probable cause for the prosecution.[44]

It was held in *Reynolds v Kennedy*[45] that no action could lie if the claimant had been convicted, even if his conviction was later reversed on appeal, the reason apparently being that the original conviction showed conclusively that there was foundation for the prosecution. In a number of modern cases, however, it was the fact that the proceedings had terminated in the claimant's favour only as the result of an appeal, but nothing was made of this.[46] The question of reasonable and probable cause for the prosecution is an independent question and should not be regarded as finally answered in the defendant's favour on the ground only that a conviction was secured in a court of first instance. *Reynolds v Kennedy* should no longer be regarded as good law.

20–009 **No claim if conviction stands.** On the other hand, if a conviction stands, then the claimant cannot succeed in an action for malicious prosecution, and this is so even if the conviction is one against which there is no right of appeal and which has been obtained by the fraud of the prosecutor. In *Basébé v Matthews*,[47] Byles J thought that if the rule were otherwise every case would have to be retried on its merits, and Montague Smith J feared that they would be turning themselves into a Court of Appeal where the legislature allowed none. The rule rests upon the more general principle that the court will strike out as an abuse of process a suit which is a collateral attack on the decision of a competent criminal court for otherwise there is a risk of inconsistent decisions.[48] *Basébé v Matthews* was followed in *Everett v Ribbands*[49] where the claimant had been bound over to find sureties to be of good behaviour. He failed in an action for malicious prosecution, for the proceedings complained of had actually been determined against him.

20–010 **May the prosecutor seek to show that the claimant was, in fact, guilty?** If the prosecution has terminated in the claimant's favour and he sues for malicious prosecution, may the prosecutor seek in his defence to show that the claimant was in fact guilty? For example, the prosecution may have presented a weak case but afterwards there may come to light much stronger evidence against the claimant.[50] Some cases hold that the prosecutor may not do this, or even use the evidence of guilt in mitigation of damages[51] relying either upon the "inconsistency" argument mentioned above or at least upon the undesirability of re-litigation of the issue of guilt. However, if D states that C has committed a criminal offence and C, having been acquitted of that offence, then sues D for defamation, we do not prevent D from justifying by trying to show that C was in

---

[44] On the relevance of the guilt of the claimant, see para.20–010.

[45] *Reynolds v Kennedy* (1784) 1 Wils. 232.

[46] *Herniman v Smith* [1938] A.C. 305; *Berry v British Transport Commission* [1962] 1 Q.B. 306; *Abbott v Refuge Assurance Co Ltd* [1962] 1 Q.B. 432; *Blaker v Weller* [1964] Crim. L.R. 311.

[47] (1867) L.R. 2 C.P. 684.

[48] The general principle may be subject to exception if there is decisive fresh evidence: *Smith v Linskills* [1996] 1 W.L.R. 763.

[49] [1952] 2 Q.B. 198; *Bynoe v Bank of England* [1902] 1 K.B. 467.

[50] At common law there were no circumstances in which he might be tried again. This can now happen where the conditions of Pt 10 of the Criminal Justice Act 2003 are fulfilled.

[51] *Commonwealth Life Assurance Society Ltd v Smith* (1938) 59 C.L.R. 527.

fact guilty, rash as that plea may perhaps be; and while there may be a general principle which treats as an abuse of process any attempt to mount a collateral attack on the decision of a competent court,[52] that is directed at the initiation of proceedings, not at the formulation of a defence.[53]

C. Lack of Reasonable and Probable Cause[54]

There does not appear to be any distinction between "reasonable" and "probable". The principal difficulty, and it is no minor one, in stating the law as to reasonable and probable cause arises from the division of function between judge and jury,[55] cases of malicious prosecution being still, typically, tried by jury. It has been recognised for centuries[56] that once a person has been acquitted by a criminal court, juries are too ready to award him damages against his prosecutor,[57] and therefore it is for the judge to decide whether the defendant had reasonable and probable cause for launching the prosecution,[58] but it is for the jury to decide any incidental questions of fact necessary for the judge's determination.[59] Moreover, this branch of the law is unusual in requiring the claimant to undertake the difficult task of proving a negative. It is for him to prove that the prosecutor did not have reasonable and probable cause, and not for the prosecutor to prove that he had.[60]

20–011

Definition of reasonable and probable cause. In *Herniman v Smith*[61] the House of Lords approved and adopted the definition of reasonable and probable cause given by Hawkins J in *Hicks v Faulkner*[62] as:

20–012

---

[52] See para.5–077.

[53] It has been held in New Zealand that proof of the guilt of the claimant is in itself a defence to a claim for malicious prosecution where the favourable termination of the proceedings was otherwise than by an acquittal on the merits, the position in that case being left open: *Van Heeren v Cooper* [1999] 1 N.Z.L.R. 731, NZCA. The *Restatement*, 2d §657 makes guilt a defence in all cases, with a civil standard of proof. The point remains open as a matter of English law: *Qema v News Group Newspapers Ltd* [2012] EWHC 1146 (QB) at [92].

[54] For a valuable review of both reasonable and probable cause and malice see *A v New South Wales* [2007] HCA 10; 233 A.L.R. 584.

[55] *Glinski v McIver* [1962] A.C. 726 at 742 per Viscount Simonds.

[56] See *Pain v Rochester and Whitfield* (1599) Cro. Eliz. 871, cited by Denning LJ in *Leibo v Buckman Ltd* [1952] 2 All E.R. 1057 at 1062.

[57] For example, *Abrath v North Eastern Ry* (1886) 11 App. Cas. 247 at 252 per Lord Bramwell; *Leibo v Buckman Ltd* [1952] 2 All E.R. 1057 at 1063 per Denning LJ; *Glinski v McIver* [1962] A.C. 726 at 741–742 per Viscount Simonds, at 777–778 per Lord Devlin; cf. at 754 per Lord Radcliffe.

[58] *Johnstone v Sutton* (1786) 1 T.R. 510; *Herniman v Smith* [1938] A.C. 305; *Reynolds v Metropolitan Police Comr* [1985] Q.B. 881. It is doubtful whether the question is one of fact or law. Probably it is best regarded as a question of fact, but one which is to be treated in the same way as if it were a question of law: *Glinski v McIver* [1962] A.C. 726 at 768 per Lord Devlin.

[59] The judge need put to the jury only questions on the salient issues of fact, for otherwise the questions would have no end: *Dallison v Caffery* [1965] 1 Q.B. 348 at 368 per Lord Denning MR.

[60] *Abrath v NE Ry* (1883) 11 Q.B.D. 440; *Stapeley v Annetts* [1970] 1 W.L.R. 20. *Green v De Havilland* (1968) 112 S.J. 766, to the contrary, cannot be relied on.

[61] [1938] A.C. 305 at 316 per Lord Atkin.

[62] (1878) 8 Q.B.D. 167 at 171, affirmed (1882) 46 L.T. 130.

> "[A]n honest belief in the guilt of the accused based upon a full conviction, founded upon reasonable grounds, of the existence of a state of circumstances, which, assuming them to be true, would reasonably lead any ordinarily prudent and cautious man placed in the position of the accuser, to the conclusion that the person charged was probably guilty of the crime imputed."

The judge's concern is essentially with the objective aspect of this definition—whether there was reasonable and probable cause in fact—but the overall question is a double one, both objective and subjective: did the prosecutor actually believe and did he reasonably believe that he had cause for prosecution?[63] Not only must there be reasonable and probable cause in fact, but the prosecutor himself must also honestly believe that he has reasonable and probable cause.[64] His belief is a matter for the jury, not the judge, to determine, but the burden of proving lack of honest belief is on the claimant[65] and the question should only be put to the jury "in the highly unlikely event that there is cogent positive evidence that, despite the actual existence of reasonable and probable cause, the defendant himself did not believe that it existed".[66] Both the objective and the subjective element are directed to the decision to set the prosecution "in motion" and not the guilt of the claimant, still less whether he will be convicted, though clearly the defendant's belief in the probable guilt of the claimant is relevant to determining whether he honestly believed that there was reasonable and probable cause to prosecute.[67]

20–013 **Relevance of advice received by the prosecutor.** In principle the fact that the prosecutor has received advice should be regarded as no more than one of the facts to be taken into account, for if the prosecutor did not himself have an honest belief in the case he put forward it is irrelevant that he received advice before doing so.[68] In practice, however, if the prosecutor believes in the facts of the case and is advised by competent counsel before whom the facts are fairly laid that a prosecution is justified, it will be exceedingly difficult to establish lack of reasonable and probable cause.[69] An opinion of counsel favourable to the prosecutor is not conclusive, but it is a potent factor to be taken into account when deciding whether to prosecute.[70]

---

[63] "[I]t would be quite outrageous if, where a party is proved to believe that a charge is unfounded, it were to be held that he could have reasonable and probable cause": *Glinski v McIver* [1962] A.C. 726 at 768 per Lord Devlin; *Abbott v Refuge Assurance Co* [1962] 1 Q.B. 432 at 453 per Upjohn LJ. See also *Moulton v Chief Constable of West Midlands* [2010] EWCA Civ 524.

[64] *Haddrick v Heslop* (1848) 12 Q.B. 268 at 274 per Lord Denman CJ; *Broad v Ham* (1839) 8 Scott 40 at 50 per Erskine J.

[65] On requests for further information (formerly further and better particulars or interrogatories) see *Stapley v Annetts* [1970] 1 W.L.R. 20 and *Gibbs v Rea* [1998] A.C. 786 at 794.

[66] *Dallison v Caffery* [1965] 1 Q.B. 348 at 372 per Diplock LJ, at 368 per Lord Denning MR; *Glinski v McIver* [1962] A.C. 726 at 743–744 per Viscount Simonds, at 745 per Lord Radcliffe, at 768 per Lord Devlin. For a disagreement as to the inference to be drawn in a case where the defendant elected to call no evidence see *Gibbs v Rea* [1998] A.C. 768 (maliciously procuring a search warrant).

[67] *Qema v News Group Newspapers Ltd* [2012] EWHC 1146 (QB) (claimant caught in a sting operation and not disputed that he committed the offences in question, but conviction set aside on grounds of non-disclosure, or abuse of process).

[68] *Glinski v McIver* [1962] A.C. 726 at 756–757 per Lord Radcliffe, at 777 per Lord Devlin.

[69] *Abbott v Refuge Assurance Co Ltd* [1962] 1 Q.B. 432, where Davies LJ dissented on the facts. See also *Ravenga v Macintosh* (1824) 2 B. & C. 693 at 697 per Bayley J; *Glinski v McIver* [1962] A.C.

Objective test alone for prosecution by the public prosecutor? It must be borne in mind that *Hicks v Faulkner* was a private prosecution and in *Herniman v Smith* the prosecution was initiated by an information sworn by the defendant. To require an "honest belief" in guilt, while perhaps still an apt test for the private prosecutor or an informant who is treated as a prosecutor, would be unrealistic if applied to a member of the CPS taking a decision on the basis of evidence placed before him by the police. It is the function of the court and jury at the criminal trial to determine the accused's guilt; the function of the prosecutor is to apply his professional judgement to the evidence before him and determine whether, as Dixon J once put it: "[T]he probability of the accused's guilt is such that upon general grounds of justice a charge against him is warranted."[71] He has not even "got to test the full strength of the defence; he is concerned only with the question of whether there is a case fit to be tried".[72]

20–014

Indeed, if the public prosecutor personally harboured serious doubts about the guilt of the accused even though the evidence was strong enough to warrant a charge, it could be said that to desist from prosecuting would be a breach of his duty as a minister of justice. The private prosecutor has no basis for making a charge in which he does not believe; the same cannot be said for a public prosecutor. It has therefore been persuasively argued that in such a case this third stage should be regarded as a purely objective one.[73]

Multiple or lesser charges. If there are several charges in the indictment, the rule as to reasonable and probable cause applies to all of them,[74] but where there is reasonable and probable cause for a prosecution on a lesser charge than that actually preferred, a question of degree may arise:[75]

20–015

> "Where there is a charge of theft of 20s. and reasonable and probable cause is shown as regards 19s. of it, it may well be that the prosecutor, when sued for malicious prosecution, is entitled to succeed, because he was in substance justified in making the charge, even though he did so maliciously. But the contrary must surely be the case if the figures are reversed and reasonable and probable cause is shown as to 1s. only out of the 20s."

---

726 at 744–745 per Viscount Simonds. A similar result will follow where a private citizen is advised by the police that the facts which he has reported constitute a particular offence: *Malz v Rosen* [1966] 1 W.L.R. 1008.

[70] *Abbott v Refuge Assurance Co Ltd* [1962] 1 Q.B. 432 at 450 per Ormerod LJ.

[71] *Commonwealth Life Assurance Society Ltd v Brain* (1935) 53 C.L.R. 343 at 382.

[72] Lord Devlin in *Glinski v McIver* [1962] A.C. 726 at 766; *Coudrat v Revenue and Customs Commissioners* [2005] EWCA Civ 616; [2005] S.T.C. 1006 at [41]. Of course, matters other than the strength of the evidence may be relevant to the overall decision of whether a prosecution would be in the public interest.

[73] *Miazga v Kvello* [2009] SCC 51; [2009] 3 S.C.R. 339.

[74] *Reed v Taylor* (1812) 4 Taunt. 616; cf. *Johnstone v Sutton* (1786) 1 T.R. 510.

[75] *Leibo v Buckman Ltd* [1952] 2 All E.R. 1057 at 1071 per Jenkins LJ, at 1073 per Hodson LJ. Cf. the dissenting judgment of Denning LJ at 1066–1067.

D. Malice

20–016   **An uncertain definition.** Judicial attempts to define malice have not been completely successful. "Some other motive than a desire to bring to justice a person whom he [the accuser] honestly believes to be guilty"[76] seems to overlook the fact that motives are often mixed. Moreover, anger is not malice, indeed it is one of the motives on which the law relies in order to secure the prosecution of criminals,[77] and yet anger is much more akin to revenge than to any desire to uphold the law. Perhaps we are nearer the mark if we suggest that malice exists where the predominant purpose of the accuser is something other than the vindication of the law.[78] The question of its existence is one for the jury[79] and the burden of proving it is on the claimant.[80]

20–017   **Distinct from lack of reasonable and probable cause.** At one time malice was not always kept distinct from lack of reasonable and probable cause, but a cogent reason for separating them is that, however spiteful an accusation may be, the personal feelings of the accuser are really irrelevant to its probable truth. The probability or improbability of X having stolen my purse remains the same, however much I dislike X, and it has long been law that malice and lack of reasonable and probable cause must be separately proved. Want of reasonable and probable cause may be evidence of malice in cases where it is such that the jury may come to the conclusion that there was no honest belief in the accusation made.[81] If there was such an honest belief, the claimant must establish malice by some independent evidence, for malicious motives may co-exist with a genuine belief in the guilt of the accused.[82]

   For the reasons explained above, however, it seems again necessary to draw a distinction between private and professional prosecutors, the question of "honest belief" being arguably irrelevant to the latter. If it is correct that lack of reasonable cause can only be established against the latter by showing that there were no objective grounds for the proceedings then to allow malice to be inferred from lack of cause would entail the risk that it would be established by proof of

---

[76] Cave J in *Brown v Hawkes* [1891] 2 Q.B. 718 at 723; *Glinski v McIver* [1962] A.C. 726 at 766 per Lord Devlin.

[77] *Brown v Hawkes* [1891] 2 Q.B. 718 at 722, but if the prosecutor's anger is aroused, not by his belief in the claimant's guilt but by some extraneous conduct of the claimant, then there may be evidence of malice: *Glinski v McIver* [1962] A.C. 726 (claimant gave evidence for X on a criminal charge which the defendant, a police officer, believed to be perjured, and X was acquitted. If this was the reason for the claimant's prosecution on a charge of fraud, the prosecutor would have been malicious). See too *Heath v Heape* (1856) 1 H. & N. 478.

[78] *Stevens v Midland Counties Ry* (1854) 10 Ex. 352 at 356 per Alderson B. "Not only spite or ill-will but also improper motive": *Gibbs v Rea* [1998] A.C. 786 at 797. A rare example of such an improper purpose in the case of a professional prosecutor can be found in *Proulx v Québec (Attorney General)* 2001 SCC 66; [2001] 3 S.C.R. 9.

[79] *Mitchell v Jenkins* (1833) 5 B. & Ad. 588; *Hicks v Faulkner* (1878) 8 Q.B.D. 167 at 175 per Hawkins J.

[80] *Abrath v NE Ry* (1886) 11 App. Cas. 247.

[81] *Brown v Hawkes* [1891] 2 Q.B. 718 at 722 per Cave J; *Hicks v Faulkner* (1878) 8 Q.B.D. 167 at 175 per Hawkins J; *Gibbs v Rea* [1998] A.C. 786 at 798.

[82] *Brown v Hawkes* [1891] 2 Q.B. 718 at 726 per Lord Esher.

negligence.[83] In all cases, however, if want of reasonable and probable cause is not proved by the claimant, the defect is not supplied by evidence of malice.[84] "From the most express malice, the want of probable cause cannot be implied."[85]

2. MALICIOUS PROCESS

For malicious prosecution the defendant must have "prosecuted", but there may also be liability if the defendant has maliciously and without reasonable and probable cause instituted some process short of actual prosecution, of which the most important example is the procuring of a warrant for the claimant's arrest. In *Roy v Prior*[86] the defendant, a solicitor, was acting for the defence of a man charged with a criminal offence. The claimant was a doctor who had attended the accused and the defendant issued a witness summons requiring him to be present to give evidence at the trial. According to the claimant, this summons was never served on him, but in any case he was not present at the trial and, on the defendant's instructions, the accused's counsel applied for a warrant for his arrest. In support of the application the defendant himself gave evidence to the effect that the claimant had been evading service of the summons. As a result the warrant was issued and the claimant was arrested at 1.00 and kept in custody until 10.30 on the same day, when he was brought before the court. The House of Lords held that if the claimant could prove that the defendant had acted maliciously and without reasonable and probable cause, as he alleged, then he was entitled to succeed.[87] On similar principles a person is also liable for procuring the issue of a search warrant.[88] In that context the European Court of Human Rights has held that to confine liability to cases where there is malice is an insufficient protection of a person's rights under art.8 of the Convention because it prevents the courts examining issues of proportionality and reasonableness.[89] Whether that has any implications for the basic tort of malicious prosecution remains to be seen.

20–018

---

[83] *Miazga v Kvello* [2009] SCC 51; [2009] 3 S.C.R. 339.

[84] *Turner v Ambler* (1847) 10 Q.B.D. 252; *Glinski v McIver* [1962] A.C. 726.

[85] *Johnstone v Sutton* (1786) 1 T.R. 510 at 545; *Glinski v McIver* [1962] A.C. 726 at 744 per Viscount Simonds.

[86] [1971] A.C. 470.

[87] It matters not that the arrest was procured in the course of civil rather than criminal proceedings, though arrest on civil process is now exceptional. See, e.g. *Daniels v Fielding* (1846) 16 M. & W. 200; *Melia v Neate* (1863) 3 F. & F. 757. The point decided by the House of Lords in *Roy v Prior* [1971] A.C. 470 was that the immunity from suit of a witness in respect of his evidence does not protect him from an action for maliciously procuring the issue of a warrant of arrest. The claimant is not suing on or in respect of the evidence. He is suing because he alleges that the defendant procured his arrest by means of judicial process which the defendant instituted both maliciously and without reasonable and probable cause: [1971] A.C. 470 at 477 per Lord Morris. See also *Surzur Overseas Ltd v Koros* [1999] 2 Lloyd's Rep. 611 (freezing injunction).

[88] *Gibbs v Rea* [1998] A.C. 786; *Reynolds v MPC* [1985] Q.B. 881; *Keegan v CC Merseyside* [2003] EWCA Civ 936; [2003] 1 W.L.R. 2187.

[89] *Keegan v UK* Application No.28867/03 (2007) 44 E.H.R.R. 83.

3. MALICIOUS CIVIL PROCEEDINGS

20–019   Historically, there was no reason why the old action upon the case for conspiracy should not be extended to malicious civil proceedings as well as to malicious criminal proceedings, and it was in fact held to apply (inter alia) to malicious procurement of excommunication by an ecclesiastical court,[90] to bringing a second writ of *fi. fa.* against a man when one had already been obtained[91] and to malicious arrest of a ship.[92] In more modern times it had been confined to malicious winding-up proceedings,[93] or the malicious procuring of ex parte interlocutory orders.[94] Where available, the same requisites must be satisfied as for malicious prosecution.[95]

20–020   **Liability for malicious civil proceedings generally?** Does the law go still further and make the malicious institution of any civil proceedings[96] actionable? The general opinion had been that it does not, and this gained considerable strength by being repeated in the House of Lords in *Gregory v Portsmouth CC*.[97] A reason commonly given has been the absence of legal damage in the great majority of cases. As Bowen LJ put it in *Quartz Hill Gold Mining Co v Eyre*:[98]

> "[T]he bringing of an ordinary action does not as a natural and necessary consequence involve any injury to a man's property, for this reason, that the only costs which the law recognises . . . are the costs properly incurred in the action itself. For these the successful defendant has already been compensated."

This is, of course, simply untrue, for the assessed costs may not amount to the total costs of the defence,[99] and it is noteworthy that any deficiency in costs awarded to the accused in a criminal case does amount to damage.[100] Further, the argument does not explain why an action will not lie in respect of a civil action

---

[90] *Hocking v Matthews* (1670) 1 Vent. 86; *Gray v Dight* (1677) 2 Show. 144.

[91] *Waterer v Freeman* (1617) Hob. 205 at 266.

[92] *The Walter D. Wallet* [1893] P. 202.

[93] *Quartz Hill Gold Mining Co v Eyre* (1883) 11 Q.B.D. 674 at 683, 689; *Brown v Chapman* (1762) 1 W.Bl. 427.

[94] See the examples referred to by Lord Sumption in *Crawford Adjusters v Sagicor General Insurance Ltd* [2013] UKPC 17; [2013] 3 W.L.R. 927 at [143], some of which are discussed in para.20–018.

[95] Thus in a claim for malicious bankruptcy there is no cause of action (and hence time does not run) until the adjudication is annulled: *Radivojevic v LR Industries Ltd* Unreported May 14, 1982 CA; *Tibbs v Islington BC* [2002] EWCA Civ 1682; [2003] B.P.I.R. 743.

[96] i.e. beyond the limited range of situations outlined in para.20–018.

[97] [2000] 1 A.C. 419. See also *Metall und Rohstoff AG v Donaldson Lufkin & Jenrette Inc* [1990] 1 Q.B. 391; *Johnson v Emerson* (1871) L.R. 6 Ex. 329 at 372; *Quartz Hill Gold Mining Co v Eyre* (1883) 11 Q.B.D. 674 at 684.

[98] (1883) 11 Q.B.D. 674 at 690.

[99] The fiction is recognised by Devlin LJ in *Berry v British Transport Commission* [1962] 1 Q.B. 306 at 323. In the US the provision for recovery of costs in civil litigation is generally a good deal more restricted and this is a major reason for the more extensive liability for malicious civil proceedings there (see *Restatement* 2d, §§674–675), but a substantial minority of courts require some "special harm" going beyond the costs and reputational harm from the suit: see Dobbs, *Torts* (2000) §437. For a review of the US cases, see the opinion of Lord Neuberger in *Crawford Adjusters v Sagicor General Insurance Ltd* [2013] UKPC 17; [2013] 3 W.L.R. 927.

[100] *Berry v British Transport Commission* [1962] 1 Q.B. 306.

which blemishes the claimant's character, such as one based on fraud. In modern conditions it is not always true that the suit will receive less publicity than a criminal charge and it will not do to say that the claimant's reputation will be cleared by his successful defence of the action,[101] for exactly the same may be said of the successful defence of a criminal charge. Furthermore, the protection afforded by other torts such as defamation, malicious falsehood or conspiracy is limited by the fact that the immunity cast around the giving and preparation of evidence in criminal cases also attaches to civil litigation,[102] so that unless there is something like the fabrication of physical evidence[103] there will be no remedy.[104] The case for extending malicious prosecution to disciplinary proceedings is weaker and what *Gregory* actually decided as a matter of precedent is that this step should not be taken.[105] In such cases there is no absolute immunity and the law of defamation and malicious falsehood[106] will come into play if malice can be proved.[107]

Crawford Adjusters v Sagicor. The criticisms of the reasoning in the *Quartz*   **20–021**
Hill case outlined above resonated with a majority of the Privy Council in *Crawford Adjusters v Sagicor General Insurance Ltd*[108] and led them to the view that the tort of malicious prosecution should be available as much for the institution of civil proceedings as for the prosecution of criminal proceedings; indeed, they also opined that in relation to both it should be extended to the infliction of general economic loss.[109] Notwithstanding that the observations to the contrary in the House of Lords in *Gregory* were obiter, the admonition that decisions of the Privy Council are not binding on the courts in England and Wales carries added weight in the light of the powerful dissenting opinions of Lord Sumption and Lord Neuberger. The differences between the majority and the minority were very fundamental indeed.

Lord Wilson, in the majority, referred to the "paradox" that there is much less chance of being a victim of a criminal prosecution brought maliciously and without reasonable cause than of a civil action so brought and was clearly influenced by the manifest injustice of leaving the claimant without a remedy where it was almost unchallenged that a claim of fraud had been brought against the claimant in circumstances which easily fulfilled all of the requirements for malicious prosecution, not least the requirement of malice given the evidence that

---

[101] *Quartz Hill Gold Mining Co v Eyre* (1883) 11 Q.B.D. 674 at 684 per Bowen LJ.
[102] *Gregory v Portsmouth CC* [2000] 1 A.C. at 432; *Surzur Overseas Ltd v Koros* [1999] 2 Lloyd's Rep. 611; para.13–058.
[103] See *Darker v CC West Midlands* [2001] A.C. 435.
[104] It might be argued that the position of the civil defendant is rather like that of the criminal defendant in the heyday of the private prosecution when the law of malicious prosecution was formed, whereas now the control of the prosecution process by the state provides a check on false accusations; see on this point the differing responses of Lord Wilson and Lord Sumption in *Crawford Adjusters v Sagicor General Insurance Ltd* [2013] UKPC 17; [2013] 3 W.L.R. 927, para.20-021. The legislature has intervened in outrageous cases, for litigious monomaniacs may be muzzled under s.42 of the Senior Courts Act 1981. See also CPR 3.11.
[105] The case concerned disciplinary action taken by a local authority against a councillor.
[106] Also, in a suitable case, misfeasance in a public office.
[107] Yet it is only defamation which provides damages for loss of reputation as such.
[108] [2013] UKPC 17; [2013] 3 W.L.R. 927.
[109] [2013] UKPC 17; [2013] 3 W.L.R. 927 at [77] per Lord Wilson.

the defendant's aim was to destroy the claimant professionally. For the majority, the overriding principle was the private law impulse that "wrongs should be remedied".[110]

Lord Sumption embarked from the same starting point when he observed that the tort in its traditional form is now "all but defunct" because the "public function" which it was intended to fulfil of deterring malicious prosecution is now largely redundant given that private prosecution hardly exists today.[111] He regarded it as one of two anomalous "malice-based" torts justified only on the basis of their public function,[112] the other being misfeasance in a public office:[113]

> "It is a tool for constraining the arbitrary exercise of the powers of public prosecuting authorities or private persons exercising corresponding functions. A malice-based tort makes no sense in the context of private litigation where the plaintiff is not exercising any public function."[114]

The introduction of the tort of malicious prosecution for civil proceedings, "outside the special case of malicious winding up petitions and a small number of analogous ex parte proceedings"[115] would also leave the law uncertain and potentially very wide and lead to real concerns about the practical consequences of offering litigants an occasion for prolonging disputes by way of secondary litigation.[116] It remains to be seen whether the courts will prefer the private law conception of the tort favoured by the majority or the public law conception of the minority.

4. ABUSE OF PROCESS[117]

20–022 Aside from liability for malicious civil proceedings the law also recognises a related tort sometimes called "abuse of process". This lies where a legal process, not itself without foundation, is used for an improper, collateral purpose, for example as an instrument of extortion in a matter not connected with the suit.[118] It is then "merely a stalking horse to coerce the defendant in some way entirely

---

[110] *X v Bedfordshire CC* [1995] 2 A.C. 633, at 663 per Sir Thomas Bingham MR, cited by both Lord Wilson (at 73]) and by Baroness Hale (at [81]).

[111] [2013] UKPC 17; [2013] 3 W.L.R. 927 at [121], [145].

[112] For the general irrelevance of malice in tort see para.3–012.

[113] See Ch.8.

[114] [2013] UKPC 17; [2013] 3 W.L.R. 927 at [145].

[115] [2013] UKPC 17; [2013] 3 W.L.R. 927 at [144].

[116] [2013] UKPC 17; [2013] 3 W.L.R. 927 at [147]-[148].

[117] We are concerned here with the tort of abuse of process. A court may stay an action where the claimant is using the process to obtain a collateral advantage (*Goldsmith v Sperrings* [1977] 1 W.L.R. 478; *Lonrho Plc v Fayed (No.5)* [1993] 1 W.L.R. 1489) though it will probably be rarely exercised because the defendant's purpose is likely to be disputed. Nowadays, however, abuse of process is also used in a broader sense as a result of the fact that part of the overriding objective of the Civil Procedure Rules is to deal with cases in ways which are proportionate to the importance of the issues and the amounts involved. A claimant may find that what is technically a perfectly good claim that he seriously intends to pursue to judgment is dismissed as an abuse of process because in the court's view the "game is not worth the candle".

[118] *Grainger v Hill* (1838) 4 Bing. N.C. 212; *Speed Seal Products Ltd v Paddington* [1985] 1 W.L.R. 1327.

outside the ambit of the legal claim upon which the court is asked to adjudicate".[119] The original case is *Grainger v Hill*[120] where the claimant, having been sued for debt, was arrested on a *capias ad respondendum* obtained by the defendant with the purpose of getting the claimant to surrender the ship's register of the *Nimble*, which was mortgaged to the defendant. The claimant surrendered the register to escape arrest and lost trade as a result of not having the register. The claimant's action succeeded even though the original proceedings for debt had not been terminated. The cases have involved the abuse of ancillary process in suits already in progress but there seems no reason why the same rule should not apply to the initiation[121] of the original proceedings as a similar instrument of extortion.[122]

The process must have been used for a collateral purpose. The liability for abuse of process is by no means the same thing as a general tort of malicious issue or use of civil proceedings. If a person presents a claim for damages in the knowledge that it is completely unfounded he is amenable to penalties for perjury[123] and perhaps to heavy costs but he does not commit the tort of abuse of process because he is using the law, albeit corruptly, for its assigned purpose, namely to recover damages against the defendant in that suit. The position is the same even if the defendant has some further purpose which will be achieved or assisted by success in the suit, for his object is still to succeed in the litigation.[124] So if D were to launch a prosecution against C, a rival for political office, in order to procure a conviction which would disqualify C from the office[125] that would be no more abuse of process than it would be for, say, a rich man to launch a civil action against a poor man with the object of ruining him because the rich man had been worsted in love by the poor man. In neither of these cases is there any element of extorting any advantage or concession from the other party. Furthermore, the tort may be committed even where the claim is in fact well founded, for a valid claim may be used as an instrument of extortion just as much as an invalid one.[126] This is why it is irrelevant in this tort, unlike malicious prosecution, that the proceedings have not been terminated in the claimant's favour. The issue is not whether the principal suit is well founded and there is

20–023

---

[119] *Varawa v Howard Smith Co* (1911) 13 C.L.R. 35 at 91 per Isaacs J.

[120] (1838) 4 Bing. N.C. 212.

[121] Not the threat of proceedings: *Pitman Training Ltd v Nominee UK* [1997] F.S.R. 797. Sed quaere, in view of the logic behind the cause of action.

[122] While the claim in *Land Securities Plc v Fladgate Fielder* [2009] EWCA Civ 1402; [2010] 2 W.L.R. 1265 failed on a number of grounds, including the unsuitability of the tort in relation to proceedings for judicial review commenced with the permission of the court, no objection seems to have been taken simply that the claim was brought on the basis of the initiation of original proceedings.

[123] Not to a civil action by his opponent in respect of the perjury: *Hargreaves v Bretherton* [1959] 1 Q.B. 45.

[124] *Goldsmith v Sperrings Ltd* [1977] 1 W.L.R. 478; *Land Securities Plc v Fladgate Fielder* [2009] EWCA Civ 1402; [2010] 2 W.L.R. 1265 at [73]. The circumstances in *Crawford Adjusters v Sagicor* [2013] UKPC 17; [2013] 3 W.L.R. 927 (see para.20-021) provide the most extreme illustration of this, but in the same case Lord Wilson was unable to concur with the view expressed by Teare J. in *JSC BTA Bank v Ablyazov* [2011] EWHC 1136; [2011] 1 W.L.R. 2996 (Comm) that any legitimate purpose negatives abuse even if an improper purpose was predominant.

[125] The example given by the majority of the HCA in *Williams v Spautz* (1992) 174 C.L.R. 509.

[126] Just as a blackmailer threatens what he has a perfect "right" to do, namely expose his victim.

therefore no risk of infringing the principle that the court seized of an issue should be the one to decide it,[127] nor of getting inconsistent results. It has been said that there must be some overt act, beyond the issue of the proceedings, demonstrating that improper purpose, such as a demand on the claimant, but the better view is that such acts only have an evidential value and are not a substantive requirement.[128] It is the abuse of the process to effect the improper purpose that is the gist of the tort.[129]

20–024   **The present position.** The tort of abuse of process was last successfully invoked 170 years ago[130] and, as a result of the decision of the Court of Appeal in *Land Securities Plc v Fladgate Fielder*,[131] it seems that it is not intended to be a growth area. The defendant started judicial review proceedings against a council over a grant of planning permission to the claimant which the claimant alleged was intended to put pressure on the claimant to help the defendant relocate offices. The Court of Appeal upheld summary judgment in favour of the defendant. After an extensive review of this area of the law, Etherton LJ said that:[132]

> "[E]ven if the tort can be committed outside circumstances of compulsion by arrest, imprisonment or other forms of duress, there is no reasonably arguable basis for extending the tort beyond the other particular heads of damage which must exist for invocation of the tort of malicious prosecution. A different conclusion would not only go beyond the factual context of *Grainger* . . . but would be inconsistent with the refusal of the House of Lords in *Gregory*[133] to extend the tort of malicious prosecution to all civil proceedings. It makes no sense severely to limit the cause of action for malicious prosecution, an essential ingredient of which is that the proceedings had been brought without reasonable or probable cause, to three particular heads of damage,[134] but to extend to all cases of economic loss a tort of abuse of process which can apply even where the alleged "abuser" had a good cause of action. The dangers of parallel litigation and deterring the pursuit of honest claims are obvious. The wider descriptions of the tort of abuse of process in cases prior to *Gregory* must be re-appraised in the light of the decision of the House of Lords in that case and the policy considerations underlying it."

Mummery LJ felt there was no "pressing need to supplement procedural law by expansive tortious liability in order to protect litigants in civil proceedings from malicious or abusive claims".[135] This must of course now be viewed in light of some of the comments of the Privy Council in *Crawford Adjusters v Sagicor General Insurance Ltd* and, in particular, the view of Lord Wilson that the main ground of the decision in *Land Securities v Fladgate*—no liability for economic loss—is wrong.[136]

---

[127] "No one shall be allowed to allege of a still depending suit that it is unjust": *Gilding v Eyre* (1861) 10 C.B.N.S. 592 at 604.
[128] *Crawford Adjusters v Sagicor General Insurance Ltd* [2013] UKPC 17; [2013] 3 W.L.R. 927 at [66], [156].
[129] *Hanrahan v Ainsworth* [1990] 22 NSWLR 73 at 120 per Clark JA.
[130] *Grainger v Hill* (1838) 4 Bing. N.C. 212 (or 150 years if *Gilding v Eyre* (1861) 10 C.B.N.S. 592 is to be regarded as an example of the tort (*Grainger* was not mentioned).
[131] [2009] EWCA Civ 1402; [2010] 2 W.L.R. 1265.
[132] *Land Securities v Fladgate Fielder* [2009] EWCA Civ 1402; [2010] 2 W.L.R. 1265 at [68].
[133] *Gregory v Portsmouth CC* [2000] 1 A.C. 419.
[134] See para.20–004.
[135] *Land Securities Plc v Fladgate Fielder* [2009] EWCA Civ 1402; [2010] 2 W.L.R. 1265 at [109].
[136] *Crawford Adjusters v Sagicor General Insurance Ltd* [2013] UKPC 17; [2013] 3 W.L.R. 927 at [77].

CHAPTER 21

VICARIOUS LIABILITY[1]

1. THE NATURE AND BASIS OF VICARIOUS LIABILITY

A relationship based liability. The expression "vicarious liability" signifies the liability which D may incur to C for damage caused to C by the negligence or other tort of a third party, A. The fact that D is liable does not, of course, insulate A from liability,[2] though in most cases[3] it is unlikely that he will be sued or that judgment will be enforced against him. It is not necessary for vicarious liability to arise that D shall have participated in any way in the commission of the tort nor that a duty owed in law by D to C shall have been broken. What is required is that D should stand in a particular relationship to A and that A's tort should be

21–001

---

[1] Atiyah, Vicarious Liability in the Law of Torts (1967).

[2] *Standard Chartered Bank v Pakistan National Shipping Corp* [2002] UKHL 43; [2003] 1 A.C. 949, para.25–033.

[3] See *Merrett v Babb* [2001] Q.B. 1174 (where the employer was insolvent) and *Shapland v Palmer* [1999] 1 W.L.R. 2068.

referable in a certain manner to that relationship.[4] D's liability is truly strict, though for it to arise in a case of negligence, there has to be fault on the part of A.[5] The commonest instance of this is the liability of an employer for the torts of his employees done in the course of their employment. The relationship required is the specific one, that arising under a contract of service, and the tort must be referable to that relationship in the sense that it must have been committed by the servant in the course of his employment. It is with this instance of vicarious liability that the first part of this chapter is principally concerned, but there are other instances some of which cannot be followed in detail in a work of this kind. Such are the liability of partners for each other's torts and, perhaps, the liability of a principal for the torts of his agent.[6] Although the great majority of the cases involve common law torts, the principle of vicarious liability is a general one which will be applied to statutory wrongs sounding in damages unless the statute indicates the contrary, expressly or by implication.[7]

21–002 **Terminology.** The traditional terminology used to describe the relationship under a contract of service was "master and servant". The phrase is now anachronistic.[8] On the other hand, there are difficulties in finding suitable alternatives for terms of art. In this chapter a compromise position is adopted. "Master" has generally[9] been replaced by "employer"; and "servant" has generally been retained: it is still in use in ordinary speech in relation to some types of employment, it is etymologically connected with the core idea of the contract of service and it is still in widespread legal use.[10] In some cases, the courts have spoken in terms of identifying a relationship "akin to employment",[11] but the essence of this relationship lies in identifying one (A) who is "serving" the interest of another (D).

21–003 **Vicarious liability distinguished from the defendant's primary liability.** It is important that we should not confuse vicarious liability with the primary liability of D for damage caused to C by the act of A. This arises where D is in breach of his own duty to C, for example where D is at fault in selecting A for the task or allowing him to continue in employment or where D has not given adequate consideration to a safe system of work: many of the cases concern the liability of

---

[4] *Catholic Child Welfare Society v Institute of the Brothers of the Christian Schools* [2012] UKSC 56; [2013] 2 A.C. 1 at [21].

[5] One finds occasional traces of an alternative theory, that the employer is in breach of his own duty via the act of the servant: *Twine v Bean's Express* (1946) 175 L.T. 131; *Broom v Morgan* [1953] 1 Q.B. 597; but this approach has now been "firmly discarded": *Majrowski v Guy's and St Thomas's NHS Trust* [2006] UKHL 34; [2007] 1 A.C. 224 at [15]. The employer may in some cases be liable for breach of his own duty in any event (see para.21–044), but the general view is that vicarious liability requires that the servant be personally liable to the claimant. See also *NHS Manchester v Fecitt* [2011] EWCA Civ 1190; [2012] I.C.R. 372.

[6] Atiyah, *Vicarious Liability in the Law of Torts* (1967), pp.99–115. See also para.21–015.

[7] *Majrowski v Guy's and St Thomas's NHS Trust* [2006] UKHL 34; [2007] 1 A.C. 224 (Protection from Harassment Act 1997).

[8] *Mahmud v BCCI* [1998] A.C. 20 at 45.

[9] Except where the historical context justified it and, of course, in quotations.

[10] For example, in contracts. "Servant or agent" is a time-honoured apposition.

[11] See para.21–014.

an employer for injury caused to one of his servants by a fellow servant.[12] The fact that there is no vicarious liability does not necessarily mean that there is no breach of the personal duty.[13]

Vicarious liability distinguished from liability for breach of a non-delegable duty. Sometimes, even though D is not in fact guilty of any negligence, he is still said to be primarily liable because the negligence of A, to whom he has entrusted a task, puts D in breach of a "non-delegable duty". This does not mean that D commits any wrong by delegating the performance of the task to an apparently competent person, nor that he is an insurer of the safe completion of the task, but simply that he stands answerable for the fault of that person in carrying it out. Such duties arise for example, where an employer is held liable for damage caused by the act of an independent contractor, for the general rule is that there is no vicarious liability for independent contractors. However, unlike the case of employer and servant, nothing in particular turns on the precise relationship between the employer and the contractor for what is said to matter is the duty owed by the employer to the claimant.[14]

21–004

History. The shape of the modern law is recognisable by the middle of the 19th century. At one time liability seems only to have arisen if the employer had expressly commanded the wrong, which is not a true vicarious liability at all, for one who orders a wrong to be committed is, in the modern law, a direct participant in the tort and any sort of antecedent relationship is, as such, unnecessary.[15] At the beginning of the 18th century it was accepted that the employer was liable not only for acts done at his express command but also for those done by his implied command, this to be inferred from the general authority he had given his servant in his employment. By the end of the 18th century, however, the idea began to grow up that some special importance attached to the relationship of master and servant as such, something more than the fact that it might supply evidence of implied authority, and by the middle of the next century it was finally accepted that the existence of that relationship was necessary for vicarious liability[16] and sufficient to make the employer liable, provided the act was done in the course of the employment. At the same time the phrase "implied authority" which had been the cornerstone of the master's primary liability gives way gradually to the modern "scope of employment", though the former phrase survives in the context of misrepresentation.

21–005

Justification. Vicarious liability is a frequent feature of legal systems and those which do not have in its "pure" form, but which in theory require some fault in

21–006

---

[12] See para.9–021. For examples outside this area see *Hartwell v Attorney General* [2004] UKPC 12; [2004] 1 W.L.R. 1273 (personal fault but no vicarious liability); *Colour Quest Ltd v Total Downstream UK Plc* [2009] EWHC 540 (Comm); [2009] 2 Lloyd's Rep 1 (failure to design safe system as well as vicarious liability); *Maga v Birmingham Archdiocese* [2010] EWCA Civ 256; [2010] 1 W.L.R. 1441 (also a true vicarious liability). As *Maga* shows, the "personal" breach of duty by D to C may arise from D's vicarious liability for the failure of X, another employee of D, to carry out his duties.

[13] *Maga v Birmingham Archdiocese* [2010] EWCA Civ 256; [2010] 1 W.L.R. 1441 at [74].

[14] *Woodland v Essex CC* [2013] UKSC 66; [2014] A.C. 537. See para.21–045.

[15] See para.22–003.

[16] *Reedie v London and North Western Ry* (1849) 4 Exch. 244.

the employer, have tended to go to considerable lengths to create a liability without fault in practice.[17] Nevertheless, given the fact that most of tort law is formally based on fault, it requires some explanation or justification. The traditional phrases *respondeat superior* and *qui facit per alium facit per se* have been criticised, the former because it, "merely states the rule baldly in two words, and the latter merely gives a fictional explanation of it."[18] However, even if they are not explanations, they probably do represent the expression of a rather deep-seated and intuitive idea that someone who, generally for his own benefit, sets a force in motion should have responsibility for the consequences even if he chooses others to carry out the task. Of course this logically leads on to a full-blown theory of enterprise liability under which an activity should bear its own costs.[19] This is not the law now because there must be some tort and that generally involves fault, but the present position is a compromise, perhaps because pure enterprise liability removes incentives from the victim to take care to avoid accidents. At any rate, if there were no vicarious liability, the employer's incentive to minimise the risks created by his activity would be reduced.

Many years ago it was observed that the employer has the deeper pocket[20] and if there were no vicarious liability much of tort law would be stultified, for it would be impracticable (and wasteful) for many employees to insure themselves against liability incurred in employment. A variant of this, though in a more sophisticated form, is that of "loss distribution". An "employer" today is normally not an individual but a substantial enterprise or undertaking, and, by placing liability on the enterprise, what is in fact achieved is the distribution of losses caused in the conduct of its business over all the customers to whom it sells its services or products. Knowing of its potential liability for the torts of its servants, the enterprise insures against this liability and the cost of this insurance is reflected in the price it charges to its customers. In the result, therefore, losses caused by the torts of the enterprise's servants are borne in small and probably unnoticeable amounts by the body of its customers, and the injured person is compensated without the necessity of calling upon an individual, whose personal fault may be slight or even non-existent, to suffer the disastrous financial consequences that may follow liability in tort. Like many things in the law, the institution is probably to be explained not by reference to any single reason but by the cumulation of several.[21] It is inconceivable that a serious proposal for the abolition of vicarious liability will be made so long as the law of tort as we know it remains alive. Indeed, the trend towards "privatisation" of activities formerly carried on by an organisation's internal, integrated work force and the increasing use of casual and part-time workers[22] may require modification of the present distinction between servants and independent contractors.

---

[17] See for example German law, where §831 B.G.B. makes the employer liable unless he shows that he exercised due care in choosing and supervising the servant. No such exculpation is possible in contract under §278 B.G.B. Hence the courts have tended to extend contractual liability.

[18] *Staveley Iron and Chemical Co Ltd v Jones* [1956] A.C. 627 at 643 per Lord Reid.

[19] See Keating (1997) 95 Mich. L.R. 1266.

[20] *Limpus v LGO Co* (1862) 1 H. & C. 526 at 539 per Willes J.

[21] *Catholic Child Welfare Society v Institute of the Brothers of the Christian Schools* [2012] UKSC 56; [2013] 2 A.C. 1 at [35].

[22] See para.21–008.

2.   The Relationship between the Defendant and the Tortfeasor

A.   In General

A relationship "capable of giving rise to vicarious liability". In *Catholic Child Welfare Society v Institute of the Brothers of the Christian Schools* Lord Phillips referred to the "first stage" of asking whether the relationship between D and A is "one that is capable of giving rise to vicarious liability".[23] The question-begging nature of this formulation is explained by the context in which it was applied, namely the liability of a religious institute for the abuse of children perpetrated by some of its members. This is dealt with in more detail below,[24] but the point being emphasised by Lord Phillips is that qualifying relationships are not confined to employment in the strict sense,[25] albeit that is still the most common instance. The criteria for a qualifying relationship are assessed in the following paragraphs, but Lord Phillips also endorsed a "simpler analysis" under which it was necessary only to ask if the member in question was acting for the "common purpose" of the institute.[26] Acting for the "common purpose" of D and A (in the case of an unincorporated association, or a partnership) or simply for the "purpose" of D (in the more typical case of an employer in the strict sense) may be seen as the essence of the qualifying relationship and what follows are merely particularised instances of that type of relationship. Thus a prisoner is not employed by the prison but when he worked in the prison kitchens, during which time he assaulted the catering manager, the Ministry of Justice enjoyed the benefit of his work and should therefore shoulder the burden of it as well.[27]

21–007

Servants and independent contractors. Since vicarious liability generally arises from a contract of service ("servant") but not from a contract for services ("independent contractor") it is necessary to determine the indicia of a contract of service.[28] This task also has to be performed for purposes totally unconnected with vicarious liability (such as employment protection and taxation), but the assumption that the question "who is a servant?" should receive the same answer almost regardless of the context in which it is asked,[29] has now been firmly

21–008

---

[23] [2012] UKSC 56; [2013] 2 A.C. 1 at [21].

[24] See para.21–014.

[25] Lord Phillips adopted the terminology of a relationship "akin to employment", first used as a matter of English law in the "lucid and bold" judgment of MacDuff J in *JGE v English Province of Our Lady of Charity* [2011] EWHC 2871 (QB); [2012] 2 W.L.R. 709 (affd [2012] EWCA Civ 938; [2013] Q.B. 722) and borrowed from Canadian law: *Doe v Bennett* [2004] SCC 17; [2004] 1 S.C.R. 436.

[26] *Catholic Child Welfare Society v Institute of the Brothers of the Christian Schools* [2012] UKSC 56; [2013] 2 A.C. 1 at [61].

[27] *Cox v Ministry of Justice* [2014] EWCA Civ 132. It is not fatal to the finding of a relationship "akin to employment" that it is not entirely voluntary: at [63]–[64] per Beatson LJ.

[28] In those cases where it is sufficient to have identified a relationship "akin to employment" (see para.21–014), a *contract* of any sort is not necessary.

[29] See Atiyah, *Vicarious Liability in the Law of Torts* (1967), pp.32–33. *Calder v H Kitson Vickers & Sons (Engineers) Ltd* [1988] I.C.R. 232 at 254.

rejected.[30] This is to be welcomed and not just in the context of relationships which are self-evidently not employment.[31] Changes in employment practices (for example, the increasing casualisation of the workforce and the growing numbers of "home workers") have produced a situation in which, for employment protection purposes, it has become difficult to continue to regard people as servants who would once routinely have been such. Without suggesting that an employer should always be vicariously liable for the torts of his independent contractors (a course which would be impracticable and probably economically inefficient) it is questionable whether a tort claimant should necessarily be affected by internal changes in the employer's employment structure[32] which have nothing to do with the nature of his activities or the risk presented by them.[33] It is perfectly sensible to say that if Company D has its goods delivered to customers by a carrier, Company A, responsibility for accidents caused in the distribution process should fall on Company A alone, for that is a specialist function which is not "characteristic" of D's business (however necessary it may be to enable that business to function) and it is reasonable to expect that Company A will make proper liability insurance provisions against that risk;[34] it by no means follows that the same result should follow, to take the facts of one Australian case, where D sets up a "bicycle courier" business and engages a number of individuals to carry out deliveries for him.[35]

21–009   **Express classification of the parties.** The express declaration of the parties, if any, is not conclusive as to the legal classification of the relationship. It has been said to be a factor to be taken into account by the court,[36] but in the context of vicarious liability[37] the better view may be that it should be disregarded altogether.[38]

21–010   **Control test.** At one time it was generally accepted that the test of the relationship of master and servant was that of control,[39] and a contract of service

---

[30] "The fluid concept of vicarious liability should not...be confined by the concrete demands of statutory construction arising in a wholly different context": *JGE v English Province of Our Lady of Charity* [2012] EWCA Civ 938; [2013] Q.B. 722 at [59] per Ward LJ.

[31] For example, the relationship between bishop and priest which was in issue in the *JGE* case.

[32] Or in the case of state activities, privatisation: *Quaquah v Group 4 Securities Ltd (No.2)*, *The Times*, June 27, 2001.

[33] See McKendrick (1990) 53 M.L.R. 770; Kidner (1995) 15 L.S. 47.

[34] If only because such insurance is required by law.

[35] The majority of the HCA, reversing the NSWCA, held that the couriers were servants in *Hollis v Vabu Pty Ltd* [2001] HCA 44; 207 C.L.R. 21. The defendant had made deductions from fees for liability insurance, but this only covered him.

[36] See, e.g. *Ferguson v John Dawson & Partners (Contractors) Ltd* [1976] 1 W.L.R. 1213; *Ready Mixed Concrete (South East) Ltd v Minister of Pensions and National Insurance* [1968] 2 Q.B. 497; *Global Plant Ltd v Secretary of State for Social Services* [1972] 1 Q.B. 139; *Calder v H Kitson Vickers Ltd* [1988] I.C.R. 232.

[37] In *Ferguson v John Dawson & Partners (Contractors) Ltd* [1976] 1 W.L.R. 1213 the context was the possible application of the Construction (Working Places) Regulations 1966

[38] Megaw LJ in *Ferguson v John Dawson & Partners (Contractors) Ltd* [1976] 1 W.L.R. 1213 at 1222 would have been prepared to go further and say that the parties' declaration ought to be wholly disregarded. This is the position where a servant is loaned by one employer to another: see para.21–018.

[39] For an early statement of the control test, see *Yewens v Noakes* (1880) 6 Q.B.D. 530 at 532–533 per Bramwell B. For its development see Atiyah, *Vicarious Liability in the Law of Tort* (1967), pp.40–44.

was thought to be one by virtue of which the employer, "can not only order or require what is to be done, but how it shall be done".[40] The control test probably retains some importance in cases to which it can be applied,[41] but in modern conditions the notion that an employer has the right to control the manner of work of all his servants, save perhaps in the most attenuated form,[42] contains more of fiction than of fact. It is clearly the law that such professionally trained persons as the master of a ship, the captain of an aircraft and the house surgeon at a hospital are all servants for whose torts their employers are responsible, and it is unrealistic to suppose that a theoretical right in an employer, who is likely as not to be a corporate and not a natural person, to control how any skilled worker does his job, can have much substance.[43] It has, therefore, been recognised that "the significance of control today is that the employer can direct what the employee does, not how he does it".[44]

"A composite approach". In an often cited statement[45] Lord Thankerton said **21–011** that there are four indicia of a contract of service: (1) the employer's power of selection of his servant; (2) the payment of wages or other remuneration; (3) the employer's right to control the method of doing the work; and (4) the employer's right of suspension or dismissal. It is respectfully suggested, however, that this does not carry the matter much further: the first and last, and perhaps also the second, are indicia rather of the existence of a contract than of the particular kind of contract which is a contract of service,[46] and some judges have preferred to leave the question in very general terms. Somervell LJ thought that one could not get beyond the question whether the contract was, "a contract of service within the meaning which an ordinary person would give under those words".[47]

---

[40] *Collins v Hertfordshire CC* [1947] K.B. 598 at 615 per Hilbery J.

[41] *Argent v Minister of Social Security* [1968] 1 W.L.R. 1749 at 1759 per Roskill LJ; *Jennings v Forestry Commission* [2008] EWCA Civ 581; [2008] I.C.R. 988.

[42] As the Special Commissioner said in *Hall v Lorimer* 1992 S.T.C. 599: "in the production of a play you must pay attention to the stage directions and the producer's directions. That applies to the leading actor and actress, but they do not for that reason become 'employees'."

[43] Kahn-Freund (1951) 14 M.L.R. 504. On ministers of religion and the distinction between employment and spiritual matters see *Percy v Church of Scotland* [2005] UKHL 73; [2006] 2 A.C. 28.

[44] *Catholic Child Welfare Society v Institute of the Brothers of the Christian Schools* [2012] UKSC 56; [2013] 2 A.C. 1 at [36] per Lord Phillips. See also: *Ready Mixed Concrete (South East) Ltd v Minister of Pensions and National Insurance* [1968] 2 Q.B. 497; *Market Investigations Ltd v Minister of Social Security* [1969] 2 Q.B. 173.

[45] *Short v J&W Henderson Ltd* (1946) 62 T.L.R. 427 at 429.

[46] *Ready Mixed Concrete (South East) Ltd v Minister of Pensions and National Insurance* [1968] 2 Q.B. 497 at 524 per MacKenna J.

[47] *Cassidy v Ministry of Health* [1951] 2 K.B. 343 at 352–353; *Argent v Minister of Social Security* [1968] 1 W.L.R. 1749 at 1760 per Roskill J.

Nowadays it is common to take a "composite" approach in which the various elements of the relationship are considered as a whole.[48] Denning LJ once said that:[49]

> "[O]ne feature which seems to run through the instances is that, under a contract of service, a man is employed as part of a business, and his work is done as an integral part of the business whereas under a contract for services, his work, although done for the business, is not integrated into it but is only accessory to it."

Employment protection cases have emphasised that there must be "mutuality" in the contractual arrangement, i.e. an obligation on the employer to provide work and on the other party to perform it when required,[50] but this is another instance where it is important to take into account the context in which the issue arises. In the employment cases the issue will normally be whether there was a contract of service with a degree of continuity, but in the context of vicarious liability the question is whether A is working as D's servant *at the time when he injures C*. It would certainly be odd if, for example, A did work for D in circumstances where A was subject to direct orders and close control over his manner of work and yet D was not liable for A's acts simply because A had the right to decline work when it suited him to do so. It is perfectly possible to say that, while there is no ongoing relationship between D and A amounting to a contract of service, A is D's servant, at least for the purposes of vicarious liability, while he is actually working.[51] A factor which, however, is likely to point away from a contract of service is the fact that the person engaged is not required to perform personally but may delegate to others if he chooses.[52]

B.   Particular Examples

21–012   **Hospitals.** It was to a substantial extent a consequence of developments in the liability of hospitals for the negligence of their staffs that dissatisfaction with the test of control developed, for while it was originally held that a hospital authority could not be liable for negligence in matters involving the exercise of

---

[48] *Lee v Cheung* [1990] 2 A.C. 374. Although the claimant worked for a number of persons the picture that emerged was: "of a skilled artisan earning his living by working for more than one employer as an employee and not as a small businessman entering into business on his own account with all its attendant risks." The case concerned a Hong Kong workmen's compensation ordinance which recognised "casual workers".

[49] *Stevenson, Jordan and Harrison Ltd v Macdonald and Evans* [1952] 1 T.L.R. 101 at 111. His Lordship gave as examples: a ship's master, a chauffeur and a staff reporter are servants but a ship's pilot, a taxi driver and a newspaper contributor are independent contractors.

[50] *Carmichael v National Power Plc* [1999] 1 W.L.R. 2042; *Stevedoring and Haulage Services Ltd v Fuller* [2001] I.R.L.R. 62.

[51] See *Muscat v Cable & Wireless Plc* [2006] EWCA Civ 220; [2006] I.C.R. 975 at [27].

[52] *Express and Echo Publications Ltd v Tanton* [1999] IRLR 367; cf. *McFarlane v Glasgow CC* [2001] I.R.L.R. 7.

professional skills,[53] this view has not been accepted since 1942. Since then it has been held that radiographers,[54] house-surgeons,[55] whole time-assistant medical officers[56] and, probably, staff anaesthetists are the servants of the authority for the purposes of vicarious liability.[57]

In some of the cases there has been a tendency to treat the question of a hospital authority's liability not as one of vicarious liability only but also as one of the primary liability of the authority for breach of its own duty to the patient[58] and this approach has received the endorsement of the Supreme Court in *Woodland v Essex CC*.[59] However, while this may save the court the task of determining whether the negligent individual is a servant of the hospital authority it will not relieve the claimant of the burden of showing negligence. In most cases his complaint will be that Dr A was negligent in his treatment and if this is so then (assuming Dr A to be a servant) to say that the hospital authority was in breach of its duty via him is to state a proposition the practical effect of which is the same as saying that it is vicariously liable for his negligence. If, however, he is not negligent (because, for example, he is given a task which is beyond the competence of a doctor holding a post of his seniority) then there is still a possibility that the hospital authority is negligent in failing to secure adequate staffing.[60] Alternatively, if A is at fault but is not a servant it now seems to be the case that, having accepted responsibility for treatment, the hospital owes a non-delegable duty to ensure that proper care is taken.[61]

Police. Until 1964 no person or body stood in the position of "master" to a police   **21–013**
officer,[62] and accordingly anyone injured by the tortious conduct of the police could have redress only against the individual officers concerned. Now, however, it is provided by s.88 of the Police Act 1996 that the chief officer of police for any police area shall be liable for torts committed by constables under his direction and control in the performance or purported performance of their functions.[63]

---

[53] *Hillyer v St Bartholomew's Hospital* [1909] 2 K.B. 820. Note that the hospital in this case was a charitable body.

[54] *Gold v Essex CC* [1942] 2 K.B. 293.

[55] *Collins v Hertfordshire CC* [1947] K.B. 598; *Cassidy v Ministry of Health* [1951] 2 K.B. 343.

[56] *Cassidy v Ministry of Health* [1951] 2 K.B. 343.

[57] *Roe v Minister of Health* [1954] 2 Q.B. 66.

[58] See, e.g. *Gold v Essex CC*[1942] 2 K.B. 293 at 301 per Lord Greene MR; *Cassidy v Ministry of Health* [1951] 2 K.B. 343 at 362–365 per Denning LJ.

[59] [2013] UKSC 66; [2014] A.C. 537 at [23] per Lord Sumption; discussed at para.21–048.

[60] See *Wilsher v Essex Area Health Authority* [1987] Q.B. 730. A claim that staffing is inadequate may face a formidable obstacle in the court's refusal to interfere with the authority's discretion over the allocation of resources: *Ball v Wirral HA* (2003) 73 B.M.L.R. 31.

[61] *X (Minors) v Bedfordshire CC* [1995] 2 A.C. 633 at 740; *A v MoD* [2004] EWCA Civ 641; [2005] Q.B. 183 at [63]; *Farraj v Kings Healthcare NHS Trust* [2009] EWCA Civ 1203; [2010] 1 W.L.R. 2139 at [88]; *Woodland v Essex CC* [2013] UKSC 66; [2014] A.C. 537 at [23].

[62] Under the Crown Proceedings Act 1947 the Crown is only liable in respect of persons who are paid wholly out of moneys provided by Parliament (s.2(6)) and this excludes the police. There is no difficulty about applying the general law of vicarious liability to members of the armed forces, though in practice what is regarded as the course of employment may extend beyond matters which are strictly in the course of duty in the military sense: *Radclyffe v MoD* [2009] EWCA Civ 635.

[63] As amended by the Police Reform Act 2002. See para.21–036. The Police Act 1997 provides for vicarious liability of the Directors-General of the National Criminal Intelligence Service and the National Crime Squad in respect of officers under their control.

This statutory liability is equated with the liability of an employer for the torts of his servants committed in the course of their employment, but the Act does not create a relationship of employer and servant, nor one of principal and agent.[64] The chief officer of police does not, of course, have to bear the damage personally. Any damages or costs awarded against him are paid out of the police fund.

21–014 **Religious institutions.** In a number of cases concerned with the abuse of children, the courts have been required to address the question of whether the relationship between the religious institution and the individual tortfeasor qualified for the purpose of vicarious liability.[65] The leading case in this respect is *Catholic Child Welfare Society v Institute of the Brothers of the Christian Schools*.[66] Children had been abused by teachers who were employed by the Society as manager of the school. The Society did not challenge the finding that it was vicariously liable but appealed against the finding that the Institute was not also vicariously liable for the abuse carried out by teachers who were brothers of the Institute. According to Lord Phillips the Institute was to be approached as a corporate body (an unincorporated association) which existed to perform the function of providing a Christian education to boys,[67] which function was carried out, in part, by the brothers who served as teachers. The Institute and the individual brothers shared a "common purpose"[68] and that was sufficient for their relationship to be regarded as sufficiently "akin to employment".[69] For the reasons given by Rix LJ in the *Viasystems* case, there was no objection to the dual liability of the Society and the Institute.[70]

21–015 **Vehicle drivers.** Thus far we have spoken of the relationship under a contract of service, or something analogous thereto. However, many cases on vicarious liability speak in the language of agency and numerous dicta can be found equating agency with a contract of service for this purpose.[71] Whatever may be

---

[64] *Farah v MPC* [1998] Q.B. 65.

[65] Whether the abuse is sufficiently connected with the relationship is dealt with at para.21–019.

[66] [2012] UKSC 56; [2013] 2 A.C. 1. See also: *JGE v English Province of Our Lady of Charity* [2012] EWCA Civ 938; [2013] Q.B. 722 (relationship between bishop and priest); cf. *Maga v Birmingham Archdiocese* [2010] EWCA Civ 256; [2010] 1 W.L.R. 1441 where employment was conceded and the court was only concerned with the "second stage" of vicarious liability, para.21–033.

[67] In both the *Child Welfare Society* case and *JGE* there is an acknowledged difficulty about the precise identity of the defendant. In *JGE* the court was concerned with the relationship between bishop and priest, but the defendants to the action were the trustees of the Diocesan Trust since the Roman Catholic Church could not be a party as it has no legal personality. Similarly, in the *Child Welfare Society* case the court looked at the relationship between the Institute (whether worldwide or only locally) and the brothers in question, but among the defendants were the trustees of two Trusts which owned significant assets on behalf of the Institute.

[68] [2012] UKSC 56; [2013] 2 A.C. 1 at [61].

[69] So far as any element of "control" was concerned, it was noted that the teaching of the brothers was undertaken because the Institute directed it and the manner in which the brothers were to conduct themselves was dictated by the Institute's rules (at [56]); cf. *E v Children's Society* [2012] EWHC 365 (QB) (no employment or anything akin to it between a charity and the son of houseparents running one of its children's homes).

[70] *Viasystems (Tyneside) Ltd v Thermal Transfer (Northern) Ltd* [2005] EWCA Civ 1151; [2005] 4 All E.R. 1181, discussed at para.21–016.

[71] See Atiyah, *Vicarious Liability in the Law of Tort* (1967), Ch.9.

the correct principle as to liability for agents, it is convenient to treat here a doctrine which fits easily into no existing legal category[72] but which developed because of the insurance position in relation to road traffic liability. The doctrine may be stated as follows. Where D, the owner[73] of a vehicle, expressly or impliedly requests or instructs A to drive the vehicle in performance of some task or duty carried out for D, D will be vicariously liable for A's negligence in the operation of the vehicle.[74] Thus in *Ormrod v Crosville Motor Services Ltd*[75] D, the owner of a car, asked A to drive the car from Birkenhead to Monte Carlo, where they were to start a holiday together. It was held that D was liable for A's negligent driving even though A might be said to be partly pursuing his own interest in driving A's car. On the other hand, liability was not imposed in *Morgans v Launchbury*[76] where the husband, who normally used his wife's car to go to work, got a third person to drive him home after visits to several public houses. In no sense was the husband acting as his wife's agent in using the car for his work and still less was the third person her agent.[77] It is now clear that mere permission to drive without any interest or concern of the owner in the driving does not make the owner vicariously liable[78] nor is there any doctrine of the "family car".[79] Where, however, the facts of the relationship between owner and driver are not fully known, proof of ownership may give rise to a presumption that the driver was acting as the owner's agent.[80]

The development of a separate head of vicarious liability for vehicle drivers was clearly prompted by a desire to ensure a claim-worthy defendant, but the House of Lords denied that the courts may go on a voyage of discovery into the insurance position in these cases and said that any alteration of the law must be left to the legislature with its superior capacity for making decisions of policy. However, to confine our attention in this context to instances of vicarious liability risks giving a false impression. If there is in force a policy of insurance covering the liability of the driver[81] there will generally be no point in suing the owner. In fact, as far as the claimant is concerned, even if the driver is not covered by the

---

[72] Winfield sought to explain the doctrine in terms of "casual delegation" of the use of a chattel, but the leading case now talks in terms of agency: *Morgans v Launchbury* [1973] A.C. 127.

[73] Ownership as such is probably not necessary: *Nottingham v Aldridge* [1971] 2 Q.B. 739. In *Morgans v Launchbury* the husband was held liable for the negligence of the driver and there was no appeal against that decision. If an owner bails his vehicle to A and A gets B to drive it, the owner is not liable for B's negligence: *Chowdhary v Gillot* [1947] 2 All E.R. 541.

[74] *Morgans v Launchbury* [1973] A.C. 127.

[75] [1953] 1 W.L.R. 1120. See also *Samson v Aitchison* [1912] A.C. 844; *Pratt v Patrick* [1924] 1 K.B. 488; *The Trust Co Ltd v De Silva* [1956] 1 W.L.R. 376, PC; *Vandyke v Fender* [1970] 2 Q.B. 292; *Candler v Thomas* [1998] R.T.R. 214.

[76] [1973] A.C. 127.

[77] Cf. the valiant attempt of Lord Denning MR and Edmund Davies LJ in the CA to fit the facts into a traditional agency framework: [1971] 2 Q.B. 245.

[78] *Morgans v Launchbury* [1973] A.C. 127; *Hewitt v Bonvin* [1940] 1 K.B. 188 (father permitting son to take girlfriends home in car); cf. *Carberry v Davies* [1968] 1 W.L.R. 1103 (owner suggesting to driver that he take owner's son out in car). A person who has "borrowed" a car, with or without the owner's permission is not acting as his agent when driving it back to him: *Klein v Caluori* [1971] 1 W.L.R. 619.

[79] Cf. the view of Lord Denning MR in *Launchbury v Morgans* [1971] 2 Q.B. 245.

[80] *Rambarran v Gurrucharan* [1970] 1 W.L.R. 556; *Morgans v Launchbury* [1973] A.C. 127 at 139 per Viscount Dilhorne.

[81] For example, under a "named driver" clause in the policy.

policy, in most cases the owner's insurer must satisfy the judgment against the uninsured driver[82] and if there is no insurance at all the claimant may proceed under the MIB Agreement.[83] The owner may be liable to indemnify his insurer or the MIB (and that will be out of his own pocket) but that is no concern of the claimant.

The question remains of the reach of this principle. While it has certainly been most prominent in the context of motor accidents, it has been applied to a boat[84] but even a special rule about "transport" seems out of tune with the style of the common law and the judgments in *Morgans v Launchbury* are couched in quite general terms of agency. On the other hand, a general principle that the owner of a chattel was liable for the negligence of anyone using it at his request would have surprising consequences.[85]

C. Lending a Servant

21–016 **Dual liability now possible.** D may be the general employer of A but X may be making temporary use of A's services.[86] If A injures some third party, who bears the vicarious liability for his acts? For long it was assumed that it must be one or the other but it could not be both.[87] The Court of Appeal rejected this proposition in *Viasystems (Tyneside) Ltd v Thermal Transfer (Northern) Ltd*.[88] Ducting was being fitted by sub-contractor X, who was making use of "labour-only" services provided by D. The negligence of A, an employee of D, caused a flood, for which the court held that both X and D were liable to the factory owner, with equal contribution between themselves under the Civil Liability (Contribution) Act 1978.[89]

21–017 **The limits of dual liability.** It does not follow that such dual vicarious liability will arise in every case. In *Viasystems* A was part of a team consisting of his superior and another skilled worker contracted to X: it was a situation of shared control of the organisation of A's work. Where, on the other hand, A's services are supplied to X on a long-term basis subject to the entire control of X, that is likely

---

[82] Road Traffic Act 1988 s.151(2)(b).

[83] It should be noted that at the time of the accident in *Morgans v Launchbury* insurance for passengers was not compulsory and therefore fell outside the scope of the MIB Agreement.

[84] *The Thelma (Owners)* v *The Endymion (Owners)* [1953] 2 Lloyd's Rep. 613.

[85] See the examples of the cricket bat and the barbecue given by Callinan J in *Scott v Davis* [2000] HCA 52; 204 C.L.R. 333 at [347]–[348] and *Moynihan v Moynihan* [1975] I.R. 192.

[86] See *MAN Nutzfahrzeuge AG v Freightliner Ltd* [2005] EWHC 2347 (Comm) at [107] (A employed by D but X puts forward A as speaking on his (X's) behalf. No reason why X should not be vicariously liable even though for other purposes only D would be).

[87] *Esso Petroleum Co Ltd v Hall Russell & Co Ltd* [1989] A.C. 643 at 686.

[88] [2005] EWCA Civ 1151; [2005] 4 All E.R. 1181.

[89] In what was only a two member Court of Appeal, May LJ adopted the stringent test of control laid down in *Mersey Docks and Harbour Board v Coggins and Griffith (Liverpool) Ltd* [1947] A.C. 1 but found that there was shared control on the facts. In *Catholic Child Welfare Society v Institute of the Brothers of the Christian Schools* [2012] UKSC 56; [2013] 2 A.C. 1 at [43], Lord Phillips preferred the approach of Rix LJ under which one looked for "a situation where the employee in question . . . is so much a part of the work, business or organisation of both employers that it is just to make both employers answer for his negligence".

to result in X alone being liable.[90] Another situation is illustrated by *Mersey Docks and Harbour Board v Coggins and Griffith (Liverpool) Ltd*.[91] D, the harbour authority, employed A as the driver of a mobile crane, and let the crane together with A as driver to X. The contract between D and X provided that A should be the servant of X but A was paid by D, and D alone had power to dismiss him. In the course of loading a ship C was injured by the negligent way in which A worked the crane. At the time of the accident X had the immediate direction and control of the operations to be executed by A and his crane, for example to pick up and move a piece of cargo, but he had no power to direct how A should work the crane and manipulate its controls. The House of Lords held that D as the general or permanent employer of A was liable to C. At that time it was assumed that it was not possible for both D and X to be liable and this was not therefore argued. However, it is suggested in the *Viasystems* case that the result might still be the same and the sole liability would be in D:[92] A was on D's premises, operating D's crane and exercising his own skill and discretion in that task, even if he was subject to the direction of X as to what loads he should lift and where he should take them.[93] Even in such a case, of course, if X, though he has no authority to do so, expressly directs A to do the act which is negligently done and causes damage, X is generally liable with A as a joint tortfeasor; whether D is vicariously liable will depend on whether A's departure from instructions given by D takes him outside the course of his employment.

Express provisions. As the *Mersey Docks* case shows, the fact that the contract between D and X expressly provided that X was to be treated as the sole employer was not determinative of the question whether that was in fact so. However, a term in the contract may entitle D to an indemnity from X in respect of any damages D has to pay to C.[94]

21–018

---

[90] See, e.g. *Hawley v Luminar Leisure Ltd* [2006] EWCA Civ 18; [2006] I.R.L.R. 817.

[91] [1947] A.C. 1.

[92] *Viasystems (Tyneside) Ltd v Thermal Transfer (Northern) Ltd* [2005] EWCA Civ 1151; [2005] 4 All E.R. 1181 at [80] per Rix LJ. It is also suggested by May LJ at [32] that *Bhoomidas v Port of Singapore* [1978] 1 All E.R. 956 would also go the same way and the stevedoring company alone would be liable.

[93] See also *Biffa Waste Services Ltd v Maschinenfabrik Ernst Hese GMBH* [2008] EWCA Civ 1257; [2009] Q.B. 725.

[94] *Herdman v Walker (Tooting) Ltd* [1956] 1 W.L.R. 209; *Spalding v Tarmac Civil Engineering Ltd* [1966] 1 W.L.R. 156. The allocation of indemnity rights between D and X is not an exclusion of liability: *Thompson v T. Lohan* [1987] 1 W.L.R. 649, but may still be regulated by the Unfair Contract Terms Act 1977 s.4. Where, however, X is also the claimant, the indemnity will operate as an exclusion of liability and s.2 of the 1977 Act applies: *Phillips Products Ltd v Hyland* [1987] 1 W.L.R. 659.

3.   THE CONNECTION BETWEEN THE RELATIONSHIP AND THE CONDUCT OF THE TORTFEASOR

A.   In General

21–019   **"Scope of employment".** In *Catholic Child Welfare Society v Institute of the Brothers of the Christian Schools* Lord Phillips referred to the "second stage" of vicarious liability as the search for the connection that links the relationship between D and A (the "first stage") and the act or omission of A which has caused harm to C. The two stages cannot therefore be considered in isolation and there is a synthesis between them.[95] In the context of employment, the question is said to be whether A's conduct fell within the "scope of his employment". If employment is understood in the broader context in which it used in vicarious liability,[96] there is no reason not to continue to employ such terminology generally, though as we will see the way in which the question has been formulated appears to have been influential in some cases and a change of language considered appropriate.[97] "Scope of employment" and "course of employment" tend to be used interchangeably, though the latter expression is often found in legislation dealing with other matters and it is dangerous to assume that authorities from such contexts can be automatically transferred to that of vicarious liability.[98] It may also be the case that statute imposes a liability for the acts of others in a particular context. Whatever form of words is used, the question under the statute is one of construction and it may lay down some wider (or narrower) principle than the common law.[99]

21–020   **A difficult question, however formulated.** It may be asked how any wrong can be in the scope of a servant's employment since no sane or law-abiding employer hires someone to tell lies, give blows or act carelessly, but that is not what scope of employment means. The focus is not so much on the wrong committed by the servant as upon the act he is doing when he commits the wrong. Traditionally it has been said that the act will be within the scope of the employment if it has been expressly or impliedly authorised by the employer[100] or is sufficiently connected with the employment that it can be regarded as an unauthorised manner of doing something which is authorised,[101] or is necessarily incidental to something which the servant is employed to do. The underlying idea is that the injury done by the servant must involve a risk sufficiently inherent in[102] the employer's business that it is just to make him bear the loss. For example, no one would think of arguing that an employer of a lorry driver should be liable for an accident caused by the driver in his own car when on holiday. In other cases, it

---

[95] [2012] UKSC 56; [2013] 2 A.C. 1 at [21].
[96] I.e. to include relationships "akin to employment": see para.21–014.
[97] See para.21–021.
[98] *Lister v Hesley Hall Ltd* [2001] UKHL 22; [2002] 1 A.C. 215 at [40] per Lord Clyde.
[99] See, e.g. *Jones v Tower Boot Co Ltd* [1997] 2 All E.R. 406 (Race Relations Act 1976 (see now Equality Act 2010)).
[100] If the act authorised is inherently wrongful (e.g. trespassing on another's land) the employer is liable because he has procured a wrong and there is no need to rely on vicarious liability.
[101] *Kirby v NCB* 1958 S.C. 514 at 533.
[102] *Lister v Hesley Hall Ltd* [2001] UKHL 22; [2002] 1 A.C. 215 at [65] per Lord Millett.

may be a difficult question to decide whether conduct is or is not within the scope of employment and, while it would not be correct to say that the question is one of fact (for it involves the application of legal principle to facts[103]) it is not one that lends itself to the imposition of mechanical or precise formulae.

A broader test: "close connection"? Since the decided cases are not amenable to any scientific classification and the issue tends to be "fact-sensitive", the best that can be done is to select and illustrate a few of the more common factual situations to see if one can discern broad trends. In *Lister v Hesley Hall Ltd*[104] the House of Lords to some extent[105] restated the "test" for scope of employment in terms of whether the act was so closely connected with the employment that it would be just to hold the employer liable. The case concerned wilful wrongdoing of an extreme kind and was intended to extend the scope of liability but it cannot necessarily be confined to that situation[106] and, despite the fact that very soon afterwards in the same court the traditional formula was used and it was said that in this area previous authorities were particularly valuable,[107] some cases cited below which have gone against the claimant are at least open to argument, even if at the end of the day most of them would probably be decided in the same way.

21–021

All acts constituting the wrong must fall within the scope of employment. It is necessary that the acts done by the servant within the scope of his employment constitute an actionable wrong in themselves: it is not enough that the wrong is constituted by some acts done by him within and some outside that relationship or that the wrong partly consists of acts done within the scope of employment by the servant and other acts committed by a third party.[108]

21–022

B. Carelessness of Servant

Employer liable provided servant is not "on a frolic of his own". By far the commonest kind of wrong which the servant commits is one due to unlawful carelessness, whether it be negligence of the kind which is in itself a tort, or negligence which is a possible ingredient in some other tort. It should be noted also that in some torts intention or negligence is immaterial: the doer is liable either way. In cases of this sort the employer may well be responsible for conduct of the servant to which no moral blame attaches;[109] but, assuming that the tort is

21–023

---

[103] *Dubai Aluminium Co Ltd v Salaam* [2002] UKHL 48; [2003] 2 A.C. 366 at [24].

[104] [2001] UKHL 22; [2002] 1 A.C. 215.

[105] However, apart from Lord Steyn and Lord Hutton it is not easy to be sure of the view of the court as a whole on the traditional test. In fact Lord Clyde seems to regard it as a correct statement of the law, but cf. *Mattis v Pollock* [2003] EWCA Civ 787; [2003] 1 W.L.R. 2158 at [19]. See also *Catholic Child Welfare Society v Institute of the Brothers of the Christian Schools* [2012] UKSC 56; [2013] 2 A.C. 1 at [74].

[106] The change of approach owes something to the Canadian case of *Bazley v Currie* (1999) 174 D.L.R. (4th) 45. However, it is said in *Sickel v Gordy* [2008] SKCA 100; 298 D.L.R. (4th) 151 that the court in that case had no intention to say anything about the straightforward case where the servant is carrying out instructions.

[107] *Dubai Aluminium Co Ltd v Salaam* [2002] UKHL 48; [2003] 2 A.C. 366 at [26] and [30]. See also *HSBC Bank Plc v So* [2009] EWCA Civ 296; [2009] 1 C.L.C. 503.

[108] *Credit Lyonnais Bank Nederland N.V. v E.C.G.D.* [2000] 1 A.C. 486.

[109] *Gregory v Piper* (1829) 9 B. & C. 591.

negligence or that it is one in which inadvertence is a possible element in its commission, it may still be in the course of employment even if the servant is not acting strictly in the performance of his duty, provided he is not "on a frolic of his own".[110] Thus a first-aid attendant at a colliery was still within the course of his employment while cycling across his employer's premises to go to an office to collect his wages,[111] and so was a person sent to work at a place away from his employer's premises who drove some distance from his place of work to get a midday meal.[112]

In *Century Insurance Co Ltd v Northern Ireland Road Transport Board*,[113] the driver of a petrol lorry, employed by the defendants, while transferring petrol from the lorry to an underground tank in the claimant's garage, struck a match to light a cigarette and threw it on the floor and thereby caused a conflagration and an explosion which damaged the claimant's property. The defendants were held liable, for the careless act of their driver was done in the course of his employment. Lord Wright pointed out that the act of the driver in lighting his cigarette was done for his own comfort and convenience; it was in itself both innocent and harmless, but the act could not be treated in abstraction from the circumstances as a separate act; the negligence was to be found by considering the time when and the circumstances in which the match was struck and thrown down, and this made it a negligent method of conducting his work.

Whether the servant is on a frolic of his own will depend on the particular nature of the employer's business and the task which the servant is required to discharge. If bailed goods have been entrusted by the employer to the care of his servant and the servant negligently damages them, his employer will be vicariously liable to their owner, for the servant has done carelessly what he was employed to do carefully, namely, to look after the goods. For this purpose it makes no difference that the servant at the time of his negligence was using the goods improperly for purposes entirely of his own, as, for example, if he uses a car, bailed to his employer and entrusted to his care, for taking his friends for a ride, and then negligently damages the car in an accident.[114] He is as much guilty of failure to *look after the car* as he would have been if the accident had occurred while he was using the car for an authorised purpose.

21–024 **Travel cases.** A number of cases are concerned with deviations by drivers from routes authorised by their employers. We have probably not advanced much beyond the test stated in the old case of *Storey v Ashton*,[115] that it is, "a question of degree how far the deviation could be considered a separate journey" divesting

---

[110] This famous phrase was coined by Parke B. in *Joel v Morison* (1834) 6 C. & P. 501 at 503.

[111] *Staton v National Coal Board* [1957] 1 W.L.R. 893.

[112] *Harvey v RG O'Dell Ltd* [1958] 2 Q.B. 78; cf. *Crook v Derbyshire Stone Ltd* [1956] 1 W.L.R. 432; *Nottingham v Aldridge* [1971] 3 W.L.R. 1.

[113] [1942] A.C. 509, approving *Jefferson v Derbyshire Farmers Ltd* [1921] 2 K.B. 281, where the facts were very similar, and for all practical purposes overruling *Williams v Jones* (1865) 3 H. & C. 602; cf. *Kirby v NCB* 1958 S.L.T. 47.

[114] *Coupe Co v Maddick* [1891] 2 Q.B. 413; *Aitchison v Page Motors Ltd* (1935) 154 L.T. 128; *Central Motors (Glasgow) Ltd v Cessnock Garage and Motor Co* 1925 S.C. 796; cf. *Sanderson v Collins* [1904] 1 K.B. 628.

[115] (1869) L.R. 4 Q.B. 476. Contrast *Whatman v Pearson* (1868) L.R. 3 C.P. 422.

the employer of responsibility.[116] It is unlikely that all the cases are reconcilable but in modern conditions one has to take account not merely of the geographical or temporal divergence from instructions, but how far the servant can still be said to be carrying out the task he was set.[117] A servant travelling between home and work will not generally be in the course of employment[118] unless he is contractually required to use a particular mode of transport[119] or comes out "on call" in his employer's time to deal with emergencies.[120] Where the employment is essentially peripatetic (for example, a travelling salesman or appliance repairer), travel from one location to another during the day will be within the course of employment[121] and the same will be true of the journey between home and the first location if the servant goes directly there rather than to his "base".[122] In these cases driving from place to place is an ordinary and necessary incident of performing the duties of the employment. This was not so in *Smith v Stages*[123] where the servants were normally employed at site A but were sent to perform an urgent job at site B over 200 miles away. Nevertheless they were held to be in the course of their employment in driving home from site B because they were paid wages (and not merely a travelling allowance) for doing so even though they were using a private vehicle[124] and had a discretion as to how and when they would travel.

C. Mistake of Servant

So far we have been dealing with the incompetent dilettante and we now pass to the misguided enthusiast. In *Bayley v Manchester, Sheffield and Lincolnshire Ry*[125] a porter working for the defendants violently pulled out of a train the claimant who said his destination was Macclesfield and who was in a train that was in fact going there. The porter mistakenly thought it was going elsewhere. The defendants were held liable. The porter was doing in a blundering way something which he was authorised to do—to see that passengers were in the right trains and to do all in his power to promote their comfort.

21–025

---

[116] *Hilton v Thomas Burton (Rhodes) Ltd* [1961] 1 W.L.R. 705.

[117] In *Angus v Glasgow Corp* 1977 S.L.T. 206 it is suggested that the real test is, "has the servant departed altogether from his master's business".

[118] *Smith v Stages* [1989] A.C. 928 ("One must not confuse the duty to turn up for one's work with the concept of already being 'on duty' while travelling to work", at 955 per Lord Lowry); but employment may commence as soon as the factory gates are passed: *Compton v McClure* [1975] I.C.R. 378.

[119] See *Nottingham v Aldridge* [1971] 2 Q.B. 739 at 747.

[120] *Blee v LNER Co* [1938] A.C. 126; *Paterson v Costain and Press (Overseas) Ltd* [1979] 2 Lloyd's Rep. 204; but as Lord Lowry admits in *Smith v Stages* [1989] A.C. 928 at 956, the concept of the "employer's time" cannot be applied to salaried workers.

[121] Yet the salesman is not in the course of his employment when he books into a hotel for the night.

[122] *Nancollas v Insurance Officer* [1985] 1 All E.R. 833 at 838.

[123] [1989] A.C. 928.

[124] The case arose because the driver was uninsured and the time limits in the MIB Agreement had not been complied with.

[125] *Bayley v Manchester, Sheffield and Lincolnshire Ry* (1873) L.R. 8 C.P. 148. See also Willes J in (1873) L.R. 7 C.P. at 420.

21–026   **Acts in protection of the employer's property.** Another application of the same principle is an act done in protection of the employer's property. The servant has an implied authority to make reasonable efforts to protect and preserve it in an emergency which endangers it. For wrongful, because mistaken, acts done within the scope of that authority the employer is liable, and it is a question of degree whether there has been an excess of the authority so great as to put the act outside the scope of authority. A carter, who suspected on mistaken but reasonable grounds that a boy was pilfering sugar from the wagon of the carter's employer, struck the boy on the back of the neck with his hand. The boy fell and a wheel of the wagon went over his foot. The employer was held liable because the blow given by the carter, although somewhat excessive, was not sufficiently so to make it outside the scope of employment.[126] However, while a servant's authority to protect his employer's goods against armed robbery extends to acts done in self-defence against the robber it does not extend to using a customer as a human shield.[127] A servant has no implied authority to arrest a person whom he suspects of attempting to steal after the attempt has ceased, for the arrest is then made not for the protection of the employer's property but for the vindication of justice.[128]

21–027   **Negligent delegation of the servant's duty to a stranger.** The existence of an emergency gives no implied authority to a servant to delegate his duty to a stranger, so as to make his employer liable for the defaults of the stranger,[129] but it may be that the servant himself was negligent in the course of his employment in allowing the stranger to do his job. In *Ilkiw v Samuels*,[130] a lorry driver in the employment of the defendants permitted a stranger to drive his lorry, and an accident resulted from the stranger's negligent driving. The defendants were held liable, not for the stranger's negligence, for he was not their servant,[131] but on the ground that the driver himself had been guilty of negligence in the course of his employment in permitting the stranger to drive without even having inquired whether he was competent to do so.[132]

21–028   **Servant usurping the job of another.** Equally, the employer may sometimes be liable even though the servant has usurped the job of another, provided that what he does is not too great a departure from the kind of thing he is employed to do. In *Kay v ITW Ltd*,[133] a storekeeper employed by the defendants needed to return

---

[126] *Poland v Parr & Sons* [1927] 1 K.B. 236; but it may be that after *Lister v Hesley Hall Ltd* [2001] UKHL 22; [2002] 1 A.C. 215 even a grossly excessive reaction would not take the servant outside the course of his employment: para.21–033.

[127] *Reilly v Ryan* [1991] 2 I.R. 247.

[128] For example, *Abrahams v Deakin* [1891] 1 Q.B. 516; *Hanson v Waller* [1901] 1 Q.B. 390; *Radley v LCC* (1913) 109 L.T. 162.

[129] *Houghton v Pilkington* [1912] 3 K.B. 308; *Gwilliam v Twist* [1895] 2 Q.B. 84. On the basis of the reasoning of Diplock LJ in *Ilkiw v Samuels* [1963] 1 W.L.R. 991 at 1003–1006 it may be that these cases would be differently decided today.

[130] [1963] 1 W.L.R. 991; *Ricketts v Thomas Tilling Ltd* [1915] 1 K.B. 644.

[131] *Ilkiw v Samuels* [1963] 1 W.L.R. 991 at 996 per Willmer LJ.

[132] See, however, the different and more complex reasoning of Diplock LJ [1963] 1 W.L.R. 991 at 1003–1006, referred to by Lord Hobhouse in *Lister v Hesley Hall Ltd* [2001] UKHL 22; [2002] 1 A.C. 215 at [58].

[133] [1968] 1 Q.B. 140; *East v Beavis Transport Ltd* [1969] 1 Lloyd's Rep. 302. Cf. *Beard v London General Omnibus Co* [1900] 2 Q.B. 530 and see the explanation of that case by Sellers LJ: [1968] 1 Q.B. 140 at 152.

a forklift truck to a warehouse but found his way blocked by a large lorry belonging to a third party. Although there was no urgency and without first inquiring of the driver of the lorry, he attempted to move the lorry himself, and by his negligence in doing so caused an injury to the claimant. The Court of Appeal considered that the case fell near the borderline, for it cannot be for every act, however excessive, that the servant may do in an attempt to serve his employer's interests that the employer is liable.[134] Nevertheless, taking into account the fact that it was clearly within the terms of the storekeeper's employment to move certain obstacles out of the way if they blocked the entrance to the warehouse, and since it was part of his normal employment to drive trucks and small vans, the court held that his act of trying to move the lorry was not so gross and extreme as to take it outside the course of his employment.

D. Wilful Wrong of Servant

When it comes to the servant's wilful wrongdoing[135] two rules are settled. First, that an act done may still be in the course of employment even if it was expressly forbidden by the employer.[136] Secondly, it does not necessarily follow that the servant is acting outside the scope of his employment because he intended to benefit himself and not his employer.[137] **21–029**

Acts expressly prohibited by the employer. The prohibition by the employer of an act or class of acts will only protect him from liability which he would otherwise incur if it actually restricts what it is the servant is employed to do:[138] the mere prohibition of a mode of performing the employment is of no avail.[139] It is a question of fact in each case whether the prohibition relates to the sphere of the employment or to the mode of performance, and "the matter must be looked at broadly, not dissecting the servant's task into its component activities . . . by asking: what was the job on which he was engaged for his employer?"[140] **21–030**

In *Limpus v London General Omnibus Co*,[141] a driver of the defendants' omnibus had printed instructions not to race with, or obstruct, other omnibuses. In disobedience to this order he obstructed the claimant's omnibus and caused a collision which damaged it. The defendants were held liable because what he did was merely a wrongful, improper and unauthorised mode of doing an act which he was authorised to do, namely, to promote the defendants' passenger-carrying

---

[134] *Kay v ITW Ltd* [1968] 1 Q.B. 140 at 151–152 per Sellers LJ.
[135] Wilful horseplay may be outside the course of employment: *Duffy v Thanet DC* (1984) 134 N.L.J. 680; *Aldred v Nacano* [1987] I.R.L.R. 292; cf. *Harrison v Michelin Tyre Co* [1985] 1 All E.R. 918, doubted in *Aldred v Nacano*. As to the employer's personal duty in such cases, see para.9–021.
[136] See paras 21–030—21–031.
[137] See paras 21–032—21–033.
[138] The servant is outside the course of employment while performing acts of precisely the character for which he is employed by the employer, if he is in fact working for someone else at the time: *Kooragang Investments Pty Ltd v Richardson & Wrench Ltd* [1982] A.C. 462.
[139] *Plumb v Cobden Flour Mills Ltd* [1914] A.C. 62 at 67 per Lord Dunedin; *LCC v Cattermoles (Garages) Ltd* [1953] 1 W.L.R. 997 at 1002 per Evershed MR; *Ilkiw v Samuels*[1963] 1 W.L.R. 991 at 1004 per Diplock LJ; *Kay v I.T.W. Ltd* [1968] 1 Q.B. 140 at 158 per Sellers LJ
[140] *Ilkiw v Samuels* [1963] 1 W.L.R. 991 at 1004 per Diplock J.
[141] (1862) 1 H. & C. 526.

business in competition with their rivals. Again, in *LCC v Cattermoles (Garages) Ltd*[142] a garage-hand was not allowed to drive vehicles, but it was part of his duty to move them by hand. His employers were held liable for his negligence while driving a vehicle. However, a fire engine crew engaging in a "go-slow" in support of a pay claim were held not to be acting in the course of their employment when they failed to arrive in time to put out a fire.[143]

21–031 **Unauthorised passengers.** The question of prohibitions by the employer has given rise to particular difficulty where the servant has given a lift in the employer's vehicle to an unauthorised passenger.[144] As Lord Greene MR put it in *Twine v Bean's Express Ltd*,[145] giving a lift to an unauthorised passenger was not merely a wrongful mode of performing the act which driver was employed to perform but was the performance of an act which he was not employed to perform at all. As always, however, this test is capable of producing divergent answers on the simplest facts and did so in *Rose v Plenty*.[146] A milkman had been warned by his employer not to allow children to assist him, nor to allow passengers on his float. In breach of these instructions he engaged the claimant, aged 13, to help him, and the claimant was injured, while a passenger on the float, by the milkman's negligent driving. To Lawton LJ the situation was indistinguishable from that in *Twine v Bean's Express Ltd*, but the majority of the Court of Appeal, while accepting the correctness of the decision in *Twine*'s case, held that the milkman was acting in the course of his employment because the engagement of the claimant was made to further the employer's business:[147] the milkman was employed to deliver milk, which was precisely what he was doing when he caused the accident. This decision is certainly in accord with the long-standing tendency to apply a very broad description to "course of employment"[148] and it was approved by three judges in *Lister v Hesley Hall Ltd*,[149] but it is questionable whether it is so easily reconcilable with the earlier passenger cases as the majority of the court asserts.[150] It may also be asked in this context whether, assuming a prohibition to limit the scope of the servant's employment, the claimant's knowledge of the prohibition is of any significance.

---

[142] [1953] 1 W.L.R. 997; *Ilkiw v Samuels* [1963] 1 W.L.R. 991; cf. *Iqbal v London Transport Executive* (1973) 16 K.I.R. 329.

[143] *General Engineering Services Ltd v Kingston and St Andrew Corp* [1988] 3 All E.R. 867; but perhaps there is no duty to get there promptly at all: *Capital & Counties Plc v Hampshire CC* [1997] Q.B. 1004: see para.5–046.

[144] This problem is now of less significance because of the compulsory insurance provisions of the Road Traffic Act 1988 but similar problems could arise in situations where the Act of 1988 is inapplicable such as use of a vehicle off the road or other forms of transport.

[145] (1946) 62 T.L.R. 458; *Conway v George Wimpey & Co Ltd* [1951] 2 K.B. 266; cf. *Young v Edward Box & Co Ltd* [1951] 1 T.L.R. 789.

[146] [1976] 1 W.L.R. 141.

[147] A supposed "benefit" which he has made it very clear he does not want, presumably because his insurers have insisted upon the prohibition.

[148] See particularly *Ilkiw v Samuels* [1963] 1 W.L.R. 991 at 1004. *Stone v Taffe* [1974] 1 W.L.R. 1575 perhaps points the same way, though in that case the employer's prohibition related not to the original entry on to their property but to the duration of the stay.

[149] [2001] UKHL 22; [2002] 1 A.C. 215 (Lords Steyn, Clyde and Millett).

[150] Surely in *Twine* and *Conway* the servants were employed to drive the vehicles, in the course of which activity they injured the claimants?

In principle, it is submitted that knowledge is not necessary[151] but that in cases where the servant has ostensible authority to invite persons into his employer's vehicle a passenger should not be affected by any prohibition of which he is unaware.[152] Whatever the present status of the earlier decisions on unauthorised passengers, it remains clear that even if the servant is acting outside the scope of his employment with regard to the passenger[153] he may still be within it with regard to other road users.[154]

Acts intended to benefit the servant. At one time it was generally thought that the servant was acting outside the scope of his employment if he intended to benefit himself and not his employer[155] but this view was displaced by *Lloyd v Grace, Smith & Co.*[156] The defendants, a firm of solicitors, employed a managing clerk who conducted their conveyancing business without supervision. The claimant was dissatisfied with the money which some cottages produced and went to the defendants' office where she saw the clerk, who induced her to give him instructions to sell the cottages and to execute two documents which he falsely told her were necessary for the sale but which in fact were a conveyance of the cottages to himself. He then dishonestly disposed of the property for his own benefit. The House of Lords unanimously held that the defendants were liable:[157] the clerk was acting as the representative of the firm and they had invited the claimant to deal with him over her property. It cannot be said, however, that as a result of *Lloyd*'s case the question of benefit is invariably irrelevant, for it will still be found in some cases that it is the fact that the servant intended to benefit himself alone that prevents his tort from being in the course of his employment. This will be so, for example, in the case of a driver who takes his employer's vehicle "on a frolic of his own". It is because the journey was made solely for the driver's benefit that the employer is not liable to a person injured by the negligence of the driver.

21–032

Abuse of children in care.[158] It is in the context of wilful wrongdoing that the approach of asking whether the servant's acts were an improper mode of doing what he was employed to do has been perceived as giving rise to most difficulty.

21–033

---

[151] See Asquith LJ in *Conway v George Wimpey & Co Ltd* [1951] 2 K.B. 266, but this point in his judgment is related to the issue of whether the claimant was a trespasser. Strictly, the issue of knowledge was irrelevant in *Rose v Plenty* because of the majority decision that the prohibition did not limit the scope of the employment but in view of the differences of opinion one may assume that it would have been mentioned if it had been regarded as possessing any significance.

[152] Cf. *Ferguson v Welsh* [1987] 1 W.L.R. 1553.

[153] The servant, of course, remains personally liable to the passenger, but his liability is not one which is required to be covered by insurance: *Lees v Motor Insurers' Bureau* [1952] 2 All E.R. 511.

[154] *Twine v Bean's Express Ltd* [1946] 62 T.L.R. 458 at 459 per Lord Greene MR; cf. *Morris v C.W. Martin & Sons Ltd* [1966] 1 Q.B. 716 at 724–725 where the doubts expressed by Lord Denning MR are, with respect, unfounded.

[155] Based on *Barwick v English Joint Stock Bank* (1867) L.R. 2 Ex. 259.

[156] [1912] A.C. 716. See also: *Uxbridge Permanent, etc. Society v Pickard* [1939] 2 K.B. 248; *United Africa Co v Saka Owoade* [1955] A.C. 130; *Morris v C.W. Martin & Sons Ltd* [1966] 1 Q.B. 716. Cases such as *Century Insurance Co Ltd v Northern Ireland Road Transport Board* [1942] A.C. 509, [21-023] can also be regarded as involving acts done by the servant for his own benefit.

[157] Equally, the servant is personally liable for fraud even if his object is solely to benefit his employer: *Thomas Saunders Partnership v Harvey* (1990) 7 Tr.L.R. 78.

[158] Cane (2000) 116 L.Q.R. 21; Feldthusen, in *Torts Tomorrow: A Tribute to John Fleming* (1998).

Many claims have been lodged against local authorities and other bodies in respect of abuse suffered by the claimants while they were children in care. In *Lister v Hesley Hall Ltd*[159] the House of Lords held that the defendant children's home was vicariously liable for the acts of the warden in abusing the claimants: the home had undertaken the care of the children and entrusted the performance of that duty to the warden and there was therefore a sufficiently "close connection" between his employment and the acts committed by him. There is a good deal of criticism of the "improper mode" approach and it is even described as "simplistic".[160] With respect this is harsh, for there seems no difficulty in accommodating the facts within the traditional test as it has been applied to matters like fraud or theft: just as the clerk's making off with Mrs Lloyd's money was an outrageous way of performing his duty to attend to her affairs, so also the conduct of the warden in indecently assaulting the children was an outrageous way of carrying out his duty to care for them.[161] What is in fact surprising is the Court of Appeal's decision to the contrary in *Lister*.

21–034   **Criticism of the "close connection" test.** Whatever view one takes, the fact remains that it may still be very difficult to determine the incidents for which the employer is responsible in these cases. It has been said that *Lister*, "provides no clear assistance on when . . . an incident is to be regarded as sufficiently work-related" to attract vicarious liability.[162] *Lister* itself was a comparatively easy case because the warden of the home was entrusted with the care of the children and an ability to influence them and take advantage was inherent in this. At the opposite extreme, if the servant had been, say, a handyman employed by a local authority who had been sent to do repairs at a home run by the authority and had taken the opportunity to commit indecent assaults, the result should be different: he is not employed to deal with children.[163] Nonetheless, there will be intermediate cases. For example, what are we to say if on facts like *Lister* the servant is the resident caretaker at the home; or where a person has the care of one inmate but uses the opportunity created by his position to abuse another?[164] In *Catholic Child Welfare Society v Institute of the Brothers of the Christian Schools*[165] Lord Phillips suggested the following approach to deal with such questions:[166]

---

[159] [2001] UKHL 22; [2002] 1 A.C. 215.

[160] *Lister v Hesley Hall Ltd* [2001] UKHL 22; [2002] 1 A.C. 215 at [20] per Lord Steyn.

[161] "Abusing the boys was diametrically opposed to [the objectives of the Institute] but, paradoxically, that very fact was one of the factors that provided the necessary close connection between the abuse and the relationship between the brothers and the Institute that gives rise to vicarious liability on the part of the latter": *Catholic Child Welfare Society v Institute of the Brothers of the Christian Schools* [2012] UKSC 56; [2013] 2 A.C. 1 at [92] per Lord Phillips

[162] *Dubai Aluminium Co Ltd v Salaam* [2002] UKHL 48; [2003] 2 A.C. 366 at [25]. See also *Catholic Child Welfare Society v Institute of the Brothers of the Christian Schools* [2012] UKSC 56; [2013] 2 A.C. 1 at [74]: "The test of 'close connection' . . . tells one nothing about the nature of the connection".

[163] *Maga v Birmingham Archdiocese* [2010] EWCA Civ 256; [2010] 1 W.L.R. 1441 at [74].

[164] No, according to *B v Jacob* (1998) 166 D.L.R. (4th) 125.

[165] [2012] UKSC 56; [2013] 2 A.C. 1 at [86].

[166] He borrowed heavily from the test formulated in the Canadian decision of *Bazley v Currie* (1999) 174 D.L.R. (4th) 45 which had also been influential in *Lister*.

"Vicarious liability is imposed where a defendant, whose relationship with the abuser put it in a position to use the abuser to carry on its business or to further its own interests, has done so in a manner which has created or significantly enhanced the risk that the victim or victims would suffer the relevant abuse. The essential closeness of connection between the relationship between the defendant and the tortfeasor and the acts of abuse thus involves a strong causative link."

The facts in the *Child Welfare Society* case itself[167] were such that Lord Phillips regarded it as "not a borderline case",[168] in particular because the risk of abuse was recognised by the prohibition on the touching of the children in the rules of the Institute and yet the brothers appointed as teachers were put in a position where they enjoyed physical proximity to their victims and the influence over them as teachers and as men of God.[169]

Other assaults. There were a number of cases before *Lister* outside the context   **21–035** of childcare but involving assaults by servants and which seemed to proceed broadly on the basis that the servant's act might be in the course of his employment if his intention was, however wrongly, to further his employer's business or assert his employer's authority,[170] but if the assault was a mere act of personal vengeance and not in pursuit of those aims, it would not.[171] After *Lister* the issue arose in *Mattis v Pollock*,[172] where a nightclub bouncer, having been assaulted by disgruntled customers in an incident at the club, went home, got a knife and, about 20 minutes after the incident, stabbed the claimant outside the club. The Court of Appeal held that the stabbing was sufficiently closely connected with the incident under *Lister* to make it within the course of his employment by the defendant. However, it was regarded as important that the defendant had encouraged the bouncer to take an aggressive attitude towards customers;[173] indeed, the court was of the opinion that the defendant was in breach of his personal duty in this respect.[174] So also in *Gravil v Carroll*[175] a rugby club was held liable for a punch by a part-time professional player in a melee which persisted after a scrum but the Court of Appeal was influenced by the fact that such attacks, though unlawful and in breach of the rules, were an

---

[167] As to which, see para.21–014.

[168] [2012] UKSC 56; [2013] 2 A.C. 1 at [93]

[169] See, to similar effect, the decisions in *Maga v Birmingham Archdiocese* [2010] EWCA Civ 256; [2010] 1 W.L.R. 1441 and *Doe v Bennett* [2004] SCC 17; [2004] 1 S.C.R. 436. In *Jacobi v Griffiths* [1999] 2 S.C.R. 570 the Supreme Court of Canada was divided on the application of *Bazley v Currie* to abuse by a youth club leader, most of which took place at his home.

[170] *Dyer v Munday* [1895] 1 Q.B. 742; *Fennelly v Connex South Eastern* [2001] I.R.L.R. 390.

[171] *Warren v Henlys Ltd* [1948] 2 All E.R. 935; *Daniels v Whetstone Entertainments Ltd* [1962] 2 Lloyd's Rep. 1; *Keppel Bus Co Ltd v Sa'ad bin Ahmad* [1974] 1 W.L.R. 1082. See Rose (1977) 40 M.L.R. 420.

[172] [2003] EWCA Civ 787; [2003] 1 W.L.R. 2158.

[173] Cf. *Brown v Robinson* [2004] UKPC 56 (security officer; pursued unruly fan offsite to teach him a lesson and shot him; no apparent evidence of encouragement of aggression by employers; liable; however, the court clearly contemplated that there could still be "private revenge" cases outside the scope of the rule—at [12]).

[174] It was left open whether the decision the other way in *Daniels v Whetstone Entertainments Ltd* [1962] 2 Lloyd's Rep. 1, where the employer had ordered the bouncer to desist, was correct.

[175] [2008] EWCA Civ 689; [2008] I.C.R. 1222.

"ordinary incident of a rugby match", leading to the conclusion that the assault was "very closely" connected with the employment.[176]

21–036   **Police.** Actions are frequently brought against chief constables in respect of acts of police officers amounting to intentional torts such as assault, false imprisonment and malicious prosecution. The statutory formula[177] is that the chief constable is liable for acts done in the performance or purported performance of the officer's functions. The powers of a police officer are conferred on him by law, by virtue of his office and do not originate in any authorisation by his superiors; it would therefore be artificial and misleading to attribute to the chief constable a "business" in the course of which he gives the officer authority to act.[178] In practice the liability of a Chief Constable for wilful acts by police officers is more extensive than the vicarious liability of an employer but it is not without limit.[179] For example, it does not extend to blackmail by an officer using information he has acquired in his work.[180] However, an officer "carries his authority about with him", so to speak, so if he purports to assert it in the course of a private quarrel when he is off duty the Chief Constable may be liable.[181] It would be a different matter if he altogether put aside his role as constable and merely used equipment provided for his police duties in order to commit a tort.[182]

E.   Theft by Servant

21–037   It was at one time the view that if a servant stole goods his employer could not be vicariously liable to their owner on the ground that the act of stealing necessarily took the servant outside the course of his employment.[183] This view was,

---

[176] The court declined to speculate how facts such as those in *Deatons Pty Ltd v Flew* (1949) 79 C.L.R. 370 would now be decided (barmaid throwing glass at customer). See also: *Wallbank v Wallbank Fox Designs Ltd* [2012] EWCA Civ 25; [2012] I.R.L.R. 307 (employer liable for spontaneous assault of one employee by another in response to a lawful instruction: cf. conjoined appeal in *Weddall v Barchester Healthcare Ltd*). Contrast *Mohamud v Wm Morrison Supermarkets Plc* [2014] EWCA Civ 116 (assault on customer by sales assistant not sufficiently closely connected to customer/sales assistant interaction).

[177] See para.21–013.

[178] *Makanjuola v MPC*, *The Times*, August 8, 1989.

[179] *Allen v Chief Constable of Hampshire* [2013] EWCA Civ 967 (facts did not reveal any, let alone a close, connection between the alleged acts and the tortfeasor's position as a police officer).

[180] *Makanjuola v MPC*, *The Times*, August 8, 1989. See also *N v CC Merseyside* [2006] EWHC 3041 (QB); [2006] Po L.R. 160 (off-duty officer raping intoxicated claimant after volunteering to take her to police station).

[181] *Weir v CC Merseyside* [2003] EWCA Civ 111; [2003] I.C.R. 708; *Bernard v Attorney General* [2004] UKPC 47; [2005] I.R.L.R. 398.

[182] *Attorney General v Hartwell* [2004] UKPC 12; [2004] 1 W.L.R. 1273 (but in view of their knowledge of the officer's previous behaviour the defendants were held in breach of their personal duty). When the "employer" provides a police officer with a gun that creates a risk of its misuse, but while the risk created by the employer is a relevant consideration in determining the scope of vicarious liability, it is not a sufficient test of it: *Brown v Robinson* [2004] UKPC 56 at [11].

[183] See, e.g. *Cheshire v Bailey* [1905] 1 K.B. 237; but even the earlier cases recognised that the employer may be primarily liable as, e.g. where the theft can be attributed to his own negligence in

however, really inconsistent with *Lloyd v Grace, Smith & Co.*[184] In *Morris v CW Martin & Sons Ltd*,[185] where some of the older cases were overruled, the claimant had sent her fur coat to X to be cleaned, and X, with her permission, sent it on to the defendants, who were specialist cleaners. The defendants handed the coat to their servant, M, for him to clean it, and M stole the coat. It was held by the Court of Appeal that on these facts the defendants were liable. Although reliance was placed on the duty owed to the claimant by the defendants themselves as bailees of the coat, so that, in effect, the theft of the coat by the servant, to whom they had delegated their own duty of reasonable care in respect of it, constituted a breach of that duty, yet the case has been regarded as illustrative of the general approach of the law to wilful wrongdoing by a servant.[186] That is not to say that in the particular context of theft the bailment was irrelevant: an essential element of the defendants' liability on any ground was that they had been entrusted with the coat and had in turn entrusted it to their servant. Had this not been the case it could not have been said that they had delegated to him their own duty as bailees, nor would the theft have been committed by him in the course of his employment. On the other hand, the principle is not confined to situations where there is a bailment to the defendant and the servant is given physical custody of the goods. There may be liability, for example, where the employer's duty is to take steps to keep property secure and this task is entrusted to the servant. Thus landlords of a block of flats were held liable when a dishonest porter employed by them used his keys to enter the claimant's flat and steal;[187] but the result would have been different if, say, the boilerman had stolen the keys and used them for the same purpose: it is not enough that the employment gives the opportunity to steal, for there is then insufficient connection between the employment and the theft.[188]

F. Fraud of Servant

Fraud within the scope of authority of the servant. Cases of fraud raise special problems because of the special character of fraud itself. Of its very nature, fraud involves the persuasion of the victim, by deception, to part with his property or in some other way to act to his own detriment and to the profit of the person practising the fraud. Thus in *Lloyd v Grace, Smith & Co*,[189] as we have seen, the defendants' clerk fraudulently persuaded the claimant to transfer her property to

21–038

---

employing a dishonest servant or if his own negligence led to the theft: *Williams v The Curzon Syndicate Ltd* (1919) 35 T.L.R. 475; *Adams (Durham) Ltd v Trust Houses Ltd* [1960] 1 Lloyd's Rep. 380.

[184] [1912] A.C. 716; see para.21–032.

[185] [1966] 1 Q.B. 716; *Mendelssohn v Normand Ltd* [1970] 1 Q.B. 177; *Port Swettenham Authority v TW Wu & Co* [1979] A.C. 580.

[186] See *Lister v Hesley Hall Ltd*[2001] UKHL 22; [2002] 1 A.C. 215 at [19] and [76] and *Photo Productions Ltd v Securicor Transport Ltd* [1980] A.C. 827 at 846.

[187] *Nahhas v Pier House Management (Cheyne Walk) Ltd* (1984) 270 E.G. 328.

[188] See *Heasman v Clarity Cleaning Co* [1987] I.C.R. 949 and *Lister v Hesley Hall Ltd* [2001] UKHL 22; [2002] 1 A.C. 215 at [45]; cf. *Brink's Global Services Inc v Igrox Ltd* [2009] EWHC 1817 (Comm).

[189] [1912] A.C. 716, para.21–032.

him, and what is significant for the purposes of vicarious liability is that it was the position in which he had been placed by the defendants that enabled him to do this. His acts were within the scope of the apparent or ostensible authority with which he had been clothed by the defendants and it is for this reason that they were liable.[190]

21-039   **Authority conferred only by the fraud of the servant.** However, there must be some statement or conduct *by the employer* which leads to the claimant's belief that the servant was acting in the authorised course of business. It is not enough that the belief has been brought about solely by reliance on the servant's misrepresentation of the scope of his authority, however reasonable, from the claimant's point of view, it may have been to have acted upon it. In *Armagas Ltd v Mundogas SA*[191] M had authority to sell a vessel belonging to the defendants on terms that it was to be chartered back to them for 12 months. As part of a fraudulent scheme he induced the claimants, the purchasers, to believe that the contract involved a 36-month charter back. Such a transaction was not within the usual class of acts which an employee in his position was entitled to do and, the claimants' belief resting solely on M's statement that he had the defendants' consent for what was being done,[192] it was held that M's employers were not liable for his fraud.

4. EMPLOYERS' INDEMNITY

21-040   **Implied undertaking of indemnity.** Vicarious liability being a form of joint liability, the provisions of the Civil Liability (Contribution) Act 1978[193] may enable the employer to recover from his servant some or all of the damages he has had to pay on account of the servant's tort.[194] Additionally, however, the employer can in some cases recover damages from his servant at common law. In

---

[190] "If the agent commits the fraud purporting to act in the course of business such as he was authorised, *or held out as authorised*, to transact on account of his principal, then the latter may be held liable for it": [1912] A.C. 716 at 725 per Earl Loreburn (emphasis added). See also at 738–739 per Lord Macnaghten and at 740 per Lord Shaw, but this does not mean that "scope of authority" is a universal substitute for "scope of employment" in statement cases: *HSBC Bank Plc v So* [2009] EWCA Civ 296; [2009] 1 C.L.C. 503. See also *Quinn v CC Automotive Group Ltd* [2010] EWCA Civ 1412; [2011] 2 All E.R. (Comm) 584.

[191] [1986] A.C. 717. See also the discussion of ostensible authority in *Freeman and Lockyer (A Firm) v Buckhurst Park Properties (Mangal) Ltd* [1964] 2 Q.B. 480 at 502–505 and in *First Energy (UK) Ltd v Hungarian International Bank Ltd* [1993] 2 Lloyd's Rep. 194 (a case of contract). Ostensible authority in the case of acts by officers of a company has been affected by the fact that the company's memorandum is a public document, but the Companies Act 2006 s.40 provides that, "in favour of a person dealing with a company in good faith, the power of the board of directors to bind the company, or authorise others to do so, is deemed to be free of any limitation under the company's constitution".

[192] Authority was also in issue in *Kooragang Investments Pty Ltd v Richardson & Wrench Ltd* [1982] A.C. 462 (a case of negligence) where the servant was "moonlighting" for X. There was no actual authority to do the acts in question, the employer in no way held out the servant as having authority and, indeed, the claimant was unaware that the servant was in the employ of the defendants. Not liable.

[193] See Ch.22.

[194] For cases in which a full indemnity was awarded to the employer under the previous legislation, the Law Reform (Married Women and Tortfeasors) Act 1935, see *Ryan v Fildes* [1938] 3 All E.R. 517; *Semtex v Gladstone* [1954] 1 W.L.R. 945; *Harvey v O'Dell Ltd* [1958] 2 Q.B. 78.

Lister v Romford Ice and Cold Storage Co,[195] L was a lorry driver employed by R who by his negligent driving in the course of his employment, had caused an injury to his father, another servant of R. R paid the father's damages and then sued L. It was held that L's negligent driving was not only a tort against his father but also a breach of an implied undertaking in his contract of service that he would exercise reasonable care, for which R were entitled to damages equivalent to the amount which they had had to pay to the father. As it has been said:[196]

> "That an employee who is negligent and causes grave damage to his employers should be heard successfully to say that he should not make any contribution to the resulting damage, is a proposition which does not in the least commend itself to me and I do not see why it should be so. I find that justice, as we conceive justice in these courts, says that the person who caused the damage is the person who must in law be called upon to pay damages arising therefrom."

Indemnity limited in practice. However, the justice of the decision in *Lister v Romford* did not commend itself so strongly to others and the matter was considered by an interdepartmental committee[197] with the result that employers' liability insurers entered into a "gentleman's agreement" not to take advantage of the principle unless there was evidence of collusion or wilful misconduct. Indeed, there are strong grounds for arguing that the *Lister* principle is unjustifiable in modern conditions: the employer would probably rarely wish to take advantage of it because of the disastrous effect on labour relations and the real claimant is likely to be an insurer acting under the doctrine of subrogation.[198] If it be objected that to deny the right of indemnity against the servant is to put him above the law, it may be replied that it is sufficient that he is liable to the victim of the tort, though admittedly judgment will rarely be enforced against him.

21–041

Indemnity limited in principle. There is an important limit to the principle of *Lister*'s case. The decision in that case constitutes, in effect, an exception to the common law rule of *Merryweather v Nixan*[199] that there can be no contribution between joint tortfeasors, for that rule was held not to apply in the case of claimants whose liability, "arose solely from the fact that they were answerable for the negligence of the defendant himself".[200] If, therefore, the employer has himself, or through some other servant, been guilty of culpable fault, the principle of *Lister's* case does not apply and the employer can only recover, if at all, under the Act of 1978.[201]

21–042

---

[195] [1957] A.C. 555. See also the judgment of the CA: [1956] 2 Q.B. 180.
[196] *Semtex v Gladstone* [1954] 1 W.L.R. 945 at 953 per Finnemore J cited with approval in *Lister v Hesley Hall Ltd* in the CA [1956] 2 Q.B. 180 at 213 per Romer LJ.
[197] Report published in 1959. See Gardiner (1959) 22 M.L.R. 652.
[198] Despite the "gentlemen's agreement" referred to above, *Lister*'s case was not killed outright: see *Morris v Ford Motor Co Ltd* [1973] Q.B. 792, where the right was sought to be exercised by a third party who was bound to indemnify the employer.
[199] (1799) 8 T.R. 186.
[200] *Lister v Romford Ice and Cold Storage Co* [[1956] 2 Q.B. 180 at 210 per Romer LJ. This aspect of the problem was not considered by the House of Lords.
[201] *Jones v Manchester Corp* [1952] 2 Q.B. 852.

5.   EMPLOYER AND INDEPENDENT CONTRACTOR

A.   General Rule

21–043   **Employer not liable for the torts of his independent contractor.** In principle an employer is not responsible for the torts of his independent contractor. It is no exception to say that he is liable for torts authorised or ratified by him or where the contractor is employed to do an illegal act, for here they are both liable as joint tortfeasors,[202] or for his own negligence, for example in failing to take care to select a competent contractor[203] or procure adequate resources. Cases of strict liability are sometimes treated as exceptions, but it is doubtful if they are so in theory and nor is it an exception that he is liable if he personally interferes with the contractor or his servants and in fact directs the manner in which the work is to be done, for he is then again liable as a joint tortfeasor.[204]

B.   Non-delegable Duty

21–044   In some cases the employer is responsible for damage caused by his contractor's fault even though there is no authorisation or misconduct on the employer's part. The conventional analysis is that in these cases the employer is liable not vicariously but because he was in breach of some duty which he himself owed to the claimant.[205] In such cases the employer is said to be under a "non-delegable" duty. Strictly speaking no duty is delegable,[206] but if my duty is merely to take reasonable care, then, if I have taken care to select a competent contractor to do the work, I have done all that is required of me.[207] If, on the other hand, my duty is "to provide that care is taken"[208] or is to achieve some actual result such as the secure fencing of dangerous parts of machinery, then my duty is not performed unless care is taken or the machinery is fenced. It is no defence that I delegated the task to an independent contractor if he failed to fulfil his duties. This is put with clarity by Lord Blackburn in *Hughes v Percival*:[209]

---

[202] *Ellis v Sheffield Gas Consumers Co* (1853) 2 El. & Bl. 767. The defendants, without authority, employed contractor to dig a trench in the street for gas pipes. Contractor's servants carelessly left heap of stones on the footpath and the claimant fell over them and was injured. The contract was to do an illegal act, a public nuisance, and defendants were liable.

[203] For the scope of this in the context of occupiers' liability see para.10–020.

[204] *M'Laughlin v Pryor* (1842) 4 Man. & G. 48; *Hardaker v Idle DC* [1896] 1 Q.B. 335. In *Brooke v Bool* [1928] 2 K.B. 578 the defendant was held liable on the basis of participation in a joint enterprise. It is respectfully submitted that *Scarbrook v Mason* [1961] 3 All E.R. 767 takes this much too far: and it was doubted in *S. v Walsall MBC* [1985] 1 W.L.R. 1150.

[205] *D&F Estates Ltd v Church Commissioners* [1989] A.C. 177 per Lord Bridge.

[206] *Cassidy v Ministry of Health* [1951] 2 K.B. 343 at 363 per Denning LJ.

[207] See *Phillips v Britannia Hygienic Laundry Co* [1923] 1 K.B. 539; *Stennett v Hancock* [1939] 2 All E.R. 578; *Salsbury v Woodland* [1970] 1 Q.B. 324.

[208] *The Pass of Ballater* [1942] P. 112 at 117 per Langton J. See also *The Lady Gwendolen* [1965] P. 294, where Winn LJ (at 350) described the duty owed by a shipowner to other ships and to persons who might be affected by the navigation of his own ships as a duty, "that all concerned in any capacity with the navigation of those ships should exercise such care as a reasonable person would exercise in that capacity."

[209] (1883) 8 App. Cas. 443 at 446.

"The law cast upon the defendant, when exercising this right, a duty towards the plaintiff. I do not think that duty went so far as to require him absolutely to provide that no damage should come to the plaintiff's wall from the use he thus made of it, but I think that the duty went as far as to require him to see that reasonable skill and care were exercised in those operations which involved a use of the party-wall, exposing it to this risk. If such a duty was cast upon the defendant he could not get rid of responsibility by delegating the performance of it to a third person. He was at liberty to employ such a third person to fulfil the duty which the law cast on himself, and, if they so agreed together, to take an indemnity to himself in case mischief came from that person not fulfilling the duty which the law cast upon the defendant; but the defendant still remained subject to that duty, and liable for the consequences if it was not fulfilled."

For this purpose, care must be taken to avoid the conclusion that because a duty owed by A to B is non-delegable, so also is a duty owed by A to C. A building contractor may well, as a matter of contract, be responsible to the building owner for deficiencies in the completed building, but it does not follow that he is responsible to third parties for damage for which they sue in tort:[210] as far as the first is concerned his duty may be to provide a building according to specifications, but to the second he owes only a duty of care.

C.   Categories of Non-delegable Duties.

Two broad categories? It is a question of law whether the duty in a given case is "non-delegable". The categories of instances do not appear to be closed, but not a great deal by way of principle appears from the cases. Indeed, in *Woodland v Essex CC* it was said by Lord Sumption that English law "does not have a single theory to explain when or why" non-delegable duties exist.[211] In the same case, he suggested that nonetheless the cases could be divided into two broad categories.[212] The first is an anomalous class of cases in which the defendant employs an independent contractor to perform some function which is either inherently hazardous or likely to become so.[213] The second, and more important category, is said to comprise cases where the common law imposes a duty which has three critical characteristics: first, the duty arises because of an antecedent relationship between the defendant and the claimant; second the duty is a positive or affirmative duty to protect a particular class of persons against a particular class of risks (and not simply a duty to refrain from acting in a way that foreseeably causes injury); and third the duty is by virtue of that relationship personal to the defendant.[214] It seems clear that Lord Sumption did not intend to suggest that every instance of a non-delegable duty could be said to fall within one or other broad category,[215] but after a brief consideration of the first we shall consider the extent to which the types of case in which such duties have arisen might be explained by the characteristics identified by Lord Sumption in the second.

21–045

---

[210] *D&F Estates Ltd v Church Commissioners* [1989] A.C. 177.

[211] *Woodland v Essex CC* [2013] UKSC 66; [2014] A.C. 537.

[212] Lords Clarke, Wilson and Toulson agreed with the speech of Lord Sumption. Baroness Hale gave a speech in similar terms with which Lords Clarke, Wilson and Toulson also agreed.

[213] See para.21–046.

[214] [2013] UKSC 66; [2013] 3 W.L.R. 1227 at [7].

[215] He subsequently referred to another "anomalous" category of "highway" cases: see para.21–050.

21-046   **Hazardous functions.** The Court of Appeal in *Honeywill and Stein Ltd v Larkin Bros Ltd*[216] stated a principle whereby there is a class of, "extra hazardous acts, that is, acts which in their very nature, involve in the eyes of the law special danger to others" such as acts causing fire and explosion, where an employer cannot escape liability by delegating their performance to an independent contractor.[217] The claimants, who procured the defendants as independent contractors to take photographs of X's cinema by flashlight, were liable for the defendants' negligence in setting fire to X's cinema. However, while some activities plainly present more hazard than others, it is extremely difficult, if not impossible, to attempt a classification based on inherent risk without at the same time taking account of the necessary precautions, which will minimise that risk. The principle stated in *Honeywill and Stein* has therefore been described by the Court of Appeal as anomalous and unsatisfactory and its application should be kept as narrow was possible.[218]

21-047   **"Assumption of responsibility".** The most obvious instance of an antecedent relationship of the type referred to by Lord Sumption in *Woodland v Essex CC* as part of his second category of cases where a duty may be non-delegable is a contract between the defendant and the claimant: "the contracting party will normally be taken to contract that the work will be done carefully by whomever he may get to do it."[219] Cases in tort which exhibit the characteristics required of this second category are those in which the defendant assumes a liability analogous to that assumed by a person who contracts to do work carefully, i.e. "the defendant can be taken not just to have assumed a positive duty, but to have assumed responsibility for the exercise of due care by anyone to whom he may delegate its performance".[220] Such an assumption of personal responsibility may indeed exist in some cases of tort, but there is no general rule and the assumption must be determined from the circumstances of the case.[221] The examples given by Lord Sumption of the public services provided in hospitals and schools are considered below,[222] but it is clear that the necessary antecedent relationship, or incidents of it, may be imposed by law[223] as in the case of a statute which imposes on the defendant a positive duty to perform some function or carry out

---

[216] [1934] 1 K.B. 191.

[217] [1934] 1 K.B. 191 at 197.

[218] *Biffa Waste Services Ltd v Maschinenfabrik Ernst Hese GMBH* [2008] EWCA Civ 1238; [2009] Q.B. 725. *Honeywill*'s case was said not to be part of Australian law in *Stevens v Brodribb Sawmilling Co Pty Ltd* (1986) 160 C.L.R. 16. See also *Transfield Services (Australia) v Hall* [2008] NSWCA 294 at [90].

[219] *Woodland v Essex CC* [2013] UKSC 66; [2014] A.C. 537 at [7], citing *Photo Production Ltd v Securicor Transport Ltd* [1980] A.C. 827 at 848.

[220] *Woodland v Essex CC* [2013] UKSC 66; [2014] A.C. 537 at [11].

[221] See *Esso Petroleum Co Ltd v Hall Russell & Co Ltd* [1988] 3 W.L.R. 730 at 759 per Lord Jauncey. Cf. *Rogers v Night Riders* [1983] R.T.R. 324 (approved in *Wong v Kwan Kin Travel Services Ltd* [1996] 1 W.L.R. 138) and *Aiken v Stewart Wrightson Members Agency Ltd* [1995] 1 W.L.R. 1281.

[222] See para.21–048.

[223] In this context, as in others, the basis of liability is not that the defendant has *voluntarily* assumed responsibility, but rather that he is treated in law as having done so: *Customs and Excise Commissioners v Barclays Bank Plc* [2006] UKHL 28; [2007] 1 A.C. 181 at [4] per Lord Bingham, para.5–052.

some operation,[224] or in the case of bailment where the bailee has a duty to procure that proper care is exercised in the custody of the goods bailed.[225]

Protection of the "vulnerable": employees, patients and pupils. The particular issue before the Supreme Court in *Woodland v Essex CC* was whether the duty of care owed by a local education authority to a school pupil was non-delegable in circumstances where the pupil suffered injury in a swimming lesson as a result of the alleged negligence of the swimming teacher and lifeguard provided by an independent contractor. Lord Sumption identified a sub-category of cases in which the personal nature of the duty imposed on the defendant is based on the vulnerability of the claimant and an antecedent relationship under which the defendant has a "degree of protective custody" over the claimant. The principal example of this category is employment and it has long been established that the employer's common law duties in respect of his servant's safety, as laid down in *Wilsons and Clyde Coal Co v English*,[226] are "non-delegable".[227] In *Woodland v Essex CC* Lord Sumption held that the time had come to recognise that the relationships between hospitals and their patients,[228] and between schools or local education authorities and their pupils fall into the same category,[229] even in the absence of a contract.[230]

21–048

It does not follow that a hospital or a school will be liable for every injury caused to a patient or a pupil by the negligence of an independent contractor who has been engaged by the hospital or school. It is essential first to identify a duty owed by the hospital or school which is personal to the hospital or school. Thus, while Lord Sumption disagreed with the views expressed in *A v Ministry of Defence*[231] as to the scope of non-delegable duties, he agreed with the decision. The Ministry was not liable for the negligence of a hospital in Germany with whom it contracted to treat soldiers and their families. Such treatment may have been "arranged" by the Ministry but it had not assumed personal responsibility to provide it.[232] Similarly, in *Farraj v King's Healthcare NHS Trust*[233] the Court of

---

[224] "Where a special duty is laid by statute on an individual or class of individuals either to take care or even to ensure safety (an absolute duty in the true sense) . . . they cannot in any way escape from or evade the full implication of and responsibility for that duty: *The Pass of Ballater* [1942] P. 112 at 117, referring to *Smith v Cammell Laird & Co Ltd* [1940] A.C. 242; *Donaghey v Boulton and Paul Ltd* [1968] A.C.1. Everything turns on the construction of the particular statute: *Rivers v Cutting* [1982] 1 W.L.R. 1146; *S. v Walsall MBC* [1985] 1 W.L.R. 1150

[225] *Morris v CW Martin & Sons Ltd* [1966] 1 Q.B. 716, at 725-728. The duty of a mortgagee or receiver to obtain the best price for property sold to meet a debt is also non-delegable so it is no answer for him to say he instructed a competent valuer: *Raja v Austin Gray* [2002] EWCA Civ 1965; 13 E.G. 117.

[226] [1938] A.C. 57.

[227] This is dealt with in Ch.9.

[228] He thus approved of the approach of Lord Greene MR in *Gold v Essex CC* [1942] K.B. 293, of Denning LJ in *Cassidy v Ministry of Health* [1951] 2 K.B. 343, and of Lord Browne-Wilkinson in *X (Minors) v Bedfordshire CC* [1995] 2 A.C.

[229] See the approach of the majority in *New South Wales v Lepore* (2003) 212 C.L.R. 511.

[230] This development has the obvious advantage of removing the anomalous distinction between fee-paying schools and hospitals where the duty of care was non-delegable because provided under a contract and state provided schools and hospitals where, hitherto, it was not, or was not understood to be, non-delegable.

[231] [2004] EWCA Civ 641; [2005] Q.B. 183.

[232] Similarly, in the context of schools, see *Myton v Woods* (1980) 79 L.G.R. 28.

Appeal was said to be correct in dismissing a claim against a hospital which had employed an independent laboratory to analyse a tissue sample for a patient who was not the custody or care of the hospital. By contrast, in *Woodland* swimming lessons were an "integral part of the school's teaching function" and the "alleged negligence occurred in the course of the very functions which the school assumed an obligation to perform and delegated to its contractors".[234] A school or education authority will not be liable for "the defaults of independent contractors providing extra-curricular activities outside school hours, such as school trips in the holidays".[235]

21–049   **Neighbouring landowners.** The rule in *Rylands v Fletcher*,[236] damage by fire,[237] and, in some cases, nuisance,[238] impose a liability for the default of an independent contractor.[239] They are explained by Lord Sumption in *Woodland v Essex CC*[240] on the basis of the antecedent relationship between neighbouring landowners. This category extends to the withdrawal of support from neighbouring land. If A, in the course of work done on his land causes subsidence on B's adjoining land and B's land is entitled to the support of A, A is liable to B, and it is no defence that the work had been entrusted to an independent contractor.[241]

21–050   **Operations affecting the highway other than normal user for the purpose of passage.** In *Tarry v Ashton*[242] the defendant employed an independent contractor to repair a lamp attached to his house and overhanging the footway. As it was not securely fastened the lamp fell on the claimant, a passer-by, and the defendant was held liable, because: "[I]t was the defendant's duty to make the lamp reasonably safe . . . the contractor has failed to do that . . . therefore the defendant has not done his duty and is liable to the plaintiff for the consequences."[243]

In *Gray v Pullen*[244] the defendant owned a house adjoining a highway and had statutory authority to cut a trench across the road to make a drain from his

---

[233] [2009] EWCA Civ 1203; [2010] 1 W.L.R. 2139.

[234] *Woodland v Essex CC* [2013] UKSC 66; [2014] A.C. 537 at [26].

[235] *Woodland v Essex CC* [2013] UKSC 66; [2014] A.C. 537 at [25]; quaere whether such trips, whether in "school hours" or not, fulfil the duty to promote a pupil's "personal development"; cf. *XVW v Gravesend Grammar School for Girls* [2012] EWHC 575; [2012] E.L.R. 417, decided before the decision of the Supreme Court in *Woodland*.

[236] See Ch.16.

[237] *Black v Christchurch Finance Co* [1894] A.C. 48; *Spicer v Smee* [1946] 1 All E.R. 489; *Balfour v Barty-King* [1957 1 Q.B. 496.

[238] *Matania v National Provincial Bank* (1936) 155 L.T. 74 (nuisance by dust and noise the inevitable consequence of extensive building operations).

[239] In *Burnie Port Authority v General Jones* (1994) 179 C.L.R. 520 the High Court declared that the rule in *Rylands v Fletcher* no longer formed part of the law of Australia, but the defendants were held liable for the activities of their contractors. However, the duty imposed seems more an enhanced duty of care than a true non-delegable duty.

[240] [2013] UKSC 66; [2014] A.C. 537 at [9].

[241] *Bower v Peate* (1876) 1 Q.B.D. 321; *Dalton v Angus* (1881) 6 App. Cas. 740; *Hughes v Percival* (1883) 8 App. Cas. 443.

[242] (1876) 1 Q.B.D. 314.

[243] (1876) 1 Q.B.D. 314 at 319 per Blackburn J.

[244] (1864) 5 B. & S. 970. See also: *Hole v Sittingbourne Ry* (1861) 6 H. & N. 488 (bridge obstructing navigation); *Hardaker v Idle DC* [1896] 1 Q.B. 335 (gas main broken by failure to pack soil round it while constructing a sewer); *Penny v Wimbledon UDC* [1899] 2 Q.B. 72 (heap of soil left unlighted in

premises to a sewer. For this purpose he employed a contractor who negligently filled in the trench improperly and the claimant, a passenger on the highway, was injured. The defendant was held liable although he was not negligent. On the other hand, in *Salsbury v Woodland*[245] the defendant had employed an apparently competent contractor to fell a tree in the front garden of his house near the highway. Done competently this would have involved no risk to anyone, but owing to the negligence of the contractor, the tree fouled some telephone wires, causing them to fall into the highway, and an accident resulted in which the claimant was injured. The Court of Appeal held that these facts did not bring the case within the special category comprising cases of work done on the highway[246] and that there was no equivalent category comprising cases in which work is done near the highway. Accordingly the general principle applied and the defendant was not liable for the negligence of the independent contractor. Cases like *Gray v Pullen* rest on the fact that they involve an obstruction of the highway which is inherent in the very nature of the act the contractor is employed to do.[247] These cases were not dealt with by Lord Sumption in *Woodland v Essex CC* but at one point he observed that, like the "hazard cases", the "highway cases" could be "put to one side",[248] suggesting that they are a further category in their own right.

D.   Collateral or Casual Negligence of Independent Contractor

In those areas where the duty owed by an employer is non-delegable, the employer is not liable for the collateral or casual negligence of an independent contractor, that is, negligence in some collateral respect, as distinct from negligence with regard to the very matter delegated to be done.[249] The distinction between the two kinds of negligence is sometimes difficult to draw[250] but is established by the cases. To take a simple case, if D employs a contractor on a construction project D would not be liable for the negligent driving of the

21–051

---

road); *Pickard v Smith* (1861) 10 C.B.(N.S.) 314 (cellar flap on railway platform left open); *Daniel v Rickett, etc.* [1938] 2 K.B. 322 (cellar flap left open on pavement); *Holliday v National Telephone Co* [1899] 2 Q.B. 392 (explosion in highway caused by dipping benzoline lamp in molten solder); *Walsh v Holst Co Ltd* [1958] 1 W.L.R. 800 (building operations adjoining highway).

[245] [1970] 1 Q.B. 324.

[246] Widgery LJ observed that the cases within this category would be found on analysis to be cases where the work done was of a character which would have been a nuisance unless authorised by statute: [1970] 1 Q.B. 324 at 338. Cf. at 348 per Sachs LJ. By statute a highway authority is liable for the negligence of contractors to which it delegates highway maintenance functions, see para.15–082.

[247] *Rowe v Herman* [1997] 1 W.L.R. 1390.

[248] *Woodland v Essex CC* [2013] UKSC 66; [2014] A.C. 537 at [23].

[249] *Pickard v Smith* (1861) 10 C.B.(N.S.) 470 at 480. See also: *Dalton v Angus* (1881) 6 App.Cas. 740 at 829, per Lord Blackburn; *Cassidy v Ministry of Health* [1951] 2 K.B. 343 at 363–364 per Denning LJ.

[250] See the criticism of Sachs LJ in *Salsbury v Woodland* [1970] 1 Q.B. 324 at 348. Keeton, Dobbs, Keeton and Prosser (eds), *Torts*, 5th edn (1984), p.516, suggests that the test of collateral negligence is not its character as a minor incident or operative detail of the work to be done, but rather its dissociation from any inherent risk created by the work itself. See also Jolowicz (1957) 9 Stanford L. Rev. 690 at 707–708.

contractor while going to get supplies.[251] More difficult is a case like *Padbury v Holliday and Greenwood Ltd*[252] where the defendants employed a sub-contractor to put metallic casements into the windows of a house which the defendants were building. While one of these casements was being put in, an iron tool was placed by a servant of the sub-contractor on the window sill, and the casement having been blown in by the wind, the tool fell and injured the claimant in the street below. It was held that the claimant's injuries were caused by an act of collateral negligence and the defendants were not liable. By contrast, in *Holliday v National Telephone Co*[253] the defendants were laying telephone wires under a street and employed an independent contractor to make certain connections. A plumber employed by the contractor dipped a blowlamp into molten solder causing an explosion which injured the claimant. In the court below Willes J, in no uncertain terms, treated this as an act of collateral negligence, but the Court of Appeal reversed his decision and held the defendants were liable. The cases are difficult to distinguish save for the delphic statement in the brief report of *Padbury* that "the tool was not placed on the window sill in the ordinary course of doing the work which the sub-contractor was employed to do". Otherwise, they both involve dangers to users of the highway and incidents in the performance of work rather than any deficiency in the finished work.

---

[251] In *Harrison v Jagged Globe (Alpine) Ltd* [2012] EWCA Civ 835 the defendant tour operator was not liable for the conduct of expedition guides in allowing a climbing stunt to go ahead which was not part of the itinerary.

[252] (1912) 28 T.L.R. 494.

[253] *Holliday v National Telephone Co* [1899] 2 Q.B. 392; cf. *Reedie v L & NW Ry* (1849) 4 Ex. 244 (railway company employed contractor to build a bridge; contractor's workman negligently caused the death of a person, passing beneath along the highway, by allowing a stone to drop on him; Ry company held not liable). "I am not liable if my contractor in making a bridge happens to drop a brick . . . but I am liable if he makes a bridge which will not open . . . The liability of the employer depends on the existence of a duty . . . it only extends to the limit of that duty. I owe a duty with regard to the structure of the bridge; I owe a duty to see that my bridge will open; but I owe no duty with regard to the disposition of bricks and hammers in the course of construction": Chapman, 50 L.Q.R. 71 at 80–81. That accords with the result of *Padbury* but not of *Holliday*.

CHAPTER 22

JOINT AND SEVERAL TORTFEASORS

1. MULTIPLE TORTFEASORS, CAUSATION AND PROOF

Where two or more people by their independent breaches of duty to the claimant   **22–001**
cause him to suffer distinct injuries, no special rules are required, for each
tortfeasor is liable for the damage which he caused and only for that damage.[1]
Where, however, two or more breaches of duty by different persons cause the
claimant to suffer a *single, indivisible* injury the position is more complicated.
The law in such a case is that the claimant is entitled to sue all or any of them for
the full amount of his loss,[2] and each is said to be jointly and severally liable for
it.[3] If the claimant sues defendant A but not B and C, it is open to A to seek
"contribution" from B and C in respect of their relative responsibility but this is a
matter among A, B and C and does not affect the claimant. This means that
special rules are necessary to deal with the possibilities of successive actions in
respect of that loss and of claims for contribution or indemnity by one tortfeasor
against the others.

No proportionate liability for single, indivisible injury. It may be greatly to the   **22–002**
claimant's advantage to show that he has suffered the same, indivisible harm at
the hands of a number of defendants for he thereby avoids the risk, inherent in
cases where there are different injuries, of finding that one defendant is insolvent
(or uninsured) and being unable to execute judgment against him. Even where all
participants are solvent, a system which enabled the claimant to sue each one
only for a proportionate part of the damage would require him to launch multiple
proceedings, some of which might involve complex issues of liability, causation

---

[1] See *Performance Cars Ltd v Abraham* [1962] 1 Q.B. 33; *Baker v Willoughby* [1970] A.C. 467,
para.7–011.

[2] Though he cannot execute judgment so as to recover more than his loss: see para.22–012.

[3] This is the general position in common law and European legal systems. See Rogers (ed.),
Unification of Tort Law: Multiple Tortfeasors (2004). The major exception is the United States, where
the position has been radically altered by statute in many states. See Green in Rogers (ed.),
Unification of Tort Law: Multiple Tortfeasors (2004), p.261. For a broader comparative overview of
divisibility issues see Oliphant (ed.), *Aggregation and Divisibility of Damage* (2009).

and proof. As the law now stands, the claimant may simply launch proceedings against the "easiest target".[4] The same picture is not, of course, so attractive from the point of view of the solvent defendant, who may end up carrying full responsibility for a loss in the causing of which he played only a partial, even secondary role. Thus a solicitor may be liable in full for failing to point out to his client that there is reason to believe that a valuation on which the client proposes to lend is suspect, the valuer being insolvent;[5] and an auditor will be likely to carry sole responsibility for negligent failure to discover fraud during a company audit. A sustained campaign against the rule of joint and several liability has been mounted in this country by certain professional bodies, who have argued instead for a regime of "proportionate liability" whereby, as against the claimant, and not merely among defendants as a group, each defendant would bear only his share of the liability.[6] While it has not been suggested here that such a change should be extended to personal injury claims,[7] this has occurred in some American jurisdictions, whether by statute or by judicial decision.[8] However, an investigation of the issue by the Law Commission on behalf of the Dept of Trade and Industry in 1996[9] led to the conclusion that the present law was preferable to the various forms of proportionate liability.[10]

22–003   **Scope of joint and several liability.** The question of the scope of joint and several liability is a difficult one and there appears to have been some narrowing of the approach in the recent case law, so that although from a medical point of view there is only one injury, there may be a greater willingness to hold that the causative contribution of each defendant can be identified and his liability confined to that. The simplest case of joint and several liability is that of two virtually simultaneous acts of negligence, as where two drivers behave negligently and collide, injuring a passenger in one of the cars or a pedestrian, but there is no requirement that the acts be simultaneous. Thus, if D1 driving too fast in icy conditions causes his lorry to "jack-knife" across the motorway and D2, also driving too fast, later comes along and, trying to avoid the obstruction, runs

---

[4] Consider for example the outcome of the Selby rail accident. A driver fell asleep on the M62, veered off the road and caused a rail crash. The driver brought (unsuccessful) contribution proceedings alleging defective design of the motorway bridge. Under the present system the victims' claim was for a simple case of driving negligence. If they had been required to sue the designers of the bridge their case would have been much more complicated: *GNER v Hart* [2003] EWHC 2450 (QB). See also *Roe v Sheffield City Council* [2004] EWCA Civ 329 at [34].

[5] See *Mortgage Express Ltd v Bowerman* [1996] 2 All E.R. 836.

[6] Which is in effect the position at sea where cargo on ship A is damaged by the concurrent fault of ship A and ship B (but not where cargo on innocent ship A is damaged by the concurrent fault of ships B and C) under the Merchant Shipping Act 1995 s.187.

[7] For an apparent exception, see the discussion of *Barker v Corus (UK) Ltd* [2006] UKHL 20; [2006] 2 A.C. 572, para.7–018.

[8] See DTI Feasibility Investigation (1996) s.6.3 and Green in Rogers (ed.), *Unification of Tort Law: Multiple Tortfeasors* (2004) p.261.

[9] See previous note. There was said to be a case in logic for proportionate liability in the case where C is at fault as well as D1 and D2 (see, e.g. *Fitzgerald v Lane* [1989] A.C. 328) though in practice a change would tend to favour defendants: see the Feasibility Study at s.4.14.

[10] The Limited Liability Partnership Act 2000 (see para.25–034) reduces the risk of personal ruin to those practising in partnerships.

down C, assisting at the scene, both D1 and D2 may be liable for C's injuries.[11] Of course on the facts it may be held that the act of D1 lost its causative effect.[12] The acts of the two defendants may be separated by a substantial period of time and yet contribute to one, indivisible injury for this purpose, as where D1 manufactures a dangerous product and D2 uses it without due care years later. In all these case there is no logical or sensible basis for dividing up the causative origin of the claimant's injury between the defendants. If, for example, he is killed in the accident one cannot say that he was half killed by D1 and half killed by D2—he was killed by the effect of the conduct of both of them.

Liability for "progressive injury". Where an injury is a progressive one it seems a different attitude may be taken. Some of these cases are concerned with the different factual situation where there is only one tortfeasor and the other contributory cause is a natural event or something for which the defendant is not responsible, but the issue is fundamentally the same as that where there are two tortfeasors. In *Holtby v Brigham & Cowan (Hull) Ltd*[13] the claimant had been exposed to asbestos during employment with several employers and each of these exposures probably made some contribution to the asbestosis which he developed, but only one employer was sued. The Court of Appeal rejected the argument that once the claimant had shown that the defendant had made a material contribution to the disease (which was a virtually inevitable inference) the defendant was liable for the whole of the loss and held that the defendant was liable only to the extent that he had contributed to the disability and that on such facts the correct approach was to attribute responsibility on the basis of the proportionate time the claimant had been exposed while in the defendant's employment. Such cases are distinguishable from the motor collision injuring the passenger (at least pragmatically) on three bases: first, the time exposure approach provides a more or less rational (though often probably unscientific) basis for allocating responsibility; secondly, it seems counterintuitive to hold second or subsequent employers liable in respect of the consequences of what happened before they took the claimant on or to hold any of them liable in respect of what happened after he left them;[14] and thirdly, conditions like asbestosis or deafness are likely to get worse with continued exposure. However, the court does not appear to have regarded the principle it was enunciating as confined to

22–004

---

[11] Based on *Rouse v Squires* [1973] Q.B. 889. If, however, C's car had been damaged by a collision with D1's lorry before the arrival of D2 on the scene then D1 alone would be responsible for that loss.

[12] This was the issue in *Rouse v Squires* [1973] Q.B. 889.

[13] [2000] 3 All E.R. 421; *Thompson v Smiths Shiprepairers (North Shields) Ltd* [1984] Q.B. 405; *Allen v BREL Ltd* [2001] EWCA Civ 242; [2001] I.C.R. 942; *Horsley v Cascade Insulation Services Ltd* [2009] EWHC 2945 (QB). In *Brookes v South Yorkshire Passenger Executive* [2005] EWCA Civ 452 the claimant was exposed by the defendant to conditions causative of vibration white finger from 1982 but the defendant was only at fault in relation to this risk from 1987. The CA declined to reduce the damages because although all exposure made some contribution to the final result, the claimant had a low susceptibility and would probably never have developed symptoms had the defendant taken proper steps in 1987. The objective of an award of damages is not to compensate the claimant for the amount of the damage suffered but for the effects of the damage on him: at [26].

[14] Cf. *Luke v Kingsley Smith & Co* [2003] EWHC 1559; [2004] P.N.L.R. 12 (lawyer D1 by dilatoriness makes C's claim vulnerable to striking out; lawyer D2 then negotiates a settlement for a fraction of C's loss; one single, indivisible loss in respect of which there can be contribution between D1 and D2).

"sequence" cases like this. In the leading case of *Bonnington Castings Ltd v Wardlaw*[15] the claimant suffered injury from exposure to silica dust in the defendants' works. One source of dust was swing grinders and the defendants were in breach of duty with regard to those (the "guilty dust") but the other source was the pneumatic hammers and there was no possible method of eliminating dust from those (the "innocent dust"). The defendants were held liable in full for the damage he suffered even though they were only to blame for part of the dust and probably substantially the lesser part of it.[16] In *Holtby* Stuart-Smith LJ noted that it was never argued that the defendants were only liable to the extent of the material contribution.

As we have seen, the court in *Fairchild v Glenhaven Funeral Services Ltd*[17] was faced with a situation where the disease might have been caused by the ingestion of asbestos fibres emitted by any one of a number of employers and held that each was liable on the basis that he had materially increased the risk; but it was not disputed for the purposes of the claim that if there was liability each was liable in full. It was later held that even though such injury was indivisible, justice required that each defendant be liable only for the extent to which he had increased the risk but that approach in turn was reversed and joint and several liability reimposed by statute.[18] However, even in that particular narrow context there was no challenge to the general rule and *Holtby* has not led to the wholesale abandonment of the proposition that each defendant is liable in full for an indivisible injury. It has been said in the Court of Appeal that the *Holtby* principle is:[19]

> "[A]n exception to the general rule intended to do justice in a particular class of case. Although at the fringes the delineation of the class of case may be debateable, in the main it has been applied and in this court at least should be limited to, industrial disease or injury cases where there has been successive exposure to harm by a number of agencies, where the effect of the harm is divisible, and where it would be unjust for an individual defendant to bear the whole of a loss when in commonsense he was not responsible for all of it."

Since the question of whether something made a causative contribution to an injury and to what extent is a question of fact and since it is not necessary that there should be precise mathematical evidence before a result may be apportioned between two causes, the courts may go quite a long way in reducing the claimant's recovery by being more willing to find that an injury is divisible.[20] The burden of proof rests on the claimant to show that the defendant was responsible for the whole or a quantifiable part of his injury, but in practice once it has been

---

15 [1956] A.C. 613.
16 *Bonnington Castings Ltd v Wardlaw* [1956] A.C. 613 at 622.
17 [2002] UKHL 22; [2003] 1 A.C. 32; para.7–015.
18 See para.7–018.
19 *Ellis v Environment Agency* [2008] EWCA Civ 1117; [2009] P.I.Q.R. P5 at [39]. See also *Wright v Stoddard International Plc* [2007] CSOH 138.
20 See the rather remarkable way in which the expert evidence in *Rahman v Arearose Ltd* [2001] Q.B. 351 attributed different aspects of the claimant's psychiatric trauma to different events (criticised by Weir [2001] C.L.J. 237). See also *Hatton v Sutherland* [2002] EWCA Civ 76; [2002] I.C.R. 613 at [41]. Cf. *Rees v Dewhirst Plc* [2002] EWCA Civ 871.

shown that what the defendant did made a material contribution he is at risk of being held liable for the whole unless he produces evidence of the contribution of other factors.[21]

2. DISTINCTION BETWEEN JOINT AND SEVERAL TORTFEASORS

Basis of the distinction. At common law tortfeasors liable in respect of the same damage were divided into "joint" tortfeasors and "several" tortfeasors.[22] This distinction, formerly of importance, has been largely eroded by statute, as we shall see in a moment, but it remains of significance for one purpose and some account of it is necessary. It has been said that: "Persons are . . . joint tortfeasors when their separate shares in the commission of the tort are done in furtherance of a common design."[23] So, in *Brook v Bool*,[24] where two men searching for a gas leak each applied a naked light to a gas pipe in turn and one of them caused an explosion, they were held to be joint tortfeasors;[25] but where two ships collided because of the independent acts of negligence of each of them, and one of them, without further negligence, collided with a third, it was held that they were several tortfeasors, whose acts combined to produce a single harm, because there was no community of design.[26] A seemingly anomalous exception to the requirement of community of design is that where an employer is liable vicariously for his servant's tort, employer and servant are joint tortfeasors. On the other hand, the parent or custodian of a child whose personal negligence enables the child to commit a tort, though he may be liable for the resulting damage, is not a joint tortfeasor with the child. He is personally negligent and his liability is for his own independent tort.[27] Mere facilitation of the commission of a tort by another does not make the defendant a joint tortfeasor and there is no tort of "knowing assistance" nor any direct counterpart of the criminal law concept of aiding and abetting: the defendant must either procure the wrongful act or act in furtherance of a common design[28] or be party to a conspiracy.[29]

22–005

---

[21] *Holtby v Brigham & Cowan (Hull) Ltd* [2000] 3 All E.R. 421.

[22] "Several or concurrent tortfeasors" is the terminology used by Auld LJ in *Jameson v CEGB* [1997] 3 W.L.R. 151 at 156. However, "concurrent tortfeasors" is a convenient phrase to describe both.

[23] *The Koursk* [1924] P. 140 at 151 per Bankes LJ at 159–160 per Sargant LJ. For the liability of company directors, see para.25–033.

[24] [1928] 2 K.B. 578. See too *Arneil v Patterson* [1931] A.C. 560; cf. *Cook v Lewis* [1952] 1 D.L.R. 1.

[25] Hence liable in respect of the damage. Note that the act of only one defendant was the physical cause of the damage. See also *Monsanto Plc v Tilly* [2000] Env L.R. 313 (reconnoitring site and being present at scene explaining matters to press sufficient to make D joint tortfeasor in relation to damage to crops); *Shah v Gale* [2005] EWHC 1087 (QB).

[26] *The Koursk* [1924] P. 140. See also *Sadler v GW Ry* [1896] A.C. 450; *Thompson v LCC* [1899] 1 Q.B. 840.

[27] See *Bebee v Sales* (1916) 32 T.L.R. 413; *Newton v Edgerley* [1959] 1 W.L.R. 1031.

[28] The act of the defendant in furthering the common design need only be more than *de minimis*; there is no requirement that it should have been an "essential part" of the commission of the tort: *Fish & Fish Ltd v Sea Shepherd UK* [2013] EWCA Civ 544; [2013] 1 W.L.R. 3700 at [58]. See also *Football Dataco Ltd v Sportradar GmbH* [2013] EWCA Civ 27; [2013] F.S.R. 30.

[29] *Credit Lyonnais Bank Nederland NV v ECGD* [2001] 1 A.C. 486. See also *CBS Songs Ltd v Amstrad Consumer Electronics Plc* [1988] A.C. 1018 at 1058.

22–006   **Relevance of the distinction.** The two principal consequences at common law of the defendants' being joint tortfeasors were: (1) judgment against one of them, even if it remained unsatisfied, barred any subsequent action, or even the continuance of the same action, against the others; and (2) the release of one operated as the release of all, even if the claimant had not recovered his full loss. In each case the reason given was that the cause of action was single and indivisible.[30] Neither rule ever applied to several tortfeasors liable for the same damage. Now, however, the first rule has been abolished by statute.[31] The second rule still exists, though the fact that even joint tortfeasors may be sued in successive actions has "heavily compromised"[32] the logic of unity of liability upon which it rests. However, if the agreement with the first joint tortfeasor can be interpreted as a covenant not to sue or (which for practical purposes amounts to the same thing) contains a reservation of the claimant's rights against the other, then the other is not discharged.[33]

Where the defendants were not true joint tortfeasors it has always been clear that if the claimant received from one damages representing his whole loss he could not proceed against the others[34] but it is now the case that the same is true wherever the settlement with the first defendant is made in full satisfaction of the claim even if the sum is less than the claimant would have received if the case had been pursued to judgment.[35] The settlement with one tortfeasor, even though other tortfeasors are not party to it, is to be taken as conclusively establishing that the sum which has been agreed represents full value for the claim,[36] despite the fact that the settlement makes no mention of the position of other tortfeasors and the sum recovered from the settlor will in practice be discounted to reflect any weaknesses in the claim. Of course the terms of the settlement may show, expressly or by implication, that it is not in full satisfaction and that the claimant is reserving his rights against other defendants. So, where C dismissed D1, its managing director, for gross misconduct amounting to fraud and he compromised their action by surrendering his shareholding, it was held in proceedings by C

---

[30] *Brinsmead v Harrison* (1872) L.R. 7 C.P. 547; *Duck v Mayeu* [1892] 2 Q.B. 511; *Cutler v McPhail* [1962] 2 Q.B. 292.

[31] Civil Liability (Contribution) Act 1978 s.3, replacing the Law Reform (Married Women and Tortfeasors) Act 1935 s.6(1)(a).

[32] Steyn LJ in *Watts v Aldington, The Times,* December 16, 1993.

[33] See *Watts v Aldington, The Times,* December 16, 1993; *Gardiner v Moore* [1969] 1 Q.B. 55; *Apley Estates Ltd v De Bernales* [1947] Ch. 217.

[34] *Clark v Urquhart* [1930] A.C. 28 at 66; *Tang Man Sit v Capacious Investments Ltd* [1996] A.C. 514 at 522; *Mason v Grogan* [2009] EWCA Civ 283; [2009] CP Rep 34.

[35] *Jameson v CEGB* [2000] 1 A.C. 455. This difficult case was a rather unsuitable vehicle on which to restate the law in this type of case, because the general rule that sums actually received would reduce the liability of other tortfeasors *pro tanto* did not apply. J recovered £80,000 in settlement from his employer, Babcock, shortly before his death from mesothelioma. After his death his widow commenced proceedings under the Fatal Accidents Act 1976 against CEGB. Although the settlement sum from Babcock passed to the widow, it is provided in s.4 of the 1976 Act that benefits accruing to the claimant (the widow) from the estate of the deceased are not to be brought into account in assessing the damages: para.24–030.

[36] *Jameson v CEGB* [2000] 1 A.C. 455 at 474.

against D2, their auditors, for failing to detect D1's wrongdoing,[37] that it was quite unrealistic to say that C was giving up its right to bring further proceedings.[38] Even where the claimant may bring successive proceedings, it is obviously desirable that a claimant should, if he reasonably can, sue in the same proceedings all the tortfeasors who are liable to him for the same damage. It is therefore provided that the claimant may not recover costs in any but the first action in respect of the damage unless the court is of the opinion that there was reasonable ground for bringing the further proceedings.[39]

3. CONTRIBUTION BETWEEN TORTFEASORS

At common law the general rule was that one concurrent tortfeasor, even if he had satisfied the claimant's judgment in full, could not recover indemnity nor contribution towards his liability from any other tortfeasor liable. The rule was laid down with regard to joint tortfeasors in *Merryweather v Nixan*[40] and was later extended to several concurrent tortfeasors.[41] The harshness of this rule was modified to a limited extent and it does not apply where the tort was not clearly illegal in itself, and the person claiming contribution or indemnity acted in the belief that his conduct was lawful;[42] nor does it apply where even though the tort was clearly illegal in itself, one of the parties has been vicariously liable for another's wrong to which he gave neither his authority nor assent and of which he had no knowledge.[43]

22–007

A. Civil Liability (Contribution) Act 1978

The rule in *Merryweather v Nixan* was for most practical purposes reversed by s.6(1)(c) of the Law Reform (Married Women and Tortfeasors) Act 1935.[44] The operation of the 1935 Act was examined by the Law Commission in the wider context of contribution generally (including contribution between contractors) and the product of its deliberations is the Act of 1978.[45] As far as contribution

22–008

---

[37] In which D2 sought contribution or indemnity from D1: one defendant cannot resist contribution proceedings by the other by saying that he has settled with C: Civil Liability (Contribution) Act 1978 s.1(3).

[38] *Cape & Dalgleish v Fitzgerald* [2002] UKHL 16; [2003] 1 C.L.C. 65, applying *Heaton v Axa Equity & Law* [2002] UKHL 15; [2002] 2 A.C. 329.

[39] Civil Liability (Contribution) Act 1978 s.4.

[40] (1799) 8 T.R. 186. The rule was regarded as resting on the maxim *ex turpi causa non oritur actio*: see para.26–062.

[41] *Horwell v LGO Co* (1877) 2 Ex.D. 365 at 379 per Kelly C.B.; *The Koursk* [1924] P. 140 at 158 per Scrutton LJ.

[42] See *Adamson v Jarvis* (1827) 4 Bing. 66 (auctioneer innocently selling X's goods at the behest of the defendant, who represented himself as owner). This exception may hold good even where the joint enterprise proves to be criminal: *Burrows v Rhodes* [1899] 1 Q.B. 816.

[43] *Romford Ice and Cold Storage Co v Lister* [1956] 2 Q.B. 180, affirmed [1957] A.C. 555, para.21–040.

[44] See Cmd. 4637 (1934). Two statutory exceptions to the rule antedated the 1935 Act: Maritime Conventions Act 1911 s.3, and Companies Act 1908 s.84. Contribution in personal injury cases at sea is now governed by the Merchant Shipping Act 1995 s.189, to the same effect as the 1911 Act.

[45] *Report on Contribution* (1977), Law Com. No.79. The Act came into force on January 1, 1979.

between tortfeasors is concerned the Act continues the same basic structure as its predecessor but there are some significant changes of detail.

22–009 **Basic scheme of the Act.** By s.1(1) of the Act, any person liable in respect of any damage suffered by another may recover contribution from any other person liable in respect of the same damage (whether jointly or otherwise) and for this purpose a person is "liable" whatever the legal basis of his liability, "whether tort, breach of contract, breach of trust or otherwise".[46] So if D1 advises C on the purchase of a computer system and as a result C buys a system from D2 which does not perform the required task satisfactorily and D1 settles C's claim, D1 may be able to seek contribution from D2, even though D2's only liability is in contract, whereas D1's sounds in contract and in tort.[47]

22–010 **The "same damage".** In order that D1 and D2 are liable in respect of the "same damage" one must generally[48] be able to say that if either of them makes a payment to C on account of his liability that will go to reduce the liability of the other to C.[49] Hence where D1 overvalued a property on the security of which C lent money to D2 and, D2 having defaulted on the loan, D1 settled C's claim for negligence for £400,000, D1 was unable to claim contribution from D2.[50] In such a case D1's liability to C is reduced by the value of D2's covenant to repay[51] but D2's liability (which is not a liability *for damage* or *in damages* at all) is not reduced by the value of the claim against the valuer. If C did recover in full from D2, no doubt it would hold £400,000 on trust for D1. Further, D1 would be subrogated to the extent of £400,000 to C's claim against D2.[52]

Considerable uncertainty has developed over the question whether, and if so how far, the Act applies where one party is liable in tort and the other liable in

---

[46] Civil Liability (Contribution) Act 1978 s.6(1). "Liability" means a liability which has been or could be established in a court in England and Wales: s.1(6). It includes a judgment, even though given on a false assumption: *BRB (Residuary) Ltd v Connex South Eastern Ltd* [2008] EWHC 1172 (QB); [2008] 1 W.L.R. 2867.

[47] Based on *Brownton Ltd v Edward Moore Inbucon Ltd* [1985] 3 All E.R. 499, a pre-1978 Act case. So also where an architect fails to supervise a builder both he and the builder are liable for the same damage, that is to say the owner being left with a defective building. But an architect whose negligent certification hampers the building owner in a claim against the builder for late completion is not liable for the same damage as the builder (*Royal Brompton Hospital NHS Trust v Watkins Gray International (UK)* [2002] UKHL 14; [2002] 1 W.L.R. 1397); nor is a builder who is exempt from liability under his contract for fire damage but required to restore the works under an insurance policy liable for the same damage as persons who also caused the fire but have no such exemption (*C.R.S. Retail Services Ltd v Taylor Young Partnership* [2002] UKHL 17; [2002] 1 W.L.R. 1419). See also *Bovis Construction Ltd v Commercial Union Assurance Co Plc* [2001] 1 Lloyd's Rep. 416; *Jubilee Motor Policies Syndicate 1231 at Lloyd's v Volvo Truck and Bus (Southern) Ltd* [2010] EWHC 3641 (QB) but cf. *Greene Wood & McClean LLP v Templeton Insurance Ltd* [2009] EWCA Civ 65; [2009] 1 W.L.R. 2013.

[48] In *Royal Brompton Hospital NHS Trust v Watkins Gray International (UK)* [2002] UKHL 14; [2002] 1 W.L.R. 1397 at [28] Lord Steyn pointed out that in the last resort it is the statutory wording which governs and that this "test" might lead to undue complexity in some cases.

[49] *Howkins & Harrison v Tyler* [2001] Lloyd's Rep. P.N. 1.

[50] *Howkins & Harrison v Tyler* [2001] Lloyd's Rep. P.N. 1: doubting Friends' *Provident Life Office v Hillier Parker & Rowden* [1997] Q.B. 85.

[51] *Eagle Star Insurance Co v Gale & Power* (1955) 166 E.G. 37.

[52] That had not been pleaded in *Howkins & Harrison* [2001] Lloyd's Rep. P.N. 1. A claim by one co-surety against another does not fall within the 1978 Act: *Hampton v Minns* [2001] 1 W.L.R. 1.

restitution, for example where D1 defrauds C of money and D2 knowingly receives it and/or disposes of it. Doubt has been expressed whether an obligation of D2 to pay C on a restitutionary basis can be described as an obligation to pay "compensation" within the meaning of the Act[53]; but at the moment there are Court of Appeal decisions accepting the applicability of the Act.[54]

Further, the defendant and the potential contributor must be liable to the same person, otherwise they are not liable for the same damage. So if D1 is liable to C, he cannot obtain contribution from D2 who is liable to some other party altogether, even if C could himself have claimed contribution from D2.[55]

On the other hand "the same damage" must not be confused with "the same damages". Where the vendor of a business is in breach of warranty the measure of damages against him may be different from that against a valuer engaged by the buyer, but that does not preclude the application of the 1978 Act.[56]

Assessment of contribution. The amount of contribution ordered is to be "such **22–011** as may be found by the court to be just and equitable having regard to the extent of that person's responsibility for the damage in question".[57] The principles are similar to those governing the apportionment of damages between claimant and defendant in the other legislation dealing with concurrent fault, the Law Reform (Contributory Negligence) Act 1945,[58] so that the court must look at both causation[59] and culpability.[60] However, it has been held, somewhat surprisingly, that culpability includes fault which is non-causative, for example attempts to cover up responsibility for the damage.[61] Where one defendant is vicariously liable to the claimant for the fault of his employee that is also the relevant fault for the purposes of a contribution claim against another defendant: the first defendant cannot say his claim should be assessed on the basis that he was free from personal blame.[62] As will be seen, in a road accident case a passenger's

---

[53] Lord Steyn in *Royal Brompton Hospital NHS Trust v Watkins Gray International (UK)* [2002] UKHL 14; [2002] 1 W.L.R. 1397 at [33].
[54] See *Charter Plc v City Index Ltd* [2007] EWCA Civ 1382; [2009] Ch. 313.
[55] *Birse Construction v Haiste Ltd* [1996] 1 W.L.R. 675.
[56] *Eastgate Group Ltd v Lindsey Morden Group Inc* [2001] EWCA Civ 1446. That does not, of course, necessarily mean that it is just and equitable that the vendor should recover contribution from the valuer.
[57] Section 2(1). The statutory right to contribution is not in the nature of a claim in tort. It has been said to resemble a quasi-contractual claim by a person who has been constrained to discharge another's liability: *Ronex Properties Ltd v John Laing Construction Ltd* [1983] Q.B. 398, but in another context the right was said to be "founded on tort": *FFSB Ltd v Seward & Kissel LLP* [2007] UKPC 16.
[58] See para.23–036. Where C, D1 and D2 are all to blame both the 1945 and 1978 Acts are applicable. The correct approach is to consider the claimant's fault against the totality of the defendants' conduct. That will give a figure for which the claimant recovers judgment against all defendants and in respect of which they may seek contribution inter se: *Fitzgerald v Lane* [1989] A.C. 328.
[59] Causation of *the damage* is what is in issue. Hence, where a collision is the fault of D1 and D2 but D1 carried C in dangerous conditions which led to the injury, D1 may carry a greater share of the responsibility than D2: *Madden v Quirke* [1989] 1 W.L.R. 702.
[60] *Jones v Wilkins* [2001] P.I.Q.R. Q12.
[61] *Re-source America International Ltd v Platt Site Services Ltd* [2004] EWCA Civ 665; 95 Con L.R. 1; *Brian Warwicker Partnership v HOK International Ltd* [2005] EWCA Civ 962; 103 Con L.R. 112 (see the doubts expressed by Arden LJ); *Furmedge v Chester-le-Street DC* [2011] EWHC 1226 (QB).
[62] *Dubai Aluminium Co Ltd v Salaam* [2002] UKHL 48; [2003] 2 A.C. 366.

failure to wear a seat belt generally leads to a 25 per cent reduction in damages for contributory negligence where the injury would have been prevented by taking that precaution[63] and in *Jones v Wilkins*[64] the Court of Appeal upheld an apportionment of 25 per cent responsibility to a passenger who failed to take adequate steps to restrain her infant child, the claimant,[65] and 75 per cent to the driver of the other car, who was responsible for the collision.

The question is one of proportion, involving an individual exercise of discretion by the trial judge and for that reason appellate courts will be reluctant to interfere with an apportionment as determined by the judge[66] unless there has been some error in his approach.[67] If it considers it appropriate, the court may exempt the defendant from any liability to make contribution[68] or direct that the contribution recoverable shall amount to a complete indemnity.[69] The Act does not cease to be applicable because the act of the defendant seeking contribution amounts to a crime[70] but where a defendant guilty of wilful wrongdoing seeks a contribution from one who has merely been negligent the latter may in some cases have a powerful and perhaps overwhelming case why it would not be just and equitable to order him to make contribution: it is unlikely that a court would accede to the request of a burglar for contribution from the security guard who fell asleep.[71] Nevertheless, there is no rule that a fraudulent defendant is required to bear the whole loss as against a negligent one.[72]

22–012   **Contribution limited to the sum which could have been recovered by the claimant.** The court's powers in any case are subject to the overriding principle

---

[63] See para.23–060.

[64] [2001] P.I.Q.R. P12.

[65] In practice, the effect (though not the theory) may be the same as identifying the child with the parent for the purposes of contributory negligence, since unless the parent is insured she may not be in a position to pay the contribution and would risk bankruptcy if the judgment were enforced in full against the driver.

[66] *Kerry v Carter* [1969] 1 W.L.R. 1372 at 1376. In determining the apportionment the court must have regard only to the parties before it and cannot take into account the possibility that some other person may also have been to blame: *Maxfield v Llewellyn* [1961] 1 W.L.R. 1119. D1 and D2 may be liable to C in respect of the same damage, but D1 may also sue D2 in respect of his own damage (and vice versa). If this happens after the conclusion of C's suit are the parties to the second action bound by the apportionment in C's suit? "Yes", said Popplewell J in *Wall v Radford* [1991] 2 All E.R. 741, reviewing conflicting lines of authority. However, a subsequent suit between D1 and D2 might not now be possible: see para.23-003.

[67] As in *Andrews v Initial Cleaning Services Ltd* [2000] I.C.R. 166 and *Alexander v Freshwater Properties Ltd* [2012] EWCA Civ 1048.

[68] Contrast the Law Reform (Contributory Negligence) Act 1945, where, once a finding has been made that the claimant is guilty of contributory negligence, the court is obliged to reduce the damages. The power to exempt a defendant from contribution is plainly directed at the case where he is nevertheless under a liability to the claimant. Cf. the curious result in *Hawley v Luminar Leisure Ltd* [2006] EWCA Civ 18; [2006] I.R.L.R. 817.

[69] As in *Semtex Ltd v Gladstone* [1954] 1 W.L.R. 945, and *K.D. v CC Hampshire* [2005] EWHC 2550 (QB); [2005] Po L.R. 253, where the first defendant's liability was only vicarious and in *Wong v Kwan Kin Travel Services* [1996] 1 W.L.R. 39 under the HK Ordinance. Cf. *Jones v Manchester Corp* [1952] 2 Q.B. 852.

[70] *K v P* [1993] Ch. 141.

[71] Counsel's example in [1993] Ch. 141.

[72] See *Downs v Chappell* [1997] 1 W.L.R. 426, where, however, some weight is placed upon the fact that it was D1's negligence rather than D2's fraud which was the direct inducement to buy and where D1's conduct was "reckless".

that one defendant cannot, by way of contribution proceedings, be liable for a greater sum than could be recovered from him by the claimant. Since the two defendants have caused indivisible damage they will often be liable for the same amount but this is not necessarily the case. Thus, if C's property worth £1,000 is destroyed as a result of the combined (and equal) negligence of D1 and D2, there being a binding contract between C and D1 whereby the latter's liability is limited to £300, the principle just mentioned means that D2 in contribution proceedings can recover no more than this amount from D1.[73] A negligent D1 may be able to rely on the claimant's contributory negligence and/or on a contractual limitation of liability; a fraudulent D2 may do neither. Let us assume that: (1) the combined conduct of D1 and D2 has produced an indivisible loss of £15 million; (2) the claimant is guilty of one-third contributory negligence; (3) D1 has validly limited his liability to £5 million and has paid that to the claimant; and (4) D2's responsibility is assessed under the Act at 75 per cent. In such a case it has been held that the correct approach is that the starting point is the total loss less the reduction for contributory negligence, i.e. £10 million, even though D2's liability to the claimant is for the full £15 million. As between D1 and D2 the £10 million would be shared in the respective sums of £2.5 million and £7.5 million. Hence since D1 has paid £5 million he is entitled to £2.5 million from D2.[74]

Contractual indemnity or contribution unaffected by the Act. It often happens   **22–013**
that one tortfeasor may be able to recover an indemnity, or damages amounting to an indemnity or contribution, from another person by virtue of a contract between them. Nothing in the 1978 Act affects the enforceability of such an indemnity[75] and it is irrelevant to this contractual claim that the extent of a tortfeasor's liability has been determined as between himself and another tortfeasor in proceedings for contribution. In *Sims v Foster Wheeler Ltd*[76] the claimant's husband was killed when defective staging collapsed, and both his employers and the constructors of the staging were liable in tort. As between these two tortfeasors it was held that the employers were 25 per cent to blame and should bear that proportion of the damages. They were, however, entitled to recover this amount from their sub-contractors by way of damages for breach of an implied warranty that the staging should be properly constructed for safe use as

---

[73] See Civil Liability (Contribution) Act 1978 s.2(3).

[74] *Nationwide Building Society v Dunlop Haywards (DHL) Ltd* [2009] EWHC 254 (Comm); [2010] 1 W.L.R. 258. Of course it may be that the fraudulent D2 is not claim-worthy, as was probably so in the case.

[75] Section 7(3) saves: (1) an express contractual right to contribution; (2) an express or implied contractual right to indemnity; (3) an express contractual provision "regulating or excluding contribution". The Act does not affect any right to recover an indemnity otherwise than by contract. This is an obscure area: see *Lambert v Lewis* [1982] A.C. 225; *The Kapetan Georgis* [1988] 1 Lloyd's Rep. 352.

[76] *Sims v Foster Wheeler Ltd* [1966] 1 W.L.R. 769; *Wright v Tyne Improvement Commissioners* [1968] 1 W.L.R. 336. Cf. *Lambert v Lewis* [1982] A.C. 225, where the person seeking indemnity was held to be the sole cause of his own loss.

scaffolding. On the other hand, the Act does not render enforceable any agreement for indemnity which would not have been enforceable had it not been passed.[77]

B. Limitation and Contribution

22–014   Under the Civil Liability (Contribution) Act 1978 a defendant may seek contribution notwithstanding that he has ceased to be liable to the claimant since the damage occurred,[78] provided he was so liable immediately before the judgment or compromise in the claimant's favour,[79] but his right to seek contribution is subject to a limitation period of two years from the time when it arises.[80] The other party likewise is liable to make contribution notwithstanding that he has ceased to be liable in respect of the damage in question,[81] unless he ceased to be liable by virtue of the expiry of a period of limitation or prescription which extinguished the right on which the claim against him in respect of the damage was based.[82] This proviso will not apply to most periods of limitation in tort since they merely bar the remedy, not the right.[83] Accordingly, suppose C is injured by the combined negligence of D1 and D2 on December 31, 2006. On December 1, 2009, C recovers judgment against D1. C's cause of action against D2 becomes statute-barred on the last day of 2009,[84] but D1 has two years from the judgment against him to seek contribution from D2. However, conversion is an exception to the principle that the expiry of a limitation period only bars the remedy, for by s.3(2) of the Limitation Act 1980, the owner's title to his chattel is extinguished six years after the conversion.[85] Thus, if C's goods are wrongfully converted by D1 and D2 on December 31, 2004, and C recovers judgment against D1 on December 1, 2010, D1 will be unable to claim contribution from D2 unless he brings proceedings before the end of 2010.

C. Settlements

22–015   **Contribution based on hypothetical liability of the defendant seeking contribution.** The vast majority of tort actions are settled (or withdrawn) before the court pronounces judgment. As we have seen, in some cases a settlement with one defendant may preclude the claimant from taking further proceedings against

---

[77] Section 7(3). This appears to refer to cases where the party seeking indemnity knew or may be presumed to have known that he was committing an unlawful act. See further *Treitel on the Law of Contract*, 13th edn (2011), para.11–022.

[78] The judgment against the defendant will, of course, extinguish the claimant's right of action against him by merger.

[79] Section 1(2).

[80] Limitation Act 1980 s.10.

[81] For example, by a settlement with the claimant: *Logan v Uttlesford DC* (1986) 136 N.L.J. 541; *Jameson v C.E.G.B.* [1998] Q.B. 323 (this point not on appeal [2000] 1 A.C. 455).

[82] Section 1(3).

[83] See para.26–096.

[84] It is assumed that there is no question of the period being extended under the Limitation Act 1980: para.26–098.

[85] There is an exception where the conversion amounts to theft: para.26–096.

others because he will be deemed to have received full satisfaction.[86] However, a defendant who has settled must have the opportunity of seeking contribution against any other person he considers liable. Under the law before the 1978 Act a defendant who settled, with or without admission of liability, could seek contribution[87] but this involved a curious reversal of the normal roles of litigation, for in the contribution proceedings he was required to show that he was liable to the claimant. What was more, if he failed to do this he could recover no contribution even though the evidence showed beyond any doubt that the person from whom he sought it was liable to the claimant.

Section 1(4) of the 1978 Act meets this point by providing that a person who has bona fide settled a claim: "[S]hall be entitled to recover contribution . . . without regard to whether or not he himself is or ever was liable in respect of the damage, provided, however, that he would have been liable assuming that the factual basis of the claim[88] against him could be established."

One objection to this is that it produces the possibility of a collusive settlement but this is probably not very great in tort actions where the real defendants will usually be insurers.[89]

Effect of judgments in favour of the defendant from whom contribution is sought. What is the position if the claimant sues one defendant (D2), fails and then successfully sues the other (D1)? Can D1 claim contribution from D2 notwithstanding the determination of C's claim in D2's favour? This would not create any issue estoppel at common law, but by s.1(5) of the 1978 Act a judgment in C's action against D2: "shall be conclusive in the proceedings for contribution as to any issue determined by that judgment in favour of the person from whom the contribution is sought." **22–016**

The effect of this is that if the action against D2 was dismissed on the merits (because C failed to make out the legal basis of his claim) D1 cannot proceed against D2 for contribution, but the position is otherwise if the dismissal was on procedural grounds (for example, for want of prosecution by C)[90] or because of the expiry of the limitation period.[91] In practice there will generally not be successive proceedings, and the issue of contribution will be disposed of in the main action. Either C will sue D1 and D2 or, if he does not and chooses to sue D1 alone, D1 may bring contribution proceedings against D2.[92]

---

[86] See para.22–005.

[87] *Stott v West Yorkshire Road Car Co Ltd* [1971] 2 Q.B. 651.

[88] Which is to be defined by reference to any pleadings: *BRB (Residuary) Ltd v Connex South Eastern Ltd* [2008] EWHC 1172 (QB); [2008] 1 W.L.R. 2867.

[89] The risk of collusion is probably considerably greater in contract actions, which are brought under the statutory contribution scheme by s.1(1) of the Act.

[90] *RA Lister & Co Ltd v EG Thompson (Shipping) Ltd (No.2)* [1987] 3 All E.R. 1032 at 1039.

[91] *Nottingham Health Authority v Nottingham CC* [1988] 1 W.L.R. 903 at 911–912. This is the only way to avoid a conflict between s.1(3) and s.1(5). The wording proposed by the Law Commission was clearer.

[92] CPR Pt 20. If the court finds that one defendant is wholly to blame and exonerates the other, that does not preclude an appeal by the first directed to placing all or part of the blame on the second: *Moy v Pettmann Smith* [2005] UKHL 7; [2005] 1 W.L.R. 581.

CHAPTER 23

REMEDIES

23–001   This chapter addresses the remedies that may be available to the victim of a tort. Remedies fall to be considered once it has been established that a tort has been committed and that no defences apply. The award of damages is the most important remedy in practice, and the first part of this chapter is devoted to the rules in this connection.[1] The second part of the chapter is concerned with the other remedies, namely, injunctive relief and an order for the specific restitution of property.

1.   DAMAGES

A.   Damages Recoverable Once Only

23–002   **Damages are awarded on a once-and-for-all basis.** The general rule is that the damages must be recovered once and for all.[2] A claimant cannot bring a second action upon the same facts simply because his injury proves to be more serious than was thought when judgment was given. The principal difficulties generated by this rule arise in relation to actions for personal injuries because in that context there will often be significant uncertainty regarding the future. Accordingly, the once-and-for-all rule has already been modified in that context.[3]

23–003   **Exception where two distinct rights are violated.** Where one act of the defendant violates two distinct rights of the claimant (such as in a case where the claimant suffers personal injury and property damage) the claimant can bring successive actions in respect of the violation of those rights.[4] However, this principle must be understood in the light of the procedural rule that it may be an abuse of process to return to court to raise issues that could have been put against the same party in earlier proceedings,[5] in which case the second claim will be struck out.[6] Lack of funds to pursue both claims in the initial proceedings is unlikely in itself to mean there is no abuse of process, though it is a relevant factor to consider.[7] Failure to raise both issues in the initial proceedings may result in the claimant having a negligence action against his lawyers, but the mere fact that he has no action in a given case will again not in itself mean that raising the issue in fresh proceedings against the defendant is not an abuse of process.[8]

23–004   **Exception where the injury is continuing.** Suppose that D wrongfully places something on C's land and leaves it there. That is not simply a single act of trespass. It is a continuing trespass that gives rise to a fresh cause of action from

---

[1] Damages for fatal accidents are considered at para.24–015.

[2] Laid down in *Fetter v Beale* (1701) 1 Ld. Raym. 339 at 692; *Fitter v Veal* (1701) 12 Mod. 542.

[3] See para.23–094.

[4] *Brunsden v Humphrey* (1884) 14 Q.B.D. 141.

[5] *Henderson v Henderson* (1843) 3 Hare 100; *Talbot v Berkshire CC* [1994] Q.B. 290; *Bradford and Bingley Building Society v Seddon Hancock* [1999] 1 W.L.R. 1482. Cf. *Sweetman v Shepherd, The Times*, March 29, 2000.

[6] See *Johnson v Gore Wood & Co* [2002] 2 A.C. 1.

[7] *Johnson v Gore Wood & Co* [2002] 2 A.C. 1.

[8] *Wain v F. Sherwood & Sons Transport Ltd* [1999] P.I.Q.R. P159.

day to day (*de die in diem*).[9] Similarly, a continuing nuisance gives rise to a fresh cause of action each time damage occurs as a result of it, and, accordingly, successive actions can be brought.[10] In fact, in a case of continuing nuisance prospective damages cannot be claimed, however probable the occurrence of future damage may be—the claimant must await the event and then bring fresh proceedings.[11] It follows that if the defendant has tortiously caused part of the claimant's land to subside, damages can be awarded only for what has already occurred, and not for the depreciation in the value of the claimant's property attributable to the risk of further subsidence.[12] However, the claimant may recover as damages the cost of remedial work to prevent further injury.[13]

B.   Damages are Awarded as a Lump Sum

Not only must damages be assessed on a once-and-for-all basis, but they must be awarded as a lump sum at the end of the case. Exceptions aside, which are discussed below,[14] no damages are paid in advance of the trial and, following the trial, damages are not paid periodically. Lump sum awards have advantages from both the claimant's and the defendant's (or, more usually, his insurer's) points of view. A lump sum payment gives the claimant closure and may help him to put the case behind him. He is given a degree of choice as to his future financial resources (e.g. he may buy a small business). The defendant's insurers, on the other hand, can shut their books on a claim and incur no further administrative costs. There is no doubt that there is force in these arguments, but there are also powerful objections to the lump sum system. In particular, there is generally no way in which the claimant's use of his damages can be controlled and if he uses his capital improvidently or engages in an unsuccessful business venture the end result may be that he is supported through social security by the community at large. Even where the claimant uses his capital wisely the lump sum system cannot protect him against an adverse investment environment.

23–005

C.   Kinds of Damages

There are six types of damages: (1) contemptuous damages; (2) nominal damages; (3) compensatory damages; (4) exemplary damages; (5) aggravated damages; and (6) gain-based damages. It is possible for more than one of these kinds of damages to be made in a single case. However, certain combinations are not possible, such as nominal and compensatory damages.

23–006

---

[9] *Hudson v Nicholson* (1839) 5 M. & W. 437; *Konskier v B Goodman Ltd* [1928] 1 K.B. 421. Distinguish the case of a single act of trespass, such as the digging of a hole on the claimant's land, where it is only the consequence of the trespass, not the trespass itself, which continues.

[10] *Darley Main Colliery Co v Mitchell* (1886) 11 App. Cas. 127; *Phonographic Performance Ltd v D.T.I.* [2004] EWHC 1795 (Ch); [2004] 1 W.L.R. 2893.

[11] Under certain conditions damages in respect of probable future harm may be awarded in lieu of an injunction under Lord Cairns's Act: see para.23–132. But see *Redland Bricks Ltd v Morris* [1970] A.C. 652.

[12] *West Leigh Colliery Co Ltd v Tunnicliffe and Hampson Ltd* [1908] A.C. 27.

[13] *Delaware Mansions Ltd v Westminster CC* [2001] UKHL 55; [2002] 1 A.C. 321.

[14] See para.23–095.

i. Contemptuous Damages

23–007 Contemptuous damages are a derisory sum of money, formerly one farthing, then one halfpenny and now, presumably, one new penny. They are awarded to indicate that while the claimant's legal rights have technically been infringed, the court has formed a very low opinion of the claimant's claim, or that his conduct was such that he deserved, at any rate morally, what the defendant did to him. Damages of this kind may imperil the claimant's chances of obtaining a costs order in his favour.[15] Although the insignificance of damages is not by itself enough to justify depriving a successful claimant of his costs, it is a material factor for the judge to consider in deciding what costs order to make.

ii. Nominal Damages

23–008 Nominal damages are awarded when the claimant's legal rights have been infringed, his conduct is not such as to attract an award of contemptuous damages, he has suffered no actual damage, but he still has a complete cause of action because the tort is actionable per se, for example, trespass to land. In *Constantine v Imperial Hotels Ltd*,[16] the defendants were guilty of a breach of their duty as common innkeepers when they unjustifiably refused accommodation in one of their hotels to the claimant, the well-known West Indian cricketer. Although the claimant was given accommodation elsewhere, he was awarded nominal damages of five guineas.[17] An award of nominal damages does not, therefore, connote any moral obliquity on the claimant's part, but even so the judge may in his discretion deprive the claimant of his costs or even make him pay the defendant's costs.

iii. Compensatory Damages

23–009 **Generally.** Compensatory damages are damages awarded in respect of the claimant's loss. The greater the claimant's loss the greater the award of compensatory damages will be. In the case of some torts, such as conversion and deceit, specific rules for the assessment of compensatory damages exist, and these have been noticed in their appropriate chapters. For the rest, the exact sum that the claimant is awarded depends upon all the detailed circumstances of the case, but this does not mean that the topic is devoid of principle.[18] On the contrary, at least where so-called pecuniary damage is concerned, some quite firm rules have developed, and even in the case of non-pecuniary damage, such as pain and suffering and what is called "loss of amenity", where precise valuation in money terms is obviously impossible, the courts now to some extent elucidate the bases of their awards.

---

[15] See, e.g. *Dering v Uris* [1964] 2 Q.B. 669.

[16] [1944] K.B. 693.

[17] Since this sum would now be at least £100, the case is perhaps better regarded as an example of "small" or "conventional" damages. The standard sum for nominal damages now seems to be £5 or £10.

[18] See the caustic observations of Lord Sumner in *Admiralty Commissioners v SS Chekiang* [1926] A.C. 637 at 643.

Restitutio in integrum. The basic principle governing the assessment of compensatory damages is that there should be *restitutio in integrum*. In *Livingstone v Rawyards Coal Co*, Lord Blackburn described this rule in the following terms:[19]

23–010

> "[W]here any injury is to be compensated by damages, in settling the sum of money to be given for reparation of damages you should as nearly as possible get at that sum of money which will put the party who has been injured, or who has suffered, in the same position as he would have been in if he had not sustained the wrong for which he is now getting his compensation or reparation."

The principle consequently calls for a comparison of the claimant's pre-tort position with his post-tort position. So, in an action for deceit, the proper starting point for the assessment of damages is to compare the position of the claimant as it was before the fraudulent statement was made to him, with his position as it became as a result of his reliance upon the statement.[20] The difference between the two situations is the measure of the damages.[21] The same approach is used in false imprisonment. In *R. (Lumba) v Secretary of State for the Home Department*,[22] the claimants were falsely imprisoned because a statutory power to detain them had been unlawfully exercised. However, it was inevitable that the claimants would have been detained even if that power had been lawfully exercised. Accordingly, they had suffered no loss and were not entitled to compensatory damages. In a case of personal injury, too, this criterion can and should be applied to the pecuniary elements of the claimant's loss such as his loss of earnings,[23] but it is difficult to see that it can be applied to the non-pecuniary elements such as pain and suffering. *Restitutio in integrum* is not possible there[24] and it may be that even compensation is not a wholly apt expression. What is given has been described as "notional or theoretical compensation to take the place of that which is not possible, namely, actual compensation".[25] There is "no medium of exchange for happiness"[26] and the exercise of converting pain and loss of function and amenity into money is an artificial one.[27]

The distinction between general and special damages. For the purposes of assessing compensatory damages, a distinction used to be drawn between

23–011

---

[19] (1880) 5 App. Cas. 25 at 39. See also *Monarch Steamship Co Ltd v Karlshamns Oljefabriker (A/B)* [1949] A.C. 196 at 221 per Lord Wright; *The Albazero* [1977] A.C. 774 at 841 per Lord Diplock.
[20] *Doyle v Olby (Ironmongers) Ltd* [1969] 2 Q.B. 158. See para.12–018.
[21] Of course one must take care that one brings into the calculation that which the claimant saves as a result of the tort. For example, if D destroys C's goods which are in the hands of X for refurbishment C can recover the cost of substitute goods less what he would have had to pay X for the refurbishment: *Re-Source America International Ltd v Platt Site Services Ltd* [2005] EWCA Civ 97; [2005] 2 Lloyd's Rep. 50.
[22] [2011] UKSC 12; [2012] 1 A.C. 245 esp at [95].
[23] *British Transport Commission v Gourley* [1956] A.C. 185; *Parry v Cleaver* [1970] A.C. 1 at 22 per Lord Morris; *Thompstone v Tameside and Glossop Acute Services NHS Trust* [2008] EWCA Civ 5; [2008] 1 W.L.R. 2207 at [47].
[24] *British Transport Commission v Gourley* [1956] A.C. 185 at 208 per Lord Goddard.
[25] *Rushton v National Coal Board* [1953] 1 Q.B. 495 at 502 per Romer LJ. See also *H. West & Son Ltd v Shephard* [1964] A.C. 326 at 346 per Lord Morris.
[26] *Andrews v Grand & Toy Alberta Ltd* (1978) 83 DLR (3d) 452 at 475 per Dickson J.
[27] *Heil v Rankin* [2001] Q.B. 272 at 293; an "essentially judgemental question": *Thompstone v Tameside and Glossop Acute Services NHS Trust* [2008] EWCA Civ 5; [2008] 1 W.L.R. 2207 at [47].

"general damages" and "special damages". This distinction was stated in several quite different ways and, as a result, its usefulness was severely limited. However, it was commonly put in terms of compensatory damages that can be quantified with precision (special damages) and those that cannot (general damages).[28] So understood, special damages related to pecuniary losses suffered before the trial, while general damages were awarded in respect of all other losses, regardless of whether they were suffered before or after the trial. The distinction used to have pleading implications: special damages had to be specifically pleaded whereas general damages did not.[29] However, the distinction no longer seems to have this consequence given that, under the Civil Procedure Rules, the claimant has to attach to his particulars of claim a schedule of details of all past and future losses which he claims.

While the divide between general damages and special damages no longer seems to have pleading implications, it has become important once again due to changes to tort law's procedural system. In an earlier chapter it was noted that success fees and ATE insurance premiums are no longer recoverable as costs.[30] In order to ensure that these changes do not eat unduly into the damages awards, with effect from April 1, 2013 general damages have been increased by 10 per cent. The Court of Appeal has explained that this reform affects general damages "for (i) pain, suffering and loss of amenity in respect of personal injury, (ii) nuisance, (iii) defamation and (iv) all other torts which cause suffering, inconvenience or distress to individuals".[31]

iv. Exemplary Damages

23–012   **Introduction.** "Exemplary damages are a controversial topic, and have been so for many years."[32] They are not compensatory but are awarded to punish the defendant and to deter him and others from engaging in similar behaviour in the future. It is for this reason that they are sometimes known as "punitive damages".[33] A claim for exemplary damages must be pleaded.[34]

23–013   **Rookes v Barnard.** In the landmark case of *Rookes v Barnard*,[35] the House of Lords, through Lord Devlin, restated the law regarding exemplary damages and severely limited their availability, and this restriction was affirmed by the House in *Cassell & Co Ltd v Broome*.[36] In Lord Devlin's view, exemplary damages are in principle objectionable because they confuse the civil and the criminal

---

[28] See, e.g. *British Transport Commission v Gourley* [1956] A.C. 185 at 206 per Lord Goddard.

[29] *Ratcliffe v Evans* [1892] 2 Q.B. 524 at 528 per Bowen LJ.

[30] See para.1–033.

[31] *Simmons v Castle* [2012] EWCA Civ 1039; [2013] 1 All E.R. 334 at [20].

[32] *Kuddus v CC Leicestershire* [2001] UKHL 29; [2002] 2 A.C. 122 at [50] per Lord Nicholls. For comparative law, see Koziol and Wilcox (eds), *Punitive Damages: Common Law and Civil Law Perspectives* (2009).

[33] "Exemplary" is now more popular than "punitive". But the Law Commission has stated a preference for "punitive": Law Com. No. 247 at [5.39].

[34] CPR 16.4(1)(c).

[35] [1964] A.C. 1129.

[36] [1972] A.C. 1027.

functions of the law[37] and, apart from cases where they are allowed by statute,[38] exemplary damages can now be awarded in only two classes of case: cases involving oppressive, arbitrary or unconstitutional action by servants of the government; and cases in which the defendant sought to profit by his tort. Of course, simply because a case falls within one of these categories does not mean that the claimant has a right to exemplary damages. It is always for the judge to decide whether exemplary damages are appropriate in the circumstances of each case.

Oppressive, arbitrary or unconstitutional action by servants of the government. The first category is where there is oppressive, arbitrary or unconstitutional action by servants of the Government. A well-known example of this, approved by Lord Devlin, is *Huckle v Money*,[39] one of the cases deciding against the legality of the search warrants which were issued against John Wilkes and others during the latter part of the eighteenth century. The claimant was detained under one of these warrants for no more than six hours and the defendant "used him very civilly by treating him with beef-steaks and beer". Yet the court refused to interfere with a verdict for £300 damages, for "To enter a man's house by virtue of a nameless warrant, in order to procure evidence, is worse than the Spanish Inquisition . . . it was a more daring public attack made upon the liberty of the subject".[40]

23–014

This class of case covers abuse of executive power. It does not therefore extend to oppressive action by individuals or corporations, no matter how powerful (though it has been suggested that it might extend to oppressive use of the law by private persons[41]). Neither does it cover acts by public bodies that are not exercising executive functions, e.g. a public body supplying water or a local

---

[37] [1972] A.C. 1027 at 1221.

[38] Lord Devlin cited the Reserve and Auxiliary Forces (Protection of Civil Interests) Act 1951 s.13(2). Lord Kilbrandon in *Cassell & Co Ltd v Broome* [1972] A.C. 1027 at 1133 doubted whether any existing statute contemplated the award of exemplary damages in the proper sense. The Copyright, Designs and Patents Act 1988 s.97, allows the award of "additional" damages. The Inner House in *Redrow Homes Ltd v Betts Brothers Plc* [1997] F.S.R. 828 held that this did not allow exemplary damages. In the House of Lords the only issue was whether such additional damages could be awarded on a claim only for an account of profits (it was held that they could not). The nature of the additional damages was left open, but in Lord Clyde's view they were probably not exemplary: *Redrow Homes Ltd v Betts Brothers Plc* [1999] 1 A.C. 197 at 209.

[39] (1763) 2 Wils. 205.

[40] (1763) 2 Wils. 205 at 207 per Pratt CJ.

[41] *Columbia Picture Industries Inc v Robinson* [1987] Ch. 38; *Moore v Lambeth County Court Registrar (No.2)* [1970] 1 Q.B. 560); cf. *Al-Rawas v Pegasus Energy Ltd* [2008] EWHC 617 (QB); [2009] 1 All E.R. 346.

authority acting in its capacity of employer of staff.[42] However, it does cover the actions of the police[43] even though police officers are not, in strict constitutional law, "servants of the government".[44]

There has been a tendency to treat the three adjectives used by Lord Devlin as synonymous, all carrying the idea of "high-handedness". But the Court of Appeal has pointed out that this is incorrect as there may be unconstitutional action which is neither "oppressive" nor "arbitrary".[45] However, the mere fact that the defendant's conduct was "unconstitutional" is not enough to attract an award of exemplary damages. Something more, such as a gross misuse of power, is needed. However, it is not necessary for the claimant to go so far as to show "malice, fraud, insolence, cruelty or similar specific conduct".[46]

23–015   **Defendant committed a tort with a view to profiting therefrom.** Lord Devlin's second category covers cases where the defendant's conduct has been calculated by him to make a profit for himself (it is not necessary, in order to come within this category, that the defendant actually made a profit). The purpose of awards in this category is to teach the defendant (and others who might be tempted to behave in the same way) that "tort does not pay". The conduct of the defendant may be a crime and since *Rookes v Barnard* there have come into existence extensive mechanisms for enabling the criminal court to make compensation orders and to confiscate the proceeds of crime[47] but these mechanisms do not preclude the making of an award of exemplary damages against the wrongdoer in a proper case,[48] nor does the gradual development of gain-based damages.[49]

The paradigm case in this category is a libel in a newspaper, but in practice it would be a rare case in which the profit attributable to the libel could be shown with anything approaching precision.[50] Furthermore, while the profit made by the defendant is a relevant consideration in arriving at the award,[51] it is not determinative and an award of exemplary damages may be made even if no profit accrues—what counts is the defendant's purpose.[52] It is not, however, sufficient to bring a case within this category that the defendant was engaged in an activity aimed at profit. There must be something more calculated and deliberate, though it is unnecessary that the defendant should have indulged in any precise balancing

---

[42] *A.B. v South West Water Services Ltd* [1993] Q.B. 507. Nor do the acts of a councillor in a local authority committee necessarily fall within this category: *Shendish Manor Ltd v Coleman* [2001] EWCA Civ 913 at [62].

[43] An award may be made against an officer who acts under colour of authority even though in the circumstances he is pursuing his own ends to such an extent that the chief constable is not vicariously liable for him: *Makanjuola v M.P.C.*, *The Times*, August 8, 1989.

[44] *Cassell & Co Ltd v Broome* [1972] A.C. 1027 at 1077–1078, 1130, 1134 per Lord Hailsham LC and Lord Diplock and Lord Kilbrandon.

[45] *Holden v CC Lancashire* [1987] Q.B. 380.

[46] *Muuse v Secretary of State for the Home Department* [2010] EWCA Civ 453 at [71].

[47] Powers of Criminal Courts (Sentencing) Act 2000; Proceeds of Crime Act 2002.

[48] *Borders (UK) Ltd v M.P.C.* [2005] EWCA Civ 197; *AT v Dulghieru* [2009] EWHC 225 (QB).

[49] *Razman v Brookwide Ltd* [2010] EWHC 2453 (Ch); [2011] 2 All E.R. 38 at [69]. Gain-based damages are discussed in para.23–030.

[50] Cf. *Attorney-General v Guardian Newspapers Ltd (No.2)* [1990] 1 A.C. 109.

[51] *John v M.G.N. Ltd* [1997] Q.B. 586 at 619.

[52] They can be awarded even though the defendant fails in his scheme to profit: *Design Progression Ltd v Thurloe Properties Ltd* [2004] EWHC 324 (Ch); [2004] 2 P. & C.R. 594.

of the chances of profit and loss. But if this profit motive is absent exemplary damages may not be awarded (unless the case falls within the other category) no matter how malicious the defendant's conduct.

Rejection of the "cause of action" test. For a time there was a further restriction on the award of exemplary damages. In *AB v South West Water Services Ltd*[53] the Court of Appeal interpreted the modern authorities in such a way that, even if the case fell within one of Lord Devlin's categories, such damages could only be awarded if they had been awarded for the tort in question prior to *Rookes v Barnard*—the "cause of action" test. This meant that such awards were not based on principle but on the accidents of past litigation;[54] however, the restriction was rejected by the House of Lords in *Kuddus v CC Leicestershire Constabulary*.[55]

23–016

Assessment. The sum awarded by way of exemplary damages should be the minimum necessary to punish the defendant, to show that tort does not pay and to deter others.[56] Relevant factors to consider include the gravity of the defendant's wrongful and his financial wealth (a larger awarded may be required where the defendant is wealthy in order to ensure that it makes an impact upon the defendant). In the case of actions against the police for trespass to the person and malicious prosecution the Court of Appeal has said that where:[57]

23–017

> "exemplary damages are appropriate they are unlikely to be less than £5,000. Otherwise the case is probably not one which justifies an award of exemplary damages at all. In this class of action the conduct must be particularly deserving of condemnation for an award of as much as £25,000 to be justified and the figure of £50,000 should be regarded as the absolute maximum, involving directly officers of at least the rank of superintendent."

The court in *John v MGN Ltd* was less prescriptive with regard to libel, and it is clear from the award of £50,000 exemplary damages in that case that libel awards may justifiably be higher, since the conduct of the defendants in that case was not the worst imaginable. But here, too, the tribunal must not cross the threshold of the "necessary minimum". Exemplary damages may, however, exceed any compensatory damages awarded by a large margin. Before making an award the tribunal should ask itself whether the sum which has been set for compensatory (including aggravated) damages is sufficient to punish the defendant.[58]

Vicarious liability. The fact that the exemplary damages will be paid not by the actual wrongdoer but by someone vicariously liable for his actions does not, as the law now stands,[59] prevent an exemplary award from being made and while the means of the defendant are in general relevant to the quantum of exemplary

23–018

---

[53] [1993] Q.B. 507.

[54] *Kuddus v CC Leicestershire Constabulary* [2001] UKHL 29; [2002] 2 A.C. 122 at [22].

[55] [2001] UKHL 29; [2002] 2 A.C. 122.

[56] *Rookes v Barnard* [1964] A.C. 1129 at 1228.

[57] *Thompson v M.P.C.* [1998] Q.B. 498 at 517.

[58] *Cassell & Co Ltd v Broome* [1972] A.C. 1027 at 1089; *John v M.G.N. Ltd* [1997] Q.B. 586 at 619; *Thompson v M.P.C.* [1998] Q.B. 498 at 517.

[59] In *Kuddus v CC Leicestershire Constabulary* [2001] UKHL 29; [2002] 2 A.C. 122 the majority of the House of Lords declined to deal with the issue of vicarious liability for exemplary damages as it was not argued. But see Lord Scott at [123].

damages[60] an award against a newspaper or a chief officer of police is not limited by the means of the journalist or constable directly responsible.[61]

23–019 **Insurance.** Where a policy of liability insurance, on its proper construction, covers an award of exemplary damages, there is no rule of public policy which prevents the insured enforcing the indemnity.[62]

23–020 **Joint tortfeasors.** Where the claimant sues more than one joint defendant in the same action, the sum that may be awarded by way of exemplary damages is the lowest that the conduct of any of the defendants deserves.[63] This rule is inapplicable where an employer and employee are jointly sued.

23–021 **Multiple claimants.** In the case of multiple claimants the court should arrive at a global sum by way of punishment and that should then be divided among the claimants. The reason for this approach is that the focus in awarding exemplary damages is the defendant and the need to punish him rather than the interests of the claimants. While a defendant may deserve more punishment, e.g. for libelling 10 than for libelling one, to fix a figure for the individual and multiply it by the number of claimants is likely to lead to an excessive award.[64]

23–022 **Punishment of the defendant via the criminal law.** Where the defendant has already been prosecuted and convicted in a criminal court for the conduct that forms the basis of the tort suit exemplary damages should ordinarily not be awarded as the defendant will already have been punished.[65] However, the Court of Appeal has upheld an award of exemplary damages where the defendant had been sentenced to imprisonment for acts that were conversion in the civil law, where very substantial loss had been inflicted on the claimant and where there was no possibility of the defendant being punished by both the exemplary damages award and by having sums of money confiscated in criminal proceedings.[66] The fact that the defendant has been fined is a "powerful factor" against the award of exemplary damages, though it may not be conclusive.[67]

23–023 **The future of exemplary damages.** The speeches in the House of Lords in *Cassell & Co Ltd v Broome*[68] disclose considerable differences of opinion about the desirability of awarding exemplary damages and had it not been for the force of history the award might have disappeared in that case or in *Rookes v*

---

[60] See para.23–017.

[61] "It is desirable as a matter of policy that the courts should be able to make punitive awards against those who are vicariously liable for the conduct of their subordinates without being constrained by the financial means of those who committed the wrongful acts in question. Only by this means can awards of an adequate amount be made against those who bear public responsibility for the conduct of the officers concerned": *Rowlands v CC Merseyside Police* [2006] EWCA Civ 1773; [2007] 1 W.L.R. 1065 at [47].

[62] *Lancashire CC v Municipal Mutual Insurance Co Ltd* [1997] Q.B. 897.

[63] *Cassell & Co Ltd v Broome* [1972] A.C. 1027.

[64] *Riches v News Group Newspapers Ltd* [1986] Q.B. 256.

[65] *Archer v Brown* [1985] Q.B. 401.

[66] *Borders (UK) Ltd v M.P.C.* [2005] EWCA Civ 197.

[67] *Devenish Nutrition Ltd v Sanofi-Aventis SA* [2007] EWHC 2394 (Ch); [2009] Ch. 390 (on appeal but not on the issue of exemplary damages [2008] EWCA Civ 1086; [2009] Ch. 390).

[68] [1972] A.C. 1027.

Barnard.[69] These differences still exist, as is evident from *Kuddus v CC Leicstershire Constabulary*,[70] where Lord Nicholls and Lord Hutton expressed the view that such damages might have a valuable role to play in dealing with outrageous behaviour and the defence of civil liberties,[71] whereas Lord Scott regarded them as anomalous.[72] The main arguments against them are that they confuse the purposes of the civil and criminal law, import the possibility of punishment into civil litigation without the safeguards of the criminal process and provide an unmerited windfall for the claimant. On the other hand, one should not too readily assume that the boundaries between the civil and the criminal law are either rigid or immutable or that the criminal law alone is an adequate mechanism to deter wilful wrongdoing, particularly in parts of tort law where the criminal law is moribund or where the wrongdoing is by the state or its agents. As Lord Wilberforce said in *Cassell & Co Ltd v Broome*:[73]

> "[O]ver the range of torts for which punitive damages may be given . . . there is much to be said
> before one can safely assert that the true or basic principle of the law of damages in tort is
> compensation, or, if it is, what that compensation is for, . . . or, if there is compensation,
> whether there is not in all cases, or at least in some, of which defamation may be an example,
> also a delictual element which contemplates some penalty for the defendant."

The acceptability of "compromising the purity of the distinction" between compensation and punishment in this way has since been confirmed in the Privy Council: "Oil and vinegar may not mix in solution but they combine to make an acceptable salad dressing."[74] Exemplary damages certainly enjoy a continuing vitality in some other common law jurisdictions, which, by and large, have rejected the various shackles imposed on them in England and extended them to situations to which they never applied here, most notably, the United States. The Law Commission has recommended that exemplary damages should be retained but the law should be restated so that they were available for any tort or equitable wrong (but not for breach of contract) where the defendant had "deliberately and outrageously disregarded the plaintiff's rights".[75] The government has so far decided not to legislate.

v. *Aggravated Damages*

Generally. There is significant disagreement over the purpose of awarding aggravated damages.[76] According to the dominant view, aggravated damages are awarded to compensate the claimant for mental distress and hurt feelings that he

23–024

---

[69] [1964] A.C. 1129.

[70] [2001] UKHL 29; [2001] 2 W.L.R. 1789.

[71] [2001] UKHL 29; [2001] 2 W.L.R. 1789 at [63] and [75] respectively.

[72] [2001] UKHL 29; [2001] 2 W.L.R. 1789 at [95].

[73] [1972] A.C. at 1027 at 1114.

[74] *The Gleaner Co Ltd v Abrahams* [2003] UKPC 55; [2004] 1 A.C. 628 at [54].

[75] Law Commission, *Aggravated, Exemplary and Restitutionary Damages*, Law Com. No. 247 (1997) at [1.57].

[76] See Murphy [2010] C.L.J 353.

suffered as a result of the way in which the defendant committed a tort.[77] They may be warranted if the defendant acted maliciously or wilfully or in a high-handed and insulting manner. Thus compensatory damages might be awarded for a serious libel published innocently with belief in its truth, a larger award of aggravated damages where the defendant published out of malice or persisted at the trial with an insupportable plea of justification[78] and a larger one still where the defendant sought to make a profit from the publication and so brought himself within the net of exemplary damages. An alternative way of understanding aggravated damages is to see them as serving a punitive function. On this view, they are a type of exemplary damages rather than a species of compensatory damages. The present law of basic compensatory, aggravated and exemplary damages was described in *Gerald v M.P.C.* as a "muddled jurisprudential amalgam of categories".[79] Arguably, however, the "muddle" arises from the fact that aggravated damages (or even basic compensatory ones) may be regarded as having the *effect* of punishing the defendant in some cases and that, as far as the purpose of aggravated damages is concerned, there is no muddle.

23–025   **Pleading.** Aggravated damages should be pleaded to avoid uncertainty as to the relief being sought, and in fairness to the defendant so that he has notice of the claim that he needs to meet.[80]

23–026   **Torts in respect of which aggravated damages may be awarded.** Awards of aggravated damages have been made in cases of trespass to the person,[81] trespass to land,[82] deceit,[83] malicious prosecution,[84] misfeasance in a public office,[85] misuse of private information,[86] and the statutory torts of discrimination.[87] Aggravated damages are probably not, however, available for negligence[88] even where the conduct of the defendant is "crass".[89]

---

[77] *Khodaparast v Shad* [2000] 1 W.L.R. 618 at 632; *Rookes v Barnard* [1964] A.C. 1129 at 1221 per Lord Devlin; *Cassell & Co Ltd v Broome* [1972] A.C. 1027 at 1124 per Lord Diplock.

[78] Usually, the claimant cannot recover damages for the indignation which he feels at the defendant's behaviour committed after the tort. The fact that the defendant's conduct in the trial in defamation proceedings is relevant is an exception to this rule.

[79] *The Times*, June 26, 1998.

[80] *Muuse v Secretary of State for the Home Department* [2010] EWCA Civ 453 at [18].

[81] *W v Meah* [1986] 1 All E.R. 935 (rape); *Appleton v Garrett* [1996] P.I.Q.R. P1 (non-consensual dental treatment).

[82] *Jolliffe v Willmett & Co* [1971] 1 All E.R. 478. See also *Columbia Picture Industries Inc v Robinson* [1987] Ch. 38 (aggravated damages available where defendant executed a search order in an excessive and oppressive manner).

[83] *Archer v Brown* [1985] Q.B. 401.

[84] *Thompson v Metropolitan Police Commissioner* [1998] Q.B. 498.

[85] *Muuse v Secretary of State for the Home Department* [2010] EWCA Civ 453.

[86] *Campbell v M.G.N. Ltd* [2004] UKHL 22; [2004] 2 A.C. 457.

[87] *Prison Service v Johnson* [1997] I.C.R. 275.

[88] In *Ashley v CC Sussex Police* [2008] UKHL 25; [2008] 1 A.C. 962 (discussed in para.1–002) the defendant conceded the availability of aggravated damages in the negligence claim against him because he was seeking to avoid trial of the battery claim: at [23]. Lord Neuberger at [101] was troubled by the idea that the parties could by agreement confer on the court power to award damages not available at law but thought it was arguable that aggravated damages might be available in some cases of negligence.

[89] *Kralj v McGrath* [1986] 1 All E.R. 54.

The need for subjective feelings on the part of the claimant that have been injured. According to the dominant understanding that aggravated damages are awarded to compensate the claimant for injury to his feelings, if the claimant's feelings have not been hurt the court should not grant aggravated damages. This logic also dictates that aggravated damages are not available where the claimant is a corporation—such corporations have no feelings that can be hurt.[90]   **23–027**

Quantum of aggravated damages. There can be no mathematical relationship between aggravated and basic compensatory damages, but ordinarily the former should not be as much as twice the latter.[91] The Court of Appeal in 1998 in *Thompson v Metropolitan Police Commissioner*[92] comprehensively restated the law on damages in actions against the police for torts like false imprisonment and malicious prosecution. In a case of false imprisonment the starting point for what the court called "basic damages" should be (in the money of 1998) about £500 for the first hour of detention, £3,000 for the first day and at a declining rate thereafter.[93] Where there are aggravating factors such as humiliation or insult the starting point for aggravated damages would be about £1,000.   **23–028**

Subsuming aggravated damages into general damages. In *Richardson v Howie*[94] the court said that in cases of assault and similar torts it should no longer be the practice to make an award of aggravated damages but to subsume the compensation for the claimant's injured feelings into the award of general damages, save in a "wholly exceptional case". In one sense this is an advance in that it recognises that "aggravated damages" *are* "injury to feelings damages": the defendant's conduct aggravates the (at large) damages beyond what they might otherwise be, rather than leads to a separate head of aggravated damages. However, the court contemplated that there may still be exceptional cases where there could be a separate award but there is no indication of what those might be. At any rate, the judges continue making separate awards under this head in the sense of identifying a separate sum.[95]   **23–029**

vi.   Gain-based Damages[96]

Generally. Gain-based damages are damages that are awarded in order to deprive the defendant of gains that he made as a result of his tort. They are known by a staggering diversity of often unilluminating and potentially confusing labels, such as "restitutionary damages".[97] They are distinct from compensatory damages since compensatory damages are concerned with the loss suffered by the claimant. The measure of damages is fundamentally different. Gain-based   **23–030**

---

[90] *Eaton Mansions (Westminster) Ltd v Stinger Compania De Inversion SA* [2013] EWCA Civ 1308 at [28].

[91] Cf. *Shah v Gale* [2005] EWHC 1087 (QB).

[92] [1998] Q.B. 498. See also *Manley v MPC* [2006] EWCA Civ 879.

[93] The starting point for malicious prosecution is about £2,000.

[94] [2004] EWCA Civ 1127; [2005] P.I.Q.R. Q3.

[95] See e.g. *Rowlands v CC Merseyside Police* [2006] EWCA Civ 1773; [2007] 1 W.L.R. 1065.

[96] Edelman, *Gain-Based Damages* (2002).

[97] Lord Nicholls in *Attorney General v Blake* [2001] 1 A.C. 268 at 284 said the phrase "restitutionary damages" is an "unhappy expression".

damages are often thought to bear some connection with exemplary damages given that exemplary damages may be awarded where the defendant sought to make a profit by committing a tort.[98] However, the overlap is apparent rather than real since the defendant need not make a profit in order to be liable for exemplary damages; a mere intention to make a profit may suffice. In contrast, unless a gain is actually made, gain-based damages are unavailable. What follows here is a very brief outline of the law regarding gain-based damages. The details must be sought in specialist works.

23–031   **Torts for which gain-based damages are available.** It is unclear for which torts gain-based damages are available. The traditional view is that they are confined to so-called "property torts", such as conversion, trespass to goods, and trespass to land.[99] Thus, a claim for gain-based damages on the basis that the defendants had operated a cartel in breach of art.81 of the EC Treaty (a breach of statutory duty in English law) failed in *Devenish Nutrition Ltd v Sanofi-Aventis SA*.[100] Other non-proprietary torts include trespass to the person, defamation, and deceit. The traditional view has come under sustained criticism,[101] and the courts might be thought to be leaning towards the position that the availability of a gain-based award should not depend on the cause of action that the claimant happens to bring.[102]

23–032   **Election.** The claimant cannot obtain both compensatory damages and gain-based damages in respect of a single wrong. The law requires him to choose between these remedies.[103] Thus, if D converts C's property and sells it, C can choose whether to recover compensatory damages or gain-based damages. The former would be calibrated to the loss suffered by the claimant as a result of D's tort. The latter would be based on the price obtained by D. When D elects to take gain-based damages he is sometimes said to "waive" the tort. That language should be avoided. The claimant does not waive his right to sue for the tort if he seeks gain-based remedy. He is free until the moment of enforcing judgment to decide the remedy that he wants to obtain.

23–033   **Licence-fee damages.** There are two general types of gain-based damages. The first is what may be called "licence-fee damages". These damages reflect a reasonable sum in respect of the benefit that the defendant obtained in being able to use the claimant's property. It is well established that where the defendant tortiously uses the claimant's property (e.g. by trespassing and dumping material on it[104] or by taking or detaining it[105]) the court will assess the damages by

---

[98] See para.23–015.
[99] *Stoke-on-Trent CC v W & J Wass Ltd* [1988] 1 W.L.R. 1406; *Devenish Nutrition Ltd v Sanofi-Aventis SA (France)* [2009] Ch. 390.
[100] [2008] EWCA Civ 1086; [2009] Ch. 390.
[101] See, e.g. Swadling in Degeling, Edelman and Goudkamp (eds), *Torts in Commercial Law* (2011).
[102] Consider *Devenish Nutrition v Sanofi-Aventis SA* [2008] EWCA Civ 1086; [2009] Ch. 390 at [4].
[103] *Attorney General v Blake* [2001] 1 A.C. 268 at 280.
[104] *Whitwham v Westminster Brymbo Coal and Coke Co* [1896] 2 Ch. 538; *Martin v Porter* (1839) 5 M & W 351; *Jegon v Vivian* (1871) L.R. 6 Ch. App. 742; *Penarth Dock Engineering Co Ltd v Pounds* [1963] 1 Lloyd's Rep. 359.
[105] *Watson, Laidlaw & Co Ltd v Pott, Cassels and Williamson* (1914) 31 R.P.C. 104 at 119; *Strand Electric and Engineering Co Ltd v Brisford Entertainments Ltd* [1952] 2 Q.B. 246.

reference to a fair rental or access payment for the use.[106] A claimant is entitled to such damages even though he has not suffered a loss[107] because, for instance, the claimant would not have made use of the property concerned even if the defendant had not tortiously interfered with it. The line between licence-fee damages and compensatory damages that are assessed by way of a "conventional" sum is not easy to draw in some cases.[108]

Disgorgement damages. The other type of gain-based damages is what may be called "disgorgement damages". Such damages provide the claimant with an account of the profits that the defendant made as a result of his tort. Disgorgement damages are different from licence-fee damages in that they can result in the defendant having to surrender the entire profit made, as opposed to merely a reasonable fee for the tortious use that he made of the claimant's property. A classic example of a situation where disgorgement damages would be available is where the defendant coverts the claimant's property by selling it for a price above its market value. The claimant would be entitled to disgorgement damages that reflect the full price received by the defendant. As Lord Nicholls remarked in *Kuwait Airways Corpn v Iraqi Airways Co (Nos 4 and 5)*:[109]   **23–034**

> "Vindication of a plaintiff's proprietary interests requires that, in general, all those who convert his goods should be accountable for *benefits* they receive. They must make restitution to the extent they are unjustly enriched. The goods are his, and he is entitled to reclaim them and any benefits others have derived from them."

vii. Vindicatory Damages?

The types of damages discussed so far may not in fact complete the tally of strands in the law of tort damages. A substantial award for libel may be spoken of as necessary to "vindicate" the claimant's right to his good reputation; a substantial award for false imprisonment may be said to "vindicate" his right to liberty. This rather imprecise word has various shades of meaning: in the libel example it means to "clear" the claimant; in the false imprisonment example the sense is decisively to uphold or defend his rights. However, there is no such thing   **23–035**

---

[106] Such damages are "readily awarded": *Pell Frischmann Engineering Ltd v Bow Valley Iran Ltd* [2009] UKPC 45 at [48].

[107] *Attorney General v Blake* [2001] 1 A.C. 268 at 279 per Lord Nicholls.

[108] Compare in *Attorney General v Blake* [2001] 1 A.C. 268 the view of Lord Nicholls at 279 and Lord Hobhouse at 299 on the example put by Lord Halsbury LC in *The Mediana* [1900] A.C. 113 involving the wrongful detention of a chair when the claimant still has enough chairs for all his needs. For Lord Nicholls the award of damages based on interest on the capital value is depriving the defendant of his gain. Conversely, for Lord Hobhouse it is simply a conventional mode of assessment of truly compensatory damages. In the "fair rental" case, although the defendant's profits are relevant to the quantification of this, the claim is not one for a share in the profits: *Severn Trent Water Ltd v Barnes* [2004] EWCA Civ 570; [2004] E.G.L.R. 95 at [41]; *Forsyth-Grant v Allen* [2008] EWCA Civ 505 at [25]. In *Experience Hendrix LLC v PPX Enterprises Inc* [2003] EWCA Civ 323; [2003] All E.R. Comm. 830 Mance LJ remarked at [26]: "Whether the adoption of a standard measure of damages represents a departure from a compensatory approach depends upon what one understands by compensation and whether the term is only apt in circumstances where an injured party's financial position, viewed subjectively, is being precisely restored."

[109] [2002] UKHL 19; [2002] 2 A.C. 883 at [79] (emphasis in original).

as an award of "vindicatory damages" in private law.[110] Common law jurisdictions with written constitutions sometimes award vindicatory damages for violation of constitutional rights because the violation may add an extra dimension to the claim.[111] Although not the exact equivalent of exemplary damages, such "constitutional" damages share the common element of deterrence and it is therefore not appropriate to combine them with an exemplary award.[112] The closest analogy here is the jurisdiction to award damages against a public authority under the Human Rights Act 1998. However, the guiding principles here are those enunciated by the European Court of Human Rights, and the awards made by that court are generally modest by English tort standards. That court quite often regards the vindication as being sufficiently provided by the declaration of violation. A bad instance of oppressive behaviour by the police might quite easily produce a tort award of £50,000 or more but would not, it seems, produce a further award under the Act.

D. Contributory Negligence[113]

23–036 **Introduction.** The doctrine of contributory negligence is of great practical significance. It is pleaded almost by default in tort actions. According to conventional wisdom, it applies where the claimant fails to take reasonable care of his own safety and that failure is causally implicated in his damage. When the doctrine is triggered, the claimant's action is not defeated, but his damages will be reduced according to what the court thinks is "just and equitable".

23–037 **Contributory negligence is part of the law of remedies.** The doctrine of contributory negligence is usually regarded as a defence. The difficulty with that understanding, however, is that the doctrine does not, when it applies, prevent liability from arising. Rather, it merely affects the remedy to which the claimant is entitled. It is for this reason that contributory negligence is treated here in the chapter on remedies.

i. The Test for Contributory Negligence

23–038 **The two-stage test.** Traditional learning holds that the doctrine of contributory negligence will be enlivened if the following two matters are established: (1) a failure by the claimant to take reasonable care for his own safety; and (2) the claimant's failure to take reasonable care for his own safety contributed to the

---

[110] *Regina (Lumba) v Secretary of State for the Home Department* [2011] UKSC 12; [2012] 1 A.C. 245 at [100]–[101].

[111] See, e.g. *Attorney General of Trinidad and Tobago v Ramanoop* [2005] UKPC 15; [2006] 1 A.C. 328; *Inniss v Attorney General of Saint Christopher and Nevis* [2008] UKPC 42.

[112] *Takitoka v Attorney-General of the Bahamas* [2009] UKPC 12; *Webster v Attorney-General of Trinidad and Tobago* [2011] UKPC 22.

[113] The definitive treatment is Williams, *Joint Torts and Contributory Negligence* (1951).

damage. This two-stage test is well-established,[114] although it is arguable that judges do not faithfully apply it in all cases and sometimes exclude the doctrine for reasons of public policy.[115]

Burden of proof. The burden of pleading and proving that the doctrine of contributory negligence applies rests with the defendant.[116]   **23–039**

a.   Failure by the Claimant to take Reasonable Care of His own Safety

The enquiry is objective. The claimant will have acted unreasonably if he took   **23–040**
less care of his own safety as the reasonable person in his position would have taken in the circumstances. The test, in other words, is objective and, rightly or wrongly, is governed by the same rules that control the enquiry into whether the defendant is guilty of negligence.[117] Thus, as with the breach element of the action in negligence, where the claimant is a child, he is judged against the standard of the reasonable child of the same age.[118] Because the test is objective, an inability to achieve the standard of the reasonable person will not insulate the claimant from the doctrine of contributory negligence. It is no answer for him to say that he did his best to take proper care of himself if the reasonable person would have taken greater care of his own safety in the circumstances.

The claimant must risk his own safety. The fact that the claimant risked the   **23–041**
defendant's safety or that of a third party is insufficient to engage the doctrine of contributory negligence. As Lord Denning MR explained in *Froom v Butcher* "Contributory negligence is a man's carelessness in looking after *his own* safety.[119] The claimant's fault must, in other words, be self-regarding.

The amount of care that the reasonable person would take varies with the   **23–042**
circumstances of each case. The lack of care that will constitute contributory negligence varies with the circumstances of each case. Thus, the greater the risk of suffering damage the more likely it will be, all other things being equal, that the reasonable person in the claimant's position would have taken precautions in respect of that risk. The reasonable person will often take into account the possibility that others around him will be careless[120] and so the claimant who does not anticipate that the defendant might be negligent may be guilty of contributory negligence. However, the law does not require the claimant to proceed like a timorous fugitive constantly looking over his shoulder for threats from others.[121]

---

[114] See, e.g. *Nance v British Columbia Electric Railway Co Ltd* [1951] A.C. 601 at 611.
[115] See Goudkamp in Pitel, Neyers and Chamberlain (eds), *Tort Law: Challenging Orthodoxy* (2013).
[116] *Heranger (Owners) v SS Diamond* [1939] A.C. 94 at 104 per Lord Wright.
[117] See Ch.6.
[118] See para.6–013.
[119] [1976] Q.B. 286 at 291 (emphasis in original).
[120] *Jones v Livox Quarries Ltd* [1952] 2 Q.B. 608 at 615 per Denning LJ.
[121] A worker is not normally put on inquiry as to whether his employer has fulfilled his duties under statutes and regulations governing industrial safety: *Westwood v Post Office* [1974] A.C. 1. So also a person is prima facie entitled to take the advice of his professional adviser at its face value: *Henderson v Merrett Syndicates (No.2)* [1996] 1 P.N.L.R. 32.

23–043 **The standard of reasonable care is sensitive to changing times and practices.** As with the standard of care to which defendants are held for the purpose of the tort of negligence, the standard of care demanded of claimants may change over time. For example, in *Froom v Butcher*[122] the Court of Appeal held that non-use of a car seat belt generally constituted contributory negligence some seven years before Parliament made the wearing of seat belts compulsory. Now that there is legislation requiring belts to be worn the correctness of this decision becomes even more obvious. For many years there has been increasing public awareness of the dangers of smoking and it has been held that a claimant who failed to give up smoking after being exposed to asbestos failed to take reasonable care of his own safety.[123] However, although public attitudes towards drinking and driving have become more severe in recent years, a person who accepts a lift from a person whom he has not seen consuming large quantities of alcohol is not obliged to interrogate him on his consumption.[124]

23–044 **Children.** While it is not possible to specify an age below which, as a matter of law, a child cannot be guilty of contributory negligence,[125] the age of the child is a circumstance that must be considered in deciding whether he has been guilty of contributory negligence. In *Yachuk v Oliver Blais Co Ltd*,[126] a boy aged nine years bought some gasoline from the defendant, falsely stating that his mother wanted it for her car. In fact, he used it to play with, and, in doing so, was badly burnt by it. It was held by the Privy Council that the defendant was negligent in supplying gasoline to so young a boy and that the boy had not been guilty of contributory negligence for he neither knew nor could be expected to know the properties of gasoline. Although Lord Denning MR said that a child should not be found guilty of contributory negligence "unless he or she is blameworthy",[127] it is not thought that the characteristics of the particular child other than his age are to be considered. The question is whether an "ordinary" child of the claimant's age—not a "paragon of prudence" nor a "scatterbrained" child—would have taken any more care than did the claimant.[128]

23–045 **Claimant confronted with emergency.** Where the defendant's negligence has put the claimant in a dilemma, the claimant will not be guilty of contributory negligence if the claimant, in the agony of the moment, tries to save himself by choosing a course of conduct which proves to be the wrong one, provided the claimant acted in a reasonable apprehension of danger and the method by which he tried to avoid it was a reasonable one. A famous illustration of the principle is

---

[122] [1976] Q.B. 286.
[123] *Badger v MoD* [2005] EWHC 2941 (QB).
[124] *Booth v White* [2003] EWCA Civ 1708.
[125] Cf. *Gough v Thorne* [1966] 1 W.L.R. 1387 at 1390 per Lord Denning MR. "The descending line measuring reasonable expectation of care rapidly approaches zero as the age diminishes, but the line is apparently asymptotic": *Beasley v Marshall* (1977) 17 S.A.S.R. 456 at 459 per Bright J. In South Australia a finding of contributory negligence was made against a child as young as six years old: *Bye v Bates* (1989) 51 S.A.S.R. 67.
[126] [1949] A.C. 386.
[127] *Gough v Thorne* [1966] 1 W.L.R. 1387 at 1390.
[128] *Gough v Thorne* [1966] 1 W.L.R. 1387 at 1391 per Salmon LJ.

Jones v Boyce,[129] where the claimant was a passenger on the top of the defendant's coach and, owing to the breaking of a defective coupling rein, the coach was in imminent peril of being overturned. The claimant, seeing this, jumped from it and broke his leg. In fact the coach was not upset. Lord Ellenborough CJ directed the jury that if the claimant acted as a reasonable and prudent man would have done, he was not guilty of contributory negligence, although he had selected the more perilous of the two alternatives with which he was confronted by the defendant's negligence. However, where all that the claimant is threatened with is mere personal inconvenience of a trifling kind, he is not entitled to run a considerable risk in order to get rid of it; so, for example, where the door of a railway-carriage was so ill-secured that it kept flying open, but the claimant could avoid the draught by sitting elsewhere, the claimant would by guilty of contributory negligence if he fell out in trying to shut it (after several earlier unsuccessful attempts) while the train was in motion.[130]

Workplace accidents. It has been suggested that in actions by employees against their employers for injuries sustained at work the courts are justified in taking a more lenient view of careless conduct on the part of the claimant than would otherwise be warranted. For example, an employee working in a factory will not be held to have fallen short of the standard of the reasonable person for every risky thing that he might do. Regard must be had to the dulling of the sense of danger through familiarity, repetition, noise, confusion, fatigue and preoccupation with work.[131] Where, however, the operation leading up to the accident is divorced from the bustle, noise and repetition that occurs in such places as factories these considerations cannot apply.   **23–046**

Deliberate self-injury. Because negligence is a type of conduct, any conduct that is conduct in which the reasonable person would not have engaged is negligence. It follows that even deliberate acts of self-harm can constitute contributory negligence. Thus, in *Reeves v Metropolitan Police Commissioner*[132] the House of Lords held that a sane detainee who was able to commit suicide due to the negligence of police officers was guilty of contributory negligence in killing himself.   **23–047**

It is unnecessary that the claimant owe a duty of care to the defendant. The existence of a duty of care is, of course, essential to a cause of action for negligence, but the doctrine of contributory negligence can be triggered without the claimant owing a duty of care to anyone, including the defendant.[133] One   **23–048**

---

[129] (1816) 1 Stark. 493. See also *The Bywell Castle* (1879) 4 P.D. 219; *United States of America v Laird Line Ltd* [1924] A.C. 286; *Admiralty Commissioners v SS Volute* [1922] 1 A.C. 129 at 136; *Sayers v Harlow Urban District Council* [1958] 1 W.L.R. 623.

[130] *Adams v L. & Y. Ry* (1869) L.R. 4 C.P. 739. Cf. *Sayers v Harlow UDC* [1958] 1 W.L.R. 623.

[131] *Flower v Ebbw Vale Steel, Iron and Coal Co Ltd* [1934] 2 K.B. 132 at 139–140 per Lawrence J, cited with approval by Lord Wright, [1936] A.C. 206 at 214; *Caswell v Powell Duffryn Associated Collieries Ltd* [1940] A.C. 152 at 166 per Lord Atkin and at 176–179 per Lord Wright; *Grant v Sun Shipping Co Ltd* [1948] A.C. 549 at 567 per Lord du Parcq; *Hawkins v Ian Ross (Castings) Ltd* [1970] 1 All E.R. 180.

[132] [2000] 1 A.C. 360.

[133] *Nance v British Columbia Electric Ry Co Ltd* [1951] A.C. 601 at 611 per Viscount Simon. Nevertheless, it will often be the case, as where there is a collision between two vehicles, that the

sometimes comes across references to the claimant owing himself a duty to take care of his own safety,[134] but strictly speaking there is no duty.

b. Causation

23–049   **The claimant's failure to take reasonable care for his own safety must be causally relevant.** The doctrine of contributory negligence will not apply unless the claimant's failure to take reasonable care of his own safety was causally implicated in his damage. Thus, contributory negligence that would have made no difference to the damage will not count against the claimant, as where a cyclist who is negligently riding without a headlight is run down from behind.

23–050   **It is not necessary that the claimant's failure to take reasonable care contribute to the accident.** In many cases where the doctrine of contributory negligence is enlivened, the claimant's negligence will have contributed to the *accident* that led to his injury (as where a driver or pedestrian fails to keep a proper look-out) but this is not necessary. What is essential is that the claimant's negligence contributes to his *damage.* Thus, the doctrine of contributory negligence may be triggered where a motorcyclist fails to wear a crash helmet,[135] where a passenger in a car does not wear his seat belt,[136] and where a man rides in a dangerous position on the outside of a dust cart,[137] or rides with a driver whom he knows to have taken substantial quantities of alcohol.[138]

23–051   **The damage suffered by the claimant should be within the scope of the risk of injury created by the claimant's carelessness.** In *Jones v Livox Quarries Ltd*[139] the claimant was riding on the towbar at the back of a "traxcavator" vehicle when the driver of another vehicle negligently drove into the back of the traxcavator and caused him injury. Although the obvious danger arising from riding on the towbar was that of being thrown off, it was held that the risk of injury from the traxcavator being run into from behind was also one to which the claimant had exposed himself and the doctrine of contributory negligence applied as a result. The outcome would have been different if, for example, the claimant had been hit in the eye by a shot from a negligent sportsman. In that case his presence on the towbar would have been only part of the history. Similarly, if a person suffering from a disease caused by smoking dies because of a negligent failure to provide him with medical treatment the doctrine of contributory negligence will not apply.[140]

---

claimant does owe a duty of care to the defendant. A duty is essential if the defendant wishes to counterclaim against the claimant in respect of his own damage.

[134] E.g. *Langley v Dray M.T. Motor Policies at Lloyds* [1998] P.I.Q.R. P314 at 320.

[135] *O'Connell v Jackson* [1972] 1 Q.B. 270; *Capps v Miller* [1989] 2 All E.R. 333. See also *Smith v Finch* [2009] EWHC 53 (QB) (pedal cyclist not wearing helmet).

[136] *Froom v Butcher* [1976] Q.B. 286.

[137] *Davies v Swan Motor Co (Swansea) Ltd* [1949] 2 K.B. 291.

[138] *Owens v Brimmell* [1977] Q.B. 859. See also *Gregory v Kelly* [1978] R.T.R. 426 (knowledge of defective brakes).

[139] [1952] 2 Q.B. 608.

[140] Consider *St George v Home Office* [2008] EWCA Civ 1068; [2008] 4 All E.R. 1039.

c. The Doctrine of Identification

In a few situations the claimant will be imputed with the contributory negligence **23–052** of another person. This occurs pursuant to what is known as the doctrine of identification. In the past, child claimants were imputed with the negligence of their parent or guardian in failing to look after them, but this rule has now been abolished.[141] Accordingly, a child who is injured due partly by the negligence of his father and partly by, say, the negligence of a motorist will not be penalised by the doctrine of contributory negligence on account of his father's fault. In a fatal accident case the dependants of the deceased are identified with his contributory negligence.[142] The claimant will also be imputed with the contributory negligence of a third-party for whom he is vicariously responsible. The rule that the negligence of an employee in the course of his employment is imputed to his employer applies whether the latter is the claimant or the defendant (equally, the contributory negligence of an independent contractor for whom the claimant is not responsible does not affect the claimant's action). Thus, if C's vehicle is damaged due to the negligence of both D and C's employee, the doctrine of contributory negligence will be applicable in proceedings against D.

ii. Apportionment of Damages

Apportionment was unavailable at common law. At common law if the **23–053** doctrine of contributory negligence applied the claimant's action would fail entirely, regardless of whether the claimant's fault was slight in comparison with the defendant's. This all-or-nothing rule was qualified by the so-called doctrine of "last opportunity".[143] This doctrine enabled the claimant to recover notwithstanding his contributory negligence if the defendant had the "last opportunity" to avoid the accident. The authorities were confused, and confusion was made worse by the extension of the doctrine, in *British Columbia Electric Ry v Loach*,[144] to cases of "constructive last opportunity". This meant that if the defendant would have had the last opportunity but for his negligence, he was in the same position as if he had actually had that opportunity.

Apportionment legislation is enacted. Apportionment of the loss between **23–054** claimant and defendant became possible in maritime collision cases under the Maritime Conventions Act 1911, but it was not until the Law Reform (Contributory Negligence) Act 1945 was passed that apportionment became available in tort law. The latter Act abolished the all-or-nothing rule and provided for damages to be apportioned where the claimant was guilty of contributory negligence. It is still open to the court to conclude that the fault of only one party was the sole cause of the loss but all the refinements of "last opportunity" have been swept away.

---

[141] *Oliver v Birmingham and Midland Motor Omnibus Co Ltd* [1933] 1 K.B. 35. A minor exception to the non-identification rule in the child/parent context is found in the Congenital Disabilities (Civil Liability) Act 1976: see para.25–018.

[142] See para.24–031.

[143] *Davies v Mann* (1842) 10 M & W 546; 152 E.R. 588.

[144] [1916] 1 A.C. 719.

23–055 **The apportionment provision.** The apportionment provision is found in s.1(1) of the 1945 Act. It provides:

> "Where any person suffers damage as the result partly of his own fault and partly of the fault of any other person or persons, a claim in respect of that damage shall not be defeated by reason of the fault of the person suffering the damage, but the damages recoverable in respect thereof shall be reduced to such extent as the court thinks just and equitable having regard to the claimant's share in the responsibility for the damage."

23–056 **"Contributory negligence" is not defined.** The Act leaves the pivotal concept of "contributory negligence" undefined. It relies on the common law to give meaning to that idea.[145] It is the common law that determines, therefore, when the gateway to apportionment is open. As discussed above, the common law adopts a two-stage test to decide when the claimant is guilty of contributory negligence.[146]

23–057 **The definition of "damage".** By s.4 the word "damage" in s.1(1) encompasses loss of life and personal injury. It also includes economic loss[147] and property damage.

23–058 **The definition of "fault".** Section 1(1) applies only when both parties are at "fault". Section 4 defines "fault" to mean "negligence, breach of statutory duty or other act or omission which gives rise to a liability in tort or would, apart from this Act, give rise to the defence of contributory negligence". It has been held that the words "negligence, breach of statutory duty or other act or omission which gives rise to a liability in tort" apply to the "original" liability-creating fault of the defendant while the words "act or omission which … would apart from this Act, give rise to the defence of contributory negligence" apply to the claimant's fault.[148] The scope of the Act is therefore wide, but not unlimited, for there were several torts where at common law the defendant could not escape liability by showing "contributory negligence" on the part of the claimant, and this is carried over into the statutory regime. Thus, the Act is inapplicable to intentional interference with goods,[149] to deceit[150] or to other claims based upon dishonesty, whether framed as conspiracy, inducing breach of contract or in some other way.[151] A fraudster cannot say that his victim should have been more cautious in relying on what he said. However, it must be borne in mind that with regard to a particular item of loss, failure by the claimant to act with common prudence when he has reason to know about the dishonesty may lead to the conclusion that he is the author of his own misfortune.[152] The courts have accepted that the Act does not apply to cases of intentional trespass to the person.[153] Neither does it apply to claims for breach of contract where the defendant's liability arises from some

---

[145] *Davies v Swan Motor Co (Swansea) Ltd* [1949] 2 K.B. 291 at 310 per Bucknill LJ and at 322 per Denning LJ.

[146] See para.23–038.

[147] See, e.g. *Platform Home Loans Ltd v Oyston Shipways Ltd* [2000] 2 A.C. 190.

[148] *Reeves v Commissioner of Police of the Metropolis* [2000] 1 A.C. 360 at 369.

[149] Torts (Interference with Goods) Act 1977 s.11.

[150] *Standard Chartered Bank v Pakistan National Shipping Corp (Nos 2 and 4)* [2002] UKHL 43; [2003] 1 A.C. 959.

[151] *Corporación Nacional del Cobre de Chile v Sogemin Metals Ltd* [1997] 1 W.L.R. 1396.

[152] *Doyle v Olby (Ironmongers) Ltd* [1969] 2 Q.B. 158 at 168.

[153] *Pritchard v Co-operative Group Ltd* [2011] EWCA Civ 329; [2012] Q.B. 320.

contractual provision which does not depend on negligence on his part[154] (e.g. the implied terms to be found in ss.12–15 of the Sale of Goods Act 1979) or from a contractual obligation which is expressed in terms of taking care but which does not correspond to a common law duty to take care that would exist in the given case independently of contract.[155] Where, however, the defendant's liability, though framed in contract, is the same as his liability in the tort of negligence independently of the existence of any contract, the Act applies.[156] This would be the case, for example, in a claim for personal injuries by a patient against a doctor giving private treatment, by passenger against carrier or by visitor against occupier,[157] and in a claim against a solicitor or valuer.[158] The difference in principles applicable to contributory fault in contract and tort has been a significant source of litigation over the boundary between those two heads of liability and the position worked out by the courts goes some way towards preventing a purely tactical approach to cases. However, it is difficult to see why a regime of apportionment should be inapplicable to a duty to take care which arises in contract only, and the Law Commission recommended legislation on similar lines for such contractual duties.[159]

Apportionment. Section 1(1) does not specify precisely how damages are to be apportioned. It simply provides that the damages recoverable by the claimant are to be reduced "to such extent as the court thinks just and equitable having regard to the claimant's share in the responsibility for the damage". The interstices in this regard have been filled by the common law and convention. The way in which apportionment works in practice is as follows. The judge identifies the parties' respective shares of responsibility for the claimant's damage as percentages. The percentages, which are normally multiples of 10 (such as 40:60 or 50:50), will add up to 100 per cent. The claimant's damages are then diminished by the percentage that is assigned to him. The process of determining each party's share of responsibility involves consideration of two factors: the parties' relative moral blameworthiness and the "causative potency" of their careless conduct.[160] The enquiry in this regard is not conducted in a scientific manner.[161] It is done in a rough-and-ready way. The judge often simply declares that a given apportionment accords with commonsense. The determination is commonly treated as one of fact, and appellate courts will only vary an assessment where the trial judge's assessment is "plainly"[162] or "fundamentally"[163] incorrect.[164]

23–059

---

[154] *Barclays Bank Plc v Fairclough Building Ltd* [1995] Q.B. 214.

[155] *Forsikringsaktieselskapet Vesta v Butcher* [1988] 3 W.L.R. 565 (affirmed [1989] A.C. 852).

[156] *Forsikringsaktieselskapet Vesta v Butcher* [1988] 3 W.L.R. 565; *Youell v Bland Welch & Co Ltd (No.2)* [1990] 2 Lloyd's Rep. 431.

[157] *Sayers v Harlow Urban District Council* [1958] 1 W.L.R. 623.

[158] *UCB Bank Plc v Hepherd Winstanley & Pugh* [1999] Lloyd's Rep. P.N. 963.

[159] Law Com. No.219 (1993).

[160] *Davies v Swan Motor Co (Swansea) Ltd* [1949] 2 K.B. 291 at 326 per Denning LJ; *Stapley v Gypsum Mines Ltd* [1953] A.C. 663 at 682 per Lord Reid.

[161] *Pride Valley Foods Ltd v Hall & Partners* [2001] EWCA Civ 1001; (2001) 76 Con. L.R. 1 at [53].

[162] *Phethean-Hubble v Coles* [2012] EWCA Civ 349 at [86].

[163] *Dixon v Clement Jones Solicitors (a firm)* [2004] EWCA Civ 1005 at [51].

[164] Nevertheless appellate courts, and especially the House of Lords, have from time to time varied apportionments of damages quite freely: *Stapley v Gypsum Mines Ltd* [1953] A.C. 663; *National Coal*

23–060   **Seatbelt cases.** In *Froom v Butcher*[165] guideline rules were laid down in seat belt cases. These rules are "ready-made" reductions that operate regardless of whether the defendant's driving was slightly or grossly negligent and irrespective of whether the failure to wear the belt was "entirely inexcusable or almost forgivable".[166] If the claimant's injuries would have been altogether avoided by wearing a seat belt there should be a reduction of 25 per cent, but if he would still have been injured, but less severely, the reduction should be only 15 per cent. The court will not encourage attempts to reduce these figures by speculative evidence as to what injuries would have been suffered if the claimant had been wearing a belt. While these are guidelines rather than absolutely rigid figures,[167] they should generally be followed[168] and will apply in the vast majority of seat belt cases. They remain valid today even though they were established over 30 years ago.[169] The courts are free to increase the discount where the claimant's failure to use a seat belt was combined with another act of contributory negligence, such as accepting a ride from an obviously intoxicated driver.

23–061   **One hundred per cent contributory negligence?**[170] It has often been held that findings of 100 per cent contributory negligence are permissible.[171] Such holdings are erroneous. A finding of 100 per cent contributory negligence would mean that the claimant is solely responsible for the damage about which he or she complains. However, if the claimant is exclusively responsible for his or her damage, no tort will have been committed. If no tort has been committed by the defendant, the issue of contributory negligence does not arise for consideration. This is because the doctrine of contributory negligence, since it is a remedial rule,[172] is relevant if and only if a tort has been committed. It follows that the idea of 100 per cent contributory negligence is illogical.

23–062   **Zero per cent contributory negligence?**[173] The courts have sometimes made findings of zero per cent contributory negligence.[174] However, the concept of zero per cent contributory negligence, like that of 100 per cent contributory negligence, is nonsensical. If a court is minded to find zero per cent contributory negligence, that would mean that the claimant was either not at fault or, if he or she was at fault, that his or her fault was not causally related to his or her damage. But unless the claimant is guilty of fault that is causally connected with his or her damage, the doctrine of contributory negligence will not be engaged and the issue

---

Board v England [1954] A.C. 403; *Quintas v National Smelting Co Ltd* [1961] 1 W.L.R. 401; *Barrett v MoD* [1995] 1 W.L.R. 1217; *Brannan v Airtours Plc, The Times*, February 1, 1999.

[165] [1976] Q.B. 286.

[166] *Froom v Butcher* [1976] Q.B. 286 at 296.

[167] *Salmon v Newland, The Times*, May 16, 1983.

[168] *Capps v Miller* [1989] 2 All E.R. 333.

[169] *Gawler v Raettig* [2007] EWCA Civ 1560; *Stanton v Collinson* [2010] EWCA Civ 81.

[170] See further Goudkamp in Pitel, Neyers and Chamberlain (eds), *Tort Law: Challenging Orthodoxy* (2013).

[171] See, e.g. *Imperical Chemical Industries Ltd v Shatwell* [1965] A.C. 656 at 672; cf. *Reeves*[2000] 1 A.C. 360 at 372, 387.

[172] See para.23–037.

[173] See further Goudkamp in Pitel, Neyers and Chamberlain (eds), *Tort Law: Challenging Orthodoxy*(2013).

[174] See, e.g. *Pankhurst v White* [2006] EWHC 2093 (QB).

of apportionment will not arise. In short, a finding of zero per cent contributory negligence is inconsistent with holdings that must be made in order for the gateway to apportionment to be opened. A finding of zero per cent contributory negligence should never be made.

Multiple defendants. If there are two or more defendants, apportionment is performed by comparing the claimant's conduct with the totality of the tortious conduct by the defendants. The relative shares of responsibility of the defendants is not relevant in this regard. Their behaviour is taken collectively. Hence, if the court concludes that the claimant is 20 per cent responsible for the loss judgment will be entered for 80 per cent of the damage against both defendants irrespective of whether the defendants are equally to blame.[175] Similarly, if, however, the court concludes that the claimant is one-third to blame for the damage, then the correct judgment is for two-thirds of the damage against both defendants, even though the claimant may be as much at fault as either defendant. Once the issue of contributory negligence has been decided, the court can in contribution proceedings[176] make adjustments as between defendants where one has paid more or less than his fair share.

23–063

E.   Mitigation of Damage

The claimant is not entitled to recover damages in respect of any part of his loss that would have been avoidable by reasonable steps on his part after the tort. Suppose, for example, that a claimant unreasonably fails to undergo surgery that would on the balance of probabilities have resolved a painful condition that was caused by the defendant's tort. That claimant will be unable to obtain damages in respect of that condition from the date on which the reasonable person would have submitted to surgery. The fine details regarding the doctrine of mitigation must be sought in specialist works. However, several points will be briefly noted about it. First, the claimant is held to an objective standard. The question is what would the reasonable person in the claimant's position have done. Secondly, because the defendant is a wrongdoer who has caused the claimant's difficulty the standard of reasonableness is not a high one.[177] Thirdly, although the courts often speak of a "duty to mitigate" there is, strictly speaking, no duty. The claimant is free not to take steps to mitigate his damage. The doctrine simply prevents the claimants from charging the consequences of his unreasonable conduct to the defendant. Fourthly, the doctrine of mitigation applies to all torts. Even victims of fraud may have their damages reduced by the doctrine of mitigation of damage.[178] Fifthly, costs incurred by the claimant in an attempt to mitigate his damage are recoverable from the defendant. For example, a claimant who reasonably spends £10,000 on surgery in an attempt to reduce pain occasioned by the defendant's tort can recover that sum from the defendant (irrespective of

23–064

---

[175] *Fitzgerald v Lane* [1989] A.C. 328.
[176] See Ch.22.
[177] *Banco de Portugal v Waterlow* [1932] A.C. 452 at 506; *Morris v Richards* [2003] EWCA Civ 232; [2004] P.I.Q.R. Q30. For cases on refusal of medical treatment, see Hudson (1983) 3 L.S. 50.
[178] *Smith New Court Securities Ltd v Citibank NA* [1997] A.C. 254 at 285.

whether the surgery is successful).[179] Sixthly, the whole of the loss that could have been avoided had the claimant taken reasonable steps to mitigate his damage will be borne by the claimant. Responsibility for the particular loss in question is not apportioned between the parties. Seventhly, unreasonable conduct by the claimant is only relevant to the extent that it made a difference to the damage about which he complains. Thus, an unreasonable failure by the claimant to follow his doctor's instructions will not count against him if, on the balance of probabilities, the claimant's condition would be unaffected by that failure. Eighthly, there is a close relationship between the doctrine of mitigation of damage and the doctrine of contributory negligence.[180] Neither rule is enlivened unless the claimant behaves unreasonably with respect to his own interests and that unreasonable conduct is causally related to the damage about which he complains. Furthermore, both doctrines judge the reasonableness of the claimant's conduct by reference to an objective standard. However, the doctrines are not the same. One important difference between them is that contributory negligence applies to pre-tort fault while the doctrine of mitigation of damage applies to post-tort fault.

F. Damages in Personal Injury Actions

i. Heads of Damage

23–065 It was for a long time customary, even after the decline of the civil jury, to make a global award that did not distinguish between the different aspects of damages. This practice was supported partly on the ground that separate assessment and addition of individual items might lead to "overlapping" and a consequently excessive award. However, judges are now compelled to itemise their award. There are many reasons for this change. One obvious reason is that appellate review of damages awards would be virtually impossible if the awards were not itemised.

a. Non-pecuniary Loss

23–066 **Two types of non-pecuniary loss.** Non-pecuniary loss consists of the two elements of: (1) pain and suffering; and (2) loss of amenity (i.e. the damaging effect of the tort upon the claimant's ability to enjoy life). In practice, in nearly all cases the two elements are lumped together in a global sum (known by the inelegant acronym of "PSLA") and it is not usual to distinguish between them in the award.[181]

23–067 **Pain and suffering.** Pain and suffering is concerned with the subjective experience of the claimant. Thus, damages should not be awarded for pain and suffering if the claimant suffered no pain because the tort rendered him

---

[179] "[T]he Claimant may recover medical ... expenses that are reasonably incurred as a result of his injury": *Crofts v Murton* [2009] EWHC 3538 (QB) at [56].
[180] See Goudkamp in Pitel, Neyers and Chamberlain (eds), *Tort Law: Challenging Orthodoxy* (2013).
[181] *Heil v Rankin* [2001] Q.B. 272 at 298.

permanently unconscious.[182] Pain and suffering includes the suffering attributable to any consequential medical treatment, and worry about the effects of the injury upon the claimant's way of life and prospects. A person is entitled to damages under this head for the mental suffering caused by his awareness that his life expectation has been shortened by his injuries.[183]

Loss of amenity. It has long been recognised that if the claimant's injuries deprive him of some enjoyment, for example, if an amateur footballer loses a leg, then he is entitled to damages on this account.[184] It has become clear, however, that loss of amenity is to a large extent an objective element of the claimant's loss and distinguishable from pain and suffering, so that even though the claimant never appreciates the condition to which he has been reduced, he may nevertheless recover substantial damages under this head. In *Wise v Kaye*[185] the claimant remained unconscious from the moment of the accident and was deprived of all the attributes of life but life itself. A majority of the Court of Appeal upheld an award of £15,000 for loss of amenity. In *H West & Son Ltd v Shephard*[186] the claimant was a married woman aged 41 at the time of her accident and sustained severe head injuries resulting in cerebral atrophy and paralysis of all four limbs. There was no prospect of improvement in her condition and her expectation of life was reduced to about five years. There was evidence that she might appreciate to some extent the condition in which she was, but she was unable to speak. A majority of the House of Lords upheld an award of £17,500 for loss of amenities. As Lord Morris said: "The fact of unconsciousness does not . . . eliminate the actuality of the deprivations of the ordinary experiences and amenities of life which may be the inevitable result of some physical injury."[187]

Powerful objections have been voiced against the decision in *West*.[188] The principal complaint is that one can no more compensate an unconscious person that a dead one and since there can be no award of damages for non-pecuniary loss in respect of the period after death, there may be a very great difference between the total sum awarded to the estate of a deceased person and that awarded to an unconscious, living one, even though the latter will be unable to use the money for his benefit and the whole sum will probably at some future date pass to his relatives.[189] On the other hand, there is a natural reluctance to treat a living claimant as if he were already dead and there are great difficulties in full and accurate diagnosis in these cases.[190] The House of Lords looked at the

23–068

---

[182] *Wise v Kaye* [1962] 1 Q.B. 638.

[183] Administration of Justice Act 1982 s.1(1)(b).

[184] *Heaps v Perrite Ltd* [1937] 2 All E.R. 60.

[185] [1962] 1 Q.B. 638.

[186] [1964] A.C. 326.

[187] [1964] A.C. 326 at 349.

[188] See the dissenting speeches of Lord Devlin and Lord Reid and the decision of the High Court of Australia in *Skelton v Collins* (1966) 115 C.L.R. 94.

[189] Against the argument based upon the ultimate destination of the damages it might be pointed out: (1) that the law has never exercised any general power to control the damages awarded to the victim of an accident; and (2) some victims who are conscious but unable to "use" their damages might feel compensated by being able to benefit their relatives.

[190] See Law Com. No.257, *Damages for Personal Injury: Non-Pecuniary Loss* (1999) at [2.14]. Furthermore, the possibility of advances in medical science bringing about some amelioration of the

matter again in *Lim v Camden and Islington Area Health Authority*[191] and refused to overrule *West*, commenting that this "should not be done judicially but legislatively within the context of a comprehensive enactment"[192] on damages.

23–069 **Objections to the award of non-pecuniary damages generally.** A more fundamental question is whether damages for non-pecuniary loss can be justified in *any* case. It has been argued: (1) that they are necessarily arbitrary in amount since there is no market by which to value a limb or brain function; (2) that they are secondary in importance to income losses and they divert limited funds from the replacement of those losses; and (3) that they represent interests which are not so highly valued by the public since the interests are not commonly insured. However, such damages are found almost without exception in developed legal systems and, judging by the responses of accident victims to a Law Commission survey,[193] they provide some sort of solace, however inadequate, for the real hurt suffered by victims of injury.

23–070 **Basis of assessment.** It is in the nature of non-pecuniary loss that it cannot be translated directly into money. However, the only type of remedy available is an award of damages, and an assessment of damages has to be made.[194] In the past their quantification was a jury question for which "no rigid rules, or rules that apply to all cases, can be laid down".[195] However, in the mid-1960s the courts practically abolished the jury in personal injury actions,[196] principally because juries were considered to be incapable of achieving sufficient uniformity in essentially similar cases. Since then it has become normal for judges to have cited to them previous awards and there is a pattern for various common kinds of injury, a tariff,[197] though one with some flexibility,[198] since no two cases are identical.[199] There is no "medical schedule" of disability, though medical evidence is of course admissible as to the extent of the claimant's disability.

23–071 **Artificiality.** As a technique the comparison of awards for non-pecuniary no doubt has drawbacks. How can a realistic comparison be made between cases involving different kinds of injury? If, for example, £87,000 is an appropriate figure for total loss by a right-handed claimant of his right arm, what guidance does that give to the damages appropriate for the loss of the sight of an eye, or for the inability to bear a child, or for loss of the sense of smell? Indeed, one might go further and ask, even assuming a suitable standard for comparison can be

---

condition may contribute to the current judicial attitude (*Croke v Wiseman* [1982] 1 W.L.R. 71 at 84) and diagnoses of permanent vegetative state may be wrong.

[191] [1980] A.C. 174.

[192] [1980] A.C. 174 at 189.

[193] Law Com. No.225, *How Much is Enough?* (1994).

[194] *The Mediana* [1900] A.C. 113 at 116 per Lord Halsbury LC.

[195] *Admiralty Commissioners v SS Susquehanna* [1926] A.C. 655 at 662 per Viscount Dunedin.

[196] *Ward v James* [1966] 1 Q.B. 273. After *H. v Ministry of Defence* [1991] 2 Q.B. 103 it seems unlikely that the discretion to order jury trial in these cases will ever be exercised again.

[197] See also the Judicial Studies Board's *Guidelines for the Assessment of General Damages in Personal Injury Cases* (11th edn). This publication delineates guides for awards of non-pecuniary loss in personal injury matters.

[198] *Wright v British Railways Board* [1983] 2 A.C. 773 at 785.

[199] The standard tariff figures assume a claimant in the prime of life. See *Nutbrown v Sheffield H.A.* [1993] 4 Med. L.R. 188 (claimant aged 76 half standard award).

found, how we justify a particular datum figure for the injury with which the comparisons are made. Why is our figure £87,000 not £870 or £870,000? As far as this latter question is concerned, one can say little more than that the choice of the right order of figure is empirical and in practice results from a general consensus of opinion of damage-awarding tribunals. As for comparisons, Diplock LJ said that the standard of comparison which the law applies "if it is not wholly instinctive and incommunicable, is based, apart from pain and suffering, upon the degree of deprivation—that is, the extent to which the victim is unable to do those things which, but for the injury, he would have been able to do".[200]

Appeals. Since the assessment of damages for non-pecuniary loss is not an exact mathematical process the Court of Appeal should not interfere with an award unless the judge has acted on a wrong principle of law, or misapprehended the facts or has for other reasons made a wholly erroneous estimate of the damage suffered.[201] That said, it has been said time and again that the Court of Appeal has general responsibility for ensuring that guidelines for awards of non-pecuniary damages are kept up to date.[202] The guidelines that it issues should be revised to take account of the changes in both the value of money and in social attitudes.   **23–072**

b. Pecuniary loss

Introduction. Pecuniary losses include a loss of earnings, medical expenses and care expenses. In the case of a serious accident, the bulk of the claimant's loss will be pecuniary. Insofar as these losses have been incurred before the trial or settlement there is unlikely to be much difficulty regarding their assessment. Complications tend to arise more frequently, however, in relation to quantifying the claimant's future pecuniary loss and reducing it to a present capital sum. This process is inevitably inexact because it involves a host of assumptions, including the claimant's future rate of earning had he not been injured, the period and extent of his disability, and the chance that his earning capacity might have been affected by some other vicissitude even if the accident had not happened.   **23–073**

Future loss of earnings. The goal here is to determine the net loss of income that the claimant has incurred because of the tort. The court will make findings about the gross income that the claimant would have earned per annum had he not been injured. The court will take into account here, for example, the claimant's prospects of promotion and the likelihood that he would have done overtime work. Where the claimant has not yet entered the workforce because of his age the court will predict the field of work that the claimant would have entered and what he would have earned. Once the gross annual income has been determined it then has deducted from it income tax,[203] social security contributions[204] and other expenditure the claimant would have had to incur to gain the income (e.g. his   **23–074**

---

[200] *Fletcher v Autocar and Transporters Ltd* [1968] 2 Q.B. 322 at 340.
[201] *Pickett v British Rail Engineering Ltd* [1980] A.C. 136; *Heil v Rankin* [2001] Q.B. 272.
[202] See, e.g. *Simmons v Castle* [2012] EWCA Civ 1039; [2013] 1 All E.R. 334 at [11].
[203] *British Transport Commission v Gourley* [1956] A.C. 185.
[204] *Cooper v Firth Brown Ltd* [1963] 1 W.L.R. 418.

contribution to a company pension scheme[205]). Logically, where the claimant is unable to work as a result of the tort, a case could be made out for deducting the claimant's travelling expenses to and from work which he will no longer incur after the accident but except perhaps in very exceptional circumstances[206] this is not done.

23-075 **Position where claimant would be disadvantaged in the employment market.** In cases of continuing disability the claimant may be able to remain in his employment but with the risk that, if he loses that employment at some time in the future, he may then, as a result of his injury, be at a disadvantage in getting another job or an equally well-paid job. The risk that the claimant would be disadvantaged has always been a compensable head of damage but it has come into more prominence in recent years. Assessment of damages under this head may be highly speculative and clearly no mathematical approach is possible but the court should be satisfied that there is a "substantial" or "real" risk that the claimant will be subject to the disadvantage before the end of his working life before it awards damages in this connection. If so satisfied, the judge must then do his best to value the "chance", taking into account all the facts of the case.[207]

23-076 **"Lost years".** In some cases the injury suffered by the claimant will reduce his expectation of life. The claimant is entitled to recover damages in respect of income that he would have earned but for the tort, including during any working years that he has lost as a result of the reduction in his life expectancy.[208] Put differently, the claimant's loss of earnings should be assessed based on his life expectancy before the accident rather than what it is as a result of the accident. However, because the claimant will not have any living expenses during the lost years, these will be deducted from the award.

23-077 **Claimant unemployed but providing domestic services.** Where a person rendered unpaid household services before the accident but is prevented from doing so due to tortiously-inflicted injuries damages will not be awarded for a loss of earnings. However, the claimant may recover the value of substitute services.[209]

23-078 **Past medical expenses.** The claimant is entitled to recover the cost of medical and similar services that he reasonably incurred as a result of his injuries. Legislation provides that in determining the reasonableness of any expenses the possibility of avoiding them by making use of the National Health Service is to

---

[205] *Dews v NCB* [1988] A.C. 1. But if as a result of the accident the claimant's employment is terminated and he suffers a reduction in pension, this is itself a compensable head of damage: *Parry v Cleaver* [1970] A.C. 1.

[206] Lord Griffiths in *Dews v NCB* [1988] A.C. 1 suggests as a possible example the case of a wealthy man who commuted daily by helicopter from the Channel Islands to London. Cf. *Eagle v Chambers* [2004] EWCA Civ 1033; [2004] 1 W.L.R. 3081 at [68].

[207] *Ashcroft v Curtin* [1971] 1 W.L.R. 1731; *Smith v Manchester Corp* (1974) 17 K.I.R. 1; *Clarke v Rotax Aircraft Equipment Ltd* [1975] I.C.R. 440; *Moeliker v A. Reyrolle & Co Ltd* [1976] I.C.R. 253; *Nicholls v NCB* [1976] I.C.R. 266; *Robson v Liverpool CC* [1993] P.I.Q.R. Q78; *Goldborough v Thompson* [1996] P.I.Q.R. Q86. Damages may be awarded under this head even though the claimant is unemployed at the date of the trial: *Cook v Consolidated Fisheries Ltd* [1977] I.C.R. 635.

[208] *Pickett v British Rail Engineering Ltd* [1980] A.C. 136.

[209] *Daly v General Steam Navigation Co Ltd* [1981] 1 W.L.R. 120.

be disregarded.[210] However, if the claimant in fact receives treatment under the National Health Service he cannot recover the notional cost of private treatment.[211] If the National Health Service is utilised, the Health and Social Care (Community Health and Standards) Act 2003 provides for the National Health Service to recover the cost of treatment from the tortfeasor's insurer up to a current maximum of £46,831.[212]

Future expenses. Determining the future expenses that the claimant will incur   **23–079**
because of the tort is largely a matter for the evidence. The claimant can recover damages in respect of liabilities that will reasonably be incurred as a result of the tort, including in respect of medication expenses, physiotherapy costs, equipment costs,[213] increased travel costs, the cost of living in a special institution[214] and care. He cannot recover damages for the cost of future private treatment if the evidence shows that he will not take that course and will instead obtain treatment via the National Health Service.[215] The fact the claimant may have a statutory right to call upon the local authority for free institutional care does not prevent him electing to pay for such services in the market and recovering the cost from the defendant.[216]

Expenses that the claimant will incur as a result of the tort will often be incurred up to the date of the claimant's death. Accordingly, in calculating the damages to be awarded for future expenses the courts will need to make a variety of guesses about what life will hold for the claimant in the future, and how things would have been for the claimant had he not been injured. In particular, the claimant's life expectancy will usually be in issue. Statistics tables are generally used to determine the claimant's life expectancy, although the courts are not bound by these tables.[217]

Care provided without charge by service provider. It may happen that care for   **23–080**
which the claimant would otherwise have to pay is rendered without payment. As shown above, the National Health Service has a statutory right to recoup the cost[218] but otherwise the provider of the services has no claim in his own right. So in *Islington London Borough Council v University College London Hospital NHS Trust*[219] the local authority was under a statutory duty to provide care for the claimant, who had suffered a stroke as a result of the defendants' negligence and although she had recovered damages, these were not available for payment of the

---

[210] Law Reform (Personal Injuries) Act 1948 s.2(4).

[211] *Harris v Brights Asphalt Contractors Ltd* [1953] 1 Q.B. 617 at 635 per Slade J.

[212] The regime does not apply to a disease which is not the result of an injury: s.150(5), (6). The system is, like that for recovery of social security payments (see para.23–091), operated by the Compensation Recovery Unit. For the background to the 2003 Act, see Law Com. No. 262 (1999).

[213] *S. v Distillers Co (Biochemicals) Ltd* [1970] 1 W.L.R. 114; *Povey v Governors of Rydal School* [1970] 1 All E.R. 841.

[214] *Shearman v Folland* [1950] 2 K.B. 43; *Oliver v Ashman* [1962] 2 Q.B. 210; *Cutts v Chumley* [1967] 1 W.L.R. 742. For the position where the claimant purchases more suitable accommodation, see *George v Pinnock* [1973] 1 W.L.R. 118; *Roberts v Johnstone* [1989] Q.B. 878.

[215] *Eagle v Chambers* [2004] EWCA Civ 1033; [2004] 1 W.L.R. 3081.

[216] *Peters v East Midlands Strategic* [2009] EWCA Civ 145; [2009] 3 W.L.R. 737.

[217] *Wells v Wells* [1999] 1 A.C. 345 at 379.

[218] See para.23–078.

[219] [2005] EWCA Civ 596; [2006] P.I.Q.R. P3.

local authority's charges. A claim for recoupment against the defendants based on negligence failed. A decision in favour of the local authority would have implications which could not be fully explored for all sorts of other bodies and persons, public and private, providing services in aid of misfortune and the specific legislation in relation to National Health Service charges pointed towards the conclusion that the matter was for Parliament.

23–081   **Gratuitous care provided by family and friends.** Where care is provided voluntarily by a relative or friend, the practical position is somewhat different from that where the care is provided by a service provider. The carer has no claim but the claimant may be able to recover damages in respect of the services even though he has not undertaken a legal obligation to pay for them. In *Donnelly v Joyce*[220] it was held that the need for the services was the claimant's own loss and hence damages for that need could be recovered by him. However, it was subsequently held in *Hunt v Severs*[221] that the claimant, having recovered the damages, held them on trust for the carer. The theory now seems to be that the loss is the carer's, but that loss is recoverable only in the action of the victim. The facts of *Hunt v Severs* were rather unusual in that the defendant (who was married to the claimant) was providing the care in respect of which the damages were being sought and the trust approach seems to have been seized on as a way of avoiding the apparent absurdity of holding that the defendant could be liable for the cost of what he was already providing gratuitously, for he could not be liable for what he would then receive back. The necessity of imposing a trust to avoid this difficulty has fallen away as the courts are now empowered under the Civil Procedure Rules to pay the damages directly to the carer.[222]

There is no hard-and-fast rule for the sum recoverable under this head. Where the carer has given up paid employment the lost wages will be recoverable provided they do not exceed the commercial rate for the services. In other cases the sum recoverable may be less than the commercial rate (if only because of the absence of tax and national insurance payments)[223] but it should be enough to ensure that the carer gets a reasonable recompense and the court should bear in mind the possibility that the carer may not be able to provide care indefinitely. There is no doubt that recovery extends to expenses reasonably incurred for the claimant's benefit, such as visits that may assist in the claimant's recovery.[224]

23–082   **Other pecuniary losses.** The recoverable pecuniary losses mentioned above are not exhaustive, nor can an exhaustive list be given, for the claimant is entitled to damages for any item of loss he may have suffered provided only that it is not too remote. The following examples provide some indication, however, of the kinds of loss that may have to be considered in any given case. If the claimant's employer provided board and lodging[225] or a car available for private use[226] and

---

[220] [1974] Q.B. 454.

[221] [1994] 2 A.C. 350.

[222] *Drake v Foster Wheeler Ltd* [2010] EWHC 2004 (QB); [2011] 1 All E.R. 63 at [43].

[223] 25 per cent below the commercial rate seems to be common: *A v National Blood Authority* [2001] 3 All E.R. 289 at 390.

[224] *Hunt v Severs* [1994] 2 A.C. 350 at 357.

[225] *Lifften v Watson* [1940] 1 K.B. 556.

[226] *Clay v Pooler* [1982] 3 All E.R. 570.

he has to give up his employment, the claimant may recover the value of those items as well as his actual loss of earnings, and if he has to give up a pensionable employment he can recover for any consequent loss of pension rights.[227] The injury inflicted by the defendant may have made it more difficult for the claimant to obtain life or health insurance.[228] In professions where reputation is significant, damages may be awarded for loss of opportunity of enhancing that reputation.[229] On a less material level, a woman may recover damages for the reduction of her prospects of marriage, which is an item of pecuniary as well as non-pecuniary loss, but it must be borne in mind that if she had married that might have reduced her earning capacity for a time. Rather than make an addition to one side of the equation and a balancing deduction on the other[230] it may be better simply to ignore marriage altogether.[231] If the claimant previously did handyman work around the house or tended to his own garden but now has to employ someone else to do this work for him because of his injuries he will be entitled to damages in respect of that expense.

The vicissitudes of life. In determining the claimant's damages for a future loss of earnings, the courts will make a reduction for the "general vicissitudes of life"—that is to say, damaging events like sickness or unemployment which might have affected the claimant even if the defendant had not injured him. Although it is justifiable to make a larger reduction for, say, a person in a hazardous occupation, the general range of reductions is modest unless there is evidence to show some special risk affecting the claimant as an individual.[232]

23–083

Discounting damages for future pecuniary loss to reflect the use value of money. Where the court makes a lump sum award for loss of future employment income the claimant receives all of the lost income when the judgment is enforced. Similarly, where a lump sum is awarded in respect of future expenses, the claimant has the enjoyment of those damages in respect of those expenses before the expenses will be incurred. To prevent the claimant from being overcompensated as a result of having the use value of money (i.e. the ability to invest and earn a return on it), these awards need to be discounted (unless inflation is running at such a high rate that it outstrips the rate of return on the capital, in which case it is necessary, instead, to increase the award[233]). The theoretical aim of the process is to provide a lump sum sufficient, when invested, to produce an income equal to the lost income when the interest is supplemented by withdrawals of capital.[234]

23–084

The discount rate is fixed at the rate of interest that it is thought that the claimant will be able to earn on the lump sum, after tax. Section 1(1) of the Damages Act 1996 provides that the court is to take account of "such rate of

---

[227] *Judd v Hammersmith, West London and St Mark's Hospital Board of Governors* [1960] 1 W.L.R. 328; *Parry v Cleaver* [1970] A.C. 1.
[228] *A v National Blood Authority* [2001] 3 All E.R. 289.
[229] Cf. *Herbert Clayton and Jack Walter Ltd v Oliver* [1930] A.C. 209.
[230] As was done in *Moriarty v McCarthy* [1978] 1 W.L.R. 155.
[231] *Hughes v McKeown* [1985] 1 W.L.R. 963; *Housecroft v Burnett* [1986] 1 All E.R. 332.
[232] *Herring v MoD* [2003] EWCA Civ 528; [2004] 1 All E.R. 44.
[233] See *Simon v Helmot* [2012] UKPC 5 at [14].
[234] *Simon v Helmot* [2012] UKPC 5 at [11].

return . . . as may from time to time be prescribed by an order made by the Lord Chancellor". The Lord Chancellor exercised that power and prescribed a rate of 2.5 per cent from June 28, 2001.[235] This rate is not binding on the courts, but it is expected that judges will depart from it only in exceptional cases.[236] The same discount rate need not be applied to all future pecuniary losses. Where the evidence shows that inflation would affect different heads of damage in different ways the courts may use different rates for different parts of the award.[237]

Whether or not a rate of 2.5 per cent is appropriate is a highly contentious issue for several reasons. First, small changes in the discount rate have a tremendous impact on the size of damages awards, especially in cases involving catastrophically injured claimants, who are likely to suffer future pecuniary loss for a lengthy period of time. Miniscule changes in the discount rate may radically alter the damages awarded. Secondly, the discount rate is set based on the assumption that the claimant is a prudent investor. However, the assumption that the claimant will expertly manage a potentially large fund over a long period for maximum advantage may not be a very accurate one.[238] Thirdly, injured claimants often cannot achieve a particularly high rate of return given that they often cannot afford to take significant risks with their capital (on which they will depend to pay for, for example, care and medical treatment).

ii. Deductions for Benefits Received[239]

23–085   **Introduction.** The claimant is not entitled to damages in respect of loss which has been avoided because he has received a countervailing benefit. The problem lies in distinguishing between those receipts[240] which go to reduce the loss and those which are "indirect" or "collateral" and do not do so. The issue is of general application in contract as well as in tort[241] and in non-personal injury cases the modern approach seems to be to ask whether the benefit received is sufficiently causally connected with the defendant's wrongdoing to require it to be brought into account. Causation is certainly a necessary element if a benefit is to be so deducted from damages in a personal injury case, too—no one would suggest that a person who received a legacy from the estate of a relative a week after being injured in an accident should have to bring that into account in a claim against the tortfeasor. However, the deduction issue in personal injury cases has generated a good deal of case law and many receipts are governed by statute so we must examine this area more closely. A distinction has to be drawn between receipts from private sources (governed by the common law) and social security benefits (governed by statute).

---

[235] Damages (Personal Injury) Order, SI 2001/2301.
[236] *Warriner v Warriner* [2002] EWCA Civ 81; [2002] 1 W.L.R. 1703.
[237] *Simon v Helmot* [2012] UKPC 5 at [52].
[238] But the Law Commission found that 84 per cent of claimants with damages of more than £100,000 had taken some investment advice: Law Com. No. 224 at [2.30].
[239] Lewis, *Deducting Benefits from Damages for Personal Injury* (1999).
[240] The principle is this area extends to savings made as well as receipts: *Salih v Enfield AHA* [1991] 3 All E.R. 400 is a macabre example.
[241] Well-known contract cases are *Erie County Natural Gas and Fuel Co Ltd v Carroll* [1911] A.C. 105 and *British Westinghouse Electric and Manufacturing Co Ltd v Underground Electric Railways Co of London Ltd* [1912] A.C. 673.

a. Receipts from Private Sources

The general rule. It has been said to be difficult to "articulate a single precise   **23–086**
jurisprudential principle by which to distinguish the deductible from the
non-deductible receipt"[242] but the basic rule is that receipts which have come to
the claimant as a result of the injury are prima facie to be set against his loss of
earnings and consequential expenses unless they fall within established
exceptions.[243]

Exception for voluntary payments prompted by the benevolence of third   **23–087**
parties. The first of these is that voluntary payments prompted by the
benevolence of third parties,[244] whether into a "disaster fund" or directly to the
claimant, are not to be brought into account to reduce the damages for the simple
reason that otherwise there would be a risk that the springs of charity would dry
up.[245] *Ex gratia* payments by the tortfeasor do not fall into this exception.[246]

Exception for insurance monies accruing to the claimant. The court will not   **23–088**
bring into account monies accruing to the claimant under policies of insurance.[247]
These must, however, be paid for by the claimant: receipts will be brought into
account if the premiums were paid for by the tortfeasor and if the claimant is, for
example, an employee of the tortfeasor he cannot say that he has paid indirectly
because the fruits of the workers' labour enabled the premiums to be paid.[248] A
reason commonly given for the insurance exception is that the claimant should
not to be disadvantaged by his own thrift and foresight. However, there is no
question of depriving the claimant of his insurance monies; the question is of his
right of recovery against the defendant, and insofar as the claimant is allowed to
recover damages and to keep the insurance payments it may be argued that he is
over-compensated for his loss. There is no such "double recovery" where the
policy is one of indemnity, for then if he sues he has to reimburse the insurer out
of the damages (though it is more likely that the insurer would sue the tortfeasor
by virtue of his subrogation to the insured's rights). It is of course another

---

[242] *Hodgson v Trapp* [1989] A.C. 807 at 820 per Lord Bridge. The views expressed to the Law
Commission were so diverse that it did not feel able to propose any general reform of this area: Law
Commission, *Damages for Personal Injury: Medical, Nursing and other Expenses; Collateral
Benefits* (1999) No.262.
[243] "It is the rule which is fundamental and axiomatic and the exceptions to it which are only to be
admitted on grounds which clearly justify their treatment as such": Buxton LJ in *Hodgson v Trapp*
[1989] A.C. 807 at 819 per Lord Bridge.
[244] The donor of the benevolence has no claim: *Esso Petroleum Co Ltd v Hall Russell & Co Ltd*
[1989] A.C. 643.
[245] *Redpath v Belfast County Down Ry* [1947] N.I. 167; *Parry v Cleaver* [1970] A.C. 1; *Naahas v
Pier House Management (Cheyne Walk) Ltd* (1984) 270 E.G. 328 (property loss).
[246] *Gaca v Pirelli General Plc* [2004] EWCA Civ 373; [2004] 1 W.L.R. 2683. In theory of course the
tortfeasor might make the payment on the terms: "This is a gift which is not to diminish any eventual
award of damages against me."
[247] *Bradburn v GW Ry* (1874) L.R. Ex. 1.
[248] *Gaca v Pirelli General Plc* [2004] EWCA Civ 373; [2004] 1 W.L.R. 2683. But it would be
surprising if insurance payments were brought into account where the premiums were paid by
someone not responsible for the tort: it is hard to believe that the damages of an injured holidaymaker
are to be reduced because another member of the party paid (otherwise than as agent) the travel
insurance premiums.

question whether the insurer's right of subrogation is justifiable, but that issue cannot be addressed solely in the context of personal injuries, where many policies (e.g. for personal accident) are not based on the indemnity principle. Where the policy is not one of indemnity the net result is that there is undoubtedly, in mathematical terms, a double recovery. Whether that is so in substance is debatable. Arguments in favour of the present position are as follows. First, that while there is no question of depriving the claimant of the benefit of his insurance, to deduct it from the damages would at least give the appearance of putting him at a disadvantage in comparison with another claimant who had chosen not to insure. No doubt there is a logical answer to this, namely that the claimant has not "wasted" the premiums for he has had the benefit of the cover, which is likely to have extended much more widely than the risk of injury in circumstances which amount to a tort. If it is thought that the defendant should not escape scot-free it would in theory be possible to require him to reimburse the claimant for all or part of the premiums paid.[249] Nevertheless, the intuitive conclusion that it is unfair to make any deduction probably has widespread appeal. Secondly, it may be thought that the traditional statement that the insurance is *res inter alios acta* does more than express a conclusion in Latin. The point about the scope of the insurance cover which is made above can be turned in support of the present regime: the claimant has taken out cover that may extend more widely than injury by tort and in non-indemnity cases the amount of that cover will be determined by the terms of the policy and need bear no necessary relationship with any objectively determined value of the interest protected. In effecting the policy the claimant may therefore fairly say that he has bought a form of security additional to and wholly different from that which the law of tort provides to him and there is no reason why the defendant should be able to take advantage of this to reduce his liability.[250]

23–089 **Sick pay.** By contrast, sick pay received is outside these exceptions and is deductible from damages for loss of earnings, whether or not it is paid by the defendant,[251] even if it takes the form of a very long-term payment which the employer has based on an arrangement with an insurance company.[252] No deduction is, of course, made if the payment to the claimant is made on condition of repayment in the event of recovery of damages.[253]

23–090 **Pension payments.** If, as a result of the injury, the claimant retires from his job and receives a payments under a pension scheme those payments are not deductible from the claim for lost earnings.[254] This is so even if the defendant provides or contributes to the pension,[255] though it is open to the defendant employer to draft the pension scheme in such a way as to negate this result. It may happen that the claim of a claimant who has to retire early includes not only loss of earnings but also loss of pension rights which he would have accumulated

---

[249] *Bristol and West B.S. v May May & Merrimans (No.2)* [1997] 3 All E.R. 206 at 226.

[250] *Parry v Cleaver* [1970] A.C. 1 at 31.

[251] *Parry v Cleaver* [1970] A.C. 1.

[252] *Hussain v New Taplow Paper Mills Ltd* [1988] A.C. 514.

[253] *Berriello v Felixstowe Dock & Ry Co* [1989] I.C.R. 467.

[254] *Parry v Cleaver* [1970] A.C. 1.

[255] *Smoker v London Fire and Civil Defence Authority* [1991] 2 A.C. 502.

had he worked until the normal retirement age. In that case the pension received is brought into account insofar as it is received in the period after the normal date of retirement.[256]

b. Social Security Benefits

Introduction. At the inception of the modern welfare state the relationship between tort damages and social security benefits was dealt with by the compromise embodied in the Law Reform (Personal Injuries) Act 1948 whereby there was a deduction from damages for loss of earnings of one-half of the value of social security benefits receivable by the claimant in the five years following the accident. The Act did not cover all benefits but the courts gradually moved towards deducting other benefits in full throughout the period of the disability.[257] This approach prevented double compensation of the victim, gave a windfall to the defendant but left the provider of the benefit, the State, the loser. In the late 1980s the government came to the conclusion that the State should not subsidise the tortfeasor in this way and the system was radically altered by the Social Security Act 1989. The current legislation is the Social Security (Recovery of Benefits) Act 1997. Under this regime benefits are deducted in full (for a period) from the claimant's damages but the deduction is used to reimburse the Secretary of State.

23–091

The legislation. A person ("the compensator"[258]) is not to make any compensation payment in consequence of an accident, injury or disease[259] until he has applied to the Secretary of State (via the Compensation Recovery Unit) for a "certificate of recoverable benefits" for the purposes of the Act. A compensation payment for this purpose is not confined to damages payable under a judgment but extends to an out-of-court settlement, whether or not proceedings have been commenced.[260] However, the Act does not extend to charitable payments made by third parties[261] for the payment must be made "by or on behalf of a person who is, or who is alleged to be, liable to any extent in respect of the accident".[262] The recoverable benefits for the purposes of the certificate are the specified social security benefits payable to the victim during the five years immediately following the accident or until the making of the compensation payment,

23–092

---

[256] *Longden v British Coal Corp* [1998] A.C. 653; *Parry v Cleaver* [1970] A.C. 1; *Cantwell v Criminal Injuries Compensation Board* [2001] UKHL 36; 2001 S.L.T. 966.

[257] Culminating in *Hodgson v Trapp* [1989] A.C. 807.

[258] In practice, in most cases the defendant's insurer.

[259] The Act was held to be inapplicable to a case where the defendants failed to inform the claimants of the risk of Down's Syndrome in their unborn child and they incurred expense (and received benefits) in looking after the child: *Rand v E. Dorset HA* [2001] P.I.Q.R. Q1.

[260] s.1(2).

[261] Payments made from a disaster fund are treated as exempt payments provided that no more than 50 per cent of the capital sum was contributed by the alleged wrongdoer. Sch.1, Pt.I.

[262] These words are not very apt to cover the Motor Insurers' Bureau since the scheme depends on an agreement between the Motor Insurers' Association and the state which is technically unenforceable by the victim. However, the statutory definition of compensation payment in s.1(2)(b) extends to a payment made "in pursuance of a compensation scheme for motor accident".

whichever is earlier.[263] This sum is to be deducted from the payment and paid to the Secretary of State. If there is a judgment the court is not concerned with the benefits, which it is to disregard—the deduction and accounting to the Secretary of State is a matter for the defendant.[264] As between the claimant and the defendant, the latter is to be treated as having fully discharged his liability to the former by paying him the difference (if any) between the amount of the damages and the recoverable benefits.[265] However, for this purpose like is only to be deducted from like. Under Sch.2 of the Act compensation payments are treated as containing up to three elements—loss of earnings, cost of care and loss of mobility—and the deduction of a particular benefit is only to be made against the equivalent element of the compensation payment. Thus if the compensation payment contains elements of £10,000 for loss of earnings and £5,000 for cost of nursing and the claimant has received £13,000 in income support and statutory sick pay and £2,000 in attendance allowance, the loss of earnings element is extinguished but he still gets £3,000 for cost of nursing. There is no deduction against damages for pain and suffering and loss of amenity,[266] there being no "equivalent" benefits. However, none of this affects the defendant's liability to reimburse the Secretary of State for all specified benefits received by the claimant. Nor is there any offset for contributory negligence, so if the defendant is only 10 per cent liable for the claimant's injuries he still has to reimburse the State for all the benefits.[267] Indeed, there is no requirement that the defendant should actually be liable to the claimant at all and it is thus dangerous to make a small payment to buy off a weak, "nuisance" claim. Fatal accident cases are entirely outside the scope of the Act.

iii. Pre-Judgement Interest on Damages

23–093 Although there is now power in certain circumstances to order an interim payment on account of damages,[268] there will always be a lapse of time between the injury and the payment of damages, and that frequently the claimant will have to wait a considerable time until his claim has been determined and the damages found due to him are paid. Unless this delay is taken into account, the claimant will be undercompensated. For many years that court had a discretionary power to award interest but it is now mandatory to award interest in an action for

---

[263] Some state benefits are not covered by the 1997 Act. If there is no indication as to their deductibility in the relevant legislation the issue must be determined under the common law: *Ballantine v Newalls Insulation Co Ltd* [2000] P.I.Q.R. Q327.

[264] s.17. The effect of this is that the claimant is entitled to interest on damages which he will not receive and which, in view of the benefits he has received, he has not (under the philosophy of the Act) been "kept out of": *Wisely v John Fulton (Plumbers) Ltd* [2000] 1 W.L.R. 820. But where the benefits exceed the damages payable a deduction may be made against any interest, too: *Griffiths v British Coal Corpn* [2001] 1 W.L.R. 1493.

[265] See s.8.

[266] Thus damages for "loss of mobility" under Sch.2 must be confined to financial costs such as having to take taxis, and does not extend to matters like sadness and frustration at being unable to get around: *Mitchell v Laing, The Times*, January 28, 1998.

[267] The justice of requiring the defendant to carry the whole burden of the claimant's support by the State when the injury is largely the claimant's fault is not apparent.

[268] CPR r.25.

personal injuries in which the claimant recovers more than £200, unless the court is satisfied that there are special reasons why interest should not be given.[269] In fatal accident claims the pecuniary loss up to the date of the trial should carry interest at half the short-term interest rates current during that period, but no interest should be awarded upon future pecuniary loss because that loss has not yet been sustained.[270] In personal injury cases pecuniary loss should be treated in the same way as in fatal accident cases.[271] As to non-pecuniary loss interest is to be awarded,[272] but only at the moderate rate of 2 per cent.[273] The reason for this low rate is that damages for non-pecuniary loss will be awarded at the rates prevailing at the time of the trial, thus covering any intervening fall in the value of money. What the claimant has therefore lost by late receipt of his damages under this head is only that element of modern interest rates which truly represent the "use value" of money.[274]

iv. Provisional Damages

As explained earlier, the common law is committed to the principle that damages **23–094** must be paid in a lump sum.[275] There are various exceptions to this principle. One exception is provided for in s.32A of the Senior Courts Act 1981. This section applies to an action for personal injuries in which there is proved or admitted to be a chance that at some time in the future the injured person will, as a result of the defendant's tort, develop some serious disease or suffer some serious deterioration in his physical or mental condition. In such a case the court has the power to make a provisional award—that is to say, award damages on the basis that the claimant will not suffer the disease or deterioration but with power to award further damages if and when he does. Obviously, this procedure is only of use in those cases where the risk of deterioration in the claimant's condition is known before judgment. The provisions have been interpreted to require a "clear and severable event" (such as, perhaps, the development of epilepsy following a head injury) rather than a gradual deterioration (such as joint degeneration or arthritis, which are common sequelae of orthopaedic injury).[276] This restriction was regarded as justifiable because an extension to gradual deterioration would vastly increase the number of cases in which provisional awards could be made and introduce a serious measure of uncertainty into the system. It should be noted that s.32A only permits damages to be increased rather than decreased.

---

[269] Senior Courts Act 1981 s.35A; County Courts Act 1984 s.69.

[270] *Cookson v Knowles* [1979] A.C. 556.

[271] *Jefford v Gee* [1970] 2 Q.B. 130; *Cookson v Knowles* [1977] Q.B. 913 (on appeal [1979] A.C. 556). There may be cases in which the award should be at the full, not the half rate: *Ichard v Frangoulis* [1977] 1 W.L.R. 556.

[272] *Pickett v British Rail Engineering Ltd* [1980] A.C. 136.

[273] *Wright v BRB* [1983] 2 A.C. 773.

[274] Arguably this should be the figure (2.5 per cent) used as the assumed rate of return on damages for future pecuniary loss, but it is not: *Laurence v CC Staffordshire* [2000] P.I.Q.R. Q349. The court may abridge the period during which interest is payable if the claimant unjustifiably delays bringing the case to trial.

[275] See para.23–005.

[276] *Willson v Ministry of Defence* [1991] 1 All E.R. 638.

v. Periodical Payments

23–095 **The provision for periodical payments.** In another departure from the principle that damages are to be paid as a lump sum,[277] s.2(1) of the Damages Act 1996 provides: "A court awarding damages in an action for personal injury may, with the consent of the parties, make an order under which the damages are wholly or partly to take the form of periodical payments."

23–096 **It is for the court to decide whether to order damages in the form of periodical payments.** It is a matter for the court to decide whether to order that damages will take the form of periodical payments irrespective of what either (or even both[278]) of the parties may want. Although, the wishes of a properly advised claimant are entitled to considerable weight, at the end of the day the question for the judge is what form of order best meets the claimant's needs and there may be cases in which he is satisfied that "he knows what is best for the claimant better than the claimant himself knows".[279]

23–097 **Order for periodical payments unlikely in high-value cases.** It is very unlikely that any personal injuries judgment will be entirely in the form of a periodical payments order even in respect of future losses. This is particularly true in the case of seriously injured claimants, for such claimants are likely to need capital to obtain equipment and accommodation.

23–098 **The parties are in principle at liberty to settle a dispute on any basis that they wish, including on terms that the defendant make periodical payments.** The court can only make an order for periodical payments if the matter comes before the court for judgment on damages or if a settlement is made on behalf of a minor or person lacking mental capacity, which requires the settlement to be approved by the court. The basic position is that it remains open for persons of full age and understanding to make what settlement they wish, whether it is for a lump sum or periodical payments on some other basis.

23–099 **Court must give indication as to whether it is minded to make an order for periodical payments.** CPR r.41.6 requires the court to indicate as soon as practicable whether it considers it appropriate for damages to be paid by way of periodical payments. Claimants may address this issue in the statement of case and may, indeed, be required to do so.

23–100 **Factors the court must take into account in deciding whether to order that damages be paid by way of periodical payments.** In deciding whether to give judgment for periodical payments the court must "have regard to all the circumstances of the case and in particular the form of award which best meets the claimant's needs".[280] By Practice Direction 41B the relevant factors include:

---

[277] See para.23–005.

[278] But if only for evidential reasons a court is unlikely to go against the wishes of both parties: *Thompstone v Tameside and Glossop Acute Services NHS Trust* [2008] EWCA Civ 5; [2008] 1 W.L.R. 2207 at [102].

[279] *Thompstone v Tameside and Glossop Acute Services NHS Trust* [2008] EWCA Civ 5; [2008] 1 W.L.R. 2207 at [103].

[280] CPR r.41.7.

"(1)   the scale of the annual payments taking into account any deduction for contributory negligence;

(2)   the form of award preferred by the claimant[281] including—

(a)   the reasons for the claimant's preference; and

(b)   the nature of any financial advice received by the claimant when considering the form of award; and

(3)   the form of award preferred by the defendant including the reasons for the defendant's preference."

An order for periodical payments may require payments at different rates in different periods of time. Periodical payments may be "stepped"—that is, made at such and such a rate for one period and at a different rate for another—to reflect anticipated changes in the claimant's circumstances.[282]   **23–101**

Court must be satisfied that the continuity of the payments will be secure. The secure continuity of the payments is obviously the matter of most critical importance and the court can only make an order for periodical payments if it is satisfied that this continuity is reasonably secure.   **23–102**

Indexation. Payments will usually be linked to the Retail Prices Index but in *Thompstone v Tameside and Glossop Acute Services NHS Trust*,[283] a long-term care case, the Court of Appeal approved indexation by reference to an index based on care costs and this will be the norm in the absence of good reason to the contrary.[284] The matter is obviously of great significance if a major element of the damages represents something likely to exceed the general rate of inflation. At least a claimant with a lump sum fund can attempt to gear his investment policy so as to meet higher costs but the periodical payments claimant cannot do this. The fact that the investment risk is taken away from the claimant also eliminates the opportunity for him to gain.   **23–103**

Variation. Periodical payments can be varied because of changed circumstances. As far as deterioration is concerned the law is modelled on the provisional damages regime[285]—that is to say, there is proved or admitted or agreed to be a chance that at some time in the future the injured person will develop some serious disease or suffer some serious deterioration. However, the variation provisions apply equally to the case where there may be some "significant improvement" in his condition,[286] a factor which would obviously influence a claimant in his attitude to the choice between a lump sum and periodical payments. Whether it is deterioration or improvement, the power to vary is confined to changes in the claimant's condition, so it will not cover, for example, changes in the availability or cost of care where these cannot be absorbed by the relevant indexation.   **23–104**

---

[281] In *Freeman v Lockett* [2006] EWHC 102 (QB) a lump sum award of £5.5 million (mostly in respect of future care) was made where the claimant had received expert advice and wished to avoid dependence on public funds.

[282] CPR r.41.8; P.D. 41.

[283] [2008] EWCA Civ 5; [2008] 1 W.L.R. 2207.

[284] [2008] EWCA Civ 5; [2008] 1 W.L.R. 2207 at [100].

[285] See para.23–094.

[286] Damages (Variation of Periodical Payments) Order, SI 2005/841, arts 2 and 9.

vi. *Structured Settlements*[287]

23–105 **Generally.** Structured settlements are a further exception to the principle that damages should be paid as a lump sum. A structured settlement involves damages for future loss being calculated as a lump sum in the traditional way. However, instead of the damages being paid to the claimant as a lump sum, the insurer responsible for compensating the claimant uses the money to purchase an annuity. The annuity provides the claimant with a guaranteed stream of income that (usually) is insulated from the effects of inflation. The duration of the annuity may exceed the claimant's life, in which case the income would go to the claimant's estate.

23–106 **Advantages and disadvantages of structured settlements to claimants.** Structured settlements have several advantages from the perspective of claimants. First, they relieve the claimant of the burden of having to invest the damages and to manage that investment. It is the insurer that is responsible for investing the lump sum and ensuring that it supplies income to the claimant. Secondly, structured settlements provide the claimant with security. The annuity will usually be a life annuity, in which case the income will be guaranteed to the claimant for his life. The insurer carries the risk that the claimant will live for longer than expected. Thirdly, there are tax advantages to structured settlements. If the claimant opts to receive a lump sum and invests it, the income generated by the investment will be taxable in the claimant's hands. However, as a result of arrangements made by the Inland Revenue Service, income flowing from a structured settlement is not taxable. The key downside of structured settlements from the viewpoint of claimants is that the capital is locked up in the annuity. The flexibility that a lump sum payment affords to claimants is lost in a structured settlement.

23–107 **Advantages and disadvantages of structured settlements to defendants.** Since claimants make a tax saving by opting for a structured settlement instead of a lump sum award the insurer should theoretically be able to negotiate a discount on the sum that would be required for a conventional lump sum settlement. In other words, the idea is that the liability of the insurer will be reduced. Downsides for the insurer include the risk, in the case of a life annuity, that the claimant will live for longer than expected.

G. Damages for Destruction of or Damage to Property[288]

23–108 As we have seen, the basic principle governing the assessment of damages is that there should be *restitutio in integrum*,[289] and in cases of loss of or damage to property this principle can be more fully applied than in cases of personal injury. It is, in fact, the dominant rule to which the subsidiary rules which follow must

---

[287] Lewis, *Structured Settlements* (1993); Law Com. No.224.
[288] For the measure of damages in conversion, see para.18–051.
[289] See para.23–010.

conform.[290] In working out these subsidiary rules the courts have been mainly concerned with cases involving ships, but the rules are the same in Admiralty and under the common law.[291]

i. Destruction of Chattels

The general principle. Where a chattel is totally destroyed as a result of the defendant's tort the normal measure of damage is its value at the time and place of the destruction. In principle the claimant is generally entitled to such a sum of money as would enable him to purchase a replacement in the market at the prices prevailing at the date of destruction[292] or as soon thereafter as is reasonable.[293] Where no precise equivalent is available the claimant may be allowed a recovery that exceeds the amount he could have obtained by selling the chattel,[294] but the cost of producing an exact replacement will be refused where it is well in excess of the value of what was destroyed and a reasonable substitute is available.[295]

23–109

Consequential loss is recoverable. The claimant may recover damages for consequential loss that are not too remote, such as the reasonable cost of hire of a substitute until a replacement can be bought.[296] When the chattel destroyed was used by the claimant in the course of his business then loss of business profits may be taken into account. Speaking of destruction of a ship, Lord Wright said: "The true rule seems to be that the measure of damages in such cases is the value of the ship to her owner as a going concern at the time and place of the loss. In assessing that value regard must naturally be had to her pending engagements, either profitable or the reverse."[297]

23–110

Avoiding double counting. Care must be taken to avoid awarding damages twice over. The market value of a profit-earning chattel such as a ship will normally recognise that the chattel will be used in a profit-earning capacity. It follows that the actual loss of prospective freights or other profits cannot, therefore, simply be added to that market value.[298] That would result in overcompensation. It is necessary to recognise in the assessment of damages of the difference between the profit-earning potential of a ship without any engagement but with the chance

23–111

---

[290] *Liesbosch Dredger v SS Edison* [1933] A.C. 449 at 463 per Lord Wright.

[291] *Admiralty Commissioners v SS Susquehanna* [1926] A.C. 655 at 661 per Viscount Dunedin; *Beechwood Birmingham Ltd v Hoyer Group UK Ltd* [2010] EWCA Civ 647; [2011] 1 All E.R. (Comm) 460 at [47].

[292] *Liesbosch Dredger v SS Edison* [1933] A.C. 449. In *Smith Kline & French Laboratories Ltd v Long* [1989] 1 W.L.R. 1 (a case of deprivation by deceit) the claimants could themselves produce a replacement at less than market cost, because with drugs most of the cost is attributable to research and development but were nevertheless entitled to recover the market value.

[293] The price the claimant paid for the article is not decisive for he may have got a bargain: *Dominion Mosaics and Tile Co Ltd v Trafalgar Trucking Co Ltd* [1990] 2 All E.R. 246.

[294] *Clyde Navigation Trustees v Bowring Steamship Co Ltd* 1929 S.C. 715. Cf. *Southampton Container Terminals Ltd v Schiffahrtsgesellschaft "Hansa Australia" MBH & Co (The Maersk Colombo)* [2001] EWCA Civ 717; [2001] 2 Lloyd's Rep. 275

[295] *Ucktos v Mazzetta* [1956] 1 Lloyd's Rep. 209.

[296] *Moore v DER Ltd* [1971] 1 W.L.R. 1476.

[297] *Dredger Liesbosch v SS Edison* [1933] A.C. 449 at 463–464. See also *Jones v Port of London Authority* [1954] 1 Lloyd's Rep. 489 (lorry).

[298] *The Llanover* [1947] P. 80.

or probability of making a profit, which will be reflected in the market value, and the actual profits that would have been made by the claimant's ship had it not been destroyed.[299] Nevertheless, if a ship is actually under charter at the time of her loss or has charters that would have commenced shortly thereafter, the loss of those charters may be allowed in some cases[300] as damages for loss of use of the ship from the time of its destruction until the time when it could reasonably be replaced.[301] In deciding whether or not these damages may be added to the market value, the manner in which the market value itself has been determined is of critical importance. If it is determined on the basis that the ship was in any case virtually certain of profitable employment, then nothing may be added for the loss of actual charters,[302] but if the market value does not assume the full employment of the ship then the loss of actual charters must be taken into account.

ii.   Damage to Chattels

23–112   **The general principle.** Where a chattel has been damaged the normal measure of damages is the amount by which its value has been diminished. The diminution in value will usually be ascertained by reference to the cost of repair,[303] simply because that is usually the only practical way to do it: there is a market in two-year-old cars of a certain type and mileage, there are no markets in such cars with dented wings or broken mirrors, we just assume that a buyer will reduce his price by the cost of repair. However, it is important to bear in mind that the loss is the diminution in value, not the cost of repair. The cost of repair is simply evidence of the diminution in value.[304]

23–113   **The consequences of the fact that the cost of repair is merely evidence of the diminution in value.** The fact that the cost of repair is of merely evidential value has several important consequences. First, the fact that the claimant can have a chattel repaired at reduced or no cost does not mean that there is no compensable loss.[305] Secondly, where the claimant has had a chattel repaired at unreasonable cost the reason why he cannot cover the cost of repair is because they do not represent the diminution in value of the chattel.[306] Thirdly, it does not matter that the repairs have not been carried out at the date of the trial,[307] or even that they are never carried out at all,[308] as where a ship is lost from other causes before the

---

[299] For this distinction, see *The Philadelphia* [1917] P. 101 at 108 per Swinfen Eady LJ.

[300] *The Kate* [1899] P. 165; *The Racine* [1906] P. 273; *The Philadelphia* [1917] P. 101.

[301] See the explanation of Greer LJ in *The Arpad* [1934] P. 189 at 217.

[302] *The Llanover* [1947] P. 80.

[303] *Coles v Hetherton* [2013] EWCA Civ 1704 at [27]. This is of course the reasonable cost of repair. Where the claimant does repairs "in house" he may be entitled to a sum for overheads as well as direct labour costs but what is relevant in causation terms may be a difficult question: *Ulsterbus Ltd v Donnelly* [1982] 13 N.I.J.B.

[304] *Coles v Hetherton* [2013] EWCA Civ 1704 at [28].

[305] *Coles v Hetherton* [2013] EWCA Civ 1704 at [29].

[306] *Coles v Hetherton* [2013] EWCA Civ 1704 at [32].

[307] *The Kingsway* [1918] P. 344.

[308] *Coles v Hetherton* [2013] EWCA Civ 1704 at [27].

repairs are done.[309] On the other hand, if a ship is damaged while on its way to the breaker's yard it is doubtful that the cost of repairing the ship could be recovered, for that cost would not necessarily represent the true reduction in the value of the ship. All that could be recovered would be the diminution, if any, in the value of the ship as scrap.[310] Fourthly, the fact that the cost of repairing the chattel exceeds its total value does not mean that more than its value can be recovered.

Loss of the use of the chattel while it is being repaired. The claimant is entitled to damages where the damage to the chattel deprived him of its use for a period of time. This is so even where he is provided with a substitute by his insurer without further charge.[311] In *The Mediana*[312] Lord Halsbury LC was of the opinion that the fact that the claimant would not have actually used the chattel was no bar to a claim for loss of use:[313]

23–114

> "Supposing a person took away a chair out of my room and kept it for twelve months, could anybody say that you had a right to diminish the damages by shewing that I did not usually sit in that chair, or that there were plenty of other chairs in the room. The proposition so nakedly stated appears to me to be absurd?"

How should the loss of use be valued? The damages for loss of use of the chair in Lord Halsbury's example do not vary according to how often he sits in it.[314] The suitable measure may vary from case to case,[315] but a calculation based on the daily cost of running a substitute plus depreciation may be suitable,[316] especially where a substitute is on stand-by. In the last resort the claimant is entitled to interest on the capital value of the chattel for the period during which it is out of use plus expenses thrown away and depreciation.[317]

Loss of profit that would have been made from the chattel. In the case of, for example, a ship that turns a profit the normal measure of damages will be the loss of profits calculated at the freight rates prevailing during the relevant period or, where the hire of a substitute is a reasonable way of avoiding such losses, the cost of that hire.[318] However, the measure based upon prevailing freight rates may in

23–115

---

[309] *The York* [1929] P. 178 at 184–185 per Scrutton LJ; *Dimond v Lovell* [2000] 2 W.L.R. 1121 at 1140.

[310] See *The London Corp* [1935] P. 70 at 77–78, where Greer LJ seems to have been in two minds on this point.

[311] *Coles v Hetherton* [2013] EWCA Civ 1704 at [46].

[312] [1900] A.C. 113.

[313] [1900] A.C. 113 at 117. See also *Attorney General v Blake* [2001] 1 A.C. 268 at 278; *Dimond v Lovell* [2000] 2 W.L.R. 1121 at 1139.

[314] *Voaden v Champion (The Baltic Surveyor and the Timbuktu)* [2002] EWCA Civ 89; [2002] 1 Lloyd's Rep. 623.

[315] In *Admiralty Commissioners v SS Susquehanna* [1926] A.C. 655 at 661 Viscount Dunedin said that these are jury-type questions on which no rigid rules are possible. Cf. *West Midlands Travel Ltd v Aviva Insurance UK Ltd* [2013] EWCA Civ 887; [2004] R.T.R. 10 at [6].

[316] *The Marpessa* [1907] A.C. 241; *Admiralty Commissioners v SS Susquehanna* [1926] A.C. 655; *The Hebridean Coast* [1961] A.C. 545.

[317] *West Midlands Travel Ltd v Aviva Insurance Ltd* [2013] EWCA Civ 887; [2014] R.T.R. 10.

[318] If a substitute is hired and the claimant is thereby enabled to make a greater profit than he would have done if his own chattel had never been damaged, credit for this must be given: *The World Beauty* [1969] P. 12; reversed without affecting this point: [1970] P. 144.

the actual case be too high or too low. It will be too high if the ship was operating at a loss at the time of the damage[319] and too low if the damage prevented the ship from fulfilling an actual charter already entered into at favourable rates.[320]

23–116   **Cost of hiring a substitute.** Where the claimant has hired a chattel to replace that which was damaged he will be entitled to damages for the cost of the hire.[321] It was held in *Giles v Thompson*[322] that where a substitute is hired it is no answer to a claim for the cost of hire that the claimant's obligation to pay for the hire is contingent upon recovery from the defendant. It was also said in that case that the fact of hire (and not merely its quantum or level) must be reasonably undertaken.[323] This may mean that if C has two cars for his sole use, C cannot recover the cost of hiring a replacement when one is damaged.

iii.   Land and Fixtures

23–117   **Generally.** The principles that have been considered thus far have been worked out in the context of damage to chattels. The rules governing the award of damages in respect of damage caused to land and buildings are not fundamentally different though their application must take account of the different character of land and fixtures thereto. For example, a claimant is more likely to recover the cost of reinstatement although the cost of reinstatement exceeds the value of the property where the property is a building than a chattel. Where a factory is burned down it may be commercially sensible to rebuild immediately on the same site rather than to move the business to a different location.[324] Ultimately, however, the reasonableness of the proposed expenditure is the issue so that where the cost of reinstatement is out of all proportion to the diminution in value the latter will be taken as the measure of damages.[325] Again, the court may allow a degree of reinstatement but refuse the claimant the extra cost of precise and meticulous restoration that will not increase the utility of the property.[326] The claimant may not claim the cost of repairs that exceed diminution in value where he has no intention of having them carried out.[327]

23–118   **Specific contexts.** What has been said above represents a broad principle which may be departed from in particular contexts. For example, the usual measure of damages for negligent survey (where the action will commonly lie concurrently

---

[319]   *The Bodlewell* [1907] P. 286. See also *SS Strathfillan v SS Ikala* [1929] A.C. 196.
[320]   *The Argentino* (1889) 14 App. Cas. 519.
[321]   *Coles v Hetherton* [2013] EWCA Civ 1704 at [46].
[322]   [1994] 1 A.C. 142.
[323]   [1994] 1 A.C. 142 at 167.
[324]   See *Harbutt's "Plasticine" Ltd v Wayne Tank and Pump Co Ltd* [1970] 1 Q.B. 447 at 467, 472, pointing out that the market in land and buildings is more limited and inflexible than in, e.g. second-hand cars.
[325]   *Jones v Gooday* (1841) 8 M. & W. 146; *Lodge Holes Colliery Co Ltd v Wednesbury Corp* [1908] A.C. 323.
[326]   *Ward v Cannock Chase DC* [1986] Ch. 546.
[327]   *Perry v Sidney Phillips & Son* [1982] 1 W.L.R. 1297; *Hole & Son (Sayers Common) v Harrisons of Thurnscoe* [1973] 1 Lloyd's Rep. 345.

in contract and tort) is the difference between the price paid by the claimant and the actual market value of the property, not the cost of putting the property in the condition described in the report.[328]

Consequential loss. Consequential losses, such as loss of rent or profits, may also be recovered.[329]

23–119

iv.   The Date of Assessment

The rapid inflation of the 1970s brought into prominence, particularly in the context of damage to buildings, the question of the date as at which damages were to be assessed, for a judgment representing the cost of repair at the time of the wrong, even with interest, would be unlikely to be sufficient to cover the work when the action came on for trial.[330] While there may still be a general rule that damages for tort are to be assessed as at the time when the tort is committed,[331] that rule is subject to exceptions and in a repair case the applicable principle is that the date for assessment of damages is the time when, having regard to all relevant circumstances, repairs can first reasonably be undertaken,[332] and in determining this question it is proper to pay regard to the claimant's financial position.[333]

23–120

v.   Benefits Received as a Result of the Tort

Whether it is a case of damage or destruction the defendant cannot rely on the fact that the claimant is entitled to claim on an insurance policy.[334] Indeed, many marine property damage claims will be brought by subrogated loss insurers and that can only happen if the claimant retains his right of action after claiming on his policy. That accords with the law on personal injuries.[335] That analogy also points to recovery where funds to replace or repair the goods are provided as, say, an act of kindness by a relative.

23–121

---

[328] *Perry v Sidney Phillips & Son* [1982] 1 W.L.R. 1297; *Patel v Hooper & Jackson* [1999] 1 W.L.R. 1792.

[329] *Rust v Victoria Graving Dock Co* (1887) 36 Ch. D. 113; *Dodd Properties Ltd v Canterbury CC* [1980] 1 W.L.R. 433 For *mesne* profits, see para.14–034.

[330] In *Dodd Properties Ltd v Canterbury CC* [1980] 1 W.L.R. 433 the cost of repair when the damage was done in 1968 was £10,817. At judgment, 10 years later, it was £30,327. Interest on a judgment at the 1968 cost would have amounted to about £5,500.

[331] *Miliangos v George Frank (Textiles) Ltd* [1976] A.C. 443 at 468.

[332] *Dodd Properties Ltd v Canterbury CC* [1980] 1 W.L.R. 433.

[333] *Dodd Properties Ltd v Canterbury CC* [1980] 1 W.L.R. 433; *Alcoa Minerals of Jamaica Incv Broderick* [2002] 1 A.C. 371.

[334] *Coles v Hetherton* [2013] EWCA Civ 1704 at [36].

[335] See para.23–086.

2. OTHER REMEDIES

A. Injunctive Relief

i. General Principles

23–122 **Definition and general principles.** Defined generally, an injunction is an order restraining the commission or continuance of some wrongful act, or the continuance of some wrongful omission. Originally only the Court of Chancery could issue an injunction, but now other courts may too in any case in which it appears to be "just and convenient" for one to be granted.[336] This does not mean that the court has a free hand to restrain conduct of which it disapproves. Ordinarily, the claimant must have some cause of action (whether for a tort or in protection of some legal or equitable right) against the defendant before an objective can be granted, for if the law were otherwise "every judge would need to be issued with a portable palm tree".[337] However, the Attorney-General has a "legal right" to bring proceedings in support of the criminal law.

23–123 **Torts for which injunctive relief can be obtained.** Injunctions are generally sought against such torts as nuisance, trespass, passing off or interference with contract but there is no theoretical reason why an injunction should not be issued to restrain the repetition or continuation of a tort of any kind. The circumstances in which injunctive relief may be granted depends somewhat on the legal context in which it is sought. What follows here is a general discussion of injunctive relief. The availability of injunctive relief in relation to certain specific torts has already been considered at appropriate points in this book.

23–124 **Injunctive relief is in the discretion of the court.** Like other equitable remedies, the issue of an injunction is in the discretion of the court and the remedy cannot be demanded as of right. However, in the context of prohibitory injunctions (i.e. those ordering the defendant to desist from wrongful conduct) it would be wrong to think that a claimant who makes out interference with his rights will face any particular difficulty in getting one. For example, a landowner is prima facie entitled to an injunction to restrain trespass by the defendant in parking his vehicle on the land[338] or running hounds across it[339] or swinging a crane jib through the air above it[340] even though he cannot produce evidence of any particular harm. Similarly, an occupier is prima facie entitled to an injunction to restrain a nuisance that is affecting his land.[341] This means that in these situations the burden lies with the defendant to show that an injunction should not be granted.[342] It is true that an injunction will not be granted where damages are an

---

[336] Senior Courts Act 1981 s.37; County Courts Act 1984 s.38.
[337] *CC Kent v V* [1983] Q.B. 34 at 45 per Donaldson LJ.
[338] *Patel v WH Smith (Eziot) Ltd* [1987] 1 W.L.R. 853. See *John Trenberth Ltd v National Westminster Bank Ltd* (1979) 39 P. & C.R. 104.
[339] *League against Cruel Sports Ltd v Scott* [1986] Q.B. 240.
[340] *Anchor Brewhouse Developments v Berkley House (Docklands Developments)* (1987) 284 E.G. 625.
[341] *Coventry v Lawrence* [2014] UKSC 13; [2014] 2 W.L.R. 433 at [100].
[342] *Coventry v Lawrence* [2014] UKSC 13; [2014] 2 W.L.R. 433 at [121].

adequate remedy[343] but this does not mean that the defendant who is willing to pay can demand to buy out the claimant's rights. In *Shelfer v City of London Electric Lighting Co* the operation of the defendant's engines seriously interfered with the enjoyment of the premises of which the claimant was occupier. Granting an injunction, Lindley LJ commented that the Court of Chancery had rejected the notion that the legislature, in allowing the award of damages in lieu of an injunction, "intended to turn that Court into a tribunal for legalising wrongful acts; or in other words, the Court has always protested against the notion that it ought to allow a wrong to continue simply because the wrongdoer is able and willing to pay for the injury he may inflict".[344] Where the injury to the claimant is trivial[345] or of a very temporary character the court may content itself with awarding nominal damages. However, an injunction will not be withheld simply because granting it will inflict more harm on the defendant than the continuance of the activity concerned will cause to the claimant.

Acquiescence. An injunction will be refused if the claimant has acquiesced in the defendant's infringement of his legal rights;[346] but mere delay is not acquiescence—the claimant must have induced the defendant to believe he does not object.[347]   **23–125**

Public interest in the continuation of the defendant's activity. A controversial matter has been the significance of the interest that the public at large may have in the continuance of the defendant's activity. The law in this regard has recently undergone a significant change. In the past it was thought that it was inappropriate to withhold an injunction simply because the wrongdoer's activity was of benefit to the public. The thought was that refusing to grant an injunction on this basis would involve judicial expropriation of the claimant's rights.[348] In *Coventry v Lawrence*, however, it was held that the effect of granting an injunction on the public was something that should be taken into account.[349]   **23–126**

ii.   Interim Injunctions

Generally. An injunction that is issued at the conclusion of a trial upon the merits is known as a perpetual injunction, but an injunction may be issued provisionally until the hearing of the case on the merits, when it is known as an interim injunction. The court on an application for an interim injunction does not profess to anticipate the final outcome of the action and since it is always possible that when the case actually comes to trial the defendant may be found to have been in the right after all, the claimant may be required, as a condition of the grant of an interim injunction, to give an undertaking in damages—that is, to undertake to pay damages to the defendant for any loss suffered by him while the injunction   **23–127**

---

[343] *London and Blackwall Ry Co v Cross* (1886) 31 Ch. D. 354 at 369 per Lindley LJ.
[344] [1895] 1 Ch. 287 at 315–316.
[345] *Llandudno U.D.C. v Woods* [1899] 2 Ch. 705; *Behrens v Richards* [1905] 2 Ch. 614; *Armstrong v Sheppard and Short Ltd* [1959] 2 Q.B. 384.
[346] *Armstrong v Sheppard and Short Ltd* [1959] 2 Q.B. 384.
[347] *Jones v Stones* [1999] 1 W.L.R. 1739.
[348] *Shelfer v City of London Electric Lighting Co* [1895] 1 Ch. 287 at 316.
[349] [2014] UKSC 13; [2014] 2 W.L.R. 433 at [124].

was in force, should it prove to have been wrongly issued.[350] In practice the parties often treat the application for an interim injunction as the trial of the action. In cases of great urgency the claimant can obtain an interim injunction in the absence of the defendant which will remain in force for a few days, until there can be a hearing.

23–128   **American Cyanamid.** The principles on which the court acts on an application for an interim injunction are to be found in *American Cyanamid Co v Ethicon Ltd*.[351] A claimant need not establish a prima facie case but merely that there is a "serious question" to be tried.[352] If so, the court must then decide whether the balance of convenience lies in favour of granting or refusing interim relief. The court should consider all the circumstances of the case, particularly whether damages are likely to be an adequate remedy for the claimant, whether the claimant's undertaking in damages gives the defendant adequate protection if the claimant fails at the trial and whether the preservation of the status quo is important enough to demand an injunction. The relative strength of each party's case is only to be considered when the other considerations leave the balance of convenience "even".

23–129   **Defamation cases.** Interim injunctions in defamation cases have always been exceedingly rare because of the public interest in freedom of expression and the fact that, historically, the question of libel or no libel was peculiarly one for the jury.[353] Under s.12 of the Human Rights Act 1998 no interim injunction is to be granted that might affect freedom of expression unless the court is satisfied that the applicant is "likely" to establish at trial that publication would not be allowed, which is a higher threshold than that prescribed by *American Cyanamid*. A claimant will be "likely" to establish at trial that publication would not be permitted if he "will probably ('more likely than not') succeed at the trial".[354]

iii.   Mandatory Injunction

23–130   Most injunctions are prohibitory—that is to say, they forbid the defendant from persisting in his wrongful conduct. But the court has power also to grant a mandatory injunction by virtue of which the defendant is actually ordered to take positive action to rectify the consequences of what he has already done. In the past, it used to be thought that these types of injunctions were governed by quite different rules. It is now clear that they are not.[355] The central issue in determining whether an injunction should be granted is what the practical

---

[350] But an undertaking in damages will not normally be required where the Crown or a local authority seeks an injunction in aid of the criminal law: *Kirklees MBC v Wickes Building Supplies Ltd* [1993] A.C. 227.

[351] [1975] A.C. 396.

[352] The same test applies whether or not the claimant is seeking a mandatory or prohibitory interim injunction: *National Commercial Bank Jamaica Ltd v Olint Corpn Ltd* [2009] UKPC 16; [2009] 1 W.L.R. 1405 at [20].

[353] *Coulson v Coulson* (1887) 3 T.L.R. 846; *Bonnard v Perryman* [1891] 2 Ch. 269.

[354] *Cream Holdings Ltd v Banerjee* [2004] UKHL 44; [2005] 1 A.C. 253 at [22].

[355] *National Commercial Bank Jamaica Ltd v Olint Corpn Ltd* [2009] UKPC 16; [2009] 1 W.L.R. 1405 at [20].

consequences of granting it or not granting it will be, and that nothing turns on whether an injunction should be classified as prohibitive or mandatory.

iv. *Quia Timet Injunction*

Injunctions are normally issued only when a tort has already been committed, and, in the case of torts actionable only on proof of damage, it is premature for the claimant to seek an injunction before any damage has actually occurred. Where, however, the conduct of the defendant is such that, if it is allowed to continue, substantial damage to the claimant is almost bound to occur, the claimant may bring a "*quia timet*" action—that is, an action for an injunction to prevent an apprehended legal wrong.[356] The existence of the court's power to grant a *quia timet* injunction is undoubted,[357] but it is not often exercised, for the claimant must show both a near certainty that damage will occur[358] and that it is imminent.[359] And even then an injunction will not be issued to compel the defendant to do something which he is willing to do without the intervention of the court.[360]

23–131

v. *Damages in Lieu of Injunction*

Lord Cairns's Act. By Lord Cairns's Act 1858[361] the Court of Chancery was enabled to award damages either in addition to, or in substitution for, an injunction, and this jurisdiction now applies to the High Court, the power being contained in s.50 of the Senior Courts Act 1981. Such damages are given in full satisfaction not only for all damage already done in the past, but also for all future damages which may occur if the injunction is not granted.[362] To say that damages may be awarded "in substitution for" an injunction is apt to mislead for it is clear that the power is not confined to cases in which the Court of Chancery would have granted the equitable relief prior to Lord Cairns's Act.[363] The power arises whenever the facts of the cases are such as to call into play the exercise of the court's general equitable discretion whether or not to grant an injunction.[364]

23–132

---

[356] *Redland Bricks Ltd v Morris* [1970] A.C. 652 at 664 per Lord Upjohn.

[357] For an example, see *Torquay Hotel Co Ltd v Cousins* [1969] 2 Ch. 106 at 120 per Stamp J.

[358] *Attorney-General v Nottingham Corp* [1904] 1 Ch. 673; *Redland Bricks Ltd v Morris* [1970] A.C. 652.

[359] *Lemos v Kennedy Leigh Developments* (1961) 105 S.J. 178. Cf. *Hooper v Rogers* [1975] Ch. 43 where the view is expressed that there is no fixed standard of certainty or imminence.

[360] *Bridlington Relay Ltd v Yorkshire Electricity Board* [1965] Ch. 436.

[361] Chancery Amendment Act 1858 (21 & 22 Vict. c.27).

[362] *Jaggard v Sawyer* [1995] 1 W.L.R. 269.

[363] *Isenberg v East India House Estate Co* (1863) 3 D. & G.J. & S. 263; *City of London Brewery Co v Tennant* (1873) 9 L.R. Ch. App. 212; *Wroth v Tyler* [1974] Ch. 30 (substitution for specific performance). The contrary is perhaps implied by Lord Upjohn in *Redland Bricks Ltd v Morris* [1970] A.C. 652.

[364] *Hooper v Rogers* [1975] Ch. 43 at 48; *Jaggard v Sawyer* [1995] 1 W.L.R. 269 at 285; *Marcic v Thames Water Utilities Ltd (No.2)* [2001] 4 All E.R. 326 at [11].

Damages may be awarded in substitution for an injunction even in a *quia timet* action.[365] This is, in effect, to allow the defendant to purchase the right to commit a tort in the future.

23–133 **Circumstances in which only damages in lieu should be awarded.** It would normally be right to refuse an injunction and to grant damages in lieu thereof if the following four conditions are satisfied: (1) it would be oppressive to the defendant; (2) the injury to the claimant's rights is small; (3) the injury is capable of being estimated in money; and (4) the injury is one that can be adequately compensated by a money payment.[366] "Laid down [over] 100 years ago [this] check-list has stood the test of time; but it needs to be remembered that it is only a working rule and does not purport to be an exhaustive statement of the circumstances in which damages may be awarded instead of an injunction."[367] This test should not be applied mechanically and does not fetter the exercise of the court's discretion.[368] Thus, it may be appropriate to grant an injunction even if this test is satisfied.[369]

There may be considerable advantage in awarding a claimant damages only where his probable future damage is likely to be much less than the cost to the defendant of preventing it, provided, of course, that the defendant has acted honestly and without the deliberate intention of hurrying on the work so as to present the court with a fait accompli. Otherwise there is a danger that proceedings for injunctions will be used by unscrupulous claimants, not to protect their rights, but to extort from defendants sums of money greater in value than any damage that is likely to occur.[370]

23–134 **The measure of damages.** There is little authority on the measure of damages in lieu of an injunction, but the Act also allows the grant of damages in lieu of a decree of specific performance of a contract, and in that context it has been held that the principles of assessment are those that apply generally at common law.[371] The same would seem to be true of damages in lieu of an injunction.[372]

B. Specific Restitution of Property

23–135 Orders for the specific restitution of property may be for the recovery of land or for the recovery of chattels. But whether it is restitution of land or of goods that is sought, the remedies are confined to cases where one person is in possession of

---

[365] *Leeds Industrial Co-operative Society Ltd v Slack* [1924] A.C. 851; *Hooper v Rogers* [1975] Ch. 43.

[366] *Shelfer v City of London Electric Lighting Co* [1895] 1 Ch. 287 at 322 per Smith LJ.

[367] *Jaggard v Sawyer* [1995] 1 W.L.R. 269 at 287 per Millett LJ. The check-list is based on the assumption that the claimant wants an injunction and the defendant resists it. It may not be suitable in a case where the claimant "only wants money" (Lindley LJ in *Shelfer v City of London Electric Lighting Co* [1895] 1 Ch. 287 at 317).

[368] *Coventry v Lawrence* [2014] UKSC 13; [2014] 2 W.L.R. 433 at [123].

[369] *Coventry v Lawrence* [2014] UKSC 13; [2014] 2 W.L.R. 433 at [123].

[370] *Colls v Home and Colonial Stores Ltd* [1904] A.C. 179 at 193 per Lord Macnaughten.

[371] *Johnson v Agnew* [1980] A.C. 367.

[372] *Jaggard v Sawyer* [1995] 1 W.L.R. 269.

another's property and this limits them to torts infringing such possession. They have been considered at appropriate points elsewhere in this book.[373]

---

[373] See paras 14–030, 18–056.

CHAPTER 24

DEATH IN RELATION TO TORT

The death of a person may affect tortious liability in two ways: **24–001**

1. It may extinguish liability for a tort. Here the question for discussion is: "If D commits a tort against C (not involving C's death), and either party dies, does C's right of action survive?"
2. Death may create liability in tort. Here the question is: "If D causes C's death, is that a tort either (a) against C, so that C's personal representatives can sue D for it or (b) against persons who have an interest in the continuance of C's life, e.g. C's spouse or children?"

1. Death as Extinguishing Liability

The position at common law. At common law the general rule was that the death **24–002** of either party extinguished any existing cause of action in tort—*actio personalis moritur cum persona.*[1] Actions in contract generally escaped the rule, and so too did those in which property had been appropriated by a deceased person and added to his own estate

---

[1] For the historical background, see Winfield (1929) 29 Col. L.R. 239.

A. Survival of Causes of Action

24–003   **The common law rule is overturned.** It was not until 1934 that the defects of the law were forced on the attention of the legislature by the growth of motor traffic and its accompanying toll of accidents. If a negligent driver was killed in the accident which he himself had caused, nothing was recoverable from his estate or his insurer by those whom he had injured. Accordingly, the Law Reform (Miscellaneous Provisions) Act 1934 was passed to provide generally for the survival of causes of action in tort.

24–004   **Actions survive the death of either party, save for actions in defamation.** By s.1(1) of the Act, all causes of action subsisting against or vested in any person on his death, except causes of action for defamation, now survive against, or, as the case may be, for the benefit of, his estate. The exclusion of actions for defamation from the 1934 Act was not so much the result of a conscious decision of policy that such actions should not survive death as of a desire to avoid potentially controversial areas and deal with the urgent issue of deaths in road accidents.[2]

B.   "Subsisting" Action

24–005   It may happen that a cause of action is not complete against a wrongdoer until after he has in fact died, as, for example, where damage is the gist of the action and no damage is suffered until after the death of the wrongdoer. In such a case no cause of action subsists against the wrongdoer at the date of his death and there is nothing to survive against his estate, so that, were there no provision in the Act to deal with the point, the person suffering the damage would be deprived of his remedy. Section 1(4) provides, however, that where damage has been suffered as a result of a wrongful act in respect of which a cause of action would have subsisted had the wrongdoer not died before or at the same time as the damage was suffered, there shall be deemed to have subsisted against him before his death such cause of action as would have subsisted if he had died after the damage had been suffered. Thus, if on facts similar to those of *Donoghue v Stevenson*,[3] D, the negligent manufacturer of noxious ginger beer, dies before the ultimate consumer, C, suffers damage from drinking it, C's cause of action against D's estate is preserved as it is regarded as arising before D's death.[4]

---

[2] See the Faulks Committee Report (1975) Cmnd.5909, Ch.15.

[3] [1932] A.C. 562, see para.5–015.

[4] A right to claim contribution from another tortfeasor is not a claim in tort and survives death without reference to the 1934 Act: *Ronex Properties Ltd v John Laing Construction Ltd* [1983] Q.B. 398.

C.   Damages Recoverable

Situation where the injured party dies. Where the injured party dies, the damages recoverable for the benefit of the estate may not include exemplary damages.[5] Nor may the award include damages for loss of income in respect of any period after the victim's death.[6] It is further provided that where death has been caused by the act or omission that gives rise to the cause of action, damages are to be calculated without reference to any loss[7] or gain[8] to the deceased's estate consequent on his death, except that funeral expenses may be included.[9] Where, however, the death of the injured party is unconnected with the act or omission that gives rise to the cause of action, it appears that substantial damages can be recovered even though the deceased himself, had he been alive when the action was brought, would only have recovered nominal damages.[10] The damages that the estate may recover include those for non-pecuniary items (such as pain and suffering and loss of amenity) during any significant[11] interval between injury and death. Also recoverable are loss of earnings suffered during this period plus any medical expenses. Damages are also available in respect of gratuitously provided services, including care provided by a hospice.[12] The court will award a reasonable sum in respect of such damages, and may order that they be held on trust for the carer or paid directly to him. Subject to any such orders, damages recovered form part of the deceased's estate, are available for payment of his debts and pass under his will or upon his intestacy. The Law Reform (Contributory Negligence) Act 1945 applies to claims by estates.

Situation where the tortfeasor dies. When the tortfeasor dies, the ordinary measure of damages applies in an action brought against his estate.

24–006

24–007

D.   Limitation

Generally, the ordinary law for the limitation of actions applies, whether the action is brought against or for the benefit of the estate.[13]

24–008

---

[5] It is hard to see why the death of the victim should bar punishment of the surviving wrongdoer, while at the same time the death of the wrongdoer does not (apparently) bar civil punishment of his estate. The Law Commission has recommended the correction of this: Law Com. No.247 at [5.275], [5.278].

[6] Law Reform (Miscellaneous Provisions) Act 1934 s.1(2)(a).

[7] For example, cessation of an annuity or life interest.

[8] For example, insurance money.

[9] Section 1(2)(c). A living claimant whose life expectancy has been shortened cannot claim "anticipatory" funeral expenses: *Watson v Cakebread Robey Ltd* [2009] EWHC 1695 (QB).

[10] *Otter v Church, Adams, Tatham & Co* [1953] Ch. 280. This was an action in contract for professional negligence, which survived at common law. It is submitted, however, that the result would have been the same even if the claimant had needed to rely upon the 1934 Act.

[11] Not momentary pain which is effectively part of the process of death itself: *Hicks v CC South Yorkshire* [1992] 1 All E.R. 65. Cf. *Beesley v New Century Group Ltd* [2008] EWHC 3033 (QB) (£72,000 for 17 months of suffering).

[12] *Drake v Foster Wheeler Ltd* [2010] EWHC 2004 (QB); [2011] 1 All E.R. 63.

[13] See para.26–098. But under the Limitation Act 1980 s.11(5), a new, fixed period of limitation arises where the victim dies during the period that commenced with his injury.

2. Death as Creating Liability

A. Position at Common Law

24–009 At common law, death could not give rise to a cause of action in other persons, even where they were dependent on the deceased. This rule was derived from the decision of Lord Ellenborough in *Baker v Bolton*[14] that "in a civil court the death of a human being could not be complained of as an injury".[15] *Baker v Bolton* was only a ruling at Nisi Prius, not a single authority was cited and the report is extremely brief, but it was nevertheless upheld in later cases and the seal of approval placed upon it by the House of Lords in *Admiralty Commissioners v SS Amerika*.[16] Long before that case, however, the legislature had intervened.

B. Fatal Accidents Act 1976[17]

24–010 **Provision for an action for dependants.** The development of railways in England led to a great upsurge in the number of accidents, fatal and non-fatal, and this made a change in the law imperative for, while those who survived an accident could recover substantial damages, the dependants of those who were killed could recover nothing. Accordingly, in 1846, the Fatal Accidents Act, otherwise known as Lord Campbell's Act, was passed and virtually overturned the common law in so far as those dependants who were specified in the Act and in later legislation were concerned.[18] The present statute is the Fatal Accidents Act 1976, which consolidates the earlier legislation. The Act provides that whenever the death of a person is caused by the wrongful act, neglect or default[19] of another, such as would (if death had not ensued) have entitled the injured person to sue and recover damages in respect thereof, then the person who would have been liable if death had not ensued shall be liable to an action for damages on behalf of the dependants, notwithstanding the death of the person injured.[20]

24–011 **Dependants.** Dependants encompass: (1) the spouse or former spouse of the deceased; (2) the civil partner or former civil partner of the deceased; (3) a person who was living as the spouse or civil partner of the deceased, in the same household, immediately before the date of the death and had been so living for at

---

[14] *Baker v Bolton* (1808) 1 Camp. 493; 170 E.R. 1033 (the claimant's wife had been killed in a stagecoach accident).

[15] The rule in *Baker v Bolton* does not apply where the claimant's cause of action is founded upon contract: *Jackson v Watson* [1909] 2 K.B. 193.

[16] *Admiralty Commissioners v SS Amerika* [1917] A.C. 38.

[17] Law Commission, *Claims for Wrongful Death*, Law Com. No.263 (1999).

[18] The historical context is detailed by Nolan in Arvind and Steele (eds), *Tort Law and the Legislature* (2013), p.131.

[19] It is now common in statutes that impose strict liability to provide that a situation giving rise to such liability is "fault" within the meaning of the Fatal Accidents Act: see, e.g. the Animals Act 1971 s.10. A breach of contract causing death is within the statute: *Grein v Imperial Airways Ltd* [1937] 1 K.B. 50.

[20] Section 1.

least two years;[21] (4) any parent or other ascendant of the deceased or person treated by the deceased as his parent; (5) any child[22] or other descendant of the deceased or any person who has been treated by the deceased as a child of the family in relation to any marriage or civil partnership of the deceased; and (6) any person who is, or is the issue of, a brother, sister, uncle or aunt of the deceased. Moreover, in deducing any relationship an adopted person is to be treated as the child of the persons by whom he was adopted,[23] a relationship by marriage or civil partnership as one of consanguinity and a relationship of the half-blood as a relationship of the whole blood. The stepchild[24] of any person is to be treated as his child and an illegitimate person as the legitimate child of his mother and reputed father.[25]

Commencing proceedings. An action under the Fatal Accidents Act must normally be brought on behalf of the dependants by the executor or administrator of the deceased[26] but where there is no personal representative, or no action is brought by him within six months, any dependant who is entitled to benefit under the Act may sue in his own name on behalf of himself and the others.[27] Subject to the court's powers under the Limitation Act 1980, the action must in any case be brought within three years of the death.[28] **24–012**

The parasitic nature of the action. The action created by the Fatal Accidents Act is "new in its species, new in its quality, new in its principles, in every way new".[29] It is not the deceased's own cause of action which survives. Rather, the dependants are given an action of their own. However, for this new cause of action to exist, the circumstances of the deceased's death must have been such that the deceased himself, had he been injured and not killed, could have sued for his injury. The dependants' action is, therefore, parasitic on the wrong committed against the deceased. **24–013**

Consequences of the parasitic nature of the action. Because the dependant's action is parasitic on the deceased's action, if the deceased would be unable to sue for any reason had he lived, the dependant will not be able to sue either. If, therefore, the deceased had been run over in the street through nobody's fault but his own, there will be no claim on behalf of his dependants. Nor will there be such a claim if by contract with the defendant the deceased had excluded any possibility of liability to himself.[30] The position is different, however, if the contract merely limited the defendant's liability. In this situation, the deceased **24–014**

---

[21] This temporal threshold on co-habitation does not violate art.8 of the European Convention on Human Rights: *Swift v Secretary of State for Justice* [2013] EWCA Civ 193; [2014] Q.B. 373.

[22] Including a posthumous child: *The George and Richard* (1871) L.R. 3 Ad. & E. 466.

[23] Where a cause of action in respect of the death of the natural parent has accrued, a subsequent adoption does not extinguish the child's claim: *Watson v Willmott* [1991] 1 Q.B. 140.

[24] Including the child of the deceased's civil partner: Civil Partnership Act 2004 Sch.21.

[25] Fatal Accidents Act 1976 s.1(5).

[26] Section 2. An executor's title to sue dates from the death, but an administrator must first obtain a grant of letters of administration.

[27] Section 2(2). If there is no executor or administrator, the dependants need not wait six months before suing: *Holleran v Bagnell* (1879) 4 L.R. Ir. 740.

[28] See para.26–098.

[29] *Seward v Vera Cruz* (1884) 10 App. Cas. 59 at 70–71 per Lord Blackburn.

[30] *Haigh v Royal Mail Steam Packet Co Ltd* (1883) 52 L.J.Q.B. 640; *The Stella* [1900] P. 161.

could have sued for some damages and, therefore, the way is open for the dependant's claim (although the dependant's will not be affected by the limitation of liability).[31] Similarly the dependants will not have a claim if the deceased, before his death,[32] had accepted compensation from the defendant[33] in satisfaction of his claim,[34] or had actually obtained judgment against the defendant,[35] or if by the date of his death his claim had become statute-barred.[36]

i. Damages that can be Recovered

24–015 **Types of damages that can be recovered.** Damages to be awarded in respect of: (1) bereavement; (2) funeral expenses; and (3) loss of support. These will be taken *seriatim*.

24–016 **Bereavement.** The spouse or civil partner of the deceased, the parents of a minor[37] who was never married,[38] or a civil partner may claim damages for "bereavement". Such damages are awarded as a fixed sum,[39] presently £12,980.[40]

---

[31] *Nunan v Southern Ry* [1924] 1 K.B. 223; *Grein v Imperial Airways* [1937] 1 K.B. 50. It is questionable whether this rule is correct since it is inconsistent with the parasitic nature of the dependency action.

[32] If there is a discontinuance of the deceased's claim after death that does not bar the dependency claim unless as a matter of construction of the agreement it is intended to do so: *Reader v Molesworths Bright Clegg* [2007] EWCA Civ 169; [2007] 1 W.L.R. 1082.

[33] Not if he has accepted a payment from another tortfeasor unless this in fact fully satisfies his claim: *Jameson v CEGB* [2000] 1 A.C. 455.

[34] *Read v GE Ry* (1868) L.R. 3 Q.B. 555. This does not contravene arts 6 or 8 of the European Convention on Human Rights: *Thompson v Arnold* [2007] EWHC 1875 (QB); [2008] P.I.Q.R. P1. The view that the dependants are barred was assumed to be correct for the purposes of the appeal in *Pickett v British Rail Engineering Ltd* [1980] A.C. 136. Whether the liability in tort is destroyed from the moment that the agreement to accept compensation is made, even before the money is actually paid, is a question of construction: *British Russian Gazette v Associated Newspapers Ltd* [1933] 2 K.B. 616.

[35] The award of provisional damages to the deceased does not bar the dependants' claim: Damages Act 1996 s.3.

[36] *Williams v Mersey Docks and Harbour Board* [1905] 1 K.B. 804.

[37] There is no claim for bereavement if the victim is injured before attaining the age of majority but dies after reaching that age: *Doleman v Deakin*, *The Times*, January 30, 1990. The Act does not apply to a stillborn child, though since the tort causing the stillbirth will be a tort against the mother she may recover substantial damages (not necessarily limited to the statutory sum) for the effect of the loss of the child on her: *Bagley v North Herts Health Authority* (1986) 136 N.L.J. 1014. Cf. *Kralj v McGrath* [1986] 1 All E.R. 54, where the emphasis seems to be on the mother's grief hindering her physical recovery, and *Kirby v Redbridge HA* [1993] 4 Med. L.R. 178.

[38] But only his mother where he was illegitimate: s.1A(2)(b).

[39] Like other damages under the Act, this sum would seem to be subject to reduction on account of the deceased's contributory negligence: see para.24–031.

[40] Fatal Accidents Act 1976 s.1A as amended by SI 2013/105. These damages are additional to any recoverable by the claimant for psychiatric trauma because there has been a tort to him: *Jones v Royal Devon etc NHS Foundation Trust* [2008] EWHC 558 (QB); 110 B.M.L.R. 154. Where the claim is made by both parents the sum is to be divided equally between them (s.1A(4)), the form of which might suggest that if one parent is the tortfeasor, the other receives the full sum but contra, *Navei v Navei* [1995] C.L.Y.

Funeral expenses. "Dependants"[41] are entitled to recover damages for funeral expenses that they have incurred.[42] The cost of a wake is irrecoverable.[43]

24–017

Loss of support: the test. The Act allows recovery for a loss of support provided by the deceased. The right to sue for this loss is given to the deceased's "dependants".[44] The Act simply says that the court may give damages proportioned to the injury resulting from the death to the dependants.[45] It does not say on what principle they are to be assessed, but Pollock CB, in 1858, adopted the test which has been used ever since. Pollock CB said that damages must be calculated: "in reference to a reasonable expectation of pecuniary benefit as of right, or otherwise, from the continuance of the life".[46]

24–018

Loss of support: the concept of a pecuniary benefit. The test established by Pollock CB means that the dependants cannot recover if they have suffered only nominal losses or none at all.[47] Nor can they recover if the deceased earned his living by crime, for then their claim arises ex turpi causa.[48] However, the courts have stretched the concept of pecuniary benefit in holding that a child may claim damages for loss of his mother's care and that in assessing this loss the court is not confined to evaluating her services as housekeeper but may take into account instruction on essential matters to do with his upbringing.[49] Where a son who worked for his father at full wages under a contract was killed his father was held to have no claim. Although he had lost the son's services, he could not prove that he had lost any pecuniary benefit since he had paid full wages for them.[50] An additional reason for rejecting the father's claim in that case was that the father could not show any benefit accruing to him from his relationship with his son, but only that he had lost an advantage derived from a contract with him, and this was insufficient.[51] "The benefit, to qualify under the Act, must be a benefit which arises from the relationship between the parties."[52] In *Malyon v Plummer*[53] the claimant widow had been in receipt of a salary of about £600 per annum for somewhat nominal services to her husband's "one-man" company. The Court of

24–019

---

[41] See para.24–011.
[42] Section 3(5).
[43] *Jones v Royal Devon etc NHS Foundation Trust* [2008] EWHC 558 (QB).
[44] See para.24–011.
[45] Section 3(1). A literal interpretation of the Act might mean that it did not apply to a case where the deceased was seriously injured but did not die for some time, for his earning capacity would be destroyed before the death. Naturally, this has been rejected: *Jameson v C.E.G.B.* [1997] 3 W.L.R. 151 (on appeal [2000] 1 A.C. 455).
[46] *Franklin v SE Ry* (1858) 3 H. & N. 211 at 213–214. Hence, the dependants are entitled to recover where the deceased has been prevented from accumulating savings that they would have received from him: *Singapore Bus Co v Lim* [1985] 1 W.L.R. 1075. It has been held that where the deceased's estate pays inheritance tax that would otherwise have been avoided, that tax is recoverable by the dependants/beneficiaries from the tortfeasor: *Davies v Whiteways Cyder Co Ltd* [1975] Q.B. 262.
[47] *Duckworth v Johnson* (1859) 29 L.J. Ex. 257.
[48] *Burns v Edman* [1970] 2 Q.B. 541. See also *Hunter v Butler*, *The Times*, December 28, 1995 (claimant aware that deceased fraudulently concealed savings) and para.26–065.
[49] *Hay v Hughes* [1975] Q.B. 790 at 802; *Regan v Williamson* [1976] 1 W.L.R. 305; *Mehmet v Perry* [1977] 2 All E.R. 529; *Beesley v New Century Group Ltd* [2008] EWHC 3033 (QB) (principle of recovery for "intangible" benefits also applicable to spouses).
[50] *Sykes v NE Ry* (1875) 44 L.J.C.P. 191.
[51] *Burgess v Florence Nightingale Hospital for Gentlewomen* [1955] 1 Q.B. 349.
[52] *Burgess* [1955] 1 Q.B. 349 at 360 per Devlin J.

Appeal estimated the value of her services to the company at £200 per annum and held that the balance, but only the balance, was attributable to her relationship as wife to the deceased. The £200 represented payment for services rendered under her contract of employment and could not therefore be recovered.

24–020   **Loss of support: reasonable expectation.** A mere speculative possibility of receiving a pecuniary benefit is insufficient, as where the person killed was aged four years and his father proved nothing except that he had intended to give the child a good education.[54] On the other hand, there may be a reasonable expectation of pecuniary benefit although the relatives had no legal claim to support by the deceased, as where a son who was killed had voluntarily assisted his father in the father's work,[55] or where he once gave him money during a period of unemployment,[56] or where a wife who was killed had gratuitously performed the ordinary household duties.[57] Indeed, it is not necessary that the deceased should have been actually earning anything or given any help, provided that there was a reasonable probability, as distinct from a bare possibility, that he would do so. A reasonable probability existed where the deceased was a girl of 16 who lived with her parents, was on the eve of completing her apprenticeship as a dressmaker, and was likely in the near future to earn a wage which might quickly have become substantial.[58] If a wife is separated from her husband at the time of his death, it is unnecessary for her to show that, on a balance of probabilities, she would have returned to live with her husband. The correct approach is for the court to determine whether there was a reasonable chance, rather than a mere speculative possibility, of reconciliation. If there was such a chance, the award should be scaled down to take account of the probability of the reconciliation taking place.[59] Where the dependant was not married to the deceased but was living with him as his wife the court is directed by statute to take into account the fact that the claimant had no enforceable right to financial support from the deceased.[60]

24–021   **Loss of support: the dependant's prospects.** In a case under the Fatal Accidents Act the court is concerned with what would have happened if the deceased had lived, but since the loss in respect of which damages are awarded is pecuniary loss that will be suffered by dependants in the future, it is also inevitably concerned with the prospects of the dependants. For example, if the dependant

---

[53] *Malyon v Plummer* [1964] 1 Q.B. 330; *Williams v Welsh Ambulance Service NHS Trust* [2008] EWC Civ 81; *Cox v Hockenhull* [2000] 1 W.L.R. 750 (loss of invalid care allowance not recoverable; claimant in effect employed by State to care for deceased).

[54] *Barnett v Cohen* [1921] 2 K.B. 461.

[55] *Franklin v SE Ry* (1858) 3 H. & N. 211.

[56] *Hetherington v NE Ry* (1882) 9 Q.B.D. 160.

[57] *Berry v Humm* [1915] 1 K.B. 627. See also *Burgess v Florence Nightingale Hospital for Gentlewomen* [1955] 1 Q.B. 349 at 361–362.

[58] *Taff Vale Ry v Jenkins* [1913] A.C. 1; *Wathen v Vernon* [1970] R.T.R. 471; *Kandalla v BEA* [1981] Q.B. 158.

[59] *Davies v Taylor* [1974] A.C. 207. See also *Wathen v Vernon* [1970] R.T.R. 471; *Gray v Barr* [1971] 2 Q.B. 554.

[60] Fatal Accidents Act 1976 s.3(4). The position is the same where there is same-sex cohabitation but no registered civil partnership.

himself has a short expectation of life the damages will be small.[61] The most controversial aspect of this matter related to the dependent widow's prospects of remarriage, but there the law has undergone a fundamental alteration by statute. The common law rule was that the court had to estimate the widow's chances of remarriage and reduce the damages accordingly, but some judges revolted against this "guessing game" and a campaign against the rule led to its reversal by the Law Reform (Miscellaneous Provisions) Act 1971. Now, in assessing the damages payable to a widow there shall not be taken into account the remarriage of the widow nor her prospects of remarriage.[62] As a result of judicial interpretation of s.4 of the Act (which deals with the offsetting of benefits received)[63] it now seems that the provision that concerns the widow's remarriage is in effect redundant and that the same result will be reached where, for example, a widower remarries or a widow cohabits without marriage.[64] The fact that remarriage is ignored means that the law strays a long way from the principle of compensation.[65] In *Cox v Ergo Versicherung AG* Lord Sumption JSC described the law in this regard as "anomalous".[66]

Loss of support: the need to establish a loss. The dependant must suffer a loss   24–022
as a result of the deceased's death. If, for example, the deceased maintained himself and his spouse solely from the income of investments and those investments pass to the spouse then the latter will have suffered no pecuniary loss except insofar as the deceased provided skill, which now needs to be replaced, in managing them.[67]

Loss of support: distinguished from need for support. It is important to   24–023
remember that loss of dependency is not the same as need. If the claimant was a successful actress who retired upon marriage to the wealthy deceased but resumed her career on his death and made even more money than she had received in support from the deceased, her claim is still based on that loss of support. "The dependency is fixed at the moment of death; it is what the dependants would probably have received as benefit from the deceased, had the deceased not died. What decisions people make afterwards is irrelevant."[68]

---

[61] See, e.g. *Haxton v Philips Electronics UK Ltd*[2014] EWCA Civ 4; [2014] 2 All ER 225 (0.7 years).Where the deceased's widow actually died before the trial damages were awarded to her estate in respect only of the period during which she actually survived him: *Williams v John I. Thornycroft Ltd* [1940] 2 K.B. 658; *Voller v Dairy Produce Packers Ltd* [1962] 1 W.L.R. 960.

[62] Section 3(3).

[63] See para.24–030.

[64] Perhaps for this reason there is no provision dealing with the contingency of a civil partner dependant entering into a new civil partnership, but there are other contexts in which a court may still have to assess a person's prospects of marriage: para.23–082.

[65] The High Court of Australia by a majority departed from the common law rule in *De Sales v Ingrilli* [2002] HCA 52; (2002) 212 C.L.R. 338.

[66] *Cox v Ergo Versicherung AG* [2014] UKSC 22; [2014] 2 W.L.R. 948 at [10].

[67] See *Wood v Bentall Simplex* [1992] P.I.Q.R. P332; *Cape Distribution Ltd v O'Loughlin* [2001] P.I.Q.R. Q73. Pensions can cause difficulties: see *Auty v NCB* [1985] 1 W.L.R. 784 (under previous legislation) and *Pidduck v Eastern Scottish Omnibuses Ltd* [1990] 1 W.L.R. 993.

[68] *Williams v Welsh Ambulance Service NHS Trust* [2008] EWCA Civ 81 at [50].

ii.   Assessment of Damages

24–024   Damages for bereavement are a fixed sum.[69] Assessing damages in respect of funeral expenses rarely causes any difficulty. Accordingly, what follows here concerns the assessment of damages for a loss of support.

24–025   **Assessment where there are multiple dependants.** Although proceedings for a loss of support are normally brought by the executor or administrator of the deceased and not by the dependants themselves, the remedy given by the statute is to individuals, not to a class.[70] In calculating the damages, therefore, the pecuniary loss suffered by each dependant should be separately assessed. In practice, however, it will frequently be necessary first of all to determine a figure for the total liability of the defendant and then to apportion the damages between the various dependants[71] and this has been said to be the more usual method.[72]

24–026   **Periodical payments.** The regime for payment of damages by way of periodical payments which has been outlined in relation to personal injury cases[73] also applies to claims under the Fatal Accidents Act.[74]

24–027   **Lump sum awards.** Where a lump sum award is made, the process of assessment is very similar to that used in assessing future loss in a personal injury action. That is to say, the court determines a multiplicand representing the net annual loss and applies to that a multiplier representing the duration of the loss scaled down for contingencies and the value of accelerated receipt in the form of a lump sum. It is, however, more complicated because the court is concerned with the prospects of the dependants as well as of the deceased (for example, whether they would have survived to enjoy the benefit of the deceased's provision[75]) and the period of dependency of individual dependants will vary (for example, that of the spouse will generally be longer than that of a child[76]), whereas in a personal injury case, as far as earnings are concerned it is generally only the claimant's working life expectancy that is in issue. As a matter of precedent the multiplier is

---

[69]   See para.24–016.

[70]   *Pym v Great Northern Ry* (1863) 4 B. & S. 396; *Avery v London & NE Ry* [1938] A.C. 613; *Jeffrey v Kent CC* [1958] 1 W.L.R. 926; *Dietz v Lennig Chemicals Ltd* [1969] 1 A.C. 170 at 183.

[71]   *Bishop v Cunard White Star Co Ltd* [1950] P. 240 at 248. Once the total liability of the defendant has been determined, the apportionment of that sum is no concern of the defendant: *Eifert v Holt's Transport Co Ltd* [1951] 2 All E.R. 655n.

[72]   *Kassam v Kampala Aerated Water Co Ltd* [1965] 1 W.L.R. 688 at 672.

[73]   See para.23–095.

[74]   Damages Act 1996 s.7.

[75]   For a full analysis see the judgment of Purchas LJ in *Corbett v Barking HA* [1991] 2 Q.B. 408.

[76]   In *Dolbey v Goodwin* [1955] 1 W.L.R. 553 it was held that the damages awarded to the widowed mother of the deceased could not be assessed on the same basis as if she had been his widow, as it was likely that the deceased would have married and that his contributions to his mother's upkeep would then have been reduced.

to be set at the date of the death, not the trial,[77] but the effect is generally to under compensate and the courts may be persuaded to change their line.[78]

Approach where deceased was the family breadwinner. Most cases fall into   **24–028** one of two broad categories. The first is where the deceased was the family breadwinner. Traditionally, the approach was to build up the multiplicand item by item by a schedule of expenditure which could be regarded as for the family benefit (mortgage payments, heating, insurance, and so on) and this may still be a valid approach in some cases. However, it is now more common simply to take the deceased's income, net of tax and other deductions, and base the multiplicand on a standard fraction of that—66.6 per cent where the only dependant is a widow, 75 per cent if there are also children.[79] These figures are intended to allow for the expenditure which the deceased incurred solely for his own benefit and recognise the fact that expenditure for joint benefit (for example heating) is not necessarily reduced by the absence of the deceased. It must, however, be stressed that the standard fractions can be varied up or down if there is evidence to justify that.

Approach where deceased provided valuable but gratuitous services. The   **24–029** other type of case is that where the deceased provided valuable but gratuitous service in looking after the home and children. Here there may be no earnings to serve as the baseline for the multiplicand and the proper approach will often be to use as a measure the cost of employing substitute domestic help, if necessary on a "live-in" basis,[80] though it may in some cases be more apt to take the earnings loss of the other parent who stays at home to look after the children.[81] The fact that commercial help is not engaged (as where the children are looked after by a relative) does not prevent the cost of such help being used as a measure but in this event it should be the net wage without tax and insurance contributions for those are items of expenditure which will never be incurred.[82] In any event, the loss by children of the services of their mother is one which is likely to be a declining one so it cannot be valued at a constant figure for the whole of the child's dependency.[83]

---

[77] *Graham v Dodds* [1983] 1 W.L.R. 808; *Cookson v Knowles* [1979] A.C. 556 at 576; *H v S* [2002] EWCA Civ 792; [2003] Q.B. 965; *Fletcher v A Train & Sons Ltd* [2008] EWCA Civ 413; [2008] 4 All E.R. 699.

[78] The alternative approach would be to set the multiplier discounted for early receipt from trial and apply to pre-trial losses the actual period between death and trial, discounted only for the risk (typically very small in the absence of specific evidence) that the deceased might anyway have died from other causes before trial.

[79] *Harris v Empress Motors* [1984] 1 W.L.R. 212. Where both spouses earned and pooled their resources, the fraction is applied to the joint income and the survivor's continuing income deducted: *H v S* [2002] EWCA Civ 792; [2003] Q.B. 965 at [31].

[80] *Jeffrey v Smith* [1970] R.T.R. 279; *Hay v Hughes* [1975] Q.B. 790. Though in principle a deduction should be made in respect of the living expenses of the deceased, this maybe offset because the courts recognise that a commercial provider may not be "as good as" the deceased: *Reagan v Williamson* [1976] 1 W.L.R. 305.

[81] *Mehmet v Perry* [1977] 2 All E.R. 529; *Cresswell v Eaton* [1991] 1 W.L.R. 1113.

[82] *Spittle v Bunney* [1988] 1 W.L.R. 847; *Corbett v Barking HA* [1991] 2 Q.B. 408.

[83] *Spittle v Bunney* [1988] 1 W.L.R. 847 (£47,500 reduced on this basis to £25,000).

24–030 **Deductions.** Section 4 of the Fatal Accidents Act provides that in "assessing damages in respect of a person's death . . . benefits which have accrued or will accrue to any person from his death or otherwise as a result of his death shall be disregarded". The law in this regard is therefore very simple: once one has assessed the dependency there is simply no deduction to be made. If the benefit does not arise as a consequence of the death it is irrelevant; and if it does so arise it is excluded from consideration by the statute. This goes even to the extent of refusing any deduction for ex gratia payments made by the defendant, though he can of course express such a payment to be on account of potential liability.[84] The law is, therefore, much more generous to the dependants of the deceased than to claimants in personal injury cases: where the breadwinner is killed the dependants are entitled to a full award based on loss of support from the deceased's earnings, even though as a result of an occupational pension, widow's benefit, insurance money and the devolution of the deceased's estate they may be better off in financial terms than they were before the death. The effect of s.4 has also been in issue where voluntary care is provided by a relative after the death of a parent. In *Stanley v Saddique*[85] the Court of Appeal held that "benefit" was to be given a wide meaning and was not confined to direct payments in money or money's worth. Hence when a child lost his mother in an accident but was then looked after by his stepmother, that was a "benefit" under s.4 and was to be ignored even if the stepmother provided better care than the natural mother (because, as in this case, the natural mother was unreliable). It follows that the child has a claim for substitute services to replace those lost and that, in line with the cases on personal injuries,[86] the damages awarded in that respect are held on trust or paid directly to the carer,[87] provided he is not the tortfeasor.[88]

iii.   Contributory Negligence

24–031 The contributory negligence of the deceased is taken into account and the damages awarded to the dependants will be reduced accordingly.[89] Although the Act is silent on the point, it is fairly clear that the contributory negligence of the dependants is also relevant. In principle the damages awarded to the contributorily negligent dependant should be reduced in proportion to his share of responsibility, but the other dependants should receive their damages in full,[90] since the remedy under the Fatal Accidents Act is given to individuals, not to the dependants as a group. In one case it was held that the damages of a non-negligent dependant were not affected by the fault of another dependant, but

---

[84] *Arnup v MW White Ltd* [2008] EWCA Civ 447; [2008] I.C.R. 1064.

[85] *Stanley v Saddique* [1992] Q.B. 1. See also *R. v Criminal Injuries Compensation Board Ex p. K* [1999] Q.B. 1131.

[86] See para.23–079.

[87] See para.24–006.

[88] *H v S* [2002] EWCA Civ 792; [2003] Q.B. 965.

[89] Section 5.

[90] *Mulholland v McRae* [1961] N.I. 135.

there the accident was held to be entirely the fault of the latter and it was conceded by counsel that she had no claim.[91]

3. RELATIONSHIP OF THE TWO ACTS

The rights of action under the two statutes are cumulative, with damages under **24–032** the Law Reform (Miscellaneous Provisions) Act 1934 going to the estate and those under the Fatal Accidents Act going to dependants. In most cases, one or more of the dependants will also be entitled to the deceased's estate. Damages under the Law Reform Act are, in the case of instantaneous death, confined to funeral expenses, and since these are anyway recoverable under the Fatal Accidents Act there is no point in bringing a Law Reform Act claim. Where there is an interval between injury and death and hence loss of amenity and earnings and so on, then no doubt a Law Reform Act claim will continue to be presented concurrently with one under the Fatal Accidents Act.

---

[91] *Dodds v Dodds* [1978] Q.B. 543. There seems no reason why the defendant should not claim contribution from a negligent dependant under the Civil Liability (Contribution) Act 1978.

CAPACITY

The title of this chapter is a compendious abbreviation of "Variation in capacity to sue, or liability to be sued, in tort". Every system of law and every branch of each system must recognise variations in favour of, or against, abnormal members of the community. Who are to be reckoned as abnormal is a question of policy. In the law of tort the chief variations in capacity are to be found with the state and its officials, minors, persons of unsound mind, corporations and trade unions.[1] Married women were abnormal for this purpose until well into the 20th century. That condition has now disappeared, but there are still some restrictions on actions between spouses.

25–001

---

[1] It is convenient to treat trade unions in the chapter on economic torts: para.19–050.

1.   THE STATE AND ITS SUBORDINATES

25–002 **The Crown and State officials: common law.** At common law no action in tort lay against the Crown[2] for wrongs expressly authorised by the Crown or for wrongs committed by its servants in the course of their employment.[3] Moreover, the head of the department or other superior official was not, and is not, personally liable for wrongs committed by his subordinates, unless he has expressly authorised them, for all the servants of the Crown are fellow servants of the Crown and not of one another.[4] On the other hand, the actual wrongdoer could, and still can, be sued in his personal capacity.[5] In practice the Treasury Solicitor usually defended an action against the individual Crown servant and the Treasury, as a matter of grace, undertook to satisfy any judgment awarded against him for a tort committed in the course of his employment. If the actual wrongdoer could not be identified the Treasury Solicitor would supply the name of a merely nominal defendant for the purpose of the action, i.e. a person who, though a Government servant, had nothing to do with the alleged wrong. However, in *Royster v Cavey*[6] it was held that the court had no jurisdiction to try the case unless the subordinate named by the Treasury Solicitor was the person who apparently had committed the tort. As the Crown had become one of the largest employers of labour and occupiers of property in the country, this system of providing compensation for the victims of torts committed by Crown servants in the course of their employment was plainly inadequate and, finally, some 20 years after it was mooted, the Crown Proceedings Act 1947 put an end to Crown immunity in tort.

25–003 **Crown Proceedings Act 1947.** Under the Act the old maxim that "the King can do no wrong" is retained to the extent that no proceedings can be instituted against the Sovereign in person,[7] and there are savings in respect of the Crown's prerogative and statutory powers,[8] but otherwise the Act went a long way towards equating the Crown with a private person of full age and capacity for the purposes of tortious liability. The Crown cannot, however, be liable in tort except as provided by the Act and this cannot be evaded by dressing up the claim as one

---

[2] Or against Government departments, for these enjoyed the immunity of the Crown unless a statute expressly provided otherwise. See *Minister of Supply v British Thomson-Houston Co* [1943] K.B. 478
[3] *Canterbury (Viscount) v Attorney General* (1842) 1 Ph. 306. The remedy by way of petition of right was available for breach of contract, and to recover property which had been wrongfully taken and withheld. *France, Fenwick & Co Ltd v R.* [1927] 1 K.B. 52. Proceedings by way of petition of right were abolished by the Crown Proceedings Act 1947 Sch.1 para.2, but only with regard to liability in respect of Her Majesty's Government in the UK. A petition of right may, therefore, still lie in certain cases, but in the common law form used prior to the Petition of Right Act 1860: *Franklin v Attorney General* [1974] Q.B. 185.
[4] *Raleigh v Goschen* [1898] 1 Ch.73 at 83; *Bainbridge v Postmaster General* [1906] 1 K.B. 178.
[5] He could not, and cannot now, plead the orders of the Crown or State necessity as a defence. *Entick v Carrington* (1765) 19 St. Tr. 1030; *Wilkes v Wood* (1763) 19 St. Tr. at 1153; *M v Home Office* [1994] 1 A.C. 337.
[6] [1947] K.B. 204, the Court of Appeal acting upon emphatic obiter dicta of the House of Lords in *Adams v Naylor* [1946] A.C. 543.
[7] Section 40(1).
[8] Section 11(1).

for a declaration that the Crown is behaving wrongfully.[9] Section 2(1) provides that the Crown shall be liable[10] as if it were a private person: (1) in respect of torts committed by its servants or agents;[11] (2) in respect of any breach of those duties which a person owes to his servants or agents at common law by reason of being their employer; and (3) in respect of any breach of the duties attaching at common law to the ownership, occupation, possession or control of property.[12] Section 2(2) makes the Crown liable for breach of statutory duty, provided that the statute in question is one which binds other persons besides the Crown and its officers. The starting point is still, apart from the Human Rights Act 1998, that the Crown can do no wrong in private law. In the second and third cases enumerated in s.2(1) and that in s.2(2) the Crown can be "institutionally" or "personally" liable;[13] but otherwise the Act makes the Crown liable for the acts of human agents who commit torts. Hence the Crown can only be liable for misfeasance in a public office if the mental element of that tort can be brought home to some individual for whose actions the Crown is answerable.[14] The apportionment provisions of the Civil Liability (Contribution) Act 1978 and the Law Reform (Contributory Negligence) Act 1945, as well as the analogous provisions of the Merchant Shipping Act 1995, apply to proceedings in which the Crown is a party.[15] There is a little doubt whether an action lies against the Crown on behalf of a deceased person's estate under the Law Reform (Miscellaneous Provisions) Act 1934 or on behalf of his dependants under the Fatal Accidents Act 1976, but it is submitted that on principle the Crown should be liable.[16]

Limitations on liability. There are certain limitations on the Crown's general liability in tort. Until 1987 it was not possible for a member of the armed forces to sue the Crown for injuries inflicted by a fellow member in the execution of his duty or arising from the condition of premises or equipment. There was a similar immunity for the actual wrongdoer.[17] These restrictions were removed by the Crown Proceedings (Armed Forces) Act 1987.[18] However, pre-1987 cases may

25–004

---

[9] *Trawnik v Lennox* [1985] 1 W.L.R. 532 (where the court had no jurisdiction to hear a claim for a nuisance in Berlin because it did not arise in respect of the Crown's activities in the UK: s.40(2)(b)).

[10] The action is brought against the appropriate government department in accordance with a list published by the Treasury, otherwise the Attorney General may be made defendant (s.17).

[11] "Agent" includes an independent contractor (s.38(2)) but the Crown is not on this account subject to any greater liability for the tort of an independent contractor employed by it than it would be if it were a private person: s.40(2)(d).

[12] The duties owed by an occupier of premises to his invitees and licensees are now contained in the Occupiers' Liability Act 1957, which binds the Crown. The liability of the Crown under the Act thus falls under s.2(2), but s.2(1)(c) continues to apply to the other duties which attach to the ownership, occupation, possession or control of property such as those in the tort of nuisance.

[13] The statement in *Chagos Islanders v Attorney General* [2004] EWCA Civ 997 at [20] seems to go too far in that it ignores these categories.

[14] *Chagos Islanders v Attorney General* [2004] EWCA Civ 997.

[15] Section 4.

[16] *Clerk and Lindsell on Torts*, 20th edn (2013), para.5–19; Treitel [1957] Pub. L. 321, 322–326.

[17] Section 10 of the 1947 Act, which applied only to death or personal injury. On its scope see *Post Traumatic Stress Disorder Litigation, Multiple Claimants v MoD, Re* [2003] EWHC 1134 (QB).

[18] It was held in *Mulcahy v MoD* [1996] Q.B. 732 that there was no duty of care in active operations during the Gulf War, even though s.10 had not been revived, as provided for by s.2. This "combat immunity" is narrowly construed: *Smith v The Ministry of Defence*[2013] UKSC 41; [2014] A.C. 52, para.5–034.

still arise (for example from diseases contracted from exposure to asbestos) and the original restriction has been declared substantive rather than procedural in nature and compatible with art.6 of the European Convention on Human Rights.[19] The remaining limitations are: (1) officers, that is, servants or Ministers of the Crown,[20] who may render the Crown liable are only those appointed directly or indirectly by the Crown and paid wholly out of moneys provided by Parliament or a fund certified by the Treasury as equivalent. This excludes liability for police officers, who are not paid out of such funds, even in the case of the Metropolitan Police,[21] and also for public corporations which are, normally, liable themselves like any other corporation;[22] (2) the Crown cannot be made liable for an act or omission of its servant unless that act or omission would, apart from the Act, have given rise to a cause of action against the servant himself.[23] This preserves such defences as act of state but does not, it is submitted, extend so far as to exempt the Crown from liability in those exceptional cases where the employer is vicariously liable even though his servant is immune from liability himself;[24] (3) the Crown is not liable for anything done by any person in discharging responsibilities of a judicial nature vested in him or any responsibilities he has in connection with execution of the judicial process.[25]

25–005   **Act of State.** It is proposed to deal with this matter briefly since it belongs much more to the realm of constitutional and international law than to the law of tort. There is no doubt that no action may be brought either against the Crown or anyone else in respect of an act of state, but there is less agreement on the meaning of this phrase. Certainly an injury inflicted upon a foreigner abroad which is done pursuant to a policy which is not justiciable by the courts[26] and which is either authorised or ratified by the Crown is for this purpose an "act of state" and cannot be made the subject of an action in the English courts,[27] but it is doubtful whether, as an answer to a claim for tort, act of state goes any further

---

[19] *Matthews v MoD* [2003] UKHL 4, [2003] 1 A.C. 1163.

[20] Section 38(2). The Crown is not expressly defined, but it appears to include all government departments, officers, servants and agents of the Crown.

[21] See now the Police Act 1996 s.88, para.21–013.

[22] *Tamlin v Hannaford* [1950] 1 K.B. 18; cf. *Glasgow Corp v Central Land Board* 1956 S.L.T. 41, HL. See also *Bank Voor Handel en Scheepvaart v Administrator of Hungarian Property* [1954] A.C. 584.

[23] Section 2, proviso. The Crown has the benefit of any statute regulating or limiting the liability of a government department or officer of the Crown: s.2(4).

[24] *Clerk and Lindsell on Torts*, 20th edn (2013), para.5–05. Contra, Glanville Williams, *Crown Proceedings*, pp. 44–45.

[25] Section 2(5). In *Quinland v Governor of Swaleside Prison* [2002] EWCA Civ 174; [2003] Q.B. 306, the failure of the Criminal Appeal office to expedite the correction of the judge's error was held to fall within s.2(5) and the suggestion that the subsection does not cover "administrative" responsibilities in *Welsh v CC Merseyside* [1993] 1 All E.R. 692 was disapproved. However, failure to deal with money paid into court is not a judicial act and outside the subsection: *Kirvek Management etc v Attorney General of Trinidad and Tobago* [2002] UKPC 43; [2002] 1 W.L.R. 2792 (similar legislation). An award of damages may be made against the Crown in limited circumstances under the Human Rights Act 1998: see para.25–012.

[26] Not merely "administrative" acts like providing accommodation for troops as in *Attorney General v Nissan* [1970] A.C. 179. There was no reliance on act of state in *Bici v MoD* [2004] EWHC 786 (QB).

[27] *Buron v Denman* (1848) 2 Ex. 167. Cf. *Carr v Francis, Times & Co* [1902] A.C. 176.

than that. It will probably not avail a defendant to plead act of State in respect of an act done within British territory,[28] whatever the nationality of the claimant.[29] There has been some dispute as to whether it may be available against a British citizen abroad, though the only case in which the point appears to have arisen decided that it may be.[30] An act of the Crown may, of course, be lawful as an act of prerogative, and s.11 of the Crown Proceedings Act preserves the Crown's rights to exercise its statutory and prerogative powers, but there is no prerogative power to seize or destroy the property of a subject without paying compensation.[31] It must be emphasised that all this concerns common law liability in tort and the Human Rights Act 1998 may have extra-territorial application to locations abroad where UK authorities are exercising effective control, thus creating an obligation not to act inconsistently with the Convention with regard to aliens as well as British subjects.[32]

Postal Services. Any potential liability in tort arising in connection with the postal service is now regulated by the Postal Services Act 2000.[33] Section 90 provides that no proceedings in tort lie against a "universal service provider"[34] in respect of loss or damage suffered by any person in connection with the provision of a universal postal service because of: (a) anything done, or omitted to be done, in relation to any postal packet in the course of transmission by post; or (b) any omission to carry out arrangements for the collection of anything to be conveyed by post.[35] Furthermore, no officer, servant, employee, agent or sub-contractor of a universal service provider nor any person engaged in or about the conveyance of postal packets is subject, except at the suit or instance of the provider, to any civil liability for: (a) any loss or damage in the case of which liability of the provider is excluded; or (b) any loss of, or damage to, a postal packet to which s.91 applies. Under s.91 the service provider is liable for loss of or damage to postal packets where he has accepted liability under a "scheme" made by it[36] and the loss or damage is due to the wrongful act, neglect or default of servants, agents or sub-contractors of the service provider, but such wrongful act, etc. is presumed unless the contrary is shown.[37]

25–006

---

[28] *Johnstone v Pedlar* [1921] A.C. 262.

[29] With the rather obvious exception of enemy aliens present in British territory without licence.

[30] *Hilal v Secretary of State for Defence* [2009] EWHC 397 (QB). This at least avoids problems arising from the fact that the old cases spoke in terms of "British subjects", a concept far wider than modern British citizenship.

[31] *Attorney General v De Keyser's Royal Hotel* [1920] A.C. 508; *Burmah Oil Co Ltd v Lord Advocate* [1965] A.C. 75; *Attorney General v Nissan* [1970] A.C. 179 at 227 per Lord Pearce. The common law right to compensation was considerably restricted by the War Damage Act 1965.

[32] *R. (on the application of Al-Skeini) v Secretary of State for Defence* [2007] UKHL 26; [2008] 1 AC 153; *Smith v The Ministry of Defence* [2013] UKSC 41; [2014] A.C. 52.

[33] As amended by the Postal Services Act 2011.

[34] Postal Services Act 2000 s.125; Postal Services Act 2011 s.65(1).

[35] The same immunity is granted to a "postal operator" (Postal Services Act 2000 s.125; Postal Services Act 2011 s.27) providing a service under a scheme made under s.89 of the 2000 Act.

[36] Under s.89.

[37] Section 92(7). This section also contains provisions governing who may sue and the amount recoverable.

25–007 **Foreign sovereigns.** English law was for long committed to the proposition (which derives from general public international law[38]) that a foreign sovereign State enjoyed absolute immunity from liability before an English court unless the immunity had been waived by submission to the jurisdiction.[39] The doctrine was not confined to "acts of state" and had become a serious problem in modern times because of the practice by many countries of carrying on ordinary trading activities through organs of state. Accordingly, attempts were made to restrict the immunity, culminating in the decision of the House of Lords in *The Congreso del Partido*[40] whereby a court was required to analyse the nature of the obligation and breach in question to determine whether it was of a private law or a "governmental" character. The law is now contained in the State Immunity Act 1978 under which a state is immune from the jurisdiction of the English courts except as provided by the Act.[41] Much of the Act concerns matters of contract, but for our purposes the principal exceptions from sovereign immunity[42] are: (1) an act or omission in this country causing death or personal injury;[43] (2) obligations arising out of the ownership, possession or use of property in this country;[44] and (3) Admiralty proceedings (whether in rem or in personam) in respect of ships used for commercial purposes.[45] The residual immunity contained in the Act does not protect an entity distinct from the executive organs of the state[46] unless the proceedings arise out of the exercise of sovereign authority and the State would have been immune.[47] However, the Act does not apply to cases involving visiting forces of a foreign power,[48] which are still governed by the common law.[49]

The law of sovereign immunity rests on the proposition that it would be an affront to the dignity and sovereignty of a state to allow it to be impleaded in a foreign court. It applies even though the acts alleged against the foreign state involve violation of a *jus cogens* or peremptory rule of international law such as the prohibition of torture.[50] That dignity may also be affronted if those who are or

---

[38] It "pursues the legitimate aim of complying with international law to promote comity and good relations between states through the respect of another state's sovereignty" and its recognition does not infringe art.6 of the European Convention on Human Rights: *Al-Adsani v United Kingdom* (2002) 34 E.H.R.R. 273 at [54].

[39] *The Cristina* [1938] A.C. 485. As to the immunity of diplomatic officials, see the Diplomatic Privileges Act 1964.

[40] [1983] A.C. 244.

[41] Section 1(1).

[42] The State may still submit to the jurisdiction: s.2.

[43] *Nigeria v Ogbonna* [2012] 1 W.L.R. 139

[44] Sections 5 and 6 respectively.

[45] Section 10. For States parties to the Brussels Convention of 1926, see s.10(6).

[46] Cf. *C Czarnikow Ltd v Centrala Handler Zagranicznego "Rolimpex"* [1979] A.C. 351.

[47] Section 14(2); but a central bank is equated with a State: s.14(4). The provisions of s.14(2) are fully examined in *Kuwait Airways v Iraqi Airways* [1995] 1 W.L.R. 1147 (a $630 million claim for conversion). The effect of s.14(2) seems to be that the issue is essentially the same as it would have been at common law under *The Congreso del Partido*.

[48] Section 16(2).

[49] See *Littrell v USA (No.2)* [1995] 1 W.L.R. 92 (treatment not actionable in US law and not justiciable here as interference with sovereign rights of USA over its military personnel) and *Holland v Lampen-Wolfe* [2000] 1 W.L.R. 1573 (provision for education of military personnel a matter within the sovereign immunity of the USA so as to bar a claim for libel).

[50] *Jones v Saudi Arabia* [2006] UKHL 26; [2007] 1 A.C. 270.

were its officials are impleaded in relation to the conduct of its affairs before the courts of another state and therefore the state can "extend the cloak of its own immunity over those officials".[51] Thus in *Grovit v de Nederlandsche Bank*[52] libel proceedings against the central bank's officers alleging malice and arising out of the refusal to register the claimant's company were struck out.

Independently of sovereign immunity, there is a principle of English law that the courts may refuse to adjudicate on acts done abroad by virtue of the sovereign authority of foreign States. In *Buttes Gas and Oil Co v Hammer*[53] the House of Lords therefore stayed litigation between private parties when it involved an examination of allegations of conspiracy between one party and a sovereign ruler and acts of assertion of territorial sovereignty by other states in the area.[54] However, this is not an absolute rule which precludes an English court from determining whether there has been a breach of international law where there are recognised standards by which the issue is justiciable.[55]

2.   JUDICIAL ACTS[56]

Acts done in the administration of justice. The law casts a wide immunity   25–008
around acts done in the administration of justice. This has been rather infelicitously styled a "privilege", but that might imply that the judge has a private right to be malicious, whereas its real meaning is that in the public interest it is not desirable to inquire whether acts of this kind are malicious or not. It is rather a right of the public to have the independence of the judges preserved rather than a privilege of the judges themselves.[57] It is better to take the chance of judicial incompetence, irritability, or irrelevance, than to run the risk of getting a bench warped by apprehension of the consequences of judgments which ought to be given without fear or favour.[58] Despite a valiant attempt by Lord Denning MR to rationalise the law into one, unified principle[59] and despite recent legislation, the law is still hard to state concisely or with precision.

High Court Judges. Judges of the High Court are immune from liability for any   25–009
act of a judicial character even though the act is in excess of or outside their jurisdiction and whether this is a result of mistake of fact or of law. If, however,

---

[51] *Jones v Saudi Arabia* in the CA at [2004] EWCA Civ [105].

[52] [2005] EWHC 2944 (QB); [2006] 1 W.L.R. 3323.

[53] [1982] A.C. 888. Similar considerations played some part in English law's long adherence to the rule that an English court had no jurisdiction over actions involving trespass to foreign land. See the discussion in *Pearce v Ove Arup Partnership Ltd* [2000] Ch. 403. That rule was abolished by the Civil Jurisdiction and Judgments Act 1982 s.30—there is still no jurisdiction if the action is principally concerned with title to, or the right to possession of such property.

[54] Nor will the English court entertain a claim *by* a foreign State which in substance amounts to an exercise of its sovereign authority: *Mbasogo v Logo Ltd* [2006] EWCA Civ 1370; [2007] Q.B. 846.

[55] *Kuwait Airways Corp v Iraqi Airways Co (Nos 4 and 5)* [2002] UKHL 19; [2002] 2 A.C. 883.

[56] The topic is dealt with at length in Winfield, *The Present Law of Abuse of Legal Procedure*, Ch.7.

[57] *Bottomley v Brougham* [1908] 1 K.B. 584 at 586–587 per Channell J.

[58] For a more sceptical view, see Olowofoyeku (1990) 10 L.S. 271 and *Suing Judges* (1993).

[59] In *Sirros v Moore* [1975] Q.B. 118.

an act is in excess of jurisdiction and is done in bad faith, then the judge would be liable in damages for what follows from the order made, for example, imprisonment or seizure of property.[60]

25–010   **Justices of the peace.** The liability of justices of the peace is now governed by the Courts Act 2003, re-enacting provisions first introduced in 1990. It is provided that no action lies for any act in the execution of the justice's duty and with respect to any matter within his jurisdiction[61] but that an action lies for an act in the purported execution of his duty and in relation to a matter which is not within his jurisdiction, if, but only if, it is proved that he acted in bad faith.[62] Putting aside the point that proceedings in magistrates' courts are amenable to review and control by the High Court, whereas a High Court judge is the sole arbiter of his jurisdiction (subject to appeal) it is difficult to see how this differs from the position of a judge of the High Court.

25–011   **Other judges.** Unfortunately, there is no legislation governing the position of the majority of professional judges (county court judges, recorders, district judges[63]) and their position has to be discovered from the older cases and by inference from what the House of Lords decided in the context of justices in *Re McC*.[64] A further complication arises from the fact that another distinction cuts across that based upon the status of the judge, namely that between courts which are and are not "courts of record". Thus, all trials on indictment are before a court of record, even though very few of them are presided over by High Court judges.[65] For acts within their jurisdiction "inferior" judges have full protection, even if they are actuated by malice.[66] What is less clear is their position with regard to acts outside their jurisdiction. The concept of jurisdiction is a difficult one and its meaning may vary from one context to another. Here what is involved is the power to decide an issue, not the method by which the decision is reached, so that procedural irregularity in reaching a result which the court has power to achieve does not take the case outside the jurisdiction.[67] According to *Re McC* this is the true explanation of *Sirros v Moore*.[68] The claimant had been convicted of an offence and recommended for deportation by a stipendiary magistrate, but without an order for his detention. The judge in the Crown Court,[69] wrongly thinking that he had no jurisdiction to hear an appeal against deportation, dismissed it but ordered the claimant to be detained. This did not amount to

---

[60] "If the Lord Chief Justice himself, on the acquittal of a defendant charged before him with a criminal offence, were to say, 'That is a perverse verdict', and thereupon proceed to pass a sentence of imprisonment, he could be sued for trespass": *Re McC* [1985] A.C. 528 at 540 per Lord Bridge.

[61] Courts Act 2003 s.31.

[62] Section 32. There are provisions for indemnity of justices in s.35, which dates from the Justices of the Peace Act 1979.

[63] Other than those of magistrates' courts.

[64] *Re McC* [1985] A.C. 541.

[65] In fact the majority of High Court *civil* actions are now heard by deputy judges, i.e. circuit judges and QCs, but there does not seem any doubt that they enjoy the same immunity as a full High Court judge.

[66] See *Hinds v Liverpool County Court* [2008] EWHC 665 (QB); [2008] 2 F.L.R. 63.

[67] Nor does error as to a collateral matter on which the jurisdiction depends: *Re McC* [1985] A.C. 541 at 544; *Johnson v Meldon* (1890) 30 L.R.Ir. 15.

[68] [1975] Q.B. 118.

[69] Not being a trial on indictment, the court was not a court of record.

trespass because he did have power to overrule the initial decision against detention and intended to do so, but implemented that decision by a "hopelessly irregular procedure". On the other hand, by analogy with *Re McC*, if a judge of an inferior court were, in good faith, to pass a sentence which he had no power to pass he would be liable. In modern conditions it is entirely unconvincing to argue as a justification for a professional judge being liable for acts done in good faith outside his jurisdiction, that he is always supposed to know the law (the state of which is in any event often a matter of opinion): if the argument has any validity at all it should surely apply, a fortiori, to judges of the High Court. What is needed, it is suggested, is a bold decision declaring the common law for inferior judges to be the same as that stated for justices in the Act.

Actions other than in tort. Enough has been said to show that it will be a rare case in which a person may recover substantial damages in respect of a judicial act. An action in tort is not, however, the only route to compensation. Where a criminal conviction is reversed on the basis of a newly-discovered fact there may be a statutory right to compensation under s.133 of the Criminal Justice Act 1988. Furthermore, an award of damages[70] under the Human Rights Act 1998 may be possible in respect of a judicial act done in good faith in order to compensate a person to the extent required by art.5(5) of the European Convention on Human Rights (which provides for compensation for arrest or detention).[71] However, the damages are awardable against the Crown and the immunity of the judge is in effect preserved.[72] **25–012**

Officers of the law. An officer of the law who executes process apparently regular, without knowing in fact the person who authorised him to do so has exceeded his powers, is protected in spite of the proceedings being ill-founded.[73] Again by the Constables Protection Act 1750,[74] no action can be brought against a constable for anything done in obedience to any warrant[75] issued by a justice of the peace until the would-be claimant has made a written demand for a copy of the warrant and the demand has not been complied with for six days. If it is complied with, then the constable, if he produces the warrant at the trial of the action against him, is not liable in spite of any defect of jurisdiction in the justice. However, if he arrests a person not named in the warrant or seizes goods of one who is not mentioned in it, he does so at his peril. His mistake, however honest, will not excuse him. In *Hoye v Bush*[76] Richard Hoye was suspected of stealing a mare. A warrant was issued for his arrest, but it described him as "John Hoye", which in fact was his father's name. Richard was arrested under this warrant and **25–013**

---

[70] The award is made against the Crown: Human Rights Act 2000 s.9(4).

[71] Section 9. Proceedings may only be brought by exercising a right of appeal, by judicial review or in such other forum as may be prescribed by rules. However, the decision of an inferior court may be subject to judicial review and a claim for damages may be presented in an application for judicial review. It is not necessarily the case that an erroneous decision gives rise to a claim under art.5: *Benham v United Kingdom* (1996) 22 E.H.R.R. 293.

[72] *Hinds v Liverpool County Court* [2008] EWHC 665 (QB); [2008] 2 F.L.R. 63.

[73] *Sirros v Moore* [1975] Q.B. 118; *London (Mayor of) v Cox* (1867) L.R. 2 H.L. 239 at 269 per Willes J. For detention under a court order based on a mistaken view of the law, see para.26–059.

[74] Section 6.

[75] For arrest without warrant see para.26–051.

[76] (1840) 1 M. & G. 775.

subsequently sued Bush, the constable, for false imprisonment. Bush was held liable, for although Richard was the man who actually was wanted, still the warrant described somebody else and it did not help Bush that John Hoye was not really wanted.[77]

3. MINORS

25–014   Since 1970 the age of majority is 18.[78] So far as the law of tort is concerned, only two questions arise concerning minors, namely their capacity to sue and to be sued for tort.

A. Capacity to Sue

25–015   **Minors.** In general no distinction falls to be taken between a minor and an adult so far as their respective capacities to sue for tort are concerned, save that a minor must sue by his "litigation friend".[79]

25–016   **Unborn children.** That a child born with a disability as a result of injuries suffered while *en ventre sa mere* could sue,[80] even though before birth it was not a legal person, was put beyond doubt by the Congenital Disabilities (Civil Liability) Act 1976, which applies to all births on or after July 22 in that year. Notwithstanding that the Limitation Act allows claims by children to be brought many years after injury is suffered, the common law is now a virtually obsolete category.[81]

25–017   **Liability under the Congenital Disabilities (Civil Liability) Act 1976.** The principal provisions of the Act may be summarised as follows. In the first place, an action only lies if the child, the claimant, is born alive and disabled.[82] Secondly, the liability to the child is "derivative", in other words it only arises if

---

[77] Contrast *McGrath v CC, RUC* [2001] UKHL 39; [2001] 2 A.C. 731 (under s.38 of the Criminal Law Act 1977 arrest of C, who was named in the warrant, was lawful, even though the person wanted was X, who had given C's name). Both cases are consistent with a policy of requiring the constable to exercise the warrant at its face value. Contrast the matter of the *timing* of the execution of the warrant, where the constable may have a discretion: *Henderson v CC Cleveland* [2001] EWCA Civ 335; [2001] 1 W.L.R. 1103.

[78] Family Law Reform Act 1969 s.1.

[79] There is no bar to a child suing a parent: see below, and para.5–042. A number of claims have been brought against parents (as opposed to those having institutional care) for sexual abuse (see, e.g. *Stubbings v Webb* [1993] A.C. 498; *Pereira v Keleman* [1995] 1 F.L.R. 428) though for obvious reasons most of them have gone to the Criminal Injuries Compensation Board. On claims by parents wrongly suspected of abuse see para.5–073.

[80] It was held at an early date that a posthumous child of a deceased father could maintain an action under the Fatal Accidents Act: *The George and Richard* (1871) L.R. 3 Ad. & E. 466.

[81] No common law liability can arise in respect of births after the commencement of the Act: s.4(5).

[82] The mother may have an action in respect of a stillbirth: *Bagley v N Herts HA* (1986) 136 N.L.J. 1014. For definition of "disabled" see s.4(1).

the defendant was under an actual or potential tort liability[83] to either parent of the child for the act or omission which led to the disability, but for this purpose: "[I]t is no answer [to a claim by the child] that there could not have been such liability because the parent suffered no actionable injury, if there was a breach of legal duty which, if accompanied by injury, would have given rise to the liability."[84]

In other words, if a pregnant woman takes a drug which has been manufactured or developed negligently or in circumstances which contravene the Consumer Protection Act 1987 and this causes her child to be born disabled, the child may recover damages from the manufacturer even though the mother suffers no injury herself from the drug.[85] In practice the commonest situation giving rise to liability[86] is likely to be that where the child is injured during its mother's pregnancy but the Act extends more widely than this to cover an occurrence which affects either parent in his or her ability to bear a normal, healthy child,[87] so that, for example, a negligent injury to the mother's reproductive system before conception could found an action by a child conceived thereafter and born disabled as a result.[88] The mother herself is not generally liable under the Act so that there is no possibility of, say, an action being brought in respect of disabilities said to have caused by the mother smoking during pregnancy.[89] The good sense of this immunity is clear: not only is the possibility of liability revolting to normal feelings but there is a risk of the liability being used as a potent weapon in husband-wife disputes. The Law Commission thought that on balance the immunity should not be extended to the father, and the Act so provides, but the Pearson Commission disagreed and proposed an amendment on this point.[90] The policy arguments in favour of immunity are nothing like so strong when the potential parental liability would be covered by insurance[91] and s.2 of the Act accordingly provides that a woman

---

[83] This liability will commonly be for negligence, but there is nothing in the Act to confine it to this. The running of time against the parent is irrelevant: s.1(3). While the child's cause of action accrues upon birth (s.4(3)) the Limitation Act would prevent time running against him until he reached majority: para.26–097.

[84] Section 1(3).

[85] In many cases it would be impossible for the mother to suffer any physical injury from the drug and it then perhaps looks odd to say that there has been any "breach of legal duty", but it is inconceivable that such a case falls outside the Act.

[86] This is not to suggest that it will be very common for the Act to be invoked at all. The Pearson Commission estimated that no more than 0.5 per cent of all severely disabled children would have grounds for claiming tort compensation. See *Royal Commission on Civil Liability and Compensation for Personal Injury* (1978), Cmnd.7054, Vol.1, Ch.26 and Annexes 12 and 13.

[87] Section 1(2)(a).

[88] In this situation there is a high likelihood that the action could be met by the defence of knowledge of the risk by the mother: s.1(4), para.25–018.

[89] Proving cause and effect in an individual case might be impossible, anyway.

[90] *Royal Commission on Civil Liability and Compensation for Personal Injury* (1978), Cmnd.7054, Vol.1, para.1471.

[91] In form the claim is one against the parent, but most people would regard the "real" defendant as the insurer (cf. *Hunt v Severs*, para.23–081). Now in motor cases there is a direct right of action against the insurer: para.1–036. Under the present law, claims by children injured as passengers in cars negligently driven by parents are not uncommon.

driving a motor vehicle when she knows or ought to know herself to be pregnant is to be regarded as under a duty of care towards her unborn child.[92]

25–018   **Defences.** The derivative nature of the child's action in cases other than those involving negligent driving by the mother is emphasised by the supplementary provisions of s.1, which "identify" the child with the parents for the purposes of defences. Thus, in the case of an occurrence preceding the time of conception, knowledge by either parent of the risk of disablement will bar the child's action;[93] where the parent affected shared responsibility for the child being born disabled, the child's damages are to be reduced according to the extent of the parent's responsibility;[94] and any contract term having the effect of excluding or restricting liability to the parent is equally effective in respect of liability to the child.[95]

25–019   **Disability caused by infertility treatment.** Since the 1976 Act was passed there have been major developments in the treatment of infertility and the possibility arises of a disability being caused by some act or omission in the course of such treatment but which would not fall within s.1, for example during the keeping of the gametes or the embryo outside the body. Section 1A of the Act, inserted by s.44 of the Human Fertilisation and Embryology Act 1990, covers these cases and provides a virtual mirror image of s.1.

25–020   **"Wrongful life" claims by the child.** So far we have been dealing with cases where, but for the defendant's wrongful act or omission, the claimant would have been born without the disability or with a lesser degree of it; but another situation presents much more acute legal problems, that is to say, where the claimant contends that he should never have been born at all, the so-called "wrongful life" case. Such a case could conceivably be advanced against a person responsible for the child's conception[96] but is more likely to arise from failure during the early stages of pregnancy to detect some deformity or disability which, if it had been detected, would have led to an abortion.[97] Such was one of the claims in *McKay v Essex Area Health Authority*,[98] decided at common law since the birth was before the 1976 Act. In striking out this claim, the court referred to various

---

[92] Should knowledge be required? Other drivers will have no means of knowing the mother is pregnant and it seems far-fetched to assume that the mother would desist from driving if she knew she was pregnant.

[93] Section 1(4); but not where the father is responsible for the injury to the mother and she does not know of the risk. If a woman is the child's other parent, under the Human Fertilisation and Embryology Act 2008 she is treated in the same way as the father: s.1(4A).

[94] Section 1(7). Cf. a case under s.2, which would follow the normal rule of non-identification (para.23–052), allowing the child to recover in full against either defendant and consigning the final allocation of loss to contribution proceedings between the defendants.

[95] Section 1(6). This provision is likely to be of very limited effect in view of the Unfair Contract Terms Act 1977 s.2(1) (para.26–017), and is anyway inapplicable to cases under the Consumer Protection Act 1987: see s.6(3)(c) of that Act.

[96] See, e.g. *Zepeda v Zepeda* 190 N.E. 2d 849 (1963).

[97] The risk of serious handicap is a ground for lawful abortion. Since the amendment of the Abortion Act 1967 by the Human Fertilisation and Embryology Act 1990 s.37, there is no specific time limit for these cases, nor is the Infant Life Preservation Act 1929 applicable (cf. *Rance v Mid-Downs HA* [1991] 1 Q.B. 587) but there might still be practical or medical grounds ruling out a late abortion.

[98] [1982] Q.B. 1166. An alternative basis of the case was unproblematical: that if the mother had received treatment the disability would have been less.

objections of a public policy nature (for example, the dangers of a legal assessment of the life of a disabled child as less valuable than that of a child without disability and the prospect of a claim against the mother where, informed of the danger, she declined to have an abortion) but that which most strongly influenced all the members of the court was the impossibility of assessing damages on any sensible basis, for the court would have to, "compare the state of the plaintiff with non-existence, of which the court can know nothing".[99] In so far as this might be taken to imply that such a comparison is impossible in all legal contexts it may have been overtaken by *Re J*,[100] in which the Court of Appeal held that in extreme circumstances it could be lawful to withhold life-sustaining treatment because of the poor quality of the life the patient would have to endure. In other words, the law accepts that there are circumstances in which it is in a person's best interests to die. However, no doubt was cast on the correctness of *McKay*'s case: the fact that the court might be compelled to engage in a comparative balancing exercise on the treatment issue did not alter the fact that the problem of assessment of damages remained insuperable.[101]

The 1976 Act replaces "any law in force before its passing, whereby a person could be liable to a child in respect of disabilities with which it might be born". This wording would appear wide enough to prevent any future cases at common law even in the unlikely event that the House of Lords were to overrule *McKay's* case and the limitation problems could be overcome. In *McKay* the Court of Appeal said, obiter, that no such claim could be made under the Act because it imports the assumption that but for the occurrence giving rise to the disabled birth, the child would have been born normal and healthy, not that it would not have been born at all. This is certainly true of s.1(2)(b),[102] which deals with the most obvious case, that where there is negligence towards the mother during pregnancy. However, no such assumption is expressly built into s.1(2)(a) dealing with pre-conception events, nor into the new s.1A. Indeed, one of the specified matters dealt with by the latter ("the selection . . . of the embryo . . . or of the gametes used to bring about the creation of the embryo") seems to point to a situation where the defect is already inherent in the "material" used. Nearly all the discussion in the English and American cases has been in terms of general damages. In some American cases damages have been allowed in respect of medical expenses caused by the disability but in practice such claims are likely to be presented by parents, whose claims are clearly not affected by the 1976 Act. It is to claims of parents that we now turn.

"Wrongful life" claims by parents. From the mid-1980s the courts faced claims **25–021** by parents (usually arising out of unsuccessful sterilisation operations) for the cost of upbringing of children. These were allowed, damages being based upon the parents' station in life and therefore sometimes amounting to very substantial sums. This line of cases was overturned by the House of Lords in *McFarlane v*

---

[99] *McKay v Essex Area Health Authority* [1982] Q.B. 1166 at 1193 per Griffiths LJ. Cf. *Cherry v Borsman* (1992) 94 D.L.R. (4th) 487 (attempted but unsuccessful abortion caused claimant's injuries).
[100] [1991] Fam. 33; but cf. Ward LJ's view of this case in *A, Re* [2001] Fam. 147.
[101] That was also the view of the majority of the High Court of Australia in *Harriton v Stephens* [2006] HCA 15; 226 C.L.R. 52.
[102] "An occurrence . . . which . . . affected the mother . . . or the child . . . so that the child is born with disabilities which would not otherwise have been present."

Tayside Health Board.[103] The reasons were various: to award damages representing the cost of upbringing was disproportionate to the wrong committed (negligent advice to the father that his vasectomy had been successful); it would fail to take account of the real (though incalculable) countervailing benefits brought to the family by the birth of a healthy child, benefits which were still present even if the parents' intention had been to have no more children; and it would offend against the idea of distributive justice, which in suitable cases had a role to play in the mosaic of tort law alongside the more usual corrective justice.[104] However, the mother was allowed to recover damages for the pain, suffering and inconvenience of pregnancy and birth and for the loss of earnings and expenses immediately attendant on those processes.[105] A little later in *Rees v Darlington Memorial Hospital NHS Trust*[106] the majority of a divided House of Lords modified the position somewhat by holding that it was necessary to do more to recognise that the mother in such a situation had suffered a legal wrong and an interference with her autonomy in being deprived of the freedom to limit her family as she wished and that this should take the form of an award of a conventional sum of damages:[107] £15,000 was awarded. This is a curious decision, which verges on judicial legislation. There have been other common law examples of such conventional awards, most notably the damages for loss of expectation of life which were formerly awarded in fatal accident cases[108] but the sum in *McFarlane* was substantially greater in real terms. Perhaps the closest analogy is the statutory sum for bereavement.[109]

Where, in such cases the child is born with a serious disability, whether mental or physical, a parent may recover as damages the extra expenses of upbringing associated with that disability, over and above the costs attached to bringing up any child.[110] It may also happen that even if the child has no disability the mother's disability makes it more difficult and expensive for her to look after the child but in that case no damages are recoverable beyond those immediately associated with the birth and the conventional sum referred to above. Such a situation was in issue in *Rees v Darlington*, where the mother was blind and had sought sterilisation because of the burden motherhood would impose on her; but this did not justify a different result, for a balance sheet of benefit and detriment still could not be drawn up—just as the law could not distinguish between the impact of an "unwanted" child on wealthy parents and poor parents, so it could not distinguish between parents who were fit and well and those whose disability

---

103 [2000] 2 A.C. 59.

104 See also *Frost v CC South Yorks* [1999] 2 A.C. 455, para.5–093.

105 The mother's loss of earnings during the upbringing of the child is not recoverable: there is no material distinction between such loss and the expenses of upbringing: *Greenfield v Flather* [2001] EWCA Civ 113, [2001] 1 W.L.R. 179 (where an attempt to rely on art.8 of the European Convention on Human Rights was also rejected).

106 [2003] UKHL 52; [2004] 1 A.C. 309.

107 In *Rees* the mother was disabled (see below) but the proposition is plainly not confined to such cases.

108 Abolished by the Administration of Justice Act 1982 s.1(1)(9).

109 See para.24–016.

110 *Parkinson v St James Hospital Trust* [2001] EWCA Civ 530; [2002] Q.B. 266.

might cause them to incur further expense.[111] Indeed, the correctness of the proposition that the "extra" cost of bringing up a disabled *child* is recoverable is a matter of controversy. In *Rees* Lord Scott said:[112]

> "The possibility that a child may be born with a congenital abnormality is plainly present to some degree in the case of every pregnancy. But is that a sufficient reason for holding the negligent doctor liable for the extra costs, attributable to the abnormality, of rearing the child? In my opinion it is not. Foreseeability of a one in 200 to 400 chance does not seem to me, by itself, enough to make it reasonable to impose on the negligent doctor liability for these costs. It might be otherwise in a case where there had been particular reason to fear that if a child were conceived and born it might suffer from some inherited disability. And, particularly, it might be otherwise in a case where the very purpose of the sterilisation operation had been to protect against that fear. But on the facts of *Parkinson* I do not think the Court of Appeal's conclusion was consistent with *McFarlane*."

B.   Liability to be Sued

No defence of infancy as such, but age not irrelevant. In the law of tort there is no defence of infancy as such and a minor is as much liable to be sued for his torts as is an adult. In *Gorely v Codd*,[113] Nield J had no hesitation in holding that a boy of 16 had been negligent when he accidentally shot the claimant with an air rifle in the course of "larking about", and it is obvious that a motorist one month short of 18 is as responsible for negligent driving as one who has reached that age. However, where a minor is sued for negligence, his age is relevant in determining what he ought reasonably to have foreseen. In an action for negligence against a young child, therefore, it is insufficient to show that he behaved in a way which would amount to negligence on the part of an adult. It must be shown that his behaviour fell below the standard of an ordinarily reasonable and prudent child of his age[114] and even though one cannot fix the age precisely, it is obvious that a tiny infant cannot be liable in tort at all.

25–022

C.   Tort and Contract

In general contracts entered into by minors are void and unenforceable, and the question arises, therefore, whether if the facts show both a breach of a (void) contract and a tort, the contract rule can be evaded by framing the claim against the minor in tort. The answer seems to be that a minor cannot be sued if the cause of action against him arises substantially *ex contractu* or if to allow the action would be to enforce the contract indirectly, but if the wrong is independent of the

25–023

---

[111] In the earlier case of *AD v East Kent Community NHS Trust* [2002] EWCA Civ 1872; [2003] 3 All E.R. 1167 the court had dismissed a claim where the child was cared for by a relative of the disabled mother.

[112] [2003] UKHL 52; [2004] 1 A.C. 309 at [147]; and Lord Bingham at [9] said that, "it is arguably anomalous that the defendant's liability should be related to a disability which the doctor's negligence did not cause and not to the birth which it did". Contra Lord Nicholls at [35] ("The legal policy on which *McFarlane* was based is critically dependent on the birth of a healthy and normal child"), Lord Hope at [57] and Lord Hutton at [91] (both dissenting on the main issue). Lord Millet at [112] left the point open.

[113] [1967] 1 W.L.R. 19; *Buckpitt v Oates* [1968] 1 All E.R. 1145 at 1149 per John Stephenson J.

[114] *Mullin v Richards* [1998] 1 W.L.R. 1304.

contract, then the minor may be sued even though but for the contract he would have had no opportunity of committing the tort.[115] In *R Leslie Ltd v Shiell*[116] a minor had fraudulently represented to the claimants that he was of full age and had thereby persuaded them to lend him money. He was held not liable for deceit or on any other ground, for a judgment against him would have amounted to the enforcement of the contract of loan in a roundabout way. On the other hand, in *Burnard v Haggis*,[117] the defendant, an undergraduate of Trinity College, Cambridge, and a minor, was held liable in the following circumstances. He hired from the claimant a mare for riding on the express stipulation that she was not to be used for "jumping or larking". He nevertheless lent the mare to a friend who, while they were galloping about fields in the neighbourhood of Cambridge, tried to jump her over a fence, on which she was staked and she died from the wound. The defendant's conduct was, as Willes J said:[118]

> "[A]s much a trespass, notwithstanding the hiring for another purpose, as if, without any hiring at all, the defendant had gone into a field and taken the mare out and hunted her and killed her. It was a bare trespass, not within the object and purpose of the hiring. It was not even an excess. It was doing an act towards the mare which was altogether forbidden by the owner."[119]

If in *R Leslie Ltd v Shiell* the minor had still been in possession of the money lent equity would have ordered its restoration on the ground of fraud. Now, under s.3(1) of the Minors' Contracts Act 1987 the court has a discretion to order the transfer back of any property acquired under the contract (or its proceeds) even without fraud, but if the money has been spent and there is nothing to show for it, nothing can be done.

D. Liability of Parent

25–024   A parent or guardian[120] is not in general liable for the torts of a child[121] but to this there are two exceptions. First, where the child is employed by his parent and commits a tort in the course of his employment, the parent is vicariously responsible just as he would be for the tort of any other servant of his. Secondly, the parent will be liable if the child's tort is due to the parent's negligent control

---

[115] *Pollock Principles of Contract*, 13th edn (1950), pp.62–63, approved by Kennedy LJ in *R. Leslie Ltd v Shiell* [1914] 3 K.B. 607 at 620.

[116] [1914] 3 K.B. 607.

[117] *Burnard v Haggis* (1863) 14 C.B.(N.S.) 45. Cf. *Jennings v Rundall* (1799) 8 T.R. 335; *Fawcett v Smethurst* (1915) 84 L.J.K.B. 473.

[118] *Burnard v Haggis* (1863) 14 C.B. (N.S.) 45 at 53.

[119] See too *Ballett v Mingay* [1943] K.B. 281.

[120] Note in this connection that it has been said that school authorities are under no greater duty than that of a reasonably careful parent: *Ricketts v Erith BC* [1943] 2 All E.R. 629; *Rich v London CC* [1953] 1 W.L.R 895, but see the comments in *Woodland v Essex CC* [2013] UKSC 66; [2014] A.C. 537, para.21–048 ("the recognition of a non-delegable duty of care owed by schools involves imputing to them a greater responsibility than any which the law presently recognises as being owed by parents", at [25] per Lord Sumption).

[121] Such liability is common in Europe. See Martin-Casals, *Children in Tort Law Part I: Children as Tortfeasors* (2006).

of the child in respect of the act that caused the injury,[122] or if the parent expressly authorised the commission of the tort, or possibly if he ratified the child's act. Thus, where a father gave his boy, about 15 years old, an airgun and allowed him to retain it after he had smashed a neighbour's window with it, he was held liable for the boy's tort in injuring the eye of another boy with the gun.[123] Where, however, a boy aged 13 had promised his father never to use his air rifle outside the house (where there was a cellar in which the rifle could be fired) and subsequently broke that promise, the Court of Appeal refused to disturb the trial judge's findings that the father had not been negligent.[124] Nor will he be liable to one who is bitten by a dog which belongs to his daughter who is old enough to be able to exercise control over it, and this is so even if the father knows of the dog's ferocious temper.[125] Where, however, the child is under the age of 16 a different rule prevails by statute.[126]

4. SPOUSES

It is 80 years since the abolition of the special rules governing a married woman's liability in tort and making her husband liable for her torts during marriage.[127] As far as third parties are concerned there are no special rules governing husband and wife and neither is liable for the other's torts, though he or she may of course be liable as a joint tortfeasor if this is in fact the case. As between themselves, the common law rule was that no action in tort was possible, but in modern times this was productive of serious anomalies and injustices and it was abolished by the Law Reform (Husband and Wife) Act 1962.[128] Each of the parties to a marriage now has the same right of action in tort against the other as if they were not married,[129] but, in order to prevent them from using the court as a forum for trivial domestic disputes, the proceedings may be stayed if it appears that no substantial benefit will accrue to either party from their continuation.[130] The proceedings may also be stayed if it appears that the case can be more conveniently disposed of under s.17 of the Married Women's Property Act 1882, which provides a summary procedure for determining questions of title or possession of property between husband and wife.

25–025

---

[122] If a juvenile court imposes a compensation order it is to be paid by the parent or guardian unless the court considers this unreasonable: see *TA v DPP* [1997] 2 F.L.R. 887.

[123] *Bebee v Sales* (1916) 32 T.L.R. 413; *Newton v Edgerley* [1959] 1 W.L.R. 1031.

[124] *Donaldson v McNiven* (1952) 96 S.J. 747.

[125] *North v Wood* [1914] 1 K.B. 629.

[126] See para.17–008.

[127] Law Reform (Married Women and Tortfeasors) Act 1935.

[128] Section 1(1). In *Church v Church* (1983) 133 N.L.J. 317, £9,605 damages were awarded in an action for battery between spouses

[129] This means, of course, that even if proceedings are not brought against the spouse, a co-tortfeasor with him may have a right of contribution.

[130] Section 1(2)(a) (there are equivalent provisions for same-sex formalised relationships in s.69 of the Civil Partnership Act 2004). See *McLeod v McLeod* (1963) 113 L.J. 420.

5. CORPORATIONS

25–026   A corporation is an artificial person created by the law. It may come into existence either by the common law, by royal charter, by Parliamentary authority, or by prescription or custom. Whatever its origin may be, a corporation is quite independent of the human beings who are its members.

A.   Capacity to Sue in Tort

25–027   **Capacity.** A corporation can sue for torts committed against it,[131] but there are certain torts which, by their very nature, it is impossible to commit against a corporation, such as assault or false imprisonment. A corporation can sue for the malicious presentation of a winding-up petition[132] or for defamation, though the precise limits of the latter are unclear. It is certain that a trading corporation may sue in respect of defamation affecting its business or property,[133] and perhaps in respect of anything affecting its conduct of its affairs[134] but a governmental authority cannot sue for defamation.[135]

25–028   **Proper claimant.** A rather different point is that the corporation (and not its members) is the only proper claimant in respect of a tort against the corporation. To some extent this is simply a reflection of the elementary principle that C cannot bring an action against D to recover damages for an injury done by D to A, C (the member) and A (the corporation) being different persons. A shareholder is not an owner of the company's assets but merely has a right to participate in them on winding up. So if the defendant infringes patents belonging to a company the company can sue but a shareholder cannot. The shareholder and the company may, of course, have separate and distinct claims arising out of the same conduct of the defendant. If D carelessly burns down the company premises and C, a shareholder who happens to be present at the time, is injured, the fact that the company has a claim for the cost of rebuilding does not affect C's claim for personal injuries. However, even though a tort has been committed against the shareholder, the loss suffered by him may be a diminution in the value of his shareholding and this is only a reflection of the loss to the company caused by the diminution of its assets. To allow both the company and the shareholder to sue would be to allow double recovery; to allow the shareholder to sue and then bar the company from further action would be to harm the company's creditors, for they are entitled to the company's assets in dissolution in priority to the

---

[131] *Semble*, even if engaged in an ultra vires undertaking at the material time: *National Telephone Co v Constable of St Peter Port* [1900] A.C. 317 at 321 per Lord Davey, obiter, a decision of the Privy Council on appeal from the Royal Court of Guernsey.

[132] *Quartz Hill Consolidated Gold Mining v Eyre* (1883) 11 Q.B.D. 674.

[133] *Metropolitan Saloon Omnibus Co v Hawkins* (1859) 4 H. & N. 87; *Jameel v Wall Street Journal Europe Sprl* [2006] UKHL 44; [2007] 1 A.C. 359.

[134] *D & L Caterers Ltd v D'Ajou* [1945] K.B. 364; *National Union of General and Municipal Workers v Gillan* [1946] K.B. 81; *Willis v Brooks* [1947] 1 All E.R. 191; *South Hetton Coal Co Ltd v NE News Association Ltd* [1894] 1 Q.B. 133, though inconclusive on the point, seems to support this view. Dicta in *Manchester Corp v Williams* (1891) 63 L.T. 805 at 806 (the fuller report) and *Lewis v Daily Telegraph Ltd* [1964] A.C. 234 at 262, seems to support the narrower view.

[135] See para.13–037.

shareholders and by allowing the shareholder to sue the company's assets would in effect be diminished. Hence English law does not allow such a "reflexive" claim. If the sole asset of a company is a box containing £100,000 and C owns 99 of the 100 shares in the company he cannot sue the thief who appropriates the contents of the box.[136] However, the same would be true in that example even if the contents were misappropriated by the thief fraudulently obtaining the key from C and thereby committing an actionable wrong against him. C has still suffered no loss other than the diminution of the value of his shareholding in the company which will arise as a result of the loss of the company's assets.[137] If, on the other hand, the value of the shareholder's holding is diminished by a tort against him which is not actionable by the company there is nothing to prevent him suing for that loss.[138]

B. Liability to be Sued

It has always been generally accepted that a chartered corporation[139] has all the powers of a natural person[140] but most companies were incorporated under statute and were expressly limited by the terms of their incorporation as to what they might lawfully do. While this is still true as far as the internal affairs of the company are concerned, s.39 of the Companies Act 2006 provides that "the validity of an act done by a company shall not be called into question on the ground of lack of capacity by reason of anything in the company's constitution". This would seem to render otiose any distinction for the purposes of the law of torts between intra vires and ultra vires acts, though the distinction had in fact been largely effaced under the old law.[141] **25–029**

Wrongs committed by servants or agents. A company will be liable for the acts of its servant committed within the course of employment[142] (and where relevant in tort, for the acts of its agent within the scope of his authority)[143] and no doubt the objects for which the company was incorporated may be very relevant in determining the limits of the employment or authority of the servant or agent.[144] **25–030**

Wrongs committed by the company itself. There are acts or omissions which, for the purposes of the law, are to be regarded as those of the company itself. Thus, it may incur a personal liability when it fails to take reasonable care for the **25–031**

---

[136] This is so even if the company chooses not to sue. However, where a wrongdoer is in control of the company a shareholder may be able to bring a "derivative" action on behalf of the company, but this is not a personal claim.

[137] *Johnson v Gore Wood & Co* [2001] 2 A.C. 1; *Prudential Assurance Co Ltd v Newman Industries Ltd (No.2)* [1982] Ch. 204.

[138] *Lee v Sheard* [1956 1 Q.B. 192; *Fischer (George) GB Ltd v Multi-Construction Ltd* [1995] 1 B.C.L.C. 260; *Gerber Garment Technology Inc v Lectra Systems Ltd* [1997] R.P.C. 443.

[139] For example, the older universities.

[140] *Case of Sutton's Hospital* (1613) 10 Co Rep. 23a.

[141] See the 13th edn of this work, p.675.

[142] See Ch.21.

[143] *New Zealand Guardian Trust Co Ltd v Brooks* [1995] 1 W.L.R. 96 (directors).

[144] Under the Companies Act 2006 s.40 (originating in 1989), "in favour of a person dealing with a company in good faith, the power of the board of directors to bind the company, or authorise others to do so, is deemed to be free of any limitation under the company's constitution".

safety of persons even if no allegation of negligence is made against any individual servant of the company[145] and it has been held, where a liability depended upon the "actual fault or privity" of the company, that this condition was satisfied if the persons who constituted the "directing mind" of the company were at fault, for the act or omission was then that of the company itself.[146] The metaphor of the "directing mind" does not, however, mean that there is a particular person or group of persons whose acts are to be regarded as those "of the company" for all purposes[147] for this question depends on the purpose for which it is sought to attribute the acts of a human being to the company, which will generally be a matter of statutory construction.[148] Thus in *The Lady Gwendolen*[149] the question was whether a collision at sea was with the "actual fault or privity" of brewers (a minor part of whose business was owning ships to carry their product to England), so that the claimants might escape the limitation of liability generally granted by statute to shipowners. For this purpose the inaction of the director who had supervision of the transport department was attributed to the brewers, but his acts and omissions would not have had this effect if the matter had been one outside his supervision under the company's organisation.[150] Contrariwise, the purpose of the statutory rule might lead to the conclusion that the act of someone well below board level should be attributed to the company.

Under this principle of "attribution" there is no legal difficulty in finding a company liable for deceit, even though it obviously has no natural capacity to be dishonest.[151] So in *Stone & Rolls Ltd v Moore Stephens*[152] it was uncontroversial that the company was liable to a bank where its sole executive director and presumed sole beneficial owner used it as a vehicle of fraud to extract money from the bank. What provoked disagreement in the House of Lords was the question whether the director's act was also to be regarded as the company's act so as to prevent it, on the basis of ex turpi causa non oritur actio,[153] suing its auditors for failure to discover the fraud, to which the majority answered that it did.[154]

25–032 **Corporate groups.** In modern conditions a business may be carried on by a group of companies, perhaps in the form of a holding company with subsidiaries in many different jurisdictions. In principle these are as much separate entities as the companies and their shareholders and directors and one is not liable for the

---

[145] See para.9–017.
[146] *Lennard's Carrying Co Ltd v Asiatic Petroleum Co Ltd* [1915] A.C. 705; *The Lady Gwendolen* [1965] P. 294 (limitation provisions in merchant shipping legislation).
[147] Though for practical purposes this may be true of a resolution of the board or of a meeting of the company.
[148] See *Meridian Global Funds Management Asia Ltd v Securities Commission* [1995] 2 A.C. 500.
[149] [1965] P. 294.
[150] These questions are less important in the context of tort than they are in crime, because vicarious liability is more extensive in the former.
[151] Or for battery: *KR v Royal & Sun Alliance Plc* [2006] EWCA Civ 1454; [2007] P.I.Q.R. P14 (where the question arose from an exclusion in a liability insurance policy in respect of the assured's deliberate acts).
[152] [2009] UKHL 39; [2009] 3 W.L.R. 455.
[153] See para.26–062.
[154] Cf. *Safeway Stores Ltd v Twigger* [2010] EWCA Civ 1472; [2011] 2 All E.R. 841.

acts of another. However, where one company in the group is involved in the management of another it may owe a duty of care to persons (for example workers or consumers) affected by the activities of the other.[155]

C. Liability of Directors[156]

As a company is a separate legal person its directors are not, apart from statute, **25–033** personally liable on contracts made by the company, nor for torts of company servants for which the company is vicariously liable. To identify the director with the company would be too great a brake on commercial enterprise and adventure, however small the company and however powerful the control of the director. Nevertheless, where directors order an act by the company which amounts to a tort they may be liable as joint tortfeasors on the ground that they have procured the wrong to be done.[157] Where the tort in question requires a particular state of mind the director must have that, but there is no general principle that a director must know that the act is tortious or be reckless as to that.[158] If a company servant were to trespass on the claimant's land believing it to belong to the company that would be trespass and there is no reason why a director who, with the same state of mind, instructed him to do the act should escape liability. The director is also, of course liable if he commits the tort himself. In some cases company law will regard an act of the directors as an act of the company itself. If the director of a company were to assault the director of a rival business in the course of a dispute about sales that could hardly be regarded as an assault by the company and any liability of the company would have to be truly vicarious, that is to say for the director qua employee. On the other hand, if the board of a company were to induce someone to make a contract by fraudulent misrepresentation that would be a fraud by the company. However, that fact does not mean that the individual directors are not also liable: "No one can escape liability for his fraud by saying: 'I wish to make it clear that I am committing this fraud on behalf of someone else and I am not to be personally liable.'"[159]

---

[155] *Chandler v Cape Plc* [2012] EWCA Civ 525; [2012] 1 W.L.R. 3111; cf. *Thompson v Renwick Group Plc* [2014] EWCA Civ 635.

[156] For a very full examination of the authorities see *Johnson Mathey (Aust) Ltd v Dacorp Pty Ltd* [2003] VSC 291; 9 V.R. 171.

[157] See, e.g. *Mancetter Developments Ltd v Garmanson and Givertz* [1986] Q.B. 1212 (waste); *Global Crossing Ltd v Global Crossing Ltd* [2006] EWHC 2043 (Ch) (incorporation of company, trade mark infringement). A company and its directors may be conspirators: para.19–042; but if C makes a contract with the D Co and the directors resolve not to perform it, C cannot sue them for inducing breach of contract: para.19–015. It has been said that there is a general principle that a director will not be liable in tort if he does no more than carry out his constitutional function in governing the company by voting at board meetings: *MCA Records v Charly Records* [2001] EWCA Civ 1441; [2002] F.S.R. 26 at [49]; *Concept Oil Services Ltd v En-Gen Group LLP* [2013] EWHC 1897 (Comm) at [53] per Flaux J ("there is no impediment to the liability of a director unless he is acting strictly and solely via the constitutional organs of the company concerned").

[158] *C Evans & Sons Ltd v Spriteband Ltd* [1985] 1 W.L.R. 317. *Joiner v George* [2002] EWHC 90 (Ch) turns on the way the case was pleaded and perhaps on the erroneous view of the CA in *Standard Chartered Bank v Pakistan National Shipping (Nos 2 and 4)* [2002] UKHL 43; [2003] 1 A.C. 959.

[159] *Standard Chartered Bank v Pakistan National Shipping (Nos 2 and 4)* [2002] UKHL 43; [2003] 1 A.C. 959 at [22].

In such a case the director would not be liable for the company's fraud but for his own fraud, as indeed would a non-director employee who participated.[160]

As far as negligence is concerned, it has been held that a director may be liable as a joint tortfeasor with the company when he sends a vessel to sea in an unseaworthy condition causing personal injury[161] but a liberal approach to director's liability will have the effect that the limited liability which is the main object of incorporation for a small, "one man" company will be set at naught. In *Williams v Natural Life Health Foods Ltd*[162] the House of Lords held that to justify liability of a director for advice there must be some special facts showing a personal assumption of responsibility,[163] which the court declined to find in the combination of the active part which the director played in preparing the financial projection in question and the representation in the company's brochure that the company's expertise in the trade was based upon the director's experience gained in a personal capacity independent of the company. There were no exchanges between the director and the claimants which could have led them reasonably to believe that he was assuming a personal responsibility to them.[164]

6. PARTNERS

25–034   In English law a partnership is not a legal person distinct from its members and consequently has no capacity to sue or be sued,[165] but each partner is liable jointly and severally with his co-partners for any wrongful act or omission committed by any of them against an outsider while acting in the ordinary course of business of the firm.[166] If a partner in a firm of solicitors were to commit fraudulent misrepresentations in the course of persuading someone to buy double glazing the other partners would not be liable for that because selling double glazing is not within the description of activities which a solicitors' firm ordinarily carries out.[167] Even where the transaction is one within that general description it may be that its details are so unusual that it is not within the ordinary course of business[168] but the mere fact that the partner intends to behave dishonestly does not take it outside the scope of vicarious liability.[169] The Limited Liability Partnerships Act 2000 introduced a new form of legal entity

---

[160] "The maxim *culpa tenet suos auctores* may not be the end, but it is the beginning of wisdom in these matters": [2002] UKHL 43; [2003] 1 A.C. 959 at [40] per Lord Rodger.

[161] *Yuille v B & B Fisheries (Leigh) Ltd* [1958] 2 Lloyd's Rep. 596. It is usually regarded as self-evident that a servant whose negligence in the course of employment causes personal injury is personally liable even though the employer is vicariously liable.

[162] [1998] 1 W.L.R. 830.

[163] Cf. *Standard Chartered Bank v Pakistan National Shipping (Nos 2 and 4)* [2002] UKHL 43; [2003] 1 A.C. 959, a case of deceit, which is not based on a duty of care.

[164] Cf. *Merrett v Babb* [2001] EWCA Civ 214; [2001] 3 W.L.R. 1, para.12–032 (employee). *Fairline Shipping Corp v Adamson* [1975] Q.B. 180 is perhaps a rather clearer case for liability.

[165] The partners may sue or be sued in the name of the firm: CPR r.5A.3.

[166] Partnership Act 1890 ss.10 and 12. See *Dubai Aluminium Co Ltd v Salaam* [2002] UKHL 48; [2003] 2 A.C. 366. The partners may, of course, also be liable for the torts of their servants or agents under ordinary principles: see, e.g. *Lloyd v Grace, Smith & Co* [1912] A.C. 716.

[167] *JJ Coughlan Ltd v Ruparelia* [2003] EWCA Civ 1057; [2004] P.N.L.R. 4 at [25].

[168] *JJ Coughlan Ltd v Ruparelia* [2003] EWCA Civ 1057; [2004] P.N.L.R. 4.

[169] See *Dubai Aluminium Co Ltd v Salaam* [2002] UKHL 48; [2003] 2 A.C. 366 especially at [120].

known as a limited liability partnership, which is a body corporate (with legal personality separate from that of its members and with unlimited capacity) and which is formed by being incorporated under the Act.

7.   CLUBS[170]

In the case of proprietary and incorporated clubs, it would seem that the ordinary rules as to the liability of employer or principal for the torts of his servants or agents apply.[171] In the case of an unincorporated club, which is not an entity known to the law and which cannot be sued in its own name, liability involves a question of substantive law and one of procedure. The first question is, who is liable for the wrongful act or breach of duty?[172] This depends on the circumstances of the particular case, and it may be the members of the committee, or someone such as a steward who is in control of the club or possibly the whole body of members. Membership of the club and even membership of the committee does not involve any special duty of care towards other members of the club nor, it seems, towards a stranger but neither is it a ground of immunity for one who has assumed a responsibility.[173] So, members of the committee (at the time when the cause of action arose) will be liable personally to the exclusion of other members, if they act personally, as by employing an incompetent person to erect a stand as the result of which a stranger is injured.[174] In the case of torts involving vicarious liability, apart from the actual wrongdoer's liability, the question depends upon whose servant or agent the wrongdoer was at the material time.[175] Where liability arises out of the ownership or occupation of property, as in nuisance or under the Occupiers' Liability Act 1957, the occupiers of the premises in question will normally be the proper persons to sue. If the property is vested in trustees they may be the proper persons to sue, but in the absence of trustees it is a question of fact as to who are the occupiers of the premises.[176] As to the procedural point, the need for a representative action only arises where it is desired to sue the whole body of members, and a representation order may be made, provided that the members whose names appear on the writ are persons

25–035

---

[170] Lloyd (1953) 16 M.L.R. 359. For the position of trade unions, see para.19–052.

[171] Halsbury, *Laws of England*, 5th edn (London: LexisNexis 2009), Vol.136; for different kinds of clubs, see para.204. In a proprietary club the property and funds of the club belong to a proprietor, who may sue or be sued in his own name or in the name of the club. The members are in contractual relation with the proprietor, and have a right to use the club premises in accordance with the rules, but they are not his servants or agents. An incorporated club may sue or be sued in its corporate name. An unincorporated members' club has no legal existence apart from its members, who are jointly entitled to the property and funds, though usually the property is vested in trustees. It cannot sue or be sued in the club name, nor can the secretary or any other officer sue or be sued on behalf of the club.

[172] For an extensive review (in the context of the Roman Catholic Church in Australia) see *Trustees of the Roman Catholic Church v Ellis* [2007] NSWCA 117.

[173] *Prole v Allen* [1950] 1 All E.R. 476; *Shore v Ministry of Works* [1950] 2 All E.R. 228; *Grice v Stourport Tennis etc. Club* Unreported February 28, 1997 CA cf. *Robertson v Ridley* [1989] 2 All E.R. 474.

[174] Halsbury, *Laws of England* (2009), Vol.136, para.231; *Brown v Lewis* (1896) 12 T.L.R. 445; *Bradley Egg Farm Ltd v Clifford* [1943] 2 All E.R. 378.

[175] Lloyd (1953) 16 M.L.R. 359.

[176] Lloyd (1953) 16 M.L.R. 359, 360.

who may fairly be taken to represent the body of club members and that they and all the other club members have the same interest in the action.[177]

8.   PERSONS OF UNSOUND MIND

25–036   **Capacity to sue.** A person suffering from mental disorder has the capacity to sue in respect of a tort against him, proceedings being conducted by his litigation friend. However, a claim in respect of action taken under the Mental Health Act 1983 will only lie if the act was done, "in bad faith or without reasonable care" and leave of the High Court is required.[178]

25–037   **Liability to be sued.** There is singularly little English authority as to the liability of persons of unsound mind for torts committed by them.[179] Sir Matthew Hale thought that dementia was one of several other forms of incapacity which might exempt a person from criminal liability, but which ordinarily do not excuse him from civil liability, for that, "is not by way of penalty, but a satisfaction of damage done to the party"[180] and there are dicta in the older cases which regard lunacy as no defence.[181] More to the purpose is a dictum of Lord Esher MR, in 1892,[182] that a mentally disordered person is liable unless the disease of his mind is so great that he cannot understand the nature and consequences of his act. In *Morriss v Marsden*[183] the defendant, who attacked and seriously injured the claimant, had been found unfit to plead in earlier criminal proceedings. He was then sued by the claimant for damages for assault and battery. Stable J found that the defendant's mind was so disturbed by his disease that he did not know that what he was doing was wrong, but that the assault was a voluntary act on his part and that the defendant was therefore liable.

Unsoundness of mind is thus certainly not in itself a ground of immunity from liability in tort, and it is submitted that the true question in each case is whether the defendant was possessed of the requisite state of mind for liability in the particular tort with which he is charged. In trespass to the person it is enough that the defendant intended to strike the claimant and the defendant in *Morriss v Marsden* was therefore rightly held liable but had his disease been so severe that his act was not a voluntary one at all he would not have been liable.[184] In defamation it is enough that the defendant published matter defamatory of the claimant and it would certainly be no defence that in his disturbed mental state he believed it to be true. Again, as Stable J said: "I cannot think that, if a person of

---

[177] *Campbell v Thompson* [1953] 1 Q.B. 445. See Lloyd (1953) 16 M.L.R. 359, 360–363 and CPR r.19.6. A representation order may also be made in favour of persons as claimants.
[178] See *Winch v Jones* [1986] Q.B. 296; *Johnston v CC Merseyside* [2009] EWHC 2969 (QB); [2009] M.H.L.R. 343.
[179] See Fridman (1963) 79 L.Q.R. 502; (1964) 80 L.Q.R. 84.
[180] 1 *History of Pleas of Crown* (ed. 1778), pp.15–16. So too, in effect Bacon (Spedding's edition of his works, pp.vii, 348).
[181] For example, *Weaver v Ward* (1616) Hob. 134.
[182] *Hanbury v Hanbury* (1892) 8 T.L.R. 559 at 569. Cf. *Mordaunt v Mordaunt* (1870) L.R. 2 P. & D. 103 at 142 per Kelly CB.
[183] [1952] 1 All E.R. 925.
[184] *Morriss v Marsden* [1952] 1 All E.R. 927 per Stable J.

unsound mind converts my property under a delusion that he is entitled to do it or that it was not property at all, that affords a defence."[185]

Negligence. The tort of negligence probably creates the greatest difficulty. The standard of negligence is said to eliminate the individual characteristics of the defendant,[186] but this does not mean, for example, that a driver who suffers a sudden, unexpected[187] and disabling illness is liable for the damage he does: even the reasonable man can have a heart attack.[188] No English court appears to have been required to deal in this context with what might be called "unsoundness of mind" in the generally accepted sense but there have been cases of inability to drive caused by a hypoglycaemic episode. In *Mansfield v Weetabix Ltd*[189] the Court of Appeal held that the defendants were not liable when their driver had a crash caused by such an episode, of the onset of which he was unaware. There was no requirement of a "sudden, disabling event" and it was wrong to bring in the criminal law test of automatism.[190] The position is still unclear where the defendant is fully conscious and has the physical capacity to control his vehicle but is suffering from an insane delusion, for example that the vehicle is subject to external control.[191] Where there is likely to be liability insurance it is perhaps tempting to judge the defendant's behaviour purely objectively, but to do that would invite the application of the same standard to a driver who was stung by a bee or who suffered a heart attack, and that would sever all connection between negligence in name and negligence in reality.[192]

25–038

9.   PERSONS HAVING PARENTAL OR QUASI-PARENTAL AUTHORITY

Parents and other persons in similar positions are necessarily immune against liability for many acts which in other people would be assault, battery or false imprisonment. They have control, usually but not necessarily, of a disciplinary character, over those committed to their charge. The nature of the control varies according to the relationship and, provided that it is exercised reasonably and moderately,[193] acts done in pursuance of it are not tortious. By s.58(3) of the

25–039

---

[185] *Morriss v Marsden* [1952] 1 All E.R. 927.

[186] See para.6–009.

[187] This is important, because if he has reason to believe that he will have an attack he may be negligent in setting out: *Jones v Dennison* [1971] R.T.R. 174.

[188] See *Waugh v James K. Allan Ltd* [1964] 2 Lloyd's Rep. 1. In *Morriss v Marsden* [1952] 1 All E.R. 925 at 927, Stable J said: "If a sleepwalker, without intention or without carelessness, broke a valuable vase, that would not be actionable." His Lordship thus evidently contemplated negligent and non-negligent sleepwalkers as legal possibilities.

[189] [1998] 1 W.L.R. 1263.

[190] *Roberts v Ramsbottom* [1980] 1 W.L.R. 823 was said to be wrong in this respect, though the decision is correct on the basis that the defendant should have been aware of his unfitness to drive before he lost control of the vehicle.

[191] In *Fiala v Cechmanek* (2001) 201 D.L.R. (4th) 680 the Alberta CA declined to impose negligence liability where the defendant could show that he did not understand what he was doing or lacked the capacity to control his actions.

[192] The *Restatement of Torts* 3d in §11 makes an allowance for physical disability but not for mental or emotional disability because it would be "one-sided" to do so. Unlike the physically disabled person, one subject to mental disability cannot take extra precautions to counter the disability.

[193] *R. v H* [2001] EWCA Crim 1024; [2002] 1 Cr.App.R. 7.

Children Act 2004 it is specifically provided that an act causing actual bodily harm (i.e. something which is more than temporary and trifling) cannot be justified.

Parental authority[194] certainly ceases when the child attains 18 years, but is a dwindling right as the child approaches adulthood and for this purpose may well cease at an earlier age.[195]

At common law a schoolteacher had power to discipline pupils and this probably rested upon the need to maintain order and discipline at the school,[196] so that a parental veto upon corporal punishment would not render its use unlawful.[197] However, by statute corporal punishment is no longer a defence to a civil action against a school, whether state or independent, even where the parent authorises the school to administer it.[198] It remains the law, however, that reasonable force may be used to avert personal injury or damage to property: that is not "punishment".

---

[194] The rights, duties and authority of father and mother of a legitimate child are equal: Children Act 1989 s.2.

[195] *Gillick v West Norfolk AHA* [1986] A.C. 112. See *R. v Rahman* (1985) 81 Cr.App.R. 349 (false imprisonment).

[196] Disciplinary powers are not necessarily confined to conduct on school premises: *Cleery v Booth* [1893] 1 Q.B. 465; *R. v Newport (Salop) JJ* [1929] 2 K.B. 416.

[197] Cf. the decision of the European Court of Human Rights (*Campbell v United Kingdom* (1982) 4 E.H.R.R.) that the European Convention on Human Rights is violated where a school administers corporal punishment against the wishes of parents.

[198] Education Act 1996 s.548, as amended. This does not conflict with the European Convention on Human Rights, one cannot apply *Campbell and Cosans v UK* (1982) 4 E.H.R.R. in reverse: *R. (on the application of Williamson) v Secretary of State for Education etc.* [2005] UKHL 15; [2005] 2 A.C. 246.

CHAPTER 26

DEFENCES[1]

---

[1] Goudkamp, *Tort Law Defences* (2013); Dyson, Goudkamp and Wilmot-Smith (eds), *Defences in Tort* (2014).

1. INTRODUCTION

26–001   **The concept of a defence.** The term "defence" is used frequently by lawyers. It is deployed to mean a great diversity of things and care is usually not taken to make it clear how it is being used. In this chapter the word "defence" refers only to arguments offered by the defendant that, if accepted, would permit the defendant to escape from liability even if all of the elements of the tort in which the claimant sues are present. Put differently, defences, for the purposes of this chapter, are rules that eliminate liability even if a complete cause of action exists. Denials of elements of the claimant's cause of action (such as a contention by the defendant that he acted reasonably in the context of proceedings in the tort of negligence) are consequently not counted as defences. Rules that do not prevent liability from arising but which merely affect the remedy to which a successful claimant is entitled (such as the doctrines of contributory negligence[2] and mitigation of damage[3]) are not counted as defences either. Such rules are fundamentally different from liability-defeating rules and should be dealt with separately.

26–002   **Classification of defences.** There are many ways in which defences can be organised. Some systems of organisation are more helpful than others. The arrangement that is adopted in this chapter is minimalistic. It organises defences into: (1) justifications; and (2) public policy defences. Justifications are defences that apply when the defendant acted reasonably in committing a tort. Conversely, public policy defences are defences that may be enlivened irrespective of the reasonableness of the defendant's conduct. This classification has the significant advantage of being exhaustive. No defences are left out in the classificatory cold since all defences are either concerned with the reasonableness of the defendant's conduct or they are not.

     It is possible to subdivide the two categories. Justifications can be split into private justifications and public justifications. The difference between these categories depends upon whose interests the defendant was advancing when he committed a tort. Private justifications are defences that are enlivened when the defendant acts reasonably in committing a tort in order to safeguard his own interests. Public justifications are defences that are triggered when the defendant acts reasonably in committing a tort in order to advance the interests of the public or a section thereof. The category of public policy defences can also be broken down into subcategories. There are two types of public policy defences: public policy defences that arise at the time of the tort; and public policy defences that arise at a later time.

---

[2] See para.23–036.
[3] See para.23–064.

Implications of this taxonomy of defences. The taxonomy of defences that is   26–003
adopted in this chapter has significant and far-reaching consequences. It is not
possible to delve into the details here. They are given elsewhere.[4] However, one
example of the taxonomy's power concerns the relevance of the defendant's
motive. In order to be justified the defendant must not be defectively motivated,
but this is not necessary in order to clinch a public policy defence. Thus, a
defendant who acts for a bad reason (e.g. hits an aggressor not in order to defend
himself but out of spite) will not be entitled to, say, the defence of self-defence
(which is a justification) but the defendant's defective motive will not affect his
entitlement to, say, an immunity (which is a public policy defence). It is arguable
that the type of defence that a defendant has can also affect whether it is
permissible for others to assist or resist him. It might be said that defendants who
are justified should not be resisted and that it is permissible for third-parties to
assist them. Likewise, one might also contend that it is permissible to resist
defendants who only have a public policy defence and that the mere fact that a
defendant has a public policy defence does not mean it is permissible for him be
assisted in his conduct by third-parties.

Defences can overlap. Just as it is possible for a single act to trigger liability in   26–004
multiple torts, so too is it possible for a defendant to have more than one defence.
For example, a defendant who is sued in battery might be able to avoid liability
on the ground that he was arresting the claimant and acting in his own defence.
However, there is probably no practical advantage that flows to the defendant in
having more than one defence.

Onus of pleading and proof. The onus of pleading and proof in respect of   26–005
defences generally rests on the defendant. This is one obvious reason why it is
critical to determine whether a given rule is a defence as opposed to a denial of
the cause of action in which the claimant sues.

Not all tort defences are addressed in this chapter. This chapter does not deal   26–006
with all defences. The number of defences known to the law of torts is
exceedingly large, although no one has ever compiled a complete list of defences.
Because of the scale of the law of tort defences, it is not practical to address all
defences. Furthermore, many defences are essentially confined to specific torts
and, for the purposes of a textbook on the law of torts generally, such defences
are more conveniently addressed in the chapters on the torts concerned.
Accordingly, this chapter sweeps together what might be thought to be fairly
general defences in the sense that they apply to more than one tort.

2.   DENIALS

This chapter is about defences. But in order to understand defences, it is   26–007
necessary to isolate them from the elements of tort in which the claimant sues.
Denials of elements of the tort in question are routinely mistaken for defences. In
this part of the chapter several pleas that function as denials are identified in order
that they can be separated clearly from defences.

---

[4] Goudkamp, *Tort Law Defences* (2013) Ch.6.

A. Consent

26–008   **Generally.** All of the varieties of trespass incorporate non-consent by the claimant to the defendant's conduct as one of their elements. If the claimant consents to the interference with his person or property the action in trespass will be incomplete. For example, a fair blow in a boxing match and a welcome embrace are not batteries because the claimant consents to them. It follows that the plea of consent is a denial and not a defence. Consistently with the fact that consent is a denial in proceedings in trespass it is for the claimant to plead and prove that he did not consent.[5]

26–009   **Consent may be implied.** Consent may be implied from conduct as well as expressed in words. The very acts of taking part in a boxing match or presenting one's arm for injection, for example, clearly conveys consent.

26–010   **Consent is objectively ascertained.** Consent is a state of mind on the part of the claimant. However, the claimant's state of mind is ascertained from his conduct. Thus, a claimant will be taken to have consented if it appears from his conduct that he consented. The fact that, secretly, the claimant did not consent is irrelevant.

26–011   **Consent must be given freely.** Consent must be freely given. "Consent" that is obtained by threats is not consent at all.[6] We have already seen that an adult of full understanding may choose whether or not to receive medical treatment even if the treatment is necessary to save his life and we have considered the capacity of minors and mentally disordered persons to give consent.[7]

26–012   **Consent must relate to the specific conduct in which the defendant engaged in order to prevent liability from arising.** C's consent must relate to the specific act done by D. For example, the fact that C has consented to one medical procedure does not justify D performing another procedure, as where a condition is discovered and treated for mere convenience during the authorised treatment of another condition.[8] In *Appleton v Garrett*[9] it was held that a dentist was liable for trespass to the person when he undertook extravagant and wholly unjustified work on patients' teeth. This result might be explained by saying that the claimants had consented only to treatment that was reasonably necessary. In *Lane v Holloway*,[10] after a verbal altercation, the elderly claimant struck the younger and stronger defendant on the shoulder and the defendant replied with an extremely severe blow to the claimant's eye. The claimant recovered damages,

---

[5] *Christopherson v Bare* (1848) 11 Q.B. 473 at 477; *Freeman v Home Office (No.2)* [1984] Q.B. 524 at 539. Cf. the position in Canada: *Non-Marine Underwriters, Lloyd's London v Scalera* [2000] SCC 24; [2000] 1 S.C.R. 551.

[6] *Latter v Braddell* (1881) 50 L.J.Q.B. 448 seems unduly narrow in insisting on threats of violence.

[7] See paras 4–014—4–015, 4–017.

[8] The terms of the consent may authorise such further treatment as the doctor considers necessary or desirable. For consideration of this, see *Brushett v Cowan* (1990) 69 D.L.R. (4th) 743.

[9] (1995) 34 B.M.L.R. 32.

[10] [1968] 1 Q.B. 379.

for although each party to a fight takes the risk of incidental injuries the claimant had not consented to the risk of a savage blow out of all proportion to the occasion.

A mistaken belief in consent will not prevent liability from arising. It seems that the fact that D mistakenly believed that C consented to the interference with his person or property has no bearing on liability. This is so even if the mistake is reasonable. Suppose that D, a doctor, performs on Patient A an operation authorised by Patient B thinking that Patient A was Patient B. Even if D's mistake is reasonable, he is clearly liable to Patient A.[11]

26–013

Fraud and concealment. What is the position where the claimant's consent is obtained by fraud? Likewise, what is the situation if the defendant fails to disclose some fact (e.g. the fact that he is suffering from a contagious disease) that would have led to the other party to withhold consent had he known the truth? The view long prevailed that the consent was valid so long as the claimant is not deceived as to the essential nature of the defendant's act or the identity of the actor. Thus, to borrow the facts of a criminal case, a defendant will be liable in battery if he falsely represents to a naïve claimant that he is performing a technique that will improve her singing when he is in fact having sexual intercourse with her and the claimant is fooled by that representation.[12] But the defendant will not be liable in battery to the claimant if he persuades the claimant to have sexual intercourse with him by promising payment or marriage when he has no intention of fulfilling such promises (but there might be liability in deceit[13]). In *R. v Richardson*[14] a criminal conviction for assault was quashed when the defendant continued to treat patients after being suspended from dental practice and it is thought that the result should have been the same in a civil action for battery. Similarly, on this approach the defendant will not be liable for battery if he has sexual intercourse with the claimant without disclosing the fact that he is suffering from a sexually transmissible disease. In the criminal law case of *R. v Dica*[15] it was held that if a person had sexual intercourse knowing he was HIV positive and concealed that fact and his partner contracted the condition, the former would be guilty of inflicting grievous bodily harm under s.20 of the Offences against the Person Act 1861 (but not of rape). The consequences of this case for the law of torts are yet to be determined.

26–014

Failure to explain risks of medical procedure. Provided that the patient understands the broad nature of what is to be done, his consent is not vitiated by a failure to explain the risks inherent in the procedure, for it would be deplorable to deal with such cases under the rubric of trespass to the person.[16] In this sense English law does not require "informed consent". However, going beyond the

26–015

---

[11] *Chatterton v Gerson* [1981] Q.B. 432.

[12] *R v Williams* [1923] 1 K.B. 340.

[13] As in *Graham v Saville* [1945] 2 D.L.R. 489 (bigamy). See also *P v B (paternity: damages for deceit)* [2001] 1 F.L.R. 1041.

[14] [1999] Q.B. 444. Cf. *R. v Tabassum* [2002] 2 Cr. App. R. 328, where D had no medical qualifications at all.

[15] [2004] EWCA Crim 1103; [2004] Q.B. 1257.

[16] *Chatterton v Gerson* [1981] Q.B. 432; *Hills v Potter* [1984] 1 W.L.R. 641n; *Sidaway v Bethlem Royal Hospital* [1985] A.C. 871. Cf. Tan (1987) 7 L.S. 149.

basic duty to give sufficient information to enable understanding of the nature of the treatment, there is a further duty, sounding in the tort of negligence, to explain the procedure and its implications in the way a careful and responsible doctor would do.

26–016   **The limits of harm to which one can consent.** The criminal law places limits on the effectiveness of consent when the public interest so requires. For example, fighting (otherwise than in the course of properly conducted sport) is unlawful if bodily harm is intended or caused, notwithstanding the consent of the participants,[17] as are activities likely to cause serious harm in the course of sadomasochistic sexual encounters.[18] Although the matter is unclear, it seems that law of torts approaches the matter differently, and that consent will always prevent liability from arising. *Lane v Holloway*,[19] which is discussed earlier, seems to support this proposition. The Court of Appeal found in favour of the claimant in that case on the basis that he had not consented to the risk of suffering such severe harm. By inference, it would seem that the claimant would have failed in his action had he agreed to run the risk of being gravely injured.

B.   Exclusion of Liability by Contract or Notice

26–017   At common law, in the absence of duress or some other vitiating factor, entry into a contract that exempted the defendant from liability for negligence prevented liability from arising. The same attitude was adopted where the claimant entered another's land by licence subject to a condition exempting the occupier from liability. The key issue at common law in this regard was usually whether the defendant had given sufficient notice to make the excluding term part of the contract or licence: if he had done so, the claimant was bound even though he might not have troubled to read the terms and hence was unaware of the excluding one. The foregoing remains the law, but in most cases it is now heavily qualified by the Unfair Contract Terms Act 1977.[20] Where the defendant acts in the course of a business or occupies premises for business purposes he cannot, by reference to any contract term or notice, exclude or restrict his liability for death or personal injury resulting from negligence,[21] and in the case of other loss or damage caused by negligence can only exclude or restrict his liability insofar as the term in the contract or notice is reasonable.[22] It is suggested that exclusion of liability by contract or notice is best understood as a denial. The claimant has no cause of action where he surrenders his rights pursuant to a contract or by proceeding in light of a notice given to him by the defendant.

---

[17] *A–G Reference (No.6 of 1980)* [1981] Q.B. 715.

[18] *R. v Brown* [1994] 1 A.C. 212.

[19] [1968] 1 Q.B. 379, see para.26–012.

[20] See also the European Community Directive on Unfair Terms in Consumer Contracts: Directive 93/13 [1993] O.J. L95/29. This Directive is given effect to by the Unfair Terms in Consumer Contracts Regulations 1999 (SI 1999/2083).

[21] Section 2(1).

[22] Section 2(2).

C. Voluntary Assumption of Risk[23]

Voluntary assumption of risk is a denial not a defence. If the claimant voluntarily assumes the risk of the defendant's negligence he cannot recover: *volenti non fit injuria*. The precise way in which this doctrine (which is often thought of as a form of the general defence of consent, which is the reason why it is dealt with in this chapter) prevents liability from arising has never been satisfactorily established. Is it a denial or is it a defence? If it is a denial, which element of the claimant's case of action does it negate? These fundamental questions have typically been ignored. It is suggested that the better view is that the plea "voluntary assumption of risk" is a denial.[24] It may deny the existence of a duty of care. If, for example, C undertakes to repair the roof of D's house and while doing so C falls off and injures himself C cannot recover. C's failure to recover might be dressed up in the language of voluntary assumption of risk but it is fairly clear that the reason why C cannot recover is not that C consented to the risk of injury but that D did not in the first place owe C any duty to instruct C on how to go safely about his task. The plea "voluntary assumption of risk" may also target the breach element of the action in negligence. Suppose that a spectator at a cricket match is struck and injured by a ball which the batsman, having little control of precisely where it will land, has hit as hard as he can. Most lawyers would agree that the claimant has no claim against the batsman and some might say that this was because the spectator had agreed to assume the risks of cricket. But the ultimate reason why there is no liability in this case is because there is no negligence. The batsman has done nothing unreasonable. *Murray v Harringay Arena Ltd*[25] is an excellent illustration of a no-breach case that is clothed in the language of voluntary assumption of risk. The claimant in this case, who was six years old at the time, was injured by an errant puck while watching an ice-hockey match. Singleton LJ, on behalf of the Court of Appeal, held that the claimant could not recover damages from the owner of the rink because he voluntarily assumed the risk of injury by attending the match. Significantly, however, in the course of reaching this conclusion, Singleton LJ focused on matters pertinent to the issue of fault. His Lordship mentioned the same factors that were decisive in the classic case of *Bolton v Stone*:[26] the low incidence with which pucks are hit out of rinks, the small risk that they will cause significant harm when they escape and the (apparent) impracticality of taking precautions to prevent pucks from escaping. Another example of a no-breach case that was dressed up in the language of voluntary assumption of risk is *Proctor v Young*.[27] The claimant in this matter suffered injury when she fell from a racehorse that she was exercising on a beach. The fall occurred because the horse stumbled in a depression in the sand. The claimant failed in her bid to recover compensation from her employer and the occupier of the beach. The judge based his decision on the voluntary

26–018

---

[23] There is a lack of high-quality scholarly analysis regarding the doctrine of voluntary assumption of risk. One thoughtful contribution is Simons (1987) 67 B.U.L Rev 213.

[24] The analysis here has been influenced by Sugarman (1997) 31 Val. U.L. Rev 833.

[25] [1951] 2 K.B. 529.

[26] [1951] A.C. 850.

[27] [2009] NIQB 56.

assumption of risk doctrine.[28] However, his reasons centred on factors relevant to the breach issue, especially the impracticality of taking preventative measures. This is perfectly understandable, since the reasonable person would not have attempted the impossible task of eliminating all variations in the beach's surface. If the foregoing is correct, the language of voluntary assumption of risk should be abandoned. It is a distraction. When it is in issue the ultimate question is whether all of the elements of the action in negligence are present. The court should engage directly with those elements, and not permit itself to be side-tracked by the voluntary assumption of risk doctrine, which, technically speaking, adds nothing to the elements of the action in negligence, since, for the reasons that have been given, it is merely a denial of one or more of those elements.

26–019   **The elements of the doctrine.** The doctrine of voluntary assumption of risk has two elements. These elements are as follows: (1) the claimant must have knowledge of the risk of injury; and (2) the claimant voluntarily agreed to incur the risk of injury. In thinking about these elements, it is important to bear in mind that they are very rarely established.[29] The voluntary assumption of risk doctrine, which once had a powerful effect on liability, now applies only exceptionally. This is principally for the reason that, when it applies, liability is defeated. The clear preference of the courts to restrict almost to vanishing point the doctrine of voluntary assumption of risk[30] and to allow partial recovery pursuant to the doctrine of contributory negligence.[31] A further point to note is that the division between the two elements of the doctrine is artificial. This is because a person cannot agree to accept a risk of injury unless he knows about it. The agreement element swallows up the knowledge element. As Scott LJ said in *Bowater v Rowley Regis Corp*: "[A] man cannot be said to be truly 'willing' unless he is in a position to choose freely, and freedom of choice predicates . . . full knowledge of the circumstances on which the exercise of choice is conditioned, so that he may be able to choose wisely."[32]

26–020   **The knowledge element.** The claimant must have information that indicates, at least in a general way, the risk of injury from the defendant's negligence. The test in this regard is subjective. Thus, the mere fact that a reasonable person would have been aware of the risk of injury is not enough to satisfy the knowledge element. This may mean that, paradoxically, a claimant who is heavily intoxicated is in a better position insofar as the voluntary assumption of risk doctrine is concerned than one who is sober. It is clear that the degree of knowledge required of the claimant before the knowledge element is satisfied is very high. In *Neeson v Acheson*[33] it was held that a claimant who was bitten by a dog that she had befriended after she put her face in proximity to its jaws did not consent to the risk of being bitten because she did not know that the dog was dangerous. In *Poppleton v Trustees of the Portsmouth Youth Activities*

---

[28] [2009] NIQB 56 at [35].

[29] For a modern case in which the doctrine was held to apply, see *Freeman v Higher Park Farm* [2008] EWCA Civ 1185; [2009] P.I.Q.R. P6.

[30] See *I.C.I. Ltd v Shatwell* [1965] A.C. 656 at 671–672.

[31] See the remarks in *Nettleship v Weston* [1971] 2 Q.B. 691 at 701.

[32] [1944] K.B. 476 at 479.

[33] [2008] NIQB 12.

Committee[34] the court held that matting on the floor of an artificial climbing venue gave the impression that it was safe to jump to the floor from a height. As a result, the claimant, who broke his neck when he fell after leaping from high on the climbing wall from a height, did not have knowledge of the risk that materialised.

The agreement element. The mere fact that the claimant is aware that the activity in which he participates carries a risk of injury does not mean that he has licensed the defendant to be negligent.[35] The maxim by which the voluntary assumption of risk doctrine is known is *volenti non fit injuria*, not *scienti non fit injuria*, and it does not follow that a person assents to a risk merely because he knows of it. For example, the knowledge that aircraft sometimes crash does not make out a case of *volenti non fit injuria* where the claimant has no reason to know of any defect in the plane or the pilot. Another illustration of this point can be found in *Slater v Clay Cross Co Ltd*.[36] In this case the claimant was lawfully walking along a narrow tunnel on a railway track owned and occupied by the defendants when she was struck and injured by a passing train owing to the negligence of the driver, Denning LJ said: "[I]t seems to me that when this lady walked in the tunnel, although it may be said that she voluntarily took the risk of danger from the running of the railway in the ordinary and accustomed way, nevertheless she did not take the risk of negligence by the driver."[37]

26–021

The agreement element will not be satisfied if the claimant is put under sufficient pressure. The claimant must be essentially free from constraints upon his decision-making processes, both in terms of constraints imposed by the defendant and from other circumstances.[38] For example, the agreement element is unlikely to be satisfied if the claimant runs a risk because avoiding it would entail considerable inconvenience or expense to him. Usually there will be economic or other pressures upon a worker, which means that the agreement element will rarely be satisfied in the workplace injury context. Indeed, some modern statements of the employer's duty of care to his workers go even further and seem inconsistent with the very existence of the doctrine in the employment context.[39]

A claimant may accept certain risks of injury in an activity but not others. This point is obvious with regard to participants in sports. As Barwick CJ said in *Rootes v Shelton*: "By engaging in a sport . . . the participants may be held to have accepted risks which are inherent in that sport . . . but this does not eliminate all duty of care of the one participant to the other."[40] The same may apply to a spectator who is injured in the course of some game or sport which he is watching. A spectator does not consent to negligence on the part of the

---

[34] [2007] EWHC 1567 (QB).
[35] The key authority in establishing this is probably the landmark decision in *Smith v Baker & Sons* [1891] A.C. 325.
[36] [1956] 2 Q.B. 264.
[37] [1956] 2 Q.B. 264 at 271.
[38] For a case where constraint was put upon an employee by someone other than his employer, see *Burnett v British Waterways Board* [1973] 1 W.L.R. 700.
[39] See para.9–028.
[40] (1967) 116 C.L.R. 383 at 385.

participants,[41] but "provided the competition or game is being performed within the rules and the requirement of the sport and by a person of adequate skill and competence the spectator does not expect his safety to be regarded by the participant".[42]

26–022 **Rescuers.** An excellent illustration of the effect of the agreement element concerns rescuers.[43] In *Haynes v Harwood*[44] the Court of Appeal affirmed a judgment in favour of a policeman who had been injured in stopping some runaway horses in a crowded street. The defendant had left the horses unattended on the highway and they had bolted. The policeman, who was on duty, not in the street, but in a police station, darted out and was crushed by one of the horses which fell upon him while he was stopping it. The agreement element of the voluntary assumption of risk doctrine was not satisfied in this case given the emergency with which the policeman was confronted. The defendant may also have considerable difficulty in establishing the knowledge element in rescue cases. It is in the nature of a rescue case that the defendant's negligence precedes the claimant's act of running the risk. The claimant may therefore be wholly ignorant of the defendant's negligence at the time of being injured. All he knows is that someone is in a position of peril and that the situation calls for his intervention as a rescuer.[45] The foregoing, incidentally, is entirely in keeping with tort law's lenient treatment of rescuers.[46] The law looks upon claims by rescuers sympathetically and is also loath to find, for example, that a rescuer is guilty of contributory negligence[47] or that his conduct constitutes an intervening act.[48] It is also worth pointing out that the generous treatment that is afforded to rescuers is extended to all rescuers, not merely to professional rescuers, such as police officers and firefighters.[49]

26–023 **Overlap with the doctrine of contributory negligence.** When, exceptionally, the doctrine of voluntary assumption of risk is engaged the doctrine of contributory negligence will usually be too. When both doctrines are enlivened the claimant will of course fail in his action, and will not be entitled to partial damages. This is because the doctrine of voluntary assumption of risk, when triggered, is fatal to the claimant's proceedings. It might be queried whether, contrary to what has been said, the overlap between the doctrines is not perfect. It

---

[41] See *Cleghorn v Oldham* (1927) 43 T.L.R. 465 and the unreported cases referred to by Sellers LJ in *Wooldridge v Sumner* [1963] 2 Q.B. 43 at 55–56.

[42] *Wooldridge v Sumner* [1963] 2 Q.B. 43 at 56 per Sellers LJ. See also at 68 per Diplock LJ.

[43] Goodhart (1934) 5 C.L.J. 192.

[44] [1935] 1 K.B. 146.

[45] *Baker v T.E. Hopkins & Son Ltd* [1959] 1 W.L.R. 966 at 976 per Morris LJ.

[46] The lenient treatment extends to cases in which the rescuer acts to protect property rather than life: *Hyett v GW Rly Co* [1948] 1 K.B. 345.

[47] See, e.g. *Brandon v Osborne, Garrett & Co Ltd* [1924] 1 K.B. 548. In *Baker v T.E. Hopkins & Son Ltd* [1959] 1 W.L.R. 966 at 976 Willmer LJ said: "Bearing in mind that danger invites rescue, the court should not be astute to accept criticism of the rescuer's conduct from the wrongdoer who created the danger."

[48] *Haynes v Harwood* [1935] 1 K.B. 146 at 163 per Maugham LJ.

[49] The fact that members of the emergency services are in a sense employed to take risks has led some American courts to deny liability to them on the part of the person whose negligence creates the danger. This, the so-called "fireman's rule", was decisively rejected by the House of Lords in *Ogwo v Taylor* [1988] A.C. 431.

is certainly the case that, almost always, when the voluntary assumption of risk doctrine applies, the doctrine of contributory negligence will too. But this will not always be so. This is because there may be cases in which voluntarily accepting certain risks of injury may be entirely reasonable.

The doctrine is excluded by statute in road traffic cases. Section 149 of the   **26–024**
Road Traffic Act 1988 eliminates the doctrine of voluntary assumption of risk as between drivers and passengers in motor vehicles. In *Pitts v Hunt*[50] Beldam LJ put it as follows:

> "[I]t is no longer open to the driver of a motor vehicle to say that the fact of his passenger travelling in a vehicle in circumstances in which for one reason or another it could be said that he had willingly accepted a risk of negligence on the driver's part, relieves him of liability for such negligence."

Section 149 has no effect on any other rules, such as the doctrines of illegality and contributory negligence. Nor does this provision apply to transport in aircraft, boats and other means.

D.   Mistake[51]

A mistake by the defendant can prevent the claimant from establishing the   **26–025**
elements of the cause of action in which he sues. It is convenient to give some examples. First, the fact that the defendant made a reasonable mistake can prevent the action in negligence from being constituted. If the injury to the claimant was the result of a mistake that the reasonable person would have committed no liability will arise in that tort. There will be no breach of any duty of care. A second example is the tort of malicious prosecution. One of the elements of that tort is a lack of reasonable and probable cause of the prosecution. Accordingly, if the defendant in proceedings in that tort mistakenly but reasonably believed that there is cause of prosecution the tort will not be constituted. Thirdly, a mistake, whether or not reasonable, can prevent the action in deceit from being made out. That tort requires an intention to defraud the claimant. Accordingly, a defendant who misrepresents a fact to the claimant because of a mistake will not possess the necessary intention to commit the tort of deceit.

There are many torts the elements of which may be satisfied even if the defendant committed a mistake, regardless of whether the mistake was a reasonable one. A good illustration is the tort of conversion. Thus, an auctioneer who innocently sells A's goods in the honest and reasonable belief that they belong to B on whose instructions he sells them will be liable to A.[52] The situation in relation to trespass to the person is the same. A surgeon who, as a result of an administrative mix-up, carries out the wrong operation[53] or who operates on the wrong patient is liable in trespass to the person. It should be

---

[50] [1991] 1 Q.B. 24 at 48.
[51] Trindade (1982) 2 O.J.L.S. 211.
[52] See para.18–041.
[53] *Chatterton v Gerson* [1981] Q.B. 432 at 443.

noted, however, that in all of these examples the "innocent" wrongdoer may be entitled to be indemnified by the person responsible for the mistake.

E. Inevitable Accident

26–026   When lawyers speak of an "inevitable accident" they mean to say that the accident could not be avoided by taking reasonable care. It follows that the plea of "inevitable accident" in, for example, a negligence case is nothing more than an attack on either the breach element.[54] Suppose that D's car crashes into C, a pedestrian, because its steering mechanism spontaneously and unforeseeably failed. This might be described as an "inevitable accident". However, because D has done nothing unreasonable the tort of negligence has not been committed. D is not at fault, and that is all that the label "inevitable accident" signifies.[55] For precisely the same reason, the plea of "inevitable accident" is a mere denial in the context of trespass to the person. That tort requires proof that the defendant was at fault.[56] Where the act complained of is due to an inevitable accident, the fault element will be missing. In truth, the phrase "inevitable accident" serves more to confuse than to illuminate. It would be better if it disappeared from the law of torts.

3.   JUSTIFICATIONS

A.   Private Justifications

i.   Self-Defence[57]

26–027   **The elements of the defence.** A person who uses no more than reasonable force in his own defence will not incur liability in trespass to the person. This defence has two elements. First, it must be necessary to use defensive force. If the unjust threat with which the defendant is confronted could reasonably be avoided by means other than using force the defendant will be expected to resort to those non-violent means. For example, the defence will be denied to a defendant if the defendant used force against an aggressor when he could have secured his safety by locking a door that was located between him and the aggressor. Secondly, the force used by the defendant must be proportionate to the threat that he faced.

26–028   **The necessity element.** The necessity element imports an imminence requirement. Unless the defendant is faced with an imminent threat it will not be

---

[54] Exceptionally, it can also constitute a denial of the causation requirement: see Goudkamp, *Tort Law Defences* (2013) p.53.

[55] "I do not find myself assisted by considering the meaning of the phrase 'inevitable accident'. I prefer to put the problem in a more simple way, namely has it been established that the driver of the car was guilty of negligence?": *Browne v De Luxe Car Services* [1941] 1 K.B. 549 at 552 per Greene MR.

[56] See para.4–004.

[57] Goudkamp (2010) 18 T.L.J 61.

necessary for him to use defensive force, as the defendant could in this situation have avoided the threat by seeking help from the police.

The proportionality element. It is a question of fact whether violence done by way of self-protection is proportionate to warding-off the threat with which the defendant was faced. The defence will be unavailable "if upon a little blow given by [C] to [D], [D] gives him a blow that maims him".[58] Not every threat will justify a blow in self-defence. Some threats and contacts must simply be tolerated and in many cases the reasonable thing to do will be nothing. The courts are generally lenient in asking whether the force used by the defendant was proportionate. It must be remembered that the defendant who acts in self-defence will often be confronted with an emergency and he will not be expected to calculate with precision the appropriate degree of force.[59] The proportionality element is not determined simply by asking whether the force used by D was less than that with which he was confronted. D may, in fact, be permitted to use greater force than that with which he was faced. For instance, it is clear that D may be permitted to kill in order to save himself from being grievously injured.

26–029

Excessive force. The proportionality element means that the defence of self-defence is unavailable where the force used by the defendant is excessive. But where the force used is excessive D may not be liable for all of the damage caused. In principle he should only be liable for the damage to the extent that it was caused by the excessive force. He should be relieved of responsibility for the damage caused insofar as the damage that he caused would have been brought about by reasonable force.

26–030

Mistaken defensive force. What if D uses force against C because of a mistake (e.g. he believes that C is about to attack him when C in fact has no intention of doing so)? The criminal law provides that D is not guilty of a crime if his action would have been justified if the facts had been as he believed them to be.[60] The mistake need not be a reasonable one. It follows that, under the criminal law D as a result of a wholly unreasonable mistake can kill a person who he thought was about to murder him without incurring any liability. Tort law adopts a different rule. In the case of a civil action D will only be entitled to the defence of self-defence where he uses defensive force as a result of a mistake if his mistake was a reasonable one.[61] The logic underpinning this rule is revealing of tort law's nature. A rule that made no allowance of mistakes is thought to be too favourable to claimants. Conversely, the criminal law rule, which makes the defence of self-defence available even where the defendant made an unreasonable mistake, is considered to be too generous to defendants in the tort law context (although it might be appropriate in the criminal law, where the defendant's interests are given priority). Allowing for mistakes but insisting that they be reasonable ones before making the defence available in the tort context is regarded as achieving a fair balance between equal parties.

26–031

---

[58] *Cockroft v Smith* (1705) 2 Salk. 642. See also *Lane v Holloway* [1968] 1 Q.B. 379.
[59] *Cross v Kirkby*, *The Times*, April 5, 2000.
[60] Criminal Justice and Immigration Act 2008 s.76. This provision restates the common law on this point.
[61] *Ashley v CC Sussex Police* [2008] UKHL 25; [2008] 1 A.C. 962.

26–032   **Pre-emption.** The defendant is not required to wait until he is struck before he is permitted to act in his own defence, for that would sometimes render the defence pointless. Thus, the defendant may be justified in using force if the claimant does no more than shake his stick at him, uttering taunts at the same time.[62] Similarly, a defendant will not be liable for assault by merely putting himself in a fighting attitude in order to defend himself.[63]

26–033   **Innocent aggressors.** Suppose that D is attacked by someone who is insane, or endangered by a baby holding a gun. Is D allowed to use defensive force against such persons in order to save himself? There is a lack of authority on this point, but the answer must be in the affirmative. It is irrelevant for the purposes of tort law that the aggressor would not incur criminal liability.

26–034   **Injury caused to bystanders.** Suppose that D in protecting himself from an unlawful attack by X, injures C, an innocent passer-by. Imagine also that D acted reasonably in the circumstances. On what principles ought D's liability to C be discussed? The situation is unclear. There are several incorrect answers to this question that must be moved out of the way. First, it is not the case that there is no tort. D has committed a battery against C by virtue of the doctrine of transferred malice. Secondly, D cannot avoid liability on the grounds of private necessity (i.e. that he inflicted a harm on a third-party in order to protect his own interests) because tort law does not recognise such a defence.[64] Arguably, D is simply liable to C.[65] Significantly, C is not like an innocent aggressor. C did not present any threat at all to D. It should be noted, however, that in this scenario, D, if he is liable to C, might be able to seek an indemnity from X.

ii.   Defence of One's Property

26–035   **Possession or right to possession.** Actual possession (whether with a good title or not), or the right to possession of property is necessary to justify force in keeping out (or, for that matter, expelling) a trespasser. Thus, in *Holmes v Bagge*[66] the claimant and defendant were both members of the committee of a cricket club. During a match in which the defendant was captain and the claimant was a spectator, the defendant asked the claimant to act as substitute for one of the 11. He did so, but being annoyed at the tone of the defendant in commanding him to take off his coat, he refused either to remove the garment or to leave the playing part of the field. He was then forcibly removed by the defendant's direction. The defendant, when sued for assault, pleaded possession of the ground, but the plea was held to be bad because possession was in the committee of the club. Note, however, that a person who does not have possession of the land may use reasonable force against persons thereon who obstruct him in carrying out statutory powers,[67] and it may be that if the defendant in *Holmes v*

---

[62] *Dale v Wood* (1822) 7 Moore C.P. 33.

[63] Lord Lyndhurst CB in *Moriarty v Brooks* (1834) 6 C. & P. 684.

[64] *Vincent v Lake Erie Transportation Co* 109 Minn. 456; 124 N.W. 221 (1910).

[65] Cf. *Scott v Shepherd* (1773) 2 Wm. Bl. 892.

[66] (1853) 1 E. & B. 782. See also *Dean v Hogg* (1834) 10 Bing. 345; *Roberts v Taylor* (1845) 1 C.B. 117.

[67] *R. v CC Devon and Cornwall, Ex p. C.E.G.B.* [1982] Q.B. 458.

Bagge had pleaded that he removed the claimant for disturbing persons lawfully playing a lawful game he would have been justified.[68] The outcome may also have been different if the defendant had been acting at the request of the committee of the club.

Other requirements. Apart from the foregoing, the defence of one's property is analogous to that of self-defence, and it is governed by equivalent rules. The key issue in relation to defence of one's property is usually that of proportionality. One is not necessarily bound to make one's premises safe for trespassers. But devices may be used to protect property only where their use is proportionate to the injuries that they are likely to inflict. Spikes on a wall or a fierce dog may be justified,[69] but not deadly implements like spring guns. The infliction of grave bodily harm is too high a price to demand for keeping one's property intact. It is an offence against the Offences Against the Person Act 1861[70] to set a spring gun or similar device. Consistently with the principle of proportion in the means of defence, more latitude may be permissible in protecting premises by night than in the daytime, or when the occupier is not in the presence of the trespasser than when he is. Thus, an intruder who injures himself on a spiked wall has no valid ground of complaint, but he certainly would have one if he, being peaceable and unarmed, had a spike thrust into him by the occupier.[71] "Presence [of the occupier] in its very nature is more or less protection . . . [P]resence may supply means [of defence] and limit what it supplies."[72] **26–036**

iii.   Abatement

Abatement is a defence, not a remedy. Abatement is often described as a "self-help" remedy. This terminology is unhelpful. A remedy is judicially sanctioned relief. Abatement is better understood as a defence because it prevents liability from arising in trespass where the defendant uses reasonable force to remove a nuisance. However, abatement is not really a distinct defence, but a manifestation of the generally applicable defence of defence of property,[73] and it is for this reason that abatement is discussed in this chapter. **26–037**

The defence of abatement is narrowly confined. The defence of abatement is kept on a tight rein because, as Sir Matthew Hale said, "this many times occasions tumults and disorders".[74] The courts have consequently taken a narrow view of what counts as reasonable force in this context. The defendant must avoid excessive acts. For example, tearing up a picture that is publicly exhibited and **26–038**

---

[68] *R. v CC Devon and Cornwall, Ex p. C.E.G.B.* [1982] Q.B. 458 per Lord Denning MR.
[69] *Sarch v Blackburn* (1830) 4 C. & P. 297. The position is now governed by the Animals Act 1971 s.5(3)(b), which is to the like effect, though the position may have been indirectly affected by the Guard Dogs Act 1975: see para.17–018.
[70] Section 31.
[71] In *Pickwick Papers*, Captain Boldwig's mode of ejecting Mr Pickwick, whom he found asleep in a wheelbarrow in his grounds, was excessive. He directed his gardener first to wheel Mr Pickwick to the devil and then, on second thoughts, to wheel him to the village pond.
[72] *Deane v Clayton* (1817) 7 Taunt. 489 at 521 per Dallas J. For the defences available to the occupier of land who kills or injures a dog, see Animals Act 1971 s.9.
[73] See para.26–035.
[74] *De Portubus Maris*, Pt.2, Ch.VII.

which is a libel on oneself is too drastic.[75] Where there are two ways of abating the nuisance, the less harmful should be followed, unless it would inflict some wrong on an innocent third party or on the public.[76]

26–039 **A request to remove the nuisance should normally be made.** Before abatement is attempted, the defendant should request the offending party to remedy the nuisance. However, a request does not need to be made if it would be pointless, where there is no time to make one because of the need for urgent action,[77] or because the nuisance can be removed by D without entry on the land from which the nuisance emanates. D may lop the branches of C's (his neighbour's) tree that project over or into his land without giving notice to C,[78] although D must not appropriate what he severs.[79]

22–040 **It must be impractical to commence legal proceedings.** The defence will be withheld unless it was urgent to abate the nuisance. If it would be reasonable to expect the defendant to wait to obtain relief via judicial proceedings the defence will not be available.

26–041 **Costs incurred in taking reasonable steps to abate the nuisance are recoverable.** Where abatement is justified, one may recover the costs reasonably incurred in carrying it out.[80]

B. Public Justifications

i. Public Necessity[81]

26–042 **Generally.** Public necessity is a defence to all forms of trespass. It is available where the defendant uses reasonable force[82] against an innocent person to avoid an imminent and greater harm to some important public interest. The defence will be lost if the situation of necessity was brought about by the defendant's own negligence.[83]

26–043 **Private necessity is not a defence.** The mere fact that the claimant used reasonable force against an innocent person (including that person's property) to protect his own private interests will not afford him any defence. In other words, tort law does not recognise a defence of private necessity.[84] Thus, to give a classic illustration, a hiker who enters a cabin in order to save himself from a storm and

---

[75] *Du Bost v Beresford* (1801) 2 Camp. 511, where the point was left open, but it may probably be regarded as settled now.

[76] Blackburn J in *Roberts v Rose* (1865) L.R. 1 Ex. 82 at 89 adopted by Lord Atkinson in *Lagan Navigation Co v Lambeg Bleaching Co Ltd* [1927] A.C. 226 at 244–246.

[77] *Lagan Navigation Co v Lambeg Bleaching Co Ltd* [1927] A.C. 226.

[78] *Lemmon v Webb* [1895] A.C. 1.

[79] *Mills v Brooker* [1919] 1 K.B. 555.

[80] *Abbahall Ltd v Smee* [2002] EWCA Civ 1831; [2003] 1 W.L.R. 1472.

[81] Virgo in Dyson, Goudkamp and Wilmot-Smith (eds), *Defences in Tort* (2014).

[82] For a case where there the requirement of reasonableness was not met see *Rigby v CC Northamptonshire* [1985] 1 W.L.R. 1242.

[83] *Southport Corp v Esso Petroleum Ltd* [1954] 2 Q.B. 182 at 194 per Singleton LJ, at 198 per Denning LJ; *Esso Petroleum Ltd v Southport Corp* [1956] A.C. 218 at 242 per Lord Radcliffe.

[84] *Vincent v Lake Erie Transportation Co* 109 Minn. 456; 124 N.W. 221 (1910).

who eats the food kept therein and burns the furniture to supply warmth is liable in tort to the cabin's owner. These types of cases are often referred as involving an "incomplete privilege".[85] The idea is as follows. Because (to continue the mountaineering example) the hiker acted reasonably he had a privilege to enter the cabin (the cabin owner could not have kept him out had he been present because he would not be acting reasonably in doing so to defend his property) but, because the privilege is incomplete, he must pay compensation. However, it is wholly unnecessary to invoke the concept of an "incomplete privilege" to explain these types of cases. The reason why the hiker has to pay compensation to the cabin owner is that he committed a tort and has no defence. There is no difficultly in holding that the hiker is liable although he acted reasonably given that the tort of trespass often attaches liability to reasonable conduct. For instance, a person who enters property reasonably but mistakenly believing that he is the owner is plainly liable to the actual owner.

Illustrations of situations where the defence of public necessity is available.   26–044
The defence will apply where the defendant pulls down a house that is on fire to prevent its spread to other property,[86] destroys a building made ruinous by fire to prevent its collapse into the highway[87] and throws goods overboard to lighten a boat in a storm.[88] A rescuer who acts to save a person in circumstances where the latter had no opportunity to consent (such as by dragging a pedestrian out of the path of a speeding car that the latter failed to notice bearing down on him) may also be within the defence.[89] More recently, and controversially, the defence was held to be available to police officers to defeat claims in trespass to the person where the officers concerned had detained suspected offenders in a police van while searching their abode for illegal firearms[90] and kept several hundred people in cramped conditions in Oxford Circus in London until safe crowd dispersal could be arranged.[91] What may be justified in one age is not necessarily justified in another. For example, considering there is today an efficient public fire service it would require an unusual case in which the defence of public necessity would apply in respect of the destruction by a private person of another's house to prevent a fire from spreading.[92] The defence was denied to environmental activists who destroyed genetically-modified crops[93] and to anti-war campaigners who damaged a military installation.[94]

Infliction of personal injury. Public necessity cases are rare, and in most of   26–045
them the thing that the defendant sacrificed was property. What is the position where it is necessary to kill or cause serious injury to a person in order to save a

---

[85] Bohlen (1926) 39 Harv. L. Rev. 307; Keeton (1959) 72 Harv. L. Rev. 401.

[86] *Saltpetre Case* (1607) 12 Co. Rep. 12 at 13.

[87] *Dewey v White* (1827) Mood. & M. 56.

[88] *Mouse's case* (1609) 12 Co.Rep. 63. It should be noted that this case took place on an inland waterway. The position as to jettison at sea may be affected by the principle of general average.

[89] *In re F (Mental Patient: Sterilisation)* [1990] 2 A.C. 1 at 74.

[90] *Connor v Chief Constable of Merseyside Police* [2006] EWCA Civ 1549; *The Times*, 4 December 2006.

[91] *Austin v Commissioner of Police of the Metropolis* [2009] UKHL 5; [2009] 1 A.C. 564.

[92] See *Burmah Oil Co (Burmah Trading) Ltd v Lord Advocate* [1965] A.C. 75 at 164–165.

[93] *Monsanto Plc v Tilly* [2000] Env L.R. 313.

[94] *Attorney-General v Leason* [2011] NZHC 1053.

greater number of people from perishing? One case that is at least obliquely relevant is the criminal law matter of *Re A (Children) (Conjoined Twins: Surgical Separation)*.[95] In this decision it was held that necessity (the criminal law does not distinguish between public and private necessity) was a justification for an operation to separate Siamese twins, where otherwise they would both have died, even though the inevitable consequence of the operation was the death of the weaker one. Presumably, the doctors would also have had a defence had a civil action been brought against them by the parents.

26–046 **Medical treatment.** Public necessity is used to afford doctors who administer medical treatment to incapable persons a defence to liability in trespass. Legislation now governs this situation,[96] although it has not technically abolished the common law.

26–047 **Relationship of public necessity to self-defence.** Because the defence of public necessity is concerned with conflicts between innocents, the maximum amount of force that is regarded as proportionate for the purpose of public necessity is less than is the case of self-defence. Thus, whereas the defence of self-defence may authorise the use of greater force than that with which one is threatened[97] it is doubtful whether the defence of public necessity allows the defendant to cause a net harm. It is not for nothing that the defence of public necessity is sometimes known as that of "lesser evils".

ii. Defence of Another Person

26–048 The rules discussed above in relation to self-defence[98] apply equally where the defendant uses force to defend a third-party. It used to be the case that it was only permissible for a defendant to come to the aid of people with whom he stood in a particular relationship (such as that of husband and wife[99] or master and servant[100]). This restriction has clearly vanished from the law. Today, one who intervenes to protect a stranger from an aggressor may be eligible for the defence.[101]

iii. Arrest

26–049 **Generally.** A person who uses no more than reasonable force to arrest another will have a defence to liability in trespass to the person. The defence is justificatory in nature because it will be lost if excessive force is used.[102]

26–050 **Arrest by a constable with a warrant.** Section 6 of the Constables Protection Act 1750 confers a defence on constables who arrest a person under a warrant.

---

[95] [2001] Fam.147.

[96] See para.4–015.

[97] See para.26–029.

[98] See para.26–027.

[99] See Blackstone, *Commentaries on the Laws of England*, Vol.4 (Clarendon Press, 1769), p.186.

[100] *Seaman v Cuppledick* (1615) Owen 150; 74 E.R. 966; *Barfoot v Reynolds* (1733) 2 Stra. 953; 93 E.R. 963.

[101] *Goss v Nicholas* [1960] Tas S.R. 133.

[102] *Simpson v CC South Yorkshire*, *The Times*, March 7, 1991.

This defence applies even if there was a "defect of jurisdiction" in the magistrate who issued the warrant. The crucial issue in the case of this defence is whether the constable obeyed the warrant. The defence will not apply if he arrests a person other than the person named in the warrant.

Arrest by a constable without a warrant pursuant to s.24 of the Police and Criminal Evidence Act. The circumstances in which an arrest by a constable may be effected without a warrant are set out in s.24 of the Police and Criminal Evidence Act 1984. This unnecessarily convoluted provision states:

> "(1) A constable may arrest without a warrant—
>   (a) anyone who is about to commit an offence;
>   (b) anyone who is in the act of committing an offence;
>   (c) anyone whom he has reasonable grounds for suspecting to be about to commit an offence;
>   (d) anyone whom he has reasonable grounds for suspecting to be committing an offence.
> (2) If a constable has reasonable grounds for suspecting that an offence has been committed, he may arrest without a warrant anyone whom he has reasonable grounds to suspect of being guilty of it.
> (3) If an offence has been committed, a constable may arrest without a warrant—
>   (a) anyone who is guilty of the offence;
>   (b) anyone whom he has reasonable grounds for suspecting to be guilty of it."

26–051

If, therefore, Constable D arrests C on reasonable suspicion that he is committing an offence then there is a defence to any action for false imprisonment even though it turns out that C was not, in fact, guilty. Under equivalent legislation[103] it was held that the arresting officer should be in possession of information that gives him reasonable cause to suspect that the claimant was about to commit or was committing an offence and that it was not enough that such information was in the possession of another officer who gave an order to arrest which the defendant officer obeyed.[104] Although it is open to debate whether this is realistic in modern conditions,[105] the legislation was founded "on the longstanding constitutional theory of the independence and accountability of the individual constable".[106] There is no reason to believe the position is different under s.24.[107]

By s.24(4) the power to arrest in s.24 is available only if the constable has reasonable grounds for believing that for any of the reasons mentioned in s.24(5) it is necessary to arrest the person in question. The reasons are:

> "(a) to enable the name or address of the person in question to be ascertained;
> (b) to prevent the person in question—
>   (i) causing physical injury to himself or any other person;
>   (ii) suffering physical injury;
>   (iii) causing loss of or damage to property;

---

[103] Prevention of Terrorism (Temporary Provisions) Act 1984.

[104] *O'Hara v Chief Constable, Royal Ulster Constabulary*[1997] A.C. 286. Cf. *Keegan v CC Merseyside*[2003] EWCA Civ 936; [2003] 1 W.L.R. 2187.

[105] *Raissi v MPC* [2008] EWCA Civ 1237; [2009] Q.B. 564 at [33].

[106] *O'Hara v Chief Constable, Royal Ulster Constabulary*[1997] A.C. 286 at 293 per Lord Steyn.

[107] The arresting officer does not, of course, have to investigate the matter himself: he may rely on apparently reliable information given to him by another officer. Any deficiencies in his briefing do not invalidate the arrest, though they may render the briefing officer liable for some other tort, e.g. misfeasance in a public office: *Alford v CC Cambridgeshire* [2009] EWCA Civ 100.

(iv)   committing an offence against public decency; or
(v)   causing an unlawful obstruction of the highway;
(c)   to protect a child or other vulnerable person from the person in question;
(d)   to allow the prompt and effective investigation of the offence or of the conduct of the person in question;
(e)   to prevent any prosecution for the offence from being hindered by the disappearance of the person in question."

26–052   **Arrest by a private citizen pursuant to s.24A of the Police and Criminal Evidence Act.** The powers of arrest of a private citizen are governed by s.24A. That section provides:

"(1)   A person other than a constable may arrest without a warrant—
(a)   anyone who is in the act of committing an indictable offence;
(b)   anyone whom he has reasonable grounds for suspecting to be committing an indictable offence.
(2)   Where an indictable offence has been committed, a person other than a constable may arrest without a warrant—
(a)   anyone who is guilty of the offence;
(b)   anyone whom he has reasonable grounds for suspecting to be guilty of it."

There are three clear differences between the powers of a constable and a private citizen. First, the citizen's power of arrest is confined to indictable offences. Secondly, the citizen has no power to make a "preventive" arrest: an offence must be in progress or he must reasonably believe that it is. Thirdly, in the case of the citizen there is no equivalent of s.24(2). An offence must actually have been committed or the defence in s.24A will not be available. Where an indictable offence has been committed any person may arrest without warrant anyone who is guilty of the offence or anyone whom he has reasonable grounds for suspecting to be guilty of it. In other words, where the offence has been committed there may be a defence even if the arrester "gets the wrong man"; but if in fact no offence has been committed by anyone the arrest is unlawful.

As in the case of the police officer, the private citizen effecting an arrest has to satisfy further alternative conditions. Three of these are similar to those applicable to constables—that he has reasonable grounds to believe that the arrest is necessary to prevent the arrestee (1) causing physical injury to himself or another, (2) suffering injury; or (3) causing loss of or damage to property.[108] He must also (4) have reasonable grounds to believe that it is necessary to prevent the arrestee "making off before a constable can assume responsibility for him".[109] Finally, in all cases it must appear to the person making the arrest (5) "that it is not reasonably practicable for a constable to make it instead".[110]

26–053   **Reasonable grounds for suspicion.** Under both s.24 and s.24A, unless it can be shown that the claimant was guilty of an offence or was about to commit it, the power of arrest depends on reasonable grounds for suspicion and in this connection it is necessary first to establish that the arrester actually did suspect the claimant;[111] but there must also be an objective basis for that state of mind. It

---

[108] Police and Criminal Evidence Act 1984 s.24A(4)(a)–(c).
[109] Police and Criminal Evidence Act 1984 s.24A(4)(d).
[110] Police and Criminal Evidence Act 1984 s.24A(3)(b).
[111] *Siddiqui v Swain* [1979] R.T.R. 454.

also seems clear as a matter of statutory language that the burden of proof lies on the arrester in respect of the presence of one of the "reasons" which justify arrest. Reasonable suspicion is less than prima facie proof[112] if only because the latter must be based on admissible evidence, whereas suspicion can take into account other matters as well.[113] Lord Devlin said that: "[S]uspicion in its ordinary meaning is a state of conjecture or surmise where proof is lacking: 'I suspect but I cannot prove.' Suspicion arises at or near the starting-point of an investigation of which the obtaining of prima facie proof is at the end."[114]

The need to inform the person arrested of the ground on which he is arrested. It was established at common law in *Christie v Leachinsky*[115] that in ordinary circumstances a person arrested must be informed of the ground on which he is arrested, otherwise the arrest is unlawful: the officer is not entitled to remain silent or to fabricate[116] a "holding charge". The law is now found in s.28 of the Police and Criminal Evidence Act 1984 and the position with regard to arrest by a police officer is as follows: where a person is arrested otherwise than by being informed that he is under arrest (e.g. where he is physically seized) he must as soon as practicable be informed[117] that he is under arrest even if the fact is obvious and also of the ground for the arrest, again even if it is obvious. The only qualification to these duties is that they do not apply if it was not reasonably practicable for the information to be given because the claimant escaped from custody before it could be given. It has been held that an arrest is a continuing state of affairs so that if the information is not given promptly but is given at a later stage the arrest becomes lawful from that point, which may affect the quantum of damages.[118] Where the arrest is by a private individual he does not have to inform the claimant of the fact of the arrest or of the ground where it is obvious. It has been said that *Christie v Leachinsky*, s.28 and art.5(2) of the European Convention on Human Rights ("everyone who is arrested shall be informed promptly, in a language which he understands, of the reasons for his arrest and of any charge against him") all express the same principle[119] and that the essential idea is that, having regard to the information available to the arresting officer, the arrested person must be told the "essential legal and factual grounds for his arrest".[120] As to what is required by way of information, technical or precise language need not be used but sufficient detail should be given to

26–054

---

[112] Where a small number of people could be identified as the only ones capable of having committed the offence, that may afford reasonable grounds for suspecting each of them, in the absence of any information that could or should enable the police to reduce the number further: *Cumming v CC Northumbria* [2003] EWCA Civ 1844; *The Times*, January 2, 2004.

[113] *Hussien v Chong Fook Kam* [1970] A.C. 942 at 949.

[114] *Hussien v Chong Fook Kam* [1970] A.C. 942 at 948. See also *Raissi v MPC* [2008] EWCA Civ 1237; [2009] Q.B. 564 at [20].

[115] [1947] A.C. 573.

[116] But if there is a charge in respect of which the officer has reasonable grounds for suspecting guilt, an arrest in respect of that is lawful even if the officer's real purpose is to investigate a more serious offence. In this sense a "holding charge" is a "well known and respectable aid to justice": *R. v Chalkely* [1998] Q.B. 848 at 873.

[117] Not necessarily by the arresting officer: *Dhesi v CC W Midlands*, *The Times*, May 9, 2000.

[118] *Lewis v CC South Wales* [1991] 1 All E.R. 206.

[119] *Taylor v CC Thames Valley* [2004] EWCA Civ 858; [2004] 1 W.L.R. 3155.

[120] *Fox, Campbell and Hartley v UK* (1990) 13 E.H.R.R. 157 at [40].

enable him to understand the factual as well as the legal nature of what he is accused of, so that, for example, "you are under the arrest for burglary" is insufficient without information of when and where.[121]

26–055 **Detention following arrest.** Where the arrest is by a private individual the arrested person must be taken before a magistrate or a police officer, not necessarily forthwith, but as soon as is reasonably possible. For example, a person arrested in the street by a store detective on suspicion of shoplifting may be taken back to the store while the matter is reported to the store manager, and may be detained there while the police are sent for.[122] It is unlikely that he would be allowed to take the suspect to the suspect's house to see whether any of the stolen property is there, though it has been held that a police officer could do so.[123] The position following a police arrest is dealt with by the Police and Criminal Evidence Act 1984. By s.30 a person arrested otherwise than at a police station must be taken to a police station as soon as practicable after his arrest, unless his presence elsewhere is necessary in order to carry out such investigations as it is reasonable to carry out immediately. The time for which and the conditions in which he may be held are then governed by Pt.IV of the Act. Section 34(1) provides that a person "shall not be kept in police detention" except in accordance with Pt.IV, and the defence of arrest will subsequently be lost if the provisions in Pt.IV are contravened.[124] These provisions are much too detailed to examine here but, very broadly, the position is that there must be periodic reviews of the detention by the police and, with the authority of a senior officer the detainee may be held for up to 36 hours without charge. Thereafter, the authority of a magistrates' court is required for further detention without charge up to 96 hours. After that period the suspect must either be released or charged and brought before a magistrates' court as soon as practicable. In any event, even if these time limits have not been exceeded, an arrested person must be released as soon as the need for detention has ceased to apply and if he is not, there is liability in false imprisonment from that time, notwithstanding that the initial arrest was lawful.[125] Various matters ancillary to detention are dealt with in Pt.V. Contravention of the provisions on searches and fingerprinting will presumably lead to liability for battery but will not render the detention unlawful. There is no damages sanction attached to the provisions dealing with the suspect's right to have someone informed of his arrest or access to legal advice. Contravention does not render the detention unlawful, and there is no claim for breach of statutory duty; nor is any right under the European Convention on Human Rights infringed unless the effect is to deprive the claimant of a fair trial.[126]

---

[121] *R. v Telfer* [1976] Crim. L.R. 562; *Newman v Modern Bookbinders Ltd* [2000] 1 W.L.R. 2559.

[122] *John Lewis & Co Ltd v Tims* [1952] A.C. 676.

[123] *Dallison v Caffery* [1965] 1 Q.B. 348.

[124] *Roberts v CC Cheshire* [1999] 1 W.L.R. 662.

[125] *Taylor v CC Thames Valley* [2004] EWCA Civ 858; [2004] 1 W.L.R. 3155.

[126] *Cullen v CC Royal Ulster Constabulary* [2003] UKHL 39; [2003] 1 W.L.R. 1763. However, if access is refused in bad faith there might be liability for misfeasance in a public office: at [71]. The case concerned s.15 of the Northern Ireland (Emergency Provisions) Act 1987 but this is modelled on the equivalent provision of the Police and Criminal Evidence Act 1984 and the reasoning would seem to apply.

Defence of arrest at common law in order to prevent an imminent breach of the peace. The common law affords a defence to people who effect an arrest in order to prevent an imminent breach of the peace by the person arrested.[127] This defence complies with art.5 of the European Convention on Human Rights.[128] In order to prevent an imminent breach of the peace there may also be detention short of arrest but there is no doctrine that such action may be justified on lesser grounds than those applicable to an arrest: in either case the apprehended breach of the peace must be happening or about to happen, not merely reasonably anticipated at some time in the future.[129]

26–056

iv. Prevention of Crime

Circumstances in which the defence applies. In addition to the powers of arrest that have been discussed above, by s.3 of the Criminal Law Act 1967 any person may use such force (which may include detention[130]) as is reasonable in the circumstances in the prevention of crime, or in effecting or assisting in the lawful arrest of offenders, suspected offenders or persons unlawfully at large. By virtue of its reasonableness requirement, this defence is justificatory in nature. Whether or not the force used is reasonable is a question of fact.[131] The offence that the defendant seeks to prevent must be an offence recognised by domestic law in order for the defence to apply. Acting to prevent breaches of international law will not enliven the defence.[132]

26–057

Overlap with other defences. The defence in s.3 of the Criminal Law Act 1967 obviously overlaps extensively with other defences. For example, it covers much of the same terrain as self-defence. But the overlap here is not perfect. An "innocent aggressor" such as an infant with a gun cannot incur criminal liability so s.3 would not be available in respect of force used against the infant. In contrast, the defence of self-defence may apply where the aggressor is not criminally responsible and, indeed, is merely perceived to be an aggressor.[133]

26–058

v. Lawful Confinement in Prison

By s.12(1) of the Prison Act 1952 "a prisoner, whether sentenced to imprisonment or committed to prison on remand pending trial" is lawfully

26–059

---

[127] *R. (Laporte) v CC Gloucestershire* [2006] UKHL 55; [2007] 2 A.C. 105.

[128] *Steel v UK* (1998) 28 E.H.R.R. 603.

[129] *R. (Laporte) v CC Gloucestershire* [2006] UKHL 55; [2007] 2 A.C. 105. In *Murray v Ministry of Defence* [1998] 1 W.L.R. 692 it is suggested that a person who restrains the movement of A for a short time if necessary to effect the lawful arrest of B will have a defence. It has also been suggested that a defence is available where the movement of occupants is restricted while premises are being searched: *DPP v Meaden* [2003] EWHC 3005 (Admin); [2004] 1 W.L.R. 945; *Connor v CC Merseyside* [2006] EWCA Civ 1549; [2007] H.R.L.R. 6.

[130] *Albert v Lavin* [1982] A.C. 546.

[131] *A–G for Northern Ireland's Reference (No.1 of 1975)* [1977] A.C. 105. It is arguable that the legislation gives insufficient guidance to persons using force as to how much force is reasonable. See generally Doran (1987) 7 L.S. 291.

[132] *R. v Jones* [2006] UKHL 16; [2007] 1 A.C. 136.

[133] See paras 26–031, 26–033.

confined in the prison. This provision confers on any prison governor or prison officer acting under his authority a defence to liability in false imprisonment.[134] This defence is probably best understood as a justification. A prison governor or prison officer acts reasonably in detaining a person ordered by a court to be confined in prison. The defence will be lost if a prison governor fails to release a prisoner at the end of his sentence. In *R. v Governor of Brockhill Prison, Ex p. Evans (No.2)*[135] the claimant was released from prison by habeas corpus when a decision of the Divisional Court disapproved earlier cases dealing with the method of calculation of the release date for prisoners with concurrent sentences, and he recovered £5,000 damages for the 59 days he had spent in prison after his proper release date. The claimant recovered even though, before the new ruling was given, the prison governor would plainly have had no authority to release him. The governor was acting in accordance with the law as it was then perceived to be, but the general rule is that decisions that are overruled are regarded as never having had legal force, subject to any issue being res judicata between parties who have previously litigated the issue. A prison governor is not guilty of false imprisonment for detaining a prisoner under a sentence which the court, it is subsequently held, had no power to impose, for he must obey an order of the court unless at that time it is invalid on its face.

vi.   Stop and Search by Police Officer

26–060   The common law gives the police no power to detain for questioning.[136] However, Pt.I of the Police and Criminal Evidence Act 1984 gives a police officer power to stop and search any person or vehicle for stolen or prohibited goods if he has reasonable grounds to believe that such goods will be found. These provisions create a defence to liability in trespass.

vii.   Statutory Authority[137]

26–061   A statute may provide that a person is authorised to engage in conduct that constitutes a tort. Such a statute creates a defence. Such statutory defences are best regarded as justifications because, usually, the protection that they confer is lost if the defendant acts unreasonably. The issue of whether or not a given piece of legislation has authorised tortious conduct is, ultimately, a matter of statutory construction, as is the scope of any such authority. However, two general points to bear in mind in this connection are as follows. First, the existence of a provision in the statute in question that provides for a person who is injured by the activity to be compensated is a material consideration. Such a provision may

---

[134] The fact that the Parole Board has acted unlawfully in administrative law terms in relation to considering the prisoner's release, or in breach of art.5(4) of the European Convention on Human Rights due to delay in considering the prisoner's case, does not render his detention actionable for the purpose of false imprisonment: *Dunn v Parole Board* [2008] EWCA Civ 374; [2009] 1 W.L.R. 728; *R. v Secretary of State for Justice, Ex p. Faulkner* [2013] UKSC 23; [2013] 2 A.C. 254.

[135] [2001] 2 A.C. 19.

[136] A person who voluntarily attends at a police station for questioning cannot be detained there unless he is lawfully arrested: Police and Criminal Evidence Act 1984 s.29.

[137] Nolan in Dyson, Goudkamp and Wilmot-Smith (eds), *Defences in Tort* (2014).

suggest that Parliament intended to create a defence. Secondly, it is for the defendant to demonstrate that Parliament intended to create a defence. Most of the cases on the defence of statutory authority have concerned liability for nuisance and the matter has been considered in that context.[138]

4. PUBLIC POLICY DEFENCES

A. Public Policy Defences that Arise at the Time of the Tort

i. The Defence of Illegality at Common Law[139]

It is a well-known principle of the law of contract that if the claimant has to found his claim on an illegal act or agreement he will fail: *ex turpi causa non oritur actio*.[140] Although that maxim may be properly confined to cases involving contracts,[141] it is clear that illegality is also a tort defence. It is a defence of general application in that it is potentially available in respect of all torts. However, its scope is heavily dependent on the context in which it is invoked. There are at least four different types of cases to consider. These will be dealt with in turn below. However, some general points are worth making about the defence at the outset. First, the defence requires unlawful (although immoral conduct may suffice) conduct.[142] The illegal conduct must be fairly serious. Trivial offending by the claimant, such as failing to wear a seatbelt, will not engage the defence.[143] Secondly, illegality by the claimant can certainly function as a defence in the sense that this word is used in this chapter, but (as will be seen), it can also eliminate recovery under particular heads of damage. Thirdly, there is a considerable overlap between the defence of illegality and the doctrine of contributory negligence. Frequently, but not always, when the illegality defence is an issue the doctrine of contributory negligence will be too. This overlap is important principally because it has made the courts fairly slow to find that the defence of illegality applies. Where they are able to do so the courts prefer to find that the doctrine of illegality is inapplicable and to take account of the claimant's conduct only by way of the doctrine of contributory negligence. This enables the claimant to recovery partially. Fourthly, the defendant bears the onus of pleading and proving that the defence of illegality is applicable. Fifthly,

26–062

---

[138] See para.15–063.

[139] The defence has spawned a large literature. For a small sample, see Weinrib (1976) 26 U.T.L.J. 28; Prentice (1995) 32 San Diego L. Rev. 53; Fordham [1998] S.J.L.S. 238; Glofcheski (1999) 19 L.S. 6; Goudkamp (2007) 29 Syd. L. Rev. 445; Goudkamp (2010) 34 M.U.L.R. 425; Goudkamp (2011) 27 L.Q.R. 354; Spencer in Dyson (ed), *Unravelling Tort and Crime* (2014), Ch.11; Virgo in Dyson (ed), *Unravelling Tort and Crime* (2014), Ch.7; Goudkamp and Mayr in Dyson, Goudkamp and Wilmot-Smith (eds), *Defences in Tort* (2014).

[140] "No cause of action may be founded upon an immoral or illegal act": *Revill v Newbery* [1996] Q.B. 567 at 576 per Neill LJ.

[141] *Smith v Jenkins* (1970) 119 C.L.R. 397 at 410 per Windeyer J.

[142] Goudkamp (2011) 27 L.Q.R. 354.

[143] It has been said repeatedly that venial wrongdoing does not enliven the doctrine: *Saunders v Edwards* [1987] 1 W.L.R. 1116 at 1134; *Vellino v Chief Constable of the Greater Manchester Police* [2001] EWCA Civ 1249; [2002] 1 W.L.R. 218 at [48]; *Currie v Clamp* 2002 S.L.T. 196 at [20]–[21]; *Griffin v UHY Hacker Young & Partners (a firm)* [2010] EWHC 146 (Ch) at [49]–[60].

where the claimant has a criminal law defence the defence of illegality will not apply, although this may depend on the type of criminal law defence that the claimant possesses.

26–063 **The claimant's illegal conduct caused his own damage.** The first type of case in which the illegality defence applies are those in which the claimant had caused his damage by his own illegal act.[144] In *Joyce v O'Brien*[145] the parties had stolen a ladder from a residential property. They loaded it onto a van which the defendant drove. The claimant rode on the back of the van but fell from it and suffered injury as the parties fled from the scene of the crime. The claimant failed in his action by virtue of the illegality defence. The Court of Appeal held that the claimant had, by his illegal act, caused his own damage. *Joyce* can be contrasted with *Delaney v Pickett*.[146] In *Delaney* the claimant passenger was injured in a car accident that was caused by the negligence of the driver of the vehicle in which he was travelling. Rescue services discovered when they attended the scene that the claimant and the driver were transporting cannabis. The defence of illegality was inapplicable on this occasion because the illegal conduct had not contributed to the accident. The offending act was not causally connected to the claimant's damage. The claimant would have suffered injury had he been acting lawfully. Query whether, in a case such as *Joyce* the claimant's illegality is operating as a defence or a denial. The court presented it as a defence but in reality it seems to be denial of the causation element of the action in negligence.

26–064 **The claimant seeks to recover damages in respect of a criminal law sanction.** The second type of case in which the defence of illegality will apply are those in which the claimant seeks damages in tort law in respect of a criminal law penalty that has been imposed on him.[147] The way in which the defence applies in this type of case is illustrated nicely by *Clunis v Camden and Islington Health Authority*.[148] The claimant in this case had a history of mental illness. The defendant health authority's officers negligently failed to follow up with him when he repeatedly missed appointments. Labouring under his mental illness the claimant stabbed a man to death on a London underground station. He was convicted of manslaughter on the basis of diminished responsibility and sentenced to detention in hospital. The claimant then sued the defendant health authority claiming that, had its officers detained him and provided him with proper treatment he would not have lost his freedom for such a lengthy period of time. The claimant's action was rejected by virtue of the illegality defence. A loss of freedom consequent upon a sentence of imprisonment is a loss inflicted by the criminal law, and the courts will not permit claimants to use tort law to "undo" that loss. A loss of earnings caused by a conviction is also part of the punishment

---

[144] This is what Lord Hoffmann called a "wide rule" case in the leading decision of *Gray v Thames Trains Ltd* [2009] UKHL 33; [2009] A.C. 1339.

[145] [2013] EWCA Civ 546; [2014] 1 W.L.R. 70, noted in Fordham [2013] S.J..L.S. 202.

[146] [2011] EWCA Civ 1532; [2012] 1 W.L.R. 2149, noted in Goudkamp (2012) 71 C.L.J. 481. The saga in this case continued in *Delaney v Secretary of State for Transport* [2014] EWHC 1785 (QB).

[147] This is what Lord Hoffmann called a "narrow rule" case in *Gray v Thames Trains Ltd* [2009] UKHL 33; [2009] A.C. 1339.

[148] [1998] Q.B. 978. See also *British Columbia v Zastowny* [2008] SCC 4; [2008] 1 S.C.R. 27.

and damages cannot, consequently, be recovered in respect of this loss.[149] Arguably, however, damages can be recovered in respect of a fine imposed where the offence committed by the claimant is merely one of strict liability, at least where the claimant was not at fault for the offence. This result might be explicable as an exception to the principle that has just been described, or on the ground that the defence of illegality is simply not triggered in the first place because the offence committed is too trivial.[150]

The claimant seeks damages in respect of lost illegal earnings. The third type of case in which the defence of illegality may apply are those where the claimant seeks damages in respect of lost illegal earnings. The leading case is *Hewison v Meridian Shipping Services Pte.*[151] The claimant committed an offence in working as a crane driver without disclosing the fact that he suffered from epilepsy. He was injured by his employer's negligence and the fact that he suffered from epilepsy then came to light. The claimant, while he was able to recover damages under all other heads, was denied recovery in respect of his earnings. Damages in that regard were withheld on the ground that this head of the claim was inextricably connected with the offence that the claimant committed. A claimant will not be barred from recovering damages for a loss of earnings simply because he would have failed to pay tax on them.[152]

26–065

The claimant seeks damages in respect of interference with a chattel his possession of which was unlawful. The operation of the defence of illegality in this type of case has been dealt with in an earlier chapter.[153]

26–066

The law regarding the defence of illegality is unsatisfactory. The law regarding the defence of illegality is a stain on the law of torts. The type of case in which the defence is most frequently in issue is the first type. The defence serves absolutely no useful function in relation to that type of case. It does not prevent the claimant from profiting from his wrong because the claimant is simply seeking damages in respect of the injuries that he suffered. He is asking to be put in the position that he would have been in but for the defendant's tort. There is, except in unusual cases, no potential for a claimant in tort law to profit from his wrong. The illegality defence equally cannot be justified on the ground that it deters offending. It is farfetched to think that a person who is considering whether to commit a serious criminal offence would be dissuaded from committing the offence in question by the risk that *if* he is injured while committing the offence he *may* be deprived of an entitlement to damages in tort. If the criminal law is insufficient to deter offending the illegality defence, which is surely not a matter of public knowledge, is unlikely to do so. In truth, far from accomplishing anything worthwhile, the defence is unhelpful because it is prone to inflict disproportionate punishment. The claimant is arguably punished when his damages are denied by virtue of the defence. However, this is a nonsensical

26–067

---

[149] *Gray v Thames Trains Ltd* [2009] UKHL 33; [2009] A.C. 1339.
[150] *Osman v J. Ralph Moss Ltd* [1970] 1 Lloyd's Rep. 313.
[151] [2002] EWCA Civ 1821; [2003] I.C.R. 766.
[152] *Hall v Woolston Hall Leisure Ltd* [2001] 1 W.L.R. 225; *Finnis v Caulfield* [2002] EWHC 3223 (QB).
[153] See para.18–037.

way of meting out punishment because the quantum of the punishment depends not on the gravity of the wrongdoing but on the quantum of the claimant's loss. The greater the loss the greater the punishment. The fact of the matter is that the claimant should be able to recover where he was injured while committing an offence even where that offending is causally related to the claimant's damages. This is the law in Canada.[154]

The defence arguably serves a useful purpose in relation to the other types of cases that have been discussed. In the second type of case the claimant seeks damages in respect of a criminal law penalty. It is probably correct that these claims are denied by the defence since otherwise the law would be restoring via tort law that which it had taken from the claimant by the criminal law. The law, in other words, would be contradicting itself. It is also likely the case that the defence properly applies so as to deny to claimants damages in respect of lost illegal earnings (the third type of case). When the claimant earns an income by committing a breach of the criminal law he is profiting from his wrong. The wrongful profiting rationale probably justifies the defence, therefore, in this type of case. Finally, in the fourth type of case, the defence might be justified on the basis that it ensure that the law is consistent. If it is illegal to possess a chattel would the law not be contradictory if it protected that possession via the law of torts?

ii. The Defence of Illegality under s.329 of the Criminal Justice Act 2003

26–068 Under s.329 of the Criminal Justice Act 2003 a defendant who is sued by a claimant who has been convicted of an imprisonable offence will have a defence to liability in trespass to the person if the following matters are satisfied. First, the act in respect of which the claimant sues was committed by the defendant on the same occasion as the conduct that led to the claimant's conviction. Secondly, the defendant acted only because he believed that the claimant was about to commit an offence (or was in the course of committing it or had committed it immediately beforehand; or that he acted to defend himself or another; or to protect or recover property; or to prevent the commission of an offence; or to apprehend the offender). Thirdly, the defendant's act was not grossly disproportionate in the circumstances. "Belief", for the purposes of the second requirement, is honest belief even if unreasonable.[155] So if the defendant (whether a police officer or a private person) arrests the claimant for, say, burglary on totally inadequate evidence but matters which later come to light lead to his conviction (for that or any other imprisonable offence) no action can be brought unless what the defendant did was "grossly disproportionate". The claimant requires the court's permission to bring proceedings and this can be given only if there is evidence that the condition as to the defendant's belief was not satisfied or that his act was grossly disproportionate.[156]

---

[154] *Hall v Hebert* [1993] 2 S.C.R. 159.

[155] Criminal Justice Act 2003 s.329(8)(b).

[156] Criminal Justice Act 2003 s.329(3). Failure to seek permission does not render the proceedings a nullity: *Adorian v MPC* [2009] EWCA Civ 18; [2009] 1 W.L.R. 1859.

iii. Immunities

Tort law recognises many immunities from liability. These immunities include **26–069** those that are afforded to certain participants in the judicial process,[157] to trade unions,[158] to the Crown (although the Crown's immunity has been severely restricted by statute),[159] to foreign states[160] and to diplomatic agents.[161] In recent decades the courts have adopted an increasingly hostile attitude towards immunities and many immunities have been removed. Immunities that have been abolished (either by judges or by Parliament) include the immunity of advocates,[162] the landlords' immunity[163] and the immunity of highway authorities for nonfeasance.[164] The erosion of immunities has been brought about by various factors, including the fact that immunities can create the impression that the law is guilty of favouritism. There is little consensus among tort lawyers as to what, precisely, the word "immunity" means. According to Hohfeld, the term "immunity" correlates with "disability" and is the opposite of "liability".[165] The nearest synonym is said to be "exemption".[166] However, it is clear that defences that attract the label "immunity" are public policy defences since their application does not depend on the reasonableness of the defendant's conduct. They arise at the time of the tort.

B.   Public Policy Defences that Arise After the Tort

i.   Waiver

When lawyers speak of "waiver" they may mean to refer to conduct by the **26–070** claimant which signifies an intention to give up a right of action for a legal wrong. Subject to the doctrine of promissory estoppel (which cannot be pursued here) a right of action for tort can only be "waived" in this sense by an agreement for valuable consideration or a release by deed.[167] Mere demand for payment of what is due is not a waiver of the right of action for the wrong[168] nor is receipt of part payment of what is due, unless it is accepted as full discharge.[169]

---

[157] See para.5–080.
[158] See para.19–055.
[159] See para.25–002.
[160] See para.25–007.
[161] See para.25–007.
[162] See para.5–007.
[163] See para.10–060.
[164] See para.15–082.
[165] Hohfeld (1913) 23 Yale L.J. 16 at 30.
[166] Hohfeld (1913) 23 Yale L. J. 16 at 57.
[167] See para.26–071.
[168] *Valpy v Sanders* (1848) 5 C.B. 886; *Morris v Robinson* (1824) 3 B. & C. 196.
[169] *Burns v Morris* (1834) 4 Tyrw. 485; *Lythgoe v Vernon* (1860) 5 H. & N. 180.

ii. Accord and Satisfaction

26–071 **Generally.** Tortious liability can be extinguished by agreement for valuable consideration between the injured party and the tortfeasor.[170] This is styled "accord and satisfaction" but is really little more than a specialised form of contract and so, to be effective, it must comply with the rules for the formation of contract.[171] "Accord" signifies the agreement, "satisfaction" the consideration which makes it operative. The satisfaction may be either executed (e.g. "I release you from your obligation in consideration of £100 now paid by you to me") or it may be executor (e.g. "I release you from your obligation in consideration of your promise to pay me £100 in six months").[172]

26–072 **Accord and satisfaction may be conditional.** A person injured in an accident brought about by the negligence of the defendant may accept an offer of compensation, reserving to himself the right to renew his claim if his injuries turn out to be worse than they were at the time of the accord.[173]

26–073 **Accord and satisfaction may extend to only part of the claimant's action.** It is also possible for the parties, by an agreement falling short of full accord and satisfaction, to limit the issues between them, as in *Tomlin v Standard Telephones and Cables Ltd*,[174] an action for damages for personal injuries, where it was agreed that the defendants would pay 50 per cent of the claimant's damages, leaving only the amount of those damages to be determined.

26–074 **Non-performance of accord and satisfaction.** What is the position of the parties if the accord and satisfaction are not carried out? Are they in the same situation as if it had never been made or must the party aggrieved sue upon the broken accord and satisfaction and upon that only? The answer is that it depends upon the construction of the agreement that embodies the accord and satisfaction.[175] If the satisfaction consists of a promise on the part of the tortfeasor, the interpretation of the agreement may be, "I accept this promise as an absolute discharge of your tortious liability". If so, all that the injured party can sue upon in the event of the tortfeasor not carrying out his promise is the contract which has been substituted

---

[170] *Peytoe's Case* (1611) 9 Co. Rep. 77b. It is important to note that since the claim will be for unliquidated damages an accord and satisfaction will be effective even though a court might have awarded more or less in the way of damages. "The agreed sum is a liquidated amount which replaces the claim for an illiquid sum. The effect of the compromise is to fix the amount of his claim in just the same way as if the case had gone to trial and he had obtained judgment": *Jameson v C.E.G.B.* [2000] 1 A.C. 455 at 474 per Lord Hope.

[171] *D & C Builders Ltd v Rees* [1966] 2 Q.B. 617.

[172] *British Russian Gazette & Trade Outlook Ltd v Associated Newspapers Ltd* [1933] 2 K.B. 616 per Scrutton LJ, at 650 per Greer LJ. On the effect of an agreement with D1 where C also has a claim against D2, see *Jameson v C.E.G.B.* [2000] 1 A.C. 455 and para.22–007.

[173] *Lee v L&Y Ry* (1871) L.R. 6 Ch. App. 527; *Ellen v GN Ry* (1901) 17 T.L.R. 453; *North British Ry v Wood* (1891) 18 R. (H.L.) 27.

[174] [1969] 1 W.L.R. 1378.

[175] Although the agreement will usually be contained in "without prejudice" correspondence, which means that the correspondence cannot be used in evidence, this correspondence can be produced to the court if the question is whether a binding agreement has actually been reached between the parties (*Tomlin v Standard Telephones and Cables Ltd* [1969] 1 W.L.R. 1378) and, presumably, also when a question of the interpretation of the agreement has to be decided.

for the tortious liability. Alternatively, the interpretation of the agreement may be, "I accept this promise as a discharge of your liability provided you carry it out". In that case, if the promise is not fulfilled, the injured party has two alternative remedies: he can either fall back upon his original claim in tort; or he can sue upon the contract which was intended to take its place. Somewhat different considerations apply to an accord and satisfaction that is expressed to be conditional in the first instance, as in the example given above of provisional acceptance of compensation in an accident. Here the injured party cannot have recourse to his action in tort unless the condition is not fulfilled. If it is fulfilled within the time specified by the agreement or, if no time is specified, within a reasonable time, then the tortious liability is extinguished. If it is not thus fulfilled, then the injured party can either rely upon his claim in tort or sue upon the conditional agreement which was substituted for it and which has been broken.

iii. Release

Closely akin to accord and satisfaction is release of tortious liability given by the injured party. In fact, there seems to be little difference between the two concepts except that a release is usually, but not necessarily, embodied in a deed and the necessity for consideration is thus avoided.[176] Release is apparently effective whether it is given before or after an action against the tortfeasor is commenced.

26–075

iv. Prior Criminal Proceedings

Statutory defence. Suppose that C brings a private prosecution against D for assault and battery. Irrespective of the outcome of the prosecution, legislation provides that the fact that the prosecution was brought will provide D with a defence to any civil liability that he might have otherwise incurred in respect of the act on which the prosecution was based.[177] The apparent rationale for this defence is that it would be wasteful and unjust to permit C to pursue D in the civil sphere in light of the prior prosecution. Because this defence presents no issue as to the reasonableness of the defendant's conduct, it is a public policy defence.[178] Several points should be noted about this defence. First, the defence will not apply if the criminal proceedings were dismissed for some technical defect. Secondly, the defence will only apply if the criminal proceedings were instituted by or on behalf of the person aggrieved, and not by someone else. Thirdly, where D has been prosecuted and convicted that fact precludes not only a civil action for assault, but also an action using the assault as the basis for some other cause of

26–076

---

[176] *Phillips v Clagett* (1843) 11 M. & W. 84.
[177] Offences Against the Person Act 1861 ss.44–45.
[178] The Criminal Law Revision Committee recommended that this defence be abolished: Criminal Law Revision Committee, *Fourteenth Report: Offences Against the Person* (Cmnd. 7844, 1980). In *Wong v Parkside Health NHS Trust* [2001] EWCA Civ 1721; [2003] 3 All E.R. 932 at [16] Hale LJ described it as "anomalous".

action.[179] Fourthly, the defence does not apply in proceedings against anyone other than the defendant, so that the conviction of an employee for an assault committed in the course of his employment is no bar to an action against his employer.[180]

v. Abuse of Process

26–077   **Generally.** The doctrine of abuse of process advances the administration of justice by preventing the court's process from being corrupted. It applies when a litigant uses a process for a purpose that is significantly different from that for which it was intended. For example, the doctrine has been invoked to stay proceedings that are an attempt to circumvent the special procedure that governs claims for judicial review[181] or which constitute a collateral attack on the verdict of a criminal court.[182] It has also been used to stay actions in defamation where the value of the damage suffered by the claimant as a result of the publication of the defendant's defamatory statement is insignificant relative to the cost of the proceedings.[183] Clearly, the doctrine of abuse of process is a defence. It is not an element of any tort that the proceedings commenced by the claimant are not an abuse of process. The doctrine is a public policy defence since it is unconcerned with the reasons that the defendant had for acting tortiously.

26–078   **Some situations where proceedings do not constitute an abuse of process.** The doctrine of abuse of process does not stand in the way of a civil action simply because the defendant had been acquitted in the criminal court: apart altogether from any substantive differences between the relevant crime and the tort in which the proceedings are brought, the standards of proof are different and a verdict of acquittal in the criminal case is quite consistent with a finding of liability in the civil action. Neither does a conviction prevent the defendant from contesting liability in a case where a civil action can be brought against him. A contrary outcome would be inconsistent with s.11 of the Civil Evidence Act 1968,[184] which provides that a criminal conviction is, in civil proceedings, prima facie but not conclusive evidence that the defendant committed the offence.[185]

vi. Judgment

26–079   **Final judgment by a court of competent jurisdiction extinguishes a right of action.** This rule has a twofold effect. First, it estops any party to the litigation

---

[179] Where D has been prosecuted and convicted this precludes not only a civil action for assault, but also an action using the assault as the basis for some other cause of action: *Wong v Parkside Health NHS Trust* [2001] EWCA Civ 1721; [2003] 3 All E.R. 932.

[180] *Dyer v Munday* [1895] 1 Q.B. 742.

[181] *O'Reilly v Mackman* [1983] 2 A.C. 237; *Clark v University of Lincolnshire and Humberside* [2000] 1 W.L.R. 1988.

[182] *Hunter v Chief Constable of the West Midlands Police* [1982] A.C. 529.

[183] See, e.g. *Jameel v Dow Jones & Co Inc* [2005] EWCA Civ 75; [2005] Q.B. 946; *Khader v Aziz* [2010] EWCA 716; [2010] 1 W.L.R. 2673.

[184] See para.6–036.

[185] *J v Oyston, The Times*, December 11, 1998. *Brinks Ltd v Abu-Saleh* [1995] 1 W.L.R. 1478 cannot be supported if it lays down any other rule: *McCauley v Hope* [1999] 1 W.L.R. 1977.

from disputing afterwards the correctness of the decision either in law or in fact. Secondly, it operates as a merger of the original cause of action in the rights created by the judgment and these are either to levy execution against the defendant or to bring a new action upon the judgment (not upon the original claim, for that has perished). There are at least two reasons for this rule. The first is that there is a strong public interest in the finality of litigation: *interest reipublicae ut sit finis litium*. The second is concerned with justice as between the litigants. It would be unfair if the parties could pursue each other repeatedly in respect of liabilities that have already been decided.[186]

vii. Assignment of Right of Action in Tort

Introduction. When a right of action in tort is transferred to another person, the defendant will have a defence to liability in respect of any proceedings that are brought by the transferror. In certain circumstances, the defendant will also have a defence to an action commenced by the transferee.   **26–080**

The general rule is that actions in tort cannot be assigned. It is a longstanding rule in the law of assignment of choses in action that, while property can lawfully be assigned, a "bare right to litigate" cannot,[187] because to allow such an assignment would be to encourage undesirable speculation in law suits.[188] Indeed, the agreement would savour of maintenance and champerty, which, formerly, were themselves torts and are still grounds for striking down a contract and providing a defence to the assignee's action.[189] This is not to say, however, that there can never be a valid assignment of a right of action in tort and the basic rule must be read in the light of the following qualifications and exceptions.[190]   **26–081**

"Proper interest of assignee". It has been held that if A transfers property to B he may also assign a right of action for breach of contract[191] (e.g. breach of covenant to repair in a lease) in relation to that property, for then, it has been said, the assignee buys the cause of action in order to protect the property he has bought.[192] Notwithstanding certain statements denying the assignability of any tort claim, it is submitted that such a case should be treated in the same way if the cause of action is in tort.[193] It is more difficult to know how far the doctrine stated in the House of Lords in *Trendtex Trading Corp v Credit Suisse*,[194] a case of   **26–082**

---

[186] Even a technically separate cause of action may now be barred by judgment if it could, with reasonable diligence, have been asserted in the original proceedings: see para.23–002.

[187] Reaffirmed in *Trendtex Trading Corp v Credit Suisse* [1982] A.C. 679.

[188] Some reasons formerly given for the rule are either unconvincing or obsolete. Thus it was said in argument in *Anon.* (1600) Godb. 81 that damages in the assigned action are too uncertain at the date of assignment, or that the assignee, "may be a man of great power, who might procure a jury to give him greater damages".

[189] *Laurent v Sale & Co* [1963] 1 W.L.R. 829.

[190] For statutory transmission on death, see Ch.24.

[191] *Ellis v Torrington* [1920] 1 K.B. 399.

[192] *Ellis v Torrington* [1920] 1 K.B. 399 at 412–413 per Scrutton LJ.

[193] See the comments of Lord Denning MR in *Trendtex Trading Corp v Credit Suisse* [1980] Q.B. 629 at 657.

[194] [1982] A.C. 679.

assignment of a claim for breach of contract, applies to tort cases.[195] It was said in that case that an assignee who has a "genuine commercial interest" in the enforcement of a claim may take a valid assignment of it so long as the transaction is not champertous and it seems that a genuine commercial interest may be present simply because the assignee is a creditor of the assignor. On this basis, unless an arbitrary line is to be drawn between contract and tort, it may be that, for example, an assignment to a bank of the assignor's claim for damages for negligent misstatement inducing a contract which the bank has financed, and on which it stands to lose, would be valid. In any event a trustee in bankruptcy and a liquidator have statutory power to sell a cause of action on terms that the assignees will pay a share of the proceeds (this statutory power necessarily precluding any challenge on the grounds of maintenance or champerty)[196] and this can extend, for example, to a tort claim for negligent advice.[197] By contrast, it is thought that the law should still refuse to give effect to the assignment of, say, a claim for libel or for personal injuries even though the assignor was indebted to the assignee.[198]

26–083   **Judgment.** No such problems arise with regard to the assignment of a judgment in an action for tort. If the judgment has already been given, the rights of the creditor are assignable like any other debt.[199] Similarly, a person may assign the fruits of an action yet to be commenced, for this is no more than the assignment of property to be acquired. Thus, in *Glegg v Bromley*[200] an assignment *pendente lite* of the fruits of an action for slander was upheld.[201]

26–084   **Subrogation.**[202] The commonest example of subrogation in this connection is in the law of insurance. An insurance company that has compensated a policyholder under an indemnity insurance policy stands in his shoes with regard to his claims against the person who caused the injury. Hence if A by negligent driving of his car damages B's car, and the X company, with whom B is insured, compensates him, the X company can exploit B's action for negligence against A. The

---

[195] But see *Brownton Ltd v Edward Moore Inbucon Ltd* [1985] 3 All E.R. 499, another contract case, at 509 per Lloyd LJ, whose statement of the principle of the *Trendtex* case applies to contract and tort alike.

[196] *Grovewood Holdings Plc v James Capel & Co Ltd* [1995] Ch. 80 at 86; *Norglen Ltd v Reeds Rains Prudential Ltd* [1999] 2 A.C. 1.

[197] *Ramsey v Hartley* [1977] 1 W.L.R. 686. There is a full review of the law in *Empire Resolution Ltd v MPW Insurance Brokers Ltd* [1999] B.P.I.R. 486.

[198] Lord Roskill in *Trendtex Trading Corp v Credit Suisse* [1982] A.C. 679 at 702 refers to the principle that "causes of action which were essentially personal in their character, such as claims fot defamation or personal injury, were incapable of assignment" but he is speaking in terms of the law 80 years ago and his general point is that the law of maintenance was then more severe. It seems that if A makes a voluntary payment to B to compensate B for loss caused by C, A may take a valid assignment of B's claim in tort against C: *Esso Petroleum Co Ltd v Hall Russell & Co Ltd* [1988] 3 W.L.R. 730 at 738.

[199] *Carrington v Harway* (1676) 1 Keb. 803; *Goodman v Robinson* (1886) 18 Q.B.D. 332.

[200] [1912] 3 K.B. 474.

[201] *Cohen v Mitchell* (1890) 25 Q.B.D. 262 can also be supported on this ground, although other reasons were given for the decision.

[202] For a statement of the principle, see *Castellain v Preston* (1883) 11 Q.B.D. 380 at 387 per Brett LJ; *Burnand v Rodocanachi, Sons & Co* (1882) 7 App. Cas. 333 at 339 per Lord Blackburn; *Morris v Ford Motor Co Ltd* [1973] Q.B. 792.

payment by the insurer under the policy does not provide the tortfeasor with a defence to a claim by the insured,[203] but if the latter recovers damages they are subject to a proprietary lien or charge in favour of the insurer.[204]

viii. Insolvency

Insolvency of the defendant. Historically, a claim for unliquidated damages in tort was not provable as a bankruptcy debt so that the claim remained alive against the bankrupt (who might acquire assets after his discharge) and liability did not pass to his trustee.[205] A similar principle applied to the winding-up of an insolvent company; however, since the company would generally then cease to exist there was no equivalent to the personal liability of the individual bankrupt. Now, by the Insolvency Act 1986, a liability in tort is a "bankruptcy debt"[206] so that the claimant may seek to share in the assets along with the other creditors and discharge from the bankruptcy provides the bankrupt person with a defence to liability in tort.[207] This defence, unless the court otherwise directs, does not apply to liability for damages for personal injuries arising from, "negligence, nuisance or breach of a statutory, contractual or other duty".[208]

26–085

Insolvency of claimant. Under the Insolvency Act 1986 the bankrupt's property[209] forms, with certain exceptions, his estate, available for distribution among creditors. If the injury is a purely personal one, like defamation, the right of action for it remains exercisable by the injured party himself and does not pass to his trustee in bankruptcy. Bankruptcy of the claimant is not a defence, therefore, in proceedings for such injuries. But when the tort is to property (e.g. conversion of goods) then the right to sue for it passes to the trustee, who can sell or assign it to anyone as he, in his discretion, thinks fit. The upshot is that the defendant will have a defence to proceedings brought by the claimant in respect of such torts.

26–086

ix. Limitation

Introduction. The defendant will have a defence—a time bar—if the claimant fails to bring his proceedings sufficiently promptly. This defence is a public policy defence since its application is unconcerned with the reasonableness of the defendant's conduct at the time the tort was committed. The law on limitation is extremely complex and of considerable practical significance. It is therefore worth dealing with it in some detail. However, what follows is far from an

26–087

---

[203] See para.1–023.

[204] *Lord Napier and Ettrick v Hunter* [1993] A.C. 713.

[205] Tort claims became provable against the insolvent estate of a deceased person by the Law Reform (Miscellaneous Provisions) Act 1934 s.1(1)(6).

[206] See s.382. By subs.(2): "in determining . . . whether any liability in tort is a bankruptcy debt, the bankrupt is deemed to become subject to that liability by reason of an obligation incurred at the time when the cause of action accrued."

[207] Proceedings might be brought by the claimant against the bankrupt's insurers pursuant to the Third Parties (Rights Against Insurers) Act 2010.

[208] Section 281(5). See also Road Traffic Act 1988 s.153.

[209] Defined in s.436 to include "things in action".

exhaustive account. It should be noted that a claimant may lose his action even if he brings proceedings within the limitation period as the court enjoys the power to strike out as an abuse of process claims within the limitation period which are pursued in a dilatory manner.

26–088   **Rationale for the defence.** There are many reasons for the existence of limitation bars. In the first place, they prevent the unfairness that would be caused to defendants if claimants could pursue them in respect of long-forgotten wrongdoing. Secondly, if limitation bars did not exist defendants might be compelled to keep evidence indefinitely to ensure that they could defend claims that may never be brought. This would be a waste of resources. Thirdly, limitation bars may help claimants to move on with their lives. Fourthly, limitation bars prevent claims from being decided on the base of stale evidence. Many types of evidence deteriorate with the passage of time (e.g. witnesses may die or leave the jurisdiction) and determining disputes on the basis of incomplete evidence is slow and there is a greater risk that the court will reach an incorrect conclusion. These considerations point to a short, definite time limit for the presentation of claims, but they have always been counterbalanced by other considerations of justice to the victim of the tort. Claimants must be given sufficient time in which to carry out investigations and to decide whether they have a claim. Furthermore, it seems fair that allowances are made—for example, for claimants who are suffering from a disability that renders them unable to pursue their claims or where they were not aware that they had an action.

26–089   **The general rules.** The principal Act today is the Limitation Act 1980,[210] with substantial amendments brought in by the Latent Damage Act 1986. Broadly speaking, actions founded on tort must be brought within six years from the date when the cause of action accrued. In the case of personal injury claims, however, the period is three years. The limitation period for defamation and malicious falsehood is one year. The strictness of these rules is ameliorated in various ways—for example, by postponing the running of time where the claimant was ignorant that he had a claim and, in personal injury cases, by giving the court a discretionary power to override the time limits altogether. Personal injury limitation will be dealt with separately.

26–090   **Burdens of pleading and proof.** The defendant must plead a limitation defence, for the court will not of its own motion take notice that the action is out of time.[211] If a limitation bar is pleaded, the claimant has the burden of showing that his claim accrued within the period.[212] Where a claimant asserts that he is entitled to the benefit of a deferred date of knowledge he also bears the onus of proof in that connection.[213] These rules are important exceptions to the general principle that the defendant bears the onus of establishing defences.

---

[210] The earliest comprehensive legislation was the Limitation Act 1623.

[211] *Dunsmore v Milton* [1938] 3 All E.R. 762. If the defendant decides to contest the case on its merits, it is not open to him to amend to plead limitation at a later stage when it becomes apparent that he is likely to lose on the merits: *Ketteman v Hansel Properties Ltd* [1987] A.C. 189.

[212] *London Congregational Union Inc v Harriss & Harriss* [1988] 1 All E.R. 15; *Crocker v British Coal* (1996) 29 B.M.L.R. 159.

[213] *AB v Ministry of Defence* [2012] UKSC 9; [2013] 1 A.C. 78 at [48].

Commencement of the limitation period. According to the Limitation Act 1980   **26–091**
the period of limitation runs "from the date on which the cause of action
accrued". No explanation of "accrued" is given, but authorities regarding earlier
legislation show that the period begins to run "from the earliest time at which an
action could be brought".[214] "Cause of action . . . means that which makes action
possible."[215] A cause of action arises, therefore, at the moment when a state of
facts occurs which gives a potential claimant a right to succeed against a potential
defendant. There must be a claimant who can succeed, and a defendant against
whom he can succeed.[216] Thus, for example, when goods belonging to a person
who has died intestate have been converted after his death, the proper party to sue
is the administrator and time does not begin to run until he has taken out letters of
administration.[217] Similarly, where the tortfeasor is entitled to diplomatic
immunity, time does not run in his favour until the termination of his period of
office, for until then no action will lie against him.[218] A merely procedural bar to
bringing a suit will not prevent time running.[219] If, however, time has begun to
run, it will continue to do so even over a period during which there is no one
capable of suing or of being sued.[220] The fact that the potential claimant is unable
to identify the defendant does not, in principle, prevent a cause of action
accruing,[221] though this is now qualified in many cases.[222] It is often the case that
the tortious conduct of the defendant will be a single act or omission that causes
damage to be suffered over a lengthy period of time. Once some damage has been
suffered time begins to run and the claimant cannot evade the limitation period by
confining his claim to losses that have occurred within the prescribed period
before he commences proceedings.[223]

Latent damage generally. In the case of torts that are actionable per se, time   **26–092**
begins to run, in general, at the moment the wrongful act was committed, whether
the injured party knows of it or not, provided that there is no fraudulent
concealment.[224] This is so even where the resulting damage (if any) does not
occur or is not discovered until a later date.[225] On the other hand, in respect of
torts of which damage is the gist time runs from the date on which the damage

---

[214] *Reeves v Butcher* [1891] 2 Q.B. 509 at 511 per Lindley LJ. The day on which the cause of action
arose is excluded: *Marren v Dawson Bentley & Co Ltd* [1961] 2 Q.B. 135. If the last day of the period
is one when court offices are closed the claimant has until the first following day when they are open
(*Kaur v S. Russell & Sons* [1973] Q.B. 336) and proceedings are started when the claim form is
received in court even if there is delay in its issue: *Barnes v St Helens MBC* [2006] EWCA Civ 1372;
[2007] 1 W.L.R. 879.
[215] *Board of Trade v Cayzer, Irvine & Co Ltd* [1927] A.C. 610 at 617. Or in terms of pleading, "Every
fact which it would be necessary for the plaintiff to prove, if traversed, in order to support his right to
the judgment of the Court": *Read v Brown* (1888) 22 Q.B.D. 128 at 131 per Lord Esher MR.
[216] *Thomson v Clanmorris* [1900] 1 Ch. 718 at 728–729.
[217] *Pratt v Swaine* (1828)8 B. & C. 285.
[218] *Musurus Bey v Gadban* [1894] 2 Q.B. 352.
[219] *Sevcon Ltd v Lucas CAV Ltd* [1986] 1 W.L.R. 462 (sealing of patent necessary before action could
be brought).
[220] *Rhodes v Smethurst* (1838) 4 M. & W. 42 affirmed in (1840) 6 M. & W. 351.
[221] *R.B. Policies at Lloyd's v Butler* [1950] 1 K.B. 76.
[222] See para.26–098.
[223] *Khan v R.M. Falvey & Co* [2002] EWCA Civ 400; [2002] P.N.L.R. 28.
[224] *Granger v George* (1826) 5 B. & C. 149.
[225] *Howell v Young* (1826) 5 B. & C. 259.

was sustained.[226] Damage may be suffered before it is apparent to the claimant. In other words, latent damage can cause time to run.[227] In *Bell v Peter Browne & Co*[228] a husband and wife upon the breakdown of their marriage in 1978 agreed that the matrimonial home should be transferred into the wife's name but that the husband's interest in the proceeds of sale should be protected by some legal mechanism. No steps were in fact taken by the husband's solicitors to effect this protection and eight years later the wife sold the house and spent all the proceeds. Time began to run for the tort claim at the latest when, after the completion of the transfer, a competent solicitor would have taken steps to protect the husband's interest, such as by lodging a Land Registry caution against the property.

26–093   **Latent Damage Act 1986.** The Latent Damage Act 1986 amended the Limitation Act 1980 by inserting into it ss.14A and 14B. These sections are generally applicable to actions for damages for negligence (other than one that includes a claim for damages for personal injury) where latent damage is involved, though not to actions for breach of contract, even though the claim is based on breach of an express or implied term to take reasonable care.[229] In very general terms, s.14A(4)(b)[230] adds to the basic period of six years that commences with the accrual of the cause of action an alternative period of three years from the earliest date on which the claimant had not only the right to sue but also knew or reasonably could have known about the damage and its attributability to the act or omission alleged to constitute negligence. This is relevant only if the alternative period expires later than the basic period of six years. Hence, if the facts of *Bell v Peter Browne & Co* were to recur, the basic six-year period would commence and finish at the same times as it did in that case but the claimant would then have three years from the point, after the sale of the house by the wife, when the problem came to light. The alternative, three-year period may commence while the initial six-year period is still running or may start time running afresh after the initial period has expired, but superimposed upon both periods is the so-called "long-stop" provision of s.14B, which bars any claim for negligence (other than in respect of personal injury) 15 years from the date of the last act of negligence to which the damage is attributable. The operation of the two sections may be illustrated in the context of a "*White v Jones*" claim[231] by a disappointed beneficiary against a solicitor who fails in 2000 to carry out his client's instructions to confer a benefit upon the beneficiary by will, the testator dying in 2007. It is unclear whether time starts running against the beneficiary when the will is executed or when the testator dies but even if it is the former, a new, three-year period will begin when the problem comes to light on the testator's death in 2007. If, however, the testator dies in 2016 the beneficiary's claim would be extinguished in any event by the long-stop provision.

---

[226] *Backhouse v Bonomi* (1861) 9 H.L. Cas. 503.

[227] There must, however, be a present loss, not merely the contingency of one at some time in the future: *Law Society v Sephton & Co* [2006] UKHL 22; [2006] 2 A.C. 543.

[228] [1990] 2 Q.B. 495.

[229] *Iron Trade Mutual Insurance Co Ltd v J.K. Buckenham Ltd* [1990] 1 All E.R. 808; *Société Commerciale de Reassurance v ERAS (International) Ltd* [1992] 2 All E.R. 82n.

[230] This provision is modelled closely on s.14, dealing with limitation in relation to personal injury proceedings. Section 14 is discussed in para.26–098.

[231] See para.5–054.

The relevant provisions of the Latent Damage Act 1986 were enacted largely in response to the problem of latent damage in the context of defective buildings. Ironically, it now seems that most of the cases upon which the provisions were intended to operate do not raise any cause of action at all since the decision of the House of Lords in *Murphy v Brentwood DC*[232] that claims for structural defects in buildings do not generally sound in tort. However, there may still be "building" cases for which s.14A has some significance. The most obvious—though probably rare in practice—are those in which operations by the defendant cause latent damage to an existing building owned by the claimant.[233] In addition, there may be cases in which the claimant can found a claim on *Hedley Byrne & Co Ltd v Heller & Partners Ltd* against someone involved in the design or building of premises that are defective from the start. Lord Keith in *Murphy v Brentwood DC*[234] thought that the decision of the House of Lords in *Pirelli General Cable Works Ltd v Oscar Faber & Partners*[235] (where the defendants were consulting engineers for a factory chimney built by a third party) might be explained in this way.[236] In *Pirelli* it was held that the cause of action arose not when the chimney was designed or built but when damage in the form of cracks appeared, even though at that stage they were neither discovered nor discoverable by any reasonable means. Where all this stands today is not easy to state.[237] The view that there was physical damage for tort purposes when the cracks occurred is irreconcilable with the view of the nature of such damage in *Murphy v Brentwood DC*; if, however, *Pirelli* is to be explained as based on *Hedley Byrne* then the liability can embrace pure economic loss. Unfortunately, that does not take us much further. In some cases of pure economic loss time has been held to run before the loss was discoverable and it is arguable that taking over a building at the end of construction is analogous to entering into the transaction in cases like *Bell v Peter Browne*. On the other hand, the Privy Council on an appeal from New Zealand (where common law liability for defective buildings is more extensive than it is in England) accepted that classification of the loss as purely economic pointed towards time running from the point where the defect became apparent to an ordinarily observant owner,[238] for it is not until then that the value of the property is depreciated. However, that decision was made in the context of the New Zealand law governing defective buildings.

Another provision of the Latent Damage Act 1986 may be yet more flotsam left behind by the wreck of the earlier building cases in *Murphy*. Property may be disposed of during the limitation period and before the defect is discovered. In *Pirelli* the House of Lords introduced the novel concept of "class limitation"

---

[232] [1991] 1 A.C. 398, see para.10–049.

[233] It is assumed that if the claimant can show negligence in fact, he is entitled to take advantage of s.14A even though the situation might fall under the rubric of nuisance, to which the Act has no application.

[234] [1991] 1 A.C. 398 at 466.

[235] [1983] 2 A.C. 1.

[236] A similar argument was rejected on the facts in *Nitrigin Eireann Teoranta v Inco Alloys Ltd* [1992] 1 W.L.R. 498.

[237] For comprehensive discussion, see McKendrick (1991) 11 L.S. 326. On facts indistinguishable from *Pirelli* the Court of Appeal in *Abbott v Will Gannon & Smith Ltd* [2005] EWCA Civ 198; [2005] P.N.L.R. 30 considered itself bound by the case.

[238] *Invercargill CC v Hamlin* [1996] A.C. 624.

whereby if time began to run against an owner it also continued to run against his successors in title. The House of Lords was not, however, directly concerned with the question of whether such successors had claims at all. If, after *Murphy*, the original owner's claim has to be based upon *Hedley Byrne* one would have thought that would be a serious obstacle to a claim by a successor in title.[239] However, s.3(1) of the Latent Damage Act 1986 provides that:

> "where—
>
> (a)   a cause of action ('the original cause of action') has accrued to any person in respect of any negligence to which damage to any property in which he has an interest is attributable (in whole or in part), and
>
> (b)   another person acquires an interest in that property after the date on which the original cause of action accrued but before the material facts about the damage have become known to any person who, at the time when he first has knowledge of those facts, has any interest in the property;
>
> a fresh cause of action in respect of that negligence shall accrue to that other person on the date on which he acquires his interest in the property."

In effect, therefore, provided the first owner had no knowledge of the defect but had a cause of action, his transferee has a new, statutory claim. Although the second owner only acquires his cause of action when he acquires the property there is no risk of extension of the limitation period because for the purpose of s.14A of the Limitation Act 1980 it is deemed to accrue at the same time as that of the first owner.

26–094   **Fraud and concealment.** Related to the problem of latent damage is s.32 of the Limitation Act 1980 dealing with fraud and concealment. The effect of s.32 is as follows. Where the claimant's action is based on the fraud of the defendant or his agent[240] or of any person through whom he (or his agent) claims time does not run until the claimant has discovered the fraud or could with reasonable diligence have discovered it.[241] This part of s.32 is limited to cases where the action is actually founded on fraud (e.g. where it is a claim for damages for deceit or to rescind a contract) and does not extend to causes of action in which "dishonest" or "fraudulent" conduct may figure (e.g. conversion).[242] However, by s.32(1)(b) the same postponement of the running of time applies where "any fact relevant to the plaintiff's right of action[243] has been deliberately concealed from him by the defendant". This includes a case of "deliberate commission of a breach of duty in circumstances in which it is unlikely to be discovered for some time".[244] Section 32(1)(b) applies where the defendant commits a tort which is not at the time known to the claimant and then, at a later date, conceals it. The ideal answer in

---

[239] See para.12–036.

[240] Which includes an independent contractor: *Applegate v Moss* [1971] 1 Q.B. 406.

[241] Section 32(1)(a). On reasonable diligence, see *Peco Arts Inc v Hazlitt Gallery Ltd* [1983] 1 W.L.R. 1315 (a s.32(1)(c) case) and *Barnstaple Boat Co Ltd v Jones* [2007] EWCA Civ 727.

[242] *Beaman v A.R.T.S. Ltd* [1949] 1 K.B. 550 at 558 per Lord Greene MR, at 567 per Somervell LJ.

[243] This has been interpreted to mean a fact that must be alleged and proved to establish a cause of action. It is not enough that the defendant has concealed facts going to the strength of the claimant's case or the availability of a defence: *Johnson v CC Surrey*, *The Times*, November 23, 1992; *C v Mirror Group Newspapers* [1997] 1 W.L.R. 131; *AIC Ltd v ITS Testing Services (UK) Ltd* [2006] EWCA Civ 1601; [2007] 1 Lloyd's Rep. 555.

[244] Section 32(2).

such a case would be to "stop the clock" at the time of the concealment and to restart it when the wrong is discovered (or becomes discoverable) by the claimant. However, the words of the Act will not bear this interpretation, so the result is that a new limitation period starts from the date of discovery.[245]

Section 32 will prevent the running of time in many cases where there is a wrongful dealing[246] with goods by a person who has custody of, or a limited interest in, them and hence the opportunity to conceal that dealing. However, it would be hard if the running of time were also suspended against defendants who were innocent purchasers. Therefore, notwithstanding that fraud or concealment will generally affect persons who claim through the actual wrongdoer, s.32(3)(b) provides that nothing in the section shall enable an action to be brought to recover property or its value against the purchaser of the property or any person claiming through him, in any case where the property has been purchased for valuable consideration by an innocent third party since the fraud or concealment.

Fiduciary obligations. Nowadays, it is not uncommon for claims based on professional liability to be run on the basis of breach of fiduciary duty as well as in contract and tort. Proceedings for breach of fiduciary duty are equitable and the Limitation Act 1980 does not provide any fixed periods in respect of equitable actions. Section 36(1) states that the periods applicable to contract and tort do not apply to any such claim "except in so far as any such time limit may be applied by the court by analogy in like manner as the corresponding time limit under any enactment repealed by the Limitation Act 1939 was applied before 1 July 1940". In *Cia de Seguros Imperio v Heath (REBX) Ltd*[247] the claim was brought in respect of alleged breaches of duty by the defendants in the operation of a "pooling" arrangement among insurers and was based on alleged breaches of fiduciary duty as well as on breach of contract and negligence. The Court of Appeal held that, the contract and tort claims being time-barred, the claim for "equitable compensation" was also time-barred by analogy since they corresponded to the common law damages claims.[248]

26–095

Extinction of title: theft. Before 1939 it was only in cases concerning title to land that expiry of the limitation period affected title. In all other cases it merely barred the claimant from pursuing his remedy before the courts so that a person wrongfully deprived of his goods whose action was time-barred might recover them by extra-judicial means and have a right of action in respect of subsequent wrongful dealings with them. The Limitation Act 1939 changed this with regard to conversion and there are further modifications in the Limitation Act 1980. Section 3(1) of the latter Act provides that once a cause of action for conversion has accrued in respect of a chattel, no action may be brought for any subsequent conversion after the expiry of six years from the accrual of the original cause of

26–096

---

[245] *Sheldon v R.H.M. Outhwaite (Underwriting Agencies) Ltd* [1996] A.C. 102. Logically this applies even if the claim was statute-barred before the concealment took place.

[246] It is assumed in this discussion that the wrongful dealing does not amount to theft. If it does, time does not run because of the provisions of s.4: see below para.26–096. Section 32 is inapplicable in the normal case of theft where the thief is unknown or untraceable: *R.B. Policies at Lloyd's v Butler* [1950] 1 K.B. 76.

[247] [2001] 1 W.L.R. 112.

[248] See also *Coulthard v Disco Mix Club Ltd* [2000] 1 W.L.R. 707.

action unless, of course, the owner has recovered possession of it in the meanwhile. Section 3(2) provides that once the period of limitation in respect of the original cause of action has expired, then the owner's title is extinguished. So, for example, if D converts C goods and later sells them to someone else, once six years have elapsed from the taking, not only has C lost the right to sue either D or the person who bought the goods from D, but the purchaser is in a position to deal with them as absolute owner notwithstanding that at the time of the sale to him D had no title which D could pass on to him. However, the Law Reform Committee was troubled at the prospect of time running in favour of a thief or receiver and we now have the further and rather complicated provisions of s.4 of the Limitation Act 1980. The effect of the section is that time does not run against the owner in respect of the theft[249] of his chattel or any conversion "related to the theft", which latter phrase means any subsequent conversion other than a purchase in good faith.[250] Thus if property is stolen and then sold by the thief to X (who is aware of its origin) and then given by X to Y, the owner's rights of action against the thief and X and Y continue indefinitely and his title will never be extinguished. However, the occurrence of a good faith purchase starts time running against the owner in favour of the good faith purchaser (and any converter from him). After six years the owner will no longer be able to sue the good faith purchaser or anyone who subsequently dealt with the goods[251] and his title to the goods will be extinguished. However, he retains his right to sue the original thief and other converters who preceded the good faith purchaser.[252]

26–097 **Disabilities.** One of the longest standing derogations from standard limitation periods occurs where the claimant is under disability. If, on the date when the right of action accrued, the person to whom it accrued was under a disability, time does not begin to run until he ceases to be under a disability or dies (whichever first occurs).[253] For these purposes, the law recognises only two forms of disability: infancy and lack of mental capacity.[254] Infancy presents no difficulty, for it means simply a person under the age of 18. The question whether a person has the mental capacity to conduct legal proceedings is to be determined by reference to the Mental Capacity Act 2005.[255]

What is the position of a claimant who had mental capacity when time began to run but later loses it; or of a claimant who was an infant when his cause of action accrued and suffered loss of mental capacity before he reached the age of 18; or of a claimant who is under a disability at the moment when he succeeds to the title of a predecessor who was under no disability? The Act provides that

---

[249] Which includes fraud and blackmail: s.4(5)(b).

[250] Any conversion following the theft is presumed to be related to the theft unless the contrary is shown: s.4(4). A purchase in good faith may itself give the purchaser a good title, but will by no means necessarily do so: para.18–041.

[251] If this person is a thief, all of the provisions of the section will apply over again vis-a-vis the good faith purchaser, who is now the owner.

[252] Section 4(1): " . . . but if his title . . . is extinguished under section 3(2) . . . he may not bring an action in respect of a theft preceding the loss of his title, unless the theft in question preceded the conversion from which time began to run for the purposes of section 3(2)."

[253] Section 28(1).

[254] Section 38(2).

[255] See para.4–015.

unless the right of action first accrues to a person who is then disabled the disability has no effect.[256] Where, however, there are successive disabilities in the same person (lack of mental capacity supervening on infancy) time does not run until the latter of the disabilities has ended, provided that there is no interval of ability between the disabilities.[257]

Special periods of limitation: personal injury and death. The law in this   **26–098**
connection is found in ss.11–14 and 33 of the Limitation Act 1980, as supplemented by common law elaboration. Section 11(1) states that the provisions apply to:

> "any action for damages for negligence, nuisance or breach of duty (whether the duty exists by virtue of a contract or of provision made by or under a statute or independently of any contract or any such provision) where the damages claimed by the claimant for the negligence, nuisance or breach of duty consist of or include damages in respect of personal injuries to the claimant or any other person."

If, therefore, the claimant claims damages for personal injury and damage to property in the same action both claims are governed by the provisions concerned. For a long while it was held that s.11 did not include actions for intentional trespass to the person,[258] and in this case the basic six-year period of s.2 applied. As we shall shortly see, although the basic period under the personal injury provisions is shorter, the fact that the claim fell under s.2 was by no means necessarily to the claimant's advantage, because there could be no extension of the period.[259] However, in *A v Hoare*[260] the House of Lords reversed this view of the law so that the provisions of ss.11–14 and 33 now apply to trespass. These provisions also capture a case where the owner of a car is sued for allowing an uninsured person to drive it, even though he has not caused the accident.[261]

The expression "personal injuries" includes any disease and any impairment of a person's physical or mental condition.[262] This covers a claim based on a failure to diagnose and treat learning difficulties such as dyslexia[263] and an unwanted pregnancy and confinement is also a "personal injury" for this purpose.[264] However, a claim in respect solely of a loss of stored substances

---

[256] Section 28(1), (2). If the claimant is rendered immediately mentally incapable by the tort itself he is disabled when the cause of action accrues, for the law takes no account of parts of a day: *Kirby v Leather* [1965] 2 Q.B. 367. Aliter if the incapacity, though caused by the tort, comes on some days later. However, that might be a pointer towards the court's exercising its discretion under s.33 of the Act, see para.26–088.

[257] This is the effect of s.28(1), which refers to the claimant's ceasing to be under a disability. See also *Borrows v Ellison* (1871) L.R. 6 Ex. 128.

[258] *Stubbings v Webb* [1993] A.C. 498.

[259] See s.33, which is discussed below in this section.

[260] [2008] UKHL 6; [2008] 1 A.C. 844.

[261] *Norman v Ali* [2000] R.T.R 107. For this liability see para.8–011. However, it seems that a claim against a solicitor for failure to pursue his client's personal injury action is not generally within the three-year period (but see *Bennett v Greenland Houchen & Co* [1998] P.N.L.R. 458 (solicitors' negligence alleged to have caused depression)).

[262] Section 38(1).

[263] *Adams v Bracknell Forest BC* [2004] UKHL 29; [2005] 1 A.C. 76.

[264] *Walkin v South Manchester HA* [1995] 1 W.L.R. 1543. Where damages for the cost of upbringing of the child are still available that claim, too, falls within this provision though whether that is

obtained from a person's body is not one for personal injury,[265] though a claim for psychiatric injury arising from such a loss is.[266]

Where s.11 applies the limitation period is three years from the date on which the cause of action accrued or the date (if later) of the claimant's "knowledge".[267] By virtue of s.14, a person has "knowledge" when he knows all the following facts (although as is explained below, knowledge may be constructive): (1) that the injury in question was significant; (2) that the injury was attributable in whole or in part to the act or omission in question which is alleged to constitute negligence, nuisance or breach of duty; (3) the identity of the defendant;[268] and (4) if it is alleged that the act or omission in question was that of a person other than the defendant,[269] the identity of that person and the additional facts supporting the bringing of an action against the defendant.

The claimant's knowledge that any acts or omissions did or did not, as a matter of law, involve negligence, nuisance or breach of duty is irrelevant.[270] An injury is "significant"[271] if the claimant would reasonably have considered it sufficiently serious to justify his instituting proceedings for damages against a defendant who did not dispute liability and was able to satisfy a judgment.[272] This has not proved easy to interpret but in *Spargo v North Essex District Health Authority*[273] the Court of Appeal distilled the earlier case law into the following guidelines:[274]

> "(1)   The knowledge required... is a broad knowledge of the essence of the causally relevant act or omission to which the injury is attributable;

---

consistent with the reasoning in *McFarlane v Tayside Health Board* [2002] 2 A.C. 59 (see para.25–021) is debatable: see *Godfrey v Gloucestershire Royal Infirmary NHS Trust* [2003] EWHC 549 (QB).

[265] *Yearworth v North Bristol NHS Trust* [2009] EWCA Civ 37; [2010] Q.B. 1.

[266] *Yearworth v North Bristol NHS Trust* [2009] EWCA Civ 37; [2010] Q.B. 1 at [18].

[267] Section 11(4).

[268] Complications can arise where there is a group of companies under common control: *Simpson v Norwest Holst Southern Ltd* [1980] 1 W.L.R. 968; *Cressey v E Timm & Son Ltd* [2005] EWCA Civ 763; [2005] 1 W.L.R. 3926.

[269] E.g. where the defendant is an employer who is vicariously liable.

[270] Section 14(1). Thus, the advice of the claimant's solicitors that the defendant's conduct does not amount to a tort does not prevent time running, although the claimant might have an action for professional negligence against them. Similarly, time runs even if the advice is correct at the time but a subsequent appellate decision makes the conduct actionable: *Robinson v St Helens MBC* [2002] EWCA Civ 1099 (QB); [2003] P.I.Q.R. P128. "To interpret section 14(1) . . . so that the three-year period runs from the date when the law first recognised such a claim by means of a judicial decision, would bring into existence a host of stale claims, some of which could be 20, 30 or more years old, and so give rise to great unfairness to defendants": *Rowe v Kingston-upon-Hull CC* [2003] EWCA Civ 1281 at [24]. See also *Awoyomi v Radford* [2007] EWHC 1671; [2008] Q.B. 793.

[271] It has been held that if the claimant knows that one injury is significant, time runs even in respect of another, of the significance of which he is unaware: *Bristow v Grout, The Times*, November 3, 1986.

[272] Section 14(2). It follows that even a quite minor injury with no long-term effects of which the claimant is then aware may justify the institution of proceedings: *A v Wirral MBC* [2008] EWCA Civ 783.

[273] [1997] P.I.Q.R. P235 at 242. See also *Haward v Fawcetts* [2006] UKHL 9; [2006] 1 W.L.R. 682 on the similar s.14A.

[274] In *AB v Ministry of Defence* [2012] UKSC 9; [2013] 1 A.C 78 at [68] it was stressed that these words should not be "treated as if they were [a] statutory text" and that "[t]he words of the 1980 Act themselves must be the starting-point".

(2)   'Attributable' in this context means 'capable of being attributed to', in the sense of being a real possibility;

(3)   A plaintiff has the requisite knowledge when she knows enough to make it reasonable for her to begin to investigate whether or not she has a case against the defendant. Another way of putting this is to say that she will have such knowledge if she so firmly believes that her condition is capable of being attributed to an act or omission which she can identify (in broad terms) that she goes to a solicitor to seek advice about making a claim for compensation;

(4)   On the other hand she will not have the requisite knowledge if she thinks she knows the acts or omissions she should investigate but in fact is barking up the wrong tree: or if her knowledge of what the defendant did or did not do is so vague or general that she cannot fairly be expected to know what she should investigate; or if her state of mind is such that she thinks her condition is capable of being attributed to the act or omission alleged to constitute negligence, but she is not sure about this, and would need to check with an expert before she could be properly said to know that it was."

A firm belief may amount to knowledge. A claimant is likely to have acquired knowledge of the facts mentioned in s.14 "when he first came reasonably to believe them".[275] A belief will be sufficient for this purpose once the claimant holds it "with sufficient confidence to justify embarking on the preliminaries to the issue of [proceedings] . . ., taking legal and other advice and collecting evidence".[276] A mere suspicion by the claimant that he might have grounds to issue proceedings is insufficient. "The focus is upon the moment when it is *reasonable* for the claimant to embark on such an investigation."[277] Once proceedings are issued, it is no longer open to the claimant to argue that he lacks the knowledge necessary to start the limitation period.[278]

"Knowledge" includes knowledge that the claimant might reasonably have been expected to acquire from facts observable or ascertainable by him and from facts ascertainable by him with the help of medical or other appropriate expert advice which it is reasonable for him to seek. However, he is not fixed with knowledge of a fact that is ascertainable only with the help of expert advice so long as he has taken all reasonable steps to obtain (and, where appropriate, to act on) this advice.[279] Thus, where the claimant suffered injury by a piece of metal flying off a hammer in 1957, the failure of the expert who later conducted a hardness test to notice the defect that was in fact the cause of the accident prevented time from running against the claimant with the result that the claimant's personal representative was able to bring a successful action in 1975.[280] Where a claimant has the requisite knowledge and then consults an expert the law will not deem that the claimant obtained the knowledge at the time at which he consulted the expert.[281] The date on which the claimant consulted an expert will not necessarily determine when he had the requisite knowledge.

---

[275] *AB v Ministry of Defence* [2012] UKSC 9; [2013] 1 A.C. 78 at [11].

[276] *Halford v Brookes* [1991] 1 W.L.R. 428 at 443 per Lord Donaldson MR, approved in *AB v Ministry of Defence* [2012] UKSC 9; [2013] 1 A.C. 78.

[277] *AB v Ministry of Defence* [2012] UKSC 9; [2013] 1 A.C. 78 at [12] (emphasis in original).

[278] *AB v Ministry of Defence* [2012] UKSC 9; [2013] 1 A.C. 78 at [67], [71].

[279] Section 14(3).

[280] *Marston v BRB* [1976] I.C.R. 124.

[281] *AB v Ministry of Defence* [2012] UKSC 9; [2013] 1 A.C. 78 at [13].

At one time the view was taken that the issue of knowledge under s.14 should be considered on a basis that was "partly subjective and partly objective",[282] taking account of matters like the claimant's intelligence and the effect on him of his injury. However, the current view is expressed by Lord Hoffmann in *A v Hoare*[283] in the following terms:

> "I respectfully think that the notion of the test being partly objective and partly subjective is somewhat confusing. Section 14(2) is a test for what counts as a significant injury. The material to which that test applies is generally 'subjective' in the sense that it is applied to what the claimant knows of his injury rather than the injury as it actually was. Even then, his knowledge may have to be supplemented with imputed 'objective' knowledge under section 14(3). But the test itself is an entirely impersonal standard: not whether the claimant himself would have considered the injury sufficiently serious to justify proceedings but whether he would 'reasonably' have done so. You ask what the claimant knew about the injury he had suffered, you add any knowledge about the injury which may be imputed to him under section 14(3) and you then ask whether a reasonable person with that knowledge would have considered the injury sufficiently serious to justify his instituting proceedings for damages against a defendant who did not dispute liability and was able to satisfy a judgment.
>
> It follows that I cannot accept that one must consider whether someone 'with [the] plaintiff's intelligence' would have been reasonable if he did not regard the injury as sufficiently serious. That seems to me to destroy the effect of the word 'reasonably'. Judges should not have to grapple with the notion of the reasonable unintelligent person. Once you have ascertained what the claimant knew and what he should be treated as having known, the actual claimant drops out of the picture. Section 14(2) is, after all, simply a standard of the seriousness of the injury and nothing more. Standards are in their nature impersonal and do not vary with the person to whom they are applied."

A reason for this shift is that even if the claimant fails on the date of knowledge issue it has since 1975 been open to the court to override the limitation period under s.33 and that is the right place to deal with, for example, the question of the impact of the injury on what the claimant could reasonably be expected to have done,[284] though it should not "be supposed that the exercise of the court's s.33 discretion will invariably replicate" the position that prevailed under the former interpretation of s.14.[285]

If the claim is under the Fatal Accidents Act 1976 in respect of a death caused by the defendant's tort the time limit is found in s.12 of the Limitation Act 1980. No action can be brought under the Fatal Accidents Act unless the deceased himself could have maintained an action at the date of his death.[286] Subject, therefore, to the court's power to override the time limit, any potential right of action under the Fatal Accidents Act will be lost three years after the accident or the date of the deceased's knowledge if later.[287] If the deceased has a cause of action at the date of his death, then the dependant may bring an action, again subject to the court's power to override the time limit,[288] within three years of the

---

[282] See *McCafferty v Metropolitan Police District Receiver* [1977] 1 W.L.R. 1073.

[283] [2008] UKHL 6; [2008] 1 A.C. 844 at [34]–[35].

[284] [2008] UKHL 6; [2008] 1 A.C. 844 at [45].

[285] [2008] UKHL 6; [2008] 1 A.C. 844 at [87] per Lord Brown.

[286] Section 12(1).

[287] Section 11. By s.12(1): "[W]here any such action by the injured person would have been barred by the time limit in section 11 . . . no account shall be taken of the possibility of that time limit being overridden under section 33."

[288] Section 33(1).

date of the death or the date of the dependant's knowledge, whichever is later.[289] In most cases of course, there is more than one dependant and in that event the provision regarding the date of knowledge is to be applied to each of them separately and anyone debarred by this is to be excluded from the action.[290]

A much more fundamental development in the law of limitation is the court's power, conferred by s.33, to override the statutory time limits if it appears to the court to be equitable to do so having regard to the degree to which the primary limitation rules prejudice the claimant and any exercise of the power would prejudice the defendant.[291] This discretion applies only to cases where the limitation period is prescribed by s.11 or s.12. Where the discretion applies, the court is directed to have regard to all the circumstances of the case and in particular to: (1) the length of, and reasons[292] for, the delay[293] on the part of the claimant; (2) the effect of the delay upon the evidence in the case; (3) the conduct of the defendant after the cause of action arose, including his response to the claimant's reasonable request for information; (4) the duration of any disability of the claimant arising after the accrual of the cause of action; (5) the extent to which the claimant acted promptly and reasonably once he knew[294] he might have an action for damages; and (6) the steps, if any, taken by the claimant to obtain medical, legal or other expert advice and the nature of any such advice as he may have received.[295]

The power in s.33 is not infrequently applied.[296] Subject to the duty to act judicially, the judge's discretion is unfettered[297] and the matters set out in s.33(3) are by way of example and not definitive.[298] Although it has been said that the greater emphasis on sticking to time limits under the Civil Procedure Rules does not fetter the court's discretion under the Act,[299] yet the question of proportionality is now important in the exercise of any discretion and courts

---

[289] Section 12(2).

[290] Section 13. This is less significant than it might seem, because the dependants will normally include children, against whom time would not run until majority.

[291] Section 33(1). "Parliament has now decided that uncertain justice is preferable to certain injustice": *Firman v Ellis* [1978] Q.B. 886 at 911 per Ormrod LJ.

[292] Which may include not only the express reasons given by the claimant, but also the subconscious factors which may have prevented him from litigating: *McCafferty v Metropolitan Police District Receiver* [1977] 1 W.L.R. 1073.

[293] Which means the delay after the primary limitation period has expired: *Thompson v Brown Construction (Ebbw Vale) Ltd* [1981] 1 W.L.R. 744 at 751; *Donovan v Gwentoys Ltd* [1990] 1 W.L.R. 472; *McDonnell v Walker* [2009] EWCA Civ 1257. But prior delay is part of the "circumstances of the case".

[294] Which means actual knowledge, not the deemed knowledge which may arise under s.14: *Eastman v London Country Bus Services, The Times*, November 23, 1985.

[295] Section 33(3). Legal advice is privileged, but the claimant may be interrogated as to whether the advice was favourable or unfavourable: *Jones v G.D. Searle & Co Ltd* [1979] 1 W.L.R. 101.

[296] Guidance on the exercise of the s.33 discretion in child abuse cases in *AB v Nugent Care Society* [2009] EWCA Civ 827; [2010] P.I.Q.R. P3.

[297] *Donovan v Gwentoys Ltd* [1990] 1 W.L.R. 472; *Horton v Sadler* [2006] UKHL 27; [2007] 1 A.C. 307.

[298] *Nash v Eli Lilly & Co* [1993] 1 W.L.R. 782.

[299] *Steeds v Peverel Management Services Ltd* [2001] EWCA Civ 419 at [9].

"should be slow to exercise their discretion in favour of a claimant in the absence of cogent medical evidence showing a serious effect on the claimant's health or enjoyment of life and employability".[300]

The exercise is essentially a balancing one and the balance will come down heavily in favour of the defendant where, for example, he is required to meet a claim that is first presented years after the wrong[301] and the longer the delay after the occurrence of the matters giving rise to the cause of action the more likely it is that the balance of prejudice would swing against the exercise of the discretion in the claimant's favour. Thus in *Adams v Bracknell Forest BC*[302] the House of Lords declined to exercise the discretion in respect of a claim alleging that the defendants were at fault in failing to diagnose and treat the claimant's dyslexia: the claim was brought 14 years after his last contact with the defendants and 12 years after he had reached majority, there were no records to enable the defendants to rebut the allegations and in view of the uncertainties of proof of causation of the claimant's current condition and its effect on his life and employment the damages would be likely to be modest. The mere fact that the exercise of the discretion will deprive the defendant of a limitation defence is not of itself "prejudice" to him: if, for example, he has had early notice of the possibility of a claim he will have had opportunity to investigate it and some delay in issuing proceedings after the expiry of the limitation period will have had no effect on his ability to defend.[303] Although the fact that the defendant is insured is a relevant consideration, it is wrong to take the line that an insured defendant cannot establish prejudice since only his insurers will suffer and they are not parties to the action. The correct approach is to treat the defendant and his insurers as a composite unit: insurers should not be penalised by being made to fight claims that an uninsured defendant would not be held bound to fight.[304] The fact that the claimant has a claim for professional negligence against his solicitors in failing to issue proceedings[305] is a highly relevant circumstance,[306] and prima facie it is the claimant, and not the defendant, who should bear the consequences of their default,[307] though the court must bear in mind the difficulty, delay and expense that may be caused to the claimant by having to change horses in

---

[300] *Robinson v St Helens MBC* [2002] EWCA Civ 1099; [2003] P.I.Q.R. P128 at [33].

[301] Even though the "delay" referred to in s.33(3) is that occurring after the expiry of the limitation period delay before then is relevant in determining the prejudice to the defendant. "A defendant is always likely to be prejudiced by the dilatoriness of the plaintiff in pursuing his claim . . . The fact that the law permits a plaintiff within prescribed limits to disadvantage a defendant in this way does not mean that the defendant is not prejudiced. It merely means that he is not in a position to complain of whatever prejudice he suffers. Once a plaintiff allows a prescribed time limit to elapse, the defendant is no longer subject to that disability": *Donovan v Gwentoys Ltd* [1990] 1 W.L.R. 472 at 479 per Lord Oliver.

[302] [2004] UKHL 29; [2005] 1 A.C. 76

[303] *Cain v Francis* [2008] EWCA Civ 1451; [2009] Q.B. 754. *Cain* is an extreme case: liability was quickly admitted, interim payments were made and proceedings were issued only one day late.

[304] *Kelly v Bastible* (1996) 36 B.M.L.R. 51.

[305] *Donovan v Gwentoys Ltd* [1990] 1 W.L.R. 472.

[306] *Thompson v Brown Construction (Ebbw Vale) Ltd* [1981] 1 W.L.R. 744 at 752; *McDonnell v Walker* [2009] EWCA Civ 1257.

[307] *Horton v Sadler* [2006] UKHL 27; [2007] 1 A.C. 307 at [53].

midstream[308] and the fact that the solicitor will have a greater knowledge of the weaknesses of the case than will the defendant.[309]

Special periods of limitation: maritime cases. The Merchant Shipping Act 1995[310] fixes two years as the period of limitation for damage to a vessel, her cargo, freight or any property on board her, or for damages for loss of life or personal injuries suffered by any person on board caused by the fault of another vessel. The court may, however, extend this period to such extent and upon such conditions as it thinks fit,[311] but the Act only applies to actions brought against ships other than that on which the damage actually occurred, and, accordingly, where an action was brought against shipowners in respect of the death of a seaman on their ship, it was held that the general law of limitation (the three-year period) applies.[312]

26–099

Special periods of limitation: liability under the Consumer Protection Act 1987. We have seen that the Consumer Protection Act 1987 imposes strict liability for defective products.[313] Although it will apply to some property damage cases it is overwhelmingly concerned with personal injury.[314] It adds a new s.11A to the Limitation Act 1980 and the main rules are identical to those generally applying in personal injury cases:[315] a primary three-year period from the damage, an alternative period running from the claimant's knowledge and a power to override the limitation period. However, there is one major difference: no action can be brought in any case more than 10 years from the date when the product was put into circulation.[316] This bar is absolute—that is to say, it cannot be overridden by the court under s.33 of the Limitation Act 1980 and it applies even if the claimant was under a disability or there was fraud, concealment or mistake, or even if no cause of action could have arisen within the 10-year period because there was no damage.[317] None of these provisions, however, affects an action for common law negligence.

26–100

Special periods of limitation: defamation and malicious falsehood. By s.4A of the Limitation Act 1980, there is a limitation period of one year from the accrual of the cause of action in cases of libel, slander and malicious falsehood. Under

26–101

---

[308] *Thompson v Brown (Ebbw Vale) Ltd* [1981] 1 W.L.R. 744 at 750; *Firman v Ellis* [1978] Q.B. 886. As has often been pointed out, the real issue in such a case is not whether the claimant will recover damages, but which liability insurer will pay them.

[309] *Hartley v Birmingham City DC* [1992] 1 W.L.R. 968.

[310] See s.190.

[311] Section 190. For a case on the exercise of the discretion, see *The Alnwick* [1965] P. 357.

[312] *The Niceto de Larrinaga* [1966] P. 80.

[313] See Ch.11.

[314] Where property damage alone is sued for the limitation period is three years, not the usual six: Limitation Act 1980 s.11A(4). The Latent Damage Act 1986 does not apply because this is not an action for negligence, but by s.5(5) of the Consumer Protection Act 1987 Act time runs from the date when the damage occurred or the earliest time at which a person with an interest in the property had knowledge of the material facts (as to which see subss.(6) and (7)).

[315] See *AB v Ministry of Defence* [2012] UKSC 9; [2013] 1 A.C. 78 at [78].

[316] This means the moment when it leaves the production process and entered a marketing process in which it was offered to the public for use or consumption: *O'Byrne v Sanofi Pasteur MSD Ltd: C-127/04* [2006] 1 W.L.R. 1606.

[317] See Limitation Act 1980 ss.11A(3), 28(7) and 32(4A).

s.32A the court may in its discretion allow a case to proceed outside this time if it would be equitable to do so having regard to the relative prejudice to the claimant and the defendant.[318]

26–102 **Special periods of limitation: contribution.** Section 10 of the Limitation Act 1980 provides that a claim to recover statutory contribution must be brought within two years of the date when the right to contribution first accrued.[319] If the tortfeasor claiming contribution has himself been sued by the victim of the tort, then the right to contribution accrues when judgment is given against him which quantifies his liability;[320] if he compromises the action the right accrues when the amount of the payment to be made by him to the victim is agreed.[321] In the case of claims for contribution between shipowners in respect of their liabilities for loss of life or personal injuries aboard ship, which are governed by the Merchant Shipping Act 1995, however, the period of limitation for contribution is one year from payment only.[322]

26–103 **Law Commission's recommendations.** The Law Commission in 2001 concluded[323] that the law of limitation should be overhauled and rationalised on the basis of a general "core regime" applicable to most causes of action (tort, contract and others) of a three-year period of limitation to run from the date when the existence of a claim was discoverable by the claimant. This would be balanced by an absolute long-stop of 10 years from the accrual of the cause of action or from the time of the act or omission giving rise to the claim. The long-stop would not apply where the defendant has dishonestly concealed relevant facts. However, in the case of personal injury (whether arising from negligence or intentional wrongdoing) the court would have a discretion to disapply the primary limitation period and there would be no long-stop. As now, there would be provision for postponement in cases of disability, though modified in several respects.

5. EXCUSES[324]

26–104 **The concept of an excuse.** A defendant who claims that he was justified asserts that he acted reasonably; in contrast, a defendant who pleads an excuse accepts that he did not achieve the same success in terms of leading a rational life as a

---

[318] This is modelled on s.33 and s.32A(2) directs the court to have regard to certain factors comparable to those listed in s.33(3). See *Steedman v BBC* [2001] EWCA Civ 1534; [2002] E.M.L.R. 318.

[319] The legislation thus gives added importance to the possibility of a common law claim between tortfeasors, e.g. by virtue of an express contract between them or under *Lister v Romford Ice and Cold Storage Co Ltd* [1957] A.C. 555 (see para.21–040) since the limitation period for such claims remains at six years.

[320] Section 10(3), as interpreted in *Aer Lingus Plc v Gildacroft Ltd* [2006] EWCA Civ 4; [2006] 1 W.L.R. 1173.

[321] Section 10(4). "Payment" includes a payment in kind (e.g. remedial work) provided a value can be placed on it: *Baker & Davies Plc v Leslie Wilks Associates* [2005] EWHC 1179 (TCC); [2005] 3 All E.R. 603.

[322] Merchant Shipping Act 1995 s.190(4).

[323] Law Com. No.270.

[324] Goldberg, "Tort Law's Missing Excuses" in Dyson, Goudkamp and Wilmot-Smith (eds), *Defences in Tort* (2014).

defendant who enjoyed a justificatory defence. Accordingly, justifications reflect more favourably on defendants than excuses. This is because an excused defendant, while still offering a rational explanation for his conduct, does not assert that his conduct was reasonable. Although there were one or more reasons for an excused defendant to do that which he did, those reasons were insufficiently strong to result in the defendant being justified in his acts.

Tort law does not recognise any excuses. According to conventional wisdom, tort law, unlike the criminal law, does not recognise any excuses. Excused defendants are liable for their torts. Three defences that are widely regarded as excuses are not tort defences. These are provocation, duress and excessive self-defence. These will be addressed in turn.

26–105

Provocation. Provocation can be dealt with quickly. It is firmly established that the fact that the defendant was provoked merely diminishes the claimant's entitlement to damages. (It is settled that provocation can reduce exemplary damages,[325] but the effect of provocation on compensatory damages is unclear.[326]) Provocation does not go to liability. Provocation is not, therefore, a defence.

26–106

Duress.[327] Duress, or threatened injury to a person unless he commits a tort, was held many years ago to be no defence if he does commit it. In *Gilbert v Stone*[328] 12 unknown armed men threatened to kill the defendant unless he entered the claimant's house with them, which he did. The defendant was held not to have any defence in an action in trespass. There are several points to note in this connection. First, actual physical compulsion, as opposed to threats, will prevent liability from arising in trespass. That is because the requirement of voluntary action will not be satisfied, and no tort will consequently be committed.[329] Secondly, a person who is subjected to threats and who commits a tort as a result will usually have an action against the person who threatened him. Thirdly, there is an obvious parallel between duress and private necessity.[330] Rightly or wrongly, duress has been said to be only a species of the genus of "necessity".[331] It might be thought that consistency demands that if private necessity is not a defence that duress should not be either.

26–107

Excessive-self-defence. Excessive self-defence is not a tort defence. As was explained earlier, if a defendant uses excessive defensive force he will not be entitled to the defence of self-defence.[332]

26–108

---

[325] *Fontin v Katapodis* (1962) 108 C.L.R. 177, applied in *Lane v Holloway* [1968] 1 Q.B. 379.
[326] Consider the apparently inconsistent positions that Lord Denning took on this issue in *Lane v Holloway* [1968] 1 Q.B. 379 at 387 and *Murphy v Culhane* [1977] Q.B. 94 at 98.
[327] Edelman and Dyer in Dyson, Goudkamp and Wilmot-Smith (eds), *Defences in Tort* (2014).
[328] (1647) Al. 35.
[329] See para.4–009.
[330] Regarding private necessity, see para.26–043.
[331] *R. v Howe* [1987] A.C. 417 at 429. In the criminal law context necessity is sometimes labelled "duress of circumstances" (as opposed to duress by threats).
[332] See para.26–030.

6.   DENIALS OF RESPONSIBILITY

26–109   **The concept of a denial of responsibility.** When a defendant denies that he is responsible in the tort law context he might simply be asserting that he is not liable in tort. But the phrase "denial of responsibility" has a second meaning which refers to the more fundamental question of whether the defendant is a rational agent. On this meaning of the phrase, a defendant who denies his responsibility contends that he is incapable of acting within the realm of reason at some relevant point in time and in some relevant aspect of his life. The fact that a defendant lacks responsibility in this basic sense will not supply him with a defence. Hence, insane defendants[333] and infant defendants[334] are liable for their torts.

---

[333] See para.25–037. See further Goudkamp (2012) 31 O.J.L.S. 727.
[334] See para.25–022.

INDEX

This index has been prepared using Sweet and Maxwell's Legal Taxonomy. Main index entries conform to keywords provided by the Legal Taxonomy except where references to specific documents or non-standard terms (denoted by quotation marks) have been included. These keywords provide a means of identifying similar concepts in other Sweet and Maxwell publications and online services to which keywords from the Legal Taxonomy have been applied. Readers may find some minor differences between terms used in the text and those which appear in the index. Suggestions to *sweetandmaxwell.taxonomy@thomson.com.*

All references are to paragraph number

INDEX